This multivolume *History* marks a new beginning in the study of American literature. It embodies the work of a generation of Americanists who have redrawn the boundaries of the field and redefined the terms of its development. The extraordinary growth of the field has called for, and here receives, a more expansive, more flexible scholarly format. All previous histories of American literature have been either totalizing, offering the magisterial sweep of a single vision, or encyclopedic, composed of a multitude of terse accounts that come to seem just as totalizing because the form itself precludes the development of authorial voice. Here, American literary history unfolds through a polyphony of large-scale narratives. Each is ample enough in scope and detail to allow for the elaboration of distinctive views (premises, arguments, and analyses); each is persuasive by demonstration and authoritative in its own right; and each is related to the others through common themes and concerns.

The authors were selected for the excellence of their scholarship and for the significance of the critical communities informing their work. Together, they demonstrate the achievements of Americanist literary criticism over the past three decades. Their contributions to these volumes speak to continuities as well as disruptions between generations and give voice to the wide range of materials now subsumed under the heading of American literature and culture.

This volume, covering the colonial and early national periods, spans three centuries and an extraordinary variety of authors: Renaissance explorers, Puritan theocrats, Enlightenment naturalists, southern women of letters, revolutionary pamphleteers, and poets and novelists of the young Republic. Myra Jehlen draws upon the multilingual literature of exploration and colonization to tell the story of how America was made up – a story of imperial expansion and imaginative appropriation. Emory Elliott traces the explosive, conflict-ridden development of the New England Way from its fractious beginnings through the tumultuous mid-eighteenth-century revivals. David S. Shields's focus is relatively narrow in time but rich in the materials it brings to light: newly uncovered collections of poems, essays, and letters that reveal a cosmopolitan network of neoclassical belles lettres extending from Philadelphia and New York to the salons of the Old South. Robert A. Ferguson examines the interconnections between the many forms of discourse that constituted the American Enlightenment and eventuated as the rhetoric of nationhood. Michael T. Gilmore describes a series of broad social and economic transformations – from republican to free-market ideology, oral to print culture, communal to individualist values – in the course of detailing the emergence of a national literary tradition.

All five narratives place the literature in international perspective; all five speak of its distinctively American characteristics, whether colonial, provincial, or national; and (in different ways) all of them demonstrate the centrality of language to the course of Americanization. Together, they offer a compelling and, for our time, comprehensive re-vision of the literary importance of early American history and the historical value of early American literature.

THE CAMBRIDGE HISTORY
OF AMERICAN LITERATURE

Volume 1
1590–1820

THE CAMBRIDGE HISTORY OF
AMERICAN LITERATURE

General editor: Sacvan Bercovitch, Charles H. Carswell Professor of
English and American Literature, Harvard University

THE CAMBRIDGE
HISTORY OF
AMERICAN LITERATURE

Volume 1
1590–1820

General Editor

SACVAN BERCOVITCH,
Harvard University

Associate Editor

CYRUS R. K. PATELL,
New York University

CAMBRIDGE
UNIVERSITY PRESS

PUBLISHED BY THE PRESS SYNDICATE OF THE UNIVERSITY OF CAMBRIDGE
The Pitt Building, Trumpington Street, Cambridge CB2 1RP

CAMBRIDGE UNIVERSITY PRESS
The Edinburgh Building, Cambridge CB2 2RU, United Kingdom
40 West 20th Street, New York, NY 10011-4211, USA
10 Stamford Road, Oakleigh, Melbourne 3166, Australia

First published 1994
Reprinted 1995 (twice)
First paperback edition 1997

Printed in the United States of America

Library of Congress Cataloging-in-Publication Data is available.

A catalog record for this book is available from the British Library.

ISBN 0-521-30105-X hardback
ISBN 0-521-58571-6 paperback

CONTENTS

v

ACKNOWLEDGMENTS

FROM THE GENERAL EDITOR

I would like to thank Harvard University for a grant that enabled the contributors to convene for three days of discussion and planning. I am grateful for the generous assistance of Andrew Brown and Julie Greenblatt of Cambridge University Press; for the steady support and advice of Daniel Aaron, Eytan Bercovitch, and Susan L. Mizruchi; and for the critical and clerical student help I received from Nancy Bentley, Michael Berthold, Lianna Farber, and Jessica Riskin. My special thanks to Margaret Reid, who helped at every stage and who prepared the index.

Sacvan Bercovitch

THE LITERATURE OF COLONIZATION

I wish to express my gratitude to the Guggenheim Foundation for a year's leave at the beginning of this project. During this leave I benefited from the hospitality of Dartmouth College, which granted me the use of its extraordinary Baker Library. I thank the University of Pennsylvania for an additional semester's leave. Robert W. Karrow, Jr., curator of maps at the Newberry Library, offered invaluable help in selecting the two American maps that illustrate my text; the Library has generously permitted their reprinting. The title of my first chapter, "Papers of Empire," is a quotation from Irwin R. Blacker's introduction to his edited volume *Hakluyt's Voyages* (New York: Viking Press, 1965), 1. Some of the translations of European texts cited in Chapter 5, as well as the title of the chapter, are borrowed from Antonello Gerbi's magisterial *The Dispute of the New World: The History of a Polemic, 1750–1900*, trans. Jeremy Moyle (Pittsburgh: University of Pittsburgh Press, 1955). Finally, I am deeply grateful to Patricia M. Spacks, Michael Warner, Emily Bartels, Marilyn Young, and Jessica Riskin for their advice and knowledge; and to Sacvan Bercovitch for his editorial guidance.

Myra Jehlen

NEW ENGLAND PURITAN LITERATURE

The following institutions provided financial support for the research and writing: the National Endowment for the Humanities, Princeton University, the University of California, and the Humanities Research Institute of the University of California. Early versions of the first chapter were presented at the University of Verona and at the Ecole Normale Superieure, and I thank my kind hosts, Professors Itala Vivan and Pierre-Yves Petillon respectively, and others who also commented on the work: Professors Viola Sachs, Dominique Marcais, Janine Dove, and Marc Chenetier. I am grateful to the director, Mark Rose, and the staff of the Humanities Research Institute at Irvine for their support, and to the other members of the 1991-2 Minority Discourse Project for reading portions of the manuscript and offering most useful suggestions: Norma Alarcon, Jose Amaya, Vincent Cheng, King-Kok Cheung, Kimberle Crenshaw, Anne Dannenberg, Abdul JanMohamed, May Joseph, Clara Sue Kidwell, Smadar Lavie, Françoise Lionnet, Haiming Liu, Lisa Lowe, Lillian Manzor-Coats, Michael Sprinker, Sterling Stuckey, David Van Leer, and Clarence Walker. At the University of California, Riverside, I have benefited from the readings and guidance of Steve Axelrod, Carol Bensick, Mark Elliott, Bruce Hagood, Deborah Hatheway, Carla Magill, and Carlton Smith. Michael Colacurcio of UCLA, Bernard Rosenthal of SUNY-Binghamton, and Heather Dubrow of the University of Wisconsin also contributed suggestions. Although there are dozens of scholars whose works have enhanced my understanding of Puritan New England, I found especially helpful for this project the work of Bernard Bailyn, Sacvan Bercovitch, Mitchell Breitwieser, Michael Clark, Pattie Cowell, Robert Daly, Edward Davidson, Andrew Delbanco, John Demos, Everett Emerson, Wendy Martin, Harrison Meserole, Robert Middlekauf, Perry Miller, Karen Rowe, Jeanne Favret-Saada, Daniel Shea, Kenneth Silverman, Alden T. Vaughan, and Larzar Ziff. I am also grateful for the support of friends, colleagues, and staff members of the English departments of Princeton and the University of California, Riverside, and to the members of my 1988 NEH Summer Seminar for their encouragement. I have appreciated the patience and help of Andrew Brown and Julie Greenblatt of Cambridge University Press, and of Elizabeth Maguire, formerly of Cambridge Press, and the confidence and suggestions of Sacvan Bercovitch and his associate editor, Cyrus Patell. As always, my wife, Georgia, provided intellectual and emotional support, and my children, Scott, Mark, Matthew, Constance, and Laura, cheerfully indulged me over many years in my preoccupation with the people and events of another time and place.

Emory Elliott

BRITISH-AMERICAN BELLES LETTRES

Although my account of British-American belles lettres owes an obvious debt to the scholarship of the persons named in the final paragraph of the section, there are influences that may not be readily apparent and that require notice. For instance, the emphasis given institutions of literary conversation owes much to Jürgen Habermas's argument concerning the central place of coffeehouses, clubs, and the republic of letters in *The Structural Transformation of the Public Sphere*. Peter Clark's work on sociability, Lawrence Klein's investigations of politeness, and Richard Bushman's explorations of gentility have instructed my readings of belles lettres as texts designed for social pleasure. Likewise, Dena Goodman's ongoing work on French salon culture greatly aided my understanding of the institutions of women's writing and conversation in British America. The path-breaking scholarship of Pattie Cowell and Carla Mulford establishing a canon of colonial women's writings is the precondition for any informed comment on the subject. My sense of British-American literature as a subject owes a good deal to the critical writings of William Spengemann.

As Samuel Foster Haven Fellow at the American Antiquarian Society, I explored the relationship of manuscript communications and print; the findings presented here should be regarded as an exercise in the new deontological history of the book advocated by David D. Hall and Michael Warner.

A National Endowment for the Humanities summer research grant enabled me to undertake archival work on Lewis Morris II and Robert Bolling. The American Philosophical Society supplied a grant to research the career and writings of Archibald Home. The Citadel Development Foundation supplied travel funds for work on Elizabeth Graeme Fergusson, James Kirkpatrick, and George Ogilvie.

I thank Robert Ferguson, J. A. Leo Lemay, Wilson Somerville, Philip Gura, and Cathy Davidson for reading and commenting on drafts of this study. I particularly thank Carla Mulford for her scrupulous critique of its argument.

Henry Brooke's manuscript poems, "A Discours on Je'sting" and "The New Metamorphosis," are quoted courtesy of the Historical Society of Pennsylvania. They appear in "Commonplace Book," Peters Collection, Historical Society of Pennsylvania.

Captain Thomas Walduck's letter of 12 November 1710 to James Petiver, Sloane MS 2302, British Library, is excerpted courtesy of the Trustees of the British Library.

Selections from "Poems on Several Occasions by Archibald Home. Esqr.

late Secretary, and One of His Majestie's Council for the Province of New Jersey: North America" are printed courtesy of the Trustees of the University of Edinburgh (Laing Manuscripts III, 452, University of Edinburgh Library).

I thank Robert Micklus for permission to quote extensively from his edition of Alexander Hamilton, *The History of the Ancient and Honourable Tuesday Club,* 3 vols. (Chapel Hill: University of North Carolina Press; Institute of Early American History and Culture, 1990).

Lewis Morris's political verse, taken from "Misc. Prose and Verse," Robert Morris Papers, is printed courtesy of Special Collections and Archives, Rutgers University Archives.

Joseph Green's letter to Captain Benjamin Pollard, 7 June 1733, Smith-Carter Papers, appears courtesy of the Massachusetts Historical Society.

Robert Bolling's "Occlusion," Collection, Br[ock] 163, appears courtesy of the Huntington Library.

Elizabeth Graeme's "The foregoing song answered by a young Lady," Juvinilia Poemata, Manuscript 13494Q, is printed courtesy of the Library Company of Philadelphia.

I thank Pattie Cowell for her permission to print the extensive quotation from Susanna Wright's verse epistle to Elizabeth Norris, "Womenkind Call Reason to Their Aid," *Signs* 6, no. 4 (1981): 800.

The Historical Society of Pennsylvania has granted permission to print Susanna Wright's "Lines written . . . in the year 1726," J. Watson Notebook, Ms Am 307, 510.

I thank Carla Mulford for permission to quote the text of Annis Boudinot Stockton's "To the Visitant," from the forthcoming edition of *The Poetry of Annis Boudinot Stockton* (Newark: New Jersey Historical Society).

David S. Shields

THE AMERICAN ENLIGHTENMENT, 1750–1820

In writing my section of this history in the present tense, I ask you to enter into a particular awareness of history as subject and as enterprise. "Presentism" is a term that historians often use to denigrate a misleading application of contemporary standards to the past, and the warning is a real one; the dangers of inappropriate application always remain with us. My own use, however, reaches for another reality. Whatever the dangers, the imposition of the present on the past is also an unavoidable construct – so unavoidable that it is well for writer and reader to recall that limitation together.

Contemporary appropriations of the American Revolution occur in every era. That is what it means, at least in part, to have a legacy. But if the Revolution changes with each succeeding generation, acknowledgment of this fact does not release the historian — even the historian as literary critic — into a realm of unbounded speculation. Indeed, the hazards of an inevitable ahistoricism should force writer and reader back upon the joined integrity and volatility of primary materials. In this sense, use of the present tense signifies both the slippage in any necessary ordering of the past and the sometimes contradictory impulse to recover history in the making.

Literary history in particular welcomes the present. It dwells upon extant texts, and I try to use the analytical convention to reach for more of the original excitement that revolutionary texts provoked. Not fixed accomplishment but the messiness of ongoing event and the related immediacies of thought and act drive the often hesitant language of the period. The now arcane genres of sermon, pamphlet, and public document — not to mention the forgotten placards of ritualized protests — are fluid forms evolving under immense cultural pressure, not rigid envelopes in a static discourse.

What do we really know about the Revolution? First and foremost, we have the writings, the related texts, and other artifacts of those figures who participated in and witnessed events. Second, we have the so-called facts gathered about those events, then and later. Third, we have the contested ground of the history of interpretation regarding the period and its thought, and fourth, we have what might more generally be called the history of ideas. Like every scholar, I seek to combine the four elements in effective and graceful ways, and I try to do so with the many previous approaches to this cumulative record in mind. My contributions to the bibliography at the end of this volume provide a partial record of my indebtedness. At the same time, and in a competing goal, I mean to remind you of uneasy simplifications in the combinations themselves. The past is always more complicated than we can know. The most basic primary text glosses underlying incident, and each new layer of writing contributes to the studied appearance of history.

I try to entertain these difficulties within several recognitions. Current awareness of cultural diversity makes this a good moment for reexamining national origins. Then, too, the writings and speeches of the period are in themselves more rhetorically complex and more fully available to critical consciousness than many have realized. I believe that we are still learning how to read the basic texts of the Revolution and that the need for scrutiny now is all the more engaging because of growing intellectual awareness of a dialectics in Enlightenment thought. This scrutiny, in turn, benefits from a singular piece of national good fortune: the federal union begins in a moment when Americans take ideas seriously — not always the case in its history. If this study opens any of these ideas to fresh inquiry for others, it will have served its most important purpose.

In the community of scholars, five have been more than communal during the course of this project. Ann Douglas and Richard Posner read and commented with care on parts of the manuscript. My immediate collaborator Michael T. Gilmore made important suggestions throughout. John Paul Russo and Priscilla Parkhurst Ferguson tested every word more than once. Separate but together, they made as fine a committee of correspondence as one could hope for.

I have been helped, as well, by the chance to place some rudimentary thoughts for this project in print, where other scholars have been able to comment and improve upon them. These items, for which I thank the editors and publishers, include: " 'We Hold These Truths': Strategies of Control in the Literature of the Founders," *Reconstructing American Literary History*, ed. Sacvan Bercovitch (Cambridge, Mass.: Harvard University Press, 1986), 1–29; "Ideology and the Framing of the Constitution," *Early American Literature* 22 (Fall 1987): 157–65; " 'We Do Ordain and Establish': The Constitution as Literary Text," *William and Mary Law Review* 29 (Fall 1987): 3–25; and " 'What is Enlightenment?' Some American Answers," *American Literary History* 1 (Summer 1989): 245–72.

Robert A. Ferguson

THE LITERATURE OF THE REVOLUTIONARY AND EARLY NATIONAL PERIODS

My contribution to the Cambridge History focuses on the flowering and decline of civic humanism in the development of American culture between the Revolution and the 1820s. This perspective derives from the writings of historians and literary critics who see the republican period as originary of our modern world but also as fundamentally different from the liberal and Romantic ethos that crystallized in the nineteenth century. Among the scholars who have strongly influenced my argument, I would like to single out Gordon Wood, J. G. A. Pocock, William Charvat, Cathy Davidson, Michael Warner, and Benedict Anderson. The rich work on the origins of the novel form, both in England and America, has been particularly important to my understanding of early national literature. In addition to Davidson's work, I wish to acknowledge the scholarship of Lennard Davis, Nancy Armstrong, and Michael McKeon. Other valuable sources – and there have been many – are listed in the bibliography. As the reader will discover, I often disagree with the conclusions of the scholars who preceded me, but I could not have written this section of the History without their pioneering investigations.

It has taken a very long time for this project to see the light, and I have accumulated many debts along the way. The manuscript was read in its entirety by Sacvan Bercovitch and Robert Ferguson; their comments led to essential revisions that gave the book its final shape. Two former colleagues at Brandeis, Allen Grossman and Anne Janowitz, acted as sounding boards for my ideas and provided penetrating critiques of several chapters. Individual chapters also benefited from the advice of Cecelia Tichi, Kenneth Silverman, Amy Lang, Donald Pease, Robert Gross, Brook Thomas, Ivy Schweitzer, Winfried Fluck, Andrew Delbanco, Eugene Goodheart, and Michael Mc-Keon. Present and former graduate students kept me on my toes by challenging and refining interpretations I first ventured in their presence. Chief among them are Steve Hamelman, Jim Keil, Ute Groenig, Marc Woodworth, Kim Hamilton, and Grant Rice. I am grateful to all these friends and colleagues; none bears any responsibility for my errors of fact and judgment.

A grant from the American Council of Learned Societies in 1987–8 enabled me to complete an initial draft, and I am thankful for the support.

On a more personal level, I owe thanks to my wife, Deborah Valenze, who supported me emotionally as well as intellectually during the years I worked on this book. She read every word, shared my excitement, and endured my frustrations. I know my prose is more lucid and accessible for her disciplining insights, my spirit more whole and resilient for her love. In the case of my two daughters, Emma and Rosa, the frustrations on their part far outweighed the satisfactions. I hope they will forgive the times when I was unavailable for outings. Their love too sustained me through the writing.

I finished revising this book not long after learning that my father had terminal cancer. His courage and relish for life, even in the face of death, were unforgettable. I dedicate this part of the Cambridge History to his memory.

Michael T. Gilmore

INTRODUCTION

THIS MULTIVOLUME *History* marks a new beginning in the study of American literature. The first *Cambridge History of American Literature* (1917) helped introduce a new branch of English writing. *The Literary History of the United States,* assembled thirty years later under the aegis of Robert E. Spiller, helped establish a new field of academic study. Our *History* embodies the work of a generation of Americanists who have redrawn the boundaries of the field and redefined the terms of its development. Trained in the 1960s and early 1970s, representing the broad spectrum of both new and established directions in all branches of American writing, these scholars and critics have shaped, and continue to shape, what has become a major area of modern literary scholarship.

Over the past three decades, Americanist literary criticism has expanded from a border province into a center of humanist studies. The vitality of the field is reflected in the rising interest in American literature everywhere, nationally and internationally, and at every level – in high schools and colleges, in graduate programs, in publications, conferences, and public events. It is expressed in the sheer scope of scholarly activity and in the polemical intensity of debate. Virtually every recent school of criticism has found not just its followers here but many of its leading exponents. And increasingly over the past three decades, American texts have provided the focus for inter- and cross-disciplinary investigation. Gender studies, ethnic studies, and popular-culture studies, among others, have penetrated to all corners of the profession, but their single largest base is American literature. The same is true with regard to controversies over multiculturalism and canon formation: the issues are transhistorical and transcultural, but the debates themselves have turned mainly on American books.

We need not endorse all of these movements, or any one of them entirely, to see in the activity they have generated the dynamics of intellectual growth. Nor need we obscure the hard facts of intellectual growth – startling disparities in quality, a proliferation of jargons, and the mixed blessings of the new, innovation and mere trendiness entwined – to recognize the benefits in this case for literary and cultural study. However we situate ourselves in current

I

polemics, it seems clear that Americanist literary criticism has proved to be a forerunner of developments in other humanistic disciplines, precisely through its openness to diversity and debate. And for much the same reason, American literature has become something of a new-found–land for teaching and research. In addition to publishing massive new editions of the nation's literary classics, scholars have undertaken an unprecedented recovery of neglected and undervalued bodies of writing. We know far more now than ever before about what some have termed (in the plural) American literatures, a term grounded in the persistence in the United States of different traditions, different kinds of aesthetics, even different notions of the literary.

These developments have substantially enlarged the meanings as well as the materials of American literature. For this generation of critics and scholars, American literary history is no longer the history of a certain, agreed-upon group of American masterworks. Nor is it any longer based upon a certain, agreed-upon historical perspective on American writing. The quests for certainty and agreement continue, as they must, but they proceed now within a climate of critical decentralization – of controversy, competition, and, at best, dialogue among different voices, different frames of explanation.

This scene of conflict has been variously described in terms of liberal–democratic process, of the marketplace, and of professionalization. In any case it signals a shift in structures of academic authority. The practice of literary history hitherto, from its inception in the eighteenth century, has depended upon an established consensus about the essence or nature of its subject. Today the invocation of consensus sounds rather like an appeal for compromise, or like nostalgia. What used to be a relatively clear division between criticism and scholarship, aesthetic and historical analysis, has blurred and then subdivided over and over again (in various combinations) into a spectrum of special interests: special branches of expertise, special kinds of investment in the materials, and special modes of argument and strategies of persuasion.

In our times, in short, the study of American literary history defines itself in the plural, through volatile focal points of a multifaceted scholarly, critical, and pedagogic enterprise. Authority in this context is a function of different but connected bodies of knowledge. The authority of difference, if it may be so termed, resides in the critic's appeal to a particular constituency, in his or her command over a particular range of materials (with their distinctive set of authorities), and in the integrative force of his or her approach. The authority of connection lies in the capacity of a particular explanation or approach to engage with, challenge, or reinforce others – in its capacity, that is, to gain substance and depth in relation to other, sometimes complementary, sometimes conflicting modes of explanation.

This new *Cambridge History of American Literature* claims authority on both counts, individual and collaborative. In a sense, this makes it representative not only of the profession it speaks for but of the culture it describes. Our *History* is fundamentally pluralist: a federated histories of American literatures. It is also an expression of ongoing debates within the profession about cultural patterns and values, including those of liberal pluralism. Accordingly, an adversarial thread runs through a number of these narratives, and it marks the *History's* most traditional aspect. The high moral stance it assumes – literary analysis as the grounds for resistance, alternative vision, or relative detachment – is implicit in the very definition of art we have inherited from the Romantic era through the genteel critics. The earlier, consensual view of literature upheld the universality of ideals embodied in great books. By implication, therefore, and often by direct assault upon social norms and practices, it fostered a broad aesthetic oppositionalism – a celebration of literature (in Matthew Arnold's words) as the criticism of life, whether in formalist terms, as in the New Critics' assault on industrial society, or in the utopian forms of left-wing cultural critique.

What distinguishes our *History* in this respect is its variety of adversarial approaches and, more strikingly, the presence throughout of revisionary, nonoppositional ways of relating text and context. One result is the emphasis on nationality as a problem. "America" in these volumes designates the United States, or the territories that were to become part of the United States; and although several of our authors adopt a comparatist framework, by and large their concerns center upon the writing in English in this country – "American literature" as it is commonly understood here and abroad in its national implications. Nonetheless, the term "American" is neither a narrative premise in these volumes nor an objective background. Quite the reverse: it is the complex subject of a series of literary–historical inquiries. "America" is a historical entity, the United States of America. It is also a declaration of community, a people constituted and sustained by verbal fiat, a set of universal principles, a strategy of social cohesion, a summons to social protest, a prophecy, a dream, an aesthetic ideal, a trope of the modern ("progress," "opportunity," "the new"), a semiotics of inclusion ("melting pot," "patchwork quilt," "nation of nations"), and a semiotics of exclusion, closing out not only the Old World but all other countries of the Americas, north and south, as well as large groups within the United States. A nationality so conceived is a rhetorical battleground.

Precisely, then, by retaining the full range of its familiar meanings, these volumes make "America" intrinsic to the *literary* history of the United States. The matter of nationhood here becomes a focal point for exploring the two most vexed issues today in literary studies: the historicity of the text and the textuality of history.

Another result of narrative diversity is the emphasis on history as the vehicle of critical revision. This is the emphasis, too, not coincidentally, of our cultural moment. At no time in literary studies has awareness of history – or more accurately, theorizing about history – been more acute and pervasive. It is hardly too much to say that what joins all the special interests in the field, all factions in our current critical dissensus, is an overriding interest in history: as the ground and texture of ideas, metaphors, and myths; as the substance of the texts we read and the spirit in which we interpret them. Even as we acknowledge that great books, a few configurations of language raised to an extraordinary pitch of intensity, transcend their time and place (and even if we believe that their enduring power offers a recurrent source of oppositionalism), it is evident upon reflection that concepts of aesthetic transcendence are themselves time-bound. Like other claims to the absolute, from ancient religion to modern science, the claims of aesthetics are shaped by history. We grasp their particular forms of transcendence (the aesthetics of divine inspiration, the aesthetics of ambiguity, subversion, and indeterminacy) through an identifiably historical consciousness.

The same recognition of contingency extends to the writing of history. Some histories are truer than others; a few histories are invested for a time with the grandeur of being "definitive" and "comprehensive"; but all are narratives conditioned by their historical moments. The claims for total description harden (because they conceal) the limitations of history: local biases, temporal assumptions, and vested interests that at once compel and circumscribe our search for absolutes. The interplay of narratives enables us to make use of such limitations in ways that open both literature and history to further and fuller inquiry. One way leads through the discovery of differ-ence: the interruptions and discontinuities through which literary history unfolds. Another way leads through the acknowledgment of connection: the shared anxieties, interests, and aspirations that underlie our perceptions of those conflicts and so impose a certain cohesion (professional, intellectual, and generational) upon difference itself.

These considerations have guided the choice of the particular format for this *History*. All previous histories of American literature have been either totalizing or encyclopedic. They have offered either the magisterial sweep of a single vision or a multitude of terse accounts that come to seem just as totalizing, if only because the genre of the brief, expert synthesis precludes the development of authorial voice. Here, in contrast, American literary history unfolds through a polyphony of large-scale narratives. Each of them is ample enough in scope and detail to allow for the elaboration of distinctive views (premises, arguments, analyses); each of them, therefore, is persuasive by demonstration (rather than by assertion) and hence authoritative in its own right; and each is related to the others through common themes and concerns.

The authors were selected first for the excellence of their scholarship and then for the significance of the critical communities informing their work. Together, they demonstrate the achievements of Americanist literary criticism over the past three decades. Their contributions to these volumes speak to continuities as well as disruptions between generations. They give voice to the wide range of materials now subsumed under the heading of American literature. They express the distinctive sorts of excitement and commitment that have led to the extraordinary expansion of the field. And they reflect the diversity of interests that constitutes literary studies in our time and that may be attributed in part to the ethnographic diversity (class background, ethnic group, and racial origin) that has come to characterize literature faculties since World War II, and especially since the 1960s.

The same qualities inform this *History*'s organizational principles. Its flexibility of structure is meant to accommodate the varieties of American literary history. Some major writers appear in more than one volume, because they belong to more than one age. Some texts are discussed in several narratives within a volume, because they are important to different realms of cultural experience. Sometimes the story of a certain movement is retold from different perspectives, because the story requires a plural focus: from the margins as well as from the mainstream, for example, or as being equally the culmination of one era and the beginning of another. In all such instances, overlap is a strategy of multivocal description. The diversity of perspectives this yields corresponds to, as it draws upon, the sheer plenitude of literary and historical materials. It also makes for a richer, more intricate account of particulars (writers, texts, movements) than that available in any previous history of American literature.

Every volume in this *History* displays these different strengths in its own way. This volume is perhaps especially notable for its diversity of historical and cultural contexts.* Together the narratives span three centuries and an extraordinary variety of authors: Renaissance explorers, Puritan theocrats, Enlighten-

---

* These include various national and linguistic contexts: e.g., exploration narratives written in Spanish, in French, and in Portuguese, as well as in English. Some of these texts are known by their original titles (e.g., the *Diario* of Christopher Columbus), and in all such cases we have preserved the original. As a rule, however, titles have been translated, and the spelling, both in titles and quotations, has been modernized. We have also modernized the spelling in all colonial texts written in English.

ment naturalists, southern women of letters, revolutionary pamphleteers, and poets and novelists of the young Republic. Myra Jehlen draws upon the multilingual literature of exploration and colonization to tell the story of how America was invented, territorially, culturally, and figuratively – a story simultaneously of imperial expansion and imaginative appropriation. Emory Elliott traces the explosive, conflict-ridden development of the New England Way from its fractious beginnings through the tumultuous mid-eighteenth-century revivals. David S. Shields's focus is relatively narrow in time but rich in the materials it brings to light: newly uncovered collections of poems, essays, and letters that reveal a cosmopolitan network of neoclassical belles lettres extending from Philadelphia and New York to the salons of the Old South and Barbados. Robert A. Ferguson examines the interconnections between the many forms of discourse, popular and elite, secular and religious, private and public, that constituted the American Enlightenment and eventuated as the rhetoric of nationhood. Michael T. Gilmore describes a series of broad social and economic transformations – from republican to free-market ideology, oral to print culture, communal to individualist values – in the course of detailing the emergence of a national literary tradition.

All five narratives place the literature in international perspective; all five speak of its distinctively American characteristics, whether colonial, provincial, or national; and (in different ways) all of them demonstrate the centrality of language to the course of Americanization. This volume might be titled "A Key to the Languages of America." Jehlen treats the languages of discovery, exploration, and settlement. Significantly, these do not include the languages of indigenous peoples,* except by proxy – through Bible translations, ethnographic reports, and dictionaries for immigrants (as in Roger Williams's *Key* to the Narraganset language) – or indirectly, through what the fact of their silence implies. Jehlen discusses the implications in both cases, but mainly she focuses on the process by which the culture that triumphed arrogated the symbology of America to itself. Her narrative unfolds in a series of cross-cultural debates – each a hybrid of fact and metaphor, encounter and interpretation – from the European invention of America to the various colonial constructions of a New World identity and thence to the aesthetic–ideological strategies that transformed the discovery of otherness into a journey toward self-knowledge and cosmic origins. Her sources are as diverse as the colonial experience: commercial, scientific, historical, cartographical, epistolary, military, agricultural. Her method is a blend of ethnographic and stylistic analysis: a cultural close reading of a procession of

---

* The proper designation for these peoples has been a matter of controversy. We have adopted the terms "Indian," "American Indian," and "Native American" as alternative designations.

representative books, from Thomas Harriot's illustrated travelogue of 1590 through major works by William Bartram and William Byrd, which (she shows) deserve to be studied as founding texts of the American imagination.

The terms of Elliott's approach are implicit in his opening scene. He begins with the confused Salem trials, rather than with the mythic Great Migration. His Puritans are not Founding Fathers but a community in crisis, internally splintered over the meaning of witchcraft — rich against poor, men against women, insider against outsider, one generation against the next, laypeople against clergy, and one clerical group against another — each faction aspiring to political power through the ritual control of language. Elliott traces the zigzag "errand" of a would-be utopia that was fragmented from the start and recurrently in danger of disintegration but that held together, and flourished, through the capacity of its leaders to negotiate between a changing set of realities and a dominant discourse they developed of covenant and destiny. That development is manifest in different, sometimes contradictory ways in Puritan writing. As Elliott proceeds through the generic forms — history, personal narrative, poetry, public exhortation — he draws out the complexities of a literature designed for crisis, nourished by anxiety and doubt, and alternately challenging the status quo and reinforcing social structures. His narrative covers the wide spectrum of literary, theological, and political issues this entailed, including issues of race and gender in early New England (for the first time in a literary history) and issues of current scholarly debate. The result is a double perspective on the period: first, a guide to the interpretation of American Puritanism; and then, more largely, an analysis of the interpretive processes through which the Puritans forged their vision of America out of the discordant (and finally uncontrollable) materials of colonial experience.

Elliott gives new drama and depth to a traditional scholarly subject; Shields's history of British-American belles lettres is the first of its kind. "Belles lettres" before 1760 denoted specific modes of writing, which Shields defines and delineates, drawing on largely unknown and often unpublished materials. In the process he re-creates the surprisingly varied, though highly ritualized, "polite" world of colonial clubs and salons. Shields introduces a number of significant writers (Dr. Alexander Hamilton, Archibald Home, Elizabeth Graeme Fergusson, and many others); he outlines the transatlantic contexts of their "literature of social pleasure" (ease, wit, decorum, and agreeableness, as distinct from edification, revelation, or memorialization); and he traces the literature's wide-ranging political and institutional implications. The story that emerges tells of a particular group of men and women — exclusive in class and outlook, distinctive in their neoclassical style and their Loyalist sympathies — and so opens up a hitherto-neglected area of early Ameri-

can life and letters. Shields also sets their achievement in context and so
provides a model of thematic continuity with other narratives in this volume
through his discussion of regional differences, "feminine" and "masculine"
modes, religious versus secular traditions, oral vis-à-vis print culture, and
most broadly the ambiguities attendant upon a literature that was both colonial and colonizing, at once a "civilized" defense against a "savage" New World
and a shaping instrument of American identity.

Ferguson's subject is the multilayered language of Enlightenment and
revolution. Interweaving aesthetic and cultural concerns – explication de
texte with explications of broad patterns of thought and expression (intellectual, political, legal, religious) – he offers a sweeping reassessment of the
country's formative decades, from the Great Awakening through the constitutional debates, and from canonical works of the Founding Fathers (whose
literary achievement he illuminates anew) to the writings of their muted
Native American and African American "children." His narrative does justice to the plenitude of its materials. Indeed, one of its contributions is to
reveal their enormous volatility (as well as variety), so that even familiar
documents reappear as the embattled statements they once were, within a
dialectic of contending claims, part of a constant interplay among popular
idiom, historical event, and crafted text. Yet Ferguson shows their coherence
as well, through his sustained analysis of the dynamics of language and
power. Historians have often noted the importance of the word, written and
spoken, in the creation of the Republic. No one has demonstrated more
cogently than Ferguson does here the crucial function of rhetoric in consolidating the era's disparate traditions, influences, and impulses: the function of
silence in formulating consensus; the verbal appositions of protest and containment, uncertainty and affirmation; and the rhetorical complexities of
texture and tone through which diverse constituencies were mobilized and
religion and politics were made to correspond. This is a story of disruption
and change that builds upon the linguistic strategies connecting pre- and
postrevolutionary America. Equally, it is a history of literary continuities
that evokes the multifarious voices of a nation born in the act of revolt.

Gilmore's narrative concerns the imaginative writing of the early Republic. The organization, appropriately, is by genre (magazines, drama, poetry,
the novel) and major authors (Charles Brockden Brown, Washington Irving,
and James Fenimore Cooper). Within this traditional framework, Gilmore
presents a radical reinterpretation of the literature, one that sets the mainstream in dialogue with the margins (women, minorities, dissidents) and
that brings the dialogue to life by demonstrating its centrality to a momentous cultural transition. The nation's first imaginative literature, he shows,
was grounded in republican thought: an ideal of public service, an emphasis

on self-denial and the common good, a civic and communal ethos that stood opposed to the basic forms (as we have come to know them) of modern professional authorship. But republican culture also carried in it the tendencies of a new era: Romantic subjectivity, the values of laissez-faire, the self-interest of a market economy. Once independence was secured, the language of liberal individualism – stressing self-expression above public concerns, the novel over the drama, print rather than oral culture – gradually eclipsed the allegiances of the past. Gilmore not only records that transformation but uncovers and accounts for the literary–historical dynamics of change. His analysis recasts the very terms of early American aesthetics. It sets out the distinctive qualities of the literature, in its full range and vitality, clarifies its differences from the literature that followed, and suggests its abiding influence on the national imagination.

Gilmore's narrative is a model of critical and scholarly recovery. And the same may be said of the other four narratives in this volume. They restore for us the formative languages of what became the United States of America, the separate but interrelated discourses of colonization and figural prophecy, of Enlightenment, revolutionary, and republican letters. Together, they offer a compelling and, for our time, comprehensive re-vision of the literary importance of early American history and the historical value of early American literature.

THE LITERATURE OF COLONIZATION

Myra Jehlen

THE PAPERS OF EMPIRE

O N THE EVE of leaving the known world to circle the globe in quest of an empire, Christopher Columbus decided to write a book. His decision foretold an important link between writing and colonizing, a link that entailed a redefinition of writing and of its relation to both the writer and history. That redefinition is the subject of this first, introductory chapter. In appropriating the New World, Europeans expropriated millions of prior inhabitants, and Chapter 2 interrogates the difficulties involved in recovering the historical substance of that expropriation today. The remaining five chapters seek to understand how the writing of books entered into the process of the conquest. Each chapter reads selected works very closely for what they reveal of the terms in which Europeans took possession of the New World, how they declared it new and yet timelessly theirs.

The emphasis throughout on the role of books and writing in the making of America does not imply a view that reality is the product of its telling. The literature of American colonization is a particular case characterized by its writers' conviction that writing could wield material power in shaping history. Only some thirty years separate the first printing of the Gutenberg Bible from Columbus's departure for the Canary Islands. In the late sixteenth century, the activities of writing and of publishing began to assume unprecedented social and political importance, and an assumption of new powers is evident in all the texts treated here. John Smith's tracts and histories intend to alter policies that the captain finds confoundingly resistant to more direct intervention. Thomas Harriot rushes out his *Brief and True Report* to ensure the continuation of the Virginia colony. William Bradford in his history hopes to control the future as well as to interpret the past. William Byrd's book walks the metes and bounds of the state of Virginia, enlarging the author's holdings in the process. Thomas Jefferson advises Meriwether Lewis and William Clark that their journals are as important or more important than their actual expedition, and that in the event of a threat to their own return, the journals should be sent back by a safer route. All along, the observation that the Indians do not have their own system of writing seems to these prolific writers to be a definitive sign that the American natives do not have a right to the land.

By the end of the colonial period, a literature of colonization has not only inscribed but helped to forge the identification of the Europeans with the continent. The word has been made land.

❦

Columbus described his resolution to write his way across the ocean in the prologue to the book whose most reliable recent edition is entitled the *Diario of Christopher Columbus's First Voyage to America*. Addressing his royal patrons, King Ferdinand and Queen Isabella of Spain, Columbus explains that to "carry out that which you had commanded me to do" (which is "to reach the Indies and give your Highnesses' message to those princes"), "for this purpose I thought of writing on this whole voyage, very diligently, all that I would do and see and experience, as will be seen further along." In the wake of many such decisions as Columbus's, it came to seem self-evident, especially to students of literature, that events fulfill themselves in their representation. It may thus take a second reading to recognize that the explanation Columbus offers hardly follows. "For this purpose," he writes, of reaching India and bringing it the message of Christianity, "I thought of writing." But how will writing about it advance the voyage to the Indies?

Navigation certainly requires a log and one can understand how a supplemental journal would also be practical. But keeping a log is a matter of course that goes unmentioned among the enterprises of the voyage listed in the prologue; and Columbus clearly does not envisage the proposed *Diario* as any kind of supplement. It is to be by itself a complete account of everything that transpires, a record of "all that I would do and see and experience," a narrative containing the voyage whole, plus the consciousness of its captain. The *Diario* will not be an ordinary diary listing events for easier recall but an account encompassing both events and their meaning. Indeed, the journal will actually contain more of the voyage than could be observed empirically. In the prologue, the *Diario* proposes another holistic representational project, a new sailing chart, upon which "I will locate all of the sea and the lands of the Ocean Sea in their proper places under their compass bearings." And "moreover," having drawn up this chart, I will "compose a book and similarly record all of the same in a drawing." The prologue of the *Diario* closes on this promise that the voyage to the Indies will produce *books*.

More precisely, the promise is that the *voyage's captain* will produce books, for both *Diario* and sailing chart are Columbus's projects exclusively. But this observation further complicates the question of why Columbus thought a book would contribute to the Indies mission. The *Diario* prologue seems not only surprisingly oriented toward representation instead of action but also rather personal to be introducing a narrative of global exploration.

The most famous account before Columbus of Europeans discovering other lands (Columbus read it carefully and took guidance from it upon first arriving in the New World) is by contrast quite impersonal. Marco Polo (1254?–1324?) appears in the prologue to his *Travels* (1298) only to testify to their objective, uninflected authenticity. "And all who read the book or hear it may do so with full confidence, because it contains nothing but the truth"; Marco Polo has either seen what he reports with his own eyes or heard about it "from men of credit and veracity." The exotic facts and events reported in the *Travels* are not fictional. Marco Polo, who has known more "of the various parts of the world" than any "man, Christian or Pagan, Tartar or Indian, or of any race whatsoever," "from the time when our Lord God formed Adam our first parent with His hands down to this day," offers only to convey the fruits of his explorations. He is himself precisely not a writer (in fact he dictated the work from notes) but a transmitter of knowledge.

As a travel reporter, Columbus has a shorter pedigree and a longer program. He promises to record "all that I would do and see and experience," a tripling of knowledge that also defines it much more actively. For Marco Polo, knowledge is a collection of wares brought back from the Orient; for Columbus, it is clear already in the *Diario,* no observation will ever be so impersonal. Thus in the four *Letters* (1493, 1494, 1498, 1503) he wrote after each of his voyages, Columbus's own presence is usually in the forefront of any scene he describes or facts he recounts. Whereas Marco Polo seems to assume that in books as in goods, the appeal of the foreign lies in its strangeness, and that therefore curiosities should be presented as starkly as possible, Columbus mediates virtually every description.

After its testimonial prologue, Polo's narrative is at once outbound: "Let me begin with Armenia." Columbus's first letter, on the other hand, opens not with a first sight of the New World but with himself and his own achievement: "Knowing that it will afford you pleasure to learn that I have brought my undertaking to a successful termination," he writes to the lord treasurer of Spain, "I have decided upon writing you this letter to acquaint you with all the events which have occurred in my voyage." In large measure, no doubt, the difference in the authors' circumstances can explain their different openings. Whereas Marco Polo writes long after his travels and is under no personal obligation, Columbus is sending a report to his employer and naturally moves at once to establish his own success. Still, the unremitting emphasis on what he has done and what reaction this should elicit from the reader is striking: "Thirty-three days after my departure from Cadiz I reached the Indian sea, where I discovered many islands, thickly peopled."

He goes on to render the islands and peoples encountered, though here glimpsed for the first time by any European, ancillary to the scene of his own activities.

In short, the center of the account lies not so much in the world out there as in the drama of Columbus's exploration. One of the islands was "so large and apparently without termination, that I could not suppose it to be an island, but the continental province of Cathay." So far, however, this Cathay has proven disappointing, containing "no towns or populous places on the sea coast, but only a few detached houses and cottages, with whose inhabitants I was unable to communicate." All in all, this conveys a rather negative first image, the New World appearing to lack interesting features of its own and deriving its animation rather from its explorer's movements. Marco Polo's accounts, on the other hand, are always positive because his ambition is first to interest us. Unpleasant conditions make as good reading as pleasant ones: since we do not expect to take possession of Armenia, its "extremely enervating climate" does not lessen its value as a foreign scene, although Polo observes that as a result, "the nobility of the country, who used to be men of valour and stalwart soldiers, are now craven and mean-spirited and excel in nothing except drinking."

Columbus's *Letter* does shortly grow more enthusiastic. But its praises are as tellingly different from Marco Polo's as its disappointments. Polo dwells on the exotic, whether in nature, like the "small animal . . . with thick hair like that of a deer, the feet and tail of a gazelle, no horns, but four slender teeth . . . about the length of three fingers, two growing upwards and two down," from which musk is derived, or in civilization, as in the magnificent palaces built by Kubilai Khan "reared on gilt and varnished pillars, on each of which stands a dragon, entwining the pillar with his tail and supporting the roof on his outstretched limbs."

Marco Polo describes "curiosities"; Columbus focuses the reader's attention on *his* curiosity. By exclaiming over the extraordinary differences between everything in the Caribbean and everything at home, he makes the foreign relative and begins to domesticate it. "I saw many trees very different from ours," he writes in the *Diario,* with branches all different from one another, "so different that it is the greatest wonder in the world how much diversity there is between one kind and another." "Here the fish are so different from ours that it is a marvel." Once more:

[A]ll the trees are as different from ours as day from night; and also the fruits and grasses and stones and everything. It is true that some trees are of the same character as others in Castile; nevertheless, there was a very great difference. And the other trees of other kinds were so many that there is no one who can tell it or compare them with others of Castile.

Incomparable these trees may be, but they appear in Columbus's texts wholly in relation to Castilian trees. The terms of Columbus's descriptions continually translate differences into such "incomparable comparability": the largest of the Caribbean isles "is exceedingly fertile . . . ; it is surrounded with many bays, spacious, very secure, and surpassing any that I have ever seen." This island is graced with "seven or eight kinds of palm trees, which, like all the other trees, herbs, and fruits, considerably surpass ours in height and beauty." The incredible is a function of the expected: "The convenience and excellence of the harbours in this island, and the abundance of the rivers, so indispensable to the health of man, surpass anything that would be believed by one who had not seen it." This is the equivalent of Marco Polo's descriptions of prodigies no one else had ever seen, but the thrust of Columbus's claim, let alone its tone, is not the same. When Columbus describes the commodiousness of the Caribbean bays as "surpassing any that I have ever seen," he is not implying that the image should tax our credulity but that these are the best harbors available anywhere. In general, throughout his writings, Columbus's use of "surpassing" is as much measure as marvel.

Or rather, "surpassing" measures the marvelous and makes wonder into a comparative response; for Marco Polo, the marvelous begins on the far side of comparison. Of course, Polo also measures the incomparable. He is, after all, a merchant of the wonders he sees, a trader whose journeys have been undertaken for quantifiable profit. Early in his travels, Polo and his brother have the occasion to make a gift of many jewels to the prince of the Tartars, who "was exceedingly pleased with them, and gave them goods of fully twice the value in return." Economic value is certainly no less important to Marco Polo than to Columbus.

But they each define it differently. The sentence cited earlier in which Columbus tells his correspondent that he has discovered many islands, thickly peopled, continues, "of which I took possession without resistance in the name of our most illustrious Monarch." He then describes naming the many islands, an act that summarizes the difference between him and his predecessor. In no position to rename, Marco Polo on the contrary finds value, including economic value, in the bizarre, gorgeous names of the extraordinary beings he encounters and their cities: Kubilai Khan, Ghinghiz Khan, Kaidu; Erguiul, Karajang, Zar-dandan. Columbus does occasionally note an indigenous name – San Salvador, he reports, was originally Guanahani – but with neither pleasure nor profit. That the islands already have Indian names seems not to interest him; he incorporates the originals into his narrative only as he renames them.

For Columbus, in other words, value is realized in possession rather than in exchange, which is another way of saying that he was not a merchant like

Marco Polo but a colonizer. Marco Polo was a traveler in the thirteenth century in Asia, where there was generally no question of Europeans appropriating the territories they crossed but only of trading. Columbus at the end of the fifteenth century makes his first stop on the way to India at "Your Highnesses' Canary Islands" and has a proprietary attitude not only toward anonymous territories but even toward what he takes to be the sovereign "continental province of Cathay," which he promptly renames Juana. In fact, his first act on landing anywhere is to take possession. Fifteenth-century merchant–colonizers would appear, on the evidence of Columbus's *Letters,* to have developed a new sense of wealth and property. Marco Polo's interest in distant lands seems to lie in discovering them to be filled with exotic commodities he can trade; Columbus's interest lies in "discovering" them. Discovery means possession to him: he seeks not so much to trade *with* as to trade *in.*

Inherent in this new development is the connection Columbus asserts between carrying out the commands of his monarchs and writing very diligently. As defined by colonization, wealth is property, an intimate aspect of the national self. Columbus is setting out to enlarge the Spanish national self and he needs a way to define his stake in that enterprise. He has already bargained for any lands he discovers during the Atlantic crossing. But when wealth is an aspect of self rather than just an external acquisition, its possession not only grants but requires a more personal engagement. Columbus needs somehow to take possession of the voyage. Moreover, to secure imperial property takes constant vigilance. One defends such property as one's self. He repeatedly insists that he was himself present at the first steps in the making of Spain's empire and that his voyage is part of that process: "I saw the Royal Standards of Your Highnesses placed . . . on the towers of the Alhambra, . . . I saw the Moorish King . . . kiss the Royal Hands . . . ; and later in the same month [after having expelled all the Jews from all of your Kingdoms and Dominions] Your Highnesses commanded me to go . . . to India." This nervous flattery expresses Columbus's continuing uneasiness over how to protect his property in the voyage. The *Diario* is at once claim and contract.

The prologue appears to have been composed during the first stage of the voyage, the crossing from the seaport of Palos to the Canary Islands, whose conquest a few years earlier had been for Spain a sort of imperial trial run. From there Columbus would carry Spanish ambitions clear around the earth. The idea of going west to come east has implications beyond cartography; Columbus's route was a gesture that encompassed the world. It traced an image of universal hegemony that would still be invoked in the nineteenth century when the English boasted that the sun never set on their empire. In the fifteenth century, the westward journey to the East figured a coveted future, a telos in the midst of utmost contingency.

The *Diario* prologue sketches three trajectories for this telos: imperial, divine, and personal. The imperial is expressed in Spain's recent territorial repossessions and expansions. The divine is explicit in the voyage's official purpose, which is to bring Christian instruction to the "Grand Khan" of the Indies. The personal is implicit in Columbus's all-encompassing writing, which actually embraces and transcends both the other plans.

Through the *Diario*, Columbus thus arrogates for himself the teleological gesture of his voyage. "For this purpose," of doing what you have commanded me to do, Columbus writes, I will not only sail but also, as important, I will consummate my sailing in the production of a book. In this new context wealth involves possession, which in turn implies self-possession (though this aspect will not be fully articulated until much later in the life of the empire); writing, then, comes into its own as the appropriation of the world – in this case of the voyage around the world.

The prologue concludes with an image of the identity of the captain with the voyage and all its enterprises: "and above all," Columbus ends his address to the king and queen, "it is very important that I forget sleep and pay much attention to navigation in order thus to carry out these purposes, which will be great labor." This is a labor not only of guidance and observation but of consciousness. He will have to remain conscious throughout; he cannot sleep because his *consciousness, his* consciousness, is at the center of the enterprise. (Much later, off the Caribbean shore, Columbus admits to having succumbed to sleep, whereupon the *Santa María* ran aground and sank.)

❦

Columbus's *Diario* thus represents writing as a kind of action, and action as a form of personal representation. The literature of the New World – the literature of discovery, exploration, and colonization – is composed of just such books. The literary history of Europe's discovery of America is the story of a literature that sought to shape history. The texts depicting the first European landings and early settlements in the Americas are almost always self-conscious participants in the events they represent.

The prologue of the *Diario* hails the efforts of King Ferdinand and Queen Isabella to build a Spanish nation and associates Columbus's voyage with that endeavor. This is quite justified, for indeed the rise of nations was simultaneously a process of domestic consolidation and of foreign expansion. What links the two explicitly in the prologue is the projected *Diario*, which will bridge the distance between Spain and the colonies Columbus establishes. Obviously informed by the recent invention of the printing press, Columbus's book is in its self-description a tangible reality, real in itself and the embodiment of the connection between monarch and deputy and between nation and empire. The written word as here defined did not create nation and empire, but it was more than a catalyst in their genesis – it was an actual component.

As Columbus was setting sail, another petitioner approached the king and queen of Spain with a plan to forward the Christian empire by means of the printed word. Elio Antonio de Nebrija (1444?–1522) wished to have the Spanish monarchy endorse and make official throughout the nation his *Gramatica de la lengua Castellana* (A Grammar of the Castilian Language, 1492), the first systematic grammar of a European vernacular language. Nebrija was a classicist who ten years earlier had published a Latin grammar. Times were changing and Latin was losing its cultural hegemony. Instead, local vernaculars were proliferating, spread by the printing press. If Ferdinand and Isabella wanted to establish and maintain central control, they needed to control language. At one time, language had been the instrument of feudal subordination, but increasingly it was becoming linked to local autonomy. Columbus's *Diario,* which seeks to appropriate the world through language, and Nebrija's *Gramatica,* projecting a concept of language as a means of control, are companion texts forging the dialectic at the center of modern thought.

In 1492, books, nations, and empires were all three emerging cultures – an observation that suggests as a starting point for this history of the New World literature in English not any single piece of writing but a collective work itself representing the appearance of a new literary culture. In 1582, Richard Hakluyt (1552?–1616) resolved to do something about what he considered the English Crown's ill-considered neglect of the possibilities of the New World. Writing would be his instrument, but not necessarily his own writing and not any particular essays or papers but a critical mass of them, a corpus describing all that had been seen, done, and experienced (as Columbus would have put it) in relation to the New World. His compilations, beginning with the *Diverse Voyages Touching the Discovery of America* (1582; dedicated to Sir Philip Sidney) and especially the two editions of his *Principal Navigations, Voyages, Traffiques, and Discoveries of the English Nation* (1589–90 and 1598–1600), define a literary form that is as representative of the literature of America's discovery and colonization as the epic is of classical Greece or the novel is of nineteenth-century Europe.

In the preface to his *Diverse Voyages,* Hakluyt wondered impatiently why it was, "since the first discovery of America . . . after so great conquests and plantings of the Spaniards and Portingales there, that we of England could never have the grace to set fast footing in such fertile and temperate places, as are left as yet unpossessed by them." Seven years later in the dedication to the *Principal Navigations,* he was still complaining that everywhere he went in Europe he heard nations extolled for their wonderful discoveries, while all the talk England seemed to inspire was of "sluggish security." Such dismissive talk would have been particularly galling to Hakluyt, who, from 1582 to his death in 1616, was the premier publisher of explorers' reports, ships' logs, commercial agreements, travel narratives, maps, geographical disquisitions, overseas legal patents and deeds, sailors' diaries, New World scientific treatises, and transatlantic letters, both business and personal. To the documents he collected from his compatriots, moreover, he added those captured or stolen from the Portuguese, Spanish, and French. In short, Hakluyt compiled "the papers of empire." He kept the books during "the palmy days of profit," as John Maynard Keynes has dubbed the period when English merchants accumulated the vast fortunes that fueled their country's predominance in commerce and lasted down the centuries to propel its industrial revolution. The backers of Francis Drake's legendary privateering voyage received a return of 4,700 percent on their investment.

In this heady atmosphere, Hakluyt urged the queen to support more forays into the Americas and especially (with an eye to the inconstant fortunes of his friend Walter Raleigh) into the Virginia territories, where the "courageous increasing youth" of the country might, with the Crusades over, find employment for their overflowing energies. Virginia, the public-spirited publisher rhapsodized, was a "great and ample country . . . the inland whereof is found of late to be so sweet and wholesome a climate, so rich and abundant in silver mines, so apt and capable of all commodities" that even the Spanish competition, whose secret map Hakluyt claims to have just acquired, acknowledged therein that Virginia was "a better and richer country than Mexico and Nueva Spania itself." This combination of homage and avidity, of sensibility and greed, is inextricably and perhaps indistinguishably both propaganda and vision.

Yet for all his lyrical nationalism and visionary imperialism, Richard Hakluyt had never been to the New World and would never go. Master of arts and student at Christchurch, Oxford, Richard Hakluyt discovered America in a book. The dedicatory epistle to his most ambitious work, *Principal Navigations,* recalls this discovery for Francis Walsingham, the queen's high secretary in charge of foreign relations. One day Hakluyt entered the study of his cousin, who taught at the Inns of Court but was far more interested in the new geography than in the law, and found, lying open on a table, a number of volumes on cosmography and a world map. When the youth expressed curiosity, his cousin, also named Richard Hakluyt, "began to instruct my ignorance." The elder Hakluyt explained the map to the younger, delighting him with the wonders of "all the known seas, gulfs, bays, straits, capes, rivers, empires, kingdoms, dukedoms and territories of each part, with declaration also of their special commodities, and particular wants, which by the benefit of traffic and intercourse of merchants, are plentifully supplied." From the map, the two moved to the Bible. There "I read, that they which go down to the sea in ships, and occupy by the great waters, they see the works of the Lord, and his wonders in the deep, etc." Overwhelmed by the combination of cosmographical and biblical scripture, Hakluyt "resolved, if ever I were preferred to the University . . . I would by God's assistance prosecute that knowledge and kind of literature, the doors whereof . . . were so happily opened before me."

Everything about the anecdote epitomizes the double occasion: on the one hand, of the publication of the *Principal Navigations* and, on the other, of the dawn of the British Empire. Hakluyt's world geography places nature (seas, straits, and rivers) and politics (kingdoms and dukedoms) in the same category. The Bible stands on higher ground: it confirms the virtues of commerce, enjoining men to go down to the sea in ships and occupy the great waters as the proper worship of the Lord's works and His wonders. But Hakluyt has one further message, more self-serving and less self-aware. At the climax of the passage, when he resolves to dedicate his life to the great tasks of travel and trade, one expects, out of the very logic of the sentence, that he means at the first opportunity to go off to sea. No; he is going to read, write, and publish. The full title of the first volume of the *Principal Navigations* will suggest the reach that he envisioned for publishing: *The principal navigations, voyages, traffiques, and discoveries of the English nation made by sea and over-land, to the remote and farthest distant quarters of the earth, at any time within the compass of these 1500 years: divided into three several volumes, according to the positions of the regions whereunto they were directed. This first volume containing the worthy discoveries, etc., of the English toward the north and northeast by sea . . . together with many notable monuments and testimonies of the ancient foreign trades, and of the warlike and other shipping of this realm of England in former ages. Whereunto is annexed also a brief commentary of the true state of Iceland, and of the northern seas and lands situated that way. And lastly, the memorable defeat of the Spanish huge Armada, anno 1588, and the famous victory achieved at the city of Cadiz, 1596, are described.*

Knowledge and literature, Hakluyt believed, are equally and as actively engaged in the imperial enterprise as are ships and voyages. In fact, Hakluyt did not really distinguish between language and action. At Oxford, he tells Walsingham, he read everything he could find on discoveries and voyages and began lecturing, whereupon he met "the chiefest captains at sea, the greatest merchants, and the best mariners of our nation." Having obtained knowledge from these men of action, he spent five years in Her Majesty's service, where he "both heard in speech and read in books" that England was behind all other nations in her overseas enterprises. "Thus both hearing and reading the obloquy of our nation," he could not stand idly by but set about his monumental project of compiling an account of England's navigations. But "these voyages lay so dispersed, scattered and hidden in several huckster's hands, that I now wonder at myself, to see how I was able to endure the delays, curiosity, and backwardness of many from whom I was to receive the originals." "Voyage" stands for both deed and report; in the lengthening list of his publications, Hakluyt saw himself building an ever-larger empire.

The preface to the 1598 edition of the *Principal Navigations* makes the incarnation explicit. Having many years labored to preserve the exploits of the English nation from oblivion, he is once again publishing his "discourse" in order "to incorporate into one body the torn and scattered limbs of our ancient and late navigations by sea, our voyages by land, and traffics of merchandise by both." Complementing the real-life character of the book, its publisher is an intrepid traveler of real roads: "what restless nights, what painful days, what heat, what cold I have endured; how many long and chargeable journeys I have travelled; how many famous libraries I have searched into." All for England: "the honour and benefit of this Commonweal wherein I live and breathe, hath made all difficulties seem easy."

In a final dedication, written in 1600 to Robert Cecil (third volume, second edition), Hakluyt lays claim to the New World by disputing its new Italian name. The lands discovered by Christopher Columbus are "more commonly than properly called America," he grumbles. As for Spain, hitherto the major colonizer of this so-called America, its dominion at least in the West Indies is now materially undermined by the publication of all its secrets in this very volume. "There is no chief river, no port, no town, no city, no province of any reckoning in the West Indies that hath not here some good description thereof, as well for the inland as the sea coast." The New World no longer belongs to the Spaniards; Hakluyt's compilations have taken it over. The "Western Atlantis or America" has been won for England: "I humbly desire you," he asks Cecil, "to receive her with your wonted and accustomed favour at my hands."

A little more poetic than Hakluyt's usual diction, "Western Atlantis" advises us that he envisioned his collection to provide through his new history a new national identity. His decision to undertake the exhausting role of the empire's publisher was prompted, he always explained, by concern as much for England's reputation, or image, as for its material advancement. Indeed, in this regard, one could think of Hakluyt's work as the historical counterpart of Edmund Spenser's (1552?–99) epic poem *The Faerie Queene* (1580–96), which was also shaped by an imperial context; Spenser wrote while serving as the queen's deputy in Ireland, the first site of the English empire's expansion. Spenser reached back to the Middle Ages for the terms to inspire a new imperial nation; Hakluyt invoked lessons from everywhere but sometimes found his compatriots frustratingly unmoved by either lofty or homely examples. "We read," he tried once to reason, "that the Bees, when they grow to be too many in their own hive at home, are wont to be led out by their Captains to swarm abroad, and seek themselves a new dwelling place. . . . If the examples of the Grecians and Carthaginians of old time, and the practice of our age may not move us, yet [he pleaded] let us learn wisdom of these small weak and unreasonable creatures." The all-encompassing range of this sentence, which associates Hakluyt's imperial case with the classical past, the urgent present, and nature's eternal truths, represents both the form and the spirit of compilations. Gathering everything at hand, all the facts, pseudofacts, impressions, and inventions it can find, it constructs a universe. Hakluyt's sentence is organized by a vision that all the lands an Englishman or, more broadly, a European discovers "of equity and right appertain unto us" — an astonishing vision made banal only by its historical fulfillment.

At the close of the twentieth century and after the fall of the European empire, however, the audacity of Hakluyt's vision is reemerging. It no longer seems obvious that the English, the French, and the Spanish would naturally take possession of two continents on the other side of the world. And once the conquest of the Americas resumes something like its original status as the outcome of a war, it becomes evident, as Edmundo O'Gorman and others have put it, that America was not "discovered" but "invented" and that the political, economic, and cultural forms that have organized social life on the North American continent express, instead of the single transcendent purpose of Nature and Nature's God, a continually and violently disputed historical process. By the light of history, the former axioms of the discovery of America, beginning with the 1492 epiphany and culminating in the founding of the United States (which has always seen itself as representing America), have lost their air of inevitability. Historians of the colonial period now refer to the "conquest" of the New World and to the "construction" of America. And they have proceeded to interrogate the documents and stories of "discovery," not as records of fulfillment, but as components of a historical process. These documents and stories themselves participated in an "encounter" whose unfolding was so far from being a natural process that at times it unfolded first in the telling.

Hakluyt's volumes are the leading English examples of this literature of action, but compilations like his had appeared earlier in Germany and Italy. Indeed, Hakluyt's initial publishing act in 1579 or 1580 was to commission a translation of the account of two Jacques Cartier voyages included in Giovanni Battista Ramusio's (1485–1557) *Navigationi et viaggi* (Navigations and Voyages, 1550–9), a collection of firsthand narratives that served generally as his model. The dissemination of knowledge about the discovery was largely the work of such collections, for the individual reports of explorers were not widely distributed and generally disappeared. Moreover, many reports were translated into Latin for publication, thus further narrowing their audience, whereas the compilers for their part brought out vernacular translations. The collections not only made the reports available, they placed them cumulatively in relation to one another; they also placed them in an interpretive context provided explicitly in prefaces and introductions and implicitly by juxtapositions. Of course, all the prefaces and introductions argued the benefits and the rectitude of European expansion.

Appropriately, in the first compilation, the *Introduction to Cosmography* (*Cosmographiae introductio,* 1507), by the German Martin Waldseemüller, the discovery fulfills itself in a linguistic act of taking possession, and the New World receives a European name. Little was known and still less understood about the voyages of Columbus or of those who followed him until Waldseemüller obtained copies of Columbus's four *Letters* to Ferdinand and Isabella of Spain. From these letters and guided by the arguments of Amerigo (Americus) Vespucci's *Letter to Soderini* (written 1504, printed 1505; translated into Latin as *Quattuor Americi navigationes* and *Mundus Novus,* or *Epistola Alberici de Novo Nuovo*), Waldseemüller derived a map of Columbus's scattered islands represented for the first time as two continents. Then, in admiration for what he saw as Vespucci's superior grasp of the geographical situation, Waldseemüller inscribed the name "Ameraca" and "Amarca" over the southern continent. Gerardus Mercator (1512–94), the Flemish cartographer who in 1569 first produced a world map that could be used directly for navigation, extended this designation to the northern continent later in the century. (Not incidentally, the "Mercator projection," a device for representing the rounded globe by a grid of straight lines, encapsulates a fundamental transformation in the way the world is, at once, envisioned, experienced, and engaged.)

In the Mediterranean countries, Peter Martyr's (1455–1526) Latin *De orbe novo . . . decades octo,* mostly letters received by churchmen (written between 1494 and 1526 and translated into English as *The Decades of the New World* by Richard Eden in 1555), like Ramusio's three volumes, was a best-seller of the age. The compilers produced a critical mass of historical knowledge that generated a sense of movement, of motion through time as well as space. To suggest that imperialism was already a hallowed tradition, they gathered materials from the past as well as the present. Thus Ramusio, gathering in all the stuff of the age of colonization, went back to its prehistory to publish in 1553 his own edition of Marco Polo's *Travels*. Ptolemy's *Geography* was restored to the European library for the first time since antiquity in Pierre d'Ailly's 1410 compilation of cosmographical texts, *Imago mundi*. At the other end of the process, the last significant compilation, though not nearly as influential as the *Principal Navigations,* was its official successor: *Hakluytus Posthumus; or, Purchas His Pilgrimes,* published in 1625 by Samuel Purchas in part from papers Hakluyt had gathered for still another collection. The heir to the whole family of compilations, *Purchas* is an opulent twenty volumes.

§

Literary forms plot their home cultures. The form of the compilation plots a culture of acquisition and expansion but one in which the things acquired and desired are not fully ordered – a culture in motion but uncertain about its map. And, in fact, as the compilations were being assembled, significant changes in the very concept of mapping also emerged. In Columbus's day, there were two radically different kinds of map in use: *mappae mundi,* "world maps," and *portolani,* "sailing charts." World maps were theoretical and drawn according to an academic geography that had little to do with observation. The world this geography projected was philosophically organized, deduced sometimes from scientific law, sometimes from scripture, but only secondarily from actual survey. The portolans were drawn by sailors in the course of navigating; they were carried about and constantly altered on board ship and in the cafés and inns of seaports.

In the Bibliothèque Nationale in Paris, there is a double map called the Christopher Columbus Chart because it is believed, on not entirely reliable evidence, to have been put together in 1492 (see Figure 1). This Christopher Columbus Chart includes a mappa mundi and a portolan, both showing the Atlantic world extending down the coast of Africa and encompassing the Portuguese discoveries. The right-hand portolan sketches the Atlantic and the Mediterranean, bounded on the north by Norway, on the east by the Black Sea, and on the South by the mouth of the Congo. Besides a number of legendary islands, the portolan also locates major cities and identifies the principal products of each region (ostrich feathers in the Sahara, pepper in Guinea, and so on). The mappa mundi, on the left, shows the world surrounded by nine celestial spheres according to the contemporary, geocentric worldview. Africa – including the Cape of Good Hope (rounded in 1488) – appears along with a suggestive inscription to the effect that "the *mappa mundi,* although drawn on a plane, should be considered to be spherical." Juxtaposed but unintegrated, the right-hand portolan and the left-hand mappa mundi enact an allegory of their era, when historical change was so fundamental that it altered the very concept of geography, transforming it from a representation of abiding cosmic relations into a theater of human mobility and mutability.

Columbus, notoriously, denied to the day of his death that the lands he had come upon on his way to the East constituted a continent hitherto unknown to Europe. When it became impossible any longer to maintain that he had arrived in Asia, he produced a new claim that he had found the site of the earthly paradise. We might understand his extraordinary resistance to acknowledging himself a discoverer as a determined effort to retain an original vision of the world: in other words, as a refusal to read a sailing chart as a mappa mundi. Columbus was a sophisticated reader of maps. It is very likely that he used a globe, possibly the one made by Martin Behaim in 1492, which displayed the most current geographical knowledge according to maps produced in the late 1480s and early 1490s. He was fully adept at deciphering portolans as well as their global equivalents; he just did not accept them as mappae mundi.

One way to describe the philosophical and historical significance of Europe's discovery of America is as a fundamental shift in the meaning and use of maps. In their historical setting, the mappae mundi served their representational purpose without having to conform to the empirical facts depicted on portolans. On the other hand, the way historical change can compel paradigmatic transformations finds its negative example in the sea captain's refusal to abandon his conceptual map of the world for his chart.

The Italian explorer Amerigo Vespucci (1451–1512), in contrast, was not averse to admitting new lands onto his conceptual map. Less sea captain than entrepreneur, he was a well-educated Florentine merchant from a family prominent in the republican aristocracy. He had been selected from among his brothers to direct the family's commercial enterprises. Over the course of either two, three, or four voyages to the New World between 1497 or 1499 and 1504, he approached the impassable land mass we now call South America as a conceptual problem, something to figure out and that might lead to reconfigurations. His *Letter to Soderini* did not yet clearly separate the New World from Asia, but it already abandoned the principle that no large landmass outside those already known could possibly exist. And although he may have invented either one or two voyages to enlarge his role in the exploration of the New World, he did understand it was new. Two events thus epitomize this period of radical change: (1) Vespucci succeeded by proclaiming that the new lands implied a new globe, and (2) Columbus, defending the old globe and unable to fit his new continents onto it, died bitter and unrewarded.

In the sixteenth century, then, the compilation and the sailing chart were the texts, the representational forms, of an ascendant worldview. Their emer-

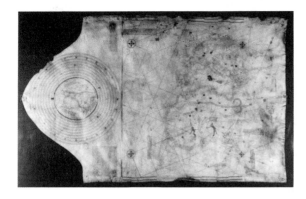

Figure 1. This combined *mappa-mundi* and portolan is commonly referred to as the "Christopher Columbus Chart" because it is believed to have been drawn up in 1492. See discussion in text, page 26.

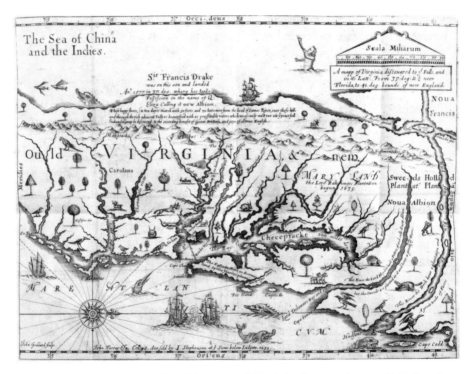

Figure 2. John Ferrar's 1651 "A mapp of Virginia discovered to ye Falls," published in the third edition of Edward Williams's *Virgo Triumphans: or Virginia Richly and Truly Valued* (London 1651), shows the Atlantic coast from Cape Cod to Cape Fear. Ferrar depicts in detail the coastal region and especially the waterways that may be followed inland – the Chesapeake Bay, the two branches of the Potomac, and the Hudson, which he shows flowing into the Pacific – but grows a little schematic when he approaches the mountains beyond. Past the mountains, however, he leaps back all the way to the terms of the mappae-mundi: "The Sea of China and the Indies" is right there, a mere "ten days march . . . from the head of the Jeames River."

Figure 3. John Mitchell's *Map of the British and French Dominions in North America,*
1755, was drawn up for the English Lords of Trade and Plantations to bolster British
territorial claims. Three features are especially interesting in our context. The first is
the pivoting of the axis of perspective since the Ferrar map drawn a century earlier.
Visually, the map of Virginia runs north–south, the eye traveling from the bottom of
the page, where European explorers land in America, up through the band of waterways to the mountains and out, back to the "Sea of China" and the route to the Indies.
Virginia is a rich find to be sure, a valuable bonus; but the main business remains as
Columbus defined it, to find a westward route to the Orient. One looks at the Mitchell
map rather from right to left. Moreover, its extension to the left and therefore the west
is exaggeratedly and indefinitely drawn out, suggesting the possibility of infinite
expansion. The colonial destination is no longer the Indies but America itself.

Empirical and practical, the Mitchell map understands the enterprise of representing the world altogether differently from the philosophical mappae-mundi. Still, lest
we forget that cartography, ancient or modern, not only depicts but interprets, there
are five islands on Mitchell's Lake Superior no one has ever seen. Robert W. Karrow,
Jr., a historian of cartography, has shown that Mitchell himself did not invent these
islands but that they surfaced on his chart intertextually, from other charts – a
caution against drawing too categorical a distinction between the mappae-mundi and
our modern maps.

One other aspect of Mitchell's map is evocative of the themes of this essay. Near
the Great Lakes is the following legend in print too small to read in this reproduc-
tion: "The Long and Barbarous Names lately given to Some of these Northern Parts
of Canada and the Lakes we have not inserted, as they are of no use, and uncertain
Authority." "Lately given" means given by the Indians of the region before the
coming of the Europeans.

gence represents in turn the development of a paradoxical new way of both being in the world and observing it. The paradox has to do with a new relation between being and observing, such that one's vision is more powerfully objective due to one's newly empowered subjectivity. Hakluyt's compilations strive above all for documentary validity and practicality. At the same time, however, the sponsors and lieutenants of America's discovery and colonization were also aggressively redefining their concept of the world to suit their notion of how it would be most profitably exploited. Masters of the portolan, they claimed the right also to redraw the mappa mundi in the image of a world they would remake.

The expression of this double ambition is an emerging style of writing whose dualism, even two-facedness, is veiled. This is the plain, reportorial, scientific style associated in its origin especially with the essays of Francis Bacon (1561–1626). These essays were addressed to aspiring young men much like those Hakluyt imagined colonizing the New World and offered analyses of concepts (like "riches" and "usury") that might illuminate their progress. To that end, the essays were written as plainly as possible, eschewing linguistic ornamentation as the expression of a wasteful and idle aristocratic culture. Increasingly the explorers' reports, letters, and narratives of colonization display the "Baconian" style.

A report on a Virginia voyage sent to Richard Hakluyt by the artist John White illustrates this style. The following passage is particularly striking because in it White describes a personal disaster, the disappearance and presumed death of his daughter and granddaughter (Virginia Dare, who was the first English child born in the New World). White, who had headed the colonizing expedition, had left them behind at Roanoke to return briefly to England. During his absence, the Roanoke colony met with a catastrophic event, to this day unknown, and when he came back to Virginia, there were no survivors. White's report, titled in Hakluyt's collection *The Fifth Voyage of M. John White into the West Indies and Parts of America called Virigina, in the Year 1590* (1593), appears intent only on establishing its trustworthiness:

I have sent you (although in a homely style, especially for the contentation of a delicate ear) the true discourse of my last voyage into the West Indies, and parts of America called Virginia, taken in hand about the end of February, in the year of our redemption 1590. And what events happened unto us in this our journey, you shall plainly perceive by the sequel of my discourse.

The report is genuinely "homely," little more than a chronological recording of daily activities and findings. Approaching the site of the plantation and finding the letters "CROATOAN" inscribed on a palisade surrounding the shells of houses, White does not pause to express dismay or anxiety. Inside the protective circle, he just continues his survey of "many bars of iron, two pigs of lead, four iron fowlers, iron sacker-shot, and such like heavy things, thrown here and there, almost overgrown with grass and weeds." The plantation has been abandoned. Leaving neither distress signals nor any intelligible indications of their destination, the colonists have disappeared, and White and his companions try to find their trail. "From thence we went along by the water side, towards the point of the creek to see if we could find any of their boats or pinnace, but we could perceive no sign of them, nor any of the last falcons and small ordinance which were left with them, at my departure from them."

Factual writing need not be so laconic or unemotional, however. Probably the best representation of the new functional style in the literature of colonization is Walter Raleigh's (1552?–1618) highly personal narrative of his voyage to Guiana in 1595. Raleigh's title would have pleased Marco Polo: *The Discovery of the Large, Rich and Beautiful Empire of Guiana, with a Relation of the Great and Golden City of Manoa (Which the Spaniards Call El Dorado)* (1596). Envious of the golden conquests of Cortés and Pizarro (over the fabled Aztecs and Incas), Raleigh thought to find deep in the Amazonian wilderness a third great aboriginal empire, the legendary El Dorado. But despite its title and its romantic inspiration, the *Discovery of the Empire of Guiana* is a thoroughly realistic chronicle – realistic, that is, in form and style, not necessarily in content. No doubt influenced by his desires, Raleigh seriously overestimated the wealth of the Indian nation he found; but he always measures it by objective standards. He clearly believes his findings are a colonizer's dream, but he presents them in the voice of sober reason: "I will promise these things that follow which I know to be true. Those that are desirous to discover and to see many nations may be satisfied within this river, . . . above 2000 miles east and west, and 800 miles south and north, and of these, the most either rich in gold, or in other merchandises." He fully means to persuade, not only to inform: "The common soldier shall here fight for gold, and pay himself instead of pence, with plates of half a foot broad, whereas he breaketh his bones in other wars for provender and penury." But the ground on which he argues is solid earth: "There is no country which yieldeth more pleasure to the inhabitants, either for these common delights of hunting, hawking, fishing, fowling, and the rest, than Guiana does."

The dualism Columbus announced as the distinguishing feature of the *Diario* – that it would report things as they were while also being an entirely personal narrative – is not specified in Raleigh's *Discovery of the Empire of Guiana;* it is fully implicit. The sentences just cited are unmistakably personal *and* they tell a story anyone can tell because it is true. When this way of telling a story makes use of an image, the image participates in the same dualism. Take this famous passage:

> Guiana is a country that hath yet her maidenhead, never sacked, turned, nor wrought, the face of the earth hath not been torn, nor the virtue and salt of the soil spent by manurance, the graves have not been opened for gold, the mines not broken with sledges, nor their images pulled down out of their temples. It hath never been entered by any army of strength, and never conquered or possessed by any Christian prince.

The sexual metaphor is consciously elaborated but it is entirely organic to the argument; it is never ornamental. Nothing appears as a result of associating conquest with rape that is not directly a fact of conquest: soil, graves, mines, and temples are real features of a real Guiana. Raleigh uses almost no adjectives; when he wants to describe the country as healthful or rich or beautiful, he makes a statement: "The soil besides is so excellent and so full of rivers, as it will carry sugar, ginger, and all those other commodities, which the West Indies have." He does not characterize the soil or the geography (as Columbus does in the "excellent soil and the commodious rivers") but describes them: "The soil . . . is . . . excellent and . . . full of rivers." A search is said to reveal "four goodly entrances" to a river, but the adjective "goodly" immediately acquires an objective measure: "whereof the least was as big as the Thames at Woolwich." Raleigh describes everything he sees and does and experiences. But he decidedly rejects conventions or ways of writing that fall into the category of the poetic or even the conventionally literary. He never develops his evocative, vivid descriptions through any of the forms of imaginative writing; the *Discovery of the Empire of Guiana* is a remarkably effective piece of writing that never acknowledges any other purpose but direct communication.

This avoidance of imaginative and poetic forms seems particularly significant when we recall that the sixteenth century in literary history is the age of the lyric. There were some lyrical accounts of the conquest certainly. And lyricism does sometimes bathe explorers' reports and shipping logs, recording a thriving commerce between poetry and power. Hakluyt included in his compilations some quite lyrical pieces, such as, for instance, Arthur Barlowe's account of his 1584 reconnoitering mission to the North American coast. Sent by Raleigh as soon as Raleigh received his patent to colonize in the area, Barlowe seems to have understood his task to be to sing the praises of Virginia. He duly evoked a land whose coastal waters "smelt so sweetly . . . as if we had been in the midst of some delicate garden, abounding with all kinds of odoriferous flowers." Landing, they find the soil "the most plentiful, sweet, fruitful, and wholesome of all the world." The people are "most gentle, loving, and faithful, void of all guile, and treason, and such as lived after the manner of the golden age." The conclusion has long been apparent: the earth in Virginia "bringeth forth all things in abundance, as in the first creation, without toil or labour."

More often, however, in the mode of Raleigh's account of El Dorado, even fantastical accounts and fanciful promotions are presented as facts. The explorer John Hawkins (1532–95) or a member of his 1564 expedition to Florida was remarkably matter-of-fact about some rather unlikely discoveries:

[T]he Floridians have pieces of unicorns' horns, which they wear about their necks, whereof the Frenchmen obtained many pieces. Of those unicorns they have many; for that they do affirm it to be a beast with one horn, which coming to the river to drink, putteth the same into the water before he drinketh. Of this unicorn's horn there are of our company, that having gotten the same of the Frenchman, brought home thereof to show.

In such accounts, the New World is wonderful without being exactly wondrous; it is marvelous not for its exoticism but for its potential to make the richest resources accessible, even familiar.

Ralph Lane, governor of Roanoke in 1585, extolled the wonders of the island less soberly than Raleigh did those of Guiana:

the goodliest soil under the cope of heaven, so abounding with sweet trees, that bring such sundry rich and most pleasant gums, grapes of such greatness, yet wild . . . the goodliest and most pleasing territory of the world (for the continent is of a huge and unknown greatness, and very well peopled and towned, though savagely) and the climate so wholesome, that we have not had one sick since we touched the land here.

But even though Lane clearly exaggerates, he does not render Roanoke fabulous.

Lane's hyperbolic "goodliest and most pleasing territory of the world" is not romance, but it *is* promotion. And in its intentions, promotion is never merely factual. It must make readers dream in order to persuade them to act. Raleigh describes El Dorado in the language of fact and avoids any semblance of romance, but his first purpose in writing the *Discovery of the Empire of Guiana* is to promote colonial voyages. Romance, which calls attention to its imaginary status, as Barlowe calls attention to his use of the myth of Eden, would not serve this purpose. A practical reader might actually be discouraged from hazarding into a country whose best qualities are patently improbable. The literature of colonial description, insisting on strict realism, conceals the distinction between fancy and fact, fuses the ideal and the real. Visions appear realistic. The plainer, more functional prose style of imperial writings does carry a new burden of scientific or factual information and also facilitates its gathering. But it is not less ideologically active than its predecessors.

In the fact-focused passages we have been reading, vision and realism confirm one another; the prose of objectivity masks an appeal to the imagination in a context ostensibly ruled by reason. The prose of objectivity can also work the other way, just as ideologically, not to evoke but to block the imagination. In the following passage, a document from the African slave trade, the sober and plain writing suppresses reader sympathy. "The Voyage Made by Mr. John Hawkins to the Coast of Guinea and the Indies of Nova Hispania, 1564" (this is the same Hawkins who reported earlier on unicorns in Florida and whose writings were published by Hakluyt) describes a raid:

The captain was advertised by the Portuguese of a town of the Negroes, where was not only great quantity of gold, but also that there were not above forty men, and an hundred women and children in the town, so that he might get an hundred slaves: he determined to stay before the town three or four hours, to see what he could do: and thereupon prepared his men in armour and weapon together, to the number of forty men well appointed, having to their guides certain Portuguese: we landing boat after boat, and diverse of our men scattering themselves, contrary to the captain's will, by one or two in a company, for the hope that they had to find gold in their houses, ransacking the same, in the meantime the Negroes came upon them, and hurt many being thus scattered whereas if five or six had been together, they had been able as their companions did, to give the overthrow to 40 of them. While this was doing the captain who with a dozen men, went through the town, returned, finding 200 Negroes at the water's side, shooting at them in the boats, and cutting them in pieces which were drowned in the water. Thus we returned back somewhat discomforted, although the captain in a singular wise manner carried himself, with countenance very cheerful outwardly: having gotten by our going ten Negroes and lost seven of our best men, and we had 27 of our men hurt.

Nothing has been left out of this account, yet little can be read in it; little, that is, of what must have been — what the account itself tells us was — the terrible devastation of the village and its people. The passage actually obscures what it describes, documenting atrocity in a way that makes the reader more or less unable to apprehend it. This opaqueness is oddly unguarded and undefensive, connoting neither denial nor a strong sense of entitlement. On the contrary, rather than the writer's nationalism, callousness, or even racism, what blocks the reader's comprehension is, ironically, the evenness and amplitude of the exposition.

The beginning of the long first sentence seems to propose the "Negroes" as candidates for the reader's sympathy by describing them in traditionally pathetic terms as mostly "women and children," one hundred of them about to become a hundred slaves. At this stage, the focus of the anecdote is on its characters and we seem to be starting a story more than a report. Almost at once, however, the human drama recedes as potential characters flatten into participants, and an incipient plot reduces to a report on strategy. The careful recorder once again provides numbers, now suggesting a balance of forces, forty against forty. But although a confrontation between men is potentially as dramatic as the capture of women, the writer does not concentrate here either but moves on equably; his main point turns out to be that their failure to keep together cost the English more casualties than was necessary. Numbers abound; precision is everywhere: the English advance on the African houses "by one or two in a company"; "if five or six had been together," they could have withstood "40 of them." The captain meets up with "200 Negroes," and finally the sum of it all: ten Africans taken slave, seven Englishmen lost, and twenty-seven injured. End of report.

It has not been all statistics, however; the rest of the story is all here: the raiders meet up with their two hundred victims not just anywhere but at the waterside, where a battle ensues that is full of circumstance and gory detail, the Africans "shooting at them in the boats, and cutting them in pieces which were drowned in the water." Yet these actual bodies are no more real than the numbers, for the major obstacle to understanding has not been abstraction but rather a totality composed indistinguishably of both bodies and numbers that literally mean nothing. They do not mean or connote; they name, describe, identify. They tell, and the very completeness of the account works to inflect all its parts equally; so that the overall clarity with which we see the forest blurs the trees.

Some considerable portion of a polity's tolerance for violence committed in its name stems from the conviction that the enemy is evil and the victims are unworthy. Hawkins's passage invokes neither judgment. And although its author might assume his readers would bring such views to their reading, one would expect, were ideology to shape their response, some appeal to imperial creeds, such as a reminder of the savagery of the Africans or of their inferior intelligence. Neither is this passage a work of apology and justification, which depend on completeness and equal time, forms one might have thought either politically neutral or, in the exercise of neutrality, possibly even subversive. On this passage, ideological content remains latent.

In fact, this story of a slave raid is so unfocused that the author has difficulty concluding it. In the penultimate sentence, the captain with his dozen men confronting two hundred Africans on shore, the Englishmen in the boats, the bodies (English? African? both?) floating in pieces on the water, are just there, disparate, unrelated. A center is needed to pull the scene together; the last sentence locates this center where a culture able to conceive of objective telling logically places it, in the person of the teller. In this disinterested world, a hero emerges, the hitherto sketchy Captain Hawkins, who now assumes enough agency to be described "carr[ying]" himself "in a singular wise manner." He will interpret the episode for us; it will derive its point from his interpretation. Until now everyone has been described not only externally but from an indeterminate distance that flattens them into the landscape. Now the captain is revealed to have not only a face but a being behind the face: the phrase "with countenance very cheerful *outwardly*" (italics added) implies an unsuspected interiority that becomes the episode's theater of meaning. Captain Hawkins's interiority implies England's; and the slave raid, of which we still know everything and nothing, achieves meaning as an episode in the evolution of an English national character. The ambition of the objective, empirical narrative reveals itself in this conclusion. The claim to tell all the truth seeks to take possession of its subject definitively and to encompass it whole. The plain factual style colonizes reality; empirical writing builds empires.

Such was Richard Hakluyt's fervent hope, although in the seventeenth century, it all remained to be done. The New World was a future so far from being already imagined, it might never come. It had to be invented: conquered, settled, and also enjoined, urged, promoted, written into being. Hakluyt's "papers of empire," like Mercator's maps, like Columbus's *Diario,* were conceived primarily as means not for depicting the world or celebrating it or speculating about it but for acting in it. Thus when one notes that a plainer, more functionalist prose style became dominant during the period of colonization, this does not mean any diminution in the status of literature. A literature emerges in Hakluyt's reports that is more powerful than ever in its ability to appropriate history on the model of, and in conjunction with, England's appropriation of foreign lands. "America" was conceived under the sign of the printing press.

2

THE NATURAL INHABITANTS

THE PEOPLE who already inhabited the North American continent had an old and richly developed oral literature; they did not write. To the diligent writers who proposed to colonize the New World the fact that its inhabitants had no system for writing was a definitive sign of their inferiority. In the eyes of the Europeans, the absence of indigenous writing among the Indians went far to vitiate their claim to the continent.

The first Native-American publication in North America, and until the nineteenth century almost the only one, was a sermon written and preached by Samson Occom (1723?–92) at the execution of a fellow Mohegan convicted of murder. Occom was a minister and worked with the educational mission of Eleazar Wheelock. The preface to the published *Sermon Preached at the Execution of Moses Paul, an Indian* (1772), begins: "The world is already full of books." Why, Occom asks, add another, "since the most excellent writings of worthy and learned men are disregarded"? But he then reflects that these writings are "in a very high and refined language" beyond the comprehension of the common people. His "plain, everyday talk" is accessible to everyone; "little children may understand it; and poor Negroes may plainly and fully understand my meaning." One last group will benefit from a simpler text: "my poor kindred the Indians." There is a final reason for Occom to publish his "broken hints" and this has to do not with the sermon's readers but with its writer: "as it comes from an uncommon quarter, it may induce people to read it because it is from an Indian." The *Sermon* derives a special force from its unexpectedness. Normally Indians do not write, and the very existence of an Indian text indicates a message of the highest inspiration. "God works where, and when he pleases . . . and he can and has used weak and unlikely instruments."

The God who made use of Samson Occom had been introduced to the American natives by the Europeans. Occom's humble claim to be this God's instrument implies a deeper self-abnegation: as an Indian, without white instruction, he would not have been even the lowliest of God's writers. From this perspective – fundamental to the way most Europeans explained the colonial project – the Indians before the arrival of Columbus lived outside the universe of understanding. It is the almost invariant thesis of the English literature of colonization in particular that the Indians lacked the components of civilization. They were wild, savage, primitive: their cultural appurtenances were rudimentary and, being unwritten, ephemeral.

This chapter differs from all the others in being unavoidably shaped by historical negation and the resulting absence of information. It begins with a discussion not of the literary history of North American Indians but of the problems and prejudices that have prevented an adequate account of this history. It turns next to what can be known of the encounter: how Europeans perceived the Indians. It then offers a reading of those Spanish texts that present a fuller account of the Indians than do any of the North American texts. This leads to a discussion of the only indigenous literature of the conquest, written under Spanish auspices. The chapter closes with a speculative coda, an effort at reading an exemplary English account differently in an attempt to bring out not the eclipsed Native-American perspective itself – an impossible ambition – but at least its presence as a shadowed other side of the encounter.

❦

Thomas Harriot (1560–1621), the mathematician and scientist who, at Hakluyt's suggestion, accompanied the second Roanoke expedition as its botanist–ethnographer, featured the continent's "Natural Inhabitants" as one of its major resources. He had the "good hope" that "they may be brought through discreet dealing and government to the embracing of the truth, and consequently to honor, obey, fear and love us." (Harriot's work is discussed in the next chapter.) For all its ostensible benevolence, this colonial marriage vow makes explicit the implied adjunct to the love, honor, and obedience clause of the marriage bond: fear. The Indian bride had better behave. Still, as metaphors of the relations between Native Americans and Europeans, there is a difference between marriage and war.

It is true that many representations of the encounter between Europeans and Americans depict the former as men, the latter as women. A famous engraving, for instance, showing Vespucci discovering America features a nude Indian woman starting up from her hammock, amazed at the appearance of an elaborately garbed and armed man bearing a cruciform banner in one hand and an astrolabe in the other. Underneath the engraving, entitled "America," is the legend "Americen Americus retextit, Semel vocauit inde semper excitam" ("Americus discovers America; once he had called her, she was forever after always awake").

Despite Harriot's conjugal idiom, however, the English colonizers of North America were more likely to see themselves ridding the territory of

Indians than rousing them. And when they cast America in a female role, they primarily thought of the land, not its inhabitants. The native population was unworthy of so fair a continent or it was an ungodly horde making her impure in their image. Generally the English preferred to imagine an empty landscape.

Picturing America as an Indian woman implied not romance but rape. The distinction between feminizing the natives and killing them is not intended here to prefer one to the other. Its usefulness lies rather in helping define the analytical problems involved in recovering a sense of the duality of the encounter, of the role of the American natives in shaping the confrontation between these essentially incommensurate cultures. Differentiating between the stance of the Vespucci engraving and another one more characteristic of the English, say William Bradford's attitude in *Of Plymouth Plantation* (1630), has to do with identifying a special problem for literary history. By and large the Indians of the English tradition are not inferior men, hence women, to be saved and enslaved; their humanity itself is in doubt.

There were certainly some who dissented, notably Roger Williams, who was expelled from Plymouth for disputing the right of Christian kings to dispose of Indian lands. (We shall examine Williams's views at length in Chapter 3.) But the dominant English colonizing stance did not merely denigrate native civilization: it denied its existence, making the natives only an aspect of an inhuman wilderness. Over the course of U.S. history, Native Americans have been melded so thoroughly with the landscape that as careful a historian as Perry Miller simply failed to see them when defining the theme of *Errand into the Wilderness* (1956), his pioneering work on the colonial period; he was writing, he said, "the massive narrative of the movement of European culture into the vacant wilderness of America." In the 1980s, Henry Nash Smith looked back at his magisterial book *Virgin Land* (1950) and was troubled to recognize that he had portrayed the West as empty space even as he analyzed texts that, like James Fenimore Cooper's Leatherstocking novels or the tales of Buffalo Bill, actually centered on Native Americans.

Like the Africans in the Hawkins slave raid discussed in Chapter 1, Native Americans are everywhere in the colonial literature, walking, talking, and going about the business of their own civilizations. Even Bradford's *Of Plymouth Plantation*, which in one chapter describes a wilderness made "hideous" by savages indistinguishable from beasts, in the next chapter recalls how the arriving colonists gratefully dug up Indian baskets filled with seed corn. Over a century and a half later, Meriwether Lewis and William Clark travel across a territory that they consider wild and unsettled but that is crowded with Indian societies.

Bradford, Lewis and Clark, Cooper, and Prentiss Ingraham, the author of the Buffalo Bill stories, render the Native American not as a presence but rather as the trace of a vanishing. The nineteenth-century phrase "the Vanishing American" identifies the Indian by lack of presence. And in line with fiction like Cooper's, much of the nineteenth-century scholarly literature praised the Indians only to bury them. The collections of Ojibwa legends the ethnologist Henry Rowe Schoolcraft (1793–1864) compiled from 1839 to 1857 inspired Henry Wadsworth Longfellow's elegy *Song of Hiawatha* (1855).

Attitudes have changed since the nineteenth century. In 1991, the National Museum of American Art mounted an exhibit of paintings by such artists as George Catlin, George Caleb Bingham, Emanuel Gottlieb Leutze, and Albert Bierstadt, entitled *The West as America: Reinterpreting Images of the Frontier, 1820–1920.* The organizers' harsh judgment of the history of western settlement drew equally harsh criticism, but their central thesis was generally accepted. In a succession of paintings the catalogue calls attention to the way Native Americans were portrayed as unseeing objects of white observation. Still, it has not been possible, at least not yet, to reconstruct the reciprocity of the first meetings of Europeans and Native Americans. At the time of this writing, the study of the colonial encounter remains essentially a Euro-American self-study.

❦

Indeed, when we emphasize the historical dimension in our studies of the encounter and seek to know what happened not overall but in the sixteenth century, it proves extraordinarily difficult and may even be impossible to reconstruct how the two cultures interacted with one another. This is because an unwritten culture is not readily identified with a precise period. Oral texts cannot be dated like written ones. Traditional tales may not reveal their form at a specific time. The incommensurability between the Europeans and the Native-American cultural materials has been pointed out by scholars who therefore question the historical bias of many current studies. Some of these scholars go farther and argue not only that a precise chronological narrative is impossible to construct but that it would at any rate present a distorted view. They refer to fundamental differences in how human beings locate themselves in the world. American Indian cultures, this argument maintains, organize themselves primarily in relation to nature rather than to society; they imagine time cyclically and stress continuity over change. How, ask the historians who embrace this view, can one write a "history" of Native Americans and the encounter without denying in the very act the validity of Native-American perceptions?

Conversely, an account of American-Indian imaginative traditions ordered by notions of cyclical time and continuity is much less hampered by the loss or lack of early texts because it is not really dependent on historical location. So considered, the difficulties of knowing the colonial situation in order to write a literary history from the native perspective may become irrelevant. The Native-American literary tradition is what it is whenever one engages it and can be grasped whole at any moment in time unlimited by the moment or its conditions.

Even if one abandons conventional history and strives rather for an ethnographic reconstruction of Indian culture, the obstacles are little less daunting. Oral texts are obviously peculiarly fragile; as fragile as human beings. In the first century of colonization, 75 to 90 percent of the indigenous population of the Americas died, most of that number in the first fifty years. Yet some of the most important forms in oral literature exist only as spoken by storytellers. Voice inflection and the temporal organization of a performance communicate the meaning of a tale at least as much as its words. In short, the indigenous literary culture that existed at the time of the first encounters was an exceptionally vulnerable body of works that we are trying to recover from a catastrophically fragmented society. Had the *Iliad* not been finally written down, what would we know of it today? For that matter, what is the relation between our *Iliad* and Homer's?

Finding a way to write a history of Native Americans in the sixteenth and seventeenth centuries without distorting basic principles of their culture, and even reconstructing an adequate ethnography, would still not eliminate peculiarly difficult problems of interpretation. The very concept of an encounter directs our attention to differences, and differences can have contradictory implications.

Take, for example, Columbus's first *Letter,* in which he observes that the Arawaks are astonishingly "liberal" with their possessions. They "give objects of great value for trifles, and content themselves with very little or nothing in return." The Spanish sailors are quick to take advantage of this, and Columbus has to intervene to prevent the Arawaks' utter despoliation. Or rather he steps in to stop what *he* understands as cheating, for the Arawaks, upon receiving "articles of no value" (such as pieces of dishes, plates, and glass) appear quite satisfied. There is no reason in this context not to trust Columbus's observation that they seemed to imagine "themselves to be possessed of the most beautiful trinkets in the world." This is a famous scene and it is generally cited as a representation of the way the Spanish exploited the natives right from the start, an interpretation that closely resembles Columbus's own view of the incident.

His conclusion that "they bartered like idiots," however, might alert us to a problem in our very condemnation of the Spanish. To reject Columbus's view one has to recognize the Arawaks' sense of value. They may be getting cheated by a European standard, but unless this standard is taken to be universal (in which case they *are* "idiots"), they are not cheated according to *their* standard. Stressing cultural difference, one finds oneself rejecting at once Columbus's contempt and, logically, the notion that the Arawaks are getting a bad deal. From this perspective, Columbus appears as ignorant of native concepts of value as the natives are of his; they become less victims than partners in mutual misunderstanding.

Not only abuse but kindness takes on other meanings when this mutuality is stressed. Columbus presents himself as the natives' champion when he forbids the exchange of broken glass for gold "as being unjust, and myself gave them many beautiful and acceptable articles which I had brought with me, taking nothing from them in return." When the difference in definitions of value is placed foremost, Columbus's forbearance recedes in importance before his ignorance. Both when he considers the Indians idiots for trading gold for glass and when he extends them a European but not necessarily an Arawak largesse, it is Columbus who may be the idiot. When Columbus looks like an idiot, his moral behavior has less force to define a situation in which the other participants also play a role.

On the other hand, we have now read the scene of the Spaniards' trading broken jars and scraps of leather for large quantities of gold and cotton as possibly benign. Few will want to stop at this reading. To restore the message of exploitation to this scene, one has to relocate difference in a larger context defined by at least some common values and issues. Columbus defines this context himself when he goes on to explain that he has made the Arawaks valuable gifts "in order that I might the more easily conciliate them, that they might be led to become Christians, and be inclined to entertain a regard for the King and Queen, our Princes and all Spaniards, and that I might induce them to take an interest in seeking out, and collecting, and delivering to us such things as they possessed in abundance, but which we greatly needed." The project of conquest and expropriation subsumes the trading scene. The issue of relative value is overridden by the issue of power. The Arawaks will not be able to imagine themselves free when they are enslaved. On the common ground of power, the Arawaks will be exploited by any standard.

The definition of history and of literature, the uses and limits of cultural ethnography, and the implications of the concept of difference are some of the fundamental issues of current literary studies that are directly engaged by attempts to restore a Native-American presence to the study of early America. Native-American studies necessarily query the nature of texts and of authors, of literature itself, and especially of language. They need to take a radical approach to meet the terms of their materials: on the one side, oral texts of obscure origin and descent and, on the other, a literature of colonization that denies outright the linguistic capability of its colonial subjects. Shakespeare's character Caliban, native of a Caribbean isle, is the prototype of the speechless Indian. Not unlike the six Arawaks Columbus captured so that they might thus "learn to speak," Caliban has no language until Prospero gives him the rudiments of one. By the same token, Caliban is not fit to rule his island. In the new European calculus we briefly surveyed in Chapter 1, his linguistic incompetence marks him as incapable of self-possession.

All through the colonial period, the natives' relation to language is delicately calibrated. They are generally considered below the threshold of effective speech. However, they may also be projected beyond the linguistic ordinary. When Occom describes his sermon as a series of "broken hints" nonetheless inspired by God, he modestly lays claim to a common view that the "silent Indians" occasionally, under inspiration, can become transcendent orators. In his *Notes on the State of Virginia* (1784–5), Thomas Jefferson cited the Mingo chief Logan, who was widely celebrated for a speech that, according to Jefferson, rivaled all the orations of Cicero and Demosthenes. Yet such reversals do not overcome quotidian incapacity. Chief Logan is almost as isolated from human conversation by his hypereloquence as Columbus's Arawaks are by their "lack" of speech.

In its radical penetration to the very ground of linguistic communication, the issue of Indians and language has affinities with problems of translation. Translation is inevitably the site of an encounter in which the comparability of the two partners is posited. Consequently, the discoverers and first colonizers faced a dilemma. Often their very survival depended on communicating with the Indians. The entry for October 12, 1492, in Columbus's *Diario* concludes with the promise that he "will take six [Arawaks] from here to Your Highnesses in order that they may learn to speak." On October 14, he could already report having seized seven Indians "to carry them away to [Your Highnesses] and to learn our language and to return them."

The linguistic situation proved more complicated, however. By November 27, Columbus was finding *his* incomprehension a problem. He has been held up in his explorations, and one important reason is that "I do not know the language, and the people of these lands do not understand me nor do I, nor anyone else that I have with me, them. And many times I understand one thing said by these Indians that I bring for another, its contrary." It has become clear that a better understanding is needed if explorations are to continue. Therefore, Columbus has decided that "I will have this tongue taught to persons of my household." This does not imply that he has come to recognize that the Arawaks have their own valid culture. Once the immediate problem of orienting to the New World has been solved and Columbus's men have learned the basic contours of the region from the Arawaks, the flow of instruction will reverse: "later the benefits will be known and efforts will be made to make all these peoples Christian." Who should teach whom is not really at issue here. The Arawaks, possessed of but a single language, are not equipped with a very complex philosophical culture either: "they have no false religion nor are they idolaters." Since they are also not Christians, they apparently have no religion at all.

Columbus does not envision learning the Arawak language as the beginning of a cultural exchange; the decision to do so has been forced upon him and he reports it with some defensiveness. Translation is the Achilles' heel of the colonizing culture; translate too much or too well and equivalences emerge, and the monologue of imperial authority — the empire's sole right to authorize — breaks down into dialogue.

Accordingly, despite Columbus's concession, which may not have been implemented, most of the translators and interpreters of colonial America were Indians rather than Europeans — or so it would seem from the literature. Throughout colonial accounts, from Doña Marina (La Malinche), the woman who translated for Cortés, to Squanto at Plymouth Colony, and Sacagawea, the chief interpreter on the Lewis and Clark expedition, native translators are described making the unintelligible intelligible, transforming a nonlinguistic "gibberish" into language — that is, into English and Spanish.

Europeans did learn native languages; the Franciscan Bernardino de Sahagún, who gathered most of the materials on Mexican culture available today, recorded them first in Nahuatl. Jesuit missionaries in North America equipped themselves first by becoming at least conversant in the Iroquois and Huron languages. But the literature, especially the English literature, does not feature European *translators;* even where there is implicit evidence in an account that Europeans understand and can speak an Indian language, this is not acknowledged. It is not difficult to understand why. Dialogue is anthropomorphic. Silent, the Indians can be relegated to the category of pernicious pests that will all disappear when the wilderness is cleared. The problem historians face today is the converse of this: unable to learn to speak like the Indians, whose voices have been all too successfully suppressed, how can we now learn their history?

❧

Reading the European side of the encounter presents by contrast very few such fundamental methodological difficulties. The colonial literature is exceptionally explicit about its concerns and in command of its terms. These concerns and terms can certainly be argued over, but their interpretation seldom entails the basic recasting of categories that seems required to treat the relationship of Native-American culture to the conventions of historical analysis or the uses of the concept of cultural difference for Native-American studies. Instead, European colonial writings are often sites of emerging visions that will shape modern literature in general. In the late sixteenth century a number of New World texts appeared that would be particularly influential. Michel de Montaigne (1533–92) wrote his two essays on the New World, "Of Cannibals" (1578–80) and "Of Coaches" (1585–8), at about the same time Jean de Léry (1534–1613) published his *Voyage to Brazil* (*Voyage au Brézil*, 1578), the work Claude Lévi-Strauss called "the breviary of the ethnologist." In Spain in the 1560s, Bernal Díaz del Castillo (1492–1584), a soldier from the army of Cortés at the conquest of Mexico, was writing his memoirs, *The Discovery and Conquest of Mexico, 1517–21* (*Historia verdadera de la conquista de la Nueva España*). One of the most striking features of all these texts is the central importance of the Native American to the definition of the New World, in contrast to the "vacant" continent featured in later English and U.S. accounts.

These Europeans are especially notable for representing the New World's indigenous inhabitants as, if anything, more civilized than themselves or as the creators of a more desirable civilization. Montaigne and Léry both find Indian social and cultural ways preferable in many respects to Europe's. Léry's *Voyage to Brazil* describes a two-year stay in the New World from 1556 to 1558, and Montaigne's essays are based on his readings and on interviews conducted in France with members of the Brazilian Guarani tribe brought to France by Vespucci. Montaigne declared himself greatly impressed by what these informants told him of their way of life, which seemed to him more rational than his own for being in better accord with nature's ways. It is we who are wild because unnatural, not the savages. They are not only more human but more humane: "I think there is more barbarity in eating a man alive than in eating him dead; and in tearing by tortures and the rack a body still full of feeling, in roasting a man bit by bit, in having him bitten and mangled by swine [as do the French in his very neighborhood "on the pretext of piety and religion"], than in roasting and eating him after he is dead."

Léry, a Swiss Huguenot acquainted with the persecutions of which "civilized" societies are capable, drew the same lesson from his acquaintance with the Tupiniki. The Brazilians might be cannibals and practitioners of the most horrific tortures on their enemies, but he suggests the reader reflect a moment. Are our everyday moneylenders, "sucking the blood and marrow and thus eating alive so many widows, orphans and other poor folk whose throats it would be kinder to slit all at once than to make them thus languish," not still more cruel?

Cannibals were and remain the greatest sensation the New World offered despite the fact that to this day their existence remains a matter of dispute. Some Native Americans appear to have been as horrified by the idea as Europeans. Cabeza de Vaca reported that when the Indians who had rescued him and his compatriots from a shipwreck discovered that five Christians on one part of the island had ended up eating one another, they "were so shocked at this cannibalism that, if they had seen it sometime earlier, they surely would have killed every one of us."

The issue is complicated by the question of how cannibalism is defined. If one defines "cannibals" as people who seek nutritional sustenance from the consumption of other people, it is not clear that there ever were such. On the other hand, many civilizations, including the Christian, feature the sacramental and ritual ingestion of token quantities of real or symbolic human flesh and blood. Montaigne's cannibals consume parts of their prisoners "and send some pieces to their absent friends," but "this is not, as people think, for nourishment . . . ; it is to betoken an extreme revenge." Whether or not they existed, sixteenth-century cannibals embody savagery itself. Whatever may be their status in the history of the discovery of the New World, they are implicit in its design. By creating the opposition of gentle, fearful Arawaks and fearsome Caribs (whom Columbus turns into "cannibales"), Columbus names the antipodal geography of the imperial promise, a world beyond Europe proffering riches to swell not only one's possessions but one's self, at the risk of the radical loss of both.

The political unconscious does not usually represent itself so explicitly. Cannibals, the focus of the sixteenth century, recede rapidly in the seventeenth; by the eighteenth, they have faded from sight like the wondrous serpents ornamenting early maps. Indian savagery, rather than reflecting the primitive impulses of all humanity, was in the sixteenth century specific to indigenous Americans and denoted their identification with the wilderness.

Arawaks and Caribs are opposite avatars of the primitive, which has been the Americas' dominant identity. But there was another set of meanings that Europe derived from the encounter. These developed in relation to an America seen, on the contrary, as extravagantly sophisticated, a magnificent civilization whose arts wrought treasures such as Europeans had only imagined. Bernal Díaz expresses this perception when describing in *The Discovery and Conquest of Mexico* (written in the 1560s) his first sight of the great capital of this civilization: "we were amazed and said that it was like the enchantments they tell of in the legend of Amadis." This reference is in no way satirical or parodic. At a loss for a comparable reality, he can describe the Aztec world only in the language of European fantasy. The first sighting of "the great City of Mexico" leaves him not exactly speechless but with his ordinary speech inadequate to the task. Firsthand chronicler of an event that he firmly believes proves Spain's right to domination, himself a participant in that event, Díaz is still linguistically overwhelmed and has to invoke the medieval past and the language of fantasy to tell his tale. Clearly, sometimes and in some areas, the balance of cultural power between Europeans and Americans was not immediately and self-evidently on the side of the conquerors.

Indeed, it was not self-evident to all the first invaders that they had the right to take over the Americas. Before it began to annex foreign territories outright, Europe had already been traveling the world in the Crusades, whose territorial goals were much debated. Planting the flag of a Christian crown in the Caribbean, especially since Columbus believed he had arrived in China, was not an altogether obvious gesture, for during the Middle Ages even the church harbored some doubts concerning whether the spiritual superiority of Christians gave them the right to appropriate the lands and goods of the infidel. At least there was no unanimity on this point; significant numbers of the Holy Roman Empire's legal scholars found that Christianity was not in all cases essential to political legitimacy. Conscious of the dangers of granting a free hand to possibly cupidinous Crusaders, these scholars argued that a secular political order could still possess authority.

In the sixteenth century, however, the problem of sovereignty came home to Europe. The first generation of Western nations became nations by becoming empires. The age of discovery and exploration was not coincidentally the age of nation building. Not only England, which actually broke with the Vatican, but France, Spain, and Portugal redefined themselves as distinct and autonomous states. The delicate case a Christian nation made for autonomy from Rome invoked a fine distinction between the spiritual, which is the province of the church, and the political, government in the name and service of Christianity but by the national authority. Spain applied to the Vatican for sanction over the discovered lands, to be granted in return for the promise to evangelize. A series of papal bulls (notably the 1493 *Inter caetera*) granted sanction over the territories but did not resolve the problematical status of their inhabitants; indeed, the missionary intent sharpened the problem of whether to consider them human beings or natural resources.

The Spanish colonists, working their plantations with forced Indian labor, rejected any distinction between land and people: Spain had full dominion over both, both were its property. The English colonists, who were never successful in harnessing native labor, drew a different conclusion from the same premise. Since the land was theirs by right of their proper use of it, the Indians could be removed from it the way forests were cleared. On the other hand, intent on saving the souls of the Indians, the Spanish missionaries found themselves contending against fellow colonizers for the Indians' physical sanctity. The church was itself interested in the riches of the New World, of course, but it favored other ways of acquiring them. The competition between colonists and missionaries quickly grew disabling and came to a head when a layman and advocate of the colonists, Juan Ginés de Sepúlveda (1490–1573), demanded that the church hear their case.

A special convocation of church authorities at Valladolid in 1550 gathered to judge an extraordinary debate that set out the basic terms of imperial ideology and language for centuries to come. Colonization itself was not at issue; there was no dispute over the virtue or the benefits of European conquest as such, just its conduct. The representative of the church in the Valladolid debate was the Dominican missionary and bishop of Central America, Bartolomé de Las Casas, who had become appalled at the colonists' brutality. Las Casas took the occasion to develop a systematic argument for Indian rights, maintaining that the Indians were reasonable men governing themselves in reasonable ways and only lacking the enlightenment of Christianity. Their primitive state did not justify depriving them of their possessions, let alone enslaving them. On the contrary, since the Indians were capable of conversion, they were already provisional members of the universal brotherhood of the church; and once they embraced Christianity they became the spiritual equals of Europeans.

On the other side, the colonists' representative was a Renaissance humanist, a friend of Erasmus and a proponent of the new secular nationalism. Sepúlveda upheld the colonizers as agents of the Crown and of national destiny, therefore having the right to subjugate the Indians. Invoking Aristotle's precept that some are born masters and others slaves, Sepúlveda denied that men were universally equal in the church and instead proposed a hierarchy of race and nation that justified the denial of sovereignty to the Indians on the very grounds of Spanish sovereignty. The church tribunal reached no clear decision but refused to grant Sepúlveda's text, *Democrates Alter,* the imprimatur. To that extent the church upheld Las Casas in this case, or at least did not deny his claim. But the principle of Christian universalism did in the end lose out to Sepúlveda's argument. In its defense of the autonomy of national and private colonization, *Democrates Alter* recorded an essential paradox of modernization: Sepúlveda's case depended on a newly stringent denial of rights to excluded groups even as it demanded expanded rights for the enfranchised community.

Only in hindsight does the ultimate outcome of the Valladolid debate seem inevitable. At the time, the debate articulated a real indeterminacy. Conducted fewer than thirty years after the conquest of Mexico in 1521, it still reverberates with the uncertain fortunes of a campaign that lasted over two years and was at least once nearly defeated. When Cortés burnt his boats to ensure that he could not retreat from the invasion of the Aztec Empire, his superiors denounced his rashness, and it was darkly predicted that his arrogance would bring him to a bad end. Ironically, this sometimes desperately uncertain campaign has become, at least since the nineteenth century, the preferred case in point for proving the inevitability of European conquest.

Montaigne did not believe the conquest inevitable, except for reasons that hardly flattered the conquerors. In his second New World essay, "Of Coaches," he protests the slaughter of the Incas in terms that complement his defense of the cannibals. The Inca civilization, he insists, is in no way inferior to the French: "if anyone had attacked them on equal terms . . . it would have been just as dangerous for him as in any other war we know of, and more so." The inequality of terms arises from the Europeans' lower morality: their lesser "devoutness, observance of the laws, goodness, liberality, loyalty, and frankness." Because of the Incas' "advantage in this [moral tone] they lost, sold, and betrayed themselves." Their defeat is tragic and implies, as do all tragedies, the at least equal force of the defeated.

One of the most striking examples of what might be called the literature of the undetermined encounter is the autobiographical story of Alvar Núñez Cabeza de Vaca entitled *La relación* (1542). Cabeza de Vaca was second in command in the ill-fated 1527 Spanish expedition to conquer Florida. Stranded and lost with four others, he wandered eight years and some six thousand miles from Florida to northern Mexico, where he finally reached the coast and a ship back to Europe. During that time, he was enslaved in a series of Indian villages until he found a way of keeping free by becoming a valued trader and purveyor of medicinal herbs and remedies. Often alone in the wilderness and at the mercy of his Indian captors, hosts, customers, and clients, Cabeza de Vaca lived the reverse adventure of Díaz and had experiences that sometimes parallel those in later English captivity narratives.

Once, for instance, after he has established himself as a trader, he and one of his companions fall in with a group of Indians who claim to have recently killed two Spaniards.

So we would know they had spoken the truth about the bad treatment of our fellows, they commenced slapping and batting Oviedo and did not spare me either. They would keep throwing clods at us, too, and each of the days we waited there they would stick their arrows to our hearts and say they had a mind to kill us the way they had finished our friends.

Not surprisingly, since he is telling the story, Cabeza de Vaca displays exemplary coolness in the face of these torments; but when he reproves Oviedo's cowardice in running away to rejoin a group of women with whom they had previously traveled, and himself elects to remain "alone with those savages," the decision bespeaks more than courage. Or rather, it defines a kind of courage that is neither the religiously inspired stalwartness characterizing the ideal seventeenth-century English captive nor defiance nor desperation. It is simply an enduring acceptance appropriate to Cabeza de Vaca's understanding of his situation as an alien wanderer among people whom he can deal with because they are not absolutely unlike him. Shortly after the departure of Oviedo, an Indian approaches Cabeza de Vaca to tell him secretly that two Christians have arrived with their captors at an accessible place. If he wishes, the man will lead Cabeza de Vaca to his compatriots. "I decided to trust him," Cabeza de Vaca explains, "since he spoke a dialect distinct from the others."

Cabeza de Vaca's admission of his ability to make that distinction reveals a vast difference between this sixteenth-century Spaniard and, for instance, the seventeenth-century English captive Mary Rowlandson. There is evidence in her narrative *The Sovereignty and Goodness of God* (1682) that she understood the native language, but she never mentions this. She almost never refers to actual exchanges on the many occasions when she describes her communication with her captors. By noting that his informant spoke a different dialect, Cabeza de Vaca endows the Indians overall with a linguistic competence that defines itself through difference and the ability to manipulate it in the constitution of a community of meaning. Projecting English or Spanish as the human lingua franca amounts to claiming that its speakers represent the universal human norm. All others are less than human: difference in this case arises at the limits of speech, between those who can speak and those who cannot. But without some sense of difference, however large or small its construction, language loses its special defining relation to communication. By bringing the Indians within the world of linguistic difference, Cabeza de Vaca makes them commensurate with himself, people with whom he can communicate, if not always actually, then potentially. In contrast, even as she does communicate, indeed negotiates, Rowlandson insists that she has been transported outside the human pale.

Like Rowlandson, Cabeza de Vaca never for a moment considers staying with the Indians. He insists that "my main purpose . . . all the while was to determine an eventual road out." However, after he succeeded in getting home, he set about planning a return expedition to try again to take possession of the rich territories he had traveled. A strong opponent of enslaving the Indians, Cabeza de Vaca was an enlightened but nonetheless determined colonizer treating with the native inhabitants and, although fully expecting to possess their land, not therefore concluding that it was never theirs. For

Rowlandson, the Indians are part of an unredeemed wilderness and thus wrongful interlopers on God's earth.

☙

There is probably a connection between Cabeza de Vaca's recognition of Indian civilization and the kind of Indian civilization that existed in Mexico, a kind more familiar to Europeans. A decade after the conquest of Mexico, even before Bernal Díaz began writing his chronicle, Indians were already writing their own story of the fall of the Aztecs. This was not an entirely independent project. It went on under the auspices of the Franciscan Bernardino de Sahagún, who arrived in Mexico after Cortés's victory to establish a seminary and generally direct the church's cultural and intellectual activities. Sahagún gathered the sons of the defeated Aztec and Mexican nobility, taught them Latin and the principles of courtly poetry, but also interviewed them about their culture, collecting texts and compiling an archive that is today one of the main sources on pre-Columbian America.

Sahagún expanded the range of cultural colonialism into a new dimension when he decided to put together his *General History of the Things of New Spain* (*Historia general de las cosas de Nueva España*), an enterprise of forty years, in Nahuatl, the main Aztec language. Only when it was finished did he undertake its Latin translation. Although Sahagún taught the Mexicans Latin (the language of European high culture), he also signaled the equal adequacy of their language by employing it for his own transcriptions, granting the Mexicans their linguistic competence and acknowledging the authority of an Aztec tongue.

In turn, this acknowledgment grants Aztec writings a voice in rendering the historical account. One of the documents Sahagún gathered into his *General History* is a set of narratives of the history of the fall of Mexico. Unsurprisingly, these describe Cortés and his men differently from the history of Bernal Díaz. For Díaz, Cortés was simply "very sagacious about everything" and always in command of exchanges. On one occasion, he describes Cortés as "in a rather grave manner, as though he were angry," scolding a group of Indians who "asked pardon for their past behavior, and said that henceforth they would be friendly." After frightening them by shooting off a cannon and, for good measure, bringing out a neighing, excited horse to paw the ground in front of them, Cortés sends the Indians away "quite contented."

Viewed from another perspective, the situation appears more complicated. Although certainly astonished by their first sightings of the bedecked and armored Spaniards, the Aztecs retain a critical distance. Thus they are cool observers of the Spanish response to their welcoming gifts.

The Spanish "picked up the gold and fingered it like monkeys," recalls an Aztec observer. "Their bodies swelled with greed, and their hunger was ravenous; they hungered like pigs for that gold. They snatched at the golden ensigns, waved them from side to side and examined every inch of them." The evocation of monkeys at the zoo (zoos were invented by the Aztecs) seems clearly deliberate.

Other narratives in the same collection accept the divine provenance of the Spaniards, their destined arrival, and their irresistible powers. Detailed accounts of ritual attacks routed by Spanish cannon and awed descriptions of Aztec chiefs who fight bravely but vainly against an enemy apparently impervious to their most powerful magic do tend to bear out the traditional view that the Indians both expected to be defeated and could do nothing about it.

Yet there are reversals of fortune. The description of "*la noche triste*" (the night of sorrows), when, after a four-day siege, the Aztecs forced the Spaniards to retreat with a loss of three-fourths of their men, pictures a humiliating defeat in which the invaders literally lose face and become mere objects of Indian wrath: "When the Spaniards reached the Canal of the Toltecs . . . they hurled themselves headlong into the water, as if they were leaping from a cliff. . . . all came to the brink and plunged over it. The canal was soon choked with the bodies of men and horses; they filled the gap in the causeway with their own drowned bodies. Those who followed crossed to the other side by walking on the corpses." This is the Aztec story.

Díaz tells the same story, but in this case the narrative conveys a somewhat different message. A series of battles has sorely tested the Spaniards, but throughout "Cortés showed himself very much of a man, as he always was." And although the fighting was fierce, "it was a memorable thing to see us all streaming with blood and covered with wounds and others slain." Then comes the retreat. Cortés is already outside the city awaiting his troops, and when he "saw that no more soldiers were coming along the causeway, tears sprang to his eyes." A lieutenant arrives at last and reports that "he and the four soldiers whom he brought with him, after their horses had been killed, crossed the bridge in great peril, over the dead bodies, horses and boxes with which that passage at the bridge was choked." Díaz elaborates, "At the bridge of sorrow . . . I assert that at the time not a single soldier stopped to see if he leaped much or little, for we could hardly save our own lives, as we were in great danger of death on account of the multitude of Mexicans charging down on us."

While describing chaos, Díaz retains authority: "I assert that at the time not a single soldier. . . ." The soldiers are running for their lives, not looking where they leap, yet their behavior makes sense; despite its horrors, the scene is actually orderly. In Sahagún's rendering of the Aztec account, the

Spaniards are wholly out of control, unable to act reasonably, "hurl[ing] themselves headlong into the water, as if they were leaping from a cliff." More precisely, they are no longer under their own control; their identities have been submerged along with their bodies, which have become inert objects. The canal is choked with bodies; "they filled the gap in the causeway with their own drowned bodies." They have at this juncture no more consciousness than the corpses on which they trample in their effort to reach safety. Much to the point, the Aztec account reports that the surviving Spaniards reached a place where, resting briefly, they "began to feel like men again." But the night's work of emasculation has been definitive; "suddenly they heard war cries and the Aztecs . . . surrounded them. . . . They also wanted . . . to complete their revenge against the Spaniards."

It is not remarkable that enemies should describe their battles differently. Rather, what is striking in the contrast presented by these two accounts is the effect of the Aztec's self-representation. In comparison, the absence of Native-American perspectives in the North American English literature appears particularly stark.

❦

To focus on this absence may actually reinforce it. The more one exposes the effacement of Native Americans from most North American texts, the more they appear indeed effaced. Their absence is thus established, but they are no more present for that. Are there other ways to read the European literature that could reveal more than absence? To repeat the question raised earlier, in the absence of Native-American histories, is there a way to recover their presence within European histories?

John Smith's *General History,* a work we shall consider in the next chapter, is a major resource for understanding the history of English colonization. For all his legendary romance with Pocahontas (1595?–1617), John Smith was wholeheartedly of the party that wished to remove the indigenous people from the land as quickly and completely as possible. He prided himself on knowing how to manage the natives and seems to have considered their point of view only in order to manipulate it. Yet in at least one encounter, his narrative lets appear the outline of an alternative vision whose relation to the English project is uncertain and whose programmatic implications are, uncharacteristically for Smith, both peripheral and vague.

In this encounter, early in the history of Virginia, the project of removing the native population is still in a preliminary phase. They have first to be brought under the colonial aegis. Indeed, the English are seeking an alliance with the powerful Algonkian chief Powhatan (1550?–1618), who was himself in the process of extending his own hegemony when the Europeans arrived in the region. The colonists dubbed him the "Great Emperor" and, hoping to transform the Indian emperor into a New World vassal, offered him a crown. John Smith, who had his doubts about the whole strategy, reported the incident in his *General History* and drew this wonderful vignette of the actual coronation:

All being met at [Powhatan's village] Werowocomoco, the next day was appointed for this coronation, then the presents were brought him, his basin and ewer, bed and furniture set up, his scarlet cloak and apparel with much ado put on him, being persuaded by [his son] Namontack they would not hurt him: but a foul trouble there was to make him kneel to receive his crown, he neither knowing the majesty nor meaning of a crown, nor bending of the knee, endured so many persuasions, examples, and instructions, as tired them all; at last by leaning hard on his shoulders, he a little stooped, and three having the crown in their hands put it on his head, when by the warning of a pistol the boats were prepared with such a volley of shot, that the king started up in a horrible fear, till he saw all was well. Then remembering himself, to congratulate their kindness, he gave his old shoes and his mantle to [the English leader] Captain Newport: but perceiving his purpose was to discover the Monacans [a non-allied tribe], he laboured to divert his resolution, refusing to lend him either men or guides more than Namontack; and so after some small complimental kindness on both sides, in requital of his presents he presented Newport with a heap of wheat ears that might contain some 7 or 8 bushels, and as much more we bought in the town, wherewith we returned to the fort.

This is a very complicated story with a foreground, background, and even underground. In the foreground, there is the astonishing spectacle of Powhatan suspiciously tolerating scarlet cloak, basin, ewer, and bed but, no matter what anyone says, absolutely drawing the line at kneeling to receive his crown, which requires three men to place on his head. Made to bend but not bow, the new king reciprocates by making the English captain a gift not just of his mantle, but of his old shoes.

In the background is the Indians' growing recognition that the English visitors are invaders rather than visitors and the attempt led by the powerful Powhatan to present a united front; while for their part the English do everything they can to divide and conquer. Underground, is Smith's untiring self-promotion, served in this instance by the manifest ineptitude of Newport, who just does not understand the natives as well as Smith.

Underground and background present no real analytical problems. That is, the emergence, as part of the process of empire building, of individual self-making has been frequently observed; and the treacheries of European–Indian relations are no surprise. In contrast, we have very little to go on in dealing with the foreground of the coronation anecdote, which is curiously out of ideological focus. The ambitious spokesman of a brand-new imperial creed, Smith describes a scene in which not just Newport but the English as a whole and their coronation ritual appear ridiculous. To be sure, Powhatan also looks silly, but that is the idea. Then why does Smith so punctiliously record a series of moves that make so solemn a white ceremony seem ludicrous? If the English expostulations and maneuvers, not to mention the culminating clapping of the crown on that stubborn head, have the aura of slapstick today, it must have been at least latent then as well. Readers may bring much of the meaning to a text; they do not bring it all. If, reading this passage, we laugh at the English, somewhere, to some degree, Smith knew they were laughable.

One current explanation for this potentially subversive description would be that it represents a sort of textual rupture, a moment in the text when Smith loses authorial control sufficiently to permit us to hear a resisting voice. But this is to assume that such texts are, by nature, wholly about control. Now, of course, they are about control, but possibly not wholly; or perhaps control itself is a divided enterprise.

There is anyway little evidence in the Smith passage of loss of control; its voice is quite firm and only characteristically impatient. Moreover, the coronation episode follows, in the *General History,* an elaborate description of a native ceremony that Smith recasts as an English masque, closing, for good measure, with two lines from Homer. The cause of Western civilization is advancing on all fronts, and the fiasco with the crown seems clearly intended to measure Powhatan's savagery. Yet, while, for the English, the chief's comic refusal does measure the limits of the savage mind, it also delimits and bounds English concepts of civilization. Mark Twain would one day perfect the mechanism in the Smith passage whereby a detailed physical description of the garb or ceremony of social dignity calls its bluff or, in the current idiom, deconstructs it.

This deconstructive effect is no transhistorical function of language as such. On the contrary, Smith's exposure of English ceremonial constructions responds to a particular historical moment, of which it offers an account whose narrative authority is limited precisely by Smith's own historical involvement. The self-deconstructing pitch of the coronation passage reflects its historical indeterminacies; Smith is simply uncertain about what is important in the situation and resorts to recording everything, in case. Such narrative moments are the very stuff of historical process and may serve as the grounds for an alternative imperial history that does not merely reverse the established account. Reversals of the imperial history may be more congenial than the original version − it is easier for us today to think that the Arawaks were Columbus's hapless victims than that they were idiots fit only for European slavery. But from the viewpoint of reconstructing the culture of the Arawaks, the new account is not much more useful than the old one. The hope is that a new approach to reading John Smith's *General History* can yield something other than either version of the same familiar story.

We have been looking for such an alternative view in passages that seem not entirely coherent with the orthodox views in the *General History*. Here is another such passage. It describes Powhatan's reaction to a number of English blandishments:

> If your king [Smith quotes Powhatan as saying] has sent me presents, I also am a king, and this is my land. . . . Your father is to come to me, not I to him, nor yet to your fort, neither will I bite at such a bait: as for the Monacans I can revenge my own injuries, and as for Atquanachuk, where you say your brother was slain, it is a contrary way from those parts you suppose it; but for any salt water beyond the mountains, the relations you have had from my people are false.

What can Smith possibly reply to such a powerful statement of the Indian position? This question represents the same paradox that emerged in the earlier passage: namely, that Powhatan's vision of the world directly counters Smith's – would in this instance leave *Smith* speechless – but it is only because Smith tells us about it that we have Powhatan's vision.

As we observed in Chapter 1, this telling, this *kind of telling,* which goes beyond the apparent needs of the writer's argument, is a new and significant phenomenon associated with the building of the European empires. The "true reports" compiled by Hakluyt are a very odd kind of writing, odd in the way the Smith passage is odd, in their apparent commitment to report what actually happened, or what they take to have actually happened. Obviously no "true report" can be strictly true: telling the truth already changes it. But the intention to tell the truth nonetheless produces a different sort of account than the intention to invent: truth-telling is a distinct kind of interpretation and one that comes into currency along with the beginnings of the European empires.

Registering Powhatan's resistance, Smith writes with political intention, to be sure, but also with considerable doubt about whether he will be able to carry out his intention – to make the natives submit to the rule of the English Crown and also to win for himself the rewards of such a victory. Uncertain, he describes to the best of his ability and as reliably as he can (because he needs not only to persuade others but also to understand for himself) all the elements of the situation, both those that will turn out – retrospectively – to predict the direction history will take and those that turn out to have been ephemeral or contrary to historical tendency.

In short, Smith's language is *not,* in the famous phrase of the bishop of Avila, the perfect instrument of empire; his *General History* is not wholly instrumental. He tries to make it so, but he is never perfectly successful. He is not wholly confident that Powhatan by this means or any other will be brought under the English aegis. John Smith does not control the history that he records; he records it in order to control it.

The colonial "true reports" and passages like Smith's description of the coronation of Powhatan are chronicles of uncertainty that bear witness to material uncertainties. These chronicles' lapses and incoherencies, their redundancies and paradoxes, represent the limits of discourse, the moments in which it does not know what to say. These are moments when it becomes evident that alternative historical paths coexist and the future is not overdetermined but *under*determined: there were never, before the fact, sufficient forces at work to *ensure* that the empire would succeed. The situation was therefore genuinely undetermined. What these moments inscribe is not historical direction but human agency. To read these moments, however, it is not enough to recognize the colonizers' limited authority over history and the text; that recognition leads only to reading textual ruptures, a practice that perversely confirms the wholeness of the reader's understanding.

If an account of the past is to include its indeterminacies, parts of it will have to remain terminally "nonproven," and others incoherent. We can say with certainty about this scene neither that the English Crown appropriated Powhatan's authority nor that it failed. In fact, the major event in these scenes is not the outcome at all but the interaction. In relation to the seventeenth century, seeing interaction on the stage of empire building reveals the empire less than destined and the empire builders less than entitled.

❦

The last word in this survey, in which the absence of Native-American texts and voices has been a constant theme, can nonetheless go to Native Americans. The Aztecs, as we saw earlier, wrote their own story, and the best-known part is also the most disturbing, for it seems to accept the defeat of their civilization without protest. According to this account, ten years before Cortés arrived, there appeared a series of eight omens clearly predicting the coming apocalypse. If we consider the Aztec omens to be artifacts of conquest, there is another way to read them than as evidence of self-abandonment. Although they prophecy doom, they also hold out a certain kind of hope; although they seal the present, they reopen the future. They do this by reaffirming a prior Aztec history as bearing its own destiny, its own authority realized in its very loss. Who knows the ways of the gods? What is lost can perhaps be regained, but if not, loss itself can become a ground on which a defeated civilization nonetheless survives – on the condition, however, that the memory of loss is not also lost but rather retained as a central component of the civilization's (defeated) identity. The last of the Aztec omens features "monstrous beings . . . : deformed men with two heads but only one body." The omens of the fall ensure that one of these heads is Aztec. But in accounts of the defeat of the North American Indians, the second head remains at best an insubstantial shadow.

3

🦋

THREE WRITERS OF EARLY AMERICA

I N CERTAIN PASSAGES of the story of America's exploration and colonization, literature has history coming and going. If, as we suggested
earlier, literature in the sixteenth century often instigated history, sometimes the major legacy of the history was the literature it produced. The
unsuccessful attempt to establish an English post on Roanoke Island left not
even a significant ruin, but it did give rise to the first book about the New
World written in English: Thomas Harriot's *A Brief and True Report of the New
Found Land of Virginia* (1588, 1590). Harriot's book is an objective account of
conditions in the New World; rather, it means to be objective. John Smith
produced the first writings in a more subjective mode, which would become
equally important in the literature. For Smith the New World was not only a
site for imperial development but a theater of self-development as well. His
major work, *The General History of Virginia, New England, and the Summer Isles*
(1624), also claims to be a "true report," but along with accounts of natural
resources and local hazards, it interweaves a narrative of Smith's career, often
told in the third person. Finally, the most likely candidate for first American
book written in English (Smith was not an American) is Roger Williams's
1643 *A Key into the Language of America*. These three works are the focus of
this chapter.

🦋

Thomas Harriot's *A Brief and True Report of the New Found Land of Virginia* was
published in haste to support Walter Raleigh's petition to the queen not to
abandon the Virginia colony, whose first settlement had just failed. A second
edition was brought out by the Flemish engraver and publisher Theodor de
Bry two years later as part of a projected series entitled *America,* and it was
multilingual (Latin, German, French, and English). Harriot had collected
notes for a much more extensive chronicle, but most of his papers were lost
on the return voyage.

The *Report* is a sort of advertising brochure. It is also a model of scrupulous
reporting whose self-effacing author is anxious to signal the limits of observation. Harriot (1560–1621) has reemerged today as a major scientist in the

company of Kepler and Galileo. His long obscurity is due to the virtual disappearance at his death of his extensive writings in mathematics and astronomy, but as the history of science comes clearer, the import of these is being reconstructed. Renaissance science was supported by aristocratic patronage, and Harriot, in the employ of Raleigh, developed mathematical principles of navigation that were essential to colonizing voyages. Raleigh sent Harriot to investigate the likelihood and the potential profitability of a Virginia plantation. ("Virginia" refers to all the land from the coast extending inward covered in Raleigh's patent.) The advice "To the gentle reader" (subtitled more pointedly "To the adventurers, favorers, and well-willers of the enterprise for inhabiting and planting in Virginia,") warns that what follows is meant for Raleigh's use in countering "diverse and variable reports with some slanderous and shameful speeches bruited abroad by many that returned from thence." Some of the aspiring settlers had returned disappointed and were counseling abandonment of the whole enterprise. Whether they were too lazy and unskilled to make it work, as Harriot contends, or, as they maintained, the expedition was ill-conceived, the "advice" reminds us that colonization is a highly competitive business and that scholarship like Harriot's entered deeply into the competition.

Harriot observes the landscape, flora, and fauna of Roanoke not only with the eye of a scientist but also with the calculation of one who has been dispatched to bring back an accounting upon which large investments depend. The *Report* plunges at once into commerce with an account of the colony's "merchantable commodities," starting with a grass he mistakenly takes to be silk grass. His discussion of this grass maps the current imperial program and makes his bid for a turn toward the western continents. "The like [of the silk grass] groweth in Persia," Harriot explains (invoking ambitions for access to the East) "which is in the selfsame climate as Virginia." The West can also serve: "by the means of sowing and planting in good ground, it will be far greater, better, and more plentiful than it is."

The catalogue is organized not by nature but by trade, from "flax and hemp" to "wapeih" (a medicinal clay), to "pitch, tar, rosin, and turpentine" (of which "the whole island [is] full"), to wine, furs, deer skins, iron, copper, pearls, and sugarcane. It ends by explicitly addressing the world of mercantile competition and piracy, for Harriot has intentionally left certain information out of the report: "Two more commodities of great value . . . I might have specified. So likewise of those commodities already set down I might have said more; as of the particular places where they are found and best to be planted and prepared . . . but because others then well-willers might be therewithal acquainted, not to the good of the action, I have wittingly omitted them."

In the background are mercantile pirates on one side and on the other merchants and noblemen competing for colonial patents. Harriot is certainly implicated in their dealings, but at the same time he begins to reflect on the living stakes of all the machinations: the New World's land and people. They begin to acquire a certain degree of autonomy for him. Having promised that well-planted the silk grass will grow even better, Harriot thinks to add something about its character prior to European intervention: "Although notwithstanding [the promise of increased fertility under cultivation] there is great store thereof in many places of the country growing naturally and wild." "Naturally and wild" are words that will occupy the center of the colonial discourse for several centuries, in play with the opposite concept of cultivation. On the surface, there is an obvious direct link between a land's inherent fertility and its promise when cultivated; and Harriot is simply establishing this link. But the relation of the wild and the cultivated, as well as the relation of both to the natural, turned out to be more complicated in ways that already begin to emerge in the *Report*.

The second part, entitled "Of such commodities as Virginia is known to yield for victual and sustenance of man's life, usually fed upon by the natural inhabitants: as also by us during the time of our abode. And first of such as are sowed and husbanded," is explicitly about cultivation. But this is para-doxical because the land described seems not to require cultivation. The inhabitants, Harriot observes, "never fatten [the ground] with muck, dung or any other thing; neither plow nor dig it as we in England." Instead of lengthy fertilizings and plowings, native farmers make few preparations before planting their crops: "A few days before they sow or set," they "only break the upper part of the ground" to rid it of weeds and dried stalks, "which after a day or two's drying in the sun being scraped up into many small heaps, to save them labour for carrying them away; they burn into ashes." This is hardly an effort, few days are spent, even the heaps of weeds are small, but the rewards are bountiful. The cultivation of maize especially has an almost Edenic quality: "Besides the manifold ways in applying it to victual, the increase is so much that small labour and pains is needful in respect that must be used for ours." The numbers — recall that Harriot was a mathematician — have a mythical cast: with fewer than twenty-four hours of labor some twenty-five square yards of ground will yield enough to sustain a man for about twelve months. But then often "they have two harvests . . . out of one and the same ground."

The cultivation required to reap these bounties is minimal. Harriot has not been describing rich plantations but rather the spontaneous plenitude of a paradisical garden. The *Report* is one of the first texts in the tradition that describes America as a garden or as the second Garden. This garden is not antithetical to cultivation. Harriot assures the potential tiller of the soil of Virginia that his success is certain: "Of the growth you need not to doubt: for barley, oats and peas, we have seen proof of, not being purposely sown but fallen casually in the worst sort of ground, and yet to be as fair as any we have seen here in England." In such accounts, the New World's exceptional fertility actually obviates the difference between cultivated and wild. But in so doing it significantly alters the definition of cultivation. The divine sentence to sweat or go hungry does not project cultivation as casually dropping seeds on the soil and lolling about until the harvest. Garden *or* farm, Virginia is a promised land.

Harriot is not elegiac throughout, however. Indeed, he has not one but two ways of representing the New World. On the one hand, Virginia is rightfully England's and the possession has only to be realized. The barley and oats are waiting to spring into prodigious growth. On the other hand, Virginia and its marvelous fertility are deeply alien, quite outside the ken of Englishmen – and already possessed by others who are themselves deeply alien. The disgruntled members of the Roanoke expeditions, whose calumny has occasioned the hurried writing of the *Report,* have failed the colonizing mission for no larger reason than laziness and want of skills. "Some . . . were of a nice bringing up, only in cities and towns, or such as never . . . had seen the world before. Because there were not to be found any English cities, nor such fair houses, nor at their own wish any of their old accustomed dainty food, nor any soft beds of down or feathers: the country was to them miserable." These dainty gentlemen cannot be taken seriously as critics of the expedition *nor as aspects of it*, because they never really took part in it; they remained outside: "they were never out of the island where we were seated, or not far, or at the leastwise in few places else." From this perspective, Virginia is not a promised land; in fact, it will not be attained without great effort.

The basis of Harriot's dualistic vision of America is his recognition that the continent is already inhabited. As we saw earlier, the "natural inhabitants" were abundantly present in Renaissance exploration narratives generally. But the *Report* makes particularly clear the way that acknowledgment of the Indian presence renders the conquest of America something other than the unilateral unfolding of a manifest destiny. It is a contest, a collision. The third part of the *Report* is almost entirely given over to a description of the "nature and manners of the people." Like the earlier descriptions, this one, Harriot warns the reader, is much abbreviated and proceeds "only so far forth, as that you may know, how that they in respect of troubling our inhabiting and planting, are not to be feared." Thus, "they shall have cause both to fear and love us, that shall inhabit with them."

The English took moral pride in distinguishing their colonizing methods from those of the Spanish, whose ferocity in Mexico and Peru had become legendary. Hakluyt, for instance, urged negotiations with the native inhabitants and peaceful barter. But there is no way finally to take away a people's land without violence. Harriot's proposition that the natives will have reason to both fear and love the colonists is more than a formality, therefore; it is the most charged expression of the dualism that pervades his entire *Report*.

Harriot is also interested in the Indians for their own sake. His vividly concrete descriptions of native life reflect his scientific orientation. For example, he explains exactly how their houses are constructed, their measurements and materials, their arrangement in villages, and how many make up an average town. These accounts are no less inflected for their precision, however. The general tenor is set by a minimalizing grammar: the towns are "but small" and "but few," made up of "but 10 or 12 houses," the largest town "but of 30." Whatever specification is not introduced by a "but" is diminished by an "if there is, then it is only": "if they be walled it is only . . . or else . . . only. . . ." Thus, even when he does not say explicitly that the Indians' manufactures are inconsequential, we assume they are. They are inconsequential or missing outright: lacking iron and steel, for instance, they are pitifully lacking in arms; and "those weapons that they have, are only bows . . . neither have they anything to defend themselves."

The message is clear: "If there fall out any wars between us and them," we can easily rout them. However, war is not the only way to deal with the Indians. They may be responsive to negotiations insofar as having "no such . . . sciences and arts as we; yet in those things they do, they show excellence of wit." White superiority can inspire as well as suppress: "by how much they shall find our manner of knowledge and craft to exceed theirs in perfection . . . by so much the more is it probable that they should desire our friendships and love, and have the greater respect for pleasing and obeying us." And from this it "may be hoped . . . that they may in short time be brought to civility, and the embracing of true religion."

Harriot's combination of attitudes springs logically and coherently from a set of premises about the desirability of an English conquest of America and from the further desirability that this conquest be executed in significant part by Harriot's own patron. They include the belief in the superiority of European civilization as this is embodied, for this Renaissance scientist, in the contemporary explosion of technological and scientific knowledge. The Indians are not the only ones impressed by the following catalogue:

Most things they saw with us, as mathematical instruments, sea compasses, the virtue of the loadstone in drawing iron, a perspective glass whereby was shown many strange sights, burning glasses, wildfire works, guns, books, writing and reading, spring clocks that seem to go of themselves, and many other things that we had, were so strange unto them, and so far exceeded their capacities to comprehend the reason and means how they should be made and done, that they thought they were rather the works of gods than of men, or at the leastwise they had been given and taught us of the gods.

Harriot, who seems without personal arrogance, nonetheless finds his own and his fellows' powers of mind and making just a little amazing.

Given those premises, the joining of carrot and stick in the program for conquest is not remarkable. What is remarkable and peculiar to the *Report* is the way force and persuasion (paralleling the arguments of Sepúlveda and of Las Casas) are deployed side by side as twin possibilities. Neither mutually necessary nor exclusive, both possibilities spring from a single, generally coherent sense both of the Native Americans and of the English. Almost at the end of his report, Harriot takes note of some unfortunate incidents:

[A]lthough some of our company towards the end of the year, showed themselves too fierce, in slaying some of the people, in some towns, upon causes that on our part, might easily enough have been borne withal: yet notwithstanding because it was on their part justly deserved, the alteration of their opinions generally and for the most part concerning us is the less to be doubted. And whatsoever else they may be, by carefulness of ourselves need nothing at all to be feared.

We were too fierce in response to insufficient provocation; they deserved their punishment and it will not change their attitude toward us. These two propositions add up to one that embraces both without transforming either: if we are careful, there is nothing to worry about.

This last passage diagrams the exceptional quality of Harriot's report. It is divided between a probing scientific spirit and an unquestioning loyalty to Raleigh's imperial project; between assurances that the most likely reaction of the Indians to white invasion will be "the turning up of their heels against us in running away" and accounts of Harriot's own apparently mutually respectful "special familiarity with some of their priests." The report is not balanced but dualistic. In this lack of fusion – not a lack of coherence but only of resolution – the latter-day reader may glimpse something of the complexity of the period of America's early exploration, when the land was a prize as well as a promise; when England's brave New World was still, even to its colonists, a world not elsewhere but just out there.

Another way to describe the unresolved dualism of Harriot's *Report* is to read it as marking the threshold of American colonization. At the other end of the process Robert Frost retrospectively resolved Harriot's dilemma by declaring, "We were the land's before the land was ours." This formulation renders the connection of whites to America organic and aboriginal – preconscious. In that case the wild and the cultivated, the indigenous Americans and the naturalized ones, are two aspects of a single unity. But for Harriot, nearly four centuries earlier, the connection to America – of cultivation to the wild, of Europeans to America – has yet to be crafted. The first step, involving disconnection of the Indians (from the land that before everything is *theirs*), implies the contingency of all such relations. The Indians are vividly there for Harriot because *their* organic presence in America, *their* preconscious belonging, argues the provisional character of white settlement. They are the "natural inhabitants"; are the English, then, unnatural inhabitants?

The organization of the *Report* reflects this question. The first section's dedication to an inventory of "merchantable" natural resources immediately annexes America to England by translating nature into a market. The presentation of the inventory is the most abstract section of the book, each "commodity" appearing out of context, with only the most basic references to its American provenance. But the subject of the second section is the ways that the New World will yield "victual and sustenance of man's life." Inevitably it plants Harriot on American soil, which now becomes the defining context rather than the market. On American soil and among Americans: if the opening of the first section identified silk grass through its relation to Persia, the second section begins with a native name, "Pagatowr, a kind of grain so called by the inhabitants." The primary identification is local; the center of the description is Virginia. In a secondary way Harriot adds that this is the grain called "maize" in the West Indies and "Guinea wheat or Turkey wheat" by the English, depending on their reference points. The depiction of nature in this agricultural section is inseparable from a relation of the ways that the natural inhabitants live in it.

The voyage continues inward in the third part, which begins with an account of indigenous building materials and moves almost at once to a final entry, introduced offhandedly as a last remark, but by most readers then and since taken as the book's culmination. "It resteth I speak a word or two of the natural inhabitants . . . leaving large discourse thereof until time more convenient hereafter," and here only saying enough to show that they are not to be feared. Native-American agricultural ways and assorted other practices have already been described, but here Harriot focuses just on them, and he proceeds to explain the rudiments of their religion and culture. It is clear that his considerable knowledge derives from the friendships he formed with Indian men. At first figured as an unincorporated assortment of goods, by the end of the book America has not only a body but a face.

Indeed the *Report* ends with a series of actual portraits, which have sometimes been considered its most important feature. The painter–illustrator–draughtsman John White had earlier accompanied the explorer Martin Frobisher to the Arctic in order to paint Eskimos. Over the nearly full year he spent at Roanoke with Harriot, White sketched the local Algonkians eating, dancing, at work, and in religious ceremonies. An unknown number of his drawings were lost along with Harriot's notes on the way back to England. But in 1587 Hakluyt had a portfolio of White's sketches to show Theodor de Bry. The deluxe edition of the *Report* was accompanied by twenty-two White drawings annotated by Harriot. The linguistically transitional character of the late sixteenth century is nicely represented by the fact that Harriot initially wrote these notes in Latin. It was the ever-mediating Hakluyt who then translated Harriot's Latin notes into English.

Ten of the sketches are of individuals, like "a weroan or great lord of Virginia" and "one of the chief ladies of Secota." Influenced by the miniaturist painting of Jacques Le Moyne, White's portraits tower over miniature landscapes in which figures can be seen in characteristic activities. A young woman said to be the daughter of Chief Secota is described as a gentlewoman. The illustration shows her twice, front and back, in order to give a complete account of her hair arrangement and clothing. She is pictured standing on the river shore, and Harriot's legend explains that such young women delight "in seeing fish taken." The text observes with ethnographical precision that the way she is holding her arms bent, so that her hands touch her shoulders, a forearm covering one naked breast, is "in token of maidenlike modesty"; the other breast remains exposed to represent the characteristic absence of upper-body clothing. In this gesture as well as in her evident interest in fishing, the woman is specifically Algonkian. But other than scientific concerns are at play. The figure's light curly hair, bow lips, and rounded face and body assimilate her to a universal myth of the human figure that evokes Greeks and Romans instead of American Indians, the Old World, not the New.

This effect is mostly the work of de Bry, whose engravings altered White's drawings presumably in the interests, as he understood them, of both art and commerce. The originals feature dark straight hair; somewhat Asiatic features; thinner, more elongated bodies; and a distinctly different way of standing and moving. A mother and child in White's illustration face forward in a matter-of-fact pose, their feet firmly planted, with no apparent message for us. De Bry has rounded and generally softened the mother's posture; markedly more fleshy, her left leg is slightly forward as she steps toward the viewer; her left hip thus arches in a curve flowing from her inclined head; she looks vaguely toward her curly-headed, chubby child, who now raises a rattle above its head and runs playfully forward. In the originals, the lips of both mother and child are parted in distinct smiles. De Bry replaced the smiles with a less defined expression. The drawing documents racial characteristics and defamiliarizes the otherwise familiar scene of mother and child. The engraving represents universal motherhood in the image European book buyers would expect.

Two things are going on here at somewhat cross-purposes. The one first likely to strike a late-twentieth-century reader is that de Bry has erased the difference between European and American Indian and projected a spuriously universal but actually European human model onto the latter. By this account, the non-Europeans are denied their identity, which White had granted them. This very loss, however, can be seen another way, as humanizing the Indians, who, in White's depiction, do look more wild (i.e., naked instead of nude, their bodies and hair rough rather than smooth). To produce as profitable a volume as possible, de Bry improves on White by making his illustrations more classically aesthetic and more ethnically sympathetic to a well-educated, enlightened European audience. On the one hand, his assimilation of the Algonkians to a mythical model of universal humanity implies that in their own guise they fall below the human form. On the other hand, it expresses a view that they can be raised up. This view makes sense of White's odd addition to the set of drawings he gave de Bry of five portraits of Picts showing "how the inhabitants of Great Britain have been in times past as savage as those of Virginia." America's natural inhabitants occupy the bottom rung on the same historical ladder as the English. Only a little elevated in de Bry's renditions, they remain clearly inferior. But they are not Calibans; the Harriot–White–de Bry trio encompasses the range of colonialist benevolence in the sixteenth and early seventeenth centuries, an unsteady, fragile benevolence that briefly qualified the ferocity of the conquest.

The legend under the introductory engraving, entitled "The arrival of the Englishmen in Virginia," captures the ambiguity of Harriot's and White's, and later de Bry's, stance. At first, when the ships approached and their occupants became visible, Harriot writes, the people on shore made "a horrible cry . . . and came away making out cries like wild beasts or men out of their wits." But upon being gently addressed by the English, they "came fawning upon us, and bade us welcome." The "Weroans or Prince" then received them "with reasonable [meaning rational] courtesy," and Harriot will now offer an account of "the stature of body of which people, their attire, and manner of living, their feasts, and banquets." This list is not only pacific but downright homely. The wild beasts and madmen have turned back into domestic human beings. The engraving itself portrays two English ships anchored off the Outer Banks, closer to which five boats half submerged can be seen to have foundered. Harriot's ship has managed to pass through to an inner harbor, in which lies Roanoke. A figure standing on the prow is addressing a fleeing Indian ashore, but the scene on the island is peaceful and orderly. Houses form a neat circle surrounded by a sort of stockade, fields of grain lie in precise rectangles outside the village, and clumps of trees dot the island, on the other side of which the inhabitants are plying canoes. The engraving is divided in half horizontally between sea and land and between English and Algonkians. It pictures an encounter between two peoples.

In sum, Harriot sells America to the English, but he also recognizes that it belongs to the Indians. The nature of this belonging does not preclude its being sold, of course; both modes of possession nonetheless obtain. The duality does not at this point move toward resolution, although it represents neither incoherence nor ambivalence. Raleigh's man Harriot is certainly not ambivalent about conquering America, which, he assures his readers, will prove more and more bounteous the deeper exploration penetrates: "the soil . . . fatter; the trees greater . . . the ground more firm and deeper mold . . . finer grass . . . more plenty of their fruits; more abundance of beasts"; and, as an aspect of this ever-expanding plenitude, "the more inhabited with people, and of greater policy and larger dominions, with greater towns and houses." Wild *and* also somehow naturally cultivated, the New World awaits European conquest *and* is the natural home of a thriving civilization.

 ❧

Harriot half recognized that America belonged to the Indians. But his readers were seldom so divided. The evolution of the concept of manifest destiny – the notion that the American continent in its extension from the Atlantic to the Pacific made manifest the destined expansion of European civilization – begins in the sixteenth and seventeenth centuries with a progressive conviction that America is meant for Europeans.

One of the first and most vigorous exponents of this view was an adventurer named John Smith (1580–1631). Smith was the ambitious son of an affluent farmer, and his first effort to climb the social ladder took him into the army of the Holy Roman Empire. Having fought the infidel in Turkey, Smith was captured and briefly enslaved. He escaped, returned to England, and enrolled in the first Jamestown colony; he set sail in 1606, this time going west to Christianity's newest battlefield. In Jamestown, Smith became the controversial but indubitably able president of the Governing Council. Despite the brevity of his stay in the New World (less than three years), Smith was one of the most influential proponents of an aggressive colonial policy, writing a multitude of influential tracts that described to England the rich advantages of its colonies and not coincidentally his own central role in securing these advantages.

Smith's *General History of Virginia, New England, and the Summer Isles* (1624) collects his own earlier writings on Virginia and New England and, on the model of his friend Purchas's compilations, adds documents and reports (including large parts of Harriot's) circulating in the community of merchants and adventurers, interspersed with classical verses as well as some written expressly to celebrate the book and its author: "Like Caesar now thou writ'st what thou hast done, / These acts, this Booke will live while there's a Sunne." It is one of the most remarkable texts, at once representative and exceptional, of the period. Indeed, Smith's claim for the book, and for himself, is to be exceptionally representative, the seventeenth century's Englishman of the hour. Nowhere are Smith's imperial exploits more timely than in establishing the absoluteness of English domination.

A passage from the *General History* encapsulates the ideology of Jamestown, as Smith was foremost in defining it, and offers something like a plot summary of the colonizing narrative. In his characteristically self-promoting way, Smith recalls the dangerous early weeks and months of the colony and how with a few decisive acts he saved the day. The London gentlemen who set up the Virginia Company lacked an appreciation of the times, which could only be had by an astute man of action. The gentlemen were too anxious to establish moral superiority over the Spanish, their traditional and despised enemy. To distinguish their imperial policy from the notorious "Black legend" of Spanish atrocities, the English dangerously constrained the colonists to a foolish pacifism. Indeed, "the command from England was so straight not to offend [the Indians]" that "they became so insolent there was no rule."

But the Indians were not dealing only with idealistic bureaucrats, and for his part Smith was a great admirer of Cortés. Soon "it chanced they meddled with Captain Smith [he typically writes about himself in the third person], who without further deliberation gave them such an encounter, as some he hunted up and down the isle, some he . . . terrified with whipping, beating, and imprisonment." It was not an easy victory, for the Indians were an obdurate lot. "For revenge they surprised two of our foraging and disorderly soldiers, and having assembled their forces, boldly threatened at our ports to force Smith to redeliver seven savages, which for their villainies he detained prisoners, or we were all dead men." In contrast to the untried gentlemen who made policy for the colonies from afar, Smith knew what had to be done. "To try their furies he sallied out amongst them, and in less than an hour, he so hampered their insolencies, they brought them his two men, desiring peace without any further composition for their prisoners."

Although his pusillanimous critics railed – wholly without reason because no Englishmen were slain – Smith's firmness ensured them all a safe future. By his decisiveness he "brought [the Indians] in such fear and obedience, as his very name would sufficiently affright them," "where before, we had sometime peace and war twice in a day, and very seldom a week, but we had some teacherous villainy or other."

Some version of this story recurs at intervals throughout Smith's writings. The only acceptable Native-American stance is "fear and obedience" when they are tolerated for their labors or contributions of food; otherwise, they are to be chased away. In another passage he castigates the administration of the Virginia colony after his departure and offers to return and set things right, promising that with but a hundred soldiers employed "only in ranging the countries, and tormenting the savages," he will "enforce the savages to leave their country, or bring them in that fear and subjection that every man should follow their business securely."

But for all this, John Smith was not only or even primarily known as an assiduous persecutor. His relations with the Indians became renowned not for war but for romance. He is today most widely known as the hero of the tale of an Indian princess, Pocahontas, who saved the life of a captured white soldier by laying her own head down in the path of the club that was to crush his skull. And in fact the passage cited just above, in which Smith boasts he has subdued the natives through shows of force and steely resolve, invokes Pocahontas as a crucial part of the strategy. From the Indian prisoners, by threats of death, he extracts the confession that they have been sent on their "villainies" by Powhatan, father of Pocahontas and sometime friend of Smith but also always potential betrayer. Seeing himself defeated in this instance, Powhatan "sent his messengers, and his dearest daughter Pocahontas with presents to excuse him of the injuries done by some rash untoward captains his subjects, desiring their liberties for this time, with the assurance of his love forever." Smith understands at once that this is tantamount to an admission of defeat, and after he "ha[s] given the prisoners what correction he thought fit, [he] use[s] them well a day or two after, and then deliver[s] them [to] Pocahontas, for whose sake only he feigned to have saved their lives, and gave them liberty." It is the return of the prisoners to Pocahontas that concludes the episode.

Does this signal a reconciliation, or less definitively, does it qualify the Indian defeat or soften it by the injection of romance into the arena of war? Rather the opposite. When in Smith's story, Powhatan sues for a return to friendly relations in the name of his daughter, he concedes not less but more than military defeat, a loss at arms and also a loss of self, in the yielding of the female representative of his nation. In the modern Western tradition emerging in Smith's time, the romantic love of a woman for a man, even when only individuals are at issue, entails the woman's self-abandonment; in the legend of Pocahontas, the Indian, cast as a woman, abandons herself and himself to white manhood. Powhatan's humiliation is more than military.

Captain John Smith's triumph, too, is more than military. He has reduced the Indian soldiers (dubbed "braves") to "fear and obedience." Thus far, however, his power over them has been external both to them and to him, a matter of imposing his will by force. Winning the heart of Pocahontas gives him access to the Indians' very being; he now annexes that self to his own. Until now, Powhatan has represented a limit to Smith's ability to define himself through his conquest of America: he can conquer it, but so long as Powhatan embodies even a conquered America, Smith cannot really claim it for himself or as a part of himself. When Powhatan's daughter is represented as abandoning herself to him – ceases to be distinct from him and becomes "his" – Smith enters into a new dominion in which America is *his,* body and soul. It is not a coincidental feature of the legend that John Smith does not love Pocahontas but only she him. Her later marriage to John Rolfe, and for that matter her untimely death in England in a state of Christian ecstasy, play out the drama of the unilateral submission of America's people to their European conquerors.

The English henceforth possess the land not unlike a husband traditionally possesses his wife, a husband who is the more wholly in command for not being a lover. The story we have been examining proffers three ways in which the whites have defeated the Native Americans: as soldiers, as fathers, and, through Pocahontas, as men. In this context, the repeated accounts by Europeans of the failure of native men to really work, so that the work of the villages was done by women, offers another instance of their unmanning. Native-American men do not farm, they do not build houses; they lounge about and occasionally hunt. For the Europeans who first explored and then settled America, hunting does not redeem the assumed effeminacy of the absence of constructive labor.

The story of La Malinche, the Mexican woman who was Cortés's mistress and translator, dramatizes the same elements of conquest while measuring the difference between the English and the Spanish conceptions of what they were about in conquering. As she is described for instance by Bernal Díaz, La Malinche contributes materially to the conquest, sometimes going beyond Cortés's speeches to add her own, better-informed arguments. She comes close to being a partner in the defeat of the Aztecs, whose downfall she too desires, for her own reasons. She is the slave of Cortés but retains a distinct identity. In a parallel way, Cortés defeated the Aztecs but did not destroy them altogether. The Spanish replaced the Aztec Empire with their own mightier and more worthy one, but the Aztecs retained an ongoing presence in Mexico after their defeat. In Mexico, La Malinche, as we have noted, signifies treachery and thus a continuing if hopeless conflict. In the United States, the self-abandoning Pocahontas stands for romance or the resolution of conflict in the absorption of one participant by the other. Pocahontas enables John Smith not only, like Cortés, to conquer the original inhabitants but to absorb them into an English America.

Far from identifying America like Harriot with its indigenous population, John Smith works constantly to define it in terms of himself. Conversely, he defines himself in terms of America. In his view, the ineffectual gentlemen of the Virginia colony came to the New World to make or improve their fortunes, and the London "lowlifes" came under duress, by and large hoping only to survive. Against both these types, Smith precociously identified making the New World with making himself.

His later reputation as a braggart and liar is anachronistic; a pioneer in the science of self-creation later systematized for Americans by Benjamin Franklin, John Smith was simply inventing and publishing himself. Or rather he invented *by* publishing himself; Smith literally published himself into fame if not always into fortune. One of the charges posterity has raised against him has been that each version of the daring tales of his life is more swashbuckling than the last. If we note, however, that he was one of the first English writers of autobiography, such progressive aggrandizement seems less gratuitous. In *The True Travels, Adventures, and Observations of Captain John Smith in Europe, Asia, Africa, and America, Beginning about the Year 1593, and Continued to This Present 1629* (1630), Smith writes of himself in the third person, telling the story of his life, beginning with his birth and concluding with a denunciation of pirates. This last is not at all quixotic but rather the appropriate conclusion to the story of a life of theft and killing in the pursuit of social status. In the last paragraph of *The True Travels,* Smith calls on "Merchants, Gentlemen, and all setters forth of ships" to pay those who man those ships a decent wage so that they need not steal; he then addresses the "seaman and soldiers," who were once honored but are now regarded as "the scum of the world," to regain their reputations by abandoning piracy to seek wealth instead in "those fair plantations of our English Nation." Although these plantations were in the beginning "scorned and condemned, yet now you see how many rich and gallant people come from thence, who went thither as poor as any soldier or sailor, and get more in one year, than you by piracy in seven." This celebration of the way to wealth was in a sense Smith's last word, for he died in 1631.

He would willingly have made it his last word, for the dereliction of the gentlemen-settlers was perhaps his favorite theme. Employing an image that was becoming a commonplace of political rhetoric, Smith complained in *A Description of New England* (1616),

If the little ant, and the silly bee seek by their diligence the good of their commonwealth; much more ought man. If they punish the drones and sting them [that] steal their labour; then blame not man. Little honey hath that hive, where there are more drones then bees: and miserable is that land, where more are idle than well employed.

The new hives of England's imperial swarming were under constant threat from the sabotage of aristocratic drones.

John Smith seems to have developed a full-blown middle-class consciousness even before the middle class was entirely acknowledged as a distinct (middle) way. *Not* a Puritan – his admiration for the solid citizens of the Massachusetts Bay Colony was somewhat tempered by their tendency to be "more precise than needs" – Smith is thus the more significant as an exponent of a class philosophy that ultimately prevailed in America. Following his retirement, when he was asked how the current defects in the Virginia government might be rectified, Smith explained that the New World (above all others) must have settlers who were prepared to work. Empire building there could not proceed as elsewhere "for there is no country to pillage as the Romans found: all you expect from thence must be by labour."

This vision of America is notably not that of the Spanish, who, having pillaged the cities of the Aztecs and the Incas, retained their imperial model and did not seek a new one even when Spanish planters established themselves not so differently from their Virginia counterparts. At a time when the English Crown and a significant portion of its capital-holding aristocracy still looked east because the traditional rewards of empire building seemed so much more abundant there, Smith promoted a new kind of empire, yielding a new kind of wealth. His New World did not compete with the old depositories of wealth; in fact, he angrily rejected suggestions that gold and precious stones might be found there. *The Proceedings of the English Colony in Virginia* (1612) includes an exasperated account of gold fever among the colonists, some of whom at one point mistakenly thought they had struck gold in and near the James River:

The worst mischief was, our gilded refiners with their golden promises, made all men their slaves in hope of recompense; there was no talk, no hope, no work, but dig gold, wash gold, refine gold, load gold, such a brute [clamor] of gold, as one mad fellow desired to be buried in the sands, least they should by their art make gold of his bones.

As he saw it, the wealth promised by the New World was better than gold, and he advised his "honourable and worthy countrymen . . . let not the meanness of the word fish distaste you, for it will afford as good gold as the mines of Guiana, or Tumbatu, with less hazard and charge and more certainty and facility." Indeed, in one apostrophe to fishing, Smith rings out the ancient model of empire and rings in the new. Fish "may seem a mean and a base commodity," he writes in the *General History,* but who doth not know that the poor Hollanders chiefly by fishing . . . are made a people so hardy and industrious, and by the venting this poor commodity to the Easterlings for as mean, which is wood, flax, pitch, tar, rosin, cordage, and such like; which they exchange again to the French, Spaniards, Portugals, and English, etc., for what they want, are made so mighty, strong, and rich, as no state but Venice of twice their magnitude is so well furnished, with so many fair cities, goodly towns, strong fortresses, and that abundance of shipping, and all sort of merchandise, as well of gold, silver, pearls, diamonds, precious stones, silks, velvets, and cloth of gold; as fish, pitch, wood, or such gross commodities?

Indeed, all the Spanish mines of silver and gold can never pay their nation's debt like "this contemptible trade of fish," for

this is the chiefest mine, and the sea the source of those silver streams of all their virtue, which hath made them now the very miracle of industry, the only pattern of perfection for these affairs: and the benefit of fishing is that Primum Mobile that turns all their spheres to this height, of plenty, strength, honor, and exceeding great admiration.

The paean to fishing continues at this pitch of excitement for another four pages.

Fish and fishermen and the merchants who realize the profits of both for everyone, these are Smith's colonizing heroes, as are planters and traders of plain and useful commodities. In this respect, he anticipates New England thinking instead of southern. His distaste for tobacco culture is especially telling. Raleigh, for instance, despite some occasional piracy, also understood the American empire in terms of merchantable goods, but his commitment to tobacco implies an understanding of the merchant life altogether different from Smith's, for whom tobacco culture is as insidious as the search for gold. Smith includes in the *General History* a description of the state of Jamestown after an interval in which the colonists had caught the tobacco fever: there were left

but five or six houses, the church down, the palizados broken, the bridge in pieces, the well of fresh water spoiled; the storehouse they used for the church, the market-place, and streets, and all other spare places planted with tobacco, the savages as frequent in their houses as themselves, whereby they were become expert in our arms, and had a great many in their custody and possession, the colony dispersed all about, planting tobacco.

Disaster impends (the natives are without fear or awe and they have guns), but the situation is even more frightening for its chaos, in which all the categories of social life have dissolved or been resolved into the common currency of a crop whose value is largely artificial. It is with deep distrust that this early entrepreneur contemplates a sort of finance capitalism in which tobacco "passes . . . as current silver, and by the oft turning and winding it, some grow rich, but many poor." In his opinion, the disparity bodes ill for both.

Smith disapproves of the "rich" as well as of the "poor." The difficulties and dangers of early Jamestown were only in part the result of natural factors. As important were the derelictions of "Gallants" sent him by the company, who were, in his view, worse than useless. His constant litany is, better "one hundred good labourers" than a thousand gentlemen. He includes in the *General History* the report of the clerk of the Jamestown council, Richard Pots, who complains of the composition of the settling party, men "more fit to spoil a commonwealth, then either begin one, or but help maintain one." And the list of these drones lumps together "rich" and "poor": "poor gentlemen [impoverished nobility, thus in class terms the rich], tradesmen, servingmen, libertines," footmen to "adventurers," and the adventurers themselves, an entire company "that never did know what a day's work was. . . . But one carpenter in the country, and three others that could do little." At one point, Smith recalls bitterly that "we were about two hundred in all, but not twenty workmen." Productive labor as the source of value was not then the truism it became; Smith's scorn for those who did not produce was wellnigh revolutionary, or rather it participated in a revolution that was still in its early days.

Harriot too inveighed against the idle gentlemen sent to Roanoke, and the preference in a new settlement for carpenters over cavaliers was inspired as much by common sense as by ideology. What is specifically ideological in Smith's repeated tirades against those who would live in "pride and idleness" is his sense that they constitute a useless *class*. The men he wants for the New World are not different from those he admires in England, men "of good estate, . . . of good credit and well-beloved in their country, not such as fly for debt, or any scandal at home."

The *General History* is punctuated by lists of new arrivals in Jamestown and these lists are always organized by class. In one party, there were "gentlemen," "labourers," "soldiers," then "tailors," "apothecaries," and some who were anathema to Smith, a jeweler, two refiners and two goldsmiths, and a perfumer. Of eleven such artisans, only three had needed skills. Solid folk of the middle classes, "gentlemen" like himself, not of noble extraction but lately risen by their own contrivance and rising further through their removal to America, enterprising artisans, and soldiers, these are the people who, ambitious to make themselves, will make America; whom, reciprocally, the making of America will make, as Captain John Smith himself is the creature of his creation of Jamestown.

With John Smith, then, America begins to imply not only quantity but quality, not only the diffusion of English or European civilization but its recreation in a different form: if the men he wants as planters of Jamestown are those he respects at home, in Virginia they will define the social scene as they do not at home. That hoped-for society will be an America that is, first, *not* the ancient world (not any crumbling Eastern kingdom to be pillaged and abandoned) and, second, *not* present-day Europe (still dominated by a parasitic aristocracy). In the act of taking possession of America, Smith envisioned that his new sort of man would also evolve an expanded sense of himself. It was a prophetic concept; in time, it would become a commonplace of the dominant national ideology that the American was an individual of unlimited potential in the image of an apparently boundless land.

Roger Williams (1603?–83) had the same reasons as John Smith to conceive of the New World as a theater for his own self-realization. He came from the same middling class as John Smith. His father was a self-made London shopkeeper who educated his son at Charterhouse and Cambridge but also apprenticed him to the Merchant Tailor's Company. As a separatist Puritan besides, Williams emigrated with the unambivalent intention to build himself a new world. Yet when the Massachusetts Bay Colony banished him in 1635, the first of the four charges Governor John Winthrop listed against Williams was that he denied the colonists' territorial rights.

Indeed, although fully supporting the project of English colonization, Williams argued that the royal charter was invalid, the king could not bestow what he did not own, and the land already belonged to the Indians. It would have to be purchased. Recognizing the rights of previous inhabitants invalidates the imperialist claim, however. The Massachusetts Bay colonists could not pay for Indian land without vitiating their transcendent right to it. Williams's proposition challenged the very basis of the imperial project.

Williams's most extensive and developed work is *A Key into the Language of America* (1643). The *Key* is virtually unique in the English literature of colonization in its projection of a developing relationship with the indigenous populations. The intent of the few other contemporary linguistic studies – notably John Eliot's (1604–90) *Primer or Catechism in the Massachusetts Indian Language* (1654) and his later *Indian Grammar Begun* (1666) and *Indian Primer* (1669) – was, not to speak with the indigenous people, but to instruct them. Williams entertains the possibility that the Europeans may also learn from the Native Americans; their ignorance of Christ does not even entirely deprive them of Christian virtues. Avoiding the form of either dictionary or grammar, he has "framed every chapter and the matter" of his study as "an implicit dialogue." Williams's notion that his book constitutes a "key" by being about language and his observation that descriptions "of the country" have been proliferating but no one has yet offered an account of "the native language of it" constitute an early alternative view of the colonial enterprise. "With this [key]," he explains, "I have entered into the secrets of those countries [of New England] . . . ; for want of this, I know what gross mistakes myself and others have run into." William Bradford and John Cotton were pleased to find translators, but they nowhere suggest that speaking the native language is key to their progress. Nor is it, because negotiating with its inhabitants is not the way they will establish themselves in the New World.

That the first book written in English by an American be about a native language is thus at once only natural and entirely anomalous. Its anomaly lies in the implication that the Indians are human beings with whom it will be important to speak. In this view, Williams resembles Las Casas, but the notion of universal humanity is more surprising coming from a Puritan than from a Catholic. And Williams's universalism, though it ultimately appeals to the Christian God, is also secular: "Nature knowes no difference between *Europe* and *America* in blood, birth, bodies, etc. God having of one blood made all mankind. Acts. 17 and all by nature being children of wrath, Ephes. 2." (Italics in quotations are in the original unless otherwise noted.) The Protestant dualism that enjoins the Puritan to be master of this world does not, for Williams, reserve the material New World for the English. "The same sun," he muses, "shines on the wilderness that doth on a garden."

Williams disputed the Puritans' royal patents; the *Key* tends to dispute their divine patent as well. Williams never doubts that New England is to be English; but he does reject the notion that the English have an a priori right to New England. That rejection is expressed organically, in the basic form of the *Key,* which features two parties engaged in exchanges. Facing lists of Narraganset and English phrases diagram an encounter. The introduction is about mutual naming. It introduces the parties: the Indians' "names are of two sorts: first, those of the English giving, as Natives, Savages, Indians, Wild-men (so the Dutch called them Wilden), Abergeny men, Pagans, Barbarians, Heathen." He notes that the Indians did not have such generic names "to difference themselves from strangers, for they knew none." Instead, they had general names, "belonging to all natives, as Ninnuock, Ninnimissinuwock, Eniskeetompauwog, which signifies men, folk, or people." Then, of course, they had proper names peculiar to their several nations, like Nanhigganeuck or Pequttoog. "They have often asked me," he concludes, why "we call them, Indians, Natives, etc., and understanding the reason they will call themselves Indians in opposition to English, etc."

Williams's most striking observation here is that the concept of generic difference is the historical product of the encounter. Prior to meeting up with the English, Native Americans had an all-embracing term for humanity. Now, having discovered a radically other people, they are subdividing "humanity" and are willing to adopt the English idiom to name the new parts. To a modern critical understanding, the fact that the English provide the names enacts their power; but in the seventeenth-century context, the exchange is perhaps not entirely one-sided, because the Native Americans enter actively into a sort of agreement whereby both sides, not just one, are different.

The logic set in motion by this simple recognition that the Indians have their own questions leads to other reversals of perspective. "This question they oft put to me," Williams reports, "Tawhich peyahettit? . . . Why come the *Englishmen* hither?" A good question, even an obvious question, yet one that appears nowhere else in the English literature. "Measuring others by themselves," Williams reports, "they say, it is because you want firing; for they having burnt up the *wood* in one place (wanting draughts to bring *wood* to them) they are fain to follow the *wood;* and so, to remove to a fresh new place for the wood's sake."

This, in fact, is the right answer, with the provision that the English sought new resources not only from necessity but for commerce. But the real revelation in this exchange is the effect of dialogue, which of itself engenders an irreducible degree of equality between the parties. Dialogue is intrinsically anthropomorphic, and the drama of Native Americans querying Englishmen casts the former as irreducibly human. It remains to be seen how human. Williams finds the Indians remarkably in harmony with classical universal principles. They demonstrate an Aristotelian "sociableness of the nature of man" for they "love society"; they share the human commitment to orderly government and justice; they demonstrate that "God hath planted in the hearts of the wildest of the sons of men, an high and honourable esteem of the marriage bed"; on a lighter note, they delight in obtaining news as much as "the *Athenians,* and all men, more or less." On a darker note, he observes that "it is a universal disease of folly in men to desire to enter into not only necessary, but unnecessary and tormenting debts." And perhaps most telling for a judgment of Indian civilization, they are fluent in numbers: " 'tis admirable how quick they are in casting up great numbers, with the help of grains of corn, instead of *Europe's* pens or counters. . . . Let it be considered," Williams wonders, "whether tradition of ancient *forefathers,* or *nature* hath taught them *Europe's arithmetic.*" In either case, the point is that the Indians are civilized.

Nevertheless, they do lack one crucial aspect of civilization: they do not write. They themselves recognize the importance of this lack. "They have no clothes, books, nor letters, and conceive their fathers never had; and therefore they are easily persuaded that the God that made Englishmen is a greater God, because He hath so richly endowed the English above themselves." Neither in their own eyes nor in Williams's is this incapacity fatal: "when they hear [presumably from Williams] that about sixteen hundred years ago, England and the inhabitants thereof were like unto themselves, and since have received from God, clothes, books, etc., they are greatly affected with a secret hope concerning themselves." The idea is the same that inspired John White to add the drawings of Picts to his album of Indian portraits, and it similarly works against the notion that the Indians are fallen Satanic brutes. The specific identification of the natives' primitive status with their lack of books is particularly powerful in the context of a book about them.

There would be other English studies of Native-American languages, but not many. Although Eliot's works display a good understanding of the language, they are true to the purpose of catechism, which is to repeat verbatim what one has been taught. The practice of catechism in itself does not necessarily preclude a larger linguistic learning. Other Christian missionaries did acknowledge the autonomy of native languages – notably, as mentioned in Chapter 2, the French Jesuits, who produced arguably the most complete and reliable accounts of native culture in North America. The journals kept by Jesuit missionaries in the interior of Canada were collected annually in the *Jesuit Relations,* a series published from 1611 to 1768 and running to even more volumes than Sahagún's compilations. Because the Jesuit priests traveled alone or in very small groups and sought nonmilitary contact, the *Jesuit Relations* may be the collection of texts that most fully represents an encounter. One citation from a report on Indian language suggests their almost unique stance.

A young Jesuit priest, Father Le Jeune, begins his 1634 journal evenhandedly by noting that the Montagnais language is "very rich and very poor, full of abundance and full of scarcity." He does not expect the scarcity of words for "piety, devotion, virtue" to surprise his Parisian readers, but, he continues, "let us now turn the tables and show that this language is fairly gorged with richness." On the other side of the table, the Montagnais lay a veritable feast of words, an "infinite number of proper nouns among them [that] I cannot explain in French, except by circumlocutions." Indeed, Le Jeune despairs of ever mastering a language so rich that it challenges his ideas about the very nature of language. For instance, the Hurons appear not to have the letter *m,* whereas "this letter seems to me almost natural." It is not clear how he is to be missionary to people whose culture as measured by their language is richer than his own, nor how he is to communicate basic principles of European belief when he is himself brought to question his own assumptions.

Le Jeune's superior, Father Jean de Brébeuf, counseled humility. He was himself the author of an important treatise on the grammatical principles of the Huron language. To Le Jeune and other new recruits bound for missions among the natives of Canada, Father de Brébeuf offered advice in which the recognition of linguistic impotence almost suspends the dominance of colonizer over colonized. Whatever high distinction a priest may have reached in Paris, the experienced Father warns, "clever man as you are, and speaking glibly among learned and capable persons, you must make up your mind to be for a long time mute among the barbarians."

As a rule, it was not the English way to fall "mute among the barbarians." Jonathan Edwards never learned the Mohegan language though he had a mission among them for many years and preached to them regularly. His son, whose work has been mentioned and is discussed just below, learned Mohegan in the course of a childhood spent among them. Later in the colonizing process, ethnographic interests inspired some, like Thomas Jefferson, to compile vocabularies; but these efforts seem unconnected to any project of speaking *with* the Native Americans. They concentrated instead on such theoretical points as whether all languages have evolved from one parent or represent the plurality of human historical paths. Jefferson and his colleagues measured rather than learned the native speech. And they were not impressed. Jefferson observed, "They have use but for few words and possess but few." He was puzzled that people with so undeveloped a linguistic culture nonetheless considered it a matter of honor to speak their own languages. This seemed perverse to many observers of white–Indian negotiations, as, for instance, to John Fontaine (1693–1767), who traveled in Virginia in the early eighteenth century. He recorded as an oddity in his *Journal* (1710–19) being present one day when a group of natives, wishing to complain to the governor, required an interpreter: "Notwithstanding some of them could speak good English, yet when they treat of anything that concerns their nation, they will not treat but in their own language, and that by an interpreter, nor will not answer to any question made to them without it be in their own tongue." There is little sense even among those who are interested in native speech that it constitutes an equivalent language.

Williams's *Key*, paralleling Le Jeune's account of the Huron language, warns at the start that the facing lists of English and Narraganset phrases will sometimes be uneven "for their language is exceeding copious, and they have five or six words sometimes for one thing." But the most telling comparison may be to John Smith's vocabulary in his *Map of Virginia* (1612). Smith lists words in no particular order and concludes with a single remarkable construction: "Kekaten pokahontas patiaquagh ningh tanks manotyens neer mowchick rawrenock audowgh," which means, "Bid Pocahontas bring hither two little baskets, and I will give her white beads to make her a chain." Whatever this is about, it is not conversation.

Williams's conception of the *Key* is radically different. The first chapter (there are thirty-two in all) already makes the expectation of communication explicit by addressing the matter of "Salutations." The book then continues to "Of Eating and Entertainment," "Concerning Sleeping and Lodging," "Of Their Persons and Parts of Body" (they believe the brain is the seat of the soul), "Of the Earth, and the Fruits Thereof, etc." (they are "very exact and punctual in the bounds of their lands. . . . And I have known them make bargain and sale amongst themselves for a small piece, or quantity of ground; nothwithstanding a sinful opinion amongst many that Christians have right to heathens' lands."), "Of Their Nakednesse and Clothing" (in which he expresses his surprise at the absence of "wantonness"), and "Of Religion, the Soul, etc." ("He that questions whether God made the world, the Indians will teach him.").

The interspersed comments are in the form of "Observations," which follow or interrupt the lists of phrases to reflect on Indian–European equivalences. Each chapter ends with a rhymed moral written from the native perspective, enacting the reflexivity of the exchange. For instance, at the end of the chapter on "Debts and Trusting," Williams imagines the Indians reflecting thus:

> Adulteries, Murthers, Robberies, Thefts,
> Wild Indians punish these!
> And hold the scales of justice so,
> That no man farthing leese.
> When Indians heare the horrid filths,
> Of Irish, English Men
> The Horrid Oaths and Murthers late,
> Thus say these Indians then,
> We wear no Cloaths, have many Gods,
> And yet our sinnes are lesse:
> You are Barbarians, Pagans wild,
> Your land's the wildernesse.

One late-eighteenth-century English study comes closest to Williams's book. This is the work of Jonathan Edwards, Jr. (1745–1801), *Observations on the Language of the Muhhekaneew Indians* (1788), a careful and scholarly account whose major thrust is to establish the comparable adequacy, both grammatical and philosophical, of the Mohegan language. Edwards takes pains to refute the reasoning of other linguists that, for instance, the absence of the verb "to be" in Mohegan reflects an absence of ontological consciousness. These linguists have concluded "that savages never abstract, and have no abstract terms," but this is a mistake, because Mohegan contains "the full proportion of abstract, to concrete terms, which is also to be found in other languages." Like Williams on behalf of the Narragansets, Edwards claims that the Mohegans are in no way linguistically inferior, with the implication that they are also equal thinkers.

Williams claims for the Indians more than participation in the universal; he also grants in surprising degree the validity of their separate ways. The *Key* opens with a complicated stipulation:

The natives are of two sorts (as the English are), some more rude and clownish, who are not so apt to salute, but upon salutation resalute lovingly. Others, and the general, are sober and grave, and yet cheerful in a mean, and as ready to begin a salutation as to resalute, which yet the English generally begin, out of desire to civilize them.

The first part of this passage asserts the universal division of humanity into the polite and the rude. But the next move separates the Indians and the English into facing camps, with the Indians having their own impulses and the English having their special motives. This division occurs rather in the form of the sentence than in its content and has the force of diagram more than statement.

Alike in embracing both civil and uncivil folks, the Americans and the Europeans manifest the universal in ways that are peculiar to their historical situations but equally cogent. Amazingly, Williams expresses no judgment when he observes that the Indians do not object to "single fornication"; nor does he assign this latitude particular weight in relation to his other observation that they participate fully in the universal respect for marriage. That they go naked seems unrelated to their general modesty; that they worship many gods appears not to diminish their virtue.

Williams believes that native religion is one of "Satan's inventions"; and he tries to teach the Indians better ways. However, he acknowledges that native ways have their own reasons. On the one hand, as a book about language, the *Key* represents the power of European literacy; on the other hand, by representing Native Americans speaking their own language, the *Key* offers to share some of this power. In the end, of course, no such sharing did or could take place, and Williams himself took back with interest whatever he had lent.

At two crucial moments in the history of European–Indian relations in New England, Williams abetted the Indians' ruin. The first was when he interceded to persuade the Narragansets against an alliance with the Pequots, whose consequent isolation was material to their massacre by the Pilgrims in 1637. That disastrous event marked the beginning of a series of armed encounters between invaders and natives ending with King Philip's War

(1675–6). During this time, Williams's knowledge of and superior relations with the Indians seem to have furnished crucial information to his compatriots. At the death of King Philip (Metacomet), Indian resistance to the English invasion was substantially over. The English had taken the land by force thanks in part to Williams.

The irony that made Williams ultimately an instrument of Native-American genocide was rooted in a contradiction he never recognized and could not have controlled. For all his goodwill, Williams simply assumed the English should and would rule America, which made negotiation and, in a sense, even land sale hypothetical issues. He reminds us of Bartolomé de Las Casas, that other good man who in the end did much evil. Still, the partial opposition of Las Casas and Williams to the dominant European mind-set deserves being remembered for its portion of morality and for its dramatization of the link between morality and history.

The dilemma of the moral man in the conquest of the New World is captured in an introductory sketch of Williams's life that accompanied the reprinting of the *Key* as the first publication of the Rhode Island Historical Society in 1827: "One fact speaks volumes of his Christian temper," writes the editor.

After he was banished, he conceived himself to be an injured, persecuted man, but with all the opportunities which his intimacy with the neighboring Indians gave him, no purpose of revenge seems ever to have been harbored by him. Instead of that, the next year after his banishment, he gave to his very persecutors, information of that Indian plot, which would have destroyed their whole settlement. He concluded treates [*sic*] for them, which ensured their peace and prosperity, employing himself continuously in acts of kindness to his persecutors, affording relief to the distressed, offering an asylum to the persecuted.

All true, and all false.

4

SETTLEMENTS

CHAPTER 9 of William Bradford's (1590–1657) *Of Plymouth Planta-tion* (written, 1630–46; published, 1857) contains perhaps the most frequently cited passage in colonial American writing. The chapter is entitled "Of Their Voyage, and How They Passed the Sea; and of Their Safe Arrival at Cape Cod." After describing the arduous Atlantic crossing that brought the Pilgrims to the New World, Bradford signals a touchstone moment: "But here I cannot but stay and make a pause, and stand half amazed at this poor people's present condition; and so I think will the reader, too, when he well considers the same." A long descent of readers has stood amazed at a vision of the Plymouth landing that long ago moved from history into myth. Bradford's immediate readers did not have to look far back; for them it was barely yet history. Indeed, Bradford *made* it history by establish-ing in it the parameters of an American legend.

Bradford began writing his history in 1630. The passage at hand comes early in the narrative, which at this point still draws heavily on a journal until recently attributed to Bradford himself and Edward Winslow (1595–1655) – author of *Good News from New England* (1624) – that had been pub-lished in London in 1622. (The current view is that the author remains uncertain.) *A Relation or Journal of the Beginning and Proceedings of the English Plantation Settled at Plymouth in New England* (generally referred to as *Mourt's Relation,* perhaps for George Morton, who saw it through the press) covers the events of the colony's first year, from September 1620 to March 1621, in a mostly matter-of-fact tone and with a good deal of concrete detail. The first entry announces the *Mayflower*'s arrival in the New World on November 11, 1620, in the Bay of Cape Cod, "which is a good harbour and pleasant bay, circled round, except in the entrance, which is about four miles over from land to land, compassed about to the very sea with oaks, pines, juniper, sassafras, and other sweet wood."

It is at this point in transforming journal into history some ten years later that Bradford paused in awed contemplation of the Pilgrims' plight. They were in "a hideous and desolate wilderness, full of wild beasts and wild men"; and the prospects were not encouraging:

Neither could they, as it were, go up to the top of Pisgah to view from this wilderness a more goodly country to feed their hopes; for which way soever they turned their eyes (save upward to the heavens) they could have little solace or content in respect of any outward objects. For summer being done, all things stand upon them with a weatherbeaten face, and the whole country, full of woods and thickets, represented a wild and savage hue.

The parallel entry in *Mourt's Relation* reads otherwise. The history's "woods and thickets" are, in *Mourt's Relation,* almost welcoming: "the wood for the most part open and without underwood, fit either to go or ride in." They offer the solace of a mercantile vision, their names already transforming them into the stuff of domestic enterprise: "oaks, pines, sassafras, juniper, birch, holly, vines, . . . some ash, walnut." The thrust of the 1622 passage is to domesticate a vista that is nowhere yet a "hideous and desolate wilderness." At first sight Cape Cod is a farming landscape, "the ground or earth, sand hills, much like the Downs in *Holland,* but much better; the crust of the earth a spit's depth, excellent black earth."

Bradford is rewriting history from *Relation* to *History.* This is the first rewriting of American history at the occasion of one of the first American writings, and it offers a remarkable opportunity to observe the formation of a communal narrative. The reader is able to observe the emergence of structuring abstractions, for at each point where Bradford adapts from the earlier text, he drops material information and, not always as explicitly as in the passage under discussion, pauses to interpret. Two major lines of interpretation emerge, both already sketched in the edited account of the landing. One line is that America was utterly savage; in the state the Pilgrims encountered it, it was virtually uninhabitable and by extension uninhabited. The second is that whatever it was and whatever it was to become had nothing to do with Europe. The comparison to the landscape of Holland in *Mourt's Relation* is replaced in *Of Plymouth Plantation* by a denial of the relevance of such comparisons.

Before the Pilgrims lay a wild and savage country such as no civilized people had ever confronted, and "if they looked behind them, there was the mighty ocean which they had passed and [which] was now as a main bar and gulf to separate them from all the civil parts of the world." Not even the ship lying at anchor qualifies this absolute separation, for the captain daily threatens to leave. "May not and ought not the children of these fathers," Bradford instructs his first readers, who are just these children, "rightly say: 'Our fathers were Englishmen which came over this great ocean, and were ready to perish in this wilderness; but they cried unto the Lord, and He heard their voice and looked on their adversity.' " The Lord is certainly a party to the Pilgrims' transcendent effort, but even His history is less dramatic: the plight of the Pilgrims is worse than that of "the Apostle and his shipwrecked company," to whom "the barbarians showed . . . no small kindness in refreshing them." The savages the Pilgrims encountered "were readier to fill their sides full of arrows than otherwise." Bradford's history differs from the generality of early American texts in featuring natives who are from the first unequivocally unfriendly.

Of Plymouth Plantation, as Bradford's call to the children of the fathers makes explicit, consciously constructs a historical tradition. It proposes some fundamental terms for organizing the experience of colonization. The most important of these terms are redefinitions of wilderness and civilization and of the opposition between them. On the one hand, the wilderness is far more absolute and horrifying in Bradford's treatment than it is, for instance, in Elizabethan pastoral. On the other hand, Bradford's wilderness, precisely in its exceptional hideousness, becomes the site of a potentially exceptional good (a potentiality manifest in *Of Plymouth Plantation*), the terrain upon which a commensurately greater virtue may be achieved. At the same time, civilization, in Bradford's account, acquires a new ambiguity.

An earlier passage in *Of Plymouth Plantation* describing the first stage of the journey, which brings the Pilgrims to Holland, foreshadows their landing at Plymouth. This passage does not have an equivalent in *Mourt's Relation,* which begins with the American landfall. In other words, the passage about arriving in Holland was conceived retrospectively, from the perspective of the subsequent arrival in America and as an aspect of the rewriting of the later event.

This recasting of the Dutch landing in the service of narrative gives it a distinctly literary air:

Being now come into the Low Countries, they saw many goodly and fortified cities, strongly walled and guarded with troops of armed men. Also, they heard a strange and uncouth language, and beheld the different manners and customs of the people, with their strange fashions and attires; all so far differing from that of their plain country villages (wherein they were bred and had so long lived) as it seemed they were come into a new world. But these were not the things they much looked on, or long took up their thoughts, for they had other work in hand and another kind of war to wage and maintain. For although they saw fair and beautiful cities, flowing with abundance of all sorts of wealth and riches, yet it was not long before they saw the grim and grisly face of poverty coming upon them like an armed man, with whom they must buckle and encounter, and from whom they could not fly. But they were armed with faith and patience against him and all his encounters; and though they were sometimes foiled, yet by God's assistance they prevailed and got the victory.

The passage evokes a country of cities. It is the opposite of the "hideous wilderness" of the New World, where the Pilgrims, exhausted by their long sea voyage, found "no friends to welcome them nor inns to entertain or refresh their weatherbeaten bodies; no houses or much less towns to repair to, to seek for succour." The landscape of the Low Countries is as if paved over with civilization.

Yet the final impression is not of contrast; the situations curiously resemble one another. The cities are walled, betokening danger; everywhere there are armed men speaking a strange "uncouth" language; and despite the country's great abundance, the Pilgrims could well starve. Indeed, civilization is possibly as dangerous as the wilderness, presenting, in different dress, many of the same dangers, such as violence, cold, and hunger. Superficially contrasting, the two landings are more deeply alike, their similarities stressed by the repetition of categories of events and dilemmas. Civilization and the wilderness are both situations that the Pilgrims have to conquer; they confront both with God's help but without that of other people and often against them.

Wilderness and civilization oppose one another in *Of Plymouth Plantation* like mirror images rather than like good and evil. When the Pilgrims arrive in the New World to confront the hideous wilderness, they leave behind not an antithetical good but another kind of evil; and the complaint that there were no houses, inns, or towns in the New World measures their problem without projecting its solution. The solution is still to be constructed, and the rest of the history describes each undertaking, whether the building of houses or the laying out of fields or the establishment of government, as from the ground up.

In Bradford's history, European civilization appears for the first time in American writing as a foreign and unwholesome creature. Europe also becomes enormously distant; the ocean once crossed becomes a "main bar and gulf" not to be recrossed except in conditions of extreme need. And what arrives from Europe (difficult settlers, interfering orders from the Council of New England, challenges to the Pilgrims' patent) is always of dubious value, often a nuisance, sometimes a dire threat. The religious doctrine that informs all aspects of the venture is crucial, but the striking innovation, whatever its provenance, in the way Bradford interpreted the colonization of America lies in his insistence that colonizing meant settling (rather than simple extraction of resources), and that the settlements were different from European civilization. They were in some manner shaped by a wilderness different from European nature.

The difference was not that celebrated by other colonizers and Europeans: by 1630, Bradford has remarkably little interest left in Plymouth's flora and fauna; he hardly responds to either beauty or oddity. Most noticeably, because of the contrast it makes with other such accounts, *Of Plymouth Plantation* shows no interest in the original inhabitants, their customs, or their culture.

The arrival in the colony one day of an Indian named Samoset, who "spoke to them in broken English" and told them about another Indian named Squanto, who had been taken as a slave to England and spoke English even better, elicits neither excitement nor reflection. Samoset, Bradford simply records, "became profitable to them in acquainting them with many things concerning the state of the country in the east parts where he lived, which was afterward profitable unto them." Although there is subsequent talk of Squanto, especially of his dishonesty in mediating between the whites and his fellow Indians, the issue of native language never comes up.

Bradford's appreciation of the problems of translation was acute enough to inspire him to learn Hebrew in his old age, but he found native speech inconsequential. Describing an early skirmish with the natives, *Mourt's Relation* had been characteristically precise: "The cry of our enemies was dreadful, especially, when our men ran out to recover their arms, their note was after this manner, *Woath woach ha ha hach woach:* our men were no sooner come to their arms, but the enemy was ready to assault them." This is the way the same incident appears in *Of Plymouth Plantation:* "The cry of the Indians was dreadful, especially when they saw their men run out of the rendezvous toward the shallop to recover their arms, the Indians wheeling about upon them." The later sentence adds an explanation of the English action, annotates the scene – they run from their shelter because their arms had been left in the boat; the Indians do not just assault, they wheel about – and it drops the phonetic account of the natives' cry. The omission is not a matter of style. It is a recasting of the incident to give all the lines to the English. The translation from journal to "history" of the first alarm preserves from the original the cry of a scout, *"They are men, Indians, Indians,"* and indeed heightens the drama: " 'Men, Indians! Indians!' "

Of Plymouth Plantation's lesser interest in the natives' language extends to the culture at large. *Mourt's Relation* takes the time to describe native houses, which were "made with long young sapling trees, bended and both ends stuck into the ground." It goes on to detail the way the houses are furnished and what the arrangements are for cooking and sleeping. *Of Plymouth Plantation* mentions one item of native culture: a bunch of arrows tied with a snakeskin "which [the Pilgrims'] interpreter told them was a threatening and a challenge." Since the interpreter was Squanto, who spoke English, one may imagine that he gave a more complete explanation. Bradford's account conveys a lack of curiosity that characterizes all his depictions of Native Americans, friendly and hostile, helpful and dangerous, without distinction.

Bradford's cuts from *Mourt's Relation* express something more positive than a lack of imagination; to delete an observation is more active than simply to fail to make it. Such deletion bespeaks policy; Bradford's *Of Plymouth Planta-*

tion is an intentionally ideological document in which the eclipsed Native Americans are replaced with an account of the English in the New World. Despite their still small numbers and dispersed situation, they fill the landscape to capacity. The narrative is crowded with English. Bradford stopped writing before midcentury; he died in 1657 and had completed *Of Plymouth Plantation* ten years earlier, but the reader is hard put to remember that in 1630 there were fewer than five thousand English colonists in all New England.

This imaginative occupation of New England is an extraordinary achievement; it required both vision and style. It is what John Smith succeeded in doing as an individual through his account of his own role in the colonizing effort. But Bradford's *Of Plymouth Plantation* identifies a whole people with that enterprise, hence its power to efface America's prior inhabitants, who in Smith's account remain present and articulate. Smith is still occupied with conquering and subjugating the Indians; Bradford moves to erase them, and not just figuratively. For Bradford, Indian attempts to prevent the English from taking over are not just inconvenient and dangerous, they are entirely unjustified. The Pequots are more than fierce enemies. They are treacherous interlopers. Bradford knew the Indian point of view in the affair. He reports that, having entered into open warfare with the English, the Pequots tried to forge an alliance embracing some tribes who were traditional enemies. In particular they "sought to make peace with the Narragansets, and used very pernicious arguments to move them thereunto." These are the arguments:

[T]he English were strangers and began to overspread their country, and would deprive them thereof in time, if they were suffered to grow and increase. And if the Narragansets did assist the English to subdue [the Pequots] they did but make way for their own overthrow, for if they were rooted out, the English would soon take occasion to subjugate them.

Bradford's unambivalent characterization of the Pequot analysis as "pernicious" measures the depth of his belief that the English were the land's rightful owners.

Two paragraphs later, Bradford unblinkingly describes the slaughter of the Pequots. Rebuffed in their attempts to unite with the Narragansets, who instead joined the English, the Pequots found themselves fighting not only whites but Indians as well. Armed men of both forces surrounded the Pequot fort one night, blocking egress. In the course of fierce fighting, houses were set afire and the flames spread quickly; "thereby more were burnt to death than [were] otherwise slain."

It burnt their bowstrings and made them unserviceable; those that scaped the fire were slain with the sword, some hewed to pieces, others run through with their rapiers, so as they were quickly dispatched and very few escaped. It was conceived they thus destroyed about 400 at this time. It was a fearful sight to see them thus frying in the fire and streams of blood quenching the same, and horrible was the stink and scent thereof.

Bradford's characteristically sober style swells with emotion. Some of those who died by the sword were hewed to pieces; others run through; they did not simply die, they were quickly dispatched. They did not just burn, they fried, and stank horribly as they did so. And finally, as he describes an infernal quenching of fire with blood, the writing acquires a biblical cadence appropriate to the moral he is about to draw. For all its horror, he writes, "the victory seemed a sweet sacrifice, and they gave the praise thereof to God, who had wrought so wonderfully for them, thus to enclose their enemies in their hands and give them so speedy a victory over so proud and insulting an enemy."

The slaughter of the Pequots (survivors were "wholly driven from their place," some of them sold as slaves in the West Indies, the rest scattered to live in varying degrees of bondage among mostly unfriendly tribes) disturbed a significant number of Bradford's contemporaries. In general there was considerable dissent over the extent of English violence against the Indians to be condoned. Though it addresses an earlier and less-horrific incident, John Robinson's condemnation of indiscriminate killing is both representative and especially telling in that Robinson had been the Pilgrims' minister in Leyden. The letter of spiritual instruction he sent along on the *Mayflower* opens *Mourt's Relation*. Barely a year after this was published, however, Robinson wrote another letter, addressed to his "Loving and Much Beloved Friend" Bradford. After an opening blessing, he got to the point:

Concerning the killing of those poor Indians, of which we heard at first by report, and since by more certain relation. Oh, how happy a thing had it been, if you had converted some before you had killed any! Besides, where blood is once begun to be shed, it is seldom staunched of a long time after. You will say they deserved it. I grant it; but upon what provocations and invitements . . . ? Besides, you being no magistrates over them were to consider . . . what you were by necessity constrained to inflict. Necessity of this, especially of killing so many (and many more, it seems, they would, if they could) I see not. Methinks one or two principals should have been full enough, according to that approved rule, The punishment to a few, and the fear to many.

There are echoes in this letter of the watershed sixteenth-century debate between Las Casas and Sepúlveda, with Bradford in the position of the secular Sepúlveda intent on establishing his plantations. From this perspective, the secular side of the Puritan enterprise emerges with unusual clarity.

The space that Bradford does not give in *Of Plymouth Plantation* to the Indians, he devotes to careful discussions of the emergence of an English culture of the New World. He describes the evolution of Plymouth's political and economic system, which involved the rapid abandonment of communal property for private and the accompanying difficulties in distributing resources and wealth between farmers and merchants. With each stage forward in that evolution, Plymouth becomes more self-referential. What distinguishes America from Europe is defined in *Of Plymouth Plantation* neither by aboriginal features nor by America's indigenous people nor by the distinctive landscape of New England. The newness of the New World lies rather in being the site for the emergence of the Pilgrims as a new people. In *Of Plymouth Plantation* Bradford tells how the Pilgrims came to America and discovered themselves.

To put this another way, the Puritans did not conceive of their plantations in America as part of the expanding European empire. In their own eyes they were not imperialists. The white society they were building in the New World constituted a new center. A center radiates, and the Puritan center of Plymouth and Massachusetts Bay not only governed itself more elaborately than Jamestown, for instance, but also projected its laws and values outward. And order, proportionately, was much more a local matter for the Puritans than for their fellow colonists. They felt much more threatened by local disorder, or by what they deemed disorder. A well-known instance of the difference is the incident at Merrymount as related in *Of Plymouth Plantation*. The protagonist here is Thomas Morton (1590?–1647), a sometime lawyer and Elizabethan cavalier of middling rank and education, a gentleman and an adventurer. Morton had come to the New World in the party of Captain Wollaston to help establish a plantation inside the Massachusetts patent and proceeded to take over what had become a failing colony.

Morton called the colony Ma-re Mount for its sea view; the Puritans quickly renamed it Merrymount to indicate their suspicion of its moral fiber. Behind this lay a fundamental disagreement about the nature of American colonization. For Morton, colonization was primarily a matter of commercial profit. He was interested in agriculture that either produced or supported the gathering of commercial goods. However long he might stay in the New World or how deeply he might come to associate himself with its possession, he would always see it as peripheral to England. Like Columbus, he wanted possession of the New World but did not identify with it. In that case, the Indians might retain it for their center, even as they constituted a part of the colony's resources. Indeed, this was the most urgent threat Morton posed in the view of the Puritans. He evidently assumed that normal relations with the natives would be peaceful, both in his plantation and in his trade, which was mostly in furs. All of the New England colonies, including the Puritan, were involved in the fur trade, since beaver skins turned huge profits in England. Morton offered an exceptional deal, guns for furs, and threatened to corner the market.

Bradford, discovering all this, was again made to pause in amazement.

"Oh, the horribleness of this villainy! How many both Dutch and English have been lately slain by those Indians thus furnished . . . Oh that princes and parliaments would . . . suppress [this mischief] by some exemplary punishment upon some of these gain-thirsty murderers . . . these evil instruments and traitors to their neighbors and country!"

In the end, it was the Puritans and not the English Parliament that in 1628 punished the gun traders. The Elizabethan maypole erected by the Ma-re Mount, or Merrymount, colonists seemed a heathen outrage to the Puritans, but it is unlikely that this of itself would have led to the decision to expel Morton from the region. His behavior in the fur trade and his refusal to stop selling the natives arms were more urgent threats. The expedition that brought Morton back to Plymouth considered that it was acting in self-defense.

Morton himself told a different story in his own book, *New English Canaan* (written, 1635; published, 1637). According to him:

The separatists envying the prosperity and hope of the plantation at Ma-re Mount (which they perceived began to come forward, and to be in a good way for gain in the beaver trade,) conspired together against mine host especially . . . and made up a party against him; and mustered up what aide they could, accounting of him, as of a great monster.

They take him prisoner when they catch him alone but rejoice prematurely, for when they begin celebrating their victory, he sneaks away. Discovering this, "[t]heir grand leader Captain Shrimp [Miles Standish] took on most furiously, and tore his clothes for anger, to see the empty nest, and their bird gone."

So Standish gives chase with eight others, "like the nine Worthies of New Canaan." At length,

[t]he nine Worthies coming before the den of this supposed monster, (this seven headed hydra, as they termed him,) and began like Don Quixote against the windmill, to beat a parley, and to offer quarter, if mine host would yield.

"The son of a soldier," Morton at first declines to surrender, but

to save the effusion of so much worthy blood, as would have issued out of the veins of these nine worthies of New Canaan, if mine host should have played upon them out at his port holes (for they came within danger like a flock of wild geese, as if they had been tailed one to another, as colts to be sold at a fair) mine Host was content to yield upon quarter.

The Worthies' promises of safe and dignified conduct are immediately broken. They beat Morton and rifle his plantation before bearing him back in triumph to Plymouth. There he is sentenced to deportation, but because no ship is available to take him, he is set on an island without gun, knife, clothing, or any other supplies. Succored by natives ("so full of humanity are these infidels before those Christians"), he eventually sails for England.

Any passage from Bradford's account will reveal a contrast with Morton's much deeper than the facts of the case. For instance, Bradford describes how Morton's captors vainly tried all means of persuasion until

they saw there was no way but to take him by force; and having so far proceeded, now to give over would make him far more haughty and insolent. So they mutually resolved to proceed, and obtained of the Governor of Plymouth to send Captain Standish and some other aid with him, to take Morton by force. The which accordingly was done. But they found him to stand stiffly in his defense, having made fast his doors, armed his consorts, set diverse dishes of powder and bullets ready on the table; and if they had not been over-armed with drink, more hurt might have been done.

Standish tries to get Morton to surrender and receives "scoffs and scorns." Morton and his men have guns, but

they were so steeled with drink as their pieces were too heavy for them. Himself with a carbine . . . had thought to have shot Captain Standish; but he stepped to him and put by his piece and took him. Neither was there any hurt done to any of either side, save that one was so drunk that he ran his own nose upon the point of a sword that one held before him, as he entered the house; but he lost but a little of his hot blood.

On one level, the two sides represent each other using similar devices. They belittle one another and accuse one another of drunkenness, of swaggering, of incompetence. They claim the same qualities for themselves: strength, sobriety, and the soldiering skill to each defeat the other with ease. Morton forswears victory so as not to shed the Worthies' blood; Bradford depicts Standish taking Morton without a shot. They also employ like rhetorical strategies, each ridiculing the other; but here, in the nature and style of the ridicule, a significant difference emerges. Morton is witty, Bradford mocking; Morton is funny, Bradford contemptuous. Bradford laughs only to scorn. (The historian Charles Francis Adams remarked of Bradford, "There is a grim solemnity in his very chuckle.") For Morton, invoking *Don Quixote,* humor is a mode of ridicule but also its own good. Morton is perhaps alone among the New England writers of his generation in having a sense of humor, an Elizabethan humor bespeaking an attitude to life and society that was deeply offensive to the Puritan colonists. Morton's satire is irreverent: Standish is simultaneously allegorized and stripped of his status as "Shrimp"; "mine host" (Morton himself) and the "nine Worthies" have blasphemous implications. His Hudibrastic humor reduces all the values it capitalizes; its constitutional levity deconstitutes authority.

Morton is serious in his own way, of course. He is serious about profiting from his plantation both in wealth and in power. In the unwholesome manipulations and conspiracies that marked the unfolding of the English conquest, he engaged in a series of patent disputes that represented in their opposing constituencies different conceptions of the imperial enterprise. The Gorges group, with whom Morton stood, was made up of men from the same general background – broadly speaking, of the class and persuasion of Raleigh. Their attention was divided between Virginia and New England, and their later careers tended south. The Massachusetts Bay Company, of which John Endecott was the chief deputy in America, represented the Puritan settlers and their kind, men rather of the middle classes than of the (generally petty) nobility or its dependents. Morton's ambition for his plantation was that it become a major trading post, one end of a thriving traffic whose metropolitan end was the indisputable terminus; the Puritans, equally avid for the beaver trade, sought from it a way to secure New England as their home base.

Morton's cultural and literary style tends to confirm the traditional elite. It is literary, allusive, based on a classical education, privileged and privileging. Morton is an indifferent practitioner of this style but he has grasped its principles; his book exudes an unmistakable cavalier air. Its prologue is a poem, and before many paragraphs have gone by, three lines of Horace appear, while Latin phrases grace the manuscript throughout. Indeed, as a curious adjunct to this claim of classical authority, Morton imparts some of it to the Indians as well. Bradford's Indians are silent; Morton's speak classical languages. "It hath been found by diverse, and those of good judgement, that the natives of this country, do use very many words both of Greek and Latin, to the same signification that the Latins and Greeks have done." Two paragraphs of etymologies follow demonstrating the similarity between such words as "*Pascopan*," which "signifieth greedy gut, this being the name of an Indian that was so of a child, through the greediness of his mind and much eating," and which seems to Morton clearly related to "*Pasco* in Latin [which] signifieth to feed, and *Pan* in Greek [which] signifieth all."

Scholars have established that Morton's transcriptions are utterly unreliable. But it may be doubted whether he trusts them himself. His case is made rather in the making than in its proof. The claim that the natives speak Greek and Latin is the crux of an early chapter in *New English Canaan* that sets out the likely origins of the first Americans. "After my arrival in those parts," he writes, "I endeavoured by all the ways and means that I could to find out from what people, or nation, the natives of New England might be conjectured originally to proceed; and by continuance and conversation amongst them, I attained to so much of their language" as to concur with the opinions of "Sir Christopher Gardiner, Knight, and able gentl. that lived amongst them, and of David Thompson, a Scottish gentl. that likewise was conversant with those people, both scholars and travellers that were diligent in taking notice of these things, . . . that the original of the natives of New England may be well conjectured to be from the scattered Trojans, after such time as Brutus departed from Latium."

This theory was widespread and would shortly receive one of its fullest treatments by John Milton, who, disclaiming any belief in it, recounts in his history of England the "modern fable" of the founding by Brutus of Troja Nova, or London. Morton speculates that not all the Trojans left with Brutus at the same time, so those who came later might have been blown off course and been as likely to land in the New World as anywhere else. Making one's way in Morton's argument from shaky premise to shifting ground, one suspects that his serious intention lies elsewhere. At the outset he describes how, arriving in the New World, he found "two sorts of people, the one Christians, the other Infidels; these I found most full of humanity, and more friendly than the other." *New English Canaan* is Morton's justification and his vengeance. The diminution he achieves explicitly in the portrait of Miles Standish as Captain Shrimp he derives as well from building up the Native Americans as equal in their patrimony to the Troy-descended English. He knows full well, of course, that the Puritans claim for themselves the transcendent status of heirs to Israel.

Morton's assertion of a classical origin was doubly damaging to the Puritan claim. First, it demoted the American Puritans from the first rank of heirs of an ancient legitimacy by claiming for England (and its deputy-cavaliers like Morton) descent from the yet more ancient Troy. Second, outrageously, it placed the Plymouth and Massachusetts colonists even behind the Indians, who in Morton's scheme are also Trojans. Indeed, by entitling his book *New English Canaan,* Morton subordinates the entire religious myth or renders it linguistically instrumental to the secular. It is not that New England *is* the promised land, he explains, but "that it is nothing inferior to Canaan of Israel . . . a kind of parallel to it, in all points." The emergence of America continues the unfolding of secular history, with God's history providing a sort of gloss — a set of images, a way of talking that the simpleminded, posturing Puritans have absurdly taken for real. Unlikely as it seems, on this topic Morton and Roger Williams have some similar views.

Tracing Morton's argument this way may lend it a sobriety it lacks in his rendition, where levity is the instrument that punctures the pretensions of his enemies. The seriousness in Morton's historical theories lies in their satire, which in its very form represents the gist of the difference between the two major ideologies competing in seventeenth-century New England. The springboard of satire is an irreverence sometimes verging on antinomianism in its denial that authority inheres in any language. Linguistically, satire often works through uncoupling word and meaning and thus permitting them to be arbitrarily or willfully recoupled. In this regard, the satirist is not unlike the creator of metaphysical conceits (also repugnant to a Puritan sensibility).

In order to compare two lovers to a pair of compasses, John Donne has first to disconnect both lovers and compasses from their conventional associations, which make up what each one usually means. Reconnecting them to one another instead, he creates a new meaning but at the cost of demonstrating that meaning is arbitrary. Morton's satire works to render colonial rule a matter not of right but of the arbitrary art of empire or the artifice of political domination. New England, he implies, was a colony acquired by force and will, a territory annexed, neither legitimately deeded to the Puritans nor redeemed by them.

Men like Morton dominated the Virginia colony and at first their behavior tended to confirm Bradford's judgment. Smith's method in the *General History* of listing the colonists by social and occupational category reflected a serious problem with the colony's population. Especially at first, Virginia had an embarrassment of riches in the nobility line; one historian has calculated that there were, proportionally, six times as many gentlemen in the Jamestown population as in England. Smith's scathing account of the behavior of these gentry is generally taken to have been justified. Many of them were young men with fancy aspirations and no qualifications. They declined to engage in agriculture or construction and instead expected to make their fortunes from the exploitation of servants and Indians. The Indians were not always complaisant, and many of the servants nursed their own ambitions for leisure or else lacked relevant skills. Each arriving ship brought only two or three useful craftsmen. Carpenters, tailors, blacksmiths, shipbuilders, experienced farmers, and fishermen were a hard-pressed minority, and they were not encouraged by the companionship of idling gentlemen at one end of the social scale and transported felons or broken-bodied and broken-spirited indigents at the other.

The problem lay both in the personnel and in the class structure itself. As in Plymouth, the original organization of the colony provided for communal ownership of the land and sharing of its yield; and like Plymouth, Jamestown abandoned this system almost at once. Some private plots existed as early as 1609, and by 1614 all land was being distributed privately. However, private property in Jamestown, unlike in Plymouth, did not quicken individual enterprise. A decade after its founding, the colony was on the verge of bankruptcy when a more powerful economic incentive finally inspired the colonists to greater efforts.

Ironically, the incentive came from a narcotic. Jamestown sent its first shipment of tobacco to England in 1617. For a short time, the Virginia Company under the relatively enlightened leadership of Edwin Sandys (brother of George Sandys, who, as a Virginia colonist, produced in 1626 the first American translation of a classical text, Ovid's *Metamorphoses*) tried to build a diversified economy. But in the 1620s, tobacco, growing everywhere, even down the center of village lanes, transformed Virginia into a theater of unexpected profits and unspeakable exploitation. The boom did not last into the thirties, but the pattern of Virginia's development had been set. The major elements were cash crops grown on large plantations and a class hierarchy. At the top a very few very rich men reigned, and at the bottom slaves solved the problem of providing sufficient numbers of laborers without creating a potentially insurrectionary class. The first ship bearing African slaves arrived in Jamestown in August 1619. The historian who took up the chronicle of Virginia after John Smith wrote sitting in his well-endowed library on the six-thousand-acre plantation he called Beverley Park.

Robert Beverley (1673–1722) admired Smith greatly and was certain that the colony would not have survived without him; he drew heavily on Smith's *General History* for his *History and Present State of Virginia* (1705; revised edition, 1722). The English colonists had traveled a great distance in the three-quarters of a century that separates the two works. The distance may be measured by the difference in their authors' signatures. Where John Smith repeatedly insists that his books are "writ by his own hand," Beverley signs himself "A Native and Inhabitant of the Place." He has made the same move as Bradford, identifying himself with the New World as an individual and as a representative of a new kind of man. Indeed, Beverley is, despite the chronological discrepancy, a likely counterpart to Bradford. Their histories of Plymouth and Virginia describe a process of colonial plantation in which not only colonies were planted but colonists as well were rooted in the land, with the effect that the imperialist project acquired an extra dimension in its agents' self-projection.

"I hope," Beverley wrote, warning the reader in the preface not to expect literary flourishes, "the plainness of my dress, will give him the kinder impressions of my honesty, which is what I pretend to. Truth desires only to be understood, and never affects the reputation of being finely equipp'd. It depends upon its own intrinsic value, and, like beauty, is rather conceal'd, than set off, by ornament." One of the connotations of "native and inhabitant of the place" is a down-to-earth, man-of-the-earth simplicity. Beverley here produces one of the first drafts of an American type that would receive its classic expression in the next century in J. Hector St. John de Crèvecoeur's *Letters from an American Farmer* (1781–2) and in Thomas Jefferson's *Notes on the State of Virginia* (1784–5). Hardly a yeoman himself (neither were Crèvecoeur and Jefferson), Beverley was known for his lack of Anglophile sophistications in manner, dress, and furnishings.

Thus far, as he begins to shape an American image out of local materials, Beverley seems very close to Bradford. Certainly, a Pilgrim could have read, might even have written, the passage just cited, but the sentence that precedes it would never have come to the pen of a New England Puritan. While ostensibly excusing his rough writing, Beverley actually boasts. He disclaims first the superfluous embellishments of cavalier cultivation and then civilization itself: "I am an *Indian*," he exults, "and don't pretend to be exact in my language." This is not the way they expounded the plain style in Massachusetts.

To Bradford, Indians are licentious, intemperate, and promiscuous. Poverty bred by laziness curbs without disciplining them; alcohol brings out their innate characteristics, which are, for human beings, degenerate. Beverley's Indians, by contrast, are idolaters full of childish superstitions. They are rudimentary men of nature from whom he expects little, either of good or of evil. Dubbing himself "Indian," he is certainly not identifying with real Indians. Rather, he seems to point toward the topos of the American man of nature and already to distinguish him from the European man of nature, for the American of whom Beverley's self-portrait is an early sketch is not a man of nature but a natural man.

The contemporary term "improvements" means bringing virgin land into cultivation. Although calling himself an Indian, Beverley does not mean that he rejects or regrets Virginia "as it is now improv'd." The real Indians did not have a claim to Virginia precisely because they did not improve it. An improved New World, however, is still the New World, and later in the eighteenth century the Americans (fusing in themselves a European genius for improvement with an "Indian" naturalness) would argue against a European view that white improvements had transformed America. The Americans would maintain instead that when they arrived, the continent was already embryonically all that it became. Jefferson would be among the foremost to argue that whites had been midwives to the New World and not its progenitors, as Europeans insisted (see Chapter 5). Beverley's self-characterization as an Indian forecasts Jefferson's argument and one major tradition in American thinking about the continent.

Improvement even at its most aggressive is not the same as redemption. Bradford's horror of the wild and his determination to redeem it engendered a different tradition, which can be traced in the nineteenth century to Henry David Thoreau's cry in the "Higher Laws" chapter of *Walden* that "Nature is hard to be overcome, but she must be overcome." Though secularized and informed by Romanticism, Thoreau's Nature is a model for human conduct only in very limited ways. As a general environment, nature is a testing ground or a base line one marks in order to pass beyond it.

There are important affinities between these traditions, of course. Both derive a special American virtue from the encounter with the wilderness. But the contrast between Bradford's explicit erasure of Native Americans from his history and Beverley's claim that he, in whatever limited way, was an Indian, significantly separates the Puritan and the cavalier traditions. When Bradford balks at assuming the Native American along with America, he projects a distinctive way of taking possession of the New World that also re-creates it. Bradford has no desire to claim an aboriginal connection. Instead, he begins his history of the New World on September 6, 1620, the day the *Mayflower* left Plymouth, and then proceeds backward to the developments that led to Plymouth, starting in 1550 with the separatist response to the Reformation. The Pilgrims do not arrive in America until Chapter 9 of the history of the Plymouth plantation, but at that point not only the plantation's history begins but so does the history of America. There is no looking back, no suggestion that America, like the Pilgrims, might have a prior history.

Beverley's history too begins and ends with the English, but including Indians has the odd effect of projecting the English themselves back into the pre-Columbian past. *The History and Present State of Virginia* begins with an outline of "Method." Book I is the history of the English in Virginia. Then, to put this process in context, Beverley offers in Book II an account of "the spontaneous productions of that country, and the original state, wherein the *English* found it at their first Arrival," apologizing for having out of ignorance "handled [Virginia's natural history] with more brevity than it deserves." From American nature, Beverley moves to the natural inhabitants. Book III "gives a true account of the *Indians,* together with their religion, customs, and government." For this section Beverley borrowed John White's Roanoke drawings, as well as some of Thomas Harriot's information, and added his own detailed observations. Book IV presents "the *English* form of government . . . and . . . likewise . . . the small improvements, that the *English* have made, since they have been in possession."

The English America this projects is continuous with a precolonial America improved but hardly remade by the colonists. The improvements have been "small" compared to the abundance of the "native perfections" detailed in Books II and III of the history. The native peoples, it is true, are the least of the New World's riches. Their government, for instance, is sadly primitive. Since they have "no sort of letters," the Indians have no written laws and obey one chief, "who is arbiter of all things among them." By contrast, the constitution and organization of Virginia's polity occupy fourteen proud chapters in which Beverley celebrates the enlightened morality and modern conveniences of civilized government.

The superiority of English ways does not prevent their juxtaposition to those of the natives, which renders the two cultures, however different, also commensurate. The native government is inferior but it exists and can be described. "Their cookery has nothing commendable in it," Beverley has found, except for its simplicity, which may prompt his comparison of a certain kind of native broth to a Spartan recipe involving the blood and innards of a hare. Their manner of building houses "is very slight and cheap"; they are beset by superstitions and terrified into veneration by the hideous garb of their priests.

Still, his vision sharpened by the exercise of comparison, Beverley's perspective reveals two aspects of native culture that directly counter the racist mythology. The first is that, lacking an alphabet, they are nonetheless able to communicate "by a sort of hieroglyphic, or representation of birds, beasts or other things, showing their different meaning, by the various forms describ'd and by the different position of the figures." Actually, Beverley, at the time he was writing the *History,* had, he confessed, only read about the hieroglyphics in "two extraordinary chapters" of Baron Lahontan's travel narrative and had not observed them directly. It is remarkable that he credits the information and even greets it with enthusiasm. The Indians, it turns out, possess a writing system in a form that not only is comparable to European writing but that performs something approaching the same function. The second unorthodox observation is that contrary to the "unjust scandal" perpetrated by "uncharitable Christians . . . upon no other ground, than the guilt of their own consciences," native women are both virginal brides and chaste wives.

The first history of the Virginia colony by "a native and inhabitant of the place" ends on a version of the myth of the noble savage:

Thus I have given a succinct account of the *Indians;* happy, I think, in their simple state of nature, and in their enjoyment of plenty, without the curse of labour. They have on several accounts reason to lament the arrival of the *Europeans,* by whose means they seem to have lost their felicity, as well as their innocence. The *English* have taken away a great part of their country, and consequently made every thing less plenty amongst them. They have introduc'd drunkenness and luxury amongst them, which have multiply'd their wants, and put them upon desiring a thousand things, they never dreamt of before.

Beverley is so moved by his own encomium to the savage life that he almost begins to doubt the colonial enterprise. The next book will describe Virginia "as it is now improv'd, (I should rather say alter'd,) by the *English*."

Beverley's interest in Native Americans is not universally shared. Between the years of Bradford's and Beverley's histories lies a series of Indian wars from which whites emerged as definite conquerors. Native Americans all but disappeared from major white settlements. "The *Indians* of *Virginia* are almost wasted," Beverley notes, "but such towns, or people as retain their names, and live in bodies. . . . All which together can't raise five hundred fighting men." He lists the native towns of Virginia:

Matomkin is much decreased of late by the smallpox, that was carried thither. . . . *Kiequotank,* is reduc'd to very few men. *Mathchopungo,* has a small number yet living. . . . *Oanancock,* has but four or five families. . . . *Chiconessex,* has very few, who just keep the name. . . . In *Charles City. Appamattox.* These Live in Colonel *Byrd*'s Pasture, not being above seven families. . . . In *Richmond. Port-Tabago,* has about five bowmen, but wasting.

Of twenty towns, four thrive. This is the scene at the turn of the seventeenth century, when the Native American begins to appear in the paradoxical role of Vanishing American.

Some twenty-five years earlier, King Philip's War, which united a number of New England tribes in an effort to at least contain English settlement, had roughly coincided with the outbreak of raids along the Potomac. The Indians of the East Coast, up to then prevented by their traditional divisions from effective resistance to white encroachments, seemed to be grouping. In part they were responding to the increasingly aggressive behavior of the Europeans, now well enough established in their coastal centers to think of expansion inland. No Europeans, as we have seen, opposed expansion, not Roger Williams and not Robert Beverley either. To be a white man or woman in America was by definition to participate in an imperial conquest. But there was considerable disagreement about how to conduct the expansion.

Those who, like Roger Williams, favored buying the land or at least negotiating for it were no more powerful in Virginia than they were in Massachusetts. Bacon's Rebellion, beginning in 1676, generally has been described as a conflict between richer and poorer Virginia planters, with Bacon challenging the authority of the royal governor over the Indian trade. But Bacon's first demand of the royal governor, William Berkeley, was not for free trade but for a free hand against the Indians.

Bacon, who was himself highborn but only lately emigrated, appealed for support among poorer border settlers by playing on their fear and hatred of the Indians. All through the rebellion, Bacon maintained that all he sought was permission to war "against all Indians in general." He proved his sincerity on one occasion when, having defeated one group of Indians with the assistance of another, he then turned on the second and killed most of them as well. Bacon and his men were responsible for numerous massacres; they ensured that henceforth relations with the Indians would always be violent.

The governor and the group of planters (including Beverley's father, also named Robert Beverley) who resisted Bacon's annihilative program did so out of strategy rather than principle. Loyalists and rebels shared a categorical disapproval of Indians as representing a way of life that constantly threatened to subvert "civilization." White men — generally servants — who ran away to live among the Indians were on recapture brutally punished and sometimes executed. The sides were drawn, and no one in a position of colonial power even came close to letting down his side: the younger Beverley's sympathy for Native Americans is a passive emotion.

The programmatic implications of this attitude toward Native Americans have more to do with class than with race. When he calls himself a plainspoken Indian, Beverley does not mean to demote himself from the rank of gentleman; nor does he thus demote the rank or blur its demarcations. In a chapter entitled "Of the Servants and Slaves in Virginia," Beverley is clear about the alterity of the entire serving class. He believes that upward mobility for servants should culminate in the rank of overseer; he has nothing to say about the possibility of an overseer becoming a planter, although this occurred with some frequency. The chapter is also distinguished by its argument, made here for what may be the first time in America and to be repeated with increasing frequency into the nineteenth century, that a slave is better off than a free laborer, "that generally [American] slaves are not worked near so hard, nor so many hours in a day, as the husbandmen, and day-labourers in *England*." The chapter following this one is entitled "Of the Other Public Charitable Works, and Particularly Their Provision for the Poor." The suggestion that servitude is one form of public charity in turn suggests a view of the world in which the incorporation of unlike groups not only does not deny but actually serves the maintenance of hierarchy.

These qualifications do not erase the difference between the ways the Massachusetts and the Virginia settlements behaved toward the Indians. On the contrary, they suggest that this difference may represent a broader one between colonial philosophies. The writings of another southerner, William Byrd II, suggest that there was indeed a distinctive southern mode of both hating Indians and loving the land. Byrd's father had supported Bacon (but ended the unsuccessful rebellion at the side of the winning governor), and Byrd himself shared neither Beverley's scruples nor his sympathies. Yet they held some important attitudes in common.

❦

William Byrd II (1674–1744) inherited an estate of some 26,000 acres, and at his death he possessed 180,000 acres of Virginia's best land. Many of these acres lay in territory that he had first seen while engaged in a survey of the boundary between North Carolina and Virginia. He described this survey in the *History of the Dividing Line Betwixt Virginia and North Carolina* (written from a journal kept in 1728–9, probably finished in 1738, and published in 1841). Byrd actually kept two journals, and the second, not published until 1929 and known as the *Secret History,* comments on the first. He was Beverley's brother-in-law but the two men seem not to have found one another congenial. In contrast to the country gentleman nativist Beverley, Byrd was a confirmed Anglophile, an avid importer of English furnishings and art for his Westover estate and a devotee of the titled and the courtly. Byrd's chief passion, however, was acquiring land, an avocation he pursued as auditor of Virginia, receiver general of quit rents, and member of the Executive Council.

It is historically appropriate that his greatest acquisitions should have followed the boundary survey. Boundary disputes began with the first colonists, who contested one another's royal patents before they even walked their territories. One such dispute contributed to the conflicts between Plymouth and Ma-re Mount. But these contests had been fought out in England rather than on native ground. A local boundary survey like the one jointly commissioned by North Carolina and Virginia marked a new era in colonization, for, in the survey, the colonists created a new legal document deriving at least part of its authority from its relation to the American land, as against the Crown-derived legitimacy of the overseas patents. This transformation in the basis of land possession was not made explicit by the survey commission, of course, for it would then constitute a challenge to royal prerogative. But it can be read everywhere in Byrd's account of walking the line that the two colonies, in the process, take possession of the territory in their own names. In further individualizing this enterprise, Byrd was pursuing its logic one more step.

The original Virginia patent issued to Raleigh in 1584–5 embraced a vast and unknown area, theoretically extending from Spanish Florida to Cape Breton. The colonized area ran from the coast to include a large part of what would be North Carolina. As colonization progressed, it also became more precise. The New England colonies received their own patents and so too did discrete territories in the south. Virginia, which had come to indicate the settlements around Jamestown, later expanded both west and north, but its coastal holdings were cut back in the Carolina charters of 1663, setting a boundary that was then reset by a second charter two years later, adding a strip of land of about thirty miles to North Carolina. The inhabitants of this area held deeds to their lands from Virginia, but they now refused to pay the higher Virginia taxes. Through a series of negotiations and standoffs, a boundary dispute simmered until in 1728 Byrd and a small group of men set off to establish the boundary once and for all. Settling the issue of governmental dominion had become both possible and pressing when much of the unoccupied land passed into private hands.

Byrd begins his *History* like Beverley by rehearsing the evolution of English colonization since Raleigh. This, in his account, culminates in the progressive dismemberment of Virginia as colony after colony is cut from her. The occasion for the *History* is one in which Virginia is once again in danger of being cheated by latecomers to the New World land auction. In the course of the survey, Byrd encounters a number of objectionable types, the worst of whom are the Carolinians. Their dubious integrity serves an inveterate laziness affecting their every activity but eating. The Carolinians, Byrd complains, "came better provided for the belly than the business. They brought not above two men . . . that would put their hands to anything but the kettle and the frying-Pan. These spent so much of their industry that way, that they had as little spirit as inclination for work." Traveling with these sluggards was often tedious business, and the Virginians several times grew restless with "the Carolina felicity of having nothing to do."

In one passage (often cited as an early example of southwestern humor) Byrd is derisively appalled by "the indolent wretches" who scrape a bare subsistence in the North Carolina backcountry. Asked about the scarcity of cornfields in one area, the locals explain that they grow grain only for their own table. They deem it too much work to feed their cattle, who are left to grub for themselves or starve, and starve they do regularly. These unwholesome people would rather do without milk than bother to climb their own trees and gather the moss that could offer a minimal provender for the cows. Indeed, the only business they *will* pursue is the "raising of hogs, which is manag'd with the least trouble, and affords the diet they are most fond of." From eating too much pork, however, the North Carolinians are "full of gross humours."

For want too of a constant supply of salt, they are commonly obliged to eat it fresh, and that begets the highest taint of scurvy. Thus, whenever a severe cold happens to constitutions thus vitiated, tis apt to improve into the yaws, called there very justly the country-distemper. This has all the symptoms of the pox, with this aggravation, that no preparation of mercury will touch it. First it seizes the throat, next the palate, and lastly shows its spite to the poor nose, of which tis apt in a small time treacherously to undermine the foundation.

This calamity is so common and familiar here, that it ceases to be a scandal, and in the disputes that happen about beauty, the noses have in some companies much ado to carry it. Nay, tis said that once, after three good pork years, a motion had like to have been made in the House of Burgesses, that a man with a nose shou'd be incapable of holding any place of profit in the province; which extraordinary motion could never have been intended without some hopes of a majority.

It is not only the Carolinians who are lazy. Having traveled through Virginia, Byrd "is sorry to say it, but idleness is the general character of the men in the southern parts of this colony as well as in North Carolina." These men are of the same type as the North Carolinians. They would rather sit on poor soil than compete for better; they are men who, "like the wild Irish, find more pleasure in laziness than luxury." Poor, idle, and Irish; these terms describe a class in the American South, already formed in the early eighteenth century, though it would be some time before it acquired its epithets of "red-neck," "clay eater," and "white trash."

The "lazy Indians" in Byrd's *History* bear a close resemblance to these improvident whites. As the white poor reject the example of their betters, so the native poor see "in what plenty a little industry enables [the English] to live, yet they choose to continue in their stupid idleness, and to suffer all the inconveniences of dirt, cold, and want, rather than to disturb their hands with care, or defile their hands with labour." The idiom in which Byrd berates the Indians is exactly that in which he deprecates the poor of his own race. In short, he locates Indians in his world on a level inhabited by all those he scorns. And although one is hard put to say of such scorn that it is "better" than outright denial, the distinction bespeaks an important ideological difference.

When, as he does in his introduction to the *History,* Byrd muses that it would have been better from the beginning to do as the French did and intermarry with the natives, he thinks as one who is at ease with feudal class structures. His tolerance for different kinds of people rests on the expectation that he and his kind will absolutely rule them. Byrd's willingness to mingle native blood with his own and his hunger for more and more American land cohabited without any apparent tension with a great ambition to shine in English aristocratic circles. Filling Westover with English furniture and art was an act of plantation, sealing the owner's possession of the American soil in which it was rooted.

In one section of the survey, the commissioners traveled through an area that so delighted Byrd he named it "The Land of Eden" (and later bought a vast tract of it). It was "exceedingly rich," he wrote; "30,000 acres at least . . . as fertile as the lands were said to be about Babylon, which yielded . . . an increase of no less than 2 or 300 for one. But this hath the advantage of being a higher and consequently much healthier, situation than that. So that a colony of 1000 families might, with the help of moderate industry, pass their time very happily there." These fortunate one thousand would find ideal grazing and tillage, they could plant vineyards that would produce the richest wines, they could have peach and apple orchards, and their rice would be the best grown anywhere. "In short everything will grow plentifully here to supply either the wants or wantonness of man."

For all this extraordinary fertility, the land has limits; but Byrd welcomes them: "Nor can I so much as wish that the more tender vegetables might grow here, such as orange, lemon and olive trees, because then we shou'd lose the much greater benefit of the brisk northwest winds, which purge the air, and sweep away all the malignant fevers, which hover over countries that are always warm." The seasonal cold that precludes oranges and olives has other benefits: "it destroys a great number of snakes, and other venomous reptiles, and troublesome insects." It is better to do without oranges, whose need for constant warmth would turn the Land of Eden into an inferno of snakes and insects. And he concludes:

There is no climate that produces everything, since the Deluge wrenched the poles of the world out of their place, nor is it fit it should be so, because it is the mutual supply one country receives from another, which creates a mutual traffic and intercourse amongst men. And in truth, were it not for the correspondence, in order to make up for each other's wants, the wars betwixt bordering nations, like those of the Indians and other barbarous people, would be perpetual and irreconcilable.

Byrd seems briefly to have contemplated an American Eden that would restore the prelapsarian wholeness. But when in the end he rejected such wholeness as actually destructive of peace and welfare, he invoked not the Fall but the Deluge, locating his argument well within human history. The Deluge functions in the passage just cited as a sort of historical Fall, a worldly debacle that has permanently shaped the *material* world. Virginia, the English colonies, America, the whole New World, compose ideally a limited world; it is so excellent a place because it does not encompass everything, for by not encompassing everything, it permits and enables a multitude of new possibilities.

Despite his aristocratic ways, Byrd is the worthy son of an upwardly mobile middle-class father. He is not just after land but after *more* land. He wants to corner the land market, have it it all, remake it all. The other property besides the Land of Eden in which he became interested after the boundary survey was the Dismal Swamp, a "doleful wilderness" so wet and overgrown that, Byrd mistakenly claims, no living creature can endure it. He proposes to drain the Dismal Swamp and sow it with hemp. It is never for him the "Slough of Despond." The "Land of Eden" and the "Dismal Swamp" are ornamented rather than informed by their allusive names. The meaning of things did not lie for Byrd in transcendent realms but on the excellent earth fast becoming his property.

This secular approach applied to understanding persons too. Alongside the official *History* Byrd wrote a *Secret History,* featuring an entire gallery of survey participants. The characters in the *Secret History* are the commissioners directing the party of surveyors; the surveyors, who actually do the work; the woodsmen directed by the surveyors; and a support staff including the aforementioned surplus of North Carolina cooks. The socially prominent commissioners are the protagonists; Byrd names the Virginians "Meanwell" and "Firebrand" and the North Carolinians "Judge Jumble," "Plausible," "Shoebrush," and "Puzzlecause." The two Virginia surveyors bear the respectful names "Orion" and "Astrolabe"; the chaplain is "Dr. Humdrum." Byrd himself is "Steddy."

The ribald episodes of the *Secret History* have earned Byrd the reputation of a refreshingly racy sense of humor. One such episode takes place on an evening when the party is encamped near a hospitable plantation. Steddy himself retires early but his colleagues stay behind to share a companionable cup:

In the gaiety of their hearts, they invited a tallow-faced wench that had sprain'd her wrist to drink with them, and when they had rais'd her in good humour, they examined all her hidden charms, and play'd a great many gay pranks. While Firebrand [a Virginian] who had the most curiosity, was ranging over her sweet person, he pick't off several Scabs as big as nipples, the consequence of eating too much pork. The poor damsel was disabled from making any resistance by the lameness of her hand; all she could do, was, to sit still, and make the fashionable exclamation of the country, "Flesh alive and tear it," and by what I can understand she never spake so properly in her life.

By sex and by class, the serving girl is outside the considerations that would make of this event an intolerable assault. Her social inferiority makes her torture humorous, as the language of the anecdote makes clear; she is placed far below the cultural level of the writer and reader. The writer's chief device is calling attention to that distance. The phrase "in the gaiety of their hearts" not only defines everything to follow as innocent fun but also invites *us* to be amused spectators. An engaged stance would be formally inappropriate. In that context, Firebrand's abuse is only the occasion for a display of literary wit that reinforces the reader's sense that the serving girl is not the sort to whom one extends sympathy. Calling her "poor damsel" works the same way: she is no fit bearer of such a chivalric title. We have already seen that and see it still more clearly now in the incongruity of the term.

Byrd's most effective turn comes at the end. The servant has been defined by her patent inability to participate in the linguistic play that produces the passage. She is incapable of wit in a situation where all value resides in wit. But she does have some language. The conclusive moment in her reduction to an object of Byrd's wit comes when he takes over her language and causes it to speak to his witty purpose. He first weakens her linguistic claim by informing us that "Flesh alive and tear it" is "the fashionable exclamation of the country." This girl does not have her own words, as Byrd does; witness the passage itself. To the extent she does speak, she does not understand what she says, or not as well as we do. "She never spake so properly" as when Byrd explicated her meaning. Byrd's command of language realizes itself in this passage in a commanding position at the top of a hierarchy of class and sex.

Wit and its devices were anathema to Bradford, who saw in them instruments for manipulating divine truth. God's altar, the Puritans repeated, needs not our polishing: even the most direct utterance is too distant from the Word. Puritan allegory shuns the wittiness that is the mainstay of Byrd's. Underlying both views – Bradford's insistence on direct utterance and Byrd's notion that a man is as good as his linguistic prowess – is a by now familiar assumption about the role of language in the constitution not only of meaning but of events. But although their differences do not negate a common ground, neither do they dissolve into it.

If we may identify the two basic components of the colonizing ideology as loving the land and hating the Indians, Bradford and Byrd represent two distinct forms of that ideology. Bradford loved the land he considered himself to have redeemed from a previously infernal state; Byrd, like Beverley, loved a land he had taken over, a land whose value was inherent. Massachusetts and Virginia embody different conceptions of the conquest of North America. Although these conceptions come together in an encompassing notion that this is a special place made so by "Nature and Nature's God," it is useful to see that this notion synthesizes two significantly divergent ideas. It is not the indivisible axiom it represents itself to be.

5

❦

THE DISPUTE OF THE NEW WORLD

B Y 1700, European empires had fully annexed the American continents; by midcentury, a debate over the value of the new acquisition
divided the literature of exploration. In that debate, one side offered a
"degenerationist" argument to the effect that nature in the New World
wilderness had fallen from its proper level, which could only be maintained
by cultivation. The other side countered that American nature had been
remarkably fertile from pre-Columbian days and that cultivation was only
bringing out, not creating, its inherent fertility. Both sides concurred on the
necessity of colonizing the New World, of course. But the degenerationists
understood colonizing as opening new territories for annexation to the existing European world; the defenders of American nature saw the newly annexed continents as constituting their own world, which might even surpass
Europe. The degenerationists were largely Europeans; most of the defenders,
already Americans.

The lines drawn in "the dispute of the New World," as this controversy is
commonly known, extend to map the world of eighteenth-century political
and scientific thought as a whole. In the arguments over the worth of New
World flora and fauna, it is possible to trace the emergence not only of ideas
of America but reciprocally of revised images of Europe as well. Reciprocity
is the key term here. It was the central dynamic in a dispute that enacted the
culminating moment of the discovery, when the New World fully entered
into the worldview of the Old. The early colonial expeditions can be understood incrementally. There was more to the world than had been known; but
because the additional portions were accruing to Europe, the enlarged world
retained its prior order. Geopolitically at least, the center still held. But the
extraordinary vigor of the eighteenth-century dispute concerning the agricultural potential and general desirability of the New World indicates that
seismic forces were at play.

The intensity of the New World dispute suggests that imperial Europe
already felt itself vulnerable even while it was rapidly ascending toward
world dominion. Paradoxically, the dispute over the desirability of the New
World as a human habitat erupted just when European civilization had

definitively established itself in America. The dispute was part of a larger debate over the general definition of a desirable human habitat, over what constituted a "good" civilization and what should be its relation to nature.

Jean-Jacques Rousseau's famous first sentence in *The Social Contract* (1762) – "Man was born free, and everywhere he is in chains" – did not imply that humanity should return to the state of nature. In the state of nature, according to Rousseau, human beings are so far from *their* proper condition that they have no language. They are animals. He even speculates about how close they are to apes, notably to orangutans, which are possibly members of the human species that never progressed beyond their first state. Some progress is necessary: nature is not a desirable habitat for human beings. However, contemporary European civilization is not desirable either because it has moved too far from nature.

Rousseau inspired a group of "primitivists" – in England, notably James Burnett, Lord Monboddo (1714–99), who published the first volume of his *Of the Origin and Progress of Language* in 1773; and Henry Home, Lord Kames (1696–1782), whose essay "Diversity of Men, and of Languages" in *Sketches of the History of Man* (1774) was especially influential. Like Rousseau, the English primitivists cite nature to criticize society, not to reject it. The optimists among them discard the neoclassical notion of a Golden Age, from which there has been steady deterioration, and turn instead to a progressive view: a rise from bestiality to civilization. Their only complaint is that, on this journey, men have been losing their way. The primitive life, as they see it, evolves at an early stage of the journey into agricultural and communal life, before the wrong turn is taken into the marketplace of Vanity Fair. But here again, on the issue of determining the ideal stage of civilized sophistication, it is difficult to draw a clear line between the exponents of nature and those of civilization. Rousseau's archadversary, Voltaire (1694–1778), was himself a scathing critic of the excesses and corruptions of the Parisian haut monde. Candide's decision to return from his world wanderings to quietly cultivate his own garden is the first wise move he makes.

The entire issue of the relation of civilization and nature is embodied, of course, in the experience of colonization. By encountering fundamentally different civilizations, it became possible for Europeans to pose radical questions about their own. One of the important venues of the argument over the right combination of nature and nurture is therefore travel. No one in the eighteenth century seemed to stay home, even those who expected nothing, or nothing good, to come from traveling. The very urban and urbane Samuel Johnson was as devoted to exploration as he was skeptical of its results. Taking a dim view of everything, he never stopped looking. In the same spirit, a profusion of mock travel narratives – Jonathan Swift's *Gulliver's*

Travels (1726), Tobias Smollett's *Travels through France and Italy* (1766), Laurence Sterne's *A Sentimental Journey through France and Italy* (1768) – all seem to have it both ways. One learns by traveling but what one learns is often absurd. Everyone is on the road or at sea, but are they going anywhere? Is there anywhere worth going?

This question may be the most succinct way of expressing the dispute of the New World, or of articulating its underlying impulse. The dispute permitted its participants, who in other respects criticized European civilization without impugning its status, to denigrate imperial acquisitions without at all implying they should be abandoned. The arguments over the value of the new European empires demonstrate with particular vividness the way in which the two sides of an era's debates, however widely separated, are united by their common situation. The situation of both primitivists and sophisticates, both defenders and attackers of the New World, is a new mobility. In this context, the definition of home (of civilization) has become disturbingly relative. Everyone, conservative stay-at-homes and adventurous travelers alike, feels the ground shaking underfoot. The problem is to figure out a new footing, to restage the world order.

One expression of the quest for a new order is the publication of numerous utopian narratives. These make up a form of travel literature that, perversely, usually condemns travel. The utopias are reached only through an arduous and unlikely voyage during which the narrator is often lost. Yet, the utopia itself, since it is a place of perfection, is a still center. Its inhabitants seldom leave home and are not enticed by new worlds. A significant percentage of the literary utopias, including the first, by Thomas More (1478–1535), are set in America. The setting of More's *Utopia* (1515) is the discovery of the New World. A Portuguese mariner sailing with Vespucci is separated from the expedition and goes on to discover the kingdom of the just king Utopus; the *Utopia* is his report. One important attribute of the kingdom of Utopia is that whenever more territory is needed, it simply takes over unused lands on its borders. This kingdom is able to grow without any of the horizon-searching hunger that for the past century had been driving less wisely governed nations to risky transoceanic voyages. When we recall that England's first imperial steps took it into Wales, Scotland, and Ireland, More's vision appears less otherworldly. He may have been suggesting only that empire begins at home.

The inhabitants of Francis Bacon's 1627 utopia, *The New Atlantis,* are contemporaries of the Virginia and Massachusetts immigrants but positively reclusive. The group of adventurers who discover the New Atlantis of Bensalem are continuing the journey of Columbus by sailing westward from Peru to China and Japan. Like him, they are possessed by global ambitions. When "in the midst of the greatest wilderness of waters in the world," they catch sight of dark shapes on the horizon, they are excited by the hope that they may be coming to "islands or continents that hitherto were not come to light." This hope sounds the leitmotiv of the Age of Exploration. But their agitation is in marked contrast to the calm of the ancient people of Bensalem, whose lives of perfect contentment unfold peacefully in place. Their immobility is in no way limiting. The Bensalemites address their Peruvian visitors in excellent Spanish and turn out to speak all the world's major languages and to have full knowledge of all nations and their current pursuits, among which is the recent great expansion of travel and exploration.

They want no part of this for themselves, however. They have remained in touch with the world by sending out "merchants of light," who travel to foreign lands to bring back neither "gold . . . nor any other commodity of matter" but only "books and all varieties of documents describing the latest inventions and discoveries." Needless to say, the book merchants are no more interested in foreign territory than in foreign goods. Far from planting the flag of their country everywhere, they come and go secretly, anxious to remain unknown.

All this they do in obedience to the teachings of Solamona, the great king and lawgiver who lived some three centuries before the birth of Christ and developed a theory of economic self-sufficiency. He sought only the happiness of his people,

taking into consideration how sufficient and substantive this land was to maintain itself without any aid at all of the foreigner, being five thousand six hundred miles in circuit and of rare fertility of soil in the greatest part thereof, and finding also the shipping of this country might be plentifully set on work both by fishing and by transportations from port to port, and likewise by sailing unto some small islands that are not far from us [trade here as in Utopia is a local enterprise] and are under the crown and laws of this state, and recalling into his memory the happy and flourishing estate wherein this land then was.

Solamona promulgated a set of antiexpansionary laws in order to prolong the present state of affairs into perpetuity. One of the most important of these laws is an interdiction against strangers, who might bring "novelties and commixture of manners." Bensalem neither exports nor imports. It shuns mercantile profits for fear of losing its wealth of spirit, preferring contentment to commerce. Wise Solamona understood the laws of economics, and Bensalem has prospered.

Mocking imperial acquisitiveness, the isolationist utopias are lands of infinite plenty. Thus the New World paradise that Voltaire's Candide visits is nothing less than Eldorado itself. Reached by shooting the fearful rapids of an underground river, the Land of Eldorado is as cut off from the world as

Bensalem and as self-sufficient. Its paths are littered with rubies and emeralds; its mud is yellow with gold. What it lacks only complements its riches: Eldorado has neither courts of law nor prisons, neither parliament nor church. The Eldoradans have everything they need and have no desire for more. They hope only "to remain forever hidden from the rapacity of European nations, who have an inconceivable rage for the pebbles and mud of our land, and who, in order to get some, would butcher us to the last man."

None of the authors of these fictions embrace stasis or reject progress, however. Bacon's departure from classical ideals of transcendent permanence is basic to his influence on the definition of modern science; his principles of inductive reasoning incorporate the idea of progress into the very process of thought. Similarly, Voltaire's skeptical rationalism implies an inductiveness that is implicitly expansive. Both the New Atlantis and Candide (1759) promote aspects of seventeenth- and eighteenth-century dynamism uncritically. They see nothing but good embodied in the new science, for instance, despite its obvious potential for changing society. The quiescent utopias criticize the imperial ethic but hardly reject it; they represent internal quarrels among the architects of a modern world whose basic principles are anti-utopian over the most effective deployment of those principles. Imperialism, the utopians insist, must have larger ideals than just economic profits or political power. Commerce is not enough. Too much commerce is counterproductive to the goal of spreading European enlightened culture over all the world. Voltaire (taunting Rousseau) applauded the destruction of the Incas for ridding the world of a disgusting tribe of man-eating savages. In this sense, the utopias compose a literature of cultural imperialism that is actually complementary to the writings Hakluyt collected, which the utopias criticize only to correct.

❦

The literature of the dispute of the New World depicts America, in varying degrees, as a dystopia. It participates in the same project of civilizing as well as conquering the empire; it creates in and through the New World a more glorious Europe. According to the Enlightenment, human beings can ascend to an ideal level already implicit in their nature. But the converse of this optimistic proposition is that these mutable human beings are also in danger of degenerating to a no less natural brutality. The fear is that they will abandon the culture of Enlightenment for a poisonous swamp, a rank wilderness, a jungle, a primeval ooze — in a word, for America.

The dispute began with, and throughout referred to, the Natural History of the Earth (Histoire naturelle) by Georges-Louis Leclerc, Comte de Buffon (1707–88). The first volume was published in 1749; other volumes appeared at regular intervals until 1788. Buffon is generally accounted to be the founder of modern natural history. Thus, along with modern anthropology, natural history is the creature of the European empire. The *Natural History* sold exceptionally well and is one of the texts most often referred to across the range of eighteenth-century philosophy, history, and literature, as well as, of course, science. Gathering reports of both animal and plant life in all the explored territories, Buffon organized them into a theory of anthropocentric but secular natural evolution (in some respects anticipating Darwin). He dismantled one world system and constructed another; he discarded divine Creation as the source of the structures of life on earth and substituted in the place of Genesis a self-evolving and self-perpetuating order, one whose organizing telos lies not in the past but in the future.

This new order is also a hierarchy of both plants and animals, and America is located very low on it. The New World appears in the following influential passage to be barely hovering above chaos. As a scientist coming after Bacon, when the Englishman's reputation was perhaps at its highest, Buffon always begins inductively with the physical evidence:

The horses, donkeys, oxen, sheep, goats, pigs, dogs, all these animals, I say, became smaller [in the New World]; . . . those which were not transported there, and which went there of their own accord, those, in short, common to both worlds, such as wolves, foxes, deer, roebuck, and moose, are likewise considerably smaller in America than in Europe, and *that without exception.*

Biological quality, he argued earlier, is indicated by size, and in America everything and everyone is small:

There is thus, in the combination of the elements and other physical causes, something antagonistic to the increase of living nature in this new world: there are obstacles to the development and perhaps even to the formation of the great seeds; those very seeds which have received their fullest form, their most complete extension, under the beneficial influence of another climate, are here reduced, shrunken beneath this ungenerous sky and in this empty land, where man, scarce in number, was thinly spread, a wanderer, where far from making himself master of this territory as his own domain, he ruled over nothing; where having never subjugated either animals or the elements, nor tamed the waters, nor governed the rivers, nor worked the earth, he was himself no more than an animal of the first order, existing within nature as a creature without significance, a sort of helpless automaton, powerless to change nature or assist her.

The rest of the passage continues to heap scorn on the American natives. Their general impotence is also, says Buffon, more particularly sexual. "The savage is feeble and small in his organs of generation; he has neither body hair nor beard, and no ardor for the female of his kind." Lacking desire, "lifeless in his soul," he has no will either: "take from him hunger and thirst, and you will destroy at the same time the active cause of all his movements; he will remain either standing stupidly or recumbent for days at a time."

This New World dystopia, however, is also an antiutopia, for Buffon has no liking for the traditional tenets of the utopia. Staying in and accepting one's place in the universe; an absence of material ambition; dispassionate calm; a life in harmony with nature, neither changing the environment nor harnessing nature's energies but rather plucking fruits from the trees and rejoicing in the earth's natural bounty even when this is rather meager – these are the conventional elements of the pastoral life, which has strong utopian affinities. The father of natural science was a passionate anti-pastoralist; he defined natural science precisely as antipastoralism.

To see what he was confronting, we might consider another of the most popular discovery texts of the period, Louis-Antoine de Bougainville's *Voyage around the World* (*Voyage autour du monde*, 1771), a popular work that boasted, as a seal of seriousness, a supplement by Denis Diderot. The *Voyage* is a collection of reports by members of an expedition that took two ships around the world from 1766 to 1769. Among other hitherto unknown beauties described is the paradisal "happy isle" that the French ship captain names Nouvelle-Cythère before learning that its indigenous name is Tahiti. The author of the Tahiti section in the work explains that he himself had wanted to name the island Utopia. The opening sentences of the description sum up the vision of the state of nature against which Buffon writes. Tahiti, explains the author, is "the only corner of the world where there live men without vices, without prejudices, without needs, without dissensions. Born beneath the most beautiful sky, nourished by the fruits of a soil that is fertile without cultivation, ruled by fathers rather than kings, they know no other god but Love."

Against this sentimental romance of the primitive, Buffon marshals science, and not only his own scientific findings but the ideology of science as it emerges in force in the eighteenth century, the age of the industrial revolution. Above all, Buffon the natural scientist believes in technology. This creed is reflected in the way he defines doing science, which has less to do with exact observations and measurements than with analysis. His relative unconcern with facts measures the distance of eighteenth-century science from twentieth. For Buffon, gathering precise data is distinct from formulating a thesis, and the real work of science lies in the formulation of powerful theses. His notorious impatience with details and individual facts expresses his refusal to be limited by nature in any way. He will not even let nature determine his evidence. The human mind is the final authority.

Buffon's love of technology is an important clue to the animosity he bears for the New World. Eighteenth-century America is precisely the world before technology. Having depicted the glooms and dooms of the American land at depressing length, Buffon, at one point in his text, has had enough and tries to take heart. He imagines man, weary of being weak and frightened, one day drawing himself upright and declaring,

"Brute nature is hideous and morbid; I and only I can make it pleasant and alive. . . . let us dry up these bogs, bring to life these dead waters by making them flow freely, forming them into streams and canals; let us employ that active, devouring element which was hidden from us and whose possession we owe only to ourselves; let us set fire to this superfluous undergrowth, to these ancient forests that are already half consumed; let us finish off with steel whatever fire will not have destroyed."

The startling violence of this passage derives from a list of verbs – dry up, bring to life, employ, use, set fire, finish off – all of which project radical transformation. Each natural condition to be addressed will end in its opposite state: wet will be dry, death will be life, stasis will be motion, full will be empty, and, once emptied, it will be refilled:

[S]oon . . . we will see appearing . . . sweet and healthful grasses; herds of animals will travel this erstwhile impassable terrain; they will find in it abundant nourishment, an ever-renewing pasture; they will multiply and multiply again; let us utilize these new resources to finish our task: let the ox be broken to the yoke, use its strength and its massive weight to furrow the earth.

Here agriculture is as much an exercise of force as was clearing the land. The human hand has yoked the ox, whose power marks the earth: the might of that hand is both measured and multiplied by the massive strength it controls. There is nothing unconscious or incidental about this assumption to global power; Buffon makes it explicit: "a new nature will emerge from our hands." The chapter, entitled "Nature in the Wild, Nature under Cultivation," envisions a transformed landscape – all "harmful" terrains, plants, and animals done away with; the whole earth become open and accessible; the wide seas now easily navigated. It ends on a hymn to human mastery: "a thousand other monuments of power and glory prove well enough that man, master of the earth, has transformed and renewed its entire surface and that for all time he shares empire over it with Nature."

This matter of sharing empire is an afterthought. Its piety is exposed by the rest of the chapter, in which Nature, far from being treated as an equal partner, is literally manhandled. (The reader will have long since noted the sexual structure of Buffon's vision, which provides an exceptionally clear illustration of the conventional concept of masculinity.) In general, the passage encapsulates at once the principles and the ethos of the modern technological relation to nature. It recalls that this age, which in its philosophy speaks so much and so highly of "Nature," is also the age that enthroned the machine in industry. One of the details in Buffon's panoramic mural of man mastering the earth is the extraction of metals: "gold and iron, more necessary than gold." The elevation of iron over gold measures the historical gulf that separates the Edenic panegyrics of Columbus from the denigrations of Buffon.

The vehemence of Buffon's disdain for American nature is partly addressed to earlier idyllic and reprehensibly unscientific accounts. His contentiousness is directed against their unrigorous method no less than their excessive enthusiasms. The writings of Buffon's disciple, Cornelius de Pauw, are even more incendiary, however. His epic subject is the "great and terrible spectacle [of] half the globe so thoroughly maltreated by Nature that everything in it was either degenerate or monstrous." De Pauw's *Recherches philosophiques sur les Américains, ou Mémoires intéréssants pour servir à l'histoire de l'espèce humaine* (Philosophical Researches on the Americans, or Interesting Memoirs for a History of Mankind, 1768) had an immediate and enormous influence on the ongoing debate over human nature. For instance, Oliver Goldsmith, though heretofore a primitivist, depicts Georgia in his 1769 poem "The Deserted Village" as a "horrid shore,"

> Where at each step the stranger fears to wake
> The rattling terrors of the vengeful snake;
> Where crouching tigers wait their hapless prey,
> And savage men, more murderous still than they.

The *Recherches* is a comparatively slim compendium of travel reports drawing heavily on Buffon. Whereas Buffon was broadly interested in the whole of American nature, de Pauw focuses on the New World's repulsive and dangerous human population. He cannot sufficiently express his disgust at the base beings that creep about America, incapable of either work or thought and just barely fit to be enslaved. He cites Sepúlveda on the American natives' weakness and lack of ambition, but his focus is different. The issue is no longer justifying the enslavement of the New World's inhabitants; in fact, they themselves do not concern de Pauw. His business is with the world of which they were unfit landlords. De Pauw argues that European civilization is America's natural master: human beings and the nature they rule have an innate potential for development, and it is a human duty to realize that potential.

This last concept may seem unexceptional and unexceptionable, but it is both new and highly charged. It defines the fulfillment of potential as an act of virtual creation. De Pauw here quotes from Buffon and offers the summary injunction, "let [Nature] be rejuvenated through cultivation." The notion that the earth grows younger under cultivation invests that human activity with much greater power than it has had hitherto. On the one hand, nature left to itself loses itself; it becomes degenerate, even unnatural. On the other hand, fulfilled nature takes the artificial form of straight furrows and solidly built barns. Man is here not only the instrument of a natural process but its source; without the art of civilization there is no nature or at most only a stunted, perverted version of it. Man is the Creator. The degeneracy thesis skirts blasphemy and forecasts Romanticism. The crux of the matter is human agency. Against fantasies like Bougainville's of Tahiti, where the only useful technology would be a basket to gather fruit plucked from self-cultivating tress, Buffon and de Pauw project a fabricated world whose most natural products are the fruit of industry. The New World is not as natural as the old; Europe will have to bring to America nature along with civilization.

The degenerationist argument, then, establishes the primacy of modern European civilization, seen now not only as the discoverer and possessor but also as the creator of the New World. This is the theme of an English work that popularized Buffon and de Pauw throughout Europe: William Robertson's 1777 *History of America*. The difference between this literature and the sixteenth- and seventeenth-century literature of New World exploration is encapsulated in Robertson's reluctance to waste his time on trifles. So deep is his sense of European superiority that he feels it is "beneath the dignity of history" to even describe the American natives.

It seems reasonable to see this enlarged claim as an expression of anxiety over the possibility of some degree of New World autonomy. But there were also other inspirations for codifying the inferiority of non-European lands and peoples. The eighteenth century saw the height of the slave trade at the same time as Enlightenment liberalism was producing a philosophy that made human slavery (the radical denial of self-possession) impossible to justify. Technology itself generated a new vulnerability in the dependence of emerging industries on colonial resources and in the threat that North America especially represented of competition in a growing world market.

At this second stage of the New World dispute, the issue of European philosophical, ideological, and economic ascendancy becomes virtually explicit. De Pauw's diatribe elicited a number of protests, notably one by a Benedictine monk and disciple of Rousseau, Aubine Joseph Pernety (1716–1801), in 1770. Among other proofs of the noble stature of the traduced American natives, Pernety revived the old legend that giants lived in the region of South America called Patagonia. In 1771, responding to this attack, de Pauw significantly modified his argument, presenting the revision as a clarification. Scoffing at fairy tales unworthy of a rational age, he dismissed Pernety as a vaporous mystic who understood nothing of the modern world, least of all its crucial principle, progress. Pernety, de Pauw argued, had completely failed to see that de Pauw was describing the New World at the time of discovery. Things had transpired since Columbus; Europeans had followed Columbus to America and materially altered the continent. Progress had begun and would continue: "After three hundred years America will as little resemble what it is today, as today it is unlike what it was at the time of the discovery."

This was a position Buffon was developing in part against de Pauw himself, whose vituperative interpretation of his work Buffon found offensive. A 1777 volume of the *Natural History* put the corrected thesis in theoretical terms. Buffon explained that he had been badly misinterpreted on the subject of degeneracy. He had used "degeneracy" as a technical term. Degeneracy identified a state of nondevelopment in which the full possibilities of the organism have not been realized, so that it falls short of, or "degenerates," from its generic potential. He had never meant to suggest that the New World was corrupt or degraded: "Nature, *far from being degenerate through old age [in America]*, is on the contrary recently born and has never existed there with the same force, the same active power as in the northern countries." By degeneracy, in short, he had meant immaturity.

With this correction, Buffon did not so much reverse as shift his stance. In order to mature, the New World would still require the treatment Buffon recommended to overcome degeneracy: a violent transformation of wilderness into the mirror image of cultivated Europe. It might take another three centuries before the New World could compare with the old.

Still, immaturity was less damning than degeneracy. It seemed to offer the ground for a compromise to the New World dispute and so had the great advantage of accommodating most of the Enlightenment, both philosophical and economic. Immaturity implied progress, and it identified progress with the New World. One of the most ardent degenerationists had been sadly perplexed by the apparent contradiction between Buffon's evaluation of American nature and the emergence in North America of a polity that seemed by its experiments in representative government and by its energetic commerce to represent an exceptional capacity for progress. In 1770, Guillaume Thomas François, the Abbé de Raynal, published an extremely popular work based on Buffon: *A Philosophical and Political History of the Settlements and Trade of the Europeans in the East and West Indies* (*Histoire philosophique et politique des établissements et du commerce des Européens dans les deux Indes*). Over the following decade, Raynal became increasingly impressed by political and economic developments, especially in the English colonies; he was eager to see good in the land as well as in its colonizers. In one passage, he grew passionate over the ways Europeans were improving America. At first, echo-

ing the biblical Creation, all was chaos and confusion. "But man appeared"
(by which he means European man) "and immediately changed the face of
North America."

He introduced symmetry by the assistance of all the instruments of the arts. The
impenetrable woods were instantly cleared, and made room for commodious dwellings. The wild beasts were driven away, and stock of domestic animals supplied their
place while thorns and briars made way for rich harvests. The waters forsook part of
their domain, and were drained off into the interior part of the land, or into the sea
by deep canals. The coasts were covered with towns, and the bays with ships; and
thus the new world, like the old became subject to man.

Thus the New World became an extension of the Old – became the Old
extended.

This representation of American evolution invoked the powerful ideology
of progress and embodied it flatteringly in the land of the New World. But
the immaturity argument also resolved the problem of European hegemony
even when that argument was put in its most challenging form, as describing
the rise and fall of empires.

By the end of the sixteenth century, one of the most problematical connotations of the discovery began to emerge in the notion that Columbus's westward journey charted the march of civilization itself. History progressed like
the sun from east to west. This notion, which had an earlier lineage in
classical thought, had at first no more disturbing meaning than that the
nations of Europe, in seizing the American continents, were working out a
universal destiny. At this point the annexation of the New World seemed
even to promise the rejuvenation of the Old. When John Frampton translated
the pharmacological study of American plants by the physician Nicolas
Monardes as *Joyful News out of the New Found World* (1577; Spanish original,
1574), he cast America as a source for "the wonderful cures of sundry great
diseases that otherwise than by these remedies, they were incurable." By the
eighteenth century, however, the historical geography of empire aroused
more urgent anxieties than Buffon's and Raynal's concept of a spatial Enlightenment could allay. Horace Walpole's vision of a transatlantic Europe drew
the sting from the decline of the original site by projecting a quintessential
Europe still in control, as transcendent cultural consciousness:

The next Augustan age will dawn on the other side of the Atlantic. There will,
perhaps, be a Thucydides at Boston, a Xenophon at New York, and, in time, a Virgil
in Mexico, and a Newton at Peru. At last, some curious traveller from Lima will visit
England and give a description of the ruins of St. Paul's.

When Goethe declared, "America, you have it better than our old continent"
("Amerika, du hast es besser / Als unser Kontinent, das alte"), it did not

occur to him that the youthful culture he envisioned was anything but European. That assumption was formulated, however, only over a period of time. There was nothing self-evidently positive in the first enunciations of the notion that America was young; the immature land of the New World was only somewhat better than the primeval slime. When Buffon, de Pauw, and Raynal granted that, under the aegis of Europe, America could rise out of that slime, this was a concession inspired by a peculiar and paradoxical mentality.

The late eighteenth century marked at once the first maturity of European imperialism and the beginning of its downfall when the English colonies in America broke away. This odd conjunction meant that for a prolonged period, when the empire was still expanding, it was also transforming itself into a new system based on commercial exploitation as much as on direct political control. In turn, that odd conjunction may be seen expressed in the paradoxical vision of an America at once less than Europe and more or, not so paradoxically, the child of Europe now and also Europe's future. In 1776, the authors of the Declaration of Independence justified breaking away on the ground that the English colonies had come of age and had reached the maturity required to be a nation. In the same year that they made this claim, Edward Gibbon (1737–94) began to publish his *Decline and Fall of the Roman Empire* (1776–88). We could read the dispute of the New World as an argument about the meaning of this coincidence.

In America the meaning seemed perfectly clear. Indeed, if any Americans at the time observed the coincidence of the Declaration and the *Decline and Fall*, they probably took it as a sign. Jerusalem was a model for the Puritan "city on a hill," but Rome became the model for Washington. The New England vision of a redeemed Garden yields, in the middle colonies and especially in the southern ones, to the image of a resurgent Rome. To those who entertained such ambitions, the idea that nature in the New World was degenerate and was being restored by Europeans implied an insulting secondariness. One of the best-known passages in Thomas Jefferson's *Notes on the State of Virginia* ("Query VI. Productions Mineral, Vegetable and Animal") rebuffs Buffon's thesis with a barrage of statistics and scientific observations intended to prove that American nature was not just the equal of Europe's but superior to it. There are, Jefferson calculates, one hundred natural species in the New World to one hundred and twenty-six in the Old World. But "the residue of the earth being double the extent of America, the exact proportion would have been but as 4 to 8." (In Jefferson's somewhat mechanical reasoning, twice as much land should accommodate twice as many species.) That the ratio is more like 4 to 5 — with one-third the world's land, America according to Jefferson has four-fifths the number of species — certainly vindicates the New World's fertility.

The rebuttal begins less dramatically with a general exposition of natural resources. After a rather plodding catalogue of mines, tree and animal species, hot springs, and kinds of earth (the *Notes* was written in answer to a questionnaire distributed by the French to all the colonies), the text grows more lively when it directly invokes Buffon's "opinion" that "nature is less active, less energetic on one side of the globe than she is on the other." Jefferson finds it hard to believe that a scientist of Buffon's distinction could credit such a thing:

As if both sides were not warmed by the genial sun; as if a soil of the same chemical composition, was less capable of elaboration into animal nutriment; as if the fruits and grains from that soil and sun, yielded a less rich chyle, gave less extension to the solids and fluids of the body, or produced sooner in the cartilages, membranes, and fibres, that rigidity which restrains all further extension, and terminates animal growth.

This exemplary piece of eighteenth-century rational—scientific prose couches an argument that actually runs counter to the ideology of Enlightenment science, for Jefferson bases his case for the equality of American nature not on progress itself but on its limits. "Every race of animals seems to have received from their Maker certain laws of extension at the time of their formation," he writes. "What intermediate station they shall take may depend on soil, on climate, on food, on a careful choice of breeders. But all the manna of heaven would never raise the Mouse to the bulk of the Mammoth." Buffon never suggested it could. His analysis had to do with intermediate "station[s]" and the *relative* sizes of plants and animals. Jefferson recasts a comparative and contingent claim into an absolute one. His own thesis too is absolute: having dismissed the possible differences as merely "intermediate," he declares nature the same on both sides of the Atlantic — universally the same, made so by the Maker according to laws "unsearchable to beings with our capacities."

Jefferson does not envision the individual making his world here but receiving it whole. Science for him had to do with deciphering the instructions for nature's use. The *Notes* was intended to convey the excellent prospects of New World trade and investment, so as to persuade the French to continue to support the colonies' independence; but it expends more pages and much more feeling on descriptions of aboriginal America than on the cultivated United States. Indeed, the present merit of American nature seems to inhere in the survival of its first conditions. Jefferson claims that mammoths, extinct elsewhere, still roam the New World wilderness. No husbandry will make a mouse into a mammoth, and Europe long ago saw its last mammoth die out. If size is to be accounted the measure of fertility, the survival of the mammoth should weigh heavily on the side of America.

Paradoxically, Jefferson's defense of America is conservative, more congenial to a neoclassical than a liberal outlook. This is the more puzzling in that his rejection of Buffon's notion of progressive colonization seems to diminish the role of Jefferson and his compatriots in the creation of the New World. Their defense of the aboriginal New World may even be said to undermine their claim to it, for the Euro-Americans are not the children of the wilderness but its conquerors, and their primary justification is the "improvement" of the New World.

Jefferson's refusal to claim for himself and his fellow conquerors the status of scientific re-creators parallels the similar demurral implicit in the Declaration of Independence. The Declaration appeals not to national autonomy but to the higher status of a natural community created by "Nature and Nature's God" and only implemented by the former colonizers, now Americans. In this parallel lies a key to Jefferson's vehement repudiation of any betterment of the sort for which Buffon and Raynal praise the Americans, for by the end of the eighteenth century, Englishmen in America no longer wish to think of themselves as colonizers. They may have come from elsewhere, but having arrived, they acquire a new identity that does not continue their old history. Rather, it recasts history altogether into a prehistory, and the American present becomes all-encompassing, recapitulating the history of the race as it culminates it. In this context, Jefferson's mammoth stands for an *American* civilization. This civilization is not just the next outpost of Europe but complete and self-sufficient in its own right. The proof of independence for American civilization lies in its possession of its *own* wilderness. Bradford saw an antithetical wilderness threatening his very identity. In the *Notes,* Jefferson signals the emergence of an apparently opposite vision of a wilderness that grounds America's transcending uniqueness.

Jefferson's contemporaries generally adopted the same stance, with surprising results. For instance, they took a particularly odd stance in relation to the American climate, which was all through the century the subject of considerable controversy. Seventeenth-century colonists arriving in New England expected to find themselves in a climate much like England's and were unhappily surprised at the harshness of the winters, which they could not explain by the country's latitude. They had not taken into account the effect of the Gulf Stream, which greatly moderates England's climate. Moreover, as we now know from meteorological studies, in the seventeenth century, New England winters were unusually severe due to a mini-ice age. When this began to pass, the weather became more temperate, but the colonists were reluctant to acknowledge the improvement.

Buffon and his fellow degenerationists claimed the change to be evidence of the benefits of settlement. They applauded the Americans for their assiduous cultivations, their drainage of swamps, and their pruning of forests. Noah Webster (1758–1843) summarized the American position in his *Dissertation on the Supposed Change of Temperature in Modern Winters* (1799). The title states the argument: there was no change, Webster assured everyone. People's memories always exaggerated past hardship. He was generally supported by other scientific observers, such as the physician Benjamin Rush (1745–1813), who similarly refused to believe any significant change had occurred. Rush and Jefferson agreed that American nature was not a historical phenomenon but a natural one and therefore in its larger designs impervious to human engineering. The Americans insisted that the weather had always been what it was and that it was not the work of settlement to try and change it.

Settlers should instead adapt: "Perhaps no climate or country is unhealthy," wrote the physician Rush, "where men acquire from experience, or tradition, the arts of accommodating themselves to it" (*Account of the Climate of Pennsylvania and Its Influence upon the Human Body,* 1790). Webster firmly concurred in his *A Collection of Papers on the Subject of Bilious Fevers, Prevalent in the United States for a Few Years Past* (1796): "If [Americans] can be convinced . . . that sources of disease and death may be found among themselves created by their own negligence, it is a great point learned." The great point was cleanliness: not to "wallow in filth," to bathe occasionally, and to clean up the cities (in this case Philadelphia, which had become an open sewer). What was wrong with the American environment had been created by disorderly settlers; in itself, the natural environment was "pure and healthy."

Webster was an unlikely defender of unimproved nature. He was a schoolteacher, a student of language, and a writer on literary and political culture; he had already published *The American Spelling Book* (1783), the famous "blue-backed speller" that would sell more than a million copies in over four hundred editions, and launched the short-lived but influential *American Magazine* (1787–8). He was a man of consummate civilization, author of the *Compendious Dictionary of the English Language* (first edition 1806 and still publishing). When he undertook his survey of the literature of epidemic diseases, he was an increasingly rigorous Federalist who worried that the new nation would suffer from an insufficiency of moral as well as physical hygiene. His colleague Benjamin Rush was a medical doctor who had interned in London. Rush wrote prolifically on matters of physical and psychological health, so that his reputation finally rested as much on his writing as on his medical practice.

Both Webster and Rush were prominent figures in a circle of men of letters and scientists that began to earn the English colonies a reputation for considerable intellectual resources. Benjamin Franklin, "the American sage," was the best-known member of this group and its major organizer, but Webster, Rush, the astronomer David Rittenhouse, the botanists James Logan, John Bartram, William Bartram, and Cadwallader Colden, along with Jared Eliot (1685–1763), a gentleman-farmer from Connecticut whose *Essays on Field Husbandry* (1748–59) exemplify the practical orientation of much of the contemporary research, were also active in the creation of an important intellectual, cultural, and scientific scene.

The seat of the circle was Philadelphia, a city of merchants with money for research and an appreciation of its uses. There Franklin and his Junto club created the Library Company, and there, by 1743, the same group drew up an appeal "That one Society be formed of virtuosi or ingenious men residing in the several Colonies, to be called *The American Philosophical Society;* who are to maintain a constant correspondence." The resistance to Buffon's notion that human beings were transforming American nature for the better through science and technology was formulated by American scientists and technological innovators, all men of a decidedly urban culture. One can understand why they took the position they did when they did. But it was nonetheless contradictory; and the contradiction outlived the occasion. Beyond permitting Americans to claim independence, embracing an aboriginal America had some dubious implications. It meant that historical process was not to be part of the essential America. The natural nation Jefferson and his colleagues invented stood outside history. The dispute of the New World was resolved, but the resolution presented its own problem.

6

TRAVELING IN AMERICA

TOWARD THE END of the eighteenth century and the beginning of
the nineteenth, during the period when the English colonies declared
themselves a nation, the enterprise of coming to the New World and
exploring it changed decisively. From a perilous journey into the unknown,
it became the civilized pursuit of traveling in America. In 1796, Timothy
Dwight (1764–1846), finding the life of a president of Yale College too
sedentary, decided "to devote [his] vacations . . . to a regular course of
traveling." During the second of these salubrious journeys, it occurred to him
while surveying the orderly countryside to wonder how these New England
landscapes had appeared eighty or even a hundred years earlier. But he found
the past impossible to recall, so swift had been the transformation. He
resolved instead to capture the fleeting present and record it for those who
would live eighty or a hundred years hence. "A country changing as rapidly
as New England must, if truly exhibited, be described in a manner resembling that in which a painter would depict a cloud," he wrote. It was an
accurate rendition of a period of transition. Dwight traveled for his health
and wrote about his travels as a literary pursuit – reflectively, speculatively,
poetically, and for an undoubted posterity.

The grandson of Jonathan Edwards and himself a prominent minister,
Dwight represents an already old New England. He recalls the persistence of
Puritan values at the founding of the Republic. Commending the decent "competence" and measured way of life of his Connecticut neighbors, he disdains the
excitements of the traditional travel narrative. Besides, he warns the reader,

adventures of all kinds must be very rare in a country perfectly quiet and orderly in
its state of society. In a series of journeys sufficiently extensive to have carried me
through two thirds of the distance round the globe, I have not met with one. Nearly
every man whom I have seen was calmly pursuing the sober business of peaceful life;
and the history of my excursion was literally confined to the breakfast, dinner, and
supper of the day.

It is not only by debunking adventure that Dwight's *Travels in New England and New York* (1821) departs from the conventions of the travel narra-

tive. The resident of New Haven has little interest in wildlife. A lyrical description of the Massachusetts landscape around Mount Holyoke depicts nothing that is not in some degree domesticated or the outright result of cultivation. This applies even to the views from the mountain top: "On the highest part of the summit, the inhabitants have cleared away the trees and shrubs so as to open the prospect in a most advantageous manner." What does he observe from this improved prospect? He sees a "variety of farms, fields, and forests, of churches and villages, of hills and valleys, of mountains and plains [that] can neither be described nor imagined."

In this panorama, the land's natural features have no priority. Dwight is not moved by natural vistas in themselves. He always prefers to gaze at a cultivated landscape, at riverbanks alternately fringed by "shrubs, green lawns and lofty trees." Everywhere he looks he finds a pleasing domestication:

The intervals, which in this view border [the river] in continual succession, are fields containing from five hundred to five thousand acres, formed like terraced gardens. . . . These fields are distributed into an immense multitude of lots. . . . One range of these lots is separated from another by a straight road, running like an alley.

There follows an apostrophe to the beauties of nature that, in organization and tone, is altogether familiar as a set piece of eighteenth-century American landscape writing. Thomas Jefferson describing a Blue Ridge Mountains pass in the *Notes on the State of Virginia,* William Bartram and Meriwether Lewis gazing out over wild vistas, are only its best-known instances. Its features are a dazzled observer and an immense view extending to a global horizon and encompassing all the possibilities of natural beauty. Dwight's version is, in this sense, quite orthodox. The scene is unparalleled:

When the eye traces this majestic stream, meandering with a singular course through these delightful fields, wandering in one place five miles to gain one . . . enclosing almost immediately beneath an island of twenty acres . . . forcing its way between these mountains, exhibiting itself like a vast canal . . . reappearing . . . in its passage to the ocean; when it marks the sprightly towns which rise upon its banks, and the numerous churches which gem the whole landscape . . . ; when it ascends higher and marks the perpetually varying and undulating arches of the hills . . . ; when last of all it fastens upon the Monadnock in the northeast, and in the northwest upon Saddle Mountain, ascending each at the distance of fifty miles in dim and misty grandeur, far above all the other objects in view; it will be difficult not to say that with these exquisite varieties of beauty and grandeur the relish for landscape if filled, neither a wish for higher perfection, nor an idea of what it is remaining in the mind.

Though its idiom and organization are commonplace, this passage, as well as the fragments cited earlier, differs from similar passages by integrating the settled into the wild – indeed, subsuming the wild into the settled. Primeval nature is the setting for domestication, not its alternative. The last phrase of Dwight's passage joins categories of nature and of mental states that are more commonly opposed. In this all-encompassing setting, "with these exquisite varieties of beauty and grandeur," Dwight declares himself so perfectly satisfied that he can form "neither a wish for higher perfection, nor an idea of what it is."

He still finds the agricultural landscape remarkable, but cultivation has cut the wilderness down to size. Other travel writers, like William Bartram, did not share Dwight's preference for domesticated vistas, but the treatment of wild landscapes in this period also reflects a rapidly changing scene in which the universe of nature is civilization, the wilderness becoming an encapsulated, figurative state within it. Bartram traveled in search of botanical knowledge, but in his literary turns and philosophical flights he seems at times only secondarily interested in reporting his findings. Dwight celebrates the cultivated landscape and Bartram the wild, but it is a sign of the times that they have more in common than separates them in their attitude to landscapes as the stuff of literature.

An ancillary purpose of Dwight's *Travels,* he explains in his preface, is to correct "the misrepresentation which foreigners, either through error or design, had published of my native country." The culminating and concluding text in the denigrating mode is Chasseboeuf de Volney's report of his journey, *A View of the Soil and Climate of the United States of America* (1804; *Tableau du climat et du sol des Etats-Unis d'Amérique* [1803]), the first volume of a projected two-volume opus that would in the second half have complemented the account of the physical continent with one of the emerging society. Volney found neither very impressive. But with American university presidents turning to the production of a native travel literature, a pattern has emerged whose basic terms announce the coming end of the period of colonization. Indeed, in disparaging the New World settlements, Volney begins to acknowledge their autonomy: they are changing from European resources to mediocre competitors on the international scene.

For their part, Dwight and his fellow travelers have no notion any longer of identifying civilization solely with Europe. Henceforth the terms are American (U.S.) civilization versus European. Alexis de Tocqueville (1805–59), during his American journey (1831–2), is not engaged in a voyage of discovery; he is traveling abroad for the classic purpose of observing how other societies conduct themselves and of criticizing one's own. He starts out knowing he will find that Americans are different, being defined as "American" by their difference. He comes to observe not the New World but American civilization. By the late eighteenth century, American travelers are also observing an established civilization, even when they survey its wilderness, even when they depict this wilderness in the wildest terms.

❧

In 1778, Jonathan Carver (1710–80), who had been a captain in the colonial troops during the French and Indian Wars, published his *Travels Through the Interior Parts of North America in the Years 1766, 1767, and 1768* and found unexpected fame and fortune. Eventually over thirty editions of the *Travels* would appear, to make this possibly the most popular American travel book ever written. Carver's route was hardly pathbreaking since, like just about everyone before him, he too sought the Northwest Passage. He was not even a particularly enlightening reporter. Often inaccurate, he mixed observation and rumor indiscriminately due to his paramount interest in telling a good story. Although later generations of critics frowned on Carver's loose relation to the truth, the scholar Jedidiah Morse (1761–1826) drew on the *Travels'* account of the frontier for his *American Geography* (1789; second edition, *The American Universal Geography,* 1793), which suggests that Carver's book was well respected in its time. It was, in fact, a book of its time whose importance today lies in representing an era when the exploration of the New World could now be undertaken with the attitude of a storyteller.

The advertisement for the 1838 American edition of Carver's *Travels* offers it first and foremost as a good read. Americans, the advertisement explains, were no sooner settled than they turned about to look upon themselves with deserved wonder, for the wonder lay in them: "There are still living," the writer of the advertisement avers, those

who recollect the impression produced by the first publication of this interesting work; the countries of which it treats, the novelty of its incidents, the peculiarities of Indian character described, gave to it the charm of Romance, and it was in the hands of all ages; but its subjects were so novel, so unknown, so incapable of realization by comparison with those which were familiar that full credence in the accuracy of its recitals, as in those of old Marco Polo, and of some other visiters of strange lands of much more modern date, remained to be established by the future.

Now, the copy goes on, the future has borne out even the most astounding of Carver's descriptions. This is not true; by 1838 many reviewers had denounced the *Travels* as wild fabrication. But the advertiser knows his book and its audience, and neither is particularly concerned about accuracy. When he claims that all of Carver's stories are true, he really means that they convey an America readers will believe in, an America that conforms to their expectations.

Carver represents popular thinking even when he is controversial, as, for instance, when he defends the benevolence and morality of the American natives. His "concise character of the Indians" would not be endorsed by all his readers but they would all recognize it as the familiar other side of the argument. "The character of the Indians," Carver writes judiciously, "like that of other uncivilized nations, is composed of a mixture of ferocity and gentleness. They are at once guided by passions and appetites, which they hold in common with the fiercest beasts that inhabit their woods, and are possessed of virtues which do honour to human nature." This may not be the majority view, but it is common sense. Carver, who has often been criticized for his irresponsible fantasizing, depicts an entirely conventional America.

❦

The more serious travel writers of the age also journeyed in a newly coherent continent. William Bartram's (1739–1823) *Travels* (1791) described the naturalist-author's peregrinations over five years from 1773 to 1778 through Florida, Georgia, and the Carolinas. Bartram's *Travels* was immediately taken up in Europe by the emerging Romantic movement. Samuel Taylor Coleridge mined it for "Kubla Khan" and "The Rime of the Ancient Mariner," William Wordsworth drew on it for his 1805 "The Prelude" and for other poems, and there are clear echoes in Robert Southey and later in Alfred, Lord Tennyson. On the Continent, the *Travels* was a primary source for one of the most popular Romantic works of the time, *Atala* (1801), a tragic tale of young love discovered and lost forever in a deep forest of the New World.

The author of *Atala,* François René de Chateaubriand (1768–1848), had himself visited America and much later published his own *Travels in America* (*Voyage en Amérique,* 1827), but it is doubtful that, in the four months or so he spent in the New World, he actually saw the Louisiana landscapes he describes in *Atala.* Arriving in Philadelphia in 1791, he was just in place and time for Bartram's book, which served as his major source for the lush savannas, the forests of giant trees twined with dripping vines, the multitudes of birds of brilliant plumage, and the riot of color and sound ("tender and savage harmonies") that stage the doomed passion of an Indian maiden and a young brave. *Atala* was followed by *Les Natchez* (1826) and the *Travels in America,* both deriving much of their local color from Bartram. *Atala* remained one of the most important texts representing America to Europe throughout the nineteenth century and into the twentieth.

America had been portrayed in Europe as utopia and dystopia, adventure story, sacred text, political document, history, scientific report, and travel narrative. It now became additionally and supremely romance, a romance of pure hearts and unadorned truths ennobled by God and His creation; simple children of forest and farm, its heroes and heroines are exalted into a spiritual aristocracy. The character Atala has diction and manners to rival those of the highest-born lady. Her eyes are as blue as the sky of her native Louisiana; her hair is golden, her skin fair, and her veins a delicate tracery. Chateaubriand was a royalist whose family had lost lives and property in the French Revolution; he returned to France along with many émigrés when Napoleon Bonaparte restored the aristocracy. Despite its transatlantic setting, the conservative and ultrapious *Atala* is, of course, about France. One expression of the reaction that followed the failure of the Revolution was the rebirth of religion. Chateaubriand was deeply religious and originally intended to include *Atala* in his equally successful *The Genius of Christianity* (*Le Génie du Christianisme*, 1802).

Chateaubriand had his own European message to convey, but he could have found at least some support for his pastoral America in Bartram's *Travels,* whose account of things is at times oddly ethereal. Bartram is, as one would expect, minutely specific about flora and fauna, but the larger setting is shadowy at best. All the writings we have considered addressed themselves to immediate situations. Bartram's world appears to exist beyond history, beyond time, even beyond place. His route takes him through a territory claimed variously by the English, the Indians, the Spanish, and the French. None of those claims are secure and all are in transition; in fact, Bartram reports his attendance at the negotiations among Creeks, Cherokees, and white settlers that led to the 1773 Treaty of Augusta. Following the meetings, surveyors set out to establish the new boundaries, and Bartram accompanied them for a time. In striking contrast to Byrd, however, Bartram sees nothing to interest him in such dividing lines. He has eyes only for natural boundaries, carefully noting the differences between one shore of a river and the other but never the political borders, with which the natural often coincide. We know where we are in his *Travels* and when, but it does not matter, or at least it matters far less than it did to Harriot, Smith, or Byrd.

The fact that the continent is more secure to white habitation now than when his predecessors traveled it does not sufficiently explain Bartram's abstraction. With the securing, new hazards and considerations have arisen that should command as much attention as ever. The area he is traveling through crosses over into the territory of the later Louisiana Purchase, and there are serious conflicts among settlers of three nationalities as well as continual skirmishes with the Indians, who are resisting the accelerating efforts to remove them.

Bartram just enjoys being out in nature. Setting off with the Treaty of Augusta surveyors, he describes a scene in which political considerations have no place:

It was now about the middle of the month of May; vegetation, in perfection, appeared with all her attractive charms, breathing fragrance everywhere; the atmo-

> sphere was now animated with the efficient principle of vegetative life; the arbustive hills, gay lawns, and green meadow . . . had already received my frequent visits; and although here much delighted with the new beauties in the vegetable kingdom . . . yet, as I was never long satisfied with present possession, however endowed with every possible charm to attract the sight, or intrinsic value to engage and fix the esteem, I was restless to be searching for more, my curiosity being insatiable.

His insatiable curiosity has no appetite for history, although history was just then exceptionally highly flavored.

Bartram's preference for nature is not unexpected. He was the son of John Bartram, perhaps the foremost naturalist of the English colonies, whose voluminous correspondence abroad constitutes the founding text of American natural history. The elder Bartram's major connection in England was with the Quaker merchant Peter Collinson, a colonial trader with an important traffic in seeds and botanical samples. Collinson's interest in the New World was inextricably economic, political, and scientific. The circle of his correspondents, who were adepts of natural and agricultural science, were deeply engaged in the discussions that led to the founding of the nation. Their observations almost always carried a political implication. Jefferson was a prominent member of this group. The younger Bartram's apparent lack of interest in the events of his time is thus especially puzzling. His journals covering the years 1773 to 1778 never so much as mention the Revolution.

Equally surprising, he never takes up the issue of slavery. A Philadelphia Quaker, Bartram could not have been unaware of the controversy over slavery, and in fact, early in the *Travels,* while describing an Indian tribe, he notes "the striking contrast betwixt a state of freedom and slavery." The enslaved Indians are pitifully tamed, abject creatures; the free are "bold, active and clamorous. They differ as widely from each other as the bull from the ox."

J. Hector St. John de Crèvecoeur, in his *Letters from an American Farmer* (1781–2), cites at length John Bartram's recommendation that former slaves be integrated into the free work force and offered every opportunity for education and advancement. Slaveholding Quakers, including John Bartram on his Schuylkill farm, had freed them and had become active proponents of abolition. Yet his son seems unmoved by the sight of slavery and in fact sketches a scene that could provide a master print for the plantation novel. Touring a large farm, Bartram and his host enter a clearing where they observe this happy prospect:

The slaves comparatively of a gigantic stature, fat and muscular, were mounted on the massive timber logs; the regular heavy strokes of their gleaming axes re-echoed in the deep forests; at the same time, contented and joyful, the sooty sons of Afric forgetting their bondage, in chorus sung the virtues and beneficence of their master in songs of their own composition.

Now, the master thus celebrated and his family are worthy folk, "educated as it were in the woods" but "no strangers to sensibility, and those moral virtues which grace and ornament the most approved and admired characters in civil society." And when he visits the "neat habitation . . . situated in a spacious airy forest" where his host's son lives, Bartram is treated to an even more enchanting view:

As we approach the door, conducted by the young man, his lovely bride arrayed in native innocence and becoming modesty, with an air and smile of grace and benignity, meets and salutes us! what a Venus! what an Adonis! said I in silent transport; every action and feature seem to reveal the celestial endowments of the mind: though a native sprightliness and sensibility appear, yet virtue and discretion direct and rule. The dress of this beauteous sylvan queen was plain but clean, neat and elegant, all of cotton, and of her own spinning and weaving.

Some part of the explanation for Bartram's grotesque embrace of the romance of slavery must lie in this pastoral, which, in the southern regions he travels, is inextricably entangled with the institution of slavery. His general disregard for the political life around him must have been mostly a matter of personal temperament. But some portion of it may be attributed to his deep engagement with the ideology of pastoralism, a view of nature that implies a social or political ideal in which revolutions have no place but to which it is quite possible to reconcile slavery.

Pastoralism is literary at its origin, and its values arise from linguistic and imagistic impulses. One might have expected Bartram to be more influenced by scientific thinking, but his naturalist science is restricted to isolated descriptions and sketches, whereas the overall scheme organizing and mobilizing his world emerges from considerations of imaginative coherence. If style can in certain instances be the man, in this instance it is the world.

Bartram was a painter as well as a writer, and his descriptions of the wildlife of the savannas and swamps he visited are sometimes strikingly visual. His description of fish in a teeming river wonderfully mingles science and artistic vision:

The blue bream is a large, beautiful, and delicious fish; when full grown they are nine inches in length, and five to six inches in breadth; the whole body is of a dull blue or indigo colour, marked with transverse lists or zones of a darker colour, scatteringly powdered with sky blue, gold and red specks; fins and tail of a dark purple or livid flesh colour; the ultimate angle of the branchiostega forming a spatula, the extreme end of which is broad and circular, terminating like the feather of the peacock's train, and having a brilliant spot or eye like it, being delicately painted with a fringed border of a fire colour.

In other descriptions, however, his scientific understanding and his artistic eye are apparently superseded by a more authoritative mode of perception:

How gently flow thy peaceful floods, O Alatamaha! How sublimely rise to view, on thy elevated shores, yon magnolian groves, from whose tops the surrounding expanse is perfumed, by clouds of incense, blended with the exhaling balm of the liquidambar, and odours continually arising from circumambient aromatic groves of illicium, myrica, laurus and bignonia.

The apostrophe to the river embraces botanical information whose scientific precision may seem incongruous glimpsed through spiritual mists, but the *Travels* frequently subsume science and direct observation into philosophical convention or into an omnipresent sense of the philosophical narrator. Even in the description of the blue bream, we see, through the detailed description, the sensitive observer almost as clearly as the fish. The fish, as it were, does the observer credit; Bartram never describes flower or beast in any but exquisite terms. Much more frequently than even in John Smith's bragging histories, it is the person of Bartram who takes the foreground; we look into his eyes as he looks upon nature. The sublime view of the Alatamaha River comes into focus upon Bartram himself:

[S]ecure and tranquil, and meditating on the marvelous scenes of primitive nature, as yet unmodified by the hand of man, I gently descended the peaceful stream, on whose polished surface were depicted the mutable shadows from its pensile banks; whilst myriads of finny inhabitants sported in pellucid floods.

This concludes the scene, as if it had now come to its point.

Bartram's descriptions often amount to a scientific version of pathetic fallacy. This is the case in perhaps the best-known interval in the *Travels,* the encounter with the alligators. Having made camp in a swamp, Bartram, while exploring in a light boat, is attacked by a whole gang of alligators, two of which, bolder than the rest, rush at him "with their heads and part of their bodies above the water, roaring terribly and belching floods of water over me." Somehow he makes it back to the land, only to discover that it is a mere spit upon which he is as much trapped as sheltered. Climbing a small promontory, he comes upon a "scene, new and surprising, which at first threw my senses into such a tumult, that it was some time before I could comprehend what was the matter." When he comes to, he is at a loss to know how to describe the scene: "How shall I express myself so as to convey an adequate idea of it to the reader, and at the same time avoid raising suspicions of my veracity?" At this point natural history moves entirely into the personal: "Should I say," he wonders, that the river was filled solid with fish fighting to pass into a lake on their way downriver and that the alligators have gathered for this annual event "in such incredible numbers . . . it would have been easy to have walked across on their heads?" It is not the naturalist who asks this, obviously, but the writer, who is less concerned with recording a reliable account than with persuading and moving his readers: "What expressions can sufficiently declare the shocking scene?"

Bartram's discussion of the alligator episode continues for about ten pages in which the naturalist material is not always as fully contained by the personal. After a time, having observed that the beasts are interested not in him but in the fish, Bartram resumes his naturalist persona and proceeds to explore this extraordinary swamp, visiting an alligator nursery full of great leathery discarded eggs. But at no point even in these calmer passages are we unaware of him, or he of us. And this is another important distinction between Bartram's *Travels* and those of his predecessors.

Reserved to the point of impersonality, Harriot's *Brief and True Report of the New Found Land of Virginia* defines its readers in the image of its author, impersonally, as a group of political and social beings. Bartram casts his readers in his own emotional, hyperreflective image – hence the possibility that the reader will be distanced and critical. Such readers are not mere perusers of documents; these are people for whom the act of reading is a primary end in itself, as the act of writing is for Bartram. They are readers for whom, in other words, the *Travels* is in the category of imaginative literature.

The *Travels* would be difficult to read without literary consciousness, given *its* literariness. The Alatamaha episode closes at sunset this way: "The glorious sovereign of day, clothed in light refulgent, rolling on his gilded chariot, hastened to revisit the western realms." The description of a passing visit to a farmer is indecipherable outside literary convention: "When I approached the house, the good man, who was reclining on a bear-skin, spread under the shade of a Live Oak, smoking his pipe, rose and saluted me: 'Welcome, stranger; I am indulging the rational dictates of nature, taking a little rest, having just come in from the chase and fishing.' " Little wonder that, looking toward the ocean from the veranda of such a man's house, Bartram exclaims, "But yet, how awfully great and sublime is the majestic scene eastward! the solemn sound of the beating surf strikes our ears; the dashing of yon liquid mountains, like mighty giants, in vain assail the skies; they are beaten back, and fall prostrate upon the shores of the trembling island." If the Romantic poets found Bartram inspiring, it was because he was himself inspired by Romanticism. Coleridge and Chateaubriand heard the poetry of the exotic New World spoken by one of their own.

Projecting the Romantic idea onto the New World led Bartram to make some odd turns. One of these we have already traced in his apologetic depiction of African slavery. Another turn involves Native Americans, who appear in the *Travels,* atypically for the period, resembling Rousseau's noble savages. Welcomed by a village of Seminoles, Bartram draws an idyllic picture:

[T]hey enjoy a superabundance of the necessaries and conveniences of life, with the security of person and property, the two great concerns of mankind. . . . They seem to be free from want or desires. No cruel enemy to dread; nothing to give them disquietude, but the gradual encroachments of the white people. Thus contented and undisturbed, they appear as blithe and free as the birds of the air, and like them as volatile and active, tuneful and vociferous. The visage, action, and deportment of the Siminoles [*sic*], form the most striking picture of happiness in this life; joy, contentment, love, and friendship, without guile or affectation, seem inherent in them, or predominant in their vital principle, for it leaves them but with the last breath of life.

This sort of passage was a cliché in eighteenth-century Europe; in America it was hardly conventional. Bartram is defensive: "I doubt not but some of my countrymen who may read these accounts of the Indians, which I have endeavoured to relate according to truth, at least as it appeared to me, will charge me with partiality or prejudice in their favour." Very well, he will examine the other side of the question and "endeavour to exhibit their vices, immoralities, and imperfections." The first vice is waging war against their own; but there "their motives spring from the same erroneous source as they do in all other nations of mankind." And what is more, "I cannot find, upon the strictest inquiry, that their bloody contests at this day are marked with deeper stains of inhumanity or savage cruelty, than what may be observed amongst the most civilized nations." He then considers such usual complaints against them as scalping, the treatment of captives generally, and sexual license; and he draws the same conclusion in regard to all these: Native Americans are no worse than others. When they seem so, it is generally at the instigation of whites who "have dazzled their senses with foreign superfluities."

The most negative account of Indians occurs at a trading post where a band of Seminoles, en route to do honorable battle with Choctaws, is seduced into breaking open the kegs of rum they are carrying for a victory celebration. Once they taste the liquor, they can no longer resist its lure, and a ten-day drunken orgy follows. It is not the Indians alone who fall into this degeneracy, however. "White and red men and women without distinction, passed the day merrily with these jovial, amorous topers, and the nights . . . as long as they could stand or move." These "ludicrous bacchanalian scenes" are hardly endemic to the Indians or their society but rather to whites, however vulnerable the Indians are to their depraved example.

One remarkable expression of Bartram's different stance toward the American natives (and of the Romantic inspiration for that stance) is his recognition that the natives have a substantial history and civilization. Such recognition is frequent in Spanish writings, as we have said, but not among English: even

Harriot, who describes the Algonkian village on Roanoke in great detail, has no sense that the society he observes has a past comparable to that of his own. Bartram, however, traveling through the region of the Savannah River, observes the extensive ruins of a vanished civilization, including what seem to be the walls of an ancient fortress, an arena, and other signs of a relatively advanced economy. At one point he sees "high pyramidal mounts with spacious and extensive avenues, leading from them out of the town, to an artificial lake or pond of water," and speculates that they were "designed in part for ornament or monuments of great magnificence, to perpetuate the power and grandeur of the nation, and not inconsiderable neither, for they exhibit scenes of power and grandeur, and must have been public edifices." This idiom of historical romance might almost assimilate the Indians to Bartram's own universe.

The description of the ruined city of the Indians occurs in a separate, last section of the *Travels,* where Bartram offers *An Account of the Persons, Manners, Customs and Government of the Muscogulges or Creeks, Cherokees, Chactaw, &c: Aborigines of the Continent of North America.* He finds that the people are "just, honest, liberal and hospitable to strangers; considerate, loving and affectionate to their wives and relations; fond of their children; industrious, frugal, temperate and persevering; charitable and forbearing." They "certainly stand in no need of European civilization." Alcohol, "this torrent of evil, which has its source in hell," is a white curse the natives are fighting to rid themselves of. Two traders who bring kegs of rum to the Nation (as the Creeks referred to themselves; Bartram grants the Indian self-nomer) are set upon by a party of Creeks. All the kegs are emptied into the road. "Do we want wisdom and virtue?" Bartram asks, "let our youth then repair to the venerable council of the Muscogulges."

Perhaps the ultimate expression of Bartram's dissent from the conventional white view comes when he projects himself into the mind of a young Indian witnessing scenes of white debauchery: he smiles, writes Bartram, "as who should say, 'O thou Great and Good Spirit! we are indeed sensible of thy benignity and favour to us red men, in denying us the understanding of white men. . . . Defend us from their manners, laws, and power.' " Putting these words in the mouth of the Seminole, Bartram not only grants speech to this representative of the other race but also alienates himself from the speech of his own.

None of this means that Bartram repudiates the conquest of America. With the wisdom and virtue of the Muscogulges relegated to the Romantic past, Bartram ends the *Travels* on a familiar note:

To conclude this subject concerning the monuments of the Americans [the ruins described above are his last topic], I deem it necessary to observe, as my opinion, that none of them that I have seen discover the least signs of the arts, sciences, or architecture of the Europeans or other inhabitants of the old world; yet evidently betray every sign or mark of the most distant antiquity.

Bartram's point is the familiar one that the indigenous populations of the New World have neither arts nor sciences, but his final assertion that the indigenous civilizations are as ancient as those of Europe adds something new. Buffon had suggested that they were much more recent; the European Romantics, including Chateaubriand, identified primitiveness with youthfulness. Bartram insists on the opposite.

Bartram's *Travels* represents a turning point in the evolution of the American concept of nature, as "nature" is an important part of the definition of "American." So considered, the pastoral romance he develops has important elements in common with Jefferson's conception in *Notes on the State of Virginia*, which also features the land itself, in its original condition before cultivation. As part of their vision of an aboriginal America, Bartram and Jefferson even agree about the first Americans, in whom the power and virtue of the continent were embodied before passing into the whites. It says a good deal for the importance of nature to definitions of national identity, however, that Jefferson, who helped establish the foundations of U.S. political thought, shared an understanding of the country's basic character with Bartram, who seems never to have noticed that there was a political discussion going on.

Bartram thus begins a long tradition of literary pastoralism in American letters. From the *Travels* it is a short step to James Fenimore Cooper's romances, where again nature seems to imply a conservative, even neofeudal, social structure and a dehistoricized history in which the continent's Native-American past is appropriated to the transcending legitimacy of an endless present. After Cooper, among those who identify "America" first of all with a mode of living on the land are Henry David Thoreau, John Muir, and Robert Frost. The naturalist Jefferson's sponsoring of the westward exploration of Meriwether Lewis and William Clark prefigures the conservationist Theodore Roosevelt's expansionism. The conquest of territory that, in modern times, has been generally associated with a progressivist ideology has additionally a paradoxically conservative pastoral cast in the American mind.

On one level, the early development of U.S. agriculture and especially industry was deplorably careless of the natural environment. The deforestation of New England by the eighteenth century and the exhaustion of the soil in the Tidewater South early in the nineteenth are outstanding examples of the first landowners' prodigal waste. But historians of U.S. thought have found a paradoxical side to this exploitative stance in its projection of exceptional resources seen as marking a nation gifted by nature. Alongside the careless attitude toward waste, therefore, and contemporary with it, could exist a conservationist vision of preserving the land in which the special character of the American people, as nature's elect, inheres. Bartram's conservationist lament contains his single allusion to the Revolution in his attack on the *British* planters' violent depredations of nature:

I have often been affected with extreme regret, at beholding the destruction and devastation which has been committed or indiscreetly exercised on those extensive fruitful Orange groves, on the banks of St. Juan, by the new planters under the British government, some hundred acres of which, at a single plantation, have been entirely destroyed, to make room for the Indigo, Cotton, Corn, Batatas [sweet potatoes], &c. or, as they say, to extirpate the musquitoes [*sic*], alleging that groves near the dwelling are haunts and shelters for those persecuting insects. Some plantations have not a single tree standing; and where any have been left, it is only a small coppice or clump, nakedly exposed and destitute; perhaps fifty or an hundred trees standing near the dwelling-house, having no lofty cool grove of expansive Live Oaks, Laurel Magnolias, and Palms to shade and protect them, exhibiting a mournful, sallow countenance; their native, perfectly formed and glossy green foliage as if violated, defaced, and torn to pieces by the bleak winds, scorched by the burning sun-beams in summer, and chilled by winter frosts.

"Nakedly exposed and destitute . . . violated, defaced, and torn to pieces . . . scorched . . . and chilled," this ravaged sentient body invites personal even more than political identification. Bartram's voyage over the land is a poetic journey, then, but of a special kind, prophetic of much that is at the heart of the U.S. literary tradition, notably the symbolism of Nathaniel Hawthorne and Herman Melville, for the *Travels* also enact a sort of physical possession. Bartram becomes materially one with an American nature whose political identity, for all that it is being forged even as he travels, is not merely historical but organic.

❧

American pastoralism in the style of Bartram and Jefferson articulates fundamental tenets of the national self-image, but Jefferson himself projects in the *Notes on the States of Virginia* another philosophy of nature that is in some important respects the opposite of pastoralism. "The chosen people of God" as well as "the most virtuous and independent citizens," Jefferson insists, are "the cultivators of the earth." However, Bartram's depiction of the devastation wrought by planting indigo, cotton, and corn or even by ridding farming settlements of insect pests suggests that, with respect to conserving nature, "labour in the earth" is an ambiguous enterprise. Buffon saw no ambiguities in it because he had no taste for nature's natural state, but Jefferson does. One odd and telling feature of the *Notes* is that despite

Jefferson's repeated commitment to an agrarian society, he never celebrates or even describes the agricultural landscape, only the wild. One reason for this omission may emerge if we look at a work that deals only with the domestic and the cultivated.

J. Hector St. John de Crèvecoeur's (1735–1813) *Letters from an American Farmer* is properly a travel narrative. It describes a foreign country to people back home, and although the first three letters, describing the idyllic condition of the American farmer, are much better known, more than half involve actual travel. In 1904, the first reissue of the *Letters* (its only American edition was in 1793, after its original publication in London in 1782) featured a preface explaining that the project had been conceived upon the editor's reading an essay in the *Sewanee Review* of February 1894 praising Crèvecoeur as a remarkable poet–naturalist. He was neither poet nor naturalist, though no doubt his rehabilitation went better for so describing him. Crèvecoeur's literary strength lies in the prosaic.

He was not a naturalist, despite some expertise in the proper conduct of a farm; he seems not to have been much interested in plant or animal nurture or in the issues of tillage. We learn from the *Letters* that the farmer takes deep pleasure in following the plow along a straight furrow, but we do not learn what he sows. In relation to farming, it is not cultivation itself he writes about but the experience of cultivating and most of all the condition of the cultivator: "My father left me," Farmer James explains, "three hundred and seventy-one acres of land, forty-seven of which are in good timothy meadow, an excellent orchard, a good house, and a substantial barn." This is America as Crèvecoeur imagines a new immigrant would observe it: "fair cities, substantial villages, extensive fields, an immense country filled with decent houses, good roads, orchards, meadows, and bridges, where an hundred years ago all was wild, woody, and uncultivated." The *Letters*, in short, are primarily political philosophy, and if their author is to be assigned a model, it would be Rousseau not Wordsworth.

The Rousseau who could be Crèvecoeur's model is not primarily a political theorist but a writer. Crèvecoeur's *Letters* are perhaps even more consciously literary than Bartram's *Travels*. His book is explicitly a work of the imagination centered on an invented protagonist. Its twelve letters purport to be the writings of a Farmer James (the advertisement for the first edition guarantees them to be "the genuine production of the American Farmer whose name they bear"). Although only the first three letters and, to a lesser degree, the last maintain the fiction of the rustic author, he is the soul of the book and bestows his personality upon it. Farmer James is a dependable, simple fellow who bears only a passing resemblance to his author. Indeed, the distance between them creates a literary problem that Crèvecoeur never resolves.

"Who would have thought," wonders the supposed American rustic addressing an imaginary correspondent, "that because I received you with hospitality and kindness, you should imagine me capable of writing with propriety and perspicuity?" This stylistic contradiction characterizes all the letters. The farmer protests his "very limited power of mind" (everywhere in the colonies there are "persons more enlightened and better educated than I am"); he describes how he received a letter inviting him to draw the picture of his rural life, and he and his wife suspect it is a hoax. How could anyone ask such a homely fellow to engage in correspondence? Yet all the while Crèvecoeur writes in polished periods, in a neoclassical prose the more remarkable for the fact that English was not his native language.

After many such self-canceling demurrals, James finally concludes his first letter with the advice of the local minister, who admits that James's writing is a rudimentary thing but urges him to write anyway for the value the reader will find in his firsthand knowledge. The patent disingenuousness of the posture underlines its double point: the rejection of European upper-class culture and the appropriation of all its strengths.

The *Letters* present themselves as both transparently plain and elegantly illuminating. The minister has counseled James to write as he speaks. However, to have him write in a local dialect would counter Crèvecoeur's argument that the farmer is equal to anyone. This includes his European correspondent, who is both the fictive and, since the book's first audience was in fact European, the real reader. Characters who speak in dialect are not the social equals of the standard-speaking author and reader. In literature, language itself provides the primary political and cultural characterization: to render his farmer as good as a prince, in a context in which an aristocratic elite still sets the cultural standard, Crèvecoeur has to make him talk like a prince or, more precisely, write so as to appear to talk like a prince. "If [your letters] be not elegant," the minister assures the farmer, "they will smell of the woods, and be a little wild." But the opening sentence of the letter, with its balanced clauses, alliterations, and elevated syntax, is hardly wild.

Any aromas wafting about the letters are most refined. James likes to have his son ride along on the beam of his plow, for the child is especially cheerful when "the odoriferous furrow exhilirates [*sic*] his spirits." The farmer himself takes intoxicating breaths of "the salubrious effluvia of the soil." He possesses no other language in which to express his delight in nature, neither the alternative conventions that were establishing themselves in his time nor the Puritan plain style nor Wordsworth's simplified diction.

The *Letters* were first published in Europe, brought out after Crèvecoeur had fled America, a persecuted Loyalist; an American edition did not appear until eleven years later. The place the *Letters* occupy today in the history of

American literature is recently acquired. In 1898 Moses Coit Tyler featured Crèvecoeur's book in his *Literary History of the American Revolution, 1763–1783* and inaugurated its latter-day career as a foundational text. Tyler meant no irony, and few readers to this day are aware that the creator of the "American farmer," the first celebrator of the yeomen who entered U.S. mythology standing by the rude bridge at Concord facing the Redcoats, opposed the Revolution, lost his farm to vengeful neighbors, and had to leave the country in fear for his life.

The last letter makes Crèvecoeur's disaffiliation inescapable. It is a document of despair entitled "Distresses of a Frontier Man." "The hour is come at last," decides an agonized James, "that I must fly from my house and abandon my farm!" But where to go? Crèvecoeur went home to France. His hero heads in the other direction and plans to seek safety among the Indians. Either way, between them, author and character make a radical departure, undoing their connection to America at America's roots. The most famous of the letters is "What Is an American?" Crèvecoeur answered the question by describing the transplantation of Europeans of many nations who breed a new race that will be indigenous twice over, once by being born on the land and the second time by planting it. An American in that letter is not a European and not an Indian: he emerges from the supplantation of both. When Crèvecoeur finds himself no longer able to be an American, he represents this loss as an undoing that returns him to Europe and/or to living in the world of the Indians.

Even earlier, in the way he defines being an American, one can see how he would have difficulty supporting what he calls "this unfortunate Revolution." The difficulty lies in the difference between his conception of an ideal relationship of the individual and the community to the land and the conception shared by Jefferson and Bartram. The difference is that Crèvecoeur's vision projects not a new world but a new society. "We are," he rejoices in the early days, "the most perfect society now existing in the world." He means a social situation defined through a relation to nature but not thereby a natural situation. It is a state *in* nature, not of it.

On one level, Crèvecoeur and Jefferson seem to envision the same perfect society, one where the yeoman farmer is the moral center. James embodies Crèvecoeur's conviction that America is to be defined as the land of farmers. A farmer is not just a person who farms; James insists proudly that he is neither "a Russian boor, [nor] an Hungarian peasant." Crèvecoeur's farmers locate themselves in society before they do so on the land. The traveler through the countryside will know that Americans are "a people of cultivators" when instead of "haughty mansion, contrasted with the clay-built hut," he beholds "a pleasing uniformity of decent competence . . . throughout our habitations." There is no one to build castle or mansion, because "lawyer or merchant are the fairest titles our towns afford." What makes this the perfect society is that "we have no princes, for whom we toil, starve and bleed." The "pleasing uniformity" of American homes reflects the "pleasing equality" of a society that makes every man a king in the castle of his own home and none a king over others. This blessed state is related to the state of nature, which ensures that social equality will not be a transitory stage by providing ever more land for equal allotments to arriving settlers. "Who can tell how far [North America] extends?" Crèvecoeur asks rhetorically. "Who can tell the millions of men whom it will feed and contain?" This amounts to an alternative definition of manifest destiny. It finds the promise of growth not for America as nation or corporate self but as the setting for an accumulation of separate individuals who inhabit America and till each one their own part of its soil.

Crèvecoeur's ideal for American society is an undifferentiated, unincorporated single grouping of persons whose individuality manifests itself without reference to others. America offers freedom from difference:

Here are no aristocratical families, no courts, no kings, no bishops, no ecclesiastical dominion, no invisible power giving to a few a very visible one; no great manufacturers employing thousands. . . . The rich and the poor are not so far removed from each other as they are in Europe.

This is possible because "we are all tillers of the earth." The land permits everyone to be equal. "We are all animated with the spirit of an industry which is unfettered and unrestrained, because each person works for himself." Although this has affinities with Jefferson's program, the divergence may be more important. Jefferson must have read with pleasure the passage where Crèvecoeur describes James as a rustic agoraphobe who never voluntarily leaves his farm because he so loves to feel his "precious soil" beneath his feet. "The instant I enter on my own land," James recalls with relief, "the bright idea of property, of exclusive right, of independence exalt my mind."

But by "independence" Crèvecoeur means something entirely different from Jefferson – not the free exercise of one's powers but freedom from the power of others. The American farmer never goes to market. The marketplace and the congressional hall are for him arenas of oppression, where some rise by lowering others. A competitive system generating inequality and its tyranny is what he fears will follow from the Revolution. The only function he admits for the state is to prevent, not to enable, competition. The law, he writes, should operate as he does in his barnyard, "a bridle and check to prevent the strong and greedy, from oppressing the timid and weak."

Crèvecoeur's democracy is an anarchist idyll that republican government

destroys because it re-creates the universal hierarchy that underlies any system of government. He complains bitterly:

The innocent class are always the victim of the few; they are in all countries and at all
times the inferior agents, on which the popular phantom is erected; they clamour,
and must toil, and bleed, and are always sure of meeting with oppression and rebuke.
It is for the sake of the great leaders on both sides, that so much blood must be spilt;
that of the people is counted as nothing. Great events are not achieved for us, though
it is *by* us that they are principally accomplished; by the arms, the sweat, the lives of
the people.

The basic organizing element in this passage is a dichotomy between two
groups of people: the innocent many and the victimizing few. This class
dichotomy crosses official political entities: the great leaders on both sides
form one group, and the people on both sides form the other. This notion of
universal class oppression is not an understanding upon which a new nation
can readily be founded.

Crèvecoeur's vision of global class conflict is cast bitterly here, but it is
already projected in the first letters in the happy description of an American
home for the simple tiller away from the predatory rich. That image, however, renders the success of American colonization contradictory, even self-
destructive. Not surprisingly, when he contemplates the possibility of living
among the Indians, Crèvecoeur finds himself questioning the very premise of
colonization. Although he believes that European civilization represents an
advance over the indigenous American culture, he nevertheless worries that
his children may find the latter way of life more appealing. This has happened
thousands of times, he reports, and not only with children. For example, two
grown men, captured in an Indian raid, never after could be persuaded to
leave the tribal village. Married to native women, "they became at last
thoroughly naturalised to this wild course of life" and refused all entreaties to
return from their white friends, who had raised a large ransom – which the
Indians refused, saying the men were free to go or stay as they wished.

Such cases were not infrequent; and others besides Crèvecoeur also pondered
their significance. Benjamin Franklin concluded predictably that they demonstrated the basic laziness of humanity, which only the strictures of white
civilization had successfully overcome. A disillusioned Crèvecoeur wonders
whether, on the contrary, white men gone native may not reflect negatively on
the so-called benefits of white civilization. Indian life, he reasons, cannot be
"so bad as we generally conceive it to be; there must be in their social bond
something singularly captivating, and far superior to any thing to be boasted
of among us; for thousands of Europeans are Indians, and we have no examples
of even one of those Aborigines having from choice become Europeans!" Here

is one more European choosing to live, though not as native, among the natives because he can no longer bear life among his own kind.

Crèvecoeur may or may not have known the tradition of narratives written by redeemed white captives; but his vision of voluntary expatriation or exculturation amounts to an anticaptivity narrative. No longer the antithesis of civilization, the Indian way of life emerges, in "Distresses of a Frontier Man," as a real though unrealistic option. Crèvecoeur's extraordinary last letter actually envisions immigration to a Native-American New World as to England or Japan, say, where he would come as an immigrant rather than as a conqueror. (Signaling his new understanding of the Indians, he dismisses the derogations of Buffon et al.: "Let us say what we will of them, of their inferior organs, of their want of bread, &c. they are as stout and well made as the Europeans.") The Revolution has emerged as the logical culmination of conquest, and conquest now contradicts the ideals Crèvecoeur originally assigned it, ideals aimed at making a new world for the common people. Earlier he had boasted that in America were no princes or aristocrats, no feudal or policing institutions, and yet Americans were uncommonly virtuous. Now, as he plans a further remove from the realms of oppression, he notes that the Indians are morally superior to the whites "without temples, without priests, without kings, and without laws."

The Indians have become the true Americans! Shortly before, in the ninth letter, another aspect of the American plantation becomes a contradiction of Americanness. This letter describes a journey to Charles-Town. The narrator explains that Charles-Town is the pride of the English colonies, the Lima of the North. "The inhabitants are the gayest in America; it is called the centre of our beau monde, and it is always filled with the richest planters of the province." We know from that moment where we are. Charles-Town is practically in Europe: "An European at his first arrival must be greatly surprised when he sees the elegance of their houses, their sumptuous furniture, as well as the magnificence of their tables can he imagine himself in a country, the establishment of which is so recent?" The reality is that this is an ambiguous sort of new country at best, one where "the three principal classes of inhabitants are, lawyers, planters, and merchants." Indeed, this country is in no way the place it seems: "While all is joy, festivity, and happiness in Charles-Town, would you imagine that scenes of misery overspread in the country?"

These scenes of misery, ignored by the fortunate of this sophisticated city, derive from slavery. The people of Charles-Town

are become deaf, their hearts are hardened; they neither see, hear, nor feel for the woes of their poor slaves, from whose painful labours all their wealth proceeds. Here the horrors of slavery, the hardship of incessant toils, are unseen; and no one thinks with compassion of the showers of sweat and of tears which from the bodies of Africans, daily drop, and moisten the ground they till.

The description is virtually contemporary with Bartram's idyllic evocation of the sons of Africa raising their voices in glad chorus as they worked in the bosom of Nature.

Two travelers from Pennsylvania, Bartram and Crèvecoeur: one a naturalist, the other an agrarian; the former entranced by the wilderness, to which human habitation is marginal, and the latter delighted by plowed fields and neat barns. For all its idealism, Bartram's pastoral romance can accommodate slavery, whereas Crèvecoeur's equally romantic agrarianism balks at it. He does renege on this in regard to slavery on northern family farms, but to slavery as a southern institution, he reacts with unmitigated horror. The episode with which the letter closes has haunted him, he claims, ever since he witnessed it.

One day, having been invited to dine with a planter outside Charles-Town, he takes his way "through a pleasant wood." Walking along, "attentively examining some peculiar plants which I had collected," he suddenly "felt the air strongly agitated." Looking up he soon discovered the source of the agitation, which was a flock of birds of prey pressing in on a cage suspended in a nearby tree. In the cage was a black man being pecked to death by the birds.

I shudder when I recollect that the birds had already picked out his eyes, his cheek bones were bare; his arms had been attacked in several places, and his body seemed covered with a multitude of wounds. From the edges of the hollow socket and from the lacerations with which he was disfigured, the blood slowly dropped, and tinged the ground beneath. No sooner were the birds flown, than swarms of insects covered the whole body of this unfortunate wretch, eager to feed on his mangled flesh and to drink his blood.

The man begs the narrator to kill him: " 'you white man, t'ank you, put some poison and give me.' " He has been in the cage two days " 'and me no die; the birds, the birds; aaah me!' " The narrator claims he would have ended the slave's ordeal had he had a gun, but without that he can only give him some water. Then he walks away. Arriving at the plantation he is told that the man is being punished for having killed his overseer. "They told me that the laws of self-preservation rendered such executions necessary."

The agony of this scene, exceedingly rare in U.S. literature in its graphic account of violence against slaves, lies in part in the fact that the narrator does nothing about it. Dining at the table of the slave's persecutor, passively listening to "the arguments generally made use of to justify the practice," he is enrolled willy-nilly in the class of the white masters. That unhappy experience confirms his idea that the world makes everyone either the oppressor or the oppressed. In the letter, as opposed to during the event described in the letter, he locates himself on the other side. The other side means being against Charles-Town, against the building in America of a more glorious Europe, since doing that has turned out to imply intolerable oppressions. Now it is the African slaves who are the true Americans.

Jefferson too deplored slavery in his writings. Like Crèvecoeur, he championed the intelligence of Native Americans if not of their civilization, and he certainly also declared the family farm the bedrock of the virtuous society. However, he did not therefore conclude that the sophistications of Virginia (of which Monticello is the epitome) should not be pursued nor that such chiefs as the eloquent Logan should be allowed to keep their lands nor even that the family farmer should rule American society. For Jefferson, independence and virtuous self-determination occur on a higher level and in larger units: official political entities transcend classes, and the social process consists in gathering the contributions of classes – some good, some bad – and distilling them into a national essence. A nation whose citizens are virtuous cultivators of the earth is thereby a virtuous nation of cultivators, and its great leaders implement this identity apparently even if they themselves are not of the virtuous class. By that logic, the owner of a large plantation and hundreds of slaves can identify himself as the representative of the yeomanry. For Crèvecoeur this is a potentially lethal fallacy.

The republican fallacy works like the pathetic fallacy to articulate a genuine relationship, in this case the relationship between small self-sufficient producers and a market society. A market society is not generally run by the majority of small businesspeople, but it depends on their presence. They generate the market that the leaders of production control. Crèvecoeur's class vision recasts this republican fallacy as betrayal and oppression. Nations as such become problematical, and Crèvecoeur rejects all nationalism: the immigrants should love America better than their homelands because America is treating them better. The only loyalty a man owes is to his family and his land.

This explains why Crèvecoeur is unmoved by the romance of the wilderness. He defines himself as "a feller of trees, a cultivator of the land, the most honourable title an American may have." Except as potential plantation, the wild woods for Crèvecoeur hardly connote nature; there is even the danger that living in wild nature may denature human beings. Against one of his primary terrors about taking refuge with the Indians, he comforts himself that "as long as we keep ourselves busy in tilling the earth, there is no fear of any of us becoming wild." The human relation to nature is inherently social;

becoming wild represents the failure of that relation, as exemplified by the licentious, idle hunters or the mongrel breed of isolated whites lurking in the neighborhoods of frontier swamps.

Jefferson and Bartram place the wild and the cultivated on a continuum, integrating them in the single category of the national nature whose converse is the natural nation. Crèvecoeur will have none of such integrations. For him America is precisely about one side in an unreconcilable opposition, the side of the cultivated against the wild (when he lives in the wilderness, he writes, he will demonstrate the virtues of cultivation), of the hardworking, poor farmer who tills his own land against the rich merchant, manufacturer, or even landowner. Crèvecoeur's America is utopia until it becomes dystopia. The proponents of the Revolution saw an independent United States bringing history to a triumphant culmination; Crèvecoeur dreamed America would be a refuge from history, a safe place for the yeomen of the world away from the world.

7

THE FINAL VOYAGE

S ENDING FARMER JAMES to the frontier to escape the terrors of the forward march of American nationalism was an unlikely move; surprisingly, Crèvecoeur seems not to have recognized that the promise of western expansion was among the major inspirations for the Revolution. Jefferson openly regarded the territories beyond the founding states as prime development sites. The last narrative we will consider, and in many ways the definitive one, emerged from a survey he commanded of the land west of the Mississippi. The expedition to the Pacific coast that was led by Meriwether Lewis and William Clark ended the era of exploration. It did so both by crossing the continent to its far coast and by demonstrating once and for all that there was no Northwest Passage through North America to the Pacific. One motive of all the previous explorations had been to fulfill the errand of Columbus by finding such a passage. It became clear that there was none just when America itself, having become the ground of an independent nation, was confirmed as a final destination in its own right. Indeed, the United States, once established as both a separate nation and as "America," was not only a final destination but a point of origin. With this development, Buffon's "ungenerous sky" and "empty land" metamorphosed conclusively into the endless horizon and vacant wilderness of manifest destiny.

The editor of the standard edition of the Lewis and Clark *Journals,* Reuben Gold Thwaites, understood this metamorphosis perfectly and dedicated his monumental work to Theodore Roosevelt:

Upon the Hundredth Anniversary of the Departure of the Trans-Mississippi Expedition of Lewis and Clark, this first publication of the Original Records of their "Winning of the West" is most respectfully dedicated.

One may wonder why documents of the national significance of the Lewis and Clark *Journals* should have waited a century for full publication. In 1814, eight years after the return of the expedition, an incomplete version did appear, much edited and glossed by Nicholas Biddle. Biddle began by cleaning up some messy details about the expedition's inception. "On the acquisition of Louisiana, in the year 1803," he explained, "the attention of the government of the United States, was early directed towards exploring and improving the new territory. Accordingly in the summer of the same year, an expedition was planned by the president." In fact, however, as Biddle knew, governmental attention had turned to the new territory well before it came under U.S. jurisdiction. When Jefferson first approached them, Lewis and Clark were to explore an area officially under Spanish rule and about to be ceded to the French. It could not be predicted at that time that the French would want to sell. The year before the Louisiana Purchase, Jefferson had been denied permission by the Spanish to "explore the course of the Missouri River," although he presented the enterprise "as a literary pursuit." Six weeks after the Spanish said no, Jefferson secretly proposed to Congress that an expedition be dispatched that would trace the Missouri to its source, a reversal of direction from the proposal he had made to the Spanish and one that now headed the exploring party west. Logically, this implied continuing all the way to the Pacific. Congress appropriated the funds, and planning was well under way when the treaty of the Louisiana Purchase was signed in May 1803, making the expedition legal.

Such an expedition offered a number of rewards. The only one officially named by Congress was the possibility of vastly increased commerce if convenient routes and agreements with the Indians could be established across a fur-rich territory now mostly exploited by Canadians. No doubt, the possibilities for territorial gain that exploration was likely to open were an equally compelling motive. Indeed, as early as 1783, three months after the signing of the Treaty of Paris, which recognized American independence and granted the United States vast new trans-Appalachian territories that projected the national borders out to the Mississippi and the Great Lakes, Jefferson proposed to George Rogers Clark, William Clark's elder brother, that he explore "the country from the Mississippi to California." Jefferson had heard that the English planned just such a trip; "they pretend it is only to promote knowledge. I am afraid they have thoughts of colonising in that quarter."

Lewis and Clark were commissioned officers in the U.S. Army reporting to the War Department, and the expedition was organized as a military detachment. Actually, in retrospect it has the air of an early national campaign, but its larger context is the history of land wars among European nations. The French and Indian Wars were as important an inspiration for Jefferson's project as the recent Revolution. The land hunger in the fledgling United States was certainly sharpened by independence and the bracing vision of self-determination; but it embodied an older appetite. Lewis and Clark bore to the Pacific coast not just the United States but Western European civilization. Their journey was remarkably smooth and well organized because it benefited from the experience of nearly four centuries of imperial expansion.

The territory covered by the Louisiana Purchase – nearly all the land between the Mississippi and the Rocky Mountains – doubled the area of the United States. In a letter to Volney, Jefferson holds out the promise of scientific advances once the Lewis and Clark route was well established. Meanwhile, "our emigration to the western country from these states the last year [1805] is estimated at about 100,000. I conjecture that about one-half the number of our increase will emigrate westwardly annually." It may be said that, as they completed Columbus's voyage, Lewis and Clark also repeated it and discovered America, this time for the United States.

On Sunday, May 13, 1804, Clark signaled the start of the expedition by making the first journal entry: "I despatched an express this morning to Captain Lewis at St. Louis, all our provisions goods and equipage on board of a boat of 22 oars." Everything was in readiness, but Clark had one worry. Was the expedition carrying a sufficient quantity of merchandise "for the multitude of Ind. thro which we must pass on our road across the continent &c. &c."? The pursuit of commerce that was the expedition's official function meant trading with the Indians. Entries like the following, two weeks into the trip, suggest its context as urgently as any description of the terrain: "as we were pushing off this morning two canoes loaded with fur &c came to from the Mahas . . . at about 10 o'clock 4 *Cajaux* or rafts loaded with furs and peltries came too, one from the Paunees . . . the others from Grand Osage."

The U.S. party variously numbered from forty-five to fifty-five. About thirty were military personnel, and the rest were support staff, including one unnamed African man who was Clark's slave and one woman, Sacagawea, a Shoshone. She was the wife of a French interpreter and served as guide, interpreter, and negotiator. Lewis and Clark took military organization seriously. Four days after the start of the trip, a court-martial was constituted to judge the case of three privates absent without leave the preceding night. All three were declared guilty of "a breach of the rules & articles of war"; one was sentenced to fifty lashes and the other two were pardoned. Such events recurred; one John Newman was convicted of "having uttered repeated expressions of a highly criminal and mutinous nature" that tended to "destroy every principle of military discipline." He was sentenced to seventy-five lashes.

Their progress was largely organized according to the disposition of Native-American tribes along the route. The expedition leaders established ongoing communications with all the large tribes of the area (Sioux, Shoshone, Mandans, and Cheyenne) and attempted a sort of census of the general population. Early in the trip, Clark listed ten nations of the prairies, all speaking different languages. At Jefferson's request, he assembled lengthy vocabularies (all later lost). Days were spent in council with the Indians – for example, with the Tetons, who had their own program to press, having to do with using the whites either to promote peace with other tribes or to gain advantage over them. The following weary entry by Clark represents the expedition's conditions far better than images of lone men in the wilderness: "I rose early after a bad night's sleep. Found the chief[s] all up, and the bank as usual lined with spectators." Usually they traveled between villages with populations of a hundred or more, and diplomatic relations figured in the expedition's program as importantly as dealing with nature. Indeed, the two activities are inseparable. The expedition could not have proceeded without the supplies it regularly obtained from the Indians. As the United States completed Europe's voyage of New World discovery, the presence of an indigenous population already occupying the land is unmistakable.

The first winter of the expedition was spent encamped among the Mandans of North Dakota. An episode during that stay illustrates the dominant stance of the explorers toward the Indians. An attack by a group of Pawnees, Ricarees, and Sioux on five Mandan hunters caused the Mandan chief to call on his white neighbors for help. Lewis and Clark had offered protection in return for hospitality, and a resulting false sense of security had betrayed the isolated hunters. The snow was now too deep to pursue the attackers, but the chief asked Clark if he would help them avenge the attack in the spring. "I told this nation," records Clark, "that we should always be willing and ready to defend them from the insults of any nation who would dare to come to do them injury during the time we would remain in the neighborhood." He was only sorry that the punishment would have to wait because of the weather. "I wished to meet those Sioux and all others who will not open their ears, but make war on our dutiful children, and let you see that the warriors of your great father will chastise the enemies of his dutiful children the Mandans, Wetersoons and Winetarees, who have open'd their ears to his advice." Then he advised caution. First, they should not jump to the conclusion that the presence of Ricarees among the attackers indicated that nation's malevolence. Perhaps the Ricarees acted out of obligation because the Sioux were their suppliers of guns. "You know yourselves," he pointed out, "that you are compelled to put up with little insults from *Christinoes and Ossinaboins* (or Stone Ind.) because if you go to war with those people, they will prevent the traders in the north from bringing you guns, powder and ball and by that means distress you very much." Then he returned to the advantages of being loyal to the United States, "when you will have certain Supplies from your great American father of all those articles you will not suffer any nation to insult you &c."

The burden of Clark's argument is clear: he meant to persuade the Mandans to depend on and defer to the whites. And Clark, who has been praised by American historians for his understanding of Native Americans, succeeds very well. After more conversation, he announces his intention to return to his fort, and the chief "thanked me very much for the fatherly protection which I shewed towards them" saying that "the village had been crying all night and day . . . but now they would wipe away their tears, and rejoice in their father's protection, and cry no more." In the language of Indian–white relations, this is the idiom of infantilization representing the pacific alternative to military rhetoric.

Despite the repeated references to dutiful children, these Native Americans were not viewed as childlike by the explorers. Being like a child has positive implications: innocence, honesty, clairvoyance. Clark's vision of infantilized Indians renders them mature but stunted. Unstable and untrustworthy, threatening treachery even as they declare dependence, primitive without the grace of simplicity, they are never innocent, even when wronged. The Native Americans whom Lewis and Clark meet lack dignity: the Mandans in Clark's tale of the Sioux attack have been humiliated by Clark and do not know it. Perhaps he does not fully know it either, intending as he does only to pacify and calm. The journal entry simply reports what he said. There may be no duplicity in a speech that is a model of opportunism, no scorn in its condescension. Clark's stance toward the Mandans is often kindly, as his frequent dispensations of medicine demonstrate. Lewis is similarly generous when he provides food for one group that appears to be starving. But kindness and generosity imply no larger recognition of common humanity; on the contrary, Lewis writes, "I really did not until now think that human nature ever presented itself in a shape so nearly allied to the brute creation. I viewed these poor starved devils with pity and compassion." The remarkable thing about the *Journals'* view of Native Americans is expressed in the absence of conflict between these two sentences, an absence that bespeaks a commensurate lack of engagement.

Fully aware of the complexities of Indian social organization and of the differences among Indian nations, the white men react matter-of-factly, without judgment, without either revulsion or identification. Of the two men, Lewis is the more speculative. The Chinooks have been very friendly, he notes at one point, and appear to be a mild people though given to petty theft. They are also "great hagglers in trade" and will bargain a whole day for a few roots if they think you want them. At first, he thinks this reflects "want of knowledge of the comparative value of articles of merchandise and the fear of being cheated," but observing that they sometimes refuse an offer only to accept a smaller one later, he concludes that they just like to bargain. Then he designs an experiment: "in order to satisfy myself on this subject I once offered a Chinook my watch two knives and a considerable quantity of beads for a small inferior sea otter's skin which I did not much want." The man turned down the offer but the next day accepted a fraction of it. "I therefore believe," Lewis reasons, "this trait in their character proceeds from an avaricious all grasping disposition." Far from generalizing, Lewis notes that Chinooks thus "differ from all Indians I ever became acquainted with, for their dispositions invariably lead them to give whatever they are possessed of no matter how useful or valuable, for a bauble which pleases their fancy."

The tone of this passage is more interesting than its content, much as in the earlier Clark passage. The objective stance of the scientist testing a hypothesis dramatizes a new detachment from the Indians that contrasts markedly with the variety of stances of earlier explorers. John Smith was abusive, Bradford horrified, Williams sympathetic and then disillusioned, Beverley and later Bartram sentimental, Byrd mocking, Crèvecoeur celebratory; even Harriot, the scientific observer, was more personally engaged than are Lewis and Clark. The issue here is not the actual judgment made of Native-American civilization or of the people themselves; it is rather the force of that judgment or its charge. The lengthy accounts of Indians in the *Journals* are curiously uncharged. Perhaps as one sign of this, native women are singularly unattractive here, even when said to be beautiful. The women of the unfortunate Chinook nation "have handsome faces low and badly made with large legs and thighs which are generally swelled from a stoppage of the circulation in the feet (which are small) by many strands of beads or curious strings which are drawn tight around the leg above the ankle." Others not so deformed are as coolly described, like the Teton women, who "are cheerful fine looking women not handsome, high cheeks dressed in skins a petticoat and robe . . . do all their laborious work and I may say perfect slaves to the men." Handsome, squat, not handsome, hardworking; the details pile up without evoking persons. The Indians in the *Journals* of Lewis and Clark are everywhere and nowhere.

The land is another matter, and is always discussed with energy and in reference to the writer. Passages describing the land constitute the *Journals'* emotional and psychic center. They are the occasion for Lewis's most personal revelations and inspire in Clark an intensity of observation expressive of deep excitement, as in this complex description of the ice on the Missouri:

[T]he water when rising forces its way thro' the cracks and air holes above the old ice, and in one night becomes a smooth surface of ice 4 to 6 inches thick, the river falls and the ice sinks in places with the water and attaches itself to the bottom, and when it again rises to its former height, frequently leaves a valley of several feet to supply with water to bring it on a level suface.

For Lewis the landscape is the face of philosophy and fate:

In the after part of the day I . . . walked out and ascended the river hills which I found sufficiently fatiguing. On arriving to the summit [of] one of the highest points in the neighborhood I thought myself well repaid for my labour; as from this point I beheld the Rocky Mountains for the first time, I could only discover a few of the most elevated points above the horizon, the most remarkable of which by my pocket compass I found bore N.65W. being a little to the N. of the N.W. extremity of the range of broken mountains seen this morning by Capt. C. These points of the Rocky Mountains were covered with snow and the sun shone on it in such manner as to give me the most plain and satisfactory view. While I viewed these mountains I felt a secret pleasure in finding myself so near the head of the heretofore conceived boundless Missouri; but when I reflected on the difficulties which this snowy barrier would most probably throw in my way to the Pacific, and the sufferings and hardships of myself and party in them, it in some measure counterbalanced the joy I had felt in the first moments in which I gazed on them; but as I have always held it a crime to anticipate evils I will believe it a good comfortable road until I am compelled to believe differently.

Like Columbus, Lewis is mistaken. The mountains are not the Rockies but a Montana chain, the Little Rocky Mountains. Like Columbus too, Lewis immediately constructs a narrative of recognition. Columbus immediately identified, named, and located San Salvador. Lewis does the same. He recognizes the Rocky Mountains and at once identifies his location as the neighborhood of the source of the Missouri, "heretofore conceived boundless" – just as the ocean was conceived to be too broad to cross westward – and now bounded by Lewis's geographical deduction. In the New World he had discovered, Columbus recognized the Old World of Asia and the primeval Garden. Lewis, looking out at the unknown expanses of the West, thinks he sees the America he already knows, which locates the Rocky Mountains at an easy four-day portage from the Missouri. But the rest of his account acknowledges a discovery. He ascends the summit, from which he gathers the objective geographical data afforded by "a plain and satisfactory view." At the same time, however, he peers within and "felt a secret pleasure" at having nearly attained a destination he had thought lay at an immense distance. Instead of finding himself dwarfed by a vast landscape, Lewis has something like the opposite experience when he stands on the rock ledge looking down at a river his vision easily encompasses. His exhilaration seems to dissolve: "but when I reflected on the difficulties which this snowy barrier would most probably throw in my way to the Pacific, . . . it in some measure counterbalanced the joy I had felt in the first moments in which I gazed on them." Then on second thought he regains his spirits: "but as I have always held it a crime to anticipate evils I will believe it a good comfortable road until I am compelled to believe differently."

It is interesting to trace the progress of this passage. It begins with Lewis crossing the landscape; at the next stage, he becomes introspective and at the same time draws the landscape toward him by seeing the head of the river unexpectedly near. At a third point, the physical force of the setting re-emerges uncontrolled and possibly uncontrollable; whereupon, at a fourth juncture, he reasserts himself, and the story ends with a heroic decision to go forth and conquer. The optimism of this ending colors the present more than the future; it is an optimism focused on the hero rather than on his situation. In retrospect each stage of the scene/story focuses on Lewis – on his view of the mountains, his feelings on seeing them, his anxiety about them, his determination not to be anxious about them. The process that began with Columbus, of personal identification with the world one is appropriating, reaches a new level of development in this passage.

Clark, on the other hand, does not share Lewis's penchant for the pathetic fallacy. His journal entry, preceding Lewis's, projects a landscape of no apparent personal meaning. "In my walk of this day I saw mounts raised on either side of the river at no great distance, those mountains appeared to be detached, and not ranges as laid down by the *Minetarrees*, I also think I saw a range of high mounts. at a great distance to the S S W. but am not certain as the horizon was not clear enough to view it with certainty." There is no story plot here, no internal drama, no progression. "The country on either side is high broken and rocky a dark brown hard rugged stone intermixed with a soft white sandstone. The hills contain coal or carbonated wood as below and some scattering pumice tone." Virtually all his accounts are equally objective.

Lewis's subjectivity and Clark's objectivity imply and complement one another. As they discover a new mountain range, Lewis sees himself climbing and Clark measures his own steps. The material rewards of exploration are now more than ever defined in terms of investment. Profit is as much a matter of the market itself as of individual sales. With Lewis and Clark, the incremental definitions of possession and expansion have been wholly subsumed into dynamic definitions. Taking possession of the land means integrating new territories into the living processes of the appropriating state.

For the explorers who represent the state, it implies a process of personal identification with the discovered lands. Lewis and Clark were an ideal team for this kind of exploration. In their collaboration, Lewis does the work of psychic and conceptual annexation, forging the conscience of the West. Clark accomplishes the other part of the task of integration by gathering something more than the discrete facts of botany and geography. He gathers the vital statistics of a new bodily limb of the United States. The West emerges from his pen an organic being.

Several times in the journey, a day's travel waited on writing up the events of the preceding day. Jefferson explicitly designated keeping journals a primary task of the expedition. His instructions to Lewis suggest that the written records themselves constitute the major find or commodity to be brought back:

Your observations are to be taken with great pains and accuracy, to be entered distinctly, and intelligibly for others as well as yourself, to comprehend all the elements necessary, with the aid of the usual tables, to fix the latitude and longitude of the places at which they were taken, and are to be rendered to the war office, for the purpose of having the calculations made concurrently by proper persons within the U.S. Several copies of these, as well as your other notes, should be made at leisure times and put into the care of the most trustworthy of your attendants, to guard by multiplying them, against the accidental losses to which they will be exposed. A further guard would be that one of these copies be written on the paper of the birch, as less liable to injury from damp than common paper.

In the *Journals* of Lewis and Clark, the literary conquest achieves its epitome as every day of the journey is covered, sometimes twice over. Besides Lewis and Clark, seven other members of the party also kept daily logs; together, the party produced some five thousand pages of precise and also reflective, speculative, meditative, and interpretive text. A principal author of the Declaration of Independence and a strong advocate of a written Constitution, Jefferson understood that writing was henceforth the seal of legitimacy. The writings that Lewis and Clark were to bring back at all costs, even at the cost of military retreat, breathe the life of contracts in the modern state of laws, not men. But they also breathe the life of modern literature, in which writing engenders not only worlds but selves.

This process is not always smooth. Lewis is immensely gratified at finding the great falls of the Missouri since they confirm the expedition's working geography; he declares them a "sublimely grand spectacle," "the grandest sight I ever beheld," and then sets out to capture them in writing. He is especially impressed by the sense of movement and transformation in the falls:

[T]he irregular and somewhat projecting rocks below receives the water in its passage down and brakes it into a perfect white foam which assumes a thousand forms in a moment sometimes flying up in jets of sparkling foam to the height of fifteen or twenty feet and are scarcely formed before large rolling bodies of the same beaten and foaming water is thrown over and conceals them.

Lewis positions himself so as to command both this movement and an encompassing quietude. "[O]pposite the center of the falls" he stands on a "butment" that separates the cascading waters from "a handsome little bottom of about three acres which is diversified and agreeably shaded with some cottonwood trees." With the waters immediately before him hurtling into the bed of the river, he surveys the land beyond, and poised against the sky between water and land, he finds himself at the center of the universal order, so that one is not surprised at the divine seal closing the description: "from the reflection of the sun on the spray or mist which arises from these falls there is a beautiful rainbow produced which adds not a little to the beauty of this majestically grand scenery."

Then Lewis's command wavers; on second thought, "after writing this imperfect description I again viewed the falls and was so much disgusted with the imperfect idea which it conveyed of the scene that I determined to draw my pen across it and begin again." Some of this is conventional. He may just be describing the scene by calling it indescribable. But he does not stop here, continuing, "I reflected that I could not perhaps succeed better than penning the first impressions of the mind." The point is not description as such but his own artistry.

I wished for the pencil of Salvator Rosa . . . or the pen of Thompson [sic], that I might be enabled to give to the enlightened world some just idea of this truly magnificent and sublimely grand object, which has from the commencement of time been concealed from the view of civilized man; but this was fruitless and vain.

Rosa was one of the best-known painters of the eighteenth century, whose canvases depict ideal landscapes of desolation; James Thomson (1700–48) was the author of the archetypal Romantic poem "The Seasons" (1726–30). With phrases like "sublimely grand," we know exactly where we are: inside the Romantic imagination.

Despair over the inadequacy of one's artistic powers is another commonplace of Romantic art. Having expressed his despair at his limited powers of representation, Lewis goes on to describe the scene in writing:

I therefore, with the assistance of my pen only endeavoured to trace some of the stronger features of this scene by the assistance of which and my recollection aided by some able pencil I hope still to give to the world some faint idea of an object which at this moment fills me with such pleasure and astonishment; and which of its kind I will venture to assert is second to but one in the known world.

Thus, the passage ends not in despair but in pride in the place. This is also a pride in oneself being of the place, a place in itself worthy of the greatest art.

Observer and landscape are inseparable on the following occasion recorded about a month later:

[T]his evening we entered the most remarkable cliffs that we have yet seen. These cliffs rise from the water's edge on either side perpendicularly to the height of (about) 1200 feet. Every object here wears a dark and gloomy aspect. The towering and projecting rocks in many places seem ready to tumble on us. The river appears to have forced its way through this immense body of solid rock for the distance of 5¾ miles and where it makes its exit below has thrown on either side vast columns of rocks mountains high.

Nothing is said here about the sublime or the magnificent, but the scene is nonetheless pervaded by a Romantic consciousness. Its dark and gloomy aspect, the rocks towering and threatening, and the river thrusting through the cleft mountain rehearse a gothic repertoire.

The passage ends well away from the realm of the gothic, however. Lewis's first reference has been to the psychic world within. "[I]t was late in the evening before I entered this place," he writes, compounding the ominous quality of the scene, "and was obliged to continue my route until sometime after dark [he emerges into the world out there] before I found a place sufficiently large to encamp my small party." The sentence concludes briskly to be followed by a similar one: "at length such a one occurred on the lar[boar]d side where we found plenty of lightwood and pitch pine. This rock is a black granite below and appears to be of a much lighter colour above and from the fragments I take it to be flint of a yellowish brown and light-cream-coloured yellow." The process of discovery, which began poetically with those dark, threatening cliffs, ends in the literal: "from the singular appearance of this place I called it the *gates of the rocky mountains*." There are no more worries here about the adequacy of language; if the earlier description seems mediated by conventional dictions, now the process of naming is direct and simple. A few days later Lewis names an island Onion Island after its major crop.

It would be a mistake to conclude that Lewis discards literary convention under pressure of reality. He retains his literary consciousness throughout. At one point on the return trip he notes that "the mountains through which the river passes nearly to the sepulchre rock, are high broken, rocky, partially covered with fir white cedar, and in many places exhibit very romantic scenes"; at another point, he observes that "the air was pleasant and a vast assemblage of little birds which crowd to the groves on the river sung most enchantingly." In diction, organization, and focus, Lewis is never far from a Romantic scene.

In Bartram's writings we saw the emergence of the American pastoral romance, rooted in the particularities of American nature but not for that any less literary. In Lewis's *Journals,* we can trace the early stages of the process that creates a distinctive American Romanticism. The Missouri falls are the occasion for a radical examination of the terms of Romanticism such as even William Wordsworth (1770–1850) does not provide. When Lewis decides that "penning the first impressions of the mind" may be the best he can do, he invokes a Romantic principle; but instead of comfort he discovers in this principle the limits of his powers. So he turns to creating a still more ambitious Romanticism. Writing alone may not be sufficient to wholly capture the imposing landscapes he crosses, but he has other relations to it that he fuses with writing.

In an earlier passage, a Romantic incarnation poses a very material danger. Near the start of the journey, the party encounters a huge brown bear. One of the expedition's hunters shoots at the bear, and the bear, too badly hurt to attack the hunter, attempts to escape. A number of the explorers follow him by his trail of blood and finally kill him with two bullets to the skull. Examining him, they discover that the hunter had shot the "monstrous beast" through the "center of the lungs, notwithstanding which he had pursued him near half a mile and had returned more than double that distance and with his talons had prepared himself a bed in the earth of about 2 feet deep and five long and was perfectly alive when we found him which could not have been less than 2 hours after he received the wound."

Lewis's bear is no poetic image; it is physically terrifying and its perils inhere in its body: "there is no other chance to conquer them by a single shot but by shooting them through the brains," Lewis observes, "and this becomes difficult in consequence of two large muscles which cover the sides of the forehead and the sharp projection of the center of the frontal bone, which is also of a pretty good thickness. The fleece and skin were as much as two men could possibly carry." But the precise physical detail has an unexpected effect. Instead of merely objectifying the bear, it intensifies the reader's sense of its formidable presence and blurs the Romantic distinction between body and spirit. Even lifeless, the bear's massive body is overwhelming. Virtually impregnable, it resists being arrogated even in death. No single individual can deal with it. It takes two men just to carry its pelt. The huge beast is irreducibly material, *and* it takes on a metaphysical resonance: "these bear being so hard to die," Lewis muses, "rather intimidates us all."

This immanent intimidation is inseparably physical and metaphysical. It is impossible to abstract Lewis's interpretation of the bear from the bear itself. By contrast, Wordsworth's emotion as he reflects upon a past vision of a field of daffodils is only indirectly linked to the flowers. The immediate presence of the daffodils is not just dispensable but even disabling. For Wordsworth, the poetic moment comes after experience. Lewis despairs of writing better later, suspecting that his best writing is instantaneous. But this is because he understands writing as capturing the thing described, not as re-creating it. This difference does not primarily reflect the roles of poet versus explorer. Rather, it is an ideological difference rooted in a disagreement about the ontological relation of the individual to nature. For Wordsworth, the human relation to nature is historically or existentially mediated. It is not only as a poet but as an Englishman surveying a long-settled landscape that Wordsworth extracts visions and memories. Lewis considers the landscape uninhabited and seeks a primary relationship to it. His collections of seeds, bones, soils, and grasses, sacks of which he is continually shipping back to Jefferson, extend his journals, which are as substantial as the samples.

Lewis's ambition is to be as one with the world he describes, rather than to relate to it through interpretation. His risk of failure is commensurate with this ambition. Beneath the conventional despair of the Missouri falls scene lies the possibility of failing not only to convey what Lewis feels about the magnificent falls but to capture the falls themselves. Wordsworth's failure would be personal and melancholy; Lewis's is potentially cosmic. When Lewis died three years after returning from his journey (Jefferson believed he committed suicide), he had not rewritten or edited any part of the *Journals* despite constant personal and political pressure to do so. The last journal entry is one line written by Clark on Friday, September 25, 1806: "a fine morning we commenced writing &c.". It was an optimistic announcement of a new beginning to mark a successful end. But, in the event, all the writing that was to be done by the explorers had ended with the journey.

❦

The West of Lewis and Clark, like the New Worlds of Harriot, Smith, Bradford, and Beverley, is a historical, rather than a literary, site. All these New Worlds are what the seventeenth century called "true reports," intended to describe reality accurately. These authors' vision of America and of its European colonization was not peculiar to them, however. The last text we will examine suggests how this vision could inform other types of writing.

The western frontier enters American fiction in Charles Brockden Brown's (1771–1810) novel *Edgar Huntly* (1799), at once a seminal and a terminal work, the first to envision a specifically American psyche and also more or less the last to represent taking possession of the continent not as a destined fulfillment but (like Harriot, Smith, and even Bradford and Beverley) as conquest.

The story takes place in 1787 at the edge of colonized America, in a territorial limbo where whites live amid lurking enemies in isolated cabins shadowed by the wilderness. The actual location is the Lehigh Valley of Pennsylvania, where the final expulsion of the original inhabitants is not entirely over and the French and Indian Wars still reverberate. *Edgar Huntly* is a wild chronicle of somnambulists wandering a nightmare landscape of horrific apparitions and bloodcurdling violence. The immediate audience for this tale was the Friendly Club, to which Brown belonged, an association of urban professionals and artists who shared twin interests in enlightened politics and dark psychology. This background and the novel's tangle of mistaken identities and character doubles have led many critics to read it psychoanalytically, as an account of terrors within. Yet the external representations of internal dramas are never incidental, and *Edgar Huntly*'s gothic horrors unravel in a recognizable landscape.

The novel is cast as a long letter from Edgar Huntly to Mary Waldegrave, whose brother, Huntly's best friend, has been found despicably murdered. Huntly has undertaken to find the killer, but at each step the investigation deepens the mystery, which soon embraces Huntly's own rather odd behavior. He walks in his sleep and on several occasions awakens in incriminating circumstances that seem to imply, if not precisely that he played a part in his friend's death, at least that he possesses a previously unsuspected capacity for violence. On one such occasion, Huntly awakens to find himself in impenetrable darkness and unable to recall anything after falling asleep in his cottage. He is "neither naked nor clothed," lying on a "stony bed" somewhere outdoors where the air is "stagnant and cold." He rises painfully and, unable to see where he is going, kicks something on the ground, which turns out to be "an Indian tom-hawk." He picks it up and inches forward to discover that he is at the bottom of a deep pit; he starts to climb out, but at the first landing, he finds himself facing a panther, which he slays with his Indian ax. He has escaped being devoured only to confront a hunger in himself that may be just as life-threatening. Feeling he must eat or die, "the first suggestion that occurred was to feed upon the carcass of this animal."

Huntly now interrupts the narrative to tell us he is filled with "loathing and horror" over his own behavior. Unable to resist the carnivorous urge, he had fallen on the panther's reeking flesh. Savagery is an omnipresent theme in accounts of the New World; going back to Columbus's accusations of the Caribs, it is frequently represented as bestial or taboo eating. Brown interprets this theme in a way that represents his fundamental stance toward what can be called the matter of colonization: he recasts external events and experiences as dramas within the white psyche. Not only is Edgar Huntly surrounded by animal-like men, but they and the need to defend himself from them rouse the beast in him. One of the major creations of the late-eighteenth-century literary imagination was a poetics of interiority. The West's first powerful representation in U.S. literature is as an objective correlative for the fragility of the civilized mind. Huntly describes eating his panther raw as "some freak of insanity."

The quintessential subject of American fiction, the West is first taken up by U.S. writers as a means to outdo their transatlantic colleagues. Brown observes in a preface to *Edgar Huntly* that the writer's main job is to evoke the reader's emotion and that "[p]uerile superstition and exploded manners;

Gothic castles and chimeras, are the materials usually employed for this end." However, "the incidents of Indian hostility, and the perils of the western wilderness, are far more suitable; and, for a native of America to overlook these, would admit of no apology."

Edgar Huntly's gothic conventions come alive in an implacable hatred of Indians that the author shares with his characters. After glutting himself on the panther, Huntly continues his groping search for an escape from the pit, which, it seems, lies inside a cave. When, after searching many blind alleys, he finds a path to the outside, he faces the direst peril yet in a group of four Indians camped at the entrance of the cave. "Most men are haunted by some species of terror or antipathy," remarks Huntly, and *his* species is Indians. As a child, he had lost his parents and an infant sibling to "these assassins," and ever since, he "never looked upon, or called up the image of a savage without shuddering." Now he finds himself confronting his nightmare. When it turns out that, besides the four Indians, the cave holds a kidnapped white girl, the die is cast. Huntly kills three of the Indians; the lone survivor drags off the "piteously shrieking" girl by the hair and levels his gun to her breast; the hero dispatches him and rescues the fair victim. "Think not," Huntly cautions his correspondent, "that I relate these things with exultation or tranquility." He has told "a bloody and disastrous tale," but "when thou reflectest on the mildness of my habits, my antipathy to scenes of violence and bloodshed, my unacquaintance with the use of fire-arms, and the motives of a soldier, thou wilt scarcely allow credit to my story."

A terrible incoherence has been born of this horror. "That one rushing into these dangers, unfurnished with stratagems or weapons, disheartened and enfeebled by hardships and pain, should subdue four antagonists, trained from their infancy to the artifices and exertions of Indian warfare, will seem the vision of fancy, rather than the lesson of truth." In conjunction with the prefatory statement that Indian hostilities are more suitable to fiction than gothic chimeras, Brown's implied warning here not to disbelieve Huntly's horrific account makes a new claim inspired by a new concern. The fictions of *Edgar Huntly* are lessons of truth; American writing, because of the peculiar conditions of its authors, has a more powerful hold on reality (and so on readers) than European. The fear is that this closer relation to reality exposes the author to exceptional dangers, *real* dangers, such as those that threaten Edgar Huntly when he awakens from sleepwalking, his worst fantasies realized, in a real wilderness where against all the qualities that define him as a man of letters and not of deeds, and certainly not of violent deeds, he is transformed into the image of the hostile Indians.

Lewis, observing starving Indians at their disgusting meal, feels pity and compassion, cathartic emotions that depend on and confirm distance. Huntly turns into a savage himself to feed upon the panther. However, this constitutes not so much an opposition as a difference of degree. Lewis and Brown share a vision of the Indians, but whereas Lewis does not consider that they have anything to do with him personally, Brown cannot readily separate himself. For Lewis, civilization is a defining trait of white men; for Brown, the line between barbarism and civilization runs hotly disputed through each individual. That all Indians are savages renders each individual Indian "of consequence, an enemy," to each individual white. Huntly insists several times that killing Indians does not come naturally to him, because he is civilized, but just because he is civilized, he is sworn to exterminate the brutes, to drive them from his surroundings and ultimately from the continent. To affirm and safeguard white civilization against the savages, Brown and his hero Huntly will go all the way to savagery. Savagery provides the occasion to transcend their European heritage but also to fall catastrophically, at once from civilized living and from literature. To be capable of writing literature, Brown and Huntly must retain a self-consciousness lacking in savages.

The entanglements of literature and history and of the personal and the racial in Brown's Indian-hating are particularly complicated in the part of the plot relating to Old Deb, an old Delaware woman living alone in "the fastnesses of Norwalk." Old Deb's tribe once inhabited a village on ground now owned by Huntly's family. When repeated harassments by the English drove the original inhabitants from the village, the old woman refused to leave. She burnt the wigwams and built herself a small cabin deep in the woods, where she has lived ever since, companioned only by three dogs "of the Indian or wolf species." She has developed a fierce symbiosis with these wild beasts and is in continual conversation with them. At the same time, "she always disdained to speak English," and her long isolation having rendered her unintelligible in her own language, she has become almost totally incapable of communication. Only Huntly has learned a little of her "jargon."

As a result, Old Deb is favorably disposed to Huntly. And he is in turn oddly interested in her:

[H]er pretensions to royalty, her shrivelled and diminutive form, a constitution that seemed to defy the ravages of time and the influence of the elements; her age, which some did not scruple to affirm exceeded an hundred years, her romantic solitude and mountainous haunts suggested to my fancy the appellation of *Queen Mab*.

The association of Old Deb with the Queen Mab of English folklore, the troublesome fairy fomenter of weird dreams, invests the Indian crone with a relevance to the story that her grunting male compatriots lack. Her incessant speech, a mad disordered torrent of wild words addressed to beasts, whom it confirms in their wildness, goes exactly against the nature of language. Her control over her three wolves and their loyalty to her subversively parody the rituals of domestication. She recalls Satan's parody of divine order. All this makes Old Deb/Queen Mab a creature of romance and of Romanticism, conceivably a heroine, if a perverse one.

Midway through the paragraph in which this possibility suggests itself, however, Brown pulls back. Perhaps, Huntly reflects, he has gone too far in seeing "some rude analogy between this personage and her whom the poets of old-time have delighted to celebrate: thou perhaps wilt discover nothing but incongruities between them." The narrator does not insist: "be that as it may, Old Deb and Queen Mab soon came into indiscriminate and general use." At first infused with the life of fantasy, the name has collapsed into a nickname. In the next paragraph the story of Old Deb is no longer romance but history. We learn that the woman's cabin has been a staging area for raiding parties like the one Huntly discovered in the cave. Refusing to accept the exile of her kind from its ancient seat, Old Deb has been conducting a guerrilla war. In that posture she is no longer a subject for Huntly's literary fantasy but the real-life confirmation of his political nightmare.

The entangled literary and historical strands were already individually twisted. As an Indian, Old Deb is a scourge to be driven out (her resistance proves the case against her), but once banished, she returns to haunt the conquerors. Huntly's psyche is a battlefield where savagery and civilization clash by night; but by day, Huntly, the citizen of Norwalk, expects to inherit a farm his uncle built on Old Deb's land. It is this explicit conjunction between the phantasmal and the real – explicit to the point that their incommensurateness is one of the novel's major themes – that distinguishes *Edgar Huntly* and makes it unique even as it sets the terms of an emerging tradition. Repeating to the point of tedium that his story defies belief, Brown at the same time ties it directly into local history. His characters are mad, but it is history that has made them so.

Edgar Huntly is thus a transitional work, doing for fiction what Bartram's *Travels* does for poetry. Brown's novel announces a new stage in the process of conceiving America. At this stage, actualities of land and history, hitherto so objectively overwhelming they compelled the service of literary discourse, now serve literature in their turn. This stage in itself constitutes a historical event. It marks the conclusive success of the European conquest of America in Europe's imaginative internalization of the New World. The most dramatic actualities of the conquest – the Native-American genocide and the appropriation of the land – emerge as the foremost images of this first literary generation. Precariously perched on the cusp of this transitional moment, Brown slides back and forth between direst invective against the Indians, who deserve mass annihilation (in the incidents we have been reading,

Huntly kills almost every Indian he meets), and internalizing them after their extinction as denizens of the white psyche.

Old Deb/Queen Mab is both real threat and subconscious specter. This duality never achieves synthesis, and at the end of the story, her fate is undecided. The Indian crone remains divided, as it were, between history and literature. When seized "on suspicion of having aided and counselled her countrymen, in their late depredations," she acts, not as they would have, but as Queen Mab. "She readily confessed and gloried in the mischief she had done. . . . and boldly defied her oppressors." However, her heroism is without substance; Brown cannot bring himself to grant her madness the sort of meaning Shakespeare invests in Lear's madness, although her characterization would readily permit it. He reduces her to a racial type, though one senses that it goes against his writerly instinct. Old Deb stands her ground, he explains, only out of "her usual obstinacy and infatuation." Brown declares her infatuated and withdraws from imagining her.

The first Native-American woman in English writing is John Smith's Pocahontas. Of noble lineage like Pocahontas, Old Deb is otherwise the antithesis of her ancestress. An ancient crone instead of a young virgin, Old Deb is also the quarry rather than the rescuer. Pocahontas loved the white man; Old Deb hates him. Pocahontas and Old Deb are Indian versions of the good woman and the bad, and an Indian good woman – young and beautiful, loving, nurturing, peacemaking, and submissive – is inconceivable in *Edgar Huntly.* However, she or her male equivalent is central to the fiction of James Fenimore Cooper (1789–1851). Cooper was writing on the other side of the definitive moment of continental conquest signaled by Lewis and Clark, and he appropriates the Native Americans along with the land. Where earlier – for Bradford, Beverley (whose "I am an Indian" nonetheless foreshadows Cooper's appropriation), Bartram, Brown, and, even to a degree, Jefferson – the Indians were contenders for possession of America, they become in Cooper's novels more or less inconvenient aspects of the geography. The good Indians facilitate white progress; the bad impede it. They are neither inanimate nor inhuman. Their fate is sad, in some instances tragic, and Cooper extends a measure of respect and sympathy even to certain "bad" Indians, like the recalcitrant and bloody Hurons in *The Last of the Mohicans* (1826) and Sioux in *The Prairie* (1827). As the title of *The Last of the Mohicans,* his best-known work, suggests, Native Americans had by then passed into the history of an accomplished colonization.

❦

Not entirely: the white imagination remains periodically terrified by visions of vengeful returns. Injun Joe, in Mark Twain's *The Adventures of Tom Sawyer*

(1876), is a creature of caves and nightmares who traces his lineage to Brown rather than to Cooper; Navajo and Apache art decorates a scene of once and future horror in Stanley Kubrick's 1980 film *The Shining,* in which the evil haunting a resort hotel is rooted in the desecrated burial ground on which the hotel is built. Still, after the Lewis and Clark *Journals,* the subject of Native Americans in writings about the continent becomes less and less charged. Detachment, as we have seen, is already evident in the *Journals,* where, at least for Lewis, the resonant topic is the land itself. After the colonial period, the U.S. imagination became overwhelmingly focused on the land, and the land became less and less historically defined.

Universal verities were to define the new nation, not history's contingencies; not human comings and goings but enduring Nature. Perhaps the notorious American disregard of history, emerging in the nineteenth century, enacts in part a suppression of historical memory. Ironically, the Indians, who, according to the arriving Europeans, were disqualified from possessing America by their lack of historical capability, became the repository of history, which the present and future Americans then transcended.

The United States shed its colonial status after it had successfully colonized America, a paradox resolved by casting the new nation as an empire to end all empires. This empire was so globally self-determining that it was beyond imperialism. As Lewis and Clark travel west, the United States unfolds under their feet both newly embodied and newly abstract. U.S. identity, in the *Journals,* is increasingly expressed through the physical continent; and the physical continent is abstracted from its past. This permits Americans to overlook the contradiction that the roots of the national imagination are planted in the soil of empire. The United States was not alone in facing this contradiction, which characterizes early modern nation building. Spain, Portugal, France, and England all established their own sovereignty in part by nullifying that of others. This country's nationhood was, however, entirely the product of empire building, rendering the contradiction between the claim of timeless natural legitimacy and the history of conquest peculiarly acute. National literatures generally work to commute discord into culture. U.S. literature has seemed from the start to display more tension than European literature in mediating between centrifugal creative impulses and the conservative needs of cultural continuity. Perhaps this comparatively greater tension reflects the difficulty of resolving so extreme a founding discord.

As England began to reshape the world, Spenser, poet and empire builder, worried that "Mutabilitie" might overturn universal order itself. Change was everywhere ascendant, and although Mutabilitie was born of Satan's seed, she had "a lovely face, / In which, faire beames of beauty did appeare." Though she blasphemously challenged him, Jove could not bring himself to smite her. In the trial to decide the condition of the world, whether it would remain wholly mutable or still under the aegis of eternity, Nature was the judge and decided in terms that effectively transformed historical process into artistic evolution:

> [While] all things steadfastnes doe hate
> And changed be: yet being rightly wayd
> They are not changed from their first estate;
> But by their change their being doe dilate:
> And turning to themselves at length againe
> Doe worke their owne perfection so by fate.

It was perhaps to be expected that this argument would be particularly persuasive to those who lived at the limits of the empire and defined themselves by extending it. Destiny has always figured large in accounts of U.S. history even though Americans are considered to be exceptionally free of prior commitments, indeed committed to change itself. And although U.S. writers repeatedly create characters who defy all restrictions on freedom of self-definition, the fates of these characters generally bear out Nature's caution that although all things change, change is itself ruled by conditions that transcend it. The United States, in the national imagination, seems oddly formal, a matter of forms to be preserved for their inherent "being," which history does not finally alter but "dilate." At the end of Spenser's debate, Jove transcends mutability. Unlike gods and monarchs, however, presidents and citizens are defined by the mutabilities of republican representation and social mobility. It is therefore the more remarkable that Spenser's transcendent Nature should have found a close descendant in Emerson's.

The implications of imperial origins for the national literary culture have yet to be fully explicated. This may be the distinctive task of the current scholarship of letters, enjoined to pay close attention to the relations of language and power. From Harriot at the close of the sixteenth century to Lewis and Clark at the dawn of the nineteenth, the authors of the New World produced a literature of colonization by taking the imperatives of territorial expansion and political domination to be universal structures of meaning. These structures were seen to be as basic to literature as to history and to enter as fully into narrative form as into the institutions of colonization. Indeed, we have seen that literature was itself a colonizing institution. "America" was the culmination of the Christian empire; it is fitting that the making of America followed the final Gospel by beginning with words.

NEW ENGLAND PURITAN LITERATURE

Emory Elliott

I

❧

THE LANGUAGE OF SALEM
WITCHCRAFT

FEW EVENTS have captured the imaginations of Americans as powerfully as the Salem Village witchcraft trials of 1692. Assessments of the
entire Puritan period have achieved their sharpest focus through an
analysis of the Salem trials, which have served as a litmus test for theories
about the nature of life in early America. Some social historians find the
reasons for the trauma in economic causes, with the jealous resentment of the
disadvantaged leading them to strike out against their circumstances as well
as against particular social enemies. One localized version of this argument
focuses upon the feuding factions of Salem Village, whose long-term battle
seems to have predetermined the would-be accused and accusers. Cultural
anthropologists and psychohistorians have read the Salem records as discursive expressions of anxieties brought on by the rapid succession of political
and economic events in the 1680s, which were exacerbated by a series of
crises, including fires, floods, disease, and Indian attacks. Other accounts
emphasize the role of the common people, who discovered demonism to be a
weapon with which to threaten the established powers. Because a high
percentage of those tried and punished were women, a number of whom
owned property under challenge, some interpretations present evidence of
the efforts of jeopardized male authorities to repress rising female independence and economic autonomy. In different ways, most interpreters share the
assumption that the Salem incident marks a critical turning point in New
England history when old religious values were in question and new secular
ones were being formed. Accordingly, the witchcraft delusion is most often
perceived as the site of a profound cultural transformation.

Although all of these arguments enliven our conversations about New
England history, each is but another attempt to re-create in our imaginations
the realities of that former time through words. Indeed, then as now, we
must turn to words and expression if we are to grasp the connections between
shadowy motivations and their often shocking and brutal public results. In
Salem Village, language and imagination were the central components in the

catastrophic events that marked the last days of an aspiring Christian utopia. Words projected a network of evil conspiracy in which anyone might be a scheming villain. The accused were suddenly transfigured in the minds of their neighbors into demons, monsters, enemies, aliens – exotic others from a dark world. Having survived, and even prospered, during decades of natural disaster, political persecution, and bloody war, the residents of Salem discovered their most terrifying menace within their borders. In a tragic summer that left twenty dead and scores imprisoned, the citizens acted out a bloody judicial process that would become paradigmatic of all subsequent forms of "witch-hunting."

No case better illustrates the crucial role of language in the formative events of Salem than that of Rebecca Nurse. During Nurse's trial, the jury at first found her innocent of witchcraft but then reversed its decision when the magistrates refused to accept the verdict. The judges declared that the jury had failed to consider a "self-incriminating" statement Nurse had made on the witness stand. In itself, the statement was actually very ambiguous: Nurse had merely questioned why two confessed witches, Abigail Hobbs and her daughter Deliverance, were allowed to testify against her when they were, in her words, people who "used to come to her." For no apparent reason, the magistrates chose to interpret her words as an admission that she saw these women regularly at witch gatherings. The jury heard differently, at least initially. The court clerk, Thomas Fitch, recorded that "after the honored court had manifest their dissatisfaction of the Verdict, several of the jury declared themselves desirous to go out again, and thereupon the honored court gave leave." When the jury appeared to not comprehend the "proper" meaning of Nurse's words, the magistrates provided them with an official interpretation. As Fitch reports, "these words were to me a principal Evidence against her."

Upon learning later about the confusion over her phrasing, Nurse petitioned the court to take into consideration what she really meant in her statement – that because Goodwife Hobbs and her daughter were imprisoned with her in the Salem jail, they were allowed to come into her company there and question her, thereby gathering incriminating material for testimony against her in court. She was incredulous that the statements of these unreliable prisoners were used as the critical evidence in her conviction. When she was questioned about this matter in court, she had been totally unaware that her words were being misinterpreted, for, as she explained, "being hard for hearing, and full of grief, none informing me how the court took up my words, and therefore, [I] had not the opportunity to declare what I intended when I said they were of our company." In spite of this plea and a petition signed by over forty citizens on her behalf, she was hanged on July 19, 1692. Words, and interpretations of them, could be fatal.

The only facts that can ever be known about the disturbing events at Salem are the words left to describe them – the verbal codes, now three centuries old, that were charged with associations and meanings that modern vocabularies have attempted to recast and make discernible for contemporary readers. The various analyses of the texts produced by those events have raised questions about a range of issues that the language of the Salem trials verbalized: questions about social and political authority, gender roles, religious order, theology, economics, and literary matters themselves – narrative structure, imagery, typology, and class-coded dialogues. Yet many questions remain: for example, before that fateful year, charges of witchcraft were nearly always treated by the clergy and the magistrates with great skepticism and dealt with in protracted proceedings that served to quell emotions and remove matters to distant courts, where they usually ended months later without resolution. In contrast, the Salem documents indicate that although many of the clergy were initially wary, especially on point of evidence, the magistrates appear to have joined forces with the accusers and confessed witches and inexplicably to have become themselves caught up in the frenzy of the hunt.

During those tumultuous months, some of the condemned citizens presented reasonable pleas to the officials imploring them to reexamine the process and the rules of evidence. In July, as he awaited execution, John Proctor desperately wrote to five Boston clergymen that "the magistrates, ministers, juries, and all the people in general, are so much enraged and incensed against us by the Delusion of the Devil, which we can term no other, by reason we know in our Consciences, we are all innocent persons." After describing in precise and deliberate terms how the accusations of confessed witches and suspicious persons had been accepted as fact and how young people, including his son, were tortured until they confessed to witchcraft, Proctor begged the Boston clergy to have "these magistrates changed and others put in their place who must conduct fair trials."

In September, knowing she was to die, Mary Easty tried to save others when she wrote:

I petition your honors not for my own life, for I know I must die and my appointed time is set, but the Lord he knows it is that if it be possible no more innocent blood may be shed which undoubtedly cannot be avoided in the way and course you go in. . . . I know that you are in the wrong way . . . and if your honors would be pleased to examine these afflicted persons strictly and keep them apart some time . . . I am confident that several of them [would have] belied themselves and others [who are lying] will appear.

Why were these reasonable requests ignored?

There are other mysteries. The texts of the accusations and the responses of the accused are quite varied and full of amplification between February and May, but the complaints during the summer months became increasingly more formulaic and the trials more theatrical, as though played out by set scripts. In these enactments, the roles of the magistrates and the bewitched accusers seem to become intertwined in a sustained effort to torment and harass the accused into confessions. Quite often the judges seem to employ verbal manipulation to obtain guilty verdicts. Indeed, what emerges from a chronological reading of the *Salem Witchcraft Papers* is an increasing similarity over several months in the tone and diction of the magistrates, the accusers, and the confessing witches, and a sharpening contrast between the tense, emotional, and strident language of those who confessed and the more objective, reasonable, and surprised tone of those who refused. The more sensible an accused person sounded, the greater the possibility that he or she would be executed, as concessions quickly became the only route to survival.

With these matters in mind, it is possible to approach the question of the vigorous engagement of the magistrates from a new historical perspective. Throughout the seventeenth century, the ministers claimed special rights and power in interpreting the language of the supernatural. In the scriptures, in nature, and even in daily events and in ordinary words, the learned clergy discerned hidden and arcane meanings of divine purpose. Through typological interpretations of the Bible, events, and various narratives, the clergy had formulated a Puritan linguistic system that gave meaning and purpose to the unknown. Law and government bestowed secular powers upon the magistrates, but the secular leaders deferred to the clergy in supernatural matters and in all things in which God's will could be discovered.

By the 1690s, however, the realities of New England life could no longer be made to conform to the symbolic projections of the ministers. Perhaps for this reason and for all of the political and economic reasons so often cited, the people and magistrates of Salem and surrounding villages were short on patience with clerical deliberations. Suddenly, the residents of the village embraced the language of witchcraft – a verbal legacy long available through the cultural heritage of Europe, where witchcraft episodes had been rampant for three centuries. In this parallel world of witchcraft, the people of Salem discovered an alternative linguistic system, and although the substance of what was being said may not have made any rational sense, the very fact that it confounded those in authority made it a source of political power. Through this form of discourse, those who embraced the language of witchcraft possessed a means of challenging the authorities in a society where such defiance had not been permitted in the churches or in the courts since the 1630s when the positions of Anne Hutchinson and Roger Williams were suppressed.

When confronted with the verbal outburst of 1692, the clergy found that their stock responses and practiced evasions would not serve, and without the support of the clergy in this supernatural matter, the magistrates were bewildered. Seeking higher secular authority for support, the magistrates turned to the newly appointed governor, William Phips, who in May authorized the Court of Oyer and Terminer (meaning literally "to hear and determine") to begin trials and later embarked on an extended trip, not to act on the matter again until October. Once testimony was being taken, the magistrates were exposed to the tremendous energy and psychic power of the accusers without the buffering devices of the clergy, who seemed temporarily stunned. As the judges were repeatedly forced to engage the accusations and denials, they themselves became locked into a discursive battle in which there was no neutral ground. Presented with no apparent alternatives, the magistrates followed the course of least resistance and appropriated to themselves the powerful vocabulary of witchcraft, thereby permanently eclipsing the clergy's privileged linguistic role in New England. So potent was the discourse of witchcraft that even a minister like the Reverend George Burroughs of Maine, who had been the minister of Salem Village from 1680 to 1682, was not safe from its destructive force; he was hanged in August 1692. Thus, the accusers and the confessed witches engaged their leaders in a new form of public drama – a primal dialogue through which the actors and audiences could speak to one another – a form of discursive exchange through which the powerless might engage, threaten, and even destroy their rulers. And before it was all over, so they did.

As events progressed under these conditions, the only way for the magistrates to maintain their authority and control the proceedings was to become unrelenting witch-hunters. Although it can never be known whether some interrogations were consciously designed to save or destroy lives, it is interesting that the pattern the magistrates followed in taking extreme measures to force the accused to confess might well have been the only method for saving the life of an accused. The defendants who tried to counter their prosecutors' charges with logic and reason and who treated the bewitched as sick or deranged were nearly all found guilty; ironically, those who defended themselves within the terms of the discourse of witchcraft survived. The psychological process that the magistrates employed for exacting confessions closely approximated the well-established linguistic formula for proving the presence of grace in religious conversions. Just as a minister might prepare the hearts of those yet to be saved and lead them in stages toward the moment of inner light, so in this inverse world of witchcraft, the magistrates might save an innocent life by coaxing a person to confess to imagined crimes.

Some of the petitions for the freedom of those still in prison in December and January, long after the panic had ended, indicate the increasing realization that confession was the only possible means for an accused to escape execution. The plea for the release of Mary Osgood and others who had confessed is quite direct on the point:

By the unwearied solicitations of those that privately discoursed with them both at home and at Salem, they were at length persuaded publicly to own what they were charged with, and so submit to that guilt which we still hope and believe they are clear of. And, it is a probability, the fear of what the event might be, that confessing was the only way to obtain favor, might be too powerful a temptation for a timorous woman to withstand, in the hurry and distraction that we have heard.

The tactful and considered term "unwearied solicitations" used here rather than some more derogatory expression may suggest awareness that such solicitations saved Osgood's life.

Along with these observations regarding the verbal tactics of the magistrates, an examination of the dynamics of the dialogues in two famous cases reveals important dimensions of the pattern. When Susannah Martin entered the courtroom on May 2, it was still early enough in the trials that she felt free to laugh when the afflicted girls cried out and fell down at her appearance. To her mind, good sense and shared adult understanding of the silliness of children would prevail over such nonsense. She quickly learns, however, that the magistrate, who is not identified but is most likely John Hathorne, is not a neutral participant; he is her prosecutor:

"Why do you laugh?"

"Well, I may at such folly."

"Is this folly? The hurt of these persons?"

Assuming that her reputation as a civil member of the community will be a valid defense, Martin answers:

"I never hurt a man, woman, or child."

At this point the drama heightens as Mercy Lewis cries out against her, and the clerk reports:

"And she laughed again."

Perhaps impatient and eager to end the proceedings quickly, Martin addresses the court with what is for her a statement of fact:

"I have no hand in witchcraft."

But to accumulate evidence against her, the magistrate ignores this declaration and pursues the issue of the children's suffering:

"What ails them?"

"I do not know."

Now that he has Martin engaged in a dialogue about what are assumed to be the results of witchcraft — assumptions that are already entertained by the audience — the magistrate springs a verbal trap. Martin is now enough on guard to try to evade it:

"What *do you think* [ails them]?" (italics in original)

Knowing that whatever answer she gives to this query will be turned against her, Martin begins to show an awareness of the danger of her situation:

"I do not desire to spend my judgement upon it."

But he persists:

"Do you think they are *bewitched?*" (italics in original)

Martin has reached a pivotal moment here because were she to say that they were bewitched and then accuse others of bewitching them and herself or were she to confess her own guilt and participation, she might still save herself, leave the anxious bench, and join the chorus in the gallery. But she disdains to engage in the language of witchcraft and bravely, but fatally, persists in declaring her innocence:

"No, I do not think they are."

Now the magistrate knows that he has enough of a verbal commitment from her to turn her words upon her:

"What *do* you think about them?" (italics in original)

At this point, Martin appears to realize her mistake, but it is too late, for she has engaged in the fatal discourse of witchcraft even by denying its effects. In one of the most interesting acknowledgements of the power of words in the records, she says:

"My thoughts are my own, when they are in, but when they are out, they are another's. I desire to lead myself according to the word of God."

In other words, the only safety is in silence. Without her own words to use against her, the magistrates would have had to concede that her case was based only on spectral evidence. Although she was naive in her initial presumption that her innocence could save her, Martin is not ignorant of the principles of Puritan theology as they apply to witchcraft cases, for she attacks the use of spectral evidence by reminding the court of past arguments against it: that when dealing with the world of the supernatural, no living person can be certain of the meaning of particular signs or appearances. She tells the magistrate:

"He that appeared in someone's shape or in a glorified shape can appear in anyone's shape."

Her argument here contends that even if the court grants the honesty of the children's report and even if it is believed they saw a vision of her that seemed to injure them, there is still no valid proof that she was involved personally and is a witch, for Satan may use the image of a goodly person as well as an evil one to do harm, and, in fact, that wily deceiver may be more likely to do so.

At this point in the proceedings, the magistrate is not about to dispute theology with a witch. Perhaps hoping to catch her off guard, he directly accuses her of dishonesty. Calmly and firmly, she responds:

"I dare not tell a lie if it would save my life."

Perhaps she understood that this is exactly what a lie would do. The magistrate's parting statement is significant both for what he says and for what he does not. His words are "Pray God discover you, if you be guilty"; however, the meaning of this coded language may be restated thus: "I hope that if you are guilty, as I think you are, God will cause you to confess your guilt, for that is the only chance you have to save your life." This seems to be the meaning that Martin takes, for she answers:

"Amen, Amen. A false tongue will never make a guilty person."

By this, she seems to mean what other condemned prisoners might have articulated to friends and loved ones from the Salem prison: "Even if I confess to being guilty, I will know that I am innocent, and the lie that will save my earthly life will condemn me to eternal damnation. Better to die and be saved than to live now and perish eternally in hell." Susannah Martin was executed two months later on July 19.

In the early weeks of the trials many of the accused were completely startled that the judges could take the absurd accusations of disturbed people seriously. The curt, straightforward replies of the accused contrast sharply with the ranting of their accusers and the verbal machinations of the magistrates. Examined on March 21, Martha Corey was one of the first to undergo interrogation. Questioned by both John Hathorne and Nicholas Noyes, Corey tried to persuade her jurors of her innocence with calm and sensible answers to the charges. Again Hathorne begins with an assumption of her guilt:

"You are now in the hands of Authority. Tell me why you hurt these persons."

"I do not."

"Who doth?"

"Pray give me leave to go to prayer. [This request was made several times.] I am an innocent person: I never had to do with witchcraft since the day I was born. I am a gospel woman."

Corey then makes a temporary verbal escape from the apparent lie against her by saying that she did not *know* how the children were injured but only *thought* or *speculated* about the matter, but a child exlaims that "there is a man whispering in her ear." Hathorne takes this assertion as truth and asks Corey:

"What did he say to you?"

Corey attempts to establish some kind of bond with Hathorne by assuming that the two of them recognize that children can be mischievous. She says:

"We must not believe all that these distracted children say."

Perhaps Hathorne does have sympathy for her at this moment, for he gives her perhaps the best advice he can under the circumstances.

"If you expect mercy of God, you must look for it in God's way by Confession."

But like Susannah Martin, she spurns the language of witchcraft by replying logically:

"Can an innocent person be guilty?"

As the rigorous questioning continues and as other members of the court join in the proceedings, the clerk records: "It was noted that she bit her lip several times and at the same time several of the afflicted bit their lips." It was also observed that when her hands were unbound, all of the afflicted girls were pinched by unseen hands, but when Corey was tied again, they were at rest. Noyes asks her: "Do you not see these women and children are rational and sober as their neighbors when your hands are fastened?" With this Corey grows weary and begins to give up the fight:

"When all are against me, what can I help it? If you will all go and hang me, how can I help it? You are all against me, and I cannot help it."

At this point, Magistrate Noyes takes up the questioning and asks her if she was in covenant with the Devil for ten years. When she laughs at this suggestion, the children cry out that they see a yellow bird with her. When Hathorne asks her about the bird, she again laughs. To provide conclusive evidence of her guilt, Noyes asks her a series of catechism questions, which she readily answers until he gets to the mystery of the Trinity:

"How many gods are there?"

"One."

"How many persons are there?"

"Three."

"Cannot you say so there is one God in three blessed persons?"

The clerk notes at this point: "She then was troubled." The sacred language of Christian theology has become a weapon in this battle of deadly words. From late spring until fall, efforts continued to persuade Martha and her husband, Giles, to confess to several crimes, but they refused to avail themselves of the language of the authorities and their accusers. Giles was pressed to death during questioning on September 19 and Martha was hung on September 22 along with six other women and one man.

During the summer of 1692, it became evident that confession – the acknowledgment of the power of the court and of the bewitched – was a defendant's only means of survival. Indeed, once it became evident that mimicry of confessed witches was the key to earthly salvation, the task for the accused was to create engaging and convincing confessional narratives. Since there seems to have been relatively little actual occult activity in New England before 1692, there were few sources for provocative details to embellish the testimony and confessions. For this reason, the testimony of Tituba, a slave woman from the Caribbean, early in March proved a fount of occult images from the African and Caribbean traditions. Her reward for her titillating testimony was not only her life but the contribution of her narrative details to many of the trials. During the summer, the confessions became more elaborate and were sprinkled with the same repeated occult phantasms: the yellow bird, the black man with the black book, pins and puppets, witch meetings in the forest, and spectral appearances of all of the previously accused witches, with a few new names usually added. The language of witchcraft also took on distinctly racial dimensions as the Devil was often identified as black and many activities of the witches occurred in the forest, where the witches interacted with Indians. Cotton Mather believed that the rise in witchcraft had "some of its Original among the *Indians,* whose chief *Sagamores* are well known unto some of our Captives, to have been horrid *Sorcerers,* and hellish *Conjurers,* and such as Conversed with *Daemons*" (italics in original).

After the horrifying event of the several executions of July 19, there commenced an orgy of confessions. On July 21, Mary Lacy, Sr., confessed to riding on a pole through the sky before falling into the water, where the Devil baptized her; on August 10, Elizabeth Johnson, Jr., confessed to using puppets to torment others; on August 30, Elizabeth Johnson, Sr., answered yes to every accusation made against her and then described a white bird and a black man who came to her; on September 1, Stephen Johnson confessed to being baptized by the Devil when he was swimming and to tormenting others himself. The most remarkable outpouring of witchcraft language came from fifteen-year-old Mary Lacy, Jr., who on July 21 – which surely must have been a day of terror for those in custody – accused her mother of making her a witch. The prolific Mary provided several pages of testimony in which she described several events: conversations with the Devil; drinking hard cider with Richard Carrier, whom she also accused; seeing black cats, which she believed sucked the body of Goody Carrier; riding on a pole above the trees; knowing of the killing of children with puppets; and attending a black mass in the forest celebrated by the Reverend George Burroughs, who served communion of brown bread and red wine from earthen cups. When asked why she and her fellow witches sought to hurt the people of the village, Mary gave an answer — cast in the jeremiad rhetoric of the Puritan pulpit — that became the standard response to this otherwise bewildering question: "The Devil would set up his Kingdom here and we should have happy days and it then be better times for me if I would obey him."

In a process that we would call today troping or parodying the establishment Puritan religious language and typology, William Barker borrowed the terms of an election day sermon in his confession: "And the design was to destroy Salem Village, and to begin at the minister's house, and to destroy the church of God and to set up Satan's Kingdoms, . . . and to destroy that place by reason of the people's being divided and their differing with their ministers." Such interweaving of the profane language of witchcraft with the sacred idiom of the Puritan sermon articulated the doom of a once vital and energizing verbal system that had been sustained for seven decades through the course of religious belief and clerical power over language. Moreover, it signaled that the trials had become the site of a dangerous discursive field in which power circulated through language.

A critical question confronts social and literary historians engaged in interrogating the experience and the discourse produced by the Salem witchcraft episode: how did it happen that such a violent verbal explosion occurred in a community that had been dedicated to fleeing persecution for the joy of Christian fellowship and peace? By 1695, the New Englanders wanted to look back upon the events at Salem as constituting a rupture, a delusion, an aberration, in an otherwise glorious history that Cotton Mather and others were steadfastly in the process of transforming into myth. Examination of the record and of the historic development of the language and literature of Puritan New England reveals that the seeds of the Salem tragedy were planted at the start and that the fruit it bore resulted from decades of cultivation of symbolic meanings, verbal inventions, and discursive descriptions. In many ways, the story of the literature of Puritan New England reads as a cautionary tale of how — through grand design, through conscious decisions and unconscious delusions, through sincere or self-serving verbal stratagems — the utopian dream of joyful fellowship metamorphosed into the realities of confusion, accusation, terror, and lamentation of 1692. Though frequently with the best of intentions, the law-makers and word-makers of Puritan New England inadvertently guided their experiment from the promise of John Winthrop's utopian dream of 1630 to the failures of the 1680s and 1690s. Along the way, Puritan authors captured in their writings the experience of a people who sought perfection in this world and salvation in the next but who, from the beginning, deeply feared that their realities were falling short of their dreams.

2

THE DREAM OF A CHRISTIAN UTOPIA

I N FASCINATING WAYS, the literature of the New England Puritans
reveals – and at times conceals – the remarkable number of contradictions in their religious, social, and political ideas, and it demonstrates
how they managed to balance opposing aspirations and ideals to sustain a
society that was from the start fragmenting from internal conflicts. Despite
their tenacious struggles to achieve clarity in their expressions of purpose and
design, the Puritans were frequently ambiguous and paradoxical. This chapter attempts to account for the compulsions, dissensions, and convergences
within their culture and to demonstrate the intellectual complexity of their
thought and writing. Language and literary forms both generated and formulated narrative expressions of the experiences of individuals and their communities as the generations journeyed from the bleak landing at Cape Cod to the
flourishing of the New England Federation in 1642 to the tragic events at
Salem in 1692.

Over the past forty years, scholarship on the American Puritans has been
so rich and various that there is hardly a statement one can make about the
Puritans today without arousing controversy. Scholars in every area of the
humanities and social sciences have employed new theories and methodologies in their studies of Puritan New England. Because many see the Puritans
as having established certain ideas and structures that are fundamental to
later American society – although even this point is much debated –
scholars are attracted to the study of seventeenth-century New England, and
interpretations of that culture frequently have larger political and ideological
implications for the United States as a whole. Competing interpretations of
complex historical or theological matters are related to arguments over
whether the Puritans were militant ideologues and the originators of all that
is problematic in America or whether they were gentle religious idealists who
earnestly sought to create a utopian community that could not be further
from the realities of modern America.

In Puritan studies, disputes begin over the very meaning of the word
"Puritan," to whom it could be applied, and for how long a period, if ever, a
recognizable "Puritanism" existed. Originally, "Puritan" was a term of deri-

sion that moderate English Christians and Catholics cast upon radical Protestants, who later embraced it as a badge of honor. Because there were so many competing reformist sects in England, however, it is difficult to determine exactly which groups "Puritan" described. In New England, the situation is somewhat clearer because the two larger gatherings of congregationalists established fairly homogeneous colonies. Still, scholars disagree over how long these New England Protestants adhered to the doctrines of "Puritanism"; some say for only six years, others say for sixty years, others say well into the eighteenth century, and still others claim that (lowercase) "puritanism" persists in America today.

The one set of statements regarding the New England Puritans that scholars do generally agree upon is that the descriptions of the "Puritan Founding Fathers" presented by historians of fifty years ago and earlier need revision. The Puritans were neither "founders," since the land was already inhabited, nor all "fathers," since mothers, sisters, and daughters played critical roles too. Nor were the Puritans the only invaders of what the Europeans called the New World in the sixteenth and seventeenth centuries; explorers and opportunists from Spain, Holland, France, Portugal, Italy, and Africa were also here, as were members of numerous other English religious groups. The mythic picture of the Pilgrims setting foot upon a pristine new land in 1620 has been categorically rejected. On Cape Cod in 1605, the French had already killed several Native Americans in hostilities over a stolen kettle.

The implications of these recently established historical perspectives are clear. A fresh approach to the literary history of the Puritans necessarily must engage with the fact of the presence of the Native-American cultures on the land that was renamed New England and the impact of the indigenous peoples upon the Europeans and the Europeans upon them. Similarly, a current survey of Puritan writing must look more closely at the complex issue of gender in the patriarchal Puritan society and the importance of women writers who persisted in writing in spite of the pervasive strictures against them. Discussions of Puritan literature must acknowledge that no single monolithic interpretation of Puritan history exists and that every statement one makes about the subject involves a choice among several competing, but not necessarily contradictory, interpretations.

Why were certain Protestant reformers labeled "Puritans" in the late sixteenth century? The answer to that question requires a brief review of their origins in the Protestant Reformation. From the time of early Christianity, church councils resolved theological disputes, defined heresies, and submitted their opinions to the pope for final judgment. Between 1378 and 1417, however, the Catholic church underwent a major split known as the Great Schism, which resulted in the election of two popes, one based in Rome and the other in Avignon, France. In 1414, the Council of Constance resolved the schism by deposing both acting popes and electing Martin V to be the one pope in Rome. The deeper effect of this period of schism, however, was the diminished power of the Roman church and the start of the Reformation, led by a number of important theologians, among them Martin Luther, John Huss, Jerome of Prague, Huldrych Zwingli, John Knox, and John Calvin. The religious programs of each of these reformers engendered independent Christian churches that separated from Rome.

Within the context of this period of rebellion, King Henry VIII rejected papal authority when he was denied the pope's permission to divorce his wife, Catherine, in order to marry Anne Boleyn. In 1534, Henry declared the autonomy of the Church of England and made himself its head. Many English Catholics objected and continued to practice their Catholic faith, and when Henry's Catholic daughter, Mary, assumed the throne in 1553, she launched a reign of terror against the Protestants that earned her the designation Bloody Mary. John Foxe recounted these persecutions in his *Book of Martyrs* (partially published in 1554, with the complete edition in 1559), which helped galvanize the Protestant movement and thus became a classic for the Puritans.

When the Protestant Elizabeth I was crowned in 1558, she reestablished the Church of England as the official state church. Throughout her long reign until her death in 1603, Elizabeth held at bay the rebellious Catholics on her political right and a growing number of radical reformers on her left who wanted the English church to discard the accoutrements of the Roman church, such as the vestments, Latin chants, rituals, statues, and other icons. Elizabeth's compromise was to encourage the reformers in theory but to retain the externals of Catholicism in practice. Those English reformers who most adamantly opposed the compromise were labeled "Puritans" for their insistence on returning to the pure forms of the early Christians.

Scholarly debate over the reasons that large numbers of people were attracted to reformist congregationalism focuses and divides primarily upon the issues of spirituality and pragmatism. The declared motives of the ministers and their followers were completely idealistic: they profoundly believed that the Church of England was wrong to retain "popish abominations"; they feared for their own and their children's souls because they were forced to practice a corrupted form of Christianity; they embraced the congregational organization of the early Christians and held that the Bible contained the actual words of God, which preachers of the English church treated cavalierly.

However, many social and economic histories support an alternative view: that the people drawn to Puritanism were those financially burdened by the sixteenth-century population growth, such as second sons disenfranchised by the laws of primogeniture and landholders of rent-controlled properties whose taxes were being increased. When Puritan ministers preached family discipline, social order, and God's spiritual and temporal calling of his saints, the disgruntled heard an empowering religious—moral—economic message. Certainly, Elizabeth I and later James I recognized that the reformers represented a political threat that exceeded the bounds of theological disputes. By 1600, those attracted to congregationalism had become a persecuted people who felt themselves martyrs in their own country. Fired by religious fervor and political anger, they sustained an underground struggle that would erupt in civil war in 1642 and regicide in 1649. Matters of landholdings, representation, taxes, and property values were very much involved in the parliamentary debates that led up to the war. Although the Puritans constantly warned themselves against materialism and punished merchants for overpricing, their mixed religious and economic motives would lead both to their financial success and to personal and communal distress.

With few doctrinal differences dividing them, the Anglicans and the Puritans actually shared many beliefs. Both postulated an ordered universe, with God heading a great chain of being of all creatures, and both believed that the Gospels contained God's word, to be interpreted by the ministry. Although the Anglicans retained some externals of Catholicism, they joined the reformers in rejecting the Latin mass, which they saw as empty performance, and in abhorring the Catholic clergy's general lack of Gospel preaching. Yet their differences, although minor in theory, were emotionally charged. The Anglicans believed in a church hierarchy, with the monarch as head, and the Puritans believed in congregations, with elected ministers and magistrates leading each church. In the early years, they insisted that each congregation be fairly independent, relying on occasional synods to check serious errors, but later, especially in England after 1649, the reformers moved toward the presbyterial structure of churches under one supreme court of elected magistrates. Ultimately, the English Puritans' inability to settle this issue of polity contributed to their demise and the Restoration of Charles II in 1660. Regarding the Bible, Anglicans believed that the scriptures were composed at different times and places and were to be construed on broad principles. They held that God gave people the power of reason for applying biblical precepts to matters of ethics and morals, which change over time. The Puritans believed that the words of the Bible literally contained all truth and that the corrupt reason of fallen humanity was unreliable. The Anglicans viewed the Puritans as narrow literalists, and the Puritans perceived the Anglicans to be blind to human corruption and ignorant of Christ's law.

Among the several major theologians whose writings influenced the English Puritans, John Calvin was preeminent. English theologians such as

John Preston, Richard Sibbes, and William Ames modified Calvin and formulated many specific doctrines of congregationalism, but the five tenets of Calvin's *Institutes of the Christian Religion* of 1536 remained basic: (1) total depravity – the complete corruption of humanity resulting from Original Sin; (2) unconditional election – the predestined salvation or damnation of every individual; (3) limited Atonement – Christ's gift of life through His death but only for those already predestined for heaven; (4) irresistible grace – necessary for conversion but which can be neither earned nor refused; (5) perseverance of the saints – the enduring justification and righteousness of the converted. Despite the assurances that the conversion experience and church membership seemed to provide, every Puritan understood that the possibility for self-delusion was strong and that even the most confident saint should constantly search his or her heart for signs of self-deception, sin, and hypocrisy.

If interpreted to their extremes, these fatalistic principles, with their emphasis upon helplessness and dependence, would appear to engender either despair or hedonism, and for that reason, the challenge for Puritan ministers was to guide believers along a spiritual and psychological middle way. When the people cried out, "What must I do to be saved?" Puritan theologians offered them Calvinism modified by the doctrine of preparationism, which held that although a person could not earn grace, the individual could prepare for grace. Certain signs in the life of the sincere penitent, such as a yearning for grace, moral and virtuous actions, and rapt attention to sermons, could provide hope of impending conversion. Although preparationism appears to contradict the doctrine of unconditional election, it eventually became a central tenet in the evolving system of spiritual nourishment and social control in the pioneer communities of Puritan New England.

To some, preparationism appeared to approach the heresy of Arminianism (that works could merit grace), and the clergy often accused one another of this error. At the other extreme, an overemphasis upon free grace moved toward antinomianism – the heresy that grace, conversion, and study of the scriptures were sufficient for salvation so that a church, a clergy, and proper conduct were superfluous. Anne Hutchinson's antinomianism was the most notorious case, but many were accused of this heresy in England and New England. Efforts to sustain the balancing act between the excesses of preparationism and conversionism correspondingly generated tortuous struggles for the clergy and engendered some of the most dramatic and engaging texts of Puritan literature.

To understand certain nuances of Puritan writings, it is necessary to examine a number of other ideas held in common by the majority of Puritans in America by 1645. With their insistence upon the need for a highly trained clergy, the Puritans considered a gift for metaphor and imagery and even a knowledge of classical literature and the arts to be valuable assets for an effective preacher. Although it is true that the Puritans valued a "plain style" of speaking and writing over the sometimes florid Anglican preaching style, they also appreciated language that could warm the affections, prepare the heart, and allude to the implicit meaning inherent in ordinary events. Language and art always had to be utilitarian, however, serving a spiritual purpose and never presuming to eclipse the Bible.

An important dimension of the Puritans' mastery of language was their use of biblical typology. In strictest terms, typological hermeneutics involved explicating signs in the Old Testament as foreshadowing events and people in the New. This produced interesting consequences; for example, Jonah's three days in the whale typologically parallels Christ's three days in the tomb, and Job's patience prefigures, or is a *figura,* of Christ's forbearance on the cross. Applied more liberally and figured more broadly, typology expanded into a more elaborate verbal system that enabled an interpreter to discover biblical forecasts of current events. Thus, the Atlantic journey of the Puritans could be an antitype of the Exodus of the Israelites; and the New England colony, a New Zion, to which Christ may return to usher in the Millennium. The first settlers were conservative, cautious typologists, but as Edward Johnson's *Wonder-Working Providence of Sion's Saviour in New England* (1654; composed c. 1650) demonstrates, by the 1640s New England's sacred errand into the wilderness and the approaching Apocalypse were accepted antitypes of sacred history. Claiming to strive for plainness, Puritan writers created instead a subtle and complex language system. The great Puritan poet Edward Taylor was the consummate typologist (see Chapter 4).

Nature was another area wherein Puritan thought made evident its affinity for the paradoxical. Along with the Bible and occasional instances of direct divine revelation, nature was for the Puritans a third channel of communication from God to humanity. An angry God might send violent storms or earthquakes to warn backsliders. Should God wish to alert a single saint to a personal failing, He might have a sparrow fall into the saint's path or even take the life of a loved one. The Puritans were living in the age of Francis Bacon, the "New Science," and the founding of the Royal Society in 1662, and their views of divine intervention into natural events might appear to be in conflict with any objective or scientific view. Science would inevitably challenge the authority of religious systems, but the Puritans discerned little conflict between the objective recording of observed natural phenomena and the discovery there of divine providences. Cotton Mather sent frequent reports to the Royal Society while searching the heavens and forests for God's messages.

For students of Puritan writing, the definition of "literature" has traditionally been broad. In addition to a relatively small corpus of self-conscious imaginative writing such as history, poetry, and captivity narratives, "Puritan literature" also includes sermons, diaries, letters, trial transcripts, religious tracts, and broadsides. Of course, most of the Puritans were reared and educated in the England of Shakespeare, Donne, Spenser, and Sidney. Thus, the Puritans did recognize and appreciate literary artistry, but their religious scruples made them suspicious of all products of the flawed human imagination. When they came to power in England, they closed the theaters, which they condemned as offering sinful entertainment that distracted people's attention from the preaching of God's word. Puritan schools emphasized the study of rhetoric to prepare for practical uses of language as in the pulpit or at the bar. Unless a poem or narrative has a pedagogical, religious purpose, its composition was seen as a waste of the author's time. Anne Bradstreet had her manuscript taken from her without her knowledge and published in England because she would never have dared publish in America; Edward Taylor did not circulate his poetry, which was not discovered until the 1930s; and Cotton Mather was forever apologizing for writing another of his over four hundred titles. Even most of the works of the great Puritan poet John Milton qualify as religious writing.

Yet, as is apparent in the imaginative works they did produce and in the richness and eloquence of much religious and political discourse, there were many Puritans who possessed literary talent. During the first three decades of colonization, the major contributors to the literary record were those in public positions who grappled with the thorny issues of church and state: William Bradford, John Winthrop, John Cotton, Roger Williams, Thomas Hooker, Thomas Shepard, and, through her powerful spoken words, Anne Hutchinson.

In England in the 1580s, Robert Browne despaired of the English government ever reforming the church along congregational lines, and he published his *Reformation without Tarrying for Any* (1582) urging nonconformity and complete separation from the Church of England. In 1609, a large number of separatists (also called Brownists) moved to Holland, but by the mid-1610s, they became convinced that all of Europe was corrupt and that the Continent provided an unfit environment for raising their children. With a charter under the title of the Plymouth Company, about one hundred separatists departed in the *Mayflower* for Virginia. In 1620, they accidentally landed to the west of Cape Cod, where they established a settlement they named Plymouth. Realizing that they had put ashore far from the territory designated in the charter, they drew up their own charter, the Mayflower Compact, which declared their loyalty to the king but established their own government by majority rule. The first governor, John Carver, died in 1621, and William Bradford assumed the post, in which he served, except for a five-year sabbatical, until his death in 1657. The colonists negotiated a treaty with Massasoit, chief of the Wampanoag tribe, and sustained tranquil relations with them for fifty years. Contacts with other tribes were not so peaceful, as when the Pilgrims used military force to appropriate lands from the Narragansets. Prospering mainly on the fur trade, which required the cooperation of the Wampanoags, the community grew and expanded. Plymouth Colony joined the New England Federation in 1643.

Following the foray of the Brownists into the New World, there came a much larger band of congregationalists of more moderate political and religious positions under the leadership of John Winthrop. Born into a landholding family in Suffolk, England, Winthrop studied at Trinity College, Cambridge, where he considered entering the ministry before deciding to become a lawyer. Establishing a prosperous practice, he retained strong religious convictions throughout his life. In 1629, he negotiated an agreement with the English government to establish the Massachusetts Bay Company and was elected its governor by its Puritan stockholders. In 1630, the group sailed the *Arbella* to New England and founded a colony that became Boston. Such a departure was dangerous, physically and emotionally arduous, and politically controversial, for they left behind their persecuted compatriots, who viewed the emigrants as escapists. But they found consolation and justifications for their flight in the scriptures, where they read that the things of this world, including parents, children, and friends, were insignificant compared to salvation.

In Boston, Winthrop and his colleagues established a theocracy in which the clergy had great political influence and the status of freeman was limited to male church members. In the original Pauline spirit, the leaders encouraged like-minded religionists from England to join them, and between fifteen and twenty thousand persons arrived during the "Great Migration" of the 1630s. Because of the considerable expense involved in making the ocean crossing, the vast majority of these early arrivals were people of wealth and status who also brought with them indentured servants and African slaves. The colonizers flourished through agriculture, fishing, and the fur trade, and soon a growing merchant class thrived as well. With their esteem for literacy and a learned clergy, they established the Boston Latin School in 1635 and Harvard College a year later.

The Massachusetts Bay Puritans differed from those at Plymouth by being nonseparating congregationalists. Clinging to some hope that the English church might yet reform, they wished to remain a loyal opposition in exile. In the interim they sought refuge from persecution and the opportunity to establish an example for their English colleagues of how model congregational communities could be formed. Indeed, many of these colonists expected their stay in America to be temporary, and hundreds did return in the early 1640s to join the English Civil War and the Puritan Commonwealth. In spite of these departures, however, the large families of the first generation and a steady flow of new immigrants rapidly increased the English population in Massachusetts by the 1650s.

Among the Native-American tribes inhabiting the territories that the Puritans eventually acquired were the Wampanoags, Massachusetts, Pokanokets, Capawicks, Mohegans, Nipmucks, Pequots, Patuxets, and Narragansets. Before the first English arrived, numerous Europeans had visited the coast of America and some had begun ill-fated settlements. During these early contacts, Europeans captured and enslaved many Native Americans and stole their food and property. Then an epidemic of smallpox in 1616 killed 75 to 90 percent of the native population along the coast between Penobscot Bay and Cape Cod. By the 1620s the plague had reduced the Pokanoket tribe of Cape Cod from twenty thousand to two thousand, and they were being tyrannized by the Narragansets, who had been spared the pox by virtue of their geographical location. When the Pilgrims' first winter claimed nearly half of the colony, the Pokanokets, who saw the Pilgrims as technologically advanced potential allies, sent the Patuxet Squanto, a prisoner of the Pokanokets who had been captured by whites years before and taken as a slave to England, to form a treaty with Bradford's group. Between 1620 and 1622, Squanto was a guide, interpreter, and diplomat for the colony, helping the English arrange treaties with other Native-American tribes and trade for food and furs. Because Squanto's entire tribe had been destroyed by smallpox when he was in England, he remained within the Plymouth Colony until his death in 1622. On his own, he would certainly have been enslaved by other tribes. The highly romanticized tale of Squanto's spontaneous aid to the Pilgrims has for many decades stood as an example of the myth of immediately friendly relations between the English and the Indians. An examination of the details of his association with the whites, however, reveals a more pragmatic and ambiguous relationship.

Before leaving for America and for some decades after, the Puritans proclaimed one of their major intentions to be the religious conversion of the native inhabitants. With the exception of the persistent missionary efforts of John Eliot and Thomas Mayhew, however, the Puritans abandoned their proselytizing attempts rather early. Since the relations between the Europeans and the native peoples were so thoroughly centered around trade, land acquisition, and political maneuvering, perhaps it appeared to the English clergy in the initial years of the settlement that there was little time for proselytizing. In addition, the Native Americans' suspicion and wariness made them rather unreceptive to the white God. Nonetheless, some were converted to Christianity, and by the 1670s there were several villages of "praying Indians." Despite these successful conversions, however, most Puritan clergy viewed the Indians as hopeless pagans. Indeed, the very attitudes and preconceptions that the Puritans brought with them prevented many from seeing the original inhabitants of the New World as human beings. For most Puritans, the "howling wilderness" outside their "enclosed gardens" was a territory under Satan's power, and amid this dangerous landscape the Indians were obviously children of the Devil. Although the English did occasionally purchase land from the native tribes, they soon began to perceive the Indians as "savages" and "animals," and this verbal and imaginative projection enabled them to conceive of the land as essentially vacant of human occupation and thus available for the taking. John Winthrop interpreted the smallpox plague as God's generous land clearing to prepare it for His saints.

In the first few years of colonization, the settlers found the native inhabitants very useful in the fur-trading business because of their knowledge of the land, their experience as hunters, and the willingness of some to sell furs cheaply to the New Englanders, who made large profits exporting them to England. As exploitation rapidly devastated the animal population near the colony, however, the fur trade became a less vital part of the English economy. Agriculture became more important, and the English began to take more land by force, leading in 1636 to the first major "Indian War," with the Pequots.

The events leading to the confrontation and the resulting massacre of between four and seven hundred Pequots is vividly described by Captain John Underhill in his *News from America* (1638), an extraordinary text depicting an early American holocaust. Beginning in 1632, the Dutch and the English were claiming ownership of the Connecticut Valley by right of discovery. The Pequots claimed prior discovery and right of conquest because they had defeated weaker tribes to gain control of the valley. While disputes and negotiations continued over the next few years, English colonists continued to move into the area. After a series of complex events about which there is much dispute among historians, the Puritans authorized an attack upon the Pequots. An army of English and their Mohegan allies surrounded the Pequot village and shot and burned the people, mostly women and children. As Underhill recounts, at the first volley of English shots, the Pequots "brake forth into a most doleful cry so as if God had not fitted the hearts of men for the service, it would have bred in them a commiseration towards them." God seems to have fitted those Puritan hearts quite well, and the English ferocity so terrified the other tribes that a general peace was sustained between the English and the native peoples until the 1670s when the Narragansets, led by Chief Sachem Metacomet, nicknamed King Philip, mounted a final stand (see Chapter 3). Because of the limited strife between the English and the Indians during the long middle period, Puritan writing may give the impression that the Indians disappeared until the war of the 1670s. Considerable interactions between the colonizers and the colonized continued, however, accompanied by sustained discussions on both sides about the nature of the troubling "other." Numerous contemporary accounts delineate the benefits and detriments of interaction with alien peoples, as the New Englanders ceaselessly interrogated the subject of the savage. Accounts of such troubling realities as these conflicts with the Indians were nearly always interwoven with myths and dreams of the possible.

So intense were the Puritan expectations that they began to generate a prophetic literature even before the English arrived at the New England site of their project. At sea on board the *Arbella* in the spring of 1630, for example, John Winthrop composed one of the most significant texts of Puritan writing, his sermon "A Model of Christian Charity," and he began another, his *Journal,* which was published in 1825–6 as *The History of New England from 1630 to 1649* (an earlier version was published in 1790). In the early years, it was not unusual for laypeople like Winthrop to deliver sermons, but the practice was forbidden after the 1636 trial of Anne Hutchinson. In 1629 in his *Reasons to be Considered . . . for the Intended Plantation in New England,* Winthrop described the "excess of riot" and the "multitude of evil examples of the licentious government" in England, and he began to formulate the framework for his own Christian government based upon the "law of the gospel." For Winthrop, these hours of composition must have been euphoric, for his text looks optimistically and hopefully toward a golden future in which the harsh New England conditions and the divisions and contentions of his governorship were as yet unimaginable.

As both an idealistic blueprint of the structure of the Puritan community and an expression of Winthrop's cherished convictions, "A Model of Christian Charity" opens by proclaiming that "God Almighty in his most holy and wise providence" has designed the human condition in such a way that social inequality is natural: "as in all times some must be rich, some poor, some high and eminent in power and dignity, others mean and in subjection." Leaving questions of social justice to the Divinity, Winthrop explains that God's plan for His community is fair and orderly and will work perfectly when His people heed the rules of the Gospel. For "every man might have need of other, and from hence they might be all knit more nearly together in the bonds of brotherly affection." Following the "two rules . . . justice and mercy," the rich will help the poor, the strong aid the weak, the people follow their leaders, and the leaders labor for their people. Imitating Christ, heeding the "law of grace or the gospel," and practicing the "duty of mercy," the community of saints will be joined into a holy unity by the love of Christ, for "Love is the bond of perfection."

Noting parallels between the Puritans and the Old Testament Hebrews, Winthrop's sermon culminates in a vision of the sacred covenant between God and His saints for this divine enterprise. With a warning that would be repeated in many sermons, Winthrop says that God "hath taken us to be his after a most strict and peculiar marriage, which will make him the more jealous of our love and obedience." Just as God told the "people of Israel" that they were the only ones he would recognize, so "God now gives a special commission" to the Puritans. If God allows the *Arbella* to reach New England, that will be the sign that "he ratified this covenant and sealed our commission," and should the people later become greedy, ambitious, and carnal – "seeking great things for ourselves and our posterity" – "the Lord will surely break out in wrath against us . . . and make us know the price of the breach of such a covenant." In his conclusion, Winthrop emblematically employs the famous image of the Puritans as the exemplary society: "The God of Israel . . . has set up this people that we shall be as a city on a hill. The eyes of all people are upon us."

Scholars disagree over whether or not at the time of their departure Winthrop and his congregation had already conceived of themselves to be embarking on a sacred errand. Some argue that the Puritans arrived with such a fully developed teleology and that Puritan ministers used typology to elaborate the biblical parallels to their present, and others insist that Winthrop was simply using stock sermon rhetoric and had no such conception of an ordained American destiny. At stake in this interpretive issue is the very foundation of what has been called "American identity." One image of these English "founders" is that Winthrop and his colleagues were, in spite of their denials of the things of this world, actually early American precapitalists who were about to initiate a process of divinely supported material progress that would lead to violent conquest, unquenchable imperialism, and self-righteous and self-obsessive nationalism. At the other extreme is a picture of a pietistic people struggling to escape a corrupt modern world to a holy utopian haven for which Winthrop's image of the "city on a hill" was really an inappropriate trope because he and his people sought a primitive medieval retreat. Debates over which of these scripts better describes the evolution of Anglo–European North America have polarized historians and literary scholars. Perhaps the only resolution is one that accepts both descriptions as somewhat accurate, that depicts Winthrop's mission as utopian in conception but necessarily flawed because of its dependence upon the language of expansionism and a teleology of perfectionism.

Winthrop's text expressed a paradox that would be a constant source of confusion and strife for the Puritans: the saints must reject the allure of this world and yet labor in their temporal callings with such diligence that they would produce material success, which, in turn, would endanger the moral integrity and spiritual perfection of the community. As another important Puritan text, *The Last Will and Testament* (1653) of the merchant Robert Keayne, makes evident, the Puritans' linking of spiritual and temporal callings was troubling. A devout member of John Cotton's church, Keayne was brought to court in 1639 for overcharging for a bag of nails. Keayne's text reveals that he was shocked and humiliated by this "deed and sharp censure," and he piously accepted God's justice since he knew that he had committed other sins that deserved penance. However, Keayne also argues that his pricing was a trivial act, compared to sins of others, and that it was only natural that merchants would follow the laws of supply and demand in setting prices. He cites the jealousy of those who envied his success as the reason for his censure. In Keayne's mind, being part of a city on the hill meant not only attending to sermons but also succeeding in the marketplace. As a result of such apparent contradictions, Winthrop's design of a loving, sharing community of saints was short-lived. Keeping their covenant would prove every bit as difficult as Winthrop had warned, perhaps even more difficult than he feared. As his *Journal* testifies, discontent and disputes would quickly and repeatedly threaten to destroy his fragile utopia.

The most frequently examined sections of Winthrop's *Journal* are those pages that record one of the Massachusetts Bay Colony's most destructive religious tumults. The trial of Anne Hutchinson is a landmark narrative in women's history. Hutchinson's New England experience began when she and her family emigrated to Boston in 1634 to follow their minister, John Cotton. Her husband, William, was elected deputy to the Massachusetts General Court, and Hutchinson continued her community service as a nurse–midwife and spiritual adviser to women. Sometime during her first years in Boston, she began to hold weekly meetings in her home to discuss the sermon of the previous Sunday. These gatherings soon grew to have sixty or more people, including the then governor, Henry Vane, and other prominent figures. After a time, Hutchinson began to criticize some of the leading clergy for preaching a covenant of works instead of grace. She accused them of being "legalists" who suggested that people could earn salvation and that the conversion process could be charted and anticipated, and she insisted upon the Calvinist doctrines of divine sovereignty and free grace. She declared: "Here is a great stir about graces [earned for works] and looking into hearts, but give me Christ; I seek not for graces, but for Christ; I seek not for promises, but for Christ; I seek not for sanctification, but for Christ; tell me not of meditation and duties, but tell me of Christ." In their efforts to offer people encouragement and promote moral order through preparationism, some of the clergy had allowed their rhetoric to slip toward Arminianism. Hutchinson keenly detected this shift, and her followers agreed. The group then began efforts to replace John Wilson, pastor of the Boston church where Cotton was the teacher, with Hutchinson's brother-in-law John Wheelwright. This move sparked support for Wilson from other parishioners and countercharges that the Hutchinson group were antinomians who were rejecting authority and the importance of law and order in every aspect of life. Some called Hutchinson and her party licentious fanatics. Convinced that the very foundation of the theocracy was at stake, the authorities convened the first synod in the colonies.

In private meetings with Hutchinson and finally during her trial, the magistrates and ministers urged her to admit her errors, but she firmly held her ground. In her view, the piety that was central to the Pauline spirit of the Puritans was being replaced by a mechanical system of social morality and rewards. So essential were these issues for her that she was prepared to be excommunicated and banished rather than to live in error in Massachusetts. The record of her trial constitutes one of the most stirring prose works in Puritan literature. Hutchinson's wit and keen intelligence are evident as are the frustrations and desperate maneuvering of her opponents. In these disputations, the intersections of discursive formations and power relations are revealed.

Although John Cotton was not on trial, many authorities were deeply suspicious of his teachings. However, since it would only further embarrass the already beleaguered government to accuse Cotton of heresy, the leaders pressured him to denounce Hutchinson. Cotton refused, but he also refused to defend her. Aware of Cotton's predicament and of the court's desire to avoid political embarrassment by separating Cotton's position from her own, Hutchinson listened as they sought grounds for condemning her teachings without implicating Cotton. She knew she could protect Cotton by claiming that her ideas came not from him but directly by divine revelation, a presumption for which she could be punished. Although it is evident throughout the trial that Hutchinson was eminently capable of eluding her questioners with complex replies and biblical citations, she finally conceded to having experienced a direct and divine revelation. In this manner she empowered herself in a way that was necessarily intolerable to the patriarchal authority. Yet, even as she confessed to the revelation, she chose her words judiciously so that they could be interpreted either as a confirmation or as a denial: she said she received the message "by the voice of his [Christ's] own spirit to my soul." By saying "soul" rather than "ear," she left the question of whether the voice was literal or constructed unanswered. However, with their own power founded upon the literal nature of language, the judges took her statement to mean that she claimed to have heard Christ speaking to her through the senses, and they condemned her. The court then urged Cotton to acknowledge her guilt, but his reply was so evasive that some members of the court remained unsatisfied. Forced to settle the matter, Governor Winthrop asserted that "Mr. Cotton is not called to answer to any thing."

The fact that Hutchinson was a woman is very important in any interpretation of the texts of the case and in later writings about her. The Puritan authorities resented all defiance, but they were doubly disturbed by her assertions of spiritual independence because of her gender, for in English society at the time women were expected to be submissive to their husbands and all other male authorities. In many contemporary and later Puritan writings, Hutchinson is referred to as a Jezebel, and much is made of her giving birth to a deformed child months after the trial as proof of her female "misconceptions." There were rumors that she was promiscuous and in love with John Cotton. After she and her family were banished in 1638, they spent five years in Rhode Island and then moved to New York, where she and all of her family but one were killed in an Indian raid. This outcome satisfied her old enemies, who saw the work of Providence both in manifesting God's judgment upon her and in confirming that events of human history are signs of the divine plan.

In the first years of the colony, Anne Hutchinson was not the only rebellious Puritan to disturb the peace of Winthrop's holy garden. Born in Smithfield, London (c. 1603), Roger Williams prepared for the ministry at Cambridge and migrated to New England in 1630. A staunch separatist, he turned down a position in a nonseparatist Boston church to accept a post in Plymouth. Strongly committed to the idea of converting the Indians, he developed close ties with the Narragansets, and unlike most other English, he recognized the natives to be people who possessed complex cultures, religions, and traditions of their own. His sympathy with them and his strict religious principles led him to challenge the legality of the charters that were being used by the whites to confiscate Indian lands. Moving to Salem in 1633, he also began to insist that the New England Way (or what has been called federal theology), which linked church and state, was fallacious. Asserting that religion was a private matter between each individual and God, he charged that laws and courts should not attempt to fuse spiritual and public issues.

When John Cotton heard Williams preach in 1633, the two ministers initiated a long debate over questions of church and state. Williams insisted that the idea of nonseparating congregationalism was absurd, for to be a congregationalist was to believe in individual church autonomy and thus to be a separatist necessarily. He perceived the nonseparationism of the Massachusetts Bay Colony to be a blatant political compromise of faith and reason in order to retain the favor of the English reformers. So unsettling were his charges that, in 1635, the Massachusetts General Court ordered Williams returned to England, but he and a dozen supporters fled to Rhode Island, where they founded Providence. There he lived among the Native Americans, learned their languages and customs, and published *A Key into the Language of America* (1643), which provides both a history of the Native Americans and information about their lives, ideas, and religion. Suggesting that the whites had much to learn from the more highly civilized natives, this work denied the myth of the native peoples as savages and heathens and shamed the Massachusetts Bay Puritans into expanding their missionary efforts.

When Williams was in England in 1644 to obtain a charter for Providence, Cotton published a letter he had written to Williams eight years before, upbraiding him for his errors. Williams responded with his essay *The Bloody Tenent of Persecution, for Cause of Conscience, Discussed* (1644), to which Cotton replied in *The Bloody Tenent, Washed, and Made White in the Blood of the Lamb* (1647), which Williams answered several years later in *The Bloody Tenent Yet More Bloody* (1652). In these works, Williams developed more fully his attack upon nonseparating congregationalism and federal theology. A stricter Calvinist than Cotton, who saw nonseparation as a liberal and generous gesture to the English church members, Williams insisted that the truest form of Christianity is that of separatist congregations where individuals and parishes can follow their own inclinations. Although not as radically individualist as Anne Hutchinson, Williams charged that the New England clergy were intolerant and persecuted those whose views varied even slightly from state-approved doctrines. Like Hutchinson, Williams also recognized in the New England Way a leaning toward Arminianism. Williams accused Cotton of "swimming with a stream of outward credit and profit, and smiting with the fist and sword of persecution such as dare not join in worship with him." Williams reasoned that government officials were elected by the people and that for them to intrude into religious affairs was a violation of the sacred world by the profane. Because he called for political authorities to stay out of religious issues, he is recognized as the first advocate in America for the principle of the separation of church and state.

From a literary viewpoint, a most interesting feature of the "Bloody

Tenent" exchanges is the key role of typology in the arguments, for the debate related to the ways that Old Testament types may or may not be applied to current political matters. Puritan ministers and magistrates frequently drew upon Old Testament texts in their arguments to justify their authority, as Cotton in his *Tenent Washed* where he draws parallels between the government of ancient Jerusalem and that of New England. Williams insists that with the establishment of Christ's new covenant and the writing of the New Testament, the Old Testament types have been fulfilled and are not applicable to secular history. Maintaining a conservative position on the use of types, Williams argues that the only valid reading of Old Testament types is as foreshadowings of New Testament antitypes. By insisting on a stricter use of typology, Williams mocks the notion of the Puritans as a chosen people; he believes that Christ's spiritual army is worldwide and not confined to a "New Israel" in New England. In a sense, Williams emerges as a true fundamentalist; for him the language of the Old Testament was not metaphorical and thus was not open to broader interpretation. The irony of his case is that he was a theological conservative who viewed all issues with narrow Calvinistic logical consistency and yet he is often remembered as the most liberal-minded Puritan New England leader.

As is already apparent from the discussions of Hutchinson and Williams, John Cotton was the most important minister of the first generation and often at the center of controversy. Born in 1584 into the family of a wealthy attorney in Derby, England, Cotton attended Cambridge and then the Puritans' Emmanuel College and became vicar of St. Botolph's in Boston, England, in 1610. At first, he gained his popularity from his elegant and ornamented preaching style, but then he fell under the influence of the reformer Richard Sibbes and henceforth emulated Sibbes's plain style. Although his nonconformity was evident early, he was protected from persecution for twenty years by family friends. He preached the farewell sermon to Winthrop's departing company in 1630, and in 1633, when he was forced to resign his post at St. Botolph's, he too migrated to America.

Cotton's sermon of 1630 *God's Promise to His Plantation* was an important political statement because of his own eminence in England and because of the suspicions among English Puritans that colonizing New England involved an abandonment of their English cause at home. Although at the time Cotton did not plan to join in the migration, his rationalization of nonseparation established him as a prominent champion for the Massachusetts Bay venture. Fending off another criticism some had made about English encroachment on Native-American territories, he also articulated the arguments for the usurpation of the American lands:

God makes room for a people in three ways: First, when he casts out the enemies of a people before them by lawful war with the inhabitants. . . . Secondly, when he gives a foreign people favor in the eyes of any native people to come and sit down with them either by way of purchase . . . or else when they give it in courtesy. . . . Thirdly, when he makes a country though not altogether void of inhabitants, yet void in the place where they reside.

Realizing that missionary work was necessary for justifying the English occupation of the natives' territories, he advises the colonists to "offend not the poor natives, but as you partake in their land, so make them partakers of your precious faith; as you reap their temporals, so feed them with your spirituals." In Cotton's rhetoric, the language of Puritan theology found resonance with the colonial project: native "others" were destined by God to be transformed and displaced.

Cotton also employs several Old Testament types to suggest parallels between the Hebrews and the colonists, but although he allows for the possibility of envisioning their journey as an errand to "the land of Canaan," he shrewdly reminds them and those remaining behind that England was also part of the New Zion: "Be not unmindful of our Jerusalem at home, whether you leave us or stay at home with us." This sort of conscious diplomacy would characterize Cotton's position in the Hutchinson trial and his preaching over the years, but it would also anger critics like Roger Williams who perceived in Cotton's language a similarity to the smooth words of the double-tongued Deceiver.

Cotton's most important works in New England include his *The Way to Life* (1641), which employs preparationist doctrine to describe how a believer moves toward salvation by way of hearing the Gospel preached, and *The Way of the Churches of Christ in New England* (1645), which is a thorough description and justification of the New England Way. By 1642, the English Civil War had begun, and Cotton was convinced that a dramatic change was occurring in the history of Christianity and that the Second Coming and the Millennium of Christ's rule on earth were at hand. In *The Pouring Out of the Seven Vials* and *The Church's Resurrection* (1642), Cotton elaborates this vision and urges New Englanders not to return to England but to keep their covenant with God in America. Although Cotton was one of three New England ministers invited to participate in the Westminster Assembly in 1642 to reform the Church of England, he declined. Instead, he reacted against the developments in English Puritanism, and at the Synod of 1646 in Boston he helped to draft the Cambridge Platform, a definition of New England congregationalism based largely upon his writings. After his death in 1652, several more of his works were published, and his influence on New England church polity remained strong for several decades.

Second only to Cotton in stature and perhaps the most effective preacher of his time in New England, Thomas Hooker was born in England in 1586 into the family of a yeoman about whom little else is known. Like Cotton, Hooker began his training at Cambridge and moved to Emmanuel College, where he remained a tutor until 1618. After serving in two churches over the next fourteen years, he fled to Holland and then New England in 1633 on the same ship with John Cotton and Samuel Stone, another leading clergyman. Hooker and Stone became the first ministers in the church in New Town, soon to be Cambridge.

In 1636, Hooker and Stone made a startling and unorthodox decision to relocate their church to Hartford, Connecticut. When Hooker's petition to the Massachusetts magistrates for permission to move was denied, he left anyway. Although Hooker explained his departure by citing the people's need for more land, some critics – then and now – have speculated that Massachusetts was not big enough for the egos of both Hooker and Cotton; the two had frequent disputes over church membership. Hooker favored a more liberal membership policy, and he devised an elaborate preparation process that involved precise psychological stages on the way to conversion. The six essential stages of this morphology of conversion were contrition, humiliation, vocation, implantation, exaltation, and possession; and these he subdivided further. He required that a prospective member demonstrate to him and then to the congregation a successful passage through these stages. This rigorous public ritual was intimidating to many later arrivals to New England because such practices never existed in England. Hooker believed, however, that his method assisted the individual to discover what to expect in the experience of grace and that this process reassured the elect and discouraged hypocrites. Most ministers agreed that the worst psychological condition was that of persons who deceived themselves about having a conversion experience only to despair later upon discovering their error. Between 1635 and 1645, many of the New England churches developed stricter tests for church membership, some requiring a lengthy public description of every detail of the conversion experience. Some historians suggest that the large influx of new colonists during the 1640s put pressure upon the towns and churches to accept new members, who, in turn, were rewarded with land and political privileges; some have suggested that economic factors, as well as religious zeal, led to more demanding membership requirements.

Hooker's sermons provide some of the best illustrations in the literature of the ways in which the Puritan inclination toward the system of logic of the French reformer Petrus Ramus affected expression and actions. It remains unclear how fully Puritan thinkers consciously embraced Ramistic logic, but the structure of many sermons suggests that many clergy found it useful. In opposition to the complex syllogistic reasoning of the Catholic Scholastics, Ramus established a Manichean strategy in which one reasoned through established sets of opposites or contraries. An example of this rhetorical strategy can be found in the much-debated question as to whether or not all who claim to be saved should be admitted into the church. Since the most liberal admission policy would result in admitting hypocrites who sought membership entirely for the political and economic advantages of franchise, then logically, it followed that it was safer to exclude some. Yet the either/or nature of Ramistic logic tended to foster polarization and extremism: a person is either saved or damned, saint or sinner, virtuous or sinful; there is no purgatory between heaven and hell. The world can be divided into the holy community of the theocracy and the "others," who are inherently and fatally flawed by the corruption of this world. The dualism of Ramus worked well enough for resolving complex theological problems quickly, but when extended into other areas of life such as race relations or politics, this Manichean logic proved to be highly problematic for the Puritans, and has remained so for Americans. Indeed, much of the history of American expansionism may be said to have been cast in similar oppositional terms.

In his work *The Application of Redemption* (1656), Hooker employs this logic to set up a series of true versus false ways of looking at sin, and he suggests that in the mind of God and in His kingdom polarization is the rule: "Imagine thou sawest the Judge of all the World sitting upon a Throne . . . the Sheep standing on his right hand, and the Goats at the left: Suppose thou heardest that dreadful Sentence, and final Doom pass from the Lord of Life (whose Word made Heaven and Earth, and will shake both) *Depart from me ye cursed;* How would thy heart shake and sink, and die within thee?" Hooker's most important works were *A Survey of the Sum of Church-Discipline* (1648), a major defense of the New England Way, and *The Soul's Preparation for Christ* (1632), a full elaboration of his conversion morphology.

Although Cotton and Hooker were much admired for their reasoning and preaching, not everyone in New England appreciated their absolutism and plain style. There were those with a sense of humor who visited New England and openly criticized the Puritans. Thomas Morton, an Anglican, established a settlement at Mount Wollaston (now Quincy), Massachusetts, but which the Puritans called Merrymount. Morton annoyed the Puritans for three years by allowing dancing and maypole festivities in his community, but he disturbed them more when he began to sell whiskey and firearms to the Indians, thereby threatening the fur trade and the incorporation of the natives into the Puritan cultural economy. In 1628, Captain Miles Standish of Plymouth led an attack upon Morton's group and arrested him, but Morton was tried and found innocent. In 1630, John Endecott arrested Morton again, burned his house, and confiscated his property. Morton was deported to England, where he attempted to have the Massachusetts charter revoked and where he published his *New English Canaan* (1637), a satiric attack upon Puritan religious practices and their tendency to compare themselves to the Israelites. He also provided descriptions of Native Americans, whom he found to be noble and superior in character to the Puritans.

A more piously motivated critic of Puritan New England was the devout English Puritan Thomas Lechford, who came to Massachusetts in 1638. He attended a congregational church in Boston and practiced law until 1641, when he returned to England. Many were repatriating at this time to support their coreligionists in the impending Civil War, but Lechford made it clear that he did so because he could not abide what he considered to be the bizarre developments in theology and church polity in New England. In 1642, he published *Plain Dealing, or News from New England,* a relatively moderate and dispassionate, but nonetheless critical, description of his experience, which he subtitled *A short View of New England's Present Government, both Ecclesiastical and Civil, compared with the anciently-received and established Government of England, in some material points fit for the gravest consideration in these times.* In particular, he was disturbed by the "public confessions and trials," which seemed to him extreme: "By what rule, I ask them, are faults of men to be so publicly handled before all the world?" He also notes that although the New Englanders claim to be congregationalists, they have already constructed a formidable state–church hierarchy. With the Civil War just beginning, Lechford's reservations about the New England Way were shared by many English Puritans. As the English revolutionaries debated the polity of the reformed church and state they hoped to establish, Boston's "city on a hill" was for them a deeply flawed model.

Not all of the satire produced from New England was aimed at the Massachusetts Puritans, however. Nathaniel Ward arrived in New England in 1634 at the age of fifty-five after he was expelled from his ministry at Essex, England. He settled at Ipswich and was drafted in 1641 to compose what became the Massachusetts Body of Liberties. Returning to England in 1645, he published *The Simple Cobbler of Aggawam in America* (Aggawam had been the Native-American name for Ipswich). A conservative Puritan, Ward satirized the emerging religious toleration of the English reformed churches, which he regarded as examples of political opportunism and compromise. Deriding the knotty theological debates being conducted in Parliament to justify such deals, he said the Devil "cannot sting the vitals of the Elect mortally" but he can "fly-blow their Intellectuals miserably." Going through four editions in its first year, this lively work is the first satire of England from the vantage point of New England, although it is clear that Ward still thought of himself as English. It also reveals a Puritan male's patriarchal views about gender identifications and his concern that established gender roles not be breached. For example, Ward repeatedly uses metaphors of female dress to talk about modern corruptions in society, and he is especially adamant that the gender divisions not be blurred. Men who lose their civil rights, he says, "are but women." For him, the fate of Anne Hutchinson is a warning to all women who overstep the boundaries of their female roles, and he advises: "Let men look to't, least women wear the Spurs." For Ward, religious tolerance – with its blurring of strict theoretical distinctions – was implicated in the tolerance of powerful women. Women who sought to expand their limited, gender-defined roles were sinners, seeking to find salvation on their own terms. To Ward, the social, religious, and political upheavals of midcentury England seemed to threaten even these most fundamental aspects of human nature and God's design.

Beginning with the confidence of Cotton's *God's Promise* and Winthrop's "Model of Christian Charity" in 1630, the Puritans rapidly found that their theological doctrines and church and civil policies were so complicated and unclear that the very sincerity and piety of believers generated such divisions and contentions that the dream of a loving fellowship soon proved unrealizable. By 1645, they had produced a substantial body of literature, but much of it is inspired by disagreement, strife, and defensiveness. Ministers debated, social idealists pleaded, juries hounded, and satirists carped. Only later would Puritan historians, such as Edward Johnson in 1654 and Cotton Mather at the turn of the century, reconstruct these first years in ways that would "spiritualize" (later readers would say romanticize) the past and transform defeat into a myth, imagining enduring and even harmonious victory. The power of language would triumph, yet again, over the "facts" of experience.

3

PERSONAL NARRATIVE AND HISTORY

A S MANY HISTORIANS ADMIT, a record of past events is the hybrid product of facts and interpretation. The Puritans, convinced of the flawed and fallen nature of humanity, distrusted all accounts of the past except those of the Bible. At the same time, they produced a host of personal narratives of individual lives and histories of the corporate New England enterprise because they believed that, even in its corrupted state, human reason is one of God's primary vehicles for communicating His lessons to humanity. A record of God's dealings with His people could be spiritually beneficial. Funeral sermons rehearsed the lives of deceased saints, and election sermons recounted the spiritual record of the community. Biographies, autobiographies, diaries, and conversion narratives recorded the saint's fulfillment of a single destiny, but histories charted the progress of God's larger design.

Although the specific focus of a particular text might be on the one or the many, Puritan authors and audiences believed that the lives of the individual and of the group were inseparable. The church represented the body of Christ, with every member such an integral part that if one person were in distress the entire body writhed. Conversely, if the spiritual community were troubled, each individual was afflicted. The spiritual journey of a single soul became a community drama that served as a paradigm for the plight of the congregation just as the well-being of the congregation was reflected in each member. With the prescribed interdependence of communal and personal history, good times would generate not only personal assurance but also the self-righteous aggression of the group against enemies and outsiders. During sunnier days in Winthrop's enclosed garden, the harmony of the saints emboldened every heart, and the fellowship of the Lord celebrated the glory of every saint. But troubled times produced paralyzing, even suicidal, doubts for the individual and communal self-castigation; during the darkest days, the people would search the depths of their souls for the causes of God's anger and scrutinize the behavior of each other for signs of spiritual offenses. Once even a single sinner or hypocrite entered the body of saints, that individual was as dangerous as a witch or an Anne Hutchinson and capable of spreading a fatal infection among them. Depending upon events and perspectives, the bond between the self and society could be empowering or it could be debilitating and destructive. The community could band together to purge the one or the few, as at Salem in 1692, or an individual like Roger Williams could excoriate the body. Given the basic corporal algorithm, imagery of sickness and death proliferated in Puritan writing.

With the conversion experience established as the essence of Puritan religious life, the spiritual relation became a basic rite of passage and verbal model that provided the psychological pattern for other genres. The psychomachy of the soul's struggle against the body, sin, and Satan and of its journey toward grace and salvation was a fundamental scenario repeated in diaries and autobiographies as well as in histories, where the subject is the whole community's trauma. Because it was one of the earliest and most powerful personal narratives, the autobiography of Thomas Shepard I (1604–49) served as an important model for the many that followed.

Shepard was born in Northampton, England, and attended Emmanuel College, where he was ordained in 1627. Silenced by Bishop Laud in 1630, he emigrated to Massachusetts Bay in 1635, where he was chosen pastor at New Town (later Cambridge). In the early 1640s, he began to publish treatises on the conversion process, notably *The Sincere Convert* (1640), and he started keeping a personal journal of his own spiritual experience, which was published much later, in 1747, under the title of *Three Valuable Pieces . . . A Private Diary* and again in Edinburgh as *Meditations and Spiritual Experiences of Mr. Thomas Shepard* (1749). In the late 1640s, he composed a retrospective account of his life in the autobiographical form, and this was published in 1832 in Boston as *The Autobiography of Thomas Shepard.*

Shepard seems to have begun his journal at the point in New England Puritan history when pressures upon the communities were moving ministers to require public tests for church membership. These tests consisted of a recounting of the details of a person's struggles toward salvation through the power of divine grace. Although Shepard had been a severe critic of Anne Hutchinson, she believed he was one of the few ministers who preached a covenant of grace. But Shepard's anger at Hutchinson, like Cotton's withdrawal of support for her, indicates the clergy's realization, perhaps unconscious, that a subtle compromise with the doctrine of grace had to be achieved to preserve ecclesiastical order and that the doctrine of preparationism was essential. In his journal Shepard charted his own preparation in order to instruct others in discovering the signs of grace. The agonizing paradox that logically one can do nothing to be saved and yet emotionally one feels the need to act is at the core of Shepard's journal. Charting the alternations between moments of ecstasy and periods of doubt, the journal demonstrates a pattern of psychological self-manipulation and emotional swings that came to characterize the conversion narrative as a genre.

Shepard's early life had been especially unsettled. When he was three, his mother died of the plague; then he lived for a time with his grandparents, who neglected him, and later with an uncle. When his father remarried, Shepard moved back home, but he said of his stepmother that she seemed "not to love me but incensed my father often against me." When he was ten, his father died in spite of Shepard's desperate prayers: "I did pray very strongly and heartily for the life of my father and made some covenant, if God would do it, to serve him [God] the better as knowing I would be left alone if he was gone. Yet the Lord took him away by death, and so I was left father less and mother less." Adding to his trials was a harsh schoolmaster whom Shepard described as being so cruel he often wished himself in "any condition to keep hogs or beasts rather than to go to school and learn." At his darkest childhood hour, however, he was saved by his older brother, John, who took him in, ensured his education, and became "both father and mother unto me." Under a new schoolmaster, he gained confidence: "it so fell out by God's good providence that this man stirred up in my heart a love and desire of the honor of learning, and therefore I told my friends I would be a scholar."

In the context of this background of emotional alternations between chaos and calm, Shepard was prepared psychologically to understand the nature of the conversion process. At college, he began to view his nature as sinful and longed to repent, but he continued his "lust and pride and gaming and bowling and drinking." The day came, however, when "[I] drank so much one day that I was dead drunk . . . and awakened late on that Sabbath and sick with my beastly carriage." Fleeing into the fields to meditate upon his condition, he experienced the presence of Christ, who did not "justly . . . cut me off in the midst of my sin [by death]" but who "did meet me with much sadness of heart and troubled my soul for this and my other sins." After this revelation, Shepard began "daily meditation about the evil of sin and my own ways" and was thereby prepared to attend to the words of John Preston's sermons in a new way: "the Lord so bored my ears that I understood what he spake and the secrets of my soul were laid upon before me . . . all the turnings and deceipts of my heart . . . my hypocrisy and self and secret sins." After the conversion experience, he resolved to become a minister, but as his narrative confirms, he never stopped doubting and searching his heart. At one point "for three quarters of a year," he was so tormented that he "had some strong temptations to run my head against walls and brain and kill myself," until finally "the Lord dropped this meditation into me: Be not discouraged therefore because thou are so vile, but make this double use of it:

(1) loathe thyself the more; (2) feel a greater need and put a greater price upon Jesus Christ."

Once he was in New England and undertook his pastorship, Shepard's external life became more settled as duties consumed much of his personal apprehension and anguish. But sainthood remained for him a process rather than a static experience, and throughout his life he continued to have what he called "renewed conversions" upon rediscovering his vile nature. The nature of God's narrative plan for the single soul and for His people was to "show his Power by the much ado of our weakness" so that "the more weak I, the more fit to be used." As Shepard observed, "When I was most empty, then by faith I was most full."

In Shepard's public works, such as *The Sound Believer. Or, a Treatise of Evangelical Conversion* (1645), he established for the colony the process by which the elect should expect to come to saving grace. Shepard preached that it is far better for a soul to face its misery now than to "perish everlastingly," and he insisted that human will plays a role in the process: "every man that perishes is his own Butcher." By the time that the Cambridge Platform was adopted in 1648, a relation of the conversion experience before the entire congregation was required of all who would join a congregational church, and ministers and church members knew exactly what they should hear from the converted. A precisely coded language and narrative text became requisite for salvation, as well as for the social and political benefits of church membership.

One remarkable document in this respect is *The Diary* (published in 1965) of the eminent minister and poet Michael Wigglesworth (1631–1705) (for Wigglesworth's poetry see Chapter 4). Born in Yorkshire, England, in 1631, Wigglesworth moved with his parents to New England in 1638 and settled in New Haven. A brilliant student, he studied with the famous schoolmaster Ezekiel Cheever and was writing compositions in Latin by the age of nine. After an interruption in his education resulting from his father's five-year illness, he went on to Harvard, where he studied medicine as well as theology, finished first in his class, obtained an A.B. and an A.M., and remained as a tutor until 1654. In 1655 he married his cousin Mary Reyner, and in 1656 he was ordained as the minister of the church at Malden. Then he entered a long period of painful and mysterious disease that so weakened him that he could not perform his clerical duties. In 1659, when Mary died, Wigglesworth's debilitation deepened. He declined the presidency of Harvard because he did not think his "bodily health and strength competent to undertake . . . such a weighty work." According to Cotton Mather, Wigglesworth turned to writing poetry because it was the only way that he could continue to serve the church and community: "that he might yet more

Faithfully set himself to Do Good, when he could not *Preach* he *Wrote* several Composures, as are for Truth's dressed up in a *Plain Meter.*"

In 1686, however, Wigglesworth experienced a remarkable rejuvenation. "It pleased God," wrote Cotton Mather, "wondrously to restore His *Faithful Servant.* He that had been for nearly Twenty years almost *Buried Alive,* comes abroad again." Wigglesworth resumed his duties in Malden, but when he shocked the community by marrying his housekeeper, Martha Mudge, who was twenty-five years younger than he and not a member of the church, his congregation reduced his salary. But, as the marriage endured and produced six children, Wigglesworth ultimately regained the respect of his congregation and of the broader Puritan community. Wigglesworth was married a third time, following Martha's death, to Sybil Avery in 1691, when he was sixty.

Wigglesworth's *Diary* for the years 1653 and 1657 documents his youthful fears of damnation brought on by sexual desire, masturbation, and nocturnal emissions and his guilt feelings over his anger toward his father, especially about his inability to feel sorrow over his father's death. Wigglesworth's *Diary* is filled with the kind of statements that have given the Puritans a reputation for obsessive gloom: "Innumerable evils compass me about, and prevail against me, wherefor I am afraid and ashamed and unable to see God still loving me with an everlasting love. I find so much of my spirit go out unto the creature, unto mirth, that there is little savour of God left in my soul." His accounts of his interactions with his students suggest that "mirth" was probably fairly rare in Wigglesworth's life: "I set myself this day to wrestle with the Lord for myself and then for my pupils . . . but still I see the Lord shutting out my prayers . . . for he whom in special I prayed for, I heard in the forenoon with ill company playing musick, though I had solemnly warned him but yesterday of letting his spirit go after pleasures." The lamentations of Puritan diaries sometimes appear forced and formulaic, but the specificity of Wigglesworth's descriptions gives convincing evidence of mental anguish.

The *Autobiography of Increase Mather* (1962) is more dispassionate than the Wigglesworth *Diary,* but it too makes clear that even those who had the strongest reasons to expect sanctification endured years of severe doubt before conversion and then experienced periodic uncertainty throughout life. Often called the "foremost American Puritan," Increase was the son of the first-generation minister Richard Mather. He graduated from Harvard in 1656, completed a master's degree at Trinity College, Dublin, married the daughter of John Cotton, and was pastor of Old North Church, Boston, for almost sixty years. A prolific author, he published over a hundred works, including histories, sermons, tracts, treatises, and a biography of his father. The most eminent minister in New England from about 1670 to the early 1700s,

Mather socialized with the highest government officials and the wealthiest merchants. From 1685 to 1701, he served as president of Harvard, which he guided through severe legal and financial crises. In 1688, he was chosen for a mission to England to entreat James II to restore the charter, and when William and Mary became the new sovereigns in 1689, Mather negotiated a new charter with them. Although he probably obtained as much for Massachusetts as was possible at the time, some criticized him for yielding too much and for using his political position to help his friends, especially his nominee for governor, Sir William Phips. After Phips's mediocre administration, Mather became embroiled in nasty political battles and suffered a decline of influence from about 1700 until his death in 1723.

Over the course of his life, Mather kept a diary, but in 1685 he decided to compose a formal autobiography from his many diary volumes. Writing for his children with no intention of publishing, he declared his purpose was to show them how his faith had been sustained through trials and doubts. One of the most interesting features of this work is the way in which the idea of God's covenant with an individual developed, at least in Mather's mind, into a two-sided agreement in which God had certain obligations. At a low point in his youth, when he was awaiting both his spiritual calling to grace and his temporal calling to the ministry, he wrote that "the Lord broke in upon my conscience with very terrible convictions and awakenings. . . . I was in extremity of anguish and horror in my soul." After reading the scriptures in search of help, Mather actually dared to threaten God:

I that day begged of God, that He would give me leave to plead with Him, (and with Tears and meltings of heart I did plead with Him) that if He should not answer me graciously, others after my decease, that should see the papers which I had written which I had kept as remembrances of my walking before God would be discouraged. For they would say "Here was one that prayed for bodily and spiritual Healing, yea and believed for it also, and yet he perished in his affliction without that Healing."

Given Mather's subsequent career, it is evident that God recognized the power of this argument and bestowed the needed grace. What is perhaps most surprising about this passage is that the forty-six-year-old pastor chose to present his children with this example of his youthful brashness.

To a great degree, Puritan diaries and autobiographies tend to be formulaic, for the individual was almost always attempting to relate each personal experience to an accepted teleology: as in John Bunyan's *Grace Abounding to the Chief of Sinners* (1666), the life of the saint follows an expected course to salvation. Many extant spiritual narrations, diaries, and autobiographies follow the paradigm rather closely. The experiences of conversion, doubt, and spiritual growth were forced to conform to narrative archetypes, gaining their authority from earlier linguistic models. Individual personality was less important than God's general ways of dealing with humanity. Given the autobiographers' inclination to record common human experiences, the unique and surprising acts of divine Providence in particular lives have special significance and give Puritan autobiographies, such as Increase Mather's, their drama. Over the course of the seventeenth century, the diaries became less formulaic so that the diaries of Cotton Mather and Samuel Sewall, for example, are more secular and express more private and individual concerns.

The *Diary of Cotton Mather for the Years 1681–1708* (published in 1911–12) and *The Diary of Cotton Mather, D.D., F.R.S. for the Year 1712* (published in 1971) show a sophisticated blending of the ritualistic and the mundane. Cotton Mather (1663–1728) was the grandson of patriarchs Richard Mather and John Cotton and the son of Increase Mather. He was educated at Harvard and assumed a post as his father's assistant in the Second Church of Boston, where he served under his father except for the five years after Increase's death in 1723 (for Cotton Mather's life, see Chapter 5). Mather's diaries are filled with what had become by the 1680s the standard laments over physical temptations and spiritual weaknesses, although they appear to have been quite genuine for him. He explains how he fights sexual temptations by fasting until he is so weak that the desire fades, and he expresses his distress over his stammering speech, which disturbed Increase and jeopardized his expected career in the pulpit. Mather also records daily observations of fashion, politics, finances, and such vanities as his longings to become a member of the Royal Society, which he did, and the president of Harvard, which he did not. The most memorable and poignant sections of Mather's diaries are those in which he reports bitter personal tragedies, such as the deaths of his closest brother, Nathaniel, and of two wives and several children. Particularly affecting are the passages on the madness of his third wife, which shocked and bewildered him, and the profligacy and finally the disappearance at sea of his favorite but rebellious son, "Creasy" (Increase II), whom he had hoped would follow him into the ministry.

Although not as famous as the frequently anthologized *Diary of Samuel Seawall* (see Chapter 5), Mather's diaries exemplify more lucidly the ways in which the convictions and passions of late Puritanism shaped a life and a writing style. With each tragedy, Mather was more determined not to abandon his faith in the divinely ordained role that he and his people had in the world. The more he suffered, the more energy he threw into his writing and his pastoral work. Every event was a sign, every adversity could be turned to good, every seeming indication of New England's demise could contain a sign that Christ was preparing His Second Coming to be in this American

New Jerusalem, where He would rule for a thousand years in glory. If Mather's grandfathers had not fully conceived of their venture in such providential terms, there is no question that Mather interpreted the Puritan experiment as a sacred mission and that he found Old Testament types being fulfilled in much of New England's history.

The move from diary and autobiography to biography is a significant step toward Puritan artistic consciousness and the creation of distinctive literary styles. As a genre, the biography occupies a middle territory between the study of the inner life of the individual recorded in personal narratives and the examination of communal progress that is the subject of Puritan history. On the surface, the purpose of biography was not very different from that of the funeral sermon – to present a holy model of one who had practiced *imitatio Christi*. As in John Bunyan's *A Pilgrim's Progress*, the life of the saint should follow the course of piety of a *figural* Christian. In Puritan biography, the narrative of the model saint also became a story of the community of saints so that inner and outer worlds were linked in the exemplary life.

Within that framework, Puritan biographers did manage to craft particular narratives that are varied in detail and remain engaging. One feature that was unique to the Puritan biographies of the first-generation saints was the unusual inclusion of a substantial discussion of why they left England. The earliest known American Puritan biography to be printed is John Norton's *Abel Being Dead Yet Speaketh* (1658) on the life of John Cotton. In his explanation of Cotton's coming to America, Norton set a pattern for later biographies by establishing several parallels between Cotton's experiences and those in the Bible: "No sooner had Christ received his mission into his public ministry, but he is led into the wilderness to be tempted by the Devil." Old Testament types foreshadow that God "transplants many of his Faithful servants into this vast Wilderness [and] giveth *Moses* the pattern of the Tabernacle in the Wilderness. *Ezekiel* seeth the forms of the House in exile. *John* receivth his Revelation in *Patmos*." Through such typologizing, England becomes Egypt, the Atlantic the Red Sea, and New England a New Zion. Despite the heavy typology and hagiography, Norton does manage to convey some glimpse of Cotton's personality by drawing upon his letters and diaries and upon anecdotes conveyed to Norton by Cotton's wife.

Twelve years after Norton's life of Cotton was published, Increase Mather advanced the form of Puritan biography with his book on his own father, *The Life and Death of That Reverend Man of God, Mr. Richard Mather* (1670). Increase not only compares Richard to the Old Testament patriarchs but praises him as one who embodied Puritan ideals that Increase feared would never be so fully represented again. Although he remains anonymous as biographer, he does sign the dedication letter that precedes the text. There he elaborates upon his father's virtues and takes the opportunity to suggest how far short Richard's congregation falls in their attempts to imitate their pastor's holiness: "Remember his Farewell Exhortation, which is now in many of your Houses, and Oh that it were in also your Hearts."

Following the formula established by Norton in the Cotton biography, Increase includes a long document by Richard in which he elaborates his reasons for leaving England. At the center of Richard's arguments are the need for a father to be able to govern his own family as he wishes and for a minister to guide his own congregation, neither of which were permitted in England. England's corruption threatened family order as well as proper religious worship. It is significant, even ironic, that Richard places such emphasis upon family order given Increase's famous defiance of his father's authority in the 1660s over church membership rules.

This family dispute was part of a generational one that gave rise to the Half-Way Covenant, as it was derisively called by its opponents. The modification in membership rules was instituted by the Boston Synod of 1662 to counter declining conversions among the children and grandchildren of the original saints. The new membership provision allowed that "if a person born and baptized in the church did not receive faith he could still continue his membership and have his own children baptized, by leading a life free from scandal, by learning and professing the doctrines of Christianity, and by making a voluntary submission to God and His church." The communion table was still reserved for full members, but the children of unregenerate parents (mostly grandchildren of the first settlers) could be baptized, and both these children and their parents could attend services. Those who favored this provision, like Richard Mather, assumed that it was very likely that the children and grandchildren of the founders would eventually receive grace and that the best environment for preparing their hearts was inside the fellowship of the church. Opponents, like Increase, perceived this accommodation to involve a serious break with the original rules and insisted that the unregenerate, regardless of family credentials, should not be worshipping among the elect. So opposed were the members of Richard's own parish at Dorchester to the change that they rejected it during Richard's lifetime in spite of his advocacy. After his death, they recanted.

Both Increase and his brother Eleazar opposed the Half-Way Covenant and opted for keeping the churches pure by granting baptism only to the children of full church members. Mather was still against it when he wrote the biography. In the text, he uses Richard's deathbed prayer as a rhetorical device for urging the new generation to avoid the need for new membership rules by finding the grace in their souls and experiencing conversion. Increase recalls his father's words: "A special thing which I would recommend to you, is Care concerning the Rising Generation in this Country, that they be under the Government of Christ in his Church; and that when grown up and qualified, they have Baptism for their Children." Increase left his position on membership unstated in the biography, employing instead a strategy of using the example of Richard's life to inspire his readers to discover the grace and salvation that would make the issue irrelevant.

However, soon after he composed the biography, Increase recognized the wisdom of his father's compromise, and he altered his position. Thus, it appears the act of writing the biography served several purposes for Increase: it helped him to clarify for himself and his readers the role of the later generations in relation to the founders, it softened his heart toward those of his own generation who lacked the spiritual confidence that had enabled him to confront the Lord, and it released some of the guilt he felt over his division with his father. The central theme of the work is that each successive generation must carry on the founders' mission by reviving the original zeal. Richard Mather's plea for spiritual continuity joins with that of every other first-generation minister in calling for all the Puritan progeny to take up the challenge of the sacred mission.

Continuing the family tradition fifty-four years later, Cotton Mather published a biography of Increase, *Parentator* (1724). Whereas Increase's biography of Richard appeared at the beginning of the watershed decade of the 1670s and is a model of the genre, Cotton's work illustrates the secularization that occurred during the five decades after Richard's death. Although he followed the general guidelines of Puritan hagiography, Cotton filled his text (several times longer than his father's work) with copious details of daily life. It is ironic that Cotton's biography of Increase stands as blatant testimony to the failure of Increase's generation to meet the challenge that Richard and the collective fathers had foreseen.

In *Parentator,* Cotton takes a defensive and self-centered posture, and his envy of his father, who had taken the reins of leadership when Puritanism was still powerful in New England, is barely masked. In Cotton's view, *Parentator* was a minor but necessary "appendix," as he called it, to his *Magnalia Christi Americana* (1702), in which he had celebrated the lives of the founders and of several of Increase's contemporaries who had already died (see Chapter 5). Cotton praises Increase's efforts but laments the decline of the spirit that Increase proved unable to prevent. Unlike Increase's celebratory narrative of Richard's life, Cotton's *Parentator,* for all of Cotton's protests to the contrary, is implicitly a study of early success and ultimate failure.

The first formal history of Puritan New England began in 1630 when William Bradford (1663–1752) began composing the manuscript that he called *Of Plimoth Plantation,* which would not be published until 1856, when it was given the title *History of Plymouth Plantation*. Bradford was born in Austerfield, England, in 1590, into the family of fairly comfortable yeoman parents. The deaths of his parents during his early years resulted in frequent moves from one relative to another. These disturbing events and a long illness led him as a boy to much private reading of the Bible and of John Foxe's *Book of Martyrs,* which prepared him for the message of the nonconformist minister Richard Clyfton, whose church in neighboring Scrooby he joined. Influenced by other congregationalists like William Brewster and later the separatist John Robinson, Bradford moved with the church in 1608 to Amsterdam and then Leyden. There he married Dorothy May, with whom he had a son, John. Dorothy and John accompanied William to Plymouth in 1620, but Dorothy drowned off Cape Cod a few days after the landing and before the passengers had disembarked. Because Bradford fails to mention this event in his history, some have speculated that the shock of the sight of the bleak winter coastline of New England drove her to suicide. Bradford soon married Alice Carpenter Southworth and had three other children: William, Mercy, and Joseph.

In his first year of writing the history, Bradford produced about one-fourth of the final work, covering the years of preparation and departure for America. During the next fifteen years, he appears to have kept a journal or diary from which he then composed a second book in 1646 covering the years between 1630 and 1646. The first book was copied into the Plymouth church records and was thereby preserved, but the second book was lost after the American Revolution and was not discovered again until 1856, when the entire work was published for the first time. Since then, it has come to be recognized not only as an important historical source but as one of the major literary texts of early New England literature. Bradford's plain-style eloquence, his vivid descriptions, his sensitivity to human nature, and the structuring of his material reflect his acute literary sensibility.

Bradford was familiar with the ancient historians such as Herodotus, Thucydides, and Tacitus, but the more important models for his Puritan conceptions of history were the two branches of historiography that emerged in the Middle Ages: the universal history inspired by Augustine's *City of God* and the chronicle. In universal history, the historian tried to discern some larger pattern of God's plan in the recorded events; the chronicle tended to be a straightforward account of details. During the Crusades, biography was blended with history to add human drama and enable the writer to group seemingly unrelated events around a life. The Puritan historians inherited these available models and added to them what they called a "spiritualized," or providential, dimension – that is, they sought to discover in past events possible divine meanings, just as a minister tried to discern the hidden truths of biblical passages. Some later Puritan historians such as Edward Johnson and Cotton Mather went further and compared current events directly with Old and New Testament types, discovering parallels that elucidated how the scriptures were being fulfilled daily.

Because Bradford did not often make such overt comparisons, discussions of his history turn upon the question of how consciously he reshaped events, selected details, and colored his textual construction to bring it subtly into alignment with implicit providential or typological patterns others would interpret. In the first book of Bradford's text, God leads his people out of a corrupt land into a new one and shields them against trials and hardships until they prosper and multiply. Though more fragmented, the chronicle of the second book enforces the biblical pattern with the depiction of the deaths of the first-generation patriarchs, the spread of sin, and the weakening of the church. No doubt Bradford was aware that his account parallels the experiences of the ancient Hebrews. From another perspective, the entire work appears structured upon alternations between success and failure. This cyclical dimension undercuts the more apocalyptic ending by suggesting that, with God's help, His chosen may go forward again.

Although Bradford was a pious believer in divine Providence and trusted in God's protection, he was also a pragmatic leader. His repeated reelection to the governorship of Plymouth demonstrates the faith others had in his good sense, and some scholars have read the two parts of his history in relation to his practical nature. The differences in the tone and structure from the first book of the history to the second, written sixteen years later, may be the result of the very different political contexts for each writing. With the arrival of the much larger Massachusetts Bay Colony in 1630, the Plymouth Colony faced one of the greatest challenges to its existence. Bradford knew that the invading thousands of nonseparatists might swallow up, persecute, or even expel the separationists. The subsequent intolerance of the Massachusetts Bay theocracy toward the views of Roger Williams and Anne Hutchinson would demonstrate that Bradford was right to be wary. Bradford's choice of this moment to begin to record Plymouth's history surely sprang, to some degree, from the clear geographical and political threat that the Winthrop colony represented. His strong emphasis upon the Pilgrims' rationale for their emigration, the foundations of their beliefs, and the role of Providence in their survival and success functions as both a self-definition of the colony and a defense against outside criticism. Once time had assured the Bradford colony of its autonomy, he could look back upon the years following 1630 differently. As he took up his pen again in 1645, his text did not need typology to support his argument justifying the Plymouth way; rather, it could be a practical man's sober accounting of the trials, pressures, and even fractures the colony had experienced. After all, with all of Boston's troubles over those years, Bradford's candid account of Plymouth's trials was no proof that Plymouth was less divinely favored.

Aboard the *Arbella,* John Winthrop began the journal that would eventually become *The History of New England from 1630 to 1649,* first published in this form in 1825–6. An earlier version, entitled *A Journal of the Transactions and Occurrences in the Settlement of Massachusetts and the Other New England Colonies from the Year 1630 to 1644,* was published in 1790. Unlike Bradford, Winthrop never attempted to turn his journal into a true history, but over the years his entries became longer and richer in their depiction of characters and circumstances, and his summaries of his own views and feelings became more revealing so that the final product is both a diary and a chronicle. Winthrop himself called his work a history; although giving no name to the first volume, he called the other two *A Continuation of the History of New England.* A striking difference between Winthrop's and Bradford's chronicles is that Bradford kept himself very much out of the account, even referring to himself in the third person, whereas Winthrop is a fully active character. Indeed, at times it seems that Winthrop's principal desire in the journal is to justify, either to himself or to posterity, his decisions and actions, especially those against his opponents.

Although the status of Winthrop's history as a literary work has never been fully settled, literary scholars are still drawn to it because of the author's personality, which alone inscribes the work with a narrative unity, and because of the unique perspective it provides on critical events. Deeply religious, Winthrop was always cognizant of the divine presence in every aspect of the New England experiment: "It is useful to observe as we go along, such especial providences of God as were manifested for the good of these plantations." Particularly suggestive are those passages in which he reflects upon the ways that the very success of the colony brought on new problems and made the people harder for him and the ministers to control: "As people increased, so sin abounded and especially the sin of uncleanness, and still the providence of God found them out." Though Winthrop sometimes feared that the experiment was destined to fail, he never doubted that the outcome would ultimately fulfill God's plan.

Although Winthrop never found a solution to this problem of the growing population and the accompanying moral pollution, he did have occasion several times during his years as governor to sharpen the definitions and applications of New England federal theology. One of the most famous passages in his *Journal* was recorded on July 3, 1645, after he had been acquitted of the charge of exceeding his authority in office. In response to this challenge, he delivered to the General Court what has come to be called his "Little Speech on Liberty," which he later recorded in the *Journal*. With a combination of general humility and total self-assurance about specifics, Winthrop provided a concise summary of the structure of authority in a theocracy. Interestingly, his use of the analogy of marriage and the submission of the wife to her husband to illustrate the nature of civil authority casts as much light on the Puritan view of gender relations as it does on political order:

The great questions that have troubled the country are about the authority of the magistrates and the liberty of the people. It is yourselves who have called us to this office, and being called by you, we have our authority from God. For the other point concerning liberty, I observe a great mistake in the country about that. There is a two-fold liberty, natural (I mean as our nature is now corrupt) and civil or federal. The first is common to man with wild beasts and other creatures. . . . It is a liberty to evil as well as to good. This liberty is incompatible and inconsistent with authority. . . . This is that great enemy of truth and peace, that wild beast which all the ordinances of God are bent against. . . . The other kind of liberty I call civil or federal, it may also be termed moral. . . . This liberty is the proper end and object of authority. . . . This liberty is maintained and exercised in a way of subjection to authority. . . . The woman's own choice makes such a man her husband; yet being so chosen, he is her lord, and she is to be subject to him, yet in a way of liberty, not of bondage; and a true wife accounts her subjection her honor and freedom, and would not think her condition safe and free, but in her subjection to her husband's authority. Such is the liberty of the church under the authority of Christ, her king and husband. . . . Even so it will be between you and your magistrates.

Given Winthrop's interpretation here, it is not surprising that he found the rebellion of Anne Hutchinson to be so unnatural. Moreover, it demonstrates the way in which Puritan gender relations were ultimately prefigured by the permanence of Puritan typology.

Because neither Bradford's nor Winthrop's histories were published during the seventeenth century, three other printed works provided several generations with the only coherent record of the English settlement of New England. The first, entitled *Mourt's Relation* (1622), was composed by a G. Mourt, which may have been a pseudonym for a person still unknown or a misprint for George Morton, who was instrumental in the work's publication and a member of one of the Leyden groups of separatists who later landed at Plymouth. Another opinion is that at least part of the work was that of Edward Winslow, with substantial contributions (perhaps two-thirds) by William Bradford, but the real identity of the author remains a mystery. Composed in the form of a history, the text is really a tract to encourage emigration, and its publication in England in 1622 was directed to prospective colonists seeking information about Plymouth. Unlike the promotional tracts of John Smith and of the Virginia colonies, *Mourt's Relation* provides a straightforward, uninflated, and undisguised account of the realities of life in New England.

Another published account of the early years of the Plymouth Colony was Nathaniel Morton's (1613–85) *New England's Memorial* (1669). Morton was one of the early settlers who arrived from Leyden on the ship *Anne* in 1623. He lived for a time in the home of William Bradford and served as his secretary before he went on to be the keeper of records for the colony from 1647 to 1685. He became one of the wealthiest men in Plymouth and drafted most of the town laws. In 1669, Morton published his history, which remained the major account of the colony's settlement until Bradford's history was discovered in the nineteenth century. In the early 1670s, Morton worked on a more complete history, which was destroyed in a fire in 1676. He then wrote another version, which was published in 1680. Morton's history is distinct from *Mourt's Relation* in being a much fuller account imbued with strongly didactic and providential elements. Even after the discovery of Bradford's history, Morton's work remains critically valuable, for it supplies certain details missing from Bradford, such as a list of the signers of the Mayflower Compact and the name of the ship that departed with the *Mayflower* but had to turn back – the *Speedwell*.

A third history published in the century is the highly controversial *A History of New England* (1654) of Edward Johnson (1598–1672). Johnson was born in England, the son of a parish clerk, and he managed to acquire land in Canterbury and to rise in the military to the rank of captain. In 1630, he visited New England, perhaps on the *Arbella* with Winthrop, and he was admitted as a freeman in 1631 but chose to return to England. In 1636, he and his wife, the former Susan Munnter, and their seven children moved to Boston, but later they settled on land he purchased in nearby Charlestown. In 1640, he was invited to participate in the building of a new community at Woburn, where he remained active in community affairs for the rest of his life, holding a variety of positions such as selectman and militia captain. Neither a clergyman nor university trained, Johnson was an unusual Puritan author.

Running to nearly three hundred pages in modern printings, Johnson's *History* stands out as the most complete and coherent report on the first twenty-five years of the colony before Cotton Mather's monumental *Magnalia Christi Americana* of 1702. Johnson considered his title to be *The Wonder-Working Providence of Sion's Saviour in New England,* which was used in the running heads, repeated in the text, and appeared on the title page of subsequent editions. Evidence suggests that he began composing the work in 1649 and that he completed it in 1651. Unified in style, tone, and voice, it is divided into three books, each of which covers a seven-year period: 1630–7,

1637–44, and 1644–51. In a lively and energetic style, Johnson's brisk narration and colorful personality convey his own enthusiasm for the Puritan experiment and his profound religious convictions. Johnson's writing and opinions have not been received with unmixed praise, however, for in his own time, and still today, some have found his work crude, strained, and unnecessarily biased. His swagger and occasional bombast sound in stark contrast to the reserve of Bradford and the subtlety of Winthrop. Puritan literary scholarship of the last twenty-five years has considered Johnson's most important contribution to be his liberal use of biblical typology to support his arguments and vision. From his perspective, New England was the New Zion, and its people's progress was the fulfillment of the divine will. Evidently, by the time Johnson was composing his work in the late 1640s, the myths and images of a divine mission were firmly enough established in the Puritan imagination that Johnson accepted them unquestioned. Guided by his prophetic sense of sacred history, Johnson gave his work an epic grandeur: the Puritans are imagined as a mighty army commissioned by Christ to battle the Antichrist and prepare a place for Christ's triumphant return to the world in New England. Forecasting the spirit of independence that would eventually inspire the American Revolution, Johnson's rhetoric explored a paradigm that would be repeated by many American presidents to come: "Here the Reader is desired to take notice of the wonderful providence of the most high God toward these his new-planted Churches, such as were never heard of . . . that in ten or twelve years there should be such wonderful alteration, a Nation born in a day, a Commonwealth orderly brought forth from a few fugitives."

In addition to articulating the Puritan vision of America, the work provides insights into more mundane attitudes of the Puritans that his "common-man" viewpoint reveals. His opinions on relations with the Indians are particularly interesting. Although he frequently expresses compassion for the Native Americans, Johnson also reiterates the accepted Puritan view, found in Winthrop, that Christ had prepared the way for His chosen by divinely causing the smallpox epidemic that devastated several tribes and weakened those potential warriors who did survive. Similarly, his account of the Pequot War describes, with sadness, the brutal killing of hundreds of native women and children, while also expressing a self-righteous pride in exercising the will of the Lord.

Correspondingly, those passages of the *History* that deal with the antinomian crisis expose a typical Puritan male's attitude toward Anne Hutchinson as a woman. An orthodox supporter of the clergy and magistrates, Johnson had deep concerns about any movements or individuals that threatened order and discipline in the colony. He had no sympathy for Hutchinson, and his descriptions of her reflect his impatience with all "erronists." For him, it made no sense for people to risk all, to transport their families across an ocean to practice their faith, and then to be caught up in dissension: "stopped and startled in their course by a kennel of devouring wolves" like those from which they fled. Of Hutchinson herself, whose name he never mentions, he says that

the weaker Sex prevailed so far that they set up a Priest of their own Profession and Sex, which was much thronged after, abominably wresting the Scriptures to their own destruction: this Master-piece of Women's wit, drew many Disciples after her . . . being much backed with the Sorcery of a second, who had much converse with the Devil. . . . This woman was wonted to give drinks to other Women to cause them to conceive . . . but sure there were Monsters born not long after.

These passages of misogynistic stereotyping of Hutchinson and her support-ers are surrounded by others that reveal the social context in which to better understand how a man like Johnson had come to such positions. More candid than the guarded expressions of the elite, Johnson's persona provides insights into the attitudes of the average, devout, but untrained layman. Besides providing a useful overview of events in early New England, Johnson's work is a prime example of spiritualized, typologized history. Johnson's *History* is the most self-consciously political history in the first fifty years of the Puritan settlements, but it would not be the last. Indeed, historiography became the subject of open public controversy in the 1670s when Increase Mather and William Hubbard (c. 1621–1704) produced two quite different kinds of histories of King Philip's War.

In February 1674, Increase Mather preached one of the sermons that would establish him as the leading minister of his generation. In a jeremiad entitled *The Day of Trouble is Near,* Mather warned his congregation that the saints were soon to pay for their sins and backsliding, for a great trial was coming that would precede the Apocalypse. Quoting Matthew, he predicted, "Ye shall hear of wars and the rumors of wars." Mather was presumably thinking of troubles in Europe and how these might affect Massachusetts, but very soon his words took on unexpected prophetic resonances. Lamenting the time that men were spending on profits instead of on family prayer – "*On this world, the World* undoeth many a man" – he envisioned a "cloud of blood . . . over our heads which begins to drop upon us." In the very next year, 1675, the devastating King Philip's War erupted. Under the leadership of the resourceful Chief Sachem Metacomet of the Wampanoags, several Native-American tribes joined in what they perceived to be their last chance to stop the whites from pushing them completely out of their homelands. During the eighteen months of fighting, both sides suffered high casualties, and the economy of the English colony underwent a complete disruption. As people fled farming villages and distant communities, Boston and other coastal towns perforce overflowed with homeless refugees. Some historians believe that this social and economic calamity, more than shifts in religious attitudes or the actions of the English Crown, was primarily responsible for dismantling the Puritan social, political, and economic structures.

From the standpoint of literary history, the war also had immediate and perhaps longer-range consequences. All that Increase Mather's *Day of Trouble* had predicted and worse had happened, and Mather repeatedly referred to the fulfillment of his prophecy. The governor of Massachusetts, John Leverett, and his deputies and military commanders understood the Indians' motives and the machinations of the war in practical, political, and financial terms, but Mather placed himself in opposition to them in a struggle for the moral and spiritual leadership of the Puritan colonies in time of peril. From the outset of the war, Mather began preaching and publishing about the real causes of the war, which he perceived to be the many sins of the English, especially of young people: disobedience to parents and ministers, drunkenness, profligacy, wantonness, swearing, Sabbath-breaking, new fashions in dress and new hairstyles, sleeping during sermons, and leaving services early. For him, the best defense against the Indians would be more fast days, stricter laws governing moral behavior, and covenant renewals in the churches. New England's sins were the "provoking evils" that God was punishing with his cloud of blood.

The governor and the members of the General Court did not agree with Mather but saw no harm in increased discipline among the English during wartime. They recognized that following Mather's proposals would at least not hurt the war effort even if they did not really believe that God would destroy the Indians if the saints repented. As a result, Mather appeared to gain political power and position during the war, influence that he built upon in the following decade. The truth was, however, that Leverett and his fellow magistrates felt little sympathy for Mather's position.

As the war seemed to go against the English, the men of Leverett's generation – twenty years older than Mather – grew weary of Mather's unrelenting accusations that they were responsible for the losses because they failed to legislate behavior more strictly. When it came time to select a preacher for the election day sermon for May 1676, the deputies and magistrates selected William Hubbard, who, twenty years Mather's senior, was his known opponent and had a reputation for good sense. Hubbard was an orthodox minister who basically shared Mather's providential view of history, but he also agreed with his pragmatic-minded brethren that other, natural factors entered into events. Hubbard was a reasonable Puritan who was skeptical of Mather's exhortations and intolerance, and his sermon that day constituted a dispassionate assessment of the crisis. He found hope in the rising generation and insisted that whatever spiritual problems existed, they could be rooted out with neither "civil nor ecclesiastic censures." Arguing that God deals with His people as individuals rather than as communities, Hubbard thereby shifted the blame for the war from the group and their leaders. For Hubbard, public events such as wars were not necessarily the direct results of divine intervention, and thus he spoke of the war more in secular than in providential terms. Entitled *The Happiness of a People in the Wisdom of their Rulers*, Hubbard's sermon looks forward to an approaching peace to be achieved more expeditiously through the people's quiet obedience to their leaders than through lamentations and fast days. When the sermon was published at the expense of the General Court, Hubbard dedicated it to Governor Leverett.

Responding to the challenge, Increase Mather countered with an essay called *An Earnest Exhortation to the Inhabitants of New England*, which argues that the people should look to the scriptures and the experience of "Israel of old" for the causes of the present war. Mather quotes the original charter of the colony, which asserts conversion of the Indians rather than land acquisition as their covenanted mission. He thereby exposes one of the most sensitive areas of their communal conscience: the communal failure to put more resources into the conversion of the Indians. As a final reminder of how far the present leadership had strayed from the aims of the founders, Mather included a woodcut of the original Massachusetts seal, which shows an Indian entreating his white brothers across the ocean to "Come over and help us."

Meanwhile, it became apparent in the summer of 1676 that the English were winning the war, especially after Metacomet was killed in August. In an act of brutal vengeance, the English dismembered his body and displayed his head on a pike in Plymouth and his hands in Boston. Such horrific displays of aggression and power were to become paradigmatic expressions of triumph and superiority in racial conflicts in the American West, and later English and American texts such as Aphra Behn's *Oroonoko* (1688), Herman Melville's "Benito Cereno" (1856), and W. E. B. Du Bois's *Autobiography* (1968) describe similar horrendous acts. Within a few weeks after Metacomet's death, Mather rushed to complete his *A Brief History of the War with the Indians in New England*, a spiritualized history that used typology to impose Mather's own interpretation upon the war. Mather's history appeared that fall in Boston and London, but he had not yet heard the last on this subject from Hubbard.

During the winter of 1676–77, Hubbard finished his own history, *A Relation of the Troubles Which Have Happened in New England, By Reason of the*

Indians There (1677). Hubbard's argument is not extraordinarily different from Mather's — for him too the war resulted from God's displeasure with the Puritans — but Hubbard's handling of many particulars differ in important ways. In making such remarks as "Time and Chance hath strangely interposed to the prolonging of our Miseries," Hubbard asserts a scientific notion of natural causes and effects that is quite contrary to Mather's spiritualized account. Hubbard's tendency to use reason and to strive for a degree of objectivity in his assessment of events looked toward a new historical methodology that would characterize later works such as Thomas Prince's *A Chronological History of New England in the Form of Annals* (1736).

The General Court was so pleased with Hubbard's more rational version of the war that they commissioned him to write a "General History of New England," which he completed in 1680. This history was not published, however, until the early nineteenth century. Historians are not certain why Hubbard's history was left unpublished for so long; most speculate that Mather blocked the work directly or indirectly. During the years following the war, Mather was busy denouncing the apostasy of the younger generation and predicting further disasters, and by the early 1680s he managed to gain control of the Boston press by becoming a member of the Board of Printers' Licensers. During the 1680s, with the political autonomy of Massachusetts under attack from England, Mather censored works that he deemed dangerous to the colony's interests. He believed that it was harmful for people to think that events occurred for natural reasons rather than by God's design because such modern notions would weaken the Puritan cause. Secularism and scientific ideas of natural causes had to be quelled, for if God's plan were called into question, even Puritan property rights were at stake. Although Hubbard's manuscript was damaged and sections were lost during the eighteenth century, it became a source for several later historians, including Cotton Mather, and was finally published in 1815. The likely suppression of Hubbard's work indicates, however, that by the latter half of the seventeenth century, the writing of history had become a highly politicized activity and that the battle between the myths of the past — which some called spiritualized history and others were beginning to call fictions — and efforts at accurate documentary was a contentious one.

In the course of fifty years, the writing of Puritan history and biography had developed from the tentative jottings of Bradford and Winthrop in their personal journals and the elaborately typologized and spiritualized narratives of Edward Johnson to become the site of academic and philosophical disputes over the processes of knowing the past and present, the legitimate methods of recording and reporting events, and the authority to reveal or conceal competing interpretations of experience. For Puritans like the Mathers, flawed human reason and memory necessarily undermined the authenticity of representations of experience and ensured the indeterminacy of history. This fallen human condition required that the inspired interpreter of the past construct narratives of events, like renderings of the scriptures, in ways that would yield the greatest spiritual benefits for the progress of God's chosen toward their temporal and heavenly callings.

4

POETRY

B ECAUSE THE New England Puritans radically distrusted the senses and the imagination and were highly suspicious of all forms of art, most literary scholars either have ignored their poems or have treated them as curiosities. The advocates of Anne Bradstreet continue to construct an image of her as a cultural rebel who produced poetry in spite of the religious and social forces against her as a woman and as a Puritan. Similarly, when the poems of Edward Taylor were discovered and published in the late 1930s, many literary historians explained that his self-conscious artistry violated Puritan doctrines and that his poetic impulses suggested that he was by temperament more Catholic or Anglican than Puritan. The long disappearance of his work prompted a conclusion that he had feared exposure of his artistry and thereby enjoined his heirs to suppress his poetry. Not only, in this view, did theology prevail against Puritan art but the harsh physical conditions of New England life left no time for aesthetic indulgences. Bradstreet's productions were attributed to the leisure available to a woman of her high social standing and Taylor's to the quiet life in his wilderness parish of Westfield, Massachusetts.

To be sure, there are many valid historical reasons for assuming the term "Puritan poetry" to be an oxymoron. In England from the late sixteenth century, Puritan theologians and ministers had warned that the senses were unreliable, that appeals to the imagination were dangerous, and that the use of figurative, imagistic, or symbolic language bordered upon idolatry. Reasoning that God had inscribed all the truth that humanity needed in the scriptures, they held that plain and direct discussion of His word was the only truly legitimate and humble mode of verbal expression. The Catholics' and Anglicans' use of graven images, emphasis on pulpit eloquence, appeals to congregations through music, and ornate vestments were further proof to the Puritans that artistry invited idolatry. The Puritans' iconoclastic destruction of religious statuary during the Civil War, their closing of the theaters, the plainness of their own churches, and their official statements condemning ornate speech and dress strongly support a view that Puritan art and poetry were all but impossible. Puritan doctrines generally forbade the use of any figurative language except for religious instruction. With all of these obvious barriers to poetic art, most scholars of the Puritans assumed that practice followed theory.

Indeed, Puritan leaders and clergy made their condemnation of literary artistry quite explicit. In 1640 a group of American Puritan clergy produced their own translation of the Psalms, *The Whole Book of Psalms Faithfully Translated into English Meter* (commonly known as *The Bay Psalm Book*), to replace what they viewed as the overly poetic translation of Thomas Sternhold and John Hopkins used by the Anglicans. John Cotton provided a preface often cited as evidence of the Puritans' firm rejection of verbal artifice:

Neither let any think, that for the meter's sake we have taken liberty or poetical license to depart from the true and proper sense of David's words in the Hebrew verses, no; but it hath been one part of our religious care and faithful endeavor to keep close to the original text. . . . If therefore the verses are not always so smooth and elegant as some may desire or expect; let them consider that God's Altar needs not our polishings.

Cotton's widely quoted assertion of Puritan literalism and plainness appears to rule out further discussion of Puritan artistry.

Yet, from the 1940s through 1960s, scholars continued to discover and publish considerable numbers of Puritan poems, many of which contain provocatively striking figurative language and allusions not only to the Bible but to classical models such as Ovid, Cicero, Virgil, Horace, and Livy. Numerous poems also contain intertextual references to the work of contemporary poets, among them Spenser, Sidney, Shakespeare, Herbert, Vaughan, and Quarles. Such evidence of an apparent gap between Puritan theory and poetic practice continues to appear. For example, one discovery revealed that at Harvard in the 1640s two sons of ministers, Seaborn Cotton and Elnathan Chauncy, copied into their commonplace books various love poems of John Cleveland as well as Robert Herrick's "Gather ye rosebuds" and Francis Beaumont's "Psyche: or Loves' Mysteries." Archives have yielded a wide variety of poems: formal elegies, lyrics, hymns, ballads, dialogues, and witty anagrams, acrostics, and epigrams. Their authors were sea captains, housewives, military men, and judges, as well as the clergy themselves. The increasing recognition of Edward Taylor's literary sophistication has led some scholars to question the relationship between narrow dogma and expressed aesthetic theory and the Puritan poetic discourse itself.

One reconsideration seeks to interrogate the artistic and imaginative inclinations of Puritans themselves as people. Those who emigrated to New England had been, after all, heirs to a rich literary tradition, and many must have cherished the beauty of the language and treasured eloquent expression in spite of religious scruples. Eventually the ministers expanded their doctrines or discovered new complexities within them that allowed an increase in the number and quality of artistic expressions. By 1650, a major shift had become evident authorizing writers to use sensual imagery more freely and even to strive consciously for eloquence. A notable sign of this change was the revised translation of *The Bay Psalm Book* undertaken in 1651 by President Henry Dunster of Harvard and Richard Lyon, who said they had "a special eye" for the "sweetness of the verse." Cotton Mather later said of this edition that "it was thought that a little more of Art was to be employed upon the verses."

This movement toward verbal artistry received its strongest official endorsement from the eminent English Puritan Richard Baxter (1615–91) in his highly popular *The Saint's Everlasting Rest* (1650). A military chaplain in the Puritan army during the Civil War and a respected antipapist, Baxter could be trusted to deal safely with such sensitive matters as the relation of meditation to conversion and salvation and the uses of the senses, imagination, and language in the meditative or poetic processes. Intended primarily as a handbook for tracking the stages of the saint's spiritual journey, Baxter's work also had important implications for legitimizing literary invention because he endorsed sensual appeals to the imagination.

Several centuries of learned debates over the meditation process and its function in religious experience had preceded Baxter's work. In fact, in England in 1632 Thomas Hooker (1586–1647) had elaborated upon the meditative process in his *The Soul's Preparation for Christ* and justified the use of the senses, imagination, and affections for making spiritual truth more compelling to the understanding. Even John Cotton, who most feared the idolatry that could result from placing sensual images between the saints and God, said that a person "may lawfully in his meditations make use of diverse Creatures or Things, that are apt and fit to represent Spiritual things unto him." Still, such a qualification as Cotton's implies that the more pious the believer, the less the need to use such "diverse Creatures."

At a key moment then in the development of New England Puritanism, the endorsement of Baxter, a poet himself, of the use of metaphor as a *positive* act, even a spiritual duty, was a significant event. Baxter argued that God gave humanity figurative language in order to enhance people's abilities to perceive His truths. Highlighting the many uses of figures in the Bible, he proposed that "these with most other descriptions of our Glory are expressed as if it were the very flesh and sense, which though they are all improper and figurative, yet doubtless if such expressions had not been best, and to us necessary, the Holy Ghost would not have so frequently used them." Not only is it permissible for the saints to use such metaphors in meditation, Baxter submitted, but people are obliged to use this God-given system and to take delight in the world of the senses, which is itself a metaphor, a vehicle of God's instruction. Although Baxter still cautioned that the meditating saint or poet must make certain that the image or figure remained a channel to the divine and not become an earthly shadow eclipsing God, he encouraged a broad range of metaphorical experimentation and even playfulness in language. Thus, the act of signification became a roving, rather than fixed, enterprise. Language became a vehicle, no longer a revealed truth.

The other developing component of Puritan thought that served to certify a Puritan poetics was the more liberal employment of biblical typology. The routine clerical explications of the fulfillment of Old Testament types in the New Testament antitypes had established a mode of symbolic expression. In the early decades of the settlements, some clergy, such as Roger Williams, warned against the extension of this hermeneutic method, but, over time, the creative impulses of Puritan ministers and other writers and the inviting vision of New England as the New Zion led to a most liberal use of typology, opening the system toward more elaborate constructs integrating biblical types with historical events, moral formulations, and even the characters of well-known individuals. Present-day reappraisals of Puritan poetry have served to reconfigure conceptions of Puritan poetics. With a new awareness that it was very possible for a Puritan poet to strive consciously for artfulness, readers have been less inclined to dismiss newly discovered productions and more open to recognizing aesthetic achievement.

Inconsistency and contradiction between Puritan aesthetic theory and poetic practice appear in the case of Roger Williams. As discussed earlier, Williams adhered to the most conservative use of types, and he displayed stubborn convictions about what he perceived as the misuse of biblical types when applied to current events in New England. But in his poetry, Williams broke with convention in significant ways. In *A Key into the Language of America* (1643), he described the characters of the Native Americans he knew and taught, and he critiqued the English, often in scathing terms, particularly in regard to their mistreatment of the natives. At the end of each chapter, he placed a poem to function as a terse summary of his prose remarks. In these poems, usually of twelve lines divided into three numbered stanzas, Williams created powerful images carefully linked to religious and moral precepts. His language is plain and direct, and his images are often homey and earthy. The rhyme is uneven and the iambic meter is rough, but the images are nonetheless remarkably effective.

In some poems, the speaker addresses his English readers directly (Roman and italic type as in the original edition):

> *Boast not proud English of thy birth and blood.*
> *Thy brother* Indian *is by birth as Good.*
> *Of one blood God made Him, and Thee and All,*
> *As wise, as faire, as strong, as personall.*

Although Williams believed that Indians could be converted and could receive saving grace, he felt that the English had a great advantage because their education and cultural heritage taught them how to prepare their hearts for grace. He preached in his poems that being so favored the English have a special obligation to have *"thy second birth, else thou shalt see, / Heaven open to* Indians *wild, but shut to thee."* In other poems, Williams used aspects of indigenous appearance or customs to form an apparent contrast to the English, which he sometimes reversed:

> *Truth is a Native, naked Beauty; but*
> *Lying Inventions are but* Indian *Paints,*
> *Dissembling hearts their Beautie's but a Lye*
> *Truth is the proper Beauty of Gods Saints.*

Here truth and the "native" exist in tandem, and the Indian's innocent application of decorative paints is far less dissembling than the false hearts of the English hypocrites. The next stanza asserts that the hair and paint of the Indian may appear *"Fowle"* to the English, but the clean faces and groomed hair of the inwardly corrupted English hypocrites look even *"More fowle"* to Christ when he sees *"such Faces in* Israel." This substitution of the biblical Israel for New England would appear to contradict Williams's position on typology, but apparently in poetry he felt types could be employed more liberally. In the final stanza, the Indians appear disordered but still genuinely innocent; in contrast, images of fire, storms, and tears depict the fate awaiting those English sinners who do not repent before Judgment:

> *Paints will not bide Christs washing Flames of fire,*
> *Fained Inventions will not bide such stormes:*
> *O that we may prevent him, that betimes,*
> *Repentance Tears may wash of all such Formes.*

In several of these poems, Williams suggests that, though lacking saving grace, the Indians are morally superior to many of the English. In one, he contrasts the serene culture of the Indians with the empty and disruptive pastimes of the English, who relentlessly violate the peace that had characterized Indian territories: *"What noise and tumults in our owne, / And eke in* Pagan *lands?"* And in one of the earliest proclamations by an English settler that the wilderness could be a source of comfort instead of threat, the speaker comments: *"Yet I have found lesse noyse, more peace / In wilde* America." This poem concludes its contrast of cultures with the obligatory religious point that, in regard to grace, both the natives and the English must remain spiritually passive *"till God's call."* In another poem, Williams contrasts the superior morals and laws of the Indians with those of the English. The speaker asserts that the natives firmly punish such crimes as adultery, murder, and theft, whereas the English treat the same crimes more lightly. When the natives learn of the English leniency, they express shock and disdain:

> *We weare no Cloths, have many Gods,*
> *And yet our sinnes are less:*
> *You are Barbarians, Pagans wild,*
> *Your Land's the Wilderness.*

Because Williams consistently asserted the spiritual equality of Native Americans, he may not have realized how using them as a metaphor for the "other," even when his images of them were positive, would function to reinforce the racial division and antagonism of the English toward them. It is likely, however, that Williams was the first English writer in English America to use the idealized image of the native, in what would become a persistent tradition, in order to berate his fellow whites to emulate more humane principles.

Writers like Williams, Edward Taylor, and John Cotton adhered to the Puritan principle of poetic didacticism, but there were other Puritans who recorded personal observations in secular verse. William Wood's (1606–post-1637) promotional work *New England's Prospect* (1634) describes the natural setting of New England and urges the English to establish trading and exploring companies in America. Little is known about Wood, but it is believed that he was a member of John Endecott's group and that he settled in Salem in 1631. Throughout the pages of his prose narrative, Wood included verses depicting his new surroundings.

Another Puritan author who wrote secular prose and poetry about America was John Josselyn (1610–post-1692). After a brief visit in 1637 to Massachusetts, where he met John Winthrop and John Cotton, he returned in 1663 and stayed until 1671. During his extended residence, he became disillusioned with the New England Way and severely criticized it in his *An Account of Two Voyages to New England* (1674). His earlier book, *New England's Rarities Discovered* (1672), describes the natural beauty and wildlife of America in prose full of wonder and some exaggeration. Interspersed among his observations are some verses on a sea storm and on springtime in New England as well as an unusual poem describing a Native-American woman.

The poem "Verses made sometime since upon the Picture of a young and handsome Gypsie, not improperly transferred upon the Indian Squaw" sets up an internal debate over whether women of fair or dark complexion are more beautiful. Anticipating the complex ways gender and race will intersect in numerous later American texts, this poem explores the erotic power of the exotic. A curious ethnic ambiguity is created by the speaker's switch to the word "Red" near the end of the poem after he had been describing the woman as "Black." This shift may indicate Josselyn's linking of all people of color into a generalized "other."

The poem's organizational principle is borrowed from the Petrarchan model, which examines a woman's charms using each of the senses in turn:

> Whether White or Black be best
> Call your Senses to the quest;
> And your touch shall quickly tell
> The Black in softness doth excel,
> And in smoothness.

With an implicit admission in the words "softness" and "smoothness" that the speaker has had physical contact with the woman, he initially mixes the senses of sight and touch in these lines. Then, he proceeds to the sense of hearing and to the quality of her mind that he can detect in her conversation:

> but the Ear,
> What, can that a Colour hear?
> No, but 'tis your Black ones Wit
> That doth catch, and captive it.

Because introducing the sense of taste would perhaps be too risqué, Josselyn's speaker both evades and underscores that omission with a pun: "Nor can ought so please the tast / As what's brown and lovely drest." This image provocatively evokes the picture of the woman in the nude since her "dress" may be brown skin. Acknowledging that the debate over complexion and beauty is endless – "Maugre then all that can be sed / In flattery of White and Red" – he then gives his own preference for darker women:

> Those flatterers themselves must say
> That darkness was before the Day;
> And such perfection here appears
> It neither Wind nor Sun-shine fears.

Although this text may be an early example of one English author's attempts to challenge racial and ethnic stereotypes regarding Native Americans and Africans, as well as "Gypsies," another possibility is presented by the recent discovery of a comic form that attained a degree of popularity in seventeenth-century English verse: the parody of the Petrarchan love sonnet. In works such as John Collop's "On an Ethiopian beauty, M.S." and his "Of the black Lady with grey eyes and white teeth," the poet mocks the extravagant praises of standard love poetry by constructing what the poet presumes to be an absurd situation in which the white male speaker expresses passion for a black woman. Since there is ample evidence of physical attraction, romantic love, and sexual relations among Native Americans, Europeans, and Africans in early America, and since little else is known of Josselyn's personal views on race and gender, the issue of the author's intention in this poem remains open to speculation.

As the broad range of Puritan poetry has come to light, one of the surprises has been the discovery of so many poems about love and desire, which seems to contrast with the popular image of Puritan reserve and restraint. The most prolific author of love poems was John Saffin (1626–1710), a prominent lawyer and judge and a member of the church at Boston. In 1665, he began his commonplace book, published in 1928 as *John Saffin, His Book,* which he continued until two years before his death. The work consists of scientific notes, philosophical contemplations, summaries of his reading, and poetry, which includes satires, elegies, characters, occasional verse, and love poems. Saffin also recorded views on the requirements of good poetry that differ rather drastically from those of most Puritan clergy: "He that would write well in verse must observe these rules . . . that it be elegant, emphatical, metaphorical, and historical; running in a fluent, and smooth channel." No mention here of the dangers of figurative language or the need for religious precepts. His "Sayle Gentle Pinnace," written during his courtship of Martha Willett, has been praised as one of the finest poems of seventeenth-century America. One of Saffin's favorite types of poem was the acrostic, which requires that the first letter of each line when read downward spell out the name of the person who is the subject of the poem. The poet also must use as many words as possible formed from the person's name. Saffin has the distinction of having written the first valentine poem in America: "On Presenting a rare Book to Madame Hull Senior: his Vallintine."

Although Saffin may have had success in his friendships with women, he had frequent disputes with male colleagues. Judge Samuel Sewall of Boston, famous for his *Diary* and for his early antislavery tract *The Selling of Joseph* (1700), was moved by an action of Saffin's to compose a poetic barb. Saffin had argued a case for reenslaving Adam, his black slave, after he had officially obtained his freedom. Sewall, who considered slavery "the most atrocious of capital Crimes," wrote in his poem "To John Saffin":

> Superanuated Squier, wigg'd and powder'd with pretence,
> Much beguiles the just Assembly by his lying Impudence.
> None being by, his sworn Attorneys push it on with
>   might and main
> By which means poor simple Adam sinks to slavery again.

It is not known whether Sewall ever presented his poem to Saffin or whether he kept it where it was eventually discovered, in the privacy of his diary.

Given the hardships of their frontier society, the Puritans had frequent occasions to compose elegies. Rather formulaic and varying greatly in quality, elegies were mainly given to family members and circulated only in limited copies, although a few, composed on prominent figures, became popular as broadsides. Usually elegies focused upon the events and accomplishments of the deceased's life, stressing the signs of grace operating in the person's character and actions. Many elegies also emphasized the bond between the individual saint and the covenanted community, first expressing regret over the group's loss and then consolation and assurance that the saint is at peace with God and His chosen. During the early decades of the colony, all of the elegies preserved were written by men about men, but beginning in the 1680s and then with greater frequency into the eighteenth century, elegies celebrating the lives of women appear as well.

The most admired Puritan elegy was produced by the Reverend Urian Oakes (1631–81) on the occasion of the death of Thomas Shepard, Jr. (1634–77), a minister and son of the first-generation Shepard. Educated at Harvard, Oakes went to England, where he was a teacher and minister for seventeen years before returning to New England in 1671. He served as president of Harvard from 1675 until his death. Composed of fifty-two stanzas of six lines each, his elegy on Shepard is one of the longest of the period. The poem's opening lines make it clear that the attitudes of ministers toward poetic artistry had changed since the 1630s, for Oakes's first seven stanzas lament his inadequacy of "Art and Fancy" to pay Shepard a fitting tribute. Beginning by proclaiming "Oh! that I were a Poet now in grain!" he restated this desire in several ways:

> Now could I wish (if wishing could obtain)
> The sprightli'est Efforts of Poetic Rage;
>
> . . . .
> And could my Pen ingeniously distill
> The purest Spirits of a sparkling wit
> In rare conceits, the quintessence of skill
> In *Elegiack Strains;* none like to it:
>
> . . . .
> Could I take highest Flights of Fancy, soar
> Aloft; If Wits Monopoly were mine:
> All would be much too low, too light, too poor
> To pay due tribute to this great Divine.
> Ah! Wits avails not, when the Heart's like to break,
> Great griefs are Toung-ti'ed, when the lesser speak.

Besides elaborating upon Shepard's qualities and his successful ministry, Oakes reads the untimely death as a possible sign of God's anger with New England: "Lord! is they Treaty with *New-England* come / To an end? And is War in thy Heart?" Near the end of the poem, Oakes explicitly places the blame for Shepard's death upon the people: "Our sins have slain our *Shepard!* we have bought / And dearly paid for our Enormities." Frequently, Puritan elegies, especially those by clergy, also became sermons, as in this case: "*New England* know that Heart-plague [for] / *With him New England fell!*" In spite of these formulas, the language also makes evident the strong personal friendship that existed between Oakes and Shepard. This personal element enables the poem to transcend the conventions and the preaching, as in the poignant final stanza:

> My Dearest, Inmost, Bosome-Friend is Gone!
> Gone is my sweet Companion, Soul's delight!
> Now in a Huddling Croud I'm all alone,
> And almost could bid all the World *Goodnight:*
>   Blest be my Rock! God lives: Oh let him be,
>   As He is All, so All in All to me.

The most prolific producer of elegies in seventeenth-century Massachusetts was Benjamin Tompson (1642–1714), whose gravestone in Roxbury bears the epitaph: "the renowned poet of New England." The son of a minister, a Harvard graduate, and a schoolmaster by profession, Tompson was the first American-born Puritan to publish a volume of poetry about the country. He composed his best-known poem, "New England's Crisis," in 1676 during King Philip's War. Like Oakes's elegy, this verse jeremiad cites backsliding as the cause of war and war itself as God's chastisement. The poem begins by recalling the early days of settlement: the "golden times (too fortunate to hold)," which "were quickly sin'd away for love of gold." Now that the people are interested only in imported chocolate and French wines, God is reducing them "so that the mirror of the Christian world / Lyes burnt to heaps." Since at the time of composition, Tompson could not know the war's outcome, he concluded that either God would destroy the Puritan experiment or else He would use the war to humble and chasten the colony and thereby prepare it for a new beginning.

Though humor is rare in Puritan poetry, Tompson also produced a small mock-epic, "On a Fortification at Boston Begun by Women" (1676), which presents a satirical, yet rather admiring, portrait of Boston women who erected a barricade around the city to defend it against native attack until the Englishmen returned from patrol:

A Grand attempt some Amazonian Dames
Contrive whereby to glorify their names,
A Ruff for *Boston* Neck of mud and turfe,
Reaching from side to side from surfe to surfe,
Their nimble hands spin up like Christmas pyes,
Their pastry by degres on high doth rise.

Although his domestic imagery defines women's "proper" sphere, it is note-worthy that, as an occasional public poet, Tompson did acknowledge their efforts and felt that they deserved a kind of formal, though begrudging, memorial.

Scholars generally agree that the three most productive and important poets in seventeenth-century New England were Anne Bradstreet, Michael Wigglesworth, and Edward Taylor. Anne Bradstreet's (c. 1612–72) *The Tenth Muse, Lately Sprung Up in America,* published in London in 1650, remains the first extant book of poetry by an inhabitant of the Americas. Born in Northampton, England, Bradstreet was educated by her father, Thomas Dudley, steward to the Earl of Lincoln, in the earl's library, where father and daughter read extensively in the classics as well as in the writers of the English Renaissance. She was especially fond of Joshua Sylvester's 1605 translation of the French poet Guillaume du Bartas's *Divine Weekes and Workes.* Dudley, a devout Puritan, saw no contradiction between his religious beliefs and the enjoyment of good literature, and he was exceptional among Puritan men in advocating the philosophical and literary education of young women. Around 1628, Anne Dudley married her father's assistant, Simon Bradstreet, and both families made plans to emigrate to America.

Sailing aboard the *Arbella* with John Winthrop in 1630, the Bradstreets and Dudleys experienced great hardships on the three-month journey, which continued during their first years in New England. Shocked at the difficult living conditions in Massachusetts and by the high rate of sickness and death among the colonists, Anne confided to her diary that she missed the comforts of England and that her "heart rose" with resistance to the "new world and new manners" of America. Bradstreet was always a devoted and dutiful Christian, but she often questioned and privately rebelled against certain dogmas of Puritanism and the strong patriarchal authority in New England. At one point, she wondered: "why may not the Popish Religion be the right? They have the same God, the same Christ, the same word: they only inter-pret it one way, we another." Such doubts infuse many of her poems with an enlivening tension that troubles the otherwise orthodox expression.

One source of personal frustration for Bradstreet and a context for illumi-nating certain subtleties of her poetry is the situation of women in seventeenth-century New England and England. From medieval times, the church and state had systematically subordinated women through both custom and law, and the Protestant revolt was especially male-centered, as demonstrated by the rejection of the Catholics' emphasis on the importance of the Virgin Mary. Most Protestant theology stressed that within the family the husband–father was the representative of God and his word was absolute, subject to neither discussion nor question. Laws in America proclaimed that wives must submit themselves to their husbands and that the husband had total authority over the family and servants. If the social and economic aspects of the Puritan revolution had provided any opportunity for women to gain in social and political status in Massachusetts, that opportunity was dashed with the antinomian affair in the 1630s, for Anne Hutchinson became a symbol for decades after of the dangers of a woman's intellectual and verbal powers. For example, in 1645 John Winthrop was certainly mindful of Hutchinson's perceived transgressions when he recorded the case of Anne Yale Hopkins in his journal:

April 13, 1645. Mr. Hopkins, the governor of Hartford upon Connecticut, came to Boston and brought his wife with him, (a goodly young woman, and of special parts) who was fallen into a sad infirmity, the loss of her understanding and reason, which had been growing upon her divers years, by occasion of her giving herself wholly to reading and writing, and had written many books. Her husband, being very loving and tender of her, was loath to grieve her; but he saw his error, when it was too late. For if she had attended her household affairs, and such things as belong to women, and not gone out of her way and calling to meddle in such things as are proper for men, whose minds are stronger, etc., she had kept her wits . . . in the place God set her.

Similar opinions about the necessarily finite role of women remained fixed well into the end of the century and found frequent expression during the Salem witchcraft trials. Given this limiting context, it is remarkable that Bradstreet was able to write poetry, have it published, and be revered for her talent during her lifetime. Perhaps her unusual degree of freedom was the ironic result of having two influential male political figures in her immediate family: her father and her husband.

After their first years of struggle in America, the Bradstreets and Dudleys began to achieve what eventually became considerable financial and social success. After several relocations, they settled in 1645 at Andover, where Thomas Dudley prospered and became the wealthiest man in Roxbury and, for a period, governor of Massachusetts. Anne's husband, Simon, became a judge, legislator, royal councillor, and finally also governor of the colony. Between 1633 and 1652, Anne had eight children, ran the household, and educated her progeny. Although it seems probable that her wealth and her servants did allow her more time for intellectual pursuits than other women had, it also seems indisputable that the many exigencies faced by an active woman in a wilderness community still put great demands on her time and energies.

As Puritans were taught to do, Bradstreet frequently examined her conscience to discover her sins and shortcomings. When she did not have a child between 1630 and 1633, she was convinced that her own spiritual failings had caused God to make her barren. Throughout her life, she frequently recorded such feelings of inadequacy: "I have often been perplexed as that I have not found that constant Joy in my Pilgrimage and refreshing which I supposed most of the servants of God have." As a highly intelligent and somewhat rebellious woman, Bradstreet by inclination frequently questioned her spiritual situation.

What is clear in her poetry, however, is a frequent tension between a passion for the material world – natural beauty, books, home, and family – and the countervailing Christian dictim that the world is corrupt and vile and vastly incomparable to the love of Christ. This textual anxiety is explicit in her poem "Contemplations":

> Then higher on the glistering Sun I gaz'd,
> Whose beams was shaded by the leavie Tree,
> The more I look'd, the more I grew amaz'd,
> And softly said, what glory's like to thee?
> Soul of this World, this Universal Eye,
> No wonder, some made thee a Deity:
> Had I not better known, (alas) the same had I.

Although she follows the convention of Puritan poetry by making a religious, even doctrinal, point, the tone of wonder and the vivid natural images suggest a competition between the love of this world and the doctrine of divine sovereignty.

Bradstreet composed her first known poem in New Town in 1632 at age nineteen, and in 1645 she first collected her poetry into an informal volume, which she dedicated to her father. These early poems tend toward a rather formulaic and dutiful presentation of religious themes. When the family moved to Andover in 1645, however, Bradstreet began to produce more mature works in which her personal voice gains strength and poetic resonance. In 1647, her brother-in-law, John Woodbridge, went to England with a copy of her poems, which he had published without her knowledge as *The Tenth Muse*. Though warmly received in London, the volume actually contained none of the poems on which Bradstreet's current reputation depends. She composed her more complex poetry over the next two decades, and these works were collected six years after her death in a volume entitled *Several Poems* (1678).

The first section of *The Tenth Muse* includes four long poems known as the quaternions and titled "The Four Elements," "The Four Humors of Man," "The Ages of Man," and "The Four Seasons." Demonstrating Bradstreet's broad learning, these works engage a range of historical and philosophical discourses and include elaborations on anatomy, astronomy, cosmology, physiology, and Greek metaphysics. As these poems graphically illustrate, Bradstreet drew upon her own personal experiences for images and illustrations to buttress her arguments. For example, in her analysis of the ages of man, she recalled her own childhood illnesses:

> What grips of wind my infancy did pain,
> What tortures I in breeding teeth sustain?
> What crudityes my stomach cold has bred,
> When vomits, fits, and worms have issued?

Although the quaternions display her erudition, the rhymed couplets, which she herself called "lanke" and "weary," sometimes become a mechanical vehicle for her learning. Indeed, she herself may have found this exercise tedious because she stopped writing before finishing the second part of the second section, called "The Four Monarchies."

In the third section, "Dialogue between Old England and New," Bradstreet adhered less to older models and allowed her own voice to emerge more forcefully. The poem presents a dialogue between Mother England and her daughter, New England, on the subject of the English political turmoil and the Civil War. Granting superior status to Old England, the speaker asserts that the survival of New England depends upon the stability of the mother country. The speaker expresses a strong attachment to England:

> O pity me in this sad perturbation,
> My plundered Towers, my houses devastation
> My weeping virgins and my young men slain;
> My wealthy trading fall'n, my dearth of grain.

Bradstreet's writing as a whole suggests that she never really felt comfortable in America and that she often yearned for the land of her birth.

Bradstreet's positions on the issue of women's status in society and on her own role as a woman writer are more ambiguous. At times, her work expresses acquiescence to women's subordination, as in the "Prologue" to her book, where the speaker says:

> Let Greeks be Greeks, and women what they are
> Men have precedency and still excell,
> It is but vain unjustly to wage warre;
> Men can do best, and women know it well

> Preheminence in all and each is yours;
> Yet grant some small acknowledgement of ours.

Even as these lines appear to express the requisite acceptance of secondary status, they also imply that men are not only dominant but are parsimonious and lack the magnanimity that should accompany power. At the same time, in the stanza preceding this apologia, Bradstreet's speaker takes a more assertive position and castigates those who held that a woman should not be a poet: "I am obnoxious to each carping tongue / Who says my hand a needle better fits." Moreover, she complains of those who, assuming that women cannot be writers, will "say it's stoln, or else it was by chance." In the final stanza, she presents an ironic and ambiguous conclusion in which she tells male poets who find her poetry worthy of laurels, "Give [me a] Thyme or Parsley wreath, I ask no bayes." In requesting domestic herbs from the kitchen instead of laurels, she seems to be subordinating herself once more, but her last two lines undercut that self-effacement with a broad hint of sarcasm when she suggests that blinding male pride must be appeased: "This mean and unrefined ure of mine / Will make your glistering gold, but more to shine." Bradstreet's choice here of the wreath of "Thyme or Parsley" may also suggest her awareness of her doubly humble status as a colonial, American woman in a land devoid of the more ornate foreign or classical rewards.

In her 1642 poem on Queen Elizabeth, "In Honor of that High and Mighty Princess Queen Elizabeth," the persona makes a more direct claim that women are the intellectual equals of men. Drawing for support upon the power that Elizabeth's memory had for nearly all the English, the speaker strongly protests male condescension:

> Nay Masculines, you have thus taxt us long,
> But she, though dead, will vindicate our wrong,
> Let such as say our Sex is void of Reason,
> Know tis Slander now, but once was Treason.

Later in the poem, the speaker praises Elizabeth for her wisdom and strength, adding "millions can testify that this is true." Emboldened by Elizabeth's example, the speaker argues that her precedent, as well as the poet's present example, should provide continuing evidence of the intellectual powers of women: "She has wip'd off th' aspersion of her Sex, / That women wisdome lack to play the Rex." Evidence suggests that both Bradstreet's father and her husband accepted her intelligence and feminist inclinations, but other families, even within the Bradstreet–Dudley circle, were less tolerant of intellectual women: Anne's sister, Sarah Cain, was rejected by her husband and finally excommunicated for prophecying and for "gross immorality." This episode is an emblematic reminder of the vulnerable position women held in the society and the great personal risk that Bradstreet knew she was taking with a poem as bold as "Mighty Princess Queen Elizabeth."

The second and expanded edition of her works, *Several Poems* (1678), provided the first publication of what have become Bradstreet's best-known poems. Although she died before this book was published, she was able to correct many errors that had appeared in those works first published in the hastily produced *Tenth Muse,* and she added a new opening, "The Author to her Book." In this poem, the speaker is a poet—mother whose children are her book and her poems. She apologizes for the fact that her child had been taken from her and sent into the world before she had a chance to prepare her properly and teach her to run with "even feet." The poem serves as an apt and witty introduction to this new book because domestic imagery is a strong component of many of the new poems, which are much more personal than the stiffer, more formal and academic works of the first edition. Further, these references to the domestic are ironic because they both embody "feminine" discourse and serve as a vehicle to transcend that limited discursive field.

In *Several Poems,* there are verses relating to her personal illnesses, elegies on the deaths of her grandchildren and daughter-in-law, love poems to her husband, and a poem on the burning of her house. These are the works that are most often anthologized, for critics consider them to be far superior to Bradstreet's earlier work because of their candor about her religious experiences, their lyrical language, and their insistence on the primacy of personal experience. For example, in "Before the Birth of One of her Children," the speaker expresses her fear that she might not survive childbirth, and she admits that she is afraid to die. Addressing her husband directly in the poem, she implores him to continue to love her after her death and prevent any harm from being done to her children by the future stepmother they are sure to have: "Love thy dead, who long lay in thine arms / . . . look to my babes my dear remains / . . . These O protect from step Dames injury."

As the century progressed, Puritan poets strayed from the didactic imperative, and Bradstreet's later poems reflect this development. Her love poems to her husband are, in fact, completely free of religious instruction and frankly acknowledge her desire for him when he is abroad: for example, "I wish my Sun may never set, but burn / Within the Cancer of my glowing breast," and in another, "I, with many a deep sad groan / Bewail my turtle true . . . Return my Dear, my joy, my only Love / . . . Let's still remain but one, till death divide." She signs this poem "Thy loving Love and Dearest Dear / At home, abroad, and every where."

Many of Bradstreet's later poems also reveal the tension and anxiety she felt when she had to accept with pious resignation the tragedy of the death of a loved one or the loss of her property. Her sense of resentment toward God is barely concealed in some of these poems although her speaker always becomes reconciled to divine justice in the end. The poem she wrote after her house burned down in 1666 reveals most clearly the conflict between human attachment to the things of this world and the indifference required by Puritan doctrine. Upon being awakened by the flames and first seeing the catastrophic destruction of the dwelling, the textual voice stoically displays the proper Christian attitude: "I blest his Name that gave and took / . . . It was his own: it was not mine." Yet she goes on to say that later, whenever she passed the ruins, she could not help thinking of the things that she had cherished:

> Here stood that Trunk, and there that chest;
> There lay that store I counted best:
> My pleasant things in ashes lye,
> And them behold no more shall I.

She also laments that no guests will be able to visit there again, where tales could be told and pleasures relived. Grief intrudes upon the textual inscription of doctrine. Drifting off into a near reverie, she speaks to the ruins, "Adeiu, Adeiu" [*sic*], but then she quickly reminds herself that "All's vanity." She chastises herself for placing such store in material existence and reassures herself that a better home awaits her with Christ. Yet the ritualistic closing – "The world no longer let me Love, / My hope and Treasure lyes Above" – is not sufficiently convincing to elude the previously expressed longing for material trappings. The reader cannot help but suspect that the next time the speaker passes the ruins she will dream again of the times and treasures she had "loved." In her meditations, Bradstreet correspondingly reflected on her difficulty in rejecting the physical world, concluding that only the knowledge of death rather than religious doctrine compels people to look forward to eternity: "for were earthly comforts permanent, who would look for heavenly?" Bradstreet often contemplated her own mortality, but until the last years of her illness, it had always been with noticeable reluctance that she anticipated her eternal peace.

In 1669, three years before her death, Bradstreet wrote what may have been her last poem, "As Weary Pilgrim, now at Rest"; the disease of her last years may have prevented her from writing more works. Here, the speaker thinks not of worldly pleasures but instead reviews life's trials: the "dangers past, and travailes done," the "bryars and thornes," "hungry wolves," "erring paths," "rugged stones," "the earth perplext / With sinns with cares and sorrows vext / By age and pain brought to decay." Longing to be "at rest / And soare high among the blest," she calls out to Christ: "Lord make me ready for that day / Then Come deare bridgrome Come away." For all of Bradstreet's personal strengths and her desire to see women on a more equal basis with men, her textual voice finally succumbs here to the dominant gender imagery of the scriptures. She imagines herself a dependent bride in the arms of the divine bridegroom. All her life she had contemplated and explored the socially restricting implications of such language, and her use of this image in her last poem seems to constitute a final, self-conscious act of submission to God, church, and her culture.

Unlike Bradstreet, the preacher–poet Michael Wigglesworth (1631– 1705) abided strictly by the rules of the Puritan aesthetic, writing always in the plain style and with a didactic message. After Bradstreet and Taylor, Wigglesworth was the third most prolific and important poet of the period. Although he was popular in his own time and even into the nineteenth century for his sermonic, orthodox *The Day of Doom* (1662) and his *Meat Out of the Eater* (1670), he has received relatively little critical attention in the twentieth century. Although biographers have been able to discover many facts of Wigglesworth's public life, they remain divided over the nature of his inner life (for biographical details, see Chapter 3). Focusing primarily on dry doctrines and Last Days, his diary and other writings present him as the stereotypical gloomy Puritan. His self-acknowledged lack of feeling regarding his father's death and his seemingly cold, but properly Puritan, reaction to the death of his first wife reinforce that image. However, sympathetic biographers suggest that his efforts to adhere dutifully to Puritan doctrines may have led to self-destructive repression and even depression, which appear to modern readers of his works as cold indifference rather than contained personal suffering.

In spite of his private turmoil, Wigglesworth's public persona and poetry project an image of the grim Puritan, and his work has often been cited as typical of Puritan verse. America's first "best-seller," *The Day of Doom* was primarily intended to teach children several doctrinal truths. Written in the ballad form with a meter of seven-foot "fourteeners," the poem consists of two hundred and twenty-four eight-line stanzas. Presented as a narrative, the action is set on Judgment Day, when, with sudden fury, Christ gathers the righteous sheep at His right hand and the sinful goats at His left. After a catalogue of the various types of sinners to be punished, the goats are allowed to plead their pitiful cases for mercy. Through this device, Wigglesworth presents the errors of doctrine and fallacious reasoning that sinners employ to justify their sins, and he illustrates how God and His righteous will demolish such false arguments and punish the wicked.

This theological instruction constitutes the thematic center of the poem, but the elements that gave the work its popular appeal are the vivid and dramatic descriptions of the shock of doom and the casting of the sinners into hell's fire. These passages appear primarily in the opening and closing stanzas. Suddenly "at midnight brake forth a Light, / Which turn'd night to day," and when Christ appears, "Skies are rent asunder," and the people hear "a mighty voice, and hideous noise, / More terrible than Thunder." As they realize that they have been caught in sin, some "do not spare their flesh to tear / Through horrible despair" while others "hide themselves in Caves." Tombs open and "Dead Bodies all rise at his call," and those whose crimes are seemingly minor, "Scoffers at Purity," are gathered together with the vilest villains: "Children flagitious, / And Parents who did them undo / by Nurture vicious" are grouped with "Murd'rers, and Men of blood / Witches, Inchanters, and Ale-house haunters." Children hearing this poem for the first time would long remember this scene and the dragons, serpents, and "Legions of Sprights unclean, / And hellish Fiends." The images at the end of the poem also seem especially designed to terrify children when they depict pious mothers and fathers rejecting their sinful offspring, who are then cast upon the burning lake for eternity.

In addition to this "verse catechism," as Cotton Mather called *The Day of Doom*, Wigglesworth also produced a verse jeremiad, *God's Controversy with New England*. Written in 1662 in the midst of a major drought, this poem warns readers that they are weakening in their commitment to their divine mission and that God's anger is evident. Joining a growing chorus of communal lamentations that would continue for the next thirty-five years, Wigglesworth mourned the loss of the zeal of the founders and the laxity of the younger generation:

> Such, O New-England, was thy first,
>   Such was thy best estate:
> But, Loe! a strange and suddain change
>   . . . .
> The brightest of our morning starrs
>   Did wholly disappeare:
> And those that tarried behind
>   With sack-cloth covered were.

Then, for the next four hundred lines, the poem describes the forms of present backsliding, the various expected punishments, and finally a formula for returning to God and hearing again His assurances for New England.

Wigglesworth also wrote several poems, and in 1670 he published his last major work, *Meat Out of the Eater*, which went to its fourth edition in 1689. More personal in tone than his others, it seems based upon his own experiences during a lengthy illness. The main purpose of the work is to console those who have endured suffering by reminding them of the goodness of

Christ and the compensations of a holy life. Some of the poems in this collection suggest that Wigglesworth possessed a gift for writing poetry that would be appealing to contemporary tastes but that his usual rigorous adherence to official Puritan poetics led him to suppress his natural talents.

Usually considered the most gifted English poet in America before the nineteenth century, Edward Taylor was born in Sketchley, Leicestershire, England, probably in 1642. He grew up on a farm, was educated at a nonconformist school, and developed strong anti-Anglican and anti-Catholic opinions. After his mother's death in 1657 and his father's in 1658, Taylor became a teacher, but the Restoration government eventually threatened to bar him from teaching unless he signed the Act of Uniformity of 1662, requiring loyalty to the Church of England. He refused, and after several years of persecution, he departed for Massachusetts in 1668. Graduating from Harvard in 1671 at the unusually advanced age of twenty-nine, Taylor accepted a post in the remote village of Westfield, where he was pastor and town physician. In 1674, he married Elizabeth Fitch and together they had eight children, five of whom died in infancy. "Upon Wedlock, & Death of Children," one of his most moving poems, expresses his suffering over these losses. In 1692, Elizabeth died, and three years later Taylor married Ruth Wyllys, who raised Elizabeth's three surviving children and the six others she herself bore. Because King Philip's War raged around Westfield in the mid-1670s, Taylor's ordination was delayed until 1679.

Once established, however, he preached tirelessly at Westfield until a few years before his death at the age of eighty-seven in 1729, and he made only a few visits to Boston and other New England towns. Over sixty of his sermons are extant, as is a long theological treatise, *The Harmony of the Gospels* (published in 1983). He completed the poems that make up *God's Determinations Touching His Elect* around 1682, and he wrote the poetry included in his *Preparatory Meditations* between 1682 and 1725. Theologically, Taylor was a pious conservative congregationalist, and over the course of his career, he engaged in several heated religious disputes with various other ministers, most notably Solomon Stoddard at nearby Northampton. Strongly opposed to innovations in church polity, Taylor composed a series of sermons attacking Stoddard's decision to open the sacrament of communion to all members of his congregation whether or not they considered themselves regenerate. Taylor argued that those awaiting grace should not fall prey to Satan's (and Stoddard's) trick of inviting them to the Lord's table while they remained in doubt. Taylor's solution was to assist the faithful to perceive more clearly the signs of their own conversions, which would likely occur for the patient.

Even Taylor's most sympathetic biographers admit that he could be a "grave, severe, stubborn, and stiff-necked" disciplinarian in his public life;

for example, when his congregation built a new meeting house in 1721–22, Taylor refused to preach there. At the time, Stephen Williams, pastor of Longmeadow Church, recorded in his diary that "Mr. Taylor is very fond of his own thoughts and I am afraid will make a very great difficulty and division in the town." Taylor was then nearing eighty years old, but this event seems representative of a life in which compromise was a rarity. Taylor's positions were always based upon his sincere convictions regarding the individual's relation to God, and no one in Puritan New England was more certain that the form of congregational Protestantism practiced in Massachusetts in the 1630s and 1640s was the one true religion.

Taylor's poetry is distinguished from that of his fellow Puritans by a strain of mysticism that infused his spiritual vision and led him to a more complex understanding of metaphor. Taylor felt a strong personal relation to God and believed that Christ was immediately present in the sacrament of communion. This mystical, or imaginative, side allowed him to conceive of language and metaphor as the bridge between the human mind and God and to perceive of death metaphorically as a glorious moment of union between this world and the next. These ideas were quite in keeping with the positions of earlier Puritan theologians such as Baxter, but Taylor embraced them with a fervor and devoted to them an abundance of rhetorical elaboration that exceeded that of his colleagues. His faith in the symbolic meaning invested in the physical universe empowered his poetic and interpretive gifts: "Natural things are not unsuitable to illustrate supernaturals by. For Christ in his parables doth illustrate supernatural things by natural, and if it were not thus, we could arrive at no knowledge of supernatural things, for we are not able to see above naturals."

Taylor's critics generally hold that he wrote poetry primarily as a form of meditation as he prepared himself to preach or that he used the composition process to put himself in the proper mental and spiritual state for receiving and administering communion. Although he may never have intended his poems for publication, he did carefully preserve them in a quarto of four hundred pages in a leather binding that was passed down from his grandson Ezra Stiles (1727–95), president of Yale, and deposited in the college library in 1883, where it was discovered by Thomas H. Johnson in 1937. Many of his preparatory meditations are directly linked to his sermons by biblical passages that serve as titles to sermons on the same texts that he preached around the time that he composed the poems. Other poems, especially the miscellaneous ones, seem to have been inspired by his observations of things in nature or daily life. It may be that he used the exercise of writing these poems to prepare himself for pastoral instruction, for often these verses use metaphors, images, and analogies based in the ordinary life of simple countryfolk.

Taylor's literary style and poetic techniques link his work to that of John Donne and the English metaphysicals, and he clearly knew and admired the poetry of George Herbert and probably Richard Crashaw. Yet, because he left England in 1668, he remained untouched by developments in post-Restoration English poetry. Some of Taylor's early critics observed that his meter and rhymes are often rough and awkward, but scholars later recognized these features to be the likely result of Taylor's conscious attempts to have the roughness in his language reflect and express the strenuous and often painful nature of religious experience and conversion. Similarly, many of Taylor's poems are difficult to read aloud, thereby suggesting that the reader must recognize that certain complex matters exceed the range of human speech. In these aspects, his techniques may be compared to attempts by modernist writers to give voice to the inarticulate. Other examples of his poetry are characterized by verbal wit and by inventive play upon biblical types and figures. He was especially fond of using sensuous images from the love poetry of the biblical Song of Songs, where images of the body, often quite erotic, function for interpreters as religious symbols, and he was also drawn to the astonishing depictions of heavenly beauty and earthly destruction in Revelation. Combining such biblical language with imagery from farm and town life, he created startling, sometimes incongruous metaphors that are in the baroque tradition of the metaphysical conceit.

What is most compelling about Taylor's poetry for modern readers is that his works repeatedly depict the conflicts between, on the one hand, human will, desire, and love of this world and, on the other, Puritan doctrine, especially of divine sovereignty and retribution. To resist temptations to doubt God's goodness, Taylor repeatedly put himself through the same spiritual and psychological process in his meditations. His poems most often duplicate the spiritual exercise: the speaker creates a metaphor as a device for understanding God's purposes and then exposes the metaphor as inadequate to this awesome task; then, as the speaker approaches the point of despair, he struggles to find a new way to rationalize the divine purpose, only to end resigned to submitting in faith to God's will, although this acceptance is often mixed with subtle hints of continued future resistance and struggle. Taylor repeated this pattern so often that some biographers have questioned his spiritual sincerity, but for Taylor, as for Thomas Shepard, spiritual peace was only a momentary hiatus in a lifelong process of painful soul-searching and conflict. He seems to have understood this human struggle as a permanent process and to have accepted it as something the mind could engage not only with genuine devotion but also with wit, play, and humor.

Taylor's *God's Determinations Touching His Elect* has been compared in form and design to Milton's *Paradise Lost* and Dante's *Divine Comedy* as an epic of salvation and conversion. The work also shares features of a medieval morality play, an Ignatian spiritual meditation, and a Puritan sermon. Rhetorical in style, it appears directed to those church members who had not yet experienced conversion and who feared that they would never be touched by grace. Analyzing the psychic operations provoked by Satan to drive the soul to despair, Taylor proposes that grace awaits those who are able to cast off the Devil's temptations of melancholia and to prepare their hearts for Christ. The remainder of the poem's full title provides an outline of its three-part structure: *and The Elect's Combat in their Conversion and Coming up to God in Christ together with the Comfortable Effects thereof.* Simply put, the message is fight Satan, pray to Christ, and receive God's grace and peace.

Perhaps for modern readers, the most singular aspect of Taylor's major work is that, orthodox Puritan though he was, he saw the individual saint's position in the world as fundamentally comic. God had already determined each soul's spiritual fate, and yet He allowed the saint to be caught up in a dramatic struggle of hope, doubt, anxiety, and ultimate joy. Taylor may not have believed that God sported with people, but he certainly suggested that from the human perspective, at least, that was how the situation sometimes appeared.

Thus, by beginning *God's Determinations* with a parody of the ways that people have tried to imagine God and His dealings with them, Taylor infused his epic of salvation with a strong element of the comic. "The Preface" sets forth in miniature the entire spiritual process that the rest of the work details. The first word, "Infinity," underscores the enormous distance between God's power and being and the finite world where humans labor futilely to grasp His nature or purpose. Although all human understanding of the supernatural is necessarily through metaphors, these vehicles are ultimately inadequate devices for imagining God, "for we are not able to see above naturals." In the first two lines, the speaker recalls that the universe is an oxymoron, an infinity of nothingness: "Infinity, when all things it beheld / In Nothing, and of Nothing all did build." Later he will return to play more upon the idea of something from nothing, but here he is setting up a list of metaphysical questions that he develops through a series of witty images. In them, the speaker uses "naturals" to try to project the idea of God. The images depict God as carpenter, blacksmith, builder, seamster, weaver, sportsman, and home decorator: the speaker asks who could make the "Globe" of the world upon his "Lath"; who "Moulds" planets in his "Furnace Vast"; who "Lac'de and Filletted the earth" with "Rivers like green Ribbons"; and who "Spread the Canopy" of the heavens and "Curtains Spun" for the skies? Then, in case the absurdity of such inadequate human projections of the divine has been lost on his audience, he asks, "Who in this Bowling Alley bowld the Sun?"

Such feeble constructions may fail, but they do have the spiritual benefit of reducing the terror of being subject to such power. While reminding himself that the Almighty "can half buy looks / Root up the rocks and rock the hills by th'roots," Taylor's speaker adds consolingly that this is a loving God whose intentions for humanity, if mysterious, are generous and merciful. Undue fear can block the soul from His saving grace and love. Thus, in the final ten lines, the speaker returns to the image of nothing and speculates about why God bothered to create the universe and humankind at all:

> Which All from Nothing fet, from Nothing, All:
> Hath All on Nothing set, lets Nothing fall.
> Gave all to nothing Man indeed, whereby
> Through Nothing then imbosst the brightest Gem
> More pretious than all pretiousness in them.

For all of His infinite power then, God seems not only to have generously given insignificant humans all of the universe to enjoy but to have engaged Himself in a kind of game with humanity: by making the most valuable thing in creation the human soul and giving one of these gems to each individual, God invites each to perform freely, like an actor, for His approval or disapproval. At present, the people of New England have "thrown down all by sin" and "darkened that lightsome Gem" so that "now his Brightst Diamond is grown / Darker by far than any Coalpit Stone." Although souls in this darkened state have reason to fear God's wrath, Taylor's imagery and logic lead to the conclusion that a loving God is ready to smile upon his creatures again if they can manage to restore the "Coalpit Stone" to a "Diamond." Many of Taylor's colleagues would have termed his use of humor blasphemous, but the poet's ludicrous portraits of God in various human occupations – sporting with people and as an audience for human performances – function to reduce the incommensurability between God and His people. The entire poetic sequence making up this book seems designed to empower the discouraged and wayward soul to return to a worthy state and to prepare for grace in the hope that against all human reason, an omnipotent God loves His people.

Consisting of two hundred and seventeen numbered poems written over forty-three years, Taylor's other work, the *Preparatory Meditations,* is divided into two series, the first written between 1682 and the end of 1692 and the second from 1693 until 1725. The full title describes them as a collection of verbal exercises, each composed *before my Approach to the Lord's Supper. Chiefly upon the Doctrine preached upon the Day of administration.* These poems vary greatly in language, tone, and subject matter, but they all appear to have the same basic purpose: to allow Taylor an opportunity to focus upon his unworthiness so that he would approach the communion table humbly. He used the meditation ritual to imagine new situations for himself and to generate new metaphors enabling him to recall that without God he is insignificant; in his "Prologue" to the first series, his speaker is a "Crumb of Dust." The first twelve poems of the first series are concerned with the spiritual pleasures of the Lord's Supper and the attraction of Christ as savior. Taylor drew upon the Song of Songs for erotic imagery to describe the love of Christ, and he used abundant imagery of food and drink to heighten the appeal of the communion table for sense-bound fallen creatures.

The frequently anthologized "Meditation Eight" illustrates effectively the poetic method of these works. As in "The Preface" of *God's Determinations,* Taylor opens this poem with images that suggest God's inaccessibility. He observes that neither the "Astronomy Divine" of theology nor his poetic metaphors can bridge the distance between God and people: "A Golden Path my Pensill cannot line, / From that bright Throne unto my Threshold ly." But while he is having "puzzled thoughts about it," he suddenly discovers that God has intervened in the natural world by putting "the Bread of Life in't at my door." Here, Taylor joins the Old Testament type of manna with the New Testament antitype of Christ as the new bread of life. The futility of human efforts to earn salvation is assuaged by God's gift of grace and eternal happiness.

The second stanza presents the image of the soul as a "Bird of Paradise put in / This Wicker Cage (my Corps)," which "in golden days" foolishly "peckt the Fruite forbad: and so did fling / Away its food." Through Original Sin, the speaker's soul is born into him already corrupt and starving from the "Celestial Famine sore" begun with the loss of Eden. Speaking to his own soul, the persona expresses his plight in being unable to get "soul bread" either from the natural world or from the angels, who show him only "An Empty Barrell" where grain for spiritual bread might normally be found. In language typical of the psychic nadir in the meditation process, the speaker cries out, "Alas! alas! Poore Bird, what wilt thou doe?" The point, clearly, is that he can do nothing. Then, in the last three stanzas, the speaker discovers God's mercy: "In this sad state, Gods Tender Bowells run / Out streams of Grace." Although the word "bowels" in the seventeenth century referred to the center of the body, which included the heart and the stomach and was considered the seat of the emotions, Taylor's digestive imagery nevertheless renders the passage rather eccentric for depicting the flow of grace. One way of viewing this imagery is that the grinding of the wheat for communion bread is like a digestive process within the body of the person who consumes it. Such a human form of dispersion and absorption, though an incongruous metaphor, is an apt and memorable emblem for people to imagine the way that God provides his grace to the starving soul.

Mixing images of liquid and solid forms to convey the conflict of grace embodied in communion bread and wine, the speaker next creates an elaborate conceit in which God takes the "Purest Wheat in Heaven, his deare-dear Son," and transforms Him into the "Bread of Life." He "Grinds, and kneads up" Christ and has him "Disht on thy Table up by Angells Hands." The speaker then asks incredulously if it is really true that God loves His people so much as to announce: "Come Eate thy fill . . . Its Heaven's Sugar Cake." Finally, in the last stanza the speaker reminds himself that "souls are but petty things" in comparison to the glory of God's grace; but even as he laments his insignificance, the speaker receives Christ and the promise of eternal life: "This bread of Life dropt in thy mouth, doth Cry. / Eate, Eate me, Soul, and thou shalt never dy." Swallowed alive and speaking, Christ becomes a part of the speaker's own body and soul.

Although Taylor's personal piety, humility, and gratitude for God's grace and communion shine through the language of his meditations, it is in many of his miscellaneous poems that particular personal experiences give the speaker's voice greater individual distinction. One of his most popular, and subtle, poems is "Upon a Spider Catching a Fly" (undated). Upon first reading, this poem appears to contain only simple, didactic moral instruction. The speaker addresses a spider as it spins its web and catches a wasp and a fly, and he observes that the spider does not attempt to kill the wasp immediately for fear of its sting and that it carefully strokes and calms the wasp lest its thrashing tear the web. In contrast, when a fly is ensnared, the spider hastily bites it dead. The speaker then elaborates the moral: just as a creature in nature avoids a direct confrontation with another of greater strength, so too should humans avoid battle with "Hells Spider," who sets his nets to "tangle Adams race," for God will send His "Grace to breake the Cord." Thus, the point seems to be that the saints should try to elude Satan's web and should pray for God's grace.

In the final stanza, however, the persona shifts oddly to a different image, that of a nightingale singing "on high / In Glories Cage . . . for joy," and this new figure throws the apparent lesson into question. The speaker claims that one lesson is that creatures in nature know better than to challenge those stronger than themselves, but his illustration really does not make that point. The fly did not seek to encounter the spider but instead flew accidentally into its web. Although the spider avoids a direct attack upon the wasp, the fate of the wasp still appears to be certain, if slow, death. If the fly represents a regenerate Christian awaiting grace, then the analogy fails, for it dies without redemption. If the fly is an unregenerate soul predestined to hell, then there is nothing to be learned from its example except that the fate of the damned is hell. Perhaps then it is the wasp that symbolizes the regenerate Christian, but in that case, the reader must ask: if the venom that saves the wasp from instant death symbolizes God's grace and if the wasp's struggling in the net represents a saint's exertions against Satan, why does God let the wasp die after prolonged agony? The speaker who pretends to explain the allegory has presented a deceptively inadequate explication.

It appears, then, that the speaker is playing a game with his imagined reader – or with himself; if so, the real lesson appears to be a warning against thoughtless acceptance of the type of simple moral instruction the poem seems to present. The student must use his or her wits to look at all sides of an analogy. The speaker himself might be the spider here, who has laid a verbal net to "tangle Adams race" by lulling readers into a false sense of confidence about the easy way to heaven only to trick them into realizing that they are "foppish" wasps who have the power of grace to "fret" Satan's net but who are too easily stroked into passivity. If the nightingale singing to God represents the poet controlling the speaker, the method of this poem is not unlike John Donne's use of the unreliable persona in many of his songs and sonnets. Like a teacher who says something absurd in order to provoke complacent students, the poet attempts to awaken readers to their own casual acceptance of easy answers or their own mistaken assumptions. Such a reading may trouble those who assume that Taylor was writing only for himself; from that standpoint, the poem could be a private exercise, a literary self-entertainment of a brilliant mind in a remote New England village.

Although Taylor's poetry usually abides by the Puritan aesthetics established early in the century and liberalized somewhat by Richard Baxter in 1649, Puritan poetry written in Boston and along the seaboard from about 1680 into the eighteenth century came under the secular influences of the Restoration and the Augustan movement in England. Clergymen such as John Danforth (1660–1730), Cotton Mather (1663–1728), Benjamin Colman (1673–1747), and Mather Byles (1707–88), as well as devoted laymen like Samuel Sewall (1652–1730), Richard Steere (1643–1721), and Roger Wolcott (1679–1767), adopted more public modes of expression and composed many poems that had no obvious religious themes and even some that seemed to defy Puritan precepts. For example, Steere, a defender of the congregational way in his religious practice and author of anti-Catholic satire, also wrote the only Nativity poem in seventeenth-century America, thereby violating the Puritan rules against the practice of "Christmas-keeping," long considered a form of Catholic idolatry.

In 1712, Cotton Mather remarked that women "have wrote such things as have been very valuable; especially relating to their own experiences." He had

Anne Bradstreet specifically in mind, but he also was aware of several other women writers of Puritan New England, whose works have only recently been discovered. No seventeenth-century Puritan women voluntarily published their writing, probably for fear of incurring a fate like that of the "insane" Anne Yale Hopkins, but several did write poetry, and in the early eighteenth century some New England women did publish their works. Those who have been recently rediscovered are Anna Hayden (1648–c. 1720), who left two elegies; Sarah Kemble Knight (1666–1727), who wrote six poems that she included in her well-known *Journal;* Mary English (c. 1652–94), who wrote an acrostic poem on her own name; Sarah Goodhue (1641–81), who wrote a poem included in a book of her writings, *Valedictory and Monitory Writing,* published in Cambridge at the time of her death; Grace Smith (c. 1685–1740), whose *The Dying Mother's Legacy* (1712) contains some poetry; and Mercy Wheeler (1706–96), who also wrote a didactic deathbed work, *An Address to Young People, Or . . . Warning from the Death* (1733), which contains some lines of verse. Single poems have survived from two other Puritan women: Susanna Rogers (b. c. 1711), who wrote an elegy for her fiancé after he was killed by Native Americans in 1725; and Mary French (c. 1685–1730), who was taken captive by Native Americans in 1703 in a raid on Deerfield, Massachusetts, and wrote a poem to her sister from captivity.

The daughters of the Reverend Benjamin Colman, Jane Colman Turell (1708–35) and Abigail (Celia) Colman Dennie (1715–45), were also poets. They were educated by their father, who himself wrote poetry. Abigail, who ran away from her parents' home in 1733 until financial need forced her to return, wrote a poem to her sister revealing her suffering:

> To you alone I venture to complain;
> From others hourly strive to hide my pain.
> But Celia's face dissembles what she feels,
> Affected looks her inward pain conceal.
> She sings, she dresses and she talks and smiles,
> But these are all spectators to beguile.

Besides Anne Bradstreet, however, the only Puritan woman to leave a substantial body of poetry appears to be Jane Colman Turell. Despite having four children and enduring the childhood deaths of each, Turell managed to keep writing regularly during her troubled twenty-seven years. Most of her prose and poetry was devoted to religious subjects, but she also wrote, in the words of her husband, Ebenezer, "pieces of wit and humor, which if publish'd would give a brighter idea of her to some of [her] readers." In addition to experimenting with the pastoral and neoclassical techniques, Turell wrote

a poem at the age of seventeen in which her poetic persona expresses a desire
to transcend the limitations that Puritanism placed upon all aspiring poets:

> O let me burn with Sappho's noble fire,
> But not like her for faithless man expire.
>
> .   .   .   .
>
> Go lead the way, my muse, nor must you stop,
> 'Til we have gain'd Parnassus shady top:
> 'Till I have view'd those fragrant soft retreats,
>
> .   .   .   .
>
> And so be worthy of a poet's name.

At her death, when her father selected some of her works to publish in
Memoirs of the Life and Death of . . . Mrs. Jane Turell, he did not include her
more humorous or rebellious works.

All Puritans with literary aspirations were aware that their religion did not
encourage literary ambitions, but women of literary talent were especially
stifled. Given the limitations of doctrine and the difficult living conditions,
it is remarkable, however, that so many Puritans wrote poetry at all and that
among their texts are some that still speak to modern readers with intensity
and passion. Although Bradstreet and Taylor far surpassed others in their
skill and energy, the works of many Puritan poets express the enduring will
to articulate desire, conflict, uncertainty, and longing even in a highly
controlled society.

5

THE JEREMIAD

B Y THE TIME of the Restoration of Charles II in England in 1660, Puritan New England had developed into a relatively prosperous, stable, and independent colony. Some who had left for England during the Protectorate returned to New England after 1660, and other English Puritans, like Edward Taylor, fled to America to escape renewed Anglican persecution. With the native tribes still traumatized by the violence of the Pequot War in the late 1630s, Puritan villages proliferated, and different local governments, customs, and economies replicated the various peasant cultures of places such as Yorkshire, Kent, East Anglia, and the West Country of England. On the whole, travelers in New England in the 1650s described flourishing agricultural communities of pious, hardworking families where the churches and the state appeared to cooperate in governance.

In larger cities such as Boston and Salem, there arose a merchant class based upon manufacturing, the fishing industry, and foreign trade, while the rural villages remained dependent upon farming. Open-field farming continued in some areas until the late seventeenth century, but most land was converted to small individual holdings. Because congregationalism encouraged village independence, forms of government were quite varied, with selectmen sometimes possessing broad powers, and in many the influence of the ministers upon civil decisions was diminishing.

This slow process of secularization was hastened and became more dramatic when two serious difficulties arose that would precipitate drastic changes in the social and religious order between 1660 and 1690: a land shortage and growing religious uncertainties among the young. Word of the prosperity of the early colonists attracted to New England growing numbers of less pious immigrants who primarily sought financial opportunities. These new arrivals pressured village governments to apportion land to them at the very time that established members had begun to desire more property for their own, often numerous, adult children. The newcomers were often denied church membership and thus land by selectmen who accused them of being opportunistic hypocrites. As church and congregational power expanded, those seeking admission had to testify publicly about their conversion experiences, and in some cases their spiritual relations had to conform to a complicated morphology of conversion established by the clergy. Such tests discouraged applicants, though perhaps not by design. This linking of language, sainthood, property ownership, and political franchise became troublesome for the established Puritans as well, however, when increasing numbers of their own adult children also failed to have or recount the requisite conversion and become full church members. The original colonists doubted that their children and grandchildren were as reprobate and deserving of exclusion as the new immigrants, and they urged authorities to find a means of distinguishing between unconverted outsiders and their spiritually inhibited offspring.

Events in the town of Sudbury in the early 1650s illustrate this crisis especially sharply. When the town had been founded, the original members set aside land for expansion, but no land was ever granted to new immigrants. By 1650, there were twenty-six adult sons of founders seeking land from the reluctant selectmen. Dissension raged for five years, and the minister Thomas Brown joined the side of the elders and preached against the degeneracy and immorality of the unconverted youths. In 1655, the frustrated young people proclaimed: "If you oppress the poor, they will cry out; if you persecute us in one city, we must fly to another." John Ruddock, an elder who supported the sons, presented a formal declaration of exodus: "God has been pleased to increase our children, which are grown to men's estates. [Their fathers] should be glad to see them settled before the Lord take us away from hence. . . . Some of us having taken some pains to view the country, we have found a place which lyeth westward." A short time later, the young people became among the first Anglo-Americans to migrate westward when they moved fifteen miles to found the town of Marlborough.

During the 1650s, a group of ministers led by Richard Mather and James Allin explored ways of modifying membership policies to respond to the problem of the unconverted children of the saints. In the 1630s, the clergy had decided that the children of the saints could be baptized in infancy on the assumption that, as children of the elect, they would surely experience conversion and become full church members. When many did not, there was the new problem of whether to baptize their children in turn. By the original rules of the 1630s, offspring of unconverted second-generation members could not be baptized. Mather and Allin argued that the grandchildren of the elect should be baptized, whereas other clergy and elders, initially including Richard's son Increase, held out fiercely for preserving the old policy. In 1662, a rancorous synod resulted in a revised doctrine, mockingly labeled the Half-Way Covenant by its opponents (see Chapter 3), that allowed the grandchildren of the founders to be baptized but still did not solve the problem of the unconverted parents. Frustration and dismay over this spiritual paralysis, whatever its cause, persisted among the elect and the clergy throughout the 1670s and 1680s.

These same conflicts recurred throughout New England during the second half of the century, and the themes of Thomas Brown's preaching against the "rising generations" were repeated in sermons now called Puritan jeremiads. Taking their texts from Jeremiah and Isaiah, these orations followed – and reinscribed – a rhetorical formula that included recalling the courage and piety of the founders, lamenting recent and present ills, and crying out for a return to the original conduct and zeal. In current scholarship, the term "jeremiad" has expanded to include not only sermons but also other texts that rehearse the familiar tropes of the formula such as captivity narratives, letters, covenant renewals, as well as some histories and biographies.

In addition to the persistent problems of landownership, several natural disasters and larger political problems between 1660 and 1690 caused the Massachusetts Bay communities to undergo a series of traumas, for which the jeremiad became the ritual response. Natural events, including fires, floods, droughts, earthquakes, and the appearances of comets; internal conflicts such as renewed fighting with the Indians, increasing occurrences of satanic possession and witchcraft, and growing secularism and materialism; external intrusions like the arrival of numbers of Quakers and Anglicans, the revocation of the Massachusetts Bay charter in 1684 by the London Court of Chancery, and finally the installation in 1686 of the Anglican royal governor, Edmund Andros – gradually, insistently, these events and the internal tensions present from the 1630s unraveled the Puritan community. Andros exacerbated the tense situation of 1686 by proceeding to nullify all land titles and to meddle in religious affairs, which sparked further lamentations over the decline of piety that, in the minds of many, had provoked God's anger and resulted in all their trials.

Whether an actual decline of religious commitment and zeal among the Puritans in these decades did occur remains one of the most debated issues in Puritan scholarship. Church membership records suggest that the decline in membership may have been a myth born of the jeremiad ritual and the compulsion to place blame for what seemed otherwise to be inexplicable disasters. Yet a shared perception of moral deterioration accrued social and political force and inspired many of the colony's most interesting literary texts, and indeed, the trope of decay or decline became central to later Puritan expressions.

The tradition of opening the annual General Court in May with an election sermon began in Boston in 1634 and continued until 1834. Most of the best-known ministers in New England gave at least one election sermon, and beginning in 1667, the sermons were printed yearly with few exceptions. When the king revoked the Massachusetts Bay charter in 1684, he banned elections and appointed Governor Edward Randolph. In defiance the clergy stopped preaching election sermons until 1691, when the new charter formulated under William and Mary allowed for the election of a body of councillors to advise the appointed governor.

From the beginning, the content of the election sermons was expected to integrate the theory of Puritan society and the current social and religious practices. The pattern created a familiar ritual: the minister summarized the larger historical picture, took stock of the past and present, and articulated a prophecy for the future, designed to inspire the people and leaders to pursue their heavenly as well as their earthly callings. The election sermon followed the standard three-part division used for most sermons. It opened with a biblical text, followed by an "Explication," which closely examined the meaning of each of the words of the text. Often the preacher would review the biblical events that foreshadowed the text, and his audience knew to look for typological parallels to the current New England situation, which the preacher would make explicit in the later "Application." In the second part of the sermon, the "Doctrine," the preacher announced the general laws and lessons that he perceived to be the basis of the text and then divided those larger principles into "Propositions" and "Reasons." The third section, the "Application," demonstrated how the Doctrine and Proposition pertained to contemporary New England. Here, the preacher expounded upon several "Uses" of the analogy between the biblical past and recent experiences. Finally, election sermons often concluded with the preacher's addressing the various groups in the audience directly: the governor, the current representatives, those standing for election, the voters, and the clergy. He might refer to former election sermons and to times of similar conditions, using the past to formulate a prophecy of what might follow, especially if the people were so foolish as to ignore his warnings.

From the late 1660s through the early 1690s, gloomy prospects and catastrophic fears of the imminent failure of the holy experiment led most ministers to construct their jeremiads as mournful dirges. In the early decades of the century, the major themes of election sermons had been the nature of good leadership, the limits of liberty and authority, the biblical roots of Puritan ideas of government, and the proper relationships between the governor and the deputies, between all leaders and the people, and between civil and ecclesiastical powers. To these themes, the jeremiads added anxiety over recent apostasy, over possible connections between tragic current events and God's design for New England, and over the danger that God would abandon his saints forever. Overall, the jeremiads had a complicated, seemingly contradictory, communal function. On the one hand, they were designed to awaken a lethargic people. On the other hand, in their repetitive and ritualistic nature, they functioned as a form of reassurance, reinscribing proof that the saints were still a coherent body who ruled New England in covenant with God and under His sometimes chastising and yet ultimately protective hand. The tension between these competing, yet finally reconciled, purposes gives the jeremiads their literary complexity and power.

Often held to be the prototype of the form is Samuel Danforth's (1626–74) *A Brief Recognition of New England's Errand into the Wilderness,* which was preached in 1670 and published the following year. Born in Framlingham, Suffolk, England, Danforth had lost his mother when he was three and came with his father to New England in 1634, when he was eight. He graduated from Harvard in 1643 and accepted a post as minister in Roxbury in 1650, where he served with John Eliot, whose missionary work among the Indians left Danforth to perform the major duties of the parish. In 1651, Danforth married Mary Wilson of Boston, and they had twelve children, several of whom died young.

Although he took his text for his famous jeremiad from Matthew 11:7–9 and not Jeremiah, Danforth announced in his preface that his theme was the "loss of first love . . . being a radical disease too tremendously growing upon us," and he declared that the "observation of that declension [was] justly calling for so meet an antidote." From a literary perspective, Danforth's project is particularly notable for its imaginative evocation of wilderness imagery and its incorporation, in the final pages, of a dramatic dialogue between Danforth and a community of fearful listeners. The text thus can be read as resonant with Christ's ironic dialogue with the followers of John the Baptist upon John's return from the desert where he began his ministry. The Doctrine that Danforth draws from the text forms a typological connection between John and the Puritan founders: both are "such as have sometimes left their pleasant cities and habitations to enjoy the pure worship of God in a wilderness." Like those who followed John and eventually lost interest in his preaching, some Puritans "are apt in time to abate and cool in their affection." At which point, "the Lord calls upon them seriously and thoroughly to examine themselves, which it was that drew them into the wilderness." Elaborating the several instances in biblical history in which the Jews forayed into the desert only to lose their fervor, Danforth introduces the prophet Jeremiah, who, "that he might reduce the people for their backslidings, cries in the ears of Jerusalem," just as Danforth himself does at the present critical moment.

In the Application, Danforth expands upon the metaphor of the wilderness. First, he recalls the journey of the first settlers "over the vast ocean into this waste and howling wilderness." Depicting their spiritual progress in terms of transforming the harsh wilderness into a fruitful garden, he recalls the times when they "Gleaned day by day in the field of God's ordinances, even among the sheaves, gathering up handfuls." In comparison, the churches today are best described in Proverbs 24:31: "the vineyard is all overgrown with thorns, and nettles cover the face thereof, and the stone wall is broken down," which is a "certain sign of calamity approaching." Instead of a fruitful vineyard, the wilderness becomes once more a threatening space where some "fall into the coal pit," others are "swallowed up alive [in] the lime pit," and "some split upon the rock of affected ostentation." Recalling that they had forsaken the pomp and riches of England for the purity of a simple pious life in the wilderness, he charges that now many, especially the "ladies of Zion," have begun to affect courtly manners and fancy dress, which are "very unsuitable to a wilderness." Linking the external physical wilderness to the internal spiritual wilderness that evil has fostered, he expands the natural imagery: "Why hast the Lord smitten us with blasting and mildew now seven years together, adding sometimes severe drought, sometimes great tempests, floods, and sweeping rains . . . blazing stars, earthquakes, dreadful thunders and lightings, fearful burnings?" In the context of his representation of New England as an enclosed garden circumscribed by wilderness, he asks why it is that so many of the founders and great ministers have died recently: "such burning and shining lights out of the candlesticks; the principal stakes of our hedges; the cornerstones of our walls? . . . breaking down our defensed cities, iron pillars?" He speculates that, like comets, the deaths too are omens: "Is it now a sign that God is making a way for his wrath?"

In his final pages, Danforth adopts a dialogue technique recalling the exchange in Matthew 12:9–13, in which Christ heals a man with a withered hand. Like this man who sought help in near despair, the people of New England should be crying out to Christ, "Alas, we are feeble and impotent; our hands are withered and our strength dried up." In a crescendo of metaphors, Danforth proclaims that the people should deplore and confess their "wound grievous," because their prejudiced hearts have provoked the "sea tempestuous," their empty fields, and the "machinations and contrivances" of their "many adversaries." For each affliction discussed, Danforth gives evidence from scripture of Christ's power and readiness to calm the waters, feed His chosen, and "restrain the rage and fury of adversaries." The key to restoring the community to the blessed state in which it was first established is "diligent attention to the ministry of the Gospel." Through this dialogic structure, Danforth suggests that the leaders of the colony recognize that in assuming their political and social tasks they must also acknowledge the central role of religion in their work, for if they do not and the tragedies continue, Danforth and the other clergy will know who to blame most severely. The citizens hear that in their spiritual lives they must strive for grace and salvation without discouragement, for the corporate survival depends upon the piety of each living soul.

Throughout the 1670s and in the early 1680s especially, preachers used election days, fast days, funerals, executions, and any special events to perform the jeremiad ritual, and more often than not the younger, or "rising," generation was the chosen target. Increase Mather proved masterful in his exploitation of the form, and with four such sermons each, he and his son Cotton preached more election sermons than any other ministers. In addition to his *Day of Trouble is Near* (1674; see Chapter 3), Increase's jeremiads included: *A Renewal of Covenant the Great Duty Incumbent on Decaying and Distressed Churches* (1677), *Pray for the Rising Generation* (1678), and *A Call from Heaven to the Present and Succeeding Generations* (1679). A few other titles of famous jeremiads convey a sense of the consistency of theme: William Adams's *The Necessity of Pouring Out of the Spirit from on High upon a Sinning Apostatizing People* (1679), Samuel Hooker's *Righteousness Rained from Heaven* (1677), Jonathan Mitchell's *Nehemiah on the Wall in Troubled Times* (1671), Urian Oakes's *New England Pleaded With* (1673), Thomas Shepard, Jr.'s *Eye-Salve, or a Watch-Word . . . To Take Heed of Apostasy* (1673), Thomas Walley's *Balm in Gilead to Heal Zion's Wounds* (1669), and Samuel Willard's *The Firey Trial No Strange Thing* (1682). Many of the ministers favored imagery of sickness to characterize the corrosive and dangerous condition of apostasy, and some of the most vivid use of such imagery appears in two jeremiads by Samuel Torrey (1632–1707). In *Exhortation Unto Reformation* (1674), he depicted New England laboring under a "heavy aggravation" that had drained "the internal, spiritual power and purity of the people," and he proposed that "if we do not speedily recover we shall let go and lose all and bury ourselves in our own ruins." Particularly vulnerable to "ill-worship" and other pernicious disorders were young people: "The sins of the Youth (which are many of them some of the most flagitious sins of the Times) are become the sins of the Churches." In *A Plea for the Life of Dying Religion* (1683), Torrey describes the "*vital decay, a decay upon the very Vitals* of Religion," which had led God to smite "us with a deadly destruction: The killing sword, a moral Contagion." And again, he pointed to the "carelessness, slothfulness, unfaithfulness" of the young, who had allowed the religion of their parents and grandparents to "decay, languish, and die away."

Whether the clergy continued to preach jeremiads in the middle to late 1680s at the rate they did in the 1670s is not certain, but fewer such sermons were printed in those years. The sermons that were published were on the whole more reassuring, less occupied with the young and with the decline of religion. Perhaps the specter of perceived external enemies in the form of the Indians and the royal governors with their Anglican brethren served to unify the congregationalists and shift blame to external scapegoats. During and after King Philip's War, most Puritan writings about Native Americans depicted them as children of Satan lurking in the wilderness, the site of evil and corruption. Then, when Andros occupied the churches and insisted that Old South Church be shared with Anglican worshippers, the unfamiliar sound of hymns pouring from the Old South may have been objectionable enough to reconcile the differences among several political factions that had formed among the New Englanders in the 1670s.

There is also evidence that some churches, although they did not go as far as Solomon Stoddard, who opened the communion table to the unconverted, did reduce the psychological pressures upon potential full members by eliminating the necessity of public confession and allowing people to give their testimony to the minister privately or simply to report that they now believed they were saved. The content of the sermons published during the late 1680s indicates that the clergy were approaching their congregations with more assurance and discussing the accessibility of communion. Even the titles convey more hopeful messages: John Bailey's *Man's Chief End to Glorify God* (1689), Ezekiel Carre's *The Charitable Samaritan* (1689), Cotton Mather's *The Call of the Gospel* (1686), Increase Mather's *Some Important Truths Concerning Conversion* (1684), Joshua Moodey's *A Practical Discourse Concerning the Choice Benefit of Communion with God in His House* (1685), Richard Standfast's *A Little Handful of Cordial Comforts for a Fainting Soul* (1690), John Whiting's *The Way of Israel's Welfare* (1686), and Samuel Willard's *Covenant-Keeping the Way to Blessedness* (1682), *A Child's Portion: or the Unseen Glory* (1684), *Mercy Magnified on a Penitent Prodigal* (1684), and *Heavenly Merchandise; or the Purchasing of Truth Recommended and the Selling of It Dissuaded* (1686). In this last sermon, Willard baldly appealed to motivations linked to the increasingly materialistic attitudes that most clergy had only recently berated. During this decade Edward Taylor preached his series of sermons on Christ as savior (collected and published as *Christographia,* 1962) partly in reply to Stoddard; Taylor believed it was proper to prepare souls for conversion by preaching of the beauty and generosity of Christ rather than by using communion as an instrument of conversion. For Taylor, language itself was a means of salvation, a bridge from the heart of the saint to grace, rather than – as it had been previously – merely a vehicle for externalizing the internal spiritual stirrings that were the signs of the presence of the spirit.

As increasing numbers of younger people became full church members in the 1680s, the clergy may have recognized that what they had perceived to be a decline in piety was more likely a myth, an appearance generated by youthful humility and spiritual temerity and by community need for internal reasons to explain difficult times. After the witchcraft delusion in the 1690s, the number of jeremiads increased again but not to the level of frequency of the earlier period or with the emphasis on the failures of the young. Indeed, one of the most notable jeremiads of the 1690s was seventy-eight-year-old Joshua Scottow's (1615–98) *Old Men's Tears for Their Own Declensions* (1693), in which he places the blame for the secularization of New England not upon the young but upon his own generation for having lost their original zeal and sense of purpose.

Although jeremiad preaching never returned to the fury of the 1670s, the ritualistic form had become firmly established in the culture, and groups of immigrants coming to America in the centuries to follow would rehearse the familiar sequence – idealism and dreams of success followed years later by feelings of disillusionment, loss, and disappointment, especially with complacent children – thereby keeping the jeremiad resonant within the American imagination. Thus, even today on every Fourth of July, speakers across the country hail the "Founding Fathers," assail present failures, and urge audiences to revive original ideals so that America can fulfill its manifest destiny. From presidential addresses to works of literary artists, the jeremiad appears as a fundamental structure in American expression. *Moby-Dick, The Narrative of the Life of Frederick Douglass, Life in the Iron Mills, Walden, The Great Gatsby, The Grapes of Wrath, Gravity's Rainbow* – these works and many others have all been called jeremiads because they seem to call for a return to a former innocence and moral strength that has been lost.

In the seventeenth century and to the present time, the jeremiad themes and structure characterize not only sermons but other writings as well. Captivity narratives usually follow the jeremiad design, with the victim reflecting upon the period of his or her life preceding the capture and discovering personal faults that had brought on God's punishment. During the time of captivity, the repentant victim searches within the self and vows to return to earlier piety, a decision that appears to be rewarded when the captive is freed. Mary White Rowlandson's captivity narrative, the first and most famous, can be read as such a jeremiad.

Mary White was born about 1637 in South Petherton, Somerset, England. Her father, John White, emigrated to Salem, Massachusetts, in 1638 and sent for the rest of the family in the following year. The family eventually moved to Lancaster, where her father, a wealthy landowner, was one of the founders. She married Reverend Joseph Rowlandson, pastor of the church at Lancaster, and the Rowlandsons had four children, one of whom died in infancy. On February 10, 1676, during King Philip's War, a Wampanoag raiding party attacked Lancaster, killing twelve citizens, including members of the Rowlandson family, burning their homes, and taking Mary and others captive. Mary's brother-in-law, eldest sister, and her sister's son were killed, and Mary's youngest daughter, Sarah, whom she held in her arms, was fatally wounded by a bullet that first passed through Mary's side. Twenty-four were taken captive, and the parents were separated from their children. Rowlandson carried her six-year-old Sarah with her until she died on February 18. Her other two children, ten-year-old Mary and thirteen-year-old Joseph, were held apart from Mary, but as she reports, she did see them briefly a few times during her captivity. All were eventually ransomed, with Mary's release coming on May 2, 1676. During her months in captivity, Mary lived with and was the servant of Weetamoo of the Pocassets and her husband, Quanopen, a chief of the Narragansets and one of the leaders of the attack on Lancaster. After her release, the Rowlandsons lived in Boston for a year before her husband became minister to the church in Wethersfield, Connecticut. Rowlandson began her narrative in either 1677 or 1678. Her husband died in November of 1678, and the last public record of her as Mary Rowlandson occurs in 1679 when she was awarded a pension and a sum for his funeral. Until very recently, historians assumed that she probably died before her narrative was published in 1682, but new evidence indicates that she married Captain Samuel Talcott on August 6, 1679, and lived in Wethersfield, Connecticut, until January 5, 1711, when she died at the age of seventy-three.

Creating, perhaps, what would become the formula for the captivity narrative, Rowlandson declares that she was moved to write of her experience because it was evident to her that God had used her for His purpose and that she wanted to convey the spiritual meaning of her experience to others. Despite this religious motive, it was a bold act for a woman to undertake a major prose work in seventeenth-century New England, and her text is the only lengthy piece of prose by a woman published in seventeenth-century America. It is likely that she was strongly encouraged to write it by Increase Mather, who had helped her husband during the ransom negotiations. Mather wrote a preface to the narrative, in which he provided the official Puritan interpretation of Mary's ordeal and of her narrative. Mather was very concerned after King Philip's War that people in New England and leaders in England should understand the reasons and meaning of the catastrophe of the war in providential terms. The war had devastated the population and the financial resources of New England at the very time that King Charles was looking for a reason to intervene in the prosperous colony's affairs. Mather's history of the war, his sermons, and Rowlandson's narrative all inscribe a "spiritualized" construction over the brutal reality of the war and allow Mather to assert that New England had been redeemed; thereby, it seemed, the colonies acquired a divine reprieve to be left politically independent.

The first part of Rowlandson's title, usually dropped in modern editions, demonstrates how her personal experience is to be subordinated to religious precepts. The full title is *The Sovereignty and Goodness of God, Together with the Faithfulness of His Promises Displayed; Being a Narrative of the Captivity and Restoration of Mrs. Mary Rowlandson, Commended by her to all that Desire to Know the Lord's Doings to, and Dealings with Her. Especially to her Dear Children and Relations.* The words pertaining to her actual experience are virtually surrounded by, contained within, and outnumbered by others that are to transform her suffering into a sign of God's "Goodness." The horror of the divine wrath presented in the text is erased in the title by God's "Faithfulness" to Mary and New England. As a Puritan and a minister's wife writing under the gaze and likely guidance of Mather and her husband, Rowlandson was certainly aware of the communal function of her narrative. To complete the holy packaging of the first publication, the text of Rowlandson's narrative was bracketed by Mather's preface and by a sermonic afterword on the war by Joseph Rowlandson. But, in spite of these devices of control and containment, Rowlandson's grief refuses to be reconstructed into an acceptance of divine will, and the emotional power of her experiences emerges through the discursive structure of the jeremiad rhetoric.

With personal feelings and Puritan rhetoric competing to control the text, the work is characterized by an internal tension resulting from the author's effort to reconstitute painful personal experiences in language and at the same time to construct her narrative in accordance with the religious expectations and demands of Mather and her fellow Puritans. In order to justify the angry God who sent the Indians into battle, Rowlandson therefore must discover in herself the signs of the failures for which God punished her, just as all of the Puritans were having to do to understand why their numbers and wealth had been so drastically diminished. She reports that on the first Sabbath of her captivity she began to recall her sins: "I then remembered how careless I had been of God's holy time, how many Sabbaths I had lost and misspent, and how evilly I had walked in God's sight." Later, she reveals, she remembered her wicked desire for smoking. For these faults, she considers that she really deserved to be killed, but that in His mercy, God had spared her: "how righteous it was with God to cut off the thread of my life and cast me out of His presence forever. Yet the Lord still showed mercy to me and upheld me; and as He wounded me with one hand, so He healed me with the other." The economic and political reasons for the attacks are either not apparent to Rowlandson or are simply perceived as irrelevant. Even the converted natives, the "Praying Indians," are dehumanized; because some of them betrayed whites during the fighting, Rowlandson concludes that no Native American can be trusted. If it ever occurred to Rowlandson that her punishment was rather harsh for her offenses or that the Native Americans had their own reasons for attacking, the pressure to narrate events in accord with Puritan ideology probably kept her from expressing those thoughts in her text.

As represented in *The Sovereignty and Goodness of God,* the captivity period thus becomes the opportunity for Mary to prepare her heart for grace, to search out the corruption in her nature, and to rediscover the glory of God in His scriptures. As it happens, a warrior who had taken a Bible during another raid gave it to Rowlandson. At first, when she attempted to read it, her spiritual torpor caused the words to seem distant and vague, but grace gradually enabled her to feel the joy of God's words again. Rowlandson conveys that the most frightening part of her experience was neither the physical suffering nor the mental anguish over her children but her lonely metaphysical passage through the dark night of her soul, during which she feared that God had abandoned her. Rowlandson thus becomes an emblematic public example or type – a New England Job – reflecting the entire community's endurance of the war. She preaches the need to remember that only things and creatures of this corrupt world were lost, to accept God's just and wise punishment, and to thank Him for His cleansing fires, deliverance, and reconciliation.

In spite of the standard rhetoric and perhaps in spite of herself, Rowlandson does manage to convey aspects of her personal experience, and where she does so, the text is most compelling for modern readers. The most passionate sections express her feelings about the loss of her loved ones and her near despair. For example, when Sarah died in the middle of the night, Mary did not tell her captors that she was dead for fear that they would discard the body in the forest without a proper burial. In her narrative she recalled how, as she kept the corpse by her through the night, she was overcome with thoughts of suicide:

I cannot but take notice how at another time I could not bear to be in the room where any dead person was; but now the case is changed – I must and could lie down by my dead babe, side by side, all night together. I have thought since of the wonderful goodness of God to me, in preserving me in the use of my reason and senses in that distressed time, [so] that I did not use wicked and violent means to end my own miserable life.

Such passages, even with the gloss of inserted religious precepts, impart the depth of Rowlandson's suffering and the degree to which her own individual narrative resists the narrative tropes of Puritan ideology.

Most interesting in this dialogue between Rowlandson's spiritualized depictions and her reports of actual, unreconstructed reactions are those passages in which she describes her interactions and experiences with the Native-American people. At the outset, she casts her narrative in the language of racist stereotypes that characterized white attitudes especially during and after the war. She describes the Indians as "atheistical, proud, wild, cruel, barbarous, brutish (in one word) diabolical creatures." Her early reactions to Algonkian culture were typical of English and European conceptions of native life. She did not recognize the people as having culture at all and saw them simply as living in senseless chaos. Soon, however, her accounts shift away from the stereotypes. The Indians cease to be merely "others" and become individuals with whom she engages in commerce and civilities. Rowlandson learns that she can use her sewing skills to make clothing and then barter for things she needs, especially food. In the text, these exchanges deconstruct Rowlandson's preconceptions and indicate implicitly that the Indians are people much like herself with different traits and temperaments. Rowlandson comes to understand savagery as a consciously constructed concept, and she even recognizes that the Indian may view her as savage. This idea finds particular emphasis when Rowlandson earns a piece of bear meat for making a shirt and a quart of peas for knitting a pair of stockings. She cooks the two foods together and offers to share her meal with an Indian couple, but the woman refuses to eat because she is repulsed to see meat and vegetables cooked together. Then, when Rowlandson returns to the wigwam of her master and tells this story, he and his wife are angry that she embarrassed them by visiting the home of another and letting it appear that she did not receive enough to eat from her master.

Perhaps Rowlandson's most striking reversal of racist stereotyping occurs in her representation of Metacomet, the hated "King Philip," who was regularly portrayed in Puritan writings as a beast of Satan. Rowlandson recounts her conversations with Metacomet, which include his request that she make a shirt for his son, his offer of a pipe of tobacco to her in friendship, and his concern about her appearance: "He asked me, When I washed me? I told him not this month, then he fetched me some water himself, and bid me wash, and gave me the glass to see how I looked." The "glass," which frequently in frontier writings reveals the savage "other," ironically here references the savagery of the intruding colonist. Contrary to Mary's and her readers' expectations, Metacomet seems more concerned with grooming and civility than she does, for she seems to have degenerated into a "primitive state."

Within the postwar atmosphere of 1676, Rowlandson could certainly not assert that she found the Indians and their leaders to be more like herself than she expected, but her account nonetheless demonstrates the subversive subtext of her narrative. This narrative is rare because of its willingness to humanize the Native American, who speaks words of human concern, self-assertion, and compassion.

Samuel Sewall (1652–1730) was surely an avid reader of Rowlandson and one who thought more seriously about questions of race and justice in his society than most. Best known as the author of the richest American Puritan diary, a major source of New England social history from 1674 to 1729, Sewall also wrote works that might be called secular jeremiads. Born in 1652 to wealthy, merchant-class parents, Henry and Jane Sewall, in Bishop Stoke, Hampshire, England, Samuel was brought to America at age nine. He attended Harvard; for two years he was the roommate of Edward Taylor, who remained a close lifelong friend. He graduated in 1673 but remained at Harvard as a tutor and took an M.A. in 1674. In 1675, Sewall married Hannah Hull, the daughter of John Hull, the colonial treasurer, master of the mint, and the wealthiest man in Boston. The Sewalls had fourteen children before Hannah died in 1717. Sewall remarried twice, in 1719 to Abigail Tilley (d. 1720) and in 1722 to Mary Gibbs. His record of his futile courtship of the widow Katherine Winthrop is the most amusing (though unintentionally so) and the most frequently anthologized section of his diary.

Although Sewall trained for the ministry, his first marriage led him to a calling in a business. He was a merchant, banker, judge, and important leader in the church and government; his diary suggests that he never doubted that his opinions were important to the community as a whole. He was elected to various political offices and was the only person to accompany Increase Mather on the crucial mission to England in 1688 to try to have the charter restored and Edmund Andros recalled. Elected to the council that was authorized to advise the governor under the new charter in 1692, Sewall served in this leading role until he retired from the position in 1725. As a friend of Governor William Phips, he was also appointed to be one of the nine judges of the Salem witchcraft trials. Although he joined in prosecuting the victims, Sewall made very few entries in his diary about the trials, perhaps feeling some anxiety about their justice. In 1697, when Samuel Willard preached that the trials had been misguided, Sewall stood up in his pew, passionately confessed his errors and guilt, and begged forgiveness from the congregation. That afternoon, he wrote a formal statement admitting his mistakes, which he gave to Willard and recorded in his diary.

In that same year, Sewall published his first book, *Phaenomena quaedam Apocalyptica Ad Aspectum Novi Orbus Configurata. Or, some few Lines towards a Description of the New Heaven, As It makes* [sic] *to those who stand upon the New Earth,* a text of sixty pages explicating the Book of Revelation as a forecast of the history of New England. At a time when some Puritan clergy were beginning to recognize that the population of New England was becoming religiously diverse and that the ideas of the city on a hill and the divine errand would remain unfulfilled dreams of a previous generation, Sewall argued strenuously that New England was still the New Heaven and New Jerusalem. In his enthusiasm, he included two prefaces reasserting this vision, one addressed to Lieutenant Governor William Stoughton, and he went throughout Boston giving copies of his book to important leaders. In this work, he recounts the history of the Protestant Reformation and the persecution of the Huguenots, and he insists that the Puritans had converted many Indians – a point attested to by the signatures of eighteen fellow citizens. With energy and eloquence not so evident in his diary, Sewall buttresses his typological arguments with natural evidence. He asserts that the physical beauty of New England, as well as biblical prophecies, proves that New England is the New Zion. His description of an island off the coast of Massachusetts is for modern readers one of the most aesthetically appealing passages in all of Puritan writing:

As long as Plum Island shall faithfully keep the command post, notwithstanding all the hectoring words and hard blows of the proud and boisterous ocean; as long as any salmon or sturgeon shall swim in the streams of the Merrimack or any perch or pickerel in Crane Pond; as long as the sea-fowl shall know the time of their coming, and not neglect seasonably to visit the places of their acquaintance; as long as any cattle shall be fed with the grass growing in the meadows, which do humbly bow down themselves before Turkey-Hill; as long as any sheep shall walk upon Old-Town Hill; and shall from thence pleasantly look down upon the River Parker, and the fruitful marshes lying beneath; as long as any free and harmless doves shall find white oak or other tree within the township, to perch, or feed, or build a careless nest upon, and shall voluntarily present themselves to perform the office of gleaners after barley harvest; as long as Nature shall not grow old and dote, but shall constantly remember to give the rows of Indian corn their education by pairs; so long shall Christians be born there, and being first made meet, shall from thence be translated to be made partakers of the inheritance of the saints in light.

The shift from the focus upon food and nature to the spiritual reaping reveals verbal skills that are not apparent in the more pedestrian writing of Sewall's diary.

It is frequently said of Sewall's diary that it reveals the gradual transformation of a staunch seventeenth-century Puritan into an eighteenth-century cosmopolitan Yankee, but even as he adapted to change in some ways, Sewall embraced religious orthodoxy until his death. However, his antislavery tract, *The Selling of Joseph* (1700), reveals a mind poised between two worlds: Sewall's Puritan tendencies toward constant introspection and scrutiny of biblical passages to support his arguments are blended with the thought of John Locke and other Enlightenment figures whose work would dominate eighteenth-century Anglo-American philosophy and ideas. The three-part structure of the argument demonstrates this fusing of modes of thought. In the first section, he depends heavily upon the scriptures to propose that whites and blacks are all children of Adam and Eve and thereby benefit equally from the contract that God made with humankind after the Fall granting them liberty. Because of this contract, the selling of Joseph by his brothers was "the most atrocious of capital Crimes." In the second part, Sewall provides a more pragmatic gloss by suggesting that the system of using indentured servants is superior to slavery because the servants are looking forward to their freedom and are thus more motivated to work hard than slaves, whose "continual aspiring after their forbidden liberty renders them unwilling servants." In the third part, he combines scriptural and pragmatic arguments in an effort to answer the objections of some that the Bible approved of slavery and that the Africans, as descendants of "Cham" (refers to Canaan, son of Ham, in Gen. 9:25–7), were condemned in the Bible to be slaves. He also replies to the thesis that because the slaves brought to America had been taken prisoner in African wars and made slaves there, they consequently may lawfully remain slaves in America. Finally, he returns to his original biblical argument and concludes that "these Ethiopians, as black as they are, seeing they are the sons and daughters of the first Adam, the brethren and sisters of the last Adam, the offspring of God; they ought to be treated with a respect agreeable."

Although Sewall is to be admired for writing the first antislavery work in New England, it must be recognized that many of his arguments are structured by cultural stereotypes. He opposes the inhumane practice of slavery but does not advocate racial integration. Rather, he urges stopping the flow of Africans into America. He argues that Africans should be kept out because "they can seldom use their freedom well" when they are free and because with the large number of African men and few African women in the community, the whites might be "obliged to find them wives." Already, he regrets, there are so many black men in the militia that "the places [are] taken up of [white] men that might make husbands of our daughters." He also argues that the Africans are a burden on the legal system and the economy: "It seems to be practically pleaded that they might be lawless; 'tis thought much of, that the law should have satisfaction for their thefts, and other immoralities." Sewall's observations necessarily reflected white racism – and white culture's inability to accept difference and the sovereign humanity of the Africans – but at least he did have the courage to take the unpopular position of denouncing slavery itself as "the most atrocious of capital Crimes."

Cotton Mather (1663–1728) was the author of the grandest, indeed epic, jeremiad and the most controversial figure of late Puritan New England. Born in Boston in 1663, the first child of Increase and Maria Cotton Mather and the grandson of the eminent founders Richard Mather and John Cotton, third-generation Cotton was practically destined from birth to go to Harvard (A.B. 1678, M.A. 1681) and to become a leading divine. Today, he is the best-known Puritan minister partly because of his prolific authorship of over four hundred publications and because of the persistent, though unjustified, myth that he was the most severe and self-righteous of Puritans. During his lifetime, however, he remained in the shadow of his father, Increase. Cotton served as the teacher of Old North Church under Increase's pastorship from Cotton's ordination in 1685 until Increase's death in 1723 at the age of eighty-four. Cotton led the church for only four years before he died in 1728. Because he tried desperately to uphold the old New England Way during the waning decades of Puritanism and because his writing style often tends toward the hyperbolic, pedantic, and shrill, many of his texts support the worst images of him as overbearing and self-righteous. He is most identified with his works on witchcraft: *Memorable Providences, Relating to Witchcrafts and Possessions* (1689) and *The Wonders of the Invisible World. Observations as well Historical as Theological, upon the Nature, the Number, and the Operations of the Devils* (1693). Even though he appears less inflamed than most of his contemporaries during the episode, Mather is remembered as the preeminent witchhunter. Recent biographers, however, have stressed other sides of his personality and have substantially revised the stereotype into a complex portrait of a brilliant and, in many ways, enlightened thinker. Some scholars have sympathetically depicted him as a victim of the familial, social, and historical circumstances that tormented him and made him appear less tolerant and rational than he actually was.

With the burden of upholding the reputations of the two most prominent clerical families of New England, precocious Cotton was a pious and studious, but unhappy, youth who mastered Latin and Greek well enough by the age of eleven to pass Harvard's entrance exam. During Cotton's childhood years, his father was cold and preoccupied, caught up in the political turmoil of the Boston Synod of 1662 and the Half-Way Covenant that divided him from his own father and led to a split in the congregation of Old North Church. Convinced that God was abandoning New England, Increase recorded in his diary his emotional distress brought on by problems with the churches, his marriage, his doubts about his own calling, and his longing to live in England. From 1669, when Richard died, to 1671, Increase experienced physical incapacities, nightmares, and depression, and he feared he was dying or going insane. Perhaps it was during this traumatic period that Cotton, who was six when Richard died, developed a stammer, about which Increase confided to his diary that he worried "lest the Hesitancy in his [Cotton's] speech should make him incapable of improvement in the work of the ministry, whereunto I had designed him." When Cotton entered Harvard, he suffered "some discouragement" as a young freshman, perhaps because of his stuttering and his inclination to correct the mistakes of others, including his older classmates. His father perfunctorily removed him from school and educated him at home that year. Cotton seems to have been abused again in his second year, but this time he stayed on to graduate.

At Cotton's graduation when he was only fifteen, President Urian Oakes praised him for his learning and declared the hope of all Puritans that he would rise to restore the churches to the happy state they had enjoyed under his forefathers: "in this youth COTTON and MATHER shall in fact as in name coalesce and revive." In Cotton's impassioned efforts to live out this charge to reverse the social, political, and intellectual forces that saw New England moving rapidly away from the world of his grandfathers, Cotton embodied the many tensions and ambiguities of late Puritanism as it fragmented around him in the storm of ideological change. With visitations of angels to inspire him and a consciousness of divine purpose to drive him, Cotton frantically wrote, preached, ministered, prayed, wept, fretted, counseled, taught, and campaigned for various causes throughout his life, winning the admiration of some and the enmity of others. For all of his seemingly ceaseless and frenetic activity, he always felt that his deeds were inadequate and that his performance failed to fulfill the promise of his name.

Although Mather did bring many hardships upon himself through his dogmatism and his sense of superiority, he also endured many unexpected personal sufferings. His first wife, Abigail Phillips, whom he married in 1686, died in 1702; and his second wife, Elizabeth Clark Hubbard, whom he married in 1703, died in 1713. In 1715, he married Lydia Lee George, but her descent into apparent mental illness caused him much worry and embarrassment; she also brought debts to the marriage incurred by her former husband, and for these Mather was nearly arrested. In 1718, he wrote in his diary that he felt "a continual Anguish of Expectation that my poor Wife, by exposing her Madness, would bring a Ruin on my Ministry." After several turbulent years together, Lydia left Mather in 1723. He also buried nine of his thirteen children, four of them and his wife Elizabeth within a few days during a measles epidemic in 1713. Always financially troubled, he supported three sisters whose husbands had died.

Though Mather is often thought of as one of the harshest and most ideologically rigid of Puritan theologians, he was actually somewhat liberal and opposed his father's conservatism on many issues. For example, while his father persistently ranted against the sins of the rising generation, Cotton convened study groups to instruct young people on Christ's free grace and to encourage their assurance of salvation. Although he was certainly orthodox and preached against sin and backsliding, he also offered many comforting sermons on New Testament texts. In a *Companion for Communicants* (1690), Mather almost approached Stoddard's radical position on open communion when he said, "Assurance is not Absolutely Necessary in order to a *worthy Coming* unto the Holy Supper." He urged uncertain members to "come with all your involuntary and unavoidable Infirmities . . . with all your Hated and your loathed Plagues . . . you shall be welcome here though you have but Faith enough to say with Tears, *Lord, help my unbelief!*"

Indeed, ambivalence and ambiguity characterized Mather's positions on many subjects. For example, he recognized and praised the contributions of women to the churches, to the education of children, and to the civilizing of society. In funeral sermons for Mary Brown, *Eureka: The Virtuous Woman Found* (1711), and for Sarah Leverett, *Monica America: Female Piety Exemplified* (1721), and in a sermon on the ideal Puritan wife, *Ornaments for the Daughters of Zion* (1692), he lauded not only these individuals but women in general. In *Ornaments,* he wrote: "There are far more *Godly Women* in the world than there are *Godly men.* . . . It seems that the *Curse* in the Difficulties both of *Subjection* and of *Childbearing,* which the *Female Sex* is doom'd unto, has been turned into a *Blessing* . . . [for] God . . . makes the *Tenderness* of their Disposition a further *Occasion* of Serious Devotion in them." In his biography of Anne Bradstreet he warmly praised her intelligence, talent, and piety. At the same time, however, in many of Mather's texts there is evidence of possible ambivalence and anxiety regarding women. He was especially disturbed by impious women and was particularly venomous toward the memory of Anne Hutchinson. Also, he often invoked imagery of the female body negatively in discussions of sin and error; doctrinal adultery, wombs of misconception, monstrous fetuses of heresy, and similar tropes appear throughout his works. These figures were common enough in Puritan sermons, but Mather's frequent employment of them may indicate an unconscious fear and disdain of women that his conscious pronouncements functioned to mask.

Certain contradictions also exist in Mather's life and writings in regard to matters involving Africans and Native Americans. Mather often publicly denounced the cruelty of the African slave trade. With Sewall, Mather recognized blacks to be equal to whites as human beings, and in his sermon *The Negro Christianized* (1706), he argued that Africans should receive a Christian education and be allowed to join the church. In spite of his financial problems, he used his own money to pay a schoolmistress to teach local Africans to read, and he entertained the religious society of blacks of his church in his home. However, he also congenially accepted a black slave, named Onesimus, given to him by his congregation. He taught the young man to read and converted him to Christianity, but his negative comments about him as being superstitious and having a "thievish Aspect" suggest that he shared the racial prejudices of his fellow whites. In regard to Native Americans, Mather learned the Iroquois language (in addition to his six other foreign languages), and he worked to integrate the local Indians into white society; of course, he did not recognize that this very process demonstrated a lack of respect for the native cultures.

Inconsistencies and contradictions also appear in many of Mather's writings on science and nature. He firmly believed that every natural event resulted from divine providence, but he saw no conflict in doing scientific research and altering nature to improve living conditions. He consistently demonstrated a desire to be a member of the international scientific community and always felt that he was intellectually confined living in provincial New England. For many years, he wrote remarkably detailed descriptions of the plants, animals, and birds of America, which he sent to the Royal Society in London. Perhaps because he hoped to impress the society's members, these letters contain some of his most evocative prose, often alternating between expressions of pride in being a New Englander and of frustration in being "in an infant country entirely destitute of philosophers." Mather also wrote the first general book on science in America, which he sent in manuscript to the society in 1714 and had published as *The Christian Philosopher* in 1721, followed in 1722 by his important medical text *The Angel of Bethesda . . . An Essay upon the Common Maladies of Mankind . . . and direction for the Preservation of Health*. His research work was admired throughout Europe, and he was elected to the Royal Society.

Perhaps Mather's most important contribution to science came in the field of medicine, a subject he pursued avidly all of his life. In 1721, during one of the smallpox epidemics that ravaged New England about every twelve years, Mather recommended the use of inoculation, which he knew was being tried in other parts of the world. For this proposal, Mather was widely attacked (including an actual assassination attempt); some of the most virulent criticism came from young Benjamin Franklin and his brother James in their newspaper, *The New England Courant*. When other ministers such as Benjamin Colman, Solomon Stoddard, and John Wise supported Mather, the public outcry against inoculation contributed to a growing anticlericalism in New England that hastened the decline of the ministry's influence in the 1720s. Mather stood firm, and successful inoculation was eventually instituted, ultimately making him a hero in the history of eighteenth-century American medicine.

Apart from the many harsh insults he received during the inoculation controversy, Mather suffered other painful professional setbacks. Throughout his life he remained hopeful that he would one day be elected president of

Harvard as his father had been, but repeatedly he was passed over for less qualified men. This obvious snub was very likely the direct result of the Mathers' persistent political conflicts with Governor Joseph Dudley. Also, although Mather's role in the witchcraft trials was not more significant than that of many others who supported the court, his publications on the subject were attacked by Robert Calef (1648–1719) in his devastating rebuttal *More Wonders of the Invisible World* (1700); as a result Mather became the scapegoat of the affair. Perhaps his greatest public humiliation came, however, in 1712 when he managed to convert success into embarrassing failure. Partly because of his liberal admission policies, the congregation of Old North Church expanded, and Mather had pews built for new parishioners. This action impinged upon the presumed privileges of many established members, who felt that the newcomers did not deserve such status. A faction of Mather's leading members split from his church in protest, elected their own minister, and built New North Church three blocks away, much reducing the size of Mathers' congregation and diminishing his influence in the city. In addition to these discouragements, Mather also complained bitterly in his diary of his failure, despite three decades of trying, to find a publisher for his twelve-volume biblical translation and commentary, "Biblia Americana," which he compiled over twenty years and which he viewed as his magnum opus. It has yet to appear in print.

Of Mather's many publications, the one that has generated the greatest number of modern interpretations is his *Magnalia Christi Americana; Or, The Ecclesiastical History of New England, from Its First Planting in the Year 1620, unto the Year of our Lord, 1698.* Written between 1694 and 1698 and published in 1702 in London, the work fulfilled his father's long-standing charge that "the memory of the great things the Lord hath done for us be transmitted to posterity." Running to over eight hundred pages, the complex work is divided into seven books: the settlement of New England; the lives of the governors; the lives of the leading ministers; Harvard College and the lives of its important graduates; Puritan church polity; "Remarkable Divine Providences"; and problems that arose with heretics, Indians, Satan, Edmund Andros, and others. It also contains several poems, notably elegies by such writers as Benjamin Tompson. In spite of this seeming fragmentation, the overall affect of the work is as a unified, epic jeremiad. In the text, Mather glorifies the Puritan founders, inflates the events of the early years, and laments the decline of fervor and purpose in the recent past. His aim, he proclaims, is to keep "*Alive,* as far as this poor *Essay* may contribute thereunto, the Interests of *Dying Religion* in our Churches."

As with so many Puritan writings, however, the *Magnalia Christi Americana* is marked by an internal tension, which doubtless arises from Mather's conflicting double motive: to celebrate the heroism of the founders in creating a New Zion and to reconcile the Puritan churches of his own time with the English Crown and with fellow English Protestants. Thus, at the outset, Mather proclaims in epic style the glories of the sacred New World: "I WRITE the *wonders* of the CHRISTIAN RELIGION, flying from the Deprivations of *Europe*, to the *American Strand*." Here, as in other textual performances, Mather embraced a chiliastic notion that Christ would soon return to earth to begin a millennium of His rule based in His chosen New England. In preparation for this event, New England must recapture the spirit of the first generation: "The *First Age* was the *Golden Age:* To return unto *that*, will make a Man a *Protestant*, and I may say, a *Puritan*." Yet in contrast to this emphasis on New England's uniqueness, Mather repeatedly stresses throughout the text that the founders of Massachusetts Bay were not separatists who had scornfully fled England; they had always loved their mother country and only sought to reform their own Anglican church: "the First Planters of *New England*, at their first coming over, did in a Public and a Printed Address, call the Church of *England*, their *Dear Mother*." In fact, Mather declares that many would have returned if only the Anglicans had removed the trappings of Catholicism. He also stresses that religious freedom was presently the rule in New England, where they "dare make no Difference between a *Presbyterian*, a *Congregational*, an *Episcopalian*, and an *Anti paedo-baptist*, where their *Visible Piety*, makes it probable, that the Lord Jesus Christ has received them." Nonetheless, given the intolerance toward Anglicans and Quakers demonstrated as late as the 1680s, some scholars read Mather's position as a disingenuous and self-serving attempt to garner political favor abroad and thereby to compensate for his own diminished influence at home.

In fairness, however, it seems necessary to remember the cultural context from which Mather produced his texts: he was born into a world of orthodox governors elected under the old charter and yet he soon found himself with a royal governor, surrounded by Anglicans, and under a new charter; in the 1690s he was himself trying to reconcile in his own mind the inherited myth of the New Jerusalem with contemporary realities. Thus, the *Magnalia Christi Americana* can be read as inscribing the myth of the New Zion upon the New England imagination while also reinterpreting it so that the present would seem to have unfolded teleologically. As his father had tried through narrative to reconstruct the devastations of King Philip's War as spiritual victory, Mather similarly attempted to mystify the shattering of the Puritan synthesis, which never really existed, as the ordained fulfillment of sacred history. Thus, he can be quite sincere in his conviction that God brought His chosen to America not to set them permanently apart from their English compatriots but rather, "*By* them, [to] give a *Specimen* of many Good Things, which He would have His Churches elsewhere aspire and arise unto." In Mather's view, providential history consists of many repeated cycles of such pious beginnings, declines of fervor, and restorations of faith. He considered his present moment in Boston to be one of the lapses, to be followed soon by the "dawning of that day" of religious revival.

This Janus-faced dimension of the *Magnalia Christi-Americana* is quite apparent in the biography of Governor Phips, who was royally appointed. In the early 1680s, Phips had been arrested in Boston for commanding a debauched ship's crew; he was known for his swearing and cursing, and at his trial he defied Governor Bradstreet. Then, a decade later, when Phips was appointed governor, Mather praised him as though his accession followed providentially from Bradford, Winthrop, Bradstreet, and other pious Puritan governors. The Phips biography stands in subtle contrast, however, to those on Bradford, Eliot, and the early leaders, for whereas Mather praises them for their piety, he lauds Phips's industry and business abilities. The Phips biography anticipates Benjamin Franklin's *Autobiography*, the Horatio Alger stories, and later fictions engaged in American self-fashioning. Moreover, it suggestively illustrates how Mather and his *Magnalia Christi Americana* performed at the intersection between two conflicting visions of America – one spiritual and one materialistic – that he was attempting to reconcile, while recognizing that each mythology threatened to dismantle the other.

Although Benjamin Franklin had attacked Mather during the smallpox epidemic, he later praised him in a famous passage of his *Autobiography* for having inspired him to live a life of moral righteousness, hard work, and good deeds. Like Franklin, Mather desperately conceived himself to be a person whose mission in life was to be of service to others. Indeed, as his son Samuel said of him: "the Ambition and Character of my Father's life was Serviceableness." This motivation correspondingly finds thematic resonance with one of Mather's most enduring works, his *Bonifacius, an Essay Upon the Good* (1710). Of all of Mather's writing, this was the text that most inspired Franklin. It also displays the liminality of Mather's intellectual situation as he slipped into an eighteenth-century mentality, recommending good works for their practical worldly value and proposing common sense as the way to salvation and wealth. This interpretive gloss appears to have been Franklin's, and the mediating subtext can easily be formulated through selective quotation from the multivalenced language of the text. Close and comprehensive reading, however, reveals Mather still to be steeped in the traditional Puritan theology that privileged grace and conversion as the only means of salvation and that commended the spiritual over the material world. Yet surrounded by wealthy merchants in a flourishing and increasingly secular society that was coming under the intellectual influences of the European Enlightenment, Mather must have been conscious of using his words in ways that permit both a conservative doctrinal reading and a more practical moral application. He may very well have felt tormented that he had to employ such terms in order to reach his generation. The New England world of 1710 was a very different one from that of 1678, when Mather had graduated from Harvard, and there was probably no other person in 1710 who wanted so much to be able "To return unto *that* [Golden Age that] will make a Man a *Protestant,* and I may say, a *Puritan."*

Mather's accomplishments and his voluminous writings testify to the persistent power of Puritan modalities of thought and of the dominating narrative of the American errand. Although Mather did not live to witness the Great Awakening of fervor that he always believed was coming, his texts suggest that he recognized that graduating from Harvard and Yale in the early 1720s were indeed several *"Excellent Young Men* who Study and Resolve their Duty, and are the *Rain-bows* of our Churches." Mather passed on to these very men the Puritan dream he had struggled to keep alive, and in 1727, just a year before Mather died, Jonathan Edwards, the grandson of the Mathers' old antagonist Solomon Stoddard, was ordained pastor of the church at Northampton. There, Edwards would lead the spiritual renewal that the Mathers had prayed for and anticipated for five decades.

6

REASON AND REVIVALISM

BEGINNING IN THE 1650S, the growing number of merchants in Boston, Salem, Cambridge, New-town, and other large towns along the seaboard began to discover themselves to be a special class. Unlike farmers, who were threatened by new immigrants seeking land, the merchants favored the growth and development of new products and international trade. During the Half-Way Covenant controversy of the 1660s, powerful merchants such as John Hull embraced those Pauline aspects of Puritan doctrines that had originally favored expansion of the fellowship, and they sided with those who supported more liberal membership standards. As disputes raged within First Church, Boston, in the 1660s, a coalition made up mainly of merchants split off to found Third Church, later known as the Old South. Under the leadership of Thomas Thatcher until 1678 and of Samuel Willard from then until his death in 1707, the Old South maintained quite lenient membership requirements.

One critical text confronting the issue of church membership was Giles Firmin's *The Real Christian* (1670). A prolific contributor to the parliamentary debates under Cromwell, Firmin lived in New England in the 1630s and 1640s and then returned to England during the Protectorate. Firmin had criticized his former New England colleagues Thomas Hooker and Thomas Shepard for being too rigid in their schematic accounts of preparation and for their discouragingly high standards for proving conversion. Firmin tried to persuade his English colleagues to advocate more tolerance, to understand "self-love" as natural, and to recognize God to be merciful and reasonable. His work found wide circulation in Boston in the 1670s, and its republication in Boston in 1742 demonstrates that the debates over conversion and church membership still continued seventy years later.

During the tumultuous 1670s and 1680s, membership issues divided old friends and often entire congregations. As a member of the Old South, Samuel Sewall noted that "one might gather by Mr. Willard's speech that there was some Animosity in him toward Mr. [Increase] Mather," and Sewall, who respected the Mathers, worried about whether he was correct to be in Willard's congregation: "I have been exceedingly tormented in my mind sometimes lest

the Third Church should not be in God's way in breaking off from the old."
Yet, despite their differences, the New Englanders remained bonded together
during the greater part of the century by their mutual interest in resisting the
intrusions of the English government. After the witchcraft delusion and the
establishment of the new charter in 1692, attention on external enemies
temporarily waned, and internal divisions arose again in the late 1690s, resulting this time in serious and permanent fragmentation.

People began to define ministers categorically as either "conservative" or
"liberal." Those termed "liberals" were usually opposed to formal narrations
of the conversion experience, reassuring about the likelihood of salvation,
tolerant of other denominations, and supportive of union between the congregationalists and the Church of England. They also practiced a more
florid and eloquent preaching style, were inclined to attend an Anglican
celebration service on Christmas Day, were approving of the Lord's Prayer,
and were unopposed to such previously transgressive pursuits as card playing, drinking alcohol for health reasons, and the wearing of periwigs.
Conservatives were likely to require public confessions of the conversion
experience, emphasize a just and wrathful God, worry over hypocrites
entering the churches, disapprove of decadent new fashions as corrupting
morals, stress New England's decline in religious fervor, and resist Anglican
presence and European influences.

These conceptual divergences became most apparent in 1699 when a
group of Boston merchants and ministers, including John Leverett, Simon
Bradstreet, and William and Thomas Brattle, became so frustrated with the
old order controlled by the Mathers and Willard that they broke from the
established churches and built the Brattle Street Church, which they passionately committed to the most liberal of theological trends. They invited the
brilliant and personally appealing young Benjamin Colman (1673–1747),
who had graduated from Harvard in 1695 and had traveled abroad and joined
the Dissenters in England, to return to Boston and assume the pulpit of the
new church. Knowing he would face stiff opposition from the Mathers and
others, Colman had himself ordained by the Presbyterians in London and
returned to Boston importing English credentials and European cosmopolitanism and elegance.

With Thomas Brattle and other reformers, Colman produced the polemical *Manifesto* (1699) and *The Gospel Order Revived* (1700), which introduced
many progressive innovations into religious practice such as offering baptism
to all children, giving communion to any who claimed to be justified,
electing ministers by the vote of the entire membership, including women,
and adopting the Anglican practice of reading the scriptures in church without comment. In general during these dynamic years, the roles of women in

the churches became increasingly important. The number of published funeral sermons on women increased, and these frequently expressed admiration for the woman's intelligent conversation, her intellectual stimulation of her husband, and her wise counsel within the church and community. For example, accompanying the publication of Nathaniel Appleton's funeral sermon on Mrs. Martha Gerrish are several of her letters, which he said had guided her many correspondents and which he asserts had been as influential as many sermons. It is not surprising that many women tended to favor those ministers who gave them more encouragement and respect, and those clergy were usually among those referred to as "modern" or "liberal."

Although Colman basically adhered to Calvinist doctrines, he and his friends challenged many established rules of church polity and liturgy. Within a few months of Colman's *The Gospel Order Revived,* Increase Mather published a seventy-page treatise, *The Order of the Gospel* (1700), steadfastly defending the old ways. In response, some members of the Brattle church wrote a satirical parody of Mather's work that they called *Gospel Order Revised* (1700). Despite Mather's efforts, Colman enjoyed immediate, strong popularity, and his tolerance and peacemaking abilities soon enabled him to repair the breach with the Mathers, in whose church he had been reared and whom he admired. Cotton Mather, who liked to fancy himself a "modernist," must have helped to persuade his father to bend with the times, although Increase, who saw New England slipping toward hell, vented his distress in his most scathing jeremiad, *Ichabod. Or, a Discourse, Showing What Cause There is to Fear that the Glory of the Lord is Departing from New England* (1702). The establishment of Brattle Street Church signaled a new phase in the evolution of Puritanism that would gradually yet inexorably push the Mathers and their supporters to the margins of early-eighteenth-century history.

One of the most significant developments at the turn of the century that contributed to the liberal movement was the shift in the control of the Board of Overseers of Harvard College and the establishment of Yale College in 1701. Complicated manipulations of local politics involving members of Brattle Street Church resulted in Increase Mather's resigning the Harvard presidency in 1701 and in the interim appointment of Samuel Willard. For six years, Willard, who sympathized with the Mathers but supported the Brattles, and Governor Dudley, who disliked the Mathers, laid the groundwork for the appointment of John Leverett of the Brattle Street faction to the Harvard presidency. As Harvard came increasingly under the control of the liberal faction, students of the ministry emulated Colman's discursive style and embraced the progressive ideology of those who called themselves "moderns" or "modernists." These included such influential figures as Joseph Sewall (1688–1769; Harvard, 1707), Thomas Prince (1687–1758; Harvard,

1707), and Charles Chauncy (1705–87; Harvard, 1721). In Connecticut, religious disputes and a reluctance to depend upon Harvard for their ministers led a conservative group who shared many of the positions of the Mathers to found Yale College, from which Jonathan Edwards (1703–58) graduated in 1720. Most scholars agree that, with many qualifications over finer points of theology, a line of theological tradition can be traced from Leverett's liberal Harvard through the Universalism of Chauncy to the Unitarianism of William Ellery Channing and the Transcendentalism of Ralph Waldo Emerson. On the other side, from Edwards's Yale, an opposing evangelical, and eventually fundamentalist, tradition evolved, which can be traced down to Timothy Dwight and Lyman Beecher in the nineteenth century and to many kinds of religious enthusiasts in the twentieth.

While squabbling among themselves, the clergy of the new century soon recognized that ministers of every party were losing favor. The leaders of all factions realized the need to act to prevent religion from becoming increasingly inconsequential for the busy, prospering colonists and to prevent the clergy from becoming so weak as to be at the mercy of the civil authorities and laypeople. The clergy reacted in two ways: they coalesced in associations and councils in an effort to strengthen their political stature and to pass legislation controlling ordination and ministerial credentials; and they preached numerous sermons stressing the importance of a trained clergy and respect for learning and scholars.

In 1704, Benjamin Colman led the Cambridge–Boston Association of ministers in a convention that drafted several proposals designed to reempower the clergy. Although the Anglican governor Joseph Dudley refused to enact their resolutions into law, the meeting of the association did embolden individual ministers to lead their congregations more firmly. In 1708, the Connecticut clergy formed the Saybrook Platform, which served the same purpose. Both conventions stirred great ferment among congregations and ministers, some of whom saw this consolidation as creating an unnecessary division between the clergy and the people by fostering clerical elitism, self-importance, and worldliness. Increase Mather opposed the association movement and held to the traditional view that the clergy possessed no more authority than laymen in ecclesiastical matters. As he saw it, the forming of associations involved "the very same path the church of Rome walked in . . . [for] their beginning was a taking of the power of privilege from the brethren."

Another result of the efforts of the clergy to regain status and influence was the emergence of special privileges and advantages for the wealthy in matters pertaining to religion and education, and such favoritism was increasingly evident in the colleges. Between 1700 and 1720, admission to the New England colleges became conspicuously dependent upon the social position of parents rather than on the piety and ability of the sons, and as a result, the quality and seriousness of the students declined. In 1722, young Benjamin Franklin wrote a scathing attack upon Harvard, where, he said, students "were little better than Dunces and Blockheads" because parents "consulted their own purses instead of their Children's Capacities." Indeed, at both Harvard and Yale in these decades, the intelligent and pious young men who would become famous ministers, such as John Cleveland, Joseph Sewall, Thomas Prince, Charles Chauncy, and Ebenezer Pemberton, formed religious clubs that were havens of serious study within the increasingly secular and often raucous settings. The growing class division between those from monied backgrounds who attended college and became ministers and the average church members resulted in increased scorn toward the clergy in general.

The congregational clergy also suffered attacks from the Anglicans, who questioned their very credentials to be ministers. The Anglicans contended that if the New England clergy considered themselves members of the Church of England, as they claimed, then they should be ordained within the English church. The rumored weaknesses of the colleges and the general clerical Anglophilia that increased in the new century led many American ministers to doubt the legitimacy of their own ordinations. In 1723, a "Great Apostasy" occurred when President Samuel Johnson of Yale and six tutors declared their intentions to be ordained again in England by Anglican bishops. Shortly thereafter, the simple congregational ordinations were replaced by more elaborate and polished ceremonies that were more like those of the Anglicans.

In spite of all the clergy's efforts at consolidating their power and improving their collective image within the shifting culture, clericalism failed. The many bitter disputes over ministers' salaries and the rise in laypeople's insistence on their equal religious authority suggest that many congregations ultimately came to resent clerical elitism. For decades, the clergy had been calling for a renewal of piety and zeal and some had heard of "awakenings" in New Jersey, but ironically, when the revival came to New England, it served to further disempower the clergy. Beginning in the early 1720s, some small revivals in Stoddard's Connecticut River domain were held, and the movement gained momentum on October 29, 1728, when a major earthquake disrupted the province with "a most violent clap of Thunder" sounding like "a sudden and sharp crack like firing a gun." The earthquake and its many aftershocks damaged homes and businesses and left many expecting to see "the Great Day of the Son of man's appearing." For weeks, ministers reported a decline in civil contentiousness and an increase in attention to sermons. Then in 1734, a larger religious revival began in Jonathan Edwards's parish in Northampton, from which it would sweep through the Connecticut River Valley. Edwards's report on these revivals, *A Faithful Narrative of the Surprising Work of God in the Conversion of Many Hundred Souls* (1737), was widely circulated and helped prepare for the Great Awakening a few years later.

In the fall of 1740, the evangelical minister Reverend George Whitefield arrived from England and embarked upon a preaching tour of the colonies. Upon hearing of his success in the middle colonies, Colman was particularly anxious to have him preach in New England. Although some ministers were dubious about whether the passions Whitefield aroused represented genuine religious zeal, those clergy who felt that religion and clerical power were languishing looked to him for help. Colman invited Whitefield to Boston, where his success prompted dozens of New England churches to welcome him. Whitefield was soon followed by the Presbyterian revivalist from New Jersey Gilbert Tennent, and then by dozens of other itinerant evangelicals. As many local ministers also generated their own awakenings, the spirit spread across the land, and for the first time in years, people, men in particular, urgently sought answers to religious questions. Ministers called for a reestablishment of family orders, and during the revivals men were converted in far greater numbers than women. This regenerated concern caused "awakened parishioners" to read and interpret the Bible for hours on end and to attempt to establish firmer discipline in both home and community.

At first, the ministers supported and led the revivals, but soon the people began to take control of the phenomenon by proclaiming visions, preaching spontaneously to congregations, and carrying on religious discussions in the absence of the minister, as Anne Hutchinson had done a hundred years before. Many clergy quickly saw that instead of buttressing their authority, the revivals were undermining it. Once again, the concept of perceived truth was an issue; the debate hinged on who was empowered to proclaim – speak – certain divine truths. Some ministers began to preach against the itinerant clergy and the effects of the movement, which was called the Great Awakening. Former alliances were destroyed, and a new division formed between the "New Lights," or "New Side," clergy, who supported evangelism, and the "Old Lights," or "Old Siders," who opposed the movement. Some of the New Lights, such as Colman, were theological liberals, and some of the Old Lights, like John Barnard, were conservatives; on the other hand, the liberal Charles Chauncy strongly opposed revivalism, and Jonathan Edwards was a conservative New Light Calvinist.

Despite all these upheavals, however, the general movement of the clergy during the first half of the eighteenth century, with some notable exceptions, was away from strict Calvinism and toward the liberal ideas of what would come to be called the Euro-American Enlightenment. Adhering to the old school and perhaps recognizing that congregations were reacting against clerical elitism, some ministers such as John Barnard (1681–1770), pastor at Marblehead from 1717 until 1770, spurned the modern ways. Barnard's image was that of the humble, unpretentious, country parson who labored on small salary in equal social standing with his parishioners. His ministerial style stood in sharp contrast to the model of Benjamin Colman, and he represented the kind of clergyman to be found more often in country villages as opposed to the urban centers, where periwigs and English fashions dominated.

A friend of the Mathers, though he outlived them by four decades, Barnard helped to preserve and extend the seventeenth-century Puritan vision into the era of the American Revolution. Barnard is known today because he published several books and because his verbose, gossipy autobiography appeared in 1836. Others like him are not so well remembered, but their parishes dotted the countryside of New England. When Thomas Paine, Thomas Jefferson, John Adams, and Benjamin Franklin invoked the discourse of the jeremiad and the rituals of fast days to arouse the passions of Americans against King George, the English Antichrist, in the 1770s, they were touching emotional chords that had remained sensitive throughout the colonies due to the work of "Old Calvinists" like Barnard rather than to the moderns such as Colman and Chauncy.

Precocious in linguistics and mathematics as a youngster, Barnard had been a pupil at Boston Latin School, where he studied under the renowned schoolmaster Ezekiel Cheever, whose extraordinarily popular *A Short History of the Latin Tongue* (1709) endured as the standard text in America well into the eighteenth century. Barnard graduated from Harvard in 1700 just before the sea change to liberalism there under the Brattles and Leverett. Shortly after arriving at Marblehead, he married Anna Woodbury; the couple had no children. Like William Hubbard before him, Barnard adhered to the early Calvinist spirit but also gave substantial place to the role of reason in all affairs except conversion. A "sweet reasonableness" was the central characteristic of his sermon style. A carpenter and shipbuilder in his spare time, Barnard was a keen observer of the economic conditions in his town, and his recommendations for improving the efficiency of the fishing and shipping industries of Marblehead contributed to its notable prosperity.

When Barnard first began to preach in Boston after his graduation, the Mathers heard in his sermons too much emphasis on works and accused him of Arminianism, but they later saw their error. Although his sermons always stressed reason and diligence, he never lost sight of divine sovereignty. In his election sermon of 1734, *The Throne Established by Righteousness,* Barnard used his plain and direct style to project his nostalgic vision of a promised land of hard work, morality, and salvation. With the type of religious–economic argument that would lead Max Weber to formulate a theory about the bond between Calvinism and the rise of capitalism, Barnard proposed that government should facilitate prosperity by "due encouragement of labor and industry, by proper premiums for serviceable manufactures, by suppressing all that tends to promote idleness and prodigal wasting and consuming of estates, by a due testimony against all fraud and deceit and unrighteousness in dealings, by cultivating frugality and good husbandry." If the government does its part, Barnard reasoned, God will fulfill His sacred promise to New England still. Barnard's holy economics was good for business and for religion. When the enthusiasm of the Great Awakening affected his congregation, he brought his parishioners to a balance of fervor and reason in his *A Zeal for Good Works, Excited and Directed* (1742), recommending a "zeal guided by knowledge, tempered with prudence, and accomplished with charity."

Another representative of these country preachers is the Reverend John Wise (1652–1725), who has been called the most original prose writer in colonial America and an early American Puritan democrat. Wise too was a conservative Calvinist and a supporter of congregational church government, but he often appealed to natural law and reason. Operating within what was already identified in Europe as a tradition of American discourse – modest, folksy, and seemingly without guile – he employed a language of homey metaphors, country humor, and commonsense examples. He was born in Roxbury, Massachusetts, to a former indentured servant, and probably would not have qualified socially to attend Harvard had he been born thirty years later. After his graduation in 1673, he served as a military chaplain during King Philip's War. From 1677 to 1682, he was pastor at Hatfield; there he married Abigail Gardner, with whom he had seven children. From Hatfield, he was called to the new Chebacco parish in Ipswich, where he became famous as a defender of the rights of the colonists against royal intrusions. In 1687 he urged the people to resist the poll and property taxes imposed by Governor Edmund Andros. When they did resist and when several other towns joined them, the government imprisoned and fined Wise and stripped him of his ministry. But when Andros was overthrown in 1689, Wise was exonerated and awarded a position as chaplain in the military expedition to Quebec, during which he distinguished himself for his sound advice and inspired preaching.

Returning to Boston just before the Salem witchcraft trials, Wise displayed courage and independence in defending his former parishioners John and Elizabeth Proctor, but to no avail (see Chapter 1). In fact, Wise may have been the only minister in the country who disavowed the proceedings from the beginning. Throughout his career, he consistently fought for democratic practices in government and the church. During the movement for clerical associations, Wise was in the opposition and wrote two books refuting the notion of a union of clergy as being narrow and undemocratic.

The first of these works, *The Churches Quarrel Espoused,* reportedly appeared in 1710, but the extant copies were published in New York in 1713 and reprinted in Boston in 1715. His second book, *A Vindication of the Government of New England Churches,* appeared in 1717 in Boston. In these tracts, Wise directs his arguments to ordinary church members, employing common images and pointed humor to sting his colleagues. Warning that the clergy's proposals "be but a Calf now, yet in time it may grow (being of a Thirsty Nature) to become a sturdy Ox that will know no Whoa," he charges that with their plan to consolidate power in associations the clergy have "Out Pope't the Pope Himself." Pretending to be making small repairs in the Cambridge Platform, the ministers, in Wise's view, were really dismantling it: they came with trowel in hand "to plaster over a chink or two, . . . but in Reality they have in their other hand a formidable *Maul* . . . to break Down the Building." Regarding one complicated proposal to emerge from the association meetings, he mocks, "a Riddle I found it, and a Riddle *I leave it.*" In response to the clergy's argument that an association was needed to help ministers resolve disagreements that might arise in particular parishes, Wise said that any decent minister should not need "a Covering of Fig-Leaves" or a "Harbor to Cowards and Fools": "if men are plac'd at Helm, to steer in all weather which Blows, they must not be afraid of the Waves, or a wet Coat." No one ever published a reply to Wise's books, and they remained the last public word against the association movement.

Like Barnard, Wise also endorsed a form of sacred economics, and in his last publication he illustrates the economic side of his equation of religion and finance. In *A Word of Comfort to a Melancholy Country; Or, the Bank of Credit Erected in Massachusetts Fairly Defended* (1721), he defends the establishment of a private land bank that would issue paper currency as a way of stimulating the economy and unifying the colony's residents in active commerce and good faith. In Wise's schema, faith in an invisible God and trust in the bank's promised reserves operate in tandem for salvation and prosperity.

Whereas men like Barnard and Wise were known for their homey, direct language and humble personal style, Benjamin Colman was urbane, witty, and sophisticated and known for his poetic constructions, variety of diction, and eloquence. Born in Boston in 1673, to Elizabeth and William Colman, Colman studied under Ezekiel Cheever at Boston Latin School and graduated from Harvard in 1692. After receiving his M.A. in 1695, he departed for England but was captured by pirates and imprisoned for several months in France. He finally arrived in England sick and destitute but was soon taken in by fellow Protestant Dissenters who arranged for him to preach at Bath, where he spent two years. During his four years in England, Colman became acquainted with poets and artists and was befriended and tutored in the manners of London society by the poet Elizabeth Singer. Later, he encouraged the poetic pursuits of his own daughters (see Chapter 4). Upon his return to Boston and the establishment of his ministry, Colman married Jane Clark, with whom he had a son, who died in infancy, Jane, the poet, and Abigail. When his first wife died, Colman married the widow Sarah Clark (no relation to Jane) in 1732, and after she died, he married another widow, Mary Frost, in 1745. In a career that spanned nearly fifty years, Colman fashioned a delicate theological and political compromise by retaining the Calvinist doctrines of the founders while allowing the external forms of the church to be adapted to the psychological needs and social desires of his eighteenth-century congregation. After the initial disturbance caused by his arrival, he formed friendships with most of the established ministers of Boston, and he even preached the funeral sermons for the Mathers and for many of their opponents, including Stoddard, Thomas Brattle, Dudley, and Leverett. He corresponded with Jonathan Edwards and welcomed Whitefield and Tennent to Boston. In the pulpit, Colman performed in a style that contemporaries called "grand and polite," and he encouraged his parishioners to think confidently of themselves as saints who had been lifted by grace above anxiety. While Increase Mather was still ranting about sin and backsliding, Colman recommended balance, calm, and assurance in Christ.

In his most famous series of sermons, *A Practical Discourse on the Parable of the Ten Virgins* (1707), Colman urged his listeners to try to "resemble virgins in purity" because then they will benefit from the joys of being with Christ in life and death. In selecting this biblical text, on which Thomas Shepard had preached a famous sermon series between 1636 and 1640, Colman shrewdly allied himself with the Puritan heritage and with Shepard's renowned balance of fervor and reason. Rather than focusing upon the evils of sin and damnation, he attempted to entice souls, with a degree of eroticism, to the beauty of Christ:

Like espoused virgins we should be expecting, desiring, waiting, and preparing for the coming of our Lord. . . . How much more should we with raptures think of and wish for heaven, the place and time of full communion and vision? In this we groan earnestly in the hope and expectance of an expecting love, the preparations against the day of the consummations of our desires, and how joyfully it is welcomed when arrived; nor is there any indecency herein. Can the bride forget to provide her ornaments and attire against the time? No more the believer his, the graces of the spirit of God, and the rightness which is through the faith in Christ. . . . Why should we not run to meet the smiling vision, as those that are found alive at Christ's second coming will fly up to meet him in the air?

Even as he apologizes for the possible "indecency" of the sexual implications of the image of the groaning, impatient bride, Colman proceeds in his balanced and melodious prose to images of comfort and safety. Ordinary emotions presented in fluid and clear language inscribed Colman's writing with an urbane grace that set it apart from the choppy and relatively crude directness of ministers such as Barnard, Wise, and Increase Mather.

Just as stylistic changes had begun to appear in the early-eighteenth-century sermons, other writers were developing new techniques in other genres. For modern readers, one of the liveliest and most delightful pieces of prose narrative of the period is *The Journal of Madam Knight,* written by Sarah Kemble Knight (1666–1727) in 1704 and 1710 and later edited and published in 1825 by Theodore Dwight, Jr. Sarah Kemble was born in Boston in 1666 to Thomas Kemble, a merchant, and Elizabeth Treice. Although it is not known to which Boston church the Kembles belonged, it is very likely that as the daughter of a successful merchant, Sarah grew up hearing Puritan sermons in one of the congregational churches. From her journal, it is evident that she had associations with several ministers, for she makes a point of visiting clergy on her journey. Sometime before 1689, she married the much older Richard Knight, who was a shipmaster and London agent for an American firm; they had one child, Elizabeth, in 1689. It is also likely that the financially comfortable Knights would have been members of one of the major Boston churches in the 1690s.

Some years before her husband died in 1706, Knight was forced to assume many of his business responsibilities. Within the context of the growing social and religious acceptance of public roles for women, she kept a shop and house on Moon Street in Boston, took in boarders, and taught children handwriting. Because she learned much about business and the law from her work, Knight decided to travel to New Haven in 1704 to help settle the estate of her cousin for his widow. Recognizing that it was rare for a woman to undertake such a journey alone, she decided to keep a narrative of her travels. Her journey covers two periods: from October 2 through October 7 and several selected days between December 6 and January 6, 1704–5.

Adopting techniques of the mock-epic and elements of the picaresque, Knight wrote a humorous, direct, and concrete account having only traces of the moral didacticism that forms the center of most Puritan autobiographies. Highly self-conscious as a narrator, even self-mocking and ironic at times, Knight demonstrates a self-reflective awareness that her narrative violates conventions. On her second night on the road, for example, she and her guide enter a dark forest. In language that anticipates the techniques of the gothic style later in the century, she recalls this frightening experience before making the religious point her contemporaries might expect:

Now returned my distressed apprehensions of the place where I was: the dolesome woods, my Company next to none, Going I knew not wither, and encompassed with Terrifying darkness; the least of which was enough to startle a more Masculine course. Added to which [were] the Reflections, as in the afternoon of the day, that my Call was very Questionable which till then I had not so Prudently as I ought considered.

Although she makes it clear here, though as an afterthought, that her fear has aroused a spiritual concern about her calling, when they reach a clearing at the top of a hill, she does not first praise God for deliverance; instead, she is enraptured with "the Sight of that fair Planet," the moon, to which she then writes a poem. When she does credit God for her safe return home at the end of the journal, she correspondingly sounds more like a Franklinian Deist than a proper Puritan: "But [I] desire sincerely to adore my Great Benefactor for thus graciously carrying forth and returning in safety his unworthy handmaid."

In earthy language and with robust energy, Knight records her experiences with her guides, saucy servants in country inns, ignorant, gruff innkeepers, and boisterous tenants who kept her awake at night. She recounts her delight in the beauty of nature but also interpolates troubling images of rural poverty:

This little Hut was one of the wretchedest I ever saw [as] a habitation for human creatures. It was supported with shores enclosed with Clapboards, laid on Length-ways, and so much asunder, that the Light come throu' every where. . . . The floor the bare earth; no windows. . . . The family were the old man, his wife and two Children; all and every part being the picture of poverty. . . . I Blest myself that I was not one of this miserable crew.

Although she tends to foreground consciousness of economics and class, she frequently displays the prejudices of her own class in her view of the world; her descriptions of country "bumpkins" are forerunners of later depictions of the backwoodsmen in works of American humor. Sharing the racial preju-dices of her white society, she accepted slavery, and she wrote with scorn of Native Americans: "There are every where in the Towns as I passed, a Number of Indians the Natives of the Country, and are the most savage of all the savages of that kind that I had ever Seen: little or no care taken (as I heard upon enquiry) to make them otherwise." The details she selected to report about Native Americans correspond to her received stereotypes of their sexual promiscuity, general immorality, and need for white supervision.

Knight often expresses her sense of moral superiority, but she also makes religion the butt of her humor. On her third day, she and her guide endure a thirty-mile stretch of highway with no accommodations. When she com-plains, her guide tells her that they would reach "Mr. Devills" in a few miles. She answers in the terminology of Puritan sermons: "But I questioned whether we ought to go to the Devil to be helpt out of affliction. However, like the rest of Deluded souls that post to ye Infernal den, We make all possible speed to this Devil's Habitation, where alighting in full assurance of good accommodations we were going in." Her description of this stop at the Devil's house mingles elements of the journey motifs of Greek mythology and the typology of spiritual passage in Christian conversion narratives that had been used in such works as *Everyman,* the *Divine Comedy,* and *Pilgrim's Progress.* In a later episode, in another comic jibe at religion, she describes the prosperity of the town of Fairfield and mocks the constant controversies over clerical salaries: "They [the townspeople] have abundance of sheep, whose very Dung brings them, great gain, with part of which they pay their Parson's salary, And they Grudge that, preferring their Dung before their minister."

It is not known if Knight produced other writings, for if she did, they have been lost. When her daughter married into the powerful Livingston family of Connecticut, Knight moved to New London in 1714, where she owned several farms and an inn. Her success as a businesswoman in these ventures, which surely must have been partly the result of her sharp wit and keen observations of society, enabled her to leave a considerable estate when she died in 1727.

Mary White Rowlandson's captivity narrative and Sarah Kemble Knight's journal both illustrate and critique dominant culture and ideology. Another substantial autobiographical text by a woman before 1750 similarly enriches early American literature. Although Elizabeth Sampson Ashbridge (1713–55) was a Quaker in the middle colonies and not a New England Puritan, her work, *Some Account of the Fore Part of the Life of Elizabeth Ashbridge* (1774), deserves mention within the context of Puritan literature because in her search for the best religion, Ashbridge explicitly considered Calvinism and rejected it, and her reasons for doing so suggest some of the problems the congregational ministers encountered during the period.

Elizabeth Sampson was born in Middlewich, Cheshire, England, in 1713 to the physician Thomas Sampson and his wife, Mary. She was the only child of this union, but her mother, a widow, had a son and daughter by her first husband. Perhaps Elizabeth inherited a propensity for travel from her father, who, she reports, "sometime after my birth, . . . took to the sea and followed his Profession on board ship, in many long voyages, till I arrived to the age of twelve years." Similar to the tales of adventure and hardship of the romances of the period such as those of Defoe's Moll Flanders, Richardson's Clarissa Harlowe, and Susanna Rowson's Charlotte Temple, Ashbridge's narrative recounts complicated events that leave her a woman on her own in the world. When she was fourteen, she eloped with a poor stocking-weaver, whom she called the "darling of my heart." When he died five months later,

Ashbridge's family exiled her to Ireland to live with Quakers, whom she initially found repulsive, a point that has ironic reverberations later in her narrative. She wanted to return home, but when her father refused to forgive and accept her, she arranged to go to America as an indentured servant.

During her years of indentureship, Ashbridge served different male masters, including a clergyman who, she reports, tried to seduce her. She observed that many ministers displayed an external righteousness whereas they were secretly corrupt and immoral. Still, on her quest for her spiritual calling, she investigated various current religions. While she was living in New Jersey, she learned of a trial of a Presbyterian minister accused of drunkenness, and she attended in the hope of learning something about that Protestant sect. Observing "great Divisions among the People about who Should be their Shepherd," she quickly grew disillusioned with the Presbyterian clergy: "I greatly Pitied their [the congregation's] Condition, for I now saw beyond the Men made Ministers, & what they Preached for." Ashbridge observes that the main interest of the clergy was to gain the highest salary but that the congregation could not see this motive because "the prejudice of Education, which is very prevalent, blinded their eyes."

In the controversy, some argued for keeping the old minister, others were for hiring "a young man had upon trial for some weeks," and "a third Party was for sending for one from New England." One member objected to the high cost of the last option: "Sir, when we have been at the Expense (which is no Small Matter) of fetching this Gentleman from New England, may be he'll not stay with us." When another answered that the way to make him stay is to "give him a good Salary," Ashbridge laments "these Mercenary creatures: they are all Actuated by one & the same thing, even the Love of Money, & not the regard of Souls." She goes on to explain the bidding war for ministers that involved hiring a famous minister away from another parish, where the people had "almost Impoverished themselves to keep him." Rejecting Presbyterianism, she says, "their Ministry all proceeded from one Cause" – "the Shepard that regards the fleece more than the flock, in whose mouths are Lies."

In a brisk and lively style, *The Life of Elizabeth Ashbridge* depicts her unusual experiences, including her brief career on the New York stage and her marriage to a schoolmaster named Sullivan who abused her. After her second husband died, Ashbridge worked as a seamstress to pay off his many debts. She then married Aaron Ashbridge in 1746, converted to Quakerism, and was ordained; with Aaron, she then returned as a Quaker missionary to Ireland, where she died in 1755. Although she moved away from Puritan New England geographically, her observations and opinions on the clergy exemplify the reasons for the increasing anticlericalism and suggest the magnitude of the problem that the New England clergy and their middle-colony colleagues faced at the time. Ashbridge's text reveals how a bold and perspicacious woman in early America could see "beyond the Men made Ministers," demystify masculine authority, and feel compassion for those whose educations had "blinded their eyes."

In the face of such critiques, one clergyman who struggled to preserve a positive image for the New England clergy both by his personal example as a temperate, sober leader devoted to the needs of his flock and through his writings was the Reverend Charles Chauncy (1705–87). Author of dozens of books and pastor of the First Church of Boston from 1727 until 1787, Chauncy played an important role in almost all of the formative events of his time: the French and Indian Wars, the resistance to an Anglican episcopacy in America, the Stamp Act controversy, the rise of science, the American Revolution, and the beginnings of Deism and Unitarianism. Whereas Edwards has been identified as a literary genius and his works have been established in the American literary canon, Chauncy's contributions as a thinker and author have remained in Edwards's shadow. In the views of some historians, however, Chauncy – along with Franklin – was much more the representative eighteenth-century American, and his career and writings bear examination in their own right.

Like Cotton Mather, Chauncy was born into a Boston family with impressive leadership and clerical credentials. He was the great-grandson of the second president of Harvard, the grandson of a controversial London minister, and the son of a leading Boston merchant. His mother, Sarah Walley, was the daughter of a Massachusetts Supreme Court judge. Chauncy graduated from Harvard in 1721, a year before Jonathan Edwards graduated from Yale, and after six more years of study and teaching, he joined Thomas Foxcroft at Boston's First Church, which people had come to call the "Old Brick." Widowed twice, he was married three times, first in 1727 to Elizabeth Hirst, with whom he had three children, then to Elizabeth Townsend in 1738, and last to Mary Stoddard in 1760.

The congregation of the Old Brick was made up of wealthy, educated, and by then long-established Boston families. Chauncy, who was by temperament and intellectual leaning a strong advocate of the New England congregational way and of Calvinism, faced the problem that had troubled New England clergy ever since the 1650s. He sought to maintain his own integrity as a strict Calvinist while preaching to a congregation that prized worldly comforts and modern ideas. Ranting sermons with images of hellfire were not to the taste of the kind of people who attended the Old Brick, yet for clergy simply to assure such people of their salvation because they were financially comfortable and performed works of charity was to approach

Arminianism. Although Chauncy believed that he avoided an Arminian doctrine of works, religious historians still debate whether Edwards was not correct in detecting that heresy in Chauncy's reassurances to his wealthy parishioners.

Advocating a "commonsense" approach to theology that would gain currency among congregationalists influenced by the Scottish Common Sense Realist philosophy in the latter decades of the century, Chauncy encouraged his congregation to "trust in Christ the Redeemer" and not to fret over the "metaphysical niceties" of theology. Within his church, he sought harmony and temperance in all things, and he tried to avoid religious disputes. In his own personal life, he also practiced a strict moderation, for which he was greatly admired. Conservative in doctrine but liberal in church polity and membership, Chauncy represented the balanced establishment ideal. As a friend admiringly described him, Chauncy was "little of stature. God gave him a slender, feeble body, a very powerful, vigorous mind, and strong passions; and he managed them all exceedingly well. His manners were plain and downright, – dignified, bold, and imposing. In conversation with his friends he was pleasant, social, and very instructive." Certainly, it was in admiration of his will and endurance and not for his physical size, that Chauncy himself came to be called Old Brick.

The New England clergy had been hoping for a renewal of religion for many decades, and perhaps for that reason Chauncy at first joined nearly all of his fellow ministers in welcoming the revivals in 1740 and 1741. By 1742, however, he had become apprehensive that those being converted "placed their Religion so much in the Heart and Fervour of their Passions, that they too much neglect their Reason and Judgement." Whereas some antirevivalist clergy opposed the movement because they feared loss of their authority to lay enthusiasts, Chauncy's motives appear to have been less self-interested. He sincerely believed that the "religious Phrenzy" and "ecstatic violence" would destroy the "reasonable peace of soul and mind" of individuals and disrupt the harmony of communities, which he cherished as the two great personal and social benefits of Christianity. He also found those converted by the revivals to be overly confident, proud, "impatient of contradiction, censorious, and uncharitable." When Edwards published *Some Thoughts Concerning the Present Revival of Religion in New England* in 1742 defending the Great Awakening, Chauncy, who had had some previous exchanges with Edwards over these issues, took up the challenge to be the spokesman of the Old Light liberals.

To gather evidence for his writing against Edwards and the Great Awakening, Chauncy traveled throughout New England in 1743 recording accounts of the "convulsions and distortions" and "quaking and trembling" that resulted from "deluded imagination[s]." Composed as a rebuttal or "antidote" to Edwards's work, Chauncy's *Seasonable Thoughts on the State of Religion in New England* attempts to reinscribe the traditional Puritan position: "there is the Religion of the Understanding and Judgment, and Will as well as of the Affections, and if little account is made of the former while great Stress is laid upon the latter, it can't be but People should run into Disorders." Chauncy's position on the perennial head versus heart debate within Puritanism seemed perfectly reasonable to many of Chauncy's congregation – but not to Thomas Foxcroft, his colleague in his own church, who continued to support the revivals. It is a mark of the even temperaments of both men that they remained cooperative over the years in spite of their opposition on this and on other divisive issues. In subsequent works against enthusiasm, Chauncy tried to expose the dangers posed by the untrained, itinerant clergy, the weaknesses of lay preachers, and the damage that religious disagreements might do to the churches in general.

In his preaching, Chauncy always advocated the plain style, and he prided himself in avoiding rhetoric and "all pomp of words, all show of learned subtlety by artful use of the scholastic, systematical, and metaphysical terms." Oratorical eloquence, he felt, had no place in the pulpit, and he said of his own sermons: "If I have wrote in a mystical, perplexed, unintelligible way, I own it is a fault not to be overlooked." Thus, one of his main objections to the New Light preachers was that they were mere performers, resorting to inflamed theatrical rhetoric and pulpit histrionics to stir the passions instead of informing the mind.

Although Chauncy believed that it was unnecessary to burden his congregation with the details of religious and philosophical thought, he held that sermons, though plain and lucid, should be founded upon deep and extensive learning. In his own constant study, he labored to reconcile the fundamental doctrines of congregationalism with new developments in philosophy and with the spiritual needs of the people. Relying heavily upon John Locke and the Scottish Common Sense philosophers such as Francis Hutcheson, Thomas Reid, and Henry Home, Lord Kames, he composed a series of theological works that reveal rather remarkable shifts in his theological positions over time. Viewing God as a benevolent "Divine Administrator," he developed quite radical ideas, such as the rejection of the arbitrary God of Calvinism and the elimination of the doctrines of election and Original Sin, which he perceived as casting infants into hell for "a sin which they certainly had no hand in." Rejecting predestination, Chauncy said: "A more shocking idea can scarce be given to the Deity than that which represents him as arbitrarily dooming the greater part of the race of men to eternal misery." Although he did not eliminate other fundamental ideas – such as the existence of hell, the need for faith and works for salvation, and the necessity that the sinner undergo painful repentance – he came to believe in universal salvation, or what came to be called Universalism, holding that Christ had died for everyone's sins and that God wants all to be saved. Thus, in doctrine and polity, Chauncy led the First Church of Boston from the seventeenth-century world of the Mathers toward the Deism of Jefferson and Franklin and the Unitarianism of Emerson. By the time of his death, Chauncy had come to be viewed as the most influential minister of his time and one of the most significant figures in eighteenth-century America. In the twentieth century, Chauncy's contributions have been much overshadowed by the luminous work of Jonathan Edwards, whose mysticism, poetic vision, and originality informed some of the most challenging and intriguing texts in American literature, which have had particular appeal to critics of the last fifty years.

Born to the Reverend Timothy and Esther Stoddard Edwards in East Windsor, Connecticut, on October 5, 1703, Jonathan was the middle child and only boy in a family of eleven children. He was the grandson of Solomon Stoddard, whose liberal church admission practices had kept him in long-standing controversies with Edward Taylor and Increase Mather. Known as the "Pope [and sometimes the 'bastard'] of the Connecticut River Valley," Stoddard was a formidable, rebellious figure for Edwards to emulate. Upon graduating from theologically conservative Yale in 1722, Edwards spent four more years there teaching and completing his M.A. before answering Stoddard's call in 1727 to be his assistant at Northampton. In the same year, Edwards married Sarah Pierrepont, with whom he had eleven children.

A devoted student of Calvin and the early Puritan theologians, Edwards was a firm believer in the religion of his ancestors in an age of its diminishing power. To increase church membership Stoddard had opened communion to all who wished for conversion as early as the 1670s, but the more theologically conservative young Edwards recognized that this tactic had only temporary positive effects and potential long-term risks. Similarly, in Edwards's view, ministers like Chauncy who preached moral propriety as a likely path to heaven were deluding their congregations in order to retain them. In contrast, Edwards always directed his philosophical gaze toward God, heaven, and eternity. Within his eschatological schema, Edwards believed the present weakened condition of Christianity in his New England to be a mere moment of lapse in sacred history. As he sought to understand God's transcendent design for humanity, Edwards investigated the writings of Locke, Newton, and other contemporary philosophers. In so doing, he formulated a synthesis of Calvinism and Enlightenment ideas that in complexity and inventiveness far eclipsed the comparatively unsophisticated thought of Chauncy and that continues to challenge theologians and intellectual historians today.

After his personal spiritual struggles with the notion of God's divine sovereignty and his subsequent conversion, Edwards became committed to the idea of salvation by faith and grace alone and to the prime importance of a personally felt and understood conversion experienced through the senses as well as the reason. Espousing a position reminiscent of the original Pauline spirit of the first-generation fathers, Edwards believed that grace empowers every saint with a daily vision of the beauty of nature, the joy of salvation, and the peace of God's heavenly glory. Thus, the sanctified Christian should not give primacy to moral duties, good works, and tests of conversion. Such conscious human efforts are useful and good, but they are secondary to the ways that the lives of the saved are conspicuously transformed by grace. In their gracious ecstasy, the converted will necessarily bring order to their families and virtue to those around them. For Edwards a congregation of such souls radiates sacred energy and assurance.

To revitalize this message for the early 1730s, Edwards invented a new language of sensory experience that stirred the passions of his country congregation. Although he actually distrusted enthusiasm and presented his sermons in a calm, deliberate manner, his use of innovative imagery to expound familiar themes struck his parishioners with a force they had never experienced. His best-known sermon, *Sinners in the Hands of an Angry God* (1741), is a jeremiad full of fire and brimstone, but that text is not typical of Edwards's style, and he reportedly delivered it in a monotone. More often he tried to make salvation and grace desirable through an invocation of positive, enticing imagery.

What Edwards's congregation also heard from him was news of the beauty and peace of the new life of grace, as in *God Glorified in the Work of Redemption, By the Greatness of Man's Dependence* (1731), which stresses human powerlessness in the process of salvation. After reading a series of scriptures depicting the saved as a "new creature," "created again," "the new man," "raising from the dead," Edwards explains:

Yea, it is a more glorious work of power than mere creation, or raising a dead body to life, in that the effect attained is greater and more excellent. That holy and happy being, and spiritual life which is produced in the work of conversion, is a far greater and more glorious effect, than mere being and life. And the state from whence the change is made – a death in sin, a total corruption of nature, and depth of misery – is far more remote from the state attained, than mere death or non-entity.

After a few years of hearing this message of humanity's dependency and God's saving grace, the people in Edwards's parish began to experience the "surprising conversions" that marked the beginning of the Great Awakening. In 1735, in response to Benjamin Colman's request for an accounting of the phenomenon, Edwards wrote a letter to Colman explaining that over the course of the last few years he had noticed that the town had "gradually been reforming," that the "contentious disposition" had quieted, that "young people . . . left off their frolicking," and that "heads of families . . . agreed every one to restrain their families." He had found a "remarkable religious concern" and new questions "about Arminianism [and] the way to salvation." He also indicates that he preached on grace and salvation, which was "found fault with by many elsewhere" but "was most evidently attended with a very remarkable blessing from heaven to the souls of the people in this town." Soon, many, including "those that were most disposed to contemn vital and experimental religion," such as the "highest families," were "affected remark-ably" by "the Spirit of God." Edwards reports that this enthusiasm spread quickly to surrounding towns, where people were "confessing their faults to one another" and "neglecting their worldly business" in order to "mind nothing but religion." So powerful were the emotions that many were weak-ened physically, as were "three young persons in this town talking together of the dying love of Christ till they all fainted away." Edwards also notes an element that must have been good news to many clergy during a time of growing anticlericalism: that since the awakenings began, the people "have greater respect to ministers" so that "there is scarcely a minister preaches here but gets their esteem and affection." Edwards concludes that his report is a true "account of this affair which Satan has so much misrepresented."

A few weeks later, Edwards wrote to Colman again but this time less confidently, for he had to report a tragic event that had soon cooled his congregation's enthusiasm for the revival. Edwards's own uncle, Joseph Hawley, had committed suicide as a result of his "deep melancholy" and "despairing thoughts," apparently stirred by his concern about "the condi-tion of his soul." But rather than becoming wary of the revival, Edwards remained committed to it: "the devil took the advantage and drove him into despairing thoughts. . . . Satan seems to be in a great rage at this breaking forth of the work of God. . . . We have appointed a day of fasting . . . by reason of . . . other appearances of Satan's rage amongst us against poor souls." Hawley's death and the other acts of "Satan's rage" seem to have stunned many, for the excitement subsided by 1736, and it would be five years before Edwards's church would experience another awakening.

In the meantime, reports of revivalism began to arrive in Massachusetts from England and from the American southern and middle colonies, where preachers such as George Whitefield, Gilbert Tennent, and James Davenport employed powerful oratory to engage and convert hundreds at a time. Re-ports of excesses of emotionalism led Edwards to repeat his earlier warnings against deliberate ministerial attempts to appeal only to the affections, yet he did invite Whitefield to preach in his parish and did himself employ terrifying rhetoric and imagery in some of his sermons of this period, including *Sinners in the Hands of an Angry God* (1741) and *The Future Punishment of the Wicked* (1741). Because of his belief in divine sovereignty and his expectation that the Apocalypse was imminent, Edwards could not conceive that the evidence of the Holy Spirit was other than the work of Providence. When critics of the revival, such as Chauncy, began to berate the emotional excesses, Edwards became the leading spokesman of the Awakening forces. Even after the revival cooled and the beginning of King George's War became the focus of public attention in 1744, Edwards continued to defend the Great Awakening in his *Treatise Concerning Religious Affections* (1746).

In a series of sermons he composed while preparing that work, Edwards presented in greater detail the ideas on church membership and salvation he had been developing. The members of his congregation were shocked to discover that he had rejected his grandfather's liberal policies of open church membership and communion. People were especially disturbed by Edwards's proposal that the church must revert to public professions of faith for full church membership. The parishioners were attached to Stoddardism, which had distinguished the Northampton parish for fifty years, and they were furious with Edwards for his arbitrary changes in the church rules. The controversy smoldered between 1744 and 1748 because no one presented themselves for membership, but the issue exploded in 1748, revealing that Edwards's congregation had turned bitterly against him. Historians and Edwards's biographers observe that other factors contributed to the break, such as local factional jealousies, various resentments, and a scandal involving a "dirty book." Edwards discovered that some young people had been circulating *Midwifery Rightly Represented,* and even though the group included some from the families of prominent church members, Edwards read their names from the pulpit and chastised them for immorality. In the months that followed, the outraged parents banded with those parishioners who had begun to doubt Edwards's spiritual leadership and formed a faction that outnumbered Edwards's supporters. While Edwards was in his study developing his most impressive ideas about psychology, nature, and God, which would bring him lasting fame, his congregation was plotting his expulsion. By 1750, Edwards's church voted for his dismissal, and after delivering his famous *Farewell Sermon,* in which he said that God would decide who was right, he stepped down.

The demise of Edwards's ministry served as resounding evidence to Chauncy and other Old Lights that Edwards and the Great Awakening were certified failures. After turning down several offers to move to other parishes, including the option of starting a second church for his supporters in Northampton, Edwards made the surprising choice of electing to take Sarah and his eleven children to the isolated frontier town of Stockbridge, where he became a missionary to the Housatonic tribe. During his seven years there, Edwards continued to experience many difficulties in the area of public relations. The Solomon Williams clan, a white family who wielded great power in Indian affairs and who antagonized the Indians, made Edwards's missionary work difficult, and the outbreak of the French and Indian Wars in 1754 made conditions dangerous. Still, in spite of his trials, Edwards spent these years of exile in his study composing the great works of his life. Although most of these books would not be published until after his death, he did manage to have his *Freedom of the Will* printed in Boston in 1754. This impressive work added so substantially to his reputation among New Light clergymen that in 1757 he was invited to be president of the College of New Jersey (later Princeton). At first Edwards resisted, saying that he lacked talent for the job, suffered poor health, and wished to remain absorbed in his studies. At that time, a college president taught a full schedule of courses in addition to his administrative duties. Offering to reduce his teaching load, the trustees persuaded him to accept, and he was inaugurated in February 1758. An outbreak of smallpox that winter led Edwards and the trustees to decide that he should be inoculated; however, soon after the inoculation, he contracted an infection and died on March 22, 1758.

Edwards's remarkable and, in many ways, regrettable public career provides an important context for understanding his towering intellectual achievement. His less public, inner narrative really began in his childhood home in East Windsor, Connecticut, where both his father, who conducted the parish grammar school, and his mother instructed their precocious son, preparing him to enter Yale at the age of twelve. From early on, Edwards seemed inclined toward scientific investigation and philosophical argumentation. Edwards's protégé and early biographer Samuel Hopkins reported that "in his second year at college, and thirteen of his age, he read Locke on the human understanding with great delight and profit." It was an important innovation that Locke and Newton were introduced in 1717 at Yale, where Edwards then studied them intensively. Edwards disagreed with Locke on many issues, but he borrowed from both thinkers and found Locke's *An Essay Concerning Human Understanding* especially valuable. Edwards's earliest known intellectual investigations were in some short scientific papers: "On Insects," "Of the Rainbow," "Of Being," "Of Atoms," a paper on light rays, a series of essays entitled "Natural Philosophy," and his "Notes on the Mind." These early writings display a fascination with nature that characterizes much of his writing. He was particularly interested in spiders, which he described with obvious delight:

Of all insects no one is more wonderful than the Spider. . . . they may be seen well enough by an observing eye at noon Day by their Glistening against the sun and what is more wonderful I know I have several times seen in a very Calm and serene Day . . . multitudes of little shining webs and Glistening Strings of a Great Length and at such a height that one would think they were tack'd to the Sky.

Although Edwards ultimately saw no conflict between such enthusiasm for physical nature and the Calvinist rejection of the world, he did think more deeply about such pleasure and would return to analyze the ambiguity of human delight in nature in his so-called *Personal Narrative,* published in *The Life and Character of The Late Reverend Mr. Jonathan Edwards* (1765).

In the *Personal Narrative,* Edwards describes his conversion experience in language through which he attempts to capture the transcendent, even mystical, quality of the effects of grace. Although the *Personal Narrative* is structured, rather like earlier Puritan conversion accounts, by his struggle to discover the truth of his calling, the work departs significantly from the traditional form in conveying passion for God in terms of human affection and love. He explains that the greatest obstacles to his conversion were his "objections to the doctrine of God's sovereignty," but he gradually came to see that "the doctrine has very often appeared exceeding pleasant, bright, and sweet." This change enabled him to read the scriptures with a "new sense," which thereby prepared his heart for grace. After talking to his father one day, he was walking in the pasture and "looking up on the sky and clouds, [when] there came into my mind so sweet a sense of the glorious *majesty* and *grace* of God that I know not how to express." Whereas before his experience he used to shrink from thunderstorms, he now "felt God, so to speak, at the first appearance of a thunder storm; . . . and [could] hear the majestic and awful voice of God's thunder. [And] while thus engaged, it always seemed natural to me to sing, or chant for my meditations; so, to speak my thoughts in soliloquies with a singing voice." Having had this awakening, he became enchanted by its beauty: "It appeared to me that there was nothing in it but was ravishingly lovely; the highest beauty and amiableness . . . a *divine* beauty." For him now, the natural world is infused with elements of the supernatural:

The soul of a true Christian . . . appeared like such a little white flower as we see in the spring of the year; low and humble on the ground, opening its bosom to receive the pleasant beams of the sun's glory; rejoicing as it were in a calm rapture; diffusing around a sweet fragrancy; standing peacefully and lovingly in the midst of other flowers . . . to drink in the light of the sun.

As an artist of language, Edwards appears to take pleasure in the words themselves as he invokes natural imagery to conflate the realms of the

worldly and the divine. He found the image of light, in particular, to be an
apt metaphor for evoking the sublime and mystical. His technique for capturing reverie in language is most evident in the famous passage he composed
about his beloved future spouse, Sarah, at about the time of his conversion.
He praises her for her love of God and also for her "sweetness, calmness, and
universal benevolence of mind," which led her to "go about from place to
place singing sweetly" and to walk in the fields and to seem "to have someone
invisible always conversing with her." After having had years of the aging
Reverend Solomon Stoddard in the pulpit, the congregation of Northampton
must have been quite startled to have young Edwards and his wife preaching,
singing, and expressing the ecstasy of the "new life" of salvation.

Edwards's first two great sermons of doctrinal analysis were *God Glorified
in the Work of Redemption, By the Greatness of Man's Dependence* (1731) and *A
Divine and Supernatural Light, Immediately Imparted to the Soul by the Spirit of
God* (1734). The first is a systematic explication of the doctrine of divine
sovereignty in which Edwards uses biblical imagery to set forth his arguments against Arminianism: "But now when fallen man is made holy, it is
from mere and arbitrary grace: God may forever deny holiness to the fallen
creature if he pleases." But in the second sermon Edwards comes close to
expressing his responses to the mystical experience of the moments of his
encounter with grace that he had recorded in his *Personal Narrative.*

Here, his language reveals a struggle for words adequate to describe the
ineffable nature of his religious experiences. His focus moves to the physical
and sensual changes after spiritual rebirth, and he distinguishes between
"natural men," who have not experienced grace, and those illuminated by it.
Using highly figurative and lyrical language, he struggles to find words
capable of conveying the complexity of his emotions. There is a vast difference,
he says, between the perception of one whose imagination has been "affected"
by "the story of Christ," which like a "romance" or a "stage play" may create
strong feelings that are "wholly graceless," and the true vision of a saint. To
describe this new life, Edwards moves to employ a poetic language that many
readers have seen as anticipating the style of the Transcendentalists:

There is a difference between having a rational judgment that honey is sweet, and
having a sense of its sweetness. . . . there is a difference between believing that a
person is beautiful, and having a sense of his beauty. . . . There is a wide difference
between mere speculative rational judging any thing excellent, and having a sense of
its sweetness and beauty. The former rests only in the head, speculation only is
concerned in it; but the heart is concerned in the latter.

The person who has grace has a "sensibleness of the excellency of divine
objects, dwells upon them with delight"; in this new state all things are

"sweet and pleasant to his soul," and the person "feels pleasure in the apprehension [of] the beauty and sweetness of the objects."

Regarding the supernatural light itself, he is at pains to make the point that the light does not depend upon reading the scriptures or upon anything in the natural world but comes entirely from the supernatural. The difference between seeing with the power of the divine light and seeing without it is like beholding "the objects on the face of the earth when the light of the sun is cast upon them" and viewing "them in a dim starlight or twilight." Edwards's use of natural imagery to emphasize the world's beauty as reflective of God's glory and his expression of what has been called his "aesthetic ecstasy" introduce original elements into Puritan theology. Edwards did understand nature to be "power" rather than substance, but he never confused God with nature, for the world consisted always, in his Christian-Platonic mode of thinking, of images and shadows of the divine real things of God. Celebrating ecstatic piety as life's true goal, Edwards's language made the more tepid moral religion being fostered in many Boston churches seem dull and legalistic by comparison.

What is the proper response of a congregation of saints struck with the supernatural light of conversion? Just as in his *Personal Narrative,* where he responded to grace by singing and chanting, so too he encouraged his congregation to sing out their joyous pleasure in their rebirth. He later reported on this time of awakening: "Our public assemblies were then very beautiful . . . there has [been] scarce any part of divine worship wherein good men amongst us have had grace so drawn forth . . . as in singing. . . . they were . . . wont to sing with unusual elevation of heart and voice." The idea that people can somehow return something to God by glorifying him in song underlies Edwards's important concept of reemanation, perhaps the most profound idea that he was to develop in subsequent works.

In making conversion so emotionally and aesthetically appealing, Edwards certainly motivated his listeners to desire grace, but he also faced the predicament that had confronted the Puritan clergy from the beginning. What can the sinner do to be saved? As a strict Calvinist who adhered to the doctrines of absolute divine sovereignty and humanity's complete helplessness, Edwards could not advise people to take actions to enable them to earn salvation, but he retained the preparationist idea that "if we would be saved, we must seek salvation" by listening to God's word preached, praying for grace, and contemplating God. For the saved, this process will be in harmony with God's predestined salvation. For the unregenerate, the attempt will necessarily fail, but their efforts will make them better members of the community.

When in 1734 and 1735, Edwards witnessed the surprising beginnings of the revival and was asked by Colman to account for those events, he began to formulate the synthesis that would explain and preserve Calvinism to modern times. This intellectual feat has earned Edwards his high place in the history of religion and philosophy. In a series of works beginning with *A Faithful Narrative of the Surprising Work of God in the Conversion of Many Hundred Souls* (1737) and continuing in *Some Thoughts Concerning the Present Revival of Religion in New England* (1742) and especially in *A Treatise Concerning Religious Affections* (1746), Edwards developed his synthesis of Calvinism and modern philosophy. While preserving some of the elements of seventeenth-century faculty psychology that was the basis for the theories of Thomas Shepard and the early divines, he used Locke's theory of human understanding to complicate the system. He retained the idea that the intellect and the will are the primary elements of the soul, but he viewed them as acting synchronically, in Locke's terms, as powers of a unified soul and understanding. Whereas the old system had depicted the affections as separate faculties sometimes in conflict with understanding, Edwards, following Locke, saw the affections not only as part of the will but as a "vigorous exercise" of the will.

In *Religious Affections,* Edwards makes one of his more important theological leaps, one that for many scholars is his most significant contribution and one that will reappear in Emerson in the idea of the genuine poet as a genius with a special higher vision. Edwards's key concept is that of reemanation. Using Locke's idea that the intellect not only receives information but has a "power" to act upon it, Edwards argued that as grace emanates from God to the saved individual, so too the saint may reemanate the grace back toward the world and to God and thereby participate actively in expressing salvation. The soul, he writes,

receives light from the Sun of Righteousness in such a manner that its nature is changed, and it becomes properly a luminous thing: not only does the sun shine in the saints, but they also become little suns. . . . The manner of their derivation of light is like that of the lamps in the tabernacle rather than a reflecting glass.

As Edwards developed this idea of active reemanation in later works, it takes on ethical and aesthetic dimensions.

After the end of the second set of revivals and his dismissal from Northampton, Edwards continued writing his major works, most of which were published after his death: *The Great Doctrine of Original Sin* (1758), *Two Dissertations: I. Concerning the End for which God Created the World. II. The Nature of True Virtue* (1765), *A History of the Work of Redemption* (1774), and *Images and Shadows of Divine Things* (1948). Resisting the human-centered elements of the Enlightenment philosophies, Edwards remained self-consciously theocentric. His aim was to keep finding intellectually convincing ways to retain God at the center of his system while developing a more complete – and more complicated – explanation of humanity's relation to God. His study of the mind led Edwards to insights in epistemology. He came to believe in the autonomy of the mind from external reality and the indeterminacy of language and of experience, concepts that would later be developed by Kant and Emerson. Yet Edwards believed in the literal truth of the Bible, in the predestined design of sacred and human history, in acts of divine Providence, in Original Sin, in the coming Millennium and Apocalypse, in angels, and in Satan's active role in the world. His work explores the nature of God, Christ, and the Trinity, and it investigates the problem of evil and the proper nature of the Christian community.

Scholars debate how attached Edwards's thought remained to his Calvinist doctrines and to what degree his writings express the potential of human power that would be fully expounded in the Romantic age. Those who see his ideas as in some ways anticipating Emerson and the Romantics argue that although Edwards insists that God has predetermined all things, he does allow that human beings have free will to make choices. The pre-Romantic Edwards may be characterized in the following terms: God has always known how a person will choose, but for Edwards, the person still has the freedom to do the choosing. Arguing that the will always motivates the understanding to choose what it perceives to be good, Edwards says that both "natural" people and saints perceive objects as good and are motivated to choose them. Others may judge the morality and ethics of those choices and praise or punish accordingly. The saint, however, sees the world with a heightened perception and will necessarily choose the good in ways that are "virtuous" and "gracious." Thus, the incandescent virtuous saint reemanates God's glory through acts of virtue that are themselves "beautiful." Beauty itself is an important concept for Edwards, one that he develops throughout his writings. When illuminated with grace, every human act of love and virtue becomes a gracious work of art, spreading God's beauty in the world. In this way, Edwards celebrates the human capability for artistic creativity and spiritual transcendence – the human power to give something back to God. There is little indication in current scholarship that the question of whether Edwards is the last great Puritan or the first American Romantic, or both at once, will soon be resolved.

The following passage on the beauty of the world does illustrate, however, why Edwards's aesthetics have earned him recognition as a literary theorist:

There are beauties that are more palpable and explicable, and there are hidden and secret beauties. . . . We find ourselves pleased in beholding the color of the violets, but we cannot know what secret regularity or harmony it is that creates that pleasure in our minds. These hidden beauties are commonly by far the greatest because the more complex the beauty is, the more hidden it is. . . . That mixture we call white is a proportionate mixture that is harmonious, as Sir Isaac Newton has shown, to each particular simple color . . . and each sort of rays play a distinct tune to the soul, besides those lovely mixtures that are found in nature. Those beauties, how lovely is the green of the face of the earth in all manner of colors, in flowers the color of the skies, and lovely tinctures of the morning and evening.

Chauncy lived thirty years beyond Edwards and helped usher in the liberal Protestantism that would dominate the American eastern seaboard for the next two centuries. But it was Edwards who had the greater impact on American culture and thought. He led the first of what would become repeated religious awakenings in America. From Princeton, where his life ended so tragically, young preachers traveled to the South and the Southwest to generate the Second Great Awakening, while New Lights from Edwards's alma mater Yale spread religious fervor across the "burned over" areas of upper New York State. Edwards's followers and admirers edited and published his books and manuscripts; his *Miscellanies,* which contains the material for his unwritten magnum opus, is only now being edited for publication; literary scholars have recognized him to be a major figure in American literature.

In our secular society, so much the product of the purely rationalist elements of the Enlightenment that Edwards resisted, it may be difficult to grasp how Edwards, who was a narrow Calvinist, in many ways looking back to the Puritan founders, could also have possessed a deep love of language, metaphor, ideas, and, thus, of the world. That, however, is one of the most arresting features of the man: the mixture of Ramistic logic with poetic visions that are at once medieval and modernist, as in the closing paragraph of "The Beauty of the World":

Corollary. Hence the reason why almost all men, and those that seem to be very miserable, love life, because they cannot bear to lose sight of such a beautiful and lovely world. The idea, that every moment whilst we live have a beauty that we take distinct notice of, brings a pleasure that, when we come to the trial, we had rather live in much pain and misery than lose.

In spite of all the theological and political disputes that racked the Puritan experiment from its earliest moments and in spite of all the pain and anxiety the Puritans inflicted upon their enemies and each other, perhaps it is their extraordinary ability to believe themselves a special people that draws readers still to their writings and to the records of their ordeals. The image of Jonathan Edwards at his desk in the frontier village of Stockbridge thinking of the awesome power of the Creator and the "lovely world" in which he would "rather live in much pain and misery than lose" in some way captures the peculiar ambiguity of Puritan literary history.

BRITISH-AMERICAN BELLES LETTRES

David S. Shields

BELLES LETTRES has become a vague term, collecting so broad a reference that it now designates the whole of "humane letters" (*litterae humaniores*) – that is, all imaginative literature or all writing evincing "literariness." Prior to the term's semantic expansion in the 1760s, it had a precise employment, naming a mode of writing that subordinated the traditional tasks of edification, revelation, and memorialization to the work of stimulating social pleasure. Belles lettres was characterized more by its effects than its forms. "Ease" and "agreeableness," qualities adjusted to the taste of the "gentle reader," were the primary belletristic virtues.

Edmund Waller imported the mode from France into the literary communications of the Stuart court. Belles lettres flourished in England in conjunction with the rise of urban sociability in the 1670s. New communities based on shared taste, friendship, or common interest formed in postfire London and in the burgeoning resorts. In the mixed-sex assemblies at the spas and in the male tavern clubs of the metropolis, aspirants to gentility embraced the court's new sociable manner of wit. Writing served talk in these circles, providing scripts for oral performance (club disquisitions, vers de société) and recording memorable sallies of wit (bon mots, toasts, impromptus, epigrams). Belles lettres disavowed writtenness, adopting the guise of conversation. Concomitantly, conversation assumed great weight in thought about society and letters. As the preamble to the 1728 constitution of the Harvard Philomusarian Club declared, conversation was "The Basis of Friendship, The fundamental Principle of Society, The Great Prerogative of Mankind." Although social pleasure might have been the immediate result of belletristic conversation, a more profound cumulative effect was the advancement of civility. Social commentators believed civil refinement to be encouraged by belles lettres' "politeness." "Belles lettres" when translated into English was usually rendered "polite letters."

The three inaugural figures of British-American belles lettres – Henry Brooke (167?–1735/6), Benjamin Colman (1673–1747), and William Byrd II (1674–1746) – were inspired by bel esprit at the English spas. Brooke, after earning his degree at Brasenose College, Oxford, in 1692, spent a decade as a beau circulating through London and the resorts before seeking his fortune in Pennsylvania. Benjamin Colman traded impromptu verse with Christian gentlewomen at Bath before returning in 1699 to direct Boston's Brattle Street Church. Byrd won his reputation as a "man of parts" at Tunbridge Wells in 1700; his verses appeared in *Tunbridgalia* (1719), a collection of the spa's finest wit and "water poetry." All three writers understood themselves to be agents of politeness upon coming to America. Henry Brooke strove to improve the conversation in the taverns of Philadelphia and Newcastle. The great local hostelries – the Blue Anchor Tavern, the Pewter Platter Inn, and the London Coffeehouse – suffered from the common afflictions of masculine society: the degeneration of wit into profane jest, political debate into malediction, and table talk into shop talk. Brooke's "A Discours upon Je'sting" (1703), a verse epistle addressed to club companion Robert Grace, demonstrated how true wit was distinguished by an ability to inspire delight upon repetition. Jest, on the other hand, was "a short-lived tho'ght / By Rodeney laughed at, & as soon forgot." In several epigrams, particularly in "On P[enn] painted in armor," Brooke illustrated how metaphor could lend point to political criticism. In "A Rule of Conversation Suggested to a Certain Club" (c. 1710), Brooke rebuked the parochial preoccupation with business among intelligent men. To dramatize the ludicrousness of a world absorbed in commerce, Brooke renovated a Philadelphia tavern tale of commercial misadventure into "The New Metamorphosis" (1702), an Ovidian travesty in which Venus punishes a greenhorn tobacco merchant, changing his sotweed into birds, for welshing on a deal with a whore. Brooke's spoof of commercial enterprise and of the sanctity of contract differed from another comic treatment of a greenhorn tobacco merchant, Ebenezer Cook's *The Sot-Weed Factor* (1708), in audience. Cook burlesqued metropolitan fantasies concerning Maryland's primitiveness; his poem was published in London. Brooke wished to ridicule the commercial anxieties of Philadelphia's taverngoers; his poems (thirty-five of which survive) circulated in manuscript in Pennsylvania. Brooke died in 1735 or 1736 a celebrity in the polite circles he had helped create. Cook died in obscurity at an unknown date. Elizabeth Magawley, Philadelphia's most trenchant critic, judged Brooke the one true poet in the province. The sons of his Quaker opponents adopted his style of satire, penning political epigrams. The sons of his club companions helped Benjamin Franklin found the most influential of American clubs, the Junto.

While Brooke injected politeness into the tavern and the club in Pennsylvania, the Reverend Benjamin Colman insinuated elegance into the pulpit, the parlor, and the college in Massachusetts. Like his friend Isaac Watts, Colman combined belletrism and Christianity to give aesthetic luster to spiritual expression. Although his cultivation of sensuous language in homiletics was dismissed by some as "syllabic idolatry," the mannerliness of his conversation in mixed company caused a sensation in Boston, and his exercise in the poetry of the religious sublime, "A Poem on Elijah's Translation" (1707), galvanized the rising generation of literati in New England.

Nicholas Bouileau-Despreaux's 1674 renovation of *Peri Hupsos* (*Of the Sublime*), a late classical tract concerning the power of certain representations to stimulate feelings of terror and ecstasy, set a generation of Western poets exploring the effects of art. With the critical encouragement of John Dennis, Christian poets in England explored how poetry might cause religious transport. Colman was the first to practice the poetics of the religious sublime in America; soon the more ambitious New England poets followed his example. Mather Byles (1707–88) declared the ambition of his generation of Harvard poets in 1744 when he spoke of desiring poetic energeia, the power to make "glitt'ring Language, and the true Sublime" collapse representations into presences: "Then should my Lines glide Languishing slow, / Or thundring roar, and rattle as they sleet" ("Written in Milton's PARADISE LOST"). Christian belletrists made language glitter by intensifying description, increasing the number of modifiers in sentences to evoke the qualities of the earthly sensorium, then amplifying them to suggest the supernatural. The religious utility of a style capable of vesting the divine with sensuous concreteness was apparent. Christian belletrism quickly became a public mode of edification. With the Reverend John Adams (1705–40), author of British America's most elaborate poetic meditation on "Society," and Matthew Adams (1694?–1753), a merchant, Byles collaborated on "The Proteus Echo Series," a vade mecum of Christian politeness published weekly in the *New England Weekly Journal* throughout 1727. Proteus Echo alternated sublime essays and poems with instructions on manners and taste. In issue 52, Matthew Adams justified the synthesis of religion and polite sociability: "The decent Ceremony of a mutual Complaisance, is . . . so near of Kind to Vertue, that I can hardly believe the want of it is reconcileable with that Religion, which is void of Offence, towards our Maker and Fellow-Creatures."

One important Christian belletrist, Jane Colman Turell (1708–35), the daughter of Benjamin Colman, did not participate in the newsprint academy of politeness. Despite the example of Elizabeth Singer Rowe ("Philomela"), an English friend of the family and popular published poet, Jane Turell avoided the public exposure ventured by her friends Adams and Byles. Her poetry, which encompassed the range of belles lettres, from biblical paraphrases in the sublime style, to Horatian imitations, to humorous verse, circulated privately in manuscript. Perhaps her reluctance can be attributed to the masculine prerogative and occasionally profane tone of Boston's newspapers. The *Boston News-Letter,* which began publication in 1704, abstracted

English and foreign news on affairs of state. The *Boston Gazette,* begun in 1719, printed political notices and an array of commercial advertisements. James Franklin's *New England Courant* (1721–7), the first American periodical to feature literary entertainment, cultivated controversy, attacked the clergy, and repeatedly satirized women. (Benjamin Franklin's adoption of the persona of "Silence Dogood" in his first essays derived much of its interest from the novelty of a sensible New England widow appearing in a paper known for featuring complaints about shrewish wives [issue 22], poetry offering "A Caution to Batchellors" [issue 8], and mock-female treatises such as Abigail Afterwit's essay on why women marry strangers rather than suitable gentlemen [issue 26].) During the 1720s, newspapers were the principal venues wherein poets could come to print. Women had to surrender something of their gentility if they sought public recognition (as a certain "Madam Staples" did in *New England Courant,* issue 10, becoming the first woman published in an American periodical). Those who cherished the principles of belletrism – taste, elegance, refinement, learned ease – generally preferred the exclusive manuscript literary communication of assemblies and tea tables.

During much of its early history belles lettres had an uneasy relation to the culture of print. A mode originally tied to the face-to-face communication of private society, belles lettres surrendered its exclusive intimacy sporadically, for instance when a wit died and admirers collected the manuscripts and put them into print. (The difficulty in determining the oeuvres of the earl of Rochester and Edmund Waller arises from their initial private circulation in manuscript.) Certain writers who operated both in the world of print and in the sociable world, Aphra Behn, for instance, segregated writings into those intended for the public and those intended for private society (Behn's "cabal"). The latter were rarely published and remained cherished tokens of one's connection with the writer. Despite the exclusivity, or perhaps because of it, a public interest attached to the conversation of the "polite world." Playwrights seized the new mode of discourse as a subject for imitation. Thomas Shadwell's *Tunbridge Wells* and William Congreve's comedies represented the conversation and the new types of conversationalists engendered by politeness: the female wit, the belle, the would-be wit, the fop, the beau. When Grub Street began to dominate the press in the 1690s, a scabrous prose rendering of the beau monde was offered the public. Ned Ward's *London Spy* caricatured clubs and spas repeatedly. These profane portraits enjoyed wide distribution and accounted for some belletrists' reluctance to venture into "vulgar print." British-American society did not escape Ward's malediction, for he concocted an account of a tour through New England: "The Inhabitants seem very Religious, showing many outward and visible

Signs of an Inward and Spiritual Grace; But tho they wear on their Faces the Innocence of Doves, you will find them in their Dealings as Subtle as Serpents. Interest is their Faith, Money their God, and Large Possessions the only Heaven they covet" ("A Trip to New England" [1704]).

Not until Joseph Addison and Richard Steele reformed the public prints by supplanting *London Spy* with the *Spectator* as monitor of social mores did politeness and the press reach a partial accommodation. Addison's immense success with the *Spectator* depended upon his transcription of the polite world in print. The frame of the periodical was a club. Like the conversation of the club, the periodical featured a variety of speaker–writers, among them men and women of the readership who operated as corresponding members of the society. Writing maintained the semblance of common speech by employing an informal, candid prose in standard vocabulary. For Addison, good manners were linked with admirable morals, so a moralized politeness became the hallmark of the periodical, a "middle style" that suited the aspirations of the developing mercantile classes.

James Franklin grasped the external devices of Addison's model when creating the *New England Courant,* as evidenced by the framing fiction that the paper was the proceedings of a club in correspondence with a readership, the employment of a figurehead persona (first Couranto, later Old Janus), and the printing of literary entertainments. However, he failed to encourage the friendly candor of tone and paid little regard to women's contributions to the social conversation. That more profound student of *Spectator,* Benjamin Franklin, learned these lessons and enacted them under the name Old Janus when brother James was jailed for offending the Massachusetts authorities. Thereafter, in the 1720s and 1730s when British-American newspapers built their subscriberships, they imitated the Addison–Franklin model. The *New England Weekly Journal* in imitation of Old Janus and his club had Proteus Echo and his circle. The *Boston Weekly Rehearsal* had its "club of young gentlemen." The *American Weekly Mercury* in Philadelphia had its Busy Body (which Franklin started) and friends. The *Virginia Gazette* had its Observator. The *South-Carolina Gazette* had its Meddlers Club.

Disparities remained between the imitations of the polite world in print and its direct expressions in manuscript. The construction of authorship was the most striking difference. In print the writer's personality could be occulted entirely by whatever voices and personae he or she wished. This duplicity was self-consciously alluded to in the choice of Old Janus (or Proteus Echo for that matter) as the presiding genius of the newsprint club. The grubstreeters, the first thralls to the print market, had realized early in the 1690s that their welfare depended on fashioning voices that could tempt people to buy their works. With an experimental daring driven by necessity, they tested and discarded personae until they hit upon one that sold. Once a writer devised a successful mask (Ned Ward's London Spy, for instance), he or she exploited it thereafter.

In British America those most closely associated with the production of print — the organizers of newspapers, printer—authors, and political pamphleteers — explored the possibilities of pseudonymity. Benjamin Franklin, for instance, was Silence Dogood, Timothy Wagstaff, Abigail Twitterfield, The Busy-Body, B. B., The Printer, Philoclerus, Betty Diligent, Anthony Afterwit, Celia Single, Alice Addertongue, Y. Z., and Blackamore, before creating Poor Richard Saunders, S. M., J. Anonymous, A. A., Veridicus, Philomath, and a host of other creatures afterward — all adapted to the purposes of the particular essay. In contrast to the reign of pseudonymity in print, the manuscript communications of the sociable world operated under the rule of cognomen. A writer adopted a name by which he or she would be known in polite conversation and spoke through an alter ego suggested by that name. The play identity never varied during one's participation in a scene of polite conversation (Aphra Behn was always "Amynta" to her cabal; Brooke was always "Sylvio" to the Philadelphia wits). One's faux-identity proved meaningful precisely because it operated in tension with the personality projected by one's proper name.

The benefits of displacing authorial identity into a fixed alter ego may be seen in the writings of William Byrd II. Byrd explored the fictionalizing of personalities in his letters. After his futile declaration of love to the Irish heiress Lady Betty Cromwell in 1703, he began incorporating narratives concerning the melancholic yearning of "Veramour" for "Facetia" into his letters to her. "Among the other sorrows he has been alarmed with, he has met with the cursed report that she was to be married to Clumsini, the very sound of which (tho he can no more believe it than the doctrine of translation) is ready to make him mad." Later in the letter: "If she should bestow her heart upon another . . . he will offer violence to himself." The tincture of fiction supplied by using cognomens permitted Byrd to express himself with an extravagance that good manners did not permit in *propria persona*. Simultaneously, it distanced the writer from his passion, sublimating desire into a game of gestures, as Lady Cromwell's cognomen, Facetia, makes clear. If violent emotion could be constrained in a sphere of aesthetic play, its expression would not endanger the civil peace of society.

Sociability depended on the moderate feeling of friendliness rather than the extravagant mutual thralldom of love. The heterosocial conversation that emerged at the spas wittily deflected ardency into amiability; indeed, the female wit (Aphra Behn/Amynta's poetic sallies with "Lysander," for instance) used her wit to deflate the amorous proclamations of beaux. By making a game of courtship and by aestheticizing feeling, the conversation of the sexes gained greater liberty while substituting social pleasure for the joy of mutual submission. This is not to gainsay that the game was played in the hope of moving from friendly converse to a more intimate joy (certainly Byrd hoped that Veramour's plight would dissolve Facetia's reserve and warm Betty Cromwell's heart), but the rules demanded that sentiment be displaced.

A consequence of belles lettres' cultivation of moderate emotions was the relative lack and mediocrity of amorous verse during the early eighteenth century. The finest love poetry published in British America, the series of twenty-eight lyrics from "a lady" to "Damon" in Barbados during the 1720s, appeared in the *Barbados Gazette* in the 1730s only because the physical separation of the lovers made the conversation a lesson in constancy, and only after the passage of nearly a decade had rendered the passion of the manuscripts a past matter. The "lady" knew that her passionate proclamations defied prevailing taste:

> My freeborn Thoughts I'll not confine,
> Tho' all *Parnassus* could be mine,
> No, let my Genius have its Way,
> My Genius I will still obey;
> Nor, with their stupid Rules, controul
> The sacred Pulse that beats within my Soul.

Noteworthy was the identification of genius as the warrant for her art. Throughout the first half of the eighteenth century, belles lettres would be indifferent to the private call of genius. Polite letters were ideally expressions of the sensus communis, that communal spirit of candid friendliness that Shaftesbury identified in *Sensus Communis; An Essay on the Freedom of Wit and Humour* (1709) as the soul of genteel society and the animating spirit of the clubs.

The rise of the clubs in Britain and America conspicuously manifested the spread of sociability. Although sodalities based on friendship existed throughout history, the club proper was created during the seventeenth century. Two models arose in the early decades: the Scots Freemasonic lodges operating under the Schaw statutes (homosocial, self-governing, hierarchical, secretive, and ritualistic) and Ben Jonson's Apollo Club (heterosocial, charismatic, self-governing, egalitarian, and aesthetic). Significant similarities existed between the organizations. Both defined their "private society" in contrast to "society at large" and marked the disparity by communal fictions – the Freemasons by their hermetic mythology, the Jonsonians by the "oracles of Apollo." Both featured a communal meal as the principal occasion of conversation. Both encouraged the production of works of art and the institution of club ceremonies to reinforce the club's identity. Both operated by codes of law. Both were exclusive in membership.

The means differed by which the models influenced subsequent associations. Freemasonry, after transmuting from a practical craft to a speculative society later in the seventeenth century, spread by replication. Its international vogue dated from the 1710s. Its table rites and social ceremonies featured songs, speeches, and secular catechisms. Many of British America's most accomplished belletrists – Benjamin Franklin, Archibald Home, Dr. Alexander Hamilton, Robert Treat Paine (the signer), Jeremiah Gridley – were Masons and active in the creation of Masonic literature. The Freemasonic model of private society also exerted an influence on other schemes of association. Daniel Defoe abstracted Freemasonry's program for privately transforming public life by means of projects in "An Essay on Projects." Defoe's tract in turn inspired the sections of Cotton Mather's *Bonifacius* (1710) encouraging the formation of young men's Christian benevolent societies. Freemasonry, Defoe, and Mather all influenced Benjamin Franklin in the design of the Junto, the signal example of a "leather-apron club" of young artisans with the aim of improving public life. It planned a library, insurance company, street maintenance scheme, academy, hospital, militia, and the American Philosophical Society.

The Apollo Club exerted influence upon the sociable world by literary means, particularly through Alexander Brome's translation of Jonson's *Leges Conviviales*. These versified laws established a pattern for club conviviality and identified the social pleasure of clubs with the play of neoclassical aesthesis. When Captain Thomas Walduck of Barbados wrote to his London friend James Petiver on November 12, 1710, about the West Indies, he could boast a sociability on the metropolitan model, bolstered by neopagan art: "At the lower end of the [club] room might be seen a large picture the whole Breadth of the room of Men societated together Some eating some drinking and dancing & playing upon Musick full of Variety of Exercise. Over head the Gods, looked down upon them Smileing – The Moral shews that when men are met together through an Innocent design, Heaven above are well pleas'd as we poor mortals below." One notes the plural "Gods."

Difficulties plague the reconstruction of the networks of British-American clubs. Fortunately, the task of identifying clubs that cultivated the arts proves less troublesome, for their productions survive in some numbers. For instance, the aesthetic development of Philadelphia subsequent to Henry Brooke's establishment of the polite world in the city taverns can be sketched by studying the literary productions of a series of circles. Aquila Rose's circle of the 1720s (a group that included poets Jacob Taylor, David French, Joseph Breintnall, and Judge Richard Hill) explored provincial identity by writing imitations of Ovid's poems of Scythian exile and promoted conviviality by composing Anacreontics. The year 1731 saw the private publication of Junto-member George Webb's paean to the club world, *Batchelors Hall*, with its recipe for convivial wit:

> The jocund tale to humour shall invite,
> And dedicate to wit a jovial night:
> Not the false wit the cheated World admires,
> The mirth of sailors, or of country 'squires;
> Nor the gay punster's, whose quick sense affords
> Nought but a miserable play on words;
> Nor the grave *Quidnunc's,* whose enquiring head
> With musty scraps of journals must be fed:
> But condescending, genuine, apt and fit;
> Good nature is the parent of true wit;
> Tho' gay, not loose; tho' learned, yet still clear;
> Tho' bold, yet modest; human, tho' severe;
> Tho' nobly thirsting after honest fame,
> In spight of wit's temptation keeping friendship's name.

Webb's discriminations specified club wit succinctly: polite, not profane; urbane, not rustic; good-natured, not artificial; friendly, not offensive. It radiated an ethos of candor, yet also of self-control. The self-governing autonomy of private society was taken up as a matter of playful reflection in the Schuylkill Fishing Company's club myth that they constituted the "State in Schuylkill." From the club's founding in 1732 through the 1740s, members elaborated a mythology around the "spirit of St. Tammany," a Delaware chief. The Tammany myth would be embraced by a network of Whiggish clubs throughout British America over the course of the century, eventually mutating in one instance into New York's infamous Tammany Hall.

Private society's fancies could become public mythologies with the proper sponsorship. Provost William Smith (1727–1803) became the foremost publicist of politeness, the mimetic arts, and the productions of private circles. During the 1750s, he superintended the rise to notice of "The Swains," a circle of protégés including Benjamin West, Thomas Godfrey, Francis Hopkinson, Nathaniel Evans, Joseph Reed, and Jacob Duché. By newspapers, magazines, letters of introduction, and booksellers, Smith brought his circle public exposure in Philadelphia and in London. He enjoyed only piecemeal success, for although West achieved world fame, and Hopkinson won some reputation for ability in literature, music, and politics, Duché, Evans, Reed, and Godfrey could never rise above the condescending notice granted provincial prodigies.

One observer of the Swains' pursuit of fame, Elizabeth Graeme Fergusson (1737?–1801), concluded that the task of Amphion – building civility –

mattered more than the accolades of London's critics. Her salon at Graeme Park in the 1760s absorbed the Swains after their failed assaults on the metropolis. Concurrently she instituted the most talented network of female belletrists to be formed in British America, including Susanna Wright, Annis Boudinot Stockton, and Hannah Griffitts – a network that favored manuscript exchange over publication. The activities of the Swains and the Graeme Park salon deserve further discussion, for as these brief characterizations of Philadelphia's literary scene indicate, the club remained the most important institutional frame for belletristic communication throughout the Colonial era.

Because of the service belles lettres performed in underwriting the sociable commerce of private society, it ran the risk of being "agreeable" to the point of conventionality and "easy" to the point of mindlessness. Jonathan Swift, a denizen of the clubs and coffeehouses, criticized the sociable style of their conversation in a series of essays, most hilariously in *A Complete Collection of Genteel and Ingenious Conversation, According to the Most Polite Mode and Method Now Used At Court, and in the Best Companies of England* (1738). Swift thought belles lettres debased because they relied upon the tarnished beauties of modish conversation to elicit pleasure. He believed politeness hindered social commerce because it often subordinated genius to system and reduced wit to formula. Swift's criticisms seem particularly apt when one surveys the great mass of vers de société generated for the delectation of circles from Bath to London, from Barbados to Halifax. Tim Vainlove's "To The Ladies in Boston, in New England" (*Boston Gazette,* November 29, 1731) supplied the same sort of gallantries employed in "The Belles of Barbados" (*Caribbeana,* 1738), Governor William Shervington's *The Antigonian and Boston Beauties* (1751?), and Charles Woodmason's song to the girls of Black Mingo, South Carolina, sung at the St. John's Hunt in 1753. The formulas of compliment and the rites of sociability differed little from locale to locale. Too often belletrists exploited the repeatability of "true wit" by repeating agreeable pieces into clichés.

Despite the tendency toward formularization, British Americans did produce several masterpieces of belles lettres – works that transcended the conventions of politeness by discovering how problematic it can be to speak through the sensus communis or by thematicizing sociability to render genteel culture comical. The most profound work to emerge from the heterosocial conversation of the polite assemblies was the 1744 "Poems on Several Occasions by Archibald Home, Esqr. late Secretary, and One of His Majestie's Council for the Province of New Jersey: North America," which collected the writings of a belletristic circle in Trenton, New Jersey, in the 1740s.

Archibald Home (1705?–44), third son of Sir John Home, baronet of Berwick, was educated privately in Scotland. He emigrated to New York in 1733 in search of a place in the imperial bureaucracy. While haunting the coffeehouses of New York City he attracted the notice of Lewis Morris II, the recently deposed chief justice of New York. When Morris procured the governorship of New Jersey in 1737, he appointed Home deputy secretary, later secretary to the provincial council, then member of His Majestie's Council. In the provincial capital, Home gathered about him a circle that cultivated music, painting, and poetry. The membership illustrated the linkage between artistic refinement and cultural cosmopolitanism. It included two Jews, Moses and Richa Franks; a Huguenot minister, the Reverend Louis Rowe; the most accomplished woman in British America (according to Benjamin Rush), Abigail Streete Coxe; Trenton's sheriff, David Martin; two pillars of the provincial government, Attorney General Joseph Warrel and Justice Robert Hunter Morris; and Home. When Home died in March 1744, his companions collected thirty-four of his poems, prefixed the collection with their elegies, and appended club writings composed under Home's tutelage. Several manuscript copies of Home's works circulated in Britain as well as in the colonies. The collections covered the range of belletristic genres – epigrams, fables, songs, verse riddles, impromptus, and classical imitations. The earliest written songs and satires give a glimpse of tavern life in 1730s New York City unequaled in vividness and memorability. These include "On a Dispute, between two Scotchmen at a S. Andrew's Feast in New-York Anno 1733," "Memoirs of a Handspike," and a sarcastic genealogy of the problem of male sexuality, "Black Joke. A Song":

> Our *Paradice Dad* ne'er had eaten the Fruit
> If that Sly *Devil Eve* had not tempted to't
> With her black Joke &ca
> He tasted the Pippen, he mounted his Bride
> He damn'd his whole race, and drove on till he dy'd
> At her coal black Joke &ca

With a grim ribaldry worthy of Robert Burns, Home confronted the Presbyterian doctrine of total depravity with the reality of human sexual appetite. The pungent humor Home derived from Scots song also found expression in a later work, "An Elegy on the much to be lamented Death of George Fraser [*sic*] of Elizabeth Town." It mockingly lamented the demise of a hail-fellow from New Jersey taverns whose hard-swearing ways made him unable to attract a spouse through love or money:

> Sae ruddy was his Face & blooming,
> That when his Head he pat the Room in,

Ye'd trud that Summer was a comming,
The melted Snaw,
Before him sat the Gait a Sooming,
Just like a Thaw.

Wha was that gae us haesome Cheer,
And waughts o'Syder and o Beer.
What was that lernt our Bairns to swear
or they could read?
George Frazer did; what need ye Speer?
But now he's dead.

The vitality with which Home portrayed Frazer's predicament may have borrowed from the poet's own romantic frustrations. Most of Home's poetry addressed the dilemma of his love for Richa Franks, the accomplished daughter of the richest Anglo-Jewish merchant in America. In the wake of her sister's elopement with a gentile and her brother's marriage to one, Richa's parents had prohibited any involvement with Home. Confronted by his ban, Home attempted to create a literary precinct in which "Florio" and "Flavia" might consort. Reimagining the Pygmalion legend, the poet confessed that "Pygmalion like I'd crave a Wife / Kneel down and pray her into Life." The poet re-created the object of his affections as "Flavia," but the pleasures he imagined with her ("Would Fate indulgent grant that I, / Might my Lov'd Flavia's Zone untye") were proscribed outside poetry. The story of Pygmalion is the classic parable about the potency of art, but Home as Pygmalion rebuked the impotence of poetry in the modern world for its inability to make the imaginary real. In the poems to Flavia, Home repeatedly projected back into the legendary eras before the world and art had fallen. In "The Four Ages of the World, from Ovid's Metamor: Lib. 1," the poet condemned the "iron age" of the present in light of a golden age *in illo tempore*. In "To Flavia" he fantasized about the possibility of an unfallen world (with no distinction between Jew and Christian because the world required no redeemer) if Flavia had only been Eve: "The Devil in vain had tempted her to sin; / Eternal joys the happy Pair had prov'd / And envying Angels wonder'd how they lov'd." In "Pandora" he imagined how the evils laid against the female sex would be canceled by Flavia's power: "A new Pandora, but without her Box; / In her fair Hands had Jove that present put, / Her soft Compassion would have kept it shut." Home's repeated invocations of a female creature possessed of an atavistic power to remake the world did not stir Richa to take charge of her fate or even to participate in the imagining of a neoclassical haven of mutual joy. Alone of the club's members she did not write. Home's early death staunched the flow of poetry to her, rendering his literary remains a testament to a problem of heterosociality – that mixed company sometimes places one in proximity with someone whom one grows to love, despite circumstances that forbid love. Against such circumstances art sometimes proves no remedy.

To forestall the frustrations of heterosexual passion, certain circles instituted homosociality. "Friendly clubs" excluded members of the opposite sex to ensure the dominion of moderate amiability. In the male world of the taverns and coffeehouses, establishing "Batchelors Hall" was no problem. The tea table societies women set up in townhouse parlors were not so insulated from male intrusion, leading Mary Astell to make her famous proposal to found a Protestant nunnery where women could enjoy a haven commensurate to those enjoyed by men. In British America the Tuesday Club of Annapolis, Maryland (1745–56), was the most richly self-conscious of homosocial organizations. Dr. Alexander Hamilton (1712–56) preserved the club's conversations and activities in minute books, refined and editorially amplified them into the "Record," then transmuted them into three magisterial volumes of fourteen books, *The History of the Ancient and Honourable Tuesday Club*.

Hamilton was superbly equipped to become the mock-historian of British-American sociability. The son of the principal of the University of Edinburgh, he enjoyed a superior education in classics, philosophy, and medicine at Edinburgh's Latin School and University. Just as Hamilton entered upon professional life, the Scottish metropolis was becoming a major center of Enlightenment intellectuality. A crucial reason for Edinburgh's emergence as a center for arts and sciences was the proliferation during the 1720s and 1730s of clubs devoted to conversation and free inquiry. Hamilton immersed himself in this society, joining the Whin-Bush Club, whose laureate, Allan Ramsay, was then engaged in reviving Scottish vernacular poetry in issues of the *Tea-Table Miscellany*. Poor health forced Hamilton to emigrate to Maryland in 1738. In 1744, on a tour from Maryland to New Hampshire, he acquainted himself with the network of British-American clubs and recorded his impressions in a travel narrative, the *Itinerarium*. In 1745 the Tuesday Club was founded in Annapolis. Hamilton was elected secretary, eventually to preside over the creation of a masterwork of mock-history. He used the incidents of his club's "rise and decline" to parody world history, imperial politics, the state of learning, the public prints, philosophic speculation, and clubbing. No capsule description communicates the variety and invention of Hamilton's fantasy. It possesses a garrulousness of address, extravagance of style, breadth of reference, and variability of humor that make it the preeminent evocation of the British-American club world. Intended for the private delectation of his society, the over-sixteen-hundred-page manuscript remained unpublished until 1990.

Hamilton's *History* may be read as the culmination of a tradition of club play lampooning public life by caricaturing it in club proceedings. The disparity between the friendly candor of private society and the gravity and contentiousness of the state permitted a parodic politics to be performed. The pretense of being mock-states depended upon clubs' understanding themselves to be authentic polities – contract societies governed by law, not appetite. (Celebrating the government of appetite became a favorite club project, leading to the republican table rites of London's Beefsteak Society, the denunciations of ragouts in the Homony odes of Maryland's Homony Club, and a host of club legislation and mythology about comestibles from Cheshire Cheese to October Ale.) With the elaboration of consent theories of government by Thomas Hobbes, James Harrington, and John Locke (all three of whom belonged to clubs) the comic tensions between the club's utopia of sympathy and the state's compromised balance of warring interests became exquisite. The first earl of Shaftesbury exploited the tensions in the Green Ribbon Club (1670s), whose code required every man to address his fellow member as "King" and whose projecting spirit inspired Whiggery and promulgated the English party system. But many clubs found that the amiable sensus communis of private society and the public spirit of the state permitted no conjunction, for no amount of projection could make a state a friendly society. Hamilton's brilliance as a comic historian lay in his inversion of the satirical premises of the club literature. Instead of the club being used as a polemical weapon to bludgeon the luxury and depraved spirit of public life, Hamilton's Tuesday Club became a microcosm of the political macrocosm. The *History* is a chronicle of a club wracked by the prerogative battles, faction fights, riots, legal provocations, and corruptions that bedeviled public life during Walpole's Robinocracy and the rule of the Pelhams. The Tuesday Club's slide into luxury and social degradation began, according to Loquacious Scribble (Hamilton's cognomen), with Nasifer Jole's violation of the club's sumptuary law restricting meals to a single dish or "bachelor's cheese." Jole's set suppers and iced cake won him election as perpetual president, ending the "Roman liberty" of the primitive club. From this minor event Hamilton constructed his comic fugue on the cycle of history, intertwining themes of the lost republic, the spread of luxury, the rise and fall of civilizations.

The Tuesday Club aestheticized political conflict by internalizing it. Rather than reflecting upon particular political situations in Maryland or London, the club abstracted the motives of political conflict and reconstituted them within the constitution and population of the club. This effectively distanced the satire. Indeed, the club's "gelastic law," requiring the company to laugh uproariously whenever a member began making passionate claims about Maryland politics or business, preserved the aesthetic distance of club play. By subordinating politics to aesthetic play, the Tuesday Club questioned the efficacy of "projecting." Social happiness was placed in the pleasure of an estranged perspective of an exclusive community.

Belles lettres' ability to articulate a sensus communis at odds with "the public spirit" and the prevailing state ideology gave them a political significance despite whatever avowals clubs might have made that they were havens of retirement from the affairs of state and business. The Kit Kat Club of London, whose secretary, Jacob Tonson, was the foremost bookseller of the metropolis, first combined belletristic aesthetics with a political program to project a public political sensibility during Queen Anne's reign. The Whiggish Kit Kats made the Tory policy appear unfashionable as well as unadvisable. With the creation of communities of political taste the meaning of belles lettres expanded to encompass writings that evoked social pleasure while projecting a public concern. Belles lettres began to impinge upon the public discourse of civic humanism. By the 1760s the once-distinct modes would be considered synonymous.

Governor Robert Hunter (1666–1734) of New York, a friend of Addison and student of the new political belletrism, imported the methods of the Kit Kat Club to the American scene. Hunter's "biographical farce," *Androboros* (1714), satirized his opponents in the Senate and local Church of England establishment, so "that the laugh was turned upon them in all companies and from this laughing humour the people began to be in good humour with their Governour." William Smith, Jr.'s contemporary assessment of the effect of Hunter's closet drama describes the institutional dynamic of political belletrism exactly: it sought to influence the people by first changing the opinions of the "companies" that made up New York society. To prosecute this end further, Hunter formed a political literary circle that included David Jamison, Robert Livingston, and Lewis Morris II. He perfected a politics that depended as much on genteel style for its popularity as on its cultivation of economic interests.

Several talented politicians emulated Hunter's example. Lieutenant Governor Sir William Keith of Pennsylvania (1680–1749) became an extraordinarily popular and effective executive during the 1720s by his charm and "open way of living." Both literature and sociability were brought to bear in creating a political mystique about his regime. Clubs of gentlemen and laborers were formed to organize his support and channel the flow of opinion. Poet Aquila Rose was recruited to serve as court laureate, celebrating Keith's treaties with the Native Americans. The lieutenant governor won the support of polite society by encouraging the theater, despite Quaker opposition. He demonstrated his own "parts" by wielding the pen repeatedly and skillfully against his opponents. His grasp of power grew so great that the Penn proprietors feared losing their control over Pennsylvania and were forced to engineer the removal of their own appointee. Keith's dissemination of the writings promoting his regime showed an understanding of their effects. The panegyrics of his court poet were handed about in manuscript to retain the exclusive aura of genteel society. Keith's polemics against James Logan and Isaac Norris were published under his name as political tracts, wholly public documents written in plain language. Keith's belletristic prose and verse satire of Andrew Hamilton, *The Life and Character of a Strange He-Monster* (1726), appeared in print anonymously, provoking a public mystery about the meaning and origin of the writing.

"He-Monster" Andrew Hamilton would win fame within the decade for successfully defending the liberty of printers to publish screeds such as that directed against him. As defense lawyer for John Peter Zenger, printer of the *New York Weekly Journal,* Hamilton vindicated the most famous literary political campaign of the early eighteenth century in British America, the River Party's attack on Governor William Cosby of New York. The junto of attackers included several ingenious and powerful men: James Alexander, Lewis Morris II, David Humphreys, and Cadwallader Colder. In libelous beast fables, ballads, and essays, the River Party junto taunted the governor into acts of repression. After Zenger's arrest and the public incinceration of two ballads and several issues of the paper at the city gibbet, the River Party junto fired popular indignation by circulating manuscript songs throughout the city. Their manuscript "publication" recalled the distribution of "court ballads" from Whig scriptoria during the 1680s, when the Stuart reaction to the Rye House plot occasioned a similar repression of the press. That expressions had to appear in manuscript ostensibly proved claims that Cosby quashed public liberties. Certain of the manuscript songs bore titles so archly unspecified as to defy libel prosecution, such as "A mournfull Elegy on the funeral pile & Execution of the ballad or ballads burnt by publick authority before a great crowd in a small town in a certain Country under the Northern hemisphere on a certain day since the year 1600." One composition, David Humphreys's "The Lamentable Story of two Fatherless & Motherless Twins which Lately Appeared in ye City of N-w-Y-k who for their Phrophetick Cires were Condemn'd to be burnt by ye Common Hangman which was Accordingly Executed &c." employed for the first time in British America Whig Sentimentalist narrative, the most effective political discourse to develop from belles lettres.

Belles lettres' concern with literary effect was redirected toward political ends in Whig Sentimentalism. An opposition discourse associated with English Country Party literature, Whig Sentimental narrative played upon audience sympathies by telling of the victimization of those lacking power.

Children (particularly orphans), the poor, the enslaved, honest provincials, and commoners were imbued with a virtue earned by undeserved suffering at the hands of the powerful – parents, courtiers, masters, kings. Thomas Otway's play *The Orphan* and Joseph Addison's *Cato* were founding texts for the discourse. The depredations of the powerful had civic, rather than personal, significance, revealing the vulnerability of the social good. Though Whig Sentimentalism would not dominate political belles lettres until the Revolution, it first emerged in America as a literary weapon in the colonial battles over prerogative power during the 1720s and 1730s. One of its ablest practitioners, Lewis Morris II, was an orphan whose inheritance was nearly wrested from him by a powerful executor who had read Otway's tragedy and from it borrowed the villain's stratagem of deceit.

Lewis Morris II (1671–1746) studied letters under George Keith, the brilliant and heretical Quaker intellectual. His political career began with his appointment as judge of the Court of Session in East New Jersey at age twenty and led rapidly to his appointment as chief justice of the Supreme Court of New York, in which post he stirred the ire of Governor Cosby, who engineered his removal. Upon Cosby's death, Morris was appointed governor of New Jersey in 1738. At every juncture of his career he employed literature to further his political aims. As a councilman he dispatched satires to colonial agents in London. In 1725 he composed a "Dialogue Concerning Trade" to counter the merchant interest under Adolph Philipse. When Governor Cosby and Philipse struck a deal to seize government power and milk the treasury for personal gain, Morris composed an allegorical account of the decline of New York's government into "The Mock Monarchy or Kingdom of Apes." He contributed one of the two ballads burnt by the hangman at Cosby's command. After Cosby's repression of the press, Morris wrote "The Last Prophetick Speech of Mr. Zengar's [*sic*] Journalls Condemn'd to be burnt by ye g – —— – r & C – —— – le." As an ironic comment upon his failed trip to London in 1735–6 to petition the Privy Council for the restoration of his office and the removal of Governor Cosby, he composed "The Dream, A Riddle," the vision of an honest provincial discovering the corruption of Old England. As governor of New Jersey he defended himself against land agitators in a reflection "On the Essex Riots." He put the legislature in good humor by spoofing the lobbying that surrounded the selection of the site of New Jersey's seat of government in "To his Excellency The Governour of New Jersie, upon the Assembly's Disiring him to fix his own Seat." Only one of his compositions was ever printed: the condemned election song. The others presumed an elite audience of opinion shapers. This audience might be located in New York's city clubs or in London's coffeehouses in the vicinity of White Hall. The allegories – "The Mock Monarchy" and "The Dream, A

Riddle" – reflected on the colonial situation with a generality that implied a metropolitan audience. Other works – "On the Death of a Late Valorous and Noble Knight" and "On the Essex Riots" – had the entre nous allusiveness of internal party documents. All operated on the assumption that the devices of belles lettres might nudge the opinions of companies toward particular political ends. Noteworthy is the semipublic character of the communications. Morris did not aspire to be his own laureate, for the declamatory style of a public oracle was inimical to his sense of how opinion became policy and then governmental action.

British America had both laureates, poets who claimed the office such as Ebenezer Cooke, and unofficial civic bards who assumed the vox populi. Benjamin Tompson, the excellent mannerist poet, spoke as a representative of Massachusetts in his "To Lord Bellamont when entering Governour of the Massachusetts" (1699). There were also poets who addressed society at large with the officious ceremony of statesmen: George Webb in Philadelphia during the regime of Governor Patrick Gordon and Mather Byles in Massachusetts during the regimes of Governor William Burnet and Governor Joseph Belcher. The proliferation of laureates and civic bards in British America marked an expansion of public discourse. Mather Byles's simultaneous assumption of the roles of minister, Massachusetts laureate, and agent of politeness shows how the once-distinct realms of individual being, public life, and private society coalesced in the wake of Addison's creation of a moralized print politeness. Magazines and newspapers were increasing popular interest in sociability and gentility. By the 1730s print's co-optation of belles lettres had become so obtrusive that a double reaction occurred. New Light evangelists seeking to reclaim the prints for Christ denounced the worldliness of polite society and its expressions. The New Lights rejected Christian belletrism and its practitioners – Reverend Mather Byles, Reverend John Adams, Nathaniel Gardner, Jr. – as Old Light. Conversely, the genteel elite persecuted evangelists for their views, jailing George Whitefield in Charleston, South Carolina for condemning social dancing in a sermon. From within the clubs the wits launched a second critique, with rum distiller Joseph Green volunteering to serve as New England's antilaureate.

Joseph Green (1706–80), who received an A.M. from Harvard College in 1729, became the chief wit in Boston's taverns during the late 1720s. His satirical manuscripts circulated in a network of merchant clubs extending from Portsmouth, New Hampshire, to Newport, Rhode Island. He specialized in skeptical reflections and parody. The growing officiousness of public life particularly provoked his wit. When obituary biographies began to appear in Boston's newspapers, Green commented ironically on their effect upon the citizenry:

Now I am upon this head of Characters I can't dismiss it, without congratulating my Country upon the pious & useful Custom of publishing Characters in the weekly Papers, which I look upon as a great Support to Religion & Virtue. Who would be at the Pains of many Actions which they now do, were it not in hopes of having them recorded, & what more proper way of doing it then this. It is what we all expect & desire; The hopes of a long Character (for the Substance & Truth of it are less regarded then the Length) thrusts us on; there is a certain stimulating Virtue in it, which pricks us on in Religion; in short like wringing a Calf by the Tail to make him go fast.

Green's sense of the significance of print in British-American culture was acute. He chose to disseminate a writing in manuscript or in print by calculating the effect that the medium would have on the message. When debunking the secrecy of the local Freemasons, he published pamphlets bearing titles lurid with Grub Street promises of wonders and revelations: *Entertainment for a Winter's Evening: Being a Full and True Account of a very Strange and Wonderful Sight seen in Boston on the Twenty-seventh of December, 1749,* and *The Grand Arcanum Detected: Or, A Wonderful Phaenomenon Explained, Which has baffled the Scrutiny of many Ages* (1755). He used manuscripts when he wished to suggest that he was conveying truths that dare not be published, such as his parodies of the addresses of Governor Joseph Belcher to the Assembly of New Hampshire in 1733–4 or his anticlerical songs and epigrams. His satires of the New Light evangelists were particularly pungent. Green inaugurated the long-lived satirical convention of linking evangelical enthusiasm with sexual misconduct. Reverend William Cooper inspired "The Disappointed Cooper," a song on the aging evangelist's loss of reputation after marrying a young redhead:

> A Cooper there was, he Work'd at his trade
> Old barrells he mended, & new one's he made
> So stiff in his way, he had *Will* for his Name
> Yet he liv'd a long while in good credit & fame
> Chorus: But his credit *Will* lost — lost how? do ye ask
> Why he put an *old bung* in a new red-oak cask.

Before the New Lights attracted Green's notice in the late 1730s, he devoted much energy to parodying the writings of Mather Byles, volunteer laureate of New England and the politest of the Old Lights. From 1728 until 1734 Mather Byles's poetic effusions would instantly be greeted by a Green parody. The coup of Green's campaign as antilaureate occurred in 1733 when the *London Magazine* printed Green's "The Poet's [i.e., Byles's] Lamentation for the Loss of his Cat, which he used to call his Muse" and a parody of an impromptu psalm Byles composed at sea on a voyage with Governor Belcher. The appearance of the parodies in the principal organ of metropolitan fashion tweaked Byles's vanity. Green realized that Byles's secret heart-sin was a lust for literary fame.

Byles was smitten by a new form of an ancient disease. Alexander Pope, the archpoet of the empire of letters, the archon of the nascent print market of literary celebrity, redefined fame for ambitious provincials. As an undergraduate Byles had saluted the "wondrous Bard! whose Numbers reach our Shore, / Tho' Oceans roll between, and Tempests roar." Books and magazines were the vehicles by which Pope managed his triumphal transit. The potency of the fiat and the press-engendered ubiquity of his presence made Pope an unprecedented phenomenon in the eyes of provincial writers. Certain belletrists who dominated particular scenes of conversation affiliated their authority with that of the imperial archpoet. Poetic pledges of allegiance survive from Benjamin Colman, Henry Brooke (one of his final poems), James Kirkpatrick of Charleston, South Carolina, and Byles. Those who sought fame without making an accommodation with Pope earned his malediction. Benjamin Franklin's friend James Ralph was mauled by Pope for *Night* and *Sawney*. But the most arbitrary stroke of Pope's power fell against Richard Lewis, the finest neoclassical poet to write in British America.

Richard Lewis (1699?–1734) understood himself to be a civic poet, but not as defined by the traditions of laureateship. Rather, he modeled himself after Addison, who not only articulated the meaning of the res publica but refined the public spirit by teaching it politeness. In Maryland, where Lewis served as Latin master of the Annapolis school, he obtained the two requisites for becoming a civic archpoet: the interest of a politically powerful patron and the trust of an able printer. His patron, Benedict Leonard Calvert, was governor of Maryland; his printer, William Parks, was the colony's official printer. Lewis performed his duties as court poet of the Calverts enthusiastically. In the poetic dedication to Benedict Calvert of *The Mouse-Trap* (1728), a translation of Edward Holdsworth's *Muscipula,* Lewis declared that "Arts Polite, shall shine in this Domain" so long as the governor maintained the civil order. The governor headed the subscription list, pledging for ten copies. Some idea of the polite polity Lewis envisioned can be had from the list. It was upper-class, cosmopolitan, and male, yet constituted something more than the company of the better Annapolis taverns. One hundred forty-eight men (no women) promised purchase of the first translation of a Latin work to be published in the colony. Twenty of these were lawyers or judges; nineteen held military rank or captained ships; nine were physicians; two were ministers; the remaining ninety-eight subscribers were either merchants or planters. Besides the comic narrative of the battle between the mice and the ancient Cambrians, readers were treated to an extensive anatomy of the virtues of Benedict Calvert and the benefits of his government.

Lewis turned from panegyrist to eulogist when Benedict Calvert died in 1732, composing two elegies: "To John Ross Esqr, Clerk of the Council" and "Verses. To the Memory of His Excelly Benedict Leonard Calvert; Late Governor of the Province of Maryland." Both elegies survive only in manuscript, but a published memorial to Benedict's rule appeared as the climax of *Carmen Seculare* (1732), a celebration of Maryland's progress to civility composed for the visit of Charles Calvert, Lord Baltimore, on the centenary of the colony's founding. *Carmen Seculare* was noteworthy for its presentation of the condition of Maryland as a historical product of political will, economic circumstance, and natural condition.

Lewis's sensitivity to American nature permitted an insight into the natural order that went beyond the Virgilian paradigms of "the war with nature" and georgic utility. His "Food for Criticks" (1731) bemoaned the depredations wrought on the wild by thoughtless utilitarians. His "Rhapsody" (1732) combined post-Newtonian physicotheology with an aesthetician's attentiveness to the qualities of nature's sensorium. Lewis's masterwork, the widely republished "A Journey from *Patapsco* to *Annapolis*, April 4, 1730," expressed the spiritual anxiety of the human subject in the post-Newtonian universe, where the physical insignificance of the human individual is manifest. At the same time, the poem demonstrated the potency of the human mind by epitomizing the design of nature in the course of a poet's journey across country over the span of a day – the variety of diurnal states, climatic conditions, topographic scenes, and social situations. The paradox of the human situation was brilliantly symbolized in descriptions of two birds: the mockingbird, whose ability to imitate any bird's song was emblematic of the power of artistic mimesis, and the hummingbird – "He mock's the *Poet*'s and the *Painter's* Skill; / Who may forever strive with fruitless Pains, / To catch and fix those beauteous changeful Stains." Both creatures were indigenous to the New World, evoking the cosmopolitan vogue for specimens of natural philosophy, while symbolizing Lewis's argument that the crises of art and human ability will be enacted more dramatically in America. Lewis's challenge to the centrality of the metropolis and his suggestion that the New World contained objects incapable of mimetic capture goaded Pope into his rebukes in Book 4 of the *Dunciad*. Pope did not know that the author of "A Journey" was Richard Lewis, but he understood the seriousness of the challenge being posed and replied with a passage describing a butterfly, to show that there were no inimitable objects for a powerful poet. Pope's critique appeared too late for Lewis, who died in 1734.

Lewis's sense of his public was imperial. Not only did he endow his province with self-understanding, but he also explained the meaning of the province – its history, economics, nature – to the metropolis. His poems appeared in the London papers and the two chief periodicals, *London Magazine* and *Gentleman's Magazine*. Because Maryland was a staple colony and because the British "empire of the seas" was a mercantilist empire that understood the significance of colonies in terms of the resources they contributed to imperial trade, Lewis's poems presented messages that commanded the interest of the metropolis. Indeed, the southern and West Indian colonies held a particular fascination for British projectors of the *imperium pelagi* that would be repeatedly exploited by writers in the decades following Lewis's death. In Charleston, South Carolina, throughout the 1730s, the physician James Killpatrick (later Kirkpatrick) labored at *The Sea-Piece: A narrative, philosophical and descriptive Poem, In Five cantos* (London, 1750). Organized as an account of a transatlantic voyage from Ireland to South Carolina, Kirkpatrick's poem was a paean to the Walpolite vision of commercial imperialism, in which trade, not conquest, constituted the way to wealth and world dominion. Endorsing Edward Young's nomination of "The British Merchant" as the hero of the empire, Kirkpatrick envisioned that Britain's global dominion of the seas would bring about the universal spread of the arts of peace. Trade's "ethical empire" would result in a utilitarian meritocracy provided that the agents of the empire – factors, merchants, seamen – could resist the lure of luxury. One of the fascinating aspects of the poem was an economics that exalted exchange over production. So thoroughly did Kirkpatrick globalize his vision of exchange, and so powerfully did he bind it to the poetic working of metamorphosis, that the entire British Empire appeared as transfigured value: the metropolis appeared as a distillation of the world's resources; the colonies, not as sites of intrinsic value, but as places where any commodity that could be desired might be produced (silk, tropical fruits, and wine, for instance, in South Carolina). The ever-changing sea served as an eloquent symbol of the transmissibility of value in the *imperium pelagi*.

Kirkpatrick fixed his attention upon land only after Oglethorpe settled Georgia in 1732. Whereas London poets hymned the colony as a philanthropic utopia, Kirkpatrick viewed it as the land of consumer wishes. In his prophecy of cornucopia published in the *South Carolina Gazette* during February 1732–3, he adorned the Georgia-to-be not only with the world's delicacies but with the luxuries celebrated in Western history and legend as well:

> [T]he fat plains with pleasant olives shine,
> And *Zaura's* date improves the barren pine.
> Fair in the garden shall the lemmon grow,
> And every grove *Hesperian* apples show.
> The almond, the delicious fruit behold
> Whose juice the feign'd immortals quaff'd of old.
> Nor haply on the well-examin'd plain
> Shall *China's* fragrant leaf be sought in vain.

A problem with prosecuting a colonial enterprise that neglected a country's intrinsic resources in favor of commodities transplanted from foreign parts was the labor entailed. Everything had to be planted from scratch. The philanthropists who founded Georgia justified the great labor involved on moral grounds. Habituation to arduous work would redeem the worthy poor transported to Georgia from indolence and poverty. Samuel Wesley's (1691– 1737) panegyric *Georgia, A Poem* (1736) celebrated the fact that the colony was one great workhouse in the wild. The colony banned slavery in order to create a working yeomanry, but the experiment failed. As Patrick Tailfer and his band of malcontents declared in *A True and Historical Narrative of the Colony of Georgia* (1741), the trustees' control of the labor market and land title drove settlers into Carolina for freehold rights and the opportunity to secure African slave labor. Georgia was eventually forced to adopt slavery and legislate freehold rights to property in order to survive.

The professional classes in the South and in the West Indies attested to their faith in an empire of trade well into the 1750s, producing works such as Reverend James Sterling's *An Epistle to the Hon. Arthur Dobbs, Esq* (Dublin, 1752) and James Abercromby's "An Examination of the Acts of Parliament Relative to the Trade and the Government of our American Colonies" (1752), but the planters who cultivated the staples upon which trade depended turned their attention toward land and the work of cultivation. Because land formed the basis of wealth for planters, their vision of empire tended to be territorial. Arthur Blackamore's "Expeditio Ultramontana," a Latin poem celebrating the trek of Governor Alexander Spottswood and "the knights of the golden horse-shoe" into the Virginia backcountry to claim land for the empire, epitomized the planter mentality. The poem's sociable spirit, its attention to topography, and its ceremoniousness in declaring the advance of civilization into unim-proved territories would be refracted in a number of Virginian works, notably Charles Hansford's "My Country's Worth" and William Byrd II's *History of the Dividing Line Betwixt Virginia and North Carolina*. These writings circulated in manuscript among planter circles, except for Byrd's *Secret History*, which was prepared for select English readership.

Byrd's histories have become the most familiar works of British-American belles lettres for current readers. Yet rarely have they been read in light of belletristic conventions. The irony pervading both of Byrd's histories should be understood not as a personal expression of Byrd's equivocal sense of society and nature but as a manifestation of the parodic candor about public matters and humane circumstances characteristic of sociable mockery. The histories belong to the same genre of mock-history as Hamilton's *History of the Ancient and Honourable Tuesday Club* and operate by similar comedic premises. Even the symbolic argument of the *Secret History* concerning the civility of Virgin-ians and the crudity of North Carolinians operates comically, with Virginians revealed in their vanity and Carolinians half-envied in their desuetude.

Whereas a serious polemic would have resolved the dialectic of Virginia and Lubberland by sublating the latter to the former in a triumph of civility, Byrd's narrative leaves the two possibilities in tension, each calling the other into question. Lubberland exerts its one fascination throughout the *Secret History* – the promise of a life without labor. That Anglo-Carolinians could adopt the simplicity/indolence of Native-American men and be sufficiently satisfied with their lot to resist the temptation of becoming Virginians suggested that the future of the South would be no progress piece toward civilization.

New Historical readers of Byrd's histories have observed that the labor maintaining Virginian civilization was not so much the planter's as the African slave's. They have argued that the invisibility of the slaves accompanying the expedition in Byrd's narratives points to the presumption that props up the planters' order. Yet Byrd's narratives do not present Virginia planters in their usual dominion, the plantation, so the applicability of this presumption can be questioned. Certainly those authors who do concern themselves with the creation of the plantation culture in the staple colonies devote exquisite attention to both the labor and the laborers needed to transform the semitropical wilderness into a productive agricultural estate.

Three belletrists made major attempts to represent the work of planting in the staple colonies: Charles Woodmason's "Indico" (1757), James Grainger's *The Sugar-Cane* (1764), and George Ogilvie's *Carolina; or, The Planter* (1776). All were georgics in form, recalling from Virgil the ethos of Roman imperial enterprise and the concern with the practical work of farming. All were civic poems with a dual audience: a local public of elite readers and the curious of Great Britain.

Woodmason's "Indico" never reached its intended audiences, for the subscription for its publication failed. However, the substantial excerpts printed in the advertisements for the proposed volume allow the poem's argument to be reconstructed. Woodmason asserted that the staple colonies afforded land "more fruitful than Britannia's own." Yet the climate of the colonies was too tropical for English laborers. Africans possessed constitutions that "temper'd to the Heat / By Situation of their native Soil, / Best bear the scorching Suns, and rustic Toil." Woodmason's justification of African labor on the grounds of climatic necessity was made in the face of extensive metropolitan criticism of the slave system. James Thomson's *Liberty* (1736) and John Dyer's metropolitan georgic *The Fleece* (1757) insisted that slavery subverted the morality of trade and would ensure future violence.

New World celebrants of plantation civilization could not ignore the problem of labor. Rather, they worried it with full attention. The culminating fourth section of James Grainger's *The Sugar-Cane* viewed the plantation culture of St. Christopher's Island in light of "The Genius of Africa." The social and material conditions of West Indian slaves were examined with unequaled thoroughness. The poem provided information on the disposition of various African tribes to plantation tasks, the diseases the tribes suffered, and the sorts of houses, gardens, dances, folk cures, and beliefs they had. When the poem was published in London it was greeted by Dr. Samuel Johnson as the first significant public poem from the New World. Johnson particularly admired Grainger's portrait of the ideal planter. Grainger (and Ogilvie after him) argued that the only moral justification for the plantation culture lay in the character of the virtuous planter. A planter's rationality, justice, and humanity stood as the only bulwarks against the future vengeance of the African slave. The message offered by *The Sugar-Cane* and *Carolina; or, The Planter* to local audiences was a warning to planters concerning the exercise of their authority. Both authors tendered their warnings doubting the inclination of planters to follow their advice. Grainger regretted the slave system sufficiently to petition the metropolis at the close of the poem to intervene in the staple colonies by imposing an English *code noir.* Ogilvie wished the failed wish of the Georgia philanthropists: the creation of a southern yeomanry that performed its own labor. The major literary presentations of southern and West Indian self-understanding repeatedly acknowledged the plantation system as a moral problem because of its dependence upon slavery. Grainger's regrets would be taken up by an entire school of West Indian civic poetry: in John Singleton's *A Description of the West Indies* (1767) and *Jamaica, a poem, in three parts* (1777), in *Poems, on subjects arising in England and the West Indies* (1783) by the rector of St. John's at Nevis, and in Edward Rushton's *West Indian Eclogues* (1788). These testimonies would be cannibalized by abolitionist poets in Britain such as Hannah More, John Marjoribanks, and William Roscoe. The wish for a southern yeomanry spoken by Ogilvie would appear most memorably in Thomas Jefferson's *Notes on the State of Virginia* (1784). Paradoxically, the fulfillment in Haiti of the prophecies of slave vengeance halted southern considerations of alternatives to the slave system. The horrors recounted by refugees frightened southern planters from any thought of lessening their control over their slaves.

Plantation society as celebrated by Grainger, Ogilvie, and Singleton operated on the old pattern of hospitality rather than on the new model of urban sociability. Social gatherings took place at rural estates under the auspices of a host family. Gatherings tended to be heterosocial; arranging social matches and contracting marital alliances were exquisite concerns of the plantation elite. Courtship took place at periodic balls or assemblies under the scrutiny of the older generation. Instead of the egalitarian spirit of the club room or city tea table, social and familial hierarchy always obtruded. Many planters knew urban sociability from seasonal residence in Annapolis, Williamsburg, Charleston, or Savannah; certain elements of spa style were taken from the city to the country. Nevertheless, plantation society retained a distinctive identity throughout the eighteenth century. Byrd's Virginia diaries supply the first extended view of this world, where the gentry circulated from plantation to plantation. The diaries of Philip Vickers Fithian, a plantation tutor, and Sally Fairfax also give vivid glimpses into plantation society. Yet the most remarkable portrait emerges in the courtship journal of Robert Bolling (1738–75). J. A. Leo Lemay's edition, *Robert Bolling Woos Anne Miller* (1990), combines Bolling's self-serving narrative of the failed courtship with the poems he composed during and after the affair. It is a proof text of the distinctively atavistic development of southern social interaction.

Robert Bolling's career as a belletrist illustrates the complexity of a talented writer's situation in British America at the end of the colonial era. Scion of one of Virginia's great planter families, he was educated in Britain at the grammar school in Yorkshire and briefly at the Inner Temple before returning to Virginia to read law in Williamsburg. A cosmopolitan, his acquaintance with French and Italian literature made him a prodigy of learning in Virginia. Poems such as his "heroitragi-comic Tale," "Neanthe" (a grotesque in the style of Francisco Berni), and "Winter" mystified local literati unread in Continental literature. Local taste was more attuned to the songs, odes, and satires that he circulated in manuscript. Certain poems he aired in the Williamsburg newspaper. Yet Bolling was never content with local approbation. He dispatched his best verse in the gallant mode to London for inclusion in the *Imperial Magazine.* When the Tidewater oligarchy's abuse of privilege resulted in the illegal bailment of Colonel John Chiswell after he committed murder, Bolling became the oracle of conscience, using his literary skill to work justice in a series of writings published in Purdie and Dixon's *Virginia Gazette.* His fame in Virginia arose from his role in this public contest, yet his ambition remained that of a virtuoso, desiring reputation as a poet, despite the fact that his ability did not run toward those genres – epic, description, meditation, progress piece, philosophical anatomy – that procured fame. Furthermore, as a Virginian, from his schooldays in Yorkshire he had felt an alienation from British opinion – a problem for one seeking fame, since London remained the place where reputation had to be won. In "Occlusion," a poem that Bolling wrote to serve as epilogue for a collection of his verse if it were ever published, he reflected humorously on the trajectory of a provincial belletrist's ambitions:

> A pert and lively Brat at Schole
> Old Carke cou'd cry This Boys no Fool

And in our annual Lays to Bess
(such Lays I weem were never known
But in her royal Praise alone)
Because my Lines had equal Pace
My Rhymes were aptly paird
Th' Old Man wou'd say – the Whelp was born a Bard
Thence thence the tuneful Rage began
What warmd the Scholeboy warms the Man
Roxanna Celia Delia heard
How horrible the Chimes I rung
How heartily their Charms I sung
In Truth the Maids plain Prose preferr'd
And what was meant as Praise
They swore was Slander in such wretched Lays
I tho't my Verses very good
And wonder'd Maids cou'd be so rude.

The poet next turned to satire, which bred trouble, then graveyard verse about "a maid, expiring in her Bloom," and finally an epic on "An Indian War" whose bathos earned universal derision.

Bolling's sketch of a poet's fate contains several details of historical interest – for instance, the lines confessing the influence of school on the formation of literary ambition. At the beginning of the century, during belles lettres' primitive glory, Swift noted that the coffeehouse, not the academies, formed the ideals of literary practice: "Several young Men at the Universities, terribly possessed with the Fear of Pedantry . . . think all Politeness to consist in reading the daily Trash sent down to them from hence: This they call *knowing the World,* and *reading Men and Manners.*" Within the colleges the undergraduates developed a mirror image of coffeehouse society. Beginning in the 1720s the students' rooms of American Colleges sprouted a succession of clubs and "juvenile associations" intent on supplementing the instruction of the classroom with their own explorations of taste, reading, and manners. Some clubs – Harvard's Philomusarians, William and Mary's F. H. C. Society, the College of New Jersey's Cliosophical Society and American Whig Society – developed into institutions within institutions, superintending the literary conversation of the students. The uninhibited indulgence in interclass and interclub paper wars or in competitive praise for local beauties honed skill as no classroom exercise in translating the classics could.

Attempts to harness these extramural exercises in belles lettres to a program of education did not take place until midcentury when Provost William Smith organized the Academy and then College of Philadelphia. In his educational tract *A General Idea of the College of Mirania* (1753), Smith justified the inclusion of study of the "mimetic arts" in the curriculum: "These studies enlarge the mind, refine and exalt the understanding, improve the temper, soften the manners, serene the passions, cherish reflection, and lead on that charming langour of soul, that philosophic melancholy, which most of all, disposes to love, friendship, and every tender emotion." Smith's justification of collegiate training in polite letters depended upon Scottish Common Sense philosophy's theoretical development of Whig Sentimentalism: public spirit would grow more compassionate if citizens were habituated to imagine themselves as other persons and in other situations. The mimetic arts made such imaginative projection pleasurable, thus encouraging the habit. Scotsman Hugh Blair's *Lectures on Rhetoric and Belles Lettres* (begun in 1759; published in a collected edition in 1783) codified aesthetic thinking on the public utility of belles lettres, emphasizing the rhetorical value of a discourse's pleasurability. In the decade after the Revolution Yale students would riot, demanding the adoption of Blair's *Lectures* as an element in their instruction. Students at the College of Philadelphia had no need to riot, for Provost Smith composed his own lectures in rhetoric that anticipated Blair's thinking in many particulars. Smith supplemented precept with example; his various literary productions – *Indian Songs of Peace* (1753), "The American Fables" (1752–3), "A Poem: Being a serious Address to the House of Representatives [of New York]" (1752) – were instances of rhetorized belles lettres, works whose pleasurable aspect "dulcified" an argument over public policy. The students at the College of Philadelphia also benefited from the example of Benjamin Franklin's writings of the late 1750s, 1760s, and 1770s, which masterfully showed the way in which a pleasant or humorous manner could render daring positions publicly palatable.

Provost Smith precluded the need for a student organization by gathering promising youths into a circle under his own direction, the so-called Swains. These included two talented persons not enrolled at the college, painter Benjamin West and poet Thomas Godfrey, who met with a student contingent including Nathaniel Evans, Joseph Reed, Francis Hopkinson, Jacob Duché, and John Green. Smith led his protégés to understand themselves as the first flowering of arts and science in the New World, the fulfillment of the long-prophecied transit of arts and empire to the new continent. Proofs of their skill were given at the college's commencement exercises, in the pages of provincial and metropolitan newspapers, and in the pages of the *American Magazine and Monthly Chronicle,* Smith's periodical designed to show the cultural adequacy of the American colonies.

Smith's magazine was the most impressive published in British America. Designed on the model of the metropolitan periodicals *London Magazine* and *Gentleman's Magazine,* it accorded to the original sense of the term "magazine," being a storehouse of miscellaneous items. It was part museum, part moral instructor, part digest of foreign news, part chronicle. Several previous attempts had been made to establish a periodical in America: Franklin's *General Magazine* in 1741, Bradford's *American Magazine, or a Monthly View of the British Colonies* in 1741, Jeremy Gridley's *American Magazine and Historical Chronicle* in 1743. Each aspired to be a British-American periodical, casting a wide net of intelligence and seeking a geographically dispersed subscribership through the network of printers and booksellers in the coastal cities. None could build a strong enough subscribership to survive more than a few months. Smith, like the earlier editors, banked on the hope that the occasion of war would give rise to a widespread need for a provincial organ treating the contest. Smith realized that the Seven Years' War gave events in America a near-global interest, since Pitt prosecuted the war on four continents. Braddock's defeat, the retaking of Louisbourg, and the death of General Wolfe at the gates of Quebec attracted international attention to the American colonies. Local authors realized that they now had an occasion commanding an interest that could bring them fame.

Robert Bolling might have joked of writing his epic on the Indian war, but an entire generation of aspiring poets plied a bellicose muse. Some, such as Joseph Shippen and James Sterling, celebrated the triumphs of British allies in Europe for an American audience. Others, such as John Beveridge, Hopkinson, Godfrey, and Alexander Martin memorialized events in the New World for an imperial audience. Perhaps the most striking indication that an interest attached to what British-American writers had to say about the struggle with the French and the Native Americans is found in the willingness of booksellers to sponsor publication of book-length works. John Maylem's *Gallic Perfidy* (1758) and *The Conquest of Louisburg* (1758) issued from Benjamin Mecom's press in Boston; George Cockings's *War; an Heroic Poem* and Benjamin Young Prime's *The Patriot Muse* appeared from London presses. In the end, one of Smith's protégés would create the definitive representation of the war. Benjamin West's *The Death of General Wolfe* eclipsed all literary comment on the war with its visual articulation of the drama of empire. The painting transformed the pictorial representation of history, asserting the commensurability of modern occasions with the great events of antiquity.

The Seven Years' War occasioned the first works of political belles lettres by women in British America. Whereas Britain from the turn of the century had its female commentators (such as Mary Pix, Susanna Centlivre, and Elizabeth Boyd) on affairs of state, politics remained a matter of privileged masculine conversation in the colonies, if we are to judge by advice such as that "To a Poetical Lady" (*Boston Weekly Magazine,* March 1743). Women were free to contribute to the literary portions of newspapers and were assured of being printed so long as they paid the printer's standard submission fee, but the preponderance of women's contributions were vers de société, reflections on courtship and marriage, or religious expressions. With the Seven Years' War, however, the *New York Mercury* began printing the civic poems of Annis Boudinot Stockton, the *Boston News-Letter* published "a Lady's" "Lines . . . upon General Amherst," and the *New Hampshire Gazette* featured a long poem "by a Female Hand in the Country" on the taking of Louisbourg. Thereafter, with increasing regularity, women treated politics, addressing a general public in print or the genteel elite in manuscript. The most extraordinary single work of political belles lettres by a British-American woman, Elizabeth Graeme Fergusson's "The Dream of the Patriotic Philosophical Farmer" (1768), a ninety-three-page poetic vision responding to John Dickinson's famous *Letters from a Farmer in Pennsylvania* (1768), remains unpublished.

Elizabeth Graeme Fergusson (1737?–1801) presided over the most brilliant literary salon in colonial America. Daughter of Dr. Thomas Graeme and inheritor of Graeme Park, a country house outside Philadelphia, she manifested her literary talent in her early teens, adopting the cognomen "Laura." Although her initial efforts were conventional pieces of sociable verse, she quickly expanded her range. The poems generated by her ill-fated romance with William Temple Franklin (Benjamin Franklin's illegitimate son) echo Aphra Behn's astute reflections on the problem of love:

> Young *Damon* came in Friendship drest
> At first spoke not of Love,
> With Fredom we our Thoughts exprest
> And Talkd of powers above,
> Of what was Right, and just, and true,
> But my own Heart I little knew.
>
> The wiser set saw the pretence
> And told me I was wrong;
> They spoke Experience backed by sense
> I deemed my Heart too strong!
> For I was pleasd to boast my Friend
> Nor thought I *Love* was at th' End.

Franklin had jilted Elizabeth Graeme in 1759 for a London belle.

The Seven Years' War prompted Graeme to communicate "sense" in her writings. Her poetical epistles to Rebecca Moore counseling feminine fortitude in the face of war were the first in a series of exchanges with talented women. When Rebecca Moore married Provost William Smith, Elizabeth was brought into contact with him and his circle. Her intellectual confidence was such that she could write a poetic assessment of Adam Smith's *Theory of Moral Sentiments* (1759). Graeme Park became a favorite resort of Provost Smith's Swains during the late 1750s. She regularly exchanged verses with Francis Hopkinson and Nathaniel Evans. By the 1760s the gatherings at Graeme Park had taken on the formality of a salon, with John Morgan and Thomas Coombe joining the company.

Salons – heterosocial gatherings for cultured conversation and the performance of arts under women's superintendence – were a French phenomenon imported into British society early in the eighteenth century. They differed from "tea table society" in their engagement with the arts. Prior to the 1750s, suggestions of the existence of a salon culture are rare. Elizabeth Magawley's poetical plantation outside Philadelphia in the late 1720s, the Trenton poets that Abigail Street Coxe presided over after Archibald Home's death in 1744, and Harriet Simons Dale's circle in Charleston during the late 1740s are the few gatherings for which evidence survives. Graeme's salon at Philadelphia and Annis Boudinot Stockton's salon at Morven in Princeton, New Jersey, formed nearly simultaneously (the late 1750s) and supply strikingly parallel histories: both incorporated college literary communities, both favored poetry above all other arts, both produced a substantial body of literary manuscript unintended for print, and both earned reputations for being the most genteel and refined companies in their colonies. Yet neither Graeme nor Stockton considered the conversation of their circles sufficient exercises of their abilities. They established a correspondence between themselves, and from it radiated a network of female literary communication that would include Hannah Griffitts, Esther Edwards Burr, Mary Read, Anna Young Smith, Rebecca Moore Smith, Elizabeth Norris, and Susanna Wright.

The female society that the Graeme–Stockton network constituted on paper distinguished itself from tea table society by its intellectuality and artistry. Reverend John Adams's portrait of a 1727 female company in Boston indicates the sort of conversation that the Graeme–Stockton network defined itself against:

If you visit the Tea-Table of some few Ladies, (to speak genteely) you have good Manners, a civil sort of Impertinence, Remarks made with excellent Judgment upon the Fashions, the Position of Some Gentlewoman's Head-dress, or fine Lectures upon the Affairs of a House, the finest way to make Sowse and Jellies, with many more Particulars of the like Advantage and Instruction, and it is very well if you escape hearing a long Roll of your Neighbour's Faults, which either are not true, or if so would better be buried in Silence.

The Graeme–Stockton network worked against the confinement of women's conversation to domestic chat, gossip, and recitations of male blandishments. As Susanna Wright said to Elizabeth Norris:

> But you, whom no seducing tales can gain
> To yield obedience, or to wear the chain,
> But set a queen, & in your freedom reign
> O'er your own thoughts of your own heart secure,
> You see what joys each erring sex allure,
> Look round the most intelligent – how few
> But passions sway, or childish joys pursue;
> Then bless that choice which led your bloom of youth
> From forms & shadows to enlight'ning truth.

The relative scarcity of well-read women and their geographical separation required that conversation among them be conducted on paper. Wright, for instance, had moved from Chester, Pennsylvania, into the wilds of the Susquehanna Valley in 1726, where,

> From all the social world estrang'd
> In desert wilds in woods
> Books and engaging friends exchang'd
> For pendant rocks and floods.

There she conducted experiments in agriculture and silk-weaving while composing poetry. A prolific and famous poet in her day, Wright is now known by a scant four poems unearthed by Pattie Cowell in her studies of British-American women's literary culture. The recovery of Wright's oeuvre should rank as one of the more important tasks now facing literary historians studying British America.

The writings of Annis Boudinot Stockton display comprehensively the concerns of the women writers in colonial networks. One finds the expected expressions of social pleasure and the polite verses and verse epistles addressed to friends and family, as well as a substantial amount of public belles lettres on political themes, such as odes to Washington and reflections on several incidents of the Revolution. Finally, one encounters polemic poems on behalf of female ability, such as "To the Visitant, from a circle of Ladies, on reading his paper. No. 3, in the Pennsylvania Chronicle" (1768):

> You, Sir, with better sense, will justly fix
> Our faults on *education,* not our *sex;*
> Will shew the source which makes the female mind
> So oft appear but puerile and blind;
> How many would surmount stern custom's laws,
> And prove the want of *genius* not the cause;
> But that the odium of a *bookish fair,*

Or *female pedant,* or *"they quit their sphere,"*
Damps all their views, and they must drag the chain,
And sigh for sweet instruction's page in vain.

With the constitution of salon culture and the projection in print of a female public voice in the 1750s and 1760s, belletrism underwent its final development as a movement of colonial culture. Having evolved from 1700 to 1760 out of an elite metropolitan conversation conducted in manuscript into a printed international discourse enjoyed by an expanding audience, it dominated notions of what was "literary" on the eve of the Revolution. Other discourses – history, natural history, homiletics, hymnody, philosophy – were forced to react to the imperial expansion of belles lettres' domain, alternately assimilating and repudiating the devices of social pleasure. The greatest resistance to belles lettres and its culture of sociability arose from evangelical Christianity. New Light pietists denounced them programmatically. Annis Boudinot Stockton would hear John Ewing, tutor of the College of New Jersey, observe that "she and the Stocktons are full of talk about Friendship and society and such stuff." Denigrating sociability or discounting women's capacity for friendship went hand-in-hand with denunciations of the theater and (later) novels.

The strong influence of reformed Christian pietism accounts for the diminished influence of the theater in British America. Even in the provincial centers where latitudinarian opinion held sway – Kingston, Charleston, Williamsburg, Annapolis, New York – the strength of disapproval prompted local belletrists to defend the theater as morally instructive. Thomas Dale in Charleston, James Sterling in Annapolis, the Reverend Mr. Johnson, rector of St. Michael's Parish in Barbados, John Barrell in Boston, and Archibald Home in New York composed prologues to plays declaring that the stage was a spur to virtue:

> Oft when the Serious admonition fails
> O'er the lov'd fault the Comick Mask prevails;
> Safe from the Bar, the Pulpit, and the Throne,
> Vice blushing yields to redicule alone,
> This Ancient Greece this the Great Romans knew,
> They held th'instructive Mirrour fair to view;
> That each his own Deformities might trace
> And smooth his features by the faithful Glass.

American belletrists devoted so much time to apologetics that they did not undertake substantial writing for the stage until Thomas Godfrey's tragedy *The Prince of Parthia* in the early 1760s. The Revolution would break out before a full-fledged theatrical literature would be established in America.

For the most part British Americans were passive recipients of metropolitan productions, awaiting the latest importation from the metropolis performed by one of the itinerant theatrical companies. As for the impression British Americans made on the London stage, Richard Cumberland's immensely popular satirical portrait *The West Indian* (1772) was the single most influential representation of a British American offered to the metropolis. It was not a flattering picture; indeed, it was ammunition for the pulpit critics of the stage.

The novel also suffered from underdevelopment during the colonial era. Tainted by the aura of Grub Street amorality, associated with subversion of the religious, civil, and familial order, the novel did not merely count pietists among its opponents. To a genteel elite its popularity identified it as vulgar. In a developing country where anxiety about the degree to which civility was manifest, the archons of politeness in the colonies did not cultivate a form that portended the decline of taste into middle-class fantasy and sentiment. The "colonial novels" known to literary history – Aphra Behn's *Oroonoko* (1688), Arthur Blackamore's *The Perfidious Brethren* (1720), and Charlotte Lennox's *The Life of Harriet Stuart* (1751) – were published in London by former residents of the colonies for a metropolitan readership. The production of novels was displaced from the colonial scene for economic and cultural reasons. A British-American readership for both novels and plays existed, but it did not exist in so coherent or serviceable a form as to permit the support of local writers. The rise of the novel in America was a postrevolutionary phenomenon tied to a host of cultural and economic circumstances that came into being after Britain's imperial autarchy was overthrown.

Just as the postrevolutionary situation gave rise to new possibilities of expression, it did away with what had gone before. The writers who came forward to speak for the new nation had little use for British-American precursors. Practitioners of civic belles lettres such as Benjamin Young Prime, Alexander Martin, and Francis Hopkinson repudiated their prerevolutionary work, either by letting it sink into oblivion or by thoroughly revising it. A substantial number of the central figures of the colonial club culture had entertained Loyalist sympathies. Many left America, and others remained to become suspect figures: Joseph Green, Mather Byles, and Benjamin Church in Boston; George Ogilvie and William Packrow in Charleston; Jonathan Boucher and Robert Ellis in Maryland; William Smith and Elizabeth Graeme Fergusson in Philadelphia. Patriot writers, declaring themselves the first manifestations of American genius, put themselves forward as the inaugurators of American literary history. With the interesting exception of William Livingston's poem *Philosophic Solitude; or, The Choice of a Rural Life* (1747), an essay in the natural sublime anticipatory of Philip Freneau's

Romanticism, the entire corpus of colonial belles lettres was expunged from the memory of the rising generation of writers.

A second development militated against the formation of an American literary tradition out of British-American belles lettres: the consolidation of the literary print market. In the wake of the Revolution, publication became the signal mark of literary worth. The manuscript literary culture of the clubs and salons disappeared, except for exchanges of manuscripts for criticism preparatory to publication. Elihu Hubbard Smith's diary descriptions of the New York Friendly Club indicate how clubs had transformed from the principal arenas of literary communication to rehearsal halls for public performances. When the first American literary historians – Samuel Knapp, Isaiah Thomas, Samuel Miller, John Neal – turned their attention (c. 1800) to the rise of belles lettres in America, they did so without a historical understanding of its institutions and imposed a standard of literary value inappropriately derived from the contemporary workings of a print culture in a market economy. Consequently, they concluded that little literary activity had occurred in British America; that the little that did occur was of low quality; and that its interest was primarily historical rather than aesthetic. This judgment prevailed well into the twentieth century, only being overcome by the painstaking work of several generations of scholars beginning with Laurence C. Wroth, Ralph Rusk, and Louis B. Wright, followed by Richard Beale Davis and C. Lennart Carlson, and culminating in Kenneth Silverman and J. A. Leo Lemay. The scholarship of these literary historians supplies the empirical grounds for understanding belles lettres in British America.

THE AMERICAN ENLIGHTENMENT, 1750–1820

Robert A. Ferguson

FINDING THE REVOLUTION

I

Understanding the American Revolution is a literary pursuit, and John Adams assumes as much in his own famous summary of the event. "The Revolution," Adams insists in 1818, "was in the minds and hearts of the people," and those who would seek it must collect and search "all the records, pamphlets, newspapers, and even handbills, which in any way contributed to change the temper and views of the people." By concentrating on this change in ideas, Adams makes *"the real American Revolution,"* as he calls it, the central event of the American Enlightenment, and he turns comprehension of it into a permanent test of cultural well-being. In urging this understanding upon "young men of letters in all of the States," he also warns them against superficial explanations that stress "the gloriole of individual gentlemen." The transformations in thought that bind Americans together in 1776 and after take place beneath the surface of events. Only by a diligent search can one hope to find the deeper truth of *"radical change in the principles, opinions, sentiments, and affections of the people."*

This challenge, already problematic in 1818, remains the challenge of today. The task is to recover as much as possible of the Revolution, itself the greatest literary achievement of eighteenth-century America, while keeping in mind the gaps between surviving word and original thought, text and lost context, assertion and expectation, story and event. If *"the real American Revolution"* resists a narrative of heroics to reside elsewhere – in the minds and hearts of the people – how does one reach that level through extant writings? The primacy of textual evidence must be balanced against the incomplete and equivocal nature of that evidence. The relation of writer to text to audience must be treated as a variable and not as a fixed sequence.

Some of the difficulties over interpretation are already clear at the time that Adams writes. In 1815, Adams and Thomas Jefferson concur that "the most essential documents, the debates and deliberations in Congress from 1774 to 1783 were all in secret, and are now lost forever." They agree further that those few speeches that have found their way into print appear "very different" from the original performances that they themselves heard. "Who shall write the history of the American revolution?" Adams asks. "Who can write it? Who will ever be able to write it?" Jefferson's response is blunt and to the point: "Who can write it? And who ever will be able to write it? Nobody; except merely its external facts." Of course, the very awareness of difficulty also stimulates a battle over approximations in interpretation.

Adams and Jefferson fully understand that the Revolution *will* be told, and they compete with each other in the knowledge that their own tellings will control subsequent thought. This process, too, is part of the literature of the Revolution – part of the later movement of ideas in the minds and hearts of the people. Adams, in particular, fears the story already being told. "The history of our Revolution," he complains to Benjamin Rush in 1790, "will be that Dr. Franklin's electric rod smote the earth and out sprung General Washington. That Franklin electrised him with his rod, and thence-forward these two conducted all the policy, negotiations, legislatures, and war." Splenetic and self-righteous, Adams nonetheless has seized upon an important truth. The electric wand in his comic fable, a fusion of science and magic, conveys the fact and the means of an enduring popular perception. Americans use this device and others like it to personify the Enlightenment in a myth of national origins, one that leads to just the kind of "gloriole of individual gentlemen" that Adams warned against.

These exchanges indicate the problems in any literary recovery of the Revolution. Whereas the intellectual historian must rediscover and contextualize ephemeral documents and forgotten speeches, the critic must assign a relative importance to each. Both attempts must qualify or at least situate the mythologies that Adams has rejected. Meanwhile, the simplest questions become difficult when answers involve the underlying change in ideas.

When did the Revolution begin? How did it begin? As early as 1743, Samuel Adams, then twenty-one, took the affirmative in a Harvard Commencement Day *Quaestio:* "Is it Lawful to resist the Supreme Magistrate, if the Commonwealth cannot otherwise be preserved?" His words, a schoolboy's exercise, were an excellent personal preparation for rebellion, but the colony, not the schoolboy, set that exercise. The theme of lawful resistance was an early preoccupation of English subjects on both sides of the Atlantic. No wonder John Adams and Jefferson concluded that the Revolution began with "the first plantation of the country." No wonder, as well, that in assigning a proximate cause a Loyalist historian like Peter Oliver could waver between the vast generality of the Reformation ("Since the emerging so suddenly from worse than Ægyptian Darkness, the human Mind was not strong enough to bear so sudden a Flash of Light") and the specificity of a single incident in 1761 (the feud between James Otis, a rising young lawyer, and Thomas Hutchinson, then lieutenant governor in Massachusetts, over the latter's appointment to the Massachusetts court). Hutchinson wrestles with the same incident and, hence, with the same problem of scale, in his own history of the times. "From so small a spark a great fire seems to have been kindled," Hutchinson marvels in retrospect. Where should the emphasis lie between the abstraction in ideas and the narrower but deeper trauma of parochial episode? Does the emphasis shift when episodes in themselves take on a larger symbolic importance in revolutionary ideology?

Questions about the influence of ideas raise another difficulty. Do the writings of revolutionary leaders transform the thought of colonial Americans, or does popular pressure dictate the pace and tenor of those writings? The catalyst of change that John Adams emphasizes, does it come from top or bottom? Answers to such questions are unavoidably provisional, but they must be kept in mind. No one, for example, would deny that Alexander Hamilton's ideas control large elements of *The Federalist* when its eighty-five numbers appear serially in 1787 and 1788, but Hamilton's essays, a distinct majority in *The Federalist,* bear little resemblance to the political preferences he expresses so passionately in Philadelphia just a few months before. Hamilton's extravagant admiration for the British Constitution on the floor of the Federal Convention is nowhere in Publius, and the reasons for the shift are in his own letters. "If a Convention is called," Hamilton writes in 1780, "the minds of all the states and the people ought to be prepared to receive its determinations by sensible and popular writings, which should conform to the views of Congress." This language of conformity, preparation, popularity, common sense, and reception reminds us that even the rigid, aristocratic-minded Hamilton engages in a flexible, consensual literature where political leadership, individual expression, and the will of the people meet.

John Adams's warnings about re-drafted writings, about the inflated roles of Washington and Franklin, and about too much emphasis on individual heroics suggest another level of concern. The success of national formation quickly clouds critical perception. The revolutionary founders are apotheosized within their own lifetimes, and many of them live long enough to gloss their own accomplishments in retrospective accounts. The combination distorts the meaning and the context of original contributions that are already difficult to interpret. The writings of the Revolution cope with issues and take aesthetic forms that have no place in modern literature, and the best of them have become the sacral objects of a national observance – icons that are more and, therefore, less than the written texts that they once were. They are, in consequence, peculiarly the property of American civilization, but Americans do not read them now as they were written or were meant to be read.

Against the difficulties in viewing the Revolution as a literary phenomenon – the product of its public records, pamphlets, newspapers, and hand-bills – are two crucial complementary strengths. From below, the Revolution takes place in one of the most generally literate cultures that ever existed, and, from above, the elite's conscious sense of itself in the act of writing is one of its few forgotten virtues. Revolutionary Americans read voraciously, and their leaders write easily and often, leaving rich, varied materials both in print and in manuscript. No generation, whether in reading or in writing, has looked more carefully to the printed word as the basis of its identity, and this reliance is all the more remarkable in a society still on the border between oral and print forms of literary and intellectual transmission.

In eighteenth-century culture, the accomplished figure demonstrates a worthiness for place and preferment by writing about the world at hand. The young Jefferson becomes a prominent Anglo-American personage overnight with one essay, *A Summary View of the Rights of British America*, in 1774. The same can be said of Thomas Paine two years later with *Common Sense*. Alexander Hamilton, James Madison, and John Adams also prosper, in part through their works on government and the Constitution. One need only compare the more limited scope of their compatriots who leave no comparable bodies of work, John Hancock and Patrick Henry, for instance. Early on, Benjamin Franklin makes a fortune as well as his reputation from printing and authorship. Even George Washington looms larger for his writings – his circular on leaving the army in 1783 and his presidential farewell in 1796.

The primacy of writing appears in crucial moments of self-assertion. John Adams, amidst the worldly tensions of 1777, distinguishes between "Kinds of Ambition," reserving for himself only those forms that are "Literary and Professional." His subsequent production in official documents, essays, treatises, letters, and diary entries more than justifies the way he gives first priority to a literary career. Jefferson's inscription for his tombstone begins "here was buried Thomas Jefferson, Author." All three sources of identification that follow – the Declaration of Independence, the Statute of Virginia for Religious Freedom, and the University of Virginia – celebrate this author's sense of creativity and immediate service. Franklin's own famous epitaph turns its subject into a work of literature with the promise that though this "old Book" itself decay, "the Work shall not be lost; For it will, (as he believ'd) appear once more, In a new and more elegant Edition." "Prose writing," Franklin confirms in his autobiography, "has been of great use to me in the course of my life, and was a principal means of my advancement."

Authorship controls identity because the leaders of the Revolution expect so much from what they write. Their major works invariably allude to their own importance as both text and historical event. Paine's *Common Sense* begins not with tales of British oppression but with a recital of the grave errors that previous writers have foisted upon the world. By correcting these errors, his own pamphlet will change history. *Common Sense* promises to turn the reader into another Noah, one who possesses the "power to begin the world over again." *The Federalist* claims to be the best discussion of the most important question of the age. In turn, Franklin's autobiography assumes for itself the praise of posterity, the attention of all future notables, and a literary niche somewhere above the contributions of Caesar and Tacitus. All three works share an important premise about writing: anything is possible when the right word receives the proper emphasis and reception. And although this presumed power of the word is biblical in its original conception, it flourishes anew as part of the timely spread of knowledge in Enlightenment thought, one of many dynamic conflations of religious and secular understanding found in eighteenth-century literary circles.

Revolutionary Americans use their faith in writing to stabilize the uncertain world in which they live. Either they accentuate perceived anxieties, problems, and unknowns on the page, to be subsumed in the substances of print, proof, style, and form, or they rigorously exclude them from what still pretends to be a "comprehensive" treatment of the subject. Jefferson's debate with the Continental Congress over the rhetorical use of slavery in the Declaration of Independence offers a clear case in point. The alternatives are either to make the horror of slavery a central theme in the document and then to make it a major grievance against the king of England *or* to remove all mention of slavery, which is done in the final draft. In a more positive variation of the same ploy, *The Federalist* responds to early republican fears of the continental wilderness by bringing all of nature under the lens of political order. "It has often given me pleasure to observe," writes Publius in *Federalist No. 2,*

that independent America was not composed of detached and distant territories, but that one connected, fertile, wide-spreading country was the portion of our western sons of liberty. . . . A succession of navigable waters forms a kind of chain round its borders, as if to bind it together; while the most noble rivers in the world, running at convenient distances, present them with highways for the easy communication of friendly aids.

The fantasy of geographical connection embodies political unity against the recurring early republican nightmare of chaos and dissension.

These devices – devices of contextualization within a theory of comprehensiveness – are conscious fabrications in the writer's search for a higher truth, and they betray a willingness, even an eagerness, to reshape and gild the cruder facts with which they must contend. As devices, they are also the counterparts of far more subtle stratagems in the literature of republican idealism. The overall tactic marks a major tendency of writing in the period. Removing a controversial subject like slavery and positing a superficially compliant natural world are attempts to forge artificial unities amidst a contentious, far-flung populace. Revolutionary writers face a deeply divided people across the 1770s and 1780s. Their assumed task is to extract consensus at all costs, and they write with a paradoxical brand of creativity in mind – a creativity of agreement.

Jefferson's account in 1825 of how he wrote the Declaration of Independence reveals the form of this aesthetic:

> Not to find out new principles, or new arguments never before thought of, not merely to say things which had never been said before; but to place before mankind the common sense of the subject, in terms so plain and firm as to command their assent. . . . Neither aiming at originality of principle or sentiment, nor yet copied from any particular and previous writing. It was intended to be an expression of the American mind.

The pronunciamiento in the statement, the Declaration as an expression of the American mind, has controlled commentary to the virtual exclusion of the many negatives that Jefferson registers here. These negatives – "Not to find out new principles . . . not merely to say things which had never been said. . . . Neither aiming at originality . . . nor yet copied" – reveal a lost distilling process and its frustrations. Where agreement dominates in literature, authorial intent and creativity willingly define themselves through the limitations of consensus.

The deft business of securing assent through language must be understood against a frequent despair in the attempt. Franklin, for one, comes to accept division as the inescapable norm of human affairs. "[Men] are generally more easily provok'd then reconcil'd," he tells Joseph Priestley in 1782, "more disposed to do Mischief to each other than to make Reparation, much more easily deceiv'd than undeceiv'd, and having more Pride and even Pleasure in killing than in begetting one another." John Adams agrees. "[N]either Philosophy, nor Religion, nor Morality, nor Wisdom, nor Interest," he warns Jefferson in 1787, "will ever govern nations or Parties against their Vanity, their Pride, their Resentment or Revenge, or their Avarice or Ambition." Ironically, the triumph of the Revolution is accompanied by a grim awareness of human limitation and continuing acrimony among those who struggle to fulfill its continuing promise.

Agreement in such a world clearly requires a manipulation beyond mere understanding. The truth may be self-evident, but those who find it must be coaxed into agreement over its meaning. "I am a sincere inquirer after truth," Adams explains in 1790, "but I find very few who discover the same truths."

The basis of this pessimism is Adams's own experience in the making of governments. "The difficulty of bringing millions to agree in any measures, to act by any rule," he observes, "can never be conceived by him who has not tried it." This comment may sound strange coming from one of the presumed architects of national formation, but the success of Adams and his generation on just this score has blunted later perception of their concern at the time. To read the works of the early Republic as they were written is to recognize that the tone, scope, meaning, and shape of those writings were forged decisively in "the difficulty of bringing millions to agree."

This consensual literature does not lend itself to a simple evolving chronology even when chronology interweaves texts with events. Chronological narratives bring their own impulses to the presumed meaning of the Revolution. British actions – from the Revenue Act, or Sugar Act, of 1764, to the Stamp Act and the Troop Quartering Act of 1765, to the Townshend Revenue Acts of 1767, to the Tea Act of 1773, to the Intolerable Acts, including the bill closing Boston Harbor, in 1774 – do indeed elicit a series of American reactions (colonial protests and pamphleteering of all kinds, nonimportation and nonconsumption agreements, the Stamp Act Congress and, later, the Continental Congress, the formation of the Sons of Liberty and of the later Committees of Correspondence, the Boston Tea Party, and so on). But this catalogue, however true and however frequently rendered, conveys too much certainty in the patterns of measure and response.

Conventional documentaries of the period assume a gradual American exasperation with British policy, one that builds from slow objection and reluctant protest to outrage and, only then, to retaliation and rupture. Yet, for all of that, violent anger, mob behavior, broad civil disobedience, and clashes between colonials and British troops are part of the Revolution from at least 1766. The Sons of Liberty, adopting their name from Isaac Barré's speech in Parliament against the Stamp Act in 1765, formed immediately and widely in that year. A break with England might have come before 1776 but for the timely repeal of parliamentary measures (the Stamp Act in 1766 and the Townshend Acts in 1770). By the same token, the conception of a slowly evolving opposition misses the spontaneity and original power of early protest writings.

American exasperation explodes into rage from the first parliamentary designs on revenue in 1764. Moreover, that rage feeds upon a spirit of opposition that long predates the shift in British monetary policies. The squabbles of colonial assemblies and their royal governors go back for generations in the volatile tradition of Anglo–American politics. Jonathan Mayhew, the liberal pastor of West Church in Boston from 1747, already sees the radical possibilities in that tradition fifteen years before the first new revenue schemes and ten before George III's succession to the British throne. Mayhew's *A Discourse Concerning Unlimited Submission and Non-Resistance to the Higher Powers* (1750) inserts in colonial dissent a curious dialectic about how Americans must "learn to be *free* and to be *loyal*." "[A] warning to all corrupt *counselors* and *ministers* not to go too far in advising arbitrary, despotic measures," this most famous of prerevolutionary sermons celebrates the 101st anniversary of the execution of Charles I and redefines the Puritan Revolution in the process; the latter is no longer a rebellion but "a most righteous and glorious stand made in defense of the natural and legal rights of the people against the unnatural and illegal encroachments of arbitrary power."

Here are most of the rhetorical tools that Americans will use to justify later rebellion. *A Discourse Concerning Unlimited Submission* remains a touchstone, a permanent literary resource against which Adams and others can test their own spirits. Thus even though Mayhew dies in 1766, well before the war between England and America, Adams, in 1818, still extols the "transcendent genius" and "great fame" that made Mayhew a "great influence in the commencement of the Revolution." *A Discourse Concerning Unlimited Submission* is read and reread into the lexicon of protest across that half century. Long after its original publication, Adams finds the Mayhew sermon to be "seasoned with wit and satire superior to any in Swift or Franklin." "It was read by everybody," he concludes, "celebrated by friends, and abused by enemies." There is a lost distinction in these comments. Mayhew's sermon is remembered within the continuum of the Revolution, but it is first written as the deepest expression of a given moment in colonial life. We need to recover the powerful initial appeal in such writings and the assumption, now bizarre, of "transcendent genius" in them.

II

Two texts can illustrate the way in which works of the moment enter into the aesthetic of a consensual literature. Although they are both minor pieces, each dramatizes major implications in revolutionary writings. The first example, an article from the *Boston-Gazette and Country Journal* for February 26, 1770, describes the death in Boston of one Christopher Seider. Seider is an eleven-year-old street urchin who, while demonstrating in favor of the colonial nonimportation agreement, is killed by a Loyalist. Indeed, Seider was so obscure in life that the *Boston-Gazette* eulogizes him as Snider. Even so, the Sons of Liberty manage to turn the occasion of his death into the largest funeral ever seen in the New World. Their success gives credence to forgotten Loyalist charges, like the one made by Peter Oliver, who writes that "Government was in the Hands of the Mob, both in Form & Substance" from the late

1760s. The elaborate orchestration of the event also shows how colonists learn from each other in their dangerous transition from English subjects to American patriots.

If this first text springs up from the grass roots of the Revolution, the second reaches down from its loftiest branches. Thomas Jefferson, in 1818, relying upon a story within a story, re-tells a Franklin anecdote from 1776 concerning Jefferson's draft of the Declaration of Independence. Together, newspaper article and anecdote span the period (from 1770 to 1818) as well as the range of revolutionary action (from mob violence to the highest political deliberation). They also share a vital awareness of spectacle and display as parts of the forgotten ritual of the Revolution. Above all, both writings deal with an unruly present, one in which spectacle, display, and ritual contend with confusion and acrimony. As such, they represent the irreducible artifacts that challenge received history.

Christopher Seider would be remembered today as the first martyr of his country were it not for Crispus Attucks, Samuel Maverick, James Caldwell, Samuel Gray, and Patrick Carr, who die more dramatically two weeks later at the hands of British soldiers when a similar mob scene becomes the Boston Massacre. In many ways, however, the death of Seider is the more instructive tragedy because so much is made at the time of its more limited political potential. In all, twenty-five hundred mourners join the Seider funeral procession, held in the coldest weather, and most of Boston's fifteen thousand residents turn out to watch. "My Eyes never beheld such a funeral," writes John Adams. Notably, Adams also draws the conclusion that the Sons of Liberty had hoped for in staging the event: "This Shewes, there are many more Lives to spend if wanted in the Service of their Country."

Benjamin Edes and John Gill, the radical editors of the *Boston-Gazette,* set the tone of the funeral as political event:

This innocent Lad is the first, whose LIFE has been a Victim, to the Cruelty and Rage of *Oppressors!* Young as he was, he died in his Country's Cause, by the Hand of an execrable Villain, directed by others, who could not bear to see the Enemies of America made the *Ridicule of Boys.* The untimely Death of this amiable Youth will be a standing Monument to Futurity, that the Time has been where *Innocence itself was not safe!*

The controlling influence of the *Boston-Gazette* appears in a detail. The motto at the end of this Edes and Gill passage, in Latin — *Innocentia ausquam tuta* — adorns Seider's coffin in its procession from the Liberty Tree on Essex Street to the Old Granary Burying Ground on the edge of Boston Common.

The actual circumstances behind the rhetoric of Edes and Gill are more complicated. On February 22, 1770, market day, always a school holiday, young Seider is part of a mob of several hundred boys who gather around the North End shop of Theophilus Lillie to protest his continuing sale of British goods. Their rallying symbols are a carved head upon a pole and a painted sign with a pointing hand and the word "importer" inscribed beneath it, and they harass anyone who enters the shop while sympathetic adults, some armed with sticks, encourage and protect them. There are accompanying acts of petty vandalism: throughout the city importers' windows are broken and their houses and shop signs smeared with filth. Lillie's shop is a target because its owner has been listed in the *Boston-Gazette* among "the Names of *those* who AUDACIOUSLY continue to counteract the UNITED SENTI-MENTS of the BODY of Merchants thro'out NORTH-AMERICA" by prefer-ring "their own little private Advantage to the Welfare of America." In noting the precise location of a dozen shops, the *Boston-Gazette* invites direct action against them. According to the newspaper, the merchants identified have "sordidly detached themselves from the public Interest" and must be treated as "Enemies to their Country, by all who are well-wishers to it."

Although the politics may seem singular, they arise out of common circum-stance and conventional social behavior in ways that help to determine Chris-topher Seider's symbolic power in eighteenth-century America. Market day, with its idle crowds, provides frequent occasion for popular disturbance in colonial cities, and it has been a particular resort of the Sons of Liberty in their campaign against importers in the months preceding Seider's death. Organized bands of boys have been the first line of intimidation against unpopular individuals since the Stamp Act crisis five years before. And the intimidation can be extreme. Mob action is an accepted communal tactic of the times, one used regularly in New England against those who deviate from social and political norms. Everything about the extraordinary event of Febru-ary 22 is ordinary for the times except for its tragic conclusion.

The pattern of familiar practice extends to the particulars. The boys' procession, their effigies, and the signs they raise in front of Lillie's store come from the insurrectionary symbols and ceremonies that neighborhood gangs have employed for generations in New England Pope Day celebrations. These colonial adaptations of the English Guy Fawkes Day celebrations will grow into regular rituals of the Revolution, with the parading of liberty poles and other totems. The Sons of Liberty are using them in 1770 to routinize defiance of authority and to articulate the scene for rioting. Of course, the virulent identification of "otherness" in Pope Day anti-Catholicism translates easily to other possibilities, in this case to Tory sympathizers.

When Ebenezer Richardson, just such a sympathizer, tries to strike down the effigies in front of Lillie's shop, his behavior parallels that of rival gangs in traditional Pope Day celebrations. The result is also the same, a riot in the streets. Followed to his house by the angry mob, Richardson eventually fires wildly from a window, killing Seider, but not before the windows and the front door of his house have been broken in. Uppermost in Richardson's mind in 1770 would have been the wanton destruction of the houses of leading citizens like Thomas Hutchinson and Andrew Oliver in the Stamp Act riots of 1765 and the near fatal mob attack on John Mein, another friend of importers, in King Street just four months before. Richardson also knows that he cannot expect help from local authorities. It is typical of the times and the situation that Sheriff Stephen Greenleaf, the responsible official, refuses a direct order from Lieutenant Governor Hutchinson to disperse the mob around Richardson's house; "he did not think it safe to attempt," Hutchinson reports.

Edes and Gill channel the anger and ambiguity of these events into the clarity and order of further ritual. They first reduce Ebenezer Richardson to stock knavery. The Richardson of the *Boston-Gazette* is a hireling and an informer, a conspirator "directed by others," and a deliberate villain who provokes the incident through inflammatory and blasphemous language and physical hostility. Biblically, he is Cain covered with "the Blood of righteous *Abel*." According to Edes and Gill, speedy vengeance, divine and otherwise, awaits this murderer and his *"Accomplices."*

The contrasting characterization of Christopher Seider, "little Hero and first Martyr to the noble Cause," is more complicated. Seider's double role of martyr and hero goes straight to the heart of a patriotic identity problem. How can the boy represent both complete innocence *and* justifiable opposition? In response, the *Boston-Gazette* carefully balances Seider's pious humility and steadfastness in death against the prospect of his *"martial Genius."* Among "the several heroic Pieces found in his Pocket" is a book entitled *Wolfe's Summit of Human Glory.* The reference is to the greatest military champion that America then knows. Seider belongs in the tradition of General James Wolfe, who, in a single embrace of victory and death at the Battle of Quebec (1759), frees the colonies from French influence, Indian attack, and Catholic corruption.

The moral contrast between Richardson and Seider does more than simplify choice. It dictates action. On the one hand, the tragedy of Seider's presumed innocence and early death is supposed to frighten and anger every American. "[W]e are fallen into the most unhappy Times," warns the *Boston-Gazette,* "when even *innocence itself is no where safe!*" On the other hand, Seider's more ambiguous "martial genius" signals the active patriotism of the bands of boys run by the Sons of Liberty. The reference is cleverly mediated through the English figure of Wolfe, but the overall meaning is clearly a radical one. Those Americans who *are* frightened and angry will be on the side of the Sons of Liberty, and the *Boston-Gazette* moves quickly to make the connection a controlling premise. Predicting that the Seider funeral "will be attended by as *numerous* a Train as was ever known here," Edes and Gill announce that only the Friends of Liberty should march in the procession. "Then," they conclude, "*all* will be hearty Mourners."

Marching in the funeral procession is necessarily a radicalizing act, and both sides of the controversy understand its political importance in this way. Like Edes and Gill, Thomas Hutchinson instantly draws the correlation to a similar funeral organized by English radicals during the John Wilkes riots of 1768. Hutchinson also comes closest to gauging the overall impact of the Seider funeral on the Boston community. Jotting in his diary, he glumly notes:

> when the boy was killed by Richardson, the sons of liberty in Boston, if it had been in their power to have brought him to life again, would not have done it but would have chosen the grand funeral, which brought many thousands together; and the solemn procession from Liberty Tree, near which the boy's father lived, to the Town House and back to the burying ground made an inconceivable impression.

But why, precisely, should the Seider funeral have made "an inconceivable impression"?

The answer requires one more level of explanation. Americans of the period, as Americans, have a very limited sense of identity. Every colony looks naturally to England rather than to its immediate neighbors, and the one visible manifestation of intercolonial consensus of the moment, the nonimportation agreement of radical merchants, is particularly uncertain in the winter of 1769–70. Although rudimentary nonimportation resolutions begin in Boston in 1764, they fail to achieve the concerted agreement of the major colonial ports until 1768, and they do so then only with a cut-off date of January 1, 1770. Renewal of the nonimportation agreements in the fall of 1769 meets with less success, and the conservative *Boston Chronicle* smugly reports the widespread breakdown in the boycotts. When the radical leadership in Boston responds by putting nonimportation on a more coercive footing, the whole question of a free and united colonial spirit becomes inextricably involved.

The tragedy of February 22, 1770, partakes of this larger battle over American identity and direction. It converts a negation (nonimportation) into a positive assertion (the patriotic recognition of heroic sacrifice). Put another way, Seider's fate ennobles nonimportation, turning it from good policy into the stuff of legend and communal glory. Phillis Wheatley seems to have grasped these implications almost as quickly as did the editors of the *Boston-Gazette*. Obviously based on Edes and Gill's newspaper account,

Wheatley's occasional poem on the death of Seider is written within days of the event, and it dwells on just how "the first martyr of the common good" brings the community together into one "Illustrious retinue" against "fair freedom's foes."

The Seider funeral enables an inventive act in communal recognition. The ritual and reportage of the event are part of a precarious search for identity. Seider dies not only as a Boston boy but, more importantly, "in his Country's Cause." The preoccupation of Edes and Gill with signs and symbols of unity, their related concern with the pageantry of events, and their shrill insistence on the combined sentiments and actions of the people all hint at the primal needs involved. The radical editors' account stresses two dimensions of the funeral: the fact of the conflict and the placards – or symbolic writings – displayed in the procession (six in all) that interpret this conflict. Distinguishing "a very numerous Train of Citizens" from "a *few*, only excepted, who have long shewn themselves to be void of the Feelings of Humanity," the *Boston-Gazette* uses participation in the funeral to create a striking numerical imbalance in the conflict at hand. The article then carefully translates the Latin inscriptions on the Seider coffin and supplies the relevant biblical quotations posted on the Liberty Tree. As the inscriptions announce Seider's struggle and innocent martyrdom, so the quotations cry for a united, social act of vengeance in the trial and punishment of Ebenezer Richardson. These sentiments, concludes the *Boston-Gazette,* "cannot easily be misapply'd."

The emphasis upon communal reading is one more symptom of the importance of ritual. In supposing signs that cannot be misapplied, Edes and Gill infer a general application and interest; to this end, they repeat each placard in print, in English as well as in Latin. The painstaking double and sometimes triple renditions insure total availability, but they also uphold the different levels of experience and education involved in each repetition. The procedure includes every possible level of participation, from the presence of the lowest urban dweller at the ceremony to the educated gentleman's private Latin reading in his study. And, underlying everything is a basic faith in universal literacy.

The funeral of Christopher Seider, in sum, is itself a text to be mastered by a community reading in unison. The *Boston-Gazette* creates a world in which the sympathetic many have to join with each other and act against the tyrannical and unfeeling few. The participants in the Seider funeral discover their identity in this collective act of understanding. Next, however, they must demonstrate their solidarity, the root of group identity, by finding and punishing the few who have acted against them. That search will be an easy one; the unjust and unfeeling few can be detected in their opposition to the people or, more concretely, in their indifference to patriotic ritual. Here, in the momentum and the calculated promise of future events, is the continuum of the Revolution.

III

Six years after Christopher Seider's death, in 1776, the writers of the Revolution understand that the problem of conflict cannot be resolved in the simple polarities of British tyranny and American rights, self-interest and popular virtue. They have begun to accept the fact of acrimony *within* the American cause and the need to impose a truth upon it. These realizations come to life in an aside between Jefferson and Franklin over the Declaration of Independence. When Jefferson complains against "depredations" and "mutilations" during congressional revision of his draft, Franklin captures the essence of a writer's dilemma:

I have made it a rule, said [Franklin], whenever in my power, to avoid becoming the draughtsman of papers to be reviewed by a public body. I took my lesson from an incident which I will relate to you. When I was a journeyman printer, one of my companions, an apprentice hatter, having served out his time, was about to open shop for himself. His first concern was to have a handsome signboard, with a proper inscription. He composed it in these words, *"John Thompson, Hatter, makes and sells hats for ready money,"* with a figure of a hat subjoined; but he thought he would submit it to his friends for their amendments. The first he showed it to thought the word *"Hatter"* tautologous, because followed by the words "makes hats," which show he was a hatter. It was struck out. The next observed that the word *"makes"* might as well be omitted, because his customers would not care who made the hats. . . . He struck it out. A third said he thought the words *"for ready money"* were useless, as it was not the custom of the place to sell on credit. . . . the inscription now stood, "John Thompson sells hats." *"Sells hats!"* says his next friend. "Why nobody will expect you to give them away, what then is the use of that word?" It was stricken out, and *"hats"* followed it, the rather as there was one painted on the board. So the inscription was reduced ultimately to "John Thompson" with the figure of a hat subjoined.

The parallels to the founding of a nation are deliberate and amusingly apt. The apprentice who opens his shop is like the colonies that declare their independence. Both have embarked on a risky enterprise that may fail. The success of a step already taken now depends upon how others respond to the signification of that event. Whether a signboard or the Declaration of Independence, the written representation is a mixed symbol of celebration and vulnerability. This is where the opinion of others enters into the success or failure of the enterprise. The hatter will lose his shop if his friends do not act upon his representation. The Revolution will be for naught without a united front behind the claim for independence. Humor flows from the thankless role of the writer or sign-maker, who must stoop to the lowest common denominator to find agreement.

Franklin's anecdote supplies four alternatives for making a text in a consensual setting. Foremost, from the perspective of modern authorship, the beleaguered writer can impose a private text on a public audience. The hatter can hang his sign without consulting anyone, hoping for acceptance of the fait accompli. This is the strategy of Jefferson's A Summary View of the Rights of British America (1774) and of Paine's Common Sense, both of which captivate in their daring. But the risk of discord from unilaterial assertion is great, particularly for eighteenth-century intellectuals with a paramount sense of community. Second, a writer can draw up a text in the marketplace of debate, as the founders are doing with the Declaration of Independence in the moment of Franklin's anecdote. This background debate in Congress actually touches a creative norm of the times. In making a finished text, the gentleman of letters distributes private drafts to a circle of equals for advice before publication – a practice that explains something of the skill and co-operation demonstrated by committees in the Continental Congress and later at the Constitutional Convention. But what of the hatter's comic inability to please his friends? What happens when agreement proves impossible?

A third alternative appears in Franklin's punch line. The writer reduces the public text into an article of faith or an icon. The sign becomes an incontestable fact when it is just a name subjoined to the figure of a hat. Many of the important writings of the Revolution have this figural quality. They have been drafted to be posted and read in public places. Of newspaper-page length, they also seek substantiating form at every turn. The founders mean the Declaration of Independence to be read aloud in every town meeting in America. They keep the document short, and they couch their language in the familiar frame of legal pleading, the *declaration* or *count* that initiates an action in common law and that is also read aloud. *The Federalist*, cut into eighty-five parts, never violates its originating form in the newspaper essay or occasional paper. Everywhere in the literature of the Revolution, from handbill to formal document, the numerology of articles, sections, and papers provides a structure to be seen to go with the words that are read.

Naming is part of this iconography, the "John Thompson" on the sign. Franklin's hatter can accept any change that leaves him in place, and the writers of the Revolution also show considerable ingenuity in this respect. The signers of the Declaration of Independence and Constitution are themselves literalized on the signboards in question. The hieroglyphic significance of those signatures is a central aspect of acceptance and ratification. Gaining agreement means engraving the separate authority of the author on the text wherever possible – a policy that easily carries beyond name, signature, and even verifiable fact. When John Dickinson writes *Letters from a Farmer in Pennsylvania* (1768), he is neither a farmer nor, strictly speaking, a Pennsylvanian but a wealthy lawyer and rising politician from tiny Delaware. The created figure on the page, strategically sequestered on a small farm in a large middle colony, does a better job of convincing British Americans that he writes for all of them. Indeed, this whole question of the crafted persona in revolutionary writings deserves more careful attention. The writer's need for posting informs a much larger quest for entitlement in the designation of founder.

Thus far, the strategies of a consensual literature are easily traced in writings that have been imposed, negotiated, reduced, and figuralized, but a fourth possibility in the anecdote is much harder to grasp. Franklin reserves that fourth alternative for himself in his imputed silence, his strategy of avoidance. "I have made it a rule," he tells Jefferson, "whenever in my power, to avoid becoming the draughtsman of papers to be reviewed by a public body." This comment frames the anecdote, creating a strange inversion. In Franklin's *telling,* sound justifies silence, verbiage praises reticence, language explains its own absence. The man behind the anecdote thrives on such ironies: *"many Words won't fill a Bushel,"* says Father Abraham at the beginning of his long speech in "The Way to Wealth" (1758). But Franklin is also serious about his larger claim. Agreement often requires the second of the thirteen virtues enumerated in his autobiography: silence.

The major source of evil in Franklin's autobiography is disputation. Because words breed only words, and then anger, Franklin the boy must learn to use them sparingly. His proper creed also comes early, from Pope's *An Essay on Criticism:*

> Men must be *taught* as if you taught them *not;*
> And Things *unknown* propos'd as Things *forgot.*

Each assumed persona in the Franklin memoirs — the printer's apprentice, the town organizer, the philosopher, the leading politician, and the renowned scientist — proves, in turn, that silence is the best policy in a dispute. Franklin's first pseudonym, Silence Dogood, proclaims the point, and so does the worst moment in the diplomat's distinguished career. Hauled before the Privy Council of Parliament as colonial agent in 1774, Franklin stands motionless, enduring the invective of the king's ministers for two hours without change of expression or reply.

Where agreement is the goal, refutation feeds what it fights. This is Franklin's assumption and is Jefferson's too, when, in his own brief autobiography, he contrasts the reserve of Franklin and Washington to "the morbid rage of debate" and "singular disposition of men to quarrel" around them. "I never heard either of them speak ten minutes at a time," observes Jefferson, explaining why he in emulation "could sit in silence" during "wordy debate." John Adams summarizes the phenomenon in his diary: "The Examples of Washington, Franklin and Jefferson are enough to shew that Silence and reserve in public are more Efficacious than Argumentation or Oratory."

Silence is the vital interstice in a consensual literature; what is spoken or written is peculiarly a function of what *cannot* be spoken or written *there.* Many Americans, to take the clearest example, object to the notion of a national federal republic in 1787, so the Constitution, in creating one, never mentions the words "national," "federal," or "republic." The language that remains communicates the possibility in less controversial terms. The radical innovations of the document are also shielded by the innovators' public silence. The fifty-five delegates of the Federal Convention agree that "nothing spoken in the House be printed, or otherwise published or communicated without leave." Despite enormous pressures to break their silence, they stick to their "rule of secrecy" from May to September. They can do so because they have come to understand the value of silence. Adams traces the mastery of this lesson to the success of 1776. The Continental Congress, he reminds Jefferson in 1815, "compared Notes, engaged in discussions and debates and formed Results by one Vote and by two Votes, which went out to the World as unanimous."

The purpose of silence is to minimize and control difference. If properly restrained, private debate can be subsumed in a public language of shared meanings. The whole thrust of such writing is to mask uglier actualities and to keep dangerous passions below the combustion point. The corresponding task of the later critic is to decipher the realities of difference that are masked by such language. Every consensual text contains distinct utterances that work against as well as with each other. There are, in consequence, two kinds of implication at work in a narrative of levels. The separate voices that author the consensual text also compete in the hierarchical process of creation. The Franklin anecdote illustrates the difference perfectly. Franklin, Jefferson, and those modifying Jefferson's draft on the floor of Congress cooperate in producing the Declaration of Independence, and their acknowledged success glosses every difference. Even so, the voices in the anecdote also work at cross-purposes. The controlling theme of Franklin's anecdote is conflict, and this conflict spills beyond the surface of the narrative in important ways.

A simple historical fact shows how conflict informs the consensual text in this case. The modern reader needs to know that the typical eighteenth-century shop sign resembles that in Franklin's anecdote; it attaches a name to an identifying shape, whether of pipe for tobacconist, boot for shoemaker, key for locksmith, or hat for hatter. But if " 'John Thompson' with the figure of a hat subjoined" supplies the correct sign, then the mutilators of Jefferson's draft appear in a different light. They become the conscientious enforcers of regular form and acceptability. Simultaneously, the amiable exchange of Franklin and Jefferson turns into a contrast. Franklin, the leather apron man, a shopkeeper himself, knows better than anyone what kind of language the people will need in order to declare their independence to themselves and to the world, and he gently admonishes his aristocratic young friend from rural Virginia about the ways of the world. In Franklin's corrective, the practicality of a nation of shopkeepers supplants the wordy idealism of the agrarian ideal.

The ultimate story, however, belongs not to Franklin in 1776 but to Jefferson in 1818, and Jefferson's retelling of it through the Philadelphia journalist Robert Walsh, and then through James Madison, should give pause. Why should the author of the Declaration of Independence want to publicize this story against himself? In effect, Jefferson's act of appropriation is part of the general refashioning of revolutionary achievement that complicates every literary and historical analysis of the period. More than forty years after the event, he suddenly needs the surfaces of the anecdote; the retelling in 1818 identifies exclusive authorship of the Declaration of Independence at exactly the moment when that authorship is being questioned. Franklin as speaker disclaims any authorship for Franklin himself, and his humor automatically separates the committee member who supports language from the drafter who creates it. The older man appears as the guiding voice in support of young Jefferson's achievement, and his benevolent tones attach every reader to Jefferson's accomplishment; they also relegate dissent to the margins of those distant and unidentified congressional voices in the background. One of those distanced voices belongs to John Adams, and therein lies another story.

Jefferson's appropriation of Franklin's anecdote is part of a remarkable debate that turns on the changing nature of literary creativity in American culture. Across the first quarter of the nineteenth century, Jefferson and Adams spar over the terms and meaning of their achievement in the Declaration of Independence. Jefferson writes the document. Adams directs its progress in congressional debate; he is, in Jefferson's phrase, "our Colossus on the floor." Early on, Adams tells Benjamin Rush that Jefferson has managed to "steal" the fame of 1776. He also claims that his own personal declaration predates Jefferson's version by at least twenty-one years. "The Declaration of Independence I always considered a theatrical show," he adds in 1811, "Jefferson ran away with all the stage effect of that . . . and all the glory of it."

By 1817 Jefferson is feeling the need to correct attacks upon an authorship "that alone was mine." When, in 1822, Adams pointedly raises the committee structure behind the Declaration and dismisses the document itself ("there is not an idea in it but what had been hackneyed in Congress for two years before"), Jefferson responds with a long letter to James Madison in formal defense of his exclusive authorship. Clearly writing for posterity, he minimizes the committee's role ("they unanimously pressed on myself alone to undertake the draught") and discounts the language changes of Adams and Franklin ("their alterations were two or three only, and merely verbal"). And once again, Jefferson gives Franklin's anecdote as conclusive external evidence for his own claim.

The striking thing about this debate is that Adams and Jefferson are both correct. Adams's stress upon the committee structure that produces the Declaration and his insistence upon the community of language behind it presuppose the consensual nature of authorship that dominates the literature of public documents in the period. Nothing could have been accomplished in 1776 and 1787 if personal pride in individual authorship had been a material consideration. Still, Jefferson's claims of authorship are substantially accurate. His colleagues do indeed choose him for the task because of his acknowledged literary capabilities. "Writings of his," Adams admitted of Jefferson in 1776, "were handed about, remarkable for the peculiar felicity of expression."

Adams finds many voices authoring a common text. Jefferson, reaching instead for hierarchical placement within the creative process, sees only the one hand in composition. Together, they dramatize the vital tension at work in a consensual literature. But those tensions suffer a distortion in time. Jefferson's claims loom larger than they should in the emerging hagiography of the founders and in the more general magnification of authorial role in the nineteenth century. As the Declaration itself becomes an icon of national culture, so its individual creator becomes a separate source of interest. Obviously, the tensions as well as the assertions in a consensual literature must be held firmly in mind. Jefferson claims no more than his due, but he must not be understood without Adams on the same subject.

IV

The comedy and tensions in Franklin and Jefferson's colloquy over the Declaration of Independence should not disguise a last overarching affinity between the two figures. Their mutual distrust of the talk around them and their concentration on the hatter's signboard are symptomatic of their larger control of and faith in the new print culture in which they live. We find them here in the very act of mastering their crafts as the most accomplished writers of the American Enlightenment. Each leaves a timeless masterpiece in a vital genre of the period (Franklin's memoirs in autobiography and Jefferson's draft of the Declaration in the literature of public documents). Both command a full range of the literary forms available to them: the political pamphlet, the epistle, the newspaper article, the scientific essay, and the broadside. Each demonstrates a peculiar capacity in still other literary forms (Franklin in the almanac and the humorous sketch or bagatelle; Jefferson in the political oration and legal document). Both leave probing analyses of the still mysterious New World, in Franklin's *Observations Concerning the Increase of Mankind, Peopling Countries, Etc.* (1751) and his *Information To Those Who Would Remove to America* (1784) and in Jefferson's *Notes on the State of Virginia* (1784–5). Finally, both write early and late, leaving prodigious outputs for scholars to decipher in ongoing but still incomplete modern editions of their works.

Yet, and this amounts to a final difficulty in studying the literature of the period, Franklin and Jefferson themselves seem to remain mysteriously aloof from or somehow outside of their writings. Neither their productivity nor their life-long fame nor the immense record of their output in relevant archives quite reveals the writers behind the works to those who now read them. Modern scholarship, as a result, is obsessed with a search for "the real Franklin" and "the real Jefferson," sometimes to the point of positing a pervasive hypocrisy or even the absence of a meaningful self at the root of their authorial writings. It helps to recognize that the elusiveness of these writings is part of their inherent literary integrity. The game of levels they so openly engaged in is part of their intention and a source of their power.

As the creators of a consensual literature for a diverse and divided citizenry, the leaders of the Revolution write to reconcile and, thereby, to control. They seek to encompass difference within a consciously communal perspective. This search for agreement makes their writing thematically simple but rhetorically complex. Their language deliberately entertains several planes of implication at a time, and it is most successful when the same utterance performs many functions. The greater appeal of mixed intellectual modes is the goal of such language, but its craft lies in bringing modes together through style, tone, symbol, and form.

Many of these characteristics apply to political language in general. The difference in the Revolution lies in a special intensity. The urgencies of rebellion and national formation bring immeasurable weight to the problems and strategies of reaching for political agreement. Anger and doubt compound the primal goal of consensus. In response, the representative texts of the period distort the nature of conflict to create order and clarity in the name of authorial calm. Order and clarity, in turn, rely upon a figural emphasis in language that attaches to the ritual and ceremony of revolutionary practice. The founders struggle to make their signs, symbols, and literary personae at once familiar, dominating, and inclusive. Agreement, after all, means agreement within the trappings of a new order. But what order? Whose order? Everywhere in their denial of British rule, the leaders of the Revolution are aware of the need for a new ruler. They express that need awkwardly and anxiously in an abstraction, "the will of the people."

It follows that effective language in the early Republic requires a basic act of mutual recognition between leaders and led. The vigor in a slogan like *E Pluribus Unum,* the motto that Franklin, Adams, and Jefferson select for the Continental Congress, consists in its simultaneous appeal above and below. Taken from the Latin of Horace, the congressional motto confirms an agenda in the separate language of a self-conscious elite. It helps a governing group to realize that it is, in fact, governing. But taken also from the epigraph of *The Gentleman's Magazine,* the same slogan reaches toward the popular and becomes a cry to the people. "From many one" represents an act of communal incorporation. It instills the consciousness in its followers of belonging to a movement – *from* many *to* one – in which their act of solidarity has created a new society.

The manner of the early republican text is about this complete interpenetration of language, belief, power, and points of view. "We hold these truths to be self evident," announce the founders in 1776. The same words that describe permanent truths everywhere in the world also introduce and impose an explicit political group, the new holders of truth in North America, the "we" of the document. Truth and its holders share self-evidence and, hence, a common security from challenge. Belief in the former implies acceptance of the latter. They appear as one: truth invested in a unified leadership. The *manner* of the literature has to do with this turning of idea and belief into a language of political assertion. Its *content,* the substance of idea and belief, are the subjects of the following chapters.

Two frameworks of belief in particular dominate eighteenth-century American thought: the Enlightenment and Protestant Reform Christianity. Chapter 2 explores the meaning and central role of the Enlightenment in America, and chapter 3 analyzes religious thought as a controlling impulse in the Revolution and in the formation of the early Republic. These frameworks come together in an American civil religion, the central expression of New World republicanism. They also compete in the making of a distinctly American mind – a mind already caught in the opposing forces of secularization and revivalism, reason and faith, knowledge and belief, individuality and community.

❦

WHAT IS ENLIGHTENMENT? SOME
AMERICAN ANSWERS

I

The Enlightenment in America is sometimes conveyed in a single phrase, the political right of self-determination realized. The reduction is possible because self-determination as a philosophical principle incorporates the basic eighteenth-century tenets of Enlightenment thought: the primacy of reason, the reliability of human understanding, the value of individual freedom, trust in method, faith in education, belief in progress, and a corresponding disregard for tradition, constituted authority, and received dogma. At the same time, the realization of self-determination in national ideology has tended to equate philosophical principle with political practice. Since the Revolution claims government by consent of the governed as the irreducible source of its achievement, self-determination becomes the sign and symptom of the Enlightenment at work in each succeeding generation. This is the legacy of the Revolution in daily life.

Not coincidentally, the Enlightenment has been a partisan concept in American historiography, one in which subsidiary notions of liberalism, progress, and rationality have shaped the character of historical reconstructions. Because the idea of an American Enlightenment coincides with national formation and a developmental sense of country, its proponents tend to dwell on the emerging prospect. They see and make use of the original aspiration of human freedom but lose all sense of the Enlightenment as a historical process with its own patterns of constraint. The result is a peculiar one-sidedness or intellectual vulnerability in critical inquiries about the subject.

The first task, then, is to put the Enlightenment into broader historical perspective, and one means to this end is the very different view of European thinkers. When Jürgen Habermas in *The Philosophical Discourse of Modernity* (1987) announces that "the permanent sign of enlightenment is domination over an objectified external nature and a repressed internal nature," he summarizes a tradition of European thought that scholars of the American Enlightenment have avoided. The differences are historically as well as philosophically based. European nations do not begin in the hope of the Enlightenment, and their modern circumstance, the direct experience of world wars and totalitarianism, has interrupted eighteenth-century legacies more obviously and decisively than in America. Continental intellectuals in particular have these devastations in mind and look less to an advance of freedom than to the threat of new kinds of institutional repression. They acknowledge scientific inquiry but emphasize the domination in scientific technologies. They think less of rational progressions and more of a reign of instrumental reason and the separation of thought from belief. For the European scholar, even self-determination can appear to be a social control as much as it is a political right, a methodology that has structured individuals into isolated monads and objects of manipulation.

The point is not to choose between American and European approaches but to use both to gain a more complete understanding. A glance at three different writings from the literature of the Enlightenment can demonstrate the need for both perspectives. First, take Thomas Jefferson's moving peroration on self-determination, written in 1826 in the last month of a long and brilliant life:

All eyes are opened, or opening, to the rights of man. The general spread of the light of science has already laid open to every view the palpable truth, that the mass of mankind has not been born with saddles on their backs, nor a favored few booted and spurred, ready to ride them legitimately, by the grace of God. These are grounds of hope for others.

Twentieth-century readers still welcome Jefferson's hope, but they see less openness all around. The light of science appears less general, the truth less palpable, the view infinitely more particularistic. Technology, the product of science, occasionally keeps "a favored few booted and spurred" in ways that Jefferson never dreamed of. Jefferson's actual language flows from another Enlightenment source, Algernon Sidney's *Discourses Concerning Government* (1698), a work that John Adams, writing to Jefferson in 1823, admires for demonstrating "the slow progress of moral, philosophical, and political illumination in the world." Neither the progress of illumination, however slow, nor the easy conjunction of moral, philosophical, and political disciplines would be such intellectual givens in describing the world today.

In effect, the results of the Enlightenment have cut across its original tenets. Enlightenment now appears as a function of what it has become and not as a philosophical frame for the advance of history. A second literary example suggests another level of problems that would have been either invisible or immaterial to eighteenth-century observers. When Samuel Johnson in 1778 expresses disdain for Benjamin Franklin's definition of a man as "a tool-making animal," readers of *The Life of Johnson,* now as then, enter into the exchange of wit at Boswell's expense. But Johnson also instinctively rejects what today would be called the instrumentalization of identity, or the reduction of thought to commodity, or, more simply, the subsuming, aggressive spirit of technologism.

A similar awareness might inform twentieth-century readings of a third example, Alexander Hamilton's brilliant *Report on Manufactures* (1791). In a remarkably prescient document, Washington's secretary of the treasury employs Enlightenment norms to sketch not just the first realistic projection of a national economy but also the first full-blown justification of child labor in American factories. The two manifestly go together. Hamilton predicts that "artificial force brought in aid of the natural force of man" together with "the genius of the people of this country, a peculiar aptitude for mechanic improvements" will bring disparate groups of workers together in a harmonious triumvirate of "cultivators, artificers, and merchants." Women and children, weak and unskilled labor, find their appropriate places in this triumvirate in the lowest levels of artificers – that is, as workers in factories. Noting the salutary example of the British cotton mills, where more than half of the labor force falls into these two categories ("many of them of a very tender age"), Hamilton proves that "women and Children are rendered more useful and the latter more early useful by manufacturing establishments, than they would otherwise be." Child labor and other forms of exploitation of factory workers follow so naturally and continue in force for so long in the American economy because they fit within a seamless or hegemonic rationale of early national identity.

Such writings make it clear that the Enlightenment must be understood in dialectical form. Reason, the original calling card, resides in both the liberation that it promises and the kinds of domination that it provokes – in both Hamiltonian prosperity and the child labor that prosperity assumes. Moreover, the original context of the Enlightenment allows for these tensions. Immanuel Kant shows his understanding of and illustrates the problem in a seminal essay, *An Answer to the Question: "What is Enlightenment?"* (1784). His treatment deserves attention because it recomplicates the original basis of Enlightenment thought and because the parallels between Kant and early republicans in America precede later cross-cultural differences on the subject. Indeed, the example of Kant offers something more. The Janus-face of enlightenment can be a means of interpretation, of joining European and American understandings together.

What is enlightenment? When Kant asks the question in 1784, the European Enlightenment already has spread over the course of the century, and its American counterpart, from its later beginnings in the 1750s, has itself just reached obvious heights with the new nation's victory in the Treaty of Paris. In other words, Kant can justifiably conceive of his answer as a description of contemporary life. That answer, perhaps in consequence, mixes negative experience with hope for change. *"Enlightenment is man's emergence from his self-incurred immaturity."* Kant thinks of it as overcoming "the inability to use one's own understanding without the guidance of another." Commentators generally avoid the clumsiness and qualifications of these constructions by leaping directly to Kant's famous motto of enlightenment (taken from Horace) − *"Sapere aude!* Have courage to use your *own* understanding!" − but in so doing they lose sight of the philosopher's essential point. The Enlightenment may trade in ringing affirmations, but its deepest meanings lie in the uncertain struggle of light against darkness. Kant underlines that struggle in a reminder to his contemporaries: you live in an age of enlightenment, he tells them, not an enlightened age. Enlightenment means process, not result.

II

Kant's idea of enlightenment as struggle and process takes on special meaning in understanding the conflict between England and America. Born in the Enlightenment, the new republic is also ripped from a previous and clearly functional context, that of colony in the Anglo-American empire. Linear notions of the Enlightenment tend to obscure the fact of disruption in metaphors of progression from colony to province to state and then to union. The notion of process, to the contrary, allows for the blood, agony, and confusion of the Revolution − an event that brought anxiety to all, extraordinary social upheaval to most, and disaster to many. And while the recognition of a dialectic instead of a linear progression does not discount the tones of measured calm and of political inevitability that dominate a work like the Declaration of Independence, it does take into account the underlying element of rupture in a Declaration that is, among other things, a declaration of war.

The Enlightenment in America is itself a manifestation of protracted conflict, and in the pressure of that conflict are the delineations of a specifically American expression. Americans receive European ideas, but they use them to express their own needs in the prolonged crisis of the Revolution and national formation. Since creativity takes place in this exchange from European models to American requisites, the important questions address the transmission of ideas, style, tone, and rhetorical emphasis. What is the appeal of the Enlightenment in American thought? What influences are paramount? Do Enlightenment ideas change in a changing American setting? What are the constitutive metaphors, and how do Americans use them? What are the dynamics of the Enlightenment text?

The import of transmission also depends on the nature of linguistic engagement. At the level of popular idiom, the Enlightenment responds to communal uncertainty. At the level of event, it supplies more complex strategies of comprehension or control. In the formalities of the intellectual text, it resituates America in a theory of history that further orders the understanding of word and event. A sustained illustration of each level of expression follows: first, in popular idiom, the mysterious appeal of the national anthem ("The Star-Spangled Banner" is an instantaneous success in 1814); next, in the volatility of event, the near revolt of the revolutionary army in 1783; and, finally, in textual assertion, the impact of General Washington's farewell address, again in 1783. At every level, these examples also explicate the turmoil of revolutionary and early republican times.

Self-recognition, the *assurance* of independence, comes only with victory in arms between 1781 and 1783, and Americans have found a primal sense of identity in acts of war ever since. The argument here is not one of an assumed militarism or special belligerence but rather of a far more intrinsic sense of definition in the possibility and outcome of military conflict. Manifestations abound in an American psyche keyed from the start to the common defense, the right to bear arms, the conquest of frontiers, and, later, to the inevitable spread and victory of republicanism. For textual evidence, however, one need look no further than the national anthem as a central artifact of violent beginnings. Written on the night of September 13–14, 1814, "The Star-Spangled Banner" presents early republican fears in the guise of a helpless prisoner, a civilian who is plunged suddenly into war and who watches the naval bombardment of Baltimore's Fort McHenry from the perspective of his captors in the invading British fleet:

> O! SAY can you see by the dawn's early light,
> What so proudly we hailed at the twilight's last gleaming,
> Whose broad stripes and bright stars through the perilous fight,
> O'er the ramparts we watch'd were so gallantly streaming?
> And the rockets' red glare, the bombs bursting in air,
> Gave proof through the night that our flag was still there.
> O! say does that star-spangled banner yet wave,
> O'er the land of the free, and the home of the brave?
>   On the shore dimly seen through the mists of the deep,
> Where the foe's haughty host in dread silence reposes,
> What is that which the breeze, o'er the towering steep,
> As it fitfully blows, half conceals, half discloses?
> Now it catches the gleam of the morning's first beam.
> In full glory reflected now shines in the stream.
> 'Tis the star-spangled banner, O! long may it wave
> O'er the land of the free, and the home of the brave.

> And where is that band who so vauntingly swore
> That the havoc of war and the battle's confusion,
> A Home and a country, shall leave us no more?
> Their blood has wash'd out their foul footsteps pollution;
> No refuge could save the hireling and slave,
> From the terror of flight, or the gloom of the grave;
> And the star-spangled banner in triumph doth wave,
> O'er the land of the free, and the home of the brave.
>   O! thus be it ever when freemen shall stand,
> Between their lov'd home, and the war's desolation,
> Blest with vict'ry and peace, may the Heav'n rescued land,
> Praise the Power that hath made and preserved us a nation!
> Then conquer we must, when our cause it is just,
> And this be our motto – *"In God is our Trust"*;
> And the star-spangled banner in triumph shall wave,
> O'er the land of the free and the home of the brave.

To rescue the original meaning of Francis Scott Key's words is to recognize that the crucial first stanza opens and closes with questions of a consuming anxiety. The proud hailing of the symbol of American identity, the flag, has taken place in the last gleaming of a previous twilight, but that affirmation is now lost in the temporal moment of the stanza, the approach of another dawn. Key's embracing questions are "Can you see?" and "Does it wave?" The only sure identification takes the form of conflict itself. Casting all of his hopes in the past tense of the battle just fought, the poet consoles himself with the remembered glare of rockets and bombs bursting; they alone "gave proof through the night that our flag was still there." Subsequent stanzas confirm these hopes in the light of morning but only after hours of dreadful uncertainty in shadows half concealing, half disclosing "on the shore dimly seen."

Dangers faced through military prowess dominate the last three stanzas. The narrative of doubts quickly raised and slowly settled can be measured in the march of grammatical modes across Key's four refrains. The star-spangled banner appears first in the interrogative mood (does it wave?), next in the subjunctive (may it wave), and only after "in triumph" in the declarative (it doth wave) and imperative (it shall wave) of stanzas 3 and 4. Throughout, Key punctuates victory with the havoc of war. Unfolding, in proper sequence, are the battle's confusion, blood, pollution, lost refuge, the terror of flight, and, finally, the gloom of the grave. Meanwhile, the poet's theme, the reiterated point of the anthem, insists upon the vital relevance of a "home of the brave" in maintaining "the land of the free." True republicans stand armed and vigilant "between their lov'd home, and the war's desolation." When they conquer in a just cause, the star-spangled flag, symbol of triumph, both receives and reflects their achievement ("In fully glory reflected now shines in the stream").

Here and everywhere in the America of the early Republic, the transference from conflict to saving knowledge takes place in the constitutive metaphor of light. Benjamin Franklin, the living symbol of the American Enlightenment, typifies this dynamic with one of his analogies from everyday life. "By the Collision of different Sentiments," he explains in his essay "The Internal State of America" (1785), "Sparks of Truth are struck out, and political Light is obtained." Two things separate American writers from their European counterparts in their use of the conventional metaphor. First, Franklin and other Americans bring tremendous confidence and authority to the fusion of science, politics, and light in their explanation of a world in conflict. Second, and paradoxically, American writers experience many more problems than Europeans in the practical matter of discerning the object so enlightened. "O! SAY can you see?" asks the anthem, where saying is patently easier than seeing. Francis Scott Key's song in 1814 is a lively type in the difficulty of perceiving an experimental republic on the edge of a vast and unformed new world.

It is worth elaborating how metaphors of light respond so readily to early republican problems of perception. Metaphors, by definition, are tropes of transference in which an unknown or imperfectly known is clarified, defined, or described in terms of a known; when metaphor succeeds, the strange and the familiar save each other. Because American intellectuals of the formative era are obsessed with the half formed, the partially visible, light is the perfect metaphor for solving their problem. Light brings unknown space under the control of experience. Its presence renders the strange familiar and the familiar more exciting.

Light in this construct is the instrument of a larger epistemology. To see is to know in eighteenth-century thought. John Locke's *Essay Concerning Human Understanding* (1690) is only the most conspicuous of a series of philosophical texts to place the visual organization of knowledge over the other senses. Strictly speaking, an epistemology of sight has its beginnings in ancient analogies of spirituality, intellect, and light. The analogy itself has functioned in every culture, but it is the Enlightenment that secularizes the notion of illumination to make vision a purely human understanding. In Johnson's *Dictionary of the English Language* (1755), "to enlighten" means to illuminate, to supply with light, to instruct, to furnish with increase of knowledge, to cheer, to exhilarate, to gladden, to supply with sight, to quicken in the faculty of vision. The same secular frame of reference enables Locke to introduce his arguments about human psychology with "the Bounds between the enlightened and dark Parts of Things." The parallel for eighteenth-century Americans is an obvious one: light spreading across the dark (because unknown) New World. Either light will reveal an order previously unseen, or it will create its own order out of an unclear(ed) wilderness.

The creators of the early Republic often resort to conventional images of light in coping with problems of perception and order. With characteristic optimism, Thomas Jefferson in 1813 sees education as the passing of light from one taper to another, and, though that passage is fraught with obstacles and even with danger, Jefferson eagerly notes that "he who lights his taper at mine, receives light without darkening mine." His more pessimistic correspondent, John Adams, gives the same image a more negative twist. "Is the Nineteenth Century to be a Contrast to the Eighteenth?" he asks Jefferson two years later. "Is it to extinguish all the Lights of its Predecessor?" Of all the founders, Adams senses the greatest difficulty in seeing his country. As vice-president he tells Benjamin Rush that the continent is a vast whispering gallery in which "the people can agree upon nothing." "[O]n what," he asks, "do you found your hopes?" Adams's own hopes depend upon filling that whispering gallery with light. His *A Defence of the Constitutions* (1787) creates an *"American Boudoir,"* a room ringed in mirrors in which "our States may see themselves in it, in every possible light, attitude and movement."

None of these standard metaphors is particularly American, but they respond to American needs by reducing complex experience to a single, manageable problem in perception. Key's "bombs bursting in air" supply light without the related intrusion of sound or the disaster of contact. Jefferson's candle replaces inchoate ignorance with the point of knowledge. Adams's room of mirrors quells the discordant voices of his whispering gallery. War, political illiteracy, and faction – major anxieties in the early Republic – give way to visual certainties. The trick, in each case, is to create a unified calm out of a noisy situation, to let the primacy of vision allay confusion. Adams gives another instance in *Defence of the Constitutions* when, in comparing the future of America to the immensity of the universe, he first creates a safe and familiar point of view:

A prospect into futurity in America is like contemplating the heavens through the telescopes of Herschell. Objects stupendous in their magnitudes and motions strike us from all quarters, and fill us with amazement! . . . that mind must be hardened into stone that is not melted into the reverence and awe.

In this passage, science, nature, history, and religion are meant to cohere. Adams joins them to give form to the unfamiliar and to hold the unimaginable in one marvelous view.

The same passage illustrates how Enlightenment norms welcome a dominating perspective. Adams's telescope controls perception even as it enables sight. By accepting the restriction of the lens, a viewer sees farther and engages in the assumption of understanding better. The technical knowledge thus gained triggers the additional assumption of more light for all. Adams, in fact, follows an eighteenth-century convention best summarized in Alexander Pope's epitaph for Isaac Newton:

> Nature and Nature's Laws lay hid in Night;
> God said, *Let Newton be!* and all was *Light.*

The telescope is the perfect heuristic device for acting out faith in the Enlightenment. Adams's simile, "A prospect into futurity in America is like contemplating the heavens," ties that faith to a central rhetorical ploy. As in virtually every other major literary work of the early Republic, singleness of vision doggedly searches for and finds sublime order.

Benjamin Franklin is the greatest American writer of the age in part because he alone understands that the obsession with perspective might be used against itself for greater literary effect. He appreciates, as Jefferson and Adams do not, that point of view can generate as well as control interest. Most of his famous sketches or bagatelles recast a familiar point of view in a bizarre or uncomprehending context. "An Edict by the King of Prussia" (1773), "Rules by Which a Great Empire May be Reduced to a Small One" (1773), "The Sale of the Hessians" (1777), "The Ephemera" (1778), and "A Petition of the Left Hand" (1785) are all cases in point. In every one, Franklin plays a game of realization between levels of perception. Appropriately, the prolific inventor seems to have been proudest of his bifocals, the device that brings contrasting views together. When skeptics question his "double Spectacles," Franklin responds in 1785 with a drawing of his invention that projects his glasses onto the page and, from there, to the very nose of his reader. "I have only to move my Eyes up or down," he observes in a claim for universal application, "as I want to see distinctly far or near, the proper Glasses being always ready."

A similar lesson in optics may have saved the Revolution two years earlier at Newburgh, New York. Now forgotten, the incident epitomizes the new nation's first attempts to see itself and illustrates the specific dialectic of reason and domination at work in the American Enlightenment. In 1783 the Continental army in camp at Newburgh comes close to rebelling over the failure of Congress to honor promises of payment. Mutinous pamphlets are circulated, and a cabal of well-connected officers orchestrate a formal meeting with the express purpose of challenging the government. General Washington, supposedly elsewhere, suddenly appears in full-dress uniform before the conspirators and steps onto the raised dais of the officers' meeting hall. Even so, his speech for the occasion, one filled with the theoretical ideals of the

Enlightenment, fails to move these thoroughly disillusioned followers, and Washington turns, instead, to a separate text, a letter from a sympathetic member of Congress who offers to seek the necessary funding.

The unfolding scene depends upon an eighteenth-century regard for spectacle and for the power of sentiment. Washington, renowned for his impeccable grace and decorum, finds himself unable to read the fine script of his congressional correspondent and pauses awkwardly. Then, fumbling in his waistcoat, he pulls into view what only his intimates have seen before, a pair of glasses. His next words end all opposition and reduce his officers to tears: "gentlemen, you will permit me to put on my spectacles. For I have not only grown gray but almost blind in the service of my country." Assured of victory, Washington then reads the letter that no one would later remember, and, without another word, slowly withdraws while his officers watch him, first, as he makes his way out, in the hall, and then, through the windows.

Visual reversals control the scene. The absent leader materializes as if by magic to dominate the situation, a not infrequent motif for Washington in revolutionary lore. (Similar advents quash a riot amongst the soldiery in 1776 and prove decisive at the battles of Princeton and Monmouth in 1777 and 1778.) Although he sees farthest in the crisis, this leader appears blind. His spectacles enable him to see, but, in the view of others, they bespeak an affecting inability – a rare personal but all too human failing. Washington's opponents once more become his followers (learn to see again as he does) only when they themselves are blinded by tears. Their aroused feelings, in an eighteenth-century understanding of the role of sentiment, then compels a new intellectual and moral awareness and, through them, a visionary rededication. In departing, the vanishing Washington grows in stature. Every eye frames him in the windows of the building from which the officers first sought to exclude him. At the heart of these reversals is the dialectic of the Enlightenment. Reason, having failed in Washington's original speech, finds another way to dominate (reason and emotion exemplified in the commanding figure) in order to obtain the consent of the governed.

It is not too much to suggest that Washington *is* the country in this moment. What exactly do we see in the midst of so many compounded ironies? At the center stands the uniformed figure, already on a pedestal or dais and then framed in the window when the example is complete. This father of his country is first and foremost a military hero, the American Cincinnatus. In its republican aspect, the Roman model in the Enlightenment embodies liberty; in its military aspect, discipline. Washington combines liberty and discipline, reason and domination. Pedestal, uniform, and the life of discipline in the service of liberty bring him into focus as a figure to be obeyed. At the same time, the notion of Cincinnatus signifies patriotic sacrifice. Washington's minor handicap in aging – "I have not only grown gray but almost blind in the service of my country" – raises that theme. It humanizes the unapproachable leader just enough to remind everyone that a living person has achieved such greatness in confirmation of the secular ideals of the Enlightenment.

Of course, the dangers in what happens at Newburgh are great. Kant's directive to have courage to do one's own thinking has been reified in the courageous individual as communal exemplum. Washington, in this sense, operates as the first figure in a hagiography that identifies America to other Americans. By the 1820s Daniel Webster and other civic orators will have arranged these beacons of light into fixed and eternal constellations that guide the nation. As the leaders of the Revolution are tied to national institutions, their writings and lives become blueprints for the history of the period. And when their words prove insufficient, the knowledge of their sacrifices in the act of founding can always be called upon. As a group, they overcome the vagaries of place and association in the emerging republic. The hagiography of transcendent individuals creates an instantaneous set of traditions, an imaginary national landscape for controlling space and understanding the world.

III

This imaginary landscape involves crucial literary questions – questions about the relation of writer, leader, text, and audience in the goals of the American Enlightenment. In Kant's essay *An Answer to the Question: "What is Enlightenment?"* the enlightened leader is a guardian who teaches that it is the duty of all citizens to think for themselves, but that guardian must also allow for "the great unthinking mass," or everything will be lost. The ideal, in Kantian terms, is *"a man of learning addressing the entire reading public."* The more frequent reality, and Kant's own example, is someone like Frederick the Great, king of Prussia, who demands obedience as an exemplary leader. The knowledge of the teacher and the status of the ruler combine in the ambiguous position of guardian. The combination is essential because a people can only achieve enlightenment slowly. Kant is quite explicit on the problem: not even a revolution, he says, can reform thought fast enough for reason alone to lead in the figure of learning. Those citizens who have not learned to think for themselves must defer to authority. Hence, when Washington's words fail to convince his officers at Newburgh, he must find ways to invest the exemplary leader in either that text or another at hand.

Just as the Enlightenment text divides in its dual attempt to command and to reason, require and educate, so the essence of literary skill in writing such a text involves the creation of unities out of divergent possibilities. This skill marks the central dynamic in American revolutionary and postrevolutionary writings; the easiest recourse, one that bolsters the hagiographical tradition, is to weave together the claims of reason with the claimants to leadership. Specifically, in literary practice, the attempt to reason insists upon its right to authority, while the attempt to command urges its own rectitude, an interplay that makes virtue in leadership the pervasive theme of the period.

Two related features also inform the nature and energy of the writings of the American Enlightenment. First, and to an unusual degree, the leaders of the Revolution believe in ideas as intrinsic repositories of meaning. Second, the source of these ideas depends heavily on the international context of the Enlightenment. Both points have often been overlooked even though they are essential to the vitality and original courage of writings that now seem timeworn and pedestrian.

Ideas are repositories of meaning in that they answer the problematics of the unknown and indeterminate in revolutionary America. The first dilemma in perception always consists in knowing where one stands. Ideas supply that knowledge of place for America's first national leaders. Thus, in 1789, Franklin expresses hope that "a thorough Knowledge of the Rights of Man, may pervade all the Nations of the Earth, so that a Philosopher may set his Foot anywhere on its Surface and say, 'This is my Country.' " In this formulation, the complexities, particularities, and frustrations of time, location, and custom give way to an easier equation in which a knowledge of rights becomes a knowledge of country.

The spread of ideas lifts the chaos of the present into the ordered spaces of the future, all of which the Enlightenment has promised. Even in the worst of times, 1799, Jefferson trusts not to politics, or to states, or to other institutions but, as he puts it in a letter to William Green Mumford, "to the American mind . . . opened." Once again, ideas are substitutes for the messiness of place. This is what the hope of the Enlightenment can mean for the architect of a new culture. In writing to Mumford, Jefferson believes, like the Marquis de Condorcet, that the human mind is formed for society and that it is "perfectible to a degree of which we cannot as yet form any conception." Jefferson's belief in human progress is a controlling lens much as is John Adams's telescope in *Defence of the Constitutions*.

The presumed advance of knowledge can reduce discord and turmoil to momentary distractions. Describing the troubled election of 1800, Jefferson writes Joseph Priestley that it has been a raging tempest in a new nation of great extent and sparse habitation. Nonetheless, all is well. The storm has broken, and "science and honesty are replaced on their high ground," proof for Jefferson that "this whole chapter in the history of man is new." The excitement in these words has to do with the power of ideas in transmission. In Europe the Enlightenment must overcome the wreckage of human history, or, as Jefferson tells Priestley, "the times of Vandalism, when ignorance put everything into the hands of power and priestcraft." Not so, in America. Freed from the tyranny of the past, ideas, even the same ideas, flourish in a different way "under the protection of those laws which were made for the wise and the good." Jefferson's convictions carry him beyond the canniness of immediate political understanding. The intellectual possibilities of the Enlightenment in America have changed the facts! Properly understood, they make history itself new.

This enthusiasm in the sophisticated politician needs to be taken at face value. Jefferson, the enlightened thinker as president in what he calls "the Revolution of 1800," seeks not so much the origins of ideas as their application in a place where ideas have the chance to be different things altogether. Historians are forgetting this orientation when they concentrate on the details of cross-cultural refraction. Does Jefferson in 1776 base the Declaration of Independence on his readings of John Locke, as some have argued, or on alternative readings of continental philosophers like Jean-Jacques Burlamaqui, or on the Scottish Enlightenment? Do the court-and-country debates of England or the Common Sense traditions of Scotland control revolutionary rhetoric in America? Can we resolve these polarities by thinking of the American Enlightenment as a progression from moderate origins in the English Enlightenment toward the radical implications of the French and then on to the conservative reaction of the Scottish? Such questions cannot be answered in the way that many historians ask them – with nationalistic orientations in mind.

The Enlightenment text as literature grows out of a commitment to the general relation and spread of ideas. Franklin runs with this theme when he associates "country" with wherever a philosopher can find "the Rights of Man." The true philosophe thinks in terms of a universal language, identifying less with nations than with the republic of letters, and revolutionary Americans are peculiarly susceptible to the international scope of these identifications. As republicans, they easily accept the republic of letters. As Americans, they reject the specific example of *every* European national history. As citizens of the New World, they are interested in the fresh application of ideas and not in the origins and details of systems of thought. Above all, as Enlightenment thinkers, they believe in the global sphere of connections and the promise of republicanism throughout the world.

These tendencies explain Jefferson's seemingly casual but actually profound faith in abstractions and in decontextualized thought as he writes the

Declaration of Independence. In the Declaration, as he tells Henry Lee in 1825, he is addressing the tribunal of the world, not from any particular and previous writing but from the harmonizing sentiments of the day as expressed "in conversation, in letters, printed essays, or in the elementary books of public right, as Aristotle, Cicero, Locke, Sidney, etc." Only in this manner can he hope to achieve what he intended: "an expression of the American mind." The creativity in this process has too often been ignored. Jefferson uproots and then harmonizes European ideas to make something specifically American out of them.

Put another way, the American Enlightenment thrives upon perceived affinities rather than on exclusive correlations. An eighteenth-century intellectual still believes in reading everything. The higher goal of that intellectual in America is to find and to apply those portions of a universal knowledge that will work best in the unprecedented setting of new world republicanism. These priorities should not be mistaken for either the rejection of intellectual traditions or utilitarianism or simple opportunism. The leaders of 1776 have better reasons than most to believe in the power of ideas, but they have come to understand ideas within the praxis of successful revolution. Their relation to an idea is one of change. Possibilities dominate their thinking. When Jefferson tells Priestley that "this whole chapter in the history of man is new," he means that ideas have succeeded in transforming the nature of revolutionary America.

Belief in a different American future qualifies the relevance of the European past. Jefferson, Adams, and Franklin, in particular, pick and choose among European frames of reference, and they do so while convinced of the limited bearing of each. They borrow ideas instead of accepting or rejecting them out of hand. Indeed, no other generation of American thinkers before the twentieth century, saving perhaps that of the first Puritans, feels and exercises such a sense of parity with its European counterparts, and the sources of this self-confidence should be clear. The success of the Revolution ratifies the independence of each additional American decision. So too, for Americans, the corresponding failure of republicanism in Europe limits the relevance of European thought and confirms the need for at least some areas of intellectual separation.

Just how widely and loosely eighteenth-century Americans select their ideas can be seen in the actual patterns that they borrow from the European Enlightenment. From the French Enlightenment of Voltaire, Montesquieu, and Buffon, they take the philosophe as international hero, a love of system, literary style within system, the uses of a philosophy of history in political science, a fascination with technology, a belief in a natural order, and a distrust of organized religion. From England comes empirical investigation in general, Newtonian science and Lockean psychology, the Whig theory of history, political oratory, and the rights of English subjects. The Continental legal philosophers (Grotius, von Pufendorf, Burlamaqui, Beccaria) contribute the primacy of natural law, the notion of a government formed in compact under law, and the essential analogy between a rule of law and the life of reason. The Scottish Enlightenment, in turn, furnishes a secular vocabulary that nevertheless keeps Providence safely in mind. It also encourages the primacy of public learning and educational institutions, the relation of economic growth to political freedom, and, not least, the justification for a colony's right of revolution.

Again, however, it is the interpenetration of these influences that counts in America. When in 1826 James Madison calls Jefferson "a 'walking Library,' " he is celebrating the capacity to apply any combination of ideas in the activity of American life. The great goal in this life of activity is to connect science (the regularity and knowability of the world) with morality (the politics of the good life) in social progress. The leaders of the Revolution, in another manifestation of the hagiography of heroes, themselves illustrate the combinations at work. Franklin can be the universal beacon for the path to be taken because he symbolizes the union of science and politics. In Turgot's phrase, "[H]e seized the lightning from the sky, and the sceptre from tyrants."

IV

The intellectual self-confidence, scope, and facility of revolutionary thought are a part of the ultimate paradox of the Enlightenment in America. For alongside these characteristics is a heightened uncertainty, leading to a strange juxtaposition of moods in representative texts of the periods. Even the most measured thought acquires an urgency in actual writings. Reason, no matter how reasonable, gives way to emotion in crucial moments. The conjunction of science and history, the spread of light, the belief in ideas all translate into a single imperative or tonal byword: "now."

Thomas Paine's *Common Sense* offers a case in point. "Now is the seed-time of continental union, faith and honor. The least fracture now will be like a name engraved with the point of a pin on the tender rind of a young oak," writes Paine. "It might be difficult, if not impossible," he adds, "to form the Continent into one government half a century hence." Delay of any kind is impossible: "the *time hath found us*"; "the *present time* is the *true time*. . . . that peculiar time, which never happens to a nation but once." Its special urgency notwithstanding, Paine's pamphlet is quite typical in its claim. The rhetoric of the Revolution reads in general like a race against time from first to last.

Stridency will dominate any revolutionary statement, but *Common Sense* achieves this tone with the deepest metaphor of the Enlightenment, and it did so in a way that suggests an American place in history. Deeper, more important than even the notion of light in the optimism of eighteenth-century thought is the concept of an approaching maturity. "Youth is the seed time of good habits, as well in nations as in individuals," Paine explains, right after claiming that "the heaviest achievements were always accomplished in the non-age of a nation." Remember that Kant defines enlightenment as humanity's emergence from a self-incurred immaturity. How are Americans to interpret this idea in a New World setting of national beginnings? How, in sum, are they to construe a condition of unavoidable cultural adolescence? Separation from the mother country can imply either a natural movement toward the control of one's own destiny or the untimely, irreparable loss of the orphan. The distinction depends not just on the worthiness of the English mother – a much debated issue in the 1770s – but also on assumptions about the maturation process in America. Only children can be orphans.

As Paine's words indicate, revolutionary writings trade constantly on the theme of youth in action as a mixture of vulnerability, necessity, and virtue. They also argue all sides of the question with considerable facility. While the newness of history in America is a favorite theme, so is the assumption that Americans have somehow outdistanced European peoples by a thousand years. The answer to this apparent contradiction lies in a new kind of maturity through education – an answer that Enlightenment norms encourage. On the other hand, the same answer increases every sense of historical urgency: the greater the presumed discrepancy between European and American peoples, the more immediate the peril of cross-cultural contamination through immigration.

The leaders of the American Revolution worry that education might not proceed fast enough to secure a virtuous republic of unified citizens. The very theme of virtue raises the danger of corruption; inevitably, foreign influence becomes every republican's first fear. Jefferson, in *Notes on the State of Virginia*, writes that immigration disturbs American principles and will reduce the populace to "a heterogeneous, incoherent, distracted mass." More pessimistic writers think it only a matter of time before ignorance and corruption from abroad overwhelm the Revolution.

The emphasis in *Common Sense* on youth in action also reduces history to a fleeting moment. Act now, says Paine over and over again, or lose the possibility forever, and the assumption is one that the leaders of the Revolution share with surprising unanimity. From their studies of the republican form of government in history, they conjecture that the people will become "careless" and "forget" their virtue. "It can never be too often repeated,"

Jefferson warns in *Notes on the State of Virginia,* "that the time for fixing every essential right on a legal basis is while our rulers are honest, and ourselves united. From the conclusion of this war we shall be going down hill." The concept of maturity translates easily into metaphors of national identity and growth, but the inevitable passage of youth translates just as easily into the rise and fall of nations. *Common Sense* is not the only paradigmatic text in 1776; the same year brings the first volume of Edward Gibbon's *The Decline and Fall of the Roman Empire.*

Their view of history also leads revolutionary writers to articulate the gravest dangers in failure. Education, exploration, and invention should unite in the general advance of humanity, but that possibility depends upon prompt action in the more immediate and unpredictable realm of politics. Progress, in other words, is not a predetermined evolution through fixed stages of history. The moment can yield permanent darkness as easily as additional light. These alternatives, in their starkness, define the fullest meaning of crisis in the eighteenth-century American mind. In the fresh dispensation of the new world, events are freighted with an extraordinary double capacity for either good or ill. The stakes are permanently high. Whatever revolutionary Americans do or do not do, they believe that their actions will change the direction of history – possibly forever.

The assumption of urgency denotes another difference between European and American Enlightenment. The conviction of a historical crisis comes late to the European Enlightenment and then only when the battle of ideas has assumed political dimensions. In America, by way of contrast, the Enlightenment *begins* in the political arena, where it unleashes the earliest recognitions of stress and disjuncture. The writers of the American Revolution always ask the same question: What should be done in the present moment? Answers aside, the strategy has its own appeal: it demands the possibility of meaningful action, and it fosters the belief, accepted by later generations of Americans, that social destiny and perhaps history itself can be controlled by recognizing and responding to crisis.

We see as much in George Washington's "Circular to the States" (1783), or, as it was then known, "Washington's Farewell to the Army." In his stoicism, Washington imparts the centrality of crisis in republican thought more convincingly than, say, the rabble-rousing Paine, or the anxious John Adams, or even Jefferson, the man of ideas. Washington's use of standard literary conventions also clarifies the impulses of the day in a way that more original writers might not. This conventionality, however, should not disguise a considerable skill. Washington's writings, as clearly as those of any other leader, make the American Revolution a literary phenomenon. "Circular to the States" is a representative text that we no longer know how to read.

Washington's "Farewell Address" as president in 1796 would rhetorically duplicate and overshadow this earlier effort, but in the 1780s there is no more important document in America except for the Constitution itself.

The four expressed goals in "Circular to the States" will dominate discussion four years later in Philadelphia. In fact, Washington's articulation of them in 1783 prefigures and, to a considerable extent, enables the agenda of 1787. The writer urges a stronger union, a sacred regard to public justice, a systematic attention to the public defense, and, lastly, a spirit of subordination and obedience to government in the sacrifice of local prejudices to the larger community. Each of these goals bespeaks the larger one of capping the Revolution by safely channeling the energies of rebellion. Not surprisingly, then, Washington's address raises a fear of potential chaos — a fear expressed variously as licentiousness, a state of nature, the extreme of anarchy, and the ruins of liberty.

Less conventional is Washington's astute resolution of the dichotomy between instruction and commandment in the Enlightenment text. Although major aspects of "Circular to the States" depend upon the writer's experience and station as General of the Army, the address rests within the reiteration of Washington's pending resignation and retreat to domestic life. His readers, as he tells them, are receiving his last official communication as a public character. It is a natural time for reflection, but Washington adds to the power of the moment by holding onto the unique relevance of his experience as commander in chief of the army. His "many anxious days and watchful nights" in that service give him a special perspective and entitle him to write "the more copiously on the subject of our mutual felicitation." Under the circumstances, he can also insist that "silence in me would be a crime." The last moment in office thus becomes the *most* public, the most assertive. The words that follow build into what Washington himself calls "the Legacy of One, who has ardently wished, on all occasions, to be useful to his Country." This conceit is well chosen. Legacies bestow, but they also stipulate and require.

The address proper opens with a paean to the Enlightenment in America: "The foundation of our Empire was not laid in the gloomy age of Ignorance and Superstition, but at an Epocha when the rights of mankind were better understood and more clearly defined, than at any former period." This prospect appears just as bountiful whether regarded from "a natural, a political or moral point of light." The metaphorical use of light typically joins different categories in a common focus or "point." Washington argues that "the free cultivation of Letters, the unbounded extension of Commerce, the progressive refinement of Manners, the growing liberality of sentiment, and above all, the pure and benign light of Revelation, have had a meliorating influence on mankind and increased the blessings of Society." These elements, taken together, have given Americans "a fairer opportunity for political happiness than any other Nation has ever been favored with" and have made them "the Actors on a most conspicuous Theatre."

The image of actors on a stage is a telling one. Theatricality is never far from either Washington's sense of persona or his prose. In this instance, his classical song of praise abruptly shifts toward eighteenth-century melodrama. Noting the many blessings that the United States enjoy, Washington warns that "if their Citizens should not be completely free and happy, the fault will be entirely their own." The conditional clause is a signal. It carries us over the edge of pleasing encomium toward sensational incident and emotional appeal. The prospect of perfect felicity raises the other possibility, of failure, and thought of the later is too awful to bear.

The swift downturn that follows represents a darker, more concrete version of what, in 1783, is only an abstract issue in European thought. Writing just a year before Kant's essay on enlightenment, Washington actually wrestles with the same subject. Both men worry most about the uncertain period between revolution and enlightenment. But where the European philosopher works out a positive solution to a perceived problem, the American soldier and man of action dwells far more on the immediate implications of failure. Practical responsibilities bring an anxiety that theory does not have. The readers of "Circular to the States" learn that "this is the time of their political probation . . . this is the moment to establish or ruin their national Character forever." Washington draws the conclusion that Kant would only hint at. "[I]t is yet to be decided," he writes, "whether the Revolution must ultimately be considered as a blessing or a curse: a blessing or a curse, not to the present age alone, for with our fate will the destiny of unborn Millions be involved."

Washington, the most phlegmatic of men, emphasizes "the importance of the Crisis, and the magnitude of the objects in discussion." Everything depends on whether or not "we have a disposition to seize the occasion and make it our own." Five times in a paragraph, Washington intones "this is the moment," either "favorable" or "ill-fated." The only options in this rhetoric of extremes are sudden victory or permanent defeat. There is no middle ground either in the moment or for the unborn millions to come. At issue is whether the United States "will stand or fall," "whether they will be respectable and prosperous, or contemptible and miserable as a Nation." Significantly, this balance in contrasting fates will appear more and more critical to Washington in retirement at Mount Vernon during the middle 1780s. Worries about "the present unsettled and deranged state of public affairs," which he expressed to Jonathan Trumbull in early 1784, soon become major anxieties; "from the high ground on which we stood," he writes James Warren by late 1785, "we are descending into the vale of confusion and darkness."

V

The American literature of the period thrives in the resonant space between the hope of blessing and the fear of curse. It defines itself in that crisis; this is where it holds its audiences. In so doing, early republican writings depend heavily upon the process of the Enlightenment. It is the struggle toward realization, not the celebration of knowledge, that creates meaning and interest. The Americans who fight for their independence on the edge of the British Empire cannot compete with European writers for centrality in any presentation of knowledge. Instead, they find their importance on the very different edge of the Enlightenment. In dramatic combinations — the hope of blessing and the fear of curse — they place themselves where light and darkness meet.

Skillful choreography of these processes epitomizes literary creativity. When Alexander Hamilton begins *Federalist No. 1* with the observation that the United States are "an empire, in many respects, the most interesting in the world," he means, first, that "the fate" of that empire hangs in the balance and, second, that American government is the greatest test of the Enlightenment ("it seems to have been reserved to the people of this country, by their conduct and example, to decide the important question, whether societies of men are really capable or not, of establishing good government from reflection and choice"). The fate of empire presents the possibility of failure; the experiment with good government establishes a context for thinking about success. In conflict, these factors, failure and success, constitute "the crisis, at which we are arrived," and a negative consequence will carry beyond the moment to "the general misfortune of mankind." Every reader has an investment in the uncertain struggle that Hamilton has sketched.

The difficulty, of course, is that the struggle remains uncertain; the outcome unclear. Process reaches only so far in the explanation of ends, and the human scale of the Enlightenment has a way of trapping every user somewhere in the broader reaches of history. Reason might clarify events, and the spread of knowledge might even make history new, but both remain entirely within the never-ending flux of circumstance — the rise and fall of nations. Time may be on the side of the Revolution, but for how long? The limits of reason and knowledge are clear even to the most optimistic early republicans when this question and others like it are asked.

In response, as well as by heritage, revolutionary writers often express their thought in spiritual terms. Washington's decision to filter the Revolution through "the pure and benign light of Revelation" and through the language of "blessing and curse" is symptomatic of a general reliance on religious forms and ideas. "Statesmen, my dear Sir, may plan and speculate for liberty," John Adams explains in 1776, writing to his cousin Zabdiel Adams, "but it is religion and morality alone which can establish the principles upon which freedom can securely stand." For most revolutionary Americans, history is still a safer subject with Providence in mind.

Providence, however, must not be misused. In his *Defence of the Constitutions of Government,* the same Adams will insist that American government has its beginnings in "the natural authority of the people alone, without a pretence of miracle or mystery," "without the monkery of priests." "It will never be pretended," he observes here, "that any persons employed in [the formation of the American governments] had interviews with the gods, or were in any degree under the inspiration of Heaven. . . . it will forever be acknowledged that these governments were contrived merely by the use of reason and the senses." In these words, Adams shares the general disdain of the Enlightenment for religious enthusiasm and superstition; yet he also knows that the natural authority of the people is a dangerous variable left to itself and that a government "merely contrived" will soon disappear in the immense scale of universal history.

It is part of Adams's American identity that he already has secured the coherence of a higher view. "The people in America," he begins *Defence of the Constitutions,* "have now the best opportunity and the greatest trust in their hands that Providence ever committed to so small a number since the transgression of the first pair; if they betray their trust, their guilt will merit even greater punishment than other nations have suffered, and the indignation of Heaven." Adams, no doubt, believes in this version of the covenant, but it is also an intellectual and political convenience, at once defining the people and placing external limits upon them. His easy mix of secular and religious explanation is everywhere in the period, and, writ large, it signifies a blend of belief and convenience that remains the single most elusive quality in the rhetoric of the times. Far from representing a loss or even a qualification in conviction, the intellectual facility of Adams and others seems to have fed upon itself. A potentially corrosive, separate faith in the Enlightenment actually explodes into fervor, and it does so precisely because it helped Americans bring their own peculiar brand of the Reformation to the Revolution.

The American Enlightenment does not quarrel with religious orthodoxies as its French counterpart does; it rests, instead, in the common or shared rhythms and patterns that the Enlightenment has taken from Christianity. The parallels in intellectual reference – salvation and progress, the health of the soul and the corresponding gauge of public interest, the regenerate

Christian and the virtuous citizen, exultation of the divine and celebration of design – are homologies in American thought rather than substitutes, one for the other, as in European philosophy. Moreover, although many eighteenth-century Americans seem to have been aware of the slippage between categories, they hold to their combinations.

The explanation lies in the still puzzling connection between Enlightenment thought and Reform Protestantism in the moment of revolutionary engagement. As the challenge of reason against mere authority supplies the broadest intellectual legitimacy and mutual recognition in American pamphleteering, so the divinely ordained mission of the primitive church motivates and justifies radical communal action. Never mind that the abstract projections of reason rob formal religion of its essential mysteries and of its retrogressive impulses toward purification! The enlightened spread of knowledge and the oppositional strategies in Congregationalism join in the idea of vigilance as patriotic virtue.

There is, in fact, no Revolution without the combination. When the Reverend Samuel Sherwood of Connecticut connects piety, public virtue, and love of country in *Scriptural Instructions to Civil Rulers and all Free-born Subjects* (1774), one of the most influential of all revolutionary sermons, he believes that only "fear of the lord" in a people "incessantly vigilant and watchful" can make a state free. A masterful conflation of divine sanctions and secular rights, *Scriptural Instructions to Civil Rulers* extols "the common cause, the public good, and general interest in the land" and seeks "to make up, unite, and gather into one common interest, all the good protestants in this land." Unmistakably, fear of the Lord and the people's vigilance over their rights do go together; a godly people, by definition, *will* discover and *will* act on the common cause. Sherwood and other ministers soon turn these stances into an involved typology of biblical text to American event. In *The Church's Flight into the Wilderness,* Sherwood's clerical counterpart to Paine's *Common Sense* in the same year, "the light of revelation" will also be "the path of the just." Here, in 1776, revelation and reason will fuse in the mission of national union.

3

RELIGIOUS VOICES

I

Religious voices speak first in the Revolution. At one level, this primacy merely restates the dominance of religious expression in early American culture. Until 1765, religious publications in the colonies outnumber all other intellectual writings combined, and they remain the single largest category of publication throughout the revolutionary era. But initial dominance only begins to explain the importance of religious expression in Anglo–American political debate. The relation between dissenting religious traditions and the growth of oppositional political discourse is a barometer of cultural modification and literary creativity throughout the era.

Steeped in the English revolutions of the seventeenth century, radical Protestants in eighteenth-century America know how to oppose a king. Jonathan Mayhew's approval of "the Resistance made to King Charles I" in *A Discourse Concerning Unlimited Submission* (1750) is shocking to his contemporaries not because it "takes the side of Liberty, the *BIBLE,* and Common Sense, in opposition to Tyranny, *PRIESTCRAFT,* and Nonsense" – standard dichotomies in eighteenth-century Protestant thought – but because, in rejecting "the slavish doctrine of passive obedience and nonresistance," it also advocates the right to judge and then act against a king as part of "the natural and legal rights of the people against the unnatural and illegal encroachments of arbitrary power."

Similar language could be heard in England, but it dominates debate in America in a different way altogether. Mayhew, after all, first preaches *Discourse Concerning Unlimited Submission* before his own congregation in the prestigious West Church of Boston. He and other American clergymen can take greater risks than their English counterparts when accused of "preaching politics instead of *CHRIST*" because they face a large and uniquely sympathetic audience for radical Protestant polemics. The single greatest factor in the evolution of a revolutionary dynamic is the religious distinctiveness of that audience. Maintained and encouraged from church congregation to church congregation across the denominational spread of reform Protantism, this distinctiveness breeds a colossal presumption. Never mind that John Adams lives on the obscurest fringe of the British Empire in February 1765; he is also an attentive reader of Mayhew's sermons, and of countless others like them, when he writes "I always consider, the settlement of America with Reverence and Wonder – as the Opening of a grand scene and Design in Providence, for the Illumination of the Ignorant and the Emancipation of the slavish Part of Mankind all over the Earth." Some have stressed the conscious art in statements like this one, but there is no chance of understanding the early American scene, either of the colonies or of the early Republic, without assessing the interplay between religion and politics as a source of liberty.

The differences from England are instructive and somewhat startling against the continuities of religious origin and influence. In the eighteenth century, at least two of every three colonial Americans place themselves somewhere within the religious dissenting tradition. England, by way of contrast, lapses into a moderate Anglicanism after the exhausting religious wars of the preceding century; dissenters dwindle to a small minority, as low as 7 percent of the total English population. By 1775, in his *Resolutions for Conciliation with the Colonies,* Edmund Burke finds it necessary to spell out the difference for an uncomprehending Parliament. Religion in America, he warns, "is a refinement on the principle of resistance" and "of that kind which is most adverse to all implicit submission of mind and opinion." Long after the fact, the Loyalist leader and historian Peter Oliver will still blame the Revolution on the dissenting clergy, "the black regiment" of rebellion in America.

But if religious dissent is a pivotal issue in the ideological formation of the Revolution, the exact nature of its influence remains the most complex and vexing puzzle in the question of national origins. Taken together, the remarks of Burke and Oliver point to one area of confusion. Did the oppositional modes of religious dissent well up into politics from the radical spirit of a Protestant people, as Burke's parliamentary speech implies, or did an organized clergy push colonial yeomanry toward rebellion, as Oliver would have it? The possibilities here often depend on the methodology of the investigator; for each preaching moderate scorned by a combative congregation, there is a "fighting pastor" just a parish away. If the ministry does lead, do rational liberal clergymen show the way, or does that honor belong more appropriately to their radical and evangelical counterparts? Nothing less than the presumed meaning and direction of American culture has been at stake in answers to these queries.

The questions themselves have been compounded by further historical investigation. It is now clear that the completed Revolution marginalizes clergymen in the political and economic life of the new nation. Ministers lose more ground in the social upheavals of the time than do any other intellectual grouping, and their downward mobility must be read in the light of a continuing vitality, unappreciated until recently, in the religious life of the people. Beyond these complications lies another mystery. How do religious conviction and the rational ideals of the secular Enlightenment come together so uncannily for certain Americans at the center of revolutionary activity? Forgotten ideological affinities explain their success. Perhaps nowhere else have the sudden and profound changes of the Revolution so obscured later understanding.

The most articulate strand in an American dissenting tradition comes, of course, from Puritanism, the legacy of seventeenth-century Anglo-American Presbyterianism and Congregationalism. The intellectual foundations of Puritanism lend themselves to oppositional discourse in ways both large and small. Among the more crucial influences are primitivism, anti-institutionalism, antiauthoritarianism, separatism and other assertions of local autonomy, the legalism of covenant theology, and biblical exegesis as regular cultural practice. The duty of reading the Bible on one's own – the Bible as the supreme guide in communal life, as the only true source of the connection between divine and human history, as the personal property of every true believer in the pious act of interpretation – appears to have been especially crucial in the evolution of a language of dissent. Because Puritanism ritually exposes the sinful heart to public judgment in a conversion experience, it also contrasts good and evil and relates individual morality to communal prosperity in compulsive ways. We are never far from the capacity to identify and resist an unworthy leadership.

Resistance to authority is, in fact, a general trait in colonial religious expression. Although most colonies follow the European model of an established church, pressure against religious uniformity represents the broadest single trait in colonial religion. Open competition among proliferating denominations and active lay involvement in church government distinguish American religion from its European origins and promote a general resistance to hierarchy. Establishmentarianism suffers in every region. William Livingston of New York is expressing an American conception when, in *The Independent Reflector* (October 11, 1753), he observes, "I Believe, that if the whole Kingdom professed one Religion, it would be of no Religion; and that the Variety of Sects in the Nation, are a Guard against the Tyranny and Usurpation of one over another." The underlying premise, toleration through the widest variation, is made famous as part of J. Hector St. John de Crèvecoeur's answer to "What is an American?" in *Letters from an American Farmer* (1782); another permutation will guard against the power of factionalism in *The Federalist No. 10* (1787).

Even in Virginia, where Anglican dominance is never in doubt, colonial leaders resist high church forms and centralization of authority. Faith in the Church of England does not prevent local vestries from controlling their own religious institutions. Later, when difficulty over Virginia's state-wide church tax erupts in the Parson's Cause of 1758, Virginians are already well on their way to a rhetoric of taxation without representation. "And what must be done with those Harpies, those Beasts of Prey, the publick Collectors?" asks Richard Bland, Virginia planter and Anglican vestryman, in his *Letter to the Clergy of Virginia* (1760). "Must they be left to feed, without Controul, upon the Vitals of the People?" The clerical response, an action to enforce payment through the Virginia courts, gives the lawyer Patrick Henry his first platform as the defender of American liberty.

The true measure of religious antiauthoritarianism can be taken in colonial fears of an America bishop. Anxiety over the prospect fuels controversy throughout the eighteenth century and leads to a major intercolonial eruption against the Church of England between 1767 and 1770. Eventually, the issue absorbs more ink than the Stamp Act dispute does and becomes a staple of radical ideological dissent – so much so that John Adams in 1815 can tell Jedediah Morse that "apprehension of Episcopacy" contributed as much as any other cause to the Revolution. The depth of this concern must also be understood against its groundlessness in fact. Establishment of an Anglican bishop in America remains an unlikely prospect at every point in the colonial period.

This discrepancy between fear and reality actually develops out of more intrinsic urgencies in early American character. Ministers like Charles Chauncy in Massachusetts, the most vocal leader in the antiepiscopacy movement of the late 1760s, do worry about the spread of Anglicanism in the New World, and for evidence to support their claims they have the growth in Anglican congregations (from three hundred to four hundred and fifty in America between 1750 and 1776) and Anglican missionary zeal (the English Society for the Propagation of the Gospel proselytizes throughout New England and the middle colonies). Even so, Anglicanism does not grow faster than other denominations in the period, and the real cause of protest lies deeper.

Colonial Americans, in effect, use their diatribes against episcopacy to recognize each other across denominational affiliations. Chauncy's *A Letter to a Friend* in 1767 is just one of many efforts in this category. Responding to John Lord Bishop of Landaff, Chauncy remonstrates against attempts "to EPISCOPISE the Colonies," but he does so in order to remind Americans of "the ERRAND of our forefathers into this Country" and of their indoctrination "in the PRINCIPLES OF CHRISTIAN LIBERTY." An embattled figure in colonial religious disputes, Chauncy can expect general agreement, even applause, on this issue. Distaste for high church ritual and practice is part of the broadest communal identification; liberty and piety are renewed in the name of the forefathers' first errand.

Almost as important in growing colonial self-recognition is the ease with which Chauncy can identify a British enemy. Distinctions between American virtue and English corruption constitute an increasing element in colonial discourse, but American leaders quickly grasp that it is safer to express these distinctions in religious rather than in political terms. Ecclesiastical differences are acceptable under liberty of conscience; political disputes raise the unacceptable prospect of faction. Not heresy but treason is the fear of the eighteenth-century Anglo-American intellectual. Accordingly, Chauncy can refer without risk to "malignity" and "the abounding growth of iniquity" in England, to English "secret back-biters and revilers" who act "through bigotry, prejudice, malice, interest, or some other lust of the flesh or mind," and, most particularly, to "that yoke of bondage" that forces the first Americans to flee England in order to "enjoy the freedom of men and christians."

The contrast in A Letter to a Friend is between British manipulation ("if Bishops should be sent to the Colonies, the people would generally turn Church-men") and American piety ("true Christianity is not *more generally* better practised in any part of the world"). When corrupt colonists do appear, they can be conveniently excluded from the purity of the American past. "Those that are so," Chauncy notes, "came to us from abroad." The moral bifurcation in this geographical scheme is a volatile ideological tool for Chauncy and others. In context, and under the pressure of language and events, the contrast slips into a conspiracy of evil against good, and the performance of unmasking British corruption appears at once an exercise in bravura and prudence. As a minister addressing his own flock, Chauncy can reject British culture and still remain free of political charges, all the while rallying Americans around their own popular standards of meaning.

Religious thought brings its own dynamic to the deepening political crisis of the 1760s and 1770s. Christian polarities contribute less to an understanding of complex problems in diplomacy and more to explanations based on an absolute difference. The identification of England with malignity and of America with virtue raises obvious biblical and historical parallels in the wars of the Lord – parallels that soon become exact in scriptural readings. By 1776, the apocalyptic "image of the beast" (Revelation 13:14–15) signifies "the corrupt system of tyranny and oppression, that has of late been fabricated and adopted by the ministry and parliament of Great-Britain." Here, in *The Church's Flight into the Wilderness,* Samuel Sherwood uses biblical typology to make the case for rebellion. "[W]e have incontestible evidence," explains Sherwood, "that God Almighty, with all the powers of heaven, are on our side." Acceptance of the premise assures victory. It also renders all thought of compromise impossible; one does not negotiate with the Antichrist.

The American revolutionary spirit owes everything to such rhetoric. In the skilled hands of the radical clergy, faintheartedness means impiety. As Samuel Langdon, preaching before the third Provincial Congress of Massachusetts, and David Jones, preaching in Philadelphia on a day of continental fast, both put the matter in 1775, "If God be with us, who can be against us?" The refrain plays upon the biblical trope of the chosen people, but it also helps many colonial minds over a political hurdle. In their respective calls to arms, even Langdon and Jones stumble over the question of royal allegiance. Like most colonial English subjects in 1775, they find it hard to fight their king.

The answer, for many of those who seek independence, comes through God's presence in colonial politics: heavenly authority supersedes an earthly king. "We must keep our eyes fixed on the supreme government of the Eternal King, as directing all events, setting up or pulling down the kings of the earth," says Langdon. Or, in the more succinct motto of Enlightenment so frequently ascribed to figures like Franklin and Jefferson, "rebellion to tyrants is obedience to God." These words demonstrate the power of belief and the limits of mere reason in the Revolution if properly understood. Interestingly enough, their source is not the secular Enlightenment but the darker side of English Puritanism. Long before Jefferson toys with the notion as an epitaph or Franklin proposes it for the Great Seal of the United States, the phrase "rebellion to tyrants is obedience to God" is already on the lips of John Bradshaw, the regicide judge who, as president of the parliamentary tribunal in 1649, refuses Charles I the right to speak before he is sentenced. Bradshaw already knows what eighteenth-century American Whigs would learn: faith, not logic, carries a rebellion.

II

Revivalism is the religious phenomenon most closely associated with the Revolution – expressly, the series of revivals at midcentury known as the Great Awakening (1734–50). Recently, however, historians have come to differ greatly over the nature, range, impact, and overall meaning of the Great Awakening; the very designation has been questioned as an unwarranted assumption about the solidarity of scattered events. Granted by some, but at issue for others, are the intercolonial character of the Awakening, its importance to lower-class protest, its relation to radical politics, and its lasting impact on social and religious institutions. And yet certain facts and assumptions remain common to all interpretations: prerevolutionary revivals take on a regional character that distinguishes them from earlier, more local communal outpourings, and their expanded scope gives them a significance that dominates religious thought and writing in America into the 1760s.

The diffuse and eclectic aspects of midcentury revivalism should not be ignored but neither should the cohesive impact of singular, affecting preachers like Jonathan Edwards among New England Congregationalists in the 1730s and 1740s, Gilbert Tennent among the Presbyterians of the middle colonies in the same decades, Samuel Davies among the Presbyterians of Virginia in the 1750s, and, above all, the English Methodist itinerant George Whitefield, who tours the colonies seven times between 1740 and his death in 1770. Their appeal is unprecedented in colonial life. Edwards counts thirty-two towns caught up in the Connecticut River Valley revival of 1734–5. Whitefield preaches in 1740 to fifteen thousand people in Boston, the largest crowd ever assembled there. Moreover, the scope of these appeals, their ability to reach across all cultural boundaries, thrives upon each preacher's recognition of broad social disjuncture.

The common thread in all prerevolutionary revivalism is its insistence upon crisis. Revivalist preachers do not have to look far to arouse the vulnerabilities of their congregations. Invasion from the wilderness remains a realistic fear in the middle third of the eighteenth century, a fear realized in the French and Indian Wars (1754–60). "The arrows of death fly unseen at noon-day," runs a characteristic warning in Edwards's *Sinners in the Hands of an Angry God* (1741). The late 1730s and 1740s are also times of enormous demographic dislocation (the colonial population moves often and rises from under three hundred thousand in 1700 to more than two million by 1770), of severe economic recession (Americans fall to their lowest standard of living in the century in 1745), and of epidemiological disaster (the diphtheria outbreak of 1735–7 alone kills as many as twenty thousand Americans; epidemics of various kinds regularly destroy between 5 and 10 percent of the population). By the same token, metaphors of communal breakdown, of rampant materialism, and of sickness dominate revivalist narratives.

One consequence is that prerevolutionary Americans already accept crisis as their accustomed frame of experience. Psychologically, they also look toward the revivalist's remedy: a dramatic change in status or conversion that separates sin and corruption from virtue and purity. Samuel Finley, a follower of Gilbert Tennent in the middle colonies, shows the way in *Christ Triumphing and Satan Raging* (1741) when he teaches his adherents how to "discern the Signs of THESE TIMES." "Why do you not either make the Tree good, and its Fruit good; or else corrupt, and its Fruit corrupt?" he asks. The true

Christian must make a choice for purity on the spot. "I tell you further," exhorts Finley, "that *the Sin against the Holy Ghost shall never be forgiven*. And I verily fear, that many, both Ministers and People, in this Generation, will be guilty of it. . . . tho' you be exalted nearer Heaven, yet woe to you, for with a more dreadful Vengeance will you be plung'd deeper into Hell."

The struggling Christian has but one comfort in this moment of extremities, but it is one filled with later social and political implications. The necessity for an immediate choice between heaven and hell is suddenly communal in its stress upon the present moment. For unlike most earlier forms of Christian exhortation, revivalism provides the assurance that no decision need ever be made alone. Its thrust toward immediate conversion within the listening group is one more sign of the desirable possibilities in union and, beyond, of a far more glorious opportunity for all.

Admonition works because it represents possibilities in the sinner's predicament, and these possibilities are immense in the fullest understanding of crisis. Revivalist writings frequently make the point that critical times are the best evidence of God's presence and coming glory. "Man's Extremity is the Lord's Opportunity," writes Samuel Davies, giving most succinct expression to the concept in *The State of Religion among the Protestant Dissenters in Virginia* (1751). Or, to take Jonathan Edwards' more complete formulation: "When [God] is about to bestow some great blessing on his church, it is often his manner, in the first place, so to order things in his providence, as to show his church their great need of it, and to bring them into distress for want of it, and so put them upon crying earnestly to him for it."

Here, in the single most influential statement on the subject, *Some Thoughts Concerning the Present Revival of Religion in New England* (1742), Edwards displays how extremity and opportunity could cohere in an explicit vision of America. Revivalism is nothing less than "a strange revolution, an unexpected, surprising overturning of things, suddenly brought to pass." Surprise, in this sense, relates directly to the "innumerable difficulties" that bring "God's dear children into great distress." The presence of distress "gives more abundant reason to hope that what is now seen in America, and especially in New England, may prove the dawn of that glorious day." *Some Thoughts Concerning the Revival* depends upon an involved antipodal reading to prove that the millennium – "when the saints shall reign on earth" – must begin in America instead of in the Old World. "When God is about to turn the earth into a Paradise," Edwards reckons, "he does not begin his work where there is some good growth already, but in a wilderness. . . . he will begin in this utmost, meanest, youngest and weakest part of it, where the church of God has been planted last of all."

Millennialist optimism, the projections of Christ's thousand-year reign on earth, pushes revivalism inexorably toward the notion of harmony and union in this world and, for that purpose, toward the need for conviction and action by a united people. *Some Thoughts Concerning the Revival* calls for "an agreement of all God's people in *America . . .* to keep a day of fasting and prayer; wherein we should all unite on the same day." By making "the union and agreement of God's people in his worship the more visible," a united America encourages God to "bow the heavens and come down, and erect his glorious kingdom through the earth." Edwards is hardly alone in these hopes. From the beginning of the century to the end, rhetoric about the future of America is about how and when heaven and earth will come together.

Five years later, in *An Humble Attempt to Promote Explicit Agreement and Visible Union of God's People,* Edwards gives further scope to a philosophical conception of union that comes out of crisis. Of England, he observes, "it looks as though the nation could hardly continue in being, but must sink under the weight of its own corruption and wickedness." Only by reiterating that "the church's extremity has often been God's opportunity," can Edwards believe "a happy change is nigh." In particular, the "remarkable religious awakenings" beginning in New England and continuing elsewhere give Edwards hope for an *"explicit agreement,* to unite in such prayer as is proposed to us." The peroration that follows will resonate in the American psyche for decades to come: "Union is one of the most amiable things that pertains to human society; yea, it is one of the most beautiful and happy things on earth, which indeed makes earth most like heaven." This "strange revolution" of Edwardsian revivalism, happiness out of distress, will be familiar enough in the Revolution proper. Actual separation from England will depend heavily on a glorious kingdom, the visible union of a godly people.

The millennialist preoccupations of revivalism also answer a central dilemma in Protestant communal life. The intolerable discrepancy between God's elect and other souls, all destined for eternal damnation, disappears in postmillennial society. Joseph Bellamy, Jonathan Edwards's most influential student, illustrates the point perfectly in a sermon on the subject that achieves an immense and lasting popularity in late-eighteenth-century circles. *The Millennium* (1758) takes as its text Revelation 20:1–3, the Angel of Heaven chaining Satan in the bottomless pit for a thousand years. Its theme is how Christ's subsequent reign on earth will change the nature and meaning of history. Conceivably, since "the glorious day is coming on," history itself may already have begun to change!

All things are suddenly possible in 1758. The incredulous question from Isaiah 66:8 ("shall a nation be born at once?") becomes a glorious statement of fact in Bellamy's hands ("a nation shall be born in a day"). The technical portions of *The Millennium,* an exhaustive typological determination of the fall of Antichrist, build slowly toward Bellamy's joy in the new dispensation. And this joy includes the inference that "the greater part of mankind may be saved." *"Many are called and few are chosen;"* Bellamy agrees, "yet it does not hence follow, that this will be the case when *a nation shall be born in a day,* and *all the people shall be righteous. . . .* it shall be quite otherwise, when *satan is bound."* Psychologically irresistible, the prospect inspires elaborate description. *The Millennium* dwells longingly on the demographics of prosperity to come: "let that universal peace and prosperity take place, which indeed will naturally result from the sincere practice of pure christianity, and mankind will naturally increase, and spread, and fill all the earth."

One does not have to be a convert to respond to this brand of talk. Bellamy's faith in a different history does not sound that different from Jefferson's. Glory out of crisis, optimism from revolutionary change, corruption in Europe, deliverance through America, the value placed on union, the miracle of sudden nationality, and the saving rewards of natural prosperity — all of these concepts transpose easily to the political debates of the 1760s and 1770s. The shift in the whole circumstance of the articulation of ideas is one more proof of the separate vitality of language in transmission. Grounded in the hope of personal salvation, the rhetoric of revivalism flatters all Americans in its cohesive approach to that end, and large numbers of colonists seem to have taken the surface of that appeal into political notions of communal identity. Salvation, the original source of that rhetoric, thus enters into a sense of general well-being that all citizens share irrespective of their religious state of mind or preference. One outcome is the widest diffusion of a rhetorical emphasis arising from the specificity of religious anxiety. (Revivalism, it should be remembered, fills a dominant role in only half of the colonies, albeit in those most active early in the Revolution — Virginia, Rhode Island, Pennsylvania, New Jersey, Connecticut, and Massachusetts.)

Two literary circumstances further magnify the impact of revivalist thought. First, by the 1770s, the available writings of figures like Edwards, Tennent, Bellamy, Davies, and Finley are known to the intellectual elite of every colony. That in itself supplies a cultural setting in which appreciation and use carry beyond the originating conditions of belief. Second, these same writings stimulate their own controversies and contention in colonial life. In one of the consummate ironies of the period, the revivalist quest for awakening and union actually causes more acrimony and division than any other phenomenon of the times. Certain tensions are intrinsic. The inroads of itinerant preaching create inevitable problems for local ministers, and these problems become acute when the concept of awakening rejects the status quo ante. It is the zeal of revivalism that then exacerbates tensions by publicizing them in both pulpit and print.

Gilbert Tennent leads the attack, establishing himself as the unquestioned leader of revivalism in the middle colonies. In the most notorious sermon of the period, *The Danger of an Unconverted Ministry* (1740), he proposes that "an ungodly Ministry is a great Curse and Judgment." Those ministers who resist the revival are likened to the biblical Pharisees; "as it was of old, so it is now." They resemble each other "as one Crow's Egg does another." "Now, what Savour have Pharisee Ministers?" asks Tennent. "In Truth, a very stinking One, both in the Nostrils of God and good men." Among other things, "they have not the Courage, or Honesty to thrust the Nail of Terror into sleeping Souls." His condemnations lead Tennent to strike at the source of conventional ministerial learning, the existing seminaries, and he also challenges the authority of established ministers through their congregations. "Let all the Followers of the Lamb stand up and act for *GOD* against all Opposers," commands Tennent, and, he then asks, "Who is upon *GOD's* Side? Who?"

Such preaching – the established clergy responds in kind – divides congregations and entire communities. "New Side" and "Old Side" factions exist in the middle colonies by 1741; "Old Lights" and "New Lights" formally separate in New England a year after. At the highest level, conflict leads to impressive exchanges on theological issues, as in Jonathan Edwards's *Some Thoughts Concerning the Present Revival* (1742) against Charles Chauncy's *Seasonable Thoughts on the State of Religion in New England* (1743). At the lowest, it brings new extremes of vituperation to American religion and American life generally. Take, for instance, the conservative minister Timothy Cutler's description of Tennent touring Boston in early 1741: "people wallowed in the snow for the benefit of his beastly brayings."

Conflict over revivalism changes the whole nature of religious thought in eighteenth-century America. The actual terms of debate are quickly summarized: the philosophical basis of the conversion experience (with more specific questions about the respective roles of reason and the affections in achieving religious conviction), the status of itinerant preaching, and the education and role of the clergy. In the heat of exchange, each of these debates shifts attention from the holiness of God's strictures toward problems in individual and communal behavior and from the mystery of Providence to assertions about human capacity.

The result is a curious paradox in the history of ideas. For if revivalism recovers a vital piety, it simultaneously carries religious thought toward a more human dimension. As revitalization assures the continuing power of religion in American thought, so a growing humanism furnishes more and more common ground for the mix of theology and Enlightenment ideology. "Our people do not so much need to have their heads stored, as to have their hearts touched," writes Edwards of revitalization in *Some Thoughts Concerning the Present Revival.* Counters Chauncy in *Seasonable Thoughts on the State of Religion.* "[T]he plain Truth is, an *enlightened Mind,* and not *raised Affections,* ought always to be the Guide of those who call themselves Men; and this, in the Affairs of Religion, as well as other Things." Bridging these differences philosophically is difficult; making rhetorical use of every possibility is not. The debate over revivalism frees American writers to blend the rational and emotional appeals available to them in the mix of religion, politics, and communal life.

Elisha Williams establishes the political potency of combining these appeals as early as 1744. A tutor and the rector of Yale College and then a judge of the superior court of Connecticut, Williams writes *The Essential Rights and Liberties of Protestants* to oppose restrictions on itineracy during revivalism. His essay traces "the Rights of *Conscience and private Judgment* in Matters of *Religion*" through biblical, legal, and philosophical traditions, verifying that in each tradition these rights "are unalterably the same." Conflating civil and religious liberty, Williams ascertains that both are "inherent," "natural and unalienable." Nevertheless, "bigotted Clergy, and arbitrary weak or popish Princes" occasionally decide otherwise. *The Essential Rights and Liberties of Protestants* already asks the crucial question in 1744. What can be done about it? What should be the response when civil authority attempts to alienate a natural right?

The answer is a step in the articulation of colonial liberties. Since the English Enlightenment, by way of John Locke and the Glorious Revolution, has confirmed that "the Rights of *Magna Charta* depend not on the Will of the Prince, or the Will of the Legislature," the same must be true of religious liberty, "a Priviledge more valuable than the civil Rights of *Magna Charta.*" Freedom of worship is, therefore, "without controul from human Laws," a right that "no Man can touch and be innocent." Conversely, to challenge religious liberty is to be absolutely guilty. There is room to blame even a king in this language.

Elisha Williams strengthens the cause of civil opposition by joining Enlightenment conceptions of law to a religious frame of reference. He does so in part because of his belief in the need for a stronger oppositional stance. Like so many other colonial writers, he fears "that Christian *Liberty,* as well as Civil, has been lost little by little." "So precious a *Jewel* is always to be watched with a careful eye; no People are likely to enjoy Liberty long," he concludes, "that are not zealous to preserve it." The mixed modes of Williams's conclusion – "a careful eye" and "zeal" in the name of liberty – develop into watchwords in later colonial discourse; they already express the tensions in revivalism. The same tensions help to make liberty an ever-pressing theme.

The religious contentions at midcentury recharge the antiauthoritarianism in American Protestanism. To fully comprehend the development one
must recognize the changing role of the clergy. Colonial ministers are
originally unrivaled cultural intermediaries in their villages and towns.
They represent unquestioned leadership and hold social and political power
far beyond their official functions. But at midcentury clerical factionalism
over revivalism erodes that status and more. When Gilbert Tennant asks
"Who is upon *GOD's* Side?" the question strikes at the authority of specific
ministerial opponents, and it also raises a previously unthinkable presumption about communal leadership in general. Suddenly, answers are conceivable that place Providence in the mass rather than in the hierarchy of civil
society.

That presumption feeds on the continuing acrimony over clerical authority. Somewhere between the extremes of the rationalist Jonathan Mayhew,
arguing in 1748 for the ascendency of a trained clergy (*The Right and Duty of
Private Judgment*), and the Baptist Isaac Backus, arguing in 1768 against
"pretended knowledge" and for the right of the people to judge religious
matters for themselves (*A Fish Caught in His Own Net*), Americans have
entered a democratic continuum that will occupy them indefinitely through
many a twist and turn. In the most significant of these transmutations, the
people themselves become the unit of meaning in religious debate.

The changing balance between clerical authority and the people's right to
choose for themselves is particularly momentous for the disenfranchised.
Anne Hutchinson's desire to instruct her Massachusetts Bay neighbors in
1636 cannot rest on their need for that instruction. By 1767, in the revivals
of Newport, Rhode Island, Sarah Osborn answers successfully with just this
argument. "I am rather as a Servant that Has a Great work assigned Him,"
she writes the Reverend Joseph Fish on March 7, 1767, after he has criticized
the prayer meetings in her home. Osborn, a housewife and schoolteacher,
resists the authority of her minister by making herself a servant of both God
and the people. The gatherings in her home are "a Sweet Sementing bond of
union that Holds us together in this critical day." Against the accusation that
she seeks "to fill a Larger sphere," Osborn even dares to pun on her minister's
name: "Dont think me obstinate then Sir if I dont know How to Let Go these
shoals of fish." Surrounding everything she writes is Osborn's excitement
about the changing world that revivalism means: "O that the Lord of the
Harvest may send forth Labourers into His Harvest and crown their Labours
with success." The tone, so in keeping with the climate of the times and her
own immediate needs, is one that no minister can safely reject.

A divided clergy, the people's growing capacity to resist both sides, the
sheer variety of religious practice, and the ideological basis of evangelical

impulses generate an assumption of freedom in religious affairs that will gradually configure similar feelings in politics. As the promise of heaven expands in millennialist thinking, so does a certain democratic right of people to be saved therein on their own terms. At the end of the century, Judith Sargent Murray will demonstrate the full ideological potential of this promise in her essay "On the Equality of the Sexes" (1790). "Is it reasonable," she asks, "that a candidate for immortality, for the joys of heaven, an intelligent being, who is to spend an eternity in contemplating the works of Deity, should . . . be allowed no other ideas, than those which are suggested by the mechanism of a pudding, or the sewing of the seams of a garnet?"

Revivalist controversies over ministerial education have consequences that are more immediate but just as unexpected by those in religious authority. New Lights found the College of New Jersey, soon to be Princeton University, in 1746. The Anglicans respond with King's College, later Columbia University, in 1754. In 1764 Baptists establish the beginnings of Brown University. Dutch New Light clergy erect Queen's College, later Rutgers University, in 1766. Ebenezer Wheelock is a New Light minister when he begins the plans for Dartmouth College in 1769. But although the impetus for all of these colleges is a seminary that will educate a doctrinally appropriate ministry, the outcome is far different.

Religious enthusiasm sparks but it does not control these educational enterprises. Enforced religious toleration and the realities of institutional growth push each college beyond its sectarian base. Each, without losing sight of its religious origins, becomes a center of general Enlightenment thought. The transition is constitutive; to be a faculty member in the third quarter of the eighteenth century means to combine religious and Enlightenment thought for the instruction of a colonial elite. Pupils like James Madison, Aaron Burr, and Hugh Henry Brackenridge of the College of New Jersey or Alexander Hamilton of King's College prove expert in their own manipulations of the combination for political purposes.

The overall spirit and contentiousness of revivalism make it an intellectual catalyst of the age and continuing source of cultural formation. In political terms that are also literary, the notion of "awakening" establishes a recognizable rhetorical stance for expressing and maintaining vigilance. Prudence and fervor, distress before joy, fear next to hope, reason within enthusiasm are some of its mixed tones. Americans at midcentury accept the appropriateness of these swings in mood and wield them to articulate communal ambivalences and anxieties. Although they wish for the unified liberty that true awakening will bring and speak of it in providential terms, they counter the very prospect (and all centralization) with other individuating principles, namely, with liberty of conscience and purification through separatism. The denominational politics of the times are full of the frustration of agreeing to disagree within a sustaining vision of higher union.

The literary work that comes closest to expressing these tensions and frustrations is Ezra Stiles's *A Discourse on the Christian Union* (1760). There may be no more prescient document of colonial confederation. Notwithstanding his conservative background as an Old Light Congregational minister, Stiles talks the language of revivalism in his zeal for pure and undefiled religion, in his stress upon the errand into America, and, above all, in his desire for "universal protestant liberty and communion." Like the revivalists, he preaches that all will "harmoniously unite in carrying on and perfecting the one same great and noble work" and that "all-prevailing TRUTH will terminate the whole in universal harmony." But there is this difference: Stiles wants union as much as he wants orthodoxy, and he espouses expediency to get it. He acknowledges the difficulties in projected union mostly to minimize them. Yet, "it is the congregation in its parochial congregational capacity that the law considers." Yes, there are a variety of sects in temporary collision. Yes, everyone must protect the unalienable right of private judgment in religion. Still, union must be made to thrive within these distinctions. "If we have any public benevolence," pleads Stiles, "any tender affection for pure and undefiled religion – by the tender mercies of Jehovah! by the love of Jesus! – let us bury and lay aside our trifling differences."

The telling analogy in *A Discourse on the Christian Union* is to the colonies themselves. Just as American churches are "distinct, ecclesiastical sovereignties, in point of power and controul. . . . So the thirteen provinces on this continent subsist independent of one another as to jurisdiction and controul over one another – yet in harmony." Stiles posits the equality and independence of churches (and colonies) as "the essential basis of the general union and confederacy." The analogy holds because "the same principles may take place in confederating a multitude of lesser bodies, as in confederating larger bodies, such as provinces, cantons, kingdoms." Stiles wants nothing to hinder "the purpose of cementing us together into a respectable body," and, to insure as much, he carefully balances parts to whole in his theory of union. The ensuing plan – "one general confederacy and public union, reserving to each part its power, liberty and proportionate influence in the mighty whole" – epitomizes American thought from colony to early Republic.

Stiles can complete this vision only by bringing religious and Enlightenment frames of reference together. He is painfully aware that religion alone has not brought harmony in revivalist America. *A Discourse on the Christian Union* expresses the hope that recent changes "made among mankind by science and letters" will keep future conflicts from dividing sects and colonies. In this way, the disputes of well-meaning Christians will give way to the benevolence of truth, and "the spirit of alienation will more and more subside." Not just faith but faith in knowledge prevails in Stiles's version of the millennium. "Such is human nature, especially enlightened with the pure light of revelation and sciences."

Whatever their differences, revivalism and the Enlightenment do meet in the colonial intellectual's favorite metaphor of light brought out of darkness. The conjunction protects the American colonies in their typological significance as a chosen people (Deuteronomy 26–8). Stiles finishes A Discourse on the Christian Union by distinguishing America from "the ruin of the Hebrew republic" under the wisest of the Jewish kings, Solomon. "We may then reap great advantage in consulting and duly applying that history, which may be in some measure typical of our own." He trusts that the corruption in Solomon's court will not repeat in a more enlightened age, though a warning remains for English subjects on both sides of the Atlantic to heed — "so fatal is the ill example of princes."

The success of Ezra Stiles's immediate plan for American Congregationalism conveys the larger relevance of his ideas. His call for a confederacy of American dissenters leads to an intercolonial organization of Congregational and Presybterian churches that meets annually, either in New Jersey or in Connecticut, between 1766 and 1775. In any given year, these so-called "congresses" have delegates from six or more of the colonies. They receive support from local Presbyterian "committees of correspondence," and their unifying theme is opposition to the spread of British episcopacy. Here are the prototypical organizational structures that will conduct many of the political acts of the Revolution. The movement from denominational politics to colonial resistance is less of a shift than it is an interaction.

Stiles, a moderate whig and president of Yale in the 1770s, writes better than he knows in 1760. The conciliatory tones of A Discourse on the Christian Union attest to a powerful colonial yearning for language that will at once individualize and unify, fulfill and purify. Stiles even lives to reformulate this paradoxical yearning in republican guise. In The Future Glory of the United States, written in 1783, the year the Treaty of Paris ratifies American independence, he reinvokes the millennial possibilities of "every man's reaping the fruits of his labor and feeling his share in the aggregate system of power." But, even as he is writing, the paradoxes deepen between reaping and sharing, between fulfillment and purification, between the Enlightenment and revivalism. "We are ardently pursuing this world's riches, honors, powers, pleasures"; observes Stiles in an amalgam of triumph and remonstrance, "[L]et us possess them, and then know that they are nothing, nothing, nothing."

Progress on these terms, living in the world with weaned affections, borrows from Puritanism and lives in revivalism, but it will not survive even Stiles's death in 1795. Nineteenth-century Americans will pursue "this world's riches" in the name of property, an unqualified possession. Prosperity will mean everything to them, in what has often been termed the Protestant Ethic, and Stiles will have shown them the way. By and large, the unknown cost of success will be more superficial success. The same appropriation of revivalism into Enlightenment thought that supplies a more amiable, inclusive theory of union necessarily qualifies reformist fervor. In the transformation of ideas, the procedural energy in "ardent pursuit" stays in "this world," and the new theory of union licenses a rampant materialism in modern American life.

III

The closer we get to the Revolution, the less satisfactory the printed text becomes as a barometer of thought, and never more so than in religious expression. As radical Protestantism privileges the spoken word, so the courage of revolutionary action depends upon the immediacy of speech. With both propensities at work in what is still an oral culture, speech dominates expression in a way that is now irreclaimable. In part, too, the problem is one of lost perception. The two controlling forms of religious expression in the Revolution, the congregational utterance and the sermon, each reflect a spontaneous emphasis in American religion; the decorums and reactive power of the independent or separate congregation meet the pivotal role of the preaching minister. Obviously, the revolutionary sermon survives in publication, though in fractional numbers and debased form. The congregational utterance, on the other hand, is a forgotten mode of expression. The most conventional and frequent sort of revolutionary participation, it survives only in the interstices of other comments; yet there is no true understanding of the sermon without it.

The congregational or communal utterance in America flows from the underlying idea of covenant. Leaders may interpret the covenant, but only God and a chosen people can make and sustain one. While God will agree to be bound, the people must give frequent voice to their understanding of divine purposes or the covenant is broken. One such moment arrives when a new congregation stands officially before God and vows to form a church. Another comes when a congregation accepts an individual convert's evidence for membership in the community of saints. Other moments include the sacraments and the declaration of creeds. Still others stipulate days to be set aside for the acknowledgment of God's mercy in a time of trial. Thanksgiving, election, and fast day observances all render public witness. Though they feature a minister's words, their purpose is to extract a collective confirmation of faith. The first duty of a people is acceptance of God's will; the second is constant vigilance in His name, protecting the covenant against transgression.

If these duties are stringent, they are also understood to be powerfully restorative; God can do much with and for a godly people. The assumption helps to reveal how the election sermon of Abraham Williams in Boston in 1762 could equate "the *Voice of the People*" with "the *Voice of God*," or how Jonathan Mayhew, a year later in *Observations on the Charter and Conduct of the Society for the Propagation of the Gospel,* could praise the American people as "philosophers and divines in comparison of the common people in England." The same assumption indicates why Charles Chauncy, celebrating repeal of the Stamp Act in a Thanksgiving sermon from 1766, could think of colonial opposition as divinely inspired: "it was under [God's] all-wise, overruling influence that a spirit was raised in all the colonies nobly to assert their freedom as men and English-born subjects." In a quieter vein, it also justifies Quaker insistence on progress through the people. "Christ knoweth the state of the people," writes John Wollman in *Essay on the Ministry* (1772), "and in the pure feeling of the gospel ministry their states are opened to His servants."

Out of such ascriptions comes a growing sense of empowerment in the people. Nathaniel Niles, preaching in Newburyport, Massachusetts, on June 5, 1774, declares that "we should all endeavour to turn the attention of our fellow members of the community on the conduct of our rulers." A student of Joseph Bellamy, he draws an instructive analogy between soul-searching in personal salvation and vigilance in politics. Members of a congregation do not depend upon their minister for redemption, why, then, should they trust political leaders for effective government? Niles expects his listeners to take "the standard of right and wrong" and apply it themselves, and he urges them to "excite others to do so likewise." "We should endeavour on every alarming occasion," he argues, "to collect the sentiments of the body, and vigorously pursue those measures that are thought the most salutary for the whole." By 1776, in Samuel West's election sermon, the people are deemed "the proper judges to determine when rulers are guilty of tyranny and oppression." They can be trusted because "by their conduct they have shown that they were regulated by the law of God written in their hearts."

Hearing the voice of the people is a more difficult proposition. There are echoes of congregational self-confidence in the local resolutions of mass meetings and instructions to legislators — not in the actual language so much as in the presumed right of the collectivity to give advice. Similar nuances emerge in political writings couched in the form of creeds. William Livingston's elaborate anticlerical parody of the Thirty-nine Articles of Religion, in *The*

Independent Reflector (October 11, 1753), creates notable controversy in New York when it glosses the convention of the Christian's "open Declaration of the Religion he professes." On the brink of Revolution in Boston, *The Massachusetts Spy* (January 19, 1775) issues "An English Patriot's" version of the Apostles' Creed. "I believe all political power to be derived originally from, and invested in the people," it reads, trusting in God to simultaneously advance His glory and the nation's welfare. Sympathetic readers would have imagined intonation in unison, a solemn justification of faith and inclination.

The religious voice enters revolutionary discourse by insisting that faith and liberty are inextricably intertwined. In possibly the most noteworthy rendition of the theme, *The Snare Broken* (1766), Jonathan Mayhew contrasts Slavery, "the deformed child of Satan," with Liberty, "celestial Maid, the daughter of God, and, excepting his Son, the first-born of Heaven." All distinction between faith and liberty disappears in this sermon. Mayhew's personal growth in liberty receives proper documentation through classical authors, but it is the scriptures that first teach him that " 'where the Spirit of the Lord is there is liberty.' " Mayhew's successor in the West Church of Boston, Simeon Howard, is one of many ministers to devote entire sermons to the idea that "loss of liberty is soon followed by the loss of all virtue and religion." *A Sermon Preached to the Ancient and Honorable Artillery Company in Boston* (1773) explicates a favorite biblical text of the Revolution in Galatians 5:1 ("Stand fast therefore in the liberty wherewith Christ hath made us free").

How the popular mind receives religious explanations of political liberty appears in the words of William Manning, a semiliterate Massachusetts farmer who sees "almost the first blood that was shed in Concord." Events – "scores of men dead, dying & wounded in the Cause of Libberty" – have forced Manning to evaluate "serious sencations" and to overcome a few doubts. His reminiscences, *The Key of Liberty* (c. 1794), catch the tenor and source of his ideas:

I have often thought it was imposable ever to seport a free Government, but firmly believing it to be the best sort & the ondly one approved off by heaven it was my unweryed study & prayers to the almighty for many years to find out the real cause & a remidy.

The recourse to heaven is a natural one. Manning is "not a man of Larning" and "no grate reader of antient history," but he has listened to countless sermons on the subject when "highly taken up with Liberty & a free Government." The oral transmission in pulpit oratory rules thought and pen, overcoming the awkwardness in both.

As the primary literary vehicle of the times, the sermon forms a dialectic with the people's voice and prepares more Americans for rebellion than do books and pamphlets. If four hundred pamphlets are published in America during the revolutionary era, more than eighteen hundred sermons emerge in the same period from Massachusetts and Connecticut alone, and these numbers do not begin to impart the weekly dimension of actual sermons, religious talks, and prayer meetings held in local communities across America. The sermon is the bellwether of rebellion; it records the Revolution in the piety of response to daily trouble.

The occasional or weekday sermon deserves particular consideration in this regard. It exists elsewhere, but, as the sermonic subgenre that officially combines religion and politics, it takes on heightened status and scope as a dominant art form in instances of early American conflict. Delivered on fast days, election days, thanksgiving days, ordinations, dedications, and other holidays, the occasional sermon takes communal well-being rather than personal salvation as its province. The emphasis naturally shifts with each occasion, but all of these sermons revolve around the people's covenant, and the minister accepts an assignment replete with vested cultural anxieties.

The formal constrictions on the speaker are part of the assignment. In the occasional sermon, the health and direction of society dominate as immediate and unavoidable generic concerns. Thus, when Samuel Davies preaches on the death of George II in 1760, his subject is not the king's death but rather the "strange, untried period" and "anxious contingency" that this death brings to a system where "the least irregularity or defect in the minutest spring, may disorder and weaken the whole machine." Davies takes his text from 2 Samuel 1:19 ("how are the mighty fallen!") and uses it first to arouse a proper fear. "When *the mighty is fallen*, shall not the feeble tremble?" he asks. "If the father of the people must cease to live, shall not the people expect to die?" As in most evangelical preaching, understanding comes only out of crisis.

On the Death of His Late Majesty, King George II astonishes the reader today mostly in the extent to which its formulaic considerations already dictate the terms of future debate. To be sure, Davies discusses the loyalty due once and future kings. But George II receives homage as a servant of the people ("the monarch himself frowned upon the principles of arbitrary power; and was an advocate for the liberties of the people"), whereas George III provokes fear as an unknown quantity ("the best of kings . . . may have evil counsellors, and evil counsellors may have the most mischievous influence"). Loyalty, as a virtue, connotes neither "servile artifice" nor "mercenary cringing" nor "complaisance of flattery" but "a disinterested love to our country" and "public spirit." Prophetic words follow. "This you must do," urges Davies, in a claim of loyalty, "or turn rebels against your own hearts and consciences."

The occasional sermons of the 1760s and 1770s push the same terminology into a reversal of implications as rebellion and loyalty change places. By the time of his Boston election day sermon in 1776, Samuel West will have proven that only God deserves full submission and that, therefore, all unquestioned authority in this world is "slavish" and "proof of a very sordid and base mind." Now the previous metaphors for limiting authority begin to disestablish it. If magistrates are really "the servants of the people," then, "in the common affairs of life," they can be replaced or dismissed as a master would any servant. For Nathaniel Niles in *Two Discourses on Liberty* (1774), public spirit is still the source of political order and virtue, but, because the source of public spirit is liberty, it always distinguishes between government and tyranny. Accordingly, "he who infringes on liberty rebels against good government, and ought to be treated as a rebel." "It matters not what station he fills; he is a traitor" reasons Niles. Instead of conveying the presumption of obedience when there is turmoil, official position now suggests the possibility of crime compounded. "He that fills an elevated station is proportionably more criminal in the same rebellion, than those in a lower state."

These rhetorical shifts, multiplied a thousand times in other sermons, cast a different light on the blemish of rebellion. The Reverend John Cleaveland of Ipswich carries them to their logical conclusion when he consigns Thomas Gage, general of the British armies, straight to hell in the *Essex Gazette* (July 13, 1775). "An aggravated damnation" applies in this case even though, officially, General Gage represents the king. As Cleaveland puts the matter directly to Gage, "[Y]ou are not only a robber, a murderer, and usurper, but a wicked Rebel: a rebel against the authority of truth, law, equity, the English constitution of government, these colony states, and humanity itself." The British commander, in sum, qualifies as one of those evil counselors who mislead a king in Samuel Davies's original nightmare. Iconographically, Gage dons the mantle of disgrace that Americans cannot tolerate on themselves, that of rebel and traitor.

Inevitably, the occasional sermon spiritualizes the theme of loyalty and rebellion as one of its charges. The proclivities are everywhere apparent in these texts: Davies's conception of loyalty in 1760 "will qualify you for both worlds"; Niles, in 1774, joins civil and spiritual liberty as body to soul and makes both together "the loan of heaven"; West's combinations of scripture and right reason, revelation and common sense, clarify the duty of obedience in 1776. Under all of these elements is a link between the Christian's doubt and the rebel's uncertainty, one that allows for a powerful similitude in responses. Superficially, the parallel means that religious sources can easily enter into a political frame of reference. "If salvation has not come from our gracious sovereign King George, we cannot expect it from the hills," Niles observes wryly. "We must look still higher." West, in turn, makes St. Paul "a strong advocate for the just rights of mankind." The special power of the occasional sermon comes from the integrity that the form itself assigns to these parallels. God holds all of the answers and offers the history of redemption to those who would decipher the present, but responses in His name must also meet the immediacy of colonial unhappiness and bewilderment. The occasional sermon serves that purpose by filtering emotional dislocation through the context of event. Generically, it tells the people how to feel and what to do in the moment.

Two Discourses on Liberty illustrates the strategy perfectly. In a Massachusetts pulpit right after the British close the port of Boston, Nathaniel Niles does not hesitate to ask the questions on everyone's mind. "What shall we do? Shall we renounce the authority of our gracious sovereign? Shall we take up arms against his troops? What shall we do?" Reiteration captures something of the helplessness and uncertainty of colonial reactions in 1774 – feelings subsequently obscured by the brag and bounce of patriotic oratory. Of course, helplessness and uncertainty are familiar impulses among the unworthy supplicants of God's grace. Niles makes the connection, and the appropriate response is also the same. "Such is the kindness of our God," Niles explains, "that, humanly speaking, it is in the power of America to save both herself and Great-Britain. . . . let us remember, that the effectual fervent prayers of the righteous avail much." Exactly how Americans are to pray opens a path toward renewed efficacy: "let us all, like Daniel of old, piously pour out our hearts before God, acknowledging our own sins, and those of our people."

Although zeal against sinfulness dominates all radical Protestant sermonology, the occasional sermon sharpens that recourse by stressing the original purity in the social covenant. God will reward or punish a covenanted group; so much more is to be gained from collective piety or to be lost in communal sinfulness. As Samuel West expresses the idea: "our cause is so just and good that nothing can prevent our success but only our sins. Could I see a spirit of repentance and reformation prevail through the land, I should not have the least apprehension." Everywhere in the occasional sermon, fear and uncertainty signal an underlying sinfulness. Niles's own version of colonial difficulties compares American uneasiness to that of the prodigal son (Luke 5:16). Unfortunately, the prodigal's specific answer is fraught with a difficult ambiguity in the American crisis. "Let us return to our father's house," he advises. But which house and which father?

The story of the eighteenth-century occasional sermon is in part about this search for proper patriarchy. Do Americans find solace in colony and king?

"George was our Father, too," Samuel Davies reminds the British in 1760. Niles still values that veneration in 1774: "let the world see that their king is dearer to the Americans than their blood." Or do Americans rely instead on a parent closer to home? "Let us learn to live in the plain manner of our fore-fathers," Niles advises in almost the same breath, associating American ancestry with purity and liberty. Simeon Howard indicates the distance to be covered when he preaches before the Boston Artillery Company in 1773: "British America, especially the northern part of it, is by its situation calcu-lated to be a nursery of heroes."

Of the occasional sermons, the annual election day sermon is the most significant for revolutionary politics and is the least accessible today. Lost is all sense of its original reception. The colonial minister who delivers an election sermon speaks before the assembled magistrates of the province in a ritual of renewal and affirmation. He is God's chosen representative as well as the designed spokesman of the community, and his words are published for all to examine. The surviving record is itself an indication of assumed merit and general dissemination. Of the two hundred twenty-two election sermons delivered in Connecticut, Massachusetts, Vermont, and New Hampshire between 1750 and 1820, two hundred and eleven appear in print, a number in multiple editions.

Reading these sermons today, a twentieth-century eye sees derivative Whig theory garnished with biblical typology, but *listening* to them, with an ear for eighteenth-century expectations, reveals a striking creativity – especially in the election sermons delivered right before the Revolution. As God's represen-tation and as his community's spokesman, the election day minister of the 1770s occupies a unique position for testing both the nature of British rule and the resolve of an American people. Realizing their position also seems to have brought out the best in these preachers. We glimpse in them a disruptive power in speech that does not belong to print. The belief required for indepen-dence literally is born in these sermons.

Gad Hitchcock, pastor of Pembroke Church in Boston, is just such a figure as he delivers the Massachusetts election sermon for 1774. General Thomas Gage, the new military governor, recently arrived from England with shiploads of British troops, is Hitchcock's nominal host. Indeed, many of Gage's supporters walk out in the middle of Hitchcock's performance – enough for the Yankee minister to quip that he preached a moving sermon. What causes this degree of offense? On the surface, Hitchcock's sermon is the usual explanation of constitutional theory in government with appropriate injunctions to colonial rulers as the trustees of society. Where Hitchcock deviates is in his creative use of the rhythms, prerogatives, and expectations of the genre. The election sermon conventionally seeks renewal and social affirmation, but Hitchcock breaks the form. He steadfastly refuses to rise above the sorrows of his people.

The biblical text of Hitchcock's sermon immediately ranges the people both for and against authority: "When the righteous are in authority, the people rejoice: but when the wicked beareth rule, the people mourn" (Proverbs 29:2). The standard triadic plan of the sermon – doctrine, reason, uses (text, explication, application) – then dramatizes the contrasting possibilities in biblical times and in the American present. Gage and his retinue could not have liked Hitchcock's opening description of "Hebrew polity," a disintegration into monarchy under the sons of Samuel with "prevailing wickedness, and corruption among some in high station." The rhetorical foreshadowing of ills in America would have been clear without Hitchcock's direct claim of parallelism; "we need not pass the limits of our own nation for sad instances of this." The tone of sadness is crucial in understanding the speaker's performance. Just as Hitchcock's opponents cannot quarrel with scripture, so they find themselves disarmed by the melancholy premise of the people mourning under evil leaders. Claims of evil are not made by Hitchcock in 1774, but he does insist over and over again on the corollary. "It is, however, certain that the people mourn!" Would they not rejoice if authority were righteous?

The goal of righteousness enhances the election day opportunity. Invited to give "counsel of God in respect to the great affairs of this anniversary, and the general conduct of government," Hitchcock uses this leverage to confront the executive officers before him. "Our danger is not visionary, but real – Our contention is not about trifles, but about liberty and property." For those who would scoff, he adds "if I am mistaken in supposing plans are formed . . . incompatible with every idea of liberty, all America is mistaken with me." Alluding next to America's "well known loyalty," Hitchcock respectfully but firmly demands "a redress of our grievances." A truly righteous authority will respond sympathetically. "Suffer me to remind you," Hitchcock admonishes Gage and the assembled officers of state, "that you act for God, and under his inspection . . . you must one day give an account to Him whose eyes are as a flame of fire, of the motives of your conduct."

The minister expresses hope for reconciliation but prepares for conflict, and his sermon raises the theoretical prospect – perhaps the necessity – of formal opposition. Only by responding to resistance, Hitchcock speculates, will the worst leaders "learn to do that out of interest, which the best constantly do out of a good principle and true love to their subjects." Certainly, the alternative, "public misery and slavery," embodies "a state of affairs infinitely worse than that of public disturbance." Once again, the theoretical and ceremonial frames of the sermon allow a clergyman to say more to British authority, face-to-face, than a mere political figure ever could.

Gad Hitchcock stretches that license to the limit in the uses of his sermon. Asking the assembled rulers "to apply the subject," he announces that "the united voice of America, with the solemnity of thunder and with accents piercing as the lightning awakes your attention, and demands fidelity." This united voice, all America, takes the first-person, plural pronominal form in Hitchcock's peroration, and it sends a final challenge to General Gage, the British governor who carries orders for disciplining the colonies. Gage must recognize the inevitable limits of colonial cooperation. While Americans revere civil government and love peace and order, they will not part with their rights and privileges. "The soil we tread on is our own, the heritage of our Fathers." An encompassing benediction will soften the exclusivity and independence of this assertion, but not before both tendencies are underscored. "We have therefore an exclusive right to it," Hitchock warns the threatening interloper.

Ministers accurately take the pulse of American anxieties in the 1770s, and, as those anxieties grow, the clergy effectively removes middle ground by reminding the faithful that God will hold everyone to a strict accounting. "If the foundations be destroyed," asks Hitchcock, "what can the righteous do?" The force of that question leads inexorably to another. If the choice be between tyranny and resistance, what then? In Hitchcock's words, "which of the two shall we chuse, for the sake of the happy effects and consequences of it?" The dynamics of the election sermon force the preacher and his followers to face these unpalatable questions squarely. Philosophically and temperamentally, the minister assumes the task of crafting answers consonant with belief. If those answers stress prudence, they are nonetheless increasingly blunt. "With respect therefore to rulers of evil dispositions," Hitchcock declares in 1774, "nothing is more necessary than that they should believe resistance, in some cases to be lawful."

Two things must happen for most Americans to choose resistance: they must believe in their solidarity, and they must believe in the rectitude of their stance in opposition. To a remarkable extent, these difficulties are questions of literary expression in the hands of the clergy. Ministers define the parameters of belief in early America, and performances like Hitchcock's incorporate "the united voice of America" and "the doctrine of resistance." Radical Whigs will need little more than British intransigence to turn these beliefs into revolutionary actions. Arguably, the clergy instills revolutionary conviction too quickly and thoroughly for its own good. Thomas Paine orchestrates "a new method of thinking" in 1776, one in which rebellion comprises "the glorious union of all things." These appropriations of evangelical language, while obvious, are already divorced from their original context. Paine insists upon it. The second edition of *Common Sense* ends with the wish that "mingling religion with politics, *may be disavowed and reprobated by every inhabitant of* AMERICA."

IV

Something vital disappears from revolutionary sermonizing once battle lines have been drawn, though it is not easy to identify the strict nature of the loss. The conviction of the people and ministerial zeal remain in place. If anything, these elements increase through the activity and success of the Revolution. They double again in the rampant revivalism of the early Republic, when, amidst broad social dislocation, evangelical preaching dominates the culture as never before. Does religious expression lose its communal thrust? Not really. Historians have demonstrated the central role of evangelical activity as a building block in emerging communities and, more generally, as one of the unifying elements in early national life. In the 1790s and after, the Second Great Awakening will turn much of America into a revivalist society. What does vanish, and very quickly, is the ministry's proprietary hold over a national covenant.

Independence reduces the occasional sermon as a major intellectual event. The preacher's most dramatic literary tool, the use of biblical typology in formulating the hypothetical case for resistance, also loses its exclusive edge. Rather than adroit rhetorical foreshadowing, the new states now need straightforward political confirmations, skills more attuned to secular oratory and governmental office. Ironically, war with England also removes the ministerial elite from the front lines; firsthand confrontation no longer colors the possibilities in the election day ceremony. Where a minister's performance once took shape in the crucible of conflict (a royal governor and his often recalcitrant legislature as one audience), it now enters upon a broad field of ideological consensus. The pressure on language is simply not the same. Finally, the doctrine of separation of church and state enters a radical new phase in 1776: where it previously signifies toleration and the discouragement of any denomination as the religion of state, the doctrine now separates all religious and governmental action. Ministers cannot assume the role of community representative on as many political topics.

The formula of the election sermon remains intact under these new handicaps; the psychological exigencies do not. A designated minister still counsels newly elected magistrates on the nature of human happiness and on the duties of rulers in achieving that goal, and he still voices alarm over a sinful people. Gone from the language, however, is the excitement of a unique burden – a minister, not selecting but selected, rising alone to articulate the needs of a culture in crisis. Others now share that burden and will soon assume it as their exclusive right.

Documenting the diminished literary power of the political sermon is a thankless task. Phillips Payson, a Chelsea pastor who leads troops from his parish in combat, delivers a Massachusetts election sermon in 1778 that is not without appeal. Yet Payson intuitively sees that his words have missed an essential balance. "I must not forget to mention religion, both in rulers and people," he reminds himself halfway through. Railleries against the British induce another cautionary note: "it is difficult to keep the passions or the tongue within the bounds of Christian moderation." If Providence has brought Americans within sight of the promised land ("We stand this day upon Pisgah's top"), Payson submits a prosaic gauge of that prospect. "We should take mankind as they are," he tells the gathered leaders of Massachusetts, "and not as they ought to be. . . . So in our searches for truth and knowledge, and in our labors for improvement, we should keep within the ken or compass of the human mind." There is good Yankee acumen in these sentiments, but Payson's election day predecessors and their audiences would have expected more.

Success and certainty make for a less interesting story than struggle and doubt. Four years after Payson, Zabdiel Adams's election sermon of 1782 dwells heavily on what he and others dub "the rising glory of America." The Reverend Adams belongs too much to the strain of his cousin John Adams to ignore dangers, but he finds himself, like Payson, "in sight of the promised land." The outcome is another version of God's glory through worldly prosperity:

Behold her seas whitened with commerce; her capitals filled with inhabitants, and resounding with the din of industry. See her rising to independence and glory. Contemplate the respectable figure that she will one day make among the nations of the earth; behold her venerable for wisdom, for counsel and for might; flourishing in science, in agriculture and navigation, and in all the arts of peace. Figure to yourself that this your native country will ere long become the permanent seat of Liberty, the retreat of philosophers, the asylum of the oppressed, the umpire of contending nations, and, we would hope, the *glory of Christ,* by a strict attachment to his gospel, and divine institutions.

In this paean to national prosperity, religion melts into the other elements of cultural well-being as one of many strengths. The passage itself could have come from any early republican intellectual; nothing about it suggests God's designated representative.

Whether converging or clashing, the optimisms of millennialism and national prosperity do not prevent election sermons from remaining good indicators of cultural anxiety. Phillips Payson, Zabdiel Adams, and Simeon Howard, who delivers an election sermon of his own in 1780, all worry about the successful completion of the Revolution. Howard also frets over the constitutional crisis in Massachusetts as he watches the state reject one constitution and debate another. The standard formula obtains. A litany of ills (covetousness, luxury, dissipation, infidelity) produces the usual consequence ("God often brings distress and ruin upon a sinful people") and the predictable solution ("Would we but reform our evil ways . . . we might then, putting our trust in God, humbly hope that our public calamities would be soon at an end"). The arrangement, though in debased form, is still that of the Puritan jeremiad.

Originality lies in the adjustment of the formula to the pressure of events. For his part, Simeon Howard turns the jeremiad into an outline for governmental reform. The dangers of "impious, immoral men at the head of government," of "weak and illiterate men," of "double-minded men," of "indecision in council," of "ineffectual exertions," and of "doubting and wavering in the supreme authority" all loom in his appeal for a stronger constitution. So does the presumed connection between religious faith and American glory. But Howard, in a move that will become reflexive in later election sermons, now worries more about the presumed connection between personal salvation and national prosperity. There is just a touch of a new fear: secular nationalism. Heaven conspicuously "owns" the Revolution, "not merely for our own families, friends, and posterity, but for the rights of humanity, for the civil and religious privileges of mankind." Still, the "eye of Heaven" will almost certainly be elsewhere on Judgment Day. Howard wants Americans to remember that national identities are ephemeral things, a "baseless fabric" in the end.

Could it be that revolutionary zeal actually encroaches on Christian piety? Any response to this question embarrasses the American clergy in 1780. Promoting patriotism takes from the chief end of glorifying God; resisting it puts the ministry against the people in a time of war. The answer of a previous time, an uncompromising injunction against the things of this world, seems somehow less appropriate in all of the excitement about republican nationalism. The equivocation in Howard's voice is an indication of changing times and lost certainties. "Whatever others may do, and however it may fare with our country," he advises, "it shall surely be well with the righteous." The focus remains on piety, but the subjunctive mode of Howard's words — "whatever others may do," "however it may fare" — allow for an audience that does not have to choose quite so directly between salvation and worldly happiness; the commitment of revolutionary ideology is to success in both worlds.

In but not *of* the world, *in* but *no longer leading* the Revolution, ministers instinctively reach for language that will bolster their flagging intellectual ascendancy in the culture at large. Their obvious resort is to the increasingly popular terminology and thought of the Enlightenment. As the Republic flourishes, so do the propensities of ministers to speak in Enlightenment terms – particularly before prestigious election day audiences. Eighty election sermons are published in America in the last quarter of the eighteenth century, and there is no better register of the link that grows between religion and the Enlightenment. But these sermons also suggest a price to be paid. Secularization has weakened original parallels between religious and civil liberty, purification and virtue, sinfulness and civic corruption. Gone as well is the initial excitement of placing Enlightenment thought in religious discourse by pre-revolutionary intellectuals like Elisha Williams and Ezra Stiles.

The Revolution itself forces more and more attention on this world over the next. When, for instance, John Tucker's election sermon of 1771 turns the voice of reason into the voice of God, orthodoxy requires that he carefully distinguish between civil and ecclesiastical arrangements. Samuel West's own election sermon in 1776 can rely on the same wording; here, too, the voice of reason is the voice of God, but West, facing the new primacy of common sense and the immediate exigency of Revolution, blurs distinctions. Right reason and revelation seem much closer together: "whatever right reason requires as necessary to be done is as much the will and law of God as though it were enjoined us by an immediate revelation from heaven, or commanded in the sacred Scriptures." And yet no eighteenth-century minister in the mainstream can really claim that reason *is* revelation. Where in these differences does God's inscrutable will end and common sense in the world begin?

There is never a straight contest over authority in these sermons. Providence conveniently supports common sense, right reason, and natural law in all of them. Samuel Langdon's election sermon in 1775 asks "the Father of Lights" to "irradiate" the minds of colonial leaders, who, as "happy instruments," will then dispel the current gloom of events. Phillips Payson decides more conventionally in 1778 that "nature has given us the claim [of independence], and the God of nature appears to be helping us to assert and maintain it." But where exactly is God in these presentations? Metaphorically, a "Father of Lights" is somehow less imminent in human affairs then the biblical flashing eye of Judgment Day. Does God now speak mainly through the design of nature? What then of scripture?

The problem with Enlightenment thought is that it invariably leaves the formulating minister somewhere on the sidelines. The history of redemption and scripture call explicitly and peculiarly on the minister's expertise; nature, science, reason, and even common sense do not. It may be that the dictates of common sense and reason are, in Samuel West's understanding, "abundantly confirmed by the sacred Scriptures," but confirmation still leaves the believer a little too firmly in this world. The already embattled minister faces an exasperating trade-off. Using the language of fashion simultaneously attracts a wider audience and undermines the speaker's authority. Dimly down the road are other difficulties. Sooner or later, the Enlightenment fixes on perfectibilities in human history and places them over a concern for salvation. Universal meanings give way to notions of empirical completeness. The autonomy of reason controls human action. The individual becomes less a soul and more a link between generations. All of these transformations work against clergymen, the first keepers of the religious voice. Significantly, each transformation also indulges a new secular leadership in the creation of an American civil religion.

V

The problems of the clergy are the solutions of the new political elite. The leaders of the Revolution immediately use separation of church and state to exclude the ministry from active roles in the republican experiment. Between 1776 and 1796, the constitutions of seven states prohibit ministers from assuming public office (Delaware, Georgia, Kentucky, New York, North Carolina, South Carolina, and Tennessee). The general aim, as Jefferson describes it in a letter to the Danbury Baptist Association in 1802, consists in "building a wall of separation between Church and State," a goal that the architects of the Republic adhere to with single-minded purpose and resolve.

The success of the doctrine of separation only intensifies secular vigilance against the clergy. For Jefferson it amounts to an obsession. He is president in 1801 when his letter to Moses Robinson inveighs against "the dominion of the clergy, who had got a smell of union between Church and State." "My opinion is that there would never have been an infidel, if there had never been a priest," he assures Mrs. Samuel Smith in 1816. A year later, as Connecticut finally abandons its state-supported church, he applauds John Adams on one more victory against "Monkish darkness, bigotry, and abhorrence": "I join you therefore in sincere congratulations that this den of the priesthood is at length broken up, and that a protestant popedom is no longer to disgrace the American history and character." Adams responds in kind. "Do you know," he warns Jefferson, "that The General of the Jesuits and consequently all his Host have their Eyes on this Country?" This vehemence, the invective of the Enlightenment, is difficult to comprehend as a question of belief or even of religious liberty. The real contest takes place over the control of civic expression on religious subjects.

Many changes in the Revolution mandate a re-articulation of values, and the role of religion in republican life is one such change. The issue is joined in the assumption, broadly shared, that republican virtue depends on religious principle. No significant secular leader would have disagreed with Jefferson's comment in *Notes on the State of Virginia* (1784–5) that national liberties depend on "a conviction in the minds of the people that these liberties are the gift of God." In fact, the standard eighteenth-century expression of the idea comes in Washington's presidential farewell (1796). For Washington and other early republicans, religion and morality are the twin pillars of human happiness and the indispensable supports of political prosperity. Clearly, religious commentary belongs in the civic realm. But who rightfully should assume responsibility for that commentary in educating a republican citizenry, and what ends should communication have in mind? If the place of religious thought in republican foundations is assured, even crucial, the context of explanation and use is not.

The ensuing battle over the proper role and expression of religion in a virtuous republic is often shrill. Secular revolutionary leaders find their enemy not in the clergy, as such, but in the political power of revivalism. They fear religious enthusiasm at least as much as they do economic inflation and factionalism, and the surge in evangelical outpourings after the Revolution increases their apprehension. Revivalism, after all, mounts a direct and formidable challenge to a conservative intellectual elite trying to cap the Revolution. Closer to the raw power of protest and closer to communal stirrings in the western territories, it offers the clearest alternative explanation to Enlightenment discourse in postrevolutionary culture.

As a result, the fear of revivalism cuts across party lines. Adams, for one, associates "Awakenings" directly with political upheaval. He draws the link for Benjamin Waterhouse in 1815: "mankind must have a crusade, a war of reformation, a French Revolution, or Anti-Revolution to amuse them and preserve them from Ennui." Jefferson also sees the danger. "The atmosphere of our country is unquestionably charged with a threatening cloud of fanaticism," he writes Dr. Thomas Cooper in 1822, "lighter in some parts, denser in others, but too heavy in all." A second comparison is to disease. Instruction "will be the remote remedy to this fever of fanaticism." Long before, Benjamin Franklin has outlined the form that instruction must take. As he tells Mary Stevenson in 1769, "[T]hose who have Reason to regulate their Actions, have no Occasion for Enthusiasm."

The political elite assigns itself the task of directing religious expression into safe channels. The underlying struggle in this enterprise is hard to see because it also takes place between conflicting and shifting genres and on unequal terms. Spontaneity, emotionalism, and personalism suit the speech in the form of revivalist sermons, but these oral performances, by definition, do not survive their own time; the cooler, abstract, universalizing rhetoric of Enlightenment discourse conforms instead to the published work. Secular leaders make their way by following the objectifying combinations of such liberal religious figures as Ezra Stiles, but their ascendancy in the public sphere is also the technical outcome of print culture over oral culture, itself another victory of the Enlightenment.

In secular postrevolutionary discourse, as in the election sermon of the period, the voice of reason is the voice of God but with a difference. Reason does not so much join revelation in the language of the political elite; it becomes revelation. These writers can make the complete, logical transition in ways that an orthodox clergy cannot. Where ministers stumble over the Enlightenment in their efforts to sustain religious dogma, the secular leaders of the Republic easily objectify both frameworks in a language of universals. They assume that religious commentary and Enlightenment discourse come together – always the goal – but that they need not come together everywhere or in every form. Delicacy of placement is the issue and a discerning test of literary skill. Two characteristic examples, both well-known, can be used to demonstrate the complexities involved: the first, from Franklin's *Autobiography,* or memoirs, the second, from Jefferson's first inaugural address.

These efforts cannot be read as simple confrontations between frames of reference; their conscious sense of their own success depends upon a conflation of alternatives. Hence, it is still possible to argue over the question of whether Franklin borrows from Congregationalist ideas or succumbs to them. His "bold and arduous project of arriving at moral perfection" has been read as both an adaptation of the Puritan objective of sanctity and a mockery of it. Franklin seems to have welcomed every possibility. In the organization of the memoirs, he carefully locates the project of moral perfection right after a claim of solitary daily worship, "a little liturgy or form of prayer for my own private use." Even so, the overall tones of this and every other section fit the calming, encompassing, and rationalizing rhetoric of the Enlightenment.

Franklin's memoirs, the first part written in 1771, tell the story of a man who succeeds despite his mistakes. The constitutive metaphor for these mistakes is the erratum, or printer's error; the narrator corrects errors in life after they happen, much as a printer would replace a defective font of type. This device deliberately contradicts the fundamental form of autobiography in Franklin's day – that of the religious conversion narrative, which moves from feelings of inadequacy in sin and helplessness toward a single dramatic transformation or influx of divine grace. There comes a moment, however, when Franklin's anticonversion narrative rises above its tactical view of error to address the larger problem. As the narrative switches from private experience toward the public figure, Franklin pauses to summarize "the then State of my Mind," and in this summary he traces his youthful mistakes to "Want of Religion." Since this defect entails an absence within the self, it requires a different corrective agency, something beyond the removal of defective fonts from experience. What, the narrator asks at this juncture, has protected me from myself?

Franklin's answer turns upon a vital triptych in Enlightenment thought: reason, Providence, and nature. Citing first his mastery of the utilitarian forms of reason, he writes that "this Persuasion, with the kind hand of Providence, or some guardian Angel, or accidental favourable Circumstances and Situations, or all together, preserved me." The interesting aspects of the passage – the things that make it so characteristic in the rhetoric of the secular elite – are the parallelism that makes the triptych possible and the stylistic ingenuity that carries it off. Reason, Providence, and nature exist on the same plane of importance in Franklin's explanation: *either* Franklin's utilitarian reason, *or* Providence, *or* circumstances and situations in the natural world, *or* "all" have preserved him. Each category exists separately, but the implied connections, the tone, and the last inclusive repetition of the conditional conjunction hold "all together" in a loose union of equal considerations.

The difficulty in the triptych is, of course, Providence. Franklin quietly brings the Ruler of the Universe down to scale, and his joined phrases, "the kind hand of Providence, or some guardian Angel," accomplish this purpose smoothly. Deity is connoted rather than named. The adjective "kind" gently dismisses the angry God of Calvinist lore, and the additional, slightly vulgar metonym for Providence, "guardian Angel," slips the concept into the less controversial world of social parlance. The point of the language is to diminish and coordinate without offending, to retain the idea of divinity while removing all particulars of dogma. No one can disagree. Franklin writes a language for everyone to believe in.

The diminishing impulse and moderating tones of this rhetoric have been misread. It is inaccurate to regard early republican leaders as detached figures who manipulate theological issues entirely for social purposes. Mere manipulation does not explain their persistent personal interest in religious questions. Most of these leaders profess their faith and engage in the tenets of Bible study. Washington and Adams are stolid but lifelong churchgoers, and the latter makes religion his primary source of investigation in his later years. Franklin and Jefferson's various theological inquiries illustrate that religion is an intellectual duty as well as a civic freedom. Franklin's "Preface to an

Abridgement of the Book of Common Prayer" (1779), his proposed new version of the Bible (1779), and his revised account of the Lord's Prayer (1779), and Jefferson's two detailed compilations from the New Testament – "The Philosophy of Jesus" (1804) and "The Life and Morals of Jesus" (1819–20) – are tangible commitments to the religious life around them.

A belief based on reason that utterly subsumes revelation may be especially hard for a modern mind to comprehend and appreciate. Jefferson can be a sincere Christian in a letter of 1803 to Benjamin Rush and then can dismiss the virgin birth, the divinity of Christ, original sin, blood atonement, and the Trinity as delirious fabrications, when writing to William Short in 1819. The uncompromising vigor of both stances has to do with Jefferson's total self-confidence in reason, his fear of revivalist excesses, and his correspondingly sharp rejection of biblical revelation ("merely the ravings of a Maniac," he tells Alexander Smyth in 1825).

In the fullest explanation of his belief, appearing in a letter to Adams from 1823, Jefferson answers some of these apparent contradictions in himself and for the culture at large. As organized Christianity is "a system of fancy absolutely incomprehensible," so there are "evident proofs of the necessity of a superintending power to maintain the Universe." Jefferson, the Enlightenment figure, rests in the appearance of order and the system of design. "I hold (without appeal to revelation) that when we take a view of the Universe, in its parts general or particular, it is impossible for the human mind not to perceive and feel a conviction of design, consummate skill, and indefinite power in every atom of its composition." The interesting aspect of this thinking in context is that it carries Jefferson back into a Christian orientation rather than away from it. His letter to Adams concludes not just with faith in "a fabricator of all things" but with acceptance of Jesus as "the most venerated reformer of human errors." The combination is a powerful one in a moment in time. Jefferson belongs to the first generation of the Enlightenment in America and therefore holds to an absolutist faith in reason, but he also belongs to a Bible culture of extraordinary vitality.

Because of that vitality, the idea of Providence always surfaces at critical times in American politics, often when other sources of explanation remain unavailable or have failed. Paine raising the millennium in the bold new hope of a continental republic, Adams summoning "rays of ravishing light and glory" in the difficult moment of independence, Jefferson warning of God's anger over slavery, Franklin asking for prayer amidst the acrimony of the Constitutional Convention – all couch their hardest problems in religious terminology. Convenience but also necessity and sometimes faith are at work in the contrivance. All three impulses encourage the instantiation of religious forms in the rituals of political life.

Because the early Republic is still a Bible culture, God appears therein as the best available symbol of order and purpose against chaos and confusion. George Washington employs traditional aspects of that symbol when he begins his first inaugural address with "fervent supplications to that Almighty Being who rules over the universe." Although stripped of teleological tensions and all thought of biblical revelation in Washington's construct, "the great Author of every public and private good" still expects "some return of pious gratitude." Notably, the benefits of order and purpose initiate a duty of worship. "No people can be bound to acknowledge and adore the invisible hand which conducts the affairs of men, more than the people of the United States," Washington intones. "Every step by which they have advanced to the character of an independent nation seems to have been distinguished by some token of providential agency."

The passage should sound familiar. Washington's first official moment as president appropriates the minister's idea of a national covenant. If Washington dilutes that covenant in abstraction and tonal quiescence, in keeping with Enlightenment discourse, he also renders it possible for every citizen to "adore the invisible hand." In the process, the doctrine separating church and state yields and then protects a distinct religious dimension within the political realm. Through such language we gain just a glimpse of what will become an elaborate, institutionalized civil religion in America. From a literary perspective, three levels of implication are at work: the writer's engagement in religious thought, the writer's tactical use of religious terminology in secular explanation, and the writer's strategic awareness of the role of religious discourse in the life of the nation.

No practitioner of this interaction (the measure of belief, the mechanics of literary skill, and the exercise of ideological awareness combined) proves cannier than Thomas Jefferson or uses it more productively in supplanting the clergy in political life. Jefferson's opposition to the clergy leaves him acutely aware of their power through ritual. In yet another diatribe against "the priests of the different religious sects" and their "holy inquisition," he fastens on that source. "We have most unwisely committed to the hierophants of our particular superstition, the direction of public opinion, that lord of the Universe," he writes to William Short in 1820. "We have given them stated and privileged days to collect and catechise us, opportunities of delivering their oracles to the people in mass, and of moulding their minds as wax in the hollow of their hands." This rejection of the occasional sermon is no more than earlier policy has dictated. In 1801, President Jefferson abruptly ends the practice previously accepted by Washington and Adams of national fast day observances, and his prohibition is followed automatically in the presidencies of his Virginia followers, James Madison and James

Monroe. By then, 1825, all formal ceremonial observances of national purpose and identity have passed from pulpit to podium.

The primary architect of the separation of church and state, Jefferson is also first to ply the language of civil religion with complete effectiveness. He supplants the clergy by succeeding them in his own inaugural address. As the new president, he consolidates "an age of revolution and reformation," outlines "the creed of our political faith," and closes with a benediction to "that Infinite Power which rules the destinies of the universe." Along the way, he enumerates the justifications for thinking of America as "a chosen country," and prominent among them is a proper sense of religion. The people are

enlightened by a benign religion, professed, indeed, and practiced in various forms, yet all of them including honesty, truth, temperance, gratitude, and the love of man; acknowledging and adoring an overruling Providence, which by all dispensations proves that it delights in the happiness of man here and his greater happiness hereafter.

These words are profoundly nonsectarian in tenor even as they sustain scriptural interpretation. They do not rule out the biblical God of history; providence still presides over the world. They also evoke a human realm of obligation to further God's will (happiness here and hereafter). At the same time, the chiefly secular virtues of "a benign religion" (honesty, truth, temperance, gratitude, and love of humanity) drain judgment of its edge and convert Jefferson's passive verb ("enlightened") into an overarching theme. By the end of the passage, an enlightened people have become the Enlightenment. More than anything, the passage is calculatedly inclusive and participatory. It inspires without requiring specific acts of faith.

Jefferson's genius as both a writer and a leader of government guide him toward a notable political truth: cohesion and well-being rather than mystery and salvation attract and drive civil worship. The inaugural address of 1801 invites Americans to bask together in providential favor as they enjoy the "dispensations" of a promised land. Future American leaders will adopt the same strategies. Occasion, language, and ritual merge in the citizen's sense of belonging to a proper celebration of republican identity. Behind such exercises, though, and essential to them, is an unspecified modicum of belief. The language holds because it once compelled, and the capacity to wield that language owes everything to earlier ceremonies. Although he does not acknowledge the fact, Jefferson fully comprehends the nature and power of the election sermon, those occasions when the clergy offer "their oracles to the people in mass." Elected, Jefferson delivers his own lay sermon. The measure of his awareness is in his language to the people in democratic union.

4

WRITING THE REVOLUTION

I

First to study the Revolution, the historian David Ramsay also first proclaims the utter centrality of its writings. "In establishing American independence," he observes in *The History of the American Revolution* (1789), "the pen and the press had merit equal to that of the sword." Writings can equal events because events, small in themselves, often take their primary significance from the symbolism that language gives them. Five people die in the Boston Massacre; just eight, in the battle of Lexington. Clearly, it is not size and scale that shake the old order but something else. The international hue and cry of the Intolerable Acts in 1774 take place over 342 chests of tea dumped in Boston Harbor. In the war, General Washington's Continental army sometimes dwindles to fewer than four thousand soldiers, and that army's arduous retreat to Valley Forge in the winter of 1777 takes it only twenty miles from the British army in Philadelphia. Numbers are even smaller in the South. The battles of King's Mountain and Cowpens, major American victories in 1780 and 1781, engage fewer than three thousand at a time. Important in themselves, such incidents take their fullest significance from revolutionary ideology or from the way they contribute to a familiar sense of story and to an understanding of occurrence. Either way, the prime value of a revolutionary event is often in the telling.

At another and prior level, the pen enables the sword. Americans write about the idea of revolution long before they can conceive of the act in realistic terms. Writing the thought inscribes the conception, which, in time, blurs the line of distinction between thought and act. Somewhere, a legitimate rhetoric of opposition grows into the outrageous possibility of revolution. Where, for example, should one place Jeremiah Dummer's *A Defence of the New England Charters* (1721) on this continuum? Dummer rejects all thought of colonial revolt as "ludicrous" in his "short digression" on the subject, and yet John Adams can properly call this pamphlet the handbook of the Revolution. As Adams tells William Tudor in 1818,

426

" '[T]he feelings, the manners and principles which produced the Revolution,' appear in as vast abundance in this work as in any that I have read."

How can Dummer and Adams both be right about *A Defence of the New England Charters?* Dummer, colonial agent for Massachusetts and Connecticut and an American lawyer in London, raises the idea of revolution only to dismiss it: "it would not be more absurd to place two of his Majesty's Beef-Eaters to watch an infant in the Cradle, that it don't rise and cuts its Father's Throat, than to guard these weak infant Colonies, to prevent their shaking off the *British* Yoke." Nevertheless, the double languages of the American and the Englishman, of the native pamphleteer and the imperial agent, do render the absurd sensible. In *A Defence of the New England Charters,* Dummer worries repeatedly about the "arbitrary" power of the Crown, the "unnatural insult" to colonial rights, and the "oppression" of royal governors. The dangers he cites are real and growing: "Oppression rushes in like a Tide, and bears down every Thing before it." To the extent that British rule appears as a burden, literally as a "yoke," it welcomes the thought of being thrown off. Dummer's metaphors belie their surface meanings. An infant cannot commit patricide, but, later and often enough, children do revolt against their parents.

The pressure that Dummer places on his own predicament shows that he grasps the uses to which his language might be put. He knows that *A Defence of the New England Charters* raises more questions than it answers. Admitting that Parliament has the *power* to revoke the colonial charters, he insists that it has no *right* to do so. To think otherwise would be "abhorrent from all Reason, Equity, and Justice." To limit Parliament, however, means that anything can happen, and, in a telling allusion, Dummer turns himself into the son of the legendary Lydian King Croesus in the *Histories* of Herodotus. The conceit plays upon a figure who, mute from birth, learns to speak only in an emergency, as invading Persians destroy both king and country. Whatever the inconsistencies in his position, Dummer writes because he believes he can hesitate no longer. Extremity has given voice to the rashest implications: "for how little so ever one is able to write, yet when the Liberties of one's Country are threaten'd, it's still more difficult to be silent."

Here, in the span between dumb silence and bold statement, is the voice of the Revolution, one that is half-English, half-American, and, in its stuttering progressions, often less than half of itself. No figure demonstrates the dynamic involved better than Patrick Henry, who seeks to embody this voice. Indeed, the great orator would later claim the Revolution for himself through his speech in the Virginia House of Burgesses against the Stamp Act in 1765:

All the colonies, either through fear, or want of opportunity to form an opposition, or from influence of some kind or other, had remained silent. . . . I determined to venture, and alone, unadvised, and unassisted, on a blank leaf of an old law book, wrote the [seven resolutions against the Stamp Act]. Upon offering them to the House violent debates ensued. . . . The alarm spread throughout America. . . . The great point of resistance to British taxation was universally established in the colonies. This brought on the war which finally separated the two countries and gave independence to ours.

While Patrick Henry, as usual, is exaggerating for effect, his description catches the flavor of revolutionary discourse. The need for bold speech comes out of the prevailing silence of a paralyzing uncertainty. Reducing that uncertainty are a series of controlling rhetorical premises: the announced thematic resistance to taxation, the spread of alarm, the sudden universality of belief through exhortation, and the notion of action following from proper language. But if Henry can think of himself as "alone, unadvised, and unassisted," he also speaks within a familiar and frequently expressed Whig tradition of legal precedents. Four of his seven resolutions against the Stamp Act reiterate the rights of English subjects. Henry may write them on the "blank leaf of an old law book," but his language owes much to the printed pages of that law book and of others like it. He writes within a coherent and established English legal theory of opposition.

Henry's actual words before the Virginia legislature in 1765 dramatize the interstices between revolutionary thought and assertion. When he proclaims that "Caesar had his Brutus, Charles the First his Cromwell, and George the Third – " the sequence prompts interrupting cries of "Treason!" in the House. "And George the Third," counters Henry above the din, "may profit by their example – if this be treason, make the most of it." The words themselves may not be exact – Henry's recorded speeches all come from spellbound listeners writing after the event – but they are true to a spirit of the times in which *the exchange* of words dominates and symbolizes action.

That exchange, at least on Henry's part, is deliberately contrapuntal. The juxtaposition of perceived meanings (a cautionary note for his king versus a plan of revolt) increases the whole by "making the most" of opposition. Henry's stock parallels of tyrants and opponents carry from a familiar past toward an uncertain present and create, along the way, an unbearable hiatus in the speaker's moment of threatened liberties. His manipulation of the Whig theory of history forces every auditor to glimpse resistance. But how much resistance and what kinds? Henry's rhetoric flows from a continuum of oppositional stances, and the perception of ongoing conflict has rendered extreme action more and more conceivable.

At the same time, the shouts of "treason" shatter the continuum of legitimate opposition. Henry's words and the reaction to them in the House of Burgesses typify a struggle to think the unthinkable in eighteenth-century

America – a struggle already glimpsed in Dummer's *A Defence of the New England Charters*. To conceive of rebellion, the extreme in resistance, is to force a strategic reconception. Suddenly, the whole subject has to be recast. Well enough do Henry's opponents grasp the notion of opposition, and well enough do they accept even the examples of previous and successful rebellion against a king, but they accept with their English heritage firmly in mind. Opposition seeks an extension of English legal rights, not the desertion of them. For colonial Americans, it is one thing to defend constitutional rights against corruption, conspiracy, and betrayal as members of the British Empire; it is quite another to act so as to reject a place in that empire altogether.

How does one defend English rights if one is no longer professedly English? Every protesting colonial American voice stumbles over the implications. Jeremiah Dummer, in the first of many attempts to face the problem, tries to solve it by making American rights more English than those of the English. In *A Defence of the New England Charters*, he writes,

the *American* Charters are of a higher Nature, and stand on a better Foot, than the Corporations in *England*. For these latter were granted upon Improvements already made, and therefore were Acts of meer Grace and Favour in the Crown; whereas the former were given as Praemiums for Services to be perform'd, and therefore are to be considered as Grants upon a *valuable Consideration;* which adds Weight and Strength to the Title.

The difficulty in this formulation is that the writer's "better foot" still rests on English soil. Dummer can put American charters over English corporations only by resorting to the Anglo-Saxon notion of consideration on a contract. The very nature of his argument leaves him entrenched "from time out of memory" in the English common-law tradition.

Dummer typifies the ways in which British Americans recognize their situation without being able to expound it fully. Again and again, protest loses its power when challenged at the sticking point, and one reason is a curious bifurcation in the perception of problems. For although the conflict between Britain and the American colonies revolves around practical questions of finance, trade, and economic imbalance, the discourse of conflict comes almost entirely from the separate sphere of constitutional theory and legal argument.

The ensuing stammer in revolutionary writings is the most significant literary characteristic of those writings; overcoming it, the first indication of revolutionary success. We need to understand this process better. A great deal has been made of the facility of colonial political writers in the 1760s and 1770s and of the convenient availability to them of an English oppositional rhetoric. Disgruntled Americans like John Dickinson, Benjamin Franklin, and Thomas Jefferson prove a literary match for the best intellects of the age in London, and their ability is one of the first things that English readers notice at the time. Mutual recognition is possible because American eloquence makes powerful use of the rhetorical devices in English politics. Even the most inflexible British reader sees familiar parallels in colonial argumentation: the restraint on power through mixed forms of government, the condemnation of standing armies, the dangers of corruption in the constitution, the fear of conspiracies against liberty, and the emphasis upon public virtue.

It may be, though, that scholars have made too much of these parallels and of an oppositional, or "country," rhetoric as the basis of interpretation. Seventeenth-century commonwealth writers like James Harrington, Algernon Sidney, and John Milton are vital influences on radical thought in both England and America, and eighteenth-century popularizers like John Trenchard and Thomas Gordon then magnify their influence in such works as *The Independent Whig* and *Cato's Letters*. But these influences in themselves stress the enabling capacities rather than the hesitations in protest, and it is the hesitations that define the evolution of colonial protest. Until 1776, the dominant Anglo-American perspective remains *against* the thought of rupture between England and America. A more formidable writer than Trenchard or Gordon — or, for that matter, than Harrington and Sidney — dramatizes this perspective in the final moment of crisis.

The sharpest single argument against independence comes in Samuel Johnson's *Taxation No Tyranny; an Answer to the Resolutions and Address of the American Congress* (1775). Properly read, *Taxation No Tyranny* conveys better than any other document of the times the immense intellectual problems that eighteenth-century Americans are facing in the act of rebellion. Johnson, the leading writer in the English-speaking world, seizes upon every embarrassing inconsistency and half-way measure in colonial claims. His well-known jibe — "how is it that we hear the loudest yelps for liberty among the drivers of negroes?" — is only the most caustic rejoinder in a systematic exposure of American contradictions and hypocrisies. Juxtaposing the creation of the Continental Congress against colonial claims of loyalty to king and country, Johnson asks, "[S]ince the Americans have discovered that they can make a parliament, whence comes it that they do not think themselves equally empowered to make a king?" To any insistence upon "all the rights of Englishmen," he responds that rights bring legal obligations. As the assertion of the one requires accountability in the other, "it seems to follow by consequence not easily avoided, that [our colonies] are subject to English government, and chargeable by English taxation."

Johnson's eloquence turns colonial protest into seeming ignorance and intractability; the Americans are being merely obstinate when they are not being dangerous and unruly. In the equivocation that taxes might be possible but not in the form that England seeks to levy them, Johnson finds administrative chaos: "dominion without authority, and subjects without subordination." When colonial rhetoric joins natural law to English rights, Johnson forces the two apart again, using the standard eighteenth-century understanding of political theory. Either the Americans are "the naked sons of Nature," or "they are no longer in a state of nature." The choice is theirs, but by resorting to English rights at all, "these lords of themselves, these kings of *Me.* these demigods of independence, sink down to colonists, governed by a charter."

These arguments also prey deliberately upon American intellectual insecurities. Johnson exposes the slipperiness and unreliability in a language of protest. "The laws of Nature, the rights of humanity, the faith of charters, the danger of liberty, the encroachments of usurpation, have been thundered in our ears, sometimes by interested faction, and sometimes by honest stupidity." Most troubling of all is the "progress of sedition" in which "those who a few years ago disputed only our right of laying taxes, now question the validity of every act of legislation." Where, Johnson wants to know, will this progression end? Indeed, the breakdown in colonial government in the protests of the 1760s and 1770s appears to many Americans to be just such an alarming sequence. Johnson sees a "delirious dream of republican fanaticism" under a "congress of anarchy." For two centuries Americans had accepted the sacred importance of their colonial charters as their source of political identity and security; now, "without their charter, there would be no power among them, by which any law could be made, or duties enjoined, any debt recovered, or criminal punished." And for what? Johnson takes pains to show that the colonists enjoy "the same virtual representation as the greater part of Englishmen." Americans have lost nothing "except that of which their sedition has deprived them."

The interesting thing about this Johnsonian remonstrance is that it summarizes what Americans already have been saying to each other piecemeal for a decade. *Taxation No Tyranny* actually echoes the radical Boston lawyer James Otis's *A Vindication of the British Colonies* (1765), where Otis calls independence a state that "none but rebels, fools, and madmen will contend for." "God forbid these colonies should ever prove undutiful to their mother country!" writes Otis, in words that Samuel Johnson would have read with approval. "Whenever such a day shall come it will be the beginning of a terrible scene. Were these colonies left to themselves tomorrow, America would be a mere shambles of blood and confusion." Despite their many differences, the conservative English Tory in Johnson and the radical American Whig in Otis express many of the same fears. The skill in Anglo-

American writings of the period lies not in the parroting of "country" rhetoric or even in the refinement of it but in the way writers handle and exploit these fears in the exchange of ideas across party lines.

A vital generic consideration also fosters exchange. *A Defence of the New England Charters, A Vindication of the British Colonies,* and *Taxation No Tyranny* are all the same kind of expression. Jeremiah Dummer, James Otis, and Samuel Johnson write within the classic era of the pamphlet, a genre that dominates the formulation of political ideas in eighteenth-century culture and in the Revolution in particular. The highly polemical and topical nature of such writing, together with the natural responsiveness of pamphlets, one to another, make them the center of the contrapuntal development in revolutionary thought. Not least in this impact is the special license that pamphlets give to writers with extreme views. Eighteenth-century newspapers remain vulnerable to prosecution for libel and breach of privilege and to direct communal pressures in ways that the pseudonymous, one-shot pamphlet does not. The lower profile, smaller publication runs, and irregularity of the pamphlet are its own protections in a time when freedom of the press is still more of a question than a right.

The exact form of the eighteenth-century pamphlet is another advantage. A few printers' sheets folded into folio, quarto, or octavo pages, depending on length, the pamphlet lends itself to easy publication, to the briefest of collaborations between author and printer, to any style or range of argumentation, to minimal expense and quick profit, and to informal modes of distribution. Each of these strengths are expressly significant in early America, where limits in technology, capitalization, and cultural attainment all favor the crude levels of performance and production that pamphleteering so easily tolerates. Of course, all of these characteristics also abet the uncertainties and relative failures in articulation already noted.

Beyond technology are ideological considerations that bring the pamphlet and the Enlightenment together with special force in revolutionary America. Insofar as the Enlightenment conceives of conflict as the struggle of knowledge against ignorance, the rapid diffusion of right information becomes a vital key to victory. Publication represents the first line of attack, and the pamphlet quickly becomes the primary medium for the new citizen reader; it will remain the clearest path to an informed public until the supremacy of the newspaper early in the nineteenth century. No revolutionary culture has ever had a higher literacy rate than do some of the politically volatile areas of the thirteen colonies. (Although accurate figures for the period are not available, approximations suggest that 85 percent of all adult males in New England are able to read compared to roughly 60 percent in England.) Political leaders, aware of the opportunities for communication that exceptional literacy provides and worried about the undeveloped nature and distance between their communities, hope that cheap, readily available commentary on important issues will in itself shape American destiny. One of the breathtaking assumptions of revolutionary intellectuals about their period and place is their belief that widespread publication of correct ideas will make all of the difference in human history. Never in the long story of printing has the ephemeral pamphlet been drafted with greater expectations.

To these high notions must be added the low and continuous irritant of conflict. Recent historical understanding of the contentiousness in colonial life indicates that clashes of all kinds are endemic and perpetual – between American and British interests, between colonial governors and their assemblies, between eastern and western needs within colonies, between colonies over border and trade problems, between North and South, between an incredible variety of religious groupings, between colonial settlers and Native-American populations, and between everyone over land everywhere. Pamphlet production thrives on these controversies because the topicality, spontaneity, and loose form of the genre allow invective and banter to compete on the same terms with rational argument. Adrift in a culture still between oral and print modes of communication, the pamphlet often comes closer than even the printed sermon to the rhythms and personal pressure of speech.

The result in the revolutionary pamphlet is often a bizarre mixture in which rectification and excoriation vie for tonal control. The frustrations involved are palpable. Knowledge should end conflict in an enlightened culture, and yet the perceptive colonial observer finds strife begetting strife on every side. The first remedy in dealing with these difficulties is writing them out, the dissemination of relevant information within the correct idea. Alexander Hamilton, at twenty in *The Farmer Refuted* (1775), seems to have believed that real differences will disappear if his opponent, in this case Samuel Seabury, will read Grotius, von Pufendorf, Locke, Montesquieu, and Burlamaqui with the right care. "I might mention other excellent writers on this subject; but if you attend, diligently, to these," Hamilton condescends to add, "you will not require any others."

The notion that the right answer can be derived from correct readings dictates a painstaking narrative style in writing after writing. Over and over, the pamphlets of the period patiently rehearse the essential connections between legal philosophy, social contract theory, and the American situation in a step-by-step presentation of the truth and its sources from the beginning of history down to the present moment. Behind the earnest insistence upon presentation is an even more earnest assumption about reception: the true narrative, if complete, will convince the rational reader. It follows, however, that continuing conflict implies more than ignorance; ignorance alone, after all, will accept refutation.

The far more likely sources of enduring conflict are willful error and the near certainty of a self-interested plan to maintain it – unforgivable blemishes on the spread of the Enlightenment. Thus, the alternative strategy in American pamphleteering, often ranged alongside the sweet rationality of the first, relies on a spirit of invective and outraged condemnation. This second response ignores failures in understanding to concentrate instead on the presence and exposure of conspiracies. The development of the pamphlet in revolutionary America is about these competing tones and the eventual mastery of them in combinations of reason and anger, explanation and vituperation – a mastery that will convince Americans of the need for Revolution when orchestrated in *Common Sense*.

II

If one document can explain the several hundred American pamphlets on the crisis in politics between 1764 and 1776, it would be John Adams's *A Dissertation on the Canon and Feudal Law* (1765). Adams begins with the assertion, taken from Bishop John Tillotson, that ignorance is the greatest cause of human misery, and he closes with the injunction that "every sluice of knowledge be opened and set a-flowing." In between comes a controlling premise: only the spread of knowledge among the people can preserve liberty. *A Dissertation on the Canon and Feudal Law* uses this framework to draw out a contrast between Adams's presumptions about European ignorance and the American Enlightenment. In Europe, a confederacy between the clergy and feudal princes has kept the people in ignorance of their rights until the Reformation, which has renewed the struggle for knowledge. The first Americans, as part of that Reformation, establish their settlements "in direct opposition to the canon and feudal systems," substituting "the Bible and common sense" for "the ridiculous fancies of sanctified effluvia from episcopal fingers." Inevitably, the Stamp Act of 1765 figures as "the first step" in a European conspiracy to introduce the canon and feudal law to America.

Three elements in Adams's argument compel him to seek the broadest popular publication of American disagreements with England. First, Adams's view of European corruption and ignorance projects "a direct and formal design on foot, to enslave all America," and colonial writers must expose that design. But if this duty to spread the alarm seems obvious enough, the compulsion to publish American views remains *whether or not* a writer shares Adams's sense of conspiracy. Since "liberty cannot be preserved without a general knowledge among the people," the American way requires "the preservation of the means of knowledge among the lowest ranks." "Care has been taken," Adams observes, "that the art of printing should be encouraged, and that it should be easy and cheap and safe for any person to communicate his thoughts to the public." Adams, right or wrong, performs a patriotic function in publishing his pamphlet in the *Boston-Gazette.* He is participating in the communal expectation that informed citizens will communicate their thoughts in writing to the waiting public.

If Adams is even partially correct in his thinking, a third overriding consideration enters into his compulsion to write out every difference with Europe. Again, no conspiracy is necessary for Americans to celebrate their separation from European forms of corruption or for them to express a fear of contamination. The perception of difference is its own threat. Adams in 1765 shares with many other colonial intellectuals a growing mission to rescue history from its European failures. As he summarizes the thought, in a journal entry from December 30th:

[Americans] think that the Liberties of Mankind and the Glory of human Nature is in their Keeping. They know that Liberty . . . has been hunted and persecuted, in all Countries, by cruel Power. But they flatter them selves that America was designed by Providence for the Theatre, on which Man was to make his true figure, on which science, Virtue, Liberty, Happiness and Glory were to exist in Peace.

This is a mighty message to convey to a fallen world, and it transforms the provincial who delivers it into a figure of international importance. Not for the last time, American identification of an external threat presumes a contingent moral superiority.

A Dissertation on the Canon and Feudal Law may be pompous, but it is never complacent. Its terms demand a new commitment to knowledge in a literary call to arms. "We have been afraid to think," Adams concludes in reviewing the failure of Americans to assert their rights against British authority. His solution is clear: "Let us dare to read, think, speak and write. Let every order and degree among the people rouse their attention and animate their resolution." Adams's agenda, properly rendered in prose, describes every major pamphlet of the period:

Let them all become attentive to the grounds and principles of government, ecclesiastical and civil. Let us study the law of nature; search into the spirit of the British constitution; read the histories of ancient ages; contemplate the great examples of Greece and Rome; set before us the conduct of our own British ancestors, who have defended for us the inherent rights of mankind against foreign and domestic tyrants and usurpers, against arbitrary kings and cruel priests, in short, against the gates of earth and hell.

It is as if these words become every writer's guide. Pamphlet after pamphlet dutifully blends the principles of government, the law of nature, the meaning of the British Constitution, and the history of classical, English, and American politics in an interpretation of the crisis at hand. Most, as well, distinguish between ecclesiastical and civil frames of reference even as they conflate religious and political rhetoric in a secular writing. The conclusions of individual investigations differ, but the methodology remains the same. Meanwhile, the tedium of repetition serves yet another purpose; the rhythms in pamphleteering gradually smooth the irregularities in revolutionary thought.

Although conflict between English and American interests is a constant in colonial politics, the year 1764 marks a significant escalation. The change can be seen in a subtle transition. After 1764, colonists prefer the term "Americans" to "Englishmen" in their newspaper descriptions of themselves, and in that year two pamphlets display a new feeling or degree of apprehension. In Virginia, continuing controversy over the payment of Anglican clergy, the Parson's Cause from 1758, reaches a new and prescient level of constitutional interpretation in 1764 in Richard Bland's *The Colonel Dismounted: or the Rector Vindicated.* In New England, Parliament's first attempt to levy additional revenue from the colonies in the Sugar Act prompts James Otis's *The Rights of the British Colonies Asserted and Proved.* Each pamphlet has been called the first paper of the Revolution. Both involved an important colonial legislative leader of the moment, and both achieve notoriety for delineating a major facet of colonial protest. Both efforts also stimulate controversy and lead to more radical writings by their authors. Taken together, they cover North and South, politics and religion, light satire and solemn assertion. Yet, between them, they also dramatize the inconsistencies in protest. Not until 1776 do colonial writers get past the intellectual problems that Bland and Otis exhibit in their most celebrated writings.

Richard Bland has been forgotten because he dies in 1776, or just as the Revolution begins, and because most of his writings have been lost. The leading expert in colonial legal history in 1764, he is also the most important member of the Virginia House of Burgesses in the generation before Patrick Henry and Thomas Jefferson; he serves in the House for thirty-three years, from 1742 until 1775. Writing to William Wirt in August of 1815, Jefferson would claim for Bland that "he wrote the first pamphlet [*The Colonel Dismounted*] on the nature of the connection with Great Britain which had any pretension to accuracy of view on that subject." Bland's effort tries to separate internal and external government – a distinction that would percolate in Anglo–American debate for a decade to come. England, the argument runs, should control matters of external government, while internal government must be left to freeborn Americans in keeping with their liberties and privileges as English subjects.

The distinction between internal and external government places a limit on the authority of king and Parliament in British America and allows for a right of resistance when that limit is passed. Bland will "upon every occasion yield a due obedience" to his king, "but submission even to the supreme magistrate is not the whole duty of a citizen. . . . Something is likewise due to the rights of our country and to the liberties of mankind." Parliament remains supreme: "I do not deny but that the Parliament, as the stronger power, can force any laws it should think fit upon us." Still, "any tax respecting our INTERNAL polity which may hereafter be imposed on us by act of Parliament is arbitrary, as depriving us of our right, and may be opposed." Later, as opposition to British authority grows, colonial theorists come to see Bland's distinction as one without a difference, but it is an important rallying cry in the 1760s.

Bland struggles to remain a good British-American subject by leaving the "something due" American rights and the license to "oppose impositions" in suspension. *The Colonel Dismounted* relies on the certainty that George III and Parliament would never extract an inordinate submission; "we have nothing of this sort of fear from those guardians of the rights and liberties of mankind." Unfortunately, Americans have everything to fear in 1764. Passage of the Stamp Act in the next year fulfills Bland's worst hypothetical case of a "tax respecting our INTERNAL polity" and places him in an untenable philosophical position. The situation demonstrates how one pamphlet, *The Colonel Dismounted*, could compel and inscribe a sequel, *An Inquiry into the Rights of the British Colonies* (1766). In a typical pattern for the period, the first decision to write now requires a second farther along the continuum of resistance; writing itself becomes a radicalizing act. Bland is one of the moderates who temporize over the thrusts of Patrick Henry in the House of Burgesses, but the Stamp Act controversy forces him away from the comfort of automatic loyalty and toward the refinement of an American theory of opposition.

An Inquiry into the Rights of the British Colonies in 1766 is unavoidably a tortured document. Bland, the legal scholar, realizes that the letter of the law can make him a traitor. He drops the satirical mode of *The Colonel Dismounted* and now agonizes in the role of colonial champion. "I must speak freely," he observes, "I am considering a Question which affects the *Rights* of above two Millions of as loyal Subjects as belong to the British Crown." Simultaneously, he fears that the actual decision to become a champion means that he will "be charged with Insolence," and, in a courageous response to that anxiety, he prints his own name, "Richard Bland, of Virginia," on the title page of the document. The gesture, unique for the times, literalizes the issue of colonial spokesman by removing the thought of mediation. Stepping from behind the conventional veil of anonymity, Bland turns himself into a living type for the writer who delivers "the Sentiments of an honest Mind with Freedom."

The pamphlet itself is a checkerboard of contrasting assertions and assurances of loyalty, on the one hand, and discussions of the right of resistance, on the other. Once again, Parliament is supreme, though once again, the colonies are not to be subject to internal taxation by authority of Parliament. "The Colonies," claims Bland, "are subordinate to the Authority of Parliament; subordinate I mean in Degree, but not absolutely so." Where, then, is the line? Bland tries to draw a distinction between the law of England and the law of Nature with recourse to the latter when the first proves insufficient, but he is too good a lawyer to rest in this conclusion. For while the usual historical review reveals the British Constitution to be in decline or worse, the rights of English subjects remain civil guarantees founded in compact, and the duty of colonists is still "to lay their Complaints at the Foot of the Throne, and to suffer patiently rather than disturb the publick Peace." But this conclusion is intolerable even to its author. And so Bland persists: "if this Justice should be denied, if the most humble and dutiful Representations should be rejected, nay not even deigned to be received, what is to be done?" The open-endedness of the question, and the way it breaks into colonial rhetoric at each crucial juncture, is one test of creativity in pamphlet writings of the period.

What *is* to be done? Bland turns away from his own natural inclinations in law for an answer in politics. *An Inquiry into the Rights of the British Colonies* recalls the debates of the Corinthians and the Corcyreans over the rights of colonies in the first pages of *The Peloponnesian War*. The actual exchange in Thucydides supports the notion of fair dealing, but the antagonism of Corinth and Corcyra ripens into conflict despite every reasonable argument; conflict, in turn, triggers general war and leads the Greeks to their ruin. Bland lets the Corcyreans speak directly from his own pages. Every colony, they tell the Corinthians, becomes an alien when treated with injury and violence.

Stymied by history and law, unwilling to end with even an indirect prediction of war ("the Subject is delicate"), Bland reaches for the framework of science. *An Inquiry* shifts suddenly into a refutation of the use of Newtonian physics by anticolonial writers. These writers construe the technical language of first movers, of revolving orbs, and of equal force to make Great Britain "the Centre of Attraction to the Colonies." To the contrary, argues Bland, "the Laws of Attraction in natural as well as political Philosophy" prove that "Bodies in Contact, and cemented by mutual Interests, cohere more strongly than those which are at a Distance and have no common Interests to preserve." The odd sudden placement of the scientific theme here is a good example of thematic breakage in revolutionary discourse. Something of a non sequitur, the passage also strangely undercuts the largest hope in Bland's pamphlet: namely, that the colonies "ever remain under a constitutional Subordination to Great Britain!" For if Bland insists repeatedly upon "the deepest loyalty" and "an unshaken Attachment to the Interest of Great Britain," the law of gravity, as he presents it, suggests a greater attachment between or among the more proximate colonies.

The discrepancy between political hope and scientific argument goes to the essence of changing colonial apprehensions. Challenges to colonial rights from England have begun to create the need for images and arguments of an American solidarity. Bland, in describing the crisis of 1766, knows that for the colonies "the closest Union becomes necessary to maintain in a constitutional Way their dearest Interests." He also realizes that the supposed objectivity of science might serve the cause, and his resort, a frequent one in the period, is to the language of astronomy. The Enlightenment habit of relating scientific knowledge to human improvement is especially clear where order in the motion of the stars presumably figure a predictability in human occurrence. A decade later, the Declaration of Independence will begin with words about the course of human events cohering in separate and equal station through the laws of nature, and Americans in 1776 will first hear these words read in the Philadelphia Observatory on the platform built to observe the transit of Venus.

For all of their differences, Richard Bland in Virginia and James Otis in Massachusetts epitomize the same larger colonial dilemma in the middle 1760s. True, in writing the most notorious pamphlet of the decade, *The Rights of the British Colonies Asserted and Proved* (1764), Otis rejects Bland's distinction between external and internal government. True again, he conflates civil and natural law where Bland finds more of a contrast, and he restricts Parliament more than Bland is willing to do, but the overriding similarities in their major writings indicate a general colonial attitude beyond personal, regional, and philosophical differences. Definitions of loyalty are the real issue in these pamphlets, and at the center of that subject is a cultural paradox.

Americans in the middle 1760s have not yet drawn a meaningful line between obedience and protest even though British attempts to tax the colonies has made protest the basis of self-definition. Hence, *The Rights of the British Colonies Asserted and Proved* assumes that "it is the duty of every good citizen to point out what he thinks erroneous in the commonwealth," and it condemns the failure of Americans to do so. "There has been a most profound and I think shameful silence," observes Otis, "till it seems almost too late to assert our indisputable rights as men and citizens." At the same time, "the power of Parliament is uncontrollable but by themselves, and we must obey. . . . let the Parliament lay what burdens they please on us, we must, it is our duty to submit and patiently bear them till they will be pleased to relieve us." In the end, Otis depends on the unilateral response of English politicians sitting in London. "And 'tis to be presumed the wisdom and justice of that august assembly always will afford us relief."

Like Bland, Otis remains hopelessly entangled in his admission that Parliament holds sovereignty over the American colonies, and, in another similarity, he writes his own sequel distinguishing between power and right. In *A Vindication of the British Colonies* (1765), Otis will discover a "difference between power and right, between a blind slavish submission and a loyal, generous, and rational obedience to the supreme authority of a state." Even so, the stridency of adjectives like "slavish" and "generous" aside, Otis's questions are also Bland's. Where does obedience end and submission begin? What should be done when power ignores rights? Bland and Otis simply cannot articulate more consistent responses in the middle 1760s, and their failures involve a weakness in logic that keeps the English world from taking them as seriously as it should have done. Why should English leaders accept the logic of colonial lawyers like Adams, Bland, and Otis when the law itself appears so decidedly against the legality of colonial assertions?

A pamphlet by Martin Howard, Jr., a prominent lawyer in Rhode Island and one of very few American Tories not intimidated into silence by communal protest, helps to clarify the colonial dilemma. Howard's reply to Otis and others in *A Letter from a Gentleman at Halifax* (1765) prefigures Samuel Johnson's more adroit exposure of colonial argumentation a decade later in *Taxation No Tyranny*. Warning that loose comparisons between England in 1641 and America in 1764 "sound like sedition," Howard shows that existing theories of sovereignty allow for no equivocation in an admission of supremacy. "The jurisdiction of Parliament being established, it will follow that this jurisdiction cannot be apportioned; it is transcendent and entire, and may levy internal taxes as well as regulate trade." Attempts to distinguish between law and rights through colonial charters and the common law prove similarly defective; one must take all of the common law or none. Then, too, the so-called American right of representation in Parliament "is but a phantom" when examined in legal terms.

It is hard to argue with these claims in the cold light of historical precedent. Howard rather than Otis presents the conventional wisdom of the times. "One cannot but smile at the inconsistency of these inherent, indefeasible [rights] men," writes the gentleman from Halifax. All the same,

Howard fully realizes that his explanations break down under "the frequent abuse poured forth in pamphlets and newspapers against the mother country." Incredibly, "the pride of some and the ignorance of others" have been victorious, and "the cry against mother country has spread from colony to colony." The irony of Howard's defeat with winning arguments hints at the refraction of truth in the history of ideas. Not logic and reason but setting and tone give credence to the writings of Bland, Otis, and others; not the theory but new forms of theorizing capture the colonial imagination.

At one level, oppositional pamphleteering in America in the 1760s involves patterns of mutual recognition and reinforcement within a new colonial leadership. It is in this decade that lawyers replace ministers and Crown administrators as the intellectual elite in America. The rhetorical patterns of the oppositional pamphlet – the conflations of natural law, political philosophy, and common law – duplicate the colonial legal profession's approach to authority and self-mastery. John Adams, writing to Hezekiah Niles in 1818, recounts this perception in a description of his mentors from the 1760s, Jeremiah Gridley and James Otis: "It was a maxim which [Otis] inculcated on his pupils, as his patron in profession, Mr. Gridley, had done before him, *that a lawyer ought never to be without a volume of natural or public law, or moral philosophy, on his table or in his pocket.*' " American pamphleteering applies just these combinations in the 1760s. One reason it is so effective politically is because it advertises the identity and merits of the colonial legal fraternity.

At another level, radical pamphleteering speaks directly to emerging communal affinities in American culture. Philosophical inconsistencies in works like *The Rights of the British Colonies Asserted and Proved* push these writers toward rhetorical extremes where their words serve a purpose beyond mere argument. In Otis's seminal pamphlet, it is not just that Americans can congratulate themselves collectively as *"the noble discoverers and settlers of a new world,"* nor that the rejection of "arbitrary" government allows them a government for "the good of *the whole,*" but that they can also hear Otis say "absolute power is *originally* and *ultimately* in the people." Patriotic identity attaches itself to the new idea that government begins – and ends – in the people.

There is a submerged, more radical discourse in such writings that begins to shape a different awareness of country. Typically, Otis's own use of astronomy – "gravitation and attraction have place in the revolution of the planets" – seeks an analogy between the physical world and the moral world, where "the first principle is *equality* and the power of the whole." Politically, the principle of equality requires "several powers properly combined," but, as the first principle, it extends to every other political consideration. Otis raises possibilities within the radical continuum that Americans will take

centuries to recognize in full. "Are not women born as free as men?" he asks
in his introductory remarks. For every colonist who heeds Otis's insistence
that Parliament is supreme, several others seem to have been listening to a
more abstract promise about human rights.

In fact, the emotional rhythms of *The Rights of the British Colonies Asserted
and Proved* have little to do with the theme of parliamentary jurisdiction.
Instead, they celebrate a fresh dispensation that the people have managed to
create for themselves. For Otis, the year 1688 represents a sharp rupture with
the past and a new constitution, not just another step in British liberties or
an extension of the old one: "by the abdication [of James II], the original
compact was broken to pieces . . . by the Revolution it was renewed and
more firmly established, and the rights and liberties of the subject in all parts
of the dominions more fully explained and confirmed." These thoughts carry
well beyond the writer's intention to prove "that no parts of His Majesty's
dominions can be taxed without their consent." The eighteenth-century
reader who accepts the fullest implication of Otis's words begins to think
that revolution might be the answer to insurmountable problems.

Plainly, much depends on whether that reader is American or English. The
impulses that appeal to colonists utterly repel their English counterparts. In
London, where literary production is still largely a matter of patronage and of
leisure and where political position still depends on aristocratic station, the
American lawyers who write out their vocationalism in political pamphleteering are vulgar upstarts at best. Virtually no one in England accepts the
constitutional arguments in American pamphlets. Even *The Annual Register*,
published there by oppositional Whigs, finds in 1766 that "advocates for the
colonies carried the idea of liberty to the highest pitch of enthusiasm" and
urges, in consequence, that an American "irregular spirit of enthusiasm
should be timely checked, by making [the colonists] sensible of their dependence." The pervasiveness of this assumption in England can be appreciated
in a single fact: Parliament passes the Stamp Act of 1765 by the resounding
margin of 245 to 49, and it does so despite strong colonial protest against
previous measures like the Sugar Act of 1764.

The emotional appeal of American pamphleteering does not translate easily into an English frame of reference, and that failure may be the clearest
indication of the growing distance between the two cultures. The same
language serves distinct purposes and has different effects on the two sides of
the Atlantic Ocean. It may even have been that similarity of language
increased acrimony by encouraging false understandings. Although English
debate over the American situation is intense and serious in 1766, most
members of Parliament summarily reject "arguments of *natural* lawyers, as
Locke, Selden, and Puffendorf, and others." Such arguments, in the language

of *The Annual Register,* "are little to the purpose in a question of constitutional law." British politicians dismiss colonial claims based on natural law through their own presumed familiarity with the theory. Missing in this familiarity, however, is the subtler understanding of a different context for ideas. Parliament misconceives the sincerity of American intentions by failing to comprehend the importance of natural-law philosophy in colonial discourse. Meanwhile, colonial leaders misconstrue parliamentary miscomprehension as a sign of corruption or worse.

These compounding failures in cultural awareness deserve elaboration. While they do not mean that the Revolution is inevitable in 1766 or after, they suggest that more is at issue in Anglo–American confrontations than conventional descriptions stress in a narrative of administrative blunders, inadequacies, instabilities, divisions, and corruption. The succession of short-lived British ministries in the 1760s compounds Anglo–American conflict without, however, being the source of it. Yes, the ministries of William Pitt, the Earl of Bute, George Grenville, the Marquis of Rockingham, Pitt again, the Duke of Grafton, and, finally, Lord North all hold power between 1761 and 1770, but every administration receives substantial support on colonial policy. Large parliamentary majorities pass the controversial colonial measures of the 1760s and 1770s, including the Intolerable Acts of 1774. Identification of the underlying sources of difference between England and America in these years would have required a truly inspired leadership; containment of them, even more. The pamphlet literature of the period is a sign of largely unrealized cultural differences and a neglected gauge, today, for measuring the range of those differences.

III

The American pamphleteer who reaches the largest audience in the world of the late 1760s is John Dickinson in *Letters from a Farmer in Pennsylvania.* Only Thomas Paine in the next decade would have a more instantaneous impact on colonial thought. Readers everywhere seem to have recognized a special contribution to the genre when Dickinson's twelve epistolary essays to "*My dear* Countrymen," first appeared in *The Pennsylvania Chronicle.* Other colonial newspapers reissue the essays as they are printed in *The Chronicle* between December 1767 and February 1768. Collected in a single pamphlet immediately after the last letter, they quickly go through seven editions in the colonies and several in England. Even today, American perceptions of the Revolution are shaped decisively by *Letters from a Farmer in Pennsylvania,* and it is important to understand why. The most detailed, sustained, learned, and ambitious pamphlet publication by an individual of the period, it also offers tonal and philosophical controls that speak directly to cultural imperatives then and now.

Intellectually, Dickinson is the most thorough and effective of the colonial lawyers who argue that Parliament cannot tax the colonies. His education at the London Inns of Court shows in the Pennsylvania Farmer's frequent citation of British law and of writers like Locke, Coke, Hume, Montesquieu, Tacitus, Harrington, and Machiavelli. These sources lead him to assume that the social compact protects the inalienable right of property; thus, any attempt to tax the property of an unrepresented citizen is contrary to English law. Emotionally, and Dickinson is a master of the transition, this intellectual assumption translates into the celebrated cry of "Letter VII": "*We are taxed* without our own consent, expressed by ourselves or our representatives. *We* are therefore – *SLAVES.*" And yet Dickinson never sacrifices his British readership to such polemics. The extraordinary balances in his prose keep everyone in place.

Education and inclination together make Dickinson the most moderate of colonial protesters, one who will actively oppose independence in 1776. The Pennsylvania Farmer always imposes careful philosophical and stylistic limitations on political opposition. He considers the Townshend Acts of 1767 (externally imposed duties on American imports of glass, paper, paint, and tea) to be as pernicious and unconstitutional as the Stamp Act before them, and he challenges these laws across the gradations of resistance from legal petition, to boycott, to force of arms. Invariably, though, the rhetoric of *Letters from a Farmer in Pennsylvania* seals off the last alternative of actual rebellion. "Letter I" detests "inflammatory measures" ("I should be sorry that any thing should be done, which might justly displease our sovereign, or our mother country"). "Letter III" terms liberty "a cause of too much dignity to be sullied by turbulence and tumult"; the colonists must be "dutiful children, who have received unmerited blows from a beloved parent." "We cannot," warns the Farmer, "act with too much caution in our disputes." "Letter IX" inveighs against popular violence and rage; "Letter XI," against popular reform; and "Letter XII," against the unseemliness of "*ill-formed zeal.*"

The right kind of restraint requires a blend of controls. Dickinson begins by asking for "a firm, modest exertion of a free spirit," but the equilibriums involved are quite complex. "Letter I" balances protest over the Townshend Acts ("a dreadful stroke aimed at the liberty of these colonies"), against a modesty of temperament ("I have waited some time, in expectation of seeing the subject treated by persons much better qualified for the task"), and the freedom of the writer's essential theme ("so should not any honest man suppress his sentiments concerning freedom") against a tougher summons of spirit in the subscript of "November 5th" (the day William of Orange confirms the Glorious Revolution by accepting Parliament's Declaration of Right). If the Farmer seems to give with one hand while taking with the other, it is because he sees that the living whole, "a free spirit," cannot be simplified – especially in America.

Meeting the problem of definition head-on in "Letter III," Dickinson explains why Americans have remained so inarticulate on the subject: "it will be impossible to determine whether an *American's* character is most distinguishable, for his loyalty to his Sovereign, his duty to his mother country, his love of freedom, or his affection for his native soil." Each element – loyalty, duty, freedom, and affection – must be kept in mind and in practice. Dickinson struggles more than any other colonial intellectual to keep these conflicting affinities aloft when they confront each other. As a result, mixed metaphors and images figure prominently in *Letters from a Farmer in Pennsylvania*. Conceptions of peace and war, of objectivity and passion, of assurance and apprehension chase each other and then mesh on the page.

Dickinson wants to bring necessary ambiguities together in a theory of union. He is certain that a proper proportion will incorporate the differences of obedience and freedom, power and law. Characteristically, "Letter II" notes that "we are as much dependent on *Great Britain,* as a perfectly free people can be on another." "The *legal authority of Great-Britain,*" runs "Letter XII," is "like the spear of Telephus, it will cure as well as wound." Dickinson chooses the simile in order to eliminate the pessimism in improbable reconciliations. As the hero Telephus receives succor from the rust of the spear that has wounded him, so the colonies can extract "surprising remedies" from parliamentary "unkindness." Everything is possible, Dickinson seems to be saying, if colonial readers will only see the truth of their multiple interests.

Americans extract more than the reluctance of the revolutionary from this vision of themselves. In Enlightenment terms, the Pennsylvania Farmer personifies the ideal life. He evinces "a contented grateful mind, (undisturbed by worldly hopes or fears, relating to myself)." The sources of his tranquillity appear in his introductory remarks: a liberal education, property, and place ("My farm is small; my servants are few, and good; I have a little money at interest"); retreat from "the busy scenes of life" after having known them; the means to pursue "a greater knowledge" ("a library, which I think the most valuable part of my small estate"); and, finally, the companionship of others like himself ("two or three gentlemen of abilities and learning, who honour me with their friendship"). From the platform of these advantages, the Farmer hopes to "have an effect greater than he could reasonably expect." Actually, the effect is greater than anyone could have expected, one reason *Letters from a Farmer in Pennsylvania* deserves closer attention.

If the Enlightenment in the eighteenth century stands for one thing, it is that proper education and free exercise of the right of property will produce independence and tranquillity of mind. The Pennsylvania Farmer functions as the crystallization of this idea in the American pamphlet tradition. In biblical terms, the idea can be reduced to a single phrase repeated over and over in litany form by colonial pamphleteers: "they shall sit every man under his vine and under his fig tree." The passage, a symbolization of the union between communal peace and individual prosperity, appears in both the First Book of Kings, where it refers to the rule of Solomon, and the Book of the Prophet Micah, where it predicts the coming of the Messiah. Dickinson takes the fuller rendition in Micah 4:4, giving it his own special emphasis in "Letter V," where "the beautiful and emphatic language of the sacred scriptures" makes the right of property "the foundation of all the rest." In his version, " 'they should sit *every man* under his vine, and under his fig-tree, and *NONE SHOULD MAKE THEM AFRAID.*' " But what if these happy property owners *are* made to be afraid? *Letters from a Farmer in Pennsylvania* is about this reversal of implications.

Dickinson's Farmer should be tranquil; manifestly, he is not. British incursions on colonial rights have robbed him of a natural equanimity. Keeping within the image of vine and tree in "Letter IX," he exclaims that "the question is not, whether some branches shall be lopt off – The ax is laid to the root of the tree; and the whole body must infallibly perish, if we remain idle spectators of the work." The impact of such words depends first on the presumption of an available happiness. Americans who are *not* happy in the 1760s should be so. As they ask themselves, in Stephen Hopkins's typical version of the question from *The Rights of Colonies Examined* (1765), "Why should the gentle current of tranquility that has so long run with peace . . . be at last obstructed, be turned out of its true course into unusual and winding channels by which many of those states must be ruined, but none of them can possibly be made more rich or more happy"?

The phraseology of ruin and obstruction that interrupts the tranquillity in Hopkins's river metaphor implies a specific difficulty of the time as well as an attitude toward it. The colonies have experienced an artificial boom based on external credit and wartime spending during the French and Indian War, but a reaction automatically sets in as the war ends in 1760, bringing a recession that continues through the middle of the decade. Buying power drops for most colonists. Though population growth continues to soar, trade declines and then fluctuates wildly. Bankruptcies of overextended merchants and a growing trade deficit add to difficulties and a general foreboding. In this atmosphere, the British decision to tax colonial imports more than increases apprehensions; it encourages Americans to blame their troubles on politics rather than the marketplace. Political unrest, it should be noted, is greatest in Virginia and the New England coastal cities, where the tobacco trade and urban mercantile centers are hardest hit.

With prosperity the assigned norm and sometimes an assumed right, comparisons of past and present in the 1760s tend to meld liberty, tranquillity, virtue, and prosperity together in the name of their opposites – tyranny, anxiety, corruption, and economic misfortune. The parallel constructions recur so frequently in colonial discourse in part because they contain the one argument that Loyalists and British writers can never counter. To the extent that the absence of tranquillity and prosperity imply a comparable loss in freedom, it is enough for colonial writers to find that Americans are, in fact, anxious. Some agency must be responsible for the facts of unhappiness and misfortune as such, and the logical candidate in the 1760s is British policy.

John Dickinson molds these patterns of protest into a concise formula in *Letters from a Farmer in Pennsylvania.* How can Americans with the best chance in the pursuit of happiness still appear to be so far from their goal? For every educated property owner who struggles to make ends meet in the recession of the 1760s and who senses a discrepancy, the Pennsylvania Farmer offers an answer in "Letter XII":

Let these *truths* be indelibly impressed on our minds – *that we cannot be HAPPY, without being FREE* – that we cannot be free, *without being secure in our property* – that *we* cannot be secure in our property, *if, without our consent, others may, as by right, take it away* – that *taxes imposed on us by parliament,* do thus take it away.

Just as the enlightened sequence of truth, freedom, happiness, security of property, and tranquillity can be entered at any point and taken in either direction, so their opposites, insecurity and external taxation, stop every virtue and pollute the entire realm.

These leaps in logic are grounded in a rhetorical claim of absolute precision. Alive to the difficulty of correct expression in "Letter III," Dickinson in "Letter IV" asks for that clarity in principle and intention that "will give certainty to our expression and safety to our conduct." The greatest identified danger in *Letters from a Farmer in Pennsylvania* is always confusion. "To suffer our ideas to be confounded by *names* on such occasions," the Farmer admonishes in his last communication, "would certainly be an *inexcusable weakness, and* probably an *irremediable error."* Dickinson prides himself on a meticulous accuracy. "I have looked over *every statute* relating to these colonies from their first settlement to this time," he announces at the beginning of "Letter II." Dickinson's learning and erudition show on every page. Singular sources of satisfaction to colonial readers, they are the hardest traits to convey to a modern audience.

To grasp the true power of this pamphlet is to realize that the Farmer's expression of his knowledge is also the source and definition of his freedom. As his peroration runs, only those people "DESERVE liberty, who so *well understand* it . . . and so *wisely, bravely,* and *virtuously assert, maintain,* and *defend* it." The capacity to assert one's understanding means everything in this context. A definition of freedom offered in "Letter VI" stresses the faculty of judging for oneself when privileges have been invaded. The exercise of that judgment *is* the exercise of freedom, just as prior knowledge is the essential prerequisite to correct judgment. The writer renders a decision based upon an understanding of country and a separate understanding of previous communal expression on the subject; his words are freedom in action.

Dickinson is the master of both understandings. He announces his true purpose, "the meaning of these letters," in "Letter III": "to convince the people of these colonies, that they are at this moment exposed to the most imminent dangers; and to persuade them immediately, vigorously, and unanimously, to exert themselves, in the most firm, but most peaceable manner, for obtaining relief." In the cause of freedom there can be no higher mission, and the Farmer underlines the charge with his last words. Although not his own, this final passage proves all the more effective for kindling emphatic recognitions in his immediate audience, "My *Dear* COUNTRYMEN."

Poignantly, Dickinson closes *Letters from a Farmer in Pennsylvania* by reclaiming the stutter in revolutionary discourse. He transforms hesitation into the loftiest eloquence by taking Jeremiah Dummer's words from *A Defence of the New England Charters* in 1721 and giving them new life in 1768. " 'How little soever one is able to write,' " says Dickinson through Dummer, " 'yet when the liberties of one's country are threatened, it is still more difficult to be silent.' " The repetition forges a literary convention out of the original statement. The right to speak extremely (because in extremity) receives fresh credence. And what is actually said increases the pressure to say more. The hesitation in oppositional discourse has shifted from the voice of the writer to the characterological surface of the speaker − to the attractive image of the peace-loving farmer. The voice, by way of contrast, is now in full cry. Its fluency in the transforming repetition signifies a larger change in the nature of American pamphleteering.

The growing urgencies of protest − the monotony of mere repetition, the demand for eloquence, the insistence upon an ever more imminent danger, above all, the need for a heightened response − these urgencies are changing the meaning and the direction of words. While Dickinson seeks to reunite colony and mother country, he also contributes to a language of separation. Resisting the danger from abroad requires a firmer sense of colonial unity, and that act of identity inexorably pushes Americans away from previous associations with Europe. "Let us consider ourselves as . . . *separate from the rest of the world,* and *firmly bound together* by the *same rights, interests* and *dangers,*" pleads the Farmer in the end. The order to unite encourages an inadvertent corollary: increasingly, the language of protest will be phrased with other Americans in mind and not with the hope of a British response.

The pamphlets of the late 1760s and early 1770s illustrate the shift in orientation. When "Britannus Americanus," writing in the *Boston Gazette* in March of 1766, finds the same love of freedom and constitutionalism in Old and New England, he might be celebrating Anglo–American ties within the British Empire but for the point of the comparison, which is to prove that Americans are "utterly unaccountable to, and uncontroulable by the *people* of Great-Britain, or any body of them whatever." Many Americans still feel uncomfortable with the notion of "standing upon *equal* footing" with England in 1766, but, having been aroused by British taxing schemes, they laugh together over the reductio ad absurdum in the *Boston Gazette* that they, in turn, might "make a law to tax their *fellow subjects* in England." British readers, including sympathetic ones, do not share in this laughter. The price of humor for Britannus Americanus is the loss of his English audience.

The more profound the opposition grows, the more it raises practical questions that Americans can ask only of themselves. Daniel Leonard, another prominent Massachusetts lawyer, will become a formidable Loyalist pamphleteer in rousing exchanges with John Adams, "Massachusettensis" against "Novanglus" in late 1774 and 1775, but earlier, in November 1773, he still wavers enough to bring the predicament of protest into stark focus. Writing for the *Massachusetts Spy,* Leonard agrees with previous commentators that British measures have been "illegal" and "intolerable," and, like them, he wonders what should be done about these encroachments. The difference in 1773 has to do with the level of response. As Leonard writes, the thought of rebellion is less shocking to all parties. Though he will stay loyal to the Crown, Leonard dwells not on the philosophical duties of the English citizen but on the practical mechanics of American politics. By 1773, "the only question is, whether it be prudent to risque resistance."

The question of probable success or failure is replacing the more agonizing quandary of freedom versus loyalty. And that question, "the only question" left, belongs less to the English-speaking world at large than it does to specific colonial leaders. Americans, Leonard urges, must measure the risk in rebellion carefully. Accordingly, his essay discriminates within its nominal audience, "*all Nations of Men,*" in order to address "*more especially the Inhabitants of British North-America.*" It narrows the field of concern and, in that process, the term "British" begins to move from intrinsic category toward descriptive appendage. The real subject of debate turns more and more on the specific American circumstance that will trigger rebellion.

The occasional dimension of the pamphlet simultaneously follows and dictates the course of change. As physical conflict becomes more and more likely in 1774 and 1775, Americans must respond more directly to the divisions in their midst. Communal pressure is forcing Loyalists into silence or flight, and colonial solidarity, always an interest, now emerges as the controlling priority in Whig writings. Two pamphlets depict the new situation: Thomas Jefferson's *A Summary View of the Rights of British America* (1774) and David Rittenhouse's *An Oration Delivered February 24, 1775, Before the American Philosophical Society.* Very different from each other, both nonetheless presage a mode of address that will erase uncertainties in the name of recognized inevitabilities. In 1776, all local discomforts – loss, displacement, confusion, violence, injury, chaos, and death – will yield to ideological horizons in the spread of the Enlightenment. Jefferson and Rittenhouse foreshadow the speed of that transformation just before the moment. Not a rupture, not even a blemish, the Revolution will be read as natural event, a part of the history and science of the New World.

A Summary View of the Rights of British America takes the bold step of making the king of England a primary adversary. The step is bold because it is also well nigh irrevocable, and its importance at this moment in 1774 cannot be overestimated. As long as Parliament remains the main target of colonial protest, Americans can qualify their opposition in the larger claim of loyalty to king and country. Jefferson, in selecting George III as his real opponent in *A Summary View,* sacrifices that safer stance; loyalty is suddenly contingent. "But can his Majesty thus put down all law under his feet?" he asks. It is the old question, but Jefferson now answers it with a direct attack on the Crown: "let him remember that force cannot give right." When he adds that "it is neither our wish nor our interest to separate from [Great Britain]," he is also announcing the negative possibility. "This, Sire," Jefferson concludes on the necessity of liberty, "is our last, our determined resolution." His words add the insult of direct address to the deepening threat of separation.

Rhetorically the same shift in address is immensely liberating – so liberating that the eloquence of Jefferson's formulation will soon secure his place as drafter of the Declaration of Independence, where again the king will figure as essential foe. Before 1774, colonial writers encounter frustrating dramatic and intellectual difficulties in making Parliament the main source of their protest. For Parliament is not only faceless and multivoiced and, therefore, hard to particularize, it also symbolizes institutional liberty in an eighteenth-century understanding of Anglo–American culture. Nothing in the legacy of

1688 welcomes an American attempt to find tyranny in parliamentary encroachment. (England is said to have regained liberty *through* Parliament and *against* the king.) Jefferson, for his part, does not absolve Parliament, but he repossesses familiar language from the Whig theory of history. In a theme that had long enthralled the English-speaking world, he concentrates instead on "the most precarious of all tenures, his Majesty's will."

The innovative alignment of the colonies against their king also figures powerfully in the dynamic of New World politics. *A Summary View of the Rights of British America* converts mundane historical fact into a vital possibility. The truism that no European king has ever stood on western shores becomes, in Jefferson's hands, a matter of conscious choice among emigrating peoples. We are close to a wholly new conception: namely, that monarchy itself might constitute an unnatural form of government on the fresh American strand. Jefferson's argument is fourfold: that all peoples have a natural right of emigration; that the first Americans, as an emigrating people, voluntarily choose to remain under the laws of England ("the emigrants thought proper to adopt that system of laws, under which they had hitherto lived in the mother country"); that the nature of this choice creates separate legal systems linked only by a common executive, the king of England; and that this king "is no more than the chief official of the people, appointed by the laws, and circumscribed with definite powers, to assist in working the great machine of government."

Jefferson is not the first to expound a theory of constitutionalism in which the Anglo–American relationship is based upon the notion of a common executive – Franklin, Adams, and James Wilson all hold similar views by 1774 – but he first converts the idea into a vivid story for Americans to believe in. The story itself thrives on a dangerous negation; none of its four main points are remotely acceptable to a British audience. The notion of a natural right of emigration has no standing in English law. Neither does the assumption of a voluntary colonial compact with England; nor of colonial legislatures free of Parliamentary jurisdiction; nor of a king who functions only as chief officer of the people. These thoughts border on treason in eighteenth-century England. Even the Virginia convention must reject them in the moment. They are, in the understatement of Jefferson's autobiography, "too bold for the present state of things."

The complex form of Jefferson's story reveals his deeper purposes. *A Summary View of the Rights of British America* takes shape as a "Draft of Instructions to the Virginia Delegates in the [First] Continental Congress." When the Convention rejects this draft, Jefferson's colleagues in Williamsburg publish and distribute it under its present title, and other publishers soon reprint it in both Philadelphia and England. As such, *A Summary View* seems to have

fallen between three stools: sometimes an official legislative document, sometimes a letter to the king, and sometimes a political pamphlet. Jefferson and
his radical colleagues manipulate all three forms to drive their compatriots
toward rebellion.

One power of the pamphlet genre is its flexibility in allowing for other
forms. As a proposed "instruction to the said deputies," *A Summary View*
partakes of official sanction even though it represents a minority view; inevitably, many who read it in 1774 assume that it represents established policy.
The form of a legislative resolution also enables Jefferson to express personal
ideas as the will of a collective presence. The first person plural pronominal
address seems to come from all Americans, and this "we" is carefully disembodied so as to obscure the possibility of particularized differences. The title
of the pamphlet, selected by Jefferson's colleagues, then reinforces this characteristic. A "summary view" implies an abridgment with overall authority; it
pretends to cover the main points, leaving aside secondary differences.

Legislative resolutions rarely reach popular audiences in the way that this
one does. It is Jefferson's letter to the king that absorbs readers then and now,
and this transition – from formal resolution to emotional letter – occurs immediately in *A Summary View*. Jefferson's "instruction . . . that an humble and
dutiful address be presented to his Majesty" merges with the idea of that
address, though without much humbleness of tone. The king is the appropriate addressee because, as Jefferson tells him, he is "the only mediatory power
between the several States of the British empire." There is no give in this letter.
As official recipient, George III can hardly accept the role assigned him, that of
a diminished "mediatory power." Neither can he have welcomed a communication so explicitly "divested of those expressions of servility, which would
persuade his Majesty that we are asking favors, and not rights." In the end,
Jefferson's language deliberately seeks to offend. "Open your breast, Sire, to
liberal and expanded thought," he orders, condescending to his king.

The artifice of a "humble and dutiful address" actually works as a political
diatribe in pamphlet form, a rallying call to the real recipients of *A Summary
View,* other Americans. And for these countrymen, apprehensive as they have
to be in 1774, Jefferson adds a veiled admonition. "Let those flatter, who
fear," he warns them; "it is not an American art." The brag and bounce in
this assertion also contains a bullying tone that should not be overlooked.
Unmistakably, those who continue to bow to their king are now somehow
less than American. The threat is veiled in a rhetoric of solidarity, but both
the reason and the high emotion of Jefferson's pamphlet are plain on the
issue. At the heart of *A Summary View* in an interpretation of law in America
that changes the king of England into an alien presence and loyalty toward
him into an unnatural act.

The most curious aspect of *A Summary View* consists in the enormous political distance that it posits between England and America. Jefferson's description of the right of emigration under natural law leaves Americans closer in spirit to their Saxon ancestors than to their contemporaries in England. So distant are the latter that parliamentary encroachments appear as "acts of power, assumed by a body of men foreign to our constitutions, and unacknowledged by our laws." Jefferson's Americans speak a different conception of law than Englishmen — a conception based on "that freedom of language and sentiment which becomes a free people claiming their rights as derived from the laws of nature." The result is a bifurcation in behaviors and understandings. While natural law cuts across English law more decisively in America, the king and his colonial governors have been carrying specific power "beyond every limit known or provided by the laws."

England and America are on a collision course, and a collision on these terms is not one that the youthful Jefferson is inclined to avoid. Much of *A Summary View* is given over to the "arbitrary measures," "despotism," "series of oppressions," and "exercises of usurped power" that kings and their ministers have employed to disturb the natural harmony of British America. Amidst the litany of accusations and implied parallels to the Norman conquest of Saxon England, Jefferson finds himself at a loss for "terms reconcilable to Majesty, and at the same time to truth." Neither does the idea of a handful of American representatives in Parliament change matters. "Can any one reason be assigned," he wonders, "why one hundred and sixty thousand electors in the island of Great Britain, should give law to four millions in the States of America, every individual of whom is equal to every individual of them in virtue, in understanding, and in bodily strength?"

The man who asks this question no longer thinks in narrow terms about the repeal of specific measures. Everywhere, on every page of *A Summary View*, America will be better off without its king and royal governors. Jefferson's mood can be gauged by the timing of his pamphlet; he drafts it just after a colony-wide day of protest. "[T]he effect of the day, through the whole colony," his autobiography notes, "was like a shock of electricity, arousing every man, and placing him erect and solidly on his centre." Only an audacious statement will suffice in this setting. "An exasperated people, who feel that they possess power," he tells George III, "are not easily restrained within limits strictly regular." The writer of these words already has pledged his life, his fortune, and his sacred honor to the American cause. Excitement over *A Summary View of the Rights of British America* flows from its tacit recognition of the need for revolution. Jefferson burns his bridges in 1774, an act of courage that will lend a practiced equanimity to his eloquence in the summer of 1776.

David Rittenhouse, the astronomer and inventor of a world-famous orrery of the solar system, seeks the same distance from Europe that Jefferson finds through politics and law. If anything, Rittenhouse's effort is the more remarkable of the two because eighteenth-century astronomy emphasizes linkages, attractions, order, proportion, and the relation of forces – all elements that overcome distance. *An Oration Delivered Before the American Philosophical Society* (1775) is a scientific treatise that cannot resist political statement. Behind the compulsion is another American intellectual's fear of European influence. Like Jefferson, Rittenhouse hopes for a separate America before the Revolution. But why should separation work so well? Both writers envisage an America somehow safe in the natural harmonies of the New World. Rittenhouse, however, comes closer to the problems in that assumption because his subject, astronomy, forces firmer articulation of inchoate though controlling assumptions about the natural world.

Eighteenth-century scientists easily posit a moral universe, and, of all the sciences in Enlightenment thought, astronomy most nearly approaches a conception of deity. Rittenhouse utilizes these conventions in his presentation of the rise and progress of astronomy. "Every enlargement of our faculties," he observes, "every new happiness conferred upon us, every step we advance towards the perfection of the divinity, will very probably render us more and more sensible of his inexhaustible shores of communicable bliss, and of his inaccessible perfections." Yet increased perceptions do not explain why new shores in themselves should involve a greater bliss. Rittenhouse finesses the problem, using metaphors of light, motion, and divinity as mutually exchangeable quantifications of universal intelligence. In his own words, "[D]ivine energy supports that universal *substratum* on which all corporal substances subsist, that the laws of motion are derived from, and that wings *light* with angelic swiftness."

The light of discovery privileges the newly discovered object. To this implied premise, Rittenhouse adds the assumption that untouched objects – untouched by human hands – reflect pure purpose. The symbol of this perfection comes, readily enough, in the stars above: "yonder radiant orbs, traversing in silent Majesty the etherial regions, are the peaceful seats of innocence and bliss. Where neither natural nor moral evil has ever yet intruded; where to enjoy with gratitude and adoration the creator's bounty, is the business of existence." These thoughts lead directly to the nearer analogy of the New World, which, like the heavens, continues relatively untouched by such evils as "British thunder impelled by British thirst of gain." Rittenhouse's conclusion is an extraordinary one. "I am ready to wish – vain wish! that nature would raise her everlasting bars between the new and old world; and make a voyage to Europe as impracticable as one to the moon."

The astronomer apologizes for this digression, one that runs against the theme of perceptual enlargement. A more appropriate parallel, as he admits, would cite "that disposition of lands and seas, which affords a communication between distant regions, and a mutual exchange of benefits." But Rittenhouse, like so many eighteenth-century Americans, fears the "unnatural advances" of a European connection, and this fear of corruption feeds upon an inverse self-confidence in natural purity. The astronomer's contrasting emotions play themselves out along geographical lines. The liveliest moment of *An Oration* comes in its narrative of tyranny and luxury "advancing like a current irresistible, whose weight no human force can stem." These vices "have long since laid in the dust, never to rise again, the glories of Asia . . . and have nearly completed their conquest of Europe." Only the untouched and, therefore, still harmonious natural world of America remains.

Division with England cannot come fast enough for those who divide the Anglo–American world between European corruption and American purity. Symbol and act of renewed purification, the Revolution will grant Rittenhouse's most extravagant wish. War accomplishes what nature cannot in reconstituting barriers between the Old and New Worlds. And if these new barriers prove less than everlasting, difficulties in transportation still discourage generations of Americans from seeking a European experience. Indeed, many republican leaders welcome the inconvenience. No less an authority than Thomas Jefferson asks "why send an American youth to Europe for education?" As he tells John Bannister in 1787, "an American coming to Europe for education, loses in his knowledge, in his morals, in his health, in his habits, and in his happiness."

War with England obviously fulfills certain intrinsic American needs. The Revolution confirms an already obsessive and often tedious internal debate over the nature of American virtue. Less conspicuously, it shelves troubling philosophical questions concerning American identity in the natural world. With such questions in abeyance – quandaries about nature and country will preoccupy the greatest writers of the next century – revolutionary discourse is left to elaborate a narrative of American purity in the New World. One consequence is a series of easy identifications. For the several generations around the Revolution, "virtue," "nature," and "America" are mutually compatible and, at times, interchangeable terms of reference.

How the story actually works toward cultural objectifications can be seen in a common symbol. David Rittenhouse might have thought little of the alternating stripes of red and white in the new flag of the United States, but he surely must have nodded assent over the rest of the design when it is announced on June 14, 1777. Congress orders "that the Union be 13 stars white in a blue field, representing a new constellation." The hieroglyph epitomizes the astronomer's hope. Joining the conviction of the Enlightenment and religious faith, the Revolution transfigures the stars into a type for new world republicanism. Under this symbol of the new constellation, amidst presumed seats of innocence and bliss, citizens are to enjoy the creator's bounty. In a secularizing vision, the land of plenty will soon be, in Rittenhouse's phrase, "the business of existence."

IV

The first catalyst of change in 1776 is literary in form. Thomas Paine's *Common Sense* appears in Philadelphia on January 10th of the year. His pamphlet runs through a first printing of one thousand copies in a week and, according to its author, one hundred twenty thousand copies in three months, a phenomenal number for the times. No one questions its impact on immediate thought. Two of its most important first readers, Benjamin Franklin and George Washington, speak of, respectively, its "prodigious" influence and its "unanswerable reasoning." Other commentators quickly assign it a unique place in the changing political scene. "[*Common Sense*]," claims a writer in *The New York Constitutional Gazette* on February 24th, "introduces a new system of politics as widely different from the old, as the Copernican system is from the Ptolemaic." Overwhelming when it is issued, *Common Sense* lives as literature today, the one pamphlet from the period that still captures the imagination of the American reader.

This success – immediate, unique, and enduring – stands somewhat in the way of interpretation. Scholars have not stressed the innate qualities of the pamphlet so much as they have interpreted its impact. Paine is said to have collared the language of the people; *or* to have established psychological equivalencies between his own situation and that of the thirteen colonies; *or* to have caught the oppositional rhetoric of colonial politics at the crucial moment; *or* to have brought the peculiar perspective of a lower-class Englishman to American problems. True enough in themselves, these assumptions linger on the surface of analysis. They have missed the deeper levels of Paine's essay, where the ultimate dynamic of the Revolution is at work.

Three elements are worth isolating in explaining the power of Thomas Paine's literary achievement: one rhetorical, one philosophical, and one political. Rhetorically, Paine ends the impasse that loyal resistance imposes on colonial argumentation. Even Jefferson feels obliged to conclude his attack in *A Summary View* with pious hopes for "love and harmony through the whole empire," and James Wilson continues to speak for most Americans when, on February 13, 1776, he repeatedly disavows any desire for independence on the part of "humble, unaspiring Colonists" in *An Address to the Inhabitants of the Colonies.* Paine cuts through these contortions at a stroke; the king of England is the acknowledged enemy of *Common Sense.* To the familiar but still intimidating cries of "Treason! Treason!," he substitutes blunt assent for the clever evasions of previous writers. Figuratively speaking, *Common Sense* refashions Patrick Henry: this *is* treason; now make the most of it.

Philosophically, Paine excels all other writers of the moment in creating political thought out of religious and scientific imagery. Jefferson will come to match his skill, but in 1776 only Paine proves truly capable of wedding a living religious voice and scientific language to secular political pamphleteering, and this accomplishment is a large part of his appeal. In *Common Sense,* nature reveals, reason explains, and God ordains that "the birth-day of a new world is at hand." This event partakes of "the glorious union of all things"; it marks the beginning of "a continental form of government" that will make America "the glory of the earth." God reigns above this creation as "the king of America." On earth, "the Word of God" appears as the rule of law in the emerging Republic. Easily, then, "in America the law is king."

Meanwhile, in Europe, the hereditary succession of kings is "unanswerably" a parallel to original sin. Since "the palaces of kings are built on the ruins of the bowers of paradise," it follows that "reconciliation and ruin are nearly related." Scientifically, monarchy is an unwanted complexity against "the simple voice of nature and of reason," where "the more simple any thing is, the less liable it is to be disordered, and the easier repaired when disordered." Reconciliation, therefore, is "*a matter exceedingly perplexed and complicated*" – "INDEPENDENCE *being a* SINGLE SIMPLE LINE." The history of religion and the geometry of science concur. In showing that "there is something very absurd, in supposing a continent to be perpetually governed by an island," Paine resorts to the conventional Newtonian metaphor of the times: "In no instance hath nature made the satellite larger than its primary planet." The entwining imagery of religion, science, and politics works to remove every hesitation, every fear of the unknown, every anxiety over the lost conveniences in British rule.

The prescience of Paine's positive vision for America also depends upon the careful conflation of religious and political imagery. *Common Sense* outlines the vital aspects of the unfolding American experiment before they happen: the continental scope of republicanism, its representative form, even its denouement in a national convention and written constitution. Significantly, Paine can suggest so much only because he possesses a set of religious ideas about what should happen. The spontaneous creation of a continental union simply cannot be conceived in strictly secular terms in 1776. The language of political reference then in use will not justify the extrapolation.

Instead, Paine describes an impending millennium of republican culture, and the contrivance of God's new Israel proves exceedingly useful in this regard. "The Reformation was preceded by the discovery of America," explains *Common Sense,* "as if the Almighty graciously meant to open a sanctuary to the persecuted in future years." Those future years have now come to pass, and they are safe only in "the distance at which the Almighty hath placed England and America." Paine, who has lived in both worlds, can insist that "the authority of the one, over the other, was never the design of Heaven." To the contrary, separation and a hatred of things English is part of God's plan. "As well can the lover forgive the ravisher of his mistress, as the continent forgive the murders of Britain," observes Paine. "The Almighty hath implanted in us these unextinguishable feelings for good and wise purposes." It is God's design, not human events, that gives this vast and largely unpopulated continent a single voice.

The third isolatable element in Paine's achievement, a peculiar politics, enables him to convert guilt over lost loyalties into anger and a new definition of country. It is here that the workings of *Common Sense* have been least understood because also least pleasant to contemplate. Critics have noted Paine's creative objectification of colonial unrest as patriotism and his corresponding articulation of the emotions of the mob. But how does he put the unrest of the moment to such explosive use, and what does it mean to articulate the emotions of the mob? Answers to such questions are difficult; they involve fault lines between the elitism of the published word and the lost emotive context of that word in the speech and will of the people. *Common Sense,* more than any other writing of the period, tries to bridge the divide.

The distinction between the anger of colonial Americans and their ability to express that anger fully in formal prose is one effect of the decorum of loyalty already noted in the pamphlet tradition. Figures like Richard Bland, James Otis, John Dickinson, and even Thomas Jefferson all mean more than they can actually say in print. Within the oral culture, however, anger is a more unbridled source of definition. Popular uprisings occur frequently enough in eighteenth-century America for the mob to operate as an intrinsic part of colonial life and as a vital extralegal arm in important communal decisions. If these upheavals are originally episodic events geared to local issues of the moment (the punishment of outlaws and other deviants, land title disputes, impressment controversies, customs enforcement, problems in local defense, and intraneighborhood conflicts of all kinds), they become a more widespread and cohesive phenomenon in the late 1760s and early 1770s. Beginning with the Stamp Act controversy, mob action is a regular and dominant force in the colonial challenge to imperial policies. It is also the clearest indication that people in every colony anticipate their leaders' opposition to British rule.

Why do we hear so little about rioting and the nature of the mob in the major literature of the Revolution? Loyalists, often the recipients of the mob's attentions, do describe their distress in private writings, but revolutionary leaders generally withhold comment in their fear that further publicity will push the people's right of resistance toward a justification of public disorder. The more chaotic events become, the less these leaders wish to discuss or write about the situation. Even radical Whigs worry about inflaming the populace. A ploy of accountability in imperial politics, their restraint in pamphleteering is also a strategy for keeping the lower orders in line.

The great exception to the rhetoric of restrained feelings is, of course, *Common Sense,* and Paine's anger finds an immediate outlet in America. When he introduces his pamphlet, Paine calls upon "every Man to whom Nature hath given the Power of feeling." He magnifies emotion in explicit contrast to those who seek to restrain it. The greatest danger in an essay obsessed with "proving enmity (or enemyship)" is not the British but rather "men of passive tempers." More than modest exertion, the American situation requires a total commitment to "those feelings and affections which nature justifies." These feelings, when most deeply probed by Paine, are almost always ones of rage. The true guardian of appropriate emotion in *Common Sense* is none other than Satan, who speaks, though unnamed, from Milton's *Paradise Lost:* "never can true reconcilement grow where wounds of deadly hate have pierced so deep." Forgiveness is an unnatural feeling in this world. "There are injuries which nature cannot forgive; she would cease to be nature if she did," Paine observes.

Paine repeatedly justifies and encourages the fact of hatred, bringing that emotion to bear first against the king of England, next against traitors in America, and only then on the positive goal of building a continental republic. "Men read by way of revenge," he explains, and his own reading in *Common Sense* is fueled by images of blood, ashes, suffering, cruelty, villainy, corruption, monstrosity, and hellishness. In April of the year, when critics call him "furious," Paine welcomes the accusation and turns it back upon them. "There are men, too," he responds as *The Forester,* "who have not virtue enough to be angry."

The point to remember is that Paine's natural and intended audience is the American mob. It is not just that Paine appropriates the language of the people. He uses anger, the natural emotion of the mob, to let the most active groups find themselves in the general will of a republican citizenry. Recognizing that "the mind of the multitude is left at random, and feeling no fixed object before them," Paine writes to give the mob specific direction in the act of independence. *Common Sense* identifies three ways of achieving independency: "by the legal voice of the people in Congress; by a military power; or by a mob." The beauty of action in the moment of 1776 is that it combines all three. Congress, soldiery, and mob can be all one if Americans will only recognize "the present time is the true time." In the moment, writes Paine, "our soldiers are citizens, and the multitude a body of reasonable men."

The explosive response to *Common Sense* comes in the mob's recognition of its own purpose and dignity. After a decade of pamphleteering on the rationality of moderate opposition – a rationality that necessarily regards the mob as a shameful by-product – Paine argues that anger and public outrage are the central vehicles of colonial identity and, hence, of cultural salvation. Recent theories about mass behavior and its modes of expression in nationalism help to illustrate the colossal effectiveness of this strategy. The cultural critic Elias Canetti has identified four central traits and a controlling activity of the mob, or crowd as he calls it, in his *Crowds and Power* (1962): the crowd wants to grow, it seeks equality within itself, it loves density, and it needs direction. Its most conspicuous activity comes in its destructiveness. Wherefore, in its early growth, the crowd or mob builds an identity by destroying representational boundary images; the doors and windows of houses are useful targets. In fact, symbolic violations of hierarchy of just this kind characterize the American mob before and during the Revolution.

Common Sense moves along these axes. Its rhetoric begins in an intellectual attack upon monarchy that culminates in a specific call to arms; the goal is to destroy all linkage with Britain. Three positive elements of cohesion then support this impulse to destroy: first, discovered mutuality in a language of equality; next, a realization of density in the projected solidarity of union; and last, a recognition of direction in group identification with an expanding continental republic. Colonial readers who accept these incentives strike a simple bargain. They sacrifice local, provincial identity, the symbol of which is their connection to England, for an enlarged American view.

There are dangers in Paine's strategy. The call for a citizen who will "generously enlarge his views beyond the present day" runs certain risks. Critics then and now have noted the cold comfort and potential isolation in Paine's abstractions of enlargement. Where are the compensating notions of attachment, the affecting and familiar links, in Paine's "the universal order of things" and "the RIGHTS OF MANKIND"? How, exactly, is the new American supposed to "hold out to his neighbour the hearty hand of friendship"? Paine's answer relies on the projected cohesion of his mob in action. For not only is the crowd the natural symbol of the isolated figure, but the crowd as nation begins to take on a special power of identity in this last part of the eighteenth century. The first to cut himself free of colonial links, Paine is also the first to recognize the absolute priority of a national argument in revolutionary America. As Elias Canetti will later elaborate on Paine's realization, "We can take it for granted that no member of a nation ever sees himself alone."

The national argument in *Common Sense* is more an expression than a formal idea, but this, too, can be a strength if taken with the realization that nationalisms are not distinguished by originality of conception or thought but by the style in which they are imagined. The style and tones in which Paine first imagines a republic of states united on the American continent are emotional rather than intellectual, and they revolve around an angry, suffering, embattled self-assertion. That self takes a ubiquitous pronominal form. The ever-present "we" of the pamphlet comprises neither colonies, nor voting citizens, nor leaderships of any kind. It concentrates, rather, on every discriminate American self in collective union. Disturbingly, this narrating self then shrinks in scope during successive stages of argumentation. Excluded by the third section of *Common Sense* are "all those who espouse the doctrine of reconciliation." The designation encompasses not just Loyalists and Tories but also "weak men who *cannot* see, prejudiced men who *will not* see," and, in a much larger category, "moderate men, who think better of the European world than it deserves."

A consummate but generally unrecognized irony emerges from the growing list of restrictions. The test of the worthy citizen narrows even as Paine insists upon the largest view of country. True Americans must declare themselves angry enough to act against England. Only colonials who have suffered "the present sorrow" of America are allowed to judge "the offences of Great Britain," and having suffered, those who seek reconciliation are unworthy of the name of citizen; they "have the heart of a coward, and the spirit of a sycophant." Paine reserves a special wrath for the inhabitant who does nothing at all in this crisis: "there is no punishment which that man doth not deserve." In the end, a defeated British soldier deserves more respect than a citizen caught on the wrong side. "The one forfeits his liberty the other his head."

Behind the threat is the unmediated commonality of *Common Sense*. Citizens gain security and transcend the limits set upon individual identity when they mass together, but the act of joining also establishes psychological patterns of exclusion; you are for the mob or it is against you. Paine is not the last to understand the power of this appeal in a democracy. Exclusionary tactics in civic membership, hidden enemies (within and abroad), melodramas of suffering and victimization, challenges against patriotic standing, the assignation of faintheartedness to identified opponents, and, above all, the anticipated communal cohesion that comes in the successful explosion of righteous anger – these are devices that Americans use in 1776 and still use to imagine their national community.

Paine realizes intuitively, as no writer before him quite does, that imagining a democratic American community requires a different series of strategies in a writer. Consider the contrast of John Adams and other radical pamphleteers meeting with three hundred and fifty supporters under the Liberty Tree at Dorchester in August 1769. Adams, jotting in his diary, wishes to "Tinge the minds of the People" and to "impregnate them with the sentiments of Liberty," but he needs simultaneously to "render the People fond of their Leaders in the Cause" and to secure the place of authority, his own included, "hearty in the Cause." Accordingly, the act of writing seeks both to inspire the people and to demonstrate a visible leadership in control of the course of events. Paine, on the other hand, offers words that address every citizen directly and without mediation of any kind, and his words have a very different purpose in mind.

Common Sense strives to empower the people, "a truly legal authority," over every group distinct therefrom. Paine takes his title from the very term in eighteenth-century politics that distinguishes between the complexity of special knowledge and the natural simplicity of the common good. Rhetorically, "common sense" operates as a check upon those men of place and learning who use their advantages to protect themselves and their class in a language of controlled differentiations. When Paine uses the idea – "nothing more than simple facts, plain arguments, and common sense" – he means three things: that anyone can understand his pamphlet, that everyone should, and that no other narrative or explanation or ceremony is necessary for action to follow comprehension. The language of common sense touches the readiest understanding; it has no literary or political tolerance for a leadership that would control thought.

In the conjunction of concept and literary work, *Common Sense* struggles against every gradation that might stand in the way of common action. "Where there are no distinctions there can be no superiority," writes Paine in his vision of the independent states, "perfect equality affords no temptation." The well-to-do are a special problem in this scheme for revolution ("The rich are in general slaves to fear, and submit to courtly power with the trembling duplicity of a spaniel"). Everything that distances the power or the importance of the people is suspect – everything. For Paine, in the first significant use of a favorite trope in American politics, even the vaunted checks and balances of the British Constitution signify "an house divided against itself."

Much more is at stake in the moment of 1776 than conflict with England. The question of home rule raises an immediate and troubling sequel: Who will rule at home? There is no more vexed query in America in the 1770s and early 1780s, and of all the leaders of the Revolution, only Tom Paine offers a completely spontaneous, ingenuous reply. In the ultimate challenge of the Revolution, he welds the relation of ruler and ruled together in the simplest of terms. The people can oppose "the unmeaning name of king" in *Common Sense* because the power of government already has been rightly and actively theirs in every moment of decision that they might want to name.

V

Other revolutionary leaders strain against the leveling spirit of Paine's pro-nouncement. They want the magic of *Common Sense* without its simplifying sweep and without its overriding anger. Yet, in straining, these leaders also see that their exertions cut across symbiotic strengths. The stark emotive power of Paine springs from his acceptance of the power of the people, and the effect of that realization on a new American elite is a mixture of fascina-tion, frustration, and dread. We glimpse all of these impulses in John Adams's famous summary. To Benjamin Waterhouse in 1805 he confides:

I know not whether any Man in the World has had more influence on its inhabitants or affairs for the last thirty years than Tom Paine. There can be no severer Satyr on the Age. For such a mongrel between Pigg and Puppy, begotten by a wild Boar on a Bitch Wolf, never before in any Age of the World was suffered by the Poltroonery of mankind, to run through such a Career of Mischief. Call it then the Age of Paine.

This invective conveys more powerfully than any argument the nature of the divide in revolutionary and postrevolutionary rhetoric. The vitality of the mongrel comes from below. How promiscuous should the role of the people be in a people's government? That is the question for every writer in 1776. Adams can be so acerbic because he instantly recognizes and articulates the threat posed. Writing James Sullivan in May of 1776, just four months after *Common Sense* appears, Adams admits that "the only moral foundation of government, is the consent of the people," but he also asks "to what extent shall we carry the principle?" The rest of his letter condemns the bottomless inclusions that the principle encourages. "Depend upon it, Sir," Adams advises, "it is dangerous to open so fruitful a source of controversy. . . . It tends to confound and destroy all distinctions, and prostrate all ranks to one common level." His personal mission in 1776 is clear, and it goes beyond the accomplishment of independence.

Adams writes a pamphlet of his own in 1776, *Thoughts on Government*. Second only to *Common Sense* in influence, it is also a direct response. At the time, Adams's autobiography reports a conversation with Paine on the subject: "I told him . . . I was as much afraid of his Work [as] he was of mine. His plan was so democratical, without any restraint or even an Attempt at any Equilibrium as Counterpoise, that it must produce confusion and every Evil Work." *Thoughts on Government,* originating in a letter to Richard Henry Lee, agrees with *Common Sense* on the need for republican government and engages in its own brand of revolutionary rhetoric, extolling the empire of laws, elective accountability, and regular rotation in office. There, however, the similarities end.

If the contrasting initiatives of *Thoughts on Government* sound familiar, it is because they supply the effective blueprint that Americans act upon after they, to use the author's delicate phrase, "are put out of the royal protection." Adams rejects Paine's notion of a single democratic assembly for a more complex bicameralism. He favors an independent judiciary, balances between branches of government, and, most important of all, the delegation of power. "The first necessary step, then," he writes, "is to depute power from the many to a few of the most wise and good." Where Paine counts on the power of the people, Adams draws upon an enlightened restriction through law. "You and I, my dear friend," he tells Richard Henry Lee, "have been sent into life at a time when the greatest lawgivers of antiquity would have wished to live."

Adams's self-confidence rides as high as Paine's, which is in itself impressive when one considers the state of government and law in America in 1776. As the Revolution begins, there are no functioning courts in North America. The separate colonies lack effective local executive authority, and depend upon an untried and fundamentally weak central government. All foundational legitimacy has been lost in the sudden irrelevance of colonial charters. It is with perfect credence that Samuel West can use his election sermon in 1776 to prove that the people, "having not the civil law to regulate themselves by, became a law unto themselves; and by their conduct they have shown that they were regulated by the law of God written in their hearts."

These weaknesses in government actually work in Adams's favor and against Paine in the long run. Stressing "the present exigency of American affairs," Adams and his allies shift the literary adventure in revolutionary thought from loose pamphleteering toward the construction of governmental institutions, an enterprise necessarily left to leadership or, in Adams's understanding, "to a few of the most wise and good." Paradoxically, the idea of a constitution as higher law – above government and derived from the people – aids this shift. The presumed special nature of constitutional writing encourages the circumvention of standard legislative institutions, where "the new men," Paine's natural allies, will gain increasing authority over the course of the Revolution. A separated enterprise, the average constitution of the period is written by a small number of men in special committee, sometimes by a single hand. John Adams will draft the Massachusetts Constitution of 1780 more-or-less on his own.

The struggle that Adams and Paine symbolize also has generic repercussions that have been forgotten. The volatility of revolutionary pamphleteering encourages radical over conservative impulses. *Thoughts on Government* may carefully gesture toward the people, but Adams also knows that his learned insistence upon "forms of government" might lead to popular censure. Quoting Milton, he begs Richard Henry Lee to protect authorial anonymity lest " 'a barbarous noise environs me / Of owls and cuckoos, asses, apes, and dogs.' " There is a subtle subversion of form in this recognition. One of the elusive shifts in early republican literature is the way Adams and other moderates use the pamphlet form to undercut its original importance. When they are finished, the age of the pamphlet is no more.

As radical forces turn against authority in western Massachusetts in 1778, the reaction of conservative pamphleteers is to regret the need for any response at all and to disclaim any claim to originality ("I pretend not to offer you any new, and cunningly devised arguments to convince you"). As "Impartial Reason" in *An Address to the Inhabitants of Berkshire County, Mass.*, William Whiting protests against anarchy and licentiousness: "I can't but take notice, how shamefully that ancient maxim, *vox populi est vox Dei* (the voice of the people is the voice of God) has been prostituted in this country." The persona of "Impartial Reason" easily distinguishes between the proper voice of elected representation and the "blasphemy and treason" of the mob, but Whiting, himself a member of the Massachusetts legislature, seems to expect more answers from the "arm of power" than from his own power of language. Curiously, he also worries that the attempt alone will replace impartial reason with anger ("ere I am aware, I should catch the epidemic disease myself, and a flame of passion, begin to rage in my own breast"). One of the growing realizations in pamphleteering is the recognition of never-ending acrimony in the act. Certainly, this writer shares a number of worries about the efficacy of his effort.

In a far more influential pamphlet from 1778, *The Essex Result,* Theophilus Parsons turns the same constitutional crisis into a noble adventure of controlled intellectual activity. Parsons, too, qualifies the meaning of *vox populi est vox Dei.* "No man will be so hardy and presumptuous," he writes, "as to affirm the truth of that proposition in its fullest extent." His candor signals changing times. Specifically, in the "arduous task" of forming a constitution, Parsons asks republicans "to look further than to the bulk of the people." Where they should look is also clear; the virtues required – wisdom, firmness, consistency, and perseverance – "will most probably be found amongst men of education and fortune." Only through these priorities will "the supreme power be so deposed and balanced, that the laws may have in view the interest of the whole." Only in this way can Americans expect a lasting constitution, "one that will smile amidst the declensions of European and Asiatic empires."

The overall impact of *The Essex Result* could not have been greater. Drafted in response to the proposed, and soon rejected, Massachusetts Constitution of 1778, this single work supplies many of the basic assumptions, gestures, and terms of American constitutionalism, including the special prominence of a bill of rights, some specifics of checks and balances, and the names and certain functions of "the house of representatives" and the "senate." But Parsons's major contribution in the moment is to lift the idea of constitution making out of the turmoil of the democratic process and away from the venue of occasional writing. Fearing that "the idea of liberty has been held up in so dazzling colours, that some of us may not be willing to submit to that subordination necessary in the freest States," Parsons finds his solutions in the idea of a correct constitution. He reduces the problems of uncertainty, chaos, and passion to the idea and unity of official and published form.

Reduction, in this case, furnishes the vision that the framers of the Federal Constitution will use to appeal to the American people. The rewards that Parsons reserves for the wise leader able to construct "the best form of government" are "a statue of gold to his memory" and "unrivalled lustre" in the annals of posterity. Well before such fame, though, this figure is already metaphorically distinct from the people:

The man who alone undertakes to form a constitution, ought to be an unimpassioned being; one enlightened mind . . . perfectly acquainted with all the alienable and unalienable rights of mankind; possessed of this grand truth, that all men are born equally free, and that no man ought to surrender any part of his natural rights, without receiving the greatest possible equivalent; and influenced by the impartial principles of rectitude and justice. . . . He ought also to be master of the histories of all the empires and states which are now existing, and all those which have figured in antiquity, and thereby able to collect and blend their respective excellencies, and avoid those defects which experience hath pointed out.

The parallels and the contrasts to John Adams's earlier description of the American writer in *A Dissertation on the Canon and Feudal Law* are instructive. Knowledge remains the same, but Adams's pamphleteer from thirteen years before "animates" and "rouses" the people, whereas this "unimpassioned" writer of constitutions uses his knowledge to overcome feeling and to resolve turmoil through skills that "possess," "master," "collect," "blend," and "avoid."

The mix of tones in works that try to both arouse and collect the people is perhaps the most palpable characteristic of early republican writing in the 1780s. Naturally geared to timeliness and excitement, the political pamphlet always exhibits these tendencies, but now more confusion enters into the choices involved. A more uncertain manic-depressive quality overtakes writers in the genre. An anonymous contributor from New Hampshire describes the phenomenon perfectly in *Address to the Public, Containing Some Remarks on the Present Political State of the American Republicks, etc.* (1786). "Amicus Republicae," as he styles himself, predicts that either virtue will make the Republic "wealthy, honorable, powerful, and happy" or vice will plunge it "into a state of the greatest calamities." He and other friends of the Republic see no middle path, no alternative to absolute success or total failure. The upshot is an obvious and active ambivalence in the observing writer: "every judicious and honest mind must, when it considers the present licentious disposition of many persons, be depressed and elated alternately by hope and fear."

Vacillation between the hope of success and the fear of failure helps constitution-makers in the 1780s and begins to erode the literary base of the more spontaneous pamphleteers. The duty of the citizen to write out a conception of country remains a literary constant still recognized by all, but, by the early 1780s, the personal attempt in pamphlet form produces mostly dismay and frustration. In performing this acknowledged "duty of a citizen," Thomas Tudor Tucker in Charleston, South Carolina, easily visualizes the ideal republic and its constitutional basis. As "Philodemus" in *Conciliatory Hints, Attempting by a Fair State of Affairs, to Remove Party Prejudice* (1784), he defines the true commonwealth as one in which "all authority is derived from the people at large, held only during their pleasure, and exercised only for their benefit" and a constitution as "a social covenant entered into by the express consent of the people, upon a footing of the most perfect equality with respect to every civil liberty." The balances in these familiar revolutionary generalizations are conventionally sound, but they no longer seem sufficient to clarify Tucker's actual situation or political agenda.

The pamphlet of the 1780s is a litany of ills. Although a talented figure like Tucker will soon enter the Continental Congress and will eventually become treasurer of the United States, a host of complexities stand in the way of his understanding and service in 1784. The "fatal influence of slavery" destroys everything, including "the boasted Characteristic of Rationality." Philodemus also wonders what to do about returning Tories, and he worries about the dangers in accepting a British conception of constitutionalism. From the other side, he fears "a government approaching to Democracy." The times are filled with "factious men assuming the mask of patriotism," with "novices in politics," with "secret combinations," with "irregularities and civil dissension," and with "a wilderness of confusion." Worst of all, Tucker knows that "our present Constitution was framed in a time of distress and confusion" and sees that it "is not founded on proper authority."

Pamphlet writing in the 1780s is about Tucker's "wilderness of confusion." It presides over a litany of ills beyond its own solution, and it looks increasingly toward another kind of writing enterprise. Salvation in Tucker's *Conciliatory Hints* means one thing: a new constitution "paramount to all acts of the Legislature, and irrepealable and unalterable by any authority but the express consent of a majority of the citizens collected by such regular mode as may be therein provided." The new challenge, shared by so many early republican intellectuals in the 1780s, lies in the framing of constitutions. Pamphleteering has begun to wait upon that eventuality.

Political writing in America has arrived at a divide – a divide that the political pamphlet will not survive intact. The volatility and immediacy of the pamphlet extend back to an oral culture, to speech and the need for protest. The desire for order, regularity, and permanence in the hope for a new constitution carry forward or toward print. The difficulties of the 1780s and time itself will place the most important revolutionary leaders of the 1770s on the side of print and constitution writing. The Philadelphia Convention of 1787, where many of these leaders will serve, brings the last flurry of pamphlets to absorb the entire nation, but the die is cast. In that flurry, the anger, frustration, localism, and rhetorical excess of the anti-Federalists give way to a new kind of pamphlet that completes even as it breaks the genre.

Alexander Hamilton will swallow his own volatile temper in *The Federalist* (1787–8) to take aim at "passions and prejudices little favorable to truth." *Federalist No. 1* gives "a lesson of moderation to those who are ever so much persuaded of their being in the right in any controversy." Dismissing the "torrent of angry and malignant passions," "the bitterness," and "the specious mask of zeal for the rights of the people" of his enemies, Publius assumes for himself "the evidence of truth" and the high ground of "a judicious estimate of our true interests, unperplexed and unbiased by considerations not connected with the public good." Hundreds of pages later, *Federalist No. 85* will conclude on the same "lesson of moderation."

The Federalist succeeds because it approaches Americans with a new act of imagination. Longer and more ponderously organized than any other pamphlet, calculated to reach from scattered and ephemeral pieces to comprehensive collection and permanent book, *The Federalist* is virtually unreadable as a pamphlet. Against the ordinary pamphleteer's embattled apologies for urgency, insufficiency, abruptness, and brevity, Publius archly promises comprehensiveness, enlargement, agreement, amiability, and candor. He does not so much raise points as, in Hamilton's opening phrase, "give a satisfactory answer to all objections." And both the nature and the source of these shifts are clear. *The Federalist* is a commentary on another sort of writing. It takes its subject, its purpose, its values, its organization, even its tone and voice from the new Federal Constitution. Publius is a successful pamphleteer, but his victory salutes a final triumph over his own genre. His gaze, also that of the country, is on the literature of public documents.

5

❦

THE LITERATURE OF PUBLIC DOCUMENTS

I

The disruptive modes in sermonizing and pamphleteering in eighteenth-century America compete with the predisposition toward consensus evident in so much writing of the period. As the first chooses perception through crisis, so the second emphasizes the possibilities in reason and progress. Separate narratives, they both contribute to revolutionary discourse – sometimes in the same breath. The skill in revolutionary writing demands the promiscuous manipulation of these tendencies in prose that often tries to be provocative and encompassing at once, but an accident of history tips the balance between them. Acrimony grows on all sides in the 1780s and, with it, an intellectual preoccupation; early republicans yearn for a better definition of their experiment in government. Constitutionalism will control that quest, and its impulses are consensual in form.

From the first, American constitutionalism differs from its English equivalent in its commitment to the written word. The biblical conjunction of sovereignty and the book of law, the need for an artificially imposed order in the wilderness, and the politics of Anglo–American relations – these factors all encourage a literal documentation of governmental forms as the reference point of communal identity. Since every act of founding a new community is also a challenge to the status quo ante, the challenge itself, however implicit, must be laid to rest in new claims of authority, placement, and acceptance. Invariably, then, community in America begins in some act of writing. If such writings tend to confirm traditional beliefs, they also reconstitute those beliefs in a moment of registered agreement, and these moments in themselves soon become a prerequisite to group identity.

This means that colonial leaders respond to the uncertainty and flimsiness of their new social forms by inscribing fundamental law more generally, more frequently, more compulsively in official documents. By way of contrast, their English counterparts put fundamental law to paper mostly in the form of individual rights and only when faced with an explicit political challenge; Magna Carta and the Bill of Rights of 1689 provide the standard examples.

In America, the need to address beginnings – instead of assuming them from time immemorial – puts a special pressure of comprehensiveness on official language, and that pressure is immediate; there is no time in the formality of colonial origins to let institutions evolve as they did in England. Instead, words and the formal presentation of them must substitute for custom and the absent past. Social compacts must also be constitutions of government. The whole artifice of colonial charters, covenants, compacts, ordinances, fundamentals, and constitutions represent a perpetual crisis in definition, a steady search for the words that will complete identity in a new moment of agreement. And the very steadiness of that search is also an underlying source as well as a symptom of developing facility.

Documents like the Mayflower Compact of 1620 and the Ordinance and Constitution for Virginia of 1621 create social and political structures as much as they assert individual rights. The desire to "covenant and combine ourselves together into a civil Body Politick," in the first instance, and "to settle such a forme of government," in the second, requires a psychology of framing. As the Mayflower Compact claims to "enact, constitute, and frame . . . just and equal Laws, Ordinances, Acts, Constitutions, and Officers," so the Ordinance and Constitution for Virginia strives "to make our Entrance, by ordaining & establishing . . . supreame Counsells." These documents and others like them also take the form of a writing upon another writing. As responses in kind to the charters of colonial incorporation (in these two cases from James I, king of England), they engender intertextual tensions, operating at once as glosses upon the king's grant and as extensions of it.

These preoccupations – faith in the written word, the psychology of framing, the specific language of ordination and establishment, and the textual mediation of power received and power assumed – are touchstones in measuring the growth of a literature of public documents. They also point to the very crux of the Revolution as literary achievement in the records of ultimate foundation, The Declaration of Independence in 1776 and the Federal Constitution of 1787. For in such methodologies of composition, collections of peoples engage in similar acts of origination from colony to colony, and the congruences allow them to unite after more than a century of limited contact and cultural divergence. Union, as such, need not have taken place; there is no single people to claim the collective identity of "American" in 1760. More to the point, union could not have taken place if "the spirit of 1776" had not received from previous generations the will and the art of reconstitution. "Many" become "one" only because colonial peoples have imbibed a confidence and a skill in political reformulation *before* the Revolution.

II

The concise uses of language in the Declaration of Independence have encouraged a search for particular sources even though the broadest influences pertain. We have seen how the nature of a consensual literature and the ideology of the Enlightenment dictate strategies of assimilation in prose. Nowhere is this characteristic more important than here, in the highest expression of the American Enlightenment. "All its authority," runs Jefferson's summary of the Declaration of Independence in 1825, "rests then on the harmonizing sentiments of the day."

Precision lies in the form of the Declaration and not in the intellectual influences upon it. If the language of self-evidence and of equality seems to come from John Locke's *Second Treatise of Civil Government* (1690), it can be found just as easily in Algernon Sidney's *Discourses Concerning Government* (1698) and, by the 1770s, everywhere in colonial America. Reference to "the pursuit of happiness" may suggest specific writers in the Scottish Enlightenment (Francis Hutcheson, David Hume, Adam Smith, Lord Kames) or, alternatively, Jean-Jacques Burlamaqui, but the idea is a general preoccupation in moral philosophy by 1776 and a regular formula in the political writings of John Adams, George Mason, James Wilson, James Otis, and others. The Declaration actually weaves three essential strands together – the constitutional writings of colonial America, Whig political theory, and English common law. Skill enters in the writer's proficient construction of a unified text from them.

Most of the Declaration, in both word and thought, follows directly from earlier documents written by Americans – more specifically, from earlier compacts, resolves, and state constitutions. All but four of the document's twenty-eight charges against the king of England appear in preceding state constitutions (specifically, the constitutions of New Hampshire, South Carolina, and Virginia). Similar lists of grievances fill colonial newspapers, and these are the elements that absorb eighteenth-century readers. The phraseology of the opening paragraphs resembles the preamble to the Virginia Constitution, adopted in June of 1776, and George Mason's Declaration of Rights for Virginia, adopted and widely circulated in the same month. Even the famous conclusion – "we mutually pledge to each other our Lives, our Fortunes, and our sacred Honor" – is a paraphrase of the Mecklenburg Resolves of North Carolina, published in May 1775.

Yet, in virtually every instance, the language of the Declaration is sharper and more succinct than its background sources. In part, these improvements reflect what John Adams, writing to Timothy Pickering in 1822, calls Jefferson's "happy talent of composition" and "peculiar felicity of expression."

In part, however, they bespeak the compressed energy and economy of understanding that occurs when form and thought truly cohere in a mastery of genre. This point needs to be properly understood. Eighteenth-century American writings are not generally known for such mastery, but they achieve an unparalleled maturity in the literature of public documents.

The blend of combinations is what counts in the Declaration. Tonally, the languages of science and politics join to convey an aura of inevitable consequence within self-evidence (the causes and constraining necessities that impel and dissolve bands in the course of human events). Thematically, the same sense of inevitability turns the Whig theory of history into a passionate source of story ("The history of the present King of Great Britain is a history of repeated injuries and usurpations, all having in direct object the establishment of an absolute Tyranny over these States"). Colonists, already familiar with extended narratives of royal despotism from *Common Sense* and other popular writings, easily blame a king for the miseries of history. The Declaration uses "a long train of abuses and usurpations" to elide troubling complexities; its self-confidence in form is never clearer than in what it decides *not* to talk about. The plan to recover lost rights from a tyrant makes use of neither the vocabulary of rebellion nor the existing debates over parliamentary jurisdiction – vexed subjects in colonial life.

Inevitability also flows from the nature of repetition in the Declaration, a characteristic that illustrates yet another level of creativity. Heavily syllogistic, the language of the document moves from major premise (the people have the right to overthrow a leader who engages in a deliberate design of tyranny) to minor premise (the king of England is such a tyrant) to conclusion (the people of the American colonies have no choice but to overthrow). There is genius in stressing the minor premise, the king as tyrant. For within the laborious proofs of the Declaration – "let facts be submitted to a candid world" – one fact remains utterly implicit: the presumption of a single people desirous of overthrow. As late as June of 1776, Jefferson, in his autobiography, sees "that the colonies of New York, New Jersey, Pennsylvania, Delaware, Maryland, and South Carolina were not yet matured for falling from the parent stem." He also reports fierce debate in America over the crucial units of meaning: colonies or citizens, representatives or constituents, "the murmurs of some" or "the opposing voice of the freer part of the people."

Does the Declaration create thirteen separate peoples who agree or one national people? The opening sentence, where "one people" dissolves bands with "another," implies a single identity, as do three other capitalized uses of the word "People" and the promiscuous mix of bare signatures at the end of the document; citizens sign the Declaration, not state representatives. But the careful title, "The Unanimous Declaration of the Thirteen United States of America," can be construed either way. Other uses of the word "people" maintain a deliberate tension; and from the other side, plural references to the states dominate syntax ("these United Colonies are, and of Right ought to be free," "as Free and Independent States, they have full power," and so on). Plainly, the psychology of opposition welcomes ambiguity: the dual principles of government – the colonies as states *and* a confederation thereof – remain deliberately uncertain. Readers of the Declaration are left with a choice within unities. Reiteration of the word "people," ten uses in all, creates identity, but the overriding definition of people *against* the king takes many forms, and all of them reinforce the common cause.

There is craft in the subtlety of such balances, but real vision lies beyond them. The document's creative integrations fuse in a powerful generic consideration. Thomas Jefferson and most of his colleagues in the second Continental Congress are eighteenth-century lawyers steeped in the English common-law tradition. They know that a *declaration* is the foremost form of pleading in a legal action and that it is the only form to be brought before a king for redress or vindication. "Pleadings," explains Blackstone in his widely read *Commentaries on the Laws of England* (1765–9), "are the mutual altercations between the plaintiff and defendent. . . . The first of these is the *declaration, narratio,* or *count,* anciently called the *tale;* in which the plaintiff sets forth his cause of complaint at length . . . with the additional circumstances of time and place, when and where the injury was committed."

Colonial Americans also know how to use a legal declaration for political ends. Both the English Petition of Right in 1628 (a demand of the House of Commons declaring essential rights and sent directly to Charles I) and the Bill of Rights of 1689 (a similar act, declaring the rights and liberties of English subjects after a listing of evils under James II) are declarations of this kind. Jefferson and his colleagues are part of an Anglo-Saxon revolutionary tradition – part of what the historian G. M. Trevelyan, describing the Revolution of 1688, calls "the triumph of the Common Law and lawyers over the king." The point is not just that English colonists in America know what to write and how to write it in 1776, but that they look upon the writing thereof as the highest patriotism, as nothing less than the whole meaning of history in their time.

The nexus of literary ingenuity and historical implication allows the drafters of the Declaration to manipulate genre without breaking the form. The long list of grievances against the king imitates common-law practice, where a declaration sets forth every conceivable cause of action "at length" to guard against a nonsuit or failure of proof in any one count. Formulaic overkill also feeds the Whig conspiratorial view of royal power as one continuous and excessive abuse of ancient rights and natural liberties. Elsewhere, appeal to "the Supreme judge of the world" evokes the modes of the courtroom and so does the final oath ("we mutually pledge to each other our Lives, our Fortunes and our sacred Honor"). In fact, the form of this conclusion is a direct parallel to the pledge of surety that every plaintiff offers against the charge of a frivolous suit in a common-law action.

The language and forms of legality carry the Declaration another step from the unseemliness of rebellion by associating legal action with "the Laws of Nature." The same maneuver solidifies "the people" in the unifying symbol of "plaintiff" and lends formality, ceremony, and credibility to conflict. Time and again, form and content work together. As the balance of plaintiff against defendant in "mutual altercation" confirms the Declaration's sweeping claim of "separate and equal station," so the whole conceit of English courtroom pleading supports "the voice of justice and consanguinity" of American protest.

The symbolism of the king as defendant is peculiarly momentous. Its crude effectiveness daunts even *The Annual Register*, which, in publishing the Declaration in England in 1776, removes the words "King of Great Britain" from the list of grievances against him. Two years later, *The Register* still speaks of how "the American declaration of independence astonished [members of Parliament] with a new, awful, and unexpected situation of public affairs." As the defendant in the Declaration, the king must "put in a *plea*," in Blackstone's explanation of the procedures, "or else the plaintiff will at once recover judgment by *default*." The transformation in colonial self-presentation is from humble suppliant to righteous accuser. All thought of political negotiation disappears in the legal charge of guilt or innocence, a determination already fixed against the king in Whig mythology.

There is genuine, explosive power in these devices, and the ensuing punch sets the English world on its heels. That power is all the greater because the originality of the conception grows out of familiar form. The document casts the basis of colonial action in a language and context that every educated member of the British Empire instantly grasps. Read aloud and then posted in every American village, the Declaration succeeds in its plea for recognition because it is so instantly recognizable. Different appreciations have come to dominate modern understanding, but this, too, is part of the lasting power of the document. Ancient accusations against a king have become timely admonitions within twentieth-century culture, reminders to every citizen that self-evident truths remain unfulfilled. Perhaps, in the resonance of language and form, there always have been two Declarations: the immediate assertion of eighteenth-century revolutionaries and the larger claim of revolution itself. The hallowed artifact is always fresh as the signifier of aspirations still unreached.

But if time-bound and timeless connotations compete, as they do in any substantial work of literature, they also meet in a more literal fascination. Americans rarely separate the universal ideas of the Declaration from specific attachment to the document itself. The conjunction seems natural because the Declaration has functioned simultaneously as the first articulation and the ultimate expression of cultural life. This language, and no other, has been accepted without question. Americans celebrate neither June 7th, the day Richard Henry Lee proposes independence to Congress, nor July 2d, when Congress actually declares independence, but July 4th, the date when Congress accepts Jefferson's modified draft of language as its own. There is relevance in this concentration on the text. The ability to write out American independence with such consummate skill is the best evidence of a cultural capacity in the moment; celebration thereof, the clearest indication of achievement in a republic of laws.

III

While one-half of the first national compact has been revered, the other half is forgotten. No one now remembers the Articles of Confederation, the first document of national government, and there is irony in the contrast because the Articles fulfill the spirit and even the intention of the Declaration. That irony deepens in the revolutionary elite's own hesitations. John Dickinson, for an assigned committee of the second Continental Congress, pens the first draft of the Articles of Confederation in June 1776, but this draft is revised and then totally transformed in long and sometimes bitter debates on the floor of Congress and in state ratifying assemblies. Not until November 1777 does Congress approve the Articles of Confederation; not until March 1781, almost five years after the Declaration, do the Articles finally go into effect.

The Articles of Confederation bend and then break because they must settle the very ambiguities that the Declaration of Independence is allowed to evade. Where does sovereignty truly lie amidst the Declaration's "Free and Independent States"? Early republicans are not prepared to answer that question as a group in 1776, or, for that matter, in 1777 or 1781. They vacillate between the relatively strong central government of Dickinson's first draft of the Articles ("The said Colonies unite themselves so as never to be divided by any Act whatever") and the final version ("Each State retains its sovereignty, freedom, and independence"). Ultimate divisions of this kind create serious problems within the understandings of a consensual literature. The Articles raise the issue of sovereignty but do not settle it in credible or agreed-upon form, a difficulty that will cause some of the same participants to try much harder in 1787 when the costs of disagreement have become clearer.

The change in expression between 1777 and 1787 is complex but quite specific. At one level, the Revolution stands for the challenge of local rights to central authority, while at another, it seeks to make the people the fundamental authority of all government. These themes enjoy a symbiotic relationship in opposition to British rule and, initially, in resistance to a strong American confederation. No one really questions or separates the issues. But the rise of "new men" in the state legislatures of the 1780s, coupled with attacks on state power from local (usually western) communities, complicates a people-based rhetoric and frightens leaders at both the national and the state levels. The response of these leaders in 1787 is to divide revolutionary impulses by subsuming one challenge into the other. They neutralize distrust of centralization by recasting, rather than displacing, a familiar rhetoric. In a word, they turn the authority of the people into a justification for national sovereignty.

The respective preambles of the Articles of Confederation and the Federal Constitution convey the shift perfectly. Compare, on the one hand, "To all to whom these Presents shall come, we the undersigned Delegates of the States affixed to our Names send greeting," with, on the other, "We the People of the United States in Order to form a more perfect Union . . . do ordain and establish this Constitution for the United States of America." The first words of the Articles of Confederation are immediately lost in distinctions and vested particularities; the first of the Federal Constitution dissolve those distinctions and particularities in the empowering presence of the people. Fully aware of previous difficulties, the framers of the Constitution turn the people themselves into the authors of the Constitution, cleverly conflating the act of writing with the process of ratification.

Note, as well, the insistence on continuity. Rhetorically, the Convention of 1787 supplies "a more perfect" consequence of union, not a new form of government, and the new document can be superior to the Articles mostly because it rests upon them. Fully one-half of what is written in the Articles appears somewhere in the Constitution. The Articles first articulate the phrase "The United States of America" in official language. They first give assurance of "perpetual union." They initiate the crucial policy (popularized by the Northwest Ordinance) of admitting new states on the same footing. They suggest the language of enumeration as a doctrine of limited powers. They outline at least the prospect of dual citizenship. They assert the equality of all citizens in privileges and immunities, and they eliminate travel limitations and trade restrictions between the states. These are not mean achievements either in initial conception or in their abiding significance.

The Articles of Confederation prove vulnerable not in their innovations but in their assent to political circumstance. The limitations that hurt most – a weak executive in a committee structure, restrictions on the taxing power, and the requirement of overwhelming majorities for confederated action – come from dominant patterns in the colonial compacts and previous plans of confederation like the Albany Plan of Union (1754). In the 1770s, Whig arguments against the king make such curbs on power politically irresistible. Soon, though, when Americans argue more among themselves than with their king, the virtues of the 1770s become the frustrations of the 1780s. Congress loses much of its ability to govern in the interim, and institutionalization of the oppositional modes in revolutionary thought is one reason.

At the same time and amidst every difficulty, the Confederation grows into more than a temporary convenience for waging war. Certainly, the Articles deserve credit for helping to expand the realm of political possibilities in the early 1780s, and the explicit nature of that achievement also demonstrates how the public document differs from other literary acts of imagination. The first rule in such writing is that the new must somehow always appear familiar; since mere plausibility in thought and language is never enough, creativity must also satisfy a stricter standard of acceptability. Minimally, the Articles of 1777 conduct the idea of union from theory into regular political discourse and practice. No longer just a hope or an idea, "union" begins to function as an answer within republican life; it can be discussed in a different way in 1787 if just because more Americans are eager to see the existing institution work.

All of these hopes and fears bring subtle changes to the writing of public documents. Between 1776 and 1787, revolutionary leaders become less convinced about the self-evidence of truth in political forums. The weakness of the Confederation, growing factionalism, Shays's Rebellion, severe land disputes, economic depression, these facts – the very facts that bring the delegates of the Constitution Convention to Philadelphia – also make Convention delegates less certain of agreement and more worried about the textual basis on which agreement might rest. While the writers of the Constitution still believe in the text as the basis or foundation of all agreement, their uncertainties within this faith create a new aesthetics of control in what is written. They work harder for agreement. These differences appear symbolically in Benjamin Franklin's famous closures as he signs first the Declaration of Independence and then, eleven years later, the Constitution.

Signing the Declaration, Franklin supposedly observes, "we must, indeed, all hang together, or most assuredly we shall all hang separately." The Declaration functions as both the artifice behind Franklin's witticism and the artifact of the solemnly sworn policy that he enunciates. The members of the Continental Congress not only "hang" together in grouped signatures, they swear to do so in the Declaration, and their oath guarantees the "facts" they submit to "a candid world." The world is "candid" because it will accept facts as given and because it will further accept a right of revolution based upon them. Facts are submitted, again in the words of the Declaration, "to prove this." Meanwhile, more than humor rides on Franklin's psychology of opposition. Colonial solidarity in 1776 depends upon the unacceptable alternative: punishment for treason in an English courtroom.

By 1787, clear enemies and incontestable facts, let alone proofs, are much harder to come by. Placed in the exact same ceremonial situation at the Constitutional Convention, Franklin achieves a similar certainty but by a far more circuitous route. James Madison describes the event in his reports of the Convention:

Whilst the last members were signing [the Constitution] Doctr. Franklin looking towards the Presidents Chair, at the back of which a rising sun happened to be painted, observed to a few members near him, that Painters had found it difficult to distinguish in their art a rising from a setting sun. I have, said he, often and often in the course of the Session, and the vicissitudes of my hopes and fears as to its issue, looked at that behind the President without being able to tell whether it was rising or setting: But now at length I have the happiness to know that it is a rising and not a setting sun.

Franklin's assumed text in this anecdote, the artist's painting, is hopelessly ambiguous without a larger context; people can and will differ over whether it depicts a rising or a setting sun, just as the delegates themselves have differed in a final argument over whether the new Constitution will mean prosperity and peace for America or anarchy and civil convulsion.

Franklin has taken a central role in these last-minute bickerings, and the substance of his contribution has been to raise an unavoidable epistemological uncertainty. "For having lived long," he tells the Convention on September 17th, "I have experienced many instances of being obliged . . . to change opinions even on important subjects, which I once thought right, but found to be otherwise. It is therefore that the older I grow, the more apt I am to doubt my own judgment." The point of this comment is to encourage his divided colleagues to settle for an "apparent unanimity" where "real" accord is impossible and to urge them to incorporate that subterfuge into the Constitution itself. Knowing that the delegates are divided, that they *cannot* hang together, Franklin successfully moves that the Constitution be approved "by the unanimous consent of *the States* present," the majority of each delegation being for ratification.

In accepting Franklin's "convenient" motion, the framers of the Constitution, as reported in Madison's *Notes of Debates in the Federal Convention,* see and welcome, "the ambiguity of the proposed form of signing." Unanimity, of

course, is less than the truth. Three leading members of the Convention –
Edmund Randolph, Elbridge Gerry, and George Mason – refuse to sign the
Constitution on the final day of the Convention, and three others – Luther
Martin, Robert Yates, and John Lansing, Jr. – withdraw earlier because of
their unhappiness with the emerging document. The unanimity injected into
the language of the Constitution is instead a useful fiction, a myth of glorious
harmony that the framers wield in the ideological struggle to elicit and then
to enforce allegiance in the fight over ratification. But unanimity can be
mobilized without hypocrisy in this fashion because the text itself has been
accepted as an inevitable repository of epistemological ambiguities. Philosophical uncertainty, in Franklin's sense, has become a vital source of political flexibility and literary creativity.

Franklin's strangely useful pessimism about human understanding might
appear idiosyncratic but for the fact that it is shared, even amplified, by a
more important leader of the Convention – by James Madison, Father of the
Constitution. At issue is how a writer turns a necessarily ambiguous text into
a tool of ideological conformity. The whole problem of consensus is a vexing
one in Madison's writings. The most famous Federalist Paper, *No. 10,* may
argue that disagreement and faction will yield to "the extent and proper
structure of the Union," but *Federalist No. 37,* also from Madison's pen,
reveals paralyzing philosophical uncertainties that call the entire realm of
human agreement into question. Here, in one of the darkest thrusts of the
American Enlightenment, Madison describes three intruding levels of chaos
in human existence: "the obscurity arising from the complexity of objects,"
"the imperfection of the human faculties," and the failure of language itself
("the medium through which the conceptions of men are conveyed to each
other adds a fresh embarrassment").

When these elements are compounded in the actual process of human
perception – "indistinctness of the object, imperfection of the organ of conception, inadequateness of the vehicle of ideas" – we are left with a world of
impenetrable "gloom," one filled with "dark and degraded pictures which
display the infirmities and depravities of the human character." This world is
so impoverished with its "discordant opinions," "mutual jealousies . . . factions, contentions, and disappointments" that Madison's "man of candor"
regards mere agreement with surprise and the presumed unanimity of the
Constitutional Convention with "wonder" and "astonishment." Only "a finger of that Almighty hand" can have supplied such a level of understanding
in mere men. As he tells Jefferson just a month after the Convention, "it is
impossible to consider the degree of concord which ultimately prevailed as
less than a miracle."

The point of *Federalist No. 37* is that real agreement becomes impossible without imposed manipulation and design — a manipulation and design that can be traced to the pen of Madison as easily as he has traced them to the finger of God. His talk of miracles and Providence may trade on the colonial tradition of unanimity in the community of saints as the human expression of God's will, and it surely echoes a covenant tradition in American constitutionalism that begins in 1629 with the transfer of the charter of the Massachusetts Bay Company to the New World ("every of us doth hereby freely and sincerely promise and bind himselfe in the word of a christian and in the presence of God who is the searcher of all hearts"). But Madison, "the man of pious reflection" in *Federalist No. 37,* is more a child of the secular Enlightenment. The substructure of his statement, and particularly the metaphor about a guiding finger, suggests how the writing of the Constitution involves an aesthetics of conscious human control, how the document itself depends upon questions of craft. The Constitution operates as a place where "theoretical propriety" and "extraneous considerations" can meet and where a molding hand resolves the difference.

How are we to know that the Constitution represents a rising and not a setting sun? What is it about the text itself that leads fallible observers to the same conclusion? The rhetoric of the framers urges us to answer these questions by thinking of the Constitution as the expression of a shared truth devised by the elected representatives of an enlightened people. We are urged, in other words, to mystify the text in question. Quite another set of answers comes to mind if we think of the text as created text, as a manipulated and manipulative work, as the imposed truth of a conscious and philosophically sophisticated elite, as the concrete product of James Madison, Edmund Randolph, James Wilson, and Gouverneur Morris — the four men who in 1787 actually write succeeding drafts from the Virginia Plan of late May, through the Report of the Committee of the Whole in mid-June, to the copy reported by the Committee of Detail in early August, to the Constitution as submitted by the Committee of Style in mid-September. The craft of the document is one of its most ignored features.

IV

National deliberations have rarely developed into intellectually impressive events. The Federal Convention stands out not just because of the oft-noted genius of its participants but because of their practiced talents as men of letters. The Constitution is a marvel of concision, emerging as it does from four months of florid effusion and often bitter debate. It contains just five thousand words of the plainest prose, cast within a one-sentence preamble and seven brief articles. Neither verbiage, nor allusion, nor admonition interrupts its prescriptive clarity; there is very little linguistic novelty, almost no philosophical innovation, and minimal elaboration. But these evasions are counterbalanced by a series of more subtle commitments. Brief rather than cryptic, the Constitution confirms a familiar past. Every word belongs to the realm of common understanding in eighteenth-century American experience, and many of them are taken directly from the constitutions of the states and from the Articles of Confederation in a reaffirmation of republican principle.

Chief among the drafters' skills is their ability to grasp and then wield a common understanding. Like John Adams, who watches anxiously from England, the framers use the state constitutions as the repositories of an American identity in the 1780s. Use, however, signifies more than a knowledge of documents; it also means making constitutional language one's own. Adams, as drafter in his own right of the Massachusetts Constitution of 1780, offers *A Defence of the Constitutions of Government of the United States of America* (1787–8) as "a specimen of that kind of reading and reasoning which produced the American constitutions." His themes are "the well-ordered constitution" as the holder of "futurity in America" and the state constitutions as the true history of an emerging republicanism.

Consensus over Adams's assumptions is a matter of practice. Between 1776 and 1784, every state except Rhode Island and Connecticut writes and adopts a new constitution. Seventeen new constitutions in all are written in America during the course of the Revolution, and the number is one key to interpretation. Even the best writer struggles through lesser works before a masterpiece becomes possible. Just so, the framers in Philadelphia prepare themselves in the workshops of congressional and state assemblies. Forty of the fifty-five delegates already have served in both. Half of that number have participated directly in the writing of state constitutions and territorial ordinances. The quantum jump in quality of language and conception between the Articles of Confederation and the Constitution actually occurs step-by-step in state convention after state convention.

The framers take the measure of their own growing ability in the very first speech of the Convention. Edmund Randolph begins his criticism of the Articles of Confederation by exonerating the authors of that document for errors made "in the then infancy of the science, of constitutions, & of confederacies." Infancy, in Randolph's terms, refers to an understanding that is just ten years old, and it includes many of the men sitting around him in Independence Hall; obviously, much has been learned in the intervening decade by American revolutionaries, many of whom are still only middle-aged. A new sophistication in the science of constitutions has reduced a series of primal uncertainties. What does it mean to write out a constitution when the ideal model of the British Constitution assumes an unwritten status? To whom does one address such a document amidst raging debates about the locus and feasibility of sovereignty? How and where, precisely, does fundamental law lie upon a page also dedicated to the artificial machinery of modern government?

The state constitutions that intervene between 1776 and 1787 curb the unfamiliar by placing it within familiar form. They, in effect, bring the framers to a greater awareness of genre. Only in repetition do possibilities become apparent. Generic skill is clearest in the framers' many shorthand references to state constitutions on the Convention floor; their mastery, in their self-confidence amidst every difficulty. Even though they are politically divided, they remain collectively committed to the sequent toil of successive drafts of the Constitution. They share a series of assumptions about the way narrative, form, and style control unruly content, and they have learned what to avoid in each other. Their borrowings from the state constitutions are, in consequence, all the more impressive because so discriminating. Witness the careful circumvention of controversial terms like "national," "republic," and "federal."

The framers' knowledge of genre is especially evident in their willingness to seek form as a primary source of meaning. Compared with the looser prolixity of the state constitutions, the generalities of the Constitution lie within a precise arrangement of tone and structure. The seven articles are clearly deployed in descending order of length, concern, and difficulty. The first three articles – on the legislative, executive, and judicial branches – give the crux of the Constitution. Each moves from description of a branch of government into issues of qualification and selection for office and then to an enumeration of powers and limits.

Each article also demonstrates that the engaged delegates have come to understand the deepest workings of constitutional language. The hardest lesson, one that the Committee of Detail articulates on July 26th, involves simplicity. Edmund Randolph and John Rutledge, for the committee, see the necessity of a scope, style, and tone that will trust to form over detail. As they draft a constitution that will be properly "fundamental," they agree "to use simple and precise language, and general propositions" and "to insert essential principles only, lest the operations of government should be clogged." This spirit of restraint, captured in Madison's *Notes of Debates in the Federal Convention,* can dominate the writing process precisely because it claims clarity of form as its goal. Randolph and Rutledge distinguish sharply between "the construction of a constitution" and the more open-ended enumeration of mere law; only the former requires "the shortest scheme that can be adopted." The accessibility of the framers' document absolutely depends upon this distinction. The Federal Constitution can be twice as clear as forerunners like the Massachusetts Constitution of 1780 in part because it is less than half as long.

The Constitution itself literalizes appropriate form. The empowering presence of the people, as the prerequisite to all government, comes first in "we, the people." This preamble is then joined by the specific articles of government to a conclusion that portrays union on the very face of the document. The signers of the Constitution appear neither in alphabetical order, nor by presumed importance or seniority, nor in haphazard fashion. They are grouped, instead, by state with the states themselves appearing in *geographical* order from north to south, starting with New Hampshire in the north and working in sequence through Georgia in the extreme south. The United States thus appear on the page in familiar map form – the perfect icon in answer to Madison's fears about indistinct objects, imperfect perception, and faulty language.

This iconicity reflects the Constitution makers' sense of their work and of themselves as "framing" and "framers." Most famously, Madison in *Federalist No. 51* uses "framing a government" to evoke the necessary controls (internal and external) that distinguish a government of men from one of angels. The metaphor of framing, a general one in the discourse of the delegates at the Convention, conjoins act and object, creation and control, regularity and contrivance with the overarching notion of order as the ultimate source of many different meanings.

In Johnson's *Dictionary of the English Language* (1755), "frame" includes "to form or fabricate by orderly construction and union of various parts," "to make," "to regulate," "to invent," and, from the noun, "a fabrick, any thing constructed of various parts or members," "any thing made so as to inclose or admit something else," "order; regularity; adjusted series or disposition," "scheme," "contrivance," "projection." The Constitution, self-consciously the fabric of union, is all of these things, but most particularly it encloses and, thereby, creates form in the midst of chaos. *Without* the weaver's fabric, the frame signifies only a void. Alexander Hamilton, no friend of the original plan, turns this opposition of order and chaos into the rallying call for ratification when he asks on September 17th, "Is it possible to deliberate between anarchy and Convulsion on one side, and the chance of good to be expected from the plan on the other?"

The frame, together with the framers' effort, insists upon what might have been thought to be missing: recognizable form. It is both a claim of accomplishment and a rejection of prevalent fears. Just how prevalent these fears have become in 1787 can be seen in George Washington's own pessimism over the "little ground on which the hope of a good establishment can be formed." "I *almost* despair of seeing a favourable issue on the proceedings of our Convention," he writes to Hamilton on July 10th, "and do therefore repent having had any agency in the business." Framing is that act of agency depersonalized, the very method of establishing common ground or good form. As noun, "frame," it is also the act accomplished, the proof of common ground.

The belief in boundaries intrinsic to the metaphor also eases the three central innovations of the Constitution, all of which involve a chilling open-endedness in conventional eighteenth-century political thought: first, the *amorphous* and *changeable* people as the foundation of all authority; second, the constitutional *separation* of powers in government; and, third, the *sharing* of sovereignty between the nation and states. None of these ideas lends unifying form to the early American mind, and all three generate uneasiness and debate. Framing is the visual aid for an assumed congruity. The eighty-five *Federalist Papers* build around these premises. They argue that the new national fabric is a uniformity woven of apposite parts and not a weak tissue, not a mere contrivance.

To be sure, the arguments themselves are easy to accept only in retrospect, but if they also require an act of faith in the troubled 1780s, the visual possibilities in framing encourage a useful personification. In the ratification process, *who the framers are* counts for as much as *what has been framed*. As Madison warns Edmund Randolph in January 1788, "[H]ad the Constitution been framed & recommended by an obscure individual, instead of a body possessing public respect & confidence . . . it would have commanded little attention from those who now admire its wisdom." The personages who enter the Convention also emerge immeasurably greater in Madison's description of what they accomplish. Their act of framing, in all of its unifying implications of craftsmanship and communal success, constructs a public body worthy of respect and confidence out of conspicuous individuals who often disagree.

Two other considerations reinforce the literary ability that the delegates bring to Philadelphia. By 1787 a majority of Americans embrace the Convention as the appropriate institutional arrangement for contemplating national union. Political legitimacy insures the high quality of its participants as well as their self-confidence and mutual awareness. In the first month of the Convention, Madison, Franklin, and George Mason all write that they can hope for much from a Convention made up of, in Madison's words to William Short, "the best contribution of talents the States could make for the occasion." Franklin, writing to Richard Price, sees "the principal people in the several states" around him. "America," adds George Mason to his son, "has certainly, upon this occasion, drawn forth her first characters."

Not uncontested, the legitimacy of the forum nonetheless brings the recognition of a golden opportunity to bear on the proceedings, and when troubles mount in late June and early July that knowledge is saving. On June 26th, Madison and Hamilton warn that, because they are "digesting a plan which in its operation wd. decide forever the fate of Republican Govt.," failure will mean "it would be disgraced & lost among ourselves, disgraced & lost to mankind forever." Three days later, Hamilton summarizes the importance of the moment. "It is a miracle that we are now here exercising our tranquil & free deliberations on the subject," he observes. "It would be madness to trust to future miracles." Then, on July 5th, Gouverneur Morris uses the theme to make his colleagues "extend their views." Each delegate, "a Representative of America," must also think as "a Representative of the whole human race; for the whole human race will be affected by the proceedings of this Convention." In these and other exhortations, the framers define a special purpose. They engage in what Herman Melville will later term "the shock of recognition," the moment in which creativity takes its own measure to move beyond itself.

The second consideration suggests a more subtle and generally forgotten influence, one that also enables Madison's "best contribution of talents" to understand and thrive upon itself. The delegates who attend the Convention conceive of themselves as eighteenth-century gentlemen of letters. Much has been made of their adept use of committee structures, their secrecy and restraint before publication, their willingness to suggest solutions without insisting upon personal investment, and their ability to compromise over language. By and large, these characteristics are exactly what one can hope for in the exemplary writers of the time. The true gentleman of letters privileges reason over emotion, writes for a small group of social peers, circulates drafts among those peers for correction, avoids publication until agreement is reached, and leaves his work unsigned. In short, the very qualities that critics have cited as weaknesses in early American fiction, poetry, and drama become strengths in the literature of public documents. The retreat to committee arrangements for compromise reveals only the most obvious of these strengths.

Surely the most remarkable trait of the Convention has to do with the delegation of sensitive writing tasks *within* committees to embattled figures like Edmund Randolph, James Wilson, and Gouverneur Morris. These men take strong stands in debate on the floor of the Convention, and yet their colleagues can trust them to express the general will when writing by assignment. The official selflessness of the man of letters is crucial in this frequent behavior pattern. Not until the 1830s do Americans learn for certain that the aristocratic, thoroughly conservative Gouverneur Morris penned the final draft of the Constitution. News of his authorship in 1787 would surely have hurt chances for ratification, but Madison, a sometime opponent of Morris, knows that the gentlemanly tradition minimizes the danger of publicity. As he tells Jared Sparks in 1831, "[A] better choice could not have been made, as the performance of the task proved."

The role of the man of letters channels authorial identity into a social or corporate orientation. Half a century later, writing to William Cogswell in 1834, Madison is still insisting on the essence of that collective spirit. "You give me a credit to which I have no claim, in calling me 'The writer of the Constitution of the U.S.,' " he explains. "This was not like the fabled Goddess of Wisdom, the offspring of a single brain. It ought to be regarded as the work of many heads and many hands." More than modesty dictates Madison's response. His notion of "many heads and many hands" is the source of all agreement in the writing of the Constitution. The aesthetic of the man of letters blends perfectly into a politics of ratification.

Unjustly ignored today, Washington's letter delivering the Constitution to Congress is a model of this convergence. Sent "By *unanimous Order of the Convention*" on September 17th, the letter uses the undifferentiated, first-person plural pronoun to incorporate every level of decorum: "In all our deliberations on this subject [differences among the several states] we kept steadily in our view, that which appears to us the greatest interest of every true American, the consolidation of our Union." A gentlemen's agreement over language is also a national consensus in spite of difference. The litany of pronominal possessives conflates framer and ordinary citizen, "our deliberations" and "our view" referring to the framers' decisions but merging with "our Union," the perspective of every true American.

Washington then alludes to differences that might have been expected but that never materialize. Again, the guiding decorum of the framers as gentlemen is also the larger decorum of the true American perspective. In Washington's words, "the Constitution, which we now present, is the result of a spirit of amity." Those who disagree must remember that the document grows out of "mutual deference and concession" and that it, therefore, "is liable to as few exceptions as could reasonably have been expected." The acceptable exceptions already have been made. By extension, a challenge to any part of the final document violates the decorum of amity, forgets "the greatest interest of every American," and endangers "our prosperity, felicity, safety, perhaps our national existence." These words follow the tactic already traced in the preamble of the Constitution, and they prefigure the framers' larger strategy in the ratification debates. The people share in the act of writing through the related act of ratification. Agreement *with* the document looms as the acceptable interpretation *of* it.

The evolution of these strategies can be seen in the framers' final debates. At sometime in the rearrangement of twenty-three loose articles into the tightened, final version of seven, a majority decides that their text should not be opened to reinterpretation. The Committee of Style presents the Constitution's ultimate amendment clause on September 12th with its stipulations on how subsequent changes are to become "part thereof," a phrase subsequently changed to "Part of this Constitution." The word "part" in this context means "extension." One need only compare such language with the relevant clause in the Articles of Confederation, which allows for the possibility of "alteration" within the articles themselves.

Amendments to the Constitution are *added on* to a document that remains intact despite every revision. The whole discussion of constitutional change takes place between September 15th and 17th, amidst the framers' rejection of calls for a second convention and their decision to resist the right of state ratifying conventions to alter language in the document. As Edmund Randolph notes, their stance leaves the people with just two alternatives regarding the Constitution, "accepting or rejecting it in toto." "Conventions," observes Charles Pinckney for the majority, "are serious things, and ought not to be repeated."

The major literary consequence of ratification is the addition of a Bill of Rights. But even these restrictive adjustments – the bargain struck after two years of debate in the first Congress and the state assemblies – have the effect of magnifying the overall document. The original framers reject the need for a Bill of Rights because, as Roger Sherman argues on September 12th, "the State Declarations of Rights are not repealed by this Constitution; and being in force are sufficient." Sherman's argument, accepted by the Convention, assumes that the Constitution must always be read in conjunction with the state constitutions. When anti-Federalists demand instead that the Constitution supply an independent guarantee of individual rights, their insistence has the ironic effect of letting the document stand on its own. The traditional Anglo–Saxon freedoms of speech, religion, press, the right to bear arms, and trial by jury lend another level of identification and allow the Constitution to emerge as an autonomous and complete expression of republican government and American politics. The first ten amendments also seal off the original document. When they are passed and then *added to* the text in 1791, they insure that all further changes will be supplementary rather than integral to the language of the framers.

Lengthy debate over the amendments in the summer of 1789 confirms the realization of form in the Constitution. Notably, Congress spends almost as much time arguing over the placement of amendments as it does discussing their substance. The strongest proponents of a Bill of Rights and perhaps an initial majority in Congress want to re-draft the preamble of the constitution, but attempts to do so please no one. Those who prefer to incorporate the amendments into the body of the document fail for similar reasons; friends deplore the loss of a separate statement on basic rights, and opponents resist alterations that would spoil an existing lucidity. James Jackson of Georgia seems to have spoken for many on the floor of Congress when he argues that the Constitution as ratified must be left untouched. To amend internally would leave the document "patched up, from time to time, with various stuffs resembling Joseph's coat of many colors." In the end, Roger Sherman, opponent of a Bill of Rights on the Convention floor in 1787, moves the successful proposal in Congress to add amendments "by way of supplement." Debate and the drafting of its own language in the amendment process drive Congress back on the original structure in framing.

Madison, for one, is quick to see that the Bill of Rights strengthens the new government. The amendments, he writes to Jefferson in December 1788, will "give to the Government its due popularity and stability." Of his own considerable role, first, in crafting those amendments so that they do not interfere with enumerated constitutional powers and, second, in shepherding them through the federal government, he is typically discreet. "I should have acted from prudence," he tells Edmund Randolph in 1789, "the very part to which I have been led by choice." There may be no more succinct gauge of creativity in the literature of public documents.

Choice is instinctively prudential in such writing; the claim of inevitability, its best defense. In keeping with these tones, the amendments themselves take the plainest, most laconic expression. They are like the Constitution itself – in direct contrast to the elaborate prose of the state constitutions and state declarations of rights. Each of the first ten amendments is a single sentence with the longest employing one hundred and six words and the shortest just sixteen; five amendments are thirty words or less. In the consensual apparatus of writing out agreement, debate means less rather than more. "Nothing of a controvertible nature," Madison explains to Edmund Pendleton during the process, "ought to be hazarded by those who are sincere in wishing for the approbation of $\frac{2}{3}$ of each House, and $\frac{3}{4}$ of the State Legislatures."

Making prudence the whole of choice must be understood against a struggle for ratification that could have gone either way. For if Delaware, New Jersey, Connecticut, Maryland, and South Carolina accept the Constitution with relative ease, the vital large states – Pennsylvania, Massachusetts, Virginia, and New York – engage in prolonged contests and pass the Constitution by narrow and bitter margins. Massachusetts ratifies by just ten votes out of a total of three hundred and fifty-five cast; Virginia, by ten out of one hundred and sixty-eight; New York, by three out of fifty-seven. North

Carolina first rejects the Constitution altogether, reconsidering a year later in 1789. When recalcitrant Rhode Island finally joins the new government in 1790, it is by two votes from a total of sixty-six. Americans are a divided people in 1788. The surprise is not in their differences but in the speed with which they resolved conflict in their first decade under the new Constitution.

V

Communal acceptance of the Constitution remains one of the mysteries of early republican life. In literary terms, the shift involves nothing less than the crystallization of a genre, the moment when decisive accomplishment transforms an art form and everyone's understanding of it. The reasons for this change of perspective in the writing and reading of constitutions are various. When John Adams, using hindsight in 1815, summarizes the period as "the age of revolutions and constitutions," the phrase contains a vital expectation. Constitutions resolve revolutions.

The assumption, one widely shared by early republicans, is that constitutional forms define revolutionary accomplishment and, thereby, American culture itself. Not for the last time, the written word is the comprehended act. But even this predilection only begins to explain the strength and scope of a new faith. In the 1790s, Americans turn their disputed document into the universal symbol of an era. The Constitution now fixes all previous aspects of revolutionary activity, especially the disruptive or chaotic parts, into a text for all to read. Aaron Hall of New Hampshire offers an early version of the controlling truism. "Till this period," he declares in an oration from 1788, "the revolution in America has never appeared to me to be completed; but this is laying on the cap-stone of the great American Empire."

The expectations in closure change how the Constitution must be regarded. If ordaining and establishing a republican form of government in America at the end of the eighteenth century possesses a universal significance in human history, as the framers in Philadelphia themselves claim so frequently, then the artifact of ordination and establishment, their document, easily becomes more than mere language. In its simplest form, these pressures turn the text of the Constitution into an independent repository of moral value. Republican virtue resides not in the act of clarification, a frequent call in the early 1780s, but in the clarifying result, the battle cry of ratification in 1788. The Constitution becomes not a symptom of virtue but the extent of virtue then possible.

Adams, writing his *Defence of the Constitutions* in the same year as the Federal Convention, shows the way by insisting that constitutionalism enables virtue and not vice versa. "The best republics will be virtuous, and have been so," he argues, "but we may hazard a conjecture that the virtues have been the effect of the well-ordered constitution, rather than the cause." Adams and other early republican intellectuals use their readings in British empirical thought to claim that institutions, not the manners and morals of a people, guarantee good government. What they add on their own in 1787 and after is the notion that a written text, the Constitution, can function as such an institution – the *central* institution.

Madison's writings play heavily on the theme. The Revolution, he explains in the *National Gazette* for January 19, 1792, distinguishes between European "charters of liberty . . . granted by power" and American "charters of power granted by liberty." As with Adams, constitutionalism defines the meaning of revolutionary action. Madison's "revolution in the practice of the world" becomes a matter of wielding and understanding official language properly. "In proportion to the value of this revolution; in proportion to the importance of instruments, every word of which decides a question between power and liberty . . . ought to be the vigilance with which they are guarded by every citizen."

Madison claims that American constitutions, as expressions of liberty rather than of power, are infinitely more precious but also inevitably more complicated than their European counterparts. This complexity "requires a more than common reverence for the authority which is to preserve order thro' the whole." The charters of government in America are the worthiest objects of reverence because "[a]s truths, none can be more sacred" and "[a]s metes and bounds of governments, they transcend all other land-marks." These public documents are the ultimate sources of definition in the culture. In consequence, texts like the Constitution require more than understanding. The citizen's highest duty is to protect and preserve "charters of government . . . superior in obligation to all others, because they give effect to all others." "How devoutly it is to be wished, then," concludes Madison, "that the public opinion of the United States should be enlightened; that it should attach itself to their governments as delineated in *great charters* . . . that it should guarantee with a holy zeal, these political scriptures from every attempt to add to or diminish from them."

The many valences of Madison's appeal – the careful balances and proportions of liberty and power, value and vigilance, effect and obligation, together with the conflated symbolism of transcendent landmarks, sacred truths, political scriptures, enlightened opinion, and holy zeal – keep the idea of constitutionalism at the center of every frame of early republican reference, whether scientific, political, economic, geographical, or religious. Individuals, society, and government are to cohere in the attachment to constitutionalism. Americans, so attached, will act out their commitment to the Revolution and define themselves accordingly through their appreciation of the documents of origination. As the ultimate spirit of consolidation in American culture, as the highest expression of the republican experiment, as a symptom of the advanced stage in the Enlightenment, and as one of the most discussed documents on the face of the earth in 1790, the Constitution must evoke the reverence that Madison stipulates.

Spontaneous and enduring, that reverence also has obscured an overall achievement in the literature of public documents. Other official writings from the period, some of consummate power, have been lost in the shadow of the Constitution. In several ways, "The Virginia Statute of Religious Liberty" (1786) provides a more moving and coherent statement of Enlightenment principles. Drafted by Thomas Jefferson, it places an awareness of mental powers ("Almighty God hath created the mind free") against darker realizations ("the impious presumptions of legislators and rulers . . . being themselves but fallible and uninspired men"). An ensuing list of injuries, incapacities, corruptions, briberies, temptations, fallacies, and intrusions represent the excesses of religious establishment. Truth alone – also gendered separately as female virtue against masculine error – stands against these dangers. Even so, "truth is great and will prevail if left to herself"; only "human interposition," literally violation, can "disarm her." Truth's natural weapons are free argument and debate. They are, however, sufficient; "errors ceasing to be dangerous when it is permitted freely to contradict them." In Jefferson's formulation, the Virginia legislature enacts its own implied marriage to truth by wrapping itself in the same protections of freedom and nature: "we are free to declare, and do declare, that the rights hereby asserted are of the natural rights of mankind."

The Northwest Ordinance from 1787, also an ignored expression of the American mind, is the cardinal achievement of Congress in the first ten years of the Republic. The clearest and most compelling picture of union in the period, the Ordinance guarantees the spread of republican government across the continent. It is drafted by Nathan Dane of Massachusetts, and its provisions mandate and orchestrate the appropriate stages of development from wilderness to territory to something like colonized status to full equality in statehood. Here, as well, are most of the central ideals of the culture rendered as practices: the assurances of due process in law, of equal inheritance, of the general availability of property, and of freedom of travel; the call for a systematic plan of public education; the protection of minorities in the promise of "utmost good faith" toward Native-American peoples; the extension of "the fundamental principles of civil and religious liberty" to all persons regardless of citizenship; and, most courageously for the times, the prohibition of slavery throughout the territory. In analyzing "the celebrated

'Ordinance' " as "the model of all subsequent territorial governments," Timothy Walker's seminal *Introduction to American Law* (1837) finds that "for brevity, comprehension, and forecast, it has no superior in the annals of legislation."

Brevity, comprehension, and forecast: these virtues mark the extraordinary general achievement in public documents by the writers of the early Republic. As works of literature, documents like the Constitution, the Statute of Religious Toleration, and the Northwest Ordinance set a standard for new generations of writers to reach for. They also assure that the tenuous bond between aspiration and realization will never be lost completely. More, as in any living literary tradition, they lend themselves to further interpretation in each additional expression, or, in this case, in the further exposition of democratic and republican principles; they sustain and guide the skills of continuing interpretation.

As with any other literary masterpiece, the Constitution encourages even as it dominates thought. All but forgotten are the first important arguments concerning strict and loose construction of constitutional language: the debate originated by George Washington, as president, but written out by his secretaries of state and of the treasury in early 1791. Jefferson, offering his opinion on February 15th of that year, and Hamilton, just a week later, take the constitutionality of the projected United States Bank as their assigned subject, and their dispute has remained the most cogent single exchange on federal power (limited or implied) across two centuries of constitutional debate. Subsequently, Hamilton's *Report on Manufactures* (1791) and Jefferson's "Kentucky Resolutions" (1798) extend their respective views. The issue they raise, central authority versus state rights, eludes resolution by the very nature of the federated Republic, but its ramifications are already clear in these four documents taken together – all from the first decade of the new government.

The loftiest of constitutional interpretations, those of John Marshall as Chief Justice of the Supreme Court, help to explain the power and excitement in all other interpretations. "[W]e must never forget," Marshall explains in *M'Culloch* v. *Maryland* (1819), "that it is a constitution we are expounding." He never does, and neither do other early republican intellectuals who wish to be heard. As the singular experiment in thought of the period, the Constitution always guarantees an audience when it is the subject. Marshall's choice of language is also instructive. "To expound" means to set forth or declare in detail; as well, "to explain" or "to interpret," especially where scripture or religious formularies are concerned, and also to offer a particular interpretation, to construe in a specified manner, chiefly in law.

Marshall's opinions resonate with all of these possibilities. Chief among all of them, however, is his assumption of a vital and absorbing enterprise, one that Americans will accept as their primary intellectual concern. When, for example, he first establishes the right of judicial review in *Marbury* v. *Madison* (1803), Marshall begins by assuming "a question deeply interesting to the United States." But why is it so interesting? After all, the question itself is a simple one and easily answered ("not of an intricacy proportioned to its interest"). No, the reader's interest in this case, and in all of Marshall's major opinions, come from the assertion that the Constitution is somehow in jeopardy. As Marshall puts the matter in converting legal principle into dramatic story, there is a danger of "doctrine [that] would subvert the very foundation of all written constitutions" and that "reduces to nothing" the Federal Constitution. Americans *must* listen because Marshall's answer to that doctrine will touch "the basis on which the whole American fabric has been erected."

Opinions like *Marbury* v. *Madison*, *M'Culloch* v. *Maryland*, *Dartmouth College* v. *Woodward* (1819), and *Gibbons* v. *Ogden* (1824) are essentially celebrations of the achievement of the framers. "Expounding" the Constitution is every citizen's link to that achievement. In the America of *Marbury* v. *Madison*, "where written constitutions have been viewed with so much reverence," the "very great exertion" of the framers signifies the "original and supreme will" of government as well as "the greatest improvement on political institutions" of the age. Any law repugnant to the Constitution is therefore necessarily void. The supreme importance of what the framers have done translates easily into the supremacy (and continuing excitement) of the document that they have rendered.

The framers, always invoked in these opinions, protect the vitality, the importance, and the simplicity of originating language. They are, in this sense, literary guardians as well as lawgivers and political leaders. In *Dartmouth College* v. *Woodward*, a "general spirit" in the Constitution excludes "unnecessary" or "mischievous" interpretations that "the framers of the constitution could never have intended to insert in that instrument." Because this spirit resides only in the strength of a common understanding, *M'Culloch* v. *Maryland* warns against turning the Constitution into "the prolixity of a legal code." Danger looms in too much complexity of interpretation. If expanded into a code, the Constitution "could scarcely be embraced by the human mind" and "would probably never be understood by the public." *Gibbons* v. *Ogden* follows with its own criticism of "powerful and ingenious minds" that "entangle and perplex understanding, so as to obscure principles which were before thought quite plain." Marshall's recurring standard, announced here, is that "the enlightened patriots who framed our constitution, and the people who adopted it, must be understood to have employed words in their natural sense, and to have intended what they have said."

These passages capture a final capacity in the literature of public documents. Marshall believes that ordinary language must encompass the most intricate of philosophical and political problems. And without exception, the leading documents of the period support his conclusion. Time and again, these formative writings subsume complexity in a narrative and form that speak directly and easily to the largest common audience. This is not to say that writers like Jefferson, Madison, Hamilton, and Marshall ignore underlying complexity; they overcome it.

Actual articulations of difficulty illustrate the point perfectly. Madison, writing to Jefferson on October 24, 1787, calls the Constitution "a task more difficult than can be well conceived by those who were not concerned in the execution of it." Franklin tells Pierre-Samuel DuPont de Nemours that the Convention should be compared to an infinitely complex game of chess in which every move is contested. From hindsight in 1818, John Adams thinks of thirteen clocks striking simultaneously, "a perfection of mechanism which no artist had ever before effected." In every case, the fact of difficulty gives way to a metaphoric projection of ease in competence and accomplishment. Madison's executor of a task, Franklin's chess player, and Adams's artist all know what to do and how to do it. Jefferson best describes the self-confidence involved. "It is a part of the American character," he writes his daughter in the anxious year of 1787, "to consider nothing as desperate; to surmount every difficulty by resolution and contrivance." The combination is illuminating: resolution (an act of will) permits contrivance (the ability to invent order in a crisis).

The literature of public documents flows out of this peculiar dynamic. Optimism, resolution, and contrivance, themselves minor literary virtues, nonetheless combine as the driving force in a creativity of almost unlimited effectiveness. They form, as Jefferson says, "part of the American character." Within the combination, we have found perhaps a dozen works of the first rank, starting with the Declaration of Independence in 1776 and extending through John Marshall's opinions in the 1820s. In fact, twelve works are a reasonable total for gauging the merit of a literary configuration, but the number becomes astonishing when the comparison drops to consider any similar time span in a civic literature. In its immediate impact, its cumulative character, its continuing importance, and its general influence, the early republican literature of public documents stands alone. There has been nothing quite like it before or since, this practiced skill in an official language that is also common to all; not in American culture nor in any other.

6

THE LIMITS OF ENLIGHTENMENT

I

A dominating frame of reference assimilates the crises in meaning and the contradictions in practice that it generates. The Enlightenment shapes early republican culture in just this way. It is both the source of ideas and the boundary placed upon them in revolutionary America, both the expression of broad aspirations and the enforcement of narrow instrumental controls. The literature of public documents offers a proximate case in point. The Federal Constitution of 1787 embodies the central aspirations of the Enlightenment. In daring to know and then in imposing their knowledge, the framers assume the capacity of reason to define and control human society. Their text, the Constitution, celebrates the association between correct human mechanism and universal improvement. Knowledge, through mechanism, forms a more perfect union that will establish justice, insure tranquillity, promote the general welfare, and secure the blessings of liberty for the people of the United States. Yet, at another level, the body and mechanics of the Constitution take back the scope and sweep of its preamble.

Not everyone in America is so insured, so promoted, so secured, so blessed. Quietly but emphatically, the Constitution eliminates whole categories from the rubric of "we, the people." In a shocking adaptation of the mathematical penchants of the Enlightenment, the Constitution, in Articles 1 and 4, perpetuates the institution of slavery and reduces all individuals who are not "free" to three-fifths of a person. Again in Article 1, it excludes Native Americans from the apportionment of representation and gives Congress an exclusive power in commerce over them. More subtly, it avoids all mention of one-half of the population under its jurisdiction, the women of the United States; all pronouns referring to gender are in the masculine form.

The calculation in such language is apparent from a simple elision. When the American woman actually finds a place in early drafts of the Constitution, it is as a fugitive slave. "If any Person bound to service or labor in any of the United States shall escape into another State," ran the original and unanimous language of August 29th, "He or *She* shall not be discharged . . .

but shall be delivered up to the person justly claiming their service or labor." Obviously pertinent in this setting, the feminine referent is altogether too singular, too solitary in its implications for the Committee of Style when it tests the appropriateness of constitutional language. Just as all explicit reference to slavery is removed from the final document, so the substitution of a simple and direct negative subject in the fugitive slave provision ("No person legally held to service") removes the subordinate conditional clause and, with it, all need for a subject pronoun that carries unsettling gender connotations.

The manipulation of language is deliberate, but how does one explain the recognition of discrepancy between theory and practice that such language implies? The simplest answer always has stressed the political needs and orientations of pragmatic statesmen. John Rutledge, representing South Carolina in the Federal Convention of 1787, reveals how bluntly a politics of interest could dominate thought. When Luther Martin of Maryland, as reported in Madison's *Notes of Debate in the Federal Convention,* argues on August 21st that "it was inconsistent with the principles of the revolution and dishonorable to the American character to have such a feature [slavery] in the Constitution," Rutledge responds that "Religion and humanity had nothing to do with this question – Interest alone is the governing principle with Nations – the true question at present is whether the Southn. States shall or shall not be parties to the Union."

Heeding Rutledge's warning, early national leaders follow a politics of interest over principle. Not one of the primary founders risks a public stance on abolition while in a position of responsibility even though most privately oppose the institution of slavery. Five of the first seven presidents (Washington, Jefferson, Madison, Monroe, and Jackson) own slaves, and all of the first seven, including John and John Quincy Adams, fully accept public silence on this issue as a price of highest office. The federal government will actually institutionalize silence, when Congress, in 1836, passes a "gag rule" to table without discussion all petitions and papers relating to slavery. These years of silence, 1789 to 1836, also mark the period of greatest expansion in American slavery; the shift from an imported African work force of four hundred thousand in the American colonies to an indigenous slave population of more than four million receives its greatest impetus in 1793 with the invention of the cotton gin.

Slavery is not the only discrepancy here. All of the major patterns of exclusion from citizenship grow stronger within the presumed benefits of an increasingly democratic culture – so much so that it is worth reexamining the conventional premise that these patterns represent "paradoxes" in the republican experiment. Black Americans, Native Americans, and women all lose ground in the first decades of the Republic even as the rights of citizenship are spreading to a broader population base: the workings of political interest and economic advantage only begin to explain these discrepancies. The discrepancies in themselves – particularly the violation of the natural rights of slaves and the subversion of Native-American property rights – receive thorough airings in public forums in the last third of the eighteenth century. Recent scholarship has documented a previously overlooked degree of protest in early republican pulpits, journals, newspapers, court records, petitions to federal and state legislatures, speeches, travel literature, pamphlets of all kinds, and the private correspondence of leading intellectuals. How then, the question remains, do early republicans justify inconsistencies that they themselves articulate?

Recognition of the contradictions in revolutionary aspiration begins in the moment of inception. "I long to hear that you have declared an independancy," Abigail Adams writes her husband, John, on March 31, 1776, " – and by the way in the new Code of Laws which I suppose it will be necessary for you to make [in the Second Continental Congress] I desire you would remember the Ladies, and be more generous and favourable to them than your ancestors." In parallels replete with mockery and irony, she appropriates the syllogisms of revolutionary rhetoric for her own purposes. Her major premise, "all Men would be Tyrants if they could," one often used by John Adams himself, supports a minor premise and direct accusation, "your Sex are Naturally Tyrannical," which, in turn, allows the standard eighteenth-century justification for Revolution as its conclusion. "If particular care and attention is not paid to the Laidies," Abigail tells John, "we are determined to foment a Rebellion, and will not hold ourselves bound by any Laws in which we have no voice, or Representation." Here, three months before the fact, are the theme, the logic, and much of the phraseology of the Declaration of Independence.

John Adams's response on April 14th deserves attention not just for its sexism ("We know better than to repeal our Masculine systems") but for its comprehensive catalogue of groupings excluded from power in the Republic. This negative catalogue, from the individual most responsible for guiding Congress toward independence, illustrates the priorities and the anxieties of revolutionary leaders caught in flux. Their question is not so much "What is an American?" as Crèvecoeur would have it in *Letters from an American Farmer* (1782) but, rather, "Who will be allowed to act as one?" In denying his wife's request, John Adams and his peers in Congress try to keep all of the margins in place:

As to your extraordinary Code of Laws, I cannot but laugh. We have been told that our Struggle has loosened the bands of Government every where. That Children and Apprentices were disobedient – that schools and Colledges were grown turbulent – that Indians slighted their Guardians and Negroes grew insolent to their Masters. But your Letter was the first Intimation that another Tribe more numerous and powerfull than all the rest were grown discontented.

Many issues are joined in this statement. The "discontented tribes" of America – workers, the poor, the young, Native Americans, blacks, and women – all enter into the universal appeal of the Revolution, while John Adams's ridicule ("I cannot but laugh"), his fear ("our Struggle has loosened the bands of Government every where"), and his pretended ignorance ("your Letter was the first Intimation") control the practical limits of achievement. It is not too much to suggest that the Republic continuously defines and redefines itself between these mixed and changing lines of hope against fear and that, in the process, the Revolution has partially fulfilled and partially reneged upon its promise each day for centuries on end.

The basic patterns in these tensions already appear in the exchange of Abigail and John Adams in 1776. Abigail argues from the premise of universal rights for a specific excluded grouping; John answers by universalizing her appeal to all excluded groupings in an exposure of special pleading. Abigail presents the basic recourse of the disenfranchised, their inclusion and participation in a "new Code of Laws," whereas John labels that expanded code "extraordinary," literally beyond the ordinary of what is to be expected. The development of the Republic in time will dictate that the extraordinary become ordinary, but in 1776 Abigail receives the answer that the disempowered regularly encounter; "be patient," John tells her. In context, this call for patience refers to the prospect of independence, but John and Abigail Adams are acutely aware that independence creates an immediate continuum of challenges, and Abigail knowingly sends another answer from out of that continuum. "I can not say that I think you very generous to the Ladies," she writes again on May 7th, "you must remember that Arbitrary power is like most other things which are very hard, very liable to be broken."

The Enlightenment supplies the lens through which both sides observe themselves in conflict, though it appeals to the powerful and to the powerless in different ways. Inasmuch as the Enlightenment emphasizes environmental conditioning over innate unchangeable character, it is radical in its thrust. And the symbol of its radicalism is an abiding faith in the efficacy of education and reason, the belief that learning transforms the present and, hence, the future forever. This is what Tom Paine means when he says in *Common Sense* that "a new method of thinking hath arisen" or that "we have it in our power to begin the world over again." It is also why Benjamin Rush, a signer of the Declaration of Independence, can expect a complete transformation simply by placing newspapers in every farmhouse. In his *Plan for the Establishment of Public Schools and the Diffusion of Knowledge in Pennsylvania* (1786), he also announces that "the golden age, so much celebrated by the poets" is already within reach; legislatures need only to establish "proper modes and places of education in every part of the state."

At the same time, the Enlightenment is a conservative force. It assumes that knowledge is harmonious in inclination, that it tends toward unity in form. The difference from Christian theology, from which it borrows much, is that it does not welcome the notion of apocalyptic conflict. Progressive in history, enlightened knowledge instinctively abhors the disobedience, turbulence, and insolence that Adams finds in discontented groups. Disruptions are the reversible signs of ignorance, symptoms of darkness that will disappear in the spread of light. Locality also gives way to universality in Enlightenment thought processes. Over and over in the period, writers and political figures strive for the largest view, and they expect to take solace in what they find there.

Conditions in the early Republic favor the conservative over the radical to the extent that the Enlightenment offers an attractive vision of unity. The virtues of progress, harmony, universality, and achieved perspective quickly attach themselves to the more concrete aspiration of political union and to its perceived concomitant, cultural homogeneity. *E Pluribus Unum,* taken from the first volume of the English *Gentlemen's Magazine* of 1731, furnishes a catch phrase for the wartime need of the whole when it is first selected by the Continental Congress for an official seal in 1776, but, six years later, when formally accepted as the national motto, it already signifies how "the many" dissolve in the solution of "the one." The radical impulses of the American Enlightenment never succumb to these homogenizing tendencies, but they are easily contained within them.

The examples of Tom Paine and Benjamin Rush convey the process of containment. For although both writers are unusually eloquent champions of minority groups, they allow the continuing urgency of the Revolution to overshadow invidious differences. As the war ends in 1783, Paine distinguishes sharply between "national character" and "local distinction" in his thirteenth *American Crisis* paper. Only the former is sacred. "Our great title is AMERICANS – our inferior one varies with the place." In the language of sacrifice, Paine argues that "something must be yielded up to make the whole secure. . . . we gain by what we give, and draw an annual interest greater than the capital." Local injustices must yield to a newly forming national identity. The goal, now that "the times that try men's souls" are over, must be to "conciliate the affections, unite the interests, and draw and keep the mind of the country together." Benjamin Rush's hopes for education in 1786 take a similar universalizing turn. His *Plan for the Establishment of Public Schools* will "convert men into republican machines." "Let our pupil be taught that he does not belong to himself," writes Rush, "but that he is public property."

The economic metaphors in these projections are indicative. Terms like "interest," "capital," "machinery," and "property" all betoken the in-strumental side of the Enlightenment. As education symbolizes the radical thrust, so property and economic value sanction the conservative side of mastery, control, and order. John Adams is the first early republican to articulate how these premises converge. Stung into expression, perhaps by his wife's charges, Adams writes to James Sullivan on May 26, 1776, of the dangers in giving too much attention and sway to "the consent of the people." Consent is the moral foundation of government, but it cannot be its agent, and Adams proposes a property qualification for the participating citizen that will keep everyone in place. Otherwise, he tells Sullivan, there will be no end of controversy and altercation. "New claims will arise"; he warns, "[W]omen will demand a vote, lads from twelve to twenty-one will think their rights not enough attended to, and every man who has not a farthing, will demand an equal voice with any other, in all acts of state."

Property can qualify and contain the spirit of equality because property itself, in the conventional triad of entitlements, is a more circumscribed natural right than life and liberty. To be sure, John Locke's *An Essay Concerning the True Original, Extent, and End of Civil Government* (1690) reserves the property of the body and its labor to each individual (slavery is against both natural and positive law), but this absolute does not apply in the same way to real or landed property. In Locke's own words, "[I]t is plain, that Men have agreed to disproportionate and unequal Possession of the Earth." The basis of that inequality is also plain:

God gave the World to Men in Common; but since He gave it them for their benefit, and the greatest Conveniences of Life they were capable to draw from it, it cannot be supposed he meant it should always remain common and uncultivated. He gave it to the use of the Industrious and Rational (and *Labour* was to be *his* Title to it;) not to the Fancy or Covetousness of the Quarrelsome and Contentious.

Much remains implicit in Locke's statement of relative capacities and disproportionate rewards. What is proper industriousness, and when does it degenerate into covetousness? Who are the rational, and why do they deserve a greater benefit? How are the wrongfully contentious to be identified, and by what means are they deprived of property? For those in the act of drawing "the greatest Conveniences of Life" from the land, the task of reason is more obvious. As the statements of both Adams and Locke suggest, reason reconciles universal human rights with "a disproportionate and unequal possession of the earth." This is part of "the right Rule of Reason." No wonder, then, that eighteenth-century conceptions of property mediate between the theory and practice of the Enlightenment.

II

The most perceptive contemporary essay on discrepancies in the Enlightenment uses property to depict the recognition and acceptance of inconsistencies. Immanuel Kant, writing in 1793 "On the Common Saying: 'This May be True in Theory, but it does not Apply in Practice' " ("Uber den Gemeinspruch: 'Das mag in der Theorie richtig sein, taugt aber nicht für die Praxis' "), begins his discussion of political right by guaranteeing certain principles as a matter of natural law. These principles are "the *freedom* of every member of society as a *human being*," "the equality of each with all others as a *subject*," and "the *independence* of each member of a commonwealth as a *citizen*." Kant's principles would seem to guarantee the basic rights of all persons in the enlightened state, but his essay immediately qualifies the meaning of freedom, equality, and independence in practice.

Each of Kant's qualifications speaks to realities in American politics. Kant argues that *freedom* thrives only within a patriotic government, where patriotism requires that "everyone in the state, not excepting its head, regards the commonwealth as a maternal womb, or the land as the paternal ground from which he himself sprang." *Equality* does not obviate "the utmost inequality of the mass in the degree of its possessions, whether these take the form of physical or mental superiority over others, or of fortuitous external property." Finally, the *independence* of the citizen must be understood within accepted limitations: "The only qualification required by a citizen (apart, of course, from being an adult male) is that he must be his *own master* (*sui iuris*), and must have some *property* . . . to support himself."

The allure of the qualifying terms themselves in early republican ideology – patriotism, available property, and the independence of the citizen – helps to explain their power when turned toward exclusionary ends. In reality, subjected Africans, dragged from their homes into slavery on another continent, could hardly have regarded themselves (or been regarded) as springing from one maternal womb or from common paternal ground with other inhabitants of the New World. Native Americans, who can make such a claim, fall instead to the charge that relative superiority rightly determines degree of possession. Meanwhile, those without land and all women disappear from Kant's a priori definition of citizenship. Kant never advocates the exclusions, but his language encourages an acceptance that his principle would deny, and his discourse of mastery palliates discrepancy by fusing theory and practice.

Kant's adult male citizen, "his own master," presides as the symbol of the Enlightenment, and his ownership of property operates as both the tangible sign and logical extension of his capacity. Moreover, this conjunction of imposed reason and ownership flourishes with special vitality in the American Enlightenment, where combinations in politics and property are readily available to all free men. In America, even more than in Europe, improving the land epitomizes a rational, virtuous, masculine, and politically necessary control of the world. To return one more time to Locke's chapter on property, "subduing or cultivating the Earth, and having Dominion, we see are joyned together"; this is "the Voice of Reason confirmed by Inspiration." But only in America does the cultivation of property become the penumbra of transcendent truths. For if the ideal of education promotes the idea of reason everywhere, the cultivation of property marks the rational working out of God's plan, a phenomenon that Americans will soon term manifest destiny. In the unfolding of that destiny, reason and order turn into the same thing; so, at times, does the ownership of property and the control of other people on the land.

Put another way, the homology between reason in thought and order in land works off of a vital presumption in Enlightenment thought. The idea of cultivation can be such a literal symbol of advancing civilization in the New World because it so directly parallels the light of reason imposing harmony and order on darkness and chaos. The appeal of the vision is matched only by the facility with which Americans manipulate its terms. Within the homology, nature instructs, but it is also there to be used and even overcome — distinctions often lost sight of in the Enlightenment. The accompanying slide between reason as universal guide (in the discovery of principle) and reason as mere tool (in the mastery of fact and circumstance) is often as imperceptible, though Benjamin Franklin, as usual, sees farther and more carefully than others. "So convenient a thing it is to be a *reasonable creature,*" he observes in his memoirs, "since it enables one to find or make a reason for everything one has a mind to do." The irony in these words touches an unarticulated battleground in Enlightenment thought: conflict is determined by who first defines and then exercises reason.

Within the rule of reason, the mechanics of exclusion find their logical place in the rational constructs of Anglo–American law. Specific restrictions on tenure in property law leave marginal groups in suspended animation. Early republican leaders, many of whom are legally trained, understand that ownership and use represent vastly different things in the possession of land. They exploit the difference, creating entrance requirements for other capacities (voting, for example) and easing the egalitarian entanglements in "life, liberty, and property." Only full title, ownership in fee simple, the capacity to devise and sell property without restriction of any kind, confers full citizenship in the early Republic, and the distinction rapidly becomes a means of filtering rights through assigned capacities.

Reconsider, for a moment, John Adams's enumeration of discontented tribes in the light of these legal restrictions on ownership. As "insolent Negroes" have "masters," so "Indians" have "guardians" in Adams's catalogue. Native Americans are wards of the state; the Indian trade and intercourse acts of 1790, 1793, 1796, 1799, and 1802 prohibit them from devising property to any other source than the government. In effect, they possess land but without title. Ultimate title resides in the United States of America, where it is a contingent remainder waiting to be fulfilled. The ensuing legal hold of early republicans over Native Americans is best expressed in Secretary of State Thomas Jefferson's record of a conversation with British Minister George Hammond on June 3, 1792: "What did I understand to be our right in the Indian soil? – 1. a right of preemption of their lands, that is to say the sole and exclusive right of purchasing from them whenever they should be willing to sell. 2. a right of regulating the commerce between them and the Whites." For President Washington a year later, Jefferson justifies the legality of preemption as "in the nature of a remainder after the extinguishment of a present right."

The impelling force of the doctrine is that possession *will* pass; a moment *will* come when the "present right" of Native Americans will be forever "extinguished," either having been relinquished by sale or lost through some failure in active possession. Politically, the doctrine accommodates the incessant demands and encroachments on Native-American lands throughout the nineteenth century. In treaty after treaty, Native Americans appear to have ceded their lands, but the technical release is much closer to a tenancy at will or a lease upon land, where a preempting and often peremptory owner expects possession sooner rather than later. Chief Justice John Marshall catches the direction of these pressures as he confirms the doctrine of preemption for the Supreme Court in *Johnson and Graham's Lessee* v. *McIntosh* (1823). The qualifiers in Marshall's assertions tell the story. "In the establishment of these regulations," he admits, "the rights of the original inhabitants were, in no instance, entirely disregarded; but were necessarily, to a considerable extent, impaired." Just how impaired is clear from another admission. "It has never been contended," Marshall finds himself saying, "that the Indian title amounted to nothing."

Adams's "insolent Negroes" come more rapidly and directly under the restriction of property. As property themselves – the property of another – slaves lose every capacity in the republic of laws. Three renowned early republicans (Patrick Henry, Benjamin Rush, and St. George Tucker) demonstrate how easily the amenities of ownership and the legal discourse of property evade the injustice of chattel slavery. When the Quaker Robert Pleasants charges Patrick Henry with owning slaves, the firebrand of American liberty responds that he cannot face "the general inconvenience of living without them." "I will so far pay my duty," writes Henry on January 18, 1773, "as to own the excellency and rectitude of [Christian] precepts, and to lament my want of conformity to them." Henry consoles himself in the hope that "a time will come, when an opportunity will be afforded, to abolish this lamentable evil," but for the moment, and for one steeped in the convenience of slavery, a lenient master is "the furthest advance towards Justice."

This convenience of ownership is not an exclusively Southern rationale. Although Benjamin Rush is a Pennsylvanian and the author of a famous essay against slavery in "An Address to the Inhabitants of the British Settlements in America upon Slave-Keeping" (1773), he still manages to own a slave throughout the revolutionary period. This slave, named William, finally wins his freedom in 1794 after eighteen years in bondage. As Rush's affidavit in May 1788 reveals, the moment of release for William comes "at such a time as will be just compensation for my having paid for him the full price of a slave for life." All paradox in the incident pales in the power of property to define behavior in American culture. At no point does the inherent injustice of slavery override the economic value of "just compensation," even though the same affidavit concludes that slavery is "contrary to reason and religion."

Inevitably, the possession of slaves as a right of property grows in power as slavery itself prospers in the early Republic. Success magnifies the conveniences and the value in ownership, and it undercuts the temporizing tones of leaders like Washington, Jefferson, and Henry, who hope that slavery somehow will disappear in the natural course of the Enlightenment. In exposing these hopes, the prosperity of the system projects a permanent institution, one that requires and receives a stiffer justification of apparent contradictions. St. George Tucker, the Virginia Blackstone, provides this harder line in deciding *Hudgins v. Wrights* in 1805 for the Virginia Supreme Court of Appeals. The Bill of Rights, observes Judge Tucker,

was meant to embrace the case of free citizens, or aliens only; and not by a side wind to overturn the rights of property, and give freedom to those very people whom we have been compelled from imperious circumstances to retain, generally, in the same state of bondage that they were in at the revolution, in which they have no *concern, agency,* or *interest.*

Yet if the right of property controls, it can never eliminate the troubling reality of people "retained" on the land. Stripped of all place in the Revolution, American slaves surface in the language of rebellion. They are the disembodied presence in their masters' litanies against enslavement, the nightmare figure behind the quest for independence. When, for example, the Virginians of 1776 devise a state seal, with "VIRTUS, the genius of the

commonwealth . . . treading on TYRANNY, represented by a man prostrate, a crown fallen from his head, a broken chain in his left hand, and a
scourge in his right," they borrow from traditional iconography, but the
image also reflects an aspect of daily life in revolutionary Virginia. The dusty
pictures of slavery that British Whigs conjure up from Roman tyranny, the
Spanish Inquisition, and Turkish despotism only begin to explain the compulsive allusions to chains in American rhetoric. "In the Southern Colonies,"
writes the South Carolinian David Ramsay in the opening chapter of *The
History of the American Revolution* (1789), "slavery nurtured a spirit of liberty,
among the free inhabitants." Revolutionary slaveowners bring special intensity to the ideological irony. "In them," adds Ramsay, "the haughtiness of
domination, combines with the spirit of liberty." Here and elsewhere, the
incongruity of tyranny next to liberty is resolved in a claim of property.

Women, as Adams's largest discontented tribe, face a restriction of similar
scope in their roles as wives and mothers. The first volume of Sir William
Blackstone's *Commentaries on the Laws of England* (1765–9) summarizes the
legal plight of the married woman in Anglo-American culture – a plight
that continues well into the nineteenth century:

By marriage, the husband and wife are one person in law: that is, the very being or
legal existence of the woman is suspended during the marriage, or at least is incorporated and consolidated into that of the husband: under whose wing, protection, and
cover, she performs every thing; and is therefore called in our law-french a *feme-covert.*

Disabilities turn into benefits in Blackstone's presentation of women. "So
great a favourite," he decides, "is the female sex of the laws of England."
Jefferson, no admirer of Blackstone's *Commentaries,* nonetheless illustrates how
the benevolent suspension of legal existence in the *feme-covert* (the "covered" or
"protected" or "hidden woman") carries into political practice. "The tender
breasts of ladies were not formed for political convulsion," he writes Angelica
Schuyler Church when she, in 1788, asks questions about the new Federal
Constitution. Women, he tells her, "miscalculate much their own happiness
when they wander from the true field of their influence into that of politicks."

The realized image of exclusion requires a description of presence without
place, a report in which restriction signals an assigned passivity. The hidden
woman, the preempted Native American (sometimes figured as the dying
Indian), and the submitting slave (without concern, agency, or interest) are
shadows in the social portrait of "every man under his vine and under his fig
tree," the republican refrain of communal happiness. As property lends a
picture of independence, so its absence renders the person without it invisible
and politically unimportant. So, too, invisibility is a verification in any
calculated evasion of Enlightenment principle.

This end point, the strange act of verifying unimportance, takes on special significance in democratic society and has unique consequence in a revolutionary one. *The Federalist* (1787–8) provides a dramatic model in the early Republic. It shows how patterns of dismissal in a hegemonic text can channel the flow of principle and, hence, the availability of rights, in a culture of consensus. Woman, as subject, appears just twice in the eighty-five papers of *The Federalist,* and the theme of each passage is a negative capacity: the dangers of female intrigue in politics in *Federalist No. 6* and the inability of married women to convey property in *Federalist No. 83.* The union may indeed represent "an empire in many respects the most interesting in the world," but the gender implications of Hamilton's summary in *Federalist No. 1* must be taken quite literally. As he tells us, "the important question [is] whether societies of men are really capable or not of establishing good government from reflection and choice."

Of the fourteen references to Native Americans in *The Federalist,* all but one concern hostility, conflict, and the need for greater federal control of the problem. The exception, curiously enough, involves an admission of failure in overall understanding. "What description of Indians are to be deemed members of a State, is not yet settled, and has been a question of perplexity and contention in the federal councils," writes Madison in *Federalist No. 42.* What is an Indian? Publius might as well ask. Earlier, *Federalist No. 24* already has imposed a working definition for policy purposes. "The savage tribes on our Western frontier," writes Hamilton, "ought to be regarded as our natural enemies." Barely visible, though portrayed as an encircling danger in *Federalist No. 25,* these tribes appear only as people of darkness in the (as yet) untamed wilderness.

Publius has more trouble with the subject of slavery, but even here his treatments remain cursory. In eighty-four of the eighty-five papers of *The Federalist,* there are but four references to American slavery; all are short, and just one, on the subject of importation in *Federalist No. 42,* takes a normative stand. Only in *Federalist No. 54* does Publius allow himself to be caught in an extensive analysis of "the mixed character of persons and of property." Elaboration here is simply inescapable. The constitutional proposal that counts slaves in the census for congressional representation has been a source of bitter national debate in 1788.

The political embarrassments that James Madison encounters in *Federalist No. 54* explain why early republican leaders resist detailed discussions of slavery whenever they can. If slaves are property, then they might enter into estimates of taxation, which are founded on property, but they should not enter into tabulations for representation, which are regulated by a census of persons. If instead slaves are "moral persons" – "if the laws were to restore

the rights which have been taken away," Publius posits in a telling phrase –
then "negroes could no longer be refused an equal share of representations
with the other inhabitants"; or, one might add, an equal share in any other
civil right.

Of the three constitutional provisions that allow for slavery without ever
mentioning the term – representation (Art. 1, Sect. 2), the importation of
slaves (Art. 1, Sect. 9) and the first fugitive law (Art. 4, Sect. 2) – only this
first reference presents an insurmountable problem for Publius. Madison
hardly mentions the fugitive law and easily handles slave importation, both
in *Federalist No. 42*. In conventional Enlightenment terms, a "barbarism of
modern policy" like the importation of slaves can be expected to disappear in
time, possibly even in 1808, when the constitutional provision protecting it
lapses. Representation, on the other hand, raises the cardinal principle of free
government and forces Publius to deal more directly with slavery in a democratic republic. In *Federalist No. 54* the mixed character of slaves as property
and as persons turns out to be "their true character" under law. It is with
"propriety" that the Constitution adopts the "compromising expedient" of
counting slaves as three-fifths of a free person.

The argument from property law is an expected one within the patterns
of marginalization just noted, and yet even Madison appears to have been
uncertain about the result. Uncertainties, in fact, are never far from the
surface in any of these arguments of exclusion. John Marshall's hesitations
over the impairment of Indian rights, St. George Tucker's vehemence in the
"imperious circumstances" of slavery, and Blackstone's complete removal of
"the very being" of the married woman all contain within them the whisper
of an opposing argument. There is the felt pressure of a righteous response,
the tacit knowledge that some republicans will find the argument a shameful one.

This realization becomes acute in *Federalist No. 54*. Madison struggles
with the ramifications of his claims, and the nature of his struggle brushes
the very edge of the Enlightenment. It is as if the two virtues of the age, the
rule of reason and universal aspiration, enter the lists against each other.
Indeed, Publius's central argument comes from another persona altogether; it
appears entirely in quotation marks that signify "the reasoning which an
advocate for the Southern interests might employ on this subject." We listen
to a voice within a voice within a voice – from Madison, to Publius, to
southern advocate:

"Let the case of the slaves be considered, as it is in truth, a peculiar one. Let the
compromising expedient of the Constitution be mutually adopted, which regards
them as inhabitants, but as debased by servitude below the equal level of free
inhabitants; which regards the slave as divested of two fifths of the *man*."

Missing in the voice of this distanced speaker is justice, where justice, in eighteenth-century terms, completes the recognitions of commonality and of right between lawgiver and subject. The language of peculiarity in *Federalist No. 54* is one of the first references to "the peculiar institution," and, as such, it violates the universal application on which the harmonies of the Enlightenment depend. Clearly, the speaker's direct association of the particular with separate verities ("as it is in truth, a peculiar one") would have jarred against the sensibilities of Madison's first readers. But why would Madison have wished to undercut his own argument? The southern advocate, after all, is his creation.

Publius is of two minds. Reaching through the mask after pages of silence, he divulges that the southern advocate "fully reconciles" him to the "propriety" of the constitutional solution, but part of him remains unconvinced, and that part wishes to be on record. If "such is the reasoning" of the southern advocate, he warns in his own voice, then "it may appear to be a little strained in some points." While failing to deter Madison's formal conclusions, this "strain" puts everyone on notice. Perhaps, as well, Publius cannot quite bring himself to mouth this shabbiest of all arguments in *The Federalist*. The greatest of early Roman consuls, Publius Valerius Poplicola is official lawgiver and first friend of the people. For this most exalted of all classical republican identifications to announce that servitude logically debases inhabitants to the degree of divesting them of two-fifths of their humanity is debasing in itself. Far better to cast the whole issue at one remove.

The interesting thing in Madison's calculated distance is his consciousness that slavery must at least acknowledge higher terms. The peculiar institution cannot stand for order and convenience in a part of republican life without some loss of principle and coherence in the whole. The philosophical distance between Madison, Publius, and the southern advocate may have been slight. All three are southern politicians on the issue of slavery, and the strain between them is "little" in *Federalist No. 54*. Even so, the deliberate invention of distance creates a tension beyond the gloss of discrepancies. We enter, however minimally, the radical hope of the Enlightenment, the insistence that humankind must use its discovered capacities to improve the lot of all people.

III

Moments of breakage in the dominant discourse indicate other ways of thinking, but they do not articulate the thought itself, and the problems in reconstructing opinions now lost are immense. Appearances and realities are substantially more difficult to decipher in the voices that speak without property behind them. The Lockean right rule of reason is a wholly different thing for those who are ruled, and the aspirations of the Enlightenment take on separate meanings among those who are barred from its dispensations. To be heard at all in eighteenth-century public forums, the defeated warrior, the debased slave, and the invisible woman must speak in fractions of themselves. They must exploit the discourse that denies them. To catch the sound of these voices (frequently no more than a murmur in translation, a decontextualized outburst, an ambiguous image, or a gesture), the joint venture of historian and critic must probe the lost circumstances, the limited vehicles, and the hidden costs of performance. Creativity in these speakers often resides in strategies of survival now taken for granted.

Some constraints on marginal voices in the early Republic are specific; others general. Eighteenth-century Native-American efforts, now in fragmentary form, contend with the near certainty of their own disappearance. Slave accounts must fight to create the sound of their own worth. The narratives of women strive against gender restrictions that dignify accommodation over assertion. Simultaneously, all of these voices suffer within the controlling aesthetic of a consensual literature. They lack the communities of auditors in the public sphere that legitimize the word in eighteenth-century literature, and the handicap is a severe one. Because literary production is profoundly social throughout the period, the circles of white male citizens that nurture and sustain the gentleman of letters can successfully reject the voices beyond their ranks or, alternatively, appropriate them for their own purposes.

Predictably, the most famous Native-American utterance is one that early republicans love to hear. Chief Logan's speech about the gratuitous murder of his family in 1774 epitomizes the vanishing Indian, first, in Thomas Jefferson's *Notes on the State of Virginia* (1784–5) and, after, in endless editions of *McGuffey's Reader*. Memorized for generations and thematized in James Fenimore Cooper's *The Last of the Mohicans* (1826), it confirms the hopes and minimizes the fears of the dominant culture. Logan, a Cayuga chieftain among the Mingos in New York, espouses a familiar Christian charity ("I appeal to any white man to say, if ever he entered Logan's cabin hungry, and he gave him not meat; if he ever came cold and naked, and he clothed him not"). He fights only when treacherously attacked by an identifiable villain ("I had even thought to have lived with you, but for the injuries of one man"), and he suffers defeat with a stoicism that limits the agony for all concerned ("Logan never felt fear"). Most memorable of all, he disappears without a trace ("There runs not a drop of my blood in the veins of any living creature. . . . Who is there to mourn for Logan? – Not one"). The truly noble savage does not complicate his story – or the stories of others – by remaining behind.

Take, however, a more practical and characteristic Native-American address: the Seneca Chief Cornplanter's speech before President Washington in Philadelphia in 1790. Cornplanter, or Kiontwogky, refers back to the military campaign of 1779, when revolutionary troops under orders from General Washington ravage and destroy Iroquois civilization in the western parts of New York and Pennsylvania, but his real preoccupation is the continuing threat to Iroquois property six years after the second Treaty of Fort Stanwix (1784) supposedly has secured all remaining Native-American lands:

When your army entered the country of the Six Nations, we called you *Caunotaucarius*, the Town Destroyer; and to this day when that name is heard, our women look behind them and turn pale, and our children cling to the knees of their mothers. Our councilors and warriors . . . are grieved with the fears of their women and children, and desire that it may be buried so deep as to be heard no more. When you gave us peace, we called you father, because you promised to secure us in possession of our lands. Do this, and so long as the lands shall remain, the beloved name will remain in the heart of every Seneca.

Cornplanter's play upon alternative nomenclature confirms the contrast in civilizations. He speaks as the political leader of a distinct people and not, like Logan, as the tragic warrior whose worthiness transcends culture boundaries in a claim of universal sympathy. The distress of living women and children, the need to overcome cultural trauma, above all, the need to secure threatened lands – these concerns dominate Cornplanter's social agenda. The fullest implication of dissimilarity appears in the juxtaposition of Washington's names: "Father of His Country" against "Town Destroyer." To understand that Washington can be both "father" and "destroyer" is to see the absolute chasm between the new American states and Native-American tribes; the development of the one means catastrophe for the other. Cornplanter brings few illusions to this unequal conflict. As he says, it is "as if our want of strength had destroyed our rights."

The creativity of Cornplanter's speech comes in the conceit that Washington must still earn the title of father. Note, in addition, that all naming depends upon the tangibility and endorsement of property for its existence. Washington first merits the designation through his promise to secure Native-American possession of Iroquois lands, but "the beloved name" lasts only "so long as the lands shall remain." Cornplanter knows that he must speak through Anglo-American norms of property to be heard at all, but he cleverly uses the device to question the fondest epithet in all of early republican lore, that of Washington as the Father of His Country. Its very effectiveness suggests why this speech cannot be memorable in the dominant culture. Cornplanter mobilizes an ignominious legacy, one in which broken republican promises devastate a helpless people. How many, in regarding that legacy, wish to contemplate George Washington as the destroyer of towns?

Native-American perceptions flicker in the clash of ideological perspectives, in the slippages of translation, in the preoccupations of transcription, and in the misunderstandings that accumulate between a literate and an oral culture. In these fragmentary records, the sign of thought is sometimes clearest in processes of reversal. Thus, although Native Americans initially fail to comprehend how the rigid binding power of a written statement might differ from the more pliant meanings that memory and oral consensus generate in tribal exchange, they soon grasp their practical disadvantage in cross-cultural debate. Deliberations over the Treaty of Fort Stanwix between the Six Nations of the Iroquois Confederacy and the Commissioners of the United States in October of 1784 take a bizarre twist when the Iroquois negotiators are the ones who want a written record of proceedings while their white counterparts refuse that record, insisting instead on the traditional Native-American exchange of wampum belts to recall provisions of speech. The Iroquois have come to realize that the legalistic and adversarial strategies of their opponents manipulate the flexibility in oral performance and prey upon the freedom of interpretation that aurality allows. They have begun to see that written evidence alone protects them in an agreement with the United States.

The thoughts of eighteenth-century Native Americans attain print mostly in translated expressions of anger, sorrow, and loss — reasonable tones for participants who are witnessing the total destruction of their way of life. Still, the overall effect in the literature is a stylistics of plaint. We are left with patterns of lamentation that convey little of the underlying vitality in tribal culture. The Shawnee Prophet, Tenskwatawa, the most eloquent exponent of Native-American nationalism in the period, typifies the strengths and weaknesses of the genre. His speech before the Tuscarora branch of the Iroquois Confederacy in 1806 supposedly rallies all tribes to action, but the published record, especially the Prophet's peroration, is more a chronicle of paralyzing declension:

They [all tribes] will vanish like a vapor from the face of the earth; their very history will be lost in forgetfulness, and the places that now know them will know them no more. We are driven back until we can retreat no farther; our hatchets are broken; our bows are snapped; our fires are extinguished; a little longer and the white man will cease to persecute us, for we shall cease to exist.

The words themselves may be a true transcription. They accurately convey the plight of Native Americans, and their predictions are fulfilled when the battles of Tippecanoe and the Thames decimate the tribes of the Northwest

Territory in 1811 and 1813, but the overall tone also evokes classical threnody and the popular eighteenth-century graveyard school of poets. That melancholy tone, which will soon achieve its American apogee in William Cullen Bryant's "Thanatopsis" (1817), stands for Anglo-American literary sensibility in the early Republic. All in all, the Prophet's mood is suspiciously conventional in its appeal, and the general effect of quiescence makes his rhetoric seem even more dubious.

Early republicans hear and report what they want to hear and report. Where, in this speech, are the radical conceptions of property and the galvanizing pride in Native-American ways that enable the Prophet and his twin brother, Tecumseh, to consolidate the tribes of the Indiana Territory against Governor William Henry Harrison? The Prophet's fatalistic description of a dying culture, with its obverse of western lands now safe from savage attack ("our hatchets are broken; our bows are snapped"), supplies an attractive image for white Americans to absorb. Shawnee hopes, in contrast, directly threaten the dominant culture. Tenskwatawa and Tecumseh seek a separate, unified Native-American nation that whites would be compelled to respect, and they begin by challenging early republican ideas of property. All tribal territory, argue the Shawnee leaders, must be held in common beyond the capacity of individual tribes to cede or otherwise alienate. Here, in principle, is a direct counter to the federal doctrine of preemption.

To the extent that the shock of devastation does dominate published Native-American oratory, it presents other problems in interpretation. The pathos of loss robs both speaker and listener of context. When, in the Philadelphia meetings of 1790, the aged Seneca chieftain Gayashuta (Kaiaghshota) "wonders at his own shadow, it has become so little," the synecdoche of personal outline for larger culture transmits nothing of the social complexity and agrarian prosperity that Gayashuta has witnessed all along the frontier in Iroquois towns of up to seven hundred people. Only a shadow is disappearing in his speech. The theme of loss feeds the expectations of the dominant culture. "We are afraid if we part with any more lands the white people will not suffer us to keep as much as will be sufficient to bury our dead," complains the Creek leader Doublehead (Chuquacuttague) at the Treaty of Colerain in June of 1796. Unfair treatment is the obvious thrust of this passage, but the language also imparts a message of breakdown, and, in Enlightenment terms, this breakdown forms part of an irresistible antithesis. Whatever the cost, Native-American disintegration computes as an acceptable price of early republican growth.

How does one sort the elements of integrity in these appropriated narratives? The task, in a sense, is to catch the separate awareness, the canniness of address, and the assertion of value that sometimes punctuate these speeches.

For instance, even though the Seneca Chief Sagoyewatha, known as Red Jacket, responds to the missionary work of Joseph Cram in 1805 with yet another sketch of Native-American decline, he manages to turn the worn theme into a powerful assertion of cultural relativity and Native-American worth. "You have got our country, but you are not satisfied," Red Jacket accuses Cram. "You want to force your religion upon us." Unanswerable questions illustrate the point. "If [the Bible] was intended for us as well as for you, why has not the Great Spirit given it to us?" "How shall we know when to believe, being so often deceived by the white people?" "If there is but one religion, why do you white people differ so much about it?" Slowly, the sarcasm in these interrogatives builds into something much greater. Red Jacket exposes the insatiable nature of white expansion in the name of a more philosophical Native-American containment and contentment:

[God] has made a great difference between his white and red children. . . . Since he has made so great a difference between us in other things, why may not we conclude that he has given us a different religion, according to our understanding? . . . We are satisfied. Brother! We do not wish to destroy your religion, or to take it from you. We only want to enjoy our own.

Victories in debate of this kind afford glimpses of a character and perception beyond pathos. In a similar flash of recognition from late 1781, the Delaware leader Captain Pipe (Hopocan) wields a single question to destroy the logic for a British alliance in the Revolution. "Who of us can believe," Pipe asks British commanders in council at Detroit, "that you can love a people of a different colour from your own, better than those who have a white skin, like yourselves?" The power of the realization should not be forgotten in its failure to change the situation. Native Americans must choose sides between white opponents in the Revolution, and they lose everything no matter how they choose. "We were struck with astonishment at hearing we were forgot [in the Treaty of Paris of 1783]," the Mohawk Thayandangea, called Joseph Brant, reminds the British secretary for colonial affairs in 1785, "we could not believe it possible such firm friends and allies could be so neglected by a nation remarkable for its honor and glory."

Occasionally, adroit minds make the most of both difference and similarity in a claim of justice. On August 13, 1793, a letter from the Seven Nations to the United States of America protests white encroachment north of the Ohio River by resisting the whole notion of money for land ("money to us is of no value, and to most of us unknown"). A better alternative, the letter continues, would be to give the money set aside for Native-American lands directly to the poor white settlers who do want it and who now steal land in search of it. The near Swiftian play upon difference does not, however, prevent another satire based on the similarity of independent cultures. The same letter infers a confusion of "common justice" in federal proposals and concessions: "[you] seem to expect that because you have at last acknowledged our independence, we should for such a favor surrender to you our country."

Communications of this sort demonstrate that the collapse of Native-American peoples does not issue from a failure in understanding; neither is the larger failure culture specific. Little Beaver, a Wyandotte speaker at the 1790 conference in Philadelphia, bluntly assigns blame where it belongs. "Do then what you said," he tells federal representatives, "restrain your people if they do wrong." Manifestly, the weak United States governments of the Confederacy and federal union cannot restrain their citizens. Early republican authorities fail to enforce even minimal policies and regulations on an exploding and acquisitive frontier population.

One ideological contribution of the Enlightenment is to imply rational controls that do not exist in white expansion and government policy. In his "Observations Concerning the Increase of Mankind" (1751), Benjamin Franklin shows how the paradigm of light can seem to stand in Nature for the rational exclusion of "all Blacks and Tawneys," where Native Americans fall under the latter category. "And while we are, as I may call it, *Scouring* our Planet, by clearing America of Woods, and so making this Side of our Globe reflect a brighter Light to the Eyes of Inhabitants in Mars or Venus," writes Franklin, "why should we in the Sight of Superior Beings, darken its People?" Less agile than the ironic Franklin, George Washington poses a rudimentary conflict between refinement and savagery. In a letter to Congressman James Duane on September 7, 1783, he explains that "the gradual extension of our Settlements will as certainly cause the Savage as the Wolf to retire; both being beasts of prey tho' they differ in shape."

Commentary of this sort keeps its speakers remote from all feeling of human obligation and away from the emotional depths in Native-American responses. "Are you determined to crush us?" Cornplanter asks Washington in 1790. "If you are, tell us so; that those of our nation who have become your children, and have determined to die so, may know what to do." The primal eloquence of this comment comes in loss realized and properly measured, but Cornplanter's words rise to another level in their recognition that republican light and refinement reflect only power and not reason. That recognition, by extension, leaves early republicans wholly *without* eloquence.

Washington simply cannot be memorable in response. His formal answer to Cornplanter, on December 29, 1790, regrets the past, promises protection, gives "suitable presents," condemns "bad Indians," and proclaims justice. But justice in the realm of cross-cultural relations already has been stripped of its philosophical foundations in eighteenth-century thought. As

Jefferson, the theorist, already has foreseen in vindicating Virginia land claims in 1773–4: "whoever shall attempt to trace the claims . . . or reconcile the invasions made on the native Indians to the natural rights of mankind, will find that he is pursuing a Chimera, which exists only in his own imagination, against the evidence of indisputable facts." The fragments that remain in the lost record of Native-American expression catch the early Republic in its least favorable light.

IV

The poignancy of the Native-American situation lies in the ephemeral moment; that of slavery, in its growing permanence. If the first is more psychologically dramatic in eighteenth-century life, the second is far more ideologically ominous. Early republicans "discover" indigenous peoples and then immediately forget them by displacing them in the destructive push of their own prosperity, but they "create" slavery in the name of that prosperity, and it flourishes as part of republican growth. Slavery also interrupts Enlightenment norms and the rhetoric of American liberty in more decisive ways. As Patrick Henry expresses these troubling divergences to Robert Pleasants in 1773, "[W]hat adds to the wonder is, that this abominable practice, has been introduced in the most enlightened Ages, Times that seem to have pretensions to boast of high improvement." "Would any one believe that I am master of Slaves," Henry muses. Belief in the presumed contradiction questions many other eventualities. "I know not where to stop," Henry tells Pleasants, "I could say many things on this subject, a serious review of which give a gloomy perspective to future times."

Just how ominously slavery hangs over the republican experiment is evident when the same awareness comes from the mouth of a slave. "I have nothing more to offer than what General Washington would have had to offer, had he been taken by the British and put to trial by them," responds a black defendant after the Gabriel Prosser slave revolt of 1800. "I have adventured my life in endeavouring to obtain the liberty of my countrymen, and am a willing sacrifice in their cause." Awareness, in fact, is doubled and inverted in transmission. These words survive through a white Virginian who witnesses the trial of the insurrectionists in a Richmond courtroom and who, years later, conveys this testimony to an outside observer, the Englishman Robert Sutcliff who, in turn, records them in *Travels in Some Parts of North America* (1811). Delay and indirection, not to mention the accident of survival, all hint at the dangers in a language of communal threat.

The logic of further rebellion is inescapable in the slave's response. The hope for a black Washington and its corollary, the fear of a black Washington, flow from Locke's premises that slaves always exist *"in a State of War"* and that this state of war is especially acute in a culture dedicated to the protection of individual rights. The practical implications for America are present as early as Arthur Lee's "Address on Slavery" in 1767. Noting for the *Virginia Gazette* that the ancients were "brought to the very brink of ruin by the insurrections of their Slaves," Lee predicts "even more fatal consequences from the greater prevalence of Slavery among us." Lee is himself of a slave-owning family. "On us, or on our posterity," he warns, "the inevitable blow, must, one day, fall." And when it falls, no excuse can or should be given. The "Bondage of the Africans" supersedes every relative moral consideration. "There cannot be in nature, there is not in all history, an instance in which every right of men is more flagrantly violated."

The mutual appreciation in master and slave of intolerable ideological contradictions has a compound effect on African American commentaries. Foremost, the awareness of contradiction in the dominant culture bends an already virulent racism into a compulsion against every human entitlement for African Americans, including the most common rights of life, liberty, and property. This compulsion must be resisted by the African-American writer at all costs. At the same time, the inevitability of the logic of further rebellion makes the logic itself dangerous and, therefore, unacceptable as a form of expression – particularly as a form of African-American expression. For while the white citizen who employs that logic is merely silenced (the *Virginia Gazette* refuses to publish a sequel to Arthur Lee's essay), African Americans are destroyed (the insurrectionist of 1800 is immediately executed as he himself, "a willing sacrifice," foresees). The eighteenth-century African-American commentator who wishes to avoid this martyrdom must resist racist impositions without attempting any sustained narrative of final consequences. The result, at its best, is a disciplined language of subordinate intentions, one that vexes the surfaces of cultural repressions by moving just below them.

The typical eighteenth-century African-American text must question through its accommodations. The petitions to state legislatures against slavery by African Americans during the Revolution draw powerfully on the negative parallels between American enslavement and British tyranny, but they do so, as a petition from New Hampshire slaves on November 12, 1779, makes apparent, "in opposing the efforts of tyranny and oppression over the country in which we ourselves have been so long injuriously enslaved," and not to create a new dimension in rebellion. A similar petition from African Americans in Massachusetts on January 13, 1777, expresses "Astonishment that It has Never Bin Consirdered that Every Principle from which Amarica has Acted in the Cours of their unhappy Deficultes with Great Briton Pleads

Stronger than A thousand arguments in favowrs of your petioners," but, once again, the rhetorical emphasis is on a common effort within "the Lawdable Example of the Good People of these States." A justified "spirit to resent" is carefully circumscribed within the framework of supplicating petitioners.

Notably, these African American accommodations are not without their own flavor and bite. Contending with the usual Anglo-American assumption of cultural superiority over peoples of color, Caesar Sarter, an ex-slave writing for the *Essex Journal and Merrimack Packet* (August 17, 1774), boldly reverses the assumption for enslaved African Americans and, by insinuation, for slave cultures everywhere:

> Though we are brought from a land of ignorance, it is as certain that we are brought from a land of comparative innocence – from a land that flows, as it were, with Milk and Honey – and the greater part of us carried, where we are, not only deprived of every comfort of life: But subjected to all the tortures that a most cruel inquisitor could invent, or a capricious tyrant execute and where we are likely, from the vicious examples before us, to become ten fold more the children of satan, than we should probably, have been in our native country.

In an ironic play upon the golden rule, Sarter inserts another reversal, that of master and slave, so that slaveowners may learn "to do to others, as you would, that they would do to you." The denouement of this section, couched in direct address that forces every reader into the role of slave, moves from uneasy feelings of conscience to the more substantial and direct sting of the body. Abduction, separation, enslavement, importation, sale and resale follow in misery after misery. "And after all this," entones Sarter, "you must be plied with that conclusive argument, that cat-o'nine tails to reduce you to what your inhuman masters would call Reason."

The key to successful assertion involves the use but not the uncritical acceptance of dominant cultural norms. Accordingly, although eighteenth-century African American commentaries and other early abolitionist texts tend to extol Christian training, they do not allow the blessings of conversion to obscure prior validations of African culture. Olaudah Equiano's *The Interesting Narrative of the Life of Olaudah Equiano or Gustavus Vassa, The African* (1789) and Broteer Furro's *A Narrative of the Life And Adventures of Venture, A Native Of Africa* (1798), along with the Quaker abolitionist Anthony Benezet's *Some Historical Account of Guinea* (1771), all insist upon the vitality, the prosperity, and general happiness of African communities before they are destroyed by slave traders. These adroit balances between African assertion and Christian acceptance represent a deliberate variation, or range of responses to racism – so much so that the balances themselves supply a gauge of literary creativity at work. As African assertion proclaims an original coherence and integrity of human identity, so Christian acceptance demonstrates intellectual, emotional, and moral capacities of adjustment that establish a claim for equal treatment in Anglo-American culture.

The all but universal embrace of Christianity in slave narratives figures on a variety of levels. Conversion not only proves capacity and gives equal access to theological claims, it commandeers the religious voice, the first voice of revolution in Anglo-American culture. Fully aware of the appropriation in 1774, Caesar Sarter's "Essay on Slavery" uses biblical lore to convey the prospect of revolt that he dare not raise directly. "Only be pleased to recollect the miserable end of Pharoah, in Consequences of his refusal to set those at Liberty, whom he had unjustly reduced to cruel servitude," Sarter reminds his real audience ("those who are advocates for holding the Africans in Slavery").

In finer hands, the same device becomes a more sophisticated critique of American slavery. Phillis Wheatley's letter to the Reverend Samson Occom on February 11, 1774, draws a parallel between the ancient Hebrews and the eighteenth-century African Americans who live and suffer under "Modern Egyptians" and "the Exercise of oppressive Power" in the United States. In the poet's account, printed widely in New England newspapers, civil and religious liberty are inseparably united. Together, they stimulate a "Love of Freedom" that is "impatient of Oppression and pants for Deliverance." Wheatley surely speaks in part from personal experience; her manumission takes place just months before her letter to Occom. But since this love of freedom is a principle "implanted" directly by God, Wheatley can raise its radical implications without the risk of counterattack. There is safety in leaving the political details to God's separate and inscrutable agenda. As Wheatley tells Occom, "God grants Deliverance in his own way and Time."

The mixture of urgency and resignation in Wheatley's letter is a source of its power, and the combination captures something of the general precariousness of African American life in the early Republic. Deliverance in her case seems to have come through a six-week stay in England in the spring and summer of 1773. "Since my return to America," she writes David Wooster on October 18, 1773, "my Master, has at the desire of my friends in England given me my freedom." The slave's dependence on external wishes and protection is one message in this letter. She can speak with such phenomenal yearning of her love of freedom precisely because freedom and life itself in eighteenth-century culture remain so tentative for African Americans. Though free, Phillis Wheatley will die in poverty at the age of thirty-one, and the identity she carries to an unknown grave will still bespeak the oppression that she pants against. Purchased "for a trifle" at the age of eight in Boston Harbor, the future poet automatically takes the surname of her masters, but John and Susanna Wheatley also mark the occasion, July 11,

1761, in a more specific manner. They name their newest possession after the *Phillis,* the slave schooner that brings her to America.

Somewhere in every slave account the scars of experience overwhelm the themes of success and acculturation. Success, after all, is the irresistible metaphor of the writer who has overcome prolonged illiteracy, and the typical slave narrative complements that triumph by accentuating the highest moments of assimilation (literacy, conversion, manumission, and marriage). Unavoidably, however, acculturation in slaves includes the domination of them. On the way to literacy, Olaudah Equiano is beaten until he will accept his Christian name Gustavus Vassa. James Gronniosaw, in *A Narrative of the Most Remarkable Particulars in the Life of James Albert Ukawsaw Gronniosaw* (1770), learns not to swear from a pious older slave who is then whipped by their master for presuming to convey the lesson. Christianity in both master and slave does not prevent flogging in *The Life, History, and Unparalleled Sufferings of John Jea, the African Preacher* (1811). Neither does manumission protect African Americans from the fixed cruelty and injustice of a racist culture. *A Brief Account of the Life, Experiences, Travels, and Gospel Labours of George White, an African* (1810) may recount another successful rise from slavery, in this instance to the vocation of Methodist minister, but the free and converted George White must still endure the regular obstruction of white Methodists, who tell him that "it was the devil who was pushing me to preach."

The starkest recognition of permanent injustice comes from Broteer Furro in his narrative as Venture Smith. Presented by his supporters and publisher as a Benjamin Franklin out of slavery, Venture Smith undercuts his own account of conversion, marriage, freedom, and material success with story after story about how white neighbors swindle him in business. These stories culminate in a New York courtroom where leading citizens cheat him and then amuse themselves by taunting their victim in his "unmerited misfortune." Not surprisingly, Venture Smith's account of this final incident has nothing to do with either the satisfaction or the reasonable tones of a Franklinian "way to wealth":

Such a proceeding as this committed on a defenceless stranger, almost worn out in the hard service of the world, without any foundation in reason or justice, whatever it may be called in a Christian land, would in my native country have been branded as a crime equal to highway robbery. But Captain Hart was a *white gentleman,* and I a *poor African,* therefore it was *all right, and good enough for the black dog.*

After sixty years and considerable success in America, Broteer as Venture remains "a defenceless stranger" in a foreign land. Racism leaves him upholding a homeland that is destroyed out from under him as a boy of seven.

Plainly, Venture is both acculturated and unacculturated as he finds himself consciously and unconsciously betwixt and between. The child who watches as his father is tortured to death by slavers in Africa is himself the father whose "lips are closed in silence and in grief" over the failures of his own children in America. Two separate standards join the traumatized child and angry man in their mutual questioning of "any foundation in reason or justice." The first standard is the sheer materiality of success. Venture, so named by a master who stamps his investment on the person of his slave, quickly accepts ownership as the primary social value. At one level, *A Narrative of the Life and Adventures of Venture* chronicles the material transformations from the first sale of Broteer for four gallons of rum and a piece of calico to the final accumulations of Venture ("more than one hundred acres of land, and three habitable dwelling houses"). Numbers and exchanges, fair and unfair, direct this narrative with bitter consequence. The rationale of the life in the value of property is vulnerable to the worst instrumentalisms of Enlightenment thought, not excluding slavery itself.

And yet a second and higher standard of success keeps Broteer and Venture together. The man from the child holds the fact of his liberty most dear. "My freedom is a privilege which nothing else can equal," concludes Venture on the last page of his narrative. Pride mixes with pain in this assessment. Personal freedom and physical accumulation form a traditional combination in America, but neither in life nor in language can Venture find rest within the combination. Nothing explains the alienation in the eighteenth-century African American text better than the way infringements on liberty and property have driven Venture Smith to reject his own success as a cultural identification. In the end, anger drives his narrative. For Venture, the sorrows of Solomon are more memorable than the joys of salvation. His last words are from Ecclesiastes: "Vanity of vanities, all is vanity."

Cognizance of the special crosscurrents, intentions, pressures, and disillusionments in eighteenth-century African American writings should aid interpretation of another work, perhaps the most misunderstood text of the entire period, Jupiter Hammon's essay to his fellow slaves in New York. *An Address to the Negroes in the State of New-York* (1787) shares many of the qualities already examined, and it, too, mirrors the dominant culture in a manner that sheds light upon its literary craft. In retrospect, we can appreciate many of the generic considerations that will dominate early African American discourse: the authenticating preface by white publishers, Hammon's occasional punning on his slave status ("I am, Gentlemen, Your Servant," he informs the African Society in the City of New York), his stress on education (most conspicuously on the capacity to read), and his resort to a double frame of reference in which "the poor, despised, and miserable state" of his auditors catches both the eternal spirit and the temporal body so as to condemn slavery within the safer condemnation of impiety.

Problems have occurred when twentieth-century readers misconstrue Jupiter Hammon's message of obedience to masters and his acceptance of slavery for himself. More attention should be given to the opening tones of the address; they are ones of overwhelming sorrow in the slave's fallen state, a sorrow that is "at times, almost too much for human nature to bear." With considerable finesse, Hammon's introduction also signifies that the price of addressing African Americans is white support. The same paragraph establishes, first, that "a number of the white people . . . thought [my writings] might do good among their servants" and, second, that the writings themselves should encourage greater solidarity among those servants. "I think you will be more likely to listen to what is said," Hammon observes, "when you know it comes from a negro, one [of] your own nation and colour, and therefore can have no interest in deceiving you, or in saying any thing to you, but what he really thinks is your interest and duty to comply with." The suggestion of a separate nation is arresting; so is the strong implication of insincerity in the dominant culture.

The prevalence of humble tones does not keep Hammon from asserting "that liberty is a great thing, and worth seeking for." The proof of the assertion lies not just in the slave's hopes but in "the conduct of the white-people, in the late war." Necessarily understated, the hypocrisy of the Revolution on slavery is nonetheless present in this essay. "I must say," notes Hammon, "that I have hoped that God would open their eyes, when they were so much engaged for liberty, to think of the state of the poor blacks, and to pity us." Interestingly, however, Hammon never relies on that pity. "If God designs to set us free," he writes late in the essay, "he will do it, in his own time, and way."

Christian humility is not without its edges. Most of the essay calls for reliance on the next world but with an immediate sociological significance. The next world, like this one, divides the free and the enslaved, but heaven and hell, an eternal division, will separate its peoples on the basis of merit rather than race. The democracy of Hammon's heaven is an impressive referent for future use. "There are some things very encouraging in God's word for such ignorant creatures as we are;" advises Hammon, "for God hath not chosen the rich of this world." Then, in an understated humor that reemphasizes the horror of the present, Hammon defines "the greatest fools" as those who become "miserable in this world, and in the world to come" by making themselves "slave here, and slaves forever." "What," he asks, at the age of seventy, "is forty, fifty, or sixty years, when compared to eternity?"

As the work of a slave, *An Address to the Negroes in the State of New-York* is doubly bound by the dictates of a consensual literature, and Jupiter Hammon's stress upon obedience to God's plan participates in a further complication of these conditions. Although he uses the scriptural injunction of St. Paul to the Ephesians (6:5–8) to remind his slave audience of the obedience of servant to master, the discussion allows a useful qualification. "Now whether it is right, and lawful, in the sight of God, for them to make slaves of us or not," Hammon reminds his slave audience, "it is our duty to obey our masters, in all their lawful commands." The matter of slavery is thus left in God's hands. Unfortunately, the overall strength of this argument has been lost because Jupiter Hammon writes out of a now forgotten shift in perspective. God's hands are tied in postrevolutionary politics in ways that they are not in the colonial period. Hammon's real energy belongs to an earlier era, when God is a more visible and active presence. When Hammon warns that God is "terrible beyond what you can think – that he keeps you in life every moment – and that he can send you to that awful Hell, that you laugh at, in an instant," his words reach back to Jonathan Edwards.

The nature of the divide is both subtle and vast. Arguably, the Revolution inflicts another disservice on the slave population of America by separating church and state with such rigor. To read the pamphlet literature of the period is to realize that the most dynamic opponents of slavery in eighteenth-century America are ministers. Moreover, the extraordinary eloquence of the clergy on the problems of slavery in the early 1770s has much to do with their political power. Preachers like Nathaniel Niles in Newburyport, Massachusetts, in 1774, Gad Hitchcock in Boston in the same year, and Levi Hart in Preston, Connecticut, in 1775 shake the foundations of the standing order because they represent communities-at-large and not just the spiritual keeping of their congregations.

Nathaniel Niles speaks for a generation of radical clergy in his masterpiece *Two Discourses on Liberty*. "God gave us liberty, and we have enslaved our fellow-men," Niles announces, putting the case as bluntly as possible. "May we not fear that the law of retaliation is about to be executed on us? What can we object against it?" The questions mount as Niles forces the contradiction on revolutionary America:

What excuse can we make for our conduct? What reason can we urge why our oppression shall not be repaid in kind? . . . Would we enjoy liberty? Then we must grant it to others. For shame, let us either cease to enslave our fellow-men, or else let us cease to complain of those that would enslave us. Let us either wash our hands from blood, or never hope to escape the avenger.

These words are close to and yet far from Thomas Jefferson's own cry over slavery in *Notes on the State of Virginia*: "I tremble for my country when I reflect that God is just: that his justice cannot sleep for ever."

One of several differences between Niles in 1774 and Jefferson in 1787 is the separation of church and state. Niles, like Phillis Wheatley and Jupiter Hammon, assumes that civil and spiritual liberty are inseparably united. "The former without the latter," he observes, "is but a body without a soul." The effect in politics of this juncture is to activate an angry God in the perception of civil injustice. Separation, the work of the Enlightenment, removes that anger from the political arena and replaces it with human reason. Jefferson sees the limits of reason in his indictment of slavery, but his comprehension does not lead to a coordination of divine and secular responses. His despairing gesture works, rather, to shift consideration of an impossible problem from human to divine hands. Even so, God remains a relatively distant figure. Sudden retribution does not shape Jefferson's rhetoric as it does the words of Niles or Hammon, and Jefferson's argument against slavery is correspondingly weaker and less convincing; gone from it is the religious voice that expects horrible and eternal punishment at any moment for the sin of slavery.

The oratorical shifts caused by the separation of church and state also protect slavery in another direction. When the clergy are removed from politics, a vital source of social protest goes with them. The peculiar right of ministers to address unpleasant and dangerous subjects in America has never extended to the other professions. (Certainly, no comparable unit replaces them in politics after 1776, and ministers have remained the most eloquent speakers in American civil rights to this day.) Benjamin Rush stumbles across the limitations imposed by this cultural truth when he writes "An Address to the Inhabitants of the British Settlements in America Upon Slave-Keeping" in 1773. "This publication . . . did me harm, by exciting the resentment of many slaveholders against me," Rush, a medical doctor, jots in his autobiography. "It injured me in another way, by giving rise to an opinion that I had meddled with a controversy that was foreign to my business." The moral issues in slavery are more intrinsic to preaching, and ministers never lose their right to comment, but their capacity to speak in politically effective forums dwindles in the early Republic, and their loss coincides with the rise of slavery. The answering rise of an effective abolitionism, thirty years later, will depend upon the reanimation of religious perspectives in the sectional debates over slavery.

These ramifications help to explain why the religious voice has been so intrinsic to African American narrratives. For more than two hundred years after the Revolution, religion has remained the surest, the safest, and the most vital source of minority protest. Psychologically, it also has allowed the expression of an anger that minimizes corrosion in the speaker. The persecuted Christian can both act and rest within God's wrath. Indeed, the

general importance of a contextualized anger cannot be sufficiently emphasized in analyzing the expanding dispensations in American life. Just as
reason is the irresistible tone of a national authority born of the Enlightenment, so anger becomes the inevitable voice of continuing change and response to that authority. Perceptive moments in early African-American
writings recognize the sign of reason as an enemy. Venture Smith, denying
any foundation in reason or justice, and Caesar Sarter, reifying reason in the
master's cat-o'nine tails, speak from experiences that are bitter beyond the
ability of ordinary emotion and language to express.

V

Anger is the necessary source of change among the disempowered because
postrevolutionary thought converts the original animus of rebellion into prospects of collective identity and manifest destiny. Nowhere is the cost of this
shift more evident than in the tonal controls placed on women's writing. The
emotion most frequently denied the educated eighteenth-century woman, or
"learned lady" as she is pejoratively termed, is anger in her own cause. Since
any strong assertion on her part runs the risk of that classification, gender
restrictions call for the most tractable tones in correct expression. Of course,
the more public the expression, the more exacting those restrictions become.

Only Tom Paine among revolutionary leaders addresses women's rights in
a sustained manner. *An Occasional Letter on the Female Sex,* written for the
Pennsylvania Magazine in 1775, summarizes the fact of injustice. "Man with
regard to [women], in all climates, and in all ages," writes Paine, "has been
either an insensible husband or an oppressor." His letter also details the
exclusion of women from the public sphere: "man, while he imposes duties
upon women, would deprive them of the sweets of public esteem, and in
exacting virtues from them, would make it a crime to aspire at honor."
Public virtues and honor are assigned to women rather than won by them,
and their general exclusion from activity in the public sphere, that unofficial
but powerful zone of influence between private discussion and formal governmental debate, sharply curtails their intellectual influence and range on every
issue.

Two factors, above others, detail the predicament of women who write in
the period. An explicit contradiction between the right of assertion and the
status of the lady – a contradiction that the eighteenth century assigns with
special weight to polite circles of literary production – traps women writers
within subordinating patterns of social and intellectual deference. Concurrently, the cultural fear of postrevolutionary America takes a gendered form
that effectively trivializes women when it does not charge them with danger-

ous behavior. Insofar as women occupy a positive space in republican ideology, it is in the figurative symbols of liberty and republican virtue, an iconography that underscores the expectation of their passivity in public forums. Liberty or virtue, often threatened in these renderings, refers to a purity of status or innocence of experience under masculine protection, categories that preclude independent female activity.

The conduct books and magazines of the period are filled with proscriptions relating to women. Virtually all spontaneous, energetic female behavior becomes suspect in them. Comparing the ideal woman to a delicate piece of porcelain in a typical treatment of the subject, *The Ladies' Pocket Library,* published in Philadelphia in 1792, argues that "greater delicacy evidently implies greater fragility; and this weakness, natural and moral, clearly points out the necessity of a superior degree of caution, retirement, and reserve." Since women "find their protection in their weakness, and their safety in their delicacy," it follows that "pretensions to that strength of intellect, which is requisite to penetrate into the abstruser walks of literature . . . they will readily relinquish." "Men, on the contrary, are formed for the more public exhibitions on the great theatre of human life" and "find their proper element" when they "appear terrible in arms, useful in commerce, shining in counsels."

The prevalence of this logic in early republican rhetoric is such that Judith Sargent Murray performs a rare act of intellectual and political courage in her total rejection of its implications. The *"apparent* superiority" of the male mind, she writes for *The Massachusetts Magazine* in "On the Equality of the Sexes" (1790), merely honors the circumstance that "the one is taught to aspire, and the other is early confined and limited." Weakness in the female is what to expect when "the sister must be wholly domesticated, while the brother is led by the hand through all the flowery paths of science." Sadly, the woman who overcomes these handicaps earns the unhappiness and maybe the scandal "of a *learned lady."* Murray adds that the role of domesticity can never occupy an active mind; presumed failings in the female character – gossip, concern with fashion, idle visiting, lavish expenditure, and so on – actually reflect the frustration of exclusion from worthier forums.

Murray's last point deliberately touches a cultural nerve. Extravagance in the female figure is a lightning rod for paranoid fears in the early Republic. A vital simplicity, perceived to be everywhere on the wane in postrevolutionary America, suffers most from a spirit of luxury, and this vice frequently assumes female form in public discussion. The conventional synecdoche for luxury in early republican life is female dress. *A Treatise on Dress, Intended as a friendly and seasonable Warning to the Daughters of America* (1783) announces that "there is no one device, in which Satan is more successful, and by which he leads people captive to his will, and plunges them into hell, than he does by charming their minds, and setting them bewitched after gay, shining, and costly apparel." *Proverbs on the Pride of Women* (1787) deplores the vanity of women "going to church with the ribs of unrighteousness round their rumple; with a displayed banner of painted hypocrisy in their right hand, to guard their faces from the sun." Charges of this nature are habitual and intense in their specificity and in their prediction of terrible outcomes. "Many of those women," thunders *Proverbs,* "are more dangerous than the mouth of devouring cannons; though they appear as angels in the church, they are as serpents in the sheets, and as Beelzebub above the blankets."

Beneath the frequency and extremity of attack is an ingrained misogyny that eighteenth-century women have to accept when they enter political discourse, a price of admission that is almost incalculable. It is one thing for George Washington, writing to James Warren on October 7, 1785, to bring "luxury, effeminacy, and corruptions" together; quite another, for Abigail Adams to warn Mercy Otis Warren on May 14, 1787, that "luxury, with ten thousand evils in her train, exiled the humble virtues" in America after the Revolution; and still another, for Warren herself to conclude her *History of the Rise, Progress, and Termination of the American Revolution* (1805) with the fear that America will someday be "effeminated by luxury." Lost somewhere in the process of gender accommodation is the capacity to meet political conflict collectively in the public sphere as gentlemen of letters frequently do. Could any circle of women writers have taken a decisive political position together in the 1780s without raising overwhelming cries of unnatural opposition and effeminacy? On politics, women write in isolation if at all. It is not until 1932 that scholars discover that Mercy Otis Warren writes *Observations on the New Constitution, And on the Federal and State Conventions* (1788), one of the most effective essays in anti-Federalist protest.

The reflexive defensiveness that women writers must bring to the subject of their own sex is just one measure of a definitive vulnerability in address. When Esther de Berdt Reed, wife of the president of Pennsylvania, organizes a Ladies Association in support of the Revolution, she must first try to exculpate women who take an active role. "Who knows if persons disposed to censure, and sometimes too severely with regard to us," asks Reed, "may not disapprove our appearing acquainted even with the actions of which our sex boasts?" Her broadside, *The Sentiments of an American Woman* (1780), lingers over the heroines of antiquity and glories "in all that which my sex has done great and commendable," but it also quietly accepts as it laments the relative limitations placed upon the modern woman: "if the weakness of our Constitution, if opinion and manners did not forbid us to march to glory by the same path as the Men, we should at least equal and sometimes surpass them in our love for the public good."

Even a formidable intellectual like Abigail Adams eschews anger when she is attacked along gender lines. Responding on February 3, 1814, to Judge F. A. Vanderkemp's complaint against "learned ladies," Adams casts her antagonist into the third person where she heaps ironies upon him: "And in the first place, to put him perfectly at his ease, I assure him that I make not any pretensions to the character of a learned lady, and therefore, according to his creed, I am entitled to his benevolence." She drolly traces "the true cause" of Vanderkemp's accusation to his fear of a rival, but the underlying tone of her letter is one of regret that softens irony and assertion. "There are so few women who may be really called learned," she ponders, "that I do not wonder they are considered as black swans." This language gently resists what it must admit. Pressing against dominant assumptions, it clarifies otherwise obscure ideological boundaries. The black swan is a blight not to itself but in the eye of the beholder — a faulty male beholder who fixes on a false incongruity between education and capacity.

Abigail Adams both welcomes and denies the power of blackness. The innate grace of the simile retains all sense of earned capacity, even as the circumstance suggests sharp limits on the progress of the Enlightenment and maybe on the very nature of the Enlightenment. What can be the importance of learning in a world where "learned" has become a pejorative term? Adams insists upon the capacity under challenge. "It is very certain," she observes, "that a well-informed woman, conscious of her nature and dignity, is more capable of performing the relative duties of life, and of engaging and retaining the affections of a man of understanding, than one whose intellectual endowments rise not above the common level." The instrumental acknowledgment of functionalism in marriage — approved by her male antagonist — marches hand in hand with the separate ideal of knowing one's own nature and dignity.

For women who live more on the margins of republican culture, the cost of suppressing and internalizing their anger is noticeably higher. The "aged matron" of *The Female Advocate,* an anonymous pamphlet printed in New Haven in 1801, "belongs to a class, whose weakness is become quite proverbial among the self sufficient lords of this lower world." She expects reproach "if she should attempt to say any thing, on behalf of her own sex, or a single word on the long exploded subject of female merit." This speaker has been "so wounded" by the "contempt" and "self distant superiority" of patriarchal structures that she must struggle to hush her thoughts on the ingratitude and reproaches of others. Fearing to give offense but bitterly "cumbered with much serving," the female advocate asks only for the merit to which she is entitled, a share in literary concerns. "I contend indeed for the honor of intellectual worth," she declares. Her aspirations and tensions are joined in this statement. Using both, the author produces the single most compelling American pamphlet on women's rights for a decade in either direction.

Many themes percolate through *The Female Advocate,* including the need for equality between the sexes for there to be real friendship, the goal of women's education to secure that equality, the type for equality in the Christian religion, the active danger of ignorance for women left alone in an unfriendly world, the arbitrary rule of "all arrogating man," the double standard in seduction, the unfair opprobrium reserved for "masculine" or active women, and the unacceptable narrowness of a life confined to domestic cares ("shall women . . . never expand an idea beyond the walls of her house?"). But every theme is informed and driven by an initial, stunned, and stunning recognition: namely, that the Enlightenment, as defined by men, utterly excludes women from its purview. If the Enlightenment signifies the capacity to know and the spread of knowledge, what can it mean, asks the female advocate, when "the arrogant assumers of male merit" believe that "our sex arrived at its zenith of improvement, at the age of twenty-one"? Is it possible, she wonders, that she has not improved since that age? "If so, what a pitiable misfortune to me, that I was born a woman!" The rest of the pamphlet is a triumphant reversal of these connotations. The "sincere Advocate for the Merits of her Sex" explains her situation through the knowledge of experience. She is the living image of the Kantian imperative "dare to know."

The anonymity of the female advocate is a reminder that every assertive woman in early republican culture needs some disguise for protection and control. For Deborah Sampson that mask is the literal one of cross dressing. Hired out as a farm employee from the age of ten, Sampson adopts men's clothing and joins the revolutionary army as Robert Shurtleff when she completes her indenture at twenty-one. It is, she decides, the one way that an impoverished but vigorous woman can satisfy her curiosity to see the world, or, in the words of her eighteenth-century biographer, "she determined to burst the bands which, it must be confessed, have too often held her sex in awe." Deborah Sampson serves for three years undetected (1781–4), sees heavy fighting at White Plains, Tarrytown, and Yorktown, and receives serious wounds before her real identity is finally discovered in Philadelphia. Passing is as much a question of performance as appearance. "Her countenance and voice were feminine; but she conversed with such ease on the subject of theology, on political subjects, and military tactics, that her manner would seem to be masculine."

This cross-gendered voice, now regrettably lost, gives way to a biography of the female soldier with more conventional purposes in mind. Herman Mann's *The Female Review; Or, Memoirs of an American Young Lady* (1797) reclaims the propriety undermined by Sampson's disguise, rejects "Female Enterprise," and extols the unblemished purity and retiring modesty of the maiden ideal. According to Mann, men and women should read Deborah Sampson's story with their separate spheres in mind. The woman soldier's "irregular" heroism, "while it deserves the applause of every patriot and veteran, must chill the blood of the tender and sensible female." Women must learn to rechannel the example of Sampson's energy back into their proper, domestic sphere. Throughout, the soldier's accomplishments remain "a great presumption in a female, on account of the inadequateness of her nature." The biography both reveres and resists the revolutionary heroism of its subject. In a unique ambivalence for the times on this theme, one that vividly confirms the exclusiveness of connection between patriotism and patriarchy in the early Republic, *The Female Review* reveals itself in reversals. Deborah Sampson may stand for patriotic heroism, but Herman Mann – the very name of the male author redoubles his theme – writes to raise the alarm of eighteenth-century men; he seeks to expose the disguise of the assertive woman.

The disguise of Eliza Lucas Pinckney (1723–93) is harder to penetrate because more conventional. A surviving letterbook shows how it worked. Scientist, farmer, businesswoman, and matriarch of the leading family in South Carolina, Pinckney masks herself in a life of service. The young Eliza Lucas is mistress of three plantations by the age of seventeen; her responsibilities include the cultivation of five thousand acres of land, commercial arrangements and correspondence in the sale and shipping of products, the direct supervision of twenty slaves and of the overseers of two other plantations, the education of a younger sister, and the management of family interests in Charleston society. "I shall begin to think my self an old woman before I am well a young one having these weighty affairs upon my hands," she wryly observes at nineteen. Her every enterprise, in the constant refrain of her letters, is the work of an "obedient and ever devoted daughter," one who mollifies the demands of an anxious and complaining absent father, George Lucas, a British army officer and the lieutenant governor in Antigua.

The school of obedience serves Eliza well in 1744 when, at twenty-one, she marries Charles Pinckney, a widower twenty-four years her senior. She resolves "next to my God, to make it my Study to please him," and when Pinckney dies suddenly in 1758, she automatically transfers all sense of service to familial honor and her three surviving children. Few accomplish as much as Eliza Lucas Pinckney in the midst of self-abnegation. Her experimentations in indigo and crop rotation earn her a name in the history of agricultural science, her letterbook of correspondence encapsulates colonial Charleston from 1738–1762, and her adroit management of economic and social assets raises the Pinckney name over all others in South Carolina.

Self-deprecation always accompanies the accomplishments of Eliza Lucas Pinckney; the device shrouds the enormous energy and intelligence that might otherwise have upset the community around her. The young girl evades an early marriage proposal by disarming the wishes of her father with self-disparaging humor. When her future husband sees "a fertile brain at schemeing" and "the little Visionary" in her agricultural experiments, she confirms his opinions without changing her course. The language of deference is her shield. "Your reasoning is convincing and unanswerable," she tells him on one occasion, "and your reproof more obliging than the highest compliment you could have made me." Typically, her reading of Richardson's *Pamela, or Virtue Rewarded* (1740–1) finds fault with the heroine for "that disgusting liberty of praising herself." Eliza Pinckney, by way of contrast, deflects attention by minimizing her role. The wealthy and cultivated young widow will avoid envy and suspicion in 1762 by mocking herself, "an old woman in the Wilds of America." Tenaciously protecting the Pinckney holdings amidst the war and devastation of 1779, she will minimize loss by telling her children "I cant want but little, nor that little long." Meanwhile, her creditors receive a careful account of extensive properties to offset the embarrassment of temporary financial inconvenience.

The rewards in these strategies coexist with a concession. The matriarch succeeds partly by muting all sense of a political voice. Eliza Pinckney can be supremely effective in negotiating for the care and release of her captured son Major Thomas Pinckney in 1780. On the other hand, the success of those negotiations has something to do with her decision to speak and write in nonpartisan terms. Fully committed to the Revolution, this mother of two army officers does not seem to have engaged in public commentary on the conflict itself; her apparent restraint, even in extant family correspondence, is part of her discipline in dealing with patriarchal authority. And the accommodation is not an unusual one. Martha Ballard, a New England midwife, supplies a parallel example in very different circumstances when she keeps a diary between 1785 and 1812 in Hallowell, Maine. A leading figure in her community, Ballard also maintains herself by avoiding political engagement and local controversy. For the successful woman of the period, political articulation on major issues is rarely part of an independent engagement in communal affairs.

The hallmarks of Pinckney's thought are piety and reason. As the first quality insures humility and sacrifice, so the second avoids enthusiasm and imbalance with all of these combinations geared toward successful endeavor. These virtues are ones to expect in the accomplished figure of neoclassical lore, but they grow into rigid prerequisites for the lady who would lead. "Consider what you owe to your self, your Country and family," Eliza Pinckney counsels a grandson in 1782. For herself and the women around her, these priorities are exactly reversed: family, then country, then self. The primary virtue of disinterestedness leads toward public service and recognition for the early republican man; toward self-effacement and the hope of private acknowledgment in the accomplished republican woman. Pinckney's achievements are all the greater for their necessary indirections, but they must also be understood in the context of fixed and sharp gender restriction.

There is no place for transforming anger to enter Eliza Lucas Pinckney's frame of reference or, for that matter, for it to legitimate the role of any other American woman as a public figure in eighteenth-century life – one reason, perhaps, why the new and still suspect form of the novel will situate anger so strongly as pathos in writings such as Susanna Rowson's *Charlotte Temple* (1791) and Hannah Foster's *The Coquette* (1797). The more covert strategies of fiction not only welcome anonymity when needed, they also establish an ideal forum for mixing private and public events and understandings.

Anger is transformative, however, when it partakes of the enabling wrath of the Revolution. By the same token, to be without it in early republican culture is to be disenfranchised. For if the Revolution comes alive in the spirit of declaration, women must still ask for their rights. It may be that Thomas Paine, as the angriest revolutionary, comes closest among men to writing out the plight of women in the revolutionary period, but he also robs them of all access to his most vital emotion. Women, unlike men, do not seize their rights in Paine's writings. They remain the supplicants of a masculine world, and they ask for the minimal justice of recognition.

" 'Be not our tyrants in all,' " runs Paine's imagined version of this supplicating voice in *An Occasional Letter on the Female Sex.* " 'Permit our names to be sometimes pronounced beyond the narrow circle in which we live. . . . deny us not that public esteem which, after the esteem of one's self, is the sweetest reward of well doing.' " The ability of the female voice to *demand* its rights, instead of pleading for them, will take centuries rather than years to develop, and central to that slow realization will be its difficulty in coming to grips with an ugly fact. Self-esteem in American culture depends upon the capacity to express public anger in a righteous cause.

VI

The dilemma of the disempowered can be read in their inability to wield that emotion within the workings of the new nation, and a number of variables are at work in the limitation. In part, the shift from participation in the

Revolution to contemplation of it forces corresponding changes in the under-standing and expression of originating angers. In part, the widely perceived fragility of early republican culture qualifies all further disruptive exercises of revolutionary spirit. In part, too, the success of revolutionary anger leads away from the solidarity of facing external enemies and toward the fragmen-tary and divisive practice of finding enemies within.

All of these variables work against Americans with limited access to the public sphere. Indeed, the same tendencies, raised in certain ways and ap-plied in given situations, channel cultural resentments directly against the disenfranchised. The hope for cohesion in republican society is a dangerous perception for those left outside. The Native American as logical opponent, the slave as feared rebel, and the woman as a symbol of luxury are only the easiest targets of early republican rage. Many other categories, essentially any group not identifiable as successfully republican, have been occasional candi-dates and sometime victims.

The loose displacement of originating communal angers appears in a strik-ing detail, the official seal of the Commonwealth of Massachusetts from 1780. In formal description, the seal shows "an Indian, dressed in his Shirt, Maggosins, belted proper, in his right hand a Bow, TOPAZ, in his left an Arrow, its point towards the Base." A crest, just above this representation, depicts "On a Wreath a Dexter Arm clothed and ruffled proper, grasping a Broad Sword, the Pummel and Hilt, TOPAZ, with this Motto: *Ense Petit Placidam Sub Libertate Quietem* [by the sword, he seeks peace under liberty]." The inscription, taken from Algernon Sidney, martyr to English liberty and author of the influential *Discourses Concerning Goverment* (1698), signals the need for willed acts of violence in the name of liberty, but the overall representation gives that meaning an additional turn, and the extent of the turn appears in a basic shift in iconography. The original seal of the Massachu-setts Bay Colony in 1675 also presents a Native American, though one who clearly symbolizes peaceful agrarian purposes and who formally salutes En-glish settlers to "come over and help us." With this salutation dropped, the added configuration of elements in 1780 is quite different in meaning.

The entirety of the new seal portrays the right arm of authority (the gentleman's arm, shirt, and sword) raised in threatening posture over an oblivious Native American. And the immediacy of this image is strength-ened by historical context. The seal of 1780 is conceived within three years of the murder of Jane McCrea, a tragedy in which the worst fears of New Englanders are fanned into wartime frenzy when the daughter of a Presbyte-rian minister is scalped and further mutilated by Native Americans as part of the British advance from Canada under General Burgoyne. The design also follows by just a year the military expedition that systematically devastates

Iroquois civilization in the western part of the northern states. Obviously, and for many republicans in 1780, more than symbolism is involved in their coat of arms; the sword of Massachusetts is poised for righteous and repeated descent.

Postrevolutionary Americans refocus the anger of their beginnings without quite recognizing the shift. Remembrance includes a mode of forgetting. Tom Paine, writing *To the People of England on the Invasion of England,* tries in 1804 to revive the original moment by reminding everyone that "the American Revolution began on untried ground" and that "some bold exertion was necessary to shock [benumbed reasoning faculties] into reflection." Not coincidentally, these views bespeak the radical side of the Enlightenment: rejection of the past with trust in the awakening power of reason. But Paine, as always, is asking for too much. No culture can long sustain itself on untried ground or bold exertions, and reason alone cannot control communal uncertainties. Republicans want to curb their fear of the unknown. Familiar ground, not untried, is what they seek, and they expect the completed success of the Revolution to provide it for them.

It is not easy, in consequence, to determine how long or in what sense the Republic remains a revolutionary culture. What is plain is how quickly the achievements of the Enlightenment (the spread of knowledge) and of the Revolution (victory) overshadow the processes of Enlightenment thought (daring to know) and distort the practices of revolutionary action (galvanizing anger in the name of liberty). Tired of years of strife and eager to create a uniform foundation out of the Revolution, early republicans want most of all to secure their achievement in time and place. They need the standard that a spirit of achievement and an appropriate sense of story can give them, and their search for heroes is the most prominent manifestation of that need.

A function of narrative expectations as well as cultural aspirations, the revolutionary hero literalizes anger by sealing it off in postrevolutionary discourse. The wrath of a Patrick Henry or of a George Washington now belongs to the highest order. A figure of this sort becomes a simulacrum of angers completed or at least stilled. Cast together in the role of founding fathers, these figures acquire the status of achievers almost before they are fully recognized as rebels. Soon enough in the popular imagination, the expectation of high-mindedness in the hero replaces the acrimony of actual wartime participation. By 1826, antebellum orators like Daniel Webster will have turned these founders into fixed and eternal constellations that guide America with "the united blaze of a thousand lights." And although it is simplicity itself to attach these motionless and mythologized figures to the victory of the Revolution, it becomes increasingly difficult to apply them with any force to the animus of further action.

The cult of the hero as a symbol system explains a great deal about early republican ideology, and the first histories of the Revolution show what is really at stake in the phenomenon. David Ramsay in *The History of the American Revolution* (1789) and Mercy Otis Warren in *History of the Rise, Progress and Termination of the American Revolution* (1805) are Federalist against anti-Federalist in politics, southerner against northerner in regional identity, male against female in domestic character, and parvenu against social pillar in society, but they agree on three things as historians: the Revolution is the struggle of American virtue against European avarice, the American historian rightly extols that virtue in a narrative of events, and, finally, virtue itself declines dangerously in the aftermath of the Revolution. All three premises dictate vigorous commemoration of the revolutionary hero, where heroism magnifies and celebrates disinterested, patriotic action. Although the conspicuous type for this figure is always George Washington, recognition of every hero helps republicans, in Ramsay's words, to "cultivate justice both public and private." The presentation of patriotic action, correctly comprehended, sustains the revolutionary victory of public interest over private feeling.

For both Ramsay and Warren, there is every reason for urgency in the personification of public virtue. Ramsay's history deplores the aftermath, "the languid years of peace, when selfishness usurped the place of public spirit." Warren begins her own work warning that principles "have been nearly annihilated. . . . the causes which involved the thirteen colonies in confusion and blood are scarcely known, amidst the rage of accumulation and the taste for expensive pleasures that have since prevailed." If the exaltation of virtuous leaders seems to have been shrill in these histories, it is because both writers think that virtue unaided will not restrain vice. The battle of good over evil, foreordained in religious discourse, unfolds with extreme uncertainty in these secular histories. "It is an unpleasing part of history," Warren concludes, "when 'corruption begins to prevail, when degeneracy marks the manners of the people, and weakens the sinews of the state.' " Ramsay, for his part, ends with the hope of progressive happiness, but he fears in the same breath that republicans will "degenerate into savages."

Employment of the revolutionary figure in patterns of emulation responds to these anxieties, but it also subverts ideological impetuses for further change. When David Ramsay writes that the victory at Yorktown produces "a social triumph and exultation, which no private prosperity is ever able to fully inspire," he locks Americans into a worthier past. The disempowered, in particular, are frozen in time when the fixed achievements of the Revolution replace all sense of a radical awareness in the people. The eighteenth-century pantheon of heroes contains no models for newer and different kinds of Americans to emulate in their struggle for equal representation. Neither does it suffice for the unrepresented to add their own heroes as eighteenth-century women writers like Esther de Berdt Reed and "the Female Advocate" of New Haven try to do.

The problems in emulation go well beyond representation. Recognition of the hero or heroine – however inspiring and however indicative of capacity – runs counter to the technical articulation and procedural protection of human rights. The timeless achievement of the one cuts across the timely process in the other. The celebration of detached or dispassionate service can easily deflect new quests for entitlement as petitioners turn into factions or interest groups under the critical gaze of those who can afford a disinterested mien. Inevitably, the retrospective tendencies in emulation resist the safeguards of formal complaint and proper redress.

Of course, the Revolution simultaneously encourages the exercise of inalienable rights, protects the right of petition, maintains the legality of formal complaint, and allows for redress. It is both radical possibility and reified monolith in early republican ideology. David Ramsay, whose Federalist leanings produce a conservative vision in 1789, can also discern and celebrate the effect of change. The Revolution brings "a vast expansion of the human mind." "It seemed," he adds, "as if the war not only required but created talents. Men . . . spoke, wrote, and acted, with an energy far surpassing all expectations which could be reasonably founded on their previous acquirements." As the conservative Ramsay is able to extol the expansive energy in expectations, so the more radical Mercy Otis Warren can worry about the "truly alarming" disturbances that threaten "civil convulsions" in the 1780s.

Closely examined, the Revolution is always both triumph and troubling event. It figures in both a radical frame and a conservative continuum, and it can be either one in Warren's insistence that it appear "the pole-star of the statesman, respected by the rising generation." At issue in the conflict of impulses is the variable and volatile revolutionary understanding of republicans caught up in constant and stressful cultural change. Then, as now, claims of a guiding uprightness, assertions of patriotic well-being, and assumptions about a place in human history are the elements of a successful public American voice. The main difference in the early Republic is that each element revolves obsessively around the suddenly colossal past.

Who will own the Revolution and to what end? The voices of postrevolutionary discourse are explosive and timid, hopeful and despairing, angry and complacent – often in the same moment – in a battleground of conflicted and conflicting voices over the meaning of the Revolution. To what extent does the disappearing past animate a claim about the future? Should revolutionary triumphs be conserved or their spirit extended? The perceptive critic can find these cautionary and expansive voices and tendencies in just about every major intellectual figure and must gauge which elements dominate and for what reasons.

Compounding these questions is a final element in postrevolutionary American expression that is so ubiquitous as frequently to be missed altogether. The universally acclaimed success of the Revolution enters into an equally omnipresent possibility of pervading loss. These tones reach an apotheosis of sorts in Abraham Lincoln's First Inaugural Address (1861), where "the mystic chords of memory" stretch back to touch "the better angels of our nature," but they exist throughout the public literature of the early Republic and antebellum culture.

Everywhere the recognition of rapid change vies with the desire to appear in control of it, and over everything looms a vague nostalgia about what is passing or missing. Loss is the elusive variable in determining voice in early republican literature. Speaker after speaker points to the fragility of what has been gained in the fact or likelihood of breakage, and in these perceptions the anger of the Revolution competes with something that comes very close to a communal sense of mourning. The American Enlightenment begins in the time of Samuel Davies's refrain over the death of George II in 1760: "George is no more!" It ends in 1826 with Daniel Webster entoning "Adams and Jefferson are no more!" How and where increasingly democratic voices place themselves within this ever-moving sense of regret is, in large measure, the story of American literature.

THE LITERATURE OF THE REVOLUTIONARY AND EARLY NATIONAL PERIODS

Michael T. Gilmore

I

❦

LETTERS OF THE EARLY REPUBLIC

FROM 1790 TO 1820, there was not a book, a speech, a conversation, or a thought in the state." So wrote Ralph Waldo Emerson in 1852, glancing back from the heyday of Romanticism to what he considered the cultural blankness of the formative years. Until the 1980s, academic criticism accepted and elaborated this pejorative assessment of postrevolutionary culture. To modern readers, there seemed little to admire in the letters of the early Republic apart from its political documents. The consensus held that the literature produced by Americans before Washington Irving and James Fenimore Cooper was derivative of English models, lacking in originality and individual expressiveness, and fatally weakened by its commitment to didacticism. In effect, the consensus concurred with the Emersonian judgment that *no* literary art existed in this country until the awakening of the Romantic spirit.

This picture has now been revised, as new interest in the writing of the early Republic has brought fuller appreciation of that writing's goals and character, but it is instructive to reflect on the reasons for the persistent neglect of postrevolutionary culture. The supposition has been that the writing of the federal era defies sympathetic understanding because it lacks intrinsic merit. This objection assumes that all literature should be held to the same standard of evaluation. It takes for granted the existence of an ahistorical notion of what constitutes literary achievement, one that gives absolute primacy to aesthetic value. Yet the privileging of the aesthetic as something desirable purely for its own sake was itself the product – at least in America – of a historical configuration that postdated the early national period.

The tradition of writing inaugurated in the 1830s and 1840s long obscured perception of previous American literature. For Emerson and the handful of his contemporaries whose works established the national canon, imaginative art was differentiated from religious, moral, and civic forms of discourse. These authors ceased to construe literature's role as instructional, as teaching readers virtue or equipping them to be better citizens. One need only think of Nathaniel Hawthorne's ambiguous "morals" to *The Scarlet Letter*

(1850) and *The House of the Seven Gables* (1851) to recognize how attenuated the idea of literary usefulness had become by the mid-nineteenth century. A heightened emphasis on private as opposed to public and collective goals accompanied this shedding of pedagogical requirement. The canonical artist strove for an original voice that communicated the author's unique personality, and this art thematized the quest for self-fulfillment. The Romantic narrative typically relates a saga of interiority in which the unfolding of the protagonist's inner being occupies center stage.

Corresponding to the uniqueness or autonomy of the artwork was a conception of the literary career as a discrete vocation. The canonical writer aspired to be a professional, someone who entered into competition with other authors for fame and money. Although artists were obliged to supplement their royalties with lecture tours or by toiling in customhouses, they thought of themselves above all as writers, as people who subsisted by the pen. Composing was not confined to moments stolen from duties as ministers, physicians, or judges; it was a full-time activity determining the very shape of working lives. Finally, the fictions, poems, and essays written and published in the antebellum era had the status of commodities. Not only were literary wares regularly put into the market to be sold for money, but the writers regarded their creations as "private" property from which they expected or at least hoped to derive a profit.

The distinctive features of Romantic art were either missing or existed only in embryo in the literature of the formative period. Most literary histories still try to recuperate the earlier writing by invoking continuities to the canon: they validate Charles Brockden Brown as a forerunner of Herman Melville and praise Joel Barlow because he wrote an epic about the United States that somehow looks ahead to Hart Crane's *The Bridge* (1930). The strategy is misconceived because it places postrevolutionary literature in the context of the history of autonomous art. A better comparison, to which we will return, would be to the domestic novelists of the 1850s, a group who shared the earlier writers' resistance to categorical differentiation; it is no wonder that these two forgotten phases of American culture have been rediscovered at the same time. In exploring postrevolutionary literature, we should take our cue from the authors themselves, for whom the belletristic was always secondary to social ends. Strictly aesthetic terms give limited access to an array of works dedicated to utility; categories drawn from outside literature have greater explanatory power. The insistent presence of "nonliterary" elements in the writings of the new Republic directs attention to the eighteenth-century matrix and to a constellation of attitudes that marked not just poetry and fiction but society and politics as well.

Early American literature was the product of a historical formation dominated by republicanism, communalism, and a preindustrial agrarian economy. Republicanism, the governing ideology of the revolutionary era, envisioned one's highest calling as active participation in the civic realm. Republicans understood virtue as the subordination of private interest to the good of the commonwealth. Benjamin Rush, a signer of the Declaration of Independence, declared that every young man in a republic must "be taught that he does not belong to himself, but that he is public property." The citizen's talents, time, "nay more, life, belong to his country." Republicans idealized economic independence but disapproved of the unfettered pursuit of gain. Many distrusted commerce because of its tendency to absorb one's energies in money-making and because of its historic associations with luxury and selfishness. Republicanism's traditional side was palpable in its deferential notion of authority. Involvement in the polity was usually restricted to white males with property, and only "the better sort," the well-off and educated minority, was presumed fit to rule. Liberalism, strongly on the rise after independence, was challenging republican assumptions and chipping away at the public–private hierarchy. But eighteenth-century Americans continued to uphold the credo of civic humanism, the belief that individuals owed their primary obligation to the collectivity.

Prevailing economic conditions reinforced these ideological biases. The postrevolutionary United States was an agrarian society with production centered in the home. The great majority of persons lived on farms and supported themselves by their own labor. They enjoyed a measure of self-sufficiency in food and in clothing. Even isolated communities relied on some outside trade, but the primitive condition of transportation tended to confine commercial dealings to within local regions and to inhibit the development of extended market networks. In rural areas, exchange retained an orientation toward use: farmers swapped produce and services and often carried on transactions without the mediation of cash. Demands for improved roads and more available currency multiplied as early as the 1780s, and growing numbers of people engaged in entrepreneurial ventures as the country entered the nineteenth century. Still, customary arrangements and imperatives remained paramount: local autonomy, allegiance to the family unit of production rather than to individual initiative, and social valuation of economic activity defined the day-to-day world of most Americans.

The legal system buttressed the communal strain in the new nation's polity and economic life. Historians of American law have shown how traditional suppositions colored understanding of property rights and imposed curbs on the freedom of owners to buy, to sell, and to develop. Custom combined with legal decisions to restrain acquisitive practices, such as usury, which were perceived as affronting the public welfare. Common-law doctrines strengthened the republican view of land as the foundation of civic independence. The principal species of property in an overwhelmingly agricultural republic, land was a possession to be worked and cherished rather than a speculative asset. Not until the nineteenth century did legal decisions dismantle customary restraints and help to transform property into an instrument geared to profit, with private rights of development superseding community standards.

The letters of the early Republic should be described as republican and communal as much as pre-Romantic. In the half century after independence, American culture reenacted on a miniaturized scale the transition in Western civilization from the epic to the novel – from a literature that was public, functional, and possessed by all to one that was subjective, individualistic, and commodified. Consider the devotion to factuality that so pervaded eighteenth-century literature. In one respect, of course, fidelity to "what happened" signaled a turn toward empiricism. Literary historicity expressed the modernizing impulse of the Enlightenment, the age of science, print, and revolution. Yet paradoxically the same aspiration to truthfulness articulated a quarrel with the modern. Historicity registered resistance to individualism and to the privatizing of narrative, and it imparted to American letters, the novel included, some of the epic's communality. The point can be grasped by glancing at two of the era's most important fictions, William Hill Brown's *The Power of Sympathy,* published in 1789 and usually designated the first American novel, and Hannah Foster's *The Coquette,* which appeared in 1797.

Both books, in the manner typical of the early novel, present themselves as founded on actual events. Both play down the role of the imagination in their making; both insist upon their practical value as moral instruction and warn against the dangers of reading novels. Paralleling its main seduction plot, Brown's tale contains several interpolated narratives, at least two of which have been shown to be closely patterned on contemporaneous incidents. One, the story of Ophelia and Mr. Martin, which is related in letters 21 through 23, was inspired by the tragic love affair of Perez Morton, a well-connected Bostonian, and his sister-in-law, Frances Apthorp, who committed suicide; the episode was public knowledge at the time Brown wrote his novel. A second nested narrative on the evils of seduction appears as a long footnote to letter 11 and concerns Elizabeth Whitman, a Connecticut woman who is identified by name and whose death had been reported only six months earlier in newspaper obituary notices. This episode also provided the basis for Foster's *The Coquette,* where the historical Elizabeth Whitman resurfaces as the barely disguised Eliza Wharton.

Neither Brown nor Foster regarded narrative as a personal possession, and neither made any claims for the distinctive individuality of the creative process. Narratives were common property, or "public knowledge," and even the appearance of a story in someone else's novel did not preclude its being recycled in a later work of fiction. On the contrary, the familiarity of a tale seems to have been in its favor, just as lack of recognition could be a strike against it; hence a reviewer of *The Power of Sympathy* objected to its putative factuality on the grounds that the main plot was not known to him personally as a resident of Boston. Foster modeled her characters after recognizable persons: the Reverend Mr. Boyer, Eliza's respectable suitor, was widely known to have been based on a prominent pastor of Portsmouth, New Hampshire, and the original for Major Sanford, the man responsible for Eliza's undoing, was Pierrepont Edwards, youngest son of the Great Awakener.

An enumeration of the reasons for the native novel's deference to "truth" would have to include the Puritan-Protestant dislike of fanciful embellishment, the suspicion of fictionality Americans acquired from their reading of Scottish Common Sense philosophy, and the luster of history writing among a people who learned much of their politics from Whiggish chronicles of ancient Greece and Rome. But the novel's documentary emphasis proclaimed a customary spirit as well as a commitment to the rational. The perception of narrative as common inheritance, as what everyone knew, firmly situated American novels in the social and political context of an agrarian republic still shaped largely by communitarian and civic humanist priorities. Fiction was not yet a display of subjectivity, not yet the private imagining of a Romantic creator. It was still entrenched in public lore and the life history of actual persons and had not achieved the status of a separate, autonomous sphere of art.

The fact-based, corporate view of narrative, often struggling to contain more inventive impulses, appeared everywhere in the literature of the young nation. In poetry, epiclike recitations of patriotic accomplishments abounded. Joseph Brown Ladd's "The Prospect of America," printed in his *Poems of Arouet* (1786), celebrates military exploits from the war with Britain and memorializes heroic officers by name. Generals Greene, Putnam, Gates, Wayne, Lincoln, Warren, Mercer, Montgomery, and Washington (the "Second Fabius" to whom Ladd inscribed the poem) parade before the reader. "Shall not the Muse record each patriot name," asked another would-be Homer, "On the rich tablet of harmonic sound?" Public events and figures provided constant inspiration for the drama, from Mercy Otis Warren's satirical farce *The Adulateur* (1773), which deals with the Boston Massacre; through William Dunlap's historical tragedy *André* (1798), in which Washington appears as a character along with the British spy he ordered hanged; to a half dozen plays about American troubles with the Barbary pirates, among them Susanna Rowson's *Slaves in Algiers* (1794) and Mordecai M. Noah's *The Siege of Tripoli* (1820).

Respect for facts in belles lettres stemmed in part from the resilience of oral discourse in the United States. The Republic was not yet the definitively print society it became in the nineteenth century. Print is usually thought of as a modernizing technology and the destroyer of oral culture, but the two media were not always distinct at this time, and factuality was an area where their proclivities initially overlapped. Print was clearly more congenial to factual retention, but in the long run, documentary superiority authorized greater imaginativeness in the arts, by relieving fictional genres from the obligation to preserve. Oral poems and narratives, at first probably reinforced in their tendencies by the spread of print, clung to facts as a way of handing down tradition and perpetuating collective memory of past events. A poem predating the revolutionary era, Lucy Terry's "Bars Fight" (1746), exemplifies oral practices. Terry's ballad endured verbally for more than a century before being printed in 1855. The opening lines meticulously record historical dates and persons:

> August, 'twas the twenty-fifth,
> Seventeen hundred forty-six;
> The Indians did in ambush lay,
> Some very valiant men to slay,
> The Names of whom I'll not leave out.
> Samuel Allen like a hero fout.

Besides esteem for facts, oral qualities that blended with eighteenth-century print culture included a commitment to usefulness. Preaching, a staple of Puritan-Protestant belief, coupled with the importance of oratory in a republican polity, accustomed Americans to think of linguistic performances as collective experiences imparting instruction. Such expectations did not vanish overnight but seeped into printed discourse; they fortified the idea that literature was a public art and that, like the epic, it belonged to and gave voice to the community. The tenacity of oral remnants discouraged originality and private insight. Oral forms depended on repetition and formulas, so that they could be memorized by speakers and easily grasped by audiences; startling with the unexpected thwarted the works' didactic and informational aims. The popularity of proverbs among all ranks in the eighteenth century reflected the hold of oral habits on the public's imagination. Anonymous and impersonal, proverbs conveyed collective wisdom and defied notions of copyright and individual inspiration.

Early American copyright law did not greatly expedite the movement toward viewing letters as private inspiration and property. Of course, the security of copyright is an essential condition for the encouragement of authorship; without it, there could be no professional class of writers. But the Copyright Act passed by Congress in 1790 afforded protection to American authors only, with consequences detrimental to the emergence of a native literature. English editions could be reissued (or rather pirated) in the United States without printers having to reimburse the writers or original publishers. The fact that native books invariably cost more made them less attractive to booksellers and readers and greatly reduced the chances of selling enough copies to compensate authors for their trouble. The first copyright statute in the Republic, adopted by Connecticut immediately after the Revolution, made clear that ownership of intellectual property retained many of the restrictions associated with the common law. The preamble invoked "the Principles of natural Equity and Justice" to defend the right of an author to receive "the Profits that may arise from the Sale of his Works." The lawmakers then proceeded to invoke the same principles to forbid either engrossing or price gouging, acquisitive practices frowned upon by the moral economy of the seventeenth and eighteenth centuries. Exclusive copyright was rescinded "whenever any such Author or Proprietor of such Book . . . shall neglect to furnish the Public with sufficient copies thereof, or shall sell the same at a Price unreasonable, and beyond what may be adjudged a sufficient Compensation for his Labour, Time, Expence, and Risque of Sale." Social good took precedence over the artist's right to unlimited returns.

The intimidating proximity of English literature bolstered the nonindividualist emphases of early culture. About three-quarters of the books published in the United States before 1820 were of English origin. Combined with the absence of an international copyright law, the availability of so many renowned authors in a common tongue created an irresistible temptation to adapt and to imitate and dampened the ambition to cultivate an original voice. James Kirke Paulding, only half tongue-in-cheek, complained that in some genres foreign competition stifled native endeavor: "Were it not for Shakespeare, Milton, Newton, Locke, Bacon, Professor Porson, and a few more illustrious English dramatic writers, the theatres in this country could not exist. Shakespeare's Tom and Jerry is played over and over again, night after night; and Bacon's Abridgement as often, if not oftener." Even books that warned against mindlessly absorbing English models, like Tabitha Tenney's send-up of romantic fictions, *Female Quixotism* (1801), borrowed heavily from foreign precursors – in Tenney's case, a popular satire by the British novelist Charlotte Lenox entitled *The Female Quixote* (1752). Behind both works, of course, stood still another foreign model, the original novel by Cervantes, which also furnished the inspiration for Hugh Henry Brackenridge's *Modern Chivalry* (1792–1815).

Calls for a distinctively American literature, commencing with the outbreak of hostilities in 1775, dramatically increased in frequency and volume
after the signing of the Treaty of Paris. "America," said Noah Webster in
1785, "must be as independent in *literature* as she is in *politics*, as famous for
arts as for *arms*." The poet Philip Freneau echoed the sentiments of many
when he urged an import tax on the works of foreign writers to teach his
compatriots that "native manufactures" deserved protection in letters as well
as in coaches and firearms. Cultural nationalism impeded appreciation of the
aesthetic as a value in its own right. Royall Tyler's advertisement for the first
edition of *The Contrast* (1790) invokes just about everything except artistic
worth in soliciting public support for his creation:

[I]t may be proper to observe that this Comedy has many claims to the public
indulgence independent of its intrinsic merits: It is the first essay of American genius
in a difficult species of composition; it was written by one who never critically
studied the rules of the drama and, indeed, had seen but few of the exhibitions of the
stage; it was undertaken and finished in the course of three weeks; and the profits of
one night's performance were appropriated to the benefit of the sufferers by the fire at
Boston.

No present-day dramatist would appeal for applause on the grounds that he
or she was a patriot, a novice, and a friend of the unfortunate.

Everyone agreed that works of literature had the duty to serve society. The
purpose of art was not to express private feelings but to advance the common
welfare; a partiality toward use predominated in culture as elsewhere. Americans shared the Aristotelian understanding of literature as giving pleasure
and instruction, but they tended to dwell on the practical side; entertainment was acceptable above all because it rendered the artwork efficacious as
teaching. Thomas Jefferson, in a famous letter to Robert Skipwith (1771),
recommended "the entertainments of fiction" for their utility in promoting
virtuous behavior through imitation. "When any signal act of charity or
gratitude," Jefferson wrote, "is presented either to our sight or imagination,
we are deeply impressed with its beauty and feel a strong desire in ourselves
of doing charitable and grateful acts also." Timothy Dwight argued a similar
case for verse in the introduction to *Greenfield Hill* (1794), his tribute to
Connecticut pastoralism. Dwight explained that by setting forth moral sentiments in a forceful and moving light, "Poetry appears to be as advantageous
an instrument of making useful impressions as can easily be conceived. It will
be read by many persons who would scarcely look at a logical discussion," and
it will affect most readers more deeply and stay with them longer than
philosophy.

A man who spent his life instructing others, as a minister and then as the
president of Yale, Dwight typified the age's didacticism. Comparable claims

for the social and moral benefits of letters can be found in countless plays, novels, magazines, and poems. According to the playwright William Dunlap, *André* was written "to impress, through the medium of a pleasing stage exhibition, the sublime lessons of Truth and Justice upon the minds of his countrymen." The most lurid fictions announced a devout wish to encourage virtue and to exhibit "the dangerous consequences of seduction," as *The Power of Sympathy* has it; earnest dedications to the impressionable "Young Ladies of Columbia" proliferated. The novels may have imparted a double message in the telling, but only modern readers would dismiss their authors' moral protests as insincere. Many of the era's best fictions were in fact guided by a commitment to bettering the public. Brackenridge's *Modern Chivalry,* presenting itself as a primer in republican principles, illustrates "the evil of men seeking office for which they are not qualified"; Royall Tyler's *The Algerine Captive* (1797) exposes the injustices of slavery; and Tenney's *Female Quixotism* advocates realism about sexual relations. As such examples underscore, belles lettres were not sharply differentiated from overtly didactic forms like the oration and the sermon. Dwight, Brackenridge, and other writers of the time found it natural to alternate educational and religious works with poetry and fiction because the lines between practical and imaginative discourses were blurred.

American writers before 1820 reached small audiences; arguably, they exercised little influence on the thinking of their countrymen. Yet artistic forms as distinguished from more expository modes clearly did assist in forming patriotic consciousness. The founding of the American polity and the creation of the native novel occurred at virtually the same moment; the Constitutional Convention gathered in 1787, and two years later the pioneering Massachusetts printer Isaiah Thomas brought out *The Power of Sympathy.* The near simultaneity of the two events points to the historical reality that nationhood and nationalism are themselves cultural artifacts forged toward the end of the eighteenth century. The nation is an act of political imagining, an artificially constructed community; in contrast to a local unit like the village, it embraces people who are widely separated geographically. Works of fiction facilitate the abstract conceptualization necessary to nationalism by dramatizing a bounded human community in which persons who may be unknown to each other perform actions at the same time and impinge on each other's lives. Genres more publicly performed and consumed than the novel exercise more immediate unifying power. Perhaps no better emblem of nationhood exists than a group of otherwise unrelated people joining together in patriotic song. Three enduring national airs either were composed or gained currency during the formative years: the anonymous "Yankee Doodle," Joseph Hopkinson's "Hail Columbia" (1798), and Francis Scott Key's

"Defense of Fort M'Henry" (1814), known to posterity as "The Star-Spangled Banner."

Togetherness or community was a keynote of literary life, at least for men. Eighteenth-century culture had a face-to-face quality, as persons of learning regularly gathered together to discuss projects and pool mental resources. Many authors belonged to social clubs – arguably the principal literary institution of the century – and produced their works in tandem with others. The country's most gifted novelist, Charles Brockden Brown; its leading dramatist and theater manager, William Dunlap; the critic Samuel Miller; and Elihu Hubbard Smith, a physician who assembled the first anthology of American verse, were all members of the Friendly Club. Three former students at Yale, John Trumbull, Joel Barlow, and David Humphreys, instituted a poetry group in Hartford and won fame collectively as the Connecticut Wits. Male authors born in the eighteenth century but active in the nineteenth continued the tradition: as late as the 1820s James Fenimore Cooper and William Cullen Bryant helped to found a New York literary club, the Bread and Cheese.

In no other period of our history has literature been so often a matter of collaboration rather than individual authorship. The series of papers called *The Federalist* (1787–8), written by Alexander Hamilton, James Madison, and John Jay and probably the most important work of political theory to issue from the United States, is but the most conspicuous instance. Brackenridge and Freneau, while classmates at Princeton, together wrote "The Rising Glory of America," a commencement poem hailing the New World's imperial promise. Royall Tyler and the editor Joseph Dennie collaborated on an essay serial, "From the Shop of Colon and Spondee" (1794–1811), and the hodgepodge of parodies, reviews, and social criticism known as *Salmagundi* (1807–8) was a cocreation of Washington Irving, his brother William, and James Kirke Paulding.

Women, consigned to a secondary position in the republic of letters, were denied access to the cultural gatherings frequented by their male contemporaries. But settings congenial to female intellect flourished in the postwar decades, above all the academies organized to improve education for women. Susanna Rowson long taught in one, and Hannah Foster employed the female academy as an emblem of mutual support and mental growth in *The Boarding School; or, Lessons of a Preceptress to her Pupils* (1798). Other women, making the most of their confinement in the family, discovered in consanguinity a source of cooperative endeavor. Some of the earliest of the familial productions that became a staple of later women's literature, testaments to the strength of kinship ties as well as to the minimizing of individualism, date from the early Republic. Margaretta V. Faugeres remembered her mother in

1793 by publishing *The Posthumous Works of Ann Eliza Bleecker, in Prose and Verse;* the second half of the volume consists of *A Collection of Essays, Prose and Poetical* written by Faugeres herself.

Republican culture discouraged specialization, and few Americans looked upon literature as a full-time occupation. Novelists and dramatists were also – or, to speak more accurately, they were primarily – housewives, state supreme court justices, or politicians. The category of author merged into other callings, and even the distinction between writer and reader was not firmly maintained. Solicitations urging readers to turn writers dotted the pages of early magazines. Editors pleaded for contributions and warned that in a country lacking professional authors, their publications could not survive without subscribers taking to their pens.

Not only were writers imperfectly differentiated from readers; authors seldom specialized in a particular branch of writing. Instead, they worked in a variety of forms, and they felt little attraction for the idea of being exclusively a poet or a novelist. One can, of course, point to examples of later artists who tried their hands at other genres; Herman Melville and Emerson composed verse, and in our own time, Robert Penn Warren has made distinguished contributions to fiction, poetry, and criticism. But diversity, or what might now be considered dilettantism, was more widely practiced by the early writers, who still subscribed to the ideal of the versatile man or woman of letters. Most shunned the familiar authorial pattern of starting with one form and then abandoning it upon the discovery of one's true métier; they were far more apt to move in and out of forms throughout their writing lives. Brackenridge, best known today for the multivolume *Modern Chivalry,* also wrote and published poetry in the 1770s and then again in 1811, when he composed an octosyllabic *Epistle to Walter Scott.* A playwright during the Revolution, he published a history of the Whisky Rebellion in 1794, and he capped his career as a justice of the Pennsylvania supreme court with the *Law Miscellanies* of 1814. Rowson is remembered as the author of the period's best-selling novel, *Charlotte Temple, A Tale of Truth* (1791; 1794). Her other works include a half-dozen plays, two volumes of poetry, nine additional novels, a speller, an edition of biblical dialogues, and books on geography and history. Any of these authors would have taken satisfaction, not offense, at Melville's intended slur against Benjamin Franklin as a "Jack of all trades, master of each and mastered by none."

The high incidence of anonymously published books in the new Republic draws attention to another aspect of American letters indicating discomfort with individualistic values: the historical circumstance that many writers literally "disowned" their works by not affixing their names to them or by not registering them as their property. Although desires for fame and money obviously existed in the eighteenth century, they often yielded to other considerations, such as patriotism, religion, or squeamishness about public disclosure. Books bearing neither an author's name nor a copyright notice were plentiful in all genres and bespeak a willingness to place individual interests second to collective goals. The customary disposition of copyright further clouded the question of ownership. Authors routinely sold or assigned their copyrights, and thus someone other than the writer would be registered as the "proprietor" of a given work. The copyright for Tyler's *The Contrast*, the first successful play in the nation, was held by Thomas Wignell, an actor who had played the role of the Yankee Jonathan; Tyler himself was identified on the dedication page solely as an "American." Books antedating the national copyright act in effect belonged to the community. In 1775, at the urging of "some friends in Congress," John Trumbull wrote and published anonymously his mock-epic *M'Fingal*, which savages the Tories; a revised and expanded edition followed in 1782. As Trumbull noted in his later "Memoir," the poem quickly acquired the status of public property:

As no author, at that period, was entitled by law to the copyright of his production, the work soon became the prey of every bookseller and printer, who chose to appropriate it to his own benefit. Among more than thirty different impressions, one only, at any subsequent time, was published with the permission, or even the knowledge of the writer; and the poem remained the property of newsmongers, hawkers, pedlars, and petty chapmen.

Disowning authorship can be seen as a republican gesture. It comported with both the self-denying and the elitist strains in civic humanist ideology. In the eighteenth and well into the first decades of the nineteenth century, it was considered beneath the dignity of a gentleman or gentlewoman to publish belles lettres under his or her own name. Ezra Stiles, later president of Yale, was uttering a commonplace when he remarked in 1775, "The lower branches of polite Literature I have an indifferent Opinion of; such as *Poetry,* the dramatic *Writings,* and the profusion of *modern Novels.*" The novel in particular had a disreputable air: its popular appeal and relative newness made it a parvenu among the arts, and respectable people did not sully themselves by identifying with it, any more than they would enter trade.

This, at least, was the patrician view of the matter, which prevailed in America even more than in England (where it was already becoming obsolete). The genteel outlook discouraged writers from regarding their publications as potentially lucrative property or indeed as property at all. Native authors commonly produced one or perhaps two books and saw themselves as amateurs who were not dependent on their pens for money. Sarah Wood voiced the preprofessional attitude of the American writer, male and female alike, when she reminded readers of the difference

between the ordinary day-labor of the common English novelist, who works for a living similar to a Mechanic, and has no other end in view than to bring forth a fashionable piece of Goods, that will suit the taste of the moment, and remunerate himself, and the Lady of refined sentiments and correct taste, who writes for the amusement of herself, her Friends, and the Public.

Publication itself was suspect in the eyes of some as an indulgence in unseemly egotism; Margaretta Faugeres observed of her mother, "[N]one but the most intimate acquaintance were ever indulged with a view of any of her performances, and *then* they were no sooner perused than she destroyed them." Many readers shared in the aristocratic idea of letters as superior to vulgar gain; subscription lists from the time highlight the patrician status of the consumers of culture. *The Spirit of the Farmer's Museum and Lay Preacher's Gazette* (1801), a collection of pieces by Joseph Dennie, prefaces its several pages of subscribers with an apologetic note: "The retention of each gentleman's title we have purposely omitted; as it would be impossible to give them all with any degree of correctness."

To be sure, gentility was not the only conception of literature in the culture, and the growing popularity of novels was undermining the social exclusivity of art. Another familiar image was the writer—husbandman, as in John Dickinson's *Letters from a Farmer in Pennsylvania* (1768) or J. Hector St. John de Crèvecoeur's *Letters from an American Farmer* (1782). But writing could be only an avocation for the busy farmer, and most novelists *had* to treat literature as a pastime because no one before Washington Irving could make it pay. The selfless notion of authorship was strengthened by the simple reality that only the rare American book returned a profit. The few writers who wanted to be professionals earning a livelihood from art – Charles Brockden Brown, Rowson, Dunlap – ended up pursuing other careers. Brown became an editor and political polemicist, Rowson spent the last half of her life as the headmistress of a young ladies' academy, and Dunlap, who went bankrupt in the theater, staved off the almshouse by painting miniatures and compiling biographies and histories.

Literary scholars sometimes single out Brown as the closest to a genuine professional that the age produced. Yet Brown behaved remarkably like his contemporaries at the outset as well as at the conclusion of his experiment in literary independence; he never quite freed himself from eighteenth-century ideas about authorial self-suppression. He signed over his first published volume, the feminist dialogue *Alcuin* (1798), to his friend Elihu Hubbard Smith, who arranged to have the book issued by subscription and was named in the copyright notice "as proprietor." Nor did Brown own his first novel, *Wieland* (1798); it belonged to the New York bookseller Hocquet Caritat, who purchased the copyright for fifty dollars. These gestures of patrician aloofness intensified as Brown experienced repeated disappointments in his efforts to support himself as a fiction writer. In 1803, having turned to periodical and pamphlet writing, he publicly repudiated the novels for which he is remembered today:

I am far from wishing . . . that my readers should judge of my exertions by my former ones. I have written much, but take much blame to myself for something [*sic*] which I have written, and take no praise for anything. I should enjoy a larger share of my own respect at the present moment, if nothing had ever flowed from my pen, the production of which could be traced to me.

In actuality, readers would have had to learn from sources other than the books themselves that Brown wrote such fictions as *Ormond* (1799) and *Edgar Huntly* (1799); the title pages do not mention him by name.

Brown's disavowals underline the gulf between the Romantic–modernist and the postrevolutionary understandings of what an "author" is and what constitutes a "text." Instead of conceiving of the author as an individual, we need to think of several people working together to produce a play, an essay, or a poem. These persons almost certainly followed nonliterary occupations or spent their time caring for families. Their names were unknown, and they had no financial stake in what they wrote. The text was a collaborative effort, belonging to an acquaintance of the authors or to the society at large, relating what everyone already knew, and doubling as a political oration, a sermon, or a guide to conduct. Neither authors nor texts were the autonomous entities that Romantic–modernist apologetics portrays them as being.

The letters of the early Republic shared features with contemporaneous African-American culture. The relatively high representation during the formative era of black writers in "imaginative" genres, especially poetry, may be attributable to the greater confluence of mainstream and minority expectations of the aesthetic. Belles lettres did not break so sharply with the qualities associated with African-American art: factuality in narrative, regard for the collectivity, and formulaic and iterative patterns evocative of oral discourse. Lucy Terry, author of the ballad "Bars Fight," was an African American, as were Jupiter Hammon and the young slave girl Phillis Wheatley, whose single book of verse, published in 1773, established her as the major African-American poet before the twentieth century. Augustan verse probably appeared less alien to Wheatley than later poetry would have. The age's preference for iambic pentameter and heroic couplets may even have facilitated her gift, for the regularity of rhymes and accents – the familiar "sing-song" of eighteenth-century poetry – was compatible with the predictability and repetitions of oral forms.

Such comparisons have to be drawn with caution; they can give a misleading impression of mainstream literature's traditionalism. The complex example of Brown, simultaneously trying to live as a professional artist and denying his art, is a reminder that postrevolutionary culture was far from being a republican monolith. Changing, and sometimes clashing, assumptions about individualism, the public and private realms, and civic responsibility characterized not only literature and the writer but the entire late-eighteenth-century phase of American history. Premodern perspectives still governed, but they were in the process of dissolution, and different authors and genres shared them to different degrees. Nor did literature evolve in lockstep with society and politics; poetry and, say, the American party system experienced unequal rates of modernization. In some ways, culture lagged behind or resisted social trends; in others, it aided in winning acceptance for innovation. Each of the various literary forms stood in a different relation to the republican and communal emphases of the period. A taxonomy of early national genres might follow these lines: the drama was the least private of the arts, the most wedded to the civic domain, whereas the more "advanced" novel edged toward abandoning the dominant but declining ethos for the ascendant values of liberalism and the marketplace. Poetry faced in both directions: public like the drama in its patriotic aspect, it also could be – as in Freneau's poems of fancy – even more inward than the novel.

In the nineteenth century, the problematics of republican culture yielded to an aesthetic paradigm that was congruent with liberal ideology and economic individualism. In the absence of a genuine aristocracy such as existed in England, a highly personalized literature, and the authorial self-definition to sustain it, did not materialize here until a new historical configuration was in place. An individualized regimen in social and economic relations was the necessary complement to the rise of Romantic art in the United States. Nor was this simply a matter of a rationalized market system facilitating the manufacturing, distribution, and sale of books. The literature of Emerson, Hawthorne, and Melville, later judged canonical, required a firmer view of the artwork as the unique production of an individual. To thrive in a postpatronage era, literary art had to belong to its creator in all the senses of the word. It had to be seen as a work of personal inspiration and creation and also as the author's property, a potentially valuable commodity to be disposed of (or not) in the marketplace. What had to happen, in other words, was that the communal and self-negating accents of eighteenth-century culture had to be inflected in the direction of an individualist aesthetics – an aesthetics predicated on the special sensibility of the artist and on the exchange value of the literary artifact.

The shift can be dated with some confidence in the decade after the War of 1812, when the fiction of Irving and Cooper and the poetry of Bryant finally secured international stature for American letters. The same years witnessed the breakdown of the premodern formation of the early Republic and the steady emergence of democratic capitalism. The republican ethos had been defined by the household economy, with its stress on production for use, organic attachments to family and community, and submission of private interest to the general good. By 1820, this amalgam of elements was disintegrating under the pressures of social and ideological change.

The War of 1812 marked the turning point. The conflict, which Cooper saw as emancipating America from "the thraldom of mental bondage" to England, consolidated national unity and weaned Americans from dependence on foreign goods. By boosting native manufactures and internal improvements, the war laid the foundation for the integrated home market of the Jacksonian period. An individualist ethos both stimulated and drew strength from economic growth. Individualism ratified entrepreneurial initiative and promoted a liberal credo favoring social mobility, self-reliance, and egalitarianism. New loyalties pushed aside republican notions of corporate obligation. The pursuit of private gain, once judged fatal to collective well-being, was now held to advance it, and virtue was redefined as a noncivic activity, comprised in the narrowly personal requirements of chastity, industry, and thrift. For many, these developments were profoundly liberating. The changes created opportunities for enterprising persons and, by subverting deference and hierarchy, hastened the democratization of American life. But residual attitudes did not simply die out in 1820. Republican ideas of virtue and community survived among a significant minority of Americans; still more people felt disquiet over the nation's burgeoning materialism. Moreover, new forms of opposition sprang up in the nineteenth century to contest the market system's dominance.

The native literature that flourished along with liberal individualism departed from the past but also preserved elements from the earlier cultural universe. The transformation should not be exaggerated: older values and patterns of behavior persisted in the arts just as they did in society. Professionalization, for instance, remained more a goal than an achieved reality, and though books became money-making commodities, none of the major Romantics consistently managed to sell enough copies to be self-supporting. Aristocratic pretensions lingered, as in Hawthorne's famous reserve and his practice of publishing his short stories anonymously – a practice he relinquished when he began to write in earnest for a livelihood. And Hawthorne was one of several writers who continued to think of narrative, at least on occasion, as a common inheritance. Not only did he pass on the germ of

Evangeline (1847) to the poet Henry Wadsworth Longfellow, he was the author of two volumes of "twice-told tales," collections of New England legends refashioned for modern readers.

Among Hawthorne's canonical contemporaries, the makers of the American Renaissance, such continuities were outweighed by a new stress on the singularity of the artist and the autonomy of the artwork; but the individualist paradigm was far from monopolizing the literary even in the antebellum period. The nineteenth-century female domestic novelists unfailingly outsold the Romantics and were successful "businesswomen of letters," yet they preserved many of the attitudes about literature held by their predecessors of both genders from the early Republic. Even when they wrote expressly in order to earn money, figures like Harriet Beecher Stowe, Catharine Maria Sedgwick, and Susan Warner continued to think of literature in social and pedagogic terms. All felt an obligation to the community – a feeling nurtured by the antebellum perception of women as moral guardians – and all justified their authorship on the grounds of service to others. Desirous of bettering their readers, they inscribed narratives about the evils of slavery, the power of moral goodness, and the importance of religious faith. The domestic novelists deprecated the uniqueness of the artist. Stowe claimed that God wrote *Uncle Tom's Cabin* (1852), and Warner collaborated with her sister on numerous books. Most women published anonymously or pseudonymously, shrank from celebrity, and portrayed their literary careers as secondary to other pursuits, notably their responsibilities as wives and mothers.

In all these respects, literary domesticity was residual, an echo of the republican past; yet in other ways, imaginative writing gave women a voice denied them in public forums and opened the possibility of self-fulfillment. This last observation also applies to women fiction writers of the eighteenth century, and we will examine the ambiguities of their situation in our chapter on the novel. But the persistence of a communal perspective from the early Republic through the 1850s dramatizes how exclusionary has been the Romantic–modernist apotheosis. The history of the United States is rich in cultural forms and traditions, only a fraction of which have endorsed the apartness of art. Enshrined in university curricula and naturalized as the sole kind of worthwhile writing, that fraction until recently seemed to define the meaning of literature itself; everything else was dismissed as sub- or extraliterary. The poetry and prose of the early Republic challenge us to rethink the uncritical elevation of the Romantic–modernist ideal. They assert that the distinction is not between literature and nonliterature, but between different types of art. And they insist that it is possible to read for and to appreciate a work's civic and didactic objectives – objectives that have to be seen as compatible with the highest standards of artistic excellence.

2

🍎

MAGAZINES, CRITICISM, AND ESSAYS

THE GENTEEL TRADITION in American letters was born in the early Republic. An active periodical culture came into being during this time, providing a forum for persons of learning to expound their thoughts on society and literature. With the pronouncements and actions of such critics, the overwhelming majority of whom were men, originates the split – or, more accurately, the obscuring of the connection – between money-making and the arts that has characterized elite literary judgment in this country well into the twentieth century. But the relation between high culture and the commercial spirit was not one just of opposition; it was also a relation of complicity. The very magazines that were airing patrician views accommodated the popular reading habits of the nascent liberal order and opened their pages to voices that disputed established hierarchies. No one more vociferously proclaimed literature's superiority to the vulgarities of American life than did the foppish editor and essayist Joseph Dennie. Yet this archconservative struggled to make authorship a vocation and helped prepare the way for Washington Irving, the nation's first financially successful writer.

Early periodicals in both England and America evolved out of newspapers and were often indistinguishable from them, a lineage that militated against the segregation of art from mundane affairs. American newspapers were an important outlet for cultural production; they welcomed poetry, literary essays, and vignettes, and their format frequently effaced the line between factual and nonfactual material. Leafing through the papers gives one a vivid sense of the interpenetration of early culture with everyday life. Thus the twice-weekly *Gazette of the United States* included in its edition for May 28, 1791, a poem, "Laura and Mary," about a coquette whose spurned lover drowns himself, an ode on reviewers, and a piece on English naval architecture, all jostling for space with dispatches from abroad, reports on commerce and politics, and lists of prices current for public securities. The juxtapositions can startle modern readers: southern newspapers regularly printed verse in columns adjacent to notices for runaway slaves and announcements of auctions of newly arrived Africans.

Some papers, more sensitive to generic differentiations, confined their cultural miscellany to the last page under headings such as "Seat of the Muses," "Poetry Corner," and "Repository of Genius." The *Farmer's Weekly Museum* of Walpole, New Hampshire, which Dennie edited during the 1790s, treated readers to a last page called "The Dessert." Besides printing poems and essays, including Dennie's celebrated "Lay Preacher" series, a subsection titled "Nuts" contained jests, curious anecdotes, and fables from Aesop. Like many other newspapers, the *Farmer's Weekly Museum* was really a hybrid; its literary content had so prominent a place that the publisher described it as "a Magazine in a minor form."

The term "magazine" refers to a repository or storehouse, and early American magazines were basically compilations drawn from native newspapers and European periodicals. In this respect, the magazines followed the lead of the London creators of the institution, such as Edward Cave, whose *Gentleman's Magazine,* launched in 1731, is believed to be the first monthly in the English-speaking world. The English pioneered other customs adopted here too, including the practice of not identifying contributors by name and the aura of gentlemanly exclusivity, a restrictiveness reinforced in Britain by the high government taxes that drove up the price of journals. The form already had a life of its own in the imperial metropole, and Americans, in developing an indigenous tradition, imitated as well as revised the foreign prototype.

British procedures frequently lent themselves to New World ideological uses. The habit of culling pieces from other sources harmonized with the ethos of republican communalism. Responsibility to the public took precedence over private advantage and individual inspiration. Because material was not copyrighted, editors saw no reason not to fill their pages with pirated selections. The Philadelphia publisher Mathew Carey was representative in viewing the convention as beneficial: he proudly identified his *American Museum, or Repository of Ancient and Modern Fugitive Pieces* (1787–92) as "a hand-maid to the newspapers" and defined its function as preserving valuable native writings that would otherwise be "thrown aside and forgotten." Carey also made available useful articles from English magazines, and, as a patriotic duty, he reprinted Thomas Paine's *Common Sense,* John Trumbull's *M'Fingal,* and other once-influential pamphlets from the revolutionary years.

The scrapbookish quality of magazines persisted into the nineteenth century, reinforced by and reinforcing the perception of literary works as belonging to all. Washington Irving briefly edited a monthly gathering of "Selections from Foreign Reviews and Magazines" entitled the *Analectic Magazine* (1813–21) and bearing the following inscription: "The wheat from these publications should, from time to time, be winnowed, and the chaff thrown away." Some journals compared their activity to gleaning, the customary right of the poor to gather the crop left behind after harvest. Judith Sargent Murray, writing under the pen name Constantia, produced one of the best-known essay serials of the postrevolutionary period in *The Gleaner,* originally printed in Isaiah Thomas's *Massachusetts Magazine* from 1792 to 1794 and then reissued as a book in 1798. No mere scissors-and-paste compendium, *The Gleaner* contained a novel, numerous articles, and several plays by Murray, but it also levied freely from other writers. By her choice of title, Murray explained, she sought to disarm accusations of plagiarism and to lay a modest claim to the overflowing granaries of the opulent. The gleaner's rights came before those of private property:

I shall ransack the fields, the meadows, and the groves; each secret haunt, however sequestered, with avidity I shall explore; deeming myself privileged to crop with impunity a hint from one, an idea from another, and to aim at improvement upon a sentence from a third. I shall give to my materials whatever texture my fancy directs; and, . . . feeling myself entitled to toleration as a Gleaner, in this expressive name I shall take shelter, standing entirely regardless of every charge relative to property, originality, and every thing of this nature, which may be preferred against me.

Original authorship, at first minimized or completely disregarded, as in Carey's *American Museum,* became more important over time but had an ambiguous status in the era's magazines. To label a piece "original" presumably meant that it had not been lifted from some other publication; in actuality, this assumption could not be taken for granted. Dennie, for example, republished an essay from the *Monthly Anthology and Boston Review* under the rubric "Original Criticism," and he justified copying pieces from British periodicals on the grounds that they were so recent as to be "in fact *original, to all intents and purposes, to a great majority of persons.*" Book reviews, even when composed expressly for the journal they appeared in, would be considered infringements of authorial property by today's standards. Most subordinated the reviewer's personal judgment to the conveying of information, and, owing to the absence of copyright restrictions, quoted immoderately from the work under review. A seven-page assessment of a newly published book might consist of as many as six pages of extracts; a typical review devoted at least half of its text to quotation.

The authors of such pieces were amateurs, for no one who wrote for the magazines made a living at it. Until 1819, payment, even to "original" contributors, was virtually unknown. Editors and publishers seldom fared any better; the incidence of business failures among the latter was appallingly high, and no literary miscellany before Dennie's *Port Folio* (1801–27) survived for as long as a decade. It has been estimated that the average lifespan for an eighteenth-century American magazine was barely fourteen months. Print, paper, and labor were all relatively costly, but by far the most daunting obstacle to financial solvency was the primitive condition of the Republic's transportation facilities. Poor roads made efficient distribution all but impossible, and the situation did not improve significantly until the completion of the Erie Canal in 1825.

Getting people to pay for their magazines was a widespread problem, further diminishing the rate of journal survival and adding to the perception that literary journalism was not a money-making pursuit. Magazines were expensive, and large numbers of readers appear to have defaulted on their subscriptions. Some journals had difficulty confronting the problem because of the code of the lettered gentleman. Carey stated in the *American Museum* that he was "almost ashamed to intimate" the subject of nonpayment, and he may have hoped that the policy of printing subscription lists would provide a discreet way of managing the matter. By publishing names, many with titles, he might embarrass delinquent readers into settling their accounts. A few publications ran dunning notices on their covers, and at least one, Isaiah Thomas's *Worcester Magazine* (1786–8), had so many delinquencies that it offered to accept produce in lieu of money. "Butter will be received for small sums," wrote Thomas, "if brought within a few days."

Genteel compunction discouraged magazine writers from making their authorship known. Articles and verses usually appeared unsigned or with the contributor's identity concealed behind a pseudonym or misleading initials, sometimes a single initial at that. Charles Brockden Brown's fastidiousness about "calling out [his] name in a crowd," as he put it in *The Literary Magazine and American Register* for 1803, was standard practice. The individual author faded from view under such circumstances, giving way, as in other works published by subscription, to the collectivity. The most conspicuous names in the *American Museum* were those of the subscribers; the second volume included ten pages of them, leading off with the Reverend Jeremy Belknap of Massachusetts and concluding with the "Honorable Thomas Jefferson, American minister to the Court of Versailles."

Another problem that troubled periodicals was the shortage of available contributors. Magazines were group productions, and most prospectuses incorporated pleas to literary friends to assist the editor by sending in their poetry and prose. Publications often advertised themselves as collective enterprises, announcing on their title pages that they were conducted by a "Society" or an "Association of Gentlemen." Indeed, no branch of early culture was more truly communal than the magazines. Few could have gotten under way without the support of the literary clubs that provided a nucleus of contributors. Brown's *Monthly Magazine and American Review* (1799–1800) could not have lasted for the short time it did without the Friendly Club, and the Tuesday Club of Philadelphia kept alive the *Port Folio*. But without the incentives of remuneration and fame, not even pooling resources could overcome the dearth of active writers. As Brown complained, "That set or class of persons, denominated authors, and which is so numerous in the European world, is, on this side of the ocean, so few as scarce to be discernible." Several numbers of Brown's *Literary Magazine* proved the justice of his lament; with one exception, he told a correspondent, he composed every article himself.

The contents of American magazines, reflecting the medium's newspaper origins, showed a diversity that could clash with the gentlemanly ethos. Many journals, including some of the most prestigious, ran short stories and published articles propounding unorthodox opinions. Because republics depended on an informed populace, efforts were made to enlarge the readership to incorporate "every class" (in the phrase of *The New-York Magazine; or, Literary Repository*). "Amelia; or The Faithless Briton – An American Tale" (1787), a narrative of seduction published in the *Columbian Magazine* of Philadelphia, was one of numerous sentimental fictions that appeared in periodicals and were aimed at a wide audience. The story, whose author is unknown, resembles Susanna Rowson's popular novel *Charlotte Temple* in portraying the despoiler of innocence as a British officer. Other stories appealed to native interest by taking economic opportunity as their subject, but the majority of the tales were pirated from English publications and betray their provenance: several, for example, deal with the evils of primogeniture. Magazines were eager to cultivate the "Columbian Fair." Articles celebrated female accomplishments and argued for the importance of knowledgeable and patriotic mothers, who served the Republic by raising public-spirited sons. The journals became vocal supporters of female education and occasionally (if rarely) printed pieces championing sexual equality.

On balance, the magazines exhibited a public and communal orientation that, like republican ideology itself, was far from egalitarian; it had a pronounced hierarchical component. Most journals were owned or edited by the "better sort" and saw their task as that of diffusing knowledge from the social and cultural epicenter to the margins. The abiding assumption was that the editors, or the "society of gentlemen" who provided literary counsel and support, would control the contents. Ordinary citizens were invited to listen and even to participate by sending in poems, essays, and letters to the editor, but there was no doubt about who exercised ultimate authority over speech.

The fate of the first postwar journal, William Billings's *Boston Magazine*, underscores this commitment to hierarchy. The magazine's remarkable career illustrates how the issue of class arose at the inception of national culture and was dealt with by a summary act of erasure. Billings, remembered today as a gifted composer, was a tanner and singing master who edited the maiden issue of the *Boston Magazine* in the fall of 1783. Eager for acceptance by the city's elite, he appealed for contributions from "gentlemen of learning and leisure," but his lack of deference in presuming to become an editor only aroused the ire of those who regarded letters as the monopoly of the pedigreed. The Reverend John Eliot, disparaging Billings as a "psalm singer," led a group of clergy and other leading citizens in seizing control of the periodical, whose contents, save for a gruesome short story, had been perfectly conventional. After securing Billings's ouster, the new editors announced a second issue promising to be "more respectable." They showed their contempt for their predecessor by repudiating the previous issue and recommending that it be expunged from memory: the refashioned magazine published under their guidance was to be "considered as the first number."

The republic of letters, at least in the city of Boston, was to be just that: a republic, not a democracy, overseen by the qualified few and thoroughly resistant to leveling innovations in politics and culture. The key figures here were the influential "Society of Gentlemen" who founded the Boston Athenaeum in 1807 and edited the *Monthly Anthology and Boston Review* from 1803 to 1811. Perhaps no group of Americans ever came closer to realizing the eighteenth-century ideal of the patrician amateur. Many were ministers, among them such distinguished individuals as Joseph Stevens Buckminster, pastor of the Brattle Street Church, William Emerson, Ralph Waldo's father, and John T. Kirkland, later president of Harvard. All held positions that freed them from the need to write for a livelihood. Their contributions, as one of them said, were "unpaid and unregulated," and they employed their pens for the sole purpose of enlightening the public. Lewis P. Simpson has fittingly described the *Anthology* men as a New England clerisy for whom literature and moral guidance were inseparable.

The members of the Boston "Society" embraced the genteel tradition by positing an irreconcilable antagonism between belles lettres on the one side and democracy and the marketplace on the other. The greatest impediments to an American culture, they agreed, were the national love of gain and the "hunting after popular favour" that spilled over from political life to contaminate literary aspiration. According to a common argument, the arts could not thrive in a country where the desire to *"get money"* overrode the humanistic values of love, friendship, charity, and the cultivation of one's intellect. Self-promotion ranked high on the *Monthly Anthology*'s list of evils; Noah Webster was ridiculed for deluging the presses with "puffs direct, puffs oblique, [and] puffs collateral." Numerous contributors attacked "a pernicious notion of equality" for crying down excellence and debasing learning to the most superficial level. The *Anthology* dismissed anyone ignorant or vain enough to suppose that American literature rivaled the immortal achievements of Britain. *The Gleaner* was but a pathetic imitation of the *Spectator,* and no reader could keep from dozing over Joel Barlow's *The Vision of Columbus.*

The *Anthology* men conceived of the critic's office as essentially political and social: like the vigilant Federalist statesman, the critic was to police the commonwealth of letters to keep out the unworthy. "It is with literature as [it is] with government," explained a contributor in 1807. Charlatans and demagogues intruded themselves into both arenas, and the critic owed it to the public to expose deceptions. More than one contributor likened reviewers to executioners meting out well-deserved punishment with "the thong of chastisement and the knout of criticism." Particularly withering barbs were reserved for those who came from modest circumstances or needed income from their writing. "Bloomfield [the English farm laborer and poet], Phillis Wheatly [sic], and many others in humble life have attracted some attention by their writings," an essayist noted, "not because they are excellent, but because they are extraordinary." After paraphrasing Dr. Johnson's quip about dogs walking on their hind legs – the wonder is not that it is done well, but that it is done at all – the essayist warned that "mendicant vagabonds" could expect no welcome in the precincts of culture.

A writer who could outdo the *Monthly Anthology* in diatribes against American barbarism was Fisher Ames, Federalist orator and member of Congress and sometime contributor to the journal. Even among Boston conservatives, Ames had a reputation as a reactionary with an almost pathological hatred of popular rule. In his eloquent essay "American Literature" (1809), he reiterated the now familiar diagnosis of native culture. The arts lacked sufficient cause to develop on these shores, Ames wrote, because nothing called forth the exertions of genius in a society devoted to worshipping the dollar and conciliating the multitude. He contrasted the United States unfavorably to ancient Greece and Rome, pointing out that the two classical cultures were anything but democratic when they produced their most enduring monuments, the Homeric epics and Virgil's *Aeneid*. America would not have a literature to speak of, Ames prophesied, until class extremes intensified to the point where a leisured and wealthy few, arising in the midst of an impoverished many, could support and cherish men of genius.

As a civic humanist, Ames hardly looked forward to this eventuality; literature would benefit, but in all likelihood liberty would perish. Moreover, such literature would necessarily fall short of the highest ideal. Ames differed from the *Anthology* group in his sense that a truly great culture could not flower without a nourishing bond between artists and their audience. His essay implicitly disputed the idea of a purified realm of letters. He devised a myth of history in which "poetry of transcendent merit," evoked by popular receptivity, appeared for two brief moments in the classical past, never to occur again. The rude warriors of Greece inspired Homer's martial epic and received its strains with rapture, and Virgil's patriotic poem was possible only because Romans loved their country with unsurpassed ardor. Art of such grandeur assumed a large and appreciative hearing; rather than aiming at "the closets of scholars," these works were written in the assurance of "reaching the hearts and kindling the fervid enthusiasm of the multitude." Ames saw modern writers as necessarily "alienated," cut off from the people, and he regarded this condition as damaging to their work. Nor, in the materialistic and democratic present, could he imagine any way of restoring the connection. Later Romantic writers like Ralph Waldo Emerson and Walt Whitman would draw quite different inferences, but they would repeat Ames's insight that a literature unable to speak to the mass public was a sterile literature, incapacitated by its isolation.

A younger contemporary of Ames, the Reverend Samuel Miller, took a more complex and benign view of the threat posed to culture by the modern era. Miller's two-volume survey, *A Brief Retrospect of the Eighteenth Century* (1803), is an invaluable resource for study of the early Republic – "the first attempt to give a general outline of the advances we have made, and the works we have produced," as it was described by a contributor to the *Monthly Anthology*. The book reviewed both the pros and the cons of the technological and cultural developments of the age. Volume I provided a sympathetic account of what has since been called the "consumer revolution" of the eighteenth century. Focusing on science and the mechanical and fine arts, Miller applauded the profusion of cheap goods – pottery, glass, stoves, clocks, and so forth – made available by recent inventions and improved methods of manufacture. He also welcomed the increased leisure brought about by the division of labor and by time-saving devices in the workplace and the home. Miller greeted these changes without moral outrage against luxury or idleness: "at no period of the world," he boasted, "was the *art of living, . . .* ever on so advantageous a footing as at present."

Volume II of *A Brief Retrospect* offered a detailed appraisal of trends in world and American literature. Miller recognized that the unprecedented cheapness and abundance of books, added to the prosperity of buyers with the time to read them, spelled a revolution in the domain of letters. His preacher side – *A Brief Retrospect* began as a sermon – got the better of the historian in his discussion of the novel and, to a lesser extent, in his remarks on the commercializing of authorship. Miller praised Charles Brockden Brown as the only American novelist "deserving respectful notice," but his overall assessment of the new genre was sharply negative. No more than one novel out of a thousand could be read for improvement; the rest were either frivolous or "seductive and corrupting." Miller saw the novel's rise as an unfortunate consequence of the invasion of letters by the commercial spirit. He noted that a new determinant of value, the market, had entered culture in the eighteenth century, leading artists away from commitment to truth and social utility and narrowing their vision to the sordid calculation of profit. All too often men and women now wrote "in accommodation to the *public taste,* however depraved, and with a view to the most *advantageous sale."* The novel, with its great circulation and shameless pandering to prurient interest, was one result; others, Miller complained, included the hasty production of worthless books and a lessening of the author's standing in public esteem.

Miller knew that he was really describing the condition of literature in more economically advanced Great Britain and not in the infant agricultural Republic. He was aware, too, that the benefits of commercialization at least equaled the abuses. Among the reasons he gave for the cultural inferiority of America was its inability to maintain a class of professional authors:

In the United States, the rewards of literature are small and uncertain. The people cannot afford to remunerate eminent talents or great acquirements. Booksellers, the great patrons of learning in modern times, are too poor to foster and reward the efforts of genius.

Miller did not look to a wealthy few to redress this situation; he had little of the *Anthology* men's faith in upper-class beneficence. Instead, he expected the change to come from an expanding market. The market would diffuse knowledge throughout the far-flung American population and stimulate an insatiable appetite for literature. It had transformed the eighteenth century into "THE AGE OF BOOKS" and enabled women, the common people, and others traditionally excluded from culture to read and "inquire to a degree that would once have been thought incredible." In a society without aristocratic patronage, only the market had the power to generate the "substantial emoluments" necessary to support artistic endeavor. Miller's confidence that "letters will flourish as much in America as in any part of the world" stemmed from his belief that authorship would be commercialized here as successfully as in Europe.

Miller's was a voice of prescience and moderation; a more radical note was struck by Judith Murray, the Republic's foremost advocate of women's rights. In some ways, Murray makes a strange dissident. She was far from being the homely gatherer of unclaimed grain she impersonated in her major work. She belonged to the same class as the Brahmins who regarded letters as a patrician indulgence and fulminated at literary bounders from the pages of the *Monthly Anthology.* A Federalist in politics, Murray dedicated *The Gleaner* to President John Adams and numbered George Washington among the book's subscribers. No American had a better claim to the title of gentlewoman of letters. Yet this cultivated and versatile writer was a maverick in religion, the wife of the British Universalist John Murray, and she held decidedly unconventional views on authorship and women. Despite publishing under a pseudonym, she repudiated republican self-effacement for an ethic of female self-assertion.

It was precisely as a woman that Murray took issue with the era's cultural priorities. Feminism underwrote her support for equality and her demand for literary recognition. She favored a healthy affirmation of the self because she felt that women's lack of esteem for their own capabilities left them vulnerable to flattery and seduction. An essay of 1784, "Desultory Thoughts upon the utility of encouraging a degree of Self-Complacency, especially in FEMALE BOSOMS," bluntly advised "self-reverence" as the best safeguard against specious adulation. Only by thinking well of herself, Murray argued, could a woman see through the false praises of the unscrupulous; only by respecting her own mental powers could she learn to aspire and to achieve. Another essay, "On the Equality of the Sexes" (1790), turned traditional disparagement of women into an argument for their intellectual parity. All agree that women excel in "exuberance of fancy" and "inventive scandal," Murray observed. This proves that women's imaginations are, if anything, naturally superior to men's; the misapplication of the faculty is attributable solely to the difference in education.

Murray wanted full credit for her own imaginative powers, and she cast aside female modesty to avow an ardent craving for literary fame. Although she donned a double male pseudonym in *The Gleaner,* Mr. Virgillius posing as Mr. Gleaner, she came forward in the book's preface as a woman, the already well-known Constantia, to lay claim to popular regard. Constantia rejected the usual apology invoked by female authors, "that the importunity of friends hath drawn me forth – certainly not." Diffidence had no part of it, nor was her principal motive a selfless wish to improve her readers. What drove her to publish, and what would be considered presumptuous by some, was an "invincible desire to present myself to [the] public" for their admiration and applause. Murray's frank ambition, uncommon for her time and class, was rarer still for her gender. Her boldness in seeking celebrity and advocating self-fulfillment as a female prerogative eluded most American women writers far into the nineteenth century, when even best-selling domestic novelists shrank from such unapologetic individualism.

Joseph Dennie, known in his lifetime as the American Addison, was a defender of literary hierarchy who, nevertheless, welcomed and forwarded liberalizing changes in republican culture. In his career and writings, Dennie pushed to their extreme limits the contradictions of the formative period. Very much an eighteenth-century gentleman in his view of literature – he chose the pseudonym "Oliver Oldschool, Esq." when he established the *Port Folio* – Dennie loved to rail against democracy and commerce and to bait the ordinary citizens who constituted the bulk of the reading public. Epithets like "the rabble" and "the malignant vulgar" came glibly off his tongue. So disenchanted did Dennie grow with American life that he regretted the Revolution and wished he had been born in England, where "men of liberality and letters" were adequately rewarded for their writings.

Dennie's first major venture was the editorship of the *Farmer's Weekly Museum*, the rural newspaper-magazine for which he composed most of his essays; here as elsewhere his allegiance to the values of the "Old School" vied with a complex, up-to-date sensibility comprising both entrepreneurial and proto-Romantic elements. During the years of his editorship, Dennie created his persona of the Lay Preacher, a self-description that links him to the Athenaeum group and palpably conveys the clerical tenor of the emergent genteel tradition. His public statements emphasized the social function of letters: the first edition of *The Lay Preacher; or Short Sermons for Idle Readers* (1796) aspired to be more "useful . . . than brilliant" and defined its "primary object" as the instruction of the villager. But the essayist as country parson was simultaneously an aspiring literary professional with a "go-getting" credo imitative of Benjamin Franklin. Never a patrician amateur – his father was a merchant who died insolvent – Dennie had no source of income other than from his writing and editing, and he pictured belles lettres quite frankly as a trade. A regular feature of the *Farmer's Weekly Museum* was "From the Shop of Colon and Spondee," a joint production of Dennie and Royall Tyler. This serial, a hodge-podge of prose and verse, purported to offer literary wares for sale. The Lay Preacher essays exhibited the same enterprising spirit: Dennie as purveyor of practical advice exhorted his compatriots to shake off sloth, practice industry, and acquire independence.

The pose of Poor Richard hardly suited Dennie, who far more often gave a dandified inflection to the image of the writer. Even in the original Lay Preacher series he admitted failing to practice the diligence he urged upon his readers: "I confess with candor that I loiter and slumber much, and while I preach industry to others, am myself a castaway." Inhabitants of the little village of Walpole could testify to the truth of this self-characterization. Dennie was notorious for sleeping late and for composing copy at the last possible moment, and he must have cut a startling figure among the busy villagers in his elegant dress, which, an acquaintance reported, always "approached the highest notch of the fashion." Among his pen names were "Meander" and "The American Lounger," and in the Lay Preacher essays written in Philadelphia, he presented himself as a precocious version of the Romantic flaneur, strolling the city streets to gather material for his literary speculations. Dennie savored the excitement and "shifting scenes" of the metropolis, and he turned refreshed from the urban panorama to his own

thoughts. Sounding like a forerunner of Edgar Allan Poe or Charles Baude-
laire, he cultivated his imagination in the midst of practical business types:

> I start a topic in High Street, and hunt it down as far as Southwark or the Northern
> Liberties. I walk through the market place as I once wandered in a wood; and while
> one is talking of his farm, and another of his merchandize, I listen to the suggestions
> of fancy, or invoke the cherub contemplation.

In actuality, Dennie was keenly conscious of tailoring his literary endeav-
ors to the needs of the active commercial civilization that the United States
was becoming, even in rural areas like New Hampshire. The new order found
its cultural organ in the same periodicals from which elite spokesmen thundered their jeremiads. Samuel Miller labeled the eighteenth century an age of
"superficial learning," a phenomenon he attributed to a commercial temper
that left people neither the time nor the inclination for study, and to "the
unprecedented circulation of Magazines, literary Journals, Abridgments,
Epitomes, &c." As early as 1792, in a serial called "The Farrago," Dennie
recognized – and delighted in – the appeal of the brief essay to the vast
majority of literate persons, those unequipped to delve into the esoteric
systems of philosophy. He acclaimed the form as one of the era's prized
inventions:

> Some work must . . . be projected to fix volatility and rouse indolence, neither too
> abstruse for the young, too prolix for the busy nor too grave for the fair. A perfor-
> mance, which should not resemble an austere monitor, . . . but a pleasant friend,
> whose conversation at once beguiles and improves the hour. The design was at length
> accomplished. Certain geniuses of the first magnitude arose, who, in the narrow
> compass of a sheet of paper, conveyed more useful knowledge to mankind than all the
> ponderous tomes of Aristotle.

This "novel species of literary entertainment" brought much-needed instruction and amusement to the middle and lower orders. According to Dennie,
people who seldom opened a book wore out the pages of the latest magazines
in their leisure moments.

Along with the short story, of which it was a nonfictional equivalent, the
periodical essay carried into literature the revolution in consumption that
marked the eighteenth century. Historians of the book speak of a change in
reading habits at this time from the intensive to the extensive: unlike the
Bible or almanacs, which were pored over repeatedly, magazines provided
fresh and expendable recreation for the industrious classes. They harmonized
with the democratic spirit of the age, enhancing the quality of life for the
many who had neither expensive educations nor unlimited leisure. Dennie
saw magazines, with their array of essays, poems, stories, and anecdotes, as
responsive to the short attention span and craving for diversity of ordinary

readers. For the inscription to the *Port Folio,* he selected lines from the English poet William Cowper: "Various, that the mind / Of desultory man, studious of change, / And pleased with novelty, may be indulged." The flaneur's relish for the heterogeneity and "many coloured life" of the urban environment, that most modern of settings, was realized in the multifarious contents of the periodical.

The first national literary weekly in the United States, with a circulation at its peak of fifteen hundred, the *Port Folio* perpetuated Dennie's pattern of protesting his elite status while striving to make literature profitable. From its first issue, the magazine proposed both to establish its creator as a man of irreproachable learning and refinement and to furnish him with a subsistence. A Prospectus invited submissions from "Men of Affluence, Men of Liberality, and Men of Letters," heaped disdain upon "the lower classes of our motley vulgar," and promised to keep monetary considerations at a distance by refusing to permit advertisements in the pages of the journal. The Prospectus bristled with erudite footnotes warning away the uninitiate; but this display, in its very excessiveness – there were twenty-one citations in the space of three pages, providing supporting quotations from Virgil, Milton, Burke, Pliny, Bolingbroke, and other authorities – pointed to the parvenu side of Dennie, the literary man on the make beset by insecurities about his credentials. This enterprising side was no less present in the Prospectus, for example in the announcement that advertisements would be accepted after all but confined to a separate sheet of paper, which would serve as a wrapping for the magazine as a whole. Calling himself "an adventurer," Dennie freely acknowledged that in starting the *Port Folio* he had the goal "of making literature the handmaid of Fortune, or, at least, of securing something like independency, by exertions, as a man of letters." A year later, perhaps fearful that his candor about his financial hopes had been misunderstood, he appended a defiant notice to subscribers vowing never to court the multitude.

Dennie edited the *Port Folio* until his death in 1812, and the conflict in his idea of literary calling sharpened rather than abated over time. In content, the magazine became more reactionary than ever, lashing out at "the general rage for *vulgar* popularity, and for amassing wealth," and denouncing Benjamin Franklin, whom Dennie used to admire, for degrading literature to the capacity of maid servants and apprentices. In presentation, there were signs of greater flexibility in accommodating the marketplace. The *Port Folio* changed to a monthly in 1809 and began to run engravings aimed at a broader range of readers; plates depicted native scenery, machines like the spinning jenny, and the latest fashions. In one breath, Dennie could appeal for popular support, as he did in the Prospectus for the new monthly format, and in the next, he could admonish readers that he approached them not in "the shape of a *fawning publican,* or a sobbing mendicant," but "with a firm step, [and] in the guise of a Cavalier." In 1811 the self-styled aristocrat of letters broke with one of the most durable mannerisms of the Old School when he dropped his pseudonym and issued the *Port Folio* under his own name. Some eminent later writers resisted such self-disclosure as too compromising; Dennie, never more the gentleman than at this moment, portrayed the change as an act of high-minded principle. Eschewing "all mystery and artifice," he wrote, would have the effect of making him "still more studiously than ever, solicitous for the reputation of his literary labours."

Dennie was succeeded as editor of the *Port Folio* by Nicholas Biddle, the Philadelphia blueblood whose later career as president of the United States Bank made him the target of the Jacksonian campaign to liberate the economy from traditional restraints. Biddle's succession encapsulates an important truth about the first generation of American literary periodicals. Most journals begun prior to the 1820s reached only a small segment of the reading public and reflected the attitudes of the "better sort" who exercised a monopoly over culture. The two leading publications established following the War of 1812, the Baltimore *Portico* (1816–18) and the *North American Review* (founded in 1815), retained a restrictive tone. William Tudor, the first editor of the *North American Review,* had been a charter member of the Anthology Society. Not until the political and social revolution of the Jackson years did literary magazines shed their upper-class air and realize, as it were, the democratic market orientation implicit in their miscellaneous structure. *Graham's Magazine, Godey's Lady's Book,* and other mass-circulation monthlies sated the popular taste for light, diverse entertainment and stamped the antebellum era as the "golden age" of periodicals.

Another "successor" of Dennie was already moving toward the new perspective in American culture. In 1802, a year after Dennie created Oliver Oldschool, a serial entitled *Letters of Jonathan Oldstyle, Gent.* began appearing in a New York newspaper, the *Morning Chronicle.* The essays heralded the arrival on the literary scene of Washington Irving. An attorney like Dennie, Irving similarly preferred writing to practicing law and thought of himself as an upholder of old-fashioned values in a frenetically modernizing world. Irving too got his start in the periodical and newspaper culture of the young Republic. Besides his *Oldstyle* letters, Irving's first major publication, *Salmagundi* (1807–8), parodied the essay serial, and he served a stint as editor of and contributor to the *Analectic Magazine* in 1813–14. The work that made him world famous, *The Sketch Book of Geoffrey Crayon, Gent.* (1819–20), was published serially both in England and in America and preserved many of the features of the miscellany. Again like Dennie, Irving insisted on the antipathy between money-making and culture; the pen names he adopted in his march to literary fortune were invariably those of "Gentlemen." But a crucial difference separated the two authors. Irving continued to employ the aristocratic pseudonyms that Dennie abandoned because he grasped what his predecessor intuited only fitfully: status itself could be sold to the public and used as an instrument, not to belabor common readers, but to cultivate and enchant them, and thus to immortalize and enrich the writer.

3

THE DRAMA

I N 1826, at the opening ceremonies of New York's Bowery Theater, a speaker voiced the hope that "the latent talents of some native Bard may here be warmed into existence, who shall emulate the growing fame, acquired in other walks, by Irving and Cooper." The statement reveals a conspicuous truth about the early American drama. As Western culture entered its Romantic phase, the American theater could not boast a single figure of international stature, a playwright who could stand comparison with the new Republic's leading fiction writers. The nearest America came to a world-famous dramatist in 1826 was John Howard Payne, a transplanted New Yorker whose adaptations of French hits played to full houses at London's Drury Lane; today, Payne is little more than a footnote to literary history.

The American drama was the most republican and propagandistic of the literary genres. Slow to accommodate the individualism that became synonymous with nineteenth-century authorship, it failed to develop Romantic talents of the highest rank. One might object that the nineteenth century, the age of the novel's apotheosis, proved remarkably inhospitable to Western playwriting generally. Although this may be an accurate appraisal, at least until the last quarter of the century, it remains true that the complex of assumptions governing the native stage was singularly uncongenial to the nurturing of Romantic inwardness and self-realization. The drama of the early Republic was intimately tied to the civic sphere. It retained a commitment to the common good long after fiction and poetry (or rather, the fictions and poems considered canonical) had modified or shed such loyalties for more private goals. The most "residual" of the arts, the theater was the closest to oratory and the world of men; it lagged behind the novel's identification with print and its receptivity to feminization.

A suggestive way of illustrating the different emphases of the early drama and the early novel would be to glance at the national hero who had the closest association with each genre. From Royall Tyler's *The Algerine Captive* (1797) and Charles Brockden Brown's *Arthur Mervyn* (1799–1800) to Herman Melville's *Israel Potter* (1854), the figure of Benjamin Franklin has exerted a special fascination for the American novel. The historical Franklin was himself strongly drawn to novels: in his *Autobiography* he praises John Bunyan, Daniel Defoe, and Samuel Richardson for mixing "Narration and Dialogue, a Method of Writing very engaging to the Reader," and in 1744 his Philadelphia printing house brought out the first novel published in America, an edition of Richardson's *Pamela*. As the title of Richardson's tale suggests, the genre had a predilection for narratives involving women — a predilection, as we shall see in our chapter on the novel, that Franklin shared. As a printer, and as someone whose career exemplified social mobility, Franklin felt a natural affinity for the literary form whose rise depended on the printing revolution and the growth of the middle class. Early American novelists in turn gave him cameo appearances or invoked him by implication in their narratives of material success and failure; many viewed him as a type of the new order of liberal individualism.

If Franklin became the patron saint of enlightened self-interest, the revolutionary leader who showed up most often in the drama, George Washington, was universally regarded as a symbol of selfless devotion to the commonweal. Washington felt little investment in print culture; a man of action, his writings were largely functional. (Only two pieces are much read today, even by scholars: the "Circular to the States" [1783] and the presidential "Farewell Address" of 1796.) The drama, a more public and oral form than the novel, appealed to Washington's republican sense of culture. He attended the theater throughout his life, even during the trying early days of the revolutionary conflict. The patriot troops, struggling to survive at Valley Forge during the bitter winter of 1776–7, entertained their commander with a performance of Joseph Addison's *Cato* (1712), his favorite play and one of the few literary works he quoted in his correspondence. As president, Washington regularly lent his prestige to the indigenous stage. His name headed the list of subscribers to the publication of Royall Tyler's *The Contrast* in 1790, and he allowed it to be announced in advance when he planned to honor a production with his presence — a form of advertisement that swelled receipts and endeared him to theater managers.

From the beginning of hostilities with Britain, American playwrights made it a common practice to portray Washington as a character. Whenever they touched on patriotic themes, they were sure to find ways of introducing him into their works. Among numerous other examples, he delivers a speech in Hugh Henry Brackenridge's *The Battle of Bunkers-Hill* (1776), appears as a character in John Leacock's *The Fall of British Tyranny* (1776) and William Dunlap's *André* (1798), and provides the model for Peter Markoe's *The Patriot Chief* (1784). Colonel Manly mentions him reverently in *The Contrast* as the paragon he has sought to imitate. For the early dramatist, the "American

Cincinnatus" (as Washington was widely known) represented the primacy of the civic, the subordination of private ends to the public good. These were imperatives especially pressing upon men, and Washington, with his austere dignity and emotional restraint, incarnated manly virtue to his compatriots. He stood for the ideals to which the theater itself aspired. When fiction, on the other hand, first utilized Washington as a character in a significant way, in James Fenimore Cooper's *The Spy* (1821), it came at the very moment when the American novel was moving away from a communal orientation. The Washington of Cooper's tale is a quasi-private figure; he appears as the mysterious spymaster Harper, not as the legendary civic hero of the drama.

Drama in the New World had always been an irreducibly social medium. Well before Americans staged plays of their own composition – the first being Thomas Godfrey's *The Prince of Parthia,* published in 1765 and professionally produced in 1767 – they attended shows by traveling players from England. The Cavalier South extended a warmer welcome than the often disapproving North, but both sections carried on a love affair with Shakespeare, and both developed a participatory notion of the stage. In contrast to the novel, the drama was consumed in a public setting. It was performed and spoken, rarely read. One could say that the drama was the cultural analogue, but also the cultural antithesis, to the present-day cinema as a popular art form. Like the cinema, it had broad appeal that overrode the distinction between elite and demotic entertainment. It assembled people from different classes to share the same verbal and visual experience. But whereas the cinema charges a single admission price, creating a sense (or illusion) of democratic equality, and demands silent attention from the spectators, the drama provided stratified seating and encouraged active involvement in the performance.

Particularly after independence, the American theater formed a discursive space that expressed the era's republican spirit – its understanding of public life as communal and engaged but socially differentiated. Going to see a play in the eighteenth and early nineteenth centuries entailed interacting with people, from players to other members of the audience. Seating arrangements physically separated the classes, with servants and slaves in the gallery, the "middling sort" in the pit, and gentlemen and their families in the costly boxes. A single building housed them all, and the more crowded sections tended to prevail in determining popular behavior. There was almost constant noise inside the theater, even when a play was in progress. Members of the public would eat, drink, chew and spit tobacco, and carry on conversations. The spectators provided part of the entertainment, and sometimes the best part, according to critics like the Anglophile fop Dimple from Tyler's *The Contrast,* who describes attending the theater in New York: "I sat with my back to the stage all the time, admiring a much better actress than any there – a lady who played the fine woman to perfection."

Applause, hisses, and other outbursts repeatedly interrupted performances. The songs and stunts presented between the acts and the farcical afterpiece that followed the main drama seemed to invite the public to join in. The system of "pointing" further contributed to the raucous atmosphere. At a celebrated moment in a play, such as Hamlet's "To be or not to be" soliloquy, the actor or actress would walk to the front of the stage and deliver the lines directly to the audience. Theatergoers would respond with either catcalls or ecstatic cries of approval and demands for an encore. A successful point, which might be repeated half a dozen times, would completely disrupt the regular business of the drama.

Other disturbances highlighted the theater's role as a kind of forum for popular political sentiment. Washington's name during a play would be greeted with applause from all sections, whereas the mention of the king of England was sure to bring forth howls of derision. James Nelson Barker's *Marmion,* written in 1812 on the eve of war with Britain, includes a speech by James of Scotland denouncing the English for treachery. The impassioned Scottish ruler vows to protect "the charter of our freedom / In glorious fields [by] our noble fathers won." The dramatist's own father, General John Barker, sprang to his feet during a performance of this scene and, brandishing his cane, led the audience in prolonged cheering. Audience disapproval of a political opinion or action could force changes in a play even if the behavior in question was clearly meant to be seen as misguided. In Dunlap's *André,* when the hotheaded Bland is unable to persuade Washington to spare André's life, he tears off his military cockade and flings it to the ground in disgust. The public was so outraged by this episode that Dunlap was obliged to rewrite it for the second performance with a contrite Bland restoring the ornament. Sometimes partisan reactions erupted into full-scale riots. Insults, real or alleged, that English actors hurled against the United States triggered the most serious clashes. The worst disturbance occurred in the antebellum period, the famous Astor Place Riot of 1849 in which some twenty people died, but the pattern was established in the early Republic: invariably taking on patriotic overtones, theatrical riots blurred the line between politics and the drama.

The riots demonstrated that the drama's relation to the civic realm could be one of antagonism and mistrust. Violent disturbances frequently led to efforts by municipal authorities to impose stricter controls upon the stage. Precisely because the theater was a more communal experience than the novel, it was perceived as more of a potential menace to the commonwealth. Plays had long been condemned as the most depraved of the arts, and in

America they came in for a greater degree of criticism and censorship than either poetry or fiction. One reason early dramatists infused their works with a didactic and moralizing strain was to combat widespread antipathy to the stage.

The Puritans had brought the antitheatrical prejudice to the New World. Pressure from English Puritans had closed the London theaters in 1642, and their coreligionists in the colonies agreed that plays were *"sinfull, heathenish, lewde, ungodly Spectacles."* During the Restoration, the monarchy's role in reopening the stage seemed proof that royalty and the drama were intertwined. Republican ideology strengthened American animus in the eighteenth century. A Genevan, Jean-Jacques Rousseau, launched the classic republican attack in his *Letter to M. D'Alembert on the Theatre* (1758). Rousseau saw the drama as an enemy of freedom because it brought a train of evils – idleness, luxury, dissipation – that destroyed the civic virtue essential to a republic. He thought the theater dangerous in its very nature because it rewarded the person who made a profession of deceiving others. A free polity, Rousseau argued, depended on persuasion and rational choice; its hero was the orator, the man who openly expressed his opinions and tried to convince others that he was right. The actor, in contrast, was a type of the demagogue; he practiced "the art of counterfeiting himself, of putting on another character than his own, of appearing different than he is."

In America, feelings against the drama ran high in the intense ideological climate of the revolutionary era. In 1774, as relations with Great Britain worsened, an anxious Continental Congress passed a resolution urging industry and frugality and censuring "every species of extravagance and dissipation, especially all horse-racing, and all kinds of gaming, cock-fighting, exhibitions of shews, plays, and other expensive diversions and entertainments." Four years later, a more stringent edict called for the dismissal of any government official "who shall act, promote, encourage, or attend such plays." It did not help the theater's standing in revolutionary America that the occupying British forces regularly staged performances in Boston and New York. The hated symbols of foreign oppression clasped the drama to them. General John Burgoyne was one of several British officers known to adore the stage; he wrote a farce deriding the patriot army as a mob of undisciplined provincials.

Aversion to theatricals as dissolute and unrepublican outlasted the conflict with Britain. Massachusetts did not get around to repealing its ban on plays until 1792; an earlier movement for repeal in Boston had been led – in what must have seemed to some a symbolic conjunction – by Perez Morton, a well-known rake and the model for one of the seducers in *The Power of Sympathy,* William Hill Brown's sentimental novel of 1789. Even Dunlap, the new nation's first theatrical professional and an ardent advocate, had to acknowledge the stage's association with licentiousness. In his *History of the American Theatre* (1832), he deplored the moral laxity of actors and the custom of reserving a portion of the boxes for prostitutes. Washington Irving was another friend of the drama who shrank from its coarser aspects. He related in his *Letters of Jonathan Oldstyle, Gent.* (1802–3) that the unruly occupants of the gallery showered food on the other theatergoers and sometimes made their wishes known by shouting and stamping until they drowned out the orchestra.

Supporters of the stage saw value in those very public qualities that were mistrusted by critics and moved to enlist the drama on the side of virtue and the common good. As Dunlap put it, "The engine is powerful for good or ill − it is for society to choose." That the theater, unlike privately consumed fiction, gathered a mass audience in one location was cited as proof of its potential for instruction. The drama's spoken, or oral, character was a related advantage: plays abounded in examples of eloquence and provided valuable training in the art of public speaking. This was a talent, as republicans from Rousseau to Thomas Jefferson argued, with exceptional importance in a free polity, where leaders had to mobilize the electorate through persuasion rather than force. Americans still inhabited a largely oral world, and a people accustomed to political oratory and weekly sermons appreciated the stage as much for its declamation and rhetoric as for its well-crafted plots. Addison's *Cato,* which enjoyed tremendous popularity throughout the eighteenth century, contains speeches that influenced both Patrick Henry's famous peroration, "Give me liberty, or give me death," and the last words of Nathan Hale, "I only regret that I have but one life to lose for my country." So close was the alliance between pedagogy and the drama that several plays were composed expressly for student performances. Brackenridge's *The Battle of Bunkers-Hill* was "drawn up for an Exercise in Oratory, to a number of young Gentlemen in a southern Academy" where he was then a teacher. The play includes a prologue and an epilogue expounding revolutionary principles and a speech of thanksgiving by Washington on his entering Boston.

Brackenridge was representative of American dramatists active during the revolutionary years: he consecrated his "muse to the great themes of patriotic virtue, bravery and heroism." The plays dating from this time are all political satires or propaganda pieces. All affirm the necessity of putting service to the commonwealth ahead of personal interests. Robert Munford's *The Candidates, or the Humours of a Virginia Election,* published in 1798 but probably written in 1770–1, assails corrupt electioneering practices and, in typical Whig fashion, advocates rule by the qualified few. One hero, Wouldbe, rejects the Mandevillean doctrine that self-interest produces public benefits, and a second, Worthy, overcomes his aristocratic reluctance to seek office in order to run against demagogues like Strutabout and Smallhopes. Two farces by Mercy Otis Warren, *The Adulateur* (1773) and *The Group* (1775), lampoon Thomas Hutchinson and the clique of Loyalist politicians who governed Massachusetts from the Stamp Act to the Revolution. Warren too condemns theorists of self-interest like Bernard Mandeville, whose *Fable of the Bees* (1714), according to the plays, is favorite reading of the Tories. "A swarm of court sycophants, hungry harpies, and unprincipled danglers," the Tories are said to have betrayed their "country for a grasp of gold." Dramatic works written after the outbreak of hostilities proclaim the union of art and arms. Leacock's *The Fall of British Tyranny* has an ironic dedication to the British army by "Dick Rifle" and a poem by the Goddess of Liberty exhorting Americans to "Wish, talk, write, fight, and die – for LIBERTY." A French visitor to Harvard in 1781, after watching undergraduates act in several of these dramas, was moved to suggest that the theater had not fulfilled such a civic role since the time of the ancient Greeks.

As a patriotic form, the drama derived its principal inspiration from current events. Playwrights vied with each other to retell great public narratives. Brackenridge chose two of the best-known early confrontations of the war for his play on Bunker Hill and for *The Death of General Montgomery at the Siege of Quebec* (1777). Later dramatists showed the same penchant for communal stories of a strongly nationalistic bent. Susanna Rowson migrated to this country as a player and had a career in the Philadelphia theater before taking up schoolteaching. With *Slaves in Algiers; or, A Struggle for Freedom* (1794), she joined the long line of playwrights who chronicled the conflict with the Barbary pirates. John Daly Burk retraced Brackenridge's territory with his flag-waving *Bunker-Hill, or The Death of General Warren.* A kind of mixed-media extravaganza with onstage troop movements, battle scenes, cannons, smoke, and fire, the piece drew record crowds when it opened in Boston and then New York in 1797. For Dunlap, the supreme moment of national self-definition occurred in the affair of the English spy, Major John André. So great was the interest in this episode that Dunlap refashioned his tragedy on the subject as a patriotic spectacle, *The Glory of Columbia: Her Yeomanry!* (1803), in a continuing effort to capitalize on André's notoriety.

Just as the American stage was shaped by public events, so the political world was colored by the drama. Again the interaction was most pronounced in the revolutionary period, particularly during the 1760s and 1770s. Americans learned their oppositional ideology from belles lettres as well as from political tracts, and the English plays performed and admired in the colonies invariably lent themselves to partisan interpretation. Works like *Cato,* John Home's Whiggish *Douglas* (1756), and John Gay's *The Beggar's Opera* (1728), which portrayed English society as thoroughly dissolute, strengthened the wish for independence. The complex of ideas known as Whig Sentimentalism, disseminated by both the novel and the drama, was another stimulus to separation from Britain. Feminizing liberty as a victim of sexual assault, this tradition enabled Americans to cast themselves as defenders of national purity against seducers intent upon violation.

Members of the revolutionary generation were acutely conscious of themselves as performers on the historical stage. Belying Rousseau's fear that the free man could not be an actor, they insisted on the congruence of liberty with self-dramatization. The protests leading up to the break with Britain had a theatrical flavor. Social life in general was more stylized in the eighteenth century, as people liked to "playact" in public through convention and gesture, and the decade of crisis following the Stamp Act saw political activity assume ritualized and highly expressive forms. Effigies were hanged, mock trials and festivals held, and demonstrators imitated mummers' plays by staging burials and resurrections of the figure of Liberty. Some orators donned togas and struck Roman poses to underscore their claim to be successors to the ancient republicans. A sense of stepping into familiar roles – those of Cicero, Cato, and Cincinnatus – built confidence in the rightness of the cause and prompted pamphleteers and newspaper writers to employ classical pseudonyms, such as the "Publius" adopted by Alexander Hamilton, James Madison, and John Jay in *The Federalist.* Something of this histrionic quality, this air of venturing before an expectant audience, comes through in the Declaration of Independence. Impelled by "a decent respect to the opinions of mankind," the document proclaiming national autonomy submits the grievances of the colonists to the judgment of "a candid world."

The drama's commitment to the collectivity militated against individualized expression and perception of the genre as private property. Canonical models, when put to patriotic uses, lent needed legitimacy, and time-honored plots and character types stood a better chance of eliciting desired responses than did experimentation. Native dramatists felt little impetus to strive for originality and little inhibition about lifting material from others. A venerable tradition of English drama – Shakespeare, as Cooper observed in 1828, was "the great author of America" – constituted an irresistible resource for borrowings. Most American plays were highly derivative, put together by rearranging episodes, characters, and dialogue from familiar English works. In Godfrey's *The Prince of Parthia,* the indigenous qualities are far less evident than are such echoes from Shakespeare as the betrayal of a king by his ungrateful child, in this case a son, the appearance of a murdered sovereign's ghost, and the bloody-mindedness of an ambitious queen. Plays more self-consciously nationalistic helped themselves just as freely to the common English stock. *The Contrast,* which warns against corrupting influences from abroad, shows the influence of George Farquhar and Richard Brinsley Sheridan. Mordecai M. Noah's *She Would Be a Soldier; or The Plains of Chippewa* (1819), a comedy of cross dressing set during the War of 1812, steals its basic situation from Thomas Shadwell's *The Woman Captain* (1680) and even owes its title to Frederick Pilon's *He Would Be a Soldier* (1786).

The lack of international copyright left these and other foreign works unprotected; recycled for American consumption, they were far more common on the early stage than were original native dramas. Besides imitating English works, American authors regularly translated and adapted Continental plays. Dunlap turned out over fifty works, only a fraction of them original. His favorite source was a German, August von Kotzebue, whose melodramas enjoyed immense success in both England and America. When Dunlap's *André* fared poorly at the box office in 1798, he was able to keep open New York's Park Theater, of which he was the manager, with a version of Kotzebue's *The Stranger* (1789). Thereafter he adapted Kotzebue so frequently that the German, anxious to get at least some returns from his popularity in the United States, offered to sell Dunlap his manuscripts ahead of publication – an offer the American, who had been reworking already existing English translations, understandably saw no reason to accept.

Even more prolific as a translator was the expatriate John Howard Payne, who relied heavily on French melodramatists such as Alexandre Duval and Guilbert de Pixérécourt. Payne wrote upwards of sixty plays, almost all of which were adaptations; only his first work, a piece called *Julia* performed in 1806 when he was just fifteen, is believed to be original. Payne made no secret of his dependence on existent sources. In the preface to *Brutus; or the Fall of Tarquin,* the tragedy that established his English reputation, he freely admits borrowing from some seven earlier treatments. The preface denies infringing private ownership and rates adaptation on a par with originality:

In the present play I have had no hesitation in adopting the conception and language of my predecessors. . . . This has been done so as to allow of no injury to personal feelings or private property. Such obligations, to be culpable, must be secret; but it may be observed, that no assistance of other writers can be available without an effort almost, if not altogether, as laborious as original composition.

The note of defensiveness in this statement can be attributed to the historical lateness of Payne's situation; Romantic ideas about creativity were already commonplace when *Brutus* was first performed in 1818.

Fiction and poetry were second to foreign plays in providing literary inspiration for the native stage. Like the cinema, the early American theater thrived on dramatizations of other genres; the better known a story was – the closer it came to being a common inheritance — the better its chances for success. The first play of Dunlap's to be produced, *The Father, or American Shandyism* (1789), indicates its debt to Laurence Sterne's novel in its title. Dunlap also reworked Ann Radcliffe's gothic thriller *Romance of the Forest* as *Fontainville Abbey* (1795), and Barker's *Marmion* was based on a popular poem by Sir Walter Scott. Cooper's *The Spy* was turned into a play, and later in the century, the actor Joseph Jefferson made a successful career out of playing Rip Van Winkle to audiences enraptured with Irving's character.

Washington Irving received nothing for these performances, but the adapters did not do much better. Remuneration for native dramatists was thoroughly unreliable and dissuaded would-be artists from viewing playwriting as a profession. Stage managers naturally preferred foreign plays because they could get them without paying a fee. Even when they accepted an American work, they made no direct payment but rather permitted the author to keep the receipts of a benefit night (minus expenses for the house). This arrangement seldom proved beneficial to the playwright; custom stipulated that the third performance belonged to the author, and few plays were sufficiently popular to warrant a three-night run. Only Dunlap and Payne among early dramatists were daring (or foolhardy) enough to try to earn a livelihood exclusively from the theater. Neither succeeded: Dunlap went bankrupt in 1805 after an unprofitable twenty-year career as a playwright, manager, and director, and Payne earned so little from his adaptations that he landed in a London debtors' prison.

American copyright statute further inhibited a proprietary view of plays. The law was far more disadvantageous for the early dramatist than for the fiction writer. Although plays could be copyrighted by individuals, in reality they belonged more to the community than to their authors. Until 1856, playwrights had no legal control over public performances of their works, and no recourse to prevent others from staging and profiting from them. Once a play was published and made generally available, anything could happen to it. Tyler's *The Contrast* was picked up by theater companies throughout the country and produced with unauthorized changes in plot and dialogue, additional songs, and revised titles like *The Contrast; or, the American Son of Liberty*. Nor did the printed version of a play necessarily show respect for the author's intentions. Several early dramas survive only as prompt copies, indicating that they were probably amended during rehearsal and were as much the creation of the company as the playwright. The holder of the copyright for the 1826 edition of Barker's *Marmion* was M. Lopez, "Prompter of the Philadelphia and Baltimore Theatres."

In a sense, the legal situation in the federal period was truer to the drama's collaborative character than more restrictive modern statutes made it. Dramas, even when technically written by a single person, are almost always joint efforts in their production. In addition to their adding or dropping lines, actors may introduce unintended inflections and gestures; directors may choose to shorten or lengthen entire scenes, or to eliminate them altogether; and the physical structures of playhouses dictate changes in setting and stage directions. The "author" of Romantic and individualist ideology, understood as a solitary creator with proprietary control over the product of his or her labor, is plainly inadequate to a cooperative venture like the theater.

Their problematic status as authorial property deterred publication of early American plays and so underlined, as it were, the genre's nature as an oral art form. In the absence of stage copyright, playwrights could best protect their interests by keeping their works in manuscript. Partly for this reason, and also because published plays were so unprofitable in general, there was a high incidence of perishability among early dramas. Again, the divergence from fiction was as pronounced as the similarity. Unlike novels, many plays never made it into print; they reached the public only as evanescent verbal performances. Countless theatrical works have consequently disappeared, among them plays by some of the leading authors of the time. *The Contrast* opened to acclaim at New York's John Street Theater in 1787 and immortalized Tyler as the Republic's first important dramatist; but the fame of his maiden effort did not lead to the publication of his later ventures into playwriting. At least two of Tyler's other plays, *May Day in Town* (1787) and *The Georgia Spec* (1797), were produced but have not been preserved, and the texts of four more remained in manuscript for a century and a half, until their discovery and publication in 1941. Rowson is known to have written a comic opera on the Whisky Rebellion, an adaptation of a Philip Massinger play, and a farce about Americans abroad. The only dramatic piece of hers to survive is *Slaves in Algiers*. Dunlap wrote his first drama, *The Modest Soldier,* in 1787, after seeing *The Contrast;* it has vanished along with most of his comedies, adaptations, and afterpieces.

Another effect of the drama's persistent amateurism was to discourage playwriting altogether. Dunlap supported himself as a painter after his bankruptcy and wrote only a few additional dramas, "receiving," as he put it in his *History of the American Theatre,* "meagre compensation for poor commodities." In the *History,* Dunlap applauded the playwriting competitions instituted by celebrated performers such as Edwin Forrest as a solution to the difficulties of native talent. But in actuality these contests, in which a star would offer prize money for the best original drama and then acquire the rights, often compounded the financial hardships of the author. Robert Montgomery Bird, the most gifted American dramatist of a slightly later generation, received but a single payment from Forrest for plays that proved enduring hits and enriched the actor. An exasperated Bird abandoned the theater for fiction, confiding to his diary, "What a fool I was to think of writing plays! To be sure, they are much wanted. But these novels are much easier sorts of things and immortalize one's pocket much sooner."

The theater's tardiness in becoming a self-supporting profession was matched by a reluctance to accept the primacy of individualistic values in theme. The genre's bond to the public sphere persisted long after independence, restricting the ennoblement of private concerns, and plays on civic subjects remained in great demand among American audiences well into the nineteenth century. Three revealing illustrations span the early national period. Composed in 1787, 1798, and 1818, respectively, the three plays are Tyler's *The Contrast*, Dunlap's *André*, and Payne's *Brutus*. As the first work by an American to achieve success on the English stage, Payne's piece can be considered the dramatic counterpart to Irving's *The Sketch Book* (1819–20) and Cooper's *The Spy*, yet it shares more in common with its generic predecessors than with those innovative fictions. The three plays exhibit remarkable continuity in their conception of exemplary character and in their allegiance to the ideal of public-spiritedness.

For all its echoes of contemporaneous English drama, *The Contrast* is a distinctively and memorably American work, "A piece," as Tyler's prologue boasts, "which we may fairly call our own." It introduces the first stage Yankee in our literature, the comic and fiercely democratic Jonathan – "I am Colonel Manly's waiter," he insists, objecting when he's called a servant – and it teems with references to the postwar scene, to Shays's Rebellion, the Marquis de Lafayette, the popular actor Thomas Wignell, revolutionary war certificates, and the latest French fashions. The play also takes up some of the leading cultural controversies of the time. It transforms the conventional drawing room comedy into a resonant satire on the debate between luxury and virtue. *The Contrast* deviates from British tradition in being a satire with a reforming spirit: although poking gentle fun at the staunchly republican Colonel Manly, Tyler admires and promotes the values he represents. Manly's speech on the fall of the Greek republics in act 3, a collapse he attributes to the erosion of civic virtue, is a summary of the early drama's central emphases. Manly warns against the idea, propounded by "the tribe of Mandevilles, . . . that a nation, to become great, must first become dissipated," and he calls upon his countrymen to shun the privatism and bickering that brought about the destruction of Greek liberty: "The common good was lost in the pursuit of private interest; and that people, who by uniting, might have stood against the world in arms, by dividing, crumbled into ruin."

Manly's fear of internal discord highlights a more topical and immediate political concern of *The Contrast,* one shaped by the circumstances surrounding the play's composition in March of 1787, just weeks before the first session of the Constitutional Convention. The catalyst for that gathering, as for Tyler's presence in New York, was the armed insurrection by a group of disaffected farmer-debtors in western Massachusetts. Respectable opinion was unanimous in seeing Daniel Shays, the rebellion's leader, as a designing demagogue who turned the heads of his followers with false promises of easy credit and the forgiveness of their debts. Luxury and foreign influence were blamed for having corrupted the rebels, many of them revolutionary war veterans; after they surrendered, they were required to take a loyalty oath renouncing "all allegiance, subjection, and obedience to the King, Queen, or Government of Great Britain." Tyler, who served with the expedition sent to quell the uprising, was in New York City on a related mission when visits to the John Street Theater inspired him to try his hand at playwriting. The figure of Daniel Shays thus stands in the background of both the new nation's first significant cultural achievement and its founding political document. (Shays also provoked several Connecticut Wits into publishing *The Anarchiad* [1786–7], a tirade in rhyming couplets that attacks the farmers as a lawless "debtor crew.") *The Contrast* uses comedy to defuse the threat that the delegates in Philadelphia countered with the federal Constitution.

For Tyler, the hypocrisy and intrigue of New York social life are the humorous metropolitan analogue to the insurrectionary plotting in the provinces. Whig Sentimentalism drew an equation between attacks on liberty and rape; and by the 1780s those who courted the multitude had replaced the British in the lexicon of sexual violation. "Democracy is Lovelace," as John Adams put it, "and the people are Clarissa. The artful villain will pursue the innocent young girl to her ruin and her death." Tyler's heroine, Maria Van Rough, similarly – if rather mysteriously at first – conflates sexual and political misconduct when she denounces the seducer Dimple as

a depraved wretch, whose only virtue is a polished exterior; who is actuated by the unmanly ambition of conquering the defenseless; whose heart, insensible to the emotions of patriotism, dilates at the plaudits of every unthinking girl; whose laurels are the sighs and tears of the miserable victims of his specious behaviour.

What becomes clear is that this "Lovelace without [the] wit" is also a Daniel Shays in dandy's garb, a dissembler who "insinuate[s]" himself into people's "good graces" with outrageous flattery while he manipulates them to his advantage. Dimple is an Anglicized version of the "new men" disliked and feared by the elite; he has changed his name from Van Dumpling to conceal his modest origins and gotten deeply into debt through his extravagance. His particular prey are the city's belles, who make easy victims because they share his relish for "invidious attacks on the rights and characters of others." Dimple woos the women as a demagogue does the masses, by paying false addresses to their faces and then abusing them behind their backs.

Just as John Adams equates the people with Clarissa, Tyler implies a comparison of the postrevolutionary populace to fickle womanhood. The analogy points to the need for commanding men and vigorous central government. "Who is it that considers the helpless situation of our sex," Maria asks rhetorically, "that does not see we each moment stand in need of a protector, and that a brave one too." *The Contrast* favors the kind of strong ruling power personified by Colonel Manly and established in the political world by the Constitution. It champions a polity of deference in which a feminized public yields authority to "manly" leaders who thwart self-seeking upstarts through the practice of Roman virtue.

Yet at the same time Tyler's play takes a trusting and optimistic view of feminine – and popular – judgment. Far from belittling the female sex, Colonel Manly believes in the "antiquated, anti-gallant" notion of speaking one's thoughts honestly to a woman. "He said once in my presence," his fashionable sister Charlotte complains, "in a room full of company – would you believe it – in a large circle of ladies, that the best evidence a gentleman could give a young lady of his respect and affection, was, to endeavour in a friendly manner to rectify her foibles." A moderate Federalist, Tyler expresses comparable faith in the public's capacity to accept and learn from constructive criticism. In the prologue to *The Contrast,* he declares to his audience:

> Let not light Censure on your faults, offend,
> Which aims not to expose them, but amend.
> Thus does our Author to your candour trust;
> Conscious, the free are generous, as just.

At the play's ending, the ladies and the people jointly vindicate such confidence by showing that they can appreciate genuine merit and tolerate correction of their shortcomings. Charlotte repents her infatuation with Dimple, and Manly secures "the good graces of his fair countrywoman" in winning the hand of Maria. In a final gesture to the audience, Tyler has Manly request "the applause of THE PUBLIC"; American theatergoers responded by making *The Contrast* the first hit play of the American stage to deal with native themes.

Manly represents the ideal leader for yet another reason: along with Maria, he is the most "feeling" of Tyler's characters, and he combines sentiment with civic-mindedness. In seduction novels like *Charlotte Temple* and *The Coquette,* the capacity for intense affect is concentrated in (though not confined to) the female. Extreme sensibility typically proves to be a wayward trait, causing the heroine to put private and individual needs ahead of others. It misleads Charlotte Temple into forsaking her filial obligations and running off with Montraville. Eliza Wharton, who similarly yields to her feelings, rejects the counsel of family and friends and strays into an illicit affair with a married scoundrel. In both cases, indulgence of emotions marks a step toward female autonomy, but independence disrupts older loyalties to the group and comes at the cost of self-destruction.

The Contrast is the first in a series of native plays that can be read as masculine rebuttals to the novel's feminizing of sentiment. By reconfiguring sensibility as a male quality, Tyler brings it into the public realm and assimilates it to the drama's civic aims. Indeed, sensibility becomes a political virtue in itself in *The Contrast,* the reassuring evidence of humanity in the otherwise austere and self-denying leader. Colonel Manly invokes George Washington as his model in selfless patriotism, and he has striven to imitate the Virginian by exposing his "health and life in the service of [his] country, without reaping any other reward than the glory of conquering in so arduous a contest." This veteran officer also has "a susceptible heart" and can speak "the language of sentiment" as fluently as anyone. He refers ardently to his parents as the "authors of my existence," thinks of the "brave old soldiers" he served with as his "family," and "has a tear for every pitiful" object. Manly is the man of virtue as the man of feeling, a figure for whom emotional intensity is compatible with the larger interests of society. He inaugurates a major dramatic trend as the public-spirited alternative to the seduced heroines of early fiction. His stage descendants include Dunlap's Washington and Payne's Junius Brutus, later hero-leaders who at once stand firm for the commonweal and weep for the human cost of single-minded devotion to the nation.

In *André* the conflict between feelings and duty, the essential matter of the seduction novel, takes an explicitly civic form. Bland – the name is an ironic misnomer – is a kind of Charlotte Temple of the public sphere. Highly emotional and often unthinking in his behavior, he allows his judgment to be clouded by affection for André, the man who saved his life when he was a British prisoner. Bland keeps pleading for clemency for his friend without weighing the consequences to the American cause. At the opposite pole stands the hardened veteran M'Donald, who regards André's execution as necessary to discourage treason and demonstrate firmness to the British. A man who unhesitatingly elevates country over personal sentiments, M'Donald has no sympathy for the condemned spy and dismisses Bland's appeal as tainted by gratitude. It is not disinterested virtue but love of self, he tells Bland, that leads you to esteem a Briton who "sav'd thy life, yet strove to damn thy country."

George Washington emerges as the play's golden mean between the extremes of Bland's emotionalism and M'Donald's pitiless sense of duty. Washington agrees with M'Donald that the national interest requires André's death, but he recognizes the young captive's merits and feels keenly the tragedy of the situation. A series of moving pleas, culminating in a particularly tearful one from André's fiancée, shakes his resolve: turning away to hide his eyes, the general confesses that his "heart is torn in twain." At this point, Washington seems about to succumb to temptation like any sentimental heroine, but Dunlap, having established his hero's compassion, has him resist the pull of the emotions and reaffirm the primacy of the communal welfare. News of a British atrocity recalls Washington to his duty – "Why, why, my country, did I hesitate?" he exclaims – and he allows the sentence of execution to be carried out. Five years later, when Dunlap rewrote *André* as the patchwork *Glory of Columbia,* he amplified the original drama's civic focus by creating a collective hero, the nation's yeomanry. The rustics who capture André move to the center of the action as the popular equivalent of Washington. In contrast to Benedict Arnold, the turncoat who betrays his country with the statement, "Perish the public good! My private welfare henceforth be my aim," the farmer-heroes show their republican virtue by decisively spurning André's bribe of gold.

Payne's *Brutus* seems still another rewrite of *André,* with the antique Roman replacing Washington as the suffering but finally unyielding patriot. Though Payne composed the play for an English audience, his protagonist had special significance for Americans as a model for their own revolutionary struggle. Republicans esteemed Brutus as the man who had overthrown the Tarquin kings and restored Rome to freedom. Like Addison's *Cato,* the comparable piece for eighteenth-century theatergoers, *Brutus* abounds in easily remembered civic aphorisms, such as "where all are slaves, / None but the fool is happy" and "Great things may yet be done, / If we are men, and faithful to our country."

Payne's Brutus is confronted with a quandary similar to but even more wrenching than that faced by Dunlap's Washington. He has to decide whether to spare or execute his own son Titus, an apolitical young man who loves Tarquinia, the tyrant's daughter, and fights on the side of Rome's enemies. Payne takes the familiar plot of the sentimental novel, with its blocking parent and frustrated lovers, politicizes it, and inverts the usual order of preferences. Instead of vindicating the young couple, the play justifies the father's sternness in opposing his son's wishes. "Let me lose / In those dear arms, the very name of son," cries Titus to his mistress; but with Rome groaning under the Tarquins, his readiness to forsake family and country in his preoccupation with love seems self-indulgent and ignoble, and he forfeits any lingering sympathy when he joins the forces of the monarchy. After

Titus's capture by the victorious republicans, Tarquinia begs for his life in speeches extolling romantic love over civic obligation. Brutus replies, "Be woman e'er so beauteous, man was made / For nobler uses than to be her slave." Again, the drama repudiates the novel's feminized sentimentalism: although Brutus proves susceptible to emotions, he masters his anguish to uphold Roman justice. "The sovereign magistrate of Rome / Condemns / A crime, thy father's bleeding heart forgives," the otherwise severe hero sobs to his son. A moment later his grief forces Brutus to turn away, "convulsed with agitation," as the curtain falls on the signal for Titus's death.

The drama's power to contain emotionalism and channel it toward civic purposes was more beleaguered in 1818 than in 1787, as the overheated final moment of Payne's play suggests. Thereafter, Payne alternated political works with tearful domestic melodramas. A collaborator with Washington Irving on *Charles the Second* (1824) and *Richelieu* (1826), he also penned the century's most popular song about domesticity, "Home, Sweet Home," an air from his musical *Clari; or, the Maid of Milan* (1823). Public life itself acquired a more histrionic coloring at this time: the first quarter of the nineteenth century saw the emergence of the Romantic style in American politics. The consanguinity between politics and the drama now assumed forms that a strict republican like Rousseau would have regarded as peculiarly troubling. Rousseau had feared that the actor's inauthenticity, his concern with performance above truthfulness, would infiltrate the civic zone if the theater were permitted in a republic. In the liberal society evolving after the War of 1812, democratic and market realities gave increased importance to a speaker's drawing power. Content receded before magnetism as the desideratum of a politician, and aspiring orators were urged to look to the stage for lessons on how to captivate an audience.

No one argued the point more vigorously than William Wirt, the biographer of Patrick Henry. The Virginia patriot had been admired by some as the country's greatest public speaker and reviled by others as a crafty rabble-rouser. Wirt sought to package Henry as a political model for the present. Because the Virginian spoke extemporaneously, few of his actual words had been preserved; Wirt's orator as actor was as much a construction of the emergent Romantic sensibility as Ahab or Uncle Tom. Wirt believed that "the pulpit, senate and bar" should draw inspiration from "master performers" like Thomas Cooper, a tragedian who had starred at Dunlap's Park Theater. Wirt praised Henry for his ability to spellbind spectators with the sure touch of an accomplished actor. According to his biographer, Henry did not so much persuade his listeners with rational demonstration as sweep them away emotionally with his electrifying delivery and eloquence. Witnesses reported that Henry's performances "made their blood run cold, and their hair to rise on end." Wirt's Henry heralded both the triumph of a perfervid oratorical style and the theatricalization of American politics. For Henry, each public occasion was "a new theatre" in which to display his talents; as Wirt put it in summarizing his subject's achievement, "he was SHAKESPEARE and GARRICK combined!"

Wirt's *Sketches of the Life and Character of Patrick Henry* appeared in 1817, near the end of the early national period, but one has to go beyond that time, to the last days of the Civil War, to appreciate fully the darker ironies of the drama—politics connection in American life. On Good Friday, 1865, Abraham Lincoln was assassinated while attending a performance of *Our American Cousin* at Washington's Ford's Theater. Lincoln's killer was John Wilkes Booth, a southern sympathizer and disaffected actor. Some witnesses claimed that as Booth leapt to the stage from the balcony where he shot the president, he cried out, "*Sic semper tyrannus!*" (Thus always to tyrants!), as though he were a latter-day Roman patriot. (The phrase is the state motto of Virginia, the leader of the Confederacy.) Booth's background suggests why such an exclamation might have resonated for him. With his brother Edwin, the foremost American actor of the antebellum years, he had performed in Shakespeare's *Julius Caesar,* a play native audiences interpreted as a defense of tyrannicide. His fiercely republican father was a distinguished actor in his own right, a popular English tragedian who had emigrated to the United States in 1821 and named John Wilkes after the London libertarian revered as a hero by the revolutionary generation. The father's name was Junius Brutus Booth; a favorite role, one he made virtually his own, was that of the title character in Payne's *Brutus; or The Fall of Tarquin.* Theater and politics were inextricable when the son chose a playhouse in which to perform the same role in reality on that April evening at the close of the Civil War.

4

☙

POETRY

L IKE THE DRAMA, eighteenth-century poetry was a public and didactic art. The practice of publishing verse in newspapers, common throughout the formative period, bespoke both the topicality of poetic discourse and, what was closely related, its embeddedness in the life of the nation. Poetry seldom dealt with private imaginings and personal emotions. Rather, it concerned itself with the kind of widely known information that was reported in the press: warfare, politics, the deaths of eminent individuals, and other public matters. Poetry had a social identity, and it shared in communal existence as a regular feature in newspapers and magazines, at college commencements and Fourth of July celebrations, and on city streets where it was hawked in broadside.

This accent on the community was strengthened by the poetic influences Americans absorbed from the English tradition. Early poets who enjoyed special popularity in the Republic included William Shakespeare and John Milton, both of whom were interpreted by Americans as writing on public themes, Shakespeare as a foe of tyranny, Milton as a friend of religious liberty and the author of the modern era's greatest epic. The Augustan, or neoclassical, style, at its height in England during the first half of the eighteenth century, held sway in the United States throughout the early years of independence. Emerging after the pietistic extremities and startling linguistic turns of the metaphysicals, neoclassicism moved away from intense and idiosyncratic expression toward "correctness" and regularity. The poetry of Alexander Pope, James Thomson, John Dryden, and Jonathan Swift – the first in particular revered in America – addressed social and political issues with the goal of inculcating proper attitudes. Satire, which assumes a community of values, replaced the personalized lyric as the age's preferred form. Americans found these emphases congenial to their own efforts to construct both a national poetry and a poetry that aimed to legitimate the nation. Although tradition, even a tradition that downplays subjectivity, can and in England obviously did nurture distinctive talents, in America neoclassical technique worked less to encourage originality than to submerge the individual voice.

Public in theme, poetry proved resistant to privatizing in other respects too. Americans acquired two dominant images of the poet from the English past: the impoverished versifier and the gentlemanly amateur composing quatrains in his leisure. Arguably, neither image was suited to an industrious people without an established nobility, but the second model was compatible with both republicanism and neoclassicism – in England, the form of "high," or elite, culture – and it remained influential in the young nation. The beggarly poet was not unknown to Americans, at least as a type, but the figure hardly recommended poetry, as we know from Benjamin Franklin's *Autobiography*. Franklin, an unwavering friend of the novel, briefly tried his hand at ballads but abandoned the effort when his father admonished him that "Verse-makers were generally Beggars." Both symbols conveyed an important truth about early verse: it adapted slowly to professionalization and never attained the market appeal of the newer and more "liberal" novel. People listened to poetry on ceremonial occasions, and they read it in newspapers, but not many of them bought it. Poets, whether patricians or beggars, had little prospect of earning money from their writings.

To be sure, other voices and other versions of the poet did emerge in this epoch to challenge the public ethos. American poetry participated, with a lag of some years, in the paradigm shift from neoclassic to Romantic that marked English verse in the second half of the eighteenth century. Even at the beginning of our period, the Augustan was far from the only available style. The cultural lag was in certain ways productive, enabling some writers to bypass prevailing models and freeing others to welcome unorthodox developments. American poetry was surprisingly pluralistic, encompassing residual forms, experimental meter, a receptivity to the sentimental and colloquial, and a private mood anticipatory of Romanticism. Women poets, African Americans, and aspiring professionals were also much in evidence, although most wrote verse shaped by the ruling orientation toward the formal. Nevertheless, the existence of this more heterogeneous and individualistic strain gives early American poetry an occasionally schizophrenic quality that prefigures the later split in the culture represented by those two originals, Emily Dickinson and Walt Whitman, on the one side, and the public and didactic Fireside Poets on the other. The infant Republic's representative poet, Philip Freneau, was typical precisely in his inability to resolve these conflicting impulses.

George Washington, the towering figure of the public sphere, had an even more extensive association with poetry than with the drama. The "American Maecenas," Washington encouraged native verse through direct patronage – he subscribed for twenty copies of Joel Barlow's *The Vision of Columbus* (1787) – by permitting authors to dedicate their works to him, and simply by being "Columbia's fav'rite son," the national soldier-statesman whose exploits could be recorded in song. Washington personified the Republic, and poems about him were collective celebrations. His death in 1799 called forth the greatest outpouring of elegies and verse orations in American history; virtually every town and newspaper in the country took poetic notice of his passing.

Verses on Washington's death resembled most contemporaneous poems in that they were pedagogic and rhetorical, summoning listeners to draw a lesson or pursue some action. Apart from being in meter and rhyme, poetry did not seek to differentiate itself from other forms of discourse. Verse was the servant of morality and politics, capable of making their precepts "more deeply felt and more lastingly remembered," in Timothy Dwight's words from the introduction to *Greenfield Hill* (1794). Barlow's directions for serving *The Hasty-Pudding* (1793) were the era's recipe for verse: "with molasses line the luscious treat, / And mix, like Bards, the useful with the sweet." (Barlow was paraphrasing Horace, whose influential *Ars Poetica* stipulated that literature should impart both amusement and instruction.) Poets insisted on the primacy of their communitarian goals. "My first wish," said Mercy Otis Warren about her verse tragedy "The Sack of Rome" (published in her *Poems, Dramatic and Miscellaneous* [1790]), "is to throw a mite into the scale of virtue"; and Barlow declared of *The Columbiad* (1807), "My object is altogether of a moral and political nature." Just as they integrated the aesthetic with the rhetorical in their writings, so poets combined their literary careers with other vocations. Among other examples, John Trumbull was a judge, Barlow and David Humphreys were diplomats, and Freneau held jobs as a postal clerk, a newspaper editor, and, for much of his life, a ship's captain.

The Washington elegies, like most poetry of the age, were composed for a specific occasion. The inspiration for rhyme usually lay outside the inner life of the poet in events of public moment or in commissions bestowed by colleges, patriotic bodies, and other institutions. Among the most popular occasions for verse were military engagements: in the wartime year of 1781, Freneau alone published poems commemorating the surrender of Lord Cornwallis, the bloody battle at Eutaw Springs, and the victory of *Le Bon Homme Richard* over the *Seraphis*. Poems written "to order" were joint fabrications of the author and his audience-purchasers, whose requirements might determine the choice of subject or theme. Such poems were further evidence of the genre's refusal to separate itself from communal experience. Robert Treat Paine, now forgotten but once celebrated among New England's Brahmins, did his writing almost exclusively at the request of others. His works include a piece commissioned by the Boston Female Asylum on the sorrows of orphan girls and an "Ode. The Street Was a Ruin" that the Massachusetts

Charitable Fire Society sponsored in 1804 to memorialize the extinguishing of a conflagration.

Audiences also took part in the production of verse through subscription publishing, which was far more common for poetry than for either drama or the novel. Because books of poetry sold poorly as a rule, such arrangements were necessary to recoup manufacturing costs. The usual practice of printing a list of subscribers, sometimes running for ten or more pages, at the front or back of the volume, conferred publicity on the buyers as patrons of the arts. Typographically, the idea of the unique creator receded; indeed, subscribers often received more billing than the poet who may have disclaimed authorship by concealing his or her name.

Audience involvement with poetry was not limited to the relatively few whose names appeared on subscription lists. In its popular oral forms, like the ballad and the song, the poetry of the early Republic helped to forge a sense of nationhood by binding people together in the common expression of patriotic sentiments. These poems were meant to be sung in groups, as collective speech; structural elements like the refrain or the use of simple repetition, as in the anonymous "Ballad of Nathan Hale" (1776), invited listeners to join in:

> Five minutes were given, short moments, no more,
> For him to repent; for him to repent.
> He prayed for his mother, he asked not another,
> To Heaven he went; to Heaven he went.

Not all popular verse originated in oral tradition or flowed from unknown pens. A signer of the Declaration of Independence, Francis Hopkinson, based a ballad, "The Battle of the Kegs" (1778), on an incident from the revolutionary war; and Susanna Rowson, as versatile a poet as a novelist, was the author of a well-known drinking song, "America, Commerce and Freedom" (1794). The air that Americans still sing together (though it is virtually unsingable) dates from a few years later: during the War of 1812, while watching a British bombardment, Francis Scott Key composed the occasional verses that became the national anthem.

Poetry in this epoch enjoyed an intimate relation to national consciousness. What became for many later writers a willed yoking together of dissimilar, or even antagonistic, categories, was for the postrevolutionary generation a natural union of allies. Poetry's duty to the Republic was twofold. First, a great people produced great poetry; they had their own literature just as they had their own political system and rulers. Verse would build pride in the United States as an independent nation equal to – or rather the superior of – the kingdoms of Europe. Poetry by Americans would vindicate the theory of *translatio,* the belief that the English Empire and its arts would be "translated" westward and that the New World would rapidly surpass the Old. The theory antedated the revolutionary war – its roots stretch back to antiquity – and it was popularized by the English themselves, most famously by George Berkeley when he announced in 1752, "Westward the Course of Empire takes its Way." Timothy Dwight was one of numerous American poets who adapted Berkeley's theme (and echoed his language):

> Columbia, Columbia, to glory arise,
> The queen of the world, and the child of the skies!
> Thy genius commands thee; with rapture behold,
> While ages on ages thy splendors unfold.
> Thy reign is the last, and the noblest of time,
> Most fruitful thy soil, most inviting thy clime;
> Let the crimes of the east ne'er encrimson thy name;
> Be freedom, and science, and virtue, thy fame.

As Dwight's lines (from "Columbia" [1778?]) suggest, poetry also had an obligation to articulate the distinctiveness of the young nation. As a newly created entity, the United States stood in urgent need of definition and legitimation. Poetry would assign meaning to the word "America"; it would explain the nation to its own citizens and to the world. In making evident and celebrating the Republic's special virtues, poetry would create a sense of national identity. It was no accident that poets ran for office and served as legislators, for they were intimately involved in formulating the nation. Poems were founding documents in meter and rhyme, belletristic analogues to the Declaration and the Constitution. Thomas Jefferson, author of the former document, also wrote an iconoclastic treatise on prosody. The transition came naturally because Jefferson regarded poetry and the polity as complementary undertakings.

Many people felt that poetry had the same kind of patriotic work to do in American culture as it had performed in the classical past. Writers wanted to produce a native epic that would immortalize the Republic's achievements and rival the *Iliad* and the *Aeneid;* hence the proliferation of poems with "iad" in the title. These works traced the history of freedom from its birth in ancient Greece and Rome to its flowering in the New World; they detailed the course of American settlement; and they reviewed the climactic events of the struggle for independence, from the Stamp Act, through the Boston Massacre and Valley Forge, to the Treaty of Paris. Barlow's was the most ambitious attempt at a heroic verse narrative: when he rewrote his *Vision of Columbus* as *The Columbiad,* he gave it the Virgilian opening, "I sing the Mariner who first unfurl'd / An eastern banner o'er the western world." Barlow saw his work as a corrective to the pernicious political doctrines propounded by Homer and Virgil, both of whom supported monarchy and "have unhappily done more harm than good." Other would-be epic poets contrasted their own fidelity to fact to the ancients' addiction to overstatement. The modern epic, like the novel, professed an allegiance to "Truth"; its aim was to honor actual persons and occurrences. Preservation of the national heritage curbed the writer's imagination. "Then hence vain *fiction* from the deathless theme," as Sarah Wentworth Morton put it in her *Beacon Hill* (1797), "And hence the rapt bard's visionary dream!"

The importance of the individual artist once again receded in such circumstances. Anticipating Joel Barlow, Richard Snowden, later to achieve recognition as a historian, published an epic titled *The Columbiad; or, A Poem on the American War* in 1795. Snowden welcomed the prospect of being overshadowed by a better poet. His work appeared without his name and without a copyright; innocent of "all vanity as an Author, Poet, or Historian," he hoped only that his slight verses on "the great events that brought about the *American Revolution*" would "prove a stimulus to some one more favoured of the Muses, who will undertake the arduous task, and carry it through upon a more extensive scale." While keeping himself out of view, Snowden gave prominence to the collectivity. In thirteen cantos, one for each state, he managed to pay tribute to literally scores of patriots who had contributed to independence, from Washington and John Adams to the "valiant" Major Samuel Hugg.

Besides the classics, Americans drew upon the Scriptures and English literature in their desire to give honorific expression to the Republic. Particularly as relations with Britain worsened, poets revived the typological narrative of the seventeenth and early eighteenth centuries in which Americans figured as a new chosen people fleeing oppression for the promised land. When Freneau and Hugh Henry Brackenridge collaborated on "A Poem on the Rising Glory of America" for the Princeton commencement of 1771, they concluded with a millennial prophecy of the kind heard routinely on this continent for one hundred and fifty years: "A *Canaan* here, / Another *Canaan* shall excel the old, / And from a fairer Pisgah's top be seen." Another poet, James Allen, was roused by the Boston Massacre to issue a biblical warning to George III: "Stay, Pharaoh, stay: that impious hand forbear, / Nor tempt the genius of our souls too far." And Dwight answered the demand for an American epic by casting Washington as Joshua and allegorizing the Revolution as the Israelite *Conquest of Canaan* (1785).

Dwight's poem borrowed its heroic couplets from the Augustans and its exalted tone from Milton, confirming that for all its nationalistic fervor, native verse remained thoroughly indebted to English models. Dwight was perhaps more oblivious than most to the paradox involved: the original plan for *Greenfield Hill,* his chauvinistic paean to New England rural life, called for him "to imitate, in the several parts, the manner of as many British Poets." No one escaped the influence of Pope, whose mastery of the rhymed couplet inspired countless American followers. Pope's hold was so far-reaching that even admirers, like a reviewer in the *Monthly Anthology and Boston Review* in 1805, protested against the prevalence of hackwork imitation: "The artisan of verses has only to resort to his work, in which . . . may be found every musical and every graceful phrase, which our language affords, and the manufacture of harmonious lines becomes the easiest thing in the world."

The overwhelming preference for the canonical in meter and rhyme went beyond the influence of any single writer. Americans did cultural work with the tools at hand, and high technique conferred some of the luster associated with past greatness. American verse tended to be as derivative in metrics as it was in subject and form. Most poets followed tradition in their adherence to rhymed couplets or to familiar quatrain schemes like *a b a b* and *a b b a.* They operated within the dominant metrical system of English-language verse, the iambic, with its alternation of unstressed and stressed syllables, and they employed the standard measures of four or five feet per line, the hexameter or the pentameter. Even when they eschewed rhyme, poets usually remained within the canonical discipline. Like other American imitators of Shakespeare, Mercy Otis Warren used blank verse in iambic pentameter to create her historical dramas "The Sack of Rome" and "The Ladies of Castile."

The group of writers known as the Connecticut Wits (also called the Hartford Wits) epitomized the reigning spirit of early American poetry. The major members were Trumbull, Dwight, Barlow, and Humphreys; lesser figures included Lemuel Hopkins, Richard Alsop, and Elihu Hubbard Smith, the friend of Charles Brockden Brown and editor of the first general anthology of native verse, *American Poems* (1793). The Wits were representative in their very identity as a group, which gave their works, even when written separately, the character of a collective enterprise. In actuality, varying combinations of them did collaborate on several poems of a topical and highly partisan nature: *The Anarchiad* (1786–7), a mock-heroic epic directed against Daniel Shays and the social unrest of postrevolutionary New England; and *The Echo* (1791–1805), a satire of contemporary newspaper style that developed into an attack on the "infidel ideas of the French Revolution." Their sense of themselves as a poetic community led the Wits to compose verse epistles to each other (Humphreys and Dwight), to paraphrase each other's language, and to incorporate praise for each other in their works (Barlow's *Vision of Columbus*).

The Wits were public poets who sought to further the common welfare through both their careers and their writings. One of them, Humphreys, was aide-de-camp to Washington during the Revolution, and a second, Barlow, gave his life to the civic realm; he died in Poland while on a diplomatic mission to Napoleon. All the Wits wrote patriotic and didactic verse in rhymed couplets, from Trumbull's *M'Fingal* (1775), a Hudibrastic satire of the Tories (and, secondarily, of the Whig rabble); to Humphreys's *A Poem Addressed to the Armies of the United States of America* (1780), an elevated verse oration designed to strengthen troop morale; to the epics of Dwight and Barlow. Trumbull was the first of the group to become known, with the publication in 1772 of Part I of *The Progress of Dulness,* a satire of higher education featuring the misadventures of a ministerial student named Tom Brainless. Trumbull, then a tutor at Yale, wanted the college curriculum to assign more weight to "useful learning" and less to unthinking idolatry of the classics:

> Oh! might I live to see that day,
> When sense shall point to youths their way
>
> . . . .
>
> Give ancient arts their real due,
> Explain their faults, and beauties too;
> Teach where to imitate, and mend,
> And point their uses and their end.

Expanded into three parts in 1773, Trumbull's poem also targeted clerical incompetence and the deficiencies of female education, which restricted women's reading to "Novels and plays, (where shines display'd / A world that nature never made)."

Trumbull brought out *The Progress of Dulness* anonymously, a patrician affectation he shared with several of the Wits. Dwight hedged on anonymity, sometimes signing his works, sometimes not; he commonly held his works back from publication for years after writing them, to maintain the pose of indifference to fame and money. With the exception of Barlow, the son of a Connecticut farmer, the Wits were gentlemen of letters with conservative politics to match. They inhabited the upper stratum of the republican, deferential, and relatively cohesive social order of New England in the late eighteenth century. This world was already showing fissures when they began writing, but the Wits remained loyal to its values and looked askance at such signs of its dissolution as individualism and the commercializing of culture. All save Barlow were ardent, life-long Federalists who combined a strong sense of regionalism with contempt for the Jeffersonians as the party of slaveholders and parvenus.

These conservative sentiments were evident as early as *M'Fingal,* whose diatribes against the revolutionary mob, though uttered by a Tory, later provided verbal ammunition for Federalists in their attacks on Shaysites and Republicans. Works like Dwight's *Greenfield Hill* and Humphreys's *A Poem on the Industry of the United States of America* (1804), celebrations of local customs and countryside, set forth the Wits' vision of a static, middling society untroubled by capitalist development. (The "industry" in Humphreys's title refers to toil or industriousness, not factory production.) Dwight hymns a Connecticut of "steady habits" and without acquisitiveness, in which the different ranks harmonize yet manage to remain distinct:

> Here every class (if classes those we call,
> Where one extended class embraces all,
> All mingling, as the rainbow's beauty blends,
> Unknown where every hue begins or ends)
> Each following each, with uninvidious strife,
> Wears every feature of improving life.

The Wits believed in a republic, not a democracy, of letters, and they disapproved of literary outsiders as well as of departures from neoclassical propriety. Humphreys, confident like his colleagues that God "ne'er design'd, / Equal conditions for the human kind," took a page from Pope and turned his wit against the intrusion of bounders into literature. In "The Monkey Who Shaved Himself and His Friends," published in 1787 during Shays's Rebellion, he moralizes on a creature that cuts its own gullet:

> Who cannot write, yet handle pens,
> Are apt to hurt themselves and friends.
> Though others use them well, yet fools
> Should never meddle with edge tools.

As these examples illustrate, the Wits' poems approximate each other in style and content, and differentiating between authors often seems impossible; the individual voice is missing.

A writer from the period who does have an aura of individuality is Robert Treat Paine. The author of monodies, odes, addresses, and two well-known pieces commissioned by Harvard University, *The Invention of Letters* (1795) and *The Ruling Passion* (1797), Paine composed public verse in Popean couplets and was much admired by his contemporaries. William Cullen Bryant, writing some years after Paine's death, described him as "a fine but misguided genius" whose work shows more "instances of the false sublime" than any other poet of the period. Bryant recognized an "exuberance of fancy" that struggled in Paine with his commitment to Augustan regularity. A stately, formal manner overlays a straining after extravagant effect. Paine's excessive images seem belatedly metaphysical or – perhaps as accurately – incipiently Romantic. One example among many of his penchant for the overwrought conceit appears in the section on foreign discord from *The Ruling Passion*. May the Atlantic forever separate America from "Europe's storms," Paine writes; or, if a convulsion should somehow send the two continents tottering toward each other, "May Fate the closing empires intervene, / And raise, when Ocean sinks, an Alps between!"

Paine's originality inhered less in his poetry than in his life. His contemporary fame stemmed chiefly from the perception of him as a dissolute, unworldly genius. He came from a distinguished Massachusetts family – his father was a signer of the Declaration and an eminent jurist – and from the time that he was suspended from college for "abusive language," he displayed an aptitude for irregular behavior that both dismayed and fascinated his admirers. After marrying an actress against his family's wishes, he neglected and then forsook a legal career to indulge his "natural indolence" and passions for wine and the theater. His aristocratic manner, air of dissipation, and "truly poetical negligence of attire," as his biographer termed it, made Paine a singular figure in turn-of-the-century Boston. Poverty and illness eventually forced him to seek shelter in his father's attic, where he died at thirty-eight, the casualty, friends believed, of his artistic sensibility.

Paine was America's first *poete maudit,* a forerunner of Edgar Allan Poe, and he performed two symbolic – albeit antithetical – functions in the culture. Most obviously, he confirmed the republican prejudice against the arts as impractical. Lacking all those qualities of industriousness the new nation prized – "no sense of duty, no desire of usefulness, no ambition of renown, could reinspire his inveterate inaction," exclaimed his biographer – Paine's example served as a warning against the danger of becoming an artist. The community had simply to look at him to be reassured about the greater social value of other careers.

Against this monitory role, one has to set the perception of Paine as an aristocrat of the spirit. His persona revealed the gentlemanly amateur mutating into the Romantic renegade, the two images united by their common distance from the material concerns of business civilization. The patriciate clearly had a stake in American culture's hospitableness to such a figure. The investment here was quite literal: Paine enjoyed the patronage of the Brahmin class long after he had forfeited any reasonable claim to it. Their institutions paid handsomely for his work: fifteen hundred dollars from Harvard for *The Invention of Letters* and seven hundred and fifty from the Massachusetts Charitable Fire Society for a Federalist song, "Adams and Liberty" (1798). Paine "proved" that the United States, even as it moved inexorably toward the democratic market society of the nineteenth century, could produce sensitive, eccentric artists who dwelt at a higher level of being than ordinary persons. "If those," his biographer wrote, "who ascend Parnassus, experience a keenness of pleasure, which none but poets know, it is to be presumed that they experience a keenness of sorrow, which none but poets feel." The elite saw in Paine a poetic analogue to their sense of themselves as a superior class – a class that held itself aloof from the scramble for gain overtaking the Republic. They needed him all the more because America, unlike Britain, could boast no actual aristocracy, and because they were proving no more immune than any other group to the lure of the market. Paine's poet as spiritual aristocrat represented the negative image of what his society was evolving into; but it was an image in which a segment of that society found self-justification.

Paine's "romantic," alienated persona, the inverse of his functional public writings, was one of several incarnations of the poet to debut in this era. Another was the professional, or rather, the would-be professional. Although few poets in England or America have ever lived off their writings alone, several in the early Republic tried to be as businesslike as possible about their art. Barlow was an anomaly among the Wits in this as he was in his politics and religious beliefs: a convert to radicalism and deism who shocked his former friends by supporting the French Revolution, he eventually became a celebrant of free-market economics. Barlow was determined to turn his poems into marketable commodities. He campaigned for the Connnecticut copyright law, the nation's first, and strongly backed the movement to give literature the status of private property. Protection for authors was imperative, he argued, in a country without "Gentlemen of fortune sufficient to enable them to spend a whole life in study, or enduce others to do it by their patronage."

In fact, Barlow's career demonstrated the persistence of the patronage system and the futility, even the impossibility, of commodifying verse. He had to spend over four years drumming up subscribers for his *Vision of Columbus* before he could secure enough advance orders to risk going into print. The poem's dedication and list of buyers reveal the mixture of aristocratic and communal elements in this method of publication. The book was dedicated "To His Most Christian Majesty, Louis the Sixteenth, King of France and Navarre," who agreed to take twenty-five copies – a most incongruous sponsor for a work of fervent republicanism. The complete subscription list figuratively encompassed almost the entire nation, in effect making the Republic the patron of *The Vision of Columbus*: in addition to Washington, 768 friends of native culture ordered copies in advance, including Franklin, Lafayette, Alexander Hamilton, Thomas Paine, Aaron Burr, and 117 officers from the revolutionary army, listed according to state. Twenty years later, a fortune made in land speculation enabled Barlow to act as his own patron. He spent lavishly to publish his revised and expanded epic in a handsome, illustrated edition. *The Columbiad* appeared without subscribers and was dedicated magnanimously to "my country," but at a prohibitive price of twenty dollars a copy, it underscored the unmarketability of poetry.

An even more interesting departure from neoclassical models of the bard was David Hitchcock, who like Barlow came from a nonpatrician background. Hitchcock was a shoemaker with little formal education, and he signified fresh possibilities for the culture. In general, one could say that whereas nineteenth-century poets like Emily Dickinson and Walt Whitman derived inspiration from archaic and popular forms, in the more deferential eighteenth century the movement was in the opposite direction, with influence filtering downward from the elite to less established figures. Hitchcock constituted a partial exception to this state of affairs. He brought the issue of class into American poetry. *The Poetical Works of David Hitchcock: Containing the Shade of Plato, Knight and Quack, and the Subtlety of Foxes* (1806) sparked a controversy with the Boston critical establishment over the propriety of admitting artisans into the republic of letters. These initial poems gave scant reason for offense: written in conventional rhymed couplets, they espoused socially conservative opinions that might have been uttered by the Wits. Hitchcock exhibited only one of the usual symptoms of artisan radicalism. In a preface attributed to the publisher but probably written by Hitchcock himself, he insists on his right to express his thoughts in verse despite the condescending objections of those who advised him "to throw away his *pen,* and stick to his *last.*" Uninhibited by gentlemanly pretensions, Hitchcock was candid about wanting to supplement his income as a shoemaker with earnings from his poems. "He appears only to wish, that the joint labours of his head and hands, may procure him a comfortable subsistence."

At this point, Hitchcock represented not so much an original voice as a new presence in American writing, a prophecy of the more democratic culture of the antebellum period, and the literary elite moved quickly to put him in his place. A reviewer for the *Monthly Anthology,* possibly the same writer who a year earlier had reproved the "artisans of verses" spawned by Pope, took exception to the sudden promiscuity of the muses. Inspiration once reserved for refined minds "nourished by solitary thought and unbroken study" was now being felt at the workbench, to the discredit of poetry. "What mysterious connexion, what secret analogy there is, between stitching shoes and making verses, we are at a loss to discover." Because "rhapsodist," the technical Greek term for a reciter of epic poetry, comes from the word for sewing or stitching together, one can only surmise that the reviewer was making a private joke – a joke that would have been appreciated by his classics-educated readers but presumably missed by an autodidact like Hitchcock, thus reemphasizing the shoemaker's unfitness to poeticize. In any case, the battle was joined over deference and democratic self-assertion. The clash reenacted the fictional strife between Captain Farrago and Teague O'Regan in Hugh Henry Brackenridge's *Modern Chivalry,* where the captain invokes the same snobbish principle as Hitchcock's detractors in quashing his servant's social aspirations: "Let the cobbler stick to his last."

Hitchcock had no intention of allowing the *Monthly Anthology* to speak the last word, and this time he did strike a fresh note in his poems, both in technique and in articulating the excluded viewpoint, that of the bogtrotter Teague or Humphreys's monkey (or Pope's dunces). Six years later he was back in print with *The Social Monitor,* a "poetical dictionary" containing versified definitions of concepts like "Happiness," "Liberty," and "Hobbling," the last a term of opprobrium used by the *Anthology* men to censure authors they considered upstarts. In witty, fluent lines, Hitchcock presents himself as a stodgy defender of the status quo, and he feigns horror at the "hobblers" pushing their way into all professions, but most scandalously into letters, "the grand market of refinement." The result, he complains, will be to degrade literature and overturn the social order:

> Suppose, for once, the following case:
> "Young *Crisp,* the cobbler's wrote a book:"
> His chums begin to stare and look:
> "He ne'er knew how to *spell* nor *read:*
> A strange phenomenon! indeed
>
> .   .   .   .
>
> Learning? 'tis all a cheat; a joke!
>
> .   .   .   .
>
> Crisp here has wrote a book, you see;
> We've got some wit as well as he;
> Like him, we'll quit our menial call,
> Abandon *leather, last,* and *awl,*
> Throw off our ordinary dress,
> And cut *across lots* to the press."

"Hobbling" registers a subversive eruption of popular speech into rhymed iambic tetrameter. The poem exemplifies the aesthetic insubordination it pretends to upbraid by conferring legitimacy on the colloquial voice. Although the lower-class speakers' words appear safely enclosed in quotation marks, their point of view spills over into the text as a whole and discredits the guardians of literature as pompous and hysterical.

Hitchcock's notes and preface eschewed irony to accuse the *Anthology* men of setting themselves up as cultural dictators. He appealed beyond them to democracy and to the marketplace – to precisely those forces that genteel critics saw as impeding the growth of American letters. Even hobbling authors, he said, "have their freedom in common with their countrymen";

they are entitled to write books and let the public decide whether to buy or not. Although little is known of Hitchcock's career, he apparently rested the case for his own poetry with the popular audience and had the satisfaction of meeting with some success. None of his books had to be published by the exclusive subscription method, and at least one of them, *The Social Monitor,* sold well enough to go into a second edition in 1814.

Another poet who broke with tradition, though in some ways remaining extremely conventional, was the slave Phillis Wheatley. The most important African-American artist of her time, Wheatley presents a series of paradoxes. Her marginalized status as a slave marked her off from contemporary white writers, but it also heightened certain of her affinities with them, and it simultaneously authorized a degree of self-assertion that confounded republican custom. The discouragement of individualism characteristic of eighteenth-century authorship applied to Wheatley with special force. Far from being a self-owning individualist, she literally belonged to someone else, John Wheatley, a prosperous Boston merchant whose wife Susanna taught the young slave girl to read and write not long after she was purchased in 1761. Even her surname was not her own possession but that of her master, and she was given her Christian name for the slave ship, the *Phillis,* that transported her to America.

Wheatley had to "speak" through the subvention of whites in order to speak at all. Because she had no property or legal identity of her own, she was completely dependent on others to get her poems into print. Her first and only book, *Poems on Various Subjects, Religious and Moral* (1773), had all the earmarks of clientship: besides being published by subscription and dedicated to an English noblewoman, the Countess of Huntingdon, it appeared with an attestation to Wheatley's authorship signed by her master and seventeen prominent Bostonians, including Thomas Hutchinson, James Bowdoin, and John Hancock. Even more than her white compatriots, Wheatley had need of the validation of the canonical, and she closely patterned her work on prevailing forms and styles. The thirty-nine poems were overwhelmingly epideictic (that is, poems of praise) and were derivative in technique, with Pope as the principal influence. The majority were written to commemorate deaths, and just two, "On Virtue" and "To the University of Cambridge in New-England," departed from rhyme for blank verse.

Where Wheatley stood apart was in her insistent emphasis on her own singularity and in her attitude toward her poetry as a potential source of income. She turned the signs of her diminished autonomy, her bondage and blackness, into affirmations of uniqueness, and she used her race in particular to publicize and sell her verses. Even in the *Poems on Various Subjects,* written while she was still a slave, the tokens of her identity are everywhere: in the engraving of her, seated at a writing desk, on the frontispiece; in the identifi-cation of her on the title page as "Phillis Wheatley, Negro Servant to Mr. John Wheatley, of Boston, in New England"; in the attestation that "PHIL-LIS, a young Negro Girl," was the actual author; and in the dozens of poems that call attention to her African origins, often with a muted but unmistak-able sense of racial pride.

These promotional devices achieved their purpose: Wheatley, technically a nonperson, whose very name on the title page was not her own, had an international reputation exceeding that of any American poet before William Cullen Bryant. Moreover, after her manumission forced her to become self-supporting in 1773, she took an active role in the sale of her book. She petitioned booksellers, sold copies herself, and advertised in newspapers, always mentioning her race. Puffing Phillis Wheatley was also promulgating the idea of black worth, and as she continued to write poems throughout the decade, Wheatley became more outspoken on behalf of liberty, championing the American cause and associating it with that of her oppressed people. Nor was she afraid to indict the hypocrisy of those who resisted British tyranny while holding slaves, as in her elegy "On the Death of General Wooster" (1777), where she imagines the patriot's final apostrophe:

> But how, presumptuous shall we hope to find
> Divine acceptance with th' Almighty mind –
> While yet, O deed ungenerous! they disgrace
> And hold in bondage Afric's blameless race?
> Let virtue reign – And thou accord our prayers
> Be victory ours, and generous freedom theirs.

The tragedy of Phillis Wheatley was that the historical movement toward political and economic freedom proved disastrous for both her life and her art. The deaths of her former master and mistress deprived her of well-connected benefactors, and her marriage in 1778 to a free black, John Peters, plunged her into indigence. The next year she advertised for subscribers to a second volume of poems, this one to be dedicated to a self-made American legend, Benjamin Franklin, with whom Wheatley must have felt some kin-ship. The "Proposals," describing her as a *rara avis in terra* and soliciting orders to "fan the sacred fire which is self-kindled in the breast of this *young African*," attracted little support. With the war on, and without wealthy backers, Wheatley no longer had the option of testing English interest – her previous book had originally been published in London – and the projected collection never materialized; twenty-eight of the thirty-three announced titles are presumed lost. A few more poems reached print in broadside and in newspapers during her lifetime, and the *Poems on Various Subjects* was reissued at least five times between 1786 and 1793. But Wheatley herself got nothing from these editions: she had died impoverished in 1784 at the age of thirty-one, a year after the American colonies won their independence.

Wheatley has fared better in literary history than she did in the postrevolutionary United States. Even before her death, she became a cultural symbol in the widening controversy over slavery and race. Although she has had unfriendly critics, readers who dismissed her verse as proof of black mental inferiority – Thomas Jefferson, as we shall see, was the most prominent detractor – she also has had articulate defenders both black and white, and has been held up as the founding "mother" of an indigenous tradition of black literature. Washington, Benjamin Rush, and the novelist Gilbert Imlay praised her warmly in the eighteenth century, and Evert Duyckinck, the antebellum critic and anthologist who was a friend of Melville's, commended her work in 1856 (with a punning reference to Alexander Pope) as a "respectable imitation of the Papal strains." African Americans adopted Wheatley as a legitimating forerunner whose example encouraged them to write. George Moses Horton paid her the tribute of binding the 1838 reissue of his *Poems: By a Slave* (1829) together with her work. And her contemporary Jupiter Hammon acknowledged Wheatley's preeminence as early as 1778 when he chose her as the subject of a broadside, "An ADDRESS to Miss Phillis Wheatly [*sic*], Ethiopian Poetess, in Boston."

Wheatley was actually the second African American to publish verse; Hammon, a slave in Long Island, New York, was the first. (Lucy Terry's ballad "Bars Fight" was composed in 1746 but not transcribed until the nineteenth century.) Hammon wrote in a pietistic and accommodationist vein. His pieces, often highly paraphrastic of the Bible, urge acceptance of Christ and never explicitly question slavery, and he acknowledges his master at the beginning or end of every poem. In the "ADDRESS," he praises Wheatley for having embraced the word of God. It is not known whether the idea for this poem originated with Hammon or with his master; arguably, its affirmation of black unity gets muffled in its preoccupation with the solidarity of the saints. But is it not possible to detect a note of criticism toward the race of owners in Hammon's emphasis on how "God's tender mercy set thee free"? Does not the poem suggest a contrast between the motives of those who abducted Wheatley from Africa for profit and the religious faith she discovered in Boston "[w]orth all the gold in Spain"? Is not Christianity, with its implication that black souls are as dear to God as white ones, a reproof to slaveholders? Wheatley herself condemns her compatriots on these grounds, and some white female poets were beginning to express a pietistic and sentimental egalitarianism that later abolitionists would mobilize effectively against slavery.

Scores of women wrote poetry in the early Republic, and most observed the social and literary conventions of their male counterparts. They published anonymously or modestly hid behind Latinate pseudonyms suggesting both classical republicanism and superior status – three favorites were Amelia, Fidelia, and Constantia – and they composed verse to each other in a display of mutual encouragement and support. One finds the usual disclaimers of ambition that appeared in the novel. Sarah Morton, known to readers by her pen name "Philenia, a Lady of Boston," says in her "Apology" for *Beacon Hill* that she never allows writing to distract her "from one occupation," the caring for others that her position as wife and mother "renders obligatory." But no more than with the novel did such protests prevent women from putting themselves forward as authors. A mother and her daughter, Ann Eliza Bleecker and Margaretta V. Faugeres, published a volume containing poems and prose pieces by both of them, as if to insist on the importance of their familial or domestic identities while simultaneously affirming their right to speak in public. The genderless nature of authorship also gave license to speak. As Morton states about her temerity in meeting "the public eye," she was emboldened to publish by "the idea, that an author should be considered of no sex, and that the individual must be lost in the writer."

Many women offered poetic homage to politics and the public sphere. In heroic couplets or otherwise familiar rhyme schemes, they sang of exploits in an arena from which they themselves were barred. A poem on the British revenue acts of the 1760s turns this exclusion into good-natured but trenchant humor. In "The Female Patriots. Address'd to the Daughters of Liberty in America, 1768," Milcah Martha Moore enjoins her countrywomen to stiffen the resolve of their "degenerate" men by boycotting tea, paper, and other commodities. Should the men, offended at their meddling in politics, "tell us to hush, / We can throw back the satire, by biding them blush." Mercy Otis Warren, in a poem she composed at the outbreak of armed hostilities, takes as her explicit theme the necessity of subordinating private and domestic matters to the common good. In "To Fidelio, Long Absent on the Great Public Cause, Which Agitated All America, In 1776," she professes love for her husband, General James Warren, but declares her willingness to yield him to the state: "The times demand exertions of the kind, / A Patriot zeal must warm the female mind."

Other pieces by female poets contested or even inverted customary binaries by addressing social and political issues from the vantage of the home. Several women wrote of the plight of slaves or other dispossessed groups in verses suffused with the sentimentality that flourished in the early novel. These works retained a belief in poetry's functionality, but they sought to enlist readers for humanitarian reform by making them feel for the sufferings of others. They appealed to the private sphere of the emotions and domesticity to solve problems afflicting the public world of men. Challenging the cultural dominance of civic humanism, the sentimental ethos elevated affect over reason, the closet over the forum, and self-indulgence over self-suppression.

The appearance of this strain in a traditional genre like poetry, as opposed to the more modern novel, was further evidence of the inroads made by liberal thought. The sentimentalist outlook undermined the hierarchical assumptions of republican ideology, for it extended the category of the fully human to persons consigned to the margins: the poor, nonwhites, women and children. Sentimentalism declared that these devalued beings were as worthy of concern as the privileged readers of verse. Morton wrote a widely reprinted antislavery poem, "The African Chief" (1792), encouraging tearful identification with the victims of injustice. After comparing a rebellious slave to George Washington and other heroes of liberty, she calls upon white readers to renounce the temperamental coldness of their race:

> While the hard race of pallid hue,
>   Unpracticed in the power to feel,
> Resign him to the murderous crew,
>   The horrors of the quivering wheel,
>
> Let sorrow bathe each blushing cheek,
>   Bend piteous o'er the tortured slave,
> Whose wrongs compassion cannot speak,
>   Whose only refuge was the grave.

Morton was also the author of a verse narrative sympathetic to Native Americans, *Ouabi; or the Virtues of Nature* (1790); and Susanna Rowson composed an "Ode to Sensibility" in which the disposition to "Exult in other's joys – or bleed at other's woe" is what separates men and women from "unfeeling brutes."

Rowson's *Miscellaneous Poems* (1804) oscillates between public, hortatory verse and a transposition into poetry of the "female" concerns of sentimental fiction. One of the salient features of the book is its multiplicity of styles and voices: whereas many pieces are epideictic and patriotic, colored by Rowson's Federalist politics, others celebrate the emotions and espouse an equivocal but genuine feminism. "Maria. Not a Fiction" is literally a versified novel, protesting its truthfulness like any other seduction narrative and imploring the reader to "drop a silent tear" for the heroine. Two other poems, "Rights of Woman" and "Women As They Are," fluctuate between assertion of female independence and submission to gender orthodoxy. "May I presume to speak? and though uncommon, / Stand forth the champion of the rights of woman?" Rowson asks in the first; the second calls for improvement in female education. Though Rowson concurs on this latter point with Mary Wollstonecraft (whose works her titles deliberately echo), she distances herself from the radicalism of her more daring contemporary. Both Rowson poems ultimately come to the temperate conclusion that "woman's proper sphere" is the home.

Rowson herself, of course, gained fame in the public world of print, and the real evidence of female individuality in her verse is its technical range and sophistication, proof of her own learning in poetic tradition and of her seriousness as a writer. A willingness to experiment, to play with formal and stylistic conventions, distinguishes the *Miscellaneous Poems* from the work of most American poets of the time. Rowson seems to have taken the freedom of the Pindaric ode as inspiration for what she calls "Irregular Poems," compositions in which she changes rhyme scheme, employs different metrical lines, and varies stanzaic length. In an ode written on John Adams's birthday, she stretches the acceptable bounds of the Pindaric, weaving blank verse amongst the odal stanzas and refusing to settle into a pattern. Skilled touches unexpectedly enliven a popular song like "America, Commerce and Freedom," which switches from rhymed hexameter in the eight-line stanzas to pentameter and internal rhymes in the refrain. Rowson circumvents neoclassical etiquette in a form presumably as standardized as the sonnet. She reaches back to the Renaissance for her models and opts for the flexible and uneven over the polished. By the late eighteenth century, the convention of the fourteen-line sonnet had been established for almost two centuries; an imitative poet like David Humphreys follows it faithfully in his sonnets on civic themes. Rowson, in contrast, persists in using the term in its archaic meaning of "little song," and the sonnets in her volume vary in length from eight to thirteen lines.

The writer whose work best exemplifies the contrary tendencies of early American verse is Philip Freneau. Efforts to explain away the inconsistencies in Freneau's biography and poetry have been unavailing for the very good reason that his contradictions were those of the age. Devotion to the commonweal warred in him with an individualistic spirit, intent upon private needs and satisfactions. For much of his life, Freneau was an ardent revolutionary and Jeffersonian partisan committed to the idea that art should serve the Republic; the bulk of his writing is didactic and politically engaged. Illustrations span his poetic career, from "The Political Litany" of 1775, asking deliverance "From a kingdom that bullies, and hectors, and swears"; to the angry broadside on his mistreatment by his captors at sea, "The British Prison Ship" (1781); to the satires and odes of the 1790s, when as a Republican journalist he lacerated Federalist policy and supported the French Revolution (see, for example, the "Ode" beginning "God save the Rights of Man!" [1795], a thrust at pro-British conservatives); to pieces written in the new century to eulogize Thomas Paine or cheer on his compatriots in the War of 1812. Freneau's versification shuns innovation and is of a piece with his communal emphasis; save for a few poetic dialogues, he writes exclusively in easily accessible rhyme.

Other verses by Freneau diverge so radically in subject and point of view that were it not for the continuity in rhyme, they scarcely would seem to issue from the same pen. Just as he physically absented himself from the civic realm at critical intervals, withdrawing to the West Indies on the eve of the Revolution and to the sea for seven years after the war ended, so in his art Freneau periodically turns away from public life to sing of personal self-fulfillment and the emancipated imagination. The attraction to retirement in such poems is not Horatian or classical republican but privatizing and proto-Romantic. The model lies in nature, in the seclusion of "The Wild Honey Suckle" (1786):

> By Nature's self in white arrayed,
> She bade thee shun the vulgar eye,
> And planted here the guardian shade,
> And sent soft waters murmuring by.

Politics looms here as the bane of poetry rather than its mainspring. "The Beauties of Santa Cruz," composed in the historically momentous year of 1776, finds Freneau culling "bright Fancy's flowers," while he leaves it to others to "Repel the Tyrant." Twelve years later, at the height of debate on the Constitution, he rebels against the imagination's duty to be useful. "An age employed in edging steel," he complains in "To an Author," "Can no poetic raptures feel."

Freneau's preoccupation with death bridges his public and private verse and marks the moment in American poetry when mortality begins to shed the communal importance it held for earlier writers and to assume the intensely personal coloring it acquired in the nineteenth century. Many of Freneau's poems pay tribute to deceased leaders like Washington and Franklin or glorify the soldiers who fell in America's wars with Britain. In these elegies, where the Republic affirms itself through recognition of its heroes, the dominant note is patriotic and social; the voice speaking belongs to the first person plural, as in the final lines of "To the Memory of the Brave Americans" (1781): "We trust they find a happier land, / A brighter sunshine of their own." Elsewhere Freneau conceives of death as a refuge from corporate commitment, from a world in which "rigid Reason" and didacticism subjugate the muse. In his gothic verse narrative "The House of Night" (1779), morbidity fixates the poet independently of its putative instructional value. The superimposed religious moral is overshadowed by fascinated talk

"Of coffins, shrouds, and horrors of a tomb"; the poem's force resides in its graphic image of death as a character expiring on the couch. "The Indian Burial Ground" (1787) specifies death's appeal for Freneau: "And Reason's self shall bow the knee / To shadows and delusions here." Fancy, banished from an America bent on nation building, holds sway in the grave, and death, which is the extinction of personhood, paradoxically becomes the site where the poet can be expressive and realize his individuality.

Freneau chose a dead man for his persona when he set forth his views on authorship in 1786, criticizing much of the preprofessionalism that turned writers into supplicants and kept American letters from gaining respect. In an essay supposedly written by the "late" Robert Slender, "a stocking and tape weaver by trade," he argues forcefully for the dignity and independence of the literary calling. He elevates the "original author" above the gentleman scholar, deprecates subscription publishing, and heaps contempt on patronage and dedications, practices that "were first invented by slaves, and have been continued by fools and sycophants." Poets may be beggars, Freneau admits, but they need not be servile; instead they can follow the example of Slender – or, one might add, of the actual artisan–poet David Hitchcock – and earn their bread by weaving stockings as well as writing verse.

In Freneau's own case, five volumes of poetry published in his lifetime and a national reputation as the "Poet of the Revolution" failed to bring him even a modicum of financial security. In his last years he was reduced to working as a common laborer on the public roads. What especially incensed him was that the American who finally made literature profitable, Washington Irving, succeeded by engaging in the very forms of flattery that brought authorship into disgrace. Whereas Freneau himself was "earning fifty cents a week," as he relates in "To a New-England Poet" (1823), Irving prospered abroad and became a best-selling author at home by fawning on British nobles and "forgetting *times* of seventy-six." For the American writer desiring popularity among his compatriots, Freneau comments bitterly, there is no more effective marketing strategy than the aristocratic aura of acceptance by the English:

> Dear Bard, I pray you, take the hint,
> In England what you write and print,
> Republished here in shop, or stall,
> Will perfectly enchant us all:
>   It will assume a different face,
>   And post your name at every place.

The step from Freneau to America's first Romantic poet, William Cullen Bryant, is a short one, not merely because Bryant sings of nature and death, but also because he remained devoted to the writer's public role both in his life and in his work. Indeed, a case could be made that of the two authors, Bryant was the more oriented toward the community. After several years of practicing law, he became a journalist and the editor of the New York *Evening Post,* actively supporting liberal causes in the half century he served the newspaper. Bryant's career contained no unaccountable flights from public affairs, and his poetry, early and late, exhibits qualities in common with the most civic-minded early American verse. Besides his monodies and his scores of poems on current events, there are nationalistic pieces such as the one commissioned by Harvard's Phi Beta Kappa Society and read at the commencement of 1821. "The Ages" seems a reversion to the epics of the revolutionary generation. In Spenserian (regular nine-line rhyming) stanzas, the poem surveys the progress of human freedom from its origin in the ancient republics to its culmination in the United States; though the piece is seldom read today, Bryant thought so well of it that he placed it first in all collected volumes of his poems. At age thirteen, when he still shared his father's Federalist politics, he even wrote a satire imitative of the Wits. Bryant's earliest publication, *The Embargo; or, Sketches of the Times* (1808), uses neoclassical couplets to hurl invective at President Jefferson for destroying New England's commerce while reclining in the arms of his "sable" mistress.

Almost all of Bryant's innovative verse appeared in the slim book published in 1821 as the *Poems of William Cullen Bryant,* and here too, at least on the level of theme, one finds little emphasis on individual as opposed to collective values. To be sure, poems like the "Inscription for the Entrance to a Wood" celebrate nature as a sanctuary from societal cares. Unlike Freneau, however, Bryant cherishes the natural world as a source of moral truths and spiritual renewal, not as an escape from communal responsibility. In "The Yellow Violet," the humble flower admonishes those who forget their friends in their "climb to wealth"; the bird's solitary flight in "To a Waterfowl" imparts "the lesson" that a benign Providence oversees every person's life. In generalized, stately diction, Bryant adopts the voice of a public teacher interpreting nature's meaning for his readers. The slightly later piece "A Forest Hymn" (1825) moves from description of a peaceful grove to reflections on the Deity in a summary statement of the physical environment's significance:

> . . . Be it ours to meditate,
> In these calm shades, thy milder majesty,
> And to the beautiful order of thy works
> Learn to conform the order of our lives.

The paradoxes behind Bryant's didactic poetic persona are multiple; they start with his politics and extend to his versification. In his editorials for the *Evening Post,* he was a vocal champion of laissez-faire capitalism and backed the Jacksonian campaign to liberate private enterprise from customary restrictions. Among his poems is an elegy for William Leggett, his assistant editor on the *Post* and perhaps the foremost advocate of free trade in the antebellum era. Bryant's writings on poetic technique reveal a similar outspokenness against traditional restraint and in favor of individual initiative. In his severe critical assessment "Early American Verse" (1818), he faults his predecessors for shunning personal feelings and practicing an unbroken "monotony of versification." The essay titled "On Trisyllabic Feet in Iambic Measure," published in 1819 but drafted as early as 1811, near the end of the reign of neoclassical models, calls for a "literary revolution" against Pope in expressly political language. It is time, Bryant says, to release native poetry from its bondage to the unvaried iambic or "see-saw" of rhymed heroic verse. He praises blank verse as freer and more natural than rhyme, and he demands "a greater license in prosody" to permit occasional irregularities such as feet of three syllables in poems of iambic measure. Throughout, he sees himself as translating the principles of American politics into art, just as free-trade liberals believed they were carrying the Revolution into the economy.

Bryant's masterpiece "Thanatopsis" best illustrates the complex mixture of loyalties in his thought. Originally published in 1817, the poem initiates the Romantic movement in American verse and was perceived as doing so by contemporaries like Bryant's friend, Richard Henry Dana, Sr., who exclaimed upon first reading it, "That [poem] was never written on this side of the water." "Thanatopsis" (the title means meditation on death) reflects Bryant's familiarity with the English landmarks of the new school, particularly William Wordsworth's *Lyrical Ballads* (1798). In its tone and versification, and to a lesser degree, in its non-Christian credo, the poem announces itself as a departure from the past. A soothing voice invites "communion" with nature's forms and offers philosophical consolation in the face of death, the promise of brotherhood with the millions who "since first / The flight of years began, have laid them down / In their last sleep." The voice speaks in blank verse, without the "restraint . . . [of] rhyme," and is conversational and prosaic, ground-breaking developments for a major American poem. Violation of the metrical smoothness inspired by Pope occurs early on, a first line in strict iambic pentameter being followed by a second with a trisyllabic foot. ("Tŏ hím whŏ iń thĕ lóve ŏf Nátŭrĕ hólds / Cŏmmúnĭŏn wíth hĕr vísĭblĕ fórms, she spéaks." Trumbull or Dwight would have contracted "vis'ble" into two syllables with an elision; Wordsworth, on the other hand, had been dispensing with contractions for two decades.)

A question exists about whether the words of the poem emanate from nature or from the bard. Intended or not, this ambiguity is revealing: it points to a conflation of the human and the natural. This merging occurs not just because the voice suggests a man speaking to other men in everyday, "natural" tones, but also because Bryant conceptualizes man as detached from external appendages. His speaker is man in his denuded essence, man cut free from both aesthetic and social entanglements. On the very threshold of the so-called take-off phase of American history, Bryant forges a free poetic subject holding forth untrammeled by the artifice of neoclassical convention and seemingly liberated from historical and communal ties. "Thanatopsis" naturalizes – makes appear normative and inevitable – the autonomous individual needed to carry forward the social and economic revolution of the antebellum era, the individual who in fact was a product of history and until recently had seen himself, above all, as a member of the community.

What should be immediately evident is that Bryant's announced theme of death's consolations clashes with, or compensates for, the ideological thrust of his tonal informality. Whereas his poetic technique works to entrench self-reliance, the unencumbered subject of "Thanatopsis" preaches the importance of the collectivity. The poem's speaker, as if to acknowledge that he clings to an obsolete ideal, transfers the hope of solidarity from social life to the grave. Among the living, community disintegrates; not even the ceremony of death binds men together any longer:

> So shalt thou rest, and what if thou withdraw
> In silence from the living, and no friend
> Take note of thy departure?

Consolation, according to Bryant's speaker, lies in the thought of mingling with "The innumerable caravan, which moves / To that mysterious realm." The poem movingly envisages a diverse humanity surrendering its differences in the unity of the grave:

> All that breathe
> Will share thy destiny. The gay will laugh
> When thou art gone, the solemn brood of care
> Plod on, and each one as before will chase
> His favorite phantom; yet all these shall leave
> Their mirth and their employments, and shall come
> And make their bed with thee. As the long train
> Of ages glides away, the sons of men,
> The youth in life's fresh spring, and he who goes
> In the full strength of years, matron and maid,
> The speechless babe, and the gray-headed man –
> Shall one by one be gathered to thy side,
> By those, who in their turn shall follow them.

Bryant's reliance in "Thanatopsis" on archaic forms of address, a striking characteristic of his work generally, reinforces the anti-individualistic moral.

Plentiful "thees," "thys," and "thous" evoke an intimacy vanished from the present and suggest a willed assertion of community in a world where people do not know each other. The hints of Quakerism are a nostalgic affectation, not a religious principle. The opening line of "Inscription for the Entrance to a Wood," "Stranger, if thou hast learned a truth which needs," captures the pathos as well as the incongruity of the poet's addressing unknown persons in familiar terms.

Bryant was never a professional author like his contemporaries Irving and Cooper, although he too eventually enjoyed international recognition. Even the dramatist John Howard Payne, who struggled in vain to live by his writing, had a firmer sense of literature as a business. There was something out-of-date about Bryant as a poet, in spite of his progressive politics. He kept his literary activities subordinate to his career as a journalist and persisted in treating verse as an avocation. (He had sound reason for this: four years after its publication, the 1821 *Poems* had netted him a scant $14.21.) His poetry ceased to explore new directions, and he never again matched the originality of his first book. Although he continued to write public art, Bryant came to feel that poetry had little relevance for the rapidly industrializing, market society of the nineteenth century. As he wrote to Dana in 1833, poems were simply not valued in the modern world:

After all, poetic wares are not in the market of the present day. Poetry may get praised in the newspapers, but no man can make money by it, for the simple reason that nobody cares a fig for it. The taste for it is something old fashioned, the march of the age is in another direction – mankind are concerned with politics, railroads and steamboats.

Bryant's words are accurate and telling, not about poetry itself – Whitman, after all, wrote great poems about technology – but rather as a revelation of the backward-looking disposition that came to dominate his verse.

From the Wits to Bryant would be one way to encapsulate the new direction in American poetry; from Elihu Hubbard Smith to Samuel Kettell would be another. As already noted, Smith was the editor of the first anthology of native verse printed in the United States, *American Poems* (1793). Thirty-five years later, Kettell would edit a collection entitled *Specimens of American Poetry, with Critical and Biographical Notices* (1829). Kettell's compilation ushered out the formative period and inaugurated the reign of the anthology in American verse. His was the first of the comprehensive gatherings, assembled most famously by Rufus Griswold, which flooded the antebellum literary market and came to dominate the consumption of poetry in the United States.

Smith's anthology had all the earmarks of the preprofessional, republican paradigm. The book was intended, according to the preface, to perform the public service of gathering and preserving American verse. A fifth of the pieces were anonymous or written under a pseudonym, and Smith's own name was mentioned nowhere in the volume. The subscribers, on the other hand, received profuse acknowledgment, with their names, many graced by titles like "Doctor" and "Esquire," occupying six pages at the end. A restrictive, hierarchical spirit governed the selections. Only one woman, "Philenia" (Sarah Morton), was included among the contributors. Smith explained that several authors who withheld their verse from newspapers – promiscuously read by "everybody" – had consented to print them in *American Poems,* where they would come "to the attention of the scientific and refined." Despite high expectations, the book's inauspicious reception demonstrated the difficulty of selling poetry in the postrevolutionary epoch. A promised second volume failed to materialize for lack of "sufficient encouragement."

Anthologies are by their nature collective phenomena, and their popularity in the nineteenth century would seem to indicate the persistence of communal ideas of poetry. There is something to this. Kettell's collection resembled Smith's in its emphasis on usefulness and patriotism. His title revealed a collector's or taxonomic aspiration, and he too defined his role as rescuing works of native talent from oblivion. Like Smith, Kettell sought to bolster pride in American achievement and to stimulate a national spirit in letters.

But the changes loomed as large as the continuities. Even though *Specimens of American Poetry* placed its authors in a corporate setting, it gave unprecedented importance to the individual artist. Each selection was prefaced by a biographical sketch of the poet, some as brief as a single paragraph, others running on for ten pages, all disclosing information that the patrician amateur of the federal period instinctively omitted. This stress on the authorial subject extended to the anthologist himself: Kettell's name appeared prominently both on the title page and in the notice of copyright on the overleaf. A democratizing impulse shaped the selections. More than a dozen women appeared in the compilation, among them Morton, Warren, Bleecker, and younger voices, like Lydia Sigourney and Sarah Hale. And *Specimens of American Poetry* consisted of three volumes, so confident was Kettell in 1829 of attracting a popular readership. Altered assumptions about ownership and the primacy of the particular person had taken hold in cultural production just as they had gained ascendancy elsewhere in American life. Kettell's anthology marked an emphatic turn toward individualism in presentation and format, a shift in the publishing of poetry that corresponded to its transformation in style.

Thomas Jefferson stands in the background of the transition to a Romantic or more individualistic sensibility in American poetry. With Freneau, Jefferson acted as governmental employer and political patron; with Bryant, he exercised a less immediate but still important influence. Bryant broke into print with a neoclassical satire of Jefferson's administration; later, while writing Romantic verse, the poet abandoned his conservatism, deserted to the Democratic party, and became an admirer of the third president. Jefferson's significance as an ally of personal expression reached beyond poetry to the two fiction writers who Americanized the new sensibility. Irving was just twenty-six when he lampooned the president in the first book he authored on his own, *A History of New York* (1809). Cooper, like Irving and Bryant the son of anti-Jeffersonian Federalists, dramatically converted to reverence at the same time that he was breaking away from English models in his fiction and establishing himself as the country's major novelist.

It may seem incongruous that Jefferson, the embodiment of the eighteenth-century gentleman of letters, functioned in the culture as a kind of guardian spirit of Romanticism. His own writings were civic, not personal. As president, and as the author of the Declaration of Independence and *Notes on the State of Virginia* (1785), Jefferson symbolized the pre-Romantic marriage of the public realm and literature. Nor was he always receptive to literary currents of change. His reaction to Phillis Wheatley in *Notes* illustrates his shortcomings. After disparaging the imaginative faculties of blacks, he dismisses her work and even casts doubt on her authorship: "Religion, indeed, has produced a Phyllis Whately [*sic*]; but it could not produce a poet. The compositions published under her name are below the dignity of criticism." This was not Jefferson at his best, either as a reader of poetry or as a friend of equality.

Yet Jefferson was the author of a brief theoretical essay on metrics that shows him to have been far in advance of the literary ethos of postrevolutionary America. The essay, *Thoughts on English Prosody*, comprises part of a letter to a Frenchman, M. de Chastellux, written around 1789; because it was left unpublished until the twentieth century, it had no impact on the course of native poetry, but it deserves to be better known as a modest poetic analogue to the Declaration. Jefferson's central insight is that the quantitative and syllabic prosodies of the eighteenth century fail to do justice to the role of accent in English-language verse. Most writers on prosody still believed that English poetry followed either the classical-language model, in which the foot consists of long and short syllables, or the Romance-language model, in which the unit of measurement is the number of syllables per line. Jefferson, disputing authorities like Samuel Johnson, insists that accent is "the basis of English verse" and determines its measure. His argument shapes itself in democratic and individualistic terms; he directs attention away from the written text and the inherent properties of language to the reader of the poem. No rules, he claims, can be formed for fixing accent, because unlike quantity or duration, usage establishes stress and is notably capricious and inconsistent. The neoclassical ideals of smoothness and uniformity fracture against the undeniable truth that different people use "different shades of emphasis" in speaking English. "No two persons will accent the same passage alike. No person but a real adept will accent it twice alike." Thus does Jefferson defy the age's worship of poetic harmony by endorsing the reader's subjective judgment and placing a principle of uncertainty or freedom at the very heart of English verse.

Although several writers in Britain and America, among them the lexicographer Noah Webster, shared Jefferson's insight about the centrality of accent, his treatise was exceptional in its forthright validation of individual experience. *Thoughts on English Prosody* prefigures the Romantic emphasis on the personal voice and had no equal in America in theoretical boldness for thirty years, until Bryant's "On Trisyllabic Feet in Iambic Measure." Not that Jefferson transcended the neoclassical prejudices of his time in all respects. He remained an Augustan, for example, in his esteem for regular meter, but even here he was ahead of most American poetic practice, for the iambic pentameter he admired was that of blank verse, not of rhymed. At the height of Pope's influence in America, he anticipated Bryant by rejecting rhyme as a regressive infringement on the poet's liberty. Freedom in versification, Jefferson believed, like freedom in the polity, unshackles human potential and produces superior results. The bard, emancipated from "those tautologies, those feeble nothings necessary to introtrude the rhyming word," is able to concentrate his or her energies on refining images and thoughts. Hence a mature taste, according to the future president, will always find blank verse more dignified and satisfying. "The fondness for the jingle leaves us with that for the baubles and rattles of childhood," until the only poets we read with pleasure are those who dispense altogether with rhyme.

Jefferson's naturalizing of blank verse paralleled his equation of political freedom with self-evidence in the Declaration; both maneuvers helped to underwrite individualism and represented revolutionary shatterings of traditional restraints. The year of the *Thoughts on English Prosody*, 1789, was also the date of the French Revolution and of William Blake's *Songs of Innocence*. Blake too saw a connection between poetic experimentation and political liberty; where Jefferson speaks of the poet being "unfettered by rhyme," the English poet declares, "Poetry Fetter'd Fetters the Human Race." (Jefferson was actually in advance of Blake, who did not get around to writing about meter until 1804, in the preface to *Jerusalem*.) Of course, the association between aesthetic and civic upheaval has a long history, going back to the ancient Greeks; Plato excluded poets from his ideal republic because he feared that the "introduction of novel fashions" in art endangered the peace of the state. In the United States, the causal relations among politics, poetry, and the social order became more complicated. Jefferson's democratic ideas had to wait for the social and political transformation of the antebellum years to reach their fulfillment in literature. Only then did the two poetic iconoclasts, Whitman and Dickinson, arise to revolutionize accepted metrical practice – Dickinson by employing an atavistic hymnal and balladic metricality, and Whitman by dispensing entirely with iambic measure.

5

❦

THE NOVEL

THE ASSOCIATION of the novel with individualism and the middle
class has been an enduring staple of literary criticism. Ample historical evidence supports the linkage. In the United States, the novel
developed in tandem with democratization and economic expansion, and
although the form did not realize its potential until the Age of Jackson, a
strong case can be made that it was complicit from its origin with the ethos
of the marketplace. Early American fiction stood out as the most privatized
and commercially viable of the literary arts, the genre most attuned to the
social order of the future. "What is a novel without novelty?" asked the first
indigenous novelist, William Hill Brown, in his posthumous *Ira and Isabella*
(1807); his question highlights the insatiable appetite for the new that
distinguished fiction from earlier forms of cultural expression. The postrevolutionary novel can be described as a prototypically "liberal" artifact. Anxious
guardians of the status quo lambasted novels as popular reading material that
pandered to mass tastes and subverted respect for traditional authority. Consumed in solitude, centered on personal ambitions and desires, and attracted,
as the name indicates, to unfamiliar experiences, novels contributed to the
undermining of a shared public sphere and encouraged the self-seeking outlook that flourished under Jacksonian democracy.

This picture, a familiar one, exaggerates the novel's collusion in the coming order; with the benefit of hindsight, it singles out the features that
became dominant rather than those that receded over time. Scholars investi-
gating the genesis of the English novel have begun to qualify the form's
identification with the middle class and to see that its retention of conservative and "romance" elements placed it in a complex relation to triumphant
individualism. A comparably nuanced picture presents itself on the American side, where native fiction contained its own volatile mixture of progressive and premodern features. If the early American novel was new, it was also
"old," enmeshed in the communitarian assumptions of its time and committed to the very systems of thought it worked to overthrow. Although it was
the first American genre to return a profit, novel writing in its infancy was
"the dullest of all trades," as Charles Brockden Brown lamented in 1800;

"the utmost that any American can look for, in his native country, is to be reimbursed for his unavoidable expenses." Imitative, unprofitable, and as intent upon collective as individualistic ends, the novel was a form in transition and at odds with itself, as much a partisan of postrevolutionary republican culture as a harbinger of nineteenth-century liberal society.

Contemporaneous mistrust of prose fiction as unrepublican often focused on its bonds to privacy and to women. And it is true that the novel had a special stake in the emerging reconfiguration of gender roles and the household. The genre gained discursive preeminence through the repositioning of women as consumers and of the home as a place of private ease. The division between dwelling and employment that became pervasive in the nineteenth century appeared in embryo in the early Republic. For postrevolutionary Americans living in or near cities – the case with most novelists – a private space of domesticity had already begun to materialize. As the household economy steadily declined over the first fifty years of the Republic, altering the home from a site of production to one of consumption, this private zone took on an identification with leisure and with women. Men left the residence daily to labor elsewhere, and the mothers and daughters who stayed behind had more free time to devote to entertainment. Increasingly, they turned to the reading of light literature.

Novels understandably headed the list of preferred books. Volumes on theology and the state dealt with areas from which women had traditionally been excluded. But novels featured women as characters and addressed matters that impinged directly on their lives, such as courtship and marriage. Moreover, women were conspicuous as the authors of such works. Some critics seized on this association with the female as proof of fiction's incompatibility with civic virtue. To them, the novel resembled a coquette who lured readers into a claustrophobic world of desire and self-indulgence, the antithesis of the public domain of rationality and men.

Certainly the novel, as a genre inseparable from print and ingested in the home, seemed an inherently private art form. Unlike the oral drama, and unlike much early poetry, which was recited on public occasions, prose fiction was – and is – experienced in isolation. People commonly were alone when they read, and if they were not physically solitary, they were imaginatively cut off from the world around them through their engagement with the printed page. Even this engagement was a form of privacy or solitude. Eighteenth-century readers frequently penned their thoughts in the margins of the novel's pages, but their relation to the events and characters described within the story was nonreciprocal. Whereas theatergoers disrupted performances and sometimes forced changes in the action, novel readers were powerless to affect what happened in the narrative. Such passivity, combined with the subjective impression of involvement, could be construed as a kind of false consciousness, an ideological illusion corrosive of the participatory outlook necessary to republicanism.

As noted in Chapter 3, the novel had a long-standing relation to Benjamin Franklin, who gave the genre its first American imprint and whose own *Autobiography,* published in a truncated version in 1793, has many of the artful qualities of fiction. The Franklin connection points once again to the novel's liberal strain. Just as Franklin represented upward mobility and the pursuit of self-interest, so the novel was itself a "rising" genre, a newcomer elbowing ahead of senior art forms in the competition for popular favor. Franklin stood for the right of the individual subject to put his or her own wishes ahead of familial obligation. The young rebel who refused to enter the family trade of chandlery, and who ran away from his indentures with his brother, could have been one of the early novel's picaresque heroes or passionate heroines. Like those fictional characters, who typically set the plot in motion by defying a parental edict, Franklin made his way through perilous adventures "remote from the Eye and Advice of my Father"; he relied on himself. His eventual transformation into a national icon conferred implicit justification on the individualism of countless novelistic protagonists.

One aspect of Franklin's experience had particular relevance for women authors. Franklin succeeded through print; he rose in the world because of his mastery of writing. As a young man, he discovered that speech could be a dangerous medium. It tempted one into unguarded expression and aroused heated contention. Franklin devised a mode of speaking that privileged indirectness, substituting reserve and hesitancy for emphatic declaration, and he gravitated to print as a technology that facilitated self-concealment. These were traits commonly linked to women, and Franklin embraced a female identity for his first appearance in print. He submitted an article to his brother's newspaper, the *New-England Courant,* under the pseudonym, "Silence Dogood." The name summarized the plight of women in the early Republic – exhorted to "do good" by remaining silent – but Franklin inverted the prescription: he did good by speaking in print. He thus set an example for the many American women, denied access to public speech, who turned to fiction writing as a way of voicing and advancing themselves through the mediation of the book.

But the Franklin connection captures only half the truth about the early novel and was itself ambiguous. Many novelists were unconvinced by the Philadelphian's claim to be an exemplary figure. As we shall see, they could not overcome their doubts about the meritocracy of those who rise through self-initiative. A similar uneasiness colored the novelists' attitude toward their own artistic powers. Uncomfortable with the very fictionality of fiction, novelists advertised their writings as based on "Fact," "Truth," or "Recent Events." They called their tales histories and retold narratives whose outlines were widely known from documentary sources such as newspapers. No genre was more insistent about its pretension to be an objective chronicle of actual occurrences.

These disavowals, a defining characteristic of the eighteenth-century novel, expressed the form's double identity, both its modernizing tendencies and its discomfort with individualism. Although authorial protests of factual accuracy reflected the scientific disposition of the age, they also conveyed mistrust of imaginative license. Artistic inventiveness was disapproved of as intrusive display of self. Prizing fidelity over creative imagination, Gilbert Imlay reversed the standard formula of modern copyright notices: "in every particular," he proudly averred in the preface to *The Emigrants* (1793), "I have had a real character for my model." The author of *The Asylum; or, Alonzo and Melissa. An American Tale, Founded on Fact* (1811), Isaac Mitchell, imagined a reader objecting to an unfortunate turn of events in the story and demanded rhetorically, "Are we not detailing facts? Shall we gloss them over with false colouring? Must we describe things as they are, or as they are not? Shall we draw with the pencil of nature, or of art? Do we indeed paint life as it is, or as it is not?"

In some hands – and Mitchell's fantastic tale belongs in this category – declarations of naive realism merely underlined the novel's generic instability. The novel's tendency, starkly on display in somewhat later works, was to oscillate between historical preservation and sentimental extravagance. Panegyrics to fact often introduced plots crammed with improbable occurrences. But the professions of historicity could betoken a genuine commitment to the community. Novelists sought to reanimate and to articulate the lessons of episodes that could have happened to anyone, because they supposedly *did* happen to someone. Truthfulness enhanced pedagogic authority for contemporaneous readers. The belief that a story really occurred meant that people would be more likely to take its moral to heart, and the genre could better serve society through its rendering of behavior to be emulated or avoided.

The iterative and formulaic qualities of eighteenth-century fictions – features that seem so tedious today – contributed to the novel's communal goals. Where the aim was to instruct, the predictable was more effective than the "novel." Here the genre, despite its dependence on print, veered toward the practices of oral storytelling. The constant repetition of familiar patterns endowed the narratives with a ritualistic air redolent of verbal discourse. No wonder modern readers find it difficult to recollect the difference between one tale and another: stock figures – the unsuspecting virgin, the dashing seducer, the distraught parents – and "twice-told" plots turn up in book after book. Contemporaries had the same trouble telling the stories apart. As Susanna Rowson remarked nearly two centuries ago, "[T]here are at the present day, about two thousand novels in existence, which begin and end in exactly the same way."

The earnest restatement of sentiments so commonplace as to approach the condition of aphorisms is another index to the early novel's proximity to oral culture. The anonymously published *Emily Hamilton* (1803; the author was identified nearly a century later as Sukey Vickery) overflows with didactic formulations that scarcely seem distinctive enough to have been uttered or thought by anyone. The following are ascribed to the eponymous heroine:

Adversity . . . is common to mortals; each one possesses a share of the misfortunes, as well as the pleasures of life.

Sorrow softens and ennobles the heart, and makes it more capable of receiving virtuous impressions.

In every enjoyment of life, some tincture of the bitter is always mingled with the most delicious sweets.

These sentences read like transcriptions of universally accepted ideas; they appear to emanate from neither the speaker nor the author. They are not so much the thoughts of an identifiable person as the received wisdom of the community.

The passing on of moral counsel, however banal, stood at the head of the novel's imperatives. To critics, of course, novelists resembled not wise mentors but seducers or temptresses; they imparted "false and romantic ideas of love," as Tabitha Tenney charged, and turned "the heads of artless young girls, to their great injury, and sometimes to their utter ruin." Tenney herself was the author of *Female Quixotism* (1801), a novel satirizing the harmful consequences of novel reading; like many another fiction writer, she exempted her own work from the indictment of the genre and pleaded a socially useful purpose. The most common analogies were to teaching and mothering, with only the rare novelist confessing to a personal ambition such as self-expression. Though she later changed her mind, Susanna Rowson even proposed to give up novel writing altogether shortly after she decided to become a full-time educator. Why instruct the young through the mediation of fiction, she reasoned in the preface to *Reuben and Rachel* (1798), when she could implant directly, "with the utmost solicitude, in their innocent minds, a love for piety and virtue."

Perhaps half the era's novels adopted the same narrative technique. These works are epistolary, told in the form of letters exchanged between two or more people. Many different voices thus go into the making of a single tale, which assumes the character of a corporate enterprise. In William Hill

Brown's *The Power of Sympathy* (1789), the principal narrative involving Harrington and Harriot emerges from the correspondence of six figures; besides the two lovers themselves, there are communications from Myra Harrington, Worthy, Mrs. Holmes, and Harrington's father. Hannah Foster's *The Coquette* (1797) comprises an even greater multiplicity of voices, with letters from Eliza Wharton, her mother, Major Sanford, the Reverend Boyer, Lucy Freeman, Mr. and Mrs. Richman, Mr. Selby, and Julia Granby. The composite epistolary narrative thoroughly subordinates the idea of individual creation; the image of storytelling it conveys is of a group of persons advising, exhorting, and confiding in each other.

In short, the novel was not preordained to assume an individualistic cast. In its formal and rhetorical emphases, the genre was often more in sympathy with republicanism than with the liberal and private values of the nineteenth century. To turn to the novel's social and cultural matrix is to reencounter this premodern aspect. The provincialism of postrevolutionary culture worked to repress early fiction's individual note. To later readers of the form, the imitation of English models is far more evident than is the faithfulness to historical fact. Written in the shadow of an established literary tradition, American tales tended to be highly derivative, content to reproduce the situations, themes, and characters of English precursors. The Richardsonian prototype dominated the seduction narrative; almost as influential were the satiric novels of Henry Fielding. Other favorites much duplicated on this side of the Atlantic included Ann Radcliffe's gothic fictions, William Godwin's novels of purpose, and Laurence Sterne's *Tristram Shandy* (1760–7), which along with the works of Jean-Jacques Rousseau acquainted Americans with the cult of sensibility.

Copyright law and economic impediments combined to delimit the native novel's status as private property. These conditions hampered salability, dissuaded authors from claiming possession of what they wrote, and prevented novel writing from becoming a vocation. In the first place, the primitive state of the economy assured that only the rare novel could achieve a profit. Books were costly to produce in postrevolutionary America, and most were priced beyond the means of ordinary citizens. Even if readers could afford a novel, booksellers had no certainty of being able to reach a wide market. Publishing was localized and distribution hindered by the lack of adequate transportation.

Legal statute created additional obstacles to profitability, benefiting neither foreign authors nor the Americans whom the law was intended to assist. Because English titles could not be copyrighted in this country, they could be issued far more cheaply than indigenous works. Enterprising printers hastened to pirate novels from abroad and felt little incentive to encourage

American writers. Royall Tyler's fictional protagonist Updike Underhill, supposedly returning to his homeland after seven years' captivity among the Algerines, remarked in 1797 on the profusion of English reprints, complaining that his compatriots had forsaken "the sober sermons and practical pieties of their fathers, for the gay stories and splendid impieties" of the foreign novelist. The vast majority of fictional narratives published and read in the United States before the antebellum era were composed by Europeans: out of some four hundred titles issued here between 1789 and 1800, only thirty-seven had American authors. As late as 1820, the number of native novels barely totaled ninety, an average of just three per year since independence.

Susanna Rowson, author of the young nation's best-selling novel, *Charlotte Temple*, was one of those who suffered from the legal disadvantages of European provenance. Rowson was a recent arrival in the United States who composed her book while still a resident of England. Because *Charlotte Temple* was originally published in London in 1791, two years before Rowson's emigration, it carried no American copyright; every region saw a flurry of pirated editions. Mathew Carey of Philadelphia, who brought out the initial American version in 1794, changed the title from the original *Charlotte. A Tale of Truth* in 1797 and was just one of several publishers to take liberties with the text. Editions appeared with chapters added or deleted and with no mention of the novelist's name. Carey informed Rowson in 1812 that sales of *Charlotte Temple* outstripped "those of any of the most celebrated novels that ever appeared in England. I think the number disposed of must far exceed 50,000 copies; and the sale still continues." Although Rowson was probably gratified at her book's popularity, she had little else to show for it; the various publishers reaped the benefits of ownership, and she herself had to find employment outside literature in order to support her family.

Copyright, the prerogative reserved for American writers, gave scant guarantee of protection against theft. Practices approximating outright plagiarism occurred routinely in the formative period, as authors appear to have had little sense that a character, an incident, or even an entire passage could be the property of an individual. Although Sarah Wood's *Dorval; or the Speculator. A Novel Founded on Recent Events* (1801) assures readers that "the character and history of Dorval are not a fiction," it is plain that the decisive "recent event" for Wood was the publication a year earlier of Charles Brockden Brown's *Arthur Mervyn*. Wood borrowed the "facts" about her villain from Brown's account of the speculator and forger Welbeck and felt no compunction about making liberal use of a story that according to law belonged to another writer. George Watterston, author of *Glencarn; or, The Disappointments of Youth* (1810), committed still more brazen acts of piracy. His novel is another retelling of *Arthur Mervyn*, focusing on a self-styled "enthusiast for virtue" who gets into difficulties because of his impetuosity and innocent trust in humanity. Watterston defends American literature against English slurs and demonstrates his patriotism by plagiarizing from a number of well-known native authors, not just novelists but playwrights and political writers as well. A scene set in a theater is lifted wholesale from Tyler's *The Contrast*, and Glencarn's description of the confluence of the Potomac and Shenandoah rivers, affording a view "grand, sublime, and picturesque beyond any thing I ever beheld," paraphrases Thomas Jefferson's account of the same location in *Notes on the State of Virginia* (1784–5).

In actuality, American authors seldom went to the trouble of applying for copyright. In Massachusetts, for example, legal protection was obtained for fewer than one-tenth of the volumes published between 1800 and 1809. Securing exclusive ownership of a cultural product that stood almost no chance of generating income must have struck many writers as more bother than it was worth. Other authors doubtless shared the upper-class aversion to writing for money and were satisfied to see their books enter the world as a species of communal possession. Similar prejudices kept most novelists from divulging their names in public. Reluctant to associate themselves with an art form deemed socially unacceptable and morally suspect, fewer than one-third of the native fiction writers published prior to 1820 revealed their names on the title pages of their works. The remaining authors either appeared anonymously or disguised their identities behind pseudonyms. Foster and Wood, both of whom announced their novels as "By a Lady of Massachusetts," exemplified the preference for rubrics that proclaimed the writer's superiority to pecuniary considerations.

The early novelist's unwillingness to acknowledge his or her productions has made it impossible, in a surprisingly large number of cases, to ascertain to whom a particular work "belongs." One fiction writer in three remains unknown; another sizable group eluded detection until the twentieth century. *The Power of Sympathy*, advertised by Isaiah Thomas as the "First American Novel" but otherwise unattributed, was long believed to have been written by the Boston poet Sarah Wentworth Morton, a sister of the original for one of the characters; even today the assignment of the book to William Hill Brown is purely circumstantial. Mitchell's *The Asylum; or, Alonzo and Melissa*, a gothic thriller whose popularity persisted into the antebellum period, has an even stranger history. Originally serialized in 1804 in the *Political Barometer* of Poughkeepsie, New York, it was reissued in 1811 as a copyrighted book with Mitchell's name on the title page. The novel went through some twenty editions by 1850, but despite the seemingly unambiguous evidence of legal ownership, these reprints were not of Mitchell's two-volume tale. They were copies of a shortened, plagiarized work in one volume that also appeared in 1811 under the altered title *Alonzo and Melissa; or, The Unfeeling Father* and was supposed to have been written by someone named Daniel Jackson. Copyright claims were never brought against Jackson, presumably because both Mitchell and his publisher died in 1812, and Mitchell's identity as the real author was not conclusively established until 1904.

Writers were not the only group who did not own their works in the early Republic; most readers did not own them either. Novels were simply too expensive to purchase; at a time when skilled workers earned about seventy-five cents a day, a single-volume novel could cost as much as a dollar, and a two-volume tale between a dollar fifty and two dollars. Wage earners with a taste for light literature generally got their novels from social or circulating libraries, which were far more affordable at about six dollars annually for a subscription. Hence the typical scene of reading in 1800, despite outward similarities, differed significantly from the comparable scene today. A contemporary reader of, say, *White Noise* (1985) would probably own the book, and the reverse side of the title page would identify Don DeLillo as the holder of the copyright. Readers of *The Power of Sympathy* would have in their hands a book that was probably not their own, the authorship of which would remain obscure for more than a hundred years.

Yet the postrevolutionary novel was above all a form in the process of change, isomorphic with neither the values of a waning social system nor those of an ascendant one. If the novel drew upon an understanding of narrative as common inheritance, it also contributed to the disintegration of that perspective. It transformed stories into marketable commodities and displaced the collectivity with the individual voice. "We are . . . rather new in the trade of novel writing," James Kirke Paulding pointed out in 1823, "having been partly induced to enter upon it, as people engage in the tobacco or grocery line, from seeing others prosper mightily in the business." A colleague of Irving and Cooper, Paulding recorded the maturation of a commercializing process begun hardly three decades earlier and inscribed, despite the form's irresolution about its nature and direction, in the first American novels. For every sign of communal, republican culture, one can adduce an apparently antithetical sign betokening the novel's growing commitment to individualism; sometimes the signs are indistinguishable.

This equivocalness crystallized in the fluctuating self-conception of the epistolary novel. It was suggested earlier that the novel of letters – which in its American avatar flourished specifically at this time – reproduces as technique the era's communal ideals. Seen from a slightly different perspective, the epistolary novel straddles the line between premodern amateurism and the commercializing of literature that marked the Jacksonian age. In one sense, epistolary fiction is clearly a residue of older, "signature" modes persisting in impersonal print culture. Letters are confidential, handwritten communications between people who know each other; and the belles lettres of the late seventeenth and early eighteenth centuries – with their limited circulation, often in manuscript rather than print, their aloofness from monetary concerns, and their preprofessional authors – retained many of the features of personal correspondence. But epistolary fictions also signal a transition toward modern commodity culture, for the letters composing such texts are addressed as much to strangers as they are to their fictional recipients. The printed words on the page are at once a noncommercial communication in letter form and a published work of fiction exchanged for money in the marketplace and pored over by unknown members of the reading public. Although the old mode is still present and visible, it has been penetrated to the core by the commodity form. In epistolary fiction, the recessive and the emergent, the not-for-sale and the vendible, inhabit the identical script; there is no difference between them.

The novel's categorical and legal equivocations are reconstituted on the level of theme. Particularly in those dozens of works dealing with seduction and marriage, one finds a similar ambivalence about communalism and the legitimacy of self-assertiveness. In at least two respects the courtship-seduction plot attempts a troubled accommodation with change. The determination of young women to make their own choices about their emotional and sexual lives, and frequently to do so in defiance of the wishes of parents and friends, is part of the history of affective individualism. Seduction becomes an absorbing problem in fiction because of the perceived reality that marriageable girls are claiming control over their own persons and refusing to regard themselves as the obedient subordinates of others. The seduction novel represents both a sincere warning against this development and a covert affirmation of it.

Marriage-seduction plots invariably tell the story of a female character's rise or fall in economic position. They tend to merge into, or to be closely allied with, narratives of social mobility. If the novelists are to be believed, sudden changes of fortune were an increasingly common occurrence in eighteenth-century America; the ethos and forms of property of an expanding economy were producing social chaos. Here, too, the novels encompass modernizing and residual energies: although they give implicit sanction to economic striving by endorsing the credo of self-reliant individualism, they also deplore the bounders and con-men of the new order and try to freeze mobility into stasis.

Charlotte Temple and *The Coquette,* the two most popular early American novels, are tales of affective transgression that deeply disapprove of the behavior they portray. Teachers by temperament, Rowson and Foster wrote to instruct young readers in the necessity of subduing unlawful desires. Pedagogy suited them so well that Rowson, the founder of a prestigious female academy, published some half-dozen textbooks in addition to her novels, and Foster donned the explicit persona of a schoolmistress in her only other book, the collection of didactic letters entitled *The Boarding School* (1798).

Charlotte Temple and *The Coquette* probably owed some of their success to the conservative recoil from the French Revolution. The reaction was already in full swing by the mid-1790s, when bloody images of the Terror produced disenchantment throughout the United States. American readers may well have interpreted Rowson's novel as an allegory of innocence betrayed by foreign seducers. The three characters who victimize the heroine all have French surnames, though two of them are English: La Rue, Montraville, and Belcour. This tale of the "temple" violated underscores the importance of internal vigilance. *The Coquette,* which takes its title from the French word for flirt, similarly permits a political reading. A spirit of license infects Americans with alien delusions. The protagonist, Eliza Wharton, becomes intoxicated with independence. She carries her desire for freedom too far and embarks on a downward course that terminates in illicit pregnancy and death.

Both novels focus on the dangers of forsaking familial responsibilities and putting the self first. Though the prolific Rowson showed remarkable independence in her own life, in her best-seller she extols filial piety and female subordination. "Oh my dear girls, for to such only am I writing," she exclaims in a characteristic passage, "listen not to the voice of love unless sanctioned by parental approbation . . . , pray for fortitude to resist the impulse of inclination when it runs counter to the precepts of religion and virtue." Rowson's manner of telling her story reinforces its emphasis on obligation to others. She starts with a chapter on Charlotte Temple at boarding school, jumps in the second chapter to Charlotte's father and his youthful acts of generosity, and shifts in the third to the misfortunes of Charlotte's maternal grandfather, Mr. Eldridge. One gets a sense of individual lives as embedded in an intergenerational network, not as isolated and autonomous. The text strongly affirms the traditional value of interdependence: Mr. Eldridge moves in with his daughter and Mr. Temple to form a "happy trio," and when Charlotte dies after giving birth to an illegitimate daughter, her parents gladly assume responsibility for the infant.

But Rowson also ratifies the female reader's sentiments, and her text's liminality inheres in its simultaneous endorsement of "parental approbation" and "the impulse of inclination." Charlotte's downfall stems from an excess of feeling; this turns out to be a trait she shares with both her creator and the novel's audience. Charlotte, who is constantly blushing and seems unable to control her emotions, is a monitory figure because she yields to her "treacherous heart" and prefers "the love of a stranger to the affectionate protection of her friends" (by whom Rowson means her family). But the hierarchy thus established between filial loyalty and affective self-fulfillment is confounded by the example of Charlotte's father. Mr. Temple is as much a prototype for his daughter's behavior as a sufferer from it: having determined at an early age "to marry where the feelings of his heart should direct him," he broke with his own father rather than submit to a loveless match.

Moreover, Rowson encourages emotional indulgence in the young women for whom she writes. She upbraids the unmoved among her readers and repeatedly summons the "heart of sensibility" to shed tears for Charlotte's fate; Chapter 33, the account of the heroine's death, carries the warning "Which People Void of Feeling Need Not Read." At such moments, the emotionalism of the authorial voice threatens to overwhelm its moral prohibitions. To critics of the genre, the educator–novelist must have seemed in league with the character most responsible for Charlotte's lapse: the French teacher, Miss La Rue, who incites her pupil's infatuation for Lieutenant Montraville.

Rowson's celebration of affectivity implicitly resituates women from the margins of the family to the center. The disposition to feel deeply and to weep is, she admits, often despised as a feminine infirmity. But because a tear "is the sacred drop of humanity," to cry is to announce one's human subjecthood, not one's failing. Miss La Rue reveals her preternatural wickedness precisely in her indifference to Charlotte's agony. And decent male characters, such as Mr. Temple and Mr. Eldridge, far from practicing a stoic self-control, regularly "sob aloud," "burst into tears," or relieve their hearts with "a friendly gush." Rowson interrupts the action to reprove any readers who might be inclined to criticize:

Should any one, presuming on his own philosophic temper, look with an eye of contempt on the man who could indulge a woman's weakness, let him remember that man was a father, and he will then pity the misery which wrung those drops from a noble, generous heart.

In Rowson's impassioned narrative, men show themselves to be fully human by emulating the behavior of women.

The Coquette, a much "cooler" fiction, utilizes the epistolary format and refrains from authorial intervention. Eliza Wharton is not a gullible innocent but a sophisticated woman in her midthirties who yearns toward a future of female emancipation. The death of her betrothed, a man chosen by her father, awakens in her a desire to direct her own life. "A melancholy event has extricated me from those shackles which parental authority had imposed on my mind. Let me then enjoy that freedom which I so highly prize." Two suitors compete for Eliza's favor: Mr. Boyer, a clergyman who offers "a decent competency" and a life of service and who embodies the rational, republican values of the past; and Major Sanford, a speculator and an apparently wealthy rake who encourages Eliza to seek her pleasure and who prefigures the atomized, acquisitive order of the nineteenth century. These two characters might be compared to the familiar fair and dark ladies of Anglo-American fiction, with Eliza assuming — or arrogating — the part of the male. Foster's heroine claims the right to choose among her admirers as she pleases, not as others advise, and she further inverts conventional gender roles by vowing not to settle down until she has "sowed all my wild oats."

The novel harshly punishes this assertion of affective autonomy. Eliza's coquetry alienates Boyer, and she eventually becomes the mistress of Sanford, who has married another woman. The desperate heroine ends up dying in childbirth in a roadside tavern "Far From Every Friend," as her tombstone has it, a stranger among strangers, her fate a grim omen of the new order's anonymity. Foster lets her plot and characters do her moralizing, especially Eliza's friend, Lucy Freeman, who counsels self-denial and, even more to the point, happily relinquishes her symbolic maiden name when she marries. And, of course, this abjuring of a freeman's status corresponded to the reality of the feminine condition. Eighteenth-century American women could neither vote nor hold office, and they were forbidden to own separate property once they married.

Foster's story serves to alert readers to the "modern" family's weakness as a moral guardian. If Eliza falls because of an excess of freedom, blame also attaches to her family for having abdicated its responsibilities. The historic transition from marriages as arranged to marriages of affection, which is telescoped in the novel's first chapter, results in a situation where parents no longer feel comfortable monitoring their children's actions. Eliza has so little fear of her mother's chastisement that she sleeps with Sanford in her own home. Mrs. Wharton is "afraid to make any inquiries into the matter" and absents herself rather than risking a scene. Nor is this simply the foible of a timid widow. The parents of Sanford's wife, Nancy, initially opposed the match because of his libertinism. "But she had not been used to contradiction, and could not bear it; and therefore they ventured not to cross her." A conservative New England Federalist, Foster agrees with Rowson on the need for filial obedience, but she sees the family in disarray and wants to revivify its traditional role of supervision over unmarried offspring.

What makes *The Coquette* a compelling reading experience today is its undeniable sympathy for the heroine. The revelation in the last chapter of Eliza's advanced age — she is thirty-seven — registers as a shock because she has seemed all along the most vibrant and youthful of the book's characters. Having previously bowed to her father's will against her own inclination, she has no wish to abridge her autonomy a second time, and one can fully understand her reluctance: neither of the men courting her seems very appealing. Sanford is shallow and vain, more in love with riches than he could ever be with a woman. The pompous Boyer acts more like a parent than a lover. Her mother, the heroine justly observes, "is better calculated to make him a good wife than I am or ever shall be." A clergyman's wife herself, Foster communicates an impression of the ministry as a declining profession – which to some extent it may have been in the 1790s – and she implies that small-town life under the watchful eyes of a congregation can be unbearably oppressive.

Foster's anti-individualistic message is at variance with her book's openness to subjectivity and desire. The novel as coquette struggles against the novel as teacher. Eliza's insistence on following her own taste gets her into trouble but also makes her the most interesting and three-dimensional of the book's characters. Her friends – who endlessly review her conduct – sense this themselves, even as they scold her for moral lapses. The many people pressing Eliza to submit to their notions of how she should behave amount to a "posse," as Sanford says, and would extinguish her personality. However much Foster favors a return to old-fashioned vigilance, she cannot help suggesting that anonymity grounds personal freedom. A future without community may be the price of independent selfhood, but at least it offers escape from the relentless scrutiny of censorious "friends."

Furthermore, though Foster's self-excision in telling her story supports its warning against emotional intemperance, the narrative, in its very restraint, encourages the intellectual freedom of the female reader. Artfulness and indirection replace lecturing, and each reader has to reach her own conclusions about Eliza's fate. Didacticism, in the most didactic of novelistic subgenres, perceptibly recedes; there is not even a preface to spell out the moral. Foster expects women to think and judge for themselves, and she is enough of a patriot to resent their exclusion from political life. The ardency of a minor character's feminist speech is clearly the author's own:

If the community flourish and enjoy health and freedom, shall we not share in the happy effects? If it be oppressed and disturbed, shall we not endure our proportion of the evil? Why, then, should the love of our country be a masculine passion only? Why should government, which involves the peace and order of the society of which we are a part, be wholly excluded from our observation?

This passage indicates the limitations of viewing the seduction novel as a privatized medium. Foster directs the reader's attention to civic affairs as surely as Royall Tyler or Hugh Henry Brackenridge. Her goal here is the political one of challenging patriarchy. Although the last sentence qualifies her passage's force, Foster, like Judith Sargent Murray and other articulate members of the revolutionary generation, found in republican rhetoric a rationale for the extension of political rights to women.

Charlotte Temple and *The Coquette* are tales haunted by social mobility as well as seduction. In both books, the villains crave position and wealth, and their pursuit of economic self-interest threatens moral order. As Charlotte Temple, abandoned by her seducer, sinks into poverty, her scheming former teacher, Miss La Rue, revels in luxury as the wife of the affluent Colonel Crayton. The rise of the guilty produces a baffled acknowledgment that "fortune is blind . . . else why do we see fools and knaves at the very top of the wheel, while patient merit sinks to the extreme of the opposite abyss."

La Rue's advancement constitutes a rebuke to new ideas of laissez faire. She prospers neither because she deserves to nor because she confers benefits on others but because her rapacity surpasses that of everyone else. Rowson cannot allow the scandal of a person's rising without merit to persist, and so she appends a concluding – and rectifying – chapter set some ten years after the principal action. In it, we learn that La Rue has been thrown out by her finally awakened husband. Reduced to begging in the streets, she serves as "a striking example that vice, however prosperous in the beginning, in the end leads only to misery and shame."

The figure in *The Coquette* who exemplifies social mobility is the dissolute Major Sanford. He too is forced to suffer for his temporary appearance of success. To Eliza, he "lives in all the magnificence of a prince," and her attraction to his opulent habits is a symptom of her moral weakness. But in reality Sanford has dissipated his wealth and has to marry an heiress to avoid impoverishment. By the story's end, he has run through his wife's fortune too and is obliged to sell everything he owns to satisfy his creditors.

The socioeconomic moralism of these two works, their insistence that corrupt persons end up destitute, calms the anxieties generated by increased mobility. As Rowson is all too aware, just deserts are seldom distributed so unerringly in the real world. The novelistic wish to compensate for this inequity often dovetails with loyalties to hierarchy and social cohesion. Many writers disapprove of the ambition to ascend to a higher class and express consternation over the more fluid conditions that prevailed after independence. These writers picture an economic environment destabilized by an expanding market and its mobile forms of wealth: wealth that can appear or disappear in an instant, created by a forger's pen – as in *Arthur Mervyn* and *Dorval* – or vanished in a shipwreck.

Rapid shifts in material condition pervade the postrevolutionary novel and register the genre's disorientation before an economy that seemed to bestow rewards and punishments on whim. Meteoric enrichments and abrupt collapses into indigence generate early fiction's endless complications of plot. Alonzo Haventon of *The Asylum* – his name plays on "have not" and "haven't one" – loses the prospect of marriage to his beloved Melissa when the senior Haventon, a merchant, suffers business reverses and the entire family is "hurled in a moment from the lofty summit of affluence to the low and barren vale of poverty." In Rebecca Rush's *Kelroy* (published anonymously in 1812), an avaricious widow is reduced to beggary by a fire and just as suddenly enriched by winning a lottery, random occurrences that darkly parody "those fatal changes to which mercantile concerns are always liable."

Numerous authors share Hannah Foster's perception of a masked and anonymous world, inhabited by people whose social origins are unknown and about whose moral characters little can be outwardly determined. In *Kelroy,* a book obsessed with economic and social disorder, the vicious Mr. Marney is described as "one of those beings who may be said to spring from nobody knows where; and rise in the world nobody can tell how; and spend the latter half of their lives in striving to erase from the minds of the community all remembrance of the former." The early novel teems with "new men," habitually cast in a negative light; it is a source of grievance that letters of reference have become as essential in social matters as in business. *Female Quixotism* turns its formidable wit on this requirement in making it an integral part of the plot. The Irish adventurer O'Connor has to forge an introduction when the heroine's father insists that someone vouch for his honor, and the discovery of the forgery leads to his exposure. In Wood's *Dorval,* which deals with speculations in public securities and Georgia lands, identity has assumed the protean shape of mobile property. Even one's name is not a secure possession: Colonel Morely changes his name from Wilson to obtain an inheritance; Dorval was christened Haland and is also known as Fowler; and the heroine Aurelia has five possible surnames in the course of the story, the last of which, Burlington, is the name she acquires when she finally marries.

Women in the courtship novel have always faced such changes of name, signifying alteration not just in marital status but often in social condition as well. An extreme though not atypical example of the entanglement of marriage and mobility occurs in *The Asylum*. Colonel Bloomfield demands that his daughter Melissa decide between her two admirers:

Happiness and misery await your choice; marry Bowman, and you roll in your coach and flaunt in your silks; your furniture and your equipage are splendid, your associates of the first character, and your family rejoice in your prosperity; marry Haventon, and you sink into obscurity, are condemned to drudgery, poorly fed, worse clothed, and your relations and acquaintance shun and despise you.

What makes this formulation unfair, according to Isaac Mitchell, is that it does not take account of economic opportunity; in a country like America, no one is condemned to permanent status as a propertyless pauper.

Here the novel's individualistic implications come to the fore. Most novelists share Mitchell's belief in economic initiative and agree that if the market breeds swindlers and speculators, it also enhances the possibility of one's advancing through personal effort: for every Thomas Welbeck, there is an Arthur Mervyn (with the proviso that Mervyn himself is an ambiguous figure). Generic leanings coalesce with the national faith in starting afresh. The novel, itself an arriviste among literary forms and a potentially lucrative speculation (or "hazard," as Mitchell terms the risk of fiction writing), harbors an irrepressible sympathy for the aspiring adventurers who throng its pages. Even Rush's deep mistrust of the newly rich does not prevent her from affirming the principle of self-reliance. Although the poet Kelroy has been impoverished by his father's speculative ventures, "his talents and industry," Rush writes, "would enable him to make his way in the world without much difficulty." Native fiction writers relished inserting Benjamin Franklin, the culture's emblem of the self-made man, into their narratives of economic striving. Franklin appears as a character in *The Algerine Captive* and *The Asylum,* and he hovers as a background presence in *Arthur Mervyn,* a paradigm for Mervyn's rise from pennilessness to wealth. In Mitchell's tale, Franklin is instrumental in disproving the supposed permanence of poverty. His intervention recoups the family fortune for the Haventons and, by restoring Alonzo to his rightful class, enables the hero to wed Melissa.

Yet the Franklin prototype failed to dispel skepticism about his representativeness as a climber who deserved success. Unpersuaded that merit invariably rises, writers could not shake their disquiet over economic fluidity. Some reverted to fantasies of a social order where change merely ruffles the surface of continuity. Alonzo's rise is in actuality no more than his reinstatement in the stratum where he began. His career updates the archetypal pattern of exile and return as a saga of declassing and of subsequent recovery of property and worldly position; the contrast to Franklin's linear experience could not be more emphatic. James Butler's *Fortune's Foot-Ball; or, The Adventures of Mercutio* (1797), a standard picaresque narrative of restless questing, traces the same circuitous route back to the beginning. The last paragraph sums up the picaro's stationary progress:

Having now completed my design, in tracing our hero through the various vicissitudes to which he was subjected in the course of his peregrinations, and, finding him at last, in his native country, surrounded by his most sincere friends and affectionate relatives, at the very summit of happiness, in the possession of the lovely Isabella, and reinstated in ease and affluence, I shall close my history.

Mercutio's fate can be taken as exemplary of a cluster of early American fictions — by no means all of them — in which the Franklin model vies with, and in the end is neutralized by, older ideals of social stability.

Tyler's *The Algerine Captive* and Brackenridge's *Modern Chivalry,* two of the stronger fictions of the period, are picaresque narratives that exhibit the novel's divergent impulses in a "masculine" form. Both works embrace the primacy of the civic sphere and retreat into insistent didacticism. Both simultaneously sanction centrifugal modern forces. Tyler's book is literally split in two: the freewheeling satire of the first volume yields to the moralizing and factual exposition of the second. Volume I relates Updike Underhill's travels in America and ridicules, among other targets, Puritan intolerance, useless classical learning, the ineptitude of doctors, and the hypocrisy of the South; the point of view is sharply critical of native foibles. Volume II provides a long account of Underhill's seizure by pirates and his six years captivity in Algiers. Descriptions of Algerine customs and history alternate with attacks on slavery to transform an irreverent novel into a pedagogic and hortatory one. The shift in tone culminates in a celebration of the United States as "the freest country in the universe" and in an appeal to uphold the federal government: "BY UNITING WE STAND, BY DIVIDING WE FALL."

Outspoken by the conclusion, Tyler's commitment to patriotism has been present all along. His preface condemns the national craving for English fictions, which intoxicate with their glamorous pictures of vice and prejudice the "young female" reader against "the homespun habits of her own country." Tyler pictures the novel reader as a woman because he aims to win her over to a revised conception of sentiment. He wants native works of literature in which the emotional or "seductive" energy of the novel is channeled to public-spirited ends. His hero, Underhill, accepts a post as a physician on a slave ship called the *Sympathy,* and whereas "the power of sympathy" incites characters to commit incest in William Hill Brown's novel of that name, in Tyler's tale sympathy produces civic benefits. Enslaved himself, Underhill experiences at first hand the anguish of those deprived of liberty. The "finer feelings of [his] heart" are awakened, and he grows into a more compassionate being and a better patriot. "Let those of our fellow citizens, who set at nought the rich blessings of our federal union, go like me to a land of slavery, and they will learn how to appreciate the value of our free government." Volume II impresses the same lesson on the novel's readers; they are jolted out of complacency by being forced to identify, through Underhill's suffering, with the slave's perspective. *The Algerine Captive,* like Tyler's comedy *The Contrast,* integrates sentiment into the world of men. The novel politicizes affectivity so that it becomes an instrument of public virtue rather than the invitation to feminine self-indulgence deplored by critics.

Paradoxically, Tyler's patriotic maneuver allies his book with historical movements that undid his republican and unionist principles. No more than William Hill Brown or Susanna Rowson could he delimit the power of feeling. Although his sometime collaborator, Joseph Dennie, reported that *The Algerine Captive* had been approved "by the few," the text's affirmations work to erode, not maintain, such elitist distinctions. Tyler's extension of full humanity to black slaves as well as to white captives admits an explosive pressure into the book, the pressure of an ascendant liberalism that grants autonomous selfhood to all persons. Liberal ideology quickened by sentiment would eventually shatter the federal unity that Tyler wrote to preserve by demanding an end to the South's "peculiar institution." The novel's unflattering portrait of the South, its appeals to that "New England staple . . . called conscience," and its horrific images of slavery (the slave traders throw ailing blacks overboard, explaining to Underhill that the creatures *"love to die"*) – these were the elements, refashioned by Harriet Beecher Stowe and other antebellum writers, many of them women, that roused abolitionist feeling and helped to bring about the Civil War.

In *Modern Chivalry,* Brackenridge's multivolume satire, republican self-denial confronts individualistic self-assertion in the persons of Captain Farrago and his Irish servant, Teague O'Regan. The book's liveliness and humor come from the conflict between these two characters, and whereas Brackenridge's sympathies clearly lie with the captain, he has a grudging admiration for Teague's unconquerable desire to make his way in the world. Brackenridge recognizes the quixotic inappropriateness of Farrago's conservatism to an increasingly egalitarian and acquisitive society. The captain, often seconded by the narrative voice, espouses an elitist brand of civic humanist ideology that proves powerless to dissuade Teague from his inexhaustible ambitions. While the illiterate "bogtrotter" pushes himself forward as a philosopher, minister, major, and congressman, Farrago counsels the importance of talent and training and the civic obligation to sacrifice personal interest to the common good. "Let the cobbler stick to his last" is his motto. To Brackenridge, the struggle between "a patrician class" represented by Farrago and "the multitude" symbolized by Teague invigorates freedom; it is the "fermentation" keeping "the spirit of democracy" alive. Farrago's intermittent success in curbing his servant stems not from persuasion but from manipulation, as in the episode where he concocts letters from a rival challenging Teague to a duel; neither character, however, definitively gains the upper hand in the novel's first half, which appeared in installments between 1792 and 1797.

The second half of *Modern Chivalry* was published in three stages between 1804 and 1815; like the second volume of *The Algerine Captive,* it brings a decrease in satire and an escalation in didacticism. The captain recedes as a character, and Brackenridge steps forward ever more frequently to reprove Teague's presumption in his own voice and to deliver lectures on the excesses of democracy. The occasional stridency and defensiveness of the authorial interventions suggest that ideas of republican virtue were under seige by liberal individualism. Satire and irony deteriorate into burlesque in Part II. Brackenridge carries his mockery of popular judgment and democratic leveling to extravagant lengths in picturing life in the western territories. The multitude who saw fit to support Teague for Congress in Part I, blithely disregarding his lack of qualification and declaring that one candidate is as good as another, now apply the same logic to animals. When the inhabitants of a frontier settlement draw up a new constitution, they decree that animals will be eligible to vote and run for government positions. Brackenridge tirelessly repeats his book's "great moral" about restraining ambition in office seekers, but his expostulations seem as quixotic as the captain's in a community where the people elect panthers to office and admit hounds to the bar.

The irony of *Modern Chivalry* is that Brackenridge's growing exasperation with popular self-assertiveness merges into individualistic display. His abandonment of the belletristic for the directive betrays his own collusion in nineteenth-century habits of thought. Almost half of Part II was written in 1815 at the threshold of the American Romantic age. As the authorial pronouncements become more overt and less mediated, one has the impression of listening to a long-winded personal voice, a voice modulated by the stirrings of the individualistic spirit in literature. The Romantic "I" strangely materializes in the republican teacher (or preacher), and self-reflexivity increases along with civic reflections.

The Brackenridge of Part II talks far more freely about himself and his feelings. He explains that he writes "to get ease, and allay pain," or he advises readers to consult his book *Incidents of the Insurrection in the Western Parts of Pennsylvania in the Year 1794.* Cavalier disruptions of the text issue from the same voice but seem incompatible with its republican catechism. Brackenridge proposes that a chapter be "omitted in the subsequent editions"; he observes at a break in the story, "There would seem here to be an hiatus in the manuscript, or the sheets misplaced. The editor cannot connect the narrative." The formal disarray of the completed novel clashes with its professed allegiance to social order and hierarchy. The book is a self-conscious hodgepodge, a farrago, but more akin to the democratic multitude, who keep eliding distinctions, than to the republican captain. *Modern Chivalry,* in the very extremity of its desperation to rebuke the present, parrots the crazed logic, self-preoccupation, and willful modern temper it decries.

The early novel's ability to hold together premodern and individualistic urges had clearly begun to unravel by the second decade of the nineteenth century. The decade's end brought the breakthroughs of Irving and Cooper, who gave fresh inflections to the form by reimagining the relation between history or fact and subjectivity. John Neal and Samuel Woodworth, a pair of writers who are unread today, anticipated the Romantic revolution even as they demonstrated the exhaustion of the older mode. Neal had a colorful if short-lived reputation in the 1820s, when he befriended Edgar Allan Poe and produced a string of historical romances using native materials; the most readable, *Rachel Dyer,* appeared in 1828. Nathaniel Hawthorne cited Neal in lamenting the tardy development of an indigenous culture: "How slowly our literature grows up! Most of our writers of promise have come to untimely ends. There was that wild fellow, John Neal, who almost turned my boyish brain with his romances; he surely has long been dead, else he never could keep himself so quiet." This was written in 1845; the prolific Neal, who continued publishing into the Gilded Age, did not die until 1875.

Woodworth wrote *The Champions of Freedom* (1816), the first genuine historical romance published by an American and a direct antecedent of Cooper's *The Spy* (1821). A literary jack-of-all-trades, he was best known to his contemporaries as a playwright and as the author of a popular song, "The Old Oaken Bucket," which became a fixture in antebellum poetry anthologies. Neither Neal nor Woodworth has endured as a novelist because, unlike Irving and Cooper, neither managed to surmount the increasing instability of the form. Their work shows early American fiction coming apart under the strain of its internal divisions, divisions exacerbated by the rise of a Romantic sensibility after the War of 1812.

Neal made his debut as a novelist in 1817 with a work that at first glance seems intent upon demolishing the past. *Keep Cool* mercilessly parodies just about every important eighteenth-century literary convention. Neal's title page mocks the authorial poses of anonymity and gentility by attributing the novel to "Somebody" – the name is a fictitious one, the reader is solemnly informed – and adding the title of "Esquire." A dedication to "His Country Women" explains that the writer will abstain from the usual protests of unworthiness – for what if his readers believed him? Next comes a review by the author of his own book in which he dismisses the idea that novels contribute to the literary prestige of the country, contending instead that "[t]rue patriotism . . . is to be quiet." The review satirizes the ostentatious erudition of upper-class journals like the *Monthly Anthology* and the *Portico* (with which Neal was associated). Its italicized opening sentence announces that *"America was discovered by Christopher Columbus, a Genoese, in the year 1492"* and supports the statement with a citation to Noah Webster's dictionary; sixteen additional footnotes, most of them equally superfluous, crowd nine pages of text. The spoofing continues into the first chapter, which features an old man who claims to be writing the novel and who utterly rejects the standard of factual accuracy: "I will *not* draw from life – my characters shall be my own." Neal's title is itself a jibe at sentimental fiction's appeal to the reader's emotions. Constantly interrupting the narrative at climactic moments, he commands his audience to "Keep Cool" and conducts them on verbose detours from the action.

Such raillery is worthy of Irving and bespeaks an imagination emancipated from republican imperatives. Despite the injunction to keep cool, the imagination at work is recognizably Romantic – impatient of convention, indifferent to social utility, fascinated by the self. Neal's high jinks keep threatening to overshadow the story with an exhibition of individual sensibility. This points to the fissured identity of *Keep Cool* as part burlesque, part courtship and adventure novel. The parodic commentary accompanies an unexceptional plot involving young lovers, their separation and trials, and their ultimate reunion. Particularly in the second volume, the parodic voice trails off, and the narrative degenerates into what it ridicules: a sentimental fiction laced with didacticism. Lectures on dueling, the plight of the Indians, and capital punishment now predominate, competing for the reader's attention with descriptions of the lovers' predicaments, and Neal's sporadic bursts of sarcasm seem wildly out of place. The effect is one of jarring incongruities, careenings between pedagogic earnestness and dismissal of it. Neal chafed at the postrevolutionary novel's procedures, but as yet he did not see how to go beyond them other than by mockery. The historical romances he subsequently wrote in an attempt to duplicate Cooper's success are distinguished chiefly by the lurid violence and sexual titillation in which they far exceed their models.

Cooper had his forerunners as well as his imitators in the writing of historical fiction, and not just on the other side of the Atlantic, where Sir Walter Scott was composing the Waverley novels. Among other indigenous examples, the Reverend Jeremy Belknap's *The Foresters* (1792) is an allegory of the dispute between the colonies and Britain, and Rowson's *Reuben and Rachel,* a fictionalized textbook written for young schoolgirls curious about "their native country," surveys American history from the voyage of Columbus to the present. Rowson's work in particular suggests how the early novel's concern with factuality and instruction could metamorphose into something approximating a historical romance. But whereas national events serve mainly as background in *Reuben and Rachel,* Woodworth purports to interweave "private events . . . with the thread of public history" in *The Champions of Freedom.* This patriotic tale carries the imposing subtitle "The Mysterious Chief. A Romance of the Nineteenth Century, Founded on Events of the War, Between the United States and Great Britain, Which Terminated in March 1815."

The Champions of Freedom can be considered the end point of the early novel, the book in which the form's conflicting allegiances erupt into open warfare. Woodworth's text reveals the difficulty, even the impossibility, of mediating any longer between the novel's communal–factual side and its commitment to individual fulfillment. According to the preface, the story is simultaneously a true memorial to civic virtue, "the most correct and complete History of the recent War, that has yet appeared," and a romance with the "sole end and aim" of expressing the artist's personality, a work so original that it resembles nothing "that has ever preceded it." Though the ensuing narrative is supposedly readable either "as a history or a novel," it defies any effort to read it as a composite work of art.

The two strains of "Love and Patriotism," as a chapter title has it, refuse to coexist amicably; their aversion becomes explicit as a theme and leads to startling divergences in style. A supernatural Indian figure known as the Mysterious Chief repeatedly warns the hero, George Washington Willoughby, not to allow his childhood sweetheart "to engross those affections which were to be devoted to your country. . . . for your country claimed you, and must have you undivided – entire." Willoughby, who spends most of his time at the front, keeps a journal in which he records the daily progress of the war; his entries, consisting of military dispatches, detailed accounts of operations, and lists of officers singled out for bravery (sometimes numbering upwards of fifty names), litter the text like inert lumps of fact. Meanwhile, the romantic narrative goes forward, a tale of courtship and seduction that seems to have strayed from some other book, perhaps *Charlotte Temple:* "The too successful villain sprang from the sofa, clasped her in his rude embrace, and for some moments held the insensible sufferer locked in his unhallowed arms, rifling her pallid lips of their sweets."

It will be apparent that Woodworth's claims to originality are highly inflated, yet there are passages not much superior to this in Cooper's historical fiction. Nor should the continuities be minimized: Woodworth is the native precursor whose failings are Cooper's magnified and whose aspirations were realized in the country's first great novelist. Beginning with *The Spy,* Cooper's works show the lesions of the early novel's identity crisis. Hybrids composed of military action and romantic entanglements, they abound in generic clashes and transfer the reader "from the hostile camp to the mansion of love" with a clumsiness that rivals *The Champions of Freedom.* Woodworth's Mysterious Chief may even have provided a hint for Cooper's enigmatic Harper from *The Spy;* the Indian unmasks in the novel's last paragraph as an allegorical embodiment of the *"Spirit of Washington."* But Cooper goes well beyond Woodworth in the privatizing of history. Whereas the author of *The Champions of Freedom* regards historical facts as a documentary record, with only tangential relation to the inner life of the characters, Cooper reconceives history as personal experience. He treats "factual truth" as a canvas on which the individual artist, emancipated from strict conformity to what actually happened, can paint as his imagination requires.

6

CHARLES BROCKDEN BROWN

I N 1 7 8 9 , when he was just eighteen, Charles Brockden Brown published a poem in honor of Benjamin Franklin, only to find that an erring printer, "from zeal or ignorance, or perhaps from both, substituted the name of Washington." The blunder, Brown relates in his journal, converted the Republic's military savior into a mere philosopher and "made the subject ridiculous. Every word of this clumsy panegyric was a direct slander upon Washington, and so it was regarded at the time."

This early incident from Brown's career can be read as a parable of his difficulties in trying to become a self-supporting author – a Franklin of letters – in a society dominated by republican ideals. Multiple lines connect the nation's first "canonical" novelist to the self-made Philadelphia printer who delighted in novels and adopted a female persona in his earliest publication. Like Franklin's *Autobiography,* Brown's fictions declare themselves to be acts of writing and hence products of print culture in contrast to the oral modes that previously held sway in America. In Brown's hands, the native novel realizes its identity as a middle-class genre overtly concerned with social mobility and individual self-fulfillment. A recurrent motif in his work, as in Franklin's, is sympathy for women and for the liberal project of female rights. Determined to treat literature as an occupation, not a gentlemanly pastime, Brown struggled to achieve independence by his pen. He was defeated in this goal most obviously because of his society's inability to support a class of professional authors, an understandable deficiency in a predominantly agricultural people. But beyond this, Brown's ambitions as a novelist foundered because he was reconceptualizing his medium as a private rather than a civic form. And in 1800, the public-spirited and corporate orientation of American culture still outweighed its individualistic side: the spirit of Washington overshadowed that of Franklin.

So formulated, the parable is too neat and does not do justice to Brown's own commitment to the idea of literary art as belonging to and serving the community. From the outset he emphasized the didactic aspect of his writing. He self-consciously sought to purify the novel of its disreputable associations in order to augment its influence for doing good. In the advertisement for his first book-length fiction, the lost *Sky Walk,* Brown describes himself as a "story-telling moralist" who aims not merely to please "the idle and thoughtless" but to engage "those who study and reflect." *Wieland; or, The Transformation* (1798), the first novel he actually published, slightly varies the image of the novelist to "moral painter" and reasserts Brown's claim to the serious reader's notice by proposing to illustrate "some important branches of the moral constitution of man."

Brown's accent on the novel's societal obligation leads him to minimize his inventiveness as an artist. The fiction writer is a purveyor of truths, not a contriver of ingenious incidents that flaunt his creativity. "Facts have supplied the foundation of the whole," Brown avers in his promotion for *Sky Walk,* a statement that could be applied to his fiction generally. *Wieland* purports to be based on "an authentic case," a gruesome murder reported in the *Philadelphia Minerva* that Brown assumes will be familiar to "most readers." He also appeals to known facts or "historical evidence" for his accounts of the senior Wieland's spontaneous combustion and Carwin's ventriloquism; and he initiates the practice, followed by later novelists like James Fenimore Cooper and Herman Melville, of supplying footnotes in the text to corroborate his narrative.

What complicates Brown's deference to historical truth and social utility is the highly problematic nature of his facts. His writing destabilizes the epistemological certainties of republican culture. *Wieland* could easily be read as a confutation, even a parody, of the early novel's proclaimed allegiance to narrative truthfulness, an allegiance that takes for granted the knowability of experience. Many of the "facts" in Brown's tale are improbable to the point of arousing disbelief, and his appeals to evidence often have the air of private jokes, as in the arcane footnote that explains the senior Wieland's death by referring the curious to the "researches of Maffei and Fontana" and to scholarly journals on medicine and on Florence. The questions, How do we know something? and, What constitutes trustworthy evidence? are at the very heart of this novel about mysterious voices and the deceptiveness of sensory data; the text provides no satisfactory answers. Brown's furnishing of a moral, or a number of morals, similarly produces more bewilderment than instruction. His narrator, Clara Wieland, variously counsels avoiding deceit, obtaining a proper upbringing, eschewing religious fanaticism, and guarding against one's own frailties. The novel's elusive and rather mercurial didacticism in effect authorizes the subjective judgment of the reader. "Make what use of the tale you shall think proper," Clara urges on the first page; "I leave you to moralize on this tale," she says on the last.

Brown's reluctance to preach to his readers reflects his belief that fictional narratives, whatever their moral benefits, are finally not synonymous with overtly didactic modes like the oration and the sermon. He has a strong sense of the novel as a new kind of cultural artifact that differs from verbal performances. Public speech involves immediacy but also formality and the subordination of the personal. The minister delivering a sermon is present to his parishioners, but his words are not a private revelation. Pervading Brown's text is an awareness of the novel as the inversion of oral practice, as a medium of distance and interiority. His art aligns itself with a far-reaching shift in American culture as a whole, a movement away from verbal forms to the constellation of values associated with writing and print.

Throughout his fiction, Brown confers conspicuous visibility on acts of speech and writing. It is as though the transition in the culture from one type of discourse to the other has brought both to consciousness and made them accessible to scrutiny in works of literature. The early novel in general shares this focus to some extent, as indicated by the widespread preference in the eighteenth century for the epistolary form, which casts the main characters in the role of writers. But Brown's work has few peers in its almost obsessive attention to speaking, hearing, reading, and writing. His novels teem with misplaced and discovered manuscripts, characters compulsively pouring out their life stories while other characters listen avidly, intercepted letters and overheard conversations, plagiarisms, forgeries, and verbal mimicries. Writing is enough of a special acquisition in his fictional world to have the status of a craft: several characters, including Arthur Mervyn and Stephen Dudley (Constantia's father in *Ormond*), find employment as scribes. People are constantly reflecting on the implications of oral versus written communication. Edgar Huntly, protagonist of the novel of the same name, begins his tale by deploring the inadequacy of writing, which is unaccompanied by the "looks and gestures" of speech. Characters in *Arthur Mervyn* express opinions ranging from mistrust of "an innocent brow and a voluble tongue" to strictures upon books as secondhand experience.

The displacement of the oral by the written figures importantly in *Wieland*. Brown's first novel suggests that attitudes originating in a verbal, face-to-face culture can be highly inappropriate, even dangerous, in the mediated, text-governed social order coming into being in the late eighteenth century. The Wieland family, along with their good friend, Pleyel, belong to a traditional world of speakers and auditors. These close-knit characters constitute a community devoted to polite conversation, theatrical performances, and the practice of "Roman eloquence." A bust of Cicero – the model of the republican orator – stands in the outdoor temple, and Clara's brother Theodore entertains the family by delivering the renowned rhetorician's speeches with suitable "gestures and cadences." For the Wielands, communication takes place not at a remove but on an interactive basis; what they value is immediacy. They have a history of hearing voices and construing them as direct utterances from an identifiable source, believed by the senior Wieland, and later by his son, to be God. Theodore's urgent pleas to the Deity – "that I might be admitted to thy presence," "that some unambiguous token of thy presence would salute my senses" – convey the family desire for unmediated access to a statement's "author."

Brown's narrative dramatizes the difficulty of knowing where voices come from and exposes the weakness in the Wielands' trust in direct experience. The family is plunged into misunderstandings and finally tragedy when Carwin, the "double-tongued deceiver," appears at the idyllic country retreat. Brown's interest in ventriloquism suggests a coded preoccupation with the nature of writing. Carwin's gift of counterfeiting voices endows him with the special power of the writer, the ability to communicate without being present to one's audience. As Clara puts it, "He is able to speak where he is not." Though Carwin's motives are far from benign, he would be harmless if the other characters did not cling to a simplified, speech-based notion of communication. They are misled by the ventriloquist's impersonations because they assume that an individual must be wherever his or her voice is. They expect all communication to exhibit the immediacy of verbal interchange.

Brown's style in *Wieland* and, indeed, in all his novels reinforces the point that writing and speech are distinct forms of utterance. His books seem almost to caricature the idea of a "writerly" text in which proximity yields to mediation. Many scholars have noticed his tendency to embed narratives in two, three, or even more additional narratives, so that stories are told at an ever greater remove from the original speaker. This pattern of removal subjects the reader to the same kind of uncertainty about authorial identity that the characters in *Wieland* too hastily try to dispel. The seemingly infinite regressions make it a daunting challenge to determine the source of the words on the page and provide a lesson in the necessity for caution. Brown's fondness for the passive voice further contributes to one's sense of being disconnected from the subject. A random page from Clara's narrative turns up this extreme but not uncharacteristic illustration: "That conscious beings, dissimilar from human, but moral and voluntary agents as we are, somewhere exist, can scarcely be denied. That their aid may be employed to benign or malignant purposes, cannot be disproved." Brown's prose in such passages is saturated with the ideology of an ascendant print culture: he produces writing that in its distance from the author proclaims its status as writing and pointedly demarcates itself from speech.

Even Brown's notorious haste in composing is consonant with the methods and values of writing as opposed to those of oral culture. Verbal art depends heavily on formulaic devices conducive to memorization. Repetition, parallelism, foreshadowing, assonance, and consonance are among the distinguish-ing features of Homeric epics and other creations of oral art. Brown's fiction is notable for both the absence and the disfigurement of such elements. His narratives have a rushed, unfinished quality, as though written at breakneck speed without attending to structural coherence. (In fact, Brown published six novels within three years.) His sentences can be overlong and convoluted but as often give an impression of being dashed off, with one short sentence following another in staccato fashion, like the jottings of an eighteenth-century Ernest Hemingway.

The headlong thrust of Brown's prose is countered by his addiction to Latin derivatives – he is anything but a colloquial writer – and by his use of techniques that impede and confuse his plots. His books abound not so much in parallels and portents as in digressions, loose strands, and subplots. He often seems to lose direction, introducing characters and incidents only to forget them. An example from *Wieland* is the story of Louisa Conway's family, which Brown mentions early on and then loses sight of until the final chapter, two hundred pages later, where he dispatches it with a quick sum-mary. What has struck almost all readers about these peculiarities is that they amount to egregiously sloppy writing. They are the faults, precisely, of bad written composition: Brown's hurried carelessness asserts the writer's free-dom from the need to remember. His prose carries the dispensations of print to extravagant lengths. The rapidity of his style and the afterthoughts and memory lapses of his plots are the antithesis of the integrated strategies of construction, the mnemonic mechanisms, necessary to oral storage.

Brown's repudiation of speech-inspired attitudes associates his fiction with the suppression of disruptive elements in the new Republic. The consolida-tion of established authority in the postrevolutionary era amounted to a print "counterrevolution." It was aimed against those persons in American society who inhabited an oral subculture where books other than the Bible and the almanac were practically unknown. These groups, which included disaffected farmers in the North and evangelicals in all regions of the country, found expression in popular verbal forms like extempore preaching and political oratory; they were people of the spoken, not the written, word. Their antideferential behavior thoroughly alarmed the elite in the turbulent de-cades after the war. The movement to check them deliberately devalued the immediacy of popular interchange; it culminated in a written document, the Constitution.

The Constitution played a key role in the entrenchment of print ideology. The federal compact is the political counterpart to *Wieland,* informed like the novel by deep suspicion of the demand for unmediated access. James Madison points out in *Federalist No. 10* that the demagogue operates most dangerously at the local, "in-person" level, and the Constitution seeks to circumvent this threat by vesting ultimate power in the national government. Against the classical republican ideal of active civic participation and the close accountability of leaders – of immediacy, one might say – the Constitution attenuates the connection between rulers and the ruled and, through its complex system of federalism, sets authority at a distance from the citizen. In effect, the Constitution reproduces in the polity the essential feature of writing as opposed to speech, the nonpresence of the author.

Brown's attraction to "printedness" as a model also links his fiction to the rise of commerce. In America, print's hegemony was historically as tied to the market as it was to politics. Trade was a vital motive – perhaps even the primary motive – for the spread of literacy and the diffusion of printed matter. Moreover, trade was closely bound up with the Republic's transition to a modern society based on mediated relations. The agricultural economy of the eighteenth century depended on face-to-face transactions. The commercial system that gradually supplanted it involved transactions at a distance and often through the mediation of commodities. Like print, and like representative government, commerce displaced direct contact with indirect dealings. As *Arthur Mervyn,* Brown's novel of the commercial city, suggests, trade put a premium on dispassionate evaluation.

After *Wieland,* Brown published three novels in rapid succession in an effort to establish himself as the Republic's foremost fiction writer: *Ormond; or The Secret Witness* (1799), *Edgar Huntly; or Memoirs of a Sleep-Walker* (1799), and *Arthur Mervyn; or Memoirs of the Year 1793* (1799–1800). He was eager to expand the subject matter of the American novel and to move the form in original directions that would enhance its standing with cultivated readers. For Brown, the "idle and thoughtless" were the addicts of sentimental love stories, most of them presumably women. The novelist had a low opinion of Samuel Richardson and of the profusion of titillating seduction tales consumed by eighteenth-century readers – tales that focused on the romantic ordeals of the heroine and that took their titles from women's names: *Pamela, Clarissa, Charlotte Temple.* Such books unwittingly confirmed the civic-humanist prejudice that whereas men aspired to public virtue – from the Latin *vir,* for man – women, as creatures of privacy and the emotions, posed a threat to republican values. The novel was a female genre that had no place in American society.

Brown's commitment to an edifying republican literature allies him to some extent with the gender binaries of his culture. His choice of titles expresses a resolve to resist the novel's feminization: the four major works of fiction he published between 1798 and 1800 are all named for men. Yet in other respects Brown dissented from the civic humanist suspicion of the female. His attachment to the modern configuration of print, individual self-realization, and the novel disposed him, much like Franklin, to identify with women. His early dialogue *Alcuin* (1798) is a plea for equality between the sexes, and two of his four major fictions, despite their titles, devote more space to female characters than to male ones. *Wieland* could easily have been called *Clara Wieland,* and his second novel, *Ormond,* is really a narrative about Constantia Dudley. This pattern of oscillation or ambivalence toward women's perspective persisted throughout Brown's career.

Ormond is a tale of female independence and political conspiracy that turns the popular seduction novel into an intellectually ambitious hybrid. Brown takes the simple plot of a maiden resisting a seducer and complicates it with unexpected turns and speculations: the quest of Constantia Dudley to achieve economic self-support, a highly unusual condition for an eighteenth-century heroine; Constantia's intense involvement, bordering on "romantic passion," with her friend, Sophia Westwyn; and reflections on a woman's plight that echo the arguments of *Alcuin.* For example, Constantia declines a marriage proposal because, as a woman living in postrevolutionary America, she would lose her separate identity by becoming a wife: "So far from possessing property, she herself would become the property of another."

The novel's eponymous villain is no ordinary seducer. A utopian schemer and Bavarian Illuminatus, Ormond opposes marriage on theoretical grounds and is a master of disguises who excels at mimicry (another example of speech aping writing's absence). He tries to seduce Constantia with rational arguments; when these fail, Ormond is so impressed by her intelligence and strength of character that he abandons his principles and proposes. His final effort to ravish her physically seems a concession to popular taste on Brown's part, and the heroine's stabbing of her attempted seducer in a deserted country residence marks a reversion to gothic melodrama. Constantia emerges as a desirable feminine mean between Helena Cleves, Ormond's dependent mistress, and his sanguinary sister, Martinette de Beauvais, an enthusiast for liberty who has donned "male dress" to fight in both the American and French revolutions.

As a novel, *Ormond* is a tissue of generic reversals or transfigurations; it replicates on the level of structure one of the most salient features of Brown's work, the mutability of his characters. Martinette's statement about her mother, "This woman was perpetually assuming new forms," holds true for just about everyone in Brown's fiction. People go mad, sleepwalk, wear disguises, and practice imposture. Doubles are everywhere, and the boundaries between persons often seem to blur or dissolve altogether. In *Ormond,* the title character exemplifies this instability, metamorphosing from political visionary to would-be rapist and murderer; along the way, he uses his "facility in imitating the voice and gestures of others" to insinuate himself into people's privacy, as when he gains access to the Dudley home by taking on the appearance of a chimney sweep.

Criticism has variously accounted for these character permutations. They have been interpreted as an index to Brown's nonmimetic, allegorical mode; as a reflex of the dislocations of postwar America; and as penetrating psychological analysis. Multiple in meaning, the metamorphoses have a social dimension that gradually moves to center stage, becoming fully visible only in the saga of Arthur Mervyn's way to wealth. But even in *Ormond,* there are repeated and chaotic examples of social mobility, alterations of a kind we have encountered elsewhere in the early novel. The Dudleys, whose history occupies much of the narrative, plunge "from the summit of affluence to the lowest indigence" and then are restored to prosperity. Helena, Martinette, and Sophia also experience "the vicissitudes of fortune." Pursuing the comparison to Benjamin Franklin, one might say that Brown's novels, along with those of his compatriots, depict the randomness and incoherence of economic life in the federal period that Franklin sought to combat through his advocacy of rational acquisitive behavior. The characters in *Ormond* are impoverished by unpredictable occurrences beyond their control – in Mr. Dudley's case, being embezzled and going blind – and they are enriched by similarly accidental events, such as catching the eye of a benefactor or receiving an unexpected inheritance.

Transformations keep piling up in *Edgar Huntly,* Brown's most self-consciously "American" novel and the only one to go into a second edition during his lifetime. Indeed, in this book Brown prophetically helped to define what an American novel would be. A prefatory note boasts of breaking new (and indigenous) ground by spurning the well-worn paraphernalia of the English horror tale – "puerile susperstition and exploded manners, gothic castles and chimeras" – in favor of "the incidents of Indian hostility, and the perils of the western wilderness." Cooper, with his Leatherstocking Tales, and Edgar Allan Poe, with his desolate landscapes and nightmarish caves, were among the later American writers to follow Brown's lead.

Edgar Huntly is a hallucinatory narrative in which the hero undergoes changes surpassing "the transitions of enchantment." Mysteriously awakening in a cave in the wilderness, Huntly enters an Ovidian realm of shifting forms where the boundaries and nature of the self are constantly in question. It turns out that he has been sleepwalking in unconscious imitation of Clithero Edny, a guilt-ridden Irishman whom he comes increasingly to resemble. In the course of his adventures, Huntly also acquires the qualities of animals and savages: "I disdained to be outdone in perspicacity by the lynx, in his sure-footed instinct by the roe, or in patience under hardship, and contention with fatigue, by the Mohawk." An interpolated story told by Clithero reinforces the novel's picture of confused and inconstant identity. Clithero's narrative concerns his benefactress, Mrs. Lorimer, and the twin brother with whom she thinks she shares a "copartnership in being." This tale culminates in the Irishman's own disintegration into madness. By the time the two narratives converge and Huntly replaces Clithero as Mrs. Lorimer's "son," completing his identification with his demented double, little remains of the idea of a distinct and knowable self.

Huntly's compulsion is clearly psychological, but it has an acquisitive side as well. He identifies with Clithero because he wants to duplicate the Irishman's rise from rural poverty. Both men are discontented sons of struggling farmers, and Clithero's tale of escaping his background rouses Huntly to crave and then literally to usurp the stranger's bettered circumstances. The theme of social mobility comes to the fore during Huntly's journey back to civilization. The hero pauses at three dwellings that summarize, as it were, his eventual career. The first is the miserable hut of Queen Mab, the second a modest farmhouse, and the third a prosperous abode betokening "beings raised by education and fortune above the intellectual mediocrity of clowns." Huntly believes he can "claim consanguinity with such beings," and the narrative vindicates his conviction by reuniting him with his former mentor, Sarsefield. Newly married to the wealthy Mrs. Lorimer, Sarsefield has returned to America to snatch his pupil "from a life of labor and obscurity." Thus does Edgar supplant Clithero in Mrs. Lorimer's protection, possibly even to seek the hand of Clarise, the look-alike niece to whom Clithero was once betrothed. Certainly Huntly has no intention of marrying his penniless fiancée, Mary Waldegrave – a change of mind that anticipates another of Brown's provincial young men on the make, Arthur Mervyn.

Arthur Mervyn is Brown's most substantial achievement and arguably the finest novel written by an American during the formative period. It is a prescient book, a harbinger of the triumph of individualism in society and of subjectivity in the novel. In two dense volumes Brown chronicles a raw youth's encounter with the metropolis and his perilous climb to success. The story, set partly in Philadelphia and partly in the surrounding countryside, calls to mind Franklin's celebrated ascent and is clearly intended as a major statement about American identity and prospects on the threshold of the new century. Here Brown turns directly to the social issues that are present but muted in his earlier fiction. He draws a graphic picture of a nation in transition from an agrarian to a commercial republic. *Arthur Mervyn* maps the social, psychological, and sexual coordinates of the emergent system, revealing how central that system is to Brown's ambitions as a novelist.

"Walstein's School of History," a critical essay Brown wrote shortly after the completion of the first volume of *Arthur Mervyn,* provides a valuable introduction to his novel. Commenting on the intellectual system of an author named Engel – a thinly disguised self-portrait – Brown declares that the most "extensive source" of human relations "is property. No topic can engage the attention of man more momentous than this. Opinions, relative to property, are the immediate source of nearly all the happiness and misery that exist among mankind." Statements about the importance of the economic were not unusual in Brown's time. The contemporaneous debate between Jefferson and Hamilton, centering on the opposition between ownership of land on the one side, and commercial and manufacturing forms of wealth on the other, looms in the background of *Arthur Mervyn.* Brown's views also resemble those of James Madison in *Federalist No. 10,* where Madison blames "the various and unequal distribution of property" as the principal cause of faction. In "Walstein's School of History," the novelist goes on to specify sex as a powerful, though secondary, determinant of human behavior. Well-being greatly depends, he says, "on the circumstances which produce, and the principles which regulate the union between the sexes."

Property and sexuality turn out to be closely related in *Arthur Mervyn,* which begins with the protagonist narrating his history to Dr. Stevens. Speech and rusticity go together here, as writing and privatized ambition are paired later. Arthur has recently arrived in Philadelphia, where he has been stricken with yellow fever, and in the novel's first half he is basically a spokesman for the Jeffersonian persuasion. Agriculture, he often insists, is the mode of life most productive of happiness; he praises "fixed property and a settled abode" as the agrarian ideal. His adventures in Philadelphia initiate him into an inverted world where everything is in motion. Unlike stable land, property in the commercial city is inherently "portable," consisting of merchandise and paper instruments that are easy to transport and convert into something else. Arthur expresses bafflement at this "floating or transferable wealth," the hallmark of which in the novel is its tendency to behave erratically. The urban setting is accordingly a scene of dramatic sociological transformations. Characters are well-off one moment and reduced to penury the next, and much of the action set in Philadelphia takes place either in sumptuous mansions or in debtors' prison. The merchant Wortley attributes these extreme swings of fortune to commercial enterprise. "Happily," he exclaims to Dr. Stevens, "you are a stranger to mercantile anxieties and revolutions. Your fortune does not rest on a basis which an untoward blast may sweep away, or four strokes of a pen demolish."

Brown holds up Thomas Welbeck as the very picture of "portable" man, as his novel develops an equation between property and temperament. Exchangeability, instability, and liability to fraud are the dominant traits both of paper money and of Welbeck's character. The son of a bankrupt Liverpool merchant, as he confides to Mervyn, he was raised in a dependent condition and acquired habits that "debarred [him] from country occupations." Unwilling to work, he turned at an early age to "dissimulation and falsehood" in order to support himself. When he appears in Philadelphia, Welbeck is a forger and con-man whose identity seems as mercurial and inauthentic as his wealth. He has Arthur accompany him to a party and astounds the hero by the startling change that comes over him in public: so pronounced is the transformation from morose to outgoing that Mervyn can "hardly persuade [himself] that it was the same person." Welbeck's sexual attachments betray a similar pattern of mutability. He is a compulsive seducer whose affections are constantly straying or "transferring" themselves to a new conquest, and he hires Arthur because he hopes that his current mistress will become infatuated with the young man and so relieve him of an embarrassment. The two most important springs of human action, property and sexuality, are in Welbeck's case contaminated by imposture: seduction is the emotional equivalent of forgery.

Volume I of *Arthur Mervyn* presents a grim vision of a city in the grip of yellow fever. Brown works with the trope of illness as moral corruption to evoke an urban environment enveloped in spiritual as well as physical disease. As the fever makes its deadly progress through the city, confidence men bilk honest merchants of their savings, and sexual predators dart from victim to victim. Philadelphia emerges as a locus of financial and erotic intrigue where property and affective life are as fickle as contagion.

To the first volume's Jeffersonian perspective, Volume II supplies a Hamiltonian correction. Brown revises the negative image of Philadelphia, in part by accentuating the benefits of urban existence and in part by discrediting the idealized version of the country put forth by advocates of agrarianism. The opposition between "fixed" and movable wealth proves to have little meaning in a society where land has always been alienable. The second volume brings the almost immediate disclosure that Arthur's father has sold the family farm and been fleeced of the money by his second wife. Nor is the rural Hadwin estate secure from predators: Eliza's rapacious uncle Philip holds a mortgage on her father's property that enables him to deprive the young woman of her inheritance. The idealization of the soil as "a settled abode" collapses before the reality of land as a ready object of purchase and sale. Moreover, fixedness as a condition diminishes in appeal for Arthur, who begins to covet geographic and social mobility and to extol the advantages of mixing with different classes and nationalities. His sympathies gravitate markedly to the metropolis as the novel progresses. On his first visit to Philadelphia, he explains to Dr. Stevens, he saw nothing save "scenes of folly, depravity, and cunning." But his second visit, in acquainting him with superior and cultivated city dwellers like Maravegli, Medlicote, and Stevens himself, produces a different impression: "If cities are the chosen seats of misery and vice, they are likewise the soil of all the laudable and strenuous productions of mind."

Arthur's transfer of allegiance to the city sets in motion a paradigm shift: landowning, public-spiritedness, and emotional stability give way to commercial transactions, individualism, and impetuosity. The revolution in the hero's thinking brings a new receptivity to urban forms of wealth. Welbeck, moments before dying, gives him Watson's bills of exchange to return, and Mervyn transports the money to Baltimore where he presents himself for the promised reward. Questioned about his readiness to be paid for simply doing his duty, the hero brushes aside such scruples as overly fastidious and insists that "the money will be highly useful" to one in his condition. In the first volume he pleaded ignorance of transferable property; here he dazzles with his knowledge of bonds and contracts and gladly accepts "a *check* for the amount" of a thousand dollars.

A significant mutation in Arthur's behavior accompanies his change in outlook. As he habituates himself to the volatile urban economy, his actions become erratic and unpredictable. Bursting into the brothel run by Mrs. Villars, he is almost killed when he provokes her into firing a pistol at him. He also enters Mrs. Wentworth's house without knocking and demands that she provide refuge for Clemenza (Welbeck's discarded mistress). An alarmed Mrs. Wentworth rebukes him, "Your language and ideas are those of a lunatic." And whereas in the first volume Arthur deplored "the folly of precipitate conclusions," the second finds him defending rashness as a principle of action. "I chuse the obvious path," he states complacently, "and pursue it with headlong expedition. . . . we must not be inactive because we are ignorant. Our good purposes must hurry to performance, whether our knowledge be greater or less."

Mervyn's growing impulsiveness, his ever-greater reliance on what he feels, signals a new absorption with the self. Volume I focused on male characters like Welbeck and Stevens, but in Volume II wives and mothers monopolize the protagonist's thoughts. He has effectively abandoned the public realm of men and duty for the private enclave of women and affectivity. Mervyn's erotic needs were initially subsumed in everyday life; prudence and concern for others restrained individual desires. Arthur deferred his marriage to Eliza because of the uncertainty of her domestic situation and because both felt obligations to family and friends. In the second volume, his happiness and sense of self-fulfillment become paramount. He conceives an infatuation for a wealthy older woman, Achsa Fielding, and openly proclaims her "the substitute of my lost mamma." A convert to Romantic sensibility, he expatiates endlessly on his feelings and is constantly taking his emotional temperature. The first volume's champion of disinterested virtue now declares himself formed for no other purpose than to "love and be loved; to exchange hearts, and mingle sentiments."

Arthur's romantic life evokes Thomas Welbeck, Brown's paradigmatic example of portable man. The upheaval in the hero's affections recalls his former employer's history of sexual indiscretions. Mervyn "transfers" his feelings from Eliza to Achsa, deciding that "the extreme youth, rustic simplicity and mental imperfections" of the farm girl no longer interest him beside the charms of the sophisticated English widow. His motives may or may not be culpable, but the image of love as promiscuous and mercenary seems, if anything, to darken in the second volume, which includes a major scene set in a whorehouse. If Welbeck is the perfect "lover" for such a world, Arthur shows considerable aptitude for a novice: the brothel is the place where he and Achsa (she has been lured there under false pretenses) first meet and discover their attraction for each other.

The hero's decision to marry Achsa is, in sum, a choice for the city over the country, for money over land, for individualism over republicanism, and for culture over rusticity. As an omen of the Republic's future, the choice is as inevitable as it seems problematic, for the static agrarianism of the first volume patently fails as an adequate response to the realities of turn-of-the-century America. Although Brown makes it more appealing to rise in the world than to remain stationary, doubts about the future linger because of the persistent ambiguities surrounding Arthur's character. The protagonist's opportunism, which many characters find offensive, seems remarkably naked toward the end, as when he betrays his eager interest in Achsa's wealth by first asking, "Has she property? Is she rich?" and only then asking, "Has she virtue?" The sequence of questions recapitulates his metamorphosis from a Jeffersonian to a Hamiltonian, from "virtue" to "commerce," and might well have been uttered by Welbeck. Mervyn freely admits that "[m]y knowledge of Welbeck has been useful to me," and the novel leaves one troubled at how faithfully in some respects the "copyist" hero takes after his mentor.

It is precisely here, in the narrative's equivocal portrait of Mervyn, that Brown mounts his most cogent defense of the culture of writing and print. Writing as an activity increases in prominence in the novel as Arthur assumes his urban identity. The erstwhile "plowman" evolves into a "penman" as well as an owner of liquid assets and a connoisseur of feelings. His first job in Philadelphia is as Welbeck's scrivener, and though he tells his adventures to Stevens in the first volume, he writes them down himself in the second. He makes a variety of pronouncements about "the pen and the book," commending them as "instruments of rational improvement" but also faulting their lack of immediacy: "they charm not our attention by mute significances of gesture and looks. They spread no light upon their meaning by cadences and emphasis and pause." Arthur furnishes his written account at the request of Mrs. Wentworth, who is moved by his direct appeal for trust but resists putting faith in his spoken assurances.

The question of Arthur's credibility was hardly raised in Volume I; it becomes a pervasive preoccupation in Volume II as skepticism about his motives proliferates. Is he truthful or deceitful, a basically honorable youth seeking to better himself or a crafty con-man hiding behind a plausible exterior? What is certain is that the reader trying to resolve this puzzle has an advantage over the characters themselves, an advantage consisting in the very distance and mediation disliked by the hero. For the proximity of verbal intercourse, Brown suggests, can hinder rational reflection. As Dr. Stevens remarks, Arthur's personal magnetism disarms the possibility of criticism: "Had I heard Mervyn's story from another, or read it in a book, I might, perhaps, have found it possible to suspect the truth; but, as long as the impression, made by his tones, gestures and looks, remained in my memory, this suspicion was impossible." For the reader, who of course encounters Mervyn's words in a book, this statement amounts to an invitation to approach the text in a detached and critical spirit. Far from being a liability, writing empowers the kind of dispassionate evaluation that speech inhibits. "Suspicion" – or, to put it more neutrally, considered judgment – is the obligation and the benefit of print culture.

Novels have a special relation to print, and Brown's novels in particular claim a bond with the ascendant world of the market. Among the imaginative arts, the novel is peculiarly a printed genre: unlike poems and plays, novels are neither recited nor performed. Brown highlights the novel's reliance on mediation by attenuating the link between words and their source and by establishing a dense, enigmatic moral universe to challenge the reader to "study and reflect." The analytic disposition his works require is, according to *Arthur Mervyn,* an essential attribute of life in an urban, commercial society. Wortley is the most outspoken of the book's characters in his reluctance to "give full credit" to the hero's story, and he imputes his habit of suspicion to his experiences as a merchant. Trade, he says to Dr. Stevens, teaches the wisdom of suspending judgment:

[Y]our confidence in smooth features and fluent accents should have ended long ago. Till I gained from my present profession some knowledge of the world, a knowledge which was not gained in a moment, and has not cost a trifle, I was equally wise in my own conceit; and, in order to decide upon the truth of any one's pretensions, needed only a clear view of his face and a distinct hearing of his words. My folly, in that respect, was only to be cured, however, by my own experience, and I suppose your credulity will yield to no other remedy.

Wortley's view of business as an investigative activity is analogous to Brown's description of the novel as a genre demanding interpretive rigor. Both the work of fiction, as Brown conceptualizes it, and the emergent social economy require an ability to interrogate the assertions and trustworthiness of others to arrive at a true estimate of character. One could say that the novel retains a revised "use" value as pedagogy: the difficulties of *Arthur Mervyn* compel readers to engage in incessant scrutiny of words and actions, a skill that can abet survival in the marketplace. The epistemologically and morally ambiguous universe of Brown's fiction, an imaginative world evocative of the nineteenth-century Romantic canon, grows out of his ambition to create a literature commensurate with the complexities of postagrarian America.

Within months after completing *Arthur Mervyn,* Brown – rather like his hero – turned his attention to the domain of women. The move represented a departure from his "major phase." Prompted by his anxious desire to succeed as a professional author, Brown decided to try his hand at the sentimental fiction he had previously dismissed as adapted to readers seeking amusement only, not mental stimulation. Although *Edgar Huntly* enjoyed a degree of popular success, none of his four novels earned much money, and his brothers were pressing him to abandon literature and enter the family mercantile business. At this juncture it is Brown's career rather than his art that forecasts the future: his venture at "popular tales," as he termed them, prefigures Melville's plan to write a domestic novel after the failure of *Moby-Dick* and Hawthorne's determination to follow *The Scarlet Letter* with works featuring happy endings. In a letter to one of his brothers, Brown conceded that "most readers" would object to the "gloominess and out-of-nature incidents" of his writing, "which alone," he continued, "is a sufficient reason for dropping the doleful tone and assuming a cheerful one." The result was a pair of epistolary romances turned out with the novelist's customary rapidity, *Clara Howard* and *Jane Talbot,* both of which appeared in 1801. The two books aspire to greater seriousness than the average sentimental narrative, but neither possesses the intellectual energy and sheer strangeness of Brown's superior fiction. A contemporary reviewer had a point when he found *Jane Talbot* so deficient in "vigour of imagination" that he wondered whether it was "an awkward imitation by some other hand."

But not the whole point. There is something fitting about Brown ending his active career as a novelist with the only two of his tales that have female names as titles. In both his support for women's rights and his quest to establish authorship as an independent vocation, Brown was in advance of republican culture, a proponent of liberalism and the market ethos. With his turn to women's subjects, he brought the two goals into harmony: the romances constituted a last appeal to the already feminized reading public and capped his attempt to earn a living as a fiction writer. But harmony, ironically, took its toll on his art: an energizing tension was lost, and without it Brown's writing could not sustain its singularity and power. When the books failed, he relinquished the goal of treating the novel as a profession. Thereafter he moved steadily away from the "Franklin" side of his thinking and reanimated the "Washington" strain. The last decade of his life saw Brown transform himself into a gentleman of letters and revert to the factual, public orientation of eighteenth-century literature.

The initial stages of this development antedated the disappointing popular response to his fiction. In 1799, Brown embarked on a second career as journal editor by founding the *Monthly Magazine and American Review*. The magazine encountered difficulties in promotion and distribution from the outset and folded after just eighteen issues. Three years later he launched a second periodical, *The Literary Magazine and American Register*, and maintained it until 1806; reborn the next year as the semiannual *American Register, or General Repository of History, Politics, and Science*, it continued until his death in 1810. The last journal, as its title suggests, was a compendium of state papers, intelligence culled from the press, and literary and scientific information, material for the most part in the public domain; reversing the direction of Brown's novels, it made a fetish of factuality. The novelist, or rather former novelist, now repudiated the ideal of the self-supporting writer. Addressing his readers in the maiden issue of *The Literary Magazine*, Brown displayed the familiar signs of amateurism. He voiced "insuperable aversion to naming himself," vowed that nobody depended on the magazine for a subsistence, and, professing shame at what he had written in the past, recanted his productions as a novelist. Several pages later, he wrapped himself in the patrician mantle of the scribbling gentleman:

While the *poor author*, that is to say, the author by trade, is regarded with indifference or contempt, the *author*, that is, the man who devotes to composition the leisure secured to him by hereditary affluence, or by a lucrative profession or office, obtains from mankind an higher, and more lasting, and more genuine reverence, than any other class of mortals. As there is nothing I should more fervently deprecate than to be enrolled in the former class, so there is nothing to which I more ardently aspire, than to be numbered among the latter.

Not long before making this statement, Brown had become a political pamphleteer speaking out on issues of national concern. In this avatar, he had less in common with the canonical Romantics of the nineteenth century than with the revolutionary statesmen who took up their pens for the specific purpose of advancing the commonweal. Having entered into a business association with his brothers, Brown embraced the Federalist politics of the commercial class to which his family belonged. In 1803, he published a widely read address calling for immediate annexation of the Louisiana territory and denouncing the Jeffersonians for supposedly dragging their feet on the matter because of their sympathy for France. Three other pamphlets criticizing Jefferson's policies followed, including a far-reaching, philosophic attack on the Embargo, *An Address to the Congress of the United States* (1809). Here Brown openly espoused the "Court" ideology that underlies *Arthur Mervyn:* he rejected agrarian self-sufficiency as an impractical goal for either individuals or nations, and he prophesied a time when the United States would equal the countries of Europe as a commercial and manufacturing power. Such a future would entail losses as well as benefits, Brown admitted, but its coming was unavoidable, dictated by the zeal with which Americans pursued trade and by the reality that they, like other peoples, were activated by the promotion of their own self-aggrandizement.

We can see, then, that the Franklin side or individualistic element in Brown's work never wholly disappeared. The public man of letters was not a classical republican counseling civic virtue but someone with a strong sense of, and respect for, the principle of self-interest. What might be called the return of the cultural repressed in Brown — his forsaking of the novel for more communal, eighteenth-century forms of writing — was an unstable process, always harboring within itself an opposing impulse toward the private. Toward the end of his life, Brown was not only editing magazines and composing polemics but also experimenting with historical fiction or fictionalized history. As early as 1799, he published two stories about historical events, "The Death of Cicero" and "Thessalonica," and at his death he left behind fragments of a massive manuscript concerning an imaginary British family named the Carrils. These works echo the skepticism about facts evident in *Wieland,* and though not dealing with native subjects, they can be said to look ahead to Irving's *History of New York* (1809) and Cooper's *The Spy* (1821), two landmarks in the evolution of American literature. Brown's stories and his unfinished saga of the Carrils rehearse the necessary ground-clearing strategy of American Romanticism. They depose history from its cultural eminence by subjectivizing it, and they defy the republican aesthetics of self-suppression by treating the realm of public events and persons as the malleable clay of the artist's imagination.

7

❦

WASHINGTON IRVING

WASHINGTON IRVING has as good a claim as anyone to the title "Father of American Literature." Born in 1783, the year the United States won its freedom, and named for the military hero venerated as the Father of His Country, Irving was the first American to make a successful vocation of authorship. Although contemporaries both at home and abroad recognized his seminal importance as the man who declared the nation's literary independence, later readers have dealt less kindly with Irving. Most have ignored his claims to precedence and dismissed him as inherently less interesting and "modern" than either James Fenimore Cooper, who followed him historically, or Charles Brockden Brown, who never attracted a popular readership. "Father of American Literature," in this sense, implies that Irving belonged to an outdated phase of culture – archaic and pre-Romantic, too remote to engage twentieth-century sensibilities.

Much in Irving's career and work lends support to this view. He portrayed himself as an antiquated gentleman and idler who felt out of place in the bustling present and had no interest in the commercial side of letters. Avoiding the novel, the genre of a modernizing civilization, he worked in forms – the essay serial, the sketch, the history – that now seem old-fashioned or somehow inappropriate for a creative artist. His writing remained imprinted with the "residual" features of eighteenth-century culture: anonymity, collaboration, regard for factuality coupled with uneasiness about originality, and an understanding of literature as communal possession.

This backward-looking man of letters, disparaged even in his own time as derivative, was nonetheless an innovator who established American writing on a new footing as a viable profession. Irving performed the essential service of assaulting from within some of the very forms and suppositions he helped to perpetuate, among them the ideas that literature had to serve a useful function and that it owed deference to facts. His achievement signals the simultaneous "disembedding" of the American artist and of literary creation, their disentanglement from surrounding matrices: he legitimated the writer as writer, someone distinct from other occupations, and he vindicated the artwork as just that, a work of art and not a vehicle for moral or civic instruction. In complicated ways, Irving's pose of obsolescence made these breakthroughs possible. His conservative allegiances both obstructed and facilitated his undeniable modernity. The regressions of his later career, when he wrote patriotic histories and biographies and sought government appointments, can be read as atonement for having dared, as he observed in 1803, to take "the *guilt of originality* upon his shoulders."

Irving emerged out of the periodical and belletristic setting of the late eighteenth century. He broke into print in 1802 with *Letters of Jonathan Oldstyle, Gent.*, an anonymous serial he contributed to a newspaper edited by his brother Peter. Here Irving comes across as a Joseph Dennie who can laugh at himself, an "Oliver Oldschool" without the venom. Though only nineteen years old, he adopted the traditional mask of an elderly bachelor and announced his opposition to "the degeneracy of the present times." The theme of estrangement from contemporary life, from innovation in manners, politics, and the arts, dominates the nine *Letters,* two-thirds of which deal with Oldstyle's experiences at New York's Park Theater. A bemused but critical picture of democratic culture takes shape, as boisterous egalitarianism and pandering to the popular taste prevail at the expense of dramatic art. The theatergoers show little capacity for sustained attention and rudely make known their wishes by "stamping, hissing, roaring, and whistling." When Oldstyle objects to the constant clamor during a performance, his friend Andrew Quoz reminds him that the patrons "*have paid their dollar,* and have a right to entertain themselves as well as they can." The problem of finding a satisfactory relation to the expanding democratic public would long vex Irving, for whom the testiness of the "Oldstyle" had a genuine appeal; his creation of an alternative persona, still a gentleman but more respectful of the common reader, lay well in the future.

Irving's next important work also grew out of periodical culture but represented a self-conscious parodying of its conventions. For several years he continued to publish anonymously in New York newspapers and to participate in an informal literary club variously known as the "Nine Worthies," the "Lads of Kilkenny," and the "Ancient and Honorable Order." A collaborative effort with two members of the club, his brother William and James Kirke Paulding, led in 1807 to *Salmagundi; or, The Whim-Whams and Opinions of Launcelot Langstaff, Esq. & Others.* Issued in twenty paperbound numbers like a magazine, *Salmagundi* satirizes the time-honored ingredients of the essay serial. It sends up fashion notes, theater criticism, and the familiar letters from a foreign visitor, and it directs mockery at the presumed didactic or use value of letters. Langstaff and his companions repeatedly avow their preference for the antique and the obsolete but reveal themselves to be forward-looking in at least this one respect, their insouciance about the betterment of the public. "[W]e write for no other earthly purpose," they state, "but to please ourselves," and they vow to discontinue the serial when they tire of it, no matter what their readers think.

Although the note of defying the audience in this passage is lighthearted, it reflects Irving's serious concern with the possible costs of success in a democratizing, capitalist society. The patrician in him recoiled from the vulgar courting of the multitude he saw as endemic to the United States, a country, he wrote, where "a man must first *descend*" before he can hope to rise. His most barbed contribution to *Salmagundi*, "On Greatness," describes a political bounder named Timothy Dabble who exemplifies the sycophancy Irving despised. Dabble toadies to party bigwigs and fawns upon the mob to get ahead, "until having gathered together a mighty mass of popularity, he mounts it in triumph, is hoisted into office, and becomes a *great man*, and a ruler in the land." The pseudonymous authors of *Salmagundi* firmly distinguish themselves as gentlemen of letters from the Dabbles of the world. They give thanks that "we are not like the unhappy rulers of this enlightened land, accountable to the mob for our actions, or dependent on their smiles for support." Even in a republic, Irving insists, literature must not imitate politics as a solicitation of popular favor.

Another piece in *Salmagundi*, "The Little Man in Black," proposes a counterimage to the mob-flattering "great man." The unnamed subject of the sketch, who goes about with a large book under his arm, "becomes a mark for injury and insult" because he fails to conform to communal norms. He keeps to himself, follows no known trade, and seems unambitious "of earning a farthing," eccentricities that arouse the fear and detestation of his neighbors. It turns out that the little man in black is a harmless antiquarian who has been studying the literary remains of an ancestor; social ostracism harries him to an impoverished death. The stirrings of Romantic sensibility are unmistakable in this portrait of a bookish outsider who represents the first fully differentiated artist in American literature. Unlike Brown's tellers and writers, Irving's scholar is purely a literary man, with no other occupation. He stands apart from and is even set against the realm of ordinary existence. The little man in black symbolizes the separateness of the aesthetic, art's emergent differentiation from the practical and social.

Irving's career developed out of the complex dynamic between Timothy Dabble and the little man in black. The two figures foreshadow his evolution into an immensely popular though seemingly unworldly artist. Dabble corresponds to the international celebrity who cultivated the patronage of Sir Walter Scott, mastered the art of promotion, and gave the public on both sides of the Atlantic what they wanted. The black-cloaked scholar, a forerunner of Diedrich Knickerbocker and Geoffrey Crayon, typifies the role Irving assumed in his writing, the quaint book lover and "very good for nothing kind of being." But reality and persona were more interdependent than this division suggests. The self-promoter and the "pure" antiquarian were both symptoms of cultural specialization: the artist as entrepreneur or professional, and the artist as artist and nothing else. The two figures flourished in tandem if nominally in opposition, and the later Irving would find it increasingly difficult to keep them compartmentalized, as he had in *Salmagundi*.

In 1807–8, though he still personified the gentlemanly dilettante, Irving was about to effect a major change in his career. Writing had been a part-time pursuit he engaged in with friends and family while casually preparing to enter the legal profession; he expected only meager returns. Assigning his copyright in *Salmagundi* to the printer–publisher, he relinquished ownership of his literary property and received a pittance for his labors. Nor was *A History of New York* (1809), the book that secured him a national reputation, originally conceived in any other way. As Irving recollected forty years later, the *History* began as a "jeu d'esprit," a parody of a New York guidebook, and was planned as a joint venture with his brother Peter. But when Peter went abroad to run the English branch of the family business, Washington cast off the restraints of eighteenth-century authorship and took calculated steps toward making letters pay. He wrote and published the *History* himself, this time retaining the copyright, and he orchestrated a clever pre- and postpublication advertising campaign in the newspapers. The result was an unprecedented success, netting Irving between two and three thousand dollars, the most money ever earned by an American for a work of prose fiction.

The *History* represented a watershed not simply because it demonstrated fiction's profitability, but also because it subverted the dominant literary categories of the past. Its target was the constellation of attitudes that conferred unrivaled prestige on history writing and that inhibited the development of the aesthetic imagination. When Irving composed his comic masterpiece – and, indeed, for years afterward – historical works lorded it over fiction, plays, and even poetry in the American cultural pantheon. Unlike these more fanciful genres, which might or might not serve a beneficial purpose, history was "philosophy teaching by examples," as Bolingbroke famously said: it inculcated virtue in its readers by holding up illustrious lives and actions for imitation. It was also believed to be objectively true, a record of factual occurrences and not an imaginary, hence a false and misleading, account of experience. History comported unusually well with the age's communitarian emphasis in that it dealt with public information and minimized the subjective or individualistic element in literature.

Works of history enjoyed a special vogue after the War of Independence, when they fostered patriotism by memorializing the Republic's distinctive

merits. Between 1783 and 1815, historical narratives recounting the struggle with Britain and exhorting the country's youth to renewed dedication
poured from American presses. Overwhelmingly celebratory, these works
told a national success story, the "Rise and Progress" of the Revolution.
Other literary forms written and published by Americans in the same period
traded on history's greater prestige by presenting themselves as truthful
chronicles. The novel in particular, with its claim to be based on "fact" or
"truth," aped history's methods. It attests to the obstinacy of these prejudices
that both Irving and Cooper, contrary to their own most original impulses,
continued to esteem histories as weightier and more worthwhile than "made
up" writings.

Irving's burlesque narrative of New York "From the Beginning of the
World to the End of the Dutch Dynasty" feigns high regard for the factuality
and usefulness identified with history writing. It incorporates genuine historical research, ostentatiously paraded before the reader with daunting footnotes, and it bears an effusive dedication from Diedrich Knickerbocker to the
New-York Historical Society. A prefatory note "To the Public" extols "faithful veracity" for its pedagogical value and pledges to maintain "the strictest
adherence to truth"; passages scattered throughout warn against the "poetic
disportings of the fancy." The circumstances surrounding the *History*'s publication reinforced its air of seeming official. The year, 1809, marked the
bicentenary of Henry Hudson's discovery of New York. The Historical Society gave a ceremonial dinner to observe the occasion at which the Reverend
Samuel Miller, author of *A Brief Retrospect of the Eighteenth Century* and a voice
of genteel culture, delivered a tribute. Miller had been compiling material
about New York for an authoritative history; Irving's book preempted him,
and he never finished it. To publicize the *History,* Irving ran notices in local
newspapers concerning Knickerbocker's disappearance from the hotel where
he supposedly lodged. An announcement from Seth Handaside, the landlord,
explained that the *History* was being published to discharge the missing
author's debts.

All this genuflecting to facts was in the service of toppling history from its
cultural preeminence and made the spoof Irving actually wrote all the more
effective. The age palmed off fictions as truthful narratives; Irving reversed
the procedure by turning history into fiction and so jumbling actual events
and sources with invented ones that it seems impossible to disentangle them.
Laughter and confusion deflate history's authority as the realm of truth.
Irving's accomplishment was at once liberating and privatizing and helped to
clear the way for American Romanticism. He freed the imagination to invent
its own version of the world, and he converted the common heritage of all
New Yorkers into the unique fantasy — the highly marketable fantasy, as it

proved – of an individual. Irving also undercut the requirement that literature had to improve the reader. Knickerbocker's claims for the utility of history swell into the ironically grandiose insistence that historians "are the benefactors of kings – we are the guardians of truth – we are the scourgers of guilt – we are the instructors of the world – we are – in short, what are we not!" Just behind this litany lurks the belief that literature is innocent of social and didactic designs, that it makes nothing happen other than to entertain its audience. Knickerbocker's inflated rhetoric implicitly renews the distinction between art and "real" life made in "The Little Man in Black" and points ahead to the overt disavowals of that self-confessed idler and aesthete Geoffrey Crayon.

Seen in another aspect, the *History* preserves a civic function as a conservative challenge to the emergent liberal consensus. Instead of glorifying national progress, Irving relates a tale of declension in which America, symbolized by the fictional New Amsterdam, begins as "a second Eden" and then succumbs to the forces of democracy and materialism represented by the Yankees. The *History* directs its sharpest satire at Thomas Jefferson as the verbose William the Testy, the Dutch governor who fatally weakens the province with "his unfortunate propensity to experiment and innovation." Part Federalist jeremiad, and part exercise in mythmaking, the book contrasts the degenerate present to an imagined moment of organic harmony located in the past. Its ideal community is the original settlement ruled over by Wouter Van Twiller and untroubled by either the "busy hum of commerce" or the insolence of the "sovereign people."

What gives the *History* its radically dissident edge is Irving's awareness that all histories are partial and reflect the viewpoint of the winners. His discussion of the seizure of Indian lands in Book I exposes the partisanship of early narratives of European settlement. Irving reduces the usual justifications of Indian displacement – the natives were infidels, agriculture was unknown to them, they lived like vagabonds, and so forth – to a simple matter of power. No claim to the soil, he writes, could be more irrefutable than the one asserted by the white settlers in practice: "the RIGHT BY EXTERMINATION, or in other words, the RIGHT BY GUNPOWDER." And he goes on to imagine a scenario in which the inhabitants of the moon, "as superior to us in knowledge, and consequently in power, as the Europeans were to the Indians," alight on this planet and, after despoiling us of our property, "graciously" allow us to reside in "the torrid deserts of Arabia, or the frozen regions of Lapland."

As this conceit suggests, Irving stands outside the national orthodoxy that sanctioned the massive Indian removals of the nineteenth century in the name of progress. He criticizes from the right, from the "Oldstyle" perspective of someone deeply skeptical about the putative advancements and moral authority of middle-class civilization. His debunking of history leads to an explicit (if fitful) rehierarchizing of the genres and to an avowal that the workings of the fancy can disclose more about the past than documented accounts. In two pieces contributed to the *Analectic Magazine* in 1814 and later reprinted in *The Sketch Book*, "Traits of Indian Character" and "Philip of Pokanoket," Irving attacks history writing at its alleged strong points, its instructional value and commitment to truth. He charges the early historians of America with "prejudice and bigotry" in their narratives of Indian warfare, and he mounts a powerful case for the greater integrity and inclusiveness of imaginative literature. The sufferings of the natives had no "friendly hand" to record them and would be lost to posterity were it not for "the romantic dreams of the poet." These alone can give access to the thoughts of a King Philip and, by redeeming the wronged warrior from the distortions of his enemies, "awaken sympathy for his fate." Elsewhere Irving would portray fiction as a category of value in its own right, not a medium competitive with history; here he sees it as besting historians on their chosen ground and creating a space for opposition to "official" versions of events.

That the intellectual and aesthetic daring of the *History* is inextricable from its conservatism, emerges finally from Irving's reliance on Diedrich Knickerbocker as narrator. Knickerbocker closely resembles the quaint old bachelors of the earlier works. He unites the penniless antiquarian of "The Little Man in Black" with the crotchety elitists of the *Letters* and *Salmagundi*. He claims to hate novelty, to revere the past, and to feel nothing but contempt for the opinions of "the mob, since called the enlightened people." Yet this upholder of tradition ushers American literature into the modern era. One of the oddities of the *History* is Knickerbocker's unwitting kinship with his apparent opposite, William the Testy, the character in the book who embodies the rage for change and who represents the disruptive Yankee element already existing within placid Dutch civilization. Like Testy, Irving's bookish persona is "a man of many words and great erudition," more than a match for the windy governor in the construction of a world out of language. He quotes ancient and modern authorities, spouts theories, and has few equals among American narrators – perhaps none until Melville's Ishmael – in his love of talk.

These affinities underline Knickerbocker–Irving's implication in the democratic, market culture of which Testy is a harbinger. They point to Irving's Testy-like "propensity to experiment and innovation" and to his use of Knickerbocker to overturn literary convention and market a best-seller. Toward the conclusion of the *History*, Knickerbocker himself softens his archconservatism and takes a more conciliatory tone with the much-despised public. In Book VI, he invites those readers who have accompanied him since the title page to "join hands, bury all differences, and swear to stand by one another, in weal or woe, to the end of the enterprize." This companionable guise accommodates market realities far better than antagonism and became Irving's trademark as a writer, placing him at the opposite end of the cultural spectrum from the combative Cooper, his fellow innovator and critic of innovation.

After the *History,* Irving went into the first of the artistic reversals or backslidings that proved a recurrent feature of his career. The enterprising publicist and literary iconoclast of 1809 forsook experimentation and reverted to the practices of the eighteenth-century man of letters. For the next decade, Irving could have been a second Joseph Dennie or another Charles Brockden Brown in the period after Brown stopped writing fiction. He accepted a sinecure in the family import business and, suppressing his individuality, became an editor of secondhand writings. In 1810, he prepared a selection of Thomas Campbell's poems for which he wrote a biographical essay; the title page identified him only as "a Gentleman of New-York." Three years later he assumed the editorship of the *Analectic Magazine* and reimmersed himself in the preprofessional world of early periodicals. A typical miscellany, the *Analectic Magazine* treated literature as public property owing an obligation to the civic welfare. It consisted mainly of reprinted − that is, pirated − extracts from English journals and patriotic pieces celebrating American exploits in the War of 1812, among the latter Francis Scott Key's "Defense of Fort M'Henry" and several sketches of military heroes contributed by Irving.

Financial necessity was the spur that drove Irving back to full-time writing and turned him into a professional. With the return of peace in 1815, he departed for England to join the ailing Peter in Liverpool, where he spent an anxious period trying to save the firm of P. & E. Irving from bankruptcy. The company's collapse in 1818 deprived him of family support and left him little choice but to resume his pen. As with the *History,* the results exceeded expectations: *The Sketch Book of Geoffrey Crayon, Gent.,* published in seven pamphletlike installments in 1819–20, lifted Irving to transatlantic renown and probably earned him ten thousand dollars in the United States alone, enough to convince him that authorship could be a means of support.

The Sketch Book is both a fulfillment and a transcendence of the past: it remains steeped in anachronistic techniques and assumptions even as it transforms them into something recognizably different. The narrator, "Geoffrey Crayon, Gent.," is another artistic amateur insisting on his social status and aloofness from commercialism. Although he has shed the irascibility of a Knickerbocker or an Oldstyle, he still professes disaffection from the present and reverence for "times gone by." *The Sketch Book* is a miscellany, and in some respects it shares the periodical world's understanding of literary works as communal property. It makes rather free use of existing sources and reworks such well-worn subjects as the traditional English Christmas and the mandatory tour of Westminster Abbey. Even Irving's best and seemingly most original tales like "Rip Van Winkle" reflect his reading in European folklore and can be described as "twice told." Irving, of course, was writing at a pivotal moment in the evolution of Anglo-American attitudes about the rights of cultural ownership. A sketch called "The Art of Book Making" reveals his sensitivity to the issue of plagiarism; it pictures modern authors as thieves piecing together their books in the British Museum by scavenging among the writings of the dead. Irving himself was perceived as doing just this by his detractors. The contemporaneous English essayist William Hazlitt had no hesitation labeling the American a literary robber, someone who has "*skimmed the cream,* and taken off patterns with great skill and cleverness, from our best known and happiest writers."

Irving the copyist – possibly a model for Melville's Bartleby – was simultaneously redefining his agenda as an artist. He saw to it that his own literary wares would be income-producing private property carefully guarded against the threat of plagiarism. Though *The Sketch Book* originally appeared in the United States in numbers like a magazine, Irving proceeded to turn this notoriously unprofitable method into a remarkably lucrative one and to secure his writing from infringement. Following his practice with the *History,* he kept the copyright and published the new work himself so as to reap the lion's share of the profits, and he charged an average of 75 cents per number, an unusually high price at the time. The total for the seven installments came to $5.37, this when an entire year's subscription to the *Port Folio* cost just $6.00, and most novels sold for less than two dollars. "If the American public wish to have literature of their own," Irving bluntly told a correspondent, "they must consent to pay for the support of authors." The complete text of *The Sketch Book* was marketed a second time as a single volume both in America and in England. Irving first brought it out in London at his own expense to prevent its being pirated; with Scott's help, he later arranged its publication by John Murray, the immensely successful "Prince of Booksellers." To his brother Ebenezer he spoke candidly of writing as an investment: "I shall be able . . . now to produce articles from time to time that will be sufficient for my present support, and form a stock of copyright property, that may be a little capital for me hereafter."

The Sketch Book makes explicit Irving's repudiation of history writing and didacticism in literature. Time and again he states his predilection for the poetical and legendary over the true. A character like Shakespeare's Jack Falstaff means more to the average reader, says Irving, than all the great men

of history, for whereas the actual hero may "have furnished examples of
harebrained prowess," the "hero of fiction" has "enlarged the boundaries of
human enjoyment." The old stress on utility has vanished completely, replaced by a notion of literature, and particularly fiction, as a locus of pure
amusement. "It is so much pleasanter to please than to instruct – to play the
companion rather than the preceptor," Irving writes, and his credo, inverting
the goal of the previous generation, signals a reconfiguring of the aesthetic as
an autonomous sphere uncontaminated by practical concerns.

Irving's persona, Geoffrey Crayon, is himself an instance of the segregation
of the aesthetic from everyday existence. In one sense, the separation is quite
literal: Crayon physically removes himself from "the commonplace realities"
of America to seek in Europe "the charms of storied and poetical association."
He is as much a type of the new Romantic artist as of the old-fashioned
gentleman of letters. Indeed, Crayon – and Irving too – can be seen as a
transitional figure in whom elements of the ascendant ideal have been grafted
onto the obsolescent one. (The transition is evident on the English side in the
more rakish person of Lord Byron, the outcast poet and nobleman born just
five years after Irving.) The patrician who merely dabbles in literature in his
leisure hours merges into the full-time sentimentalist idly "following the
bent of his vagrant inclination." What joins the two poses, the aristocratic
and the Romantic, is a common aversion to the habits of market civilization:
Crayon could not be more unlike the rational, purposeful nineteenth century.
Against the age's materialism and social and geographic mobility, he proclaims his admiration for the antique, the customary, the unregulated. The
pseudonym "Crayon" and the title "Sketch Book" underline his impractical-
ity: drawing and painting were fine arts many Americans still viewed with
suspicion as useless luxuries in 1820.

Alienation from the restless modern world permeates *The Sketch Book* as an
obsessive fascination with death. Sketch after sketch belongs to the graveyard
school of literature: "The Widow and Her Son," "Rural Funerals," "London
Antiques," "The Pride of the Village" – all find Crayon musing over the
departed and reflecting on the grave as "a place of rest." Nor is a cemetery
needed to elicit his morbidity: simply crossing the ocean turns his thoughts
to the drowned. Death appeals to Crayon as an occasion for meditation and
the indulgence of feeling. It offers escape from the repressions and competitiveness of early industrial capitalism; in his own words, death is "a realm of
shadows," a quiet bye lane of the fancy where he can "turn aside from the
high way of busy money seeking life."

The independence of art and its alliance with death figure centrally in
Irving's two most memorable stories, "Rip Van Winkle" and "The Legend
of Sleepy Hollow"; both also expose the inadvertent collusion of the imagi-

nation with cash-conscious modernity. As happens so often in Irving's work, the opposition between the aesthetic and sordid "reality" is articulated as a clash between the Dutch past and the Yankee present. "Rip Van Winkle" announces itself as "A Posthumous Writing of Diedrich Knickerbocker"; the association with death is reiterated in the twenty-year sleep of the protagonist, a metaphorical passing away (and possibly in the letters of his given name as well). The story has been read as a parable of Irving's own feelings of estrangement from nineteenth-century America. A portrait of the artist as an old man, Rip is an idler with "an insuperable aversion to all kinds of profitable labor." His family sinks into poverty while he wastes his time rambling over the countryside and telling stories to the village gossips. When he falls into his deathlike sleep, Rip's ancient village in the Kaatskills still bears the marks of its Dutch origins; awakening into the postrevolutionary United States, he discovers that the "very nature of the people seemed changed." The "busy, bustling disputatious tone" of the Yankees has supplanted the easy-going tranquillity of the Dutch, and Rip feels out of place and unsure of his identity. A note appended by Diedrich Knickerbocker continues the contrast between art and antiart by satirizing the convention of literature's truthfulness. Knickerbocker's straight-faced claims to have spoken with Rip and seen documents authenticating his veracity highlight the absurdity of expecting fiction to imitate history and be something other than what it is.

In "The Legend of Sleepy Hollow," the clash between the imagination and the enterprising modern world is played out in the rivalry of Brom Bones and Ichabod Crane for the hand of Katrina Van Tassel. Death again casts a shadow over the narrative, which is said to have been "Found among the Papers of the late Diedrich Knickerbocker"; Sleepy Hollow abounds in gothic tales and shadowy superstitions, none more frightening than the story of a Hessian soldier's ghost that rides forth nightly in search of its head. Ichabod Crane, a native of Connecticut, is a restless Yankee intruder into the "enchanted region" inhabited by the Dutch. He possesses the "consuming" habit of thought prevalent in the new century: his "devouring mind's eye" perceives the physical environment as objects to be ingested or as property to be "turned into cash, and the money invested in immense tracts of wild land, and shingle palaces in the wilderness." Brom Bones, by posing as the Headless Horseman, succeeds in expelling his rival from Sleepy Hollow and preserving the domain of art from the predatory materialism of the Yankees. A postscript attributed to Knickerbocker reaffirms the victory of the aesthetic. The original storyteller, an unnamed "pleasant, shabby, gentlemanly old figure," employs a nonsense syllogism to confound a listener who suspiciously demands to "know the moral of the story, and what it went to prove."

Literature, in short, has no practical purpose or lesson to teach; its value is that it entertains without regard to use.

Irving is unable to maintain the division between the creative spirit and the money-grubbing, utilitarian present. The two spheres he strives to hold apart keep overlapping and interpenetrating to reveal that they are not after all antithetical but complementary and even dependent on each other. In "Rip Van Winkle," things have not changed so drastically as it first appears in the transition from colony to nation. Images of likeness and doubling suggest that Dutch and Yankee are counterparts: Rip's son is as much a sluggard as the father ever was, "the ditto of himself," and though George Washington now governs in lieu of George III, the painted figure on the tavern sign has the same face. Moreover, business culture proves far more hospitable to the storyteller than was the somnolent past. Reverenced as a village patriarch, Rip now enjoys special favor "among the rising generation" for his vivid chronicles of "the old times." Viewed in this light, he seems less an emblem of alienation than a prophecy of Irving's growing acceptance by the reading public. His success calls attention to the historical reality, which his creator was the first to exploit, that not until the nineteenth century did Americans possess sufficient affluence and leisure to support a class of professional writers.

Many of the same ambiguities recur in "The Legend of Sleepy Hollow," which qualifies the positive estimate of the Dutch and shows Irving to be more of a Yankee than he liked to think. Tarrytown, the village nearest Sleepy Hollow, is identified in the opening paragraph as a market town that got its name because people lingered there on market days; as in the *History,* the Yankee disposition is already present in the Dutch world, long before Ichabod Crane takes up residence there. Irving's peaceful Dutch valley makes a poor enclave of the imagination. The natives are contemptuous of reading and writing, and the Headless Horseman that protects the community's insularity also advertises its mindlessness. Crane, the ostensible enemy, seems a composite version of the artist Irving actually was. He resembles both Timothy Dabble and the little man in black and brings together in a single character Irving's two sides as antiquarian and ambitious man of the world. The calculating schoolteacher who ends up as a politician and justice of the city courts is at the same time a book lover and storyteller referred to by the narrator as "[o]ur man of letters." His habit of moving on is a reminder that Irving, far from remaining stationary like his admired Dutch, boasted of his gypsylike temperament and spent much of his life in travel.

Certainly Irving's fiction *needs* the Yankee mentality symbolized by Crane. One of the things the schoolteacher devours with so much gusto is literature: his "appetite" for marvelous tales and his "powers of digesting" them are reported to be prodigious. From this perspective, he can be understood as a type of the greatly expanded reading public that had come into being by 1820, as part of the consumer revolution accompanying the spread of capitalism − a public with money to spend on books and free time in which to read them. In the envoy to *The Sketch Book,* Irving compares his own writings to food and hopes that the miscellany of dishes he has prepared will include something to gratify every taste. The fact that his book *is* a miscellany represents an accommodation with the new "extensive" style of reading. *The Sketch Book* is the prototypical work by an American to transpose the market strengths of the magazine − its variety and the brevity of its articles − into a volume unified by the sensibility of a persona−narrator and written and copyrighted in its entirety by an individual.

Irving's instrumentality in validating and commodifying the autonomous aesthetic helps to explain his fascination with death. In breaking with the past, he allied his writing with two key historical developments that involved recession from presence. Irving accelerated the trend away from orality to the impersonal values of print. Not only did he rewrite and copyright popular tales and legends, but he also discredited such residual features of narrative as the commitment to a "moral" and the passing on of factual information, features integral to the oral art of the storyteller. Though Irving's fictions invariably employ narrators, they eliminate the last traces of living speech by portraying the teller as dead, vanished, or separated from the audience by an ocean. *The Sketch Book* in particular internalizes the modalities of print as an integral aspect of its identity. Print substitutes space and time, or distance and durability, for the proximity and evanescence of oral performance. *The Sketch Book* foregrounds these qualities in its self-presentation as a work of exoticism and antiquarianism, a voice from a distant land haunting libraries and gravesites to collect touching anecdotes about the past.

That Irving composed his masterpiece in England but marketed it in America is a reminder of the transportation revolution of the early nineteenth century. This was the second historical development with which his writing was affiliated, one that again entailed the recession of human agency. The contemporaneous explosion in consumption occurred in part because of technological advances in moving goods − by road, canal, steamboat, improved sailing ship, and, eventually, by rail − from one location to another. *The Sketch Book* appeared at precisely the moment when the American system of transportation was entering a major phase of modernization. A boom in turnpike and canal building occurred between 1815 and 1825, with the Erie Canal, then the largest canal in the country, completed in the latter year. Many Americans were growing accustomed to merchandise produced not locally but at a distance. Increasingly, they encountered objects, including books, magazines, and newspapers, whose producers they never saw. Though few of these more generally available goods were made in factories, their long-range distribution diminished their aura of human presence.

The aesthetics of production and reception of Irving's fiction grows out of this commercial and technological circumstance. Both externally and internally, the fiction reproduces the fundamental characteristic of modern consumer society: consumption at a distance from the source. *The Sketch Book* announces itself as the work of an American living abroad, and it first becomes a best-seller in the United States, on the other side of the Atlantic from the scene of its composition. Within the text, Irving's narratives make a fetish of mediation. To read the stories is to be made aware of one's removal from a departed or inaccessible point of origin. The best pair of tales are "posthumous," and "The Art of Book Making" generalizes this condition by equating the manufacture of literary wares with stealing from the dead. Story after story is filtered through a dizzying sequence of narrators. "The Legend of Sleepy Hollow" provides an extreme example of distancing: before it can reach the reader, the narrative has to migrate from the original teller, to Diedrich Knickerbocker, who copies it down, to Geoffrey Crayon, the putative author of *The Sketch Book,* to Washington Irving. This imaginary process of dissemination recapitulates the fate of the word in American culture: from communal, verbal forms, to handwritten manuscripts passed around a circle of like-minded gentlemen, to the printed text before us, a widely distributed commodity bought and sold on the market.

The instability of boundaries in Irving's work – between past and present, Dutch and Yankee, art and money-making – suggests that his antibourgeois pose as Romantic aristocrat itself constitutes a stroke of commercial acumen. The incongruity between literary tradesman and indolent aesthete can be resolved by posing the question, What would be the most effective means of marketing fiction and the fiction writer in 1820? The new abundance of print, the growth of the reading public, the revolution in consumption – these developments did not signify that culture and appreciation of the beautiful had lost their upper-class prestige; on the contrary, it was now possible for ordinary men and women to enjoy access to activities once reserved for the privileged few. Although letters became a commodity, they retained much of their high status as a priceless badge of gentility; the currency, even today, of the phrase "belles lettres" captures something of their inherent refinement. In a sense, Irving was selling the unsalable – confirmation of entrance into the rarefied world of culture – and one can imagine no more perspicacious marketing strategy than to portray literature and its creator as superior to the sordid concerns of business. The buyers of *The Sketch Book* were raised above commerce in the very act of purchase, and Irving had the double satisfaction of attracting a popular readership and maintaining his self-respect as a gentleman of letters.

That the pose was sincere, and that Irving genuinely believed in the gentility of authorship, can be seen in the subsequent pattern of his career. He had been an instigator of radical changes in the arts, a kind of literary "Son of Liberty." As he settled into the role of "Father of American Literature," Irving came to feel deeply uncomfortable with his erstwhile insurgency. He spoke of "the *guilt of originality*" in his first publication, and behind his retreat from novelty after *The Sketch Book* lay repentance for having aligned himself with the most advanced currents in cultural life. Though the remainder of his work falls outside the time frame of this discussion, a glance at the aptly titled "Author's Apology" to the 1848 revision of the *History* palpably conveys his contrition. It was far from his object, Irving claims, to have committed "any grievous historical sin" by blending facts with fictitious persons and incidents. Rebukes from "men of soberer minds" awoke him to his error, but he still takes satisfaction in his youthful effort because the *History* accomplished two highly meritorious ends. The Knickerbocker satire fostered respect for historical truth; it stimulated interest in "forgotten archives" and "provoked research" into New York's past. Moreover, by making the early history of the province come alive, the book succeeded in its "main" purpose: the patriotic objective of attaching the heart of the citizen to his or her native habitat. Thus did the iconoclast of 1809 recant his inventiveness and represent himself as a defender of the identical literary practices he had led the way in undermining.

8

JAMES FENIMORE COOPER

N O AMERICAN WRITER was ever more conscious of founding a
national tradition in letters than James Fenimore Cooper. As early
as his second book, *The Spy* (1821), Cooper realized that in constituting himself the novelist equivalent of the Founding Fathers, he was
making his principal bid for immortality. Yet few of Cooper's contemporaries
in that era of new beginnings felt as uncertain as he did about the act of
origination. In part his problem was the relatively simple one of finding a
form and a setting for his fiction. But this problem encoded the more vexing
one of whether Cooper — to schematize for the moment — was to be a "republican" or a "liberal" novelist, an author whose goals were social and patriotic
or one who pursued primarily aesthetic ends. Behind this question lay the
related issue of professionalization. How would Cooper accommodate himself
to the commercial processes transforming the identity of the writer?

This literary pioneer reconceptualized his genre. Much like Irving, he
reversed the emphases of the civic-humanist paradigm that governed the
writing of fiction for the first quarter century of the Republic's existence. To
the preceding generation, fiction was "truth" or history; to Cooper, history
was fiction. By reimagining the novel as a subjective art form that would
appeal to postrepublican readers, not as a moral discourse in narrative, Cooper affiliated his writing with the new social order.

Yet Cooper never tired of belaboring his compatriots for deserting the
values of the republican past. Again like Irving, he was profoundly at odds as
well as fervently in sympathy with the acquisitive civilization coming into
being during the first decades of the nineteenth century. A speculator and
capitalist farmer who was in constant need of money, he deplored the materialistic spirit of the age and maintained a lifelong image of himself as an
eighteenth-century gentleman standing censoriously aloof from his compatriots' scramble for riches and position. And he had a gentleman's disdain for
novel writing, an activity that he regarded as beneath his dignity even as he
became the first American to succeed at it professionally.

This chapter will focus on Cooper's early novels through *The Pioneers*
(1823), which can be read as complex meditations on his anxious effort, as a

contemporary reviewer put it, to lay "the foundations of American romance." The legend preserved by his family was that he tried his hand at fiction on a dare: having declared that he could do better than the English domestic novels then in vogue, he took up his pen when his wife and her cousin challenged him to make good on the boast. Whatever the truth of this account, it has the virtue of conveying not only Cooper's studied insouciance about authorship but his competitiveness as well. At this point, he wanted to emulate and to outdo the popular women writers of his day. Above all, he hoped to rival their sales, for he had pressing motives for publishing his first novel, *Precaution* (1820). Although he had inherited a fortune from his father, Judge William Cooper, the founder of Cooperstown, by 1820 he was experiencing severe financial difficulties. He had exhausted a cash bequest and gotten himself deeply into debt through a series of ill-fated business ventures, including speculating in land and investing in a whaling vessel. (Three years later, in 1823, Cooper was forced to sell the remainder of his father's estate to satisfy the claims of creditors.) Fiction appealed to him as a way out of his troubles; by writing a novel of manners modeled on Jane Austen's *Persuasion* (1818), he hoped to produce a best-seller that would enable him to escape insolvency.

Thus at the beginning of his career as a novelist, Cooper thought of the genre in private and "feminine" terms – as a courtship tale that would rescue him financially. He evidently believed that the key to salability in America lay not simply in copying English novels but in taking England as his setting and in pretending to be English. He speaks of Great Britain familiarly as "this country," as though it were his own, and he places a noble, the Earl of Pendennyss, at the center of his narrative, giving prominence to the sort of titled character he soon repudiated as unsuitable for an American novel. Cooper did not go so far as to pose as a female author – "the writer of these pages is a man," he confesses – but knowing that women composed the bulk of his audience, he tried to please potential readers by choosing love and its perils as his subject and paying effusive tribute to "female purity and female truth."

Cooper's sensitivity to the market did not extinguish his fidelity to the republican model of authorship, already well in decline by 1820. He offers perfectly conventional views on the snares and usefulness of fiction. *Precaution* warns against overindulging the imagination and defines literature as worthwhile only when it puts aesthetic pleasure at the service of moral edification. Books are said to have the power "to save or to destroy," and the difference in judgment between the heroine and her unthinking sister is summed up in the statement, "Books were the entertainers of Jane, and instructors of Emily."

On the publishing side, *Precaution* was a typically amateurish performance.

Cooper brought out the novel at his own risk, demonstrating the prickly independence for which he later became notorious. Despite his wish to sell, he refused to puff the book out of pride and insisted on observing the gentleman's code of anonymity: "take care of my *name*," he admonished his bookseller, "do not let it appear in any manner." The typography was unprofessional and unaesthetic, filled with errors in grammar, punctuation, and paragraphing. Although some blunders were owing to the incompetence of the printers, others stemmed from Cooper's nonchalance and haste.

In short, Cooper did not really know what kind of novelist he was or indeed whether he was a novelist at all. No sooner did he complete his first work of fiction than he began work on a second and seemingly very different one, dashing off sixty pages of *The Spy* within two weeks and assuring his bookseller that the new tale, "an American novel professedly," was far superior to its predecessor. In addition to its native setting, *The Spy* marked a change in Cooper's temporal focus: it takes place during an epoch of the recent past, the revolutionary conflict, and represents a turn away from the novel of manners to historical romance. The transatlantic renown of Sir Walter Scott may have influenced Cooper in these choices; he undoubtedly hoped to imitate, and to Americanize, Scott's historical tales of the Border country. A remarkably combative man, Cooper may also have been motivated by a wish to upstage Washington Irving, a New Yorker like himself, whose acclaimed *Sketch Book* reaffirmed American literature's dependence on English subjects. *The Spy* was to be a patriotic making of amends for the Anglophilism of *Precaution*.

The signs that Cooper had suddenly discovered his true vocation as a chronicler of the nation's past are misleading, however. Irving's success, after all, underlined the difficulty of interesting American readers in the scenes and manners of their own country, and Cooper doubted if his new work would have sufficient popular appeal to make a profit. He actually abandoned *The Spy* for several months after finishing the first volume, only to begin a third fictional work that is also set in America but otherwise resembles *Precaution* in its focus on "the matrimonial speculations." This third literary effort, a collection of stories, bore the provisional title *American Tales,* and here Cooper did impersonate a female writer by allowing his publishers to announce the book as "by a Lady." The novelist still had not made up his mind about the kind of literary model he would have to follow if he were going to sell enough books to justify his continued writing. He literally kept vacillating between a female, sentimental formula and a republican and "male" notion of the writer's calling. The former model had a record of selling well; civic and historical fictions, at least in America, not only failed to sell but were predicated on aloofness from the market. The tepid response to *Precaution* may have helped Cooper to resolve his dilemma by diminishing the courtship novel's economic attractions. In any case, not long after commencing the stories about marriage, he abandoned them as well.

The Spy, which Cooper resumed writing at this point and completed without further delays, inaugurates a process of "defeminization" in his self-image as artist. It signals the shift toward masculine subjects and preoccupations that culminated in the Leatherstocking Tales. The book differentiated its author from Irving, who cultivated an epicene persona, and from the women competitors whose monopoly of the market imparted to all fiction writing a feminized aura. Cooper's gravitating toward Scott and military–historical adventure was a means of fending off the derogation of novelists as unmanly.

Yet if *The Spy* registers the beginning of this development, the work remains strongly marked throughout by the uncertainties still troubling Cooper as he felt his way toward a self-conception, a genre, and an audience. The novel is as much about the founding of an American literature as about the establishment of American independence. Although Cooper professed a wish "to induce love" of his homeland, the preface to the first edition of 1821 reveals a defensive and problematic attitude toward the use of native materials. The preface opens by reviewing the arguments for and against an American selecting his country for the scene of his story; it quickly reaches the conclusion that the drawbacks outnumber the advantages. Cooper observes that national loyalty should insure brisk sales for an American novel, then admits that this hope may "prove to be like the book itself – a fiction." There is the advantage of novelty, he says, Charles Brockden Brown being the only previous native novelist to achieve any fame; but Brown had to die before winning recognition, and his writing – Cooper specifically mentions the cave scene from *Edgar Huntly* – constitutes more of an obstacle than a precedent because it lacks verisimilitude. English critics expect Americans to write exclusively about Indians, and women readers, on whom the novelist is most dependent for support, are predisposed against any book that does not feature lords and castles, none of which exist in America. By the end of the preface Cooper's tone has turned openly truculent and his objectives crudely mercenary, as he belittles female readers for their literary tastes and sends his "compliments to all who read our pages – and love to those who buy them."

Cooper's doubts about *The Spy*'s reception unfold within the narrative proper as a conflict about the generic identity of the American novel. Set during the Revolution and subtitled "A Tale of the Neutral Ground," the book traces the struggle for control of New York's Westchester County, a no-man's-land situated between the British and American armies. But *The Spy* is not merely about war in the sense that *Precaution* is about marriage; it is about marriage as well as war, combining episodes and conventions that seem to belong in different stories and constantly negotiating awkward shifts from one level of the plot to the other. The novel is a "neutral ground" in its own right, a fiction torn between the two models Cooper had at his disposal. On one side are the incidents of history and warfare Cooper had in mind when he described his goal as patriotism: the appearance of George Washington as the mysterious Harper; the intrigues of the peddler–spy, Harvey Birch, who acts as Washington's secret agent; and the raids by the lawless bands of partisans, the prorebel Skinners and the Loyalist Cowboys. On the other side are the romantic complications and close observation of manners likely to appeal to women readers: the courtship between Frances Wharton and Major Dunwoodie; the subplot involving Isabella Singleton, who loves Dunwoodie without encouragement and has humiliated herself by betraying her emotions; and the scheming of the two lower-class women, Katy Haynes and Betty Flanagan, to get Harvey Birch and Sergeant Hollister to marry them.

To be sure, romantic elements are also present in Scott's historical novels. But the clash of genres in *The Spy* exceeds anything in Scott for sheer incongruity and comic effect. "War," Cooper states during a lull in the action, "was a dreadful enemy to love," and what ensues from those hostilities are some of the earliest instances of narrative improbability in a body of work not known for realism. Two examples will have to stand for many: marauders and cavalrymen battle each other in the Wharton home, the Locusts, while Sarah Wharton, her mind shattered by an English officer's duplicity, plays out an Ophelia-like mad scene; and the Americans, in hot pursuit of Henry Wharton, call a time out from war so that Frances and Dunwoodie can marry.

The salience of these incongruities recalls Cooper's immediate American precursor, Samuel Woodworth. But Cooper is as much in advance of Woodworth as he lags behind Scott. *The Spy* is a masterful novel in spite of its defects because Cooper has begun to reconceive history as a kind of personalized fiction. He draws upon real people and occurrences from the revolutionary period, but he never allows his work to become a mere documentary record of facts in the public domain. What interests him is the way great events and trends impinge on the lives of ordinary men and women. Fictional characters and "made-up" incidents occupy the center of his tale, and even the principal "fact" – Washington's employment of a peddler–spy – has an aura of fabrication. It is not common knowledge but confidential disclosure, fragmentary information supposedly passed on to Cooper, as he reveals in the 1849 introduction, by "an illustrious man" who had been active in the struggle with Britain. *The Spy*'s very title intimates the novelty of Cooper's perspective on historical knowledge: once a common heritage, past deeds are now secrets known only to a few. The fiction writer himself seems more like a spy than a historian, a trafficker in privileged stories, not a compiler of data belonging to the community. In effect, Cooper is privatizing or subjectivizing history, a development he will carry further in *The Pioneers,* where he turns to his family's experience in settling Cooperstown for the factual basis of his narrative.

Cooper's literary strategy was in keeping with the temper of an ever more buoyant and individualistic society. The liberal order of 1821 gave greater leeway to personal initiative. An ethic of self-making was pushing aside communal loyalties. Many Americans began to feel that they could shape the world around them as individuals, not as members of a group. Cooper's imaginative manipulation of history in *The Spy* reflected the era's growing confidence in the power of the sovereign agent. (Emerson called it the age of the "first person singular.") Like William Cullen Bryant's "Thanatopsis," published four years earlier, *The Spy* assumes an autonomous subject – in Cooper's case, the novelist – who is unconstrained by external forms. He is able to impose his will on his material and to amend the past as he chooses. The republican paradigm, with its privileging of the collectivity, has yielded to the wishes of the individual.

Despite breaking fertile new ground in his revision of historical romance, Cooper remained a typical postrevolutionary man of letters with a conviction of the novel's civic utility. The War of 1812, popularly styled the Second War of American Independence, had quickened national self-awareness. Cooper intended *The Spy* to demonstrate to American readers that their own country afforded a rich field for the writing of historical fiction. Irving located asethetic value in Europe, where it had always been; Cooper performed the patriotic service of showing that authentic works of art could grow in indigenous soil too. His book quickly became a best-seller here and in Europe and inspired an array of native imitators.

Cooper saw the novelistic genre as giving form and definition to the Republic. He had specifically political ambitions for his tale and wanted to influence the question, Who is fit to participate in the American experiment? *The Spy* reflects the agenda of a republican gentleman with a firm commitment to hierarchical arrangements. A series of exclusions defines an acceptable community composed of a social elite and selfless, deferential representatives of the humble orders like Harvey Birch. Those banished from the Neutral Ground include the British aristocrat Wellmere and the lower-class leader of the Skinners, a grasping man on the make whose greed determines his allegiances and who meets his end by hanging.

Significantly, Cooper's ideal community is intersectional. The marriage of Frances and Major Dunwoodie, who are cousins, unites New York and Virginia, North and South, and affirms a national identity that transcends regional differences. In 1821, a year after the Missouri Compromise, the need to preserve the federal union was very much on the minds of Cooper's contemporaries. *The Spy* seeks to forestall a recurrence of the divisions that had erupted into armed conflict in 1775 – the Revolution, the novelist states in the 1849 introduction, "had many of the features of a civil war" – and that were now threatening to revive over the explosive slavery issue. Consolidating nationhood was essential to complete the break with England; slavery troubled Cooper but little. His portrait of Caesar Thompson, the Whartons' family retainer – and, evasively, a northern slave – is one of the earliest stereotypes in our fiction of the comical, subservient black.

For all his patrician self-conception, Cooper is deeply invested in Harvey Birch, his plebeian protagonist and precursor of Natty Bumppo. With his hut on the pinnacle of a hill from which he can survey the whole of the Neutral Ground, and with his wardrobe of disguises, Birch seems an apt image of the artist in his workshop, able to don different identities and to manipulate the action from above. Combining devotion to the commonweal with attentiveness to the interests of the female public, the peddler–spy bridges the sentimental and historical novels and incarnates in his person the generic alloy of Cooper's fiction. He is first seen displaying his wares to the women at the Locusts and haggling over the price of various articles, all the while passing on information to Washington under the pretext of giving the latest news about the war. The mixture of monetary and patriotic motives evident in this scene evokes the 1821 preface, and one senses in Cooper's portrayal of Birch an effort to come to terms with his own feelings about engaging in the commerce of literature.

Birch is a version of the artist as high-minded trader and dedicated patriot. Particularly toward the end of the story, he crystallizes Cooper's mixed feelings about the professionalizing of authorship. Or rather he provisionally resolves Cooper's ambivalence, for he simultaneously manages to sell and to serve his country. Birch justifies his creator for "peddling" fiction. Like Cooper, the spy has suffered a decline in economic condition; having known "better fortunes," he now appears "absorbed in the one grand object of amassing money." He maintains a thriving trade in wartime, avidly accepts payment for his services to Henry Wharton, and keeps a hoard of gold hidden beneath the floorboards in his cottage. But as the penultimate chapter demonstrates, money is not the real object of Birch's activities: patriotism is. In his dramatic final interview with Washington, he proudly refuses the offer of a cash reward and announces that his sole aim has been to advance the welfare of his country.

Birch's sacrifice will not be rightly estimated by his compatriots, Cooper grouses. "It is seldom that either popular condemnation or applause falls where it is merited," he writes about the misperception of his hero, and Washington, in their last meeting, tells the spy that the veil concealing his true character "cannot be raised for years – perhaps never." Birch's situation is uncannily prophetic of Cooper's own fate as a novelist. The spy is the figure in whom Cooper came increasingly to see himself: a disinterested patriot whose contribution to his country is unacknowledged. Cooper anticipates at the very outset of his career the indifference and outright antipathy he was to suffer from the public. Indeed, given Cooper's abrasive relations with his publishers and readers, one is tempted to view Harvey Birch as a self-fulfilling prophecy. The preface to *The Spy*, which bristles with a prospective sense of injury, virtually embraces a Birch-like obscurity as the inevitable lot of the American novelist. According to the novel's final chapter, Birch's name is completely forgotten after the Revolution. No one knows of his exploits until he perishes in the War of 1812 and Washington's note divulging his true identity is discovered on his body.

A paradox arises at this point to further complicate the problem of Cooper's aggrieved attitude toward his audience. Even as he craved honor for his achievement, Cooper regarded both spying and novel writing as ungentlemanly and persisted in seeking *not* to be recognized by publishing *The Spy* anonymously. He could not overcome his prejudice against the novelist's practice of "disguising" himself in his characters and dealing in imaginary occurrences, in "deceit" rather than the historian's facts. His upper-class figures, with whom a part of him strongly identified, insist that persons of superior breeding should always be absolutely truthful. Major Dunwoodie voices Cooper's own sentiments when he exclaims at Henry Wharton's trial for spying, "I have known this gentleman from a boy; deceit never formed part of his character. He is above it." Cooper himself refused to permit his name to appear on new works of fiction long after his vocation as a novelist was known to everyone. His title pages carry the line "By the author of . . . " and list two or three earlier novels; there is no mention of James Fenimore Cooper. In contrast, works of nonfiction such as *The American Democrat* (1838) and *The History of the Navy of the United States of America* (1839), works Cooper considered serious and respectable, identify him openly by name.

The prohibition against dealing in falsehood by gentlemen is relaxed toward the conclusion of *The Spy*, as if Cooper were becoming more reconciled to an instrumental rather than moralistic conception of his fiction writing. Henry Wharton discovers that wearing disguises can have positive consequences. Sentenced to hang for having visited the Locusts in wig and eye patch, he effects his escape from jail by masquerading as his black servant Caesar. Even the blameless George Washington, in Cooper's portrait of him, disguises himself as Harper so that he can consult with Birch about the movements of the enemy. Rewriting history in this way allows a great public figure plausibly to enter the story; it also seems a covert defense of Cooper's own activity of fictionalizing.

Almost in spite of himself, Cooper was beginning to accept his position as a professional novelist, as someone who makes a living by trafficking in stories. He was simultaneously moving away from the customary subordination of the novel to social purposes and coming to see the imaginary as having a value equal or superior to factual accuracy. This shift in emphasis — for it was never more than that, as Cooper never abandoned the idea of literary production for use — is evident in even a minor work like the *Tales for Fifteen*, the version of *American Tales* that the novelist finally published in 1823. The preface to the collection disavows didactic function. Originally, Cooper says, he intended the stories to have "moral advantage" for the readers of them; now he "only hopes that if they do no good," they will, "at least, do no harm." In another piece dating from this time, a review of Catharine Maria Sedgwick's *A New-England Tale* (1822), Cooper challenges the stigmatizing of fiction as a less worthwhile genre than history. A storyteller like Sedgwick, he argues, has at least as good a claim on our attention as the recorder of "true names and dates," for she deals with "that higher truth, the truth of nature and of principles, which is a primitive law of the human mind."

Cooper's growing appreciation for the aesthetic as an autonomous realm of value had a formative influence on his next major work of fiction, *The Pioneers*. Subtitled "A Descriptive Tale," and filled, as D. H. Lawrence enviously noted, with "some of the loveliest, most glamorous pictures in all literature," *The Pioneers* is the first self-consciously "beautiful" novel written by an American. The opening volume of the Leatherstocking Tales, it renounces the postrevolutionary paradigm by firmly differentiating fiction from fidelity to fact. Cooper aims merely to convey "a general picture," according to the introduction (added in 1832); "rigid adherence to truth," whereas indispensable in travel writing and history, would destroy "the charm of fiction." Moreover, history verges on autobiography in *The Pioneers*. The "literal facts" are derived not from the public record, but from the novelist's background and memory; "brought an infant into this valley," he ascribes the "faithfulness" of his picture to childhood experience. In thus personalizing history, Cooper is able to circumvent the problems of *The Spy*. The generic conflicts of the earlier book decline in intensity in the new novel. If the realms of "love" and "war," sentiment and civic life, are not completely integrated in *The Pioneers*, they are handled with greater assurance, and the tension between them recedes to the minor but chronic irritant it remains throughout Cooper's work.

Cooper's individualistic slant on history opened his art to its discordances and complexities. *The Pioneers* is a classic instance of the historical novel as a genre of becoming. The book treats history as an unfinished and strife-ridden process, an arena of struggle between a rising and a doomed nation, the expanding American Republic and the beleaguered society of the natives. But in *The Pioneers* the disappearance of indigenous peoples, which became the paramount theme of the later Leatherstocking Tales, is less central than the antagonism between two stages in the growth of American civilization. The novel provides a fitting conclusion to the formative phase of our national literature: it concerns itself with the shift from the use-oriented culture of the postrevolutionary years to the market outlook that came to dominate the Age of Jackson. Although Cooper renders the change as a confrontation between his frontiersman—hero and Judge Marmaduke Temple, in actuality the two viewpoints were increasingly difficult to tell apart. Cooper's own novelistic program blurs the difference between them. His accurate sense that representations of American nature and customs would be avidly consumed by American readers demonstrates that function can be made to serve exchange and that the two attitudes are not necessarily incompatible, or at least are no longer so at the time he was writing.

Certainly the tale's original preface of 1823 evokes the acquisitive ethos of the Jacksonian era. Traces of *The Spy*'s belligerence remain, but Cooper now suggests that the best gauge of an artwork's value is its marketability. Everything betrays his keen interest in his book's material fortunes. Not only does he dedicate the preface to his bookseller, Charles Wiley, he reduces a "true account" of the work's reception to the number of copies purchased by the public. "The critics," Cooper declares, "may write as obscurely as they please, and look much wiser than they are; the papers may puff or abuse, as their changeful humours dictate; but if you [Wiley] meet me with a smiling face, I shall at once know that all is essentially well."

Prefaces, especially when addressed to one's bookseller, are a form of advertisement; and self-promotion is one of the principal themes of *The Pioneers,* part of the novel's meticulous attention to American mores. The book's first paragraph refers to a stable settlement in which the son lingers "around the grave of his father," but it quickly becomes evident that the more representative pattern in early Templeton is set by those like Jotham Riddel who buy and sell farms for profit. Cooper depicts the formation of a liberal society marked by geographic and economic mobility and ceaseless striving to advance oneself. In a country where birth confers no rank and status is so fluid, a person can make of himself whatever his talents, energy, and luck permit. Traditional fitness and training have little application. Though "it might make a Templar smile," Marmaduke Temple has been appointed a judge in the community he founded, his habit of ruling and "native clearness of mind" taking the place of legal knowledge. Elnathan Todd, who has no formal education but learned medicine by practicing it, is the settlement's physician, and Richard Jones occupies the offices of architect and sheriff, thanks to the circumstance of his being the judge's cousin.

With worldly position up for grabs, people in Templeton struggle to set themselves apart from each other by constantly publicizing their merits. The opening episode shows that even Judge Temple participates in the rage for self-inflation: he offers to buy the deer shot by Natty and Oliver Effingham because he craves "the honour" of having killed it and wishes to "make a good story about its death." As Richard Jones observes, the judge "is a prodigious bragger about any small matter like this." Jones of course is the most vocal self-promoter in the book and more than the judge's match in the rivalry for bragging rights. Confident that "genius will supply the place of learning," he proclaims his aptitude for languages, medicine, law, architecture, mining — for "any thing and every thing."

Cooper is as much a competitive individualist as his characters and joins them in trumpeting his own abilities and deprecating those of others. Repressing his disdain for newspaper puffs, he agreed to the advance publication of two excerpts from his novel in the *Commercial Advertiser*. Moreover, he contrives several scenes with the deliberate intention of outperforming the two writers most commonly mentioned as his rivals for "the palm as an American novelist" (as a reviewer phrased it in 1822), Washington Irving and Charles Brockden Brown. His detailed narrative of the Christmas festivities at Templeton, including New World customs like the turkey shoot, is an American rejoinder to the widely praised account of an English Christmas in Irving's *Sketch Book*. In the preface to *The Spy*, Cooper spoke slightingly of the panther episode in *Edgar Huntly;* he gets the better of Brown in *The Pioneers* with his vivid description of the panther attack on Elizabeth Temple and Louisa Grant.

Closely related to the theme of self-promotion in *The Pioneers* is the question of property, its ownership and uses. The opening scene, which centers on a dispute about who is entitled to the slain buck, is symptomatic of the novel's lines of division. The incident introduces the sensitive issue of rightful ownership, pitting Natty, Indian John, and young Effingham against Judge Temple in a miniature version of the larger quarrel (or misunderstanding, as it turns out) about the true owner of the land around Templeton. Whereas Natty and his friends desire the deer for food, the judge is only secondarily interested in its use as venison, and his immediate impulse is to give them money in exchange for it, just as he then proceeds to offer Oliver a hundred dollars when he realizes that his errant shot has wounded the young man.

Cooper draws a balanced if rather acerbic portrait of the judge, possibly expressing feelings of resentment toward his own father, an overbearing man who founded Cooperstown and speculated aggressively in land. The judge appears to believe that money can purchase almost anything. He has applied his fortune to buying up some hundred thousand acres of virgin soil, prompting Jones to ask him rhetorically, "Do you not own the mountains, as well as the valleys? Are not the woods your own?" The judge is thoroughly identified with a conception of the physical environment as commodity. He started out as a merchant, and he invests in the landscape with the same shrewdness that he displayed in his commercial ventures. Where others see "nothing but a wilderness," the judge's eye summons up "towns, manufactories, bridges, canals, [and] mines," future improvements that will not only multiply the value of his holdings but extend the dominion of the market over nature.

Judge Temple differs from the townspeople whose wastefulness he condemns, but Cooper makes clear that he resembles them too. Whereas they waste because they see no way to exchange, the judge's "bias to look far into futurity" disposes him to conserve so that exchange value can be generated at a later time. Cooper devotes several chapters to the settlers' heedless consumption of the wilderness, and he makes Temple a spokesman for the conservationist argument that natural resources should be protected rather than indiscriminately exploited. On this matter the judge claims to be of Natty's mind: "Your reasoning is mine: for once, old hunter, we agree in opinion." But Natty quickly dismisses the notion of any such alliance. He feels that the judge, like his neighbors, fails to appreciate nature for itself. Although the judge is not indifferent to the physical environment's beauty and usefulness, he invariably seeks to convert nature into wealth. He opposes the wholesale destruction of the maple trees because he contemplates improvements in the manufacture of sugar, anticipating the day "when farms and plantations shall be devoted to this branch of business," and because even the butts of the trees felled so carelessly by the settlers "would have sold in the Philadelphia market for twenty dollars." The settlers are unable to get their logs to Philadelphia at present, as Jones points out derisively, but the judge's imagined canals and bridges are the developments that will make transportation to the metropolis possible. To Judge Temple, the maples are "treasures," "jewels of the forest," and "mines of comfort and wealth." As his language indicates, he has as strong an interest in extracting profit from them as in mining the surrounding mountains for coal and precious metals.

Against the ascendant commercial order represented by the judge, Cooper places the Leatherstocking as an advocate for the residual values of an older society. Natty is interested not in conservation but in reversing or at least halting the course of history; he pines for the time before humans and nature came under the sway of economic calculation. The Otsego area was "a second paradise," he contends, and "would have been so to this day, but for the money of Marmaduke Temple." Natty is the novel's spokesman for a world based on use rather than on exchange; he gives voice both to the Indian understanding of the proper relation of humans to the environment and to the ideals of the household regime. Various characters in *The Pioneers* refer to "the native owners of the soil," but this designation is purely metaphoric because the Indians had no conception of the land as private property. They thought in terms of usufruct rights, not the ownership of real estate; what they "owned" was the use of the land, including the privilege of hunting and fishing on it.

Natty, who has lived among the Indians, shares their emphasis on the usefulness of things. A man in his seventies in 1793, when the story opens, he abhors the "wasty ways" of the settlers and believes that "the least thing was . . . made for use, and not to destroy." He protests against the slaughter of wildlife like the passenger pigeons and the Otsego bass because "God made them for man's food, and for no other discernable reason," and it is "sinful and wasty to catch more than can be eat." Similarly he opposes the destruction of the maple trees, not, like Judge Temple, in order to harvest them more efficiently someday, but because they were "made for the beasts and birds to harbour in, and when man wanted their flesh, their skins, or their feathers, there's the place to seek them."

Natty's stress on use has an analogue in Cooper's continued concern for literature's social benefits. Like *The Spy, The Pioneers* constructs a microcosm of the Republic, enabling readers to conceptualize the nation as a distinct community. The epigraph from James Kirke Paulding's *The Backwoodsman,* referring to habits, manners, and contrasts "[t]hat other lands and ages never knew," prepares for the wealth of almost sociological notation. Cooper mounts an elaborate case for the "melting pot" thesis of American identity. His Templeton is a "composite order" – the phrase is his – consisting of immigrants drawn from all the countries of Europe, all living together in relative harmony. The settlement's immense "variety in character and nations" emerges vividly from the cultural idiosyncrasies, multiple dialects, and differences in accent of its inhabitants. Cooper takes special care to distinguish American language – to some, proof of the Republic's cultural dependency – from that of England. He peppers the text with minilectures on the singularities of native speech, explaining the derivation and nuances of "clearing," "Yankee," "sleigh," and of phrases like "make their pitch."

It is above all the physical environment that demarcates the United States from the Old World. Instead of Irving's cemeteries and cathedrals, Cooper provides extended descriptions of landscape and climate. His graphic word-pictures of existence in the wilderness link him once again to the ancient woodsman who feels so much reverence for the natural world. *The Pioneers* abounds in stunning visual images of humans interacting with their surroundings; scenes like the chase of the deer on the lake, the nighttime fishing for the bass, the shooting of the pigeons, whose numbers darken the heavens as far as the eye can see, and the visit to the woodchopper, Billy Kirby, while he is manufacturing maple sugar in the mountains – "no unreal picture of human life in its first stages of civilization," as Cooper calls the last episode – these and other scenes are among the most fully realized descriptive passages in American Romantic fiction. Anticipating Joseph Conrad's famous prescription for the novel – "before all, to make you *see!*" – they impart to the book a static, painterly quality.

It should be apparent that function has ceased to govern literary craft in *The Pioneers;* the wish to celebrate American uniqueness is unmistakably there, but it is subsumed in the goal of creating artistically satisfying moments. The preface of 1823 implicitly acknowledges as much. Omitting any reference to civic or didactic purposes, Cooper speaks of his delight in representing the scenes of his youth; the book, he says, "has been written, exclusively, to please myself." The effect of this relish for pure aesthetic pleasure is to push the novel in the direction of the visual arts. Contemporaries noticed this immediately; they hailed Cooper's book as a natural ally of painting and illustration. The New York periodical press reported that *The Pioneers* "excited a sensation among the artists, altogether unprecedented in the history of our domestic literature." Cooper, who has Elizabeth Temple call the fishing scene "a subject for the pencil," told a correspondent that he hoped to "rouse the sleeping talents of the nation," and he must have felt gratified by the outpouring of visual artworks based on his narrative. The panther scene inspired numerous engravings as well as oil paintings by John Quidor and George Loring Brown, and there were original canvases or drawings devoted to the forest fire, Natty's defense of his hut, the death of Mohegan, and many other incidents.

A landscape painter in words, Cooper furthered a major realignment of the American novel or rather of that strain of novels decreasingly committed to the role of teacher. Just a few years earlier, it had been customary to associate fiction with rhetorical discourses on morality and politics. Much like Irving's revealingly titled *Sketch Book,* authored by "Geoffrey Crayon," *The Pioneers* encouraged an association with the fine arts, which is to say with the aesthetic in its purest, least functional form. Literature was no longer to be situated in a discursive field with orations, histories, and sermons. Instead, it was to be constellated with the nonpragmatic realm of painting, with a medium whose capacity to "say" was considerably less salient than its ability to "be."

The alliance of fiction with the pictorial arts had advantages for both. The novel, that latecomer among literary forms, lost some of its moral justification, but it gained in other ways; association with traditional high culture conferred instant prestige. The genre's desirability as an object of consumption was enhanced. The expanding, modernizing economy that emerged after the War of 1812 created wealth and an appetite for home-grown products. People had more disposable income and more leisure time in which to spend it. Many felt a new willingness to read for entertainment, to purchase literature for its beauty and excitement regardless of any message it might impart. Here Cooper diverges from the Leatherstocking: in his Judge Temple-like awareness of the exchange value of his text's artful evocations of nature. He knew that the passages of exceptional beauty were powerful inducements to buy the novel, and he gave two of them, Natty's killing of the deer and the Christmas turkey shoot, to the *Commercial Advertiser* to arouse prepublication interest among potential readers. The strategy succeeded so well that thirty-five hundred copies of *The Pioneers* were sold within a day of its publication.

The fine arts, for their part, gained in acceptance and dissemination from their union with the novel. Until recently, Americans had regarded paintings as superfluous and unrepublican. To the revolutionary generation, visual artworks were expensive luxuries that filled no real need. Native-born painters like Benjamin West and John Singleton Copley had been forced to settle abroad to find the financial support and critical appreciation missing in their homeland. Even history painting, which was supposed to promote nationalism, failed to overcome these prejudices: West's famous *Death of General Wolfe* was executed in London, not in New York or in Philadelphia. By the 1820s, the situation was changing, thanks in part to the waning of the functionalist requirement, but the fine arts remained foreign to the experience of most Americans. Cooper's novel helped to dispel that exoticism by encouraging receptivity to visual representation, metaphorically through language but also quite literally by providing artists with well-known characters and scenes to reproduce.

The country's first successful professional novelist played a key role in establishing the visual arts as a viable profession. The celebrity of *The Pioneers* meant that painters and illustrators could be sure of an already existing market for their works. Along with the fiction of Irving and the poetry of Bryant, Cooper's novels contributed to the emergence of the Hudson River School, the first native community of artists and the creators of a distinctive style of American landscape painting. One of the most gifted members of the group, Thomas Cole, painted forest and mountain scenes from several of the Leatherstocking Tales, including *The Pioneers*. Engravers and illustrators in particular found Cooper's book a rich vein to mine. Thanks to improved technologies, such as steel engraving, they could realistically expect to earn a living by illustrating books and magazines (as well as by engraving bank notes, a major source of employment in the 1820s). Cooper's "Descriptive Tale" offered a range of possibilities: engravings of its characters and settings appeared in later editions of the novel, in journals like *The Columbian Magazine* and *The Port Folio,* and in a separate volume entitled *Illustrations from The Spy, The Pioneers, and the Waverley Novels, with Explanatory and Critical Remarks* (1826). Just as the prestige of the fine arts rubbed off on fiction, so the arts themselves were democratized, made available in inexpensive copies for which Americans were now prepared to pay.

One thing the beautiful helped to "sell" was nature, and in this respect too *The Pioneers* had an almost immediate impact. To be sure, people who read the book did not flock to the mountains and woods after wealth; they went there in search of visual appropriations of the wilderness. In Chapter 26 Natty delivers a rapturous speech describing the view from Pine Orchard in the Catskills. As he launches into his description, he begins to sound more like a travel guide interested in promotion than a solitary frontiersman. "I can recommend the spot," he effuses to Effingham, adding that "it is a spot to make a man solemnize," "the best piece of work that I've met with in the woods." Effingham, who is greatly impressed by Natty's eloquence, remarks that he has "never heard of this spot before; it is not mentioned in the books," but, of course, it is mentioned in Cooper's book, and the description of it not only inspired a painting by Cole but was instrumental in publicizing the site's attractions. Natty's account was believed to be so accurate that one could locate the very place where he stood. Nearby was a large resort hotel, the Catskill Mountain House, which, as James Franklin Beard, Cooper's modern editor, relates, became "a world-famous Mecca for lovers of fine scenery from the 1820s to the end of the nineteenth century." Moved by *The Pioneers,* tourists came from as far away as Europe to savor the picturesque view; they brought business to the Mountain House and enjoyed themselves in aesthetic consumption of nature.

The title of Cooper's novel contains a significant ambiguity: the word "pioneers" refers both to Natty, who flees the settlements for the woods, and to Judge Temple, who leads the march of civilization into the untamed regions of the country. D. H. Lawrence believed that Cooper was of Natty's party without knowing it. On our reading, it is the other way around: Cooper's real allegiance is to the judge and to the society he heads. *The Pioneers* pointed the way into the wilderness for seekers after beauty, and it made profits out of nature for its author as well as for others. But in another sense the very opposition between the Leatherstocking and the judge has to be questioned. Although the tale posits an antithesis between use and exchange, between the woodsman's viewpoint and the magistrate's, it also works to elide that contrast by lending Natty's words and presence to the commodifying of beautiful places like Pine Hill. By 1823, *The Pioneers* suggests, the two perspectives were not so much opposites as part of a continuum; Cooper may lean to one pole or the other, but use has become a pretext or rationale for exchange in a society undergoing rapid commercialization. Perhaps the most telling index of collusion between Natty's party (if not Natty himself) and the judge's involves the Effinghams. The novel's representatives of proud if frayed gentility – and in this they resemble Cooper himself – the Effinghams once employed the Leatherstocking and now act as his allies, but they turn out to be in league with the Temples. It is not merely that Oliver, after siding with Natty and Mohegan, ends up marrying Elizabeth and inheriting the judge's lands. Before the Revolution the Effinghams had entered into a secret partnership with Judge Temple. Although they looked down on commerce as "a degrading pursuit" and kept their connection to the judge concealed, they were implicated in his mercantile enterprises from the beginning and "entitled to an equal participation in the profits."

Yet a share of the profits was never enough to allay Cooper's discomfort about partnership with the judge. Lawrence's interpretation seems more defensible if the Leatherstocking series – and Cooper's career – is considered as a whole. Even in *The Pioneers,* residual values engross Cooper's imagination. The ending of the book, in which Natty holds his final interview with Elizabeth and Effingham before departing for the West, can be read as a farewell to the whole constellation of attitudes marginalized or rendered obsolete by the transformation of the United States in the first quarter of the nineteenth century; the emotional force of the text lies with the defeated elements. More than that, the novel's concluding scene suggests a dour judgment on the emergent order's historical amnesia. The tombstone erected by Oliver to commemorate Chingachgook – a figure from a vanishing America – contains a significant error: the inscription for the Indian warrior misspells his name as "Chingagook," a distortion, Natty complains, that obliterates the name's meaning. It seems reasonable to interpret this erasure as emblematic of the Romantic age's repression of republican culture. And the point is underscored when Oliver makes the spectacularly inappropriate gesture of offering Natty bank notes to carry with him into the wilderness.

In his later writings, the nonfiction as well as the novels, Cooper became ever more vociferous in his disaffection from the present. Something of a cranky reactionary by the 1840s, he wrote novels extolling the organic, elitist communities of his childhood and berating his compatriots for their avarice and disrespect for traditional ways. Nor did Cooper ever relinquish his understanding of letters as serving a socially useful purpose. *The Crater,* his anti-utopian novel of 1847 and one of the last works he published, sounds "a timely warning" that "those who now live in this republic" face destruction unless they amend their behavior. And of course the subsequent volumes of the Leatherstocking Tales stage a steady retreat from the judge's world. Cooper, as a professional author, belonged to the specialized market society of the Jacksonian era, but the books in which he solidified his position as the country's greatest historical romancer follow Natty in turning from the clearings to the woods.

CHRONOLOGY
1590–1820

Cyrus R. K. Patell

	Important Texts In and Concerning the New World	Historical Events in the New World	Historical and Literary Events in the Old World
1590	**Hakluyt, Richard** (1552–1616), *The Principal Navigations, Voyages, Traffiques, and Discoveries of the English Nation* (1589–90) **Harriot, Thomas** (1560–1621), *A Brief and True Report of the New Found Land of Virginia* (edition with de Bry engravings, published in Latin, English, French, and German as the first installment in a projected series entitled *America*; an unillustrated edition was published in 1588)		Sidney, *Arcadia* (written c. 1580–2) Spenser, *The Faerie Queene*, Books I–III
1591			Henry IV of France excommunicated by Pope Gregory XIV. Sidney, *Astrophel and Stella* (posth.)
1592			Michel de Montaigne dies (b. 1533). Kyd, *The Spanish Tragedy*
1593	**White, John** (*fl.* 1585–93), *The Fifth Voyage of M. John White into the West Indies and Parts of America called Virginia, in the Year* 1590		Henry IV of France becomes a Roman Catholic. George Herbert born (d. 1633). Christopher Marlowe dies (b. 1564). Nicholas Poussin born (d. 1665).

1594	Henry IV crowned king, enters Paris. Tintoretto dies (b. 1518).
1595	Henry IV absolved by Pope Clement VIII. Torquato Tasso dies (b. 1544).
1596	**Raleigh, Walter** (1552?–1618), *The Discovery of the Large, Rich, and Beautiful Empire of Guiana, with a Relation of the Great and Golden City of Manoa (which the Spaniards call El Dorado)*	Pacification of Ireland by British. Spenser, *The Faerie Queene*, Books IV–VI
1597	Second Spanish Armada leaves for England and is scattered by storms at sea.
1598	**Hakluyt, Richard** (1552–1616), *The Principal Navigations, Voyages, Traffiques, and Discoveries of the English Nation* (second edition, 1598–1600)	René Descartes born (d. 1650). Bacon, *Essays, Civil and Moral*
1599	Fyodor I of Russia dies; Boris Godunov seizes throne and is formally elected czar by national assembly.
1600	Edmund Spenser dies (b. 1552).

	Important Texts In and Concerning the New World	Historical Events in the New World	Historical and Literary Events in the Old World
1601			Earl of Essex leads a revolt against Elizabeth I; he is tried for treason and executed.
1603			Death of Elizabeth I; accession of James I to the English throne.
1604			Guy Fawkes plot against James I.
1605		French hostilities with Indians.	Cervantes, *Don Quixote*, Part I Spenser, *The Mutabilitie Cantos* (posth.)
1606		Virginia Company of London is granted royal charter and sends 120 colonists to Virginia.	Rembrandt van Rijn born (d. 1669). Jonson, *Volpone* Shakespeare, *King Lear*
1607		Founding of Jamestown, Virginia, first English settlement on the American mainland.	"Flight of Earls" from Ireland to Spain to escape arrest for attempted insurrection. Monteverdi, *Orfeo*
1608	**Smith, John** (1580–1631), *A True Relation of Virginia*		Galileo constructs astronomical telescope.

1609		Henry Hudson discovers the Hudson River, claims New Netherlands.	Separatists (called "Brownists") move from England to Holland.
1610		Henry Hudson discovers Hudson's Bay.	Michelangelo Caravaggio dies (b. 1579).
1611	*Jesuit Relations* (New World diaries published annually until 1768)		James I dissolves Parliament. Shakespeare, *The Tempest*
1612	**Smith, John** (1580–1631), *A Map of Virginia, with a Description of the Country, the Commodities, People, Government and Religion; The Proceedings of the English Colony in Virginia*	Tobacco planted in Virginia.	Webster, *The White Devil*
1613			Fire destroys Globe Theater, London.
1614		Pocahontas, a Native-American princess, marries John Rolfe.	
1615			Cervantes, *Don Quixote*, Part II
1616	**Smith, John** (1580–1631), *A Description of New England*	Smallpox epidemic kills 75–95 percent of the native population along the coast between Penobscot and Cape Cod.	William Shakespeare dies (b. 1564).
1617			Ben Jonson becomes poet laureate of England.

	Important Texts In and Concerning the New World	Historical Events in the New World	Historical and Literary Events in the Old World
1618			Sir Walter Raleigh returns to England and is executed.
1619		First Africans arrive in Virginia. First representative assembly in North America meets in Virginia under Governor Sir George Yeardley.	
1620		Signing of Mayflower Compact; Puritans land at Cape Cod and establish a settlement named Plymouth.	
1621		First Puritan governor, John Carver, dies; William Bradford (1590–1657) assumes post and serves until his death.	Bacon, *Novum organum* Burton, *The Anatomy of Melancholy*
1622	*A Relation or Journal of the Beginning and Proceedings of the English Plantation Settled at Plymouth in New England* (commonly known as *Mourt's Relation*; attrib. to **William Bradford** and **Edward Winslow**; short title refers to George Morton who saw it through the press) **Smith, John** (1580–1631), *New England's Trials*		

1623		New Netherland in America formally organized as a province. First English settlement in New Hampshire.	The First Folio: *Mr. William Shakespeares Comedies, Histories and Tragedies Published According to the True Originall Copies*
1624	**Smith, John** (1580–1631), *The General History of Virginia, New England, and the Summer Isles* **Winslow, Edward** (1595–1655), *Good News from New England* (pamphlet)	Virginia becomes crown colony; Virginia Company dissolved; Sir Francis Wyatt made governor.	Poussin, *Rape of the Sabine Women*
1625	**Purchas, Samuel** (1575?–1626), *Hakluytus Posthumus; or Purchas His Pilgrimes, containing a History of the World in Sea Voyages and Land Travels, by Englishmen and others*		Death of James I; accession of Charles I.
1626		Peter Minuit arrives in New Netherland, buys Manhattan Island, and renames it New Amsterdam.	
1627			Bacon, *The New Atlantis*
1628		Captain Miles Standish of Plymouth leads an attack upon Thomas Morton and his group; Morton tried but acquitted.	Petition of Right sent by the House of Commons to Charles I.

	Important Texts In and Concerning the New World	Historical Events in the New World	Historical and Literary Events in the Old World
1629	Winthrop, John (1588–1649), *Reasons to be Considered . . . for the Intended Plantation in New England* (pamphlet)	John Winthrop negotiates an agreement with English government to establish Massachusetts Bay Company and is elected its governor by its Puritan stockholders.	
1630	Bradford, William (1590–1657), Begins to write "Of Plymouth Plantation"; continues after hiatus in 1646; preserved in church records (published in 1856 as *The History of Plymouth Plantation*)	John Endecott arrests Thomas Morton, who returns to England. Members of Massachusetts Bay Company sail aboard the *Arbella* to New England and found a colony that becomes Boston. Beginning of the "Great Migration."	
	Cotton, John (1584–1652), *God's Promise to His Plantation* (sermon)		
	Smith, John (1580–1631), *The True Travels, Adventures, and Observations of Captain John Smith in Europe, Asia, Africa, and America, beginning about the year 1593, and continued to this present 1629*		
	Winthrop, John (1588–1649), "A Model of Christian Charity" (lay sermon); begins keeping his *Journal* (published in 1825–6 as *The History of New England from 1630 to 1649*)		

702

1631	**Smith, John** (1580–1631), *Advertisements: Or, The Path-Way to Experience to Erect a Plantation*		John Donne dies (b. 1572?).
1632	**Díaz del Casillo, Bernal** (1496–1584), *The True History of the Conquest of New Spain* (written in the 1560s)	Boston becomes capital of Massachusetts. Cecilius Calvert, Lord Baltimore, receives charter for Maryland colony.	John Locke born (d. 1704).
	Hooker, Thomas (1586–1647), *The Soul's Preparation for Christ* (tract)		
1633		John Cotton resigns his post at St. Botolph in Boston, England, and sails to America with Thomas Hooker and Samuel Stone.	
1634	**Wood, William** (1606–post-1637), *New England's Prospect* (nonfiction)	First settlements in Maryland.	
1635		Boston Latin School established. Roger Williams ordered by Massachusetts General Court to return to England; flees with followers to Rhode Island, where they found Providence.	
1636		First "Indian War" (against Pequots). Harvard College founded.	

	Important Texts In and Concerning the New World	Historical Events in the New World	Historical and Literary Events in the Old World
1637		Thomas Hooker and Samuel Stone relocate their congregation to Hartford, Connecticut, in defiance of Massachusetts authorities.	
1638	**Morton, Thomas** (1590?–1647), *New English Canaan* (pamphlet)	Antinomian Crisis: Anne Hutchinson and her husband are banished from Massachusetts and flee to Rhode Island.	
	Underhill, John (c. 1597–1672), *News from America* (pamphlet)		
1639			
1640	**Mather, Richard** (1596–1669), *The Whole Book of Psalms Faithfully Translated into English Meter* (trans. with **John Eliot** and **Thomas Weld**; commonly known as *The Bay Psalm Book*)		Charles I summons the "Long Parliament" (1640–60).
	Shepard, Thomas (1604–49), *The Sincere Convert, Discovering the Paucity of True Believers* (tract)		
1641	**Cotton, John** (1584–1652), *The Way of Life* (tract)		

1642	Cotton, John (1584–1652), *The Pouring Out of the Seven Vials*; *The Church's Resurrection* (sermons) Lechford, Thomas (?), *Plain Dealing, or News from New England* (pamphlet)	Basic literacy law passed in Massachusetts. Sir William Berkeley becomes governor of Virginia.	English Civil War (1642–6). Cardinal Richelieu dies (b. 1585); succeeded as first minister of France by Cardinal Mazarin.
1643	Williams, Roger (1603?–83). *A Key into the Language of America*	Massachusetts Bay, Plymouth, Connecticut, and New Haven colonies form the New England Federation.	
1644	Williams, Roger (1603?–83), *The Bloody Tenent of Persecution, for Cause of Conscience, Discussed* (tract)		
1645	Cotton, John (1584–1652), *The Way of the Churches of Christ in New England* (tract) Shepard, Thomas (1604–49), *The Sound Believer. Or, a Treatise of Evangelical Conversion*		Milton, "L'Allegro" and "Il Penseroso"
1646	Ward, Nathaniel (1578?–1652), *The Simple Cobbler of Aggawam in America* (tract) Bradford, William (1590–1657) writes the second book of his history of Plymouth Plantation from his journals; it is lost after the American Revolution until 1865, when both books are published together for the first time		Surrender of Charles I.

	Important Texts In and Concerning the New World	Historical Events in the New World	Historical and Literary Events in the Old World
1647	Cotton, John (1584–1652), *The Bloody Tenent, Washed, and Made White in the Blood of the Lamb* (tract)	Peter Stuyvesant becomes governor of New Netherland. Law requiring towns to maintain schools passed in Massachusetts Bay Colony. Thomas Hooker dies (b. 1586).	
1648	Hooker, Thomas (1586–1647), *A Survey of the Sum of Church Discipline* (tract)	Massachusetts and Connecticut Congregationalists adopt the Cambridge Platform.	George Fox founds first Quaker society in England (1648–50). Peace of Westphalia ends Thirty Years War.
1649		John Winthrop dies (b. 1588).	Charles I executed at Whitehall. Commonwealth formed. Oliver Cromwell becomes commander in chief of the army.
1650	Baxter, Richard (1615–91), *The Saint's Everlasting Rest* (tract) Bradstreet, Anne (c. 1612–72), *The Tenth Muse, Lately Sprung Up in America* (verse)	First export of iron from Massachusetts to England.	Charles II proclaimed king in Scotland.

1651			Charles II defeated by Cromwell; escapes to France. Hobbes, *Leviathan*
1652	Williams, Roger (1603?–83), *The Bloody Tenent Yet More Bloody* (tract)	Maine declared legal part of the Massachusetts Bay Colony. John Cotton dies (b. 1584).	
1653	Keayne, Robert (?), *The Last Will and Testament* Wigglesworth, Michael (1631–1705) begins his *Diary* (published in 1965)	Peter Stuyvesant forced to grant self-government to New Amsterdam.	Oliver Cromwell becomes Lord Protector of the Commonwealth.
1654	Eliot, John (1604–90), *Primer or Catechism in the Massachusetts Indian Language* Johnson, Edward (1598–1672), *A History of New England* (better known as *The Wonder-Working Providence of Zion's Saviour in New England*)		
1655		Dutch occupy Fort Casimir (now Newcastle) on the Delaware River, ending Swedish rule in North America.	Cromwell dissolves Parliament.

	Important Texts In and Concerning the New World	Historical Events in the New World	Historical and Literary Events in the Old World
1656	Hooker, Thomas (1586–1647), *The Application of Redemption* (posth.)	English Quakers arrive in Boston, but are arrested and deported.	
1657		Quakers arrive in New Amsterdam and are sent to Rhode Island.	
1658	Norton, John (1606–63), *Abel Being Dead Yet Speaketh; or, The Life and Death of . . . John Cotton*		Death of Oliver Cromwell; his son Richard becomes Lord Protector.
1659		Two Quakers executed in Boston.	Richard Cromwell forced to resign; Commonwealth reestablished.
1660			Restoration of Charles II to the English throne. Theaters reopened in London.
1661			Charles II calls first Parliament (known as "Cavalier Parliament").
1662	Wigglesworth, Michael (1631–1705), *The Day of Doom; or, A Poetical Description of the Great and Last Judgement* (verse); *God's Controversy with New England* (verse)	Half-Way Covenant: Boston Synod modifies rules for church membership to counter declining conversions.	Founding of the Royal Society.

1663	Carolina charter granted to eight proprietors. Rhode Island granted charter.	Butler *Hudibras* (1663–78)
1664	British troops seize New Amsterdam (renamed New York) and Fort Orange (renamed Albany) from the Dutch. Charter for New Jersey granted to two proprietors.	
1665	**Danforth, Samuel** (1626–74), *An Astronomical Description of the Late Comet*	Colony of New Jersey founded.
1666	**Eliot, John** (1604–90), *The Indian Grammar Begun*	Great Fire of London. Bunyan, *Grace Abounding to the Chief of Sinners* Molière, *The Misanthropist*
1667		End of Anglo-Dutch War in America. Milton, *Paradise Lost*
1668		John Dryden named poet laureate of England. Dryden, *Essay on Dramatick Poesie* La Fontaine, *Fables* (1668–94)

	Important Texts In and Concerning the New World	Historical Events in the New World	Historical and Literary Events in the Old World
1669	Eliot, John (1604–90), *The Indian Primer* Morton, Nathaniel (1613–85), *New England's Memorial* (history) Walley, Thomas (1616–79), *Balm in Gilead to Heal Zion's Wounds* (sermon)		
1670	Firmin, Giles (?), *The Real Christian* (tract) Mather, Increase (1639–1723), *The Life and Death of that Reverend Man of God, Mr. Richard Mather* Wigglesworth, Michael (1631–1705), *Meat Out of the Eater* (verse)	British colony established at Charleston, South Carolina.	Pascal, *Pensées*
1671	Danforth, Samuel (1626–74), *A Brief Recognition of New England's Errand into the Wilderness* (sermon) Mitchell, Jonathan (1624–68), *Nehemiah on the Wall in Troubled Times* (sermon)		Milton, *Paradise Regained; Samson Agonistes*

1672	**Josselyn, John** (1610–post-1692), *New England's Rarities Discovered* (travel)	Third Anglo-Dutch War. Anne Bradstreet dies (b. 1612).	Royal African Company founded (slave trade).
1673	**Oakes, Urian** (1631–81), *New England Pleaded With, and Pressed to Consider the Things Which Concern Her Peace* (sermon)	French expedition finds upper Mississippi.	Parliament passes Test Act (against Roman Catholics).
	Shepard, Thomas, Jr. (1605–49), *Eye-Salve, or a Watch-Word from Our Lord Jesus Christ unto His Churches to Take Heed of Apostasy* (sermon)		
1674	**Josselyn, John** (1610–post-1692), *An Account of Two Voyages to New England*	Treaty of Westminster returns New York to the British. Sir Edmund Andros appointed governor of New York.	Holy Roman Empire declares war on France. John Milton dies (b. 1608).
	Mather, Increase (1639–1723), *The Day of Trouble is Near* (sermon)		
	Torrey, Samuel (1632–1707), *An Exhortation Unto Reformation* (sermon)		
1675		King Philip's War (Iroquois Confederacy against New England Confederacy), 1675–6.	
1676	**Mather, Increase** (1639–1723), *An Earnest Exhortation to the Inhabitants of New England* (essay)	Nathaniel Bacon's Rebellion, in Virginia.	

Important Texts In and Concerning the New World	Historical Events in the New World	Historical and Literary Events in the Old World
Hubbard, William (c. 1621–1704), *The Happiness of a People in the Wisdom of their Rulers* (sermon)		
Mather, Increase (1639–1723), *A Brief History of the War with the Indians in New England*		
Tompson, Benjamin (1642–1714), "New England's Crisis. Or a Brief Narrative, of New England's Lamentable Estate at Present" (verse); "On a Fortification at Boston Begun by Women" (mock epic)		
1677 **Hooker, Samuel** (1635–97), *Righteousness Rained from Heaven* (sermon)	English Quakers settle in New Jersey.	Racine, *Phaedra*
Hubbard, William (c. 1621–1704), *A Relation of the Troubles Which Have Happened in New England, By Reason of the Indians There*		
Mather, Increase (1639–1723), *A Renewal of Covenant the Great Duty Incumbent on Decaying and Distressed Churches* (sermon)		

	Literature	American History	World Events
	Oakes, Urian (1631–81), "An Elegie on the Death of the Reverend Mr. Thomas Shepard" (verse)	Sieur Duluth claims the upper Mississippi for France.	Popish Plot (supposed threat to Charles II).
1678	Bradstreet, Anne (c. 1612–72), *Several Poems* (posth.) Mather, Increase (1639–1723), *Pray for the Rising Generation* (sermon)		
1679	Adams, William (?), *The Necessity of Pouring Out of the Spirit from on High upon a Sinning Apostatizing People* (sermon) Mather, Increase (1639–1723), *A Call from Heaven to the Present and Succeeding Generations*	New Hampshire proclaimed separate colony.	Cavalier Parliament dissolved. Habeas Corpus Act passed in England. Thomas Hobbes dies (b. 1588).
1680	Hubbard, William (c. 1621–1704), *General History of New England from the Discovery to MDCLXXX* (published 1815)		British "penny post" established. Comédie Française founded.
1681	Goodhue, Sarah (1641–81), *Valedictory and Monitory Writing* (nonfiction)	William Penn given charter for Quaker colony of Pennsylvania by Charles II.	
1682	Mather, Cotton (1663–1728), "A Poem Dedicated to the Memory of . . . Urian Oakes"	Philadelphia becomes capital of William Penn's colony.	Orway, *Venice Preserv'd*

	Important Texts In and Concerning the New World	Historical Events in the New World	Historical and Literary Events in the Old World
	Rowlandson, Mary White (c. 1637–1711?), *The Sovereignty and Goodness of God, Together with the Faithfulness of His Promises Displayed; Being a Narrative of the Captivity and Restoration of Mrs. Mary Rowlandson . . .* (pamphlet)	Sieur de La Salle claims lower Mississippi Valley for France, names it Louisiana after Louis IV.	
	Taylor, Edward (1644?–1729), *God's Determinations Touching His Elect* (verse; approximate completion date; published 1939)		
	Willard, Samuel (1640–1707), *The Firey Trial No Strange Thing* (sermon); *Covenant-Keeping the Way to Blessedness* (sermon)		
1683	Torrey, Samuel (1632–1707), *A Plea for the Life of Dying Religion* (sermon)		Rye House Plot to assassinate Charles II. Turks besiege Vienna.
1684	Mather, Increase (1639–1723), *Some Important Truths Concerning Conversion* (sermon)	Revocation of the Massachusetts Charter by the Land Court of Chancery; Edward Randolph appointed governor.	Pierre Corneille dies (b. 1606).
	Willard, Samuel (1640–1707), *A Child's Portion: or the Unseen Glory* (sermon); *Mercy Magnified on a Penitent Prodigal* (sermon)		

1685	Mather, Cotton (1663–1728), "An Elegy . . . on Nathanael Collins"	La Salle explores east Texas. Edict of Nantes revoked; French Huguenots settle in America.	Death of Charles II; accession of James II.
	Mather, Increase (1639–1723) begins to compose a formal autobiography from his many diary volumes (published 1962)		J. S. Bach born (d. 1750).
	Moodey, Joshua (1633–97), *A Practical Discourse Concerning the Choice Benefit of Communion with God in His House* (sermon)		
1686	Mather, Cotton (1663–1728), *The Call of the Gospel* (sermon)	Installation of Anglican Royal Governor of Massachusetts, Sir Edmund Andros.	
	Whiting, John (1635–89), *The Way of Israel's Welfare* (sermon)		
	Willard, Samuel (1640–1707), *Heavenly Merchandise; or the Purchasing of Truth Recommended and the Selling of It Dissuaded* (sermon)		
1687		First Anglican church service held in Boston. Yamasee Indian revolt in Florida.	Newton, *Principia mathematica*
1688			"Glorious Revolution": Whigs and Tories invite Prince William of

	Important Texts In and Concerning the New World	Historical Events in the New World	Historical and Literary Events in the Old World
			Orange to seize the English throne; James II flees to France.
			Behn, *Oroonoko*
1689	Bailey, John (1644–97), *Man's Chief End to Glorify God* (sermon)	Colonists in Boston rebel against Andros, causing his recall.	Accession of William and Mary as joint British monarchs.
	Carre, Ezekiel (?), *The Charitable Samaritan* (sermon)		English Bill of Rights.
			Louis XIV declares war on England; beginning of "King William's War" in America (until 1697).
	Mather, Cotton (1663–1728), *Memorable Providences, Relating to Witchcrafts and Possessions* (tract)		Samuel Richardson born (d. 1761).
			Charles-Louis de Secondat (later Baron de Montesquieu) born (d. 1755).
	Wigglesworth, Michael (1631–1705), *Riddles Unriddled; or, Christian Paradoxes* (verse; published in the 4th edition of *Meat Out of the Eater*)		Locke, *A Letter Concerning Toleration*
1690	Mather, Cotton (1663–1728), *Companion for Communicants* (sermon)		Locke, *Essay Concerning Human Understanding*; *Two Treatises of Government*
	Standfast, Richard (1608–84), *A Little Handful of Cordial Comforts for a Fainting Soul* (sermon)		
1691			

1692	**Mather, Cotton** (1663–1728), *Ornaments for the Daughters of Zion* (sermon) **Taylor, Edward** (c. 1644–1729), *Christographia* (sermons)	Sir Edmund Andros appointed governor of Virginia. New Massachusetts Charter. Salem witchcraft trials.	Purcell, "The Fairy Queen"
1693	**Mather, Cotton** (1663–1728), *The Wonders of the Invisible World. Observations as well Historical as Theological, upon the Nature, the Number, and the Operations of the Devils* (tract) **Scottow, Joshua** (1615–98), *Old Men's Tears for Their Own Declensions* (sermon)	Postal service between New York and Philadelphia. College of William and Mary founded.	
1694			Death of Mary II. François Marie Arouet [Voltaire] born (d. 1778).
1695			
1696			Samuel Johnson born (d. 1772).
1697	**Sewall, Samuel** (1652–1730), *Phaenomena quaedam Apocalyptica Ad Aspectum Novi Orbis Configurata. Or, some few Lines towards a Description of the New Heaven, As It makes to those who stand upon the New Earth* (tract)	Second recall of Andros to England.	

	Important Texts In and Concerning the New World	Historical Events in the New World	Historical and Literary Events in the Old World
1698			A. Sidney, *Discourses Concerning Government*
1699	**Colman, Benjamin** (1673–1747) and others, *Manifesto* **Tompson, Benjamin** (1642–1714), "To Lord Bellamont when entering Governour of the Massachusetts" (verse)	John Leverett, Simon Bradstreet, William and Thomas Brattle, and others establish the Brattle Street Church and bring Benjamin Colman from England to become minister. "Captain Kidd," pirate, arrested in New England, returned to England and executed in 1701.	
1700	**Calef, Robert** (1648–1719), *More Wonders of the Invisible World* (tract) **Colman, Benjamin** (1673–1747) and others, *The Gospel Order Revived* (treatise) **Mather, Increase** (1639–1723), *The Order of the Gospel* (treatise; response to *The Gospel Order Revived*; parodied in *The Gospel Order Revived* [1700] by members of the Brattle church) **Sewall, Samuel** (1652–1730), *The Selling of Joseph* (antislavery tract)	Catholic priests banned in Massachusetts.	John Dryden dies (b. 1631).

1701	**Mather, Cotton** (1663–1728), "Consolations" (verse)	Establishment of Yale College.	War of the Spanish Succession (England against France and Spain).
1702	**Brooke, Henry** (167?–1735/6), "The New Metamorphosis" (verse) **Mather, Cotton** (1663–1728), *Magnalia Christi Americana; or, The Ecclesiastical History of New England* (written 1694–8)	"Queen Anne's War": colonial phase of the War of the Spanish Succession (1702–13).	Death of William III; accession of Anne to British throne.
1703	**Mather, Increase** (1639–1723), *Ichabod. Or, a Discourse, Showing What Cause There is to Fear that the Glory of the Lord is Departing from New England* **Brooke, Henry** (167?–1735/6), "A Discours upon Je'sting" (verse)		
1704	**Knight, Sarah Kemble** (1666–1727), *The Journal of Madam Knight* (includes six poems; published 1825) *Boston News-Letter* (first successful American newspaper; ceases publication 1776)	French and Indians attack Deerfield, Massachusetts.	John Locke dies (b. 1632). Swift, *A Tale of the Tubs*; *The Battle of the Books*
1705	**Beverley, Robert** (c. 1673–1722), *The History and Present State of Virginia* (revised edition 1722); *An Essay upon the Government of the English Plantations on the Continent of America*	Michael Wigglesworth dies (b. 1631).	

	Important Texts In and Concerning the New World	Historical Events in the New World	Historical and Literary Events in the Old World
1706	Mather, Cotton (1663–1728), *The Negro Christianized* (sermon)	Benjamin Franklin born (d. 1790).	
1707	Colman, Benjamin (1673–1747), "A Poem on Elijah's Translation"; *A Practical Discourse on the Parable of the Ten Virgins* (sermon)		England and Scotland united to form Great Britain. Henry Fielding born (d. 1754).
1708	Cook, Ebenezer (fl. 1708–32), *The Sot-Weed Factor* (verse) Saffin, John (1626–1710), *John Saffin, His Book* (1665–1708) (commonplace book, published 1928)	Saybrook Platform adopted in Connecticut.	
1709	Tompson, Benjamin (1642–1714), "The Grammarian's Funeral" (verse) Cheever, Ezekiel (1615–1708), *A Short History of the Latin Tongue*		
1710	Mather, Cotton (1663–1728), *Bonifacius, an Essay Upon the Good* Wise, John (1652–1725), *The Churches Quarrel Espoused* (tract)		First English copyright laws.

1711	**Mather, Cotton** (1663–1728), *Eureka: The Virtuous Woman Found* (sermon)	Tuscadora War (settlers in North Carolina against Indians), 1711–13.	David Hume born (d. 1776). Pope, *An Essay on Criticism*
1712	**Smith, Grace** (?), *The Dying Mother's Legacy* (verse)		Addison, *Cato* Jean-Jacques Rousseau born (d. 1778).
1713			Treaty of Utrecht ends Queen Anne's War. Laurence Sterne born (d. 1768).
1714	**Danforth, John** (1660–1730), "A Poem, Upon the Much Honoured . . . Mrs. Maria Mather" **Hunter, Robert** (1666–1734), *Androboros: A Biographical Farce* (drama)		End of the War of the Spanish Succession. Death of Anne; accession of George I to English throne. Mandeville, *Fable of the Bees*
1715		Yamassee Indians massacre settlers in South Carolina.	Death of Louis XIV; accession of Louis XV to French throne.
1716			
1717	**Wise, John** (1652–1725), *A Vindication of the Government of New-England Churches* (tract)		Horace Walpole born (d.1797). Handel, "Water Music"

	Important Texts In and Concerning the New World	Historical Events in the New World	Historical and Literary Events in the Old World
1718	**Mather, Cotton** (1663–1728), *Psalterium Americanum* (verse)	New Orleans founded.	
1719	**Byrd, William, II** (1674–1746), *Tunbridgalia* (verse) *Boston Gazette* (ceases publication 1798)	French Mississippi Company begins to found settlements in America.	Defoe, *Robinson Crusoe*
1720			
1721	**Dummer, Jeremiah** (1681–1739), *A Defence of the New England Charters* **Mather, Cotton** (1663–1728), *The Christian Philosopher* (treatise); *Monica America: Female Piety Exemplified* (sermon) **Wise, John** (1652–1725), *A Word of Comfort to a Melancholy Country; Or, the Bank of Credit Erected in Massachusetts Fairly Defended* (tract) *New England Courant*, first American publication to feature literary entertainment, founded by James Franklin (1721–7)	First smallpox inoculations, in Boston.	Sir Robert Walpole becomes first prime minister of England (1721–42). Tobias Smollett born (d. 1771). J. S. Bach, "The Brandenburg Concertos" Montesquieu, *Lettres persanes*

1722	**Beverley, Robert** (c. 1673–1722), *The History and Present State of Virginia* (revised edition) **Mather, Cotton** (1663–1728), *The Angel of Bethesda . . . An Essay upon the Common Maladies of Mankind . . . and direction for the Preservation of Health* (treatise)	Iroquois Confederation of Six Nations signs treaty with settlers in Virginia. Samuel Adams born (d. 1803).	Defoe, *Moll Flanders; A Journal of the Plague Year, 1665*
1723		"Great Apostasy," in which President Samuel Johnson of Yale and six tutors declared their intentions to be ordained again in England by Anglican bishops. Christ Church ("Old North Church") built in Boston. Increase Mather dies (b. 1639).	Bach, *St. John Passion*
1724	**Mather, Cotton** (1663–1728), *Parentator* (biography of Increase Mather) **Morris, Lewis, II** (1671–1746), "Dialogue Concerning Trade"	First permanent white settlement in Vermont.	Defoe, *Roxana*
1725	**Taylor, Edward** (1644–1729), *Preparatory Meditations* (verse; published 1960) **Wolcott, Roger** (1679–1767), *Poetical Meditations, Being the Improvement of Some Vacant Hours*		Peter the Great of Russia dies.

	Important Texts In and Concerning the New World	Historical Events in the New World	Historical and Literary Events in the Old World
1726	**Keith, William** (1680–1749), *The Life and Character of a Strange He-Monster* (satire); *A Modest Reply to the Speech of Isaac Norris*; *Remarks upon the Advice to Freeholders*		Voltaire banished from France Swift, *Gulliver's Travels*
1727	**Byles, Mather** (1707–88), "A Poem on the Death of His Late Majesty King George . . ."; with **Rev. John Adams** (1705–40) and **Matthew Adams** (1694?–1753), "The Proteus Echo Series" (verse; *The New-England Weekly Journal*, 1727–8)	Benjamin Franklin founds Junto Club.	Death of George I; accession of George II to the English throne. Edmund Burke born (d. 1797). Sir Isaac Newton dies (b. 1642).
1728	**Lewis, Richard** (1699?–1734), *The Mouse-Trap* (trans. of Edward Holdsworth's *Muscipula*)	John Bartram plants first botanical gardens, near Philadelphia. Cotton Mather dies (b. 1663).	Gay, *Beggar's Opera* Pope, *The Dunciad*
1729		Separate royal colonies created in North and South Carolina. Founding of Baltimore. Edward Taylor dies (b. c. 1644).	J. S. Bach, "St. Matthew Passion" Swift, *A Modest Proposal*
1730			Colley Cibber becomes poet laureate of England. Thomson, *The Seasons* (1726–30)

	Authors and works	Historical events	Cultural events
1731	**Edwards, Jonathan** (1703–58), *God Glorified in the Work of Redemption By the Greatness of Man's Dependence* (sermon)	Benjamin Franklin founds first circulating library, in Philadelphia.	*The Gentleman's Magazine* founded in London (ceases publication 1910). Oliver Goldsmith born (d. 1774).
	Lewis, Richard (1699?–1734), "Food for Criticks" (verse)		
	Vainlove, Tim (?), "To The Ladies in Boston, in New England" (verse)		
	Webb, George (1708–32), *Batchelors Hall* (verse)		
1732	**Lewis, Richard** (1699?–1734), *Carmen Seculare* (verse); "Rhapsody" (verse)	English settlers arrive in Georgia. George Washington born (d. 1799).	Franz Joseph Hayden born (d. 1809).
1733	**Green, Joseph** (1706–80), "The Poet's Lamentation for the Loss of his Cat, which he used to call his Muse" (verse satire)	Molasses Act restricts colonial importation of sugar goods from the French West Indies.	Pope, *Essay on Man*
	Morris, Lewis II (1671–1746), "The Mock Monarchy, or Kingdom of Apes" (verse)		
	Wheeler, Mercy (1706–96), *An Address to Young People, Or . . . Warning from the Death* (verse)		

	Important Texts In and Concerning the New World	Historical Events in the New World	Historical and Literary Events in the Old World
1734	**Barnard, John** (1681–1770), *The Throne Established by Righteousness* (election sermon)	Jonathan Edwards leads an evangelical revival in Northampton, Massachusetts, and in the Connecticut River Valley ("The Great Awakening").	
	Edwards, Jonathan (1703–58), *A Divine and Supernatural Light, Immediately Imparted to the Soul by the Spirit of God* (sermon)		
1735	**Turell, Jane Colman** (1708–35), Poems included in *Memoirs of the Life and Death of . . . Mrs. Jane Turell*	John Peter Zenger acquitted of seditious libel on the ground that printing the truth does not constitute libel.	Thomson, *Liberty* (1735–6)
1736	**Byles, Mather** (1707–88), "To His Excellency Governeur Belcher, on the Death of His Lady. An Epistle" (verse)		
	Morris, Lewis, II (1671–1746), "The Dream, A Riddle" (verse)		
	Prince, Thomas (1687–1758), *A Chronological History of New England in the Form of Annals*		
	Wesley, Samuel (1691–1737), *Georgia, A Poem*		

1737	**Edwards, Jonathan** (1703–58), *A Faithful Narrative of the Surprising Work of God in the Conversion of Many Hundred Souls*		
1738	**Byles, Mather** (1707–88), "On the Death of the Queen" (verse) **Byrd, William, II** (1674–1744), *History of the Dividing Line betwixt Virginia and North Carolina* (written from journals kept in 1728–9; probably finished in 1738; published 1841)	English evangelical minister George Whitefield's first visit to American Methodists.	J. S. Bach, B-Minor Mass (full version) Voltaire, *Discourse on Man*
1739			Hume, *A Treatise on Human Nature*
1740	**Tennent, Gilbert** (1703–64), *The Danger of an Unconverted Ministry*	Whitefield embarks on preaching tour of the colonies.	Richardson, *Pamela, or Virtue Rewarded* (1740–1)
1741	**Edwards, Jonathan** (1703–58), *Sinners in the Hands of an Angry God* (sermon); *Future Punishment of the Wicked* (sermon) **Finley, Samuel** (1715–66), *Christ Triumphing and Satan Raging* **Tailfer, Patrick** (?), *A True and Historical Narrative of the Colony of Georgia*	Danish navigator Capt. Vitus Bering discovers Alaska.	

	Important Texts In and Concerning the New World	Historical Events in the New World	Historical and Literary Events in the Old World
1742	**Barnard, John** (1681–1770), *A Zeal for Good Works, Excited and Directed* (sermon) **Edwards, Jonathan** (1703–58), *Some Thoughts Concerning the Present Revival of Religion in New England*	Faneuil Hall built in Boston (1740–2).	Fielding, *Joseph Andrews* Handel, *Messiah* Young, *A Complaint, or Night Thoughts* (1742–8)
1743	**Chauncy, Charles** (1705–87), *Seasonable Thoughts on the State of Religion in New England* **Franklin, Benjamin** (1706–90), *A Proposal for Promoting Useful Knowledge Among the British Plantations in America* *The American Magazine and Historical Chronicle* founded by Jeremy Gridley (ceases publication 1746)	American Philosophical Society founded, in Philadelphia. Thomas Jefferson born (d. 1826).	
1744	**Byles, Mather** (1707–88), *Poems on Several Occasions*; "The Comet" (verse) **Hamilton, Dr. Alexander** (1712–56), *Itinerarium* (travel narrative)	"King George's War": colonial phase of the War of the Austrian Succession, between British and French (1744–8). William Byrd dies (b. 1674).	Alexander Pope dies (b. 1688).

	Home, Archibald (1705?–44), "Poems on Several Occasions by Archibald Home, Esqr." (posth. private publication) **Williams, Elisha** (1694–1755), *The Essential Rights and Liberties of Protestants* Benjamin Franklin's Philadelphia printing house brings out the first novel published in America, an edition of Richardson's *Pamela*	Jonathan Swift dies (b. 1667).
1745		
1746	**Edwards, Jonathan** (1703–58), *A Treatise Concerning Religious Affections* **Terry, Lucy** (?), "Bars Fight" (verse)	College of New Jersey (now Princeton University) founded.
1747	**Edwards, Jonathan** (1703–58), *An Humble Attempt to Promote Explicit Agreement and Visible Union of God's People* **Livingston, William** (1723–90), *Philosophic Solitude; or, The Choice of a Rural Life: A Poem* **Shepard, Thomas** (1604–49), *Three Valuable Pieces . . . A Private Diary* (posth.)	Richardson, *Clarissa* (1747–8)

	Important Texts In and Concerning the New World	Historical Events in the New World	Historical and Literary Events in the Old World
1748	**Eliot, Jared** (1685–1763), *Essays on Field Husbandry* (1748–59) **Mayhew, Jonathan** (1720–66), *The Right and Duty of Private Judgment*	Treaty of Aix-la-Chapelle ends King George's War, restores balance of power in French and British colonies.	Hume, *Philosophical Essays Concerning Human Understanding* Montesquieu, *The Spirit of the Laws* Smollett, *Roderick Random*
1749	**Buffon, Comte Georges-Louis Leclerc de** (1707–88), *Natural History of the Earth* (first volume; 36 volumes published at regular intervals until 1778) **Shepard, Thomas** (1604–49), *Meditations and Spiritual Experiences of Mr. Thomas Shepard* (posth.)	Ohio Company formed by Virginia planters to extend westward settlements.	Fielding, *Tom Jones* Handel, "Music for the Royal Fireworks" Johnson, *The Vanity of Human Wishes*; *Irene*
1750	**Edwards, Jonathan** (1703–58), *Farewell Sermon* **Green, Joseph** (1706–80), *Entertainment for a Winter's Evening: Being a Full and True Account of a very Strange and Wonderful Sight seen in Boston on the Twenty-seventh of December, 1749* (pamphlet) **Kirkpatrick, James** (1692?–1770), *The Sea-Piece: A narrative, philosophical and descriptive Poem, In Five cantos*	Jonathan Edwards dismissed from Northampton church. Iron Act restricts production of finished iron goods in the British colonies.	J. S. Bach dies (b. 1685).

	Mayhew, Jonathan (1720–66), *A Discourse Concerning Unlimited Submission and Non-Resistance to the Higher Powers*		
1751	**Davies, Samuel** (1724–61), *The State of Religion among the Protestant Dissenters in Virginia* **Franklin, Benjamin** (1706–90), *Observations Concerning the Increase of Mankind, Peopling Countries, Etc.*	Currency Act restricts issuance of paper money in New England.	Diderot et al., *Encyclopédie* (1751–80)
1752	**Smith, William** (1727–1803), "A Poem: Being a serious Address to the House of Representatives [of New York]" (verse); "The American Fables" (1752–3)	Philip Freneau born (d. 1832).	Gregorian Calendar adopted in Great Britain. Muzio Clementi born (d. 1832). Lenox, *The Female Quixote*
1753	**Smith, William** (1727–1803), *A General Idea of the College of Mirania, with a Sketch of the Method of Teaching Science and Religion* (educational tract); *Indian Songs of Peace* (verse)	Benjamin Franklin becomes fellow of the Royal Society of London.	
1754	**Edwards, Jonathan** (1703–58), *Freedom of the Will* (treatise)	Albany Congress and Plan of Union. Beginning of "French and Indian War" (1754–63). French build Fort Duquesne (now Pittsburgh). King's College chartered (now Columbia University).	Henry Fielding dies (b. 1707).

	Important Texts In and Concerning the New World	Historical Events in the New World	Historical and Literary Events in the Old World
1755	**Green, Joseph** (1706–80), *The Grand Arcanum Detected: Or, A Wonderful Phaenomenon Explained, Which has baffled the Scrutiny of many Ages* (pamphlet)		Baron de Montesquieu dies (b. 1689). Johnson, *A Dictionary of the English Language*
1756			Britain declares war on France. Wolfgang Amadeus Mozart born (d. 1791). Home, *Douglas*
1757	**Dyer, John** (1700?–58), *The Fleece* (verse) **Woodmason, Charles** (c. 1720–c. 1776), "Indico" (verse)		William Whitehead named poet laureate of England. Burke, *Origin of Our Ideas of the Sublime and Beautiful*
1758	**Bellamy, Joseph** (1719–90), *The Millennium* (sermon) **Edwards, Jonathan** (1703–58), *The Great Doctrine of Original Sin* (posth., tract) **Franklin, Benjamin** (1706–90), "The Way to Wealth"	"Parson's Cause": dispute in Virginia over statewide church tax. First Indian reservation established, in New Jersey.	Rousseau, *Letter to M. D'Alembert on the Theatre*

1759	Maylem, John (1739–?), *The Conquest of Louisburg* (verse); *Gallic Perfidy* (verse) Eliot, Jared (1685–1763), *Essays on Field Husbandry* (pub. begins 1748)	Wolfe defeats Montcalm at Plains of Abraham; Quebec falls to British.	Smith, *Theory of Moral Sentiments* Voltaire, *Candide*
1760	Bland, Richard (1710–76), *Letter to the Clergy of Virginia* (pamphlet) Davies, Samuel (1724–61), *On the Death of His Late Majesty, King George II* Stiles, Ezra (1727–95), *A Discourse on the Christian Union*	Canada is surrendered to the British.	Death of George II; accession of George III to the British throne. Sterne, *Tristam Shandy* (1760–7)
1761			Samuel Richardson dies (b. 1689).
1762		Treaty of Fontainebleau transfers Louisiana Territory from France to Spain.	Peter III becomes czar of Russia and is assassinated shortly thereafter; accession of Catherine the Great. Rousseau, *The Social Contract*
1763	Mayhew, Jonathan (1720–66), *Observations on the Charter and Conduct of Society for the Propagation of the Gospel*	Treaty of Paris ends French and Indian War. Pontiac's Rebellion, Indian uprising in Ohio Valley (1763–5).	Peace of Paris ends Seven Years' War.

	Important Texts In and Concerning the New World	Historical Events in the New World	Historical and Literary Events in the Old World
1764	**Bland, Richard** (1710–76), *The Colonel Dismounted: or the Rector Vindicated* (pamphlet)	Proclamation line drawn by British along the Appalachians forbids western settlement by whites.	Samuel Johnson founds Literary Club in London (with Burke, Gibbon, Goldsmith, Reynolds, and others).
	Grainger, James (1721–66), *The Sugar-Cane. A Poem in Three Books*	St. Louis founded. Rhode Island College founded (now Brown University).	
	Otis, James (1725–83), *The Rights of the British Colonies Asserted and Proved*	Sugar Act reduces duty on foreign molasses.	
	Prime, Benjamin Youngs (1733–91), *The Patriotic Muse* (verse)		
1765	**Adams, John** (1735–1826), *A Dissertation on the Canon and Feudal Law*	Stamp Act passed by Parliament: first direct tax levied on the colonies by Great Britain.	Blackstone, *Commentaries on the Laws of England*
	Cockings, George (17??–1802), *War; an Heroic Poem*	Patrick Henry speaks against Stamp Act in the Virginia House of Burgesses.	Percy, *Reliques of Ancient English Poetry*
	Edwards, Jonathan (1703–58), *Personal Narrative* (posth., written c. 1740); *Two Dissertations: I. Concerning the End for which God Created the World. II. The Nature of True Virtue* (posth.)	Stamp Act Congress meets in New York and adopts Declaration of Rights and Grievances.	Walpole, *The Castle of Otranto*

	Literature	History
	Godfrey, Thomas (1736–63), *The Prince of Parthia* (play)	Sons of Liberty formed.
	Hopkins, Stephen (1707–85), *The Rights of Colonies Examined* (pamphlet)	
	Howard, Martin, Jr. (fl. 1765–81), *A Letter from a Gentleman at Halifax* (pamphlet)	
	Otis, James (1725–83), *A Vindication of the British Colonies* (pamphlet)	
1766	Bland, Richard (1710–76), *An Inquiry into the Rights of the British Colonies* (pamphlet)	Parliament repeals Stamp Act, but passes the Declaratory Act, asserting its authority to enact colonial laws.
	Mayhew, Jonathan (1720–66), *The Snare Broken* (sermon)	Dutch New Light clergy erect Queen's College (later Rutgers University).
1767	Chauncy, Charles (1705–87), *A Letter to a Friend*	Townshend Acts levy import duties on the colonies.
	Lee, Arthur (1740–92), "Address on Slavery"	Daniel Boone begins explorations west of Appalachia.
	Singleton, John (?–1791), *A Description of the West Indies* (verse)	

Thomas Malthus born (d. 1834).

Goldsmith, *The Vicar of Wakefield*

Haydn, *Great Mass in E-Flat*

Lessing, *Laocoön*

Smollett, *Travels through France and Italy*

	Important Texts In and Concerning the New World	Historical Events in the New World	Historical and Literary Events in the Old World
1768	**Backus, Isaac** (1724–1806), *A Fish Caught in His Own Net*	Secretary of State of the Colonies established in England. British troops sent to Boston.	Laurence Sterne dies (b. 1713). Sterne, *A Sentimental Journey through France and Italy* (posth.)
	De Pauw, Cornelius (1739–99), *Recherches philosophiques sur les Américains, ou Mémoires intéressantes pour servire à l'histoire de l'espèce humaine*		
	Dickinson, John (1732–1808), *Letters from a Farmer in Pennsylvania*		
	Fergusson, Elizabeth Graeme (1737?–1801), "The Dream of the Patriotic Philosophical Farmer" (verse)		
	Moore, Milcah Martha (1740–1829), "The Female Patriots. Address'd to the Daughters of Liberty in America," 1768" (verse)		
	Stockton, Annis Boudinot (1738–1801), "To the Visitant, from a circle of Ladies, on reading his paper. No. 3, in the Pennsylvania Chronicle" (verse)		
1769		American Philosophical Society reorganized, with Benjamin Franklin as president. Dartmouth College chartered.	

1770	François, Guillaume Thomas, Abbé de Raynal, (?), *A Philosophical and Political History of the Settlements and Trade of the Europeans in the East and West Indies* Gronniosaw, James (?), *A Narrative of the Most Remarkable Particulars in the Life of James Albert Ukawsaw Gronniosaw*	Establishment of Lord North's ministry. Townshend duties repealed, with symbolic exception of tax on tea. Boston Massacre.	Ludwig von Beethoven born (d. 1827). William Wordsworth born (d. 1850). Goldsmith, *The Deserted Village*
1771	Benezet, Anthony (1713–84), *Some Historical Account of Guinea* Bougainville, Louis Antoine de (1729–1811), *Voyage Around the World*	Battle of the Alamance in North Carolina over lack of representation in colonial government. Charles Brockden Brown born (d. 1810).	Tobias Smollett dies (b. 1721).
1772	Brackenridge, Hugh Henry (1748–1816) and Philip Freneau (1752–1832), "A Poem on the Rising Glory of America" Evans, Nathaniel (1742–67), *Poems on Several Occasions, with Some Other Compositions* [Trumbull, John (1750–1831)], *The Progress of Dulness*, part one (verse) Occom, Samson (1723–92), *Sermon Preached at the Execution of Moses Paul, an Indian* Woolman, John (1720–93), *Essay on the Ministry*	British customs schooner *Gaspee* burned off Rhode Island. Boston Committee of Correspondence led by Samuel Adams.	Samuel Taylor Coleridge born (d. 1834).

	Important Texts In and Concerning the New World	Historical Events in the New World	Historical and Literary Events in the Old World
1773	Franklin, Benjamin (1706–90), "An Edict by the King of Prussia"; "Rules by Which a Great Empire May be Reduced to a Small One" Howard, Simeon (1733–1804), A Sermon Preached to the Ancient and Honorable Artillery Company in Boston Rush, Benjamin (1745–1813), "An Address to the Inhabitants of the British Settlements in America upon Slave-Keeping" Warren, Mercy Otis (1728–1814), The Adulateur (drama) Wheatley, Phillis (1753?–84), Poems on Various Subjects, Religious and Moral	Boston Tea Party in response to the Tea Act asserts colonists' refusal to be taxed.	Burnett, Of the Origin and Progress of Language Goldsmith, She Stoops to Conquer
1774	Ashbridge, Elizabeth Sampson (1713–55), Some Account of the Fore Part of the Life of Elizabeth Ashbridge Duché, Jacob (1737–98), Observations on a Variety of Subjects, Literary, Moral, and Religious (commonly known as Casapipina's Letters)	Parliament passes Coercive Acts to punish colonists. (commonly called the "Intolerable Acts" in the colonies). First Continental Congress meets in Philadelphia. Edmund Burke's oration on American taxation.	Louis XVI becomes king of France. Oliver Goldsmith dies (b. 1731). Goethe, The Sorrows of Young Werther Home, Sketches of the History of Man

Important Texts In and Concerning the New World	Historical Events in the New World	Historical and Literary Events in the Old World
Warren, Mercy Otis (1728–1814), *The Group* (drama)		
1776 **Adams, John** (1735–1826), *Thoughts on Government*	The Declaration of Independence. Congress calls on colonies to establish new governments under the authority of the people.	David Hume dies (b. 1711). Gibbon, *Decline and Fall of the Roman Empire* (1776–88)
Anonymous, "The Ballad of Nathan Hale"	New Hampshire, New Jersey, Pennsylvania, Delaware, Maryland, Virginia, North Carolina, and South Carolina write state constitutions;	Smith, *The Wealth of Nations*
Brackenridge, Hugh Henry (1748–1816), *The Battle of Bunkers-Hill* (drama)	Rhode Island and Connecticut alter their colonial charters.	
Freneau, Philip (1752–1832), "The Beauties of Santa Cruz" (verse)	George Mason's "Declaration of Rights for Virginia" adopted and widely circulated.	
Leacock, John (1729–1802), *The Fall of British Tyranny* (drama)		
Ogilvie, George (1740?–1801), *Carolina; or, The Planter* (verse)		
Paine, Thomas (1737–1809), *Common Sense*		
Sherwood, Samuel (1730–83), *The Church's Flight into the Wilderness* (sermon)		

	Warren, **Mercy Otis** (1728–1814), "To Fidelio, Long Absent on the Great Public Cause, Which Agitated All America, In 1776"		Sheridan, *The School for Scandal*
	Wilson, **James** (1742–98), *An Address to the Inhabitants of the Colonies*		
1777	Anonymous, *Jamaica, a poem, in three parts*	Washington defeated at Brandywine, Pennsylvania; British occupy Philadelphia (September); Washington retires to Valley Forge for the winter (December).	
	Brackenridge, **Hugh Henry** (1748–1816), *The Death of General Montgomery at the Siege of Quebec* (drama)		
	Franklin, **Benjamin** (1706–90), "The Sale of the Hessians"		
	Robertson, **William** (1721–93), *History of America*		
	Wheatley, **Phillis** (1753?–84), "On the Death of General Wooster" (verse)		
1778	Carver, **Jonathan** (1710–80), *Travels Through the Interior Parts of North America in the Years 1766, 1767, and 1768*	Articles of Confederation adopted by Congress (ratified 1781).	Jean-Jacques Rousseau dies (b. 1712). Voltaire dies (b. 1694).
	Dwight, **Timothy** (1752–1817), "Columbia" (verse, c. 1778)		Burney, *Evelina*

	Important Texts In and Concerning the New World	Historical Events in the New World	Historical and Literary Events in the Old World
	Franklin, Benjamin (1706–90), "The Ephemera"		
	Hopkinson, Francis (1737–91), "The Battle of the Kegs" (ballad)		
	Parsons, Theophilus (1754–1813), The Essex Result (pamphlet)		
	Whiting, William (1730–92), An Address to the Inhabitants of Berkshire County, Mass.		
1779	Franklin, Benjamin (1706–90), "Preface to an Abridgement of the Book of Common Prayer"	Capt. John Paul Jones and the Bonhomme Richard defeat the Serapis off the coast of England.	Johnson, The Lives of the English Poets (1779–81)
	Freneau, Philip (1752–1832), "The House of Night" (verse narrative)		
1780	Humphreys, David (1752–1818), A Poem Addressed to the Armies of the United States of America	British troops capture Charleston. Benedict Arnold defects and joins the British.	Haydn, "Toy" Symphony
	Reed, Esther de Berdt (1747–80), The Sentiments of an American Woman		

1781	Freneau, Philip (1752–1832), "The British Prison Ship"; "To the Memory of the Brave Americans" (verse)	Siege of Yorktown; Cornwallis surrenders to Washington. Articles of Confederation ratified.	Kant, *Critique of Pure Reason* Rousseau, *Confessions*
1782	Crèvecoeur, J. Hector St. John de (1735–1813), *Letters from an American Farmer*	Peace talks begin in Paris. Netherlands recognizes American independence.	Fall of Lord North's ministry. Niccolò Paganini born (d. 1840). Giacchino Antonio Rossini born (d. 1868). Laclos, *Les liaisons dangereuses*
1783	Anonymous, *A Treatise on Dress, Intended as a friendly and seasonable Warning to the Daughters of America* Blair, Hugh (1718–1800), *Lectures on Rhetoric and Belles Lettres* Rector of St. John's at Nevis, *Poems, on subjects arising in England at the West Indies* Stiles, Ezra (1727–95), *The Future Glory of the United States* Washington, George (1732–99), "Circular to the States" ("Washington's Farewell to the Army")	Treaty of Paris ends American Revolution.	William Pitt named prime minister (1783–1801).

	Important Texts In and Concerning the New World	Historical Events in the New World	Historical and Literary Events in the Old World
	Webster, Noah (1758–1843), *The American Spelling Book*		Samuel Johnson dies (b. 1709).
			Beaumarchais, *The Marriage of Figaro*
	Boston Magazine founded by William Billings		Kant, *An Answer to the Question: "What is Enlightenment?"*
1784	Franklin, Benjamin (1706–90), *Information to Those Who Would Remove to America*	New York becomes temporary capital of the U.S.	
		North Carolina cedes its western territories to the U.S.	
	Jefferson, Thomas (1743–1826), *Notes on the State of Virginia* (1784–5, private edition; also French edition)		
	Markoe, Peter (c. 1752–92), *The Patriot Chief* (drama)		
	Murray, Judith Sargent (1751–1820), "Desultory Thoughts upon the utility of encouraging a degree of Self-Complacency, especially in FEMALE BOSOMS" (essay)		
	Tucker, Thomas Tudor (1745–1828), *Conciliatory Hints, Attempting by a Fair State of Affairs, to Remove Party Prejudice*		
1785	Dwight, Timothy (1752–1817), *The Conquest of Canaan* (verse)		

744

	Franklin, Benjamin (1706–90), "The Internal State of America"; "A Petition of the Left Hand"	Frederick the Great dies. Mozart, *The Marriage of Figaro*
1786	*The Anarchiad* (verse satire, 1786–7)	
	Anonymous, *Address to the Public, Containing Some Remarks on the Present Political State of the American Republicks, etc.*	
	Freneau, Philip (1752–1832), "Wild Honey Suckle" (verse)	Virginia Statute for Religious Freedom. Shays's Rebellion.
	Jefferson, Thomas (1743–1826), "The Virginia Statute of Religious Liberty"	
	Ladd, Joseph Brown (1764–86), *The Poems of Arouet*	
	Rush, Benjamin (1745–1813), *Plan for the Establishment of Public Schools and the Diffusion of Knowledge in Pennsylvania*	
	Worcester Magazine founded by Isaiah Thomas (ceases publication 1788)	
1787	Adams, John (1735–1826), *A Defence of the Constitutions of Government of the United States of America*	Constitution of the United States signed in Philadelphia. Pennsylvania admitted to statehood. Mozart, *Don Giovanni*

Important Texts In and Concerning the New World	Historical Events in the New World	Historical and Literary Events in the Old World
Anonymous, "Amelia; or The Faithless Briton – An American Tale" (published in *Columbian Magazine*)	Northwest Ordinance enacted by Congress.	
Anonymous, *Proverbs on the Pride of Women*		
Barlow, Joel (1754–1812), *The Vision of Columbus* (verse)		
Dane, Nathan (1752–1835), "The Northwest Ordinance"		
Dunlap, William (1766–1839), *The Modest Soldier* (drama, now lost)		
Edwards, Jonathan, Jr. (1745–1801), *Observations on the Language of the Muhhekaneew Indians* (1788, according to *Annals*)		
Federalist Papers published (through 1788), written by **Alexander Hamilton** (1757–1804), **John Jay** (1745–1829) and **James Madison** (1751–1836)		

1788

Freneau, **Philip** (1752–1832), "The Indian Burial Ground" (verse)

Hammon, **Jupiter** (1711?–1800), *An Address to the Negroes in the State of New York*

Jefferson, **Thomas** (1743–1826), *Notes on the State of Virginia* (first authorized public edition in English)

Madison, **James** (1751–1836), *Notes on Debates in the Federal Convention* (first published 1843)

Tyler, **Royall** (1757–1826), *May Day in Town* (drama, now lost)

American Magazine launched by Noah Webster (ceases publication 1788)

The American Museum, or Repository of Ancient and Modern Fugitive Pieces founded by Mathew Carey in Philadelphia; ceases publication in 1892

[Warren, **Mercy Otis** (1728–1814)], *Observations on the New Constitution, And on the Federal and State Conventions* (essay)

Rowson, **Susanna** (c. 1762–1824), *Poems on Various Subjects*

Kant, *Critique of Practical Reason*

Mozart, Three "great" symphonies (E-flat, G minor, "Jupiter")

U.S. Constitution in force after ratification by ninth state, New Hampshire.

	Important Texts In and Concerning the New World	Historical Events in the New World	Historical and Literary Events in the Old World
	Rushton, Edward (1756–1814), *West Indian Eclogues* (verse)		
1789	**Brown, William Hill** (1765–93), *The Power of Sympathy* (novel)	First U.S. Congress meets in New York.	Storming of Bastille begins French Revolution.
	Dunlap, William (1766–1839), *The Father, or American Shandyism* (drama)	Washington inaugurated as president of U.S.	Blake, *Songs of Innocence*
	Equiano, Olaudah (1745–?), *The Interesting Narrative of the Life of Olaudah Equiano or Gustavus Vassa, The African*	Bill of Rights proposed by Congress. John Jay appointed first chief justice of the Supreme Court.	Goethe, *Torquato Tasso* Kotzebue, *The Stranger*
	Jefferson, Thomas (1743–1826), *Thoughts on English Prosody* (essay)	James Fenimore Cooper born (d. 1851).	
	Morse, Jedidiah (1761–1826), *The American Geography; or, A View of the Present Situation of the United States of America* (2d ed. 1793 as *The American Universal Geography*)		
	Ramsay, David (1749–1819), *The History of the American Revolution*		

1790

Benjamin Rush (1745–1813), *Account of the Climate of Pennsylvania and Its Influence Upon the Human Body*

Morton, Sarah Wentworth (1759–1846), *Ouâbi; or the Virtues of Nature* (verse narrative)

Murray, Judith Sargent (1751–1820), "On the Equality of the Sexes" (essay)

Tyler, Royall (1757–1826), *The Contrast* (drama, written 1787)

Warren, Mercy Otis (1728–1814), *Poems, Dramatic and Miscellaneous*

Winthrop, John (1588–1649), *A Journal of the Transactions and Occurrences in the Settlement of Massachusetts and the Other New England Colonies from the Year 1630 to 1644*

Philadelphia becomes nation's capital (until 1800).
First American copyright law passed.
Washington, D.C., founded.
First session of the U.S. Supreme Court.

Benjamin Franklin dies (b. 1706).

Adam Smith dies (b. 1723).

Blake, *The Marriage of Heaven and Hell*
Burke, *Reflections on the Revolution in France*

1791

Bartram, William (1739–1823), *Travels Through North & South Carolina, Georgia, East & West Florida, The Cherokee Country, the Extensive Territories of the Muscolges, or Creek Confederacy, and The Country of the Chactaws*

The Echo (satire; through 1805)

Vermont admitted to the Union.
Bill of Rights ratified.
First Bank of the U.S. incorporated.

Wolfgang Amadeus Mozart dies (b. 1756).

Boswell, *Life of Samuel Johnson*
Sade, *Justine*
Schiller, *History of the Thirty Years' War* (1791–3)

	Important Texts In and Concerning the New World	Historical Events in the New World	Historical and Literary Events in the Old World
	Hamilton, Alexander (1757–1804), *Report on Manufactures*		
	Rowson, Susanna (c. 1762–1824), *Charlotte Temple, A Tale of Truth* (novel)		
	First issue of *Gazette of the United States*		
1792	**Belknap, Jeremy** (1744–98), *The Foresters* (novel)	Kentucky admitted to the Union. Militia Act addresses Indian unrest in Northwest Territory.	British prime minister Pitt attacks slave trade. France declared a republic.
	Brackenridge, Hugh Henry (1748–1816), *Modern Chivalry* (novel, completed 1815)	New York Stock Exchange opens. Cornerstone of White House laid.	Francis II becomes last Holy Roman Emperor.
	Dennie, Joseph (1768–1812), "The Farrago" (essay serial)	Dollar coinage minted.	Wollstonecraft, *A Vindication of the Rights of Women*
	Hamilton, Alexander (1757–1804), *Letters by "An American"*		
	Hopkinson, Francis (1737–91), *The Miscellaneous Essays of Francis Hopkinson* (posth.)		
	Morton, Sarah Wentworth (1759–1846), "The African Chief" (antislavery poem)		

1793	Barlow, Joel (1754–1812), *The Hasty-Pudding* Bleecker, Ann Eliza (1752–83), *The Posthumous Works of Ann Eliza Bleecker, in Prose and Verse* (with Margaretta V. Faugeres [?], *A Collection of Essays, Prose and Poetical*) Crèvecoeur, J. Hector St. John de (1735–1813), *Letters from an American Farmer* (first American edition) Imlay, Gilbert (1754?–1828?), *The Emigrants* (novel) Smith, Elihu Hubbard (1771–98), ed., *American Poems* (first anthology of native verse) *Farmer's Weekly Museum* (Walpole, N.H.; ceases publication 1810)	Washington inaugurated for second term. Washington's "Proclamation of Neutrality" in French-British War. Citizen Genet affair. Fugitive Slave law passed. Eli Whitney applies for patent on cotton gin.	Execution of Louis XVI and Marie Antoinette; outbreak of war in Europe. Reign of Terror in France (1793–4). Kant, "Theory and Practice"
1794	Dwight, Timothy (1752–1817), *Greenfield Hill: A Poem in Seven Parts* Manning, William (?), *The Key of Liberty* (memoirs, c.1794) Paine, Thomas (1737–1809), *The Age of Reason* (tract)	Whisky Rebellion quelled (Pennsylvania farmers against excise tax). Jay's Treaty results in British evacuation of Northwest military posts. U.S. Navy established.	French occupy Belgium. Blake, *Songs of Experience* Fichte, *Foundation of the Complete Theory of Knowledge* Godwin, *Caleb Williams* Radcliffe, *The Mysteries of Udolpho*

	Important Texts In and Concerning the New World	Historical Events in the New World	Historical and Literary Events in the Old World
	Rowson, Susanna (c. 1762–1824), "America, Commerce and Freedom" (drinking song); Slaves in Algiers; or, A Struggle for Freedom (drama)		
	Tyler, Royall (1757–1826), and Joseph Dennie (1768–1812), "From the Shop of Colon and Spondee" (essays, through 1811)		
1795	Dunlap, William (1766–1839), Fountainville Abbey (drama, adaptation of Ann Radcliffe's Romance of the Forest)	Treaty of San Lorenzo between U.S. and Spain establishes boundaries of Florida.	French occupy Netherlands. End of Reign of Terror.
	Paine, Robert Treat (1773–1811), The Invention of Letters (verse)	Naturalization Act sets requirements for citizenship.	John Keats born (d. 1821). Thomas Carlyle born (d. 1881).
	Snowden, Richard (1753–1825), The Columbiad; or, A Poem on the American War		Goethe, Wilhelm Meister's Apprenticeship (1795–6)
1796	Dennie, Joseph (1768–1812), The Lay Preacher; or Short Sermons for Idle Readers	Tennessee admitted to the Union. John Adams defeats Thomas Jefferson in U.S. presidential election; Jefferson elected vice-president.	Napoleon wages Italian campaign (1796–7). Spain allies itself with France against Britain.
	Tucker, St. George (1752–1827), Dissertation on Slavery	William Hickling Prescott born (d. 1859).	Burke, Letters to a Noble Lord Burney, Camilla

Coleridge, *Poems on Various Subjects*
Goethe and Schiller, *Xenien*
Goya, *Los Caprichos* (painting)
Matthew Lewis, *The Monk*
Southey, *Joan of Arc*

Edmund Burke dies (b. 1727).
Franz Schubert born (d. 1828).
Horace Walpole dies (b. 1717).

Coleridge, "Kubla Khan" (written)
Hölderlin, *Hyperion*
Radcliffe, *The Italian*
Sade, *Juliette*
Southey, *Poems*

John Adams inaugurated second president of the U.S.
Relations with France deteriorate due to Jay's Treaty.
XYZ Affair (Talleyrand attempts to extort money from U.S. commissioners).

Washington, George (1732–99), "The Speech of George Washington, Esq., Late President of the United States of America: on His Resignation of That Important Office" (commonly known as the "Farewell Address")

Webster, Noah (1758–1843), *A Collection of Papers on the Subject of Bilious Fevers, Prevalent in the United States for a Few Years Past*

1797 **Bingham, Caleb** (1757–1817), *The Columbian Orator* (manual)

Bleecker, Ann Eliza (1752–83), *The History of Maria Kittle* (captivity narrative)

Burk, John Daly (?–1808), *Bunker-Hill, or the Death of General Warren* (drama)

Butler, James (1755?–1842), *Fortune's Foot-Ball; or, The Adventures of Mercutio* (novel)

Foster, Hannah (1759–1840), *The Coquette* (novel)

Mann, Herman (1772–1833), *The Female Review; Or, Memoirs of an American Young Lady*

	Important Texts In and Concerning the New World	Historical Events in the New World	Historical and Literary Events in the Old World
	Morton, Sarah Wentworth (1759–1846), *Beacon Hill: A Local Poem, Historic and Descriptive*		
	Paine, Robert Treat (1773–1811), *The Ruling Passion* (verse)		
	Tyler, Royall (1757–1826), *The Algerine Captive: or, The Life and Adventures of Doctor Updike Underhill* (novel); *The Georgia Spec* (drama, now lost)		
1798	**Brown, Charles Brockden** (1771–1810), *Alcuin: A Dialogue* (nonfiction); *Wieland; or, The Transformation* (novel)	Congress amends Naturalization Act; passes Alien and Sedition Acts. Mississippi Territory created. Beginning of undeclared naval war with France (1798–1800).	French troops occupy Rome. Napoleon's Campaign in Egypt (1798–9). Lord Nelson defeats French fleet near Alexandria.
	Dunlap, William (1766–1839), *André* (drama)		
	Foster, Hannah (1759–1840), *The Boarding School; or, Lessons of a Preceptress of her Pupils*		
	Furro, Broteer (?), *A Narrative of the Life and Adventures of Venture, A Native of Africa*		
	Hopkinson, Joseph (1770–1842), "Hail Columbia" (verse)		

Jefferson, Thomas (1743–1826), "Kentucky Resolutions"

Manning, William (1747–1814), *The Key of Liberty, Showing the Causes Why a Free Government has Always Failed, and a Remedy Against it; Written in the Year 1798* (pamphlet)

Munford, Robert (?–1784), *The Candidates, or the Humours of a Virginia Election*

Murray, Judith Sargent (1751–1820), *The Gleaner* (miscellany, originally published in Isaiah Thomas's *Massachusetts Magazine* from 1792–4)

Paine, Robert Treat (1773–1811), "Adams and Liberty" (song)

Rowson, Susanna (c.1762–1824), *Reuben and Rachel* (novel)

1799   **Brown, Charles Brockden** (1771–1810), *Ormond; or The Secret Witness* (novel); *Edgar Huntly; or Memoirs of a Sleep-Walker* (novel); *Arthur Mervyn; or Memoirs of the Year 1793* (novel, 1799–1800); "The Death of Cicero" (story); "Thessalonica" (story)

George Washington dies (b. 1732).

Honoré de Balzac born (d. 1850).

	Important Texts In and Concerning the New World	Historical Events in the New World	Historical and Literary Events in the Old World
1800	Webster, Noah (1758–1843), *Dissertation on the Supposed Change of Temperature in Modern Winters* *Monthly Magazine and American Review* founded by Charles Brockden Brown (ceases publication 1800)	Washington, D.C., becomes capital of the U.S. Northwest Territory divided into Ohio and Indiana Territories. Library of Congress founded.	Spain cedes Louisiana Territory to France. Napoleon occupies Italy.
1801	Anonymous, *The Female Advocate* (pamphlet) Brown, Charles Brockden (1771–1810), *Clara Howard* (novel); *Jane Talbot* (novel) Dennie, Joseph (1768–1812), *The Spirit of the Farmer's Museum and Lay Preacher's Gazette* Tenney, Tabitha (1762–1837), *Female Quixotism* (novel)	U.S. at war with Tripoli.	United Kingdom of Great Britain and Ireland established. Csar Paul I assassinated; Alexander I crowned emperor of Russia. Vincenzo Bellini born (d. 1835). Chateaubriand, *Atala*

Wood, Sarah (1759–1855), *Dorval; or the Speculator. A Novel founded on Recent Events*

Port Folio, literary miscellany, founded by Joseph Dennie (ceases publication 1827)

1802   Irving, Washington (1783–1859), *Letters of Jonathan Oldstyle, Gent.* (newspaper serial, 1802–3)

The Literary Magazine and American Register founded by Charles Brockden Brown; ceases publication 1806; revived as *American Register, or General Repository of History, Politics, and Science* until Brown's death in 1810

Georgia cedes its western territory to U.S.

Chateaubriand, *The Genius of Christianity*

1803   Dunlap, William (1766–1839), *The Glory of Columbia: Her Yeomanry!* (drama)

Miller, Samuel (1769–1850), *A Brief Retrospect of the Eighteenth Century* (2 vols.)

[Vickery, Sukey (1799–1821)], *Emily Hamilton* (novel)

Wirt, William (1772–1834), *Letters of the British Spy* (nonfiction)

Monthly Anthology and Boston Review (1803–11)

Ohio admitted to the Union.
Louisiana Purchase: Napoleon sells Louisiana Territory to U.S. for $15 million.
Marbury v. Madison affirms right of judicial review.

Hector Berlioz born (d. 1869).

	Important Texts In and Concerning the New World	Historical Events in the New World	Historical and Literary Events in the Old World
1804	**Humphreys, David** (1752–1818), *A Poem on the Industry of the United States of America*	Aaron Burr kills Alexander Hamilton in a duel.	Napoleon crowned emperor of France.
	Jefferson, Thomas (1743–1826), "The Philosophy of Jesus"	Meriwether Lewis (1774–1809) and William Clark (1770–1838) lead their expedition to the Pacific Coast; return 1806. *Original Journals of the Lewis and Clark Expedition* collected by R. G. Thwaites and published in 8 volumes from 1904–5.	Johann Strauss, Sr., born (d. 1849).
	Paine, Thomas (1737–1809), *To the People of England on the Invasion of England* (pamphlet)		
	Rowson, Susanna (c. 1762–1824), *Miscellaneous Poems*	Nathaniel Hawthorne born (d. 1864).	
	Vanderlyn, John (1775–1852), *Death of Jane McCrea*		
1805	**Warren, Mercy Otis** (1728–1814), *History of the Rise, Progress, and Termination of the American Revolution*	Michigan Territory created. Zebulon Pike explores upper Mississippi River.	Napoleon crowned king of Italy. Lord Nelson defeats French at Trafalgar.
1806	**Hitchcock, David** (1773–1849), *The Poetical Works of David Hitchcock: Containing the Shade of Plato, Knight and Quack, and the Subtlety of Foxes*	President Jefferson orders arrest of Aaron Burr. William Gilmore Simms born (d. 1870).	Francis II renounces title of Holy Roman Emperor. John Stuart Mill born (d. 1873). Elizabeth Barrett born (d. 1861).
	Payne, John Howard (1791–1852), *Julia* (drama)		

	Tenskwatawa (?), Speech before the Iroquois Confederacy		
	Webster, Noah (1758–1843), *Compendious Dictionary of the English Language*		
1807	Barker, James Nelson (1784–1858), *The Indian Princess; or, La Belle Sauvage* (play)	Embargo Act passed by Congress. Aaron Burr tried for treason and acquitted.	Napoleon signs treaties with Russia and Prussia.
	Barlow, Joel (1754–1812), *The Columbiad* (verse)	Steamboat *Clermont* launched by Robert Fulton.	Charles and Mary Lamb, *Tales from Shakespeare*
	Brown, William Hill (1765–93), *Ira and Isabella; or, The Natural Children* (novel, posth.)	Henry Wadsworth Longfellow born (d. 1882).	Hegel, *The Phenomenology of Mind*
	Irving, Washington (1783–1859), William Irving (1766–1821), and James Kirke Paulding (1778–1860), *Salmagundi; or, The Whim-Whams and Opinions of Launcelot Langstaff, Esq. & Others* (satiric serial, through 1808)	John Greenleaf Whittier born (d. 1892).	
	Wilson, Alexander (1766–1813), *American Ornithology*		
1808	Bryant, William Cullen (1794–1878), *The Embargo; or, Sketches of the Times* (verse)	Importation of African slaves outlawed by Congress.	Napoleon occupies Spain; abolishes the Inquisition in Spain and Italy.
			Beethoven, Symphonies No. 5 and 6 ("Pastoral")

	Important Texts In and Concerning the New World	Historical Events in the New World	Historical and Literary Events in the Old World
1809	**Ames, Fisher** (1758–1808), "American Literature" (essay) **Brown, Charles Brockden** (1771–1810), *An Address to the Congress of the United States* (anti-Embargo pamphlet) **Irving, Washington** (1783–1859), *A History of New York* (fiction)	James Madison becomes fourth president of the U.S. Embargo Act repealed by Congress. Illinois Territory created. Thomas Paine dies (b. 1737). Abraham Lincoln born (d. 1865). Edgar Allan Poe born (d. 1849).	Goethe, *Faust, Part 1* Ingres, *La Grande Baigneuse* (painting) Charles Lamb, *Specimens of English Dramatic Poets* Russia annexes Finland. Napoleon annexes Papal States. Charles Darwin born (d. 1882). Nikolai Gogol born (d. 1852). Franz Joseph Haydn dies (b. 1732). Felix Mendelssohn born (d. 1847). Alfred, Lord Tennyson born (d. 1892). Beethoven, *Emperor Concerto* Byron, *English Bards and Scotch Reviewers* Schlegel, *On Dramatic Art and Literature*
1810	**Pike, Zebulon Montgomery** (1779–1813), *Account of Expeditions to the Sources of the Mississippi and Through the Western Parts of Louisiana*	U.S. annexes West Florida. Population of U.S. is 7.2 million.	Napoleon annexes Holland; his power at its apex.

Watterston, George (1783–1854), *Glencarn; or, The Disappointments of Youth* (novel)

White, George (?), *A Brief Account of the Life, Experiences, Travels, and Gospel Labours of George White, an African*

Charles Brockden Brown dies (b. 1771).
Margaret Fuller born (d. 1850).

Frédéric Chopin born (d. 1849).
Robert Schumann born (d. 1856).

1811 Brackenridge, Hugh Henry (1748–1816), *Epistle to Walter Scott* (verse)

Jea, John (?), *The Life, History, and Unparalleled Sufferings of John Jea, the African Preacher*

Mitchell, Isaac (1759?–1812), *The Asylum; or, Alonzo and Melissa. An American Tale, Founded on Fact* (novel)

Trumbull, Henry (1781–1843), *History of the Indian Wars* (revised 1841; nonfiction)

Gen. William Henry Harrison defeats native American tribes at the battle of Tippecanoe.
First steamboat service on the Mississippi River.
John Jacob Astor sends a ship around Cape Horn to build Fort Astoria on the Columbia River; launches overland expeditions led by Wilson Price Hunt and Robert Stuart.

Harriet Beecher Stowe born (d. 1896).

George III of England declared insane; Prince of Wales becomes Prince Regent.
"Luddites" destroy industrial machines in North England.
Franz Liszt born (d. 1886).
William Makepeace Thackeray born (d. 1863).

Austen, *Sense and Sensibility*

1812 Barker, James Nelson (1784–1858), *Marmion* (drama, adapted from a poem by Walter Scott)

Cuffee, Paul (1759–1817), *A Brief Account of the Settlement and Present Condition of the Colony of Sierra Leone in Africa*

U.S. declares war on Great Britain (1812–14).
Louisiana admitted to the Union.
Missouri Territory created.

Napoleon invades Russia, destroys Smolensk, occupies Moscow, but is forced to retreat.

Beethoven, Symphonies No. 7 and 8

	Important Texts In and Concerning the New World	Historical Events in the New World	Historical and Literary Events in the Old World
	Paulding, James Kirke (1778–1860), *The Diverting History of John Bull and Brother Jonathan* (nonfiction)	British navy blockades U.S. ports.	Duke of Wellington invades France. Mexico declares its independence. Robert Southey named poet laureate of England.
	[**Rush, Rebecca** (?)], *Kelroy* (novel)		
1813	**Bryan, Daniel** (1795–1866), *The Mountain Muse* (poem)		Giuseppe Verdi born (d. 1901). Richard Wagner born (d. 1883).
	Paulding, James Kirke (1778–1860), *The Lay of the Scotch Fiddle* (poem)		Austen, *Pride and Prejudice*
	Analectic Magazine (briefly edited by Washington Irving, ceases publication 1821)		
1814	**Biddle, Nicholas** (1786–1844), *History of the Expedition Under the Command of Captains Lewis and Clark to the Sources of the Missouri*	British burn the White House and the Capitol, attack Baltimore. Creek Indian War ends.	Napoleon abdicates and is exiled to Elba. Restoration of Louis XVIII to French throne.
	Brackenridge, Hugh Henry (1748–1816), *Law Miscellanies*		Austen, *Mansfield Park* Beethoven, *Fidelio* (opera, final version)
	Key, Francis Scott (1779–1843), "Defense of Fort M'Henry" ("The Star-Spangled Banner")		Goya, *The Second of May 1808* and *The Third of May 1808* (paintings) Scott, *Waverly*

1815	**Brackenridge, Hugh Henry** (1748–1816), *Modern Chivalry* (final edition)	Andrew Jackson defeats British at New Orleans.	Napoleon's "Hundred Days." Wellington defeats Napoleon at Waterloo.
	Drake, Daniel (1785–1852), *Picture of Cincinnati in 1815* (nonfiction)	Benjamin Latrobe begins rebuilding the White House (1815–17).	Napoleon's second exile, to St. Helena.
	Paulding, James Kirke (1778–1860), *The United States and England* (poem)	Paul Cuffee leads a group of colonists to Sierre Leone.	
	Porter, David (1780–1843), *Journal of a Cruise Made to the Pacific Ocean*		
	North American Review founded (ceases publication 1939)		
1816	**Boudinot, Elias (Sr.)** (1740–1821), *Star in the West* (nonfiction)	Indiana admitted to the Union. Second Bank of the United States (1816–36).	Austen, *Emma* Rossini, *Il Barbiere di Siviligia*
	Tucker, George (1775–1861), *Letters from Virginia* (nonfiction)	Establishment of American Colonization Society and its journal, the *African Repository*.	
	Woodworth, Samuel (1784–1842), *The Champions of Freedom* (novel)	Hugh Henry Brackenridge dies (b. 1748).	
	Portico founded in Baltimore (ceases publication 1818)		

	Important Texts In and Concerning the New World	Historical Events in the New World	Historical and Literary Events in the Old World
1817	Bryant, William Cullen (1794–1878), "Thanatopsis" (verse) Delano, Amasa (1763–1823), *Narrative of Voyages in the Northern and Southern Hemispheres* Neal, John (1793–1876), *Keep Cool* (novel) Paulding, James Kirke (1778–1860), *Letters from the South* (travel sketches, rev. ed. 1835) Riley, James (1777–1840), *Sufferings in Africa* (autobiography) Wirt, William (1772–1834), *Sketches of the Life and Character of Patrick Henry* (biography)	James Monroe inaugurated as fifth president of the U.S. Mississippi admitted to the Union. Alabama Territory created. Construction of Erie Canal begins. Henry David Thoreau born (d. 1862).	*Blackwood's Edinburgh Magazine* founded (ceases publication 1980). Jane Austen dies (b. 1775). Byron, *Manfred* Coleridge, *Biographia Literaria*
1818	Bryant, William Cullen (1794–1878), "Early American Verse" (essay); "On Trisyllabic Feet in Iambic Measure" (essay) Heckewelder, John G. (1743–1823), *History, Manners, and Customs of the Indian Nations* (nonfiction)	Illinois admitted to the Union. Canadian boundary established by U.S. and Great Britain. First Seminole War begins when Andrew Jackson invades Florida.	Hegel succeeds Fichte (d. 1814) as professor of philosophy in Berlin. Karl Marx born (d. 1883). Austen, *Northanger Abbey*; *Persuasion* M. Shelley, *Frankenstein*

Neal, John (1793–1876), *The Battle of Niagara* (verse)

Paulding, James Kirke (1778–1860), *The Backwoodsman* (poem)

Payne, John Howard (1791–1852), *Brutus; or, The Fall of Tarquin* (drama)

Narrative of the Captivity and Sufferings of Mrs. Mary Smith

1819   Channing, William Ellery (1780–1842), "A Sermon Delivered at the Ordination of the Rev. Jared Sparks" (commonly known as "Unitarian Christianity")

Halleck, Fitz-Greene (1790–1867), *Poems, by Croaker, Croaker & Co., and Croaker Jun.* (with Joseph Rodman Drake [1795–1820])

Irving, Washington (1783–1859), *The Sketch Book of Geoffrey Crayon, Gent.* (1819–90)

Jefferson, Thomas (1743–1826), "The Life and Morals of Jesus" (1819–20)

Neal, John (1793–1876), *Otho* (verse)

Alabama admitted to the Union.
East Florida ceded to U.S. by Spain in Adams-Onís Treaty.
Arkansas Territory organized.
Financial panic in U.S.
Stephen Long's "Yellowstone Expedition."
Anti-Slave Trade Act passed.
M'Culloch v. Maryland: on the constitutionality of the Second Bank.

Dartmouth College v. Woodward: on jurisdiction of state legislatures over private corporate charters.

Herman Melville born (d. 1891).
Walt Whitman born (d. 1892).

Future Queen Victoria of England born (d. 1901).
Simón Bolívar becomes president of Venezuela.

Byron, *Don Juan* (1819–24)
Scott, *Ivanhoe*
Shelley, *The Cenci*

Important Texts In and Concerning the New World	Historical Events in the New World	Historical and Literary Events in the Old World
Noah, Mordecai M. (1785–1851), *She Would Be a Soldier; or, The Plains of Chippewa* (drama)		George IV crowned king of England.
Paulding, James Kirke (1778–1860), *Salmagundi: Second Series* (1819–20)		Keats, *Lamia and Other Poems* Malthus, *Principles of Political Economy* Shelley, *Prometheus Unbound*
Schoolcraft, Henry Rowe (1793–1864), *A View of the Lead Mines of Missouri*		
Channing, William Ellery (1780–1842), *The Moral Argument Against Calvinism* (essay)	Missouri Compromise outlaws slavery north of latitude 36° 30′. Maine admitted to the Union as the twenty-third state. President Monroe reelected.	
Cooper, James Fenimore (1789–1851), *Precaution* (novel)	Susan B. Anthony born (d. 1906).	
Eastburn, James W. (1797–1819), *Yamoyden, A Tale of the Wars of King Philip* (poem)		
Noah, Mordecai M. (1785–1851), *The Siege of Tripoli* (drama)		
Symmes, John [Adam Seaborn] (1780–1829), *Symzonia: Voyage of Discovery*		

1820

BIBLIOGRAPHY

This selected bibliography is drawn from lists provided by the contributors to this volume. It represents works that they have found to be especially influential or significant. The bibliography does not include dissertations, articles, or studies of individual authors. We have also excluded primary sources, with the exception of certain collections that present materials that have been generally unknown or inaccessible to students and scholars.

Adair, Douglass. *Fame and the Founding Fathers: Essays.* Edited by Trevor Colbourn. New York: Norton, 1974.

Ahlstrom, Sydney E. *A Religious History of the American People.* New Haven, Conn.: Yale University Press, 1972.

Aldridge, Alfred Owen, ed. *The Ibero-American Enlightenment.* Urbana: University of Illinois Press, 1971.

Anderson, Benedict. *Imagined Communities: Reflections on the Origin and Spread of Nationalism.* London: Verso, 1983.

Andrews, William L., ed. *Journeys in New Worlds: Early American Women's Narratives.* Madison: University of Wisconsin Press, 1990.

Appleby, Joyce. *Capitalism and a New Social Order: The Republican Vision of the 1790s.* New York: New York University Press, 1984.

Arendt, Hannah. *On Revolution.* New York: Viking, 1963.

Armstrong, Nancy. *Desire and Domestic Fiction: A Political History of the Novel.* New York: Oxford University Press, 1987.

Axtell, James. *The Invasion Within: The Contest of Cultures in Colonial North America.* New York: Oxford University Press, 1985.

Bailyn, Bernard. *Education in the Forming of American Society.* Chapel Hill: University of North Carolina Press, 1960.

    The Ideological Origins of the American Revolution. 1967. Enl. ed. Cambridge, Mass.: Harvard University Press, 1992.

    The New England Merchants in the Seventeenth Century. Cambridge, Mass.: Harvard University Press, 1955.

    ed. *Pamphlets of the American Revolution.* Cambridge, Mass.: Harvard University Press, 1965.

Bailyn, Bernard, and John B. Hench, eds. *The Press and the American Revolution.* Worcester, Mass.: American Antiquarian Society, 1980.

Banning, Lance. *The Jeffersonian Persuasion: Evolution of a Party Ideology.* Ithaca, N.Y.: Cornell University Press, 1978.

Barish, Jonas. *The Antitheatrical Prejudice.* Berkeley and Los Angeles: University of California Press, 1981.

Beeman, Richard, Stephen Botein, and Edward D. Carter II, eds. *Beyond Confederation: Origins of the Constitution and American National Identity.* Chapel Hill: University of North Carolina Press, 1987.

Bercovitch, Sacvan. *The American Jeremiad.* Madison: University of Wisconsin Press, 1978.

   The Puritan Origins of the American Self. New Haven, Conn.: Yale University Press, 1975.

   ed. *The American Puritan Imagination: Essays in Revaluation.* Cambridge University Press, 1974.

   ed. *Typology and Early American Literature.* Amherst: University of Massachusetts Press, 1972.

Berens, John F. *Providence and Patriotism in Early America, 1640–1815.* Charlottesville: University Press of Virginia, 1978.

Bloch, Ruth H. *Visionary Republic: Millennial Themes in American Thought, 1756–1800.* Cambridge University Press, 1985.

Bonomi, Patricia U. *Under the Cope of Heaven: Religion, Society, and Politics in Colonial America.* New York: Oxford University Press, 1986.

Boorstin, Daniel J. *The Americans: The Colonial Experience.* New York: Random House, 1958.

   The Americans: The National Experience. New York: Random House, 1965.

Boyer, Paul, and Stephen Nissenbaum. *Salem Possessed: The Social Origins of Witchcraft.* Cambridge, Mass.: Harvard University Press, 1974.

Bozeman, Theodore Dwight. *To Live Ancient Lives: The Primitivist Dimensions in Puritanism.* Chapel Hill: University of North Carolina Press, 1988.

Breen, T. H. *The Character of the Good Ruler: A Study of Puritan Ideas in New England, 1630–1730.* New Haven, Conn.: Yale University Press, 1970.

   Puritans and Adventurers: Change and Persistence in Early America. New York: Oxford University Press, 1980.

Breitwieser, Mitchell Robert. *American Puritanism and the Defense of Mourning: Religion, Grief, and Ethnology in Mary White Rowlandson's Captivity Narrative.* Madison: University of Wisconsin Press, 1990.

   Cotton Mather and Benjamin Franklin: The Price of Representative Personality. Cambridge University Press, 1984.

Brown, Herbert Ross. *The Sentimental Novel in America, 1789–1860.* Durham, N.C.: Duke University Press, 1940.

Brown, Richard D. *Modernization: The Transformation of American Life, 1600–1865.* New York: Hill & Wang, 1976.

Brumm, Ursula. *American Thought and Religious Typology.* Translated by John Hooglund. New Brunswick, N.J.: Rutgers University Press, 1970.

Bruns, Roger, ed. *Am I Not a Man and a Brother: The Antislavery Crusade of Revolutionary America, 1688–1788.* New York: Chelsea House, 1977.

Buel, Richard, Jr. *Securing the Revolution: Ideology in American Politics, 1789–1815*. Ithaca, N.Y.: Cornell University Press, 1972.

Buell, Lawrence. *New England Literary Culture: From Revolution through Renaissance*. Cambridge University Press, 1986.

Caldwell, Patricia. *The Puritan Conversion Narrative: The Beginnings of American Express*. Cambridge University Press, 1983.

Campbell, Mary B. *The Witness and the Other World: Exotic European Travel Writing, 400–1600*. Ithaca, N.Y.: Cornell University Press, 1988.

Canetti, Elias. *Crowds and Power*. Translated by Carol Stewart. New York: Viking Press, 1962.

Carroll, Peter N. *Religion and the Coming of the American Revolution*. Waltham, Mass.: Ginn-Blaisdell, 1970.

Cassirer, Ernst. *The Philosophy of the Enlightenment*. Translated by Fritz C. A. Koelln and James P. Pettegrove. Princeton, N.J.: Princeton University Press, 1951.

Charlton, D. G. *New Images of the Natural in France: A Study of European Cultural History, 1750–1800*. Cambridge University Press, 1984.

Charvat, William. *The Origins of American Critical Thought, 1810–1835*. Philadelphia: University of Pennsylvania Press, 1936.

The Profession of Authorship in America, 1800–1870: The Papers of William Charvat. Edited by Matthew Bruccoli. Columbus: Ohio State University Press, 1966.

Cheyfitz, Eric. *The Poetics of Imperialism: Translation and Colonization from* The Tempest *to* Tarzan. New York: Oxford University Press, 1991.

Chiappelli, Fredi, ed. *First Images of America: The Impact of the New World on the Old*. Berkeley and Los Angeles: University of California Press, 1976.

Clark, Harry Hayden, ed. *Transitions in American Literary History*. New York: Octagon, 1975.

Clendinnen, Inga. *Ambivalent Conquests: Maya and Spaniard in Yucatan, 1517–1570*. Cambridge University Press, 1987.

Cohen, Charles Lloyd. *God's Caress: The Psychology of Puritan Religious Experience*. New York: Oxford University Press, 1986.

Cohen, Lester H. *The Revolutionary Histories: Contemporary Narratives of the American Revolution*. Ithaca, N.Y.: Cornell University Press, 1980.

Coolidge, John S. *The Pauline Renaissance in England: Puritanism and the Bible*. Oxford: Clarendon, 1970.

Cott, Nancy. *The Bonds of Womanhood: "Woman's Sphere" in New England, 1780–1835*. New Haven, Conn.: Yale University Press, 1977.

Cowell, Pattie. *Women Poets in Pre-Revolutionary America: An Anthology*. Troy, N.Y.: Whitson, 1981.

Cronon, William. *Changes in the Land: Indians, Colonists, and the Ecology of New England*. New York: Hill & Wang, 1983.

Daly, Robert. *God's Altar: The World and the Flesh in Puritan Poetry*. Berkeley and Los Angeles: University of California Press, 1978.

Davidson, Cathy N. *Revolution and the Word: The Rise of the Novel in America*. New York: Oxford University Press, 1986.

ed. *Reading in America: Literature and Social History.* Baltimore: Johns Hopkins University Press, 1989.

Davidson, James West. *The Logic of Millennial Thought.* New Haven, Conn.: Yale University Press, 1977.

Davies, Horton. *Worship and Theology in England.* Princeton, N.J.: Princeton University Press, 1961–75.

The Worship of the American Puritans, 1629–1730. New York: Lang, 1990.

Davis, Lennard J. *Factual Fictions: The Origins of the English Novel.* New York: Columbia University Press, 1983.

Davis, Richard Beale. *Intellectual Life in the Colonial South, 1585–1763.* 3 vols. Knoxville: University of Tennessee Press, 1978.

Intellectual Life in Jefferson's Virginia. Chapel Hill: University of North Carolina Press, 1964.

Delbanco, Andrew. *The Puritan Ordeal.* Cambridge, Mass.: Harvard University Press, 1989.

Demos, John Putnam. *Entertaining Satan: Witchcraft and the Culture of Early New England.* New York: Oxford University Press, 1982.

A Little Commonwealth: Family Life in Plymouth Colony. New York: Oxford University Press, 1970.

Dowling, William C. *Poetry and Ideology in Revolutionary Connecticut.* Athens: University of Georgia, 1990.

Dunn, Richard S. *Puritans and Yankees: The Winthrop Dynasty of New England, 1630–1717.* Princeton, N.J.: Princeton University Press, 1962.

Easthope, Antony. *Poetry as Discourse.* London: Methuen, 1983.

Elliott, Emory. *Power and Pulpit in Puritan New England.* Princeton, N.J.: Princeton University Press, 1975.

Revolutionary Writers: Literature and Authority in the New Republic. New York: Oxford University Press, 1982.

ed. *Puritan Influences in American Literature.* Urbana: University of Illinois Press, 1979.

Ellis, Joseph J. *After the Revolution: Profiles of Early American Culture.* New York: Norton, 1979.

Ellis, Richard E. *The Jeffersonian Crisis: Courts and Politics in the Young Republic.* New York: Oxford University Press, 1971.

Emerson, Everett H. *Puritanism in America.* Boston: Twayne, 1977.

ed. *Major Writers of Early American Literature.* Madison: University of Wisconsin Press, 1972.

Faust, Langdon Lynne. *American Women Writers: A Critical Reference Guide from Colonial Times to the Present.* 4 vols. New York: Ungar, 1979–82.

Favret-Saada, Jeanne. *Deadly Words: Witchcraft in the Bocage.* Translated by Catherine Cullen. Cambridge University Press, 1980.

Ferguson, Robert A. *Law and Letters in American Culture.* Cambridge, Mass.: Harvard University Press, 1984.

Fliegelman, Jay. *Prodigals and Pilgrims: The American Revolution against Patriarchal Authority, 1750–1800.* Cambridge University Press, 1982.

Foster, Stephen. *The Long Argument: English Puritanism and the Shaping of New England Culture, 1570–1700*. Chapel Hill: University of North Carolina Press, 1991.
Their Solitary Way: The Puritan Social Ethic in the First Century of Settlement in New England. New Haven, Conn.: Yale University Press, 1971.

Franklin, Wayne. *Discoverers, Explorers, Settlers: The Diligent Writers of Early America*. Chicago: University of Chicago Press, 1979.

Furtwangler, Albert. *American Silhouettes: Rhetorical Identities of the Founders*. New Haven, Conn.: Yale University Press, 1987.
The Authority of Publius: A Reading of the Federalist Papers. Ithaca, N.Y.: Cornell University Press, 1984.

Gaustad, Edwin S. *Faith of Our Fathers: Religion and the New Nation*. New York: Harper & Row, 1987.
A Religious History of America. Rev. ed. New York: Harper & Row, 1990.

Gay, Peter. *The Enlightenment: An Interpretation*. 2 vols. New York: Knopf, 1966–9.

Gerbi, Antonello. *The Dispute of the New World: The History of a Polemic, 1750–1900*. Translated by Jeremy Moyle. Pittsburgh, Pa.: University of Pittsburgh Press, 1973.

Gildrie, Richard P. *Salem, Massachusetts, 1626–1683: A Covenant Community*. Charlottesville: University Press of Virginia, 1975.

Gilmore, Michael T., ed. *Early American Literature: A Collection of Critical Essays*. Englewood Cliffs, N.J.: Prentice-Hall, 1980.

Gilmore, William J. *Reading Becomes a Necessity of Life: Material and Cultural Life in Rural New England, 1780–1835*. Knoxville: University of Tennessee Press, 1989.

Granger, Bruce. *American Essay Serials from Franklin to Irving*. Knoxville: University of Tennessee Press, 1978.

Greenblatt, Stephen. *Learning to Curse: Essays in Early Modern Culture*. New York: Routledge, 1990.
Marvelous Possessions: The Wonder of the New World. Chicago: University of Chicago Press, 1991.

Greene, Jack P., ed. *The American Revolution: Its Character and Limits*. New York: New York University Press, 1987.
ed. *The Reinterpretation of the American Revolution, 1763–1789*. New York: Harper & Row, 1968.

Greven, Phillip J. *Four Generations: Population, Land and Family in Colonial Andover, Massachusetts*. Ithaca, N.Y.: Cornell University Press, 1970.
The Protestant Temperament: Patterns of Child-Rearing, Religious Experience, and the Self in Early America. New York: Knopf, 1977.

Grimsted, David. *Melodrama Unveiled: American Theater and Culture, 1800–1850*. Chicago: University of Chicago Press, 1968.

Gummere, Richard M. *The American Colonial Mind and the Classical Tradition: Essays in Comparative Culture*. Cambridge, Mass.: Harvard University Press, 1963.

Gura, Philip F. *A Glimpse of Sion's Glory: Puritan Radicalism in New England, 1620–1660*. Middletown, Conn.: Wesleyan University Press, 1984.

Habermas, Jürgen. *The Structural Transformation of the Public Sphere: An Inquiry into a*

Category of Bourgeois Society. Translated by Thomas Burger with the assistance of
Frederick Lawrence. Cambridge Mass.: MIT Press, 1989.

Hall, David D. *The Faithful Shepherd: A History of the New England Ministry in the
Seventeenth Century.* Chapel Hill: University of North Carolina Press, 1972.

Worlds of Wonder, Days of Judgment: Popular Religious Belief in Early New England.
New York: Knopf, 1989.

ed. *The Antinomian Controversy, 1636–1638: A Documentary History.* 2d ed. Durham, N.C.: Duke University Press, 1990.

Hambrick-Stowe, Charles. *The Practice of Piety: Puritan Devotional Disciplines in
Seventeenth-Century New England.* Chapel Hill: University of North Carolina
Press, 1982.

Hansen, Chadwick. *Witchcraft at Salem.* New York: Braziller, 1969.

Hatch, Nathan A. *The Sacred Cause of Liberty: Republican Thought and the Millennium in
Revolutionary New England.* New Haven, Conn.: Yale University Press, 1977.

Heimert, Alan. *Religion and the American Mind: From the Great Awakening to the
Revolution.* Cambridge, Mass.: Harvard University Press, 1966.

Heimert, Alan, and Perry Miller, eds. *The Great Awakening: Documents Illustrating the
Crisis and Its Consequences.* Indianapolis: Bobbs-Merrill, 1967.

Henderson, Katherine Usher, and Barbara F. McManus, eds. *Half Humankind: Contexts and Texts of the Controversy about Women in England, 1540–1640.* Urbana:
University of Illinois Press, 1985.

Henretta, James A., and Gregory H. Nobles. *Evolution and Revolution: American
Society, 1600–1820.* Lexington, Mass.: Heath, 1987.

Higonnet, Patrice. *Sister Republics: The Origins of French and American Republicanism.*
Cambridge, Mass.: Harvard University Press, 1988.

Hill, Christopher. *Reformation to Industrial Revolution: A Social and Economic History of
Britain, 1530–1780.* London: Weidenfeld & Nicolson, 1967.

Hobsbawm, E. J. *Nations and Nationalism since 1780: Programme, Myth, Reality.*
Cambridge University Press, 1990.

Hoffman, Ronald, and Peter J. Albert, eds. *Women in the Age of the American Revolution.* Charlottesville: University Press of Virginia, 1989.

Holifield, E. Brooks. *The Covenant Sealed: The Development of Puritan Sacramental
Theology in Old and New England, 1570–1720.* New Haven, Conn.: Yale University Press, 1974.

Holstun, James. *A Rational Millennium: Puritan Utopias of Seventeenth-Century England
and America.* New York: Oxford University Press, 1987.

Horkheimer, Max, and Theodor Adorno. *Dialectic of Enlightenment.* Translated by
John Cumming. New York: Continuum, 1972.

Hulme, Peter. *Colonial Encounters: Europe and the Native Caribbean, 1492–1797.*
London: Methuen, 1986.

Hyneman, Charles S., and Donald Lutz, eds. *American Political Writing during the
Founding Era, 1760–1805.* 2 vols. Indianapolis: Liberty, 1983.

Jackson, Blyden. *A History of Afro-American Literature.* Vol. 1, *The Long Beginning,
1746–1895.* Baton Rouge: Louisiana State University Press, 1989.

Jacobs, Wilbur R. *Dispossessing the American Indian: Indians and Whites on the Colonial Frontier.* 1972. Reprinted. Norman: University of Oklahoma Press, 1985.

Jantz, Harold S. *The First Century of New England Verse.* Worcester, Mass.: American Antiquarian Society, 1944.

Jehlen, Myra. *American Incarnation: The Individual, the Nation, and the Continent.* Cambridge, Mass.: Harvard University Press, 1986.

Jennings, Francis. *The Invasion of America: Indians, Colonialism, and the Cant of Conquest.* Chapel Hill: University of North Carolina Press, 1975.

Jensen, Merrill. *The Founding of a Nation: A History of the American Revolution, 1763–1776.* New York: Oxford University Press, 1968.

Jones, Howard Mumford. *O Strange New World: American Culture: The Formative Years.* New York: Viking, 1964.

Revolution and Romanticism. Cambridge, Mass.: Harvard University Press, 1974.

Jordan, Cynthia S. *Second Stories: The Politics of Language, Form, and Gender in Early American Fictions.* Chapel Hill: University of North Carolina Press, 1989.

Jordan, Winthrop. *White over Black: American Attitudes toward the Negro, 1550–1812.* Chapel Hill: University of North Carolina Press, 1968.

Joyce, William L., David D. Hall, Richard D. Brown, and John B. Hench, eds. *Printing and Society in Early America.* Worcester, Mass.: American Antiquarian Society, 1983.

Kammen, Michael. *Mystic Chords of Memory: The Transformation of Tradition in American Culture.* New York: Knopf, 1991.

People of a Paradox: An Inquiry Concerning the Origins of American Civilization. New York: Knopf, 1972.

A Season of Youth: The American Revolution and the Historical Imagination. New York: Knopf, 1978.

Karlsen, Carol F. *The Devil in the Shape of a Woman: Witchcraft in Seventeenth-Century New England.* New York: Norton, 1987.

Karsten, Peter. *Patriot-Heroes in England and America: Political Symbolism and Changing Values over Three Centuries.* Madison: University of Wisconsin Press, 1978.

Kerber, Linda K. *Federalists in Dissent: Imagery and Ideology in Jeffersonian America.* Ithaca, N.Y.: Cornell University Press, 1970.

Women of the Republic: Intellect and Ideology in Revolutionary America. Chapel Hill: University of North Carolina Press, 1980.

Kibbey, Ann. *The Interpretation of Material Shapes in Puritanism: A Study of Rhetoric, Prejudice, and Violence.* Cambridge University Press, 1986.

Koch, Adrienne, ed. *The American Enlightenment: The Shaping of the American Experiment and a Free Society.* New York: Braziller, 1965.

Koehler, Lyle. *A Search for Power: The "Weaker Sex" in Seventeenth-Century New England.* Urbana: University of Illinois Press, 1980.

Kolodny, Annette. *The Lay of the Land: Metaphor as Experience and History in American Life and Letters.* Chapel Hill: University of North Carolina Press, 1975.

Kupperman, Karen Ordahl. *Settling with the Indians: The Meeting of English and Indian Cultures.* Totowa, N.J.: Rowman & Littlefield, 1980.

Lancaster, Bruce. *The American Revolution*. New York: American Heritage, 1971.

Lang, Amy Schrager. *Prophetic Woman: Anne Hutchinson and the Problem of Dissent in the Literature of New England*. Berkeley and Los Angeles: University of California Press, 1987.

Lawson-Peebles, Robert. *Landscape and Written Expression in Revolutionary America: The World Turned Upside Down*. Cambridge University Press, 1988.

Leach, Douglas Edward. *Flintlock and Tomahawk: New England in King Philip's War*. New York: Macmillan, 1958.

Leary, Lewis. *Soundings: Some Early American Writers*. Athens: University of Georgia Press, 1975.

Lemay, J. A. Leo. *A Calendar of American Poetry in the Colonial Newspapers and Magazines and in the Major English Magazines through 1765*. Worcester, Mass.: American Antiquarian Society, 1972.

  Men of Letters in Colonial Maryland. Knoxville: University of Tennessee Press, 1972.

Leon-Portilla, Miguel. *The Aztec Image of Self and Society: An Introduction to Nahuatl Culture*. Edited and with an introduction by J. Jorge Klor de Alva. Salt Lake City: University of Utah Press, 1992.

  ed. *The Aztec Account of the Conquest of Mexico*. Boston: Beacon, 1972.

Lestringant, Frank. *Le Huguenot et le sauvage: L'Amérique et la controverse coloniale, en France, au temps des Guerres de Religion*. Paris: Aux Amateurs de livres, 1990.

Leverenz, David. *The Language of Puritan Feeling: An Exploration in Literature, Psychology, and Social History*. New Brunswick, N.J.: Rutgers University Press, 1980.

Levernier, James, and Douglas Wilmes, eds. *American Writers before 1800: A Biographical and Critical Dictionary*. 3 vols. Westport, Conn.: Greenwood, 1983.

Levin, David. *In Defense of Historical Literature: Essays on American History, Autobiography, Drama, and Fiction*. New York: Hill & Wang, 1967.

Levine, Lawrence W. *Highbrow/Lowbrow: The Emergence of Cultural Hierarchy in America*. Cambridge, Mass.: Harvard University Press, 1988.

Lewalski, Barbara Kiefer. *Protestant Poetics and Seventeenth-Century Religious Lyric*. Princeton, N.J.: Princeton University Press, 1979.

Lewis, Gordon K. *Main Currents in Caribbean Thought*. Baltimore: Johns Hopkins University Press, 1983.

Lipset, Seymour Martin. *The First New Nation: The United States in Historical and Comparative Perspective*. New York: Basic, 1963.

Lockridge, Kenneth A. *A New England Town: The First Hundred Years, Dedham, Massachusetts, 1636–1736*. Exp. ed. New York: Norton, 1985.

Lovejoy, Arthur O. *Essays in the History of Ideas*. Baltimore: Johns Hopkins University Press, 1948.

Lowance, Mason I. *The Language of Canaan: Metaphor and Symbol in New England from the Puritans to the Transcendentalists*. Cambridge, Mass.: Harvard University Press, 1980.

Lukács, Georg. *The Historical Novel*. Translated by Hannah Mitchell and Stanley Mitchell. 1937. Lincoln: University of Nebraska Press, 1983.

Lutz, Donald. *The Origins of American Constitutionalism*. Baton Rouge: Louisiana State University Press, 1988.

Maier, Pauline. *The Old Revolutionaries: Political Lives in the Age of Samuel Adams*. New York: Knopf, 1980.

Main, Jackson Turner. *The Social Structure of Revolutionary America*. Princeton, N.J.: Princeton University Press, 1965.

Martin, Calvin, ed. *The American Indian and the Problem of History*. New York: Oxford University Press, 1987.

Martin, Terence. *The Instructed Vision: Scottish Common Sense Philosophy and the Origins of American Fiction*. Bloomington: Indiana University Press, 1961.

Martin, Wendy. *An American Triptych: Anne Bradstreet, Emily Dickinson, Adrienne Rich*. Chapel Hill: University of North Carolina Press, 1984.

May, Henry F. *The Enlightenment in America*. New York: Oxford University Press, 1976.

McDonald, Forrest. *Novus Ordo Seclorum: The Intellectual Origins of the Constitution*. Lawrence: University Press of Kansas, 1985.

McKeon, Michael. *The Origins of the English Novel, 1600–1740*. Baltimore: Johns Hopkins University Press, 1987.

McWilliams, John P., Jr. *Political Justice in a Republic: James Fenimore Cooper's America*. Berkeley and Los Angeles: University of California Press, 1972.

Meinig, D. W. *The Shaping of America: A Geographical Perspective on 500 Years of History*. Vol. 1, *Atlantic America, 1492–1800*. New Haven, Conn.: Yale University Press, 1986.

Merrell, James H. *The Indians' New World: Catawbas and Their Neighbors from European Contact through the Era of Removal*. Chapel Hill: University of North Carolina Press, 1989.

Meserole, Harrison T., ed. *Seventeenth-Century American Poetry*. New York: New York University Press, 1968.

Meserve, Walter J. *An Emerging Entertainment: The Drama of the American People to 1828*. Bloomington: Indiana University Press, 1977.

Middlekauff, Robert. *The Mathers: Three Generations of Puritan Intellectuals, 1596–1728*. New York: Oxford University Press, 1971.

Miller, Perry. *Errand into the Wilderness*. Cambridge, Mass.: Harvard University Press, 1956.

The New England Mind: From Colony to Province. Cambridge, Mass.: Harvard University Press, 1953.

The New England Mind: The Seventeenth Century. New York: Macmillan, 1939.

Orthodoxy in Massachusetts, 1630–1650. Cambridge, Mass.: Harvard University Press, 1933. Reprinted, with a new preface, Boston: Beacon, 1959.

Morgan, Edmund S. *American Slavery, American Freedom: The Ordeal of Colonial Virginia*. New York: Norton, 1975.

The Birth of the Republic, 1763–1789. Rev. ed. Chicago: University of Chicago Press, 1977.

Inventing the People: The Rise of Popular Sovereignty in England and America. New York: Norton, 1988.

The Meaning of Independence: John Adams, George Washington, Thomas Jefferson. Charlottesville: University Press of Virginia, 1976.

The Puritan Dilemma: The Story of John Winthrop. Boston: Little, Brown, 1958.

The Puritan Family: Religion and Domestic Relations in Seventeenth-Century New England. Rev. ed. New York: Harper & Row, 1966.

Visible Saints: The History of a Puritan Idea. Ithaca, N.Y.: Cornell University Press, 1963.

Morison, Samuel Eliot. *Harvard College in the Seventeenth Century.* 2 vols. Cambridge, Mass.: Harvard University Press, 1936.

The Intellectual Life of Colonial New England. 2d ed. New York: New York University Press, 1956.

Morris, Richard B. *The Forging of the Union, 1781–1789.* New York: Harper & Row, 1987.

Mott, Frank Luther. *A History of American Magazines.* 5 vols. Cambridge, Mass.: Harvard University Press, 1930–68.

Murdock, Kenneth B. *Literature and Theology in Colonial New England.* Westport, Conn.: Greenwood Press, 1949.

Murray, David. *Forked Tongues: Speech, Writing, and Representation in North American Indian Texts.* Bloomington: Indiana University Press, 1991.

Nash, Gary B. *Race and Revolution.* Madison, Wis.: Madison House, 1990.

Nelson, Dana D. *The Word in Black and White: Reading "Race" in American Literature, 1638–1867.* New York: Oxford University Press, 1992.

New, John F. H. *Anglican and Puritan: The Basis of Their Opposition.* Stanford, Calif.: Stanford University Press, 1964.

Norton, Mary Beth. *Liberty's Daughters: The Revolutionary Experience of American Women, 1750–1800.* Boston: Little, Brown, 1980.

Nye, Russel Blaine. *American Literary History: 1607–1830.* New York: Knopf, 1970.

The Cultural Life of the New Nation, 1776–1830. New York: Harper & Row, 1960.

O'Gorman, Edmundo. *The Invention of America: An Inquiry into the Historical Nature of the New World and the Meaning of Its History.* Bloomington: Indiana University Press, 1961.

Ostriker, Alicia Suskin. *Stealing the Language: The Emergence of Women's Poetry in America.* Boston: Beacon, 1986.

Pagden, Anthony. *European Encounters with the New World: From Renaissance to Romanticism.* New Haven, Conn.: Yale University Press, 1993.

The Fall of Natural Man: The American Indian and the Origins of Comparative Ethnology. Cambridge University Press, 1982.

Palmer, Stanley H., and Dennis Reinhartz, eds. *Essays on the History of North American Discovery and Exploration.* College Station: Texas A&M University Press, 1988.

Parry, J. H. *Europe and a Wider World, 1415–1715.* Edited by Sir Maurice Powicke. 1949. Reprinted as *The Establishment of the European Hegemony, 1415–1715: Trade and Exploration in the Age of the Renaissance.* New York: Harper & Row, 1961.

Pearce, Roy Harvey. *Savagism and Civilization: A Study of the Indian and the American*

Mind. Berkeley and Los Angeles: University of California Press, 1988. (First published as *The Savages of America,* 1953.)

Peterson, Merrill D. *The Jefferson Image in the American Mind.* New York: Oxford University Press, 1960.

Petter, Henri. *The Early American Novel.* Columbus: Ohio State University Press, 1971.

Pettit, Norman. *The Heart Prepared: Grace and Conversion in Puritan Spiritual Life.* New Haven, Conn.: Yale University Press, 1966. 2d ed. Middletown, Conn.: Wesleyan University Press, 1989.

Piercy, Josephine K. *Studies in Literary Types in Seventeenth-Century America (1607–1710).* New Haven, Conn.: Yale University Press, 1939.

Plumstead, A. W., ed. *The Wall and the Garden: Selected Massachusetts Election Sermons, 1670–1775.* Minneapolis: University of Minnesota Press, 1968.

Pocock, J. G. A. *The Machiavellian Moment: Florentine Political Thought and the Atlantic Republican Tradition.* Princeton, N.J.: Princeton University Press, 1975.

    Politics, Language, and Time: Essays on Political Thought and History. 1971. Reprinted. Chicago: University of Chicago Press, 1989.

Pope, Robert G. *The Half-Way Covenant: Church Membership in Puritan New England.* Princeton, N.J.: Princeton University Press, 1969.

Porterfield, Amanda. *Female Piety in Puritan New England: The Emergence of Religious Humanism.* New York: Oxford University Press, 1992.

Potter, Janice. *The Liberty We Seek: Loyalist Ideology in Colonial New York and Massachusetts.* Cambridge, Mass.: Harvard University Press, 1983.

Powell, Sumner Chilton. *Puritan Village: The Formation of a New England Town.* Middletown, Conn.: Wesleyan University Press, 1963.

Prucha, Francis Paul. *American Indian Policy in the Formative Years: The Indian Trade and Intercourse Acts, 1790–1834.* Cambridge, Mass.: Harvard University Press, 1962.

Quinn, Arthur Hobson. *A History of the American Drama from the Beginning to the Civil War.* 2d ed. New York: Appleton-Century-Crofts, 1951.

Quinn, David Beers. *North America from Earliest Discovery to First Settlements: The Norse Voyages to 1612.* New York: Harper & Row, 1977.

    Set Fair for Roanoke: Voyages and Colonies, 1584–1606. Chapel Hill: University of North Carolina Press, 1985.

    ed. *New American World: A Documentary History of North America to 1612.* 5 vols. New York: Arno, 1979.

Rakove, Jack N. *The Beginnings of National Politics: An Interpretive History of the Continental Congress.* New York: Knopf, 1979.

Reid, John Phillip. *Constitutional History of the American Revolution.* Madison: University of Wisconsin Press, 1986.

Richardson, Lyon. *A History of Early American Magazines, 1741–1850.* New York: Nelson, 1931.

Rodgers, Daniel T., trans. *Contested Truths: Keywords in American Politics since Independence.* New York: Basic, 1987.

Rossiter, Clinton. *1787: The Grand Convention.* 1966. Reprinted. New York: Norton, 1987.

Rubin, Louis D., Jr. *A Bibliographical Guide to the Study of Southern Literature*. Baton Rouge: Louisiana State University Press, 1969.

Ruether, Rosemary Radford, and Rosemary Skinner Keller, eds. *Women and Religion in America: The Colonial and Revolutionary Periods*. San Francisco: Harper & Row, 1981–6.

Rutland, Robert Allen. *The Birth of the Bill of Rights, 1776–1791*. Chapel Hill: University of North Carolina Press, 1955. Rev. ed. Boston: Northeastern University Press, 1983.

Rutman, Darrett B. *American Puritanism: Faith and Practice*. Philadelphia: Lippincott, 1970.

Sandoz, Ellis. *A Government of Laws: Political Theory, Religion, and the American Founding*. Baton Rouge: Louisiana State University Press, 1990.

    ed. *Political Sermons of the American Founding Era*. Indianapolis, Ind.: Liberty, 1991.

Scheick, William J. *Design in Puritan American Literature*. Lexington: University Press of Kentucky, 1992.

Schweitzer, Ivy. *The Work of Self-Representation: Lyric Poetry in Colonial New England*. Chapel Hill: University of North Carolina Press, 1991.

Seelye, John. *Prophetic Waters: The River in Early American Life and Literature*. New York: Oxford University Press, 1977.

Selement, George. *Keepers of the Vineyard: The Puritan Ministry and Collective Culture in Colonial New England*. Lanham, Md: University Press of America, 1984.

Sennett, Richard. *The Fall of Public Man*. New York: Knopf, 1977.

Shaw, Peter. *American Patriots and the Rituals of Revolution*. Cambridge, Mass.: Harvard University Press, 1981.

Shea, Daniel B., Jr. *Spiritual Autobiography in Early America*. Princeton, N.J.: Princeton University Press, 1968.

Shields, David S. *Oracles of Empire: Poetry, Politics, and Commerce in British America, 1690–1750*. Chicago: University of Chicago Press, 1990.

Silverman, Kenneth. *A Cultural History of the American Revolution*. New York: Thomas Y. Crowell, 1976.

Simpson, David. *The Politics of American English, 1776–1850*. New York: Oxford University Press, 1986.

Simpson, Lewis P. *The Brazen Face of History: Studies in the Literary Consciousness in America*. Baton Rouge: Louisiana State University Press, 1980.

    The Dispossessed Garden: Pastoral and History in Southern Literature. Athens: University of Georgia Press, 1975.

    The Man of Letters in New England and the South. Baton Rouge: Louisiana State University Press, 1962.

    ed. *The Federalist Literary Mind*. Baton Rouge: Louisiana State University Press, 1962.

Sisson, Dan. *The American Revolution of 1800*. New York: Knopf, 1974.

Slotkin, Richard. *Regeneration through Violence: The Mythology of the American Frontier, 1600–1860*. Middletown, Conn.: Wesleyan University Press, 1974.

Smith, Henry Nash. *Virgin Land: The American West as Symbol and Myth.* New York: Random House, 1950. Rev. ed. Cambridge, Mass.: Harvard University Press, 1978.

Smith, James Ward, and A. Leland Jamison, eds. *Religion in American Life.* 4 vols. Princeton, N.J.: Princeton University Press, 1961–.

Somkin, Fred. *Unquiet Eagle: Memory and Desire in the Idea of American Freedom, 1815–1860.* Ithaca, N.Y.: Cornell University Press, 1967.

Spengemann, William. *A Mirror for Americanists: Reflections on the Idea of American Literature.* Hanover, N.H.: University Press of New England, 1989.

Stone, Lawrence. *The Family, Sex and Marriage in England, 1500–1800.* New York: Harper & Row, 1977.

Stout, Harry S. *The New England Soul: Preaching and Religious Culture in Colonial New England.* New York: Oxford University Press, 1986.

Swann, Brian, and Arnold Krupat, eds. *Recovering the Word: Essays on Native American Literature.* Berkeley and Los Angeles: University of California Press, 1987.

Takaki, Ronald. *Iron Cages: Race and Culture in Nineteenth-Century America.* 1979. Reprinted. New York: Oxford University Press, 1990.

Tebbel, John. *A History of Book Publishing in the United States.* Vol. 1. *The Creation of an Industry, 1630–1865.* New York: Bowker, 1972.

Thickstun, Margaret Olofson. *Fictions of the Feminine: Puritan Doctrine and the Representation of Women.* Ithaca, N.Y.: Cornell University Press, 1988.

Thomas, Isaiah. *The History of Printing in America with a Biography of Printers & an Account of Newspapers.* Edited by Marcus A. McCorison. New York: Weathervane, 1970.

Tichi, Cecilia. *New World, New Earth: Environmental Reform in American Literature from the Puritans through Whitman.* New Haven, Conn.: Yale University Press, 1979.

Todorov, Tzvetan. *The Conquest of America: The Question of the Other.* Translated by Richard Howard. New York: Harper & Row, 1984. (Translation of *La Conquête de l'Amérique.* Paris: Editions du Seuil, 1982.)

Tompkins, Jane. *Sensational Designs: The Cultural Work of American Fiction, 1790–1860.* New York: Oxford University Press, 1985.

Toulouse, Teresa. *The Art of Prophesying: New England Sermons and the Shaping of Belief.* Athens: University of Georgia Press, 1987.

Truettner, William H., ed. *The West as America: Reinterpreting Images of the Frontier, 1820–1920.* Washington, D.C.: Smithsonian, 1991.

Tyler, Moses Coit. *The Literary History of the American Revolution, 1785–1812.* 2 vols. New York: Putnam, 1898.

Ulrich, Laurel Thatcher. *Good Wives: Image and Reality in the Lives of Women in Northern New England: 1650–1750.* New York: Knopf, 1982.

Vaughan, Alden T. *New England Frontier: Puritans and Indians, 1620–1675.* Rev. ed. New York: Norton, 1979.

Vaughan, Alden T., and Francis J. Bremer, eds. *Puritan New England: Essays on Religion, Society, and Culture.* New York: St. Martin's, 1979.

Vaughan, Alden T., and Edward W. Clark, eds. *Puritans among the Indians: Accounts of Captivity and Redemption, 1624–1674*. Cambridge, Mass.: Harvard University Press, 1981.

Wall, Helena M. *Fierce Communion: Family and Community in Early America*. Cambridge, Mass.: Harvard University Press, 1990.

Warner, Michael. *The Letters of the Republic: Publication and the Public Sphere in Eighteenth-Century America*. Cambridge, Mass.: Harvard University Press, 1990.

Washburn, Wilcomb E. *The Indian in America*. New York: Harper & Row, 1975.

Watt, Ian. *The Rise of the Novel: Studies in Defoe, Richardson, and Fielding*. Berkeley and Los Angeles: University of California Press, 1957.

Watts, Emily Stipes. *The Poetry of American Women from 1632 to 1945*. Austin: University of Texas Press, 1977.

Watts, Steven. *The Republic Reborn: War and the Making of Liberal America, 1790–1820*. Baltimore: Johns Hopkins University Press, 1987.

Weber, Donald. *Rhetoric and History in Revolutionary New England*. New York: Oxford University Press, 1988.

White, Morton. *Philosophy, The Federalist, and the Constitution*. New York: Oxford University Press, 1987.

The Philosophy of the American Revolution. New York: Oxford University Press, 1978.

White, Peter, ed. *Puritan Poets and Poetics: Seventeenth-Century American Poetry in Theory and Practice*. University Park: Pennsylvania State University Press, 1985.

Wilson, Garff B. *Three Hundred Years of American Drama and Theatre: From* Ye Bare and Ye Cubb *to* Chorus Line. 2d ed. Englewood Cliffs, N.J.: Prentice-Hall, 1982.

Woloch, Isser. *Eighteenth-Century Europe: Tradition and Progress, 1715–1789*. New York: Norton, 1982.

Wood, Gordon S. *The Creation of the American Republic*. Chapel Hill: University of North Carolina Press, 1969.

The Radicalism of the American Revolution. New York: Knopf, 1991.

Wright, Louis B. *The Cultural Life of the American Colonies, 1607–1763*. New York: Harper & Row, 1957.

Tradition and the Founding Fathers. Charlottesville: University Press of Virginia, 1975.

Wright, Thomas G. *Literary Culture in Early New England, 1620–1730*. New Haven, Conn.: Yale University Press, 1920.

Youngs, J. William T. *God's Messengers: Religious Leadership in Colonial New England, 1700–1750*. Baltimore: Johns Hopkins University Press, 1976.

Zakai, Avihu. *Exile and Kingdom: History and Apocalypse in the Puritan Migration to America*. Cambridge University Press, 1992.

Ziff, Larzer. *Puritanism in America: New Culture in a New World*. New York: Viking, 1973.

Writing in the New Nation: Prose, Print, and Politics in the Early United States. New Haven, Conn.: Yale University Press, 1991.

Zuckerman, Michael. *Peaceable Kingdoms: New England Towns in the Eighteenth Century*. New York: Knopf, 1970.

INDEX

419; gender imagery in, 242–3; and history,
394; Hutchinson's use of, 196; imagery from,
302; and individual rights, 401; and interpretation, 174, 199, 284, 392, 425; law in,
470; and liberty, 408; Cotton Mather on,
275; in oral culture, 648; and preparationism,
200; in Protestantism, 390; Puritan uses of,
185–8, 190, 194, 199, 203, 205, 228; and
reason, 410, 418; and slavery, 270; sovereignty in, 470
Bible, texts and figures from: Abel, 357; Acts,
77; Adam, 252, 270; Babylon, 105; Cain,
357; Canaan, 92, 95, 200, 270, 596; chosen
people, 395, 405; Creation, 120; Daniel,
411; David, 227; the Deluge, 106; Deuteronomy, 405; Ecclesiastes, 521; Eden, 33, 61–2,
105–7, 117, 250, 666; Egyptians, 212, 519;
Ephesians, 77, 523; Eve, 270; Exodus, 188;
Ezekiel, 212; the Fall, 106; Galatians, 408;
the garden, 61, 77, 121, 155, 260; Genesis,
114, 270; Ham, 270; Hebrews, 194, 200,
216, 405, 413, 519; Isaiah, 257, 398; Israel,
95, 188, 194, 199, 203, 230, 596; Jeremiah,
257, 259; Jerusalem, 121, 199, 200, 212,
259, 269, 276; Jews, 259; Jezebel, 197; Job,
188, 266; John, 212; John the Baptist, 259;
Jonah, 188; Joseph, 489; Joshua, 596; Judgment Day, 230, 243, 417–18; Kings, 466;
Micah, 446; Luke, 411; New Testament,
188, 199, 216, 229, 250, 273, 423; Noah,
351; Old Testament, 188, 194, 199, 200,
212, 216, 229, 250; Paradise, 397; Paul,
411, 523; Pharisees, 400; Pisgah, 85, 416,
596; promised land, 62, 95, 121, 285, 416,
425; Proverbs, 260, 413; Psalms, 227; Red
Sea, 212; Revelation, 247, 268, 394, 398;
Samuel, 409, 413; Second Coming, 200,
211, 288; Solomon, 405, 446, 521; Song of
Songs, 247, 250; Zion, 188, 200, 212, 220,
229, 260, 269, 276; see also typology, biblical
Bibliothèque Nationale (Paris), 26
bicameralism, 464
Biddle, Nicholas, 149, 571
Bierstadt, Albert, 40
Billings, William, 562–3
Bill of Rights: English, 470, 474; United States,
466, 488–9, 505
Bingham, George Caleb, 40
biography, Puritan, 209, 213; communal func-
tion of, 205; development of, 224; formula of,
212–13; heroic, 275–6; and history, 215;
and jeremiad rhetoric, 257; by Cotton
Mather, 273, 275–7; secularization of, 214
Bird, Robert Montgomery, 583–4
Bishop Stoke (England), 268
Blackamore, Arthur: "Expeditio Ultramontana,"
331; The Perfidious Brethren, 342
Black legend, 69

Black Mingo (South Carolina), 318
"black regiment," 391
Blackstone, William: Commentaries on the Laws of
England, 474–5, 505–6, 508
Blair, Hugh: Lectures on Rhetoric and Belles Lettres,
336
Blake, William: Jerusalem, 618; Songs of Innocence,
618
Bland, Richard, 458; The Colonel Dismounted,
436–8; An Inquiry into the Rights of the British
Colonies, 437–9; Letter to the Clergy of Virginia,
393
Bleecker, Ann Eliza, 607, 616; The Posthumous
Works of Ann Eliza Bleecker, 551
Bloomfield, Robert, 564
Blue Anchor Tavern, 310
Blue Ridge Mountains, 127
Board of Printers' Licensers (Boston), 224
Bolingbroke, Henry St. John, 570
Bolling, Robert, 337; "An Indian War," 335;
"Neanthe," 334; "Occlusion," 334; "Winter,"
334
Bonaparte, Napoleon, 131
Le Bon Homme Richard (ship), 593
books, 566, 622, 646; as commodities, 556, 674;
as communal possessions, 627; and copyright,
554; costs and distribution of, 625; historians
of, 569; illustrators of, 691; and market, 553,
555
booksellers, 554; and authors, 605, 685; and copyright law, 547, 552, 554; and distribution,
337; and market, 625; as patrons, 337, 566
Booth, Edwin, 590
Booth, John Wilkes, 590
Booth, Junius Brutus, 590
Boston (England), 199
Boston (Massachusetts), 120, 190, 219, 237,
245, 259, 264, 269, 342, 544, 548, 593,
604, 607, 627; Common, 355; conservatism
in, 563–4; churches in, 209, 211, 233, 262,
271, 275, 279–80, 289, 293–4, 296, 303,
310, 353, 390, 408, 412, 563; clergy in,
173, 280, 286–8; clubs in, 326, 339, 563;
conditions of life in, 216–17; Dorchester,
213, 462; election sermons in, 257, 407,
410; Essex Street, 355; Harbor, 353, 411,
426, 519; in King Philip's War, 222–3;
King Street, 357; Liberty Tree, 355, 358–9,
462; literary establishment in, 563, 600,
602; in literature, 235–6, 318, 545, 595–6,
606–7; Mather family in, 209, 270–1, 277,
288; merchant class in, 255, 279–80, 389,
293; mob uprisings in, 354–60; Moon Street,
389; newspapers and magazines in, 311–13,
318, 326, 337–8, 354–9, 435, 449, 562–4,
566, 597, 602–3; North End, 356; Old Granary Burying Ground, 355; publishing in,
206, 224, 300; radicalism in, 358; religious